Performing with Microsoft® Office 2003

Introductory Course

Iris Blanc

New York City Board of Education

Cathy Vento

Computer Education Consultant

COURSE TECHNOLOGY
25 THOMSON PLACE
BOSTON, MA 02210

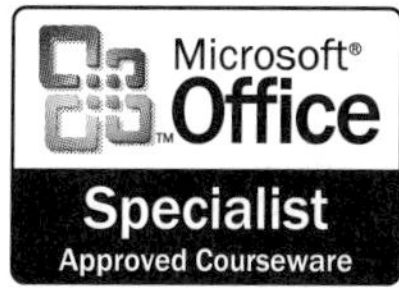

Australia • Canada • Mexico • Singapore • Spain • United Kingdom • United States

Performing with Microsoft Office 2003: Introductory Course

by Iris Blanc and Cathy Vento

Executive Director:
Cheryl Costantini

Senior Editor:
Alexandra Arnold

Product Manager:
David Rivera

Development Editor:
Rose Marie Kuebbing
Custom Editorial Productions, Inc.

Senior Marketing Manager:
Kim Ryttel

Director of Production:
Patty Stephan

Production Editor:
Jean Findley
Custom Editorial Productions, Inc.

Senior Manufacturing Coordinator:
Trevor Kallop

Senior Designer:
Abby Scholz

Illustrations:
Ferruccio Sardella

Compositor:
GEX Publishing Services

Printer:
Banta Menasha

Printed in the United States of America

2 3 4 5 6 7 8 9 BM 07 06 05

For more information, contact Course Technology, 25 Thomson Place, Boston, Massachusetts, 02210.

Or find us on the World Wide Web at:
www.course.com

ISBN 0-619-18381-0

ISBN 0-619-18382-9

PREFACE

The *Performing with Microsoft® Office 2003* series teaches Office tools through a unique set of task-oriented exercises and project-based applications built around a business theme. Students focus on the skills they need to know to complete practical, realistic applications and create materials suitable for portfolio evaluation. In this Introductory Course text, the software skills developed meet Specialist level Microsoft Office Specialist certification requirements for Office 2003. XP users may also use this text since XP procedures are noted where they differ from Office 2003.

Performing with Microsoft® Office 2003 is a new and different approach based on the premise that students successfully assimilate and retain computer skills when they understand why the skills are useful. *Performing with Microsoft® Office 2003* presents skill sets within the framework of engaging projects and tasks that teach the software and business competencies needed to succeed in the workplace, thus providing a real-life context for learning. Through this task- and project-based approach, students develop critical thinking, analysis, problem solving, and information and resource management skills. With the Internet activities that appear throughout the text, they learn research and communication skills—essential tools for today's workplace. College or college-bound students will find that these software, business, and thinking skills will serve them in their coursework, internships, and professional careers.

Rather than focus solely on software features, this series emphasizes the project or task and develops those software skill sets needed to accomplish it.

OBJECTIVES

Performing with Microsoft® Office 2003: Introductory Course is intended for a one-year Computer Applications course. No experience with this software is assumed. The objectives of this book are:

- To use a three-phased approach to develop Office Specialist competencies:
  - **Tryouts:** Learners practice software skills using a step-by-step tutorial approach.
  - **Rehearsals:** Learners apply software skills to an illustrated business task.
  - **Performances:** Learners use technology to complete a business project.
- To use tasks and projects to develop SCANS competencies:
  - Acquire and evaluate data
  - Organize and maintain files
  - Interpret and communicate information
  - Apply technology to specific tasks
  - Apply critical thinking and problem solving
  - Work with members of a team
- To provide a text that may be used for independent study.

When students complete a Computer Applications course using this text, they will have Specialist level skills and workplace competencies.

ORGANIZATION OF THE TEXT

Performing with Microsoft® Office 2003: Introductory Course begins with a computer concepts unit that gives the foundation for an understanding of computers. Following that is the Performance Basics unit, which teaches Internet basics and the features found in all Office applications, such as opening, saving, and printing files. Subsequent units are devoted to each application in the Office suite: Word, Excel, PowerPoint®, and Access. Outlook Basics is covered in Appendix I, and some Outlook features are covered within the Word and Excel units.

Each application unit is organized by a series of project categories. For example, the Word unit is organized into lessons that cover the following document-based projects:

- Correspondence
- Reports and Long Documents
- Meeting Documents and Schedules
- Sales and Marketing Documents
- Integration/Word and the Web

The Excel projects include:

- Business Forms
- Accounting Records
- Data Analysis
- Budgets and Financial Reports
- Charts
- Integration/Excel and the Web

Lessons use a three-phased pedagogy. The first phase, **Tryout,** introduces the software features necessary to complete document production in the lesson category (e.g., correspondence). It also includes software concepts, illustrations, step-by-step directions, and short, easy exercises called **Try it Out**, which provide practice with software features. Students should read all software concepts on a topic before completing the related **Try it Out!** exercise.

In the second phase, **Rehearsal,** students apply the software skills practiced in the Tryout phase to a series of tasks in which they produce model professional documents. **What You Need to**

Know information and **Cues for Reference** guide learners in completing the activities on their own, thus helping them build skills and confidence in accomplishing the Rehearsal activity. The Rehearsal phase produces tangible results that represent actual professional documents within the lesson category.

In the third phase, **Performance,** students complete challenging work-related projects (either independently or as a team) for one of nine companies. In this phase, students must apply critical thinking and problem-solving skills and integrate the software skills and business concepts learned to produce the documents required by the company-related scenarios. This phase can be used as evidence of lesson mastery.

This text is an innovative approach to teaching software skills through a project-based, applied learning process. This approach is unique because it teaches the Specialist level skills by applying software features in various work-based contexts. The opportunity to use the skills independently and creatively will enable students to survive and thrive in a high-performance workplace.

SPECIAL FEATURES

- **Keyboarding Reinforcement Unit** (found on the Data CD) contains 18 exercises of drill and practice material covering the entire alphabet for those who wish to learn the keyboard or improve their keyboarding skills quickly.
- **End-of-Lesson Performance activities** use a project-based approach to reinforce the concepts and applications learned in the lesson and require critical thinking and Internet skills.
- **Final Capstone Project** applies the skills learned throughout the text.
- **Data files** (found on the Data CD) allow learners to complete many of the activities without keyboarding lengthy text.
- **Directories** list file names alphabetically with corresponding lesson numbers, as well as document sample pages.
- **Vocabulary words**—both software and project-related—for each lesson.
- **Portfolio-building projects** found in the Performance sections of each lesson.
- **Multiple-Choice, True/False, Matching and Completion Objective test questions** as part of the Encore review can be found on the Data CD.
- **Appendices** that include the following:
  - Microsoft® Office Specialist Correlation Chart
  - File Management
  - Using the Mouse
  - Toolbars, Menus, and Dialog Boxes
  - Selection Techniques
  - Portfolio Basics
  - Proofreader's Marks
  - Task Reference
  - Outlook Basics
- **Glossary**

As part of this series, there are stand-alone, comprehensive texts on Microsoft Word and Excel. Since Microsoft Expert certification is available only for Word and Excel with this new version of Office, these comprehensive texts can be used to develop Expert Microsoft Office Specialist certification skills. The advanced skills sets identified in the previous version of Access and PowerPoint are now incorporated into Specialist level competencies in Office 2003.

To help with additional projects, there is *Performing with Microsoft® Office: Projects for the Entrepreneur.*

ACKNOWLEDGMENTS

For the many people who have played a role in the production of this quality book, we owe our gratitude and appreciation. First and foremost among them are Cheryl Costantini, Executive Director; Kim Ryttel, Senior Marketing Manager; Patty Stephan, Director of Production; Alexandra Arnold, Senior Editor; David Rivera, Product Manager; Trevor Kallop, Senior Manufacturing Coordinator; and Abby Scholz, Senior Designer for their professionalism, guidance, and support throughout this project.

Our heartfelt thanks go to those who have made significant contributions and assisted us with the production of this book:

- To the production team at Custom Editorial Productions: Rose Marie Kuebbing, Jean Findley, and Beckie Middendorf, who kept everyone on track and on time, and did so with support and guidance all along the way.
- To Marie Michele for her wonderful illustrations.
- To our families for their love, encouragement, inspiration, and above all, for their patience.

Iris Blanc
Cathy Vento

ABOUT THE AUTHORS

Iris Blanc is currently the Director of Virtual Enterprises, International, a New York City Department of Education program. Formerly, Ms. Blanc was assistant principal/ department chair of Business Education at Tottenville High School, a New York City public high school.

Ms. Blanc has taught business education and computer applications at the high school and college levels for over 30 years. Ms. Blanc conducts seminars, workshops, and short courses in applied learning strategies and methods of teaching and integrating technology at conferences nationwide.

Catherine Vento is currently working as a consultant for the New York City Department of Education and as a staff developer for the district. She was formerly the assistant principal/department chair of Business Education at Susan Wagner High School, a New York City public high school.

Ms. Vento has taught business education, accounting, and computer applications at the high school level. She has presented seminars, workshops, and mini-courses at conferences, colleges, and business schools nationwide.

Ms. Blanc and Ms. Vento have co-authored numerous computer application texts and reference guides for over 20 years. The Performing series represents their combined pedagogical talents in an innovative, new approach to develop workplace skills and competencies. Over their many years as educators and authors, they have discovered that students learn best what they need to know!

HOW TO USE THIS BOOK

LESSON 2

Lesson Outcome
Indicates the workplace-related goal for learning software skills.

Correspondence

In this lesson, you will learn to use features found in Word to format correspondence, create an envelope and labels, and send e-mail. Correspondence includes written communications such as letters, memos, and e-mails. You will complete the following projects:

- a business letter
- a personal letter and envelope
- a memorandum using a template
- a business letter using a Wizard

Upon completion of this lesson, you should have mastered the following skill sets:

- Set margins
- Insert the date and time
- Use Smart Tags
- Use AutoText
- Use horizontal text alignments
- Create envelopes and labels
- Use templates
- Open existing templates
- Create your own template
- Use wizards
- Send e-mail
- Create a new message
- Send a Word document as e-mail

Terms

Software-related

Portrait orientation
AutoText
Template
Placeholder
Wizard
E-mail

Document-related

Full-block business letter
Enclosure notation
Personal letter
Justified text
Delivery address
Letterhead
Logo

Terms
Lists software-related and document/ file-related terms. Terminolgy is introduced on a need-to-know basis.

Lesson Summary
Summarizes the lesson's objectives and workplace-related applications.

Lesson Skills Sets
Lists skills sets that the learner needs to know to complete the work-related activities.

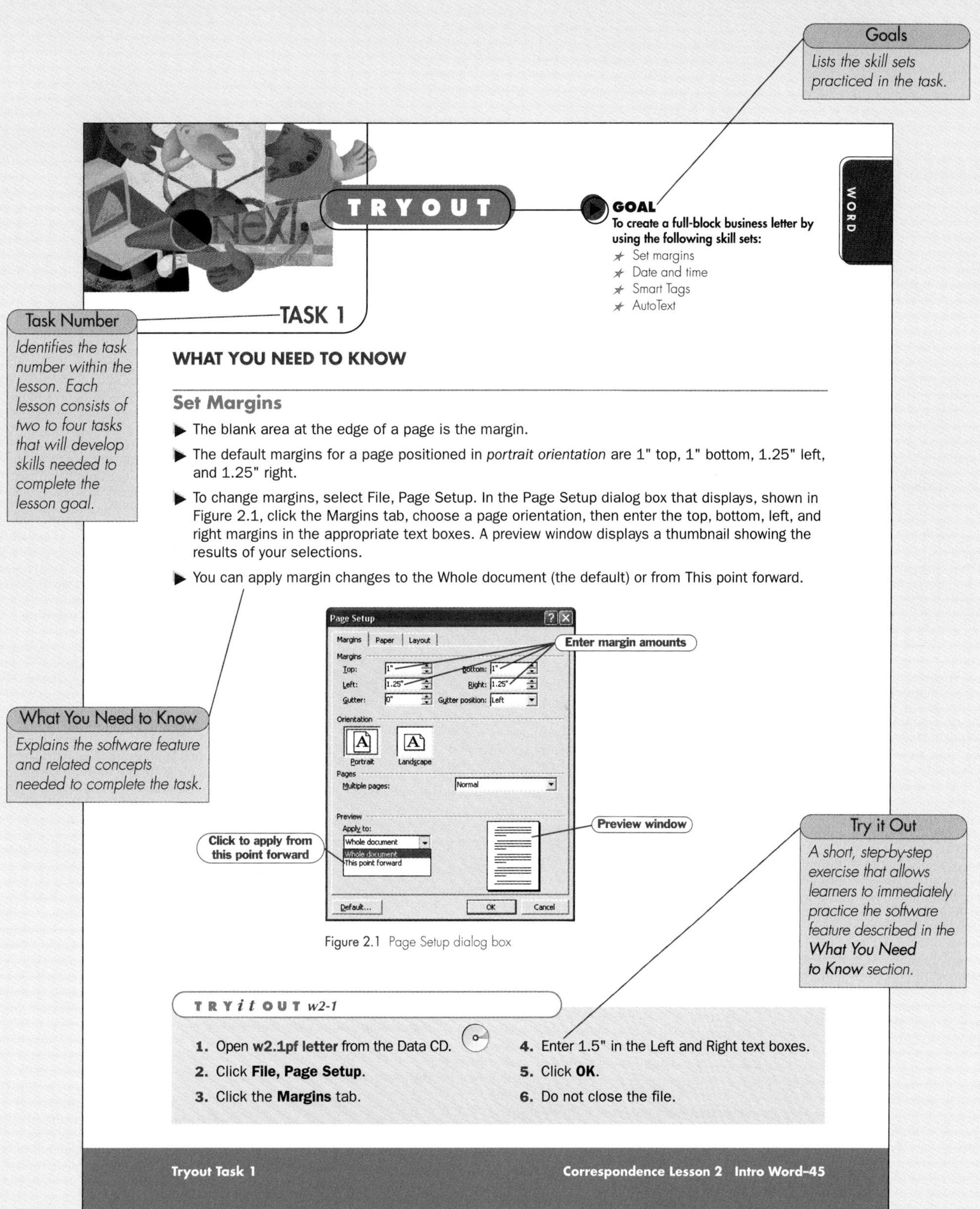

Goals

Lists the skill sets practiced in the task.

TRYOUT

TASK 1

Task Number

Identifies the task number within the lesson. Each lesson consists of two to four tasks that will develop skills needed to complete the lesson goal.

GOAL
To create a full-block business letter by using the following skill sets:

- Set margins
- Date and time
- Smart Tags
- AutoText

WORD

WHAT YOU NEED TO KNOW

Set Margins

- The blank area at the edge of a page is the margin.
- The default margins for a page positioned in *portrait orientation* are 1" top, 1" bottom, 1.25" left, and 1.25" right.
- To change margins, select File, Page Setup. In the Page Setup dialog box that displays, shown in Figure 2.1, click the Margins tab, choose a page orientation, then enter the top, bottom, left, and right margins in the appropriate text boxes. A preview window displays a thumbnail showing the results of your selections.
- You can apply margin changes to the Whole document (the default) or from This point forward.

What You Need to Know

Explains the software feature and related concepts needed to complete the task.

Figure 2.1 Page Setup dialog box

Try it Out

A short, step-by-step exercise that allows learners to immediately practice the software feature described in the ***What You Need to Know*** *section.*

TRY *it* OUT *w2-1*

1. Open **w2.1pf letter** from the Data CD.
2. Click **File, Page Setup**.
3. Click the **Margins** tab.
4. Enter 1.5" in the Left and Right text boxes.
5. Click **OK**.
6. Do not close the file.

Tryout Task 1 Correspondence Lesson 2 Intro Word–45

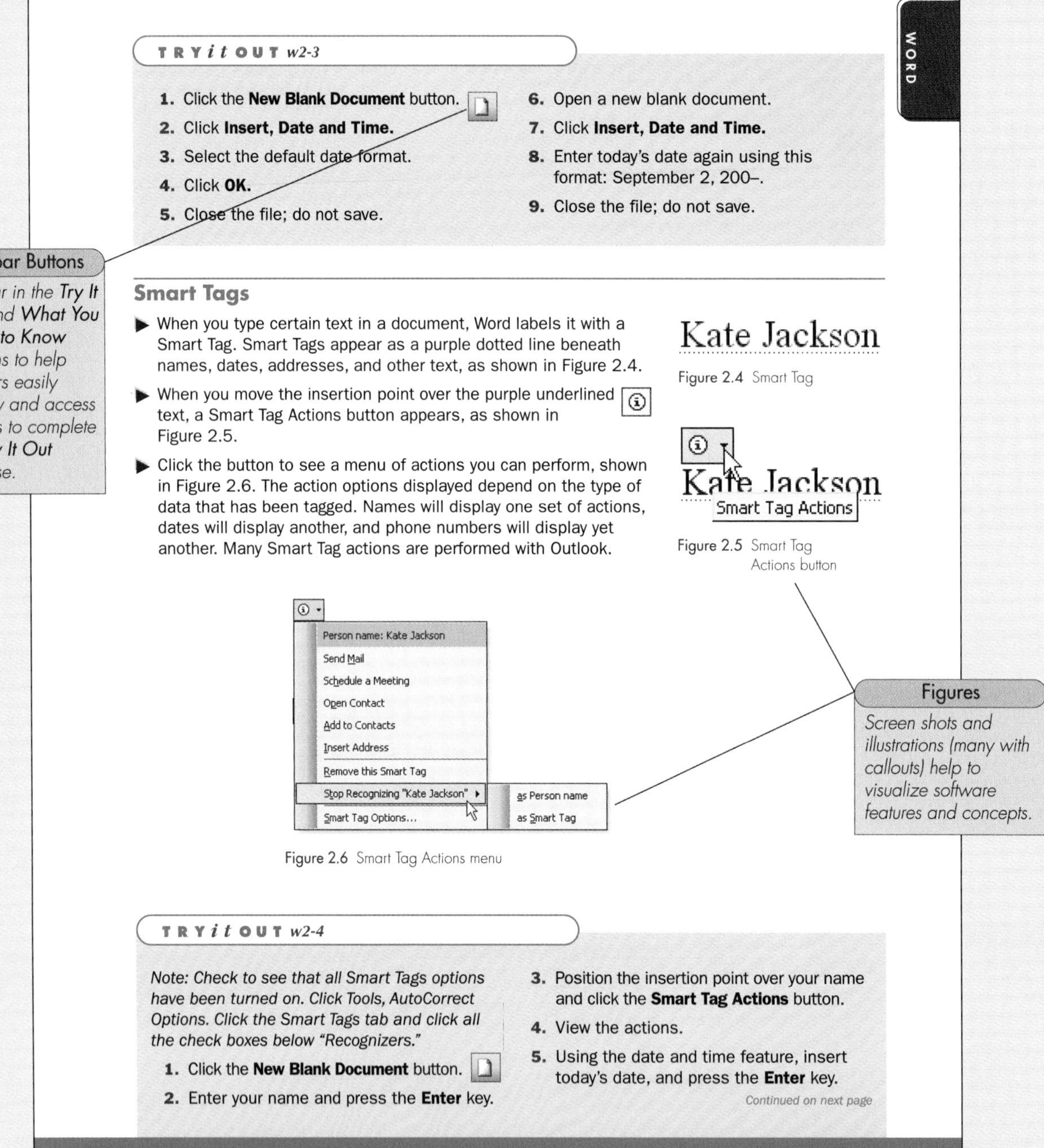

WORD

TRY *it* OUT *w2-3*

1. Click the **New Blank Document** button.
2. Click **Insert, Date and Time.**
3. Select the default date format.
4. Click **OK.**
5. Close the file; do not save.
6. Open a new blank document.
7. Click **Insert, Date and Time.**
8. Enter today's date again using this format: September 2, 200–.
9. Close the file; do not save.

Toolbar Buttons

Appear in the Try It Out and What You Need to Know sections to help learners easily identify and access buttons to complete the Try It Out exercise.

Smart Tags

- ▶ When you type certain text in a document, Word labels it with a Smart Tag. Smart Tags appear as a purple dotted line beneath names, dates, addresses, and other text, as shown in Figure 2.4.
- ▶ When you move the insertion point over the purple underlined text, a Smart Tag Actions button appears, as shown in Figure 2.5.
- ▶ Click the button to see a menu of actions you can perform, shown in Figure 2.6. The action options displayed depend on the type of data that has been tagged. Names will display one set of actions, dates will display another, and phone numbers will display yet another. Many Smart Tag actions are performed with Outlook.

Kate Jackson

Figure 2.4 Smart Tag

Kate Jackson

Smart Tag Actions

Figure 2.5 Smart Tag Actions button

Person name: Kate Jackson
Send Mail
Schedule a Meeting
Open Contact
Add to Contacts
Insert Address
Remove this Smart Tag
Stop Recognizing "Kate Jackson"
Smart Tag Options...
as Person name
as Smart Tag

Figure 2.6 Smart Tag Actions menu

Figures

Screen shots and illustrations (many with callouts) help to visualize software features and concepts.

TRY *it* OUT *w2-4*

Note: Check to see that all Smart Tags options have been turned on. Click Tools, AutoCorrect Options. Click the Smart Tags tab and click all the check boxes below "Recognizers."

1. Click the **New Blank Document** button.
2. Enter your name and press the **Enter** key.
3. Position the insertion point over your name and click the **Smart Tag Actions** button.
4. View the actions.
5. Using the date and time feature, insert today's date, and press the **Enter** key.

Continued on next page

Tryout Task 1 Correspondence Lesson 2 Intro Word–47

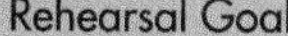

Rehearsal Goal

Identifies the outcome of the applications.

GOAL
To create a one-page report with indented text using the skill sets learned

SETTING THE STAGE/WRAPUP
Margins: Default
Start line: At 2.5"
File name: **3.1car**

Setting the Stage

*Identifies file names and/or settings needed to begin the **Rehearsal** application.*

TASK 1

Task Number

*Each task includes a **Rehearsal** that applies all the software features practiced in the **Try It Out** phase.*

WHAT YOU NEED TO KNOW

- A *report* or *manuscript* communicates information about a topic. The topic may be formal or informal. Although most reports require research, others include the writer's opinion or position on the topic.
- The margins for a report depend on how the report is bound. The recommended margin requirements for different bindings are as follows:
  - Unbound—1" or 1.25" left and right, 2" or 2.5" top, 1" bottom
  - Left-bound—1.5" left, 1" right, 2" or 2.5" top, 1" bottom
  - Top-bound—1" left and right, 2" or 2.5" top, 1" bottom
- The start line for the first page is generally 2" or 2.5".
- The title of the report is centered and in all caps.
- A report is generally double-spaced. Each paragraph starts 0.5" or 1" from the left margin.
- In this Rehearsal activity, you will create a one-page report with indented paragraphs.

What You Need to Know

Explains business-related concepts and provides information needed to complete the application.

DIRECTIONS

The illustration on the facing page is shown on one page; however, the final document will span two pages.

1. Click the **New Blank Document** button. Switch to Print Layout view if you are not already in that view mode.
2. Use the default margins.
3. Begin the document at **2"** (from the top edge of the page).
4. Key the report as shown or open **3.1car** from the Data CD. Format the title and the first two paragraphs as follows:
   a. Center the title and set it to a sans serif 14-point bold font.
   b. Insert any desired symbol before and after the title as shown.
   c. Set a **1"** first-line indent and line spacing to **Exactly 20 point.**
5. Format the side headings and paragraphs below the side headings as follows:
   a. Set side headings to a sans serif 10-point bold font. (Use **Format Painter** to copy the formatting from the first side heading to the second side heading.)
   b. Set a **0.5"** left and right indent on the paragraphs shown.
   c. Create a hanging indent and bold the first sentence on the paragraphs shown.
   d. Set paragraph spacing before and after each paragraph to **6 pt.** for the entire document. Note the soft page break; the document now spans two pages.
6. Spell check.
7. Save the file; name it **3.1buycar.**
8. Preview both pages.
9. Print.
10. Close.

Directions

*Clear instructions that guide learners to complete the application. These instructions are less detailed than those in the **Try It Out** phase, requiring students to build skills and confidence.*

82–Intro Word Lesson 3 Reports and Long Documents **Rehearsal Task 1**

WORD

❖❖❖ HOW TO PURCHASE A USED CAR ❖❖❖

For many people, the thought of purchasing a car is scary. Buying a car, whether new or used, is a huge investment. With new car prices at an all-time high, many are choosing to purchase used cars, but the unknowns in such a purchase are often intimidating.

The following are important questions to think about and some tips for the beginner who is in the early stages of buying a used car.

ASK YOURSELF THESE QUESTIONS

What is the condition of the car I currently own? Why do I want to replace it? If I do not presently own a car, what are my primary reasons for wanting to purchase one?

Do I want to buy a used car from a dealership or would I prefer to go through a private owner? What are the advantages and disadvantages of both?

How will I finance my purchase? How will my current transportation costs compare with owning my own vehicle?

What kind of car am I looking for? What functions does the car need to serve (i.e., daily transportation vs. weekend trips or both)?

0.5" left indent

0.5" right indent

THE FIRST FEW STEPS

Research, research, research. The most successful purchaser of a used car is one who is empowered with knowledge. Read consumer guides and books. Find the resources available to you online. Learn to speak "car talk." Look through the newspaper to get a sense of the used car market and to understand what car sellers are advertising.

Enlist the help and support of a friend or family member who knows about cars and is familiar with the process of purchasing a used car. Experience can be the best teacher.

Formulate a realistic budget so that you can arrive at a definite price range from which you will not waver when shopping and negotiating. Set up a meeting with a financial manager if necessary.

Dream a little. With knowledge, hard work, and a definite purpose, finding the used car of your dreams at the right price is possible.

Hanging indent

Illustrated Application

A model of the document or final product to guide learners as they create the application. Callouts and proofreaders' marks are sometimes included to help learners complete the activity.

Cues for Reference

A concise reference tool that reviews the keystrokes and actions students will need to complete the Rehearsal activity.

Cues for Reference

Line Spacing

1. Place insertion point where new line spacing is to begin or select paragraphs to receive line-spacing change.
2. Click **Format, Paragraph.**
3. Click the **Indents and Spacing** tab.
4. Click the **Line Spacing** list arrow.
5. Click the option you want.
   Or use a shortcut method:
   Press **Ctrl + 2** = double spacing;
   press **Ctrl + 1** = single spacing;
   press **Ctrl + 5** = 1.5 spacing.

Paragraph Spacing

1. Place the insertion point in paragraph or select paragraphs to format.
2. Click **Format, Paragraph.**
3. Click the **Indents and Spacing** tab.
4. Click **Before** and/or **After** text box.
5. Enter a spacing amount and click **OK.**

Indent Text

1. Click **Format, Paragraph.**
2. Click **Indents and Spacing** tab.
3. Make your selections and/or enter amount of the indent.
4. Click **OK.**

Hanging Indents

1. Place the insertion point in affected paragraph or select desired paragraphs.
2. Drag hanging indent marker on ruler to appropriate position, or press **Ctrl + T.**

or

1. Click **Format, Paragraph.**
2. Click the **Indents and Spacing** tab.
3. Click the **Special** list arrow and select **Hanging.**
4. Click increment arrow in the **By** text box to enter hanging indent amount.
5. Click **OK.**

Rehearsal Task 1 — Lesson 3 Reports and Long Documents Intro Word–83

SETTING THE STAGE/WRAPUP
Act I File name: **2.p1dallas**
Act II File names: **2.p2alslet**
2.p2sanfran
Act III File name: **2.p3osha**

Setting the Stage
Identifies file names and/or settings needed to begin the activities, which are listed as Acts. There may be two to four Acts in this phase.

WHAT YOU NEED TO KNOW

In the Performance phase of each lesson, it is assumed that you work or correspond with one of the companies listed on pages xv–xvii of this textbook. A description of the company, its logo, and the company's communication information is indicated there. In subsequent exercises, only the logo will be presented, so if you need to review company information, you will have to refer to the front of this textbook. Your performance in preparing documents and projects typically used in business will apply the skills you developed in previous phases of this lesson.

Act I

Scenario
Introduces the business problem.

You are interested in traveling to Dallas, Texas, in May. Write a personal letter to Ms. Robin Byron of the Air Land Sea Travel Group in New York. Request that they send you the famous *Travel Guide 2005*. Tell them you are particularly interested in visiting the Arts District, Civic Center, and the Farmer's Market and would like any additional information they might have about those areas.

Follow these guidelines:

- Use your own name, address, and phone information for the letterhead.
- Use any desired margins, an appropriate letter style, and an appropriate closing.
- Save the file; name it **2.p1dallas.**
- Prepare an envelope.
- Print one copy of the letter and envelope.

travel group

Guidelines
Lists the requirements, specifications, and/or tips needed to complete the project.

Company Logo
Identifies the company that the students are "working for" in the scenario. The company information is outlined on the ***To the Student*** *pages and may be used for reference.*

70–Intro Word Lesson 2 Correspondence Performance

WHAT'S NEW AND IMPROVED IN MICROSOFT® OFFICE 2003

Microsoft Office 2003 has many powerful new features as well as significantly improved interfaces to the features with which you are already familiar. Complex operations such as mail merge are now much easier. Improved Web access from all applications means you can integrate Web resources with your Office files. Sharing the information or data in your Office applications via the Web is now practically seamless. Office 2003 includes improved tools to enhance collaboration when you work on projects with other people. Some of the new features are covered in this Introductory Course. Other features are taught in the *Performing with Microsoft® Office Word 2003* and *Performing with Microsoft® Office Excel 2003* comprehensive texts.

The many new and improved Office 2003 features include:

- New and improved task panes to improve access to special features.
- Research task pane offering a wide variety of reference information.
- Support for ink devices such as a Tablet PC.
- Better integration of Microsoft Office Online site features.
- Shared workspace task pane.

Microsoft® Word 2003 includes the following new features:

- Compare documents side by side.
- Improved readability using the new Reading Layout view.
- Improved document protection for formatting and content.
- Support for XML documents.

Microsoft® Excel 2003 includes the following new features:

- Compare workbooks side by side.
- Improved statistical functions.
- Improved list functions.
- Support for import and export of XML data.

Microsoft® PowerPoint® 2003 includes the following new features:

- Updated PowerPoint viewer for opening presentations without software installation.
- New Slide Show navigation tools.
- Ink feature to mark slides in a presentation.
- New SmartTag support.

Microsoft® Access 2003 includes the following new features:

- Can view information on object dependencies.
- Error checking for forms and reports.
- Back-up database feature.
- Improved sorting functions.
- Field properties can be propagated from tables to forms.

Start-up Checklist

HARDWARE

Minimum Configuration

- PC with Pentium 233 MHz or higher; Pentium III recommended.
- Microsoft Windows 2000, Service Pack 3 or later, or Windows XP or later (recommended)
- 64 MB RAM (minimum) 128 MB RAM (recommended)
- Hard disk with 350 MB free for typical installation
- CD-ROM drive
- Super VGA monitor (800 × 600) or higher resolution with 256 colors
- Microsoft Mouse, Microsoft IntelliMouse, or compatible pointing device
- 33,600 bps or higher modem
- Printer

Before you start to work, please read this introduction. Spending this time before you begin will enhance your learning experience.

Conventions: Different type styles have special meaning. You will save time by recognizing the nature of the text from the type style.

Type Style	Color	Use	Example
Bold Italics	Black	Key terms	***word processing***
Bold	Black	Action items	Press the **Enter** key
Bold	Red	File names	**2.2to.xls** **3.3pf styles.doc**

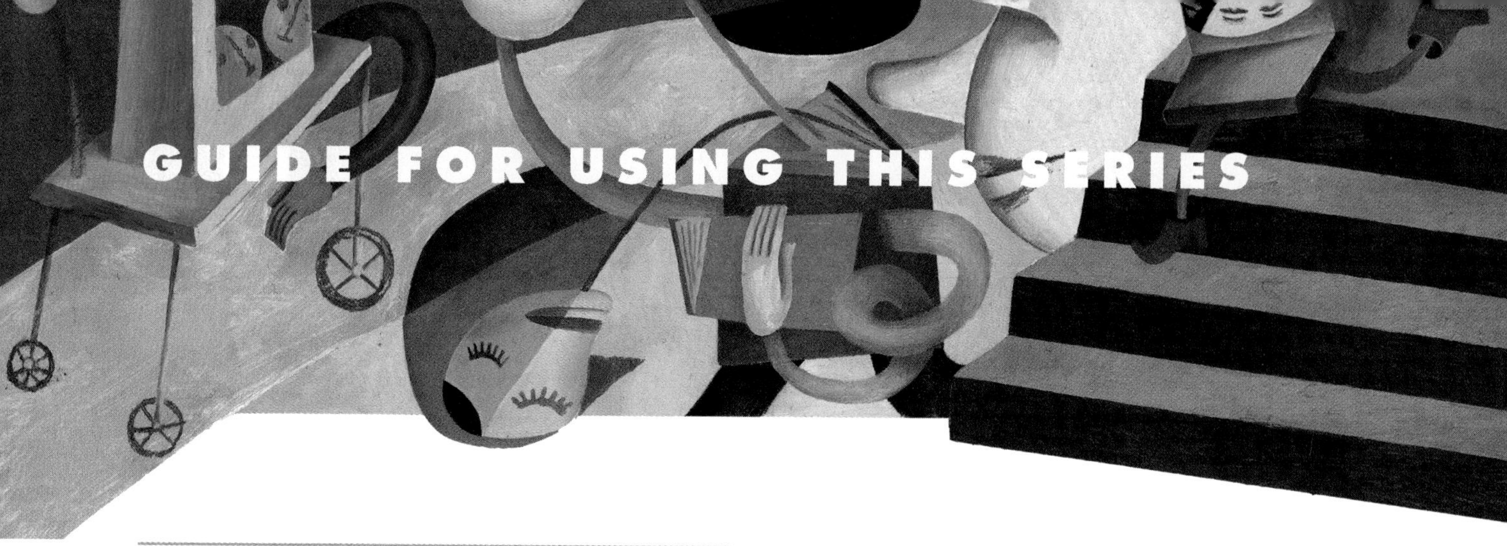

ANCILLARIES

Student Data Files: All data files mentioned in the text that are needed to complete the exercises for this book are located on on a separate CD called a Review Pack. They can also be downloaded for each title on www.course.com.

Instructor Resources (IR) CD-ROM: The Instructor Resources CD-ROM contains a wealth of instructional material you can use to prepare for and aid in your teaching of Office 2003. On the CD, you will find:

- Data files for the course.
- Solution files for the course.
- Answers to all exercises.
- Lesson plans for each lesson.
- Copies of the figures that appear in the student text, which can be used to prepare transparencies.
- A correlation grid that shows skills required for Microsoft Office Specialist certification.
- A correlation grid that shows the SCANS workplace competencies skills.
- PowerPoint presentations showing Office 2003 features for Word, Excel, Access, and PowerPoint®.
- Keyboarding Reinforcement unit.
- Multiple-Choice, True/False, Matching and Completion Objective test questions.

ExamView®

This textbook is accompanied by ExamView®, a powerful testing software package that allows instructors to create and administer printed, computer (LAN-based), and Internet exams. ExamView® includes hundreds of questions that correspond to the topics covered in this text, enabling students to generate detailed study guides that include page references for further review. The computer-based and Internet testing components allow students to take exams at their computers, and also save the instructor time by grading each exam automatically.

TO THE STUDENT

The Rehearsal and Performance phases of each lesson use various types of companies to demonstrate the kinds of documents that a real business might produce. A description of each company used in this text is outlined below. The Performance phase of each unit will identify the company you "work for" by the company logo illustrated. Use these pages as a reference if you need to find information about the company as you complete the project at hand.

Company Name and Contact Information	***Description of Company***	***Logo***
Air Land Sea Travel Group *New York* 505 Park Avenue New York, NY 10010 Phone 212-555-5555 Fax: 212-666-6767 E-mail: als@net.com *Boston* One Main Street Boston, MA 11111 Phone: 617-666-6666 Fax: 617-777-7777 E-mail: alsbos@net.com *California* Los Angeles 46 Beverly Drive Beverly Hills, CA 90210 Phone: 310-555-5555 Fax: 310-555-4444 E-mail: alsbh@net.com San Francisco 35 Market Street San Francisco, CA 99876 Phone: 415-888-8888 Fax: 415-222-2222 E-mail: alssf@net.com	The Air Land Sea Travel Group, also known as the ALS Travel Group, has offices in Boston, New York, and two in California. ALS specializes in both corporate and leisure travel packages. The Corporate Travel Department services business clients throughout the country. The company has been in business for over 40 years and is known for its reliable service, great prices, and exclusive offers. The president of the company is Ms. Janice Pierce. The director of the Corporate Travel Department in New York is Mr. Wilson Jones. The director of the Leisure Travel Department is Ms. Robin Byron.	

Company Name and Contact Information	***Description of Company***	***Logo***
Green Brothers Gardening 32 Braddock Road Fairfax, VA 22030 Phone: 703-555-0005 Fax: 703-555-0015 E-mail: gbg@network.com Web: www.grenbros.com	Green Brothers Gardening, a full-service landscaping and nursery business, has three locations in and around Fairfax, Virginia. Calvin Green, the president and CEO, runs the business with his brother, Ralph Green, the chief financial officer. Maria Torres is their director of Marketing and Sales. They have an office and nursery staff in each store. They also employ workers on a daily basis. The firm handles lawn maintenance programs, tree and shrub planting, pruning, masonry, snow plowing, sanding, and landscape contracting. They carry unique specimen plants and cater to corporate as well as residential markets. They have a reputation for creating natural, lush landscaping.	GREEN BROTHERS GARDENING
Odyssey Travel Gear 445 Michigan Avenue Chicago, IL 60611 Phone: 630-222-8888 Fax: 630-666-8787 E-mail: otg@networld.com Web: www.otg.com	Odyssey Travel Gear offers products that make travel easier, such as luggage and luggage carts, garment bags, rain gear, money belts, sleep sacks, etc. The company has several retail stores, but most of their business comes from catalog and Internet sales. The retail stores are located in Chicago, Miami, Boston, Dallas, and San Diego. The company's headquarters are located in Chicago, Illinois. Ms. Jane McBride is the president and CEO. The Web site features new products, dozens of reduced-priced items from past catalogs, and lots of valuable information.	OTG odyssey travel group
Trilogy Productions California 101 Sunset Boulevard Beverly Hills, CA 90210 Phone (310) 505-0000 Fax (310) 606-0000 E-mail tpc@world.com *New York* 350 West 57 Street New York, NY 10106 Phone (212) 555-9999 Fax (212) 555-8900 E-mail: tpny@world.com	Trilogy Productions is a motion picture and television production company. John Alan, the current CEO (chief executive officer) and president, and Andrew Martin, the current CFO (chief financial officer) formed the company in 1990. Trilogy Productions deals with a number of Hollywood's top talent, including writers, directors, and filmmakers. They have released roughly 50 feature films and numerous Emmy-winning television programs. The Motion Picture and Television Divisions are located in the same building in Beverly Hills, California. Trilogy also maintains a small office in New York, which primarily handles all marketing and sales distribution. The director of Marketing and Sales is Christopher Manning. Ms. Cindy Napster is the manager of the Human Resources Department. She handles all employee-related matters for the New York and California offices.	TRILOGY PRODUCTIONS 3
In-Shape Fitness Centers 54 Cactus Drive Phoenix, AZ 85003 Phone: 602-555-1001 Fax: 602-555-1005 E-mail: inshape@net.com	In-Shape Fitness Centers began in Phoenix, Arizona with one location and quickly grew to four other locations within the Phoenix area. In-Shape Fitness is a high-quality health and fitness facility, which offers a wide range of exercise and fitness programs. The company's successful growth over a short time has been the result of its innovative fitness programs, well-trained staff, and dedication to quality and service. Mr. Robert Treadmill, president, retired this year and Ms. Alivea James has replaced him.	

Company Name and Contact Information	Description of Company	Logo
Occasions Event Planning *New York* 675 Third Avenue New York, NY 10017 Tel: 212-555-1234 Fax: 212-555-1230 *New Jersey* 1045 Palisades Avenue Fort Lee, NJ 07024 Phone: 201-555-4322 Fax: 201-555-4323 E-mail: oep@world.com	Occasions Event Planning offers full service gourmet catering, DJ's, live bands, recreational rentals, entertainment for children, vending machines, appliance rental, and more. Located in New York City, the Occasions Event Planning Company plans conferences, parties, seminars, and meetings. Recently, it opened a New Jersey office. Jane McBride is the president of the company.	
Four Corners Realty 450 Flora Boulevard Hollywood, FL 30025 Phone: 954-555-4433 Fax: 954-555-4412 E-mail: 4corners@world.net	Four Corners Realty is a real estate company located in Hollywood, Florida. It specializes in the sale and rental of residential and commercial properties. Dennis Halpern is the president and CEO (chief executive officer). The company has a large staff of associates servicing the Hollywood, Florida area and has been selling fine properties for more than 25 years.	
Time Out Sporting Goods *Barkely Store* 1412 Barkely Street Chicago, IL 60004 Phone: 874-555-1200 Fax: 874-555-1201 *Montrose Store* 235 Parsons Boulevard Chicago, IL 60075 Phone: 847-555-1950 Fax: 847-555-1951 E-mail: tosg@aom.com Web: www.timeout.com	Time Out Sporting Goods is a family-owned-and-operated retailer of sporting equipment, sporting apparel, and athletic footwear. Time Out has two stores in the Chicago area. The Barkely store is located in downtown Chicago, while the Montrose store is located in a suburb west of the city.	
Sutton Investment Group 34562 Corona Street Los Angeles, CA 90001 Phone: 213-555-6660 Fax: 213-555-6623 E-mail: Sutton@money.com Web: www.Sutton.com	Sutton Investment Group is a full-service investment company located in downtown Los Angeles. They service corporate and individual clients and provide investment, financial planning, and brokerage services. They offer their employees a full benefits package and have been in business for ten years.	

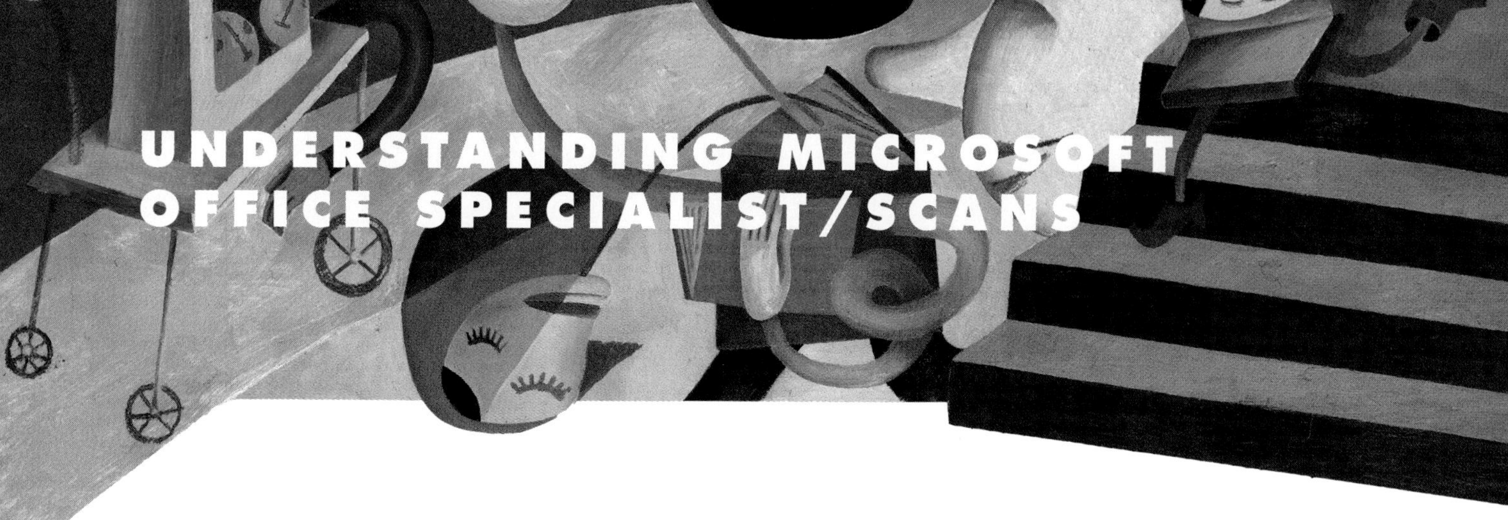

UNDERSTANDING MICROSOFT OFFICE SPECIALIST CERTIFICATION

What is certification?

The logo on the front cover indicates that the Microsoft Corporation has officially certified the book at the Specialist skill level for Office 2003 in Word, Excel, Access, and PowerPoint. This certification is part of the **Microsoft Office Specialist** program that validates your Office skills. For more information about the program, visit www.microsoft.com/learning/mcp/OfficeSpecialist/. Appendix A provides a chart that lists skill sets and activities, and references the page numbers in this text where the skill sets are discussed.

Why would I want to become certified?

- The Microsoft Office Specialist Program provides an industry-recognized standard for measuring an individual's mastery of Office applications.
- By passing one or more Microsoft Office Specialist Program certification exams, you demonstrate your proficiency in a given Office application to employers.
- Individuals who pass one or more exams can gain a competitive edge in the job marketplace.

Where does testing take place?

To be certified, you will need to take an exam from a third-party testing company called an Authorization Certification Testing Center. Call **800-933-4493** at Nivo International to find the location of the testing center nearest you. Learn more about the criteria for testing and what is involved. Tests are conducted on different dates throughout the calendar year. Course Technology, a division of Thomson Learning, has developed an entire line of training materials.

Skills Assessment Software

Use SAM 2003, our skills assessment software, to gauge students' readiness for the Microsoft Office Specialist certification exams for Microsoft Office 2003. Through predefined prep exams that map back to skills taught in Course Technology textbooks, your students will have the tools they need to pass the certification exam with flying colors. For more information, visit www.course.com.

UNDERSTANDING SCANS: SECRETARY'S COMMISSION ON ACHIEVING NECESSARY SKILLS

The Secretary's Commission on Achieving Necessary Skills (SCANS) from the U.S. Department of Labor was asked to examine the demands of the workplace and whether new learners are capable of meeting those demands. Specifically, the Commission was directed to advise the Secretary on the level of skills required to enter employment. In carrying out this charge, the Commission was asked to do the following:

- Define the skills needed for employment.
- Propose acceptable levels of proficiency.
- Suggest effective ways to assess proficiency.
- Develop a dissemination strategy for the nation's schools, businesses, and homes.

SCANS research verified that what we call workplace know-how defines effective job performance today. This know-how has two elements: competencies and a foundation. The SCANS report defines five competencies and a three-part foundation of skills and personal qualities that lie at the heart of job performance. These eight requirements are essential preparation for all students, whether they are entering the workforce, continuing in a present work environment, or planning further education.

SCANS workplace competencies and foundation skills have been integrated into Microsoft Office 2003. The workplace competencies are identified as: 1) ability to use resources, 2) interpersonal skills, 3) ability to work with information, 4) understanding of systems, and 5) knowledge and understanding of technology. The foundation skills are identified as 1) basic communication skills, 2) thinking skills, and 3) personal qualities.

Please refer to the correlation document on the Instructor Resources CD-ROM for specifics on how the topics in this text meet these requirements.

TABLE OF CONTENTS

PREFACE

INTRODUCTION TO COMPUTERS

PERFORMANCE BASICS

LESSON 1 Office Basics

LESSON 2 Internet Basics

PERFORMING WITH WORD

LESSON 1 Word Basics

PERFORMING WITH WORD

PERFORMING WITH EXCEL

PERFORMING WITH EXCEL

PERFORMING WITH ACCESS

PERFORMING WITH POWERPOINT

FINAL PROJECT

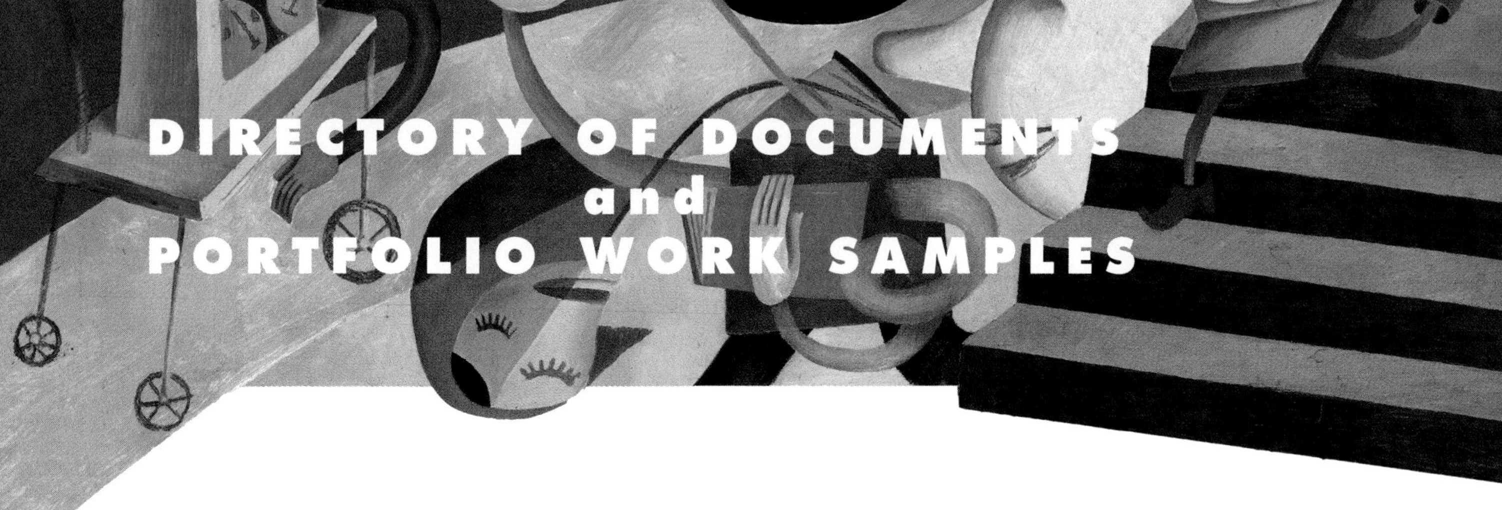

DIRECTORY OF DOCUMENTS and PORTFOLIO WORK SAMPLES

DIRECTORY OF DOCUMENTS

The document types indicated on the left can be found in the Units and Pages noted on the right.

PORTFOLIO WORK SAMPLES

You may use the documents that you produce in the Performance Phase of each Lesson and the Final Project as your portfolio work samples. Include all rough (first) copies along with the final document.

A
1
2
3

DIRECTORIES

Directory of Word Files

Lesson	Section	Task No.	Data	Solution
1	Tryout	1	w1.4pf spelling	
	Rehearsal	1	1.1correct	
			w1.6marina views	
	Tryout	2	w1.6pf move	
			w1.7marina views	
	Rehearsal	2		s1.2wordwrap
	Tryout	3	w1.8pf	
			w1.10 edit	
			w1.12pf move	
			w1.14of spelling & grammer	
			w1.16marina views	
			w1.17pf print	
	Rehearsal	3	1.3wordwrap	s1.3wordwrap
	Tryout	4	w1.18 font practice	
			w1.20pf painter	
			w1.21pf highlighter	
	Rehearsal	4	1.4ad	s1.4ad
2	Tryout	1	w2.1pf letter	
	Rehearsal	1		s2.1employment
	Tryout	2	w2.6alignments	
			w2.7pf letter	
	Rehearsal	2		s2.2apply
	Rehearsal	3		s2.3memo
	Tryout	4	w2.13 pf letter	
	Rehearsal	4		s2.4followup
	Performance	Act I		s2.p1dallas
		Act II		s2.p2alslet
				s2.p2sanfran
		Act III		s2p.3osha
3	Tryout	1	w3.1pf2	
			w3.2pf	
			w3.3pf	
			w3.4pf	
	Rehearsal	1	3.1car	s3.1buycar
	Tryout	2	w 3.5pf2	
			w 3.6pf2	
			w 3.8pf	
			w 3.9pf	
	Rehearsal	2		s3.2jobsearch
				s3.2jobsearch cover
			3.2jobsearch	s3.2jobsearch biblio
	Tryout	3	w3.12pf styles	
			w3.14pf thesaurus	
			w3.15pf letter	
			w3.16pf realty	
			w3.16pf insert	
	Rehearsal	3	3.3benefits text	s3.3benefits
			3.3education	s3.3benefits.1

Directory of Word Files

Lesson	Section	Task No.	Data	Solution
	Tryout	4	w3.17pf comments	
			w3.18 track changes	
			w3.19pf compare documents	
			w3.19pf compare documents1	
			w3.20pf compare documents	
	Rehearsal	4	3.4draft document	s3.4draft document1
	Performance	Act I		s3p.travel guide
		Act II	3p.maps	s3p.travel guide1
			s3p.guide cover	
4	Tryout	1		s4.1pf outline
			w4.3 outline	
	Rehearsal	1		s4.1inshape
				s4.1inshape1
	Tryout	2	w4.7pf table	
	Rehearsal	2		s4.2minutes
				s4.2feedback form
				s4.2feedback form1
	Tryout	3	w4.8pf table	
			w4.10pf table	
			w4.11pf table	
	Rehearsal	3	4.3minutes	s4.3minutes
				s4.3minutes1
			4.3.feedback form1	s4.3.feedback form
	Tryout	4	w4.14pf table tabs	
	Rehearsal	4		s4.4 itinerary
				s4.4fitness schedule
				s4.4hearings
	Performance	Act I		s4.p1 expense form
		Act II		s4.p2 agenda
		Act III		s4.p3 brussels
		Act IV		s4.p4 conference
5	Tryout	1	w5.1pf letter spacing	
			w5.6pf text wrap	
	Rehearsal	1		s5.1press release
				s5.1 flyer
	Tryout	2	w5.15pf text wrap	
			w5.16pf shapes	
	Rehearsal	2	5.2ad text	s5.2 advertisement
				s5.2 catalog page
			5.2 newsletter text	s5.2 newsletter
	Performance	Act I		s5.p1 barbeque
		Act II	5.p2 airlines	s5.p2 airlines ad
		Act III	5.p3 als newstext	s5.p3 als news
6	Tryout	1	6.1pf ski table1	
	Rehearsal	1		s6.1invite final
			6.1ALS letterhead	s6.1ski vacation letter
			6.1table	

Continued on next page

Directory of Word Files

Lesson	Section	Task No.	Data	Solution
	Tryout	2	w6.3pf golf	
			w6.4pf golf outing	
			w6.7fitness	
	Rehearsal	2	6.2 catalog page	s6.2 catalog
			6.2fitness locations	
			6.2weekend schedule	
			6.2inshape newsletter	
			6.2new employee meeting	s6.2fitness web
	Tryout	3	6.3themes	
			6.3 occasions price list	
	Rehearsal	3	6.3 occasions web text	s6.3occasions home page
	Rehearsal	4	6.4siglet	
				s6.4support
				s6.4support final
	Performance	Act I		s6.p1alsradio
				6.p1als clients
		Act II	6.p2ski week	
			6.1pf ski table1	6.p2als web

Directory of Excel Files

Lesson	Section	Task No.	Data	Solution
2	Tryout	1	E2-2	
			E2-3	
			E2-4	
			E2-5	E2-5
				E2-5a
	Rehearsal	1		s.2.1proinv
				s.2.1solution
	Tryout	2	E2-6	
			E2-7	
			E2-8	
			E2-9	
			E2-10	
			E2-11	
			E2-12	
			E2-13	
			E2-14	s.E2-14
	Rehearsal	2		s.2.2purord
	Tryout	3	E2-16	
	Rehearsal	3		s.2.3invoice (xlt)
				s.2.3invoice (xls)
				s.2.3timeout
	Performance	Act I	2p1.proinv	2p1.bill
		Act II		s.2p2.otginv (xlt)
				s.2p2.bertle
		Act III		s.2p3.quote (xlt)
				s.2p3.quote (xls)
				s.2p3.quotecarson
3	Tryout	1	E3-1	
			E3-2	
			E3-3	
			E3-4	s.E3-4
			E3-5	s.E3-5
	Rehearsal	1	3.1account	s.3.1account
			3.1statement	s.3.1statement
	Tryout	2	E3-6	
			E3-7	
			E3-8	E3-8
	Rehearsal	2	3.2journal	s.3.2journal
	Tryout	3	E3-9	
			E3-10	

Directory of Excel Files

Lesson	Section	Task No.	Data	Solution
			E3-11	
			E3-12	s.E3-12
	Reherasal	3	3.3payroll	s.3.3payroll
	Tryout	4	E3-13	
			E3-14	
			E3-15	
			E3-16	s.E3-16
	Rehearsal	4	3.4expense	s.3.4expense
	Performance	Act I	3p1.salejour	s.3p1.salejour
		Act II	3p2.payroll	s.3p2.payroll
		Act III	3p3.expense	s.3p3.expense (xlt)
				s.3p3.exp1012
4	Tryout	1	E4-1	
			E4-2	
			E4-3	s.E4-3
			E4-4	
			E4-5	
			E4-5a	
	Rehearsal	1	4.1budget	s.4.1budget
	Tryout	2	E4-6	
			E4-7	
			E4-8	
			E4-9	s.E4-9
			E4-10	s.E4-10
			E4-11	s.E4-12
	Rehearsal	2	4.2is	s.4.2is
				s.4.2is (html)
	Tryout	3	E4-13	
			E4-14	s.E4-14
			E4-15	
			E4-16	
			E4-17	
			E4-18	s.E4-18
	Rehearsal	3	4.3revenue	s.4.3revenue
	Tryout	4	E4-19	
			E4-20	s.E4-20
			E4-21	
			E4-22	
			E4-23	
			E4-24	s.E4-24
	Rehearsal	4	4.4options	s.4.4options
	Performance	Act I	4p1.budget	s.4p1.budget
		Act II	4p2.incomebk	s.4p2.incomebk
		Act III	4p3.warehouse	s.4p3.warehouse
5	Tryout	1	E5-1	s.E5-1
			E5-2a	
			E5-2	s.E5-2
			E5-3	s.E5-3
			E5-3a	s.E5.3a
			E5-4	s.E5-4
			E5-4a	s.E5-4a
			E5-5	s.E5-5
			E5-5a	s.E5-5a
	Rehearsal	1	5.1sched	s.5.1sched
			5.1tb	s.5.2tb
	Tryout	2	E5-8	
			E5-9	
			E5-10	
			E5-11	s.E5-11
			E5-12	
			E5-13	s.E5-13

Continued on next page

Directory of Excel Files

Lesson	Section	Task No.	Data	Solution
	Rehearsal	2	5.2bonus	s.5.2bonus
			5.2worksheet	s.5.2worksheet
	Tryout	3	E5-14	
			E5-15	
			E5-13logo	
			E5-16	s.E5-16
	Rehearsal	3	5.3income	s.5.3income
	Tryout	4	E5-17	
			E5-18	
			E5-19	
			E5-20	s.E5-20
			E5-21	
			E5-22	s.E5-22
	Rehearsal	4	5.4balsheet	s.5.4balsheet
	Performance	Act I	5p1.sched	s.5p1.sched
			5p1.trialbal	s.5p1.trialbal
		Act II	5p2.cis	s.5p2.cis
		Act III	5p3.worksheet	s.5p3.worksheet
			5p3.balsheet	s.5p3.balsheet
6	Tryout	1	E6-1	
			E6-2	
			E6-3	
			E6-4	
			E6-5	s.E6-5
			E6-6	
			E6-7	s.E6-7
	Rehearsal A	1	6.1salechart	s.6.1salechart
	Rehearsal B	1	6.1expchart	s.6.1expchart
	Tryout	2	E6-8	s.E6-8
			E6-9	s.E6-9
			E6-10	s.E6-10
			E6-11	s.E6-11
			E6-12	s.E6-12
	Rehearsal	2	6.2portfolio	s.6.2portfolio
	Performance	Act I	6p1.income	s.6p1.income
		Act II	6p2.expense	s.6p2.expense
		Act III	6p3.stock	s.6p3.stock
7	Tryout	1	E7-1	
			E7-1WD	
			E7-2	
			E7-2WD	s.E7-2WD
			E7-3	
			E7-3WD	s.E7-3WD
			E7-4	s.E7-4
			E7-4WD	s.E7-4WD
			E7-5WD	s.E7-5WD
	Rehearsal	1	7.1benefits	s.7.1benefits
			7.1rates	s.7.1rates
			7.1calcmemo	s.7.1calcmemo
	Tryout	2	E7-6	
			E7-6WD	
			E7-7	s.E7-7
			E7-7WD	s.E7-7WD
			E7-8	s.E7-8
			E7-8WD	s.E7-8WD
			E7-9	s.E7-9
			E7-10	s.E7-10
			E7-11	s.E7-11
				s.E7-11txt
				s.E7-11csv
			E7-12	s.E7-12
				s.E7-12txt
				s.E7-12csv
	Rehearsal	2	7.2stocks	s.7.2stocks
				s.7.2stocks (txt)
				s.7.2stockscsv
			7.2broker	
	Performance	Act I	7p1.tips	s.7p1.tips
			7p1.currency	s.7p1.currency
			7p1.travel guide	s.7p1.travel guide
		Act II	7p1.income	s.7p1.income
			7p1.quarterly	s.7p1.quarterly

Directory of PowerPoint Files

Lesson	Section	Task No.	Data	Solution
1	Tryout	1	1.1latte	
	Rehearsal	1	1.losangelestv	
	Tryout	2	1.2vienna	
			1.1admissions	
	Rehearsal	2	1.2traveltips	
2	Rehearsal	1		2.1isstrategy
	Tryout	2	p2.10latte	
			p2.11entreport	
	Rehearsal	2		s.2.2houseplant
	Tryout	3	p2.15neworleans	
			p2.16neworleans	
	Rehearsal	3		s.2.3overview
	Performance	Act I		s.pp2trilogy
		Act II		s.pp2madrid
3	Tryout	1	p3.1admissions	s3.1Admissions
			p3.3membership	
			p3.4retire401k	
	Rehearsal	1		s3.1retire401
	Rehearsal	2	3.2summerproposal	s3.2summerproposal
				s3.2summertemplate
	Tryout	3	p3.10inshape	
			p3.11customshows	
			p3.12customshows	
	Rehearsal	3		s.3.3landscaping
	Tryout	4	p3.21neworleans	
	Rehearsal	4		s3.4goldstar
			3.4agenda	
			3.4wedcake	
			3.4present	
				s3.4creative sales
	Performance	Act I		s.pp3undercover
		Act II		s.pp3partnership
4	Tryout	1	p4.7training	
	Rehearsal	1		s4.1realty
	Tryout	2	p4.8neworleans	
			p4.11charts	
			p4.13neworleans	
			p4.14devon	
			p4.15wedcake	
			p4.15paris	
			p4.15iceberg	
	Rehearsal	2		s4.2training
				s4.2broker
				s4.2photoalbum
				s4.2brokeralbum
	Tryout	3	p4.16devon	
	Rehearsal	3		s4.3seniors
	Performance	Act I		spp4recruit
		Act II		spp4odysseyoutdoors

Continued on next page

Directory of PowerPoint Files

Lesson	Section	Task No.	Data	Solution
5	Tryout	1	p5.1pfmeeting	
			p5.1pfoutline	
			p5.2membership	
			p5.3pfbudget	
			p5.4pftable	
			p5.5pfundercover	
			p5.5pfstation	
	Rehearsal	1	5.1ooutline	
			5.1highlightstable	
			5.1salechart	
			5.1yearahead	s5.1tofinancial
	Tryout	2	p5.6collegeplan	
			p5.7collegeplan	
			p5.8brand	
			p5.9collegeplan	
			p5.9brand	
	Rehearsal	2	5.2realty	s5.3realty
	Tryout	3	p5.10devon	
	Rehearsal	3	5.3greenbros	s5.3newproducts
				s5.3newproducts (mhtml)
	Performance	Act I		spp5trilogy
			pp5undercover	
			pp5boxoffice	
			pp5releaseschedule	
		Act II	pp5income	
			pp5outline	
				spp5airlandsea
			pp5competition	spp5competition
			pp5recommendation	

Directory of Access Files

Lesson	Section	Task No.	Data	Solution
1	Tryout	1	A1-3	
			A1-4	
			A1-5	
	Rehearsal	1	Members	
2	Tryout	1		A2-1
			A2-3	
			A2-4	
			A2-5	
			A2-6	A2-6
	Rehearsal	1		2EMP
	Tryout	2		A2-7
			A2-8	
			A2-9	A2-9
			A2-10	
			A2-11	A2-11
	Rehearsal	2	2EMP2	2EMP2
	Performance	Act I		s.trilogy employees1
				s.trilogy employees2
3	Tryout	1	Members	
			A3-5	
			A3-6	
			A3-7	s.A3-7members
			A3-8	
	Rehearsal	1	Four Corners Realty	s.Four Corners Realty
	Tryout	2	Members2	
			A3-11	
			A3-12	
			A3-13	
			A3-14	s.A3-14members
				s.A3-15members
			Product	s.Product

Directory of Access Files

Lesson	Section	Task No.	Data	Solution
	Rehearsal	1	Four Corners Realty2	s.Four Corners Realty2
	Performance	Act I/ Act II	Green Brothers Gardening	s.Green Brothers Gardening
4	Tryout	1	Members	
			A4-3	
			A4-4	
			A4-5	
			A4-6	s.A4-6
	Rehearsal	1	Four Corners Realty	
	Tryout	2	A4-7	
			A4-9	
			A4-10	
			A4-11	
			A4-12	
			A4-13	
	Rehearsal	2	Four Corners Realty.2	s.Four Corners Realty.2
	Tryout	3	A4-14	s.A4-14
			A4-15	s.A4-15
			A4-16	s.A4-16
			A4-17	
			A4-19	s.A4-19
	Rehearsal	3	Four Corners Realty.3	Four Corners Realty.3
	Performance	Act I	ALS	s.ALS
		Act II	ALS2	s.ALS2
5	Tryout	1	A5-1	
			A5-2	
			A5-3	
			A5-4	
			A5-5	
	Rehearsal	1	Four Corners Realty	s.Four Corners Realty
	Tryout	2	A5-6	
			A5-7	
			A5-8	s.A5-8
			A5-9	
			A5-10	s.A5-10
	Rehearsal	2	Four Corners Realty1	s.Four Corners Realty1
	Performance	Act I	ALS	s.ALS
		Act II	ALS2	s.ALS2
6	Tryout	1	A6-1	s.A6-1
			FourCornersRealty	
			A6-2	
			Members (xls)	
			A6-3	s.A6-3
			New Members (xls)	
			A6-4	
			Suppliers	s.Suppliers
			A6-5	ALL MEMBERS (xls)
			A6-6	ALL MEMBERS (rtf)
			ALL MEMBERS (rtf)	
	Rehearsal	1	FourCornersRealty1	s.Four Corners Realty1
			Rental Listings (xls)	Rental Listings
				Rental Listings_files
				s.Listings (xls)
				Agents (doc)
	Tryout	2	A6-7	s.A6-7BU
			A6-8	
			A6-9	s.A6-9
			A6-10	
			A6-11	ALL MEMBERS (html)
			A6-12	s.A6-12

Continued on next page

Directory of Access Files

Lesson	Section	Task No.	Data	Solution
	Rehearsal	2	FourCornersRealty2	s.Four Corners Realty2
				FCRBackup
				Listings (html)
				Listings_files
	Performance	Act I	ALS	s.ALS
			Prospects (xls)	Prospects (rtf)
				Prospects (html)
				Prospects_files
				Customers (rtf)
				Customers (html)
				Customers_files
		Act II	ALS2	s.ALS2
				s.ALSBU

Directory of Final Performance Files

Lesson	Section	Task No.	Data	Solution
			Conference Details	
				s.pressrelease
				s.flyer
			chofcom	s.chofcom
			chcomlet	s.mergelet
				s.web page home
				s.web page exhibitors1
				s.web page events
				s.web page breakout
				s.web page registration
			data	s.data
			map	s.conference program
			finalbud	s.finalbud
				s.presentation

1
2
3

Introduction to Computers

NOTE TO STUDENTS Read this section carefully so you have an understanding of the computer, its history, hardware and software applications, the Internet, telecommunications, and related topics.

INTRODUCTION

Thirty-five years ago, few people handled computers. Computer users were limited to specially trained operators and engineers.

No one ever anticipated that today every office worker must work with computers and that most people use computers in their everyday lives—both at home and at school.

Therefore, it is important to learn about the parts of a computer, how a computer operates, some of the tasks a computer can perform, and the many responsibilities of being a computer user. It is also important to understand how the computer you are using today evolved and how this incredible tool can give you access to one of the greatest sources of information—the Internet.

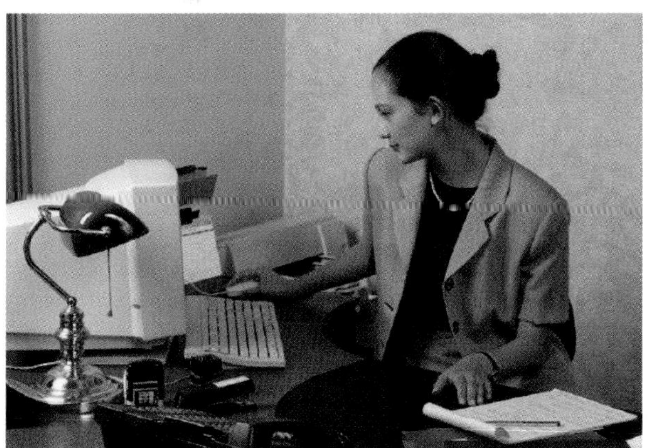

BRIEF HISTORY OF COMPUTERS

Although the microcomputer, or *PC* (personal computer), was developed in the early 1980s, computers have been around for a long time. A major step in computer technology was the development in the early 1800s of machines that could be programmed. The operation was controlled by cards with holes punched in them. In 1886, an electric punch-card machine was developed that could be used with electricity. In 1890, the U.S. Census results were tabulated for the first time with this new electrically driven punch-card tabulator.

In 1944, engineers from IBM and Howard Aiken of Harvard University developed a 50-foot-long, 8-foot-high machine that was able to add, subtract, multiply, divide, and refer to data tables using punched cards.

In 1945, a team from the University of Pennsylvania developed a machine for the U.S. Army's Ballistics Research Lab. This machine could make calculations a thousand times faster than earlier devices. The machine weighed in at approximately 30 tons and covered about 1,000 square feet of floor space.

In 1947, a method was developed for storing programs electronically. This invention of storing programs led the way for the development of today's computers. Before this invention, computers were wired to perform only certain tasks. If you wanted to change the task, the computer had to be rewired.

The first machine to be called a computer was completed in 1948. In 1951, the first commercial computer was completed. Eight of them were sold.

Besides becoming more versatile, computers were becoming faster, cheaper, and smaller. Computers were designed to perform tasks that responded to machine instructions. One of the original IBM computers could perform about 2,000 instructions per second. By the mid-1970s, operating speed had increased by more than 2,000%, to 43,000 instructions per second. By the late 1980s, computers had begun to be rated in ***MIPS (millions of instructions per second).*** Today's fastest supercomputers can handle well over a billion instructions per second.

The development of tiny silicon chips led the way for desktop microcomputers, or PCs. Microcomputers were first introduced in the mid-1970s. At that time, these small computers had limited memory and storage ability. Two major developments occurred in the early 1970s that led the way for the incredible growth of the computer industry. In 1975, Steve Jobs and Steve Wozniak started Apple Computer in the Jobs' family garage and, also in 1975, Paul Allen and Bill Gates established their own company, Microsoft.

Today's modern PC is the direct result of the advancements made by Apple Computer and IBM in hardware and software development, Microsoft in software development, and chip manufacturers such as Motorola and Intel in processor development. These advancements have brought us computers that have thousands of times the capability of those much larger computer systems of years ago—and at a fraction of the cost.

THE COMPUTER SYSTEM

A ***computer*** is an electronic device that can perform tasks and calculations based on the instructions that have been given to it.

How a Computer System Works

Although computers amaze us with their apparent "intelligence," all of their functions are based on these three very simple tasks:

- Compare numbers or symbols to see if they are the same
- Add two numbers together
- Subtract one number from another

Computers can perform these tasks with great speed, accuracy, and reliability. Data is entered into the computer, the computer processes the data, and displays the desired information. How does the computer know what to do with the data? A ***software program,*** a detailed set of computer instructions installed in the computer, tells the computer what to do.

There are two types of computer software programs. One is *system program software,* which controls the way computer parts work together. The other is *application program software,* which tells the computer to perform a specific task. (See later section on software.)

Types of Computers

Computers vary in type, size, speed, and capability. The most common type of computer used in homes, offices, and schools is the ***personal computer*** (more commonly known as the ***PC***), a computer that is small enough to fit on a desk, is relatively inexpensive, and is designed for an individual user. ***Laptop computers*** (also called *notebooks*), which are portable, also fall into this category.

Other types of computers include the following:

- *Supercomputer*
  The ***supercomputer*** is the fastest type of computer. It can store data and perform numerous tasks simultaneously at incredible speeds. This type of computer is used for specialized tasks that require vast amounts of mathematical calculations such as weather forecasting and medical and weapons research. Usually comprising many computers working in unison, the supercomputer is used only by government agencies, educational institutions, and large corporations.

- *Mainframe*
  Mainframe computers are less powerful and less expensive than supercomputers, but they are still capable of storing and processing large amounts of data. Several hundred individuals can use a mainframe, with their own terminals, at the same time. These computers are used most often by universities, medical institutions, and large companies such as banks and brokerage houses, where it is necessary

to complete millions of daily transactions and save corresponding amounts of data.

- *Minicomputer*
  The ***minicomputer***, also called a ***server,*** is smaller than a mainframe, is larger than a microcomputer, and can support multiple users, with their own terminals, at the same time. Medium-sized companies, such as accounting, advertising, and manufacturing firms, use these computers.

Computer Memory

Computer memory is composed of circuits that are contained in tiny computer chips. The number of memory locations is stated in terms of bytes. A ***byte*** is a unit of storage capable of holding a single character. A byte is equal to 8 bits. Large amounts of memory are indicated in terms of ***kilobytes*** (K or KB), ***megabytes*** (M or MB), and ***gigabytes*** (G or GB). A ***kilobyte*** is equal to 1,024 bytes, a ***megabyte*** is equal to 1,048,576 bytes, and a ***gigabyte*** is equal to 1,073,741,824 bytes. Twenty megabytes of memory can hold data equivalent to what could be saved on one box of floppy disks.

Every computer comes with a certain amount of physical memory, usually referred to as main memory or ***random access memory (RAM)***. Think of main memory as an array of boxes, each of which can hold a single byte of information. A computer that has 1 megabyte of memory, therefore, can hold about 1 million bytes (or characters) of information.

Read-only memory, or ***ROM,*** is computer memory on which data has been prerecorded. Data recorded on a ROM chip can only be read; it cannot be deleted. Unlike RAM, ROM preserves its contents even when the computer is shut down. Personal computers contain some ROM memory that stores critical programs, such as those needed for system start-up, for example.

Processing Power

A computer's procesing speed (also known as clock speed) is measured in ***megahertz*** (mHz) and ***gigahertz*** (gHz). In 1993, the average computer processing speed was 25 mHz. By the end of 1994, processing speed increased to 66 mHz for the PC. The 486DX2 chip was new, and there was talk about two new revolutionary chips from Motorola and IBM—the PowerPC and Pentium chips.

The PowerPC was developed by 1996 and its chip speed started at 60 mHz and was capable of running at 120 mHz—unheard of in 1996. The Pentium matched these speeds. Within a year, chip speeds increased exponentially. Today, the PowerPC can run in excess of 1 gHz, and the current speed for a Pentium 4 is over 3 gHz.

Although processor speed is one of the major factors of computer speed, several other significant factors give a computer a greater operating speed. In addition to faster RAM (the memory chips that hold data when the computer is running), computers now take advantage of a data buffer called ***cache*** (pronounced "cash"). Cache is a series of superfast RAM chips that allow the processor to communicate more quickly and efficiently with the rest of the computer.

As for the future, both Motorola and Intel are working on the next-generation processor, again exceeding current processing speeds. These advancements in technology will be a step toward computers 100 billion times as fast as today's most powerful personal computers.

PARTS OF A COMPUTER

A computer system is made up of two principal components: hardware and software.

Computer hardware

Hardware

Hardware refers to the physical parts of the computer and includes four main components: input devices, processing unit, output devices, and storage devices.

Input Devices ***Input devices*** transport data into the computer.

- *Keyboard*
  The ***keyboard*** is the most commonly used input device. It contains typewriter-like keys as well as specialized keys for entering data.

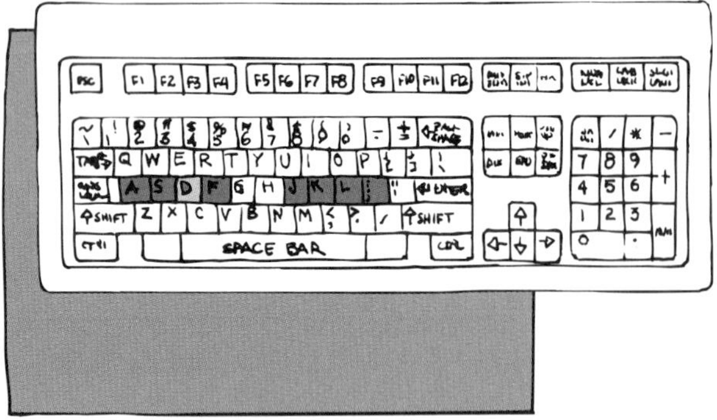

- *Mouse, pointing stick, trackball, light pen, puck, and touchpad*
  These small alternative input devices direct the movement of the pointer on the screen.

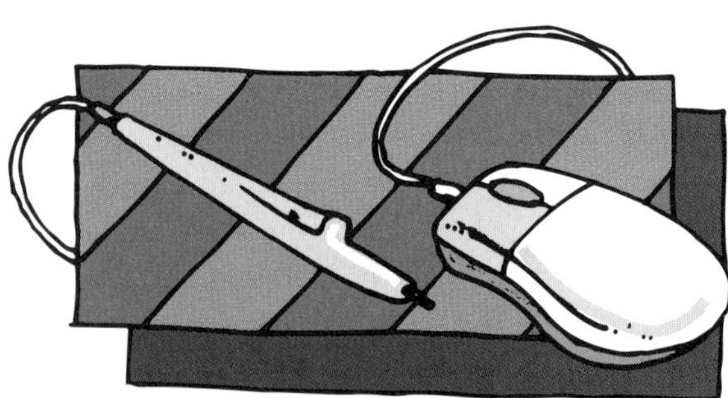

- *Optical character recognition (OCR) system*
  This device scans the printed page and translates characters and images into a computer file that can be edited (by a word processing application, for example).

- *Scanner*
  A ***scanner*** is a device that can read text or illustrations and transmit them in a digitized format to the computer screen. Scanners can be handheld or as large as a photocopy machine.

- *Digital camera*
  This is a filmless camera that captures images into memory storage. A ***digital camera's*** images can be transferred to a computer and edited or inserted into a document.

- *Video input camcorder*
  A ***video input camcorder*** is a digital video camera that can record live audio and video, which can then be downloaded into a computer for multimedia applications.

- *Microphone*
  A ***microphone*** accepts voice input to enter data or execute commands.

Processing Unit The processing unit, also referred to as microprocessor or ***CPU*** (***central processing unit***), is the "brains" of the computer. This piece of hardware contains the computer chips and circuits that control and manipulate data to produce information.

Output Devices ***Output devices*** allow the user to see or hear the information the computer compiles.

- *Printers*
  Printers are devices that print text or graphics on paper. Printers come in a variety of types and are categorized as either impact or nonimpact. An *impact printer* uses a device that strikes a ribbon on paper; *nonimpact printers* use laser

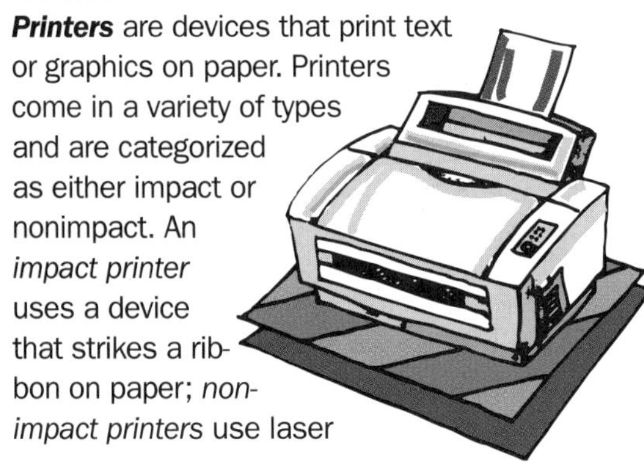

and inkjet technology. The quality of the print and the printing speed determine the cost of a printer.

- *Monitor*
  A ***monitor,*** also known as a ***display, CRT*** (cathode ray tube), ***VDT*** (video display terminal), or simply ***computer screen,*** allows the user to view computer information. Computer screens vary in size and cost depending on their ***resolution,*** which is the clarity and sharpness of an on-screen image. If you look closely at a computer screen, you will see that it is made up of a series of ***pixels,*** which is a series of dots. The more closely packed the pixels, the higher the resolution of the image.

- *Speakers*
  Speakers are devices that amplify sound. Speakers can be internal or external to the computer.

Storage Devices ***Storage devices*** allow instructions and data to be saved. Some storage devices are housed within the computer; others are removable and thus allow data to be transported from one computer to another.

- *Hard drive*
  A ***hard drive,*** an internal storage device, is also known as a "fixed" disk. Hard drives can hold huge amounts of information. The size of the drive, that is, how much information it can save, affects the price of the computer. A computer that has one "gig" (gigabyte) of storage capacity can hold 1 billion bytes of information.

- *Floppy disks*
  Floppy disks (often called *diskettes*) are bendable, oxide-coated, magnetic plastic with a hard cover that can be inserted and removed from a disk drive. The 3½" floppy disk can store 1.4 MB of data.

- *Zip disks*
  Zip disks are larger versions of floppy disks. Each Zip disk holds as much information as 80 floppy disks (about 100 megabytes). Zip disks require a Zip drive, which can be connected inside or outside of the computer.

- *CD-ROM disks*
  These disks can store huge amounts of data (approximately 650 megabytes, or about 500 floppy disks). Because of their large storage capability, ***CD-ROMs*** are often used to save graphics, video, and audio. CD-ROM disks require a CD-ROM drive.

- *DAT (digital audio tape)*
  Digital audio tape is a standard magnetic tape that resembles basic audiocassettes. DATs have the ability to hold tremendous amounts of information on a tape much smaller than an audiocassette. DAT devices can hold up to 10 separate DAT tapes, each of which can hold up to 26 gigabytes of information.

Software

Software is a set of instructions written by programmers in a machine (or programming) language that tells the computer what to do, how to do it, and how to perform tasks based on input from the user. The numerous ***programming languages*** include FORTRAN, COBOL, BASIC, C, C++, Java, JavaScript, Visual Basic, Visual C++, and RPG.

The words "software," "program," and "application" are used interchangeably. There are two types of software: operating system software and application software. Application software (like Microsoft Office) can run only when operating system software (like Windows XP) is installed and running on a computer. Operating system software can be compared to the foundation of a house; application software can be compared to the rooms within the house.

Operating System Software The basic operation of the computer is controlled by ***operating system software.*** This type of software manages the computer's files and programs and acts as a graphic interface that translates mouse and keyboard actions into appropriate programming code. There are many types of operating systems, each having different capabilities. Some operating systems can run only a single application at a time; others can multitask and run several at once. The most popular operating systems include Microsoft Windows and Apple Computer's Mac OS. Others include IBM's OS/2 Warp, Microsoft DOS (Disk Operating System), Linux, and UNIX, a text-based command-line interface operating system.

Some operating systems were created specifically for use on a network. These include Novell NetWare, AppleShare IP, Microsoft Windows for Workgroups, and Microsoft Windows NT Server.

Application Software Sometimes referred to as "tool" software, ***application software*** provides the tools needed to complete a task. Tool software is widely used by business, government, schools, and individuals for anything from financial management, Web surfing, and word processing to sound engineering, graphic design, and cooking.

These are the most common types of application software:

- *Word processing*
  Word processing software is used to create and print documents such as letters, memos, and reports. This type of software allows for easy editing of text. Microsoft Word is an example of word processing software.

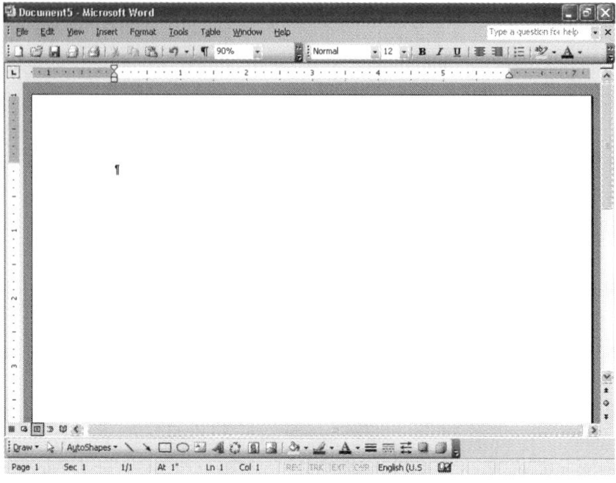

- *Spreadsheet*
  Spreadsheet software is used for analysis and reporting of statistical or numerical data to complete such tasks as preparing budgets, payroll, balance sheets, and profit and loss statements. Spreadsheet software can create charts from statistical information. Microsoft Excel and Lotus 1-2-3 are examples of spreadsheet software.

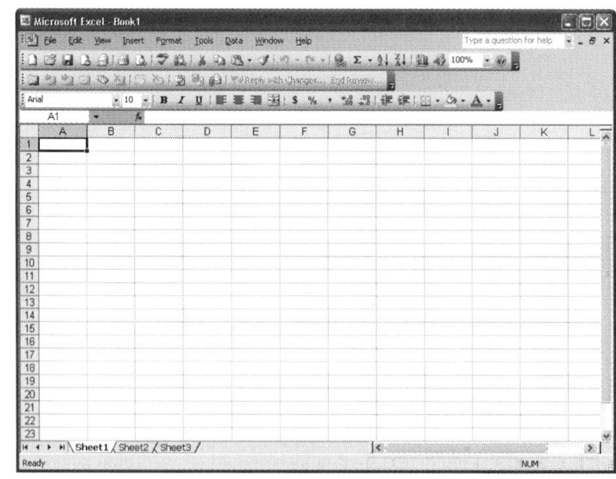

- *Database*
  Database software allows the user to collect, store, organize, modify, and extract data. Microsoft Access is an example of database software.

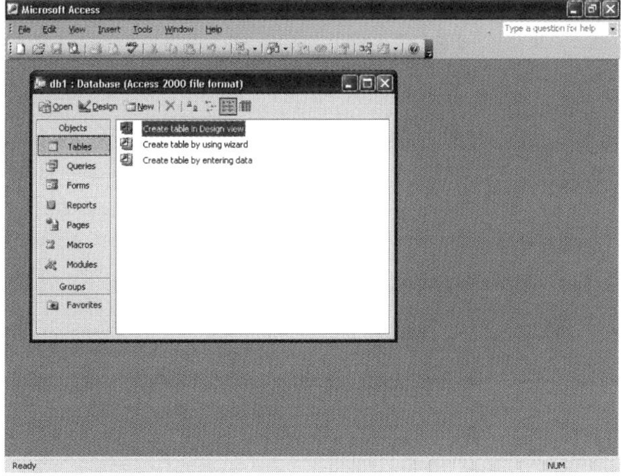

- *Accounting*
  Accounting software is used for organizing and managing money and finances. QuickBooks is an example of this type of software.
- *Groupware*
  Groupware is software that helps groups of users communicate and organize activities, meetings, and events through one common interface. For example, group software is used within corporations so all employees can share the same common screens on their computers. Lotus Notes is an example of groupware.
- *Communication*
  Communication software is used to transmit and receive information from one computer to another. For the transfer to take place, both the receiver and the sender must have the software installed.
- *Internet browser*
  Internet browser software is used to locate and display Web pages. The most popular Internet browsers are Netscape Navigator and Microsoft Internet Explorer.

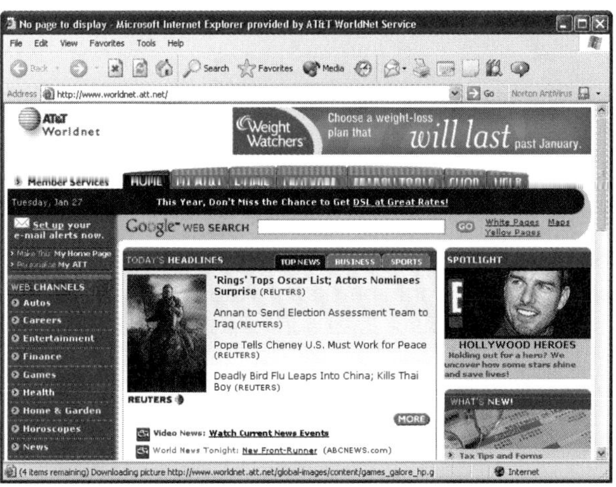

- *E-mail program*
  E-mail program software is used to send and retrieve e-mail from a mail server. Outlook is an example of an e-mail program. Many e-mail programs (like Outlook) are now part of other software applications. For example, you can e-mail from within all Microsoft Office 2003 applications.
- *Online service*
  Online service software provides subscribers with the ability to communicate with one another, through e-mail, for example, as well as connect with unlimited third-party information providers, such as news, weather, and sports bureaus. America Online and MindSpring are examples of online service software. Access to this information also requires communications equipment. (See section on Telecommunications.)

- *Presentation*
  Presentation software is used to create slides that can be shown while an oral report is given. The slides often summarize report data and emphasize report highlights. Microsoft PowerPoint is an example of presentation software.

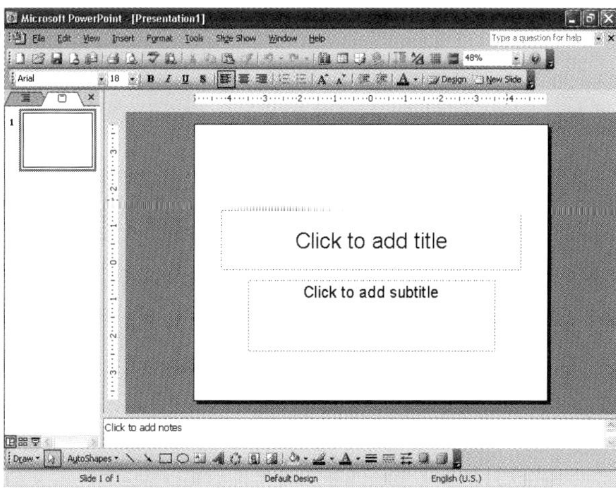

- *Voice recognition*
  Voice recognition software is used to create, edit, and format documents by speaking into a microphone (which is attached to the computer). The dictation is transcribed directly on the computer. Dragon Naturally Speaking and Point and Click are two popular voice recognition software products.
- *Web page*
  Web page software is used to create and manage professional-quality Internet Web sites. Microsoft FrontPage and Adobe PageMill are examples of Web page design software.

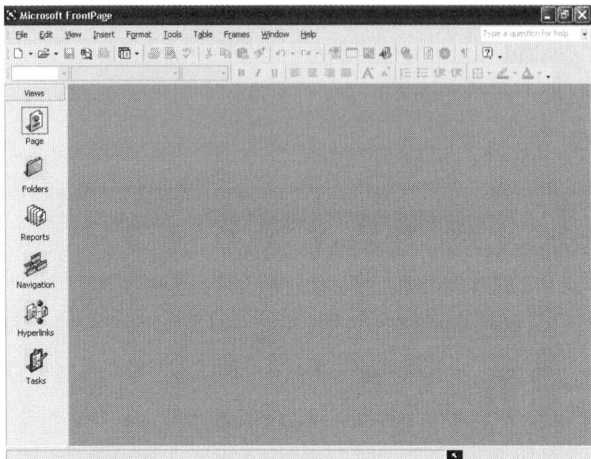

- *Graphics*
  A variety of ***graphics*** software packages are used to create charts, pictures, illustrations, drawings, and 3D images. Included in this category are the following types of programs:
  - Paint
  - Illustration/design
  - Photo-editing
  - Desktop publishing

THE INTERNET

The ***Internet*** is a worldwide network of smaller computer networks all linked together by unique ***IP*** (***Internet Protocol***) addresses. These computers may be located in businesses, schools, research foundations, hospitals, and/or individuals' homes. The Internet has unlimited uses. Businesses use the Internet to share information and to advertise their services and products. Students use the Internet for research and to share information with fellow students and professors. The Internet can be used to book airline flights, buy movie tickets, check your savings account, buy and sell stocks, order a pizza, shop for a gift, apply to a college, find a job, and buy a home. Internet users can also share personal information about themselves through chat groups, bulletin boards, and e-mail.

To access the Internet, a user must sign up with an ***Internet Service Provider*** (***ISP***), which sells access to the Internet for a monthly charge. Some popular ISPs include the Microsoft Network, America Online, EarthLink, net.com, MindSpring, and AT&T Worldnet. Connecting via modem to an ISP allows a user access to the ***World Wide Web,*** a service of the Internet on which pages, or ***Web sites,*** display information. These Web sites are created by companies, individuals, schools, religious institutions, government agencies—just about anybody.

By subscribing to an ISP, a user is offered much more than access to the Web. Other ISP services include e-mail, news on demand, personal Web site hosting, and much more.

Some ISPs offer specific online content such as Dow Jones News Retrieval and Lexis/Nexis. These ISPs provide financial and business news that is updated daily. The cost to use these services depends on how long a user stays online and how much of the information is downloaded.

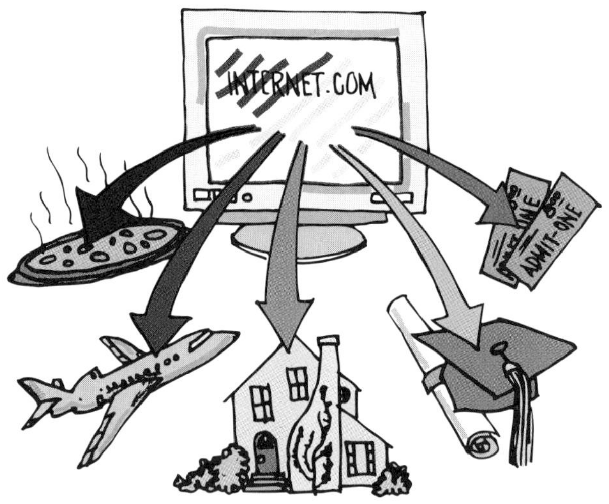

Web sites reside on a ***Web server,*** a dedicated computer that delivers Web pages. Every Web server has an IP address and possibly a ***domain name.*** Domain names are used in URLs (Uniform Resource Locators), to identify particular Web sites. (A URL is also referred to as a Web address.) For example, in the URL http://www.microsoft.com, the domain name is ***microsoft.com***. A domain suffix identifies the Web site as commercial (.com), noncommercial (.org), government (.gov), educational (.edu), U.S. military (.mil), or network (.net) organization.

Information on the Web is created using a programming language called ***HTML*** (***hypertext markup language***). A Web browser translates HTML into a readable format. The Internet user can choose to use one of several dozen different Web browsers. Some popular Web browsers include Netscape Navigator and Microsoft Internet Explorer. Certain Web sites have a different look when viewed with different Web browsers due to translation inconsistencies. A Web browser can locate a specific site by its ***uniform resource locator (URL)***.

You can transmit files between a computer workstation and a file server (a dedicated computer) or a Web server. File transfer protocol, or FTP, is a format for transmitting data from one device to another in order for the files to be available on the Internet. When "ftp" appears in a URL, it means that the user is connecting to a file server and not a Web server.

HTTP is a protocol used to transfer files from a Web server onto a browser in order to view a Web page that is on the Internet. Using FTP, entire files are transferred from one computer device to another; HTTP only transfers the contents of a Web page into a browser for viewing. When "http" appears in a URL, it means that the user is connecting to a Web server and not a file server.

TELECOMMUNICATIONS

To transmit data over a phone line, you need a modem. A ***modem*** (modulator/demodulator) is a device that connects a computer to a phone line, allowing data to be transmitted from one computer to another. For the transmission to work, both computers must have modems and the appropriate communications software. A modem can be internal (inside the computer in the form of a circuit board) or external.

Modems have various speeds at which they transmit data. Downloading files and transmitting data requires fast modem speeds. Otherwise, tasks can be very time consuming. Traditional dial-up modems provide online access through telephone lines at speeds up to 57.6 bits per second (bps). A cable modem, however, gives users high-speed Internet access through a cable line at more than 1 million bits per second. A bit is a single binary unit of measurement.

A *fax modem* not only transmits data, but allows graphics and documents to be sent as well. In this respect, the modem is similar to a real facsimile machine; however, the computer, unlike the fax machine, can receive faxes while it is turned off. To transmit faxes via the computer, you need to have the appropriate communications software package installed.

There are various ways to transmit data, sound, and video electronically. Here are some of the more common options:

- *Electronic mail (e-mail)*
  This method of transmitting electronic messages does not necessarily use a telephone line or assistance from an ISP. It may also use a ***network system*** known as an *intranet*. If they have Internet access, users are able to send messages to one or more Internet mailboxes simultaneously. They can also retrieve messages. Access to an electronic mailbox is exclusive and limited. Generally, users of the mailbox must know a ***password,*** or code, to send or retrieve messages. Messages can be transmitted 24 hours a day to anyone around the world who has an e-mail address. E-mail addresses are usually formatted in a specific way: user@domain.com. For example, John Doe works for the Pixie Soda Company. His e-mail address might be: john.doe@pixiesoda.com

- *Fax*
  A term derived from the word "facsimile" (which means "duplicate" or "copy"), a ***fax*** is a machine connected to a telephone, that scans

a document and translates the visual image into electronic impulses. These impulses are then transmitted along telephone lines to another fax machine at a different location. The remote machine receives the electronic impulses, reconstructs the visual image of the document, and prints out an exact copy of the original document.

- *Electronic bulletin board*
  Information on a variety of topics can be placed on or accessed from an ***electronic bulletin board.*** Through a computer connected to a telephone line, it is possible to "talk" with other users, "discussing" or exchanging information on topics ranging from zoology to taxes, stocks and bonds to medical issues. Access to some bulletin boards is free; others charge a subscription fee.

- *Teleconferencing*
  Teleconferencing allows persons in different locations to see and hear one another. A videoconference is accomplished by using a television camera and microphone to transmit voice and video signals through satellite networks.

WIDE AREA NETWORK

Networks

A computer ***network*** is a linked group of computers. Networks allow computers to share information, programs, printers, or scanners, or to facilitate communication between people via e-mail. There are two principal kinds of networks: ***intra*** networks and ***inter*** networks. An ***intranet*** refers to an internal network confined within a specific location, usually one particular office or building. An intranet is sometimes referred to as a ***LAN (local area network).*** An intranet can also include several interlinked LANs.

The main purpose of an intranet is to share files and records within a company. An intranet can also be used to facilitate group collaboration and for teleconferences. For example, a law office might set up its own intranet so that every computer in the office can access the same files and case information and every computer prints to the same printer. An intranet can connect users to a common *file server* (minicomputer) that allows all of the computers connected to the network to access the same hard drive, the Internet, or to go outside the company to a *WAN* (wide area network).

Regardless of whether you are connected to a LAN or a WAN, you must always enter a password to access, or "log in to," the network. Network connections transmit data at a much faster speed than does a modem or a telephone line.

In addition to networked computers, businesses have the ability to communicate with workers outside the office as well as with overseas co-workers through telecommunication and access to the Internet. Developing computer video and sound technology makes it possible for business meetings to take place entirely through computers (video conferencing). This is known as the "virtual office." Because the Internet provides 24-hour access to information, businesses that operate in multiple locations and time zones can continue to work even when one workday is ending and another is just beginning. Workers no longer need to share office space or have a networked computer to share important information and accomplish team projects.

Many households with more than one computer are establishing networks so that the computers can share an Internet connection, printers, and data files. There are four main technologies that allow a user to set up a home computer network:

Ethernet technology requires an Ethernet card that slips into one of the computer's slots. Each computer must be linked with cables to its Ethernet connectors. If you have more than two computers in your network, you need to connect them all to either a hub (a common connection point for devices in a network) or, for a little more money, a router (a connection device that connects any number of LANS, or local area networks). The advantage of a router is that it lets each computer in the network connect to the Internet without having to have another computer turned on. The disadvantage of this type of setup is cabling, which can involve running cables through walls and ceilings.

Phone line technology uses your home's existing phone wires to link computers. Each computer connects to the network via a phone jack.

Power line technology uses your home's electrical wiring to link computers. Each computer connects to the network through an electrical wall outlet.

Wireless technology works like a cordless phone. A wireless base station broadcasts to a special card inside, or to a small device attached to, each desktop or laptop. Heavy walls, aluminum siding, or brickwork can block transmissions.

To summarize, the major components needed to assemble a home network include the following:

- ***Ethernet cable***—connects computers to networking devices such as routers or hubs.
- ***Hub***—connects several computers so they can "see" each other.
- ***Network card*** (also known as an Ethernet card)—provides an outlet for networking or for directly connecting to a DSL or cable modem. (DSL, an acronym for Digital Subscriber Line, is a high-speed transmission line used for sending data).
- ***Printer server***—resides near a printer and connects the printer directly to the network so you can use the printer without having to keep any particular computer turned on.
- ***Router***—has outlets for computers, high-speed modems, and print servers. Once a router is connected to the Internet, any computer connected to it can go online, even if other computers are turned off.
- ***Wireless access***—lets you wirelessly connect multiple devices, such as laptops or printers, to a network that is otherwise connected by wires.

Telecommuting

Telecommuting is a term used to describe employees using technology to perform regular work activities from a remote location. Telecommuting moves the work to the worker instead of vice versa, almost completely eliminating the need for a downtown business office. The typical telecommuter has a personal computer (usually a laptop) with a fax/cellular modem. Once dialed into the company network as a remote user, the telecommuter has full use of the company's intranet, including the e-mail system, server files, and, in some cases, Internet capability as well.

Wireless Computing

Wireless computing allows you to work from almost anywhere, and gives you access to all kinds of information when you are on-the-go by maintaining a data connection with a remote network. Some popular wireless communication devices are the PDA (personal digital assistant), cellular phones, and mobile e-mail devices.

The PDA is a handheld device that combines computing, telephone/fax, and networking features. Information can be input into a PDA using a keyboard, a stylus (a pen-like device), or your own voice. Today, Palm Pilots are one of the most popular PDA brands.

Cellular phones allow for text messaging. Text messaging can be used for short messages, which are usually sent between two or more mobile devices.

Mobile e-mail devices provide access to e-mail accounts, allowing users to read and send e-mails, as well as view calendars and contact information, which exist on their Internet-connected PCs. Blackberry is a popular line of mobile e-mail devices that includes airtime and software.

COMPUTERS AND SOCIETY

At home, computers perform many functions. Application software can be used to calculate an individual's taxes, the household budget, and interest on a personal loan, or to determine an amount owed on a mortgage. More and more banks, through the use of ATMs (automatic teller machines), offer individuals the opportunity to do their banking without ever having to leave their homes. Financial transactions can be performed on one's personal computer which, through the Internet, can be linked with a bank's computers.

In addition, many home computers have Internet access and more and more home users are able to use the World Wide Web to shop. Internet credit card purchasing has increased significantly. Now you can book a flight to Walt Disney World, reserve a hotel room, order a pizza, and buy books, clothing, vitamins, or even concert tickets with very little effort.

Tired of television? Then play games! Computer-based video games have become increasingly popular among young and old alike. The types of games available range from traditional games—such as chess, backgammon, and poker, which are adapted to video screens—to more complex, interactive games, such as flight simulation and strategy games in which the computer is a challenging opponent.

Computers are often present in the household in less visible ways. Home heating thermostats, watches, cars, and even children's toys all contain complicated computer systems. Washing machines, microwave ovens, answering machines, and dishwashers are just a few of the household appliances containing small computers that greatly reduce manual household labor.

Future Technologies

Computer technology is developing at an extraordinary rate. It has been said that the state of technology doubles in efficiency and speed every year. Computer hardware and software become obsolete within months of their initial development, while at the same time new products with extraordinary capabilities become available to the general market. For example, ***DVDs (digital versatile or video discs)*** have seven times the storage capacity of CD-ROMs without taking up any more space. In addition, DVD players are backward compatible and thus able to support the soon-to-be-outdated CD-ROM technology. DVD will eventually replace laser discs, CD-ROMs, and traditional VHS videotape.

Another example of a rapidly developing technology is virtual reality. ***Virtual reality*** (***VR***) software uses three-dimensional graphics and special devices such as a data glove and VR goggles to allow the user to interact with a computing environment in "real space." Although many people are familiar with VR in relation to computer simulation games, the development of VR technology has had a significant impact on many professions and fields of research.

Voice recognition software technology is making incredible advancements in perfecting the computer's ability to carry out voice commands and take dictation. It is now possible to purchase software for as little as $200 that allows the user to speak naturally into the computer up to 160 words per minute without pausing between words. The words appear immediately on the computer's screen.

An up-and-coming technology known as ***intercasting*** is the merging of the personal computer with the television. Web TV is a television that can be used to surf the Internet. Computer data must still be converted into signals that can be understood by the television. With the development of digital television and cable modems, however, complete intercast, with high-quality resolution, will be a definite reality.

Your Responsibility Using a Computer

In business, workers mostly deal with public information; however, a great deal of private information (e.g., phone numbers, social security numbers, tax records, credit card information, medical histories, and legal records) is also stored on computers. Access to this information usually requires knowledge of passwords and/or codes. Therefore, a computer database may be a secure place to keep private, extremely important, or secret records. Computer databases can be a more secure storage medium than a piece of paper. Some of the U.S. government's top secret records and research are entered into computers. In the wrong hands, such information could do great damage.

When irresponsible or unethical individuals, sometimes referred to as ***hackers,*** discover ways to break codes and gain access to classified files, not only personal, but also national security may be threatened.

A great deal of responsibility goes along with personal computing. Working in an office allows you to obtain confidential information only when you are authorized to do so. It is a criminal offense to retrieve or view information from a private or limited-access computer or database without permission. It is also illegal to make copies of software programs. In addition, information provided on the World Wide Web is usually copyrighted and protected by the creators and Webmasters of the site. Copying software or duplicating information from the Web for public business is a violation of U.S. copyright infringement regulations. Violators are subject to prosecution and imprisonment. Finally, when using information from the Internet for independent research, cite the Web site, author, and original source where applicable. Failure to do so is considered plagiarism.

CARE OF YOUR COMPUTER, PERIPHERALS, AND DATA

To maximize the use of your computer, take steps to maintain its operation. Some maintenance is required periodically; other care is required each time you use your computer. It is also critical to take positive, proactive steps to reduce the risk of data loss.

Care of Computer and Peripherals

System Care The system case should be cleaned, both inside and out, on a regular basis to prevent buildup of dust.

- Wipe the outside case clean with a damp cloth. Never spray liquids directly on the casing.
- The inside of the computer can be cleaned by using a compressed-air can to blow out dust, or by using a small handheld vacuum to remove the dust.
- Check the power supply fan periodically to be sure that it has good ventilation and is free of dirt and dust buildup.

Monitors

- Clean monitors using a soft, damp cloth to remove the dust, which accumulates rather quickly. This should be done at least once a week.
- Be sure to check that the monitor's cooling vents are never blocked.
- Do not keep monitors turned on for extended periods of time, and certainly not overnight. This will minimize safety risks and increase the monitor's life span.

Floppy Disk Drives Unlike hard disk drives, which are sealed within the central processing unit of the computer, floppy drives are exposed to the outside air. The drive's read/write heads should be cleaned every few months using alcohol or special cleaning kits.

Keyboards Keyboards are somewhat resistant to abuse, but over time they will develop keys that stick or repeat if they are not maintained. To avoid these problems, keep food and liquids away from the keyboard.

- Develop a "no eating and drinking" policy while using the computer. Should liquids spill into the keyboard, it is likely you will need to replace it.
- Clean the key caps at least once every six months, and use compressed air to blow out dust from between the keys.

Mice Like keyboards, mice are handled all the time and tend to accumulate a good deal of dirt. If the ball becomes dirty, it will not roll properly and the pointer will not react on the screen's surface. Using a damp cloth, clean the mouse and the rollers inside the mouse unit at least once a month.

Care of Media

Floppy Disks

- Do not subject disks to temperatures above 120°F, because they will warp and all data on them will be lost. Keep disks in a cool, dry place.
- Do not touch the surface of the disk, because fingerprints or dirt can cause problems reading the disk.
- Do not expose disks to moisture or liquid.
- Do not expose disks to magnetic fields (magnets, stereo speakers, home appliances). This too can cause data loss.
- Although disks are called "floppy," the magnetic tape within the jacket should not be bent. Doing so will damage the disk.
- Airport X-ray machines do not affect disks.

Compact Discs (CDs) Compact discs are more durable than floppies and they do not require as much special care.

- CDs should not be subjected to temperatures above 100°F.
- Do not handle the surface of a CD. Doing so causes the surface to become scratched, which will interfere with the computer's ability to read the disc.
- Moisture and liquids will not harm a CD. If a CD becomes wet, simply wipe it off with a soft cloth.
- CDs are not affected by magnetic fields.
- CDs can be cleaned using a damp, soft cloth.
- Airport X-ray machines do not affect CDs.

Care of Data

To prevent data loss, perform daily backup of your data from your hard drive to a floppy disk, Zip disk, tape drive, or CD.

To avoid losing data in an unexpected shutdown of your computer, be sure to:

- Save data frequently in all applications.
- Close all open applications.
- Shut down your operating system according to the instructions given to you by the system.

Install a virus-scan program on your computer to protect data from becoming infected.

Delete unwanted files from your hard drive monthly to increase hard drive performance.

PERFORMANCE BASIC

LESSON 1
Office Basics

LESSON 2
Internet Basics

LESSON 1

Office Basics

In the first part of this lesson, you will learn about the Microsoft Office 2003 suite of programs, including how to start a program, navigate program windows, work with multiple programs, close programs, and use the Help options. In the last part of this lesson you will learn to use the basic features common to all Office programs. Word will be used to demonstrate these features.

Upon completion of this lesson, you should have mastered the following skill sets:

- Start an Office program
- Switch between programs
- Explore Office screen elements
- Get Help
- Start a new file
- Save a file
- Close a file
- Open a file
- Search a file
- Undo/Redo
- Quick Print

Terms

Software-related

- Desktop
- Taskbar
- Title bar
- Window control buttons
  - Minimize button
  - Restore button
  - Maximize button
  - Close button
- Menu bar
- Ellipsis points
- Dialog box
- Shortcut menu
- Toolbar
- Standard toolbar
- Formatting toolbar
- Hyperlink
- Task pane
- ScreenTip
- Scroll arrow
- Scroll bar
- Scroll box
- Office tool
- File name
- Search criterion
- Undo
- Redo
- Quick print

TASK 1

GOALS

To explore Office screen parts and use the Help feature

To practice using the following skill sets:

- Start an Office program
- Switch between programs
- Explore Office screen elements
  - Title bar
  - Menu bar
  - Toolbars
  - Task pane
- Get Help

WHAT YOU NEED TO KNOW

About Office 2003

- Office 2003, professional edition, is a suite of software programs that provides a full range of powerful computer tools that you can use independently or in an integrated fashion. Office 2003, professional edition, includes Word (word processing), Excel (spreadsheet), Access (database), PowerPoint (presentations), Publisher (desktop publishing), and Outlook (desktop information manager). Publisher will not be covered in this book.
- To use the features found in Office, you must be comfortable using the mouse. If you are not familiar with mouse actions and terminology, refer to Appendix C.

Start an Office Program

- The first window you see when you start your computer is the *desktop*, the area that displays program and file icons. You can customize the desktop to include buttons for those programs you use most frequently. Therefore, your opening screen may vary from the illustration shown in Figure 1.1. The following program icons represent each application found in Office 2003.

Word   Excel   Access 

PowerPoint    Outlook    Publisher 

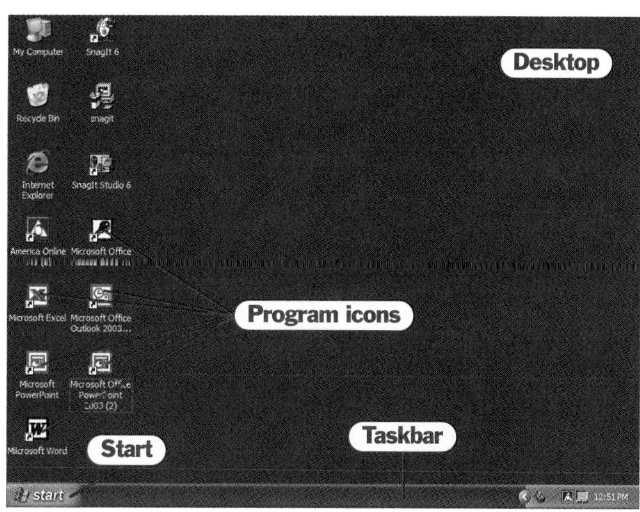

Figure 1.1 Desktop

BASICS

▶ You also see the *taskbar,* located at the bottom of the Windows screen, which displays the Start button, as well as open documents and programs. When clicked, the Start button displays menu options to start programs and work with aspects of your computer. You can customize the start options to include quick access to Office applications.

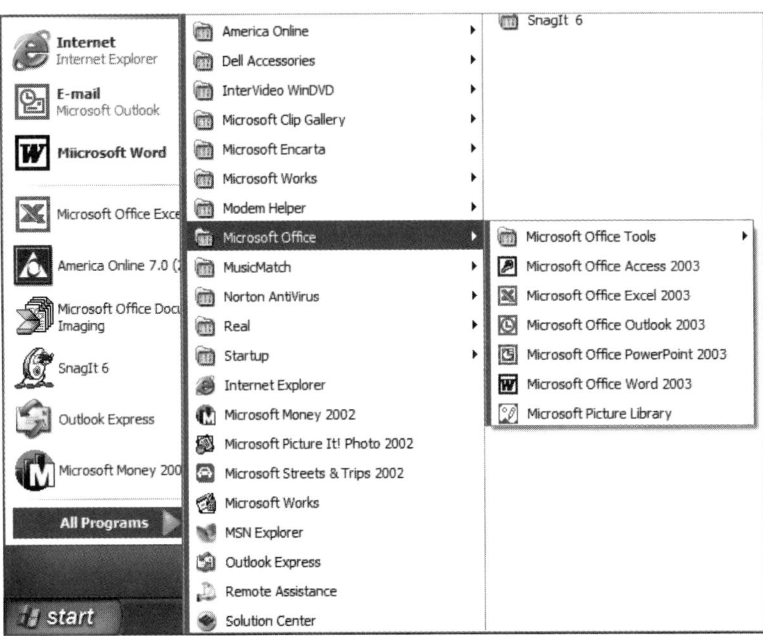

Figure 1.2 All Programs menu

▶ There are two basic ways to start an Office program:

1. Click the Start button on the taskbar, point to All Programs, point to Microsoft Office, and select the program you want on the submenu, as shown in Figure 1.2.

2. Double-click the program icon on the deskop, if you customized it to include program icons as shown in Figure 1.1.

TRY *it* OUT *pb1-1*

1. Click **Start,** point to **All Programs,** point to **Microsoft Office,** and click **Microsoft Office Excel 2003** to start the program.
2. Click **Start,** point to **All Programs,** point to **Microsoft Office,** and click **Microsoft Office Word 2003.**
3. Click **Start,** point to **All Programs,** point to **Microsoft Office,** and click **Microsoft Office PowerPoint 2003.**
4. Click **Start,** point to **All Programs,** point to **Microsoft Office,** and click **Microsoft Office Access 2003.**

Switch Between Programs

▶ When you start a program, a button appears on the taskbar, showing a program icon and the document name (the program name will truncate if many buttons are displayed). When you point to a program button, a pop-up window known as a ScreenTip displays the full document and program name. (Office provides a generic name until you provide one during the save process. See Task 2 to save a document.)

▶ To switch between programs on the taskbar, click the button for the program you to want to display, as shown in Figure 1.3.

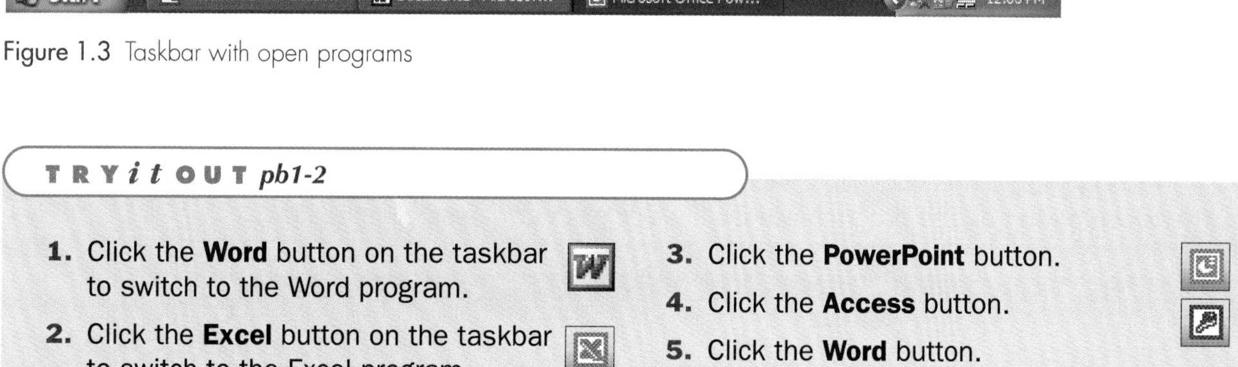

Figure 1.3 Taskbar with open programs

TRY *it* OUT *pb1-2*

1. Click the **Word** button on the taskbar to switch to the Word program.
2. Click the **Excel** button on the taskbar to switch to the Excel program.
3. Click the **PowerPoint** button.
4. Click the **Access** button.
5. Click the **Word** button.

Explore Office Screen Elements

▶ After launching an Office program, you see its opening screen. The common parts of all Office program windows are illustrated and discussed using the Word window, as shown in Figure 1.4. The screen parts that apply specifically to an Office program are discussed in the related units of this book. Each program window contains the following common elements: title bar, menu bar, toolbars, and task pane. *Note: Scroll boxes, bars, and arrows allow you to move a window horizontally or vertically. Scrolling techniques will be detailed and practiced in each Office program.*

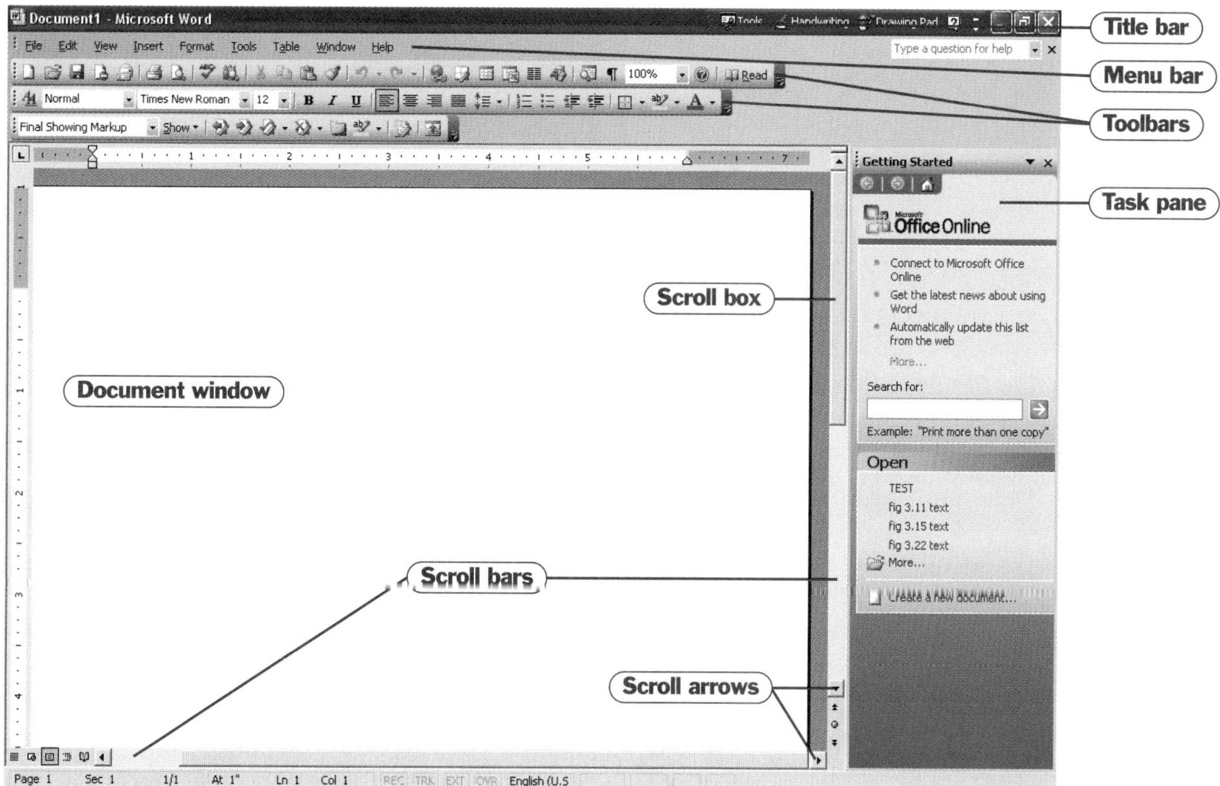

Figure 1.4 Word window

BASICS

Title Bar

- The *title bar*, located at the top of the program window, as shown in Figure 1.5, displays the document name, followed by the program name. A program-specific generic name will be displayed until you provide a name during the save process.
- The title bar also includes *window control buttons*, which have the functions listed below:

  The Minimize button reduces the window to a button on the taskbar.

  The Restore button returns a window to its previous size.

  A Maximize button replaces the Restore button after you click the Restore button.

  The Close button on the program window quickly exits or closes the program.

Figure 1.5 Title bar

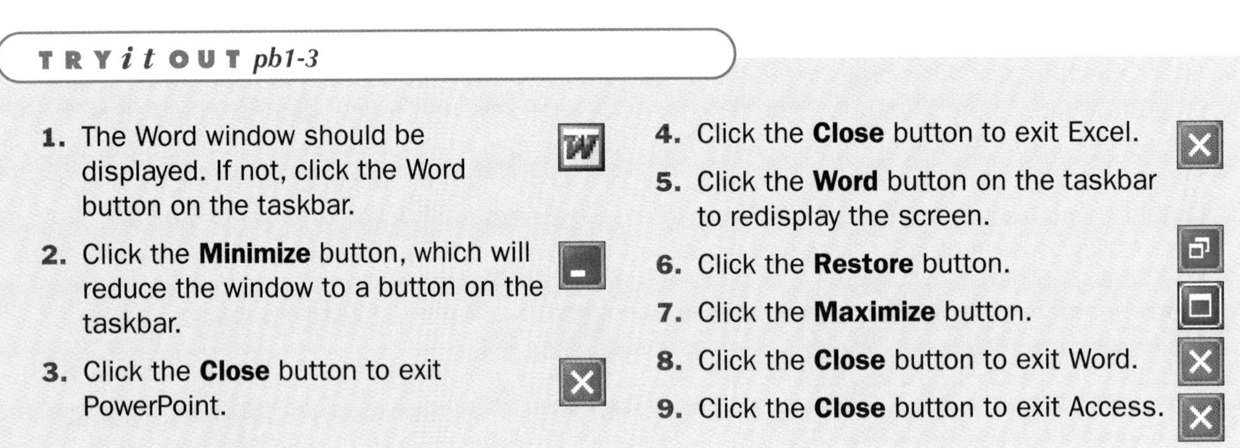

TRY it OUT *pb1-3*

1. The Word window should be displayed. If not, click the Word button on the taskbar.
2. Click the **Minimize** button, which will reduce the window to a button on the taskbar.
3. Click the **Close** button to exit PowerPoint.
4. Click the **Close** button to exit Excel.
5. Click the **Word** button on the taskbar to redisplay the screen.
6. Click the **Restore** button.
7. Click the **Maximize** button.
8. Click the **Close** button to exit Word.
9. Click the **Close** button to exit Access.

Menu Bar

- The *menu bar*, located below the title bar, displays items that you click to execute commands. The Type a Question for help box and the Close button on the document window appear on the right. *The Close button on the menu bar closes the current document; the close button on the title bar exits the program.* To close a program using the menu, click File, Exit. The Word menu bar is illustrated in Figure 1.6.

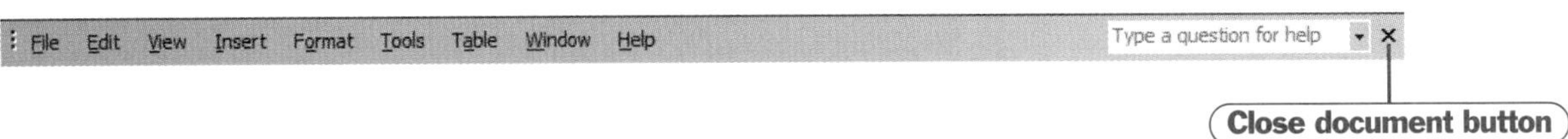

Figure 1.6 Word menu bar

- You can choose menu bar items (File, Edit, View, etc.) using the mouse or the keyboard. With the mouse, point to an item on the menu bar and click once. On the keyboard, press the Alt key plus the underlined letter in the menu name.
- When you select a menu bar item, a submenu appears with additional options. The menu that appears when you click View is illustrated in Figure 1.7.

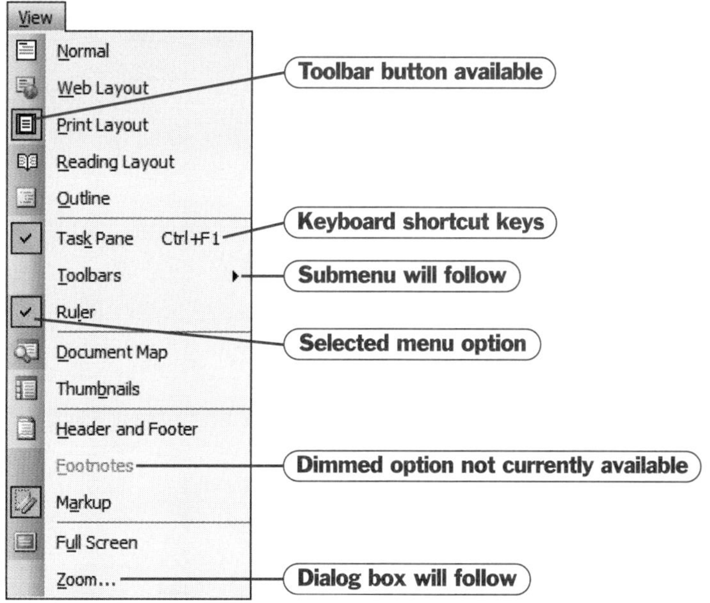

Figure 1.7 Word View menu

- Notice the following about submenu items:
  - Some options are dimmed, whereas others appear black. Dimmed options are not available for selection at the present time.
  - A check mark next to a menu item means the option is currently selected.
  - Some menu items display shortcut keys to also allow access to the feature using the keyboard.
  - An arrow next to a menu item means another submenu will be forthcoming.
  - Some menu items display a toolbar button, which means there is a toolbar button available to access this feature. You might, however, have to customize the toolbar to display a particular button.
  - A menu item followed by ellipsis points (...) indicates that a dialog box will be forthcoming.
    - A *dialog box* presents information about the current settings for a command and allows you to have a "dialog" with it—that is, to change the settings. The Print dialog box, shown in Figure 1.8, appears after clicking File, Print. The parts of a dialog box are described in detail in Appendix D. To close a dialog box, click its Close button.

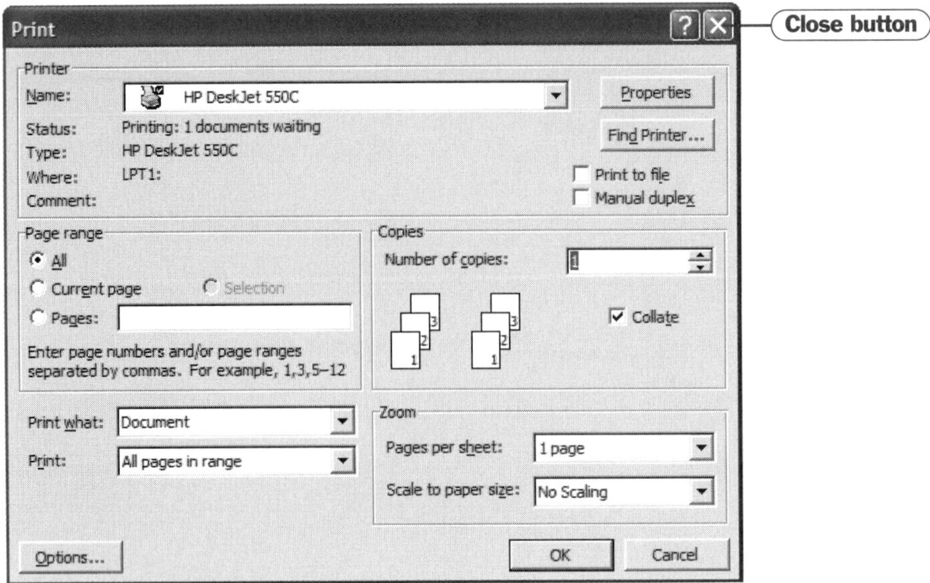

Figure 1.8 Print dialog box

- A *Shortcut menu* appears when you click the right mouse button. The menu options will vary, depending on where the mouse is pointing and what task you are performing. Figure 1.9 illustrates the Shortcut menu that displays when you right-click the document window in Word.

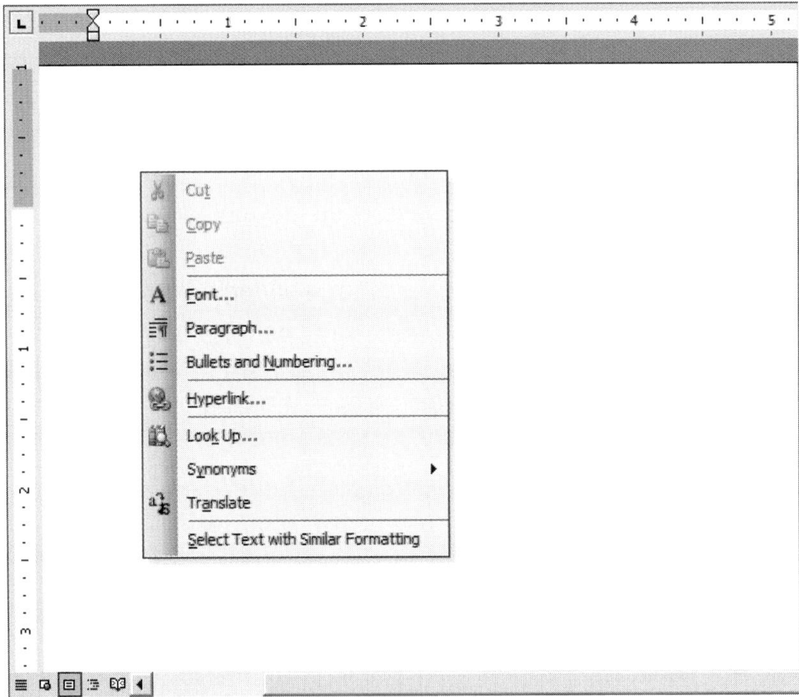

Figure 1.9 Shortcut menu

TRY it OUT pb1-4

1. Click **Start,** point to **All Programs,** point to **Microsoft Office** and click **Microsoft Office Word 2003.**
2. Click **Edit.** Notice the menu selections that appear.
3. Rest the mouse pointer on the other menu items. Notice the selections that appear.
4. Position the mouse pointer in the middle of the document window and right-click. Notice the Shortcut menu that appears. Click off the Shortcut menu to close it.
5. Click **File, Print.** Notice the Print dialog box displays.
6. Click the **Close** button on the dialog box. 
7. Click **Close** on the document window. Notice that the document window closes. 
8. Click **File, Exit** to close the program.

Toolbars

- A *toolbar*, located below the menu bar, provides quick access to features you use frequently. There are more buttons on the bar than will fit across the screen. To display the hidden buttons, click the Toolbar Options list arrow and choose Show Buttons on Two Rows. These two rows constitute the Standard and Formatting toolbars.
- The *Standard* and *Formatting toolbars* appear in every program. These toolbars contain common buttons, as well as program-specific buttons, and are shown in Figures 1.10 and 1.11.
- Other toolbars are available within each program and are displayed by clicking View, Toolbars. When working on certain tasks, it is convenient to have task-specific toolbars displayed.

Figure 1.10 Word Standard and Formatting toolbars

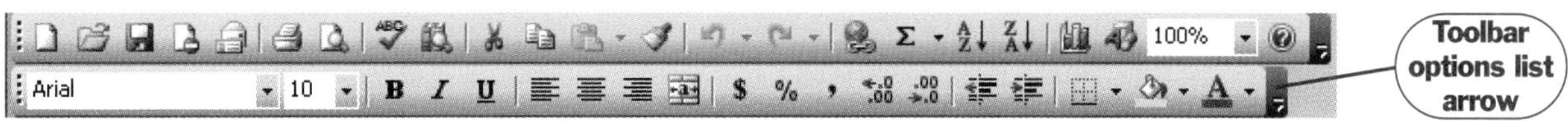

Figure 1.11 Excel Standard and Formatting toolbars

TRY it OUT pb1-5

1. Click **Start,** point to **All Programs,** point to **Microsoft Office** and click **Microsoft Office Word 2003.**
2. Point to and rest the pointer on a toolbar button to display its name. Do this for all buttons on the toolbar.
3. Click the **Toolbar Options** list arrow and choose **Show Buttons on Two Rows.** If the buttons are already on two rows, notice the available options.
4. Click **View, Toolbars.** Notice the toolbars available in Word.

Continued on next page

BASICS

TRY it OUT pb1-5 Continued

5. Click **Formatting** to deselect it. Notice that the Formatting toolbar is no longer displayed.
6. Click **View, Toolbars.**
7. Click **Formatting** to select it. Notice that the Formatting toolbar is redisplayed.

Task Pane

- A Getting Started task pane, located on the right side of the screen, appears when a program is launched (see Figure 1.4). Task panes provide easy access options for working with documents and files. There are numerous task panes available specific to each Office program.
- You can open and display other task panes by clicking the Other Task Panes list arrow on the task pane title bar. The New Document task pane is shown in Figure 1.12. The navigation arrow buttons allow you to move forward and back between open task panes. The home button returns you to the Getting Started task pane.
- To close the task pane, click the Close button in the top-right corner of the task pane. If the task pane is not displayed, you can display it by clicking View, Task Pane.

- When you position the mouse pointer over a task pane option, a *hyperlink* appears. A hyperlink is an underlined word that provides a shortcut to other information. To access a task pane option, click its hyperlink.

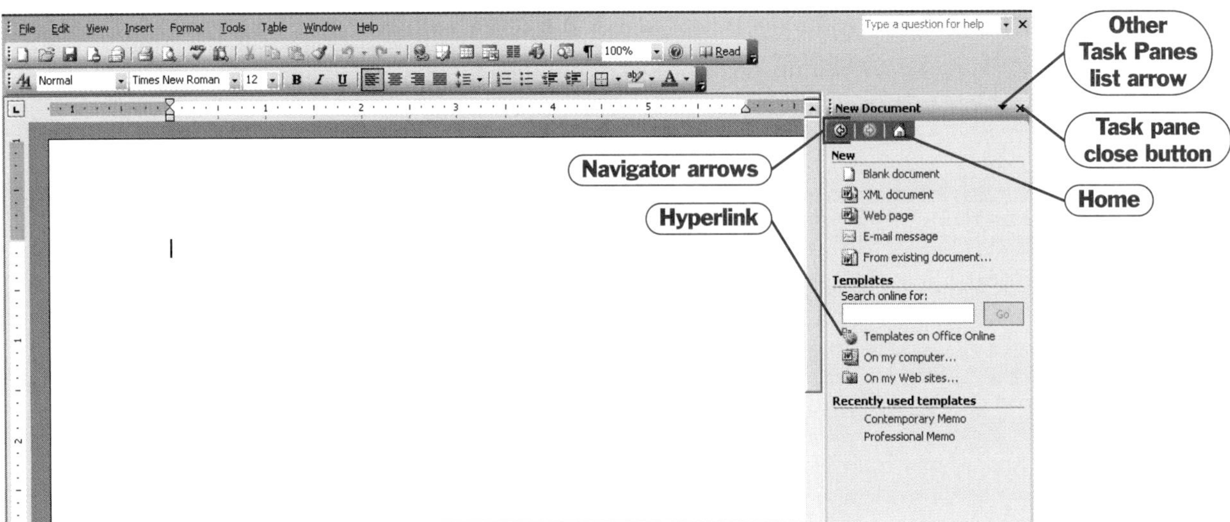

Figure 1.12 New Document task pane in Word window

TRY it OUT pb1-6

1. Click **File, New** to display the New Document task pane.
2. Position the insertion point over **Blank Document** to display its hyperlink and click. Notice that a new blank document appears and the task pane disappears.
3. Click **View, Task Pane** to redisplay the task pane.
4. Click the **Other Task Panes** list arrow.
5. Click **Clip Art.**

Continued on next page

TRY it OUT *pb1-6 Continued*

6. Click the **Back** arrow button to return to the Getting Started task pane. 

7. Click the **Close** button on the task pane. 

Get Help

▶ Several forms of Help are available in each Office program:

- Help task pane.
- Type a Question for Help box.
- Office Assistant.
- ScreenTips.
- Office on Microsoft.com.

The Help Task Pane

▶ The Microsoft Help task pane, shown in Figure 1.13, displays after clicking the Microsoft Office Help button on the Standard Toolbar, by clicking the Other task panes list arrow and choosing the Help option, or by pressing F1. In the Help task pane, enter a topic to search on in the Search for box. Press Enter or click the green Start searching arrow to begin the search process. You can also click the Connect to Microsoft Office Online link to search topics online.

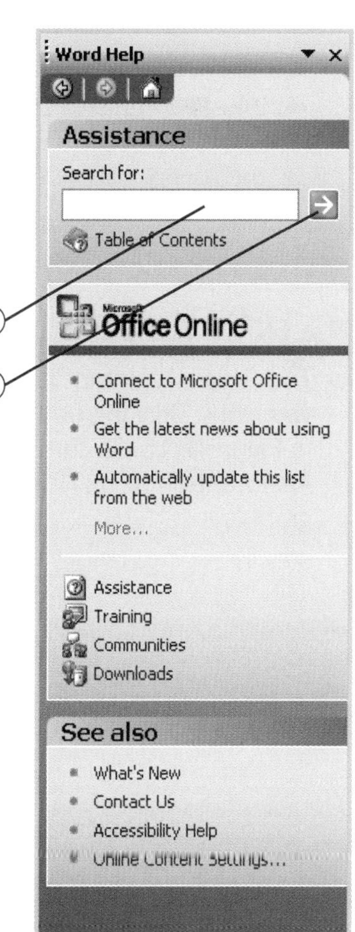

Figure 1.13 Help task pane

BASICS

Type a Question for Help Box

▶ The Type a Question for Help box, shown in Figure 1.14, appears on the menu bar in every program. Enter a question in the box, press the Enter key, and the Search Results task pane displays a list of topics that responds to your question. Click on a topic to view an explanation. You can print the topic by clicking the Print icon on the help screen.

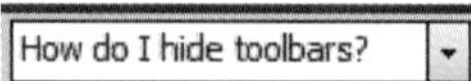

Figure 1.14 Type a Question for Help box

TRY *it* OUT *pb1-7*

1. Press **F1.** Notice the Word Help task pane displays.
2. Click the **Close** button on the task pane. 
3. Click the **Microsoft Office Help** button on the Standard toolbar. 
4. Enter **Margins** in the search box, and click the **Start** searching arrow. Click on one of the topics and view the help screen.
5. Click the **Close** button on the help screen; click the **Close** button on the Search Results task pane.
6. Enter the following question in the Type a Question for Help box: `How do I hide toolbars?`
7. Press the **Enter** key, and notice the topics that display.
8. Click the **Close** button on the Search Results task pane.

The Office Assistant

▶ The Office Assistant is an animated graphic that provides Help topics on tasks you perform as you work. Clicking on the Assistant displays a What would you like to do? question box, as shown in Figure 1.15. To turn the Assistant on, click Help, Show the Office Assistant. To turn the Assistant off, click Help, Hide the Office Assistant. To change Assistant options, right-click on the graphic.

Figure 1.15 Office Assistant question box

TRY*it*OUT *pb1-8*

1. Click **Help, Show the Office Assistant.** Note: If you are prompted to install the Office Assistant, click **Yes**.
2. Click on the **Office Assistant** graphic.
3. Enter `Print a document` in the What would you like to do? question box.
4. Click **Search.**
5. Click **Print a document.** Notice the information that appears in the Help window. Close the Help window.
6. Right-click the **Office Assistant.**
7. Click **Options.**
8. On the Gallery tab, click the **Next** button to view a different assistant graphic. Click **OK** to select it. Note: Click **Yes** if prompted to install additional assistants.
9. Click **Help, Hide the Office Assistant.**

ScreenTips

- *ScreenTips* are notes that pop up on the screen to provide information about different Microsoft features. ScreenTips may be turned on and off by clicking Tools, Options. On the View tab, click to enable or disable the feature.

Help on the Web

- You can get help on the World Wide Web within any Office program by clicking Help, Microsoft Office Online. See Lesson 2 in this unit for Internet Basics.

BASICS

REHEARSAL

GOALS
To explore Office screen parts (using Word) and to use the Help feature

TASK 1

WHAT YOU NEED TO KNOW

- When many programs are open at once, the buttons on the taskbar become smaller.
- In this Rehearsal activity, you will open several Office programs, change the windows, and use the Help feature.

DIRECTIONS

1. Start **Word,** if necessary.
2. Close the task pane.
3. Start **Excel.**
4. Start **PowerPoint.**
5. Start **Access.**
6. Switch to **Excel.**
7. Click to minimize the Excel window.
8. Switch to **PowerPoint**.
9. Hide the Formatting toolbar.
10. Click to minimize the PowerPoint window.
11. Display the Office Assistant, if it is not already displayed.
12. Press the **F1** key to access Help.
13. Enter `Office Assistant` in the Search text box, as shown on the following page, and begin the search.
14. Find information about selecting a different Office Assistant.
15. Print the topic.
16. Follow the directions on the printout to change the Assistant.
17. Turn off the Office Assistant.
18. Switch to **PowerPoint.**
19. Close all programs.

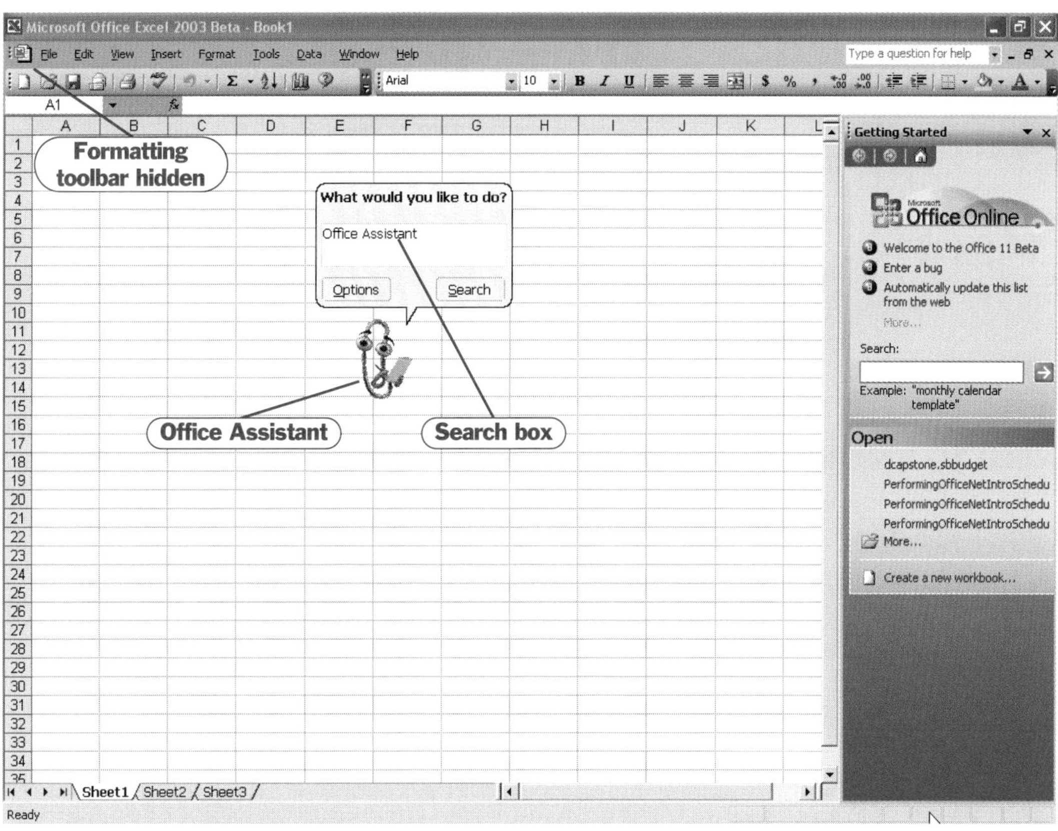

BASICS

Cues for Reference

Start Office

1. Click **Start** on the taskbar.
2. Point to **All Programs.**
3. Point to **Microsoft Office**.
4. Click the program name.

   or

   Double-click the program icon on the desktop.

   or

   Office XP: Click **Start, Programs, Microsoft Word.**

Switch Between Programs

- Click the desired program/ document button on the taskbar.

Close a Program

- Click the Close button on the program window. 

Change Toolbars

1. Click **View**, **Toolbars**.
2. Select or deselect toolbars as desired.

Close the Task Pane

- Click the **Close** button on the task pane title bar. 

Use Help

- Press **F1.**

  or

  Click the **Microsoft Office Help** button. 

  or

  Click **Help, Microsoft Office Word Help.**

Show/Hide the Office Assistant

1. Click **Help.**
2. Click **Show** or **Hide** the Office Assistant.

Turn Off the Office Assistant

1. Right-click the **Office Assistant**.
2. Click **Options.**
3. Click the **Use the Office Assistant** check box to deselect the option.

GOALS

To create new documents, enter text, and work with multiple files

To practice using the following skill sets:

- Start a new file
- Save a file
- Close a file
- Open a file
- Search for a file
- Undo/Redo
- Quick Print

WHAT YOU NEED TO KNOW

About Files and Folders

- It is important to understand files and folders and how they are organized on your computer. See Appendix B, File Management, to review file management procedures before starting this unit.

Start a New File

- When you launch an *Office application*, an opening screen appears showing a work window and a task pane.
- Once you open an Office tool, you have actually created a new file in that application. The file is assigned a generic name until you provide a name during the save process.
- Using Word as an example, the opening screen is a blank document, which has been assigned the name **Document1**, as shown in Figure 1.16. To create another new file, click Blank Document on the New Document task pane or click the New Blank Document button on the Standard toolbar. A new blank document will appear with **Document2** as its name. Note: If the New Document task pane is not displayed, click the Other Task Panes list arrow on the Task Pane toolbar and select the New Document task pane.
- As each new file is opened, a corresponding button will appear on the taskbar. To switch between open documents, click the desired button.

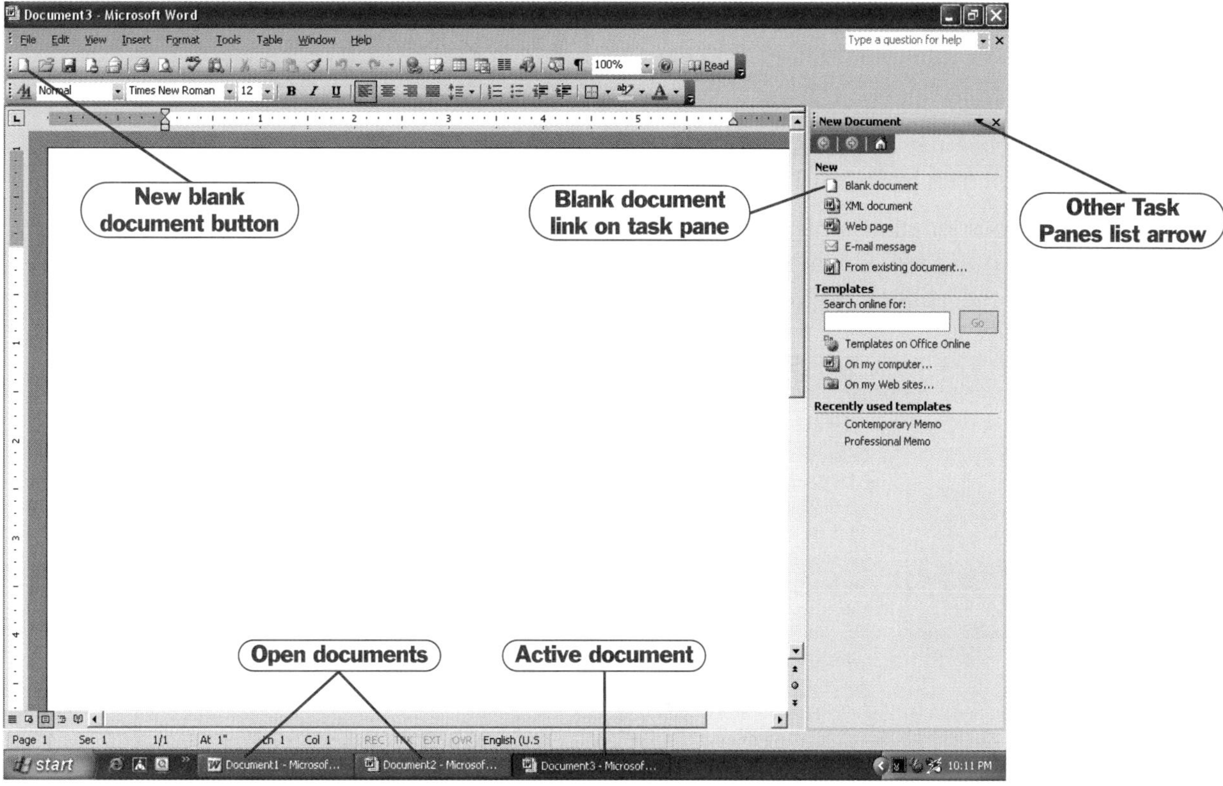

Figure 1.16 Opening Word screen

TRY it OUT *pb1-9*

1. Start **Word**.
2. Enter your first and last name in **Document1.**
3. Click **File**, **New**, then click the **Blank Document** link on the New Document task pane. Notice that you have created **Document2.**
4. Enter your home address, city, and state in **Document2.**
5. Click the **New Blank Document** button on the toolbar. Notice that you have created **Document3.**
6. Enter your telephone number in **Document3.** Notice the buttons on the taskbar for the three open documents.
7. Switch to **Document1.**
8. Do not close any open files.

BASICS

Save a File

▶ To save a new file you created, you must name it for identification. A *file name* may contain a maximum of 255 characters and can include spaces. File names may not include certain characters found on the keyboard:

\ (backslash)	* (asterisk)	: (colon)	< (less than)
[] (brackets)	; (semicolon)	/ (slash)	? (question mark)
| (vertical bar)	> (greater than)	= (equal)	, (comma)
" (quotation mark)	. (period)		

- To save a file for the first time, you must:
  - Provide a unique file name.
  - Determine where on your computer you wish to save the file.
- To save a file, click the Save button on the Standard toolbar or click File, Save. In the Save As dialog box, shown in Figure 1.17, enter the name of the file in the File name text box. 
- To save a file to a location other than the default (My Documents is the default save-in folder), click the Save in list arrow and choose another location. You can also choose a location by clicking one of the options on the Places bar.

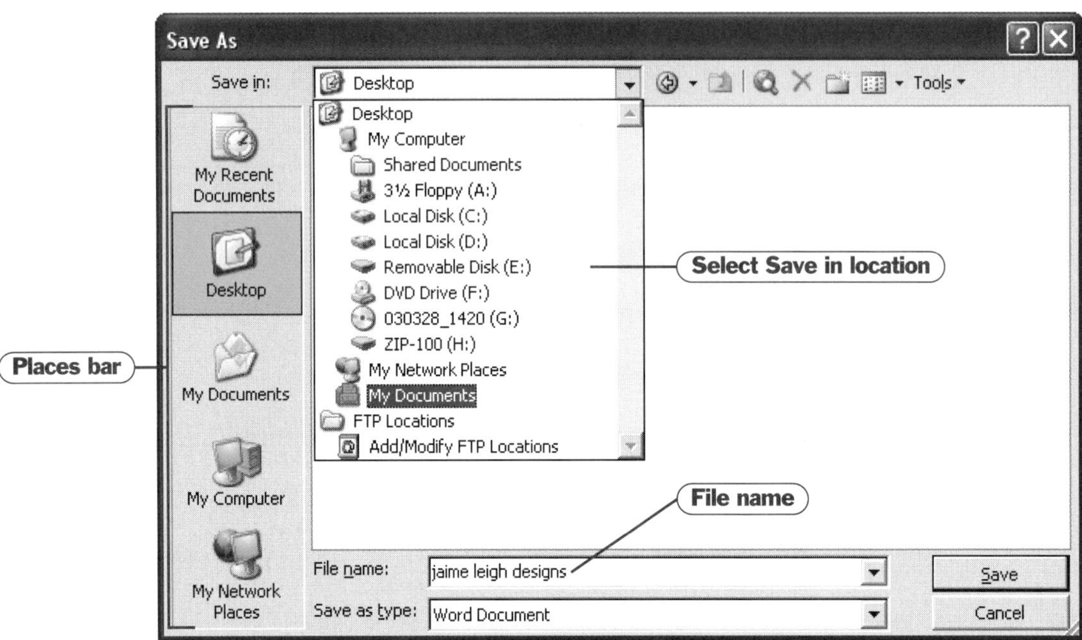

Figure 1.17 Save As dialog box

- After choosing a save location and entering a file name, click Save. Once the file is saved, the file name appears on the title bar and the document remains on screen.
- To update changes to a saved document, click the Save button on the Standard toolbar. 

Save As

- To save a document under a different file name or to a different location, click File, Save As. In the Save As dialog box, you can enter the new file name and/or location. The original file will remain intact.

TRY *it* OUT *pb1-10*

1. Click **File, Save** on **Document1.**
2. Click the **Save in** list arrow and choose a location to save the file, if necessary. Check with your teacher.
3. Enter `testfile` in the File name text box.
4. Click **Save.**
5. Switch to **Document2.**
6. Click the **Save** button on the Standard toolbar.

Continued on next page

TRY it OUT *pb1-10 Continued*

7. Enter `testfile2` in the File name text box.
8. Click **Save.**
9. Switch to **testfile.**
10. Click **File, Save As,** and name the file `testfile4.`
11. Click **Save.** Do not close Word.

Close a File

- As indicated earlier, when you save a file it remains on the screen. To clear the screen, click File, Close, or click the Close button on the document window, as shown in Figure 1.18. If you attempt to close a file you have not yet saved, you will be prompted to save it.

- When several files are open at once, you can save or close all of them simultaneously by holding down the Shift key and clicking File, Save All or File, Close All.

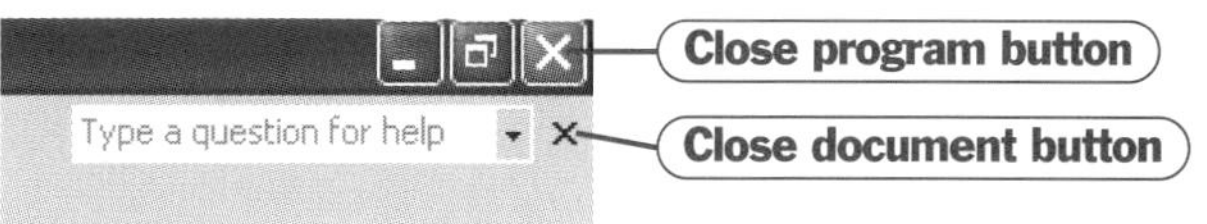

Figure 1.18 Close button on the document window

TRY it OUT *pb1-11*

1. Display **testfile4** if it is not already displayed.
2. Click **File, Close.**
3. Display **Document3** if it is not already displayed.
4. Click **File, Close** to close **Document3.** You will be prompted to save it.
5. Click **Yes** and name the file **testfile3**, then click **Save**. The file is saved and closed.
6. Click the **Close** button on the **testfile2** document window. Do not close the Word program.

7. Click the **New Blank Document** button on the Standard toolbar and enter the name of your school.
8. Click the **New Blank Document** button again and enter today's date.
9. Hold down the **Shift** key and click **File.**
10. Click **Close All.** Do not save.

BASICS

Open a File

- The last four saved files are listed at the bottom of the Getting Started task pane, shown in Figure 1.19, as well as at the bottom of the File menu, shown in Figure 1.20.

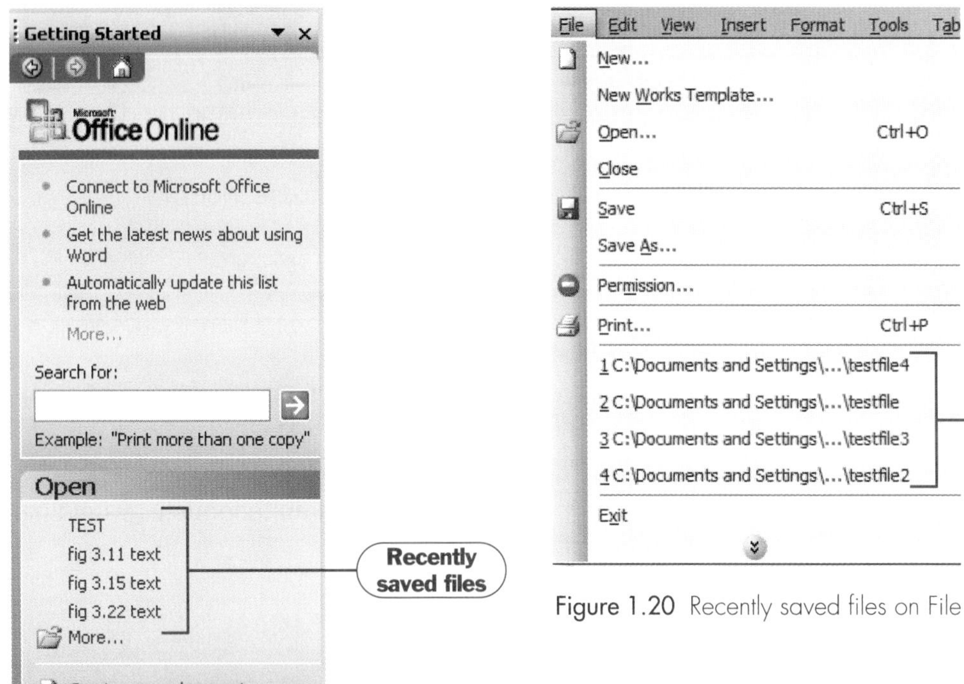

Figure 1.19 Recently saved files in task pane

Figure 1.20 Recently saved files on File menu

▶ To open a recently saved file:

- click the file name in the task pane or
- click File on the menu bar and choose a document from those listed at the bottom of the menu.

▶ To open a file that has not been recently saved:

- click File, Open or
- click the Open button on the Standard toolbar or 
- click More in the Getting Started task pane (see Figure 1.19). In the Open dialog box, shown in Figure 1.21, double-click the file name to be opened from those documents listed. If the desired file is not shown, click the Look in list arrow and choose the drive or folder where the document was saved.

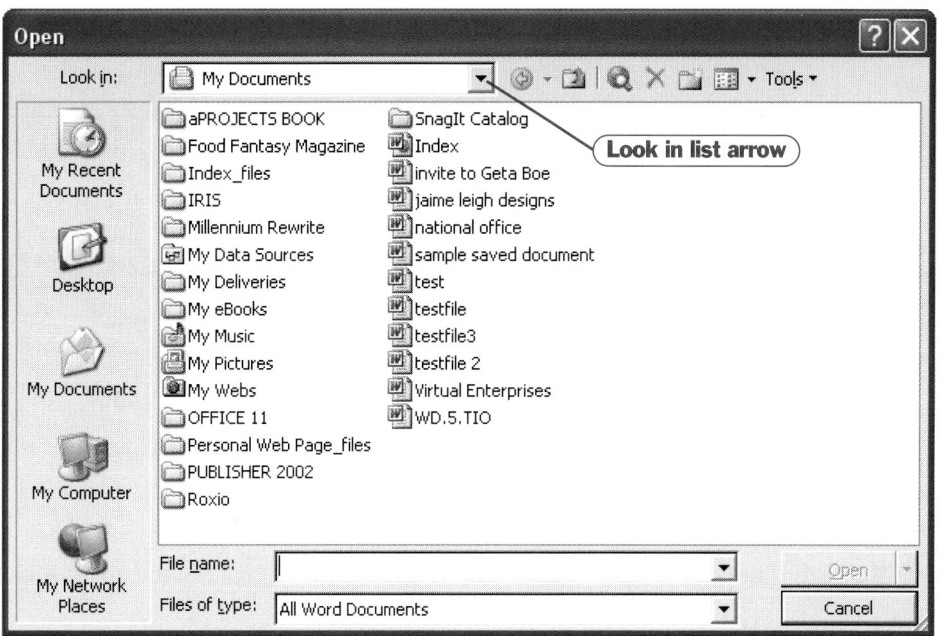

Figure 1.21 Open dialog box

▶ To use an existing document as a basis for a new document, click the From existing document link in the New Document task pane, shown in Figure 1.22. This opens the New from Existing Document dialog box, where you can choose an existing document on which to base the new file. You can then edit this file and save it under a new name.

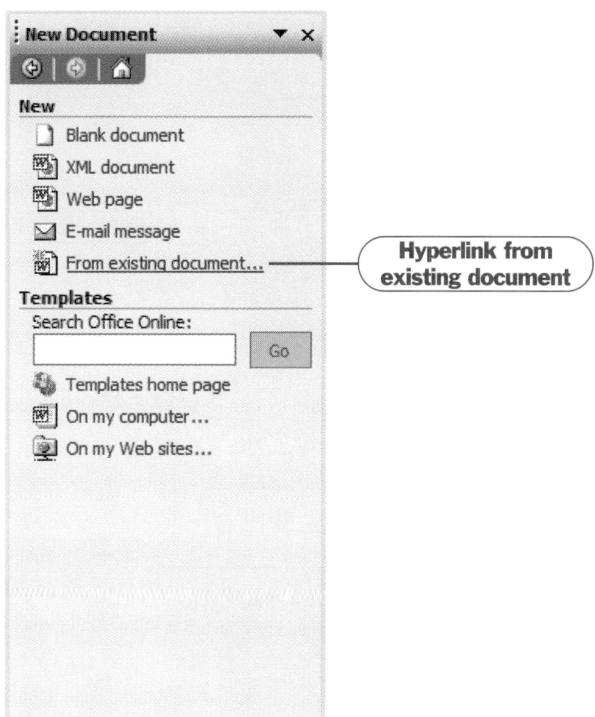

Figure 1.22 New Document task pane

BASICS

TRY it OUT *pb1-12*

1. Click **File.**
2. Click **testfile** at the bottom of the **File** menu.
3. Click **View, Task Pane** to display the task pane.
4. Click **testfile2** in the task pane.
5. Click **File, Open.**
6. Click **testfile3.** If the file name is not listed in the Open dialog box, click the **Look in** list arrow and choose the directory/folder where the file has been saved. Click **Open.**
7. Click **View, Task Pane** to display the task pane.
8. Click **Create a new document** in the Getting Started task pane.
9. Click **From existing document** in the New document task pane, then choose **testfile3** in the **New from Existing Document** dialog box.
10. Press the **Enter** key once.
11. Enter your first and last name.
12. Click **File, Save As,** and name the document **testfile5.**
13. Click **Save.** 
14. Hold down the **Shift** key and click **File.**
15. Click **Close All.**

Search For a File

- You can search for a saved file by its file name or, if you don't remember the file name, you can search for it using unique text contained in the file.
- To search for a file, click File, File Search on the menu, which displays the Basic File Search task pane, shown in Figure 1.23.

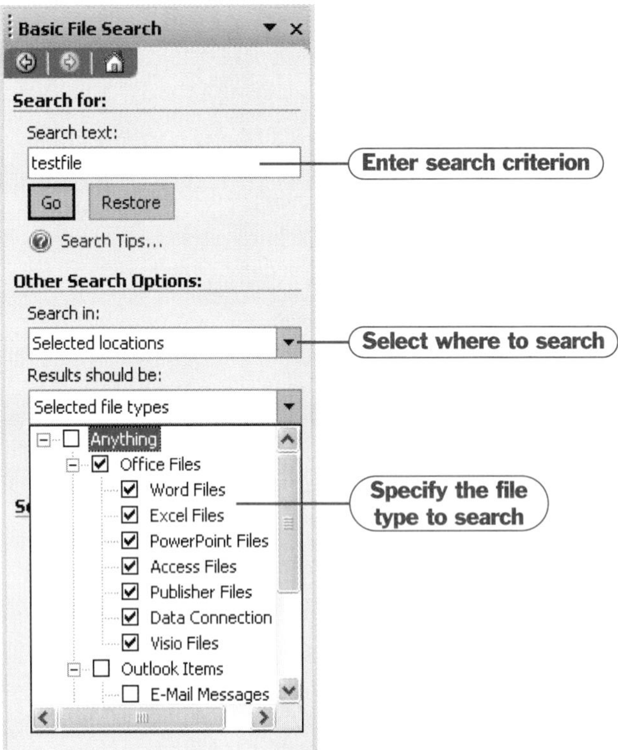

Figure 1.23 Basic File Search task pane

- Begin the search by entering the *search criterion* in the Search text box. In the Other Search Options section, you can specify where to search and the file type. Click Go to start searching.
- A Search Results task pane displays files that contain the search text whether it is in the body of the file or in the file name. For example, a search for the file name "Letter" would return files named Letter, Letterhead, Letter to Mr. Jones, or any file in which the word "letter" was used in the document.
- Once you find the file, click to open it.

TRY *it* OUT *pb1-13*

1. Click **File, File Search.**
2. Enter `testfile` in the Search text box in the Basic File Search task pane.
3. Click the **Search in** list arrow and click the folder in which your test files are located. *Note: To do this, click the plus sign next to My Computer to view your folders. Then deselect the My Computer checkbox and select the checkbox of the folder in which you saved the test files.* Click a blank part of the task pane to close the list.
4. Click the **Results should be** list arrow and click the **Office Files** checkbox to deselect it, if necessary.
5. Click the **Word Files** checkbox to select it, if necessary.
6. Click **Go.** All the testfile documents will display.
7. Click **testfile** to open it.
8. Click **File, Close** to close testfile.

Undo/Redo

- The *Undo* feature lets you reverse an action. If you delete a word by mistake, click the Undo button on the Standard toolbar and you will reverse the action. If you click the Undo button repeatedly, you will reverse a series of actions. An application creates a list of actions as you work. To undo a group of actions, click the Undo list arrow and select the group of actions to be reversed. The most recent action appears at the top of the list.
- The *Redo* feature lets you reverse the previous Undo action. If you undo an action by mistake, click the Redo button on the toolbar. As with Undo, you can redo one or a series of Undo actions.

Quick Print

- To print a file quickly, click the Print button on the Standard toolbar. This *quick print* method sends your document directly to the printer; it does not allow for setting of print options. You will learn to set print options in each program application unit.

TRY *it* OUT *pb1-14*

1. Click the **New Blank Document** button on the toolbar.
2. Type `Summer` and press the **Enter** key.
3. Click the **Undo** button once. *Summer* should no longer be on your screen.

4. Click the **Redo** button once. *Summer* should be back on your screen.

5. Type your first and last name.
6. Click the **Print** button.

7. Close the file; do not save.

GOAL
To create new documents, enter text, and work with multiple files

SETTING THE STAGE
Margins: Default
Start line: At 1"
File names: **1.2names**
1.2foods
1.2colors
1.2colorsall

WHAT YOU NEED TO KNOW

- To create a list, press Enter after each item on the list.
- In this Rehearsal activity, you will create and save several documents, then print and close them. You will also open and search for documents that were previously saved.

DIRECTIONS

1. Start **Word,** if necessary, and open a new blank document.
2. Create a list of names by entering your name and the names of three other people. Press the **Enter** key after each name.
3. Save the file; name it **1.2names.**
4. Display the task pane (if it is not already displayed).
5. Open a new blank document from the task pane.
6. Create a list of your five favorite colors.
7. Save the file; name it **1.2colors.**
8. Switch to **1.2names** and close it.
9. Click the **New Blank Document** button to open a new file. 
10. Make a list of your four favorite foods.
11. Close the file. When prompted, save the file as **1.2foods.**
12. Open **1.2names** and add one additional name to the list.
13. Click **Undo.**
14. Click **Redo.**
15. Save the file.
16. Use the **Basic File Search** task pane to search for a file. Enter a food name you used previously as the search text.
17. Open **1.2foods** from the search results list.
18. In the New Document task pane, create a new document from an existing document by choosing the **1.2colors** file.
19. Add five other colors to the list.

Continued on next page

20. Save the file as **1.2colorsall.**
21. Print the document.
22. Close all files.

Your Name Friend's name Friend's name Friend's name	Red Blue Green Yellow Purple	Pizza Hamburger Ice cream Salad	Red Blue Green Yellow Gray Orange Pink Black Brown
1.2names	1.2colors	1.2foods	1.2colorsall

Cues for Reference

Start a New File

- Click the **New Blank Document** button on the Standard toolbar.

or

Click **Blank Document** in the New Document task pane.

or

1. Click **File, New.**
2. Click **Blank Document.**

Save a File

To save a file for the first time

1. Click the **Save** button.
2. If necessary, click the **Save in** list arrow to select a drive or folder.
3. Enter the file name in the File name text box.
4. Click the **Save** button.

To overwrite or update a previously saved file

- Click the **Save** button.

To save a file with a new name or to a new location

1. Click **File, Save As.**
2. If necessary, click the **Save in** list arrow to select a drive or folder.
3. Enter the file name in the File name text box.
4. Click **Save.**

Save All/Close All Open Documents

1. Press **Shift.**
2. Click **File.**
3. Click **Save All** and/or **Close All.**

Open a File

1. Click the **Open** button.

or

Click **File, Open.**

or

In the Getting Started task pane, click the file name or click **More.**

Office XP: In the New Documents task pane, click the file name or click **More documents**.

2. If necessary, click the **Look in** list arrow box to select a drive or folder.
3. Double-click the file name.

Close a File

- Click the **Close** button on the document window.

or

Click **File, Close.**

Search for a File

1. Click **File, File Search.**
2. Click in the Search text box and enter the search word(s).
3. Set other search options as desired.
4. Click **Go.**

Undo/Redo

1. Click the **Undo** button.
2. Click the **Redo** button.

Quick Print

- Click the **Print** button on the Standard toolbar.

BASICS

LESSON 2

Internet Basics

In this lesson, you will learn the basic concepts of the Internet. You will also learn to use a Web browser to access the World Wide Web, copy text and graphics from Web site pages, print Web site pages, and use search techniques to find information on the Internet.

Upon completion of this lesson, you should be able to use the following skill sets:

- Launch Internet Explorer
- Navigate the browser window
- Access a Web site using a Web address (URL)
- Print Web pages
- Save Web pages
- Copy from a Web site
- Exit the browser
- Search the Internet
  - Use search engines and directories
  - Use Boolean operators to refine a search

Terms

Software-related

World Wide Web
Web browser
Internet Explorer
Home page
Web site
Download
Hyperlink
Web address
URL (uniform resource locator)
Domain name
Search engine
Directory
Text string
Boolean operators: AND, OR, NOT

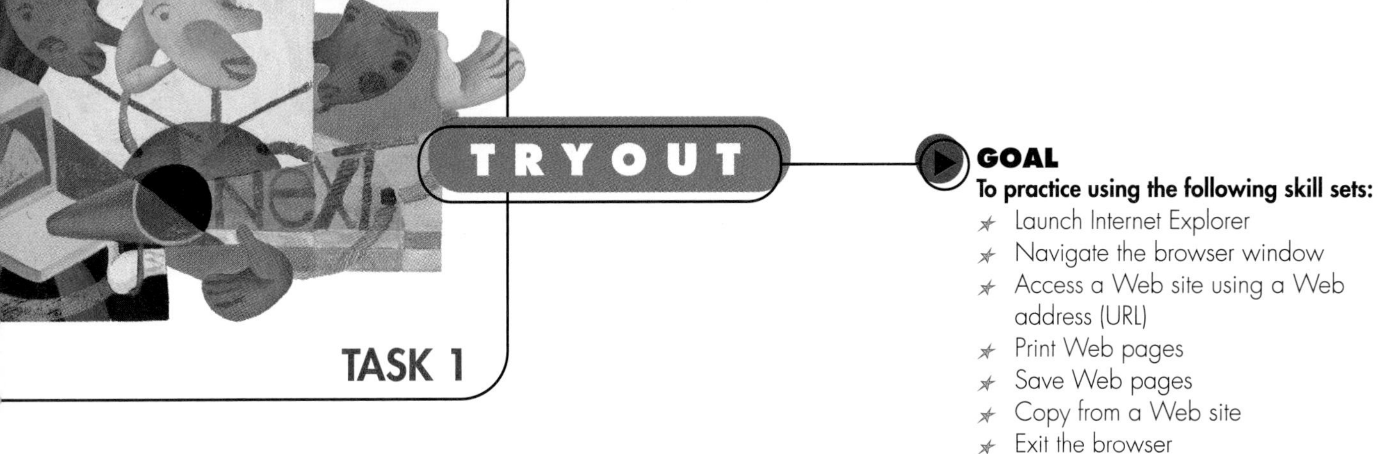

GOAL

To practice using the following skill sets:

- Launch Internet Explorer
- Navigate the browser window
- Access a Web site using a Web address (URL)
- Print Web pages
- Save Web pages
- Copy from a Web site
- Exit the browser

WHAT YOU NEED TO KNOW

Launch Internet Explorer

- The *World Wide Web* is a service of the Internet, in which pages, created by companies, individuals, schools, and government agencies around the world, are linked to one another.
- A *Web browser* is a software program that displays the information you retrieve from the Internet in a readable format. *Internet Explorer* is the Web browser that is included in the Office suite.
- After you connect to the Web with your Internet Service Provider, to start Internet Explorer, click the Search the Web button on the Web toolbar, which contains the same buttons in any Office program, or click the Explorer button on the taskbar, as shown in Figure 2.1.

Figure 2.1 Taskbar

TRY it OUT *pb2-1*

1. Start **Word.**
2. Click **View, Toolbars, Web.**
3. Click the **Search the Web** button to start Internet Explorer.

BASICS

Navigate the Browser Window

- When you start Internet Explorer, the browser window replaces the program window, and a home page is displayed. The *home page* is the start page of any Web site. A *Web site* is a collection of Web pages.
- The Internet Explorer window, shown in Figure 2.2, displays a menu bar, toolbar, Address line, and the page area where the Web page displays. The Status bar displays the status of the information being processed and indicates how much of the page has been downloaded. *Downloading* is the process of copying files from the Internet to your own computer.

▶ The Toolbar found on the Explorer window contains navigation buttons, which are explained in the table below.

BUTTON	EXPLANATION
Back (Back)	Returns you to the previous page
Forward	Advances you to the next page
Stop	Interrupts the search
Refresh	Reloads the Web page
Home	Returns you to the home page

▶ Web pages contain hyperlinks. A *hyperlink* (also referred to as *link*) appears as underlined or colored text or as a graphic. When clicked, a hyperlink takes you to a new page with related information. The mouse pointer changes to a hand when it finds a link.

Figure 2.2 Internet Explorer window with MSN home page displayed

TRY *it* OUT *pb2-2*

1. Click a **hyperlink** on the home page. Click another link.
2. Click the **Back** button to return to the previous page. (Back)

Continued on next page

TRY it OUT *pb2-2 Continued*

3. Click the **Forward** button to advance to the next page. 
4. Click the **Refresh** button to reload the page. 
5. Click the **Home** button to return to the start page. 

Access a Web Site Using a Web Address (URL)

- Every Web site has a unique *Web address,* which is referred to as a *URL (uniform resource locator).* A URL suffix is called a domain name. A *domain name* identifies the Web site as a commercial (.com), noncommercial (.org), government (.gov), educational (.edu), U.S. military (.mil), or network (.net) organization. A typical Web address might look like the ones shown in Figure 2.3.
- Each time a Web page downloads, its address appears on the Address line of the Internet Explorer window. To go to another Web page, click a link or enter the correct address on the Address line and press Enter or click Go to activate the search. An icon to the right of the Menu bar rotates while information is being sought or processed.

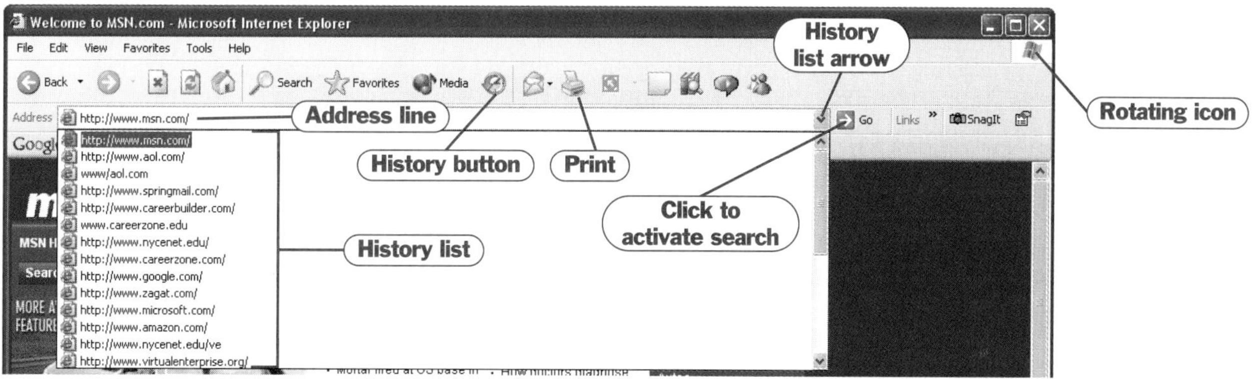

Figure 2.3 Explorer menu bar, toolbar, address line, and history list

- Internet Explorer records a history list of the sites you have visited and allows you to jump back to a recently visited site. To view a history list, click the list arrow to the right of the Address line as shown in Figure 2.3. You can also click the History button on the toolbar to view a history of the sites you visited on specific days of the week.

Print Web Pages

- Printing Web pages enables you to keep information you research for future reference. To print the current Web page, click the Print button on the Explorer toolbar (see Figure 2.3), or click File, Print on the Explorer menu bar. 

TRY it OUT *pb2-3*

1. Click another link on the displayed Web page and note the address that displays on the Address line.
2. Enter the following URL on the Address line: `www.dell.com`.

Continued on next page

BASICS

TRY it OUT *pb2-3 Continued*

3. Press **Enter.**
4. Enter the following URL on the Address line: `www.nasa.gov.`
5. Click **Go.**
6. Click the **Address** list arrow and view the list of the sites visited. Click off the menu to close the list.
7. Click **File, Print.** View the print options, then click Cancel.

Save Web Pages

- Because Web sites change constantly, it is a good idea to save a page that you find valuable. To do so, click File, Save As on the Explorer menu bar. The process of saving a Web page is the same as that for saving a file. A saved Web page displays the Explorer icon next to its file name.

Copy from a Web Site

- You can copy text or a picture from a Web site and paste it into an Office application. Select the Web site text or picture to be copied, right-click, and choose Copy from the Shortcut menu, as shown in Figure 2.4. Position the insertion point in the Office document to receive the copied text or picture and click Edit, Paste.

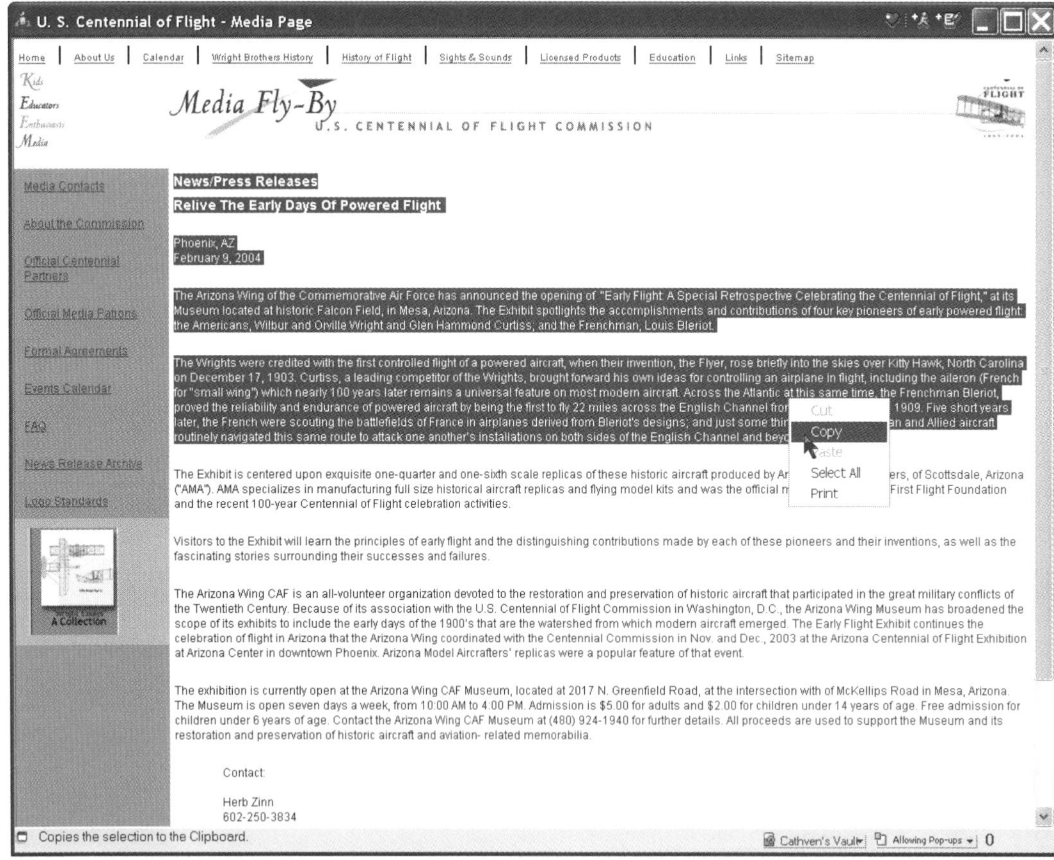

Figure 2.4 Copying text from a Web site

▶ To save a picture, right-click the picture and choose Save Picture As from the Shortcut menu, as shown in Figure 2.5. (You can also e-mail and print the picture from this menu.)

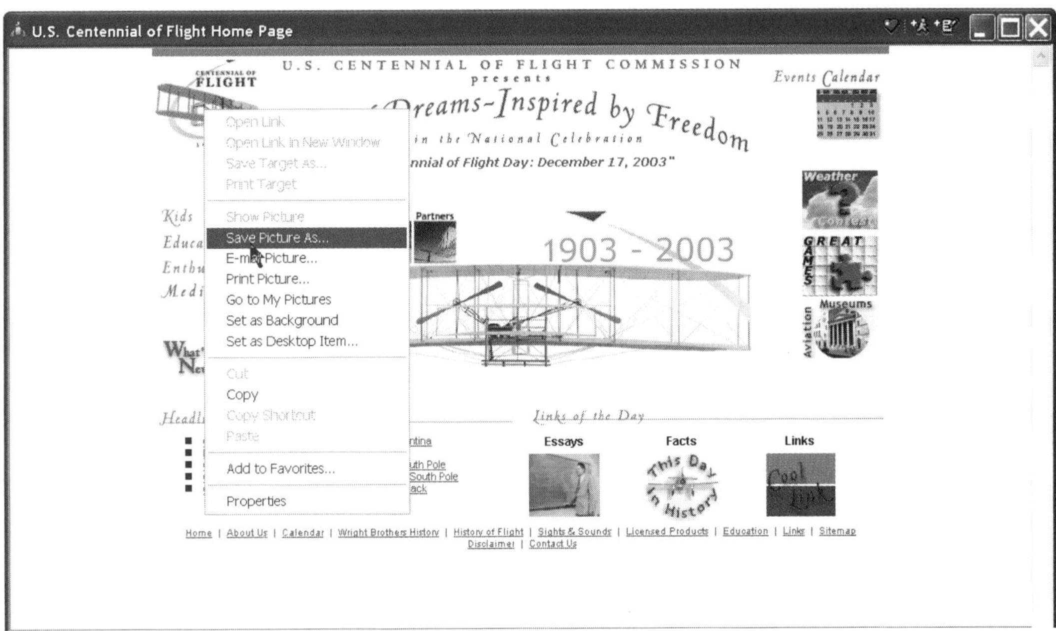

Figure 2.5 Copying a picture from a Web site

▶ In the Save Picture dialog box, shown in Figure 2.6, choose the folder in which to save the file, enter a name for the picture, and click Save.

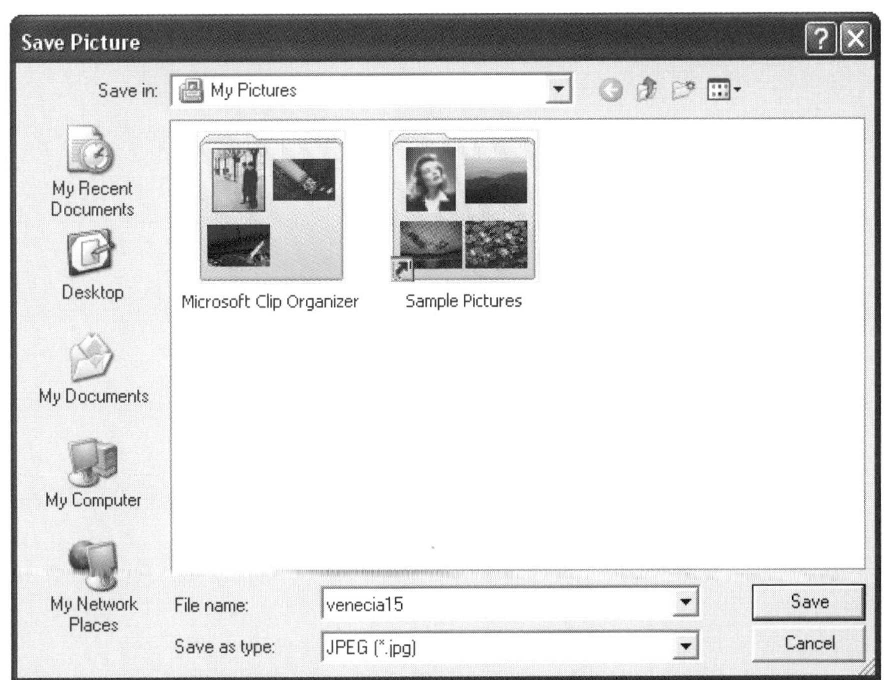

Figure 2.6 Save Picture dialog box

▶ Saved picture files may be inserted into a document. You will learn more about inserting pictures into a document in the Word unit of this text.

TRY*it* OUT *pb2-4*

1. Open a new blank document in Word, if necessary.
2. Open **Internet Explorer.**
3. Enter `www.centennialofflight.gov` on the Address line. Click **Go.**
4. Click a link to an article or essay.
5. Select the first paragraph of text on that page.

Note: Web sites change constantly, so the page you see when you access this Web site may not resemble Figure 2.4.

6. Right-click and choose **Copy.**
7. Click the **Word** button on the taskbar to switch to the blank document.
8. Click **Edit, Paste** on the Word menu bar.
9. Click the **Explorer** button on the taskbar to return to the browser window.
10. Find a picture to copy.
11. Right-click the picture and choose **Save Picture As.**
12. Select a folder in which to save the file; enter `flight` as the file name.
13. Click **Save.**
14. Click **File, Close** to close Explorer. Close Word without saving the file.

Exit the Browser

▶ To exit Internet Explorer, click File, Close on the menu bar. Exiting the browser does not necessarily mean that you are exiting from your Internet Service Provider (the service that gives you access to the Internet). Check to see that you have disconnected from your service provider so that you are not charged for additional time online.

A
1
2
3

GOAL
To access Web sites using a Web address, print Web site pages, and exit the browser

TASK 1

WHAT YOU NEED TO KNOW

- Because Web sites can change often, a Web site may display a different home/start page each time you access it.
- If the Standard and Address toolbars are not visible when you start Internet Explorer, click View, Toolbars and choose the toolbars you want to display.
- Be sure to cite the source of any Internet material you use in a document. Failing to do so is called plagiarism. See Word, Lesson 3, to learn how to cite from the Internet.
- If you try to copy a picture and find you are having difficulty, it may be that the picture is not available to you because it has been copyrighted. A copyrighted picture has legal protection and cannot be used unless you obtain written permission from the publisher. Be sure to read Web pages carefully for this information.
- In this Rehearsal activity, you will access a Web site, copy text and a picture, print Web pages, and exit the browser.

DIRECTIONS

1. Start Internet Explorer, if it is not already running.
2. Display the toolbar, if it is not already displayed.
3. Enter the following Web address (URL) on the address line, then press the **Enter** key or click **Go:** `www.microsoft.com/`. See the home page in Illustration A. Scroll down and click **Careers.**
4. Print one copy of the page(s). Read the information and keep the printed copy as a reference.
5. Click the **Back** button.

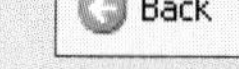

6. Click the **Forward** button.

7. Click the **Home** button.

8. Access the following Web site: `www.nba.com`. See the home page in Illustration B.
   - Click the **Teams** list arrow.
   - Click a team you are interested in learning more about.
9. Print one copy of the team page.
10. Click the **History** button.
11. Return to the home page. Close the **History** pane.
12. Return to the NBA home page.
13. Access the following Web site: `www.nasa.gov`.
14. Wait for the page to load and click **GO TO MAIN NASA SITE.**
15. Print one copy of the page.
16. Copy a picture from the page and paste it into a new blank Word document.
17. Return to Internet Explorer.
18. Save the NASA site; name it **nasa.**
19. Access the following Web site: `www.bloomberg.com`.
20. Click **About Bloomberg.**
21. Click **About Bloomberg** on this page.
22. Scroll through the page, and copy the paragraph about Bloomberg.

Continued on next page

23. Paste it into a new blank Word document.
24. Close the browser and all files; do not save.

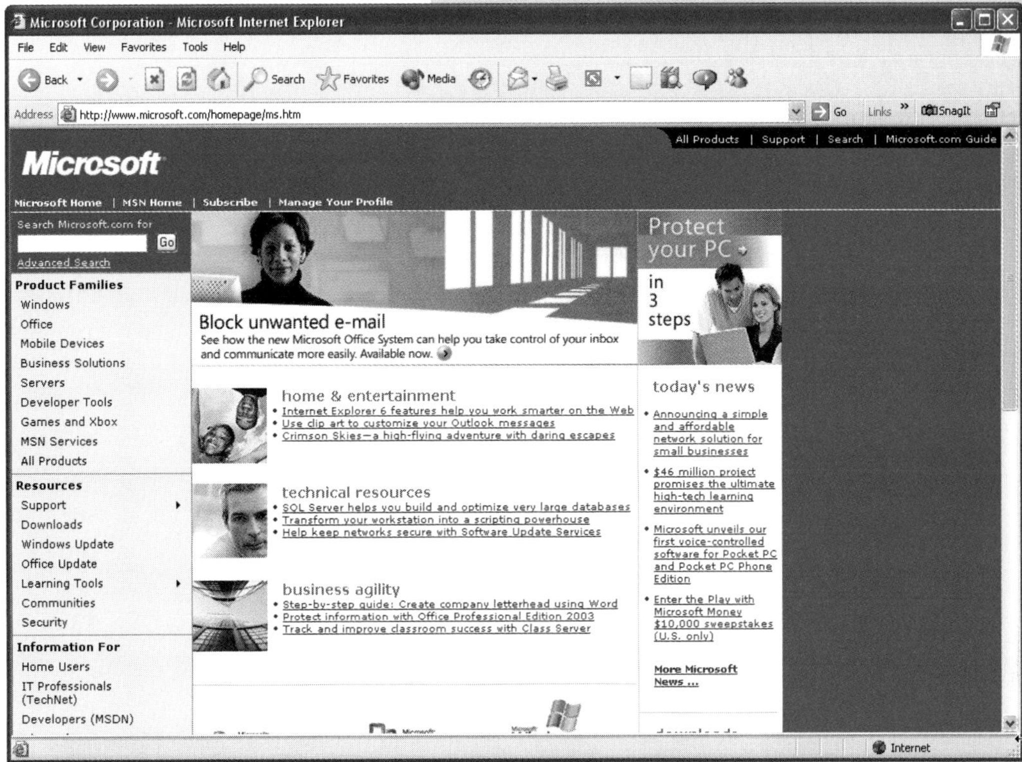

Illustration A

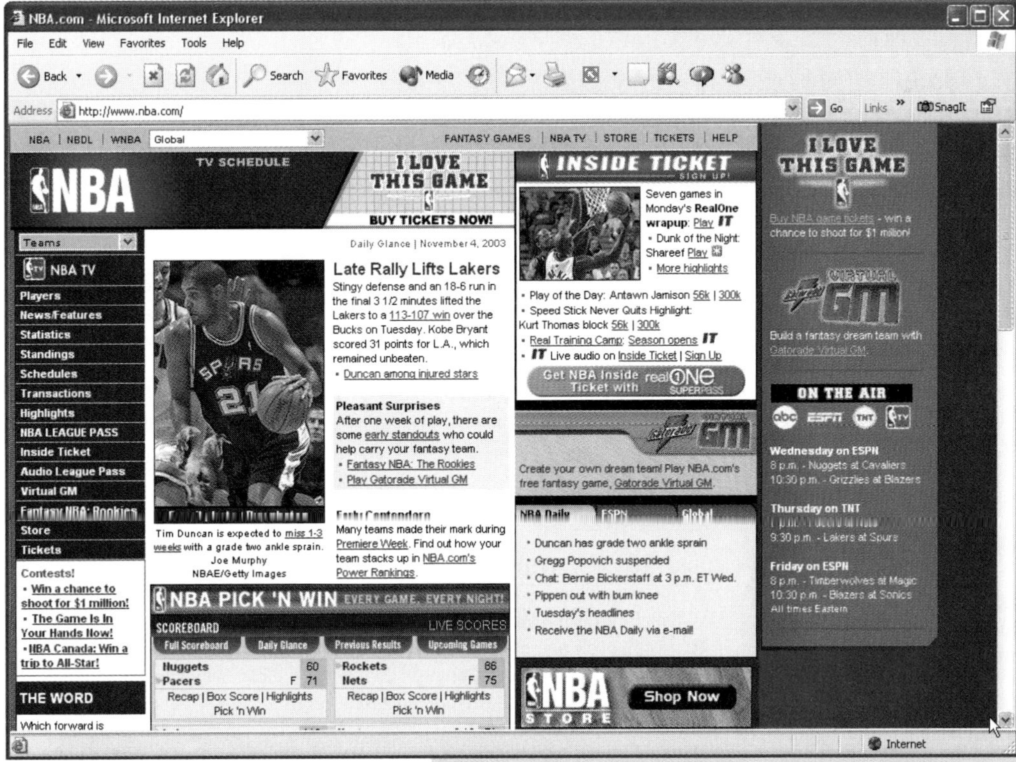

Illustration B

BASICS

Cues for Reference

Start Internet Explorer

- Click the **Explorer** button on the taskbar.

  or

1. Start an Office application such as Word or Excel.
2. Click **View, Toolbars, Web.**
3. Click the **Search the Web** button. 

Display Internet Explorer Toolbar (if necessary)

1. Click **View.**
2. Point to **Toolbars.**
3. Click **Standard Buttons.**

Access a Web Site

1. Enter the URL on the Address line.
2. Press **Enter** or click **Go.**

   or

- Click a link on the displayed Web page.

Print Web Pages

- Click the **Print** button on the Explorer toolbar. 

Copy from a Web Site

1. Highlight the text or point to the picture on the Web page to copy.
2. Right-click and choose **Copy.**
3. Position the insertion point in the document to paste the copied text or picture.
4. Click **Edit, Paste** on the menu bar.

Save a Picture

1. Right-click the picture to save.
2. Click **Save Picture As** from the short-cut menu.
3. Select a folder to save, enter a file name, and click **Save.**

Save a Web Site

1. Click **File.**
2. Click **Save As.**
3. Select a folder to save, enter a file name, and click **Save.**

Exit the Browser

1. Click **File.**
2. Click **Close.**

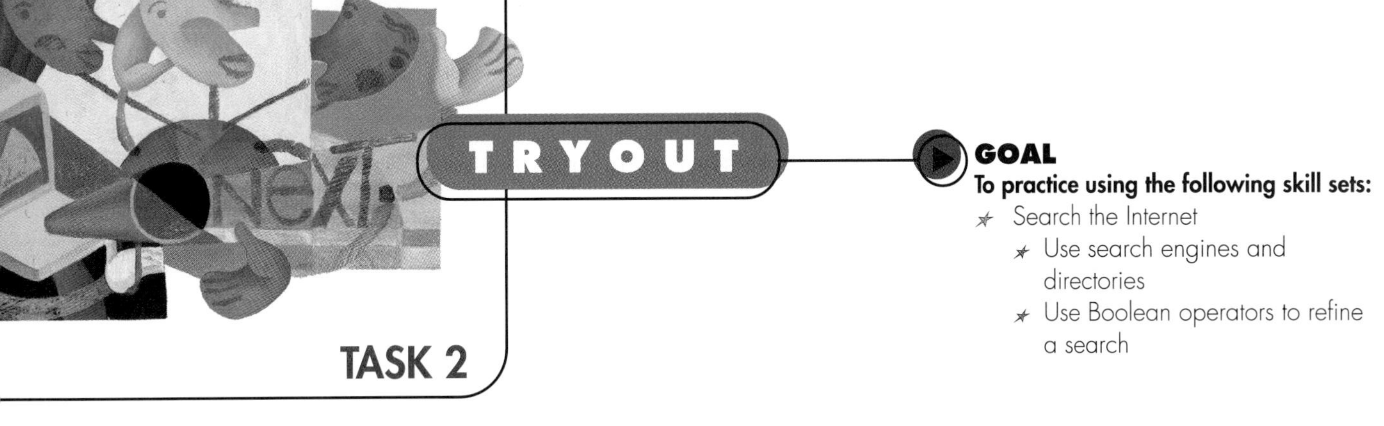

GOAL

To practice using the following skill sets:

- Search the Internet
  - Use search engines and directories
  - Use Boolean operators to refine a search

WHAT YOU NEED TO KNOW

Search the Internet

- The Internet contains enormous amounts of information. You learned in the previous task that you could enter the Web address in the Address line and find information on that site. It would be impossible, however, to know every site where specific information can be found. Therefore, you must search the Internet to locate Web sites with the information you want. To find the information most efficiently, you need to use the tools that have been developed for this purpose.
- It is important to note the following when working with the Internet:
  - Anyone can publish information on the Internet—not all information is accurate.
  - Anything downloaded from the Internet can have a virus. Be sure that the computers you are using have virus-protection software installed.

Use Search Engines and Directories

- One of the tools you can use to search for information is a *search engine*—a software program that searches the Web and automatically indexes home pages. The index displays keywords with hyperlinks to new pages. Popular search engines include HotBot, AltaVisa, and Lycos. The term "search engine" is often used to describe both true search engines as well as directories. They are not the same.
- A *directory* displays information by major topic headings, which are broken down into smaller topics that are then broken down further. A search looks for matches only in the descriptions submitted. Yahoo, Magellan, and Infoseek are examples of popular directories.
- Both search engines and directories are often called "Web crawlers" or "spiders," because they crawl the Web looking for information.

BASICS

TRY *it* OUT *pb2-5*

1. Start **Internet Explorer.**
2. Enter the following directory Web address in the Address line: `www.yahoo.com`. Click **Go.**
3. Enter `British` in the Search the Web box and click **Yahoo! Search.** Notice the results.
4. Enter the following search engine Web address in the Address line: `www.altavista.com`. Press **Enter.**
5. Enter `British` in the **SEARCH box** and click **FIND.** Notice the results.
6. Do not close the browser.

- To start a search, access a search engine or directory, such as Yahoo, AltaVista, or Google. Search engine sites always provide a Search box in which to enter the word, words, or phrase you wish to use in your search. This is often referred to as a *text string*. Text strings that contain a single word or phrase are simple; text strings that contain operators (see below) can be more complex. After entering a text string in the Search box, press **Enter** or click the **Search button**, as shown in Figure 2.7; the button is sometimes named Go, Go Get It, Google Search, or Find.

Figure 2.7 Search engine home page

Use Boolean Operators to Refine a Search

- A search can return vast amounts of information that match your request. You can refine your search to return fewer sites by entering more words in the text string or by using advanced search techniques. One such technique is to use Boolean operators as part of the search string.
- A *Boolean operator* is a word or symbol that narrows a search to give you more specific information. Although operators do help filter sites, they are not perfect. The most common Boolean operators are AND, OR, and NOT.
  - Use *AND* or a plus sign (+) when you want the results to include all the words in the text string. ("Kansas AND City Hotels" will find sites that contain all three words in the search results.)
  - Use *OR* when you want the results to include one of the words in the text string. ("Kansas OR City Hotels" will find sites that contain either "Kansas" *or* "City Hotels.")
  - Use *NOT* or a minus sign (–) when you want the results to include only the words preceding the NOT operator. (New York NOT City will find sites that contain New York but not sites that contain New York City.) In Figures 2.8 and 2.9, note how the search for British novels was narrowed by using the AND operator in the second search.
- Not all search sites support the use of operators.

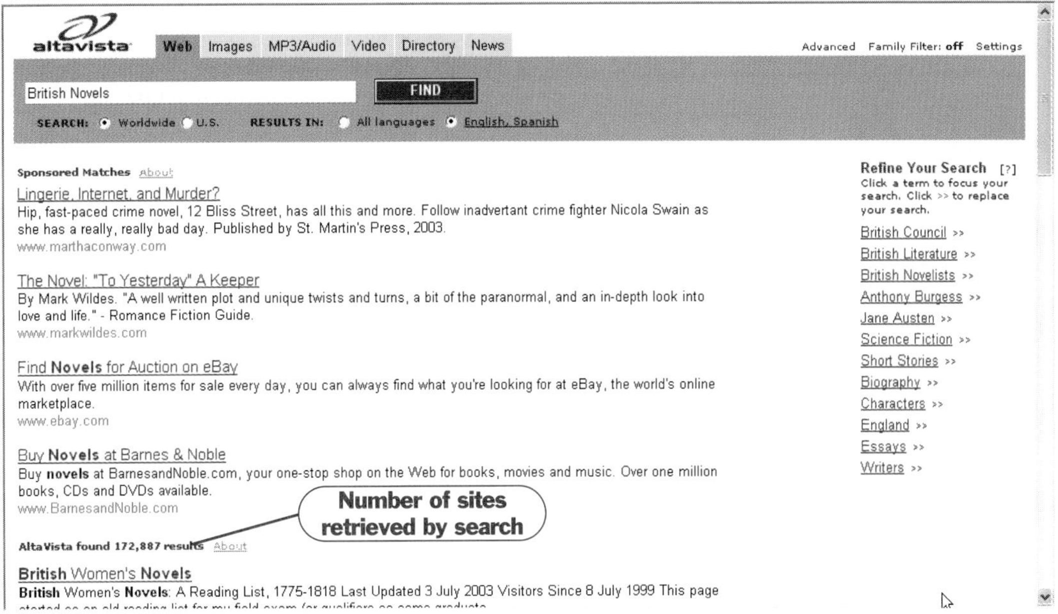

Figure 2.8 Search string in AltaVista

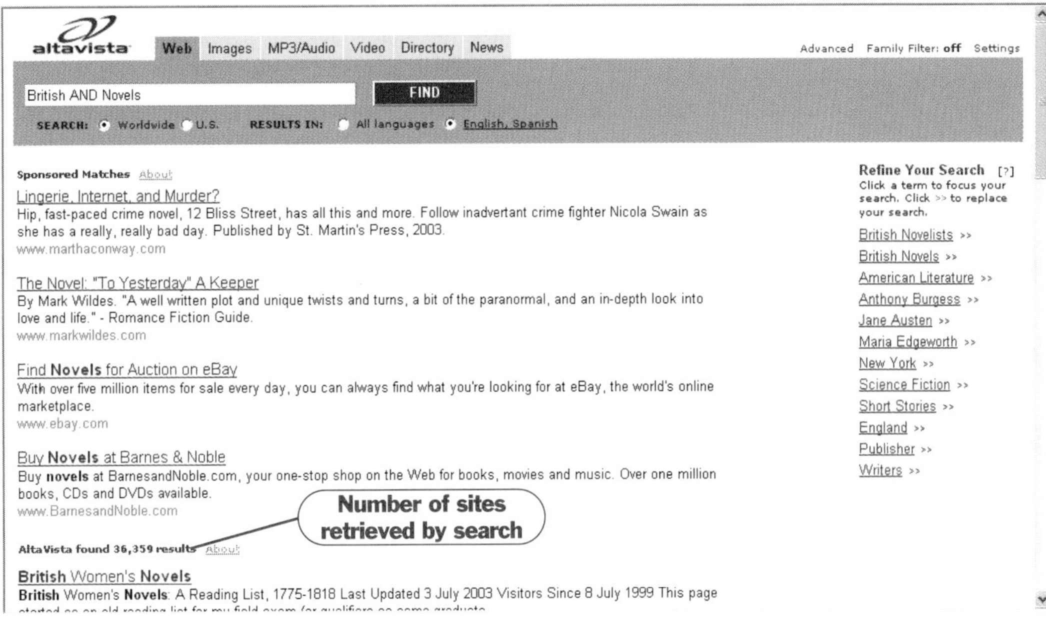

Figure 2.9 Search string using a Boolean operator in AltaVista

BASICS

TRY *it* OUT *pb2-6*

1. Return to Internet Explorer and click the **Back** button.
2. Enter `British AND Novels` in the **SEARCH box.**
3. Click **FIND** or press the **Enter** key.
4. Enter `British OR Novels`. Press **Enter**. Notice how the results are different from those of the previous search.
5. Click **File, Close.**

GOAL
To search the Internet using search engines/directories and Boolean operators

WHAT YOU NEED TO KNOW

- Seek out multiple sites when you research a topic. Directories and search engines vary in their content and accuracy and will often yield different results. Therefore, use a directory when you have a broad topic to research; use a search engine when you have a narrow topic to research.
- In this Rehearsal activity, you will search the Internet and print Web pages.

DIRECTIONS

1. Start **Internet Explorer.**
2. Enter `www.yahoo.com` in the Address line and press **Enter.** See this home page on the next page.
3. Enter `www.google.com` in the Address line and press **Enter.**
4. Enter the text string `Kansas AND City Hotels` in the Search box and press **Enter.**
5. Notice the results and the number of sites this search has yielded. Print one copy of the page.
6. Enter the text string `Kansas OR City Hotels` in the Search box and press **Enter.**
7. Notice the results and the number of sites this search has yielded. Print one copy of the page.
8. Enter the text string `Kansas NOT City` in the Search box and press **Enter.**
9. Notice the results and the number of sites this search has yielded. Print one copy.
10. Use the History list to return to yahoo.com.
11. Repeat steps 4 through 9.
12. Click the **Home** button. 
13. Compare the printouts and note the difference between the results when the search is narrowed using Boolean operators.
14. Close the browser.

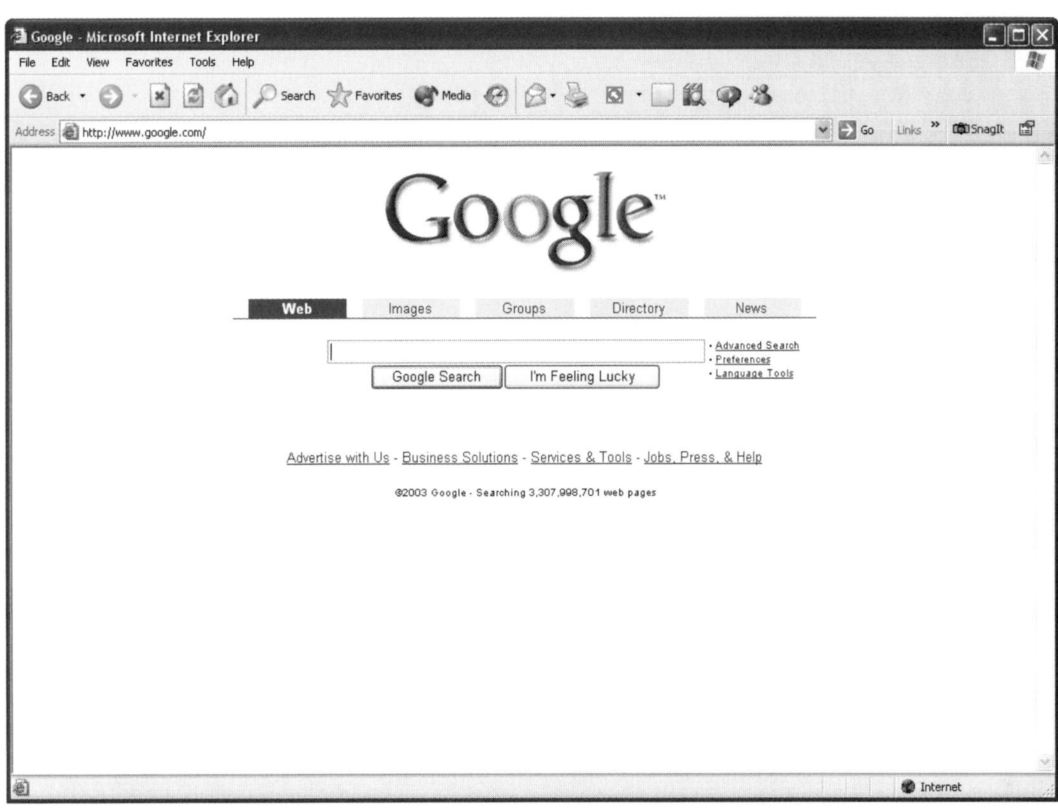

BASICS

Cues for Reference

Access a Search Engine or Directory

1. Start Internet Explorer.
2. Enter a search engine or directory site in the Address line.
3. Press **Enter.**

Use a Search Engine or Directory to Refine the Search

1. Enter a text string in the Search box.

Note: You can use a simple text string or one that contains the operators AND, NOT, or OR.

2. Press **Enter** or click the **Search** button.

1
2
3

PERFORMING WITH WORD
INTRODUCTORY UNIT

LESSON 1
Word Basics

LESSON 2
Correspondence

LESSON 3
Reports and Long Documents

LESSON 4
Meeting Documents, Schedules, and Forms

LESSON 5
Sales and Marketing Documents

LESSON 6
Integration/Word and the Web

LESSON 1

Word Basics

In this lesson, you will be introduced to Word and its basic features.

Upon completion of this lesson, you should have mastered the following skill sets:

- Start Word
- Explore the Word screen
- AutoCorrect
- AutoFormat as you type
- Automatic spell check
- Automatic grammar check
- Create new documents
- Switch between open documents
- Arrange multiple documents
- Change document views
- View two parts of document at once
- Zoom
- Navigate through a document
- Select text/data
- Insert, overwrite and delete text
- Show/hide codes
- Hide text
- Office Clipboard
- Move and copy text
- Spelling and grammar check
- Save and Save As
- Print preview
- Print
- Work with fonts
  - Change font
  - Change font size
  - Change font style
  - Change font color
- Apply font effects
- Highlight text
- Change case
- Use symbols
- Format painter

Terms

Software-related

Active document
AutoCorrect
AutoFormat as you type
Click and type
Clipboard
Cut and paste
Drag and drop
Insert mode
Landscape orientation
Nonbreaking space
Normal view
Outline view
Overtype mode
Portrait orientation
Print layout view
Reading layout view
Save as
Show/hide codes
Task pane
Web layout view
Word-wrap
Zoom

GOAL
To open a document and practice using the following skill sets:

- Start Word
- Explore the Word screen
- AutoCorrect
- AutoFormat as you type
- Automatic spell check
- Automatic grammar check

WHAT YOU NEED TO KNOW

About Word

Word is the word processing application within the Office suite that enables you to create letters, memos, reports, and other text-based documents. The features found in Word allow you to perfect and enhance your document and share it among workgroups. In addition, Word provides you with quick access to the Internet to support and communicate the documents you create.

Start Word

- There are two basic ways to start Word:
    1. Click the **Start** button on the taskbar, point to **All Programs,** point to **Microsoft Office,** then click **Microsoft Office Word 2003,** as shown in Figure 1.1.

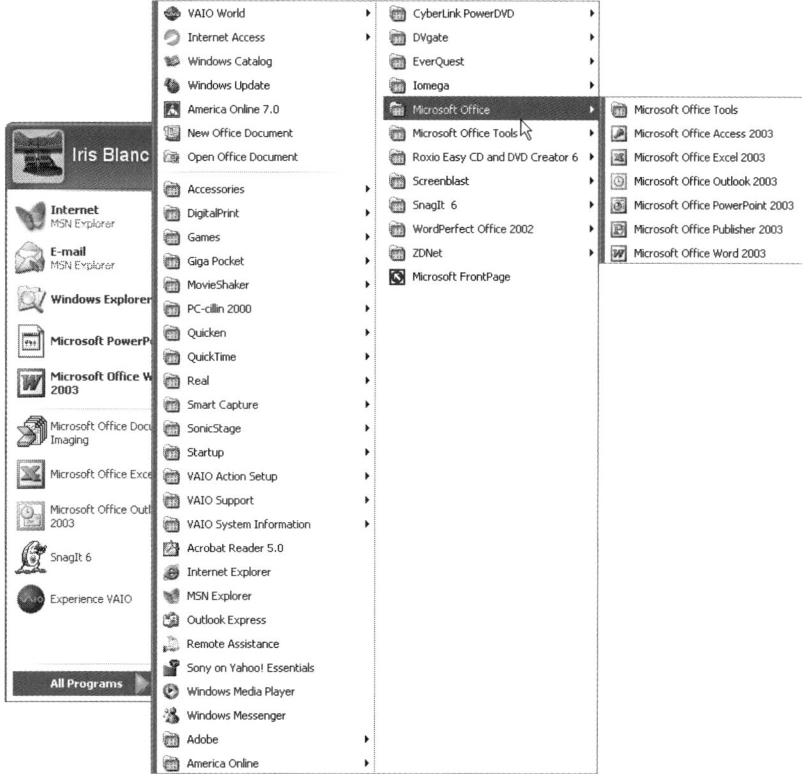

Figure 1.1 Start Word from Taskbar

2. Double-click the Microsoft Word program icon on the desktop as shown in Figure 1.2.

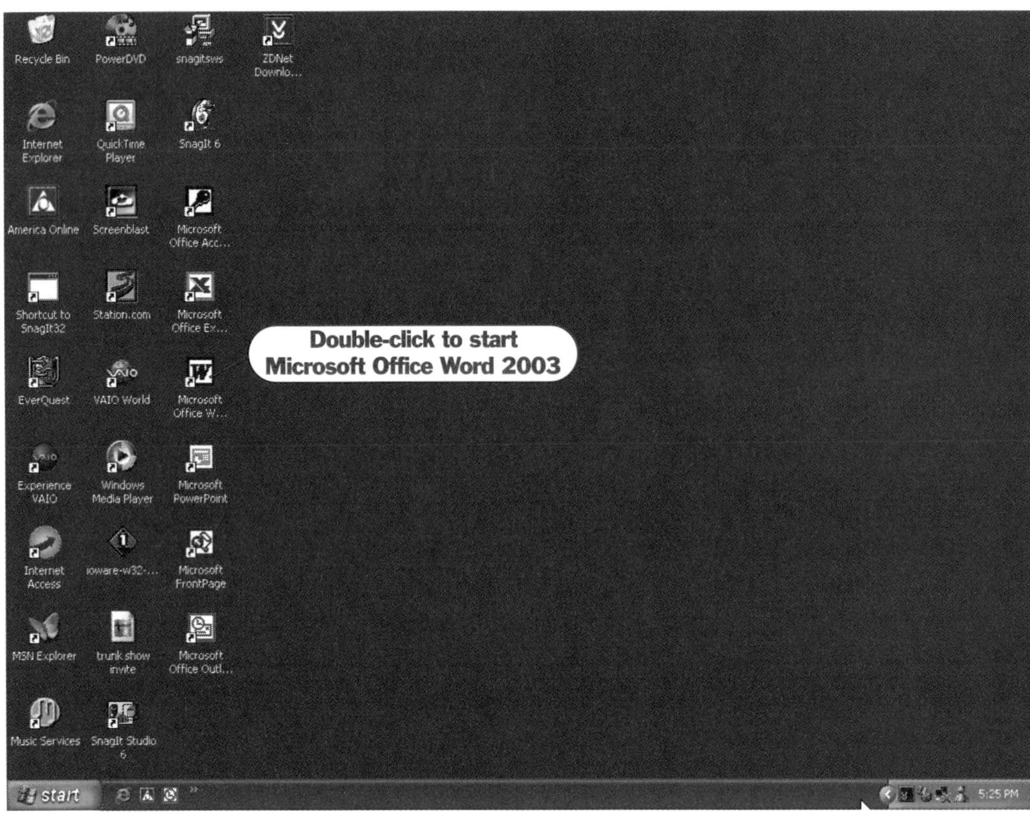

Figure 1.2 Start Word from Desktop

TRY *it* OUT *w1-1*

1. Click **Start.**
2. Point to **All Programs.**
3. Point to **Microsoft Office**.
4. Click **Microsoft Office Word 2003.**
5. Click the Close Window button on the program window. 

Explore the Word Screen

- After Word starts, a new blank page appears, ready for you to create a new document. A *task pane* may also appear to the right of the blank page, providing quick access to opening, creating, formatting, and sharing documents. A thumbnail pane may also appear to the left of the page, showing a miniature of each page that you create. If you do not see the task pane, click View, Task Pane. If you do not see the thumbnail pane, click View, Thumbnails.
- The Word screen that appears when the application starts is shown in Figure 1.3. A brief review of each screen element follows.

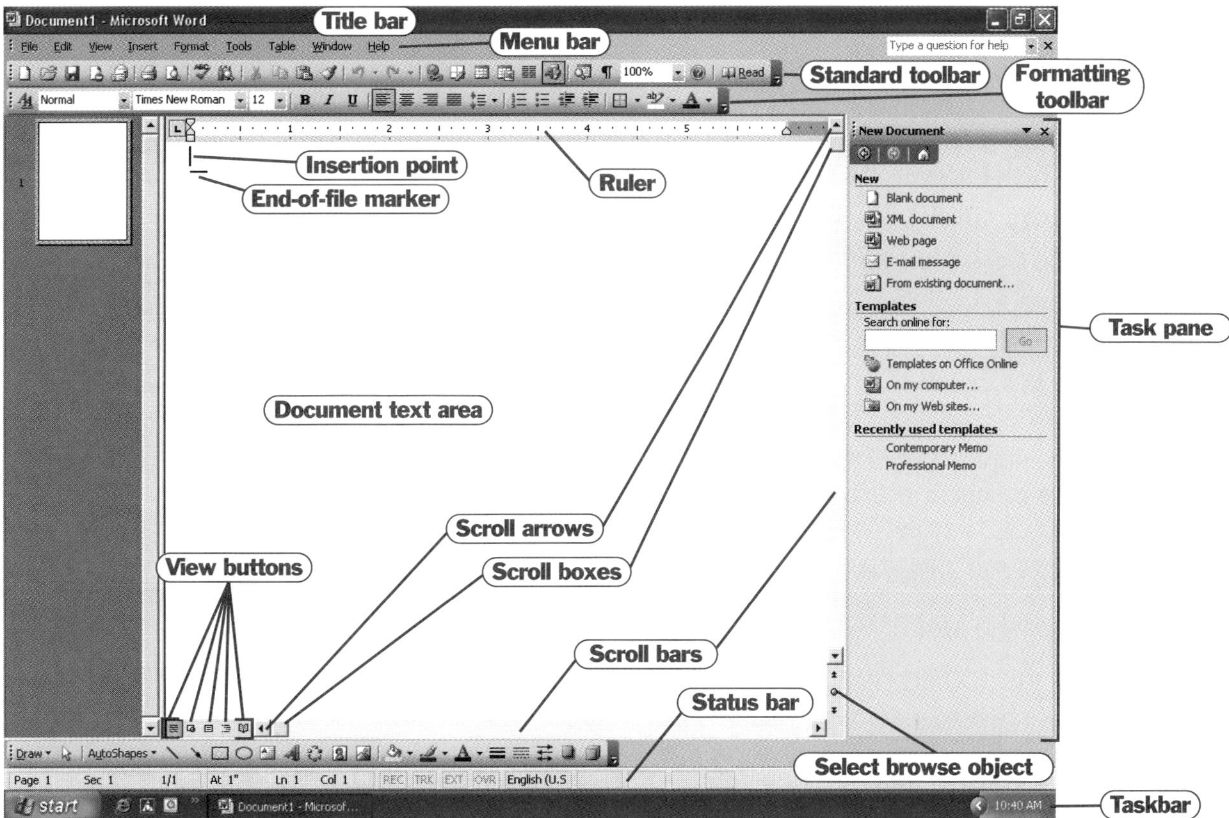

Figure 1.3 Word screen

- The **Title bar** displays the document and program names.
- The **Menu bar** displays items that you select to execute commands.
- The **Standard toolbar** contains buttons to accomplish many common word processing tasks, such as printing and saving a document.
- The **Formatting toolbar** contains buttons to help change the appearance of text in a document such as text alignment and font styles.
- The **Ruler** displays the horizontal measurement of the page. The vertical ruler displays only in print layout view (see Document views).
- The **Document text area** is the blank area where you enter document text.
- The **Insertion point** is the vertical blinking line that indicates where text will be entered.
- The **End-of-file marker** is a horizontal line that indicates the end of a document.
- **Scroll bars**, **Scroll boxes**, and **Scroll arrows** move the screen view horizontally or vertically. (The use of these navigation options will be covered in Task 2).
- The **Select browse object button** allows you to search a document by a specific page, table, graphic, or other item.
- The **View buttons** allow you to change document views.
- The **Status bar** displays the page number (Page 1), section (Sec 1), the current page and total number of pages (1/1 indicates page one of a one-page document), the measurement in inches from the top edge of the page (At 1"), the line number at which the insertion point is currently located (Ln 1), and the distance of the insertion point from the left margin in number of characters (Col 1). The status bar also contains mode buttons. Double-clicking a mode button provides easy access to some of Word's features.

- The **Taskbar** displays the Start button and the Quick-Launch toolbar, as well as open documents and programs.

▶ To display more of the document text area, you can do one of the following:

a. *Close the task pane:* Click the Close button on the task pane title bar or click View and deselect Task Pane.

b. *Hide toolbars:* Click View, Toolbars and deselect those you want to hide.

c. *Display the full screen without any elements of the Word window:* Click View, Full Screen.

TRY *it* OUT *w1-2*

Note: While the initial Word screen may show toolbar buttons on one row, you need to display toolbar buttons on two rows to correlate your computer screen with subsequent figures in the Word unit. These rows constitute the Standard and Formatting toolbars.

1. Open Microsoft Office Word 2003.
2. Click the toolbar options arrow and select **Show Buttons on Two Rows.** If buttons are already on two rows, skip this step.
3. Click each menu bar item. Notice the submenu commands.
4. Move the mouse pointer over each toolbar button to display its ScreenTip.
5. Click **View, Ruler** to hide the rulers.
6. Click **View, Ruler** to redisplay the rulers.
7. Click the **Close** button on the task pane. 
8. Click **View, Task Pane** to redisplay the task pane.
9. Click **View, Toolbars, Standard** to hide the Standard toolbar.
10. Click **View, Toolbars, Standard** to redisplay the Standard toolbar.
11. Click **View, Full Screen.**
12. Click **Close Full Screen.**
13. Click **View, Thumbnails** to hide the thumbnail pane, if necessary.
14. Click **View, Thumbnails** to redisplay the thumbnail pane.

AutoCorrect

▶ The *AutoCorrect* feature automatically corrects common capitalization, spelling, and grammatical errors as you type.

▶ You can also set this feature to insert specific words by entering an abbreviation. For example, you can enter "Mr" and have AutoCorrect replace it with "Mr. Snufulufougus."

▶ You can also enter words you commonly misspell into the AutoCorrect dictionary. To do so, click Tools, AutoCorrect Options. In the AutoCorrect dialog box, shown in Figure 1.4, make the changes you want.

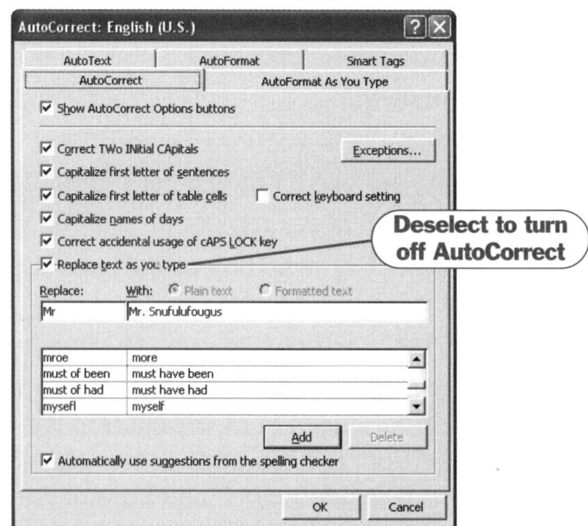

Figure 1.4 AutoCorrect dialog box

WORD

- When a word is corrected by the AutoCorrect feature, a blue horizontal line appears below the corrected word. Placing your insertion point on the line displays an AutoCorrect options button shown in Figure 1.5. Clicking it displays options related to the corrected word.
- The AutoCorrect feature is on by default. If you find this feature annoying, deselect the Replace text as you type check box within the AutoCorrect dialog box to turn the feature off.

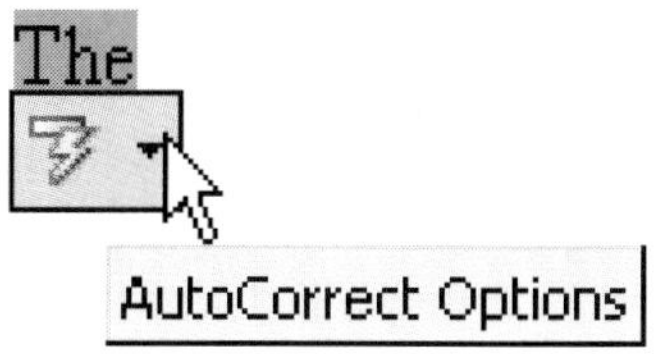

Figure 1.5 AutoCorrect options button

AutoFormat As You Type

- The *AutoFormat As You Type* feature allows you to set formatting options that are applied automatically as you type your document. For example, you can choose to automatically change two hyphens (--) to a dash (–), fractions such as 1/2 to ½ , and ordinals (2nd) with a superscript 2nd. To set formatting options as you type, click Tools, AutoCorrect Options. In the AutoCorrect dialog box, click the AutoFormat As You Type tab as shown in Figure 1.6, and select the options you want.

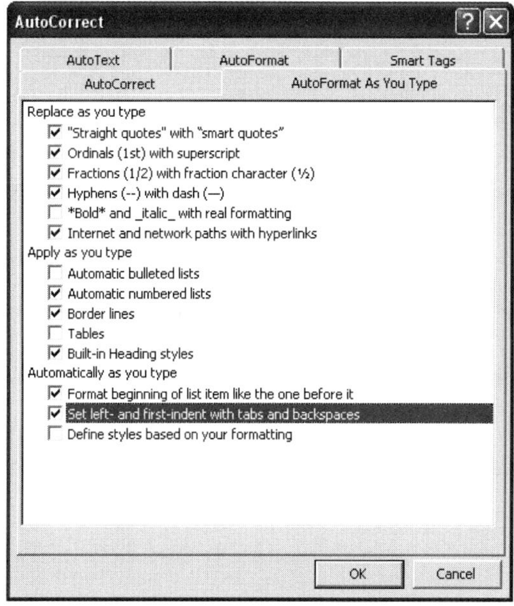

Figure 1.6 AutoFormat As You Type options

TRY *it* OUT *w1-3*

Note: A blank document should be open on screen.

1. Enter each word exactly as shown and note that the correct spelling will appear after pressing the spacebar.

   `teh accomodate adn acheive`

2. Click **Tools, AutoCorrect Options**. Click the **AutoCorrect tab**.
3. Enter **`usa`** in the Replace text box.
4. Enter **`United States of America`** in the With text box.
5. Click the **AutoFormat As You Type** tab, if the tab is not already selected.
   a. Select the following options, if they have not already been selected: *Ordinals (1st) with superscript* and *Fractions (1/2) with fraction character (½).*
   b. Deselect the following option if it is selected: *Set left- and first-indent with tabs and backspaces.*
6. Note the other options.
7. Click **OK**.
8. Enter: **`On May 1st I will be going to the usa. I will be there for 6 1/2 months.`**
9. Close the file; do not save.

Automatic Spell Check

- The *automatic spell check* feature underlines spelling errors with a wavy red line as you type. To correct a misspelled word that is underlined, right-click the word, and a Shortcut menu, shown in Figure 1.7, displays a list of suggested corrections. Click the correctly spelled word on the menu to replace the incorrectly spelled word in the document.
- You can add the word you misspelled to the application's dictionary or to AutoCorrect.

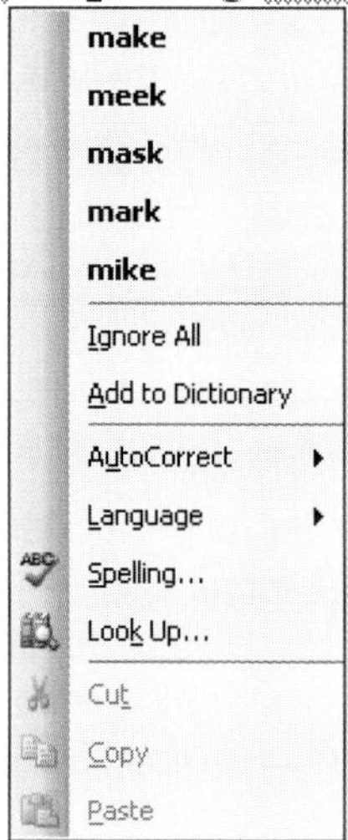

Figure 1.7 Spelling shortcut menu

Automatic Grammar Check

- The *automatic grammar check* feature checks for correct word usage and style and underlines usage and style errors with a green wavy line as you type. To correct a grammatical error that is underlined, right-click the word, and a shortcut menu, shown in Figure 1.8, displays suggested corrections. You can click a listed suggestion or choose to ignore it.
- You can turn the automatic spell and grammar check features on and off by clicking Tools, Options, choosing the Spelling and Grammar tab, and making the desired selections.

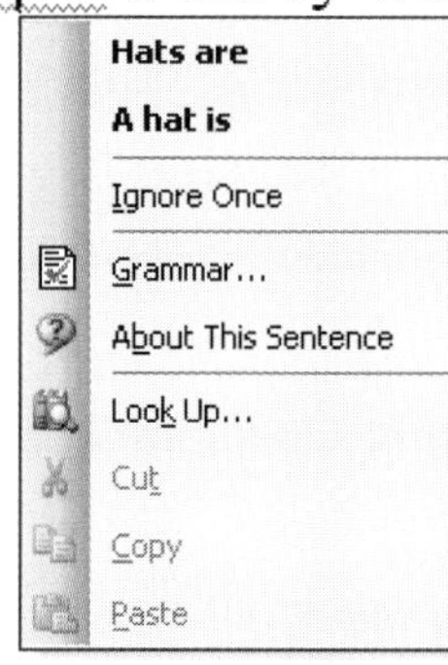

Figure 1.8 Grammar shortcut menu

TRY *it* OUT *w1-4*

1. Open **w1.4pf spelling** from the Data CD.
2. Right-click "visitt," then click the correctly spelled word on the list.
3. Right-click "community," then click the correctly spelled word on the list.
4. Correct the remaining spelling errors.
5. Right-click the first grammatical error, then click "yachts are" on the list.
6. Correct any remaining grammatical errors.
7. Close the file; do not save.
8. Click **File, Exit** to exit Word.

1
2
3

GOAL
To open a document, practice using AutoCorrect, and make basic spelling and grammar corrections

SETTING THE STAGE/WRAPUP
Margins: Default
Start line: At 1"
File name: **1.1correct**

WHAT YOU NEED TO KNOW

- In this Rehearsal activity, you will open a document that contains numerous spelling and grammatical errors. You will make basic spelling and grammar corrections and practice using the AutoCorrect feature.

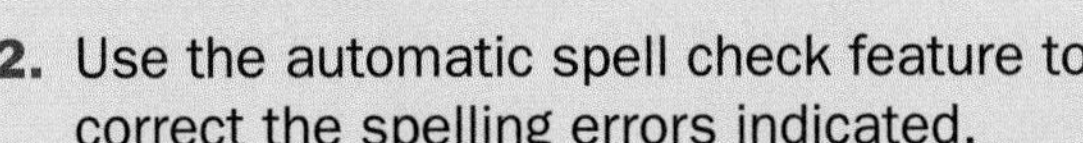

DIRECTIONS

1. Open **1.1correct** from the Data CD.
2. Use the automatic spell check feature to correct the spelling errors indicated.
3. Use the automatic grammar check feature to correct the grammatical errors indicated.
4. Click **Tools, AutoCorrect** options.
   a. Click the **AutoFormat as You Type** tab. Be sure all the options are checked.
   b. Click the **AutoCorrect** tab.
   c. Enter `ac` in the Replace text box. Enter `AutoCorrect` in the With text box.
5. Click **OK.**
6. Double-click below "Using AutoCorrect." Enter the following paragraph exactly as shown, including the misspelled words that are highlighted.

   `THe ac feature corrects common capitalization, spelling and grammatical errors as you type once you press teh spacebar. You must be sure the ac menu has been set to make the corrections yuo want. The AutoFormat as You Type option (which is part of the ac feature) allows you to set formatting options. Try typing these fractions and ordinals: 1/2, 1/4, 1ST, 2ND. did the ac feature work for you?`

7. Close the file; do not save.

Grammar Check Limitations
Grammar check, just liike spell check, is not alwaays correct correct and can be misleeading.

Language is complex. It is difficult for a programm to identify everything that is incorrect in a documment. In fact, Grammar check can be totally wrong. You MUST proofread a document and not depend on the computer to flagg errors for you.

Use grammar check to correct the following sentences:

1. She wore two hat.
2. The girl are from a city near the ocean.
3. The book were written by an author.
4. A painting were stolen from the museum.

Using AutoCorrect

Cues for Reference

Start Word (and Open a New Blank Document)

1. Click **Start.**
2. Point to **All Programs.**
3. Point to **Microsoft Office.**
4. Click **Microsoft Office Word 2003.**

Office XP: Click **Start, Programs, Microsoft Word.**

Add to the AutoCorrect Dictionary

1. Click **Tools, AutoCorrect Options.**
2. In the Replace text box, enter an incorrectly spelled word.
3. In the With text box, enter the correctly spelled word.
4. Click **OK.**

Automatic Spell and Grammar Check

- Right-click the misspelled word or usage error and choose a correctly spelled word or usage correction from the Shortcut menu.

Turn Automatic Spell and Grammar Check On/Off

1. Click **Tools, Options.**
2. Click the **Spelling and Grammar** tab.
3. Make desired changes.
4. Click **OK.**

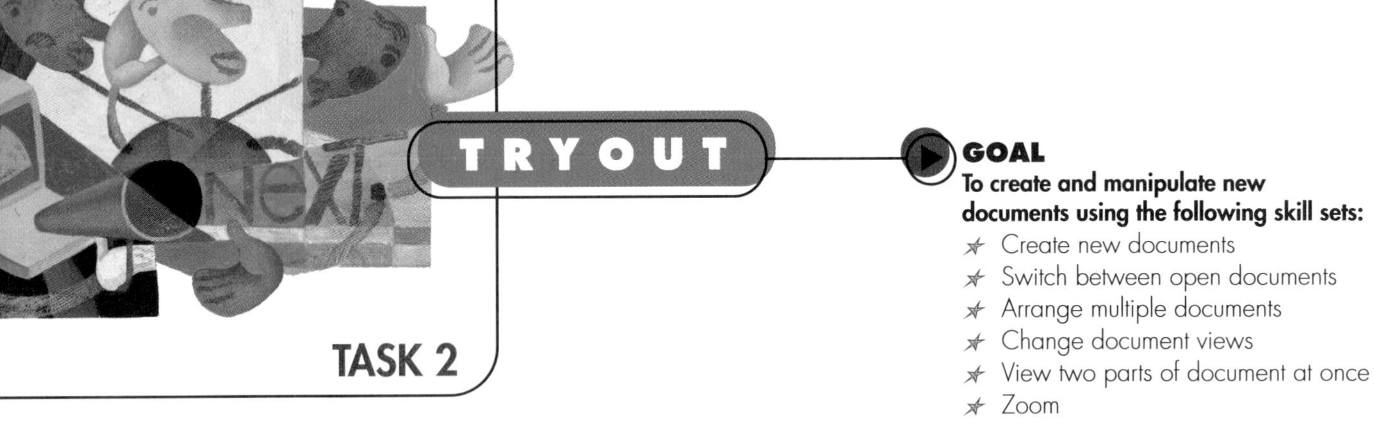

GOAL

To create and manipulate new documents using the following skill sets:

- Create new documents
- Switch between open documents
- Arrange multiple documents
- Change document views
- View two parts of document at once
- Zoom

WHAT YOU NEED TO KNOW

Create New Documents

Enter Text Using Wordwrap

- When the blank screen appears, Word assigns (Document1) on the title bar as the document name until you provide a name during the save process. As you enter text, the Column and Line indicators on the status bar change to show the current location of the insertion point. Text entered beyond the right margin automatically advances to the next line. This is called *wordwrap.* Press the Enter key *only* at the end of a short line or to begin a new paragraph.
- You can create additional new documents without closing or exiting Word by clicking the Blank Document link in the New Document task pane or by clicking the New Blank Document button on the toolbar.
- When you create second and subsequent blank documents, the task pane closes. You can redisplay it by clicking File, New or by clicking View, Task Pane. Word numbers each new document consecutively (Document2, Document3, etc.) until you provide each with a name during the save process.

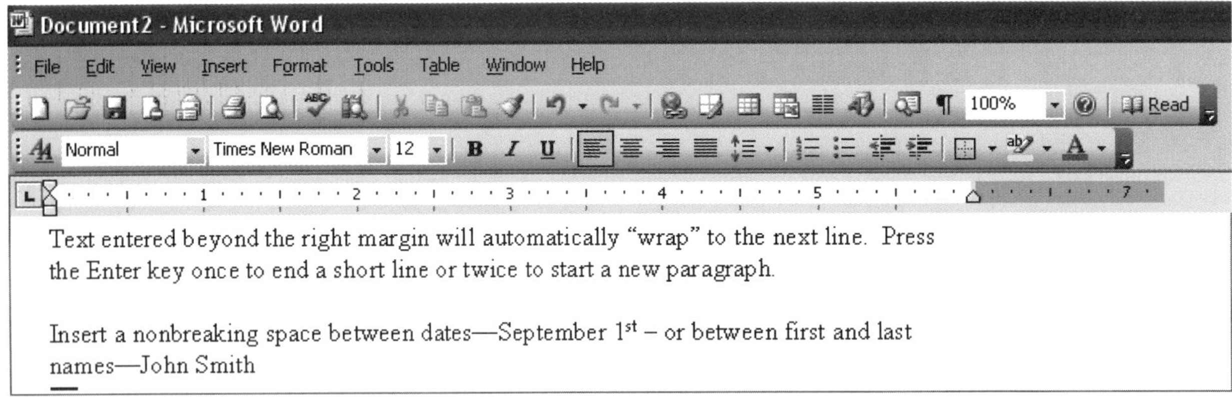

Figure 1.9 Unsaved document showing word-wrapped text

Insert Nonbreaking Spaces

- To prevent dates, names with titles, times, equations, or first and last names from splitting during wordwrap, you can insert a *nonbreaking space* between words. To do so, enter the first word, press Ctrl + Shift + spacebar at the same time, and type the next word.

TRY it OUT w1-5

1. Start Word. *Note that Document1 is displayed on the title bar.*
2. Click the **New Blank Document** button on the toolbar. *Note that Document2 is displayed on the title bar and the task pane closes.*
3. Click **File, New.** Note that the task pane reappears.
4. Click the **Blank Document** link on the task pane. *Note that Document3 is displayed on the title bar and the task pane closes.*
5. Enter the following, allowing the text to wrap to the next line. Do not stop to correct spelling errors at this time. Insert a nonbreaking space between parts of the date and John Smith's first and last names. Press the enter key twice to begin a new paragraph.

   Text entered beyond the right margin will automatically "wrap" to the next line. Press the Enter key once to end a short line or twice to start a new paragraph.

   ¶Insert a nonbreaking space between dates-September 1st-or between first and last names-John Smith.

   Notice the position of the insertion point by checking the At, Ln, and Col indicators on the status bar.
6. Use the Automatic Spell check to correct any spelling or grammatical errors that you might have made during text entry. Click Ignore for other underlined words that are flagged as errors.
7. Do not close the file.

Switch Between Open Documents

- A button on the taskbar with the Word icon indicates each open document, as shown in Figure 1.10. When you place the insertion point on a document button, a ScreenTip appears, showing the document name. The highlighted button indicates the *active document* (the document containing the insertion point). Click on a button to display a document.

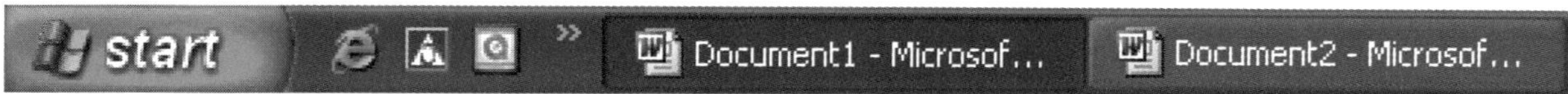

Figure 1.10 Taskbar showing open documents

- When many documents are open, the buttons cannot fit on the taskbar. This causes the document buttons to consolidate under one Microsoft Word button. This button indicates how many Word documents are open. Clicking on the consolidated Word button displays a pop-up menu with the open documents listed as shown in Figure 1.11. Click on a listed document to display it. You can also press the Ctrl + F6 keys to cycle between open Word documents.
- Remember that you can close a document by clicking the Close button on the document window. You can save or close several documents at once by holding down the Shift key and clicking File, Save All or File, Close All.

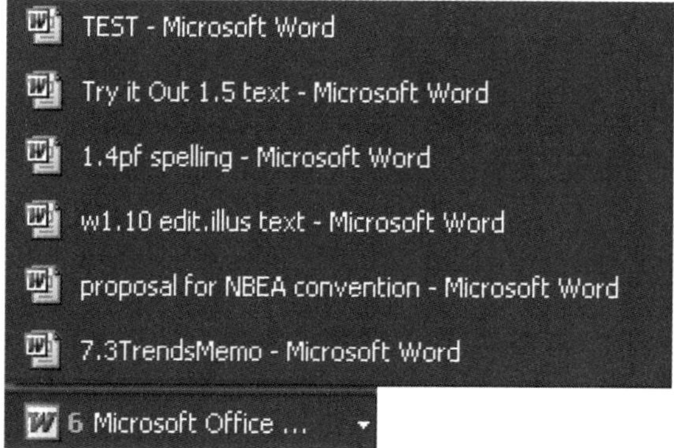

Figure 1.11 Toolbar showing consolidated Word button with open documents

Arrange Multiple Documents

▶ When several documents are open, you can arrange them so you can view them at one time. To do so, open the documents you wish to view. Then, click Window, Arrange All. This will tile your documents top to bottom as shown in Figure 1.12. The active document contains the insertion point and displays a darkened title bar.

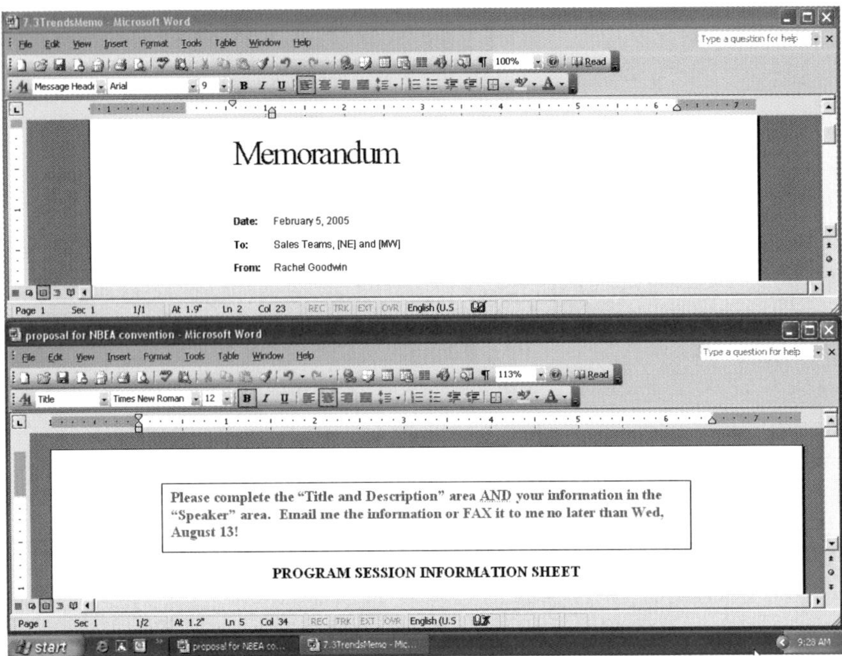

Figure 1.12 Arranged documents top to bottom

▶ To view your documents side by side rather than top to bottom as shown in Figure 1.13, click Window, Compare Side by Side. To close side-by-side view, click the appropriate button on the menu that displays.

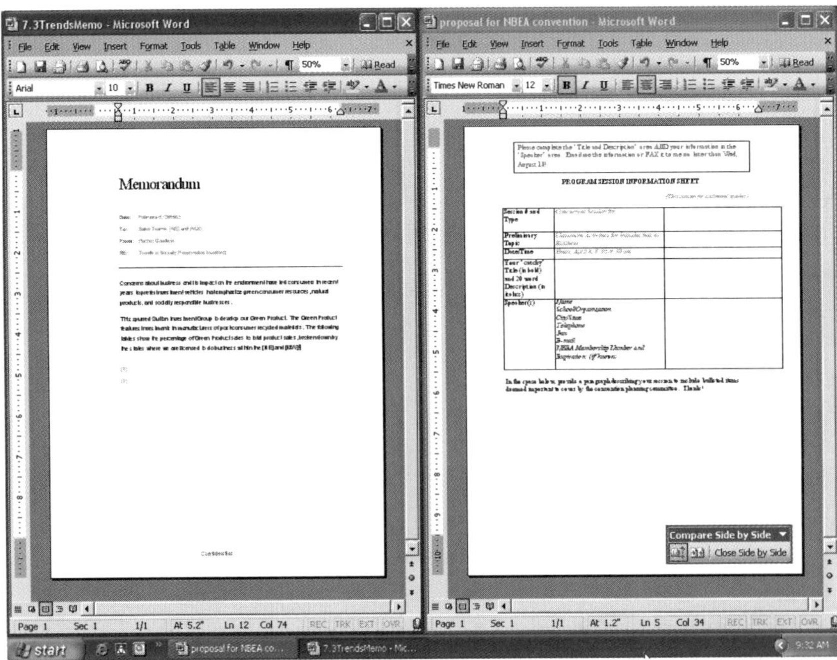

Figure 1.13 Arranged documents side by side

TRY it OUT *w1-6*

Note: Document3 should be open and three buttons should display on the taskbar, indicating three open documents.

1. Click the **Document1** button on the taskbar.
2. Click **Window, Document2.**
3. Press the **Ctrl** + **F6** keys twice to cycle between the open documents.
4. Click the **Document1** button on the taskbar.
5. Hold down the **Shift** key and click **File, Close All;** do not save.
6. Open the following documents from the Data CD: **w1.6marina views** and **w1.6pf move.**
7. Click **Window, Arrange All.**
8. Click in the document area of **w1.6marina views** to make it the active document.
9. Click **Window, Compare Side by Side with w1.6pf move.**
10. Click the **Close Side by Side with** button on the Compare Side-by-Side toolbar to close this view.
11. Maximize **1.6marina views.**
12. Hold down the **Shift** key and click **File, Close All;** do not save.

Change Document Views

- Word provides several ways to view a document on screen. You can change views by clicking a view button at the bottom of the screen, as shown in Figure 1.14, or by clicking View on the menu and choosing an option.

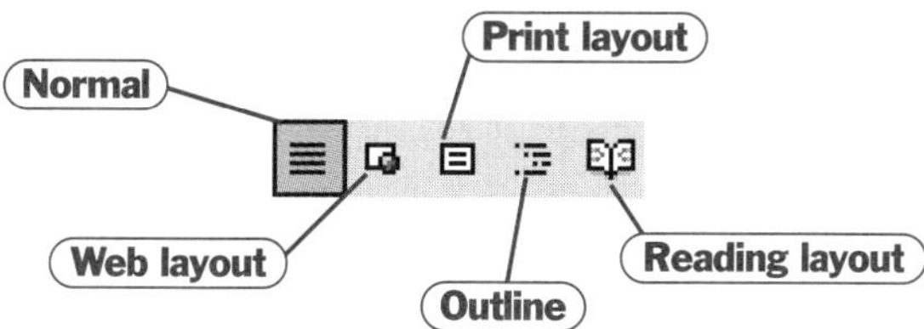

Figure 1.14 View buttons

▶ There are five views in Word:

- *Normal view* is used for most typing, editing, and formatting and is illustrated in Figure 1.15. 

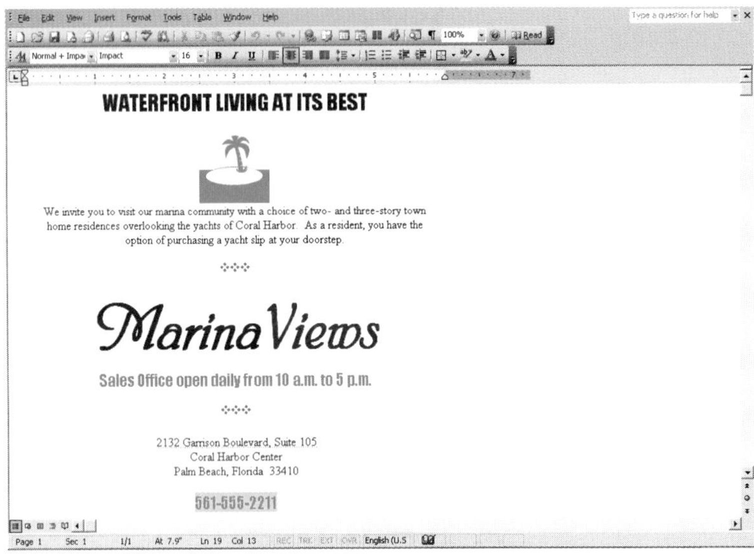
WATERFRONT LIVING AT ITS BEST
We invite you to visit our marina community with a choice of two- and three-story town home residences overlooking the yachts of Coral Harbor. As a resident, you have the option of purchasing a yacht slip at your doorstep.
Marina Views
Sales Office open daily from 10 a.m. to 5 p.m.
2132 Garrison Boulevard, Suite 105
Coral Harbor Center
Palm Beach, Florida 33410
561-555-2211

Figure 1.15 Document in Normal view

- *Web layout view* shows how a document will look as a Web page and is illustrated in Figure 1.16. 

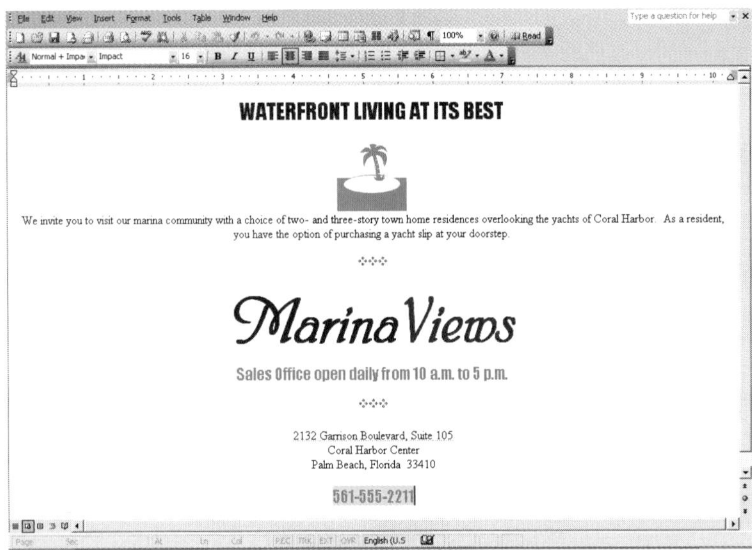
WATERFRONT LIVING AT ITS BEST
We invite you to visit our marina community with a choice of two- and three-story town home residences overlooking the yachts of Coral Harbor. As a resident, you have the option of purchasing a yacht slip at your doorstep.
Marina Views
Sales Office open daily from 10 a.m. to 5 p.m.
2132 Garrison Boulevard, Suite 105
Coral Harbor Center
Palm Beach, Florida 33410
561-555-2211

Figure 1.16 Document in Web Layout view

- *Print layout view* shows how a document will look when it is printed. This view allows you to see headers and footers, columns, and drawing objects. This view displays the vertical ruler and is shown in Figure 1.17.

▶ In this view, you can save screen space by hiding the white space on the top and bottom of each page. Move the insertion point to the top or bottom of the page and click the Show White Space or Hide White Space button that displays.

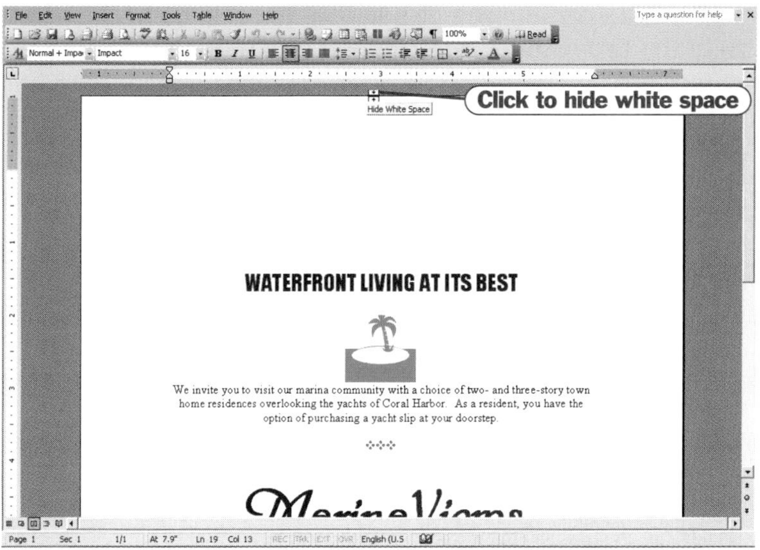
Click to hide white space
WATERFRONT LIVING AT ITS BEST
We invite you to visit our marina community with a choice of two- and three-story town home residences overlooking the yachts of Coral Harbor. As a resident, you have the option of purchasing a yacht slip at your doorstep.

Figure 1.17 Document in Print Layout view with Hide White Space pop-up displayed

- *Outline view* allows you to see heading levels in an outline. Use this view when you are creating and editing an outline. (Outlines will be covered in Lesson 4.) This view is illustrated in Figure 1.18.

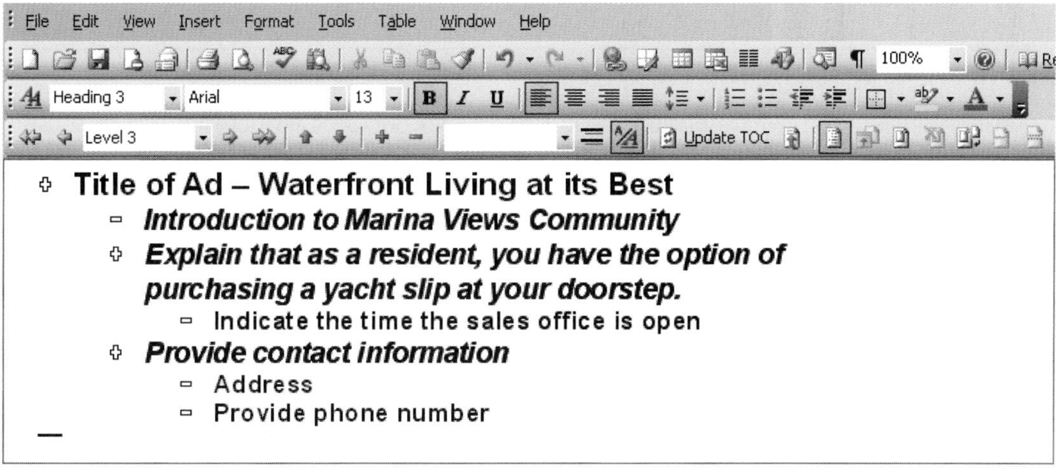
File Edit View Insert Format Tools Table Window Help
Heading 3
Arial
13
Level 3
Update TOC
Title of Ad – Waterfront Living at its Best
Introduction to Marina Views Community
Explain that as a resident, you have the option of purchasing a yacht slip at your doorstep.
Indicate the time the sales office is open
Provide contact information
Address
Provide phone number

Figure 1.18 Document in Outline view

- *Reading layout view*, shown in Figure 1.19, maximizes the reading experience by hiding all toolbars and increasing the size of the text without affecting the size of the font in the document. The entire document may not be visible in this view. Thumbnails appear to help you navigate through the document. You can edit text in this view.

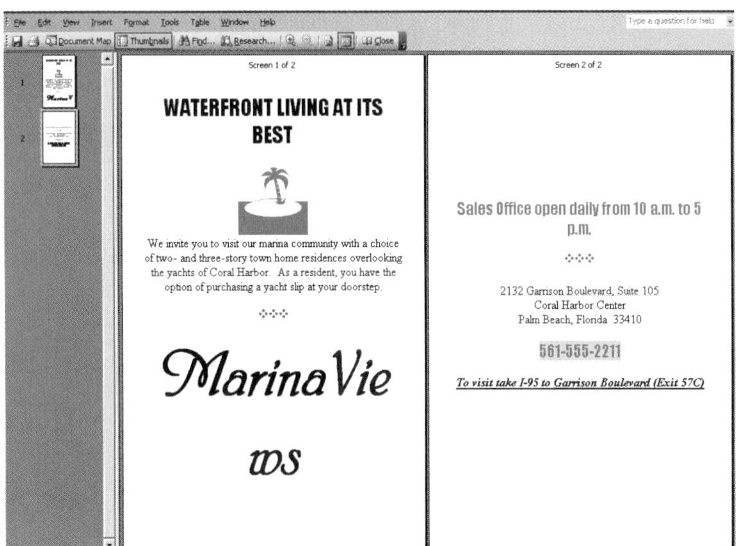
Screen 1 of 2
WATERFRONT LIVING AT ITS BEST
We invite you to visit our marina community with a choice of two- and three-story town home residences overlooking the yachts of Coral Harbor. As a resident, you have the option of purchasing a yacht slip at your doorstep.
MarinaVie
ws
Screen 2 of 2
Sales Office open daily from 10 a.m. to 5 p.m.
2132 Garrison Boulevard, Suite 105
Coral Harbor Center
Palm Beach, Florida 33410
561-555-2211
To visit take I-95 to Garrison Boulevard (Exit 57C)

Figure 1.19 Document in Reading Layout view

View Two Parts of a Document At Once

▶ You can split a document screen, which enables you to see two parts of a document at one time. To split a document, click Window, Split. A heavy grey line displays. Move your insertion point where you want the split to occur and click the left mouse button. To remove a split, click Windows, Remove Split. Figure 1.20 displays a document that has been split.

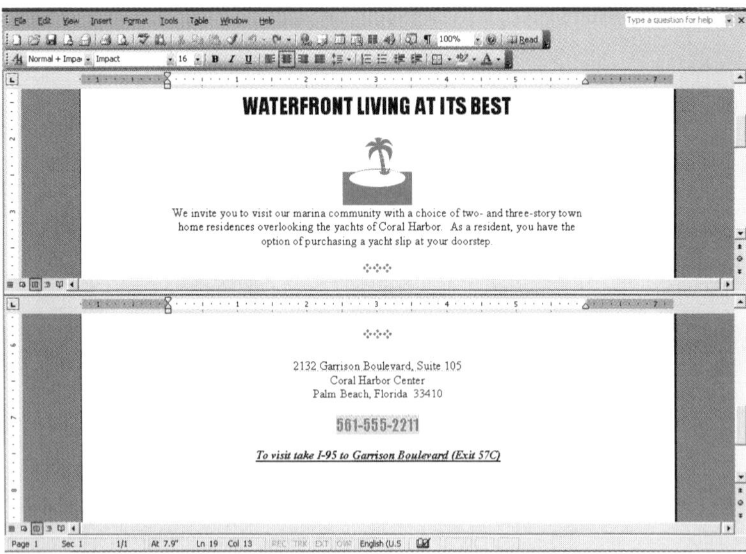
WATERFRONT LIVING AT ITS BEST
We invite you to visit our marina community with a choice of two- and three-story town home residences overlooking the yachts of Coral Harbor. As a resident, you have the option of purchasing a yacht slip at your doorstep.
2132 Garrison Boulevard, Suite 105
Coral Harbor Center
Palm Beach, Florida 33410
561-555-2211
To visit take I-95 to Garrison Boulevard (Exit 57C)

Figure 1.20 Split document

Zoom

▶ The *Zoom* feature allows you to magnify data or to reduce data to see more of a page. To change the magnification of data on the screen, click the Zoom list arrow on the Standard toolbar and choose a percentage. You can also click View, Zoom and choose a magnification option in the Zoom dialog box that displays, shown in Figure 1.21.

114%

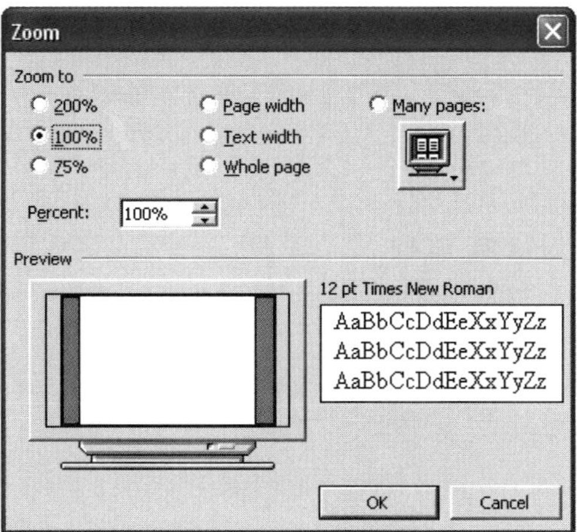

Figure 1.21 Zoom dialog box

TRY *it* OUT *w1-7*

1. Open **w1.7marina views.**
2. Click the **Normal View** button.
3. Click the **Outline View** button. *Notice that the Outline toolbar appears.*
4. Click the **Print Layout View** button. *Notice that the vertical ruler appears.*
5. Move the insertion point to the top of the page. When the Hide White Space button displays, click it.
6. Click the **Reading Layout View** button. Click the **Close** button on the toolbar to exit Reading layout view.
7. Click the **Zoom** list arrow and choose 50%.
8. Click **View, Zoom,** choose 100%, and click **OK.**
9. Click **Window, Split.** Scroll to the middle of the page and left-click. Scroll the page in each window.
10. Click **Window, Remove Split.**
11. Close the file; do not save.

REHEARSAL

AGAIN

TASK 2

GOAL

To create new documents, enter text using wordwrap and AutoCorrect, make basic spelling and grammar corrections, change document views, and switch between open documents

SETTING THE STAGE/WRAPUP

Margins: Default
Start line: At 1"
File name: **1.2wordwrap**

WHAT YOU NEED TO KNOW

- A document is also called a file.
- Space twice after punctuation that ends a sentence.
- In this Rehearsal activity, you will open several new documents, enter text using the wordwrap feature, change document views, and switch between open documents. You will save one of the documents, which you will use again in Task 2.

DIRECTIONS

1. Start Word, if it is not already open.
2. Open a new blank document. You should be in Normal view.
3. Display the task pane (if not already displayed).
4. Click **Tools, AutoCorrect Options.** Enter `oep` in the Replace text box. Enter `Occasions Event Planning` in the With text box.
5. Enter the paragraphs shown on the facing page.
6. Press the **Enter** key only to start a new paragraph.
7. Insert a nonbreaking space within the times and between Jean McDonald's first and last name.
8. Correct spelling errors using the shortcut menu (right-click the misspelled word, then choose the correct spelling).
9. Save the document; name it **1.2wordwrap.** Do not close.
10. Change to Print Layout view.
11. Open a new blank document from the task pane. (This will be Document2.)
12. Enter: `This is practice text for Document2.` This text will not be saved.
13. Open a new blank document from the task pane. (This will be Document3.)
14. Enter: `The shirts is blue.` Use the automatic grammar check to correct the flagged error.
15. Open a new blank document from the task pane. (This will be Document4.)
16. Enter: `She is a selfmade woman and can do more in 1/2 minute than most people can do in 1 3/4 hours.` Use the automatic spelling check to correct the flagged error.

Continued on next page

17. Switch to the saved document (**1.2wordwrap**).
18. Arrange the documents top to bottom.
19. Redisplay **1.2wordwrap** as a full document.
20. Change the magnification to **150%.**
21. Cycle between the open documents.
22. Switch to Document2.
23. Close all documents at once; do not save.

Event planning requires much of your time and energy. It requires a dependable network of suppliers. Assigning an inexperienced person to this type of work can be time-consuming.

oep will help you with your event-planning needs. We coordinate all aspects of the event to ensure that is it is ON TIME, and ON BUDGET. Let oep plan your next party. Our commitment to 100% satisfaction is the basis of our service.

Time is money. In the time it takes for an inexperienced person to plan an event, you may end up spending more money than it would have cost you to hire a professional.

Hiring an event planner to manage an event means you can relax and enjoy the party. Call us at 222-555-5555, Monday through Friday, from 8:00 a.m. to 5:30 p.m. Ask for Jean McDonald.

Cues for Reference

Create a New Document

- Click the **New Blank Document** button on the toolbar.

  Or

1. Click **File, New** on the Menu bar.

   Or

2. Click the **Blank Document** link on the New Document task pane.

Insert a Nonbreaking Space

1. Enter the first word.
2. Press **Ctrl** + **Shift** + **spacebar.**
3. Enter the next word.

Switch between Open Word Documents

- Press **Ctrl** + **F6.**

  Or

- Click a Word document button on the taskbar.

  Or

1. Click **Window.**
2. Click the document to display.

Arrange Multiple Documents

1. Open the documents you wish to work with.
2. Click **Window, Arrange All** to arrange documents vertically.
3. Click **Window, Compare side by side with...** to arrange documents horizontally (only works with two open documents).
4. Maximize each window to redisplay the entire document.

Change Document Views

- Click a view button at the bottom of the screen:

  Normal

  Web Layout

  Print Layout

  Outline

  Reading Layout

Office XP: Reading Layout not available.

Or

1. Click **View.**
2. Choose a document view.

View Two Parts of a Document at Once

1. Click **Window, Split.**
2. Move the insertion point where you want the split to occur.
3. Click the left mouse button.
4. Click **Window, Remove Split** to redisplay entire document.

Save All/Close All Open Documents

1. Hold down the **Shift** key.
2. Click **File.**
3. Click **Save All** or **Close All.**

Zoom

- Click the Zoom list arrow on the Standard toolbar and choose a magnification percentage.

  114%

  Or

- Click **View, Zoom** and choose a magnification percentage.

TASK 3

GOAL
To edit, save and print a document using the following skill sets:

- Navigate through a document
- Select text/data
- Insert, overwrite, and delete text
- Show/hide codes
- Hide text
- Move and copy text
- Office Clipboard
- Spelling and grammar check
- Save and Save As
- Print Preview
- Print

WHAT YOU NEED TO KNOW

Navigate through a Document

- The easiest way to move the insertion point around a document is to place the I-beam where you want it and click. (This is called *click and type.*) If you are working on long documents, however, you must be able to scroll through the pages quickly. To quickly display a page, click on its thumbnail. A border around the thumbnail indicates the displayed page. Once you display a page, you can use the keyboard and/or mouse movements described in the table below to navigate through it.

EXPRESS KEYBOARD MOVEMENTS		EXPRESS MOUSE MOVEMENTS	
Press:	***To Move:***	***Do This:***	***To:***
Ctrl + left or right arrow	One word to the left or to the right	Click above or below the scroll box	Scroll up or down one screen
Ctrl + up or down arrow	One paragraph up or down	Drag the scroll box	Scroll to a specific page
End key	To the end of a line	Hold Shift key and click the left scroll arrow	Scroll left, beyond the margin
Home key	To the beginning of a line	Click the Select Browse Object button on the vertical scroll bar Click Go To Enter page number and click Go To	Go to a specific page
Page up or Page down key	Up or down one screen	Click on a thumbnail	Quickly display a page
Ctrl + Page Down	To the top of the next page	Rotate the center wheel forward or backward through a document	Scroll up or down using the IntelliMouse
Ctrl + Page Up	To the top of the previous page	Press down on the center wheel When you see the scroll symbol, move the mouse up or down Press down on the center wheel to stop AutoScroll	Quickly scroll up or down using AutoScroll on the IntelliMouse
Ctrl + End	To the end of the document		
Ctrl + Home	To the beginning of the document		

TRY it OUT *w1-8*

1. Open **w1.8pf** from the Data CD.
2. Display Thumbnails (View Thumbnails) if they are not already displayed.
3. Click on the thumbnail of page two, then click the thumbnail of page one.
4. Drag the vertical scroll box down to view the entire document.
5. Press the **Ctrl** + **Home** keys to return to the top of the document.
6. Press the **Ctrl** + **End** keys and the **Ctrl** + **Home** keys again.
7. Click at the beginning of paragraph 1.
8. Press the **End** key, then press the **Home** key.
9. Press the **Ctrl + PageDown** keys, then the **Ctrl** + **PageUp** keys.
10. Click the arrow below the vertical scroll box.
11. Click at the beginning of paragraph 2.
12. Press the **Ctrl** + **Home** keys.
13. Click the **Select Browse Object** button (located on the vertical scroll bar), and roll your mouse pointer over each option to view its purpose.
    a. Click the **Go To** button.
    b. Enter page 2, click **Go To,** then click **Close.**
14. If you have an IntelliMouse, click the center wheel and watch the document scroll down.
    a. Slide the mouse downward to scroll the document faster.
    b. Click the center wheel to stop AutoScroll.
15. Do not close the file.

Select Text/Data

- Before you can edit text or data (format, delete, move, or copy it), you must first select it. Selecting text highlights a character, word, or block of text or data.
- There are numerous ways to select text. The most frequently used selection techniques are outlined below:

TO SELECT:	ACTION:
A word	Double-click the word.
A sentence	Press and hold Ctrl as you click in the sentence
A paragraph	Triple-click anywhere in the paragraph
Entire document	Triple-click in the left margin, or click Edit, Select All from the menus

- There are many other shortcuts, which are detailed in Appendix E.

TRY *it* OUT *w1-9*

Note: ***w1.8pf*** *should still be displayed on your screen. If it is not, open it again.*

1. Double-click "Scrolling" in the title to select the word.
2. Double-click "Through" in the title to select the word.
3. Click and drag the mouse over the first paragraph to select it.
4. Position the insertion point in the second paragraph. Triple-click in rapid succession to select the paragraph.
5. Position the insertion point in the first sentence of the first paragraph. Press the **Ctrl** key and click once to select a sentence.
6. Click **Edit, Select All** to select the entire document.
7. Close the file; do not save.

Insert, Overwrite, and Delete Text

Insert text

▶ To insert text, position the insertion point to the left of the character that will follow the inserted material. When you enter inserted text, the existing text moves to the right.

Overwrite text

▶ You can overwrite existing text with new text using two methods:

1. Use *Overtype mode.* Using this method, existing text does not move to the right; it is typed over. By default, Word is in *Insert mode.* To switch to Overtype mode, double-click the OVR indicator on the status bar. Use this method when you are replacing one word(s) with another word(s) of the same length.
2. *Select the old text and begin typing*. Using this method, the new text will overwrite the highlighted selection.

Delete text

▶ The *Delete* feature allows you to remove text, graphics, or codes from a document. To delete a character or close up spaces to the left of the insertion point, press the Backspace key. To delete blocks of text, you must first select the text you want to delete, then press the Delete key or click the Cut button on the toolbar. (See Appendix E for selection techniques.)

TRY *it* OUT *w1-10*

1. Open a new blank document.
2. Enter the following without pressing the Enter key:

   `Admission to all Conference events is free. Please join us.`
3. Double-click the word "all" and press the **Delete** key.
4. Double-click the word "events" and enter `sessions`.
5. Position the insertion point anywhere in the sentence "Please join us." Press **Ctrl + click** to select it, then press the **Delete** key.
6. Open **w1.10edit** from the Data CD. Insert and delete words as shown in the illustration below (insert underlined words; delete words that are crossed out).

We now have growth opportunities ~~available~~ in our ~~new~~ company for managers ~~and associate managers~~ who are ~~very~~ interested in a ~~fast-track~~ career with an industry leader. ~~in the industry~~. Please ~~send a~~ fax your resume to me as soon as possible.

7. Close the files; do not save.

Show/Hide Codes

- As you create a new document, Word inserts nonprinting codes. When you click the Show/Hide button on the toolbar, codes for paragraph marks (¶), tabs (↔), spaces (•), and nonbreaking spaces (°) are visible in a document, as shown in Figure 1.22. Use this show/hide codes feature when editing a document.

¶

→ To·learn·more·about·the·benefits·of·this·exciting·opportunity,·call· Joanna°Newman·at·(212)°555-5555.¶
¶
→ I·will·set·up·an·appointment·to·discuss·these·opportunities.¶

Figure 1.22 Document with show/hide codes displayed

- The *Reveal Formatting* feature allows you to review the formatting that you apply to selected text.
- To use this feature, select the text on which you wish to reveal formatting and click Format, Reveal Formatting. The formatting information appears in the Reveal Formatting task pane, as shown in Figure 1.23. To change any formatting items in the task pane, click the blue underlined link and change any options in the dialog box that opens.
- You can also show/hide codes in a document by clicking the Show all formatting marks option at the bottom of the task pane.

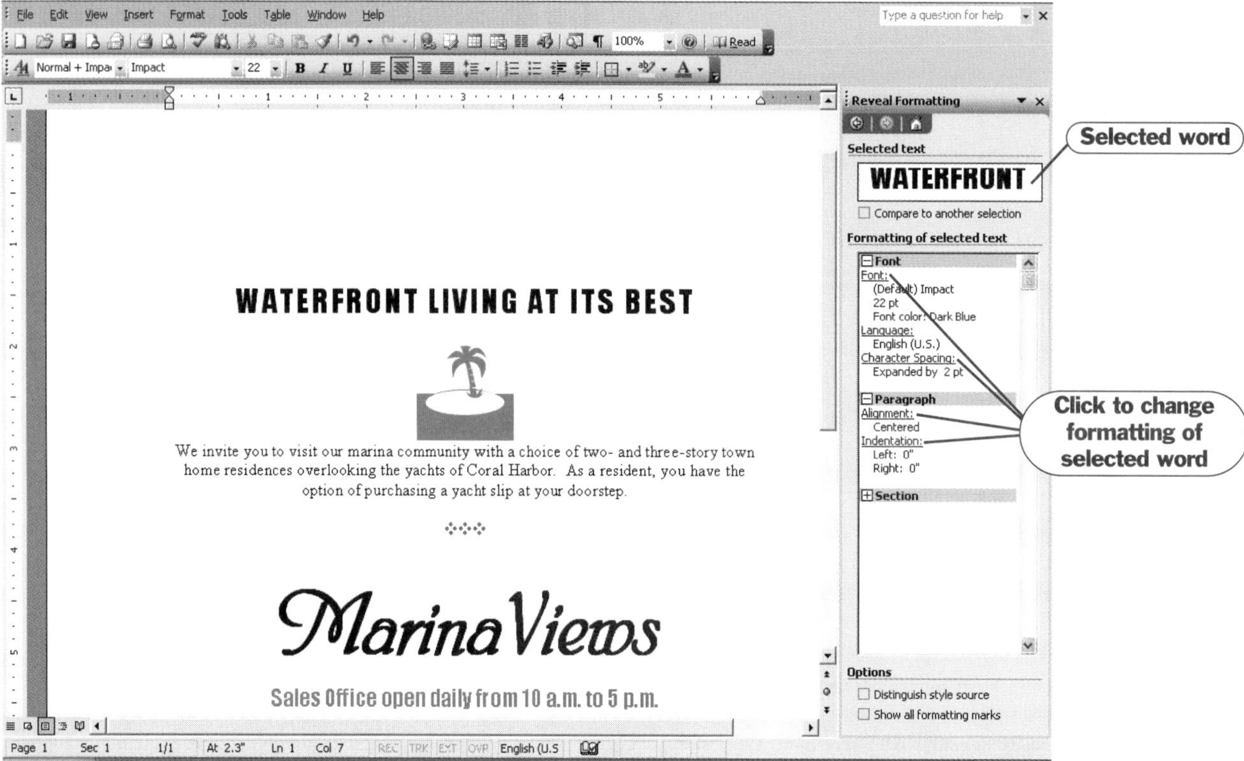

Figure 1.23 Reveal Formatting task pane

TRY it OUT w1-11

Note: This Try it Out refers to Figure 1.22.

1. Open a new blank document.
2. Click **Tools, AutoCorrect Options, AutoFormat as You Type** tab. Deselect Set left-and first-indent with tabs and backspaces, if it is not already deselected, and click **OK**.
3. Enter the text shown in Figure 1.22.
   a. Press the **Tab** key to indent each paragraph.
   b. Insert a nonbreaking space where you see the nonbreaking space symbol (°).
4. Click the **Show/Hide button** on the toolbar. *Notice the screen codes, which should match those in Figure 1.22.* ¶
5. Delete the paragraph symbols between the first and second paragraphs to create a single paragraph.
6. Click the **Show/Hide** button again to hide the codes.
7. Insert the word `investment` before the word "opportunity" in the first sentence.
8. Delete the word "exciting" in the first sentence.
9. Insert the words `with you` after "appointment" in the second sentence.
10. To change the phone number using Overtype mode:
    a. Position the insertion point to the immediate left of the phone number.
    b. Double-click the **OVR** indicator on the status bar.
    c. Enter `444-4444` in bold.
    d. Double-click the **OVR** indicator on the status bar to return to Insert mode.
11. Select **444-4444,** click **Format, Reveal Formatting.**
12. Click **Font** in the Reveal Formatting task pane.
13. Click **Regular** in the Font style box and click **OK.**
14. Close the file; do not save.

Move and Copy Text

Move Text

- Moving text allows you to remove text from one location and reinsert it in another. The easiest way to accomplish moving text is to use the *Cut and Paste* feature. First, select the text you wish to move, then click the Cut button on the toolbar. Click in the location where you want to insert the text, then click the Paste button on the toolbar
- Text cut from the screen is placed temporarily on the Office Clipboard, a temporary storage area in the computer's memory. (See the Office Clipboard section below).
- When moving text, it is recommended that you display screen codes. This will help you select the space following a word or sentence, and/or the paragraph mark following a paragraph or line that you plan to move or copy, as shown in Figure 1.24. (The paragraph mark stores the formatting you apply to a paragraph; therefore, it is particularly important to include the paragraph marks in your selected text to ensure that the paragraph formatting is moved or copied along with the text.)

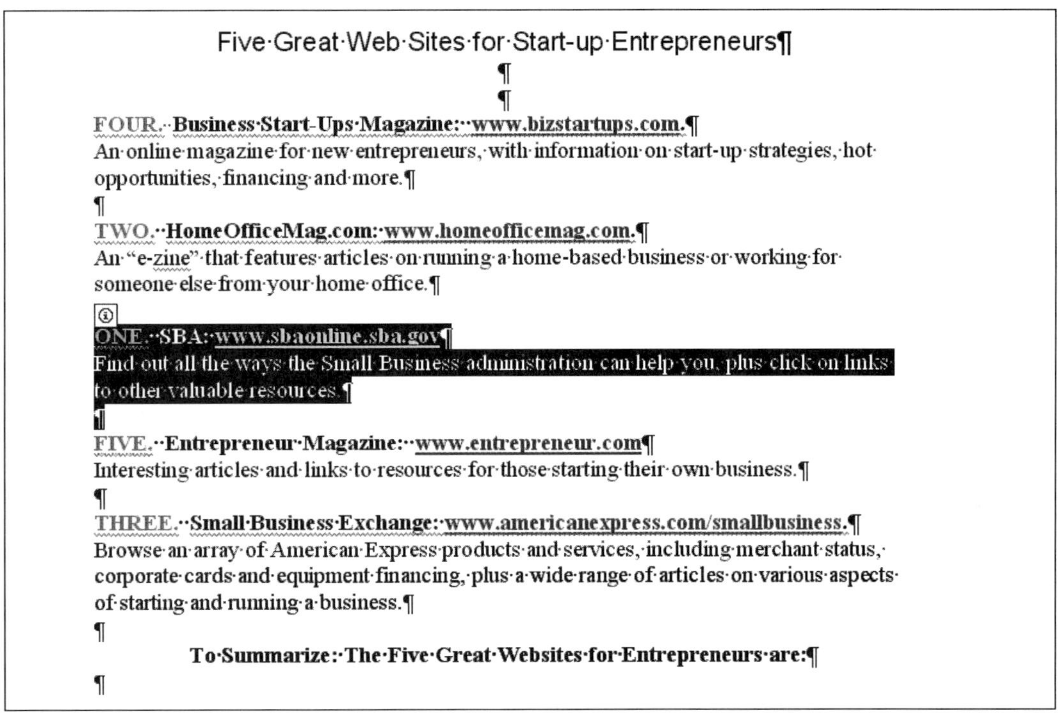

Five Great Web Sites for Start-up Entrepreneurs¶
¶
¶
FOUR. **Business Start-Ups Magazine: www.bizstartups.com.**¶
An online magazine for new entrepreneurs, with information on start-up strategies, hot opportunities, financing and more.¶
¶
TWO. **HomeOfficeMag.com: www.homeofficemag.com.**¶
An "e-zine" that features articles on running a home-based business or working for someone else from your home office.¶
ONE. SBA: www.sbaonline.sba.gov¶
Find out all the ways the Small Business administration can help you, plus click on links to other valuable resources.¶
¶
FIVE. **Entrepreneur Magazine: www.entrepreneur.com**¶
Interesting articles and links to resources for those starting their own business.¶
¶
THREE. **Small Business Exchange: www.americanexpress.com/smallbusiness.**¶
Browse an array of American Express products and services, including merchant status, corporate cards and equipment financing, plus a wide range of articles on various aspects of starting and running a business.¶
¶
To Summarize: The Five Great Websites for Entrepreneurs are:¶
¶

Figure 1.24 Selected paragraph to be moved

- *Drag and drop* is another method by which you can move text. Place the pointer on the selected text, drag the selected text to its new location, then release the mouse button. This method *does not* place text on the Office Clipboard.

Copy Text

- Copying text leaves text or data in its original location while placing a duplicate in another location.
- To copy text, select the text to copy and click the Copy button on the toolbar. Click in the location where the you want to insert the text and click the Paste button on the toolbar.

- To copy text using the drag-and-drop method, hold down the Ctrl key as you drag a selection.

▶ You can also access the Cut, Copy, and Paste commands using their shortcut methods: Cut = Ctrl + X, Copy = Ctrl + C, Paste = Ctrl + V

TRY it OUT w1-12

Note: This Try it Out refers to Figure 1.24.

1. Open **w1.12pf move** from the Data CD.
2. Click the **Show/Hide** button.
3. Move the paragraphs into numerical order as follows:
   a. Select the paragraph numbered ONE, including the two paragraph marks following the paragraph, as shown in Figure 1.24.
   b. Click the **Cut** button.

   c. Position the insertion point to the left of FOUR.

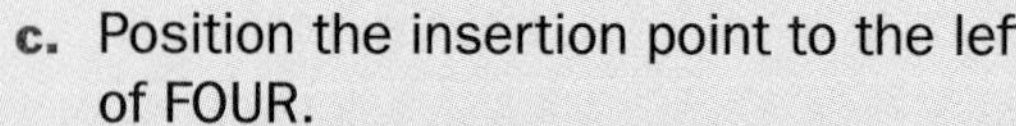

   d. Click the **Paste** button.
   e. Select the paragraph numbered THREE, including the two paragraph marks following the paragraph.
   f. Drag and drop it in front of the FIVE.
   g. Move the remaining paragraphs into order using any method you prefer.
4. Do not close the file.

Office Clipboard

▶ As indicated above, when you cut or copy text, it is temporarily placed on the *Clipboard.* The Clipboard is a temporary storage area that can hold up to 24 items. To view the Clipboard contents after you cut or copy more than one item, click Edit, Office Clipboard. The Clipboard task pane, shown in Figure 1.25, lists each copied or cut item.

▶ Position the insertion point where you wish to reinsert the cut or copied item and click the item in the Clipboard task pane. A list box next to each item gives you a delete option.

▶ To paste all or clear all of the selections, click the appropriate button in the Clipboard task pane (see Figure 1.25).

▶ If you want to display the task pane automatically after you have cut or copied more than one selection, click Options at the bottom of the task pane and choose Show Office Clipboard Automatically.

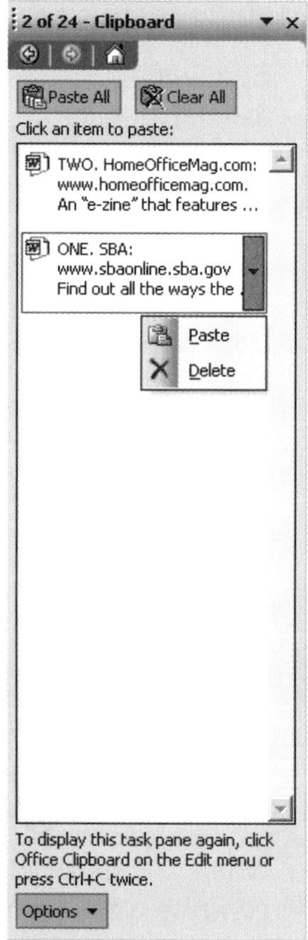

Figure 1.25 Clipboard task pane

TRY it OUT *w1-13*

Note: ***w1.12pf move*** *should still be displayed on your screen. If it is not, repeat Try it Out w1-12 before completing this one.*

1. Click **Edit, Office Clipboard** from the menu to display the Clipboard.
2. Copy the first line of each paragraph (multiple-copy these items).
3. Paste each line individually below the words "To Summarize..."
4. Press the **Enter** key after each pasted item. Close the file; do not save.

Spelling and Grammar Check

- You learned earlier that you can correct individual spelling and grammatical errors as you type using the shortcut method (right-clicking the word containing a red or green wavy line and choosing a suggested correction). You can also check your entire document or parts of the document using the Spelling and Grammar feature.
- To access this feature, click the Spelling and Grammar button on the toolbar or click Tools, Spelling and Grammar from the menus. A spelling error will open the Spelling and Grammar dialog box, as shown in Figure 1.26. You can then choose a correction option, each of which is explained in the table below.

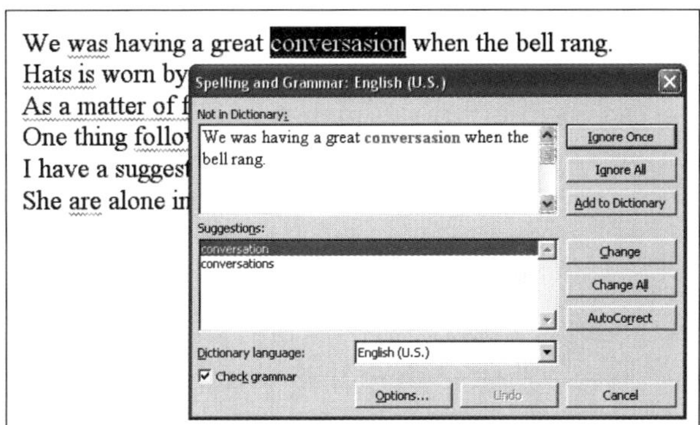

Figure 1.26 Spelling and Grammar dialog box with flagged spelling error

OPTION	EXPLANATION
Ignore Once	Ignores this error.
Ignore All	Ignores all instances of this error.
Add to Dictionary	Adds the highlighted word to Word's custom dictionary.
Change	Changes the flagged error to the selected suggestion.
Change All	Changes all instances of the error to the selected suggestion.
AutoCorrect	Adds the word to the AutoCorrect dictionary.

Note: Because language is complex, it is difficult for a computer to identify everything that is incorrect in a document. Remember that neither the grammar nor the spelling check eliminates the need for you to carefully proofread a document.

- When you start typing, a book icon appears in the lower-right corner of the status bar. As you continue typing, a check mark moves from page to page on the book. When you stop typing, a red check mark remains, indicating that the Spelling and Grammar feature detected no spelling or grammatical errors. If an X appears, it indicates that errors exist in the document. Double-click the book icon, and Word advances to an error and opens a shortcut menu with suggested corrections.

TRY *it* OUT *w1-14*

1. Open **w1.14pf spelling & grammar** from the Data CD.
2. Right-click the first misspelled word and choose the correct spelling from the shortcut menu.
3. Right-click the first grammatical error and choose the correct usage from the shortcut menu.
4. Double-click the **book icon** on the status bar. Choose the correction from the shortcut menu.
5. Click the **Spelling and Grammar** button on the toolbar and correct the remaining errors.
6. Close the file; do not save.

Use Save and Save As

- Word automatically names documents Document1, Document2, etc., until you save them with specific file names. Click the Save button to save a new file or to overwrite an existing file. If you are saving a new file, the Save As dialog box displays, as shown in Figure 1.27. Specify where you want to save the file and enter a filename.
- The *Save As* feature allows you to save a file as a new name, as a different file type, or in a different location. Select File, Save As from the menu. In the Save As dialog box that appears, enter the save options you want.

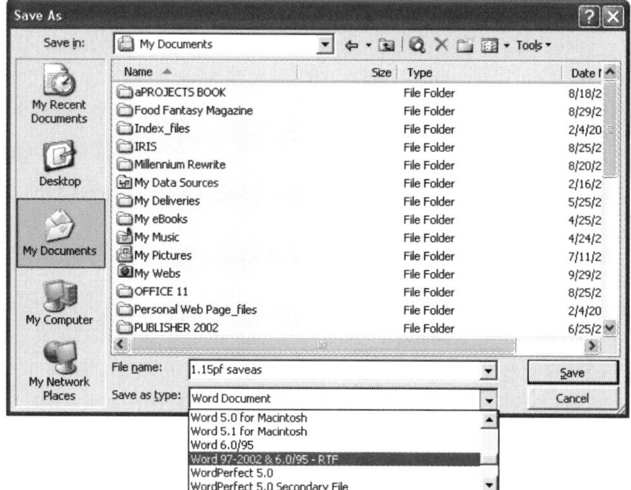

Figure 1.27 Save As dialog box

TRY *it* OUT *w1-15*

1. Open **w1.14pf spelling & grammar** from the Data CD.
2. Click **File, Save As.**
3. Enter the file name: **1.15pf saveas.yi** (your initials).
4. Click the **Save as type** list arrow.
5. Scroll down and select **Word 97–2003 & 6.0/95 – RTF** as the file type.
6. Click **Save.**
7. Close the file.

Print Preview

- The Print Preview feature allows you to see how a document will look on the page before printing it. To preview a document, Click File, Print Preview, or click the Print Preview button on the Standard toolbar.
- The Print Preview window, shown in Figure 1.28, has its own toolbar that includes buttons for the Preview mode. The buttons and their functions are described below:

CLICKING THIS BUTTON...		....WILL CAUSE THIS ACTION
Print		Prints the document on screen
Magnifier		Enlarges a portion of the document
One page		Shows one page of the document
Multiple Pages		Displays multiple pages
Zoom	114%	Sets a magnification percentage
View Ruler		Shows/hides the Ruler on the Print Preview window
Shrink to Fit		Fits text data onto one page
Full Screen		Removes all screen elements except the Preview toolbar
Close	Close	Closes the Print Preview window

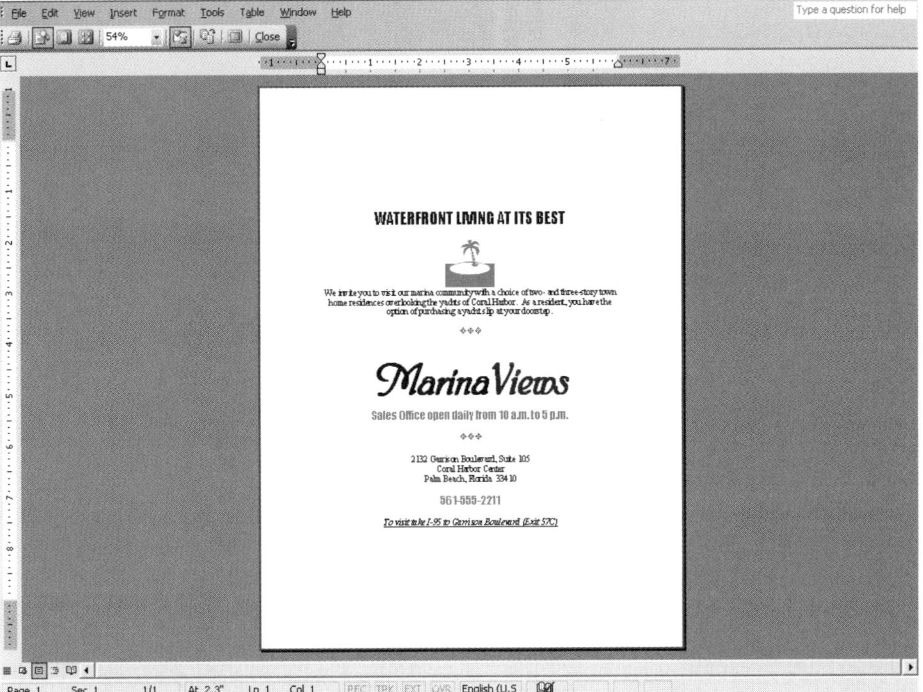

Figure 1.28 Print Preview window

TRY*it* OUT *w1-16*

1. Open **w1.16marina views** from the Data CD. 
2. Click the **Print Preview** button on the Standard toolbar.
3. Position the mouse pointer, which appears as a magnifying glass, on the smallest text, and click to enlarge it.
4. Click again to reduce the page.
5. Click the **Zoom** list arrow.
6. Change the magnification to **100%.**
7. Click the **View Ruler** button to hide the ruler.
8. Click the **View Ruler** button to show the ruler.
9. Click the **Full Screen** button.
10. Click the **Close Full Screen** button.
11. Click the **Close** button on the Preview toolbar.

Print

Print with Options

▶ You learned earlier that you can quickly print a document by clicking the Print button on the Standard toolbar. This method sends your document directly to the printer without giving you any printing options.

▶ To print a document with options, click File, Print. In the Print dialog box that follows, shown in Figure 1.29, you can choose from the following options. Clicking OK will send the document to the printer with the selected options.

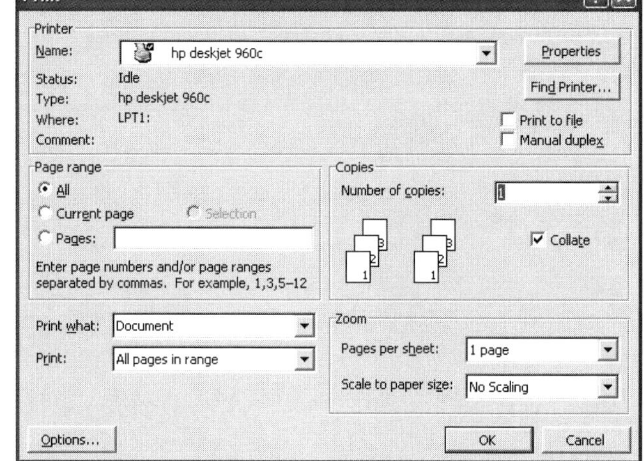

Figure 1.29 Print dialog box with options selected

- *Page range*—print part or all of a document by choosing the appropriate button in the Page range area.
  - To print *consecutive pages*, click the Pages option and enter the pages you want printed, separated by a hyphen. (To print pages 1 through 3, for example, you would enter 1-3 in the text box.)
  - To print *individual pages*, enter the page numbers, separated by a comma (1,5).
  - To print the *current page* (the page containing the insertion point), click the Current page option.
  - To print a *portion of the document*, select the text you want, click File, Print, then click the Selection option button.
- *Copies*—print a single copy or multiple copies of a document by entering the number you want in the Number of copies text box.
- *Print*—print all pages or just odd- or even-numbered pages by clicking the Print list arrow and choosing an option.
- *Collate*—specify how you want the document collated by selecting or deselecting the Collate check box.

TRY *it* OUT *w1-17*

1. Open **w1.17pf print** from the Data CD.
2. Select the summary information, including the heading "To Summarize...."
3. Click **File, Print.**
4. Click the **Selection** option to print the selected text.
5. Click **Cancel.**
6. Click **File, Print.**
7. Click to deselect the **Collate** check box to view the other collate options.
8. Click the **Print** list arrow to view the options.
9. Click **Cancel.**
10. Close the file; do not save.

Print in Landscape Orientation

- By default, a standard page prints in portrait orientation. *Portrait orientation* positions a page so that it is taller than it is wide, as shown in Figure 1.30. You can also print a page in *landscape orientation,* which positions a page so that it is wider than it is tall, as shown in Figure 1.31.

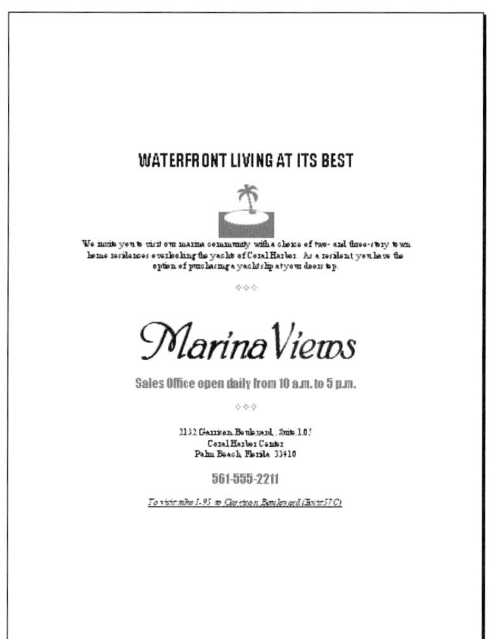

WATERFRONT LIVING AT ITS BEST
Marina Views
Sales Office open daily from 10 a.m. to 5 p.m.
561-555-2211

Figure 1.30 Portrait orientation

Figure 1.31 Landscape orientation

- To print in landscape orientation, click File, Page Setup. In the Page Setup dialog box, shown in Figure 1.32, click the Landscape orientation option. Then, print your document.

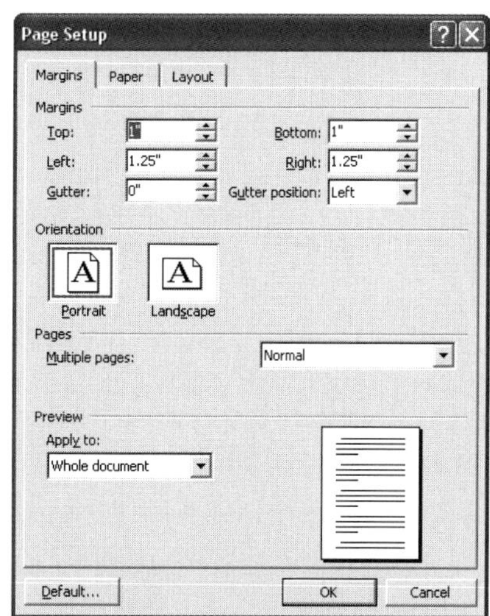

Figure 1.32 Page Setup dialog box

GOAL

To edit a document using basic editing features and document navigation techniques, then print the final version.

SETTING THE STAGE/WRAPUP

Margins: Default
Start Line: At 1"
File name: **1.3wordwrap**

WHAT YOU NEED TO KNOW

- An edited document contains proofreader's marks, which indicate corrections that need to be made to the text.
- The proofreader's mark to indicate a new paragraph is ¶
- The proofreader's mark to indicate an insertion is ∧
- The proofreader's mark to indicate a deletion is ℓ
- The proofreader's mark to indicate a move is ○→
- Remember, click the Undo button immediately after an edit to reverse the action and restore the text to its unedited form.
- In this Rehearsal activity, you will edit the document you created in Task 2 of this lesson, then print the final version.

DIRECTIONS

1. Open **1.2wordwrap** (if you completed it in the previous Rehearsal activity).
2. Save as **1.3wordwrap** or open **1.3wordwrap** from the Data CD. 
3. Click the **Show/Hide button** on the toolbar to show the screen codes, if necessary.
4. Make the revisions shown in the illustration on the facing page.

Note: Use any move method you want to move the paragraphs into the order indicated by the numbers to the left of each paragraph (do not type the numbers). Use Overtype mode to replace the phone number.

5. Correct spelling, if necessary.
6. Print one copy.
7. Close the file; save the changes.

② Event planning requires ~~much of your~~ time, ~~and~~ energy, dedication, and ~~It requires~~ a dependable network of suppliers. Assigning an inexperienced person to this type of work can be time-consuming, and costly

① Occasions Event Planning will help you with all your event-planning needs. We coordinate all aspects of the event to ensure that is it is ON TIME ON TARGET and ON BUDGET. ~~Let Occasions Event Planning plan your next party.~~ Our commitment to 100% satisfaction is the basis of our service.

copy Time is money. In the time it takes for an novice ~~inexperienced person~~ to plan an event, you may end up spending double what ~~more money than~~ it would have cost you to hire a professional. move

③ Hiring an event planner to manage an event means everyone ~~you~~ can relax and enjoy the party. Call us at ~~222-555-5555~~, Monday through Friday, from 8:00 a.m. to 5:30 p.m. Ask for Jean McDonald. 202-555-2222

¶ Remember, [lowercase "t" for "time"]

Cues for Reference

Insert Text
1. Position the insertion point to the left of the character where you want to insert text.
2. Click and enter the new text.

Overwrite Text
1. Click where Overtype is to begin.
2. Double-click the **OVR** indicator on the status bar.
3. Enter the text.
4. Double-click the new **OVR** indicator on the status bar to return to Insert mode.

Delete Text
Character(s)
1. To delete a character, position the insertion point to the right of the character to delete.
2. Press **Backspace.**

Blocks of Text
1. Select the text to delete.
2. Press **Delete** or click the **Cut** button or Press **Ctrl** + **X.** 

Show/Hide Codes
- Click the **Show/Hide** button on the toolbar. 

Move and Copy Text
Cut/Copy-and-Paste Method
1. Select the text to move.
2. Click the **Cut** button (to move) or the **Copy** button (to copy). 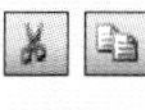
   or
   Press **Ctrl** + **X** (cut) or **Ctrl** + **C** (copy).
3. Position the insertion point where you want the text inserted.
4. Click the **Paste** button. 
   or
   Press **Ctrl** + **V.**

Drag-and-Drop Method
1. Select the text to move or copy.
2. Point to the selected text.
3. To move, hold down the left mouse button and drag the text to the new location. To copy, hold down the **Ctrl** key and the left mouse button as you drag the text to the new location.
4. Release mouse button.

Display Clipboard Task Pane
- Click **Edit, Office Clipboard.**

Spelling and Grammar Check
1. Click the **Spelling and Grammar** button. 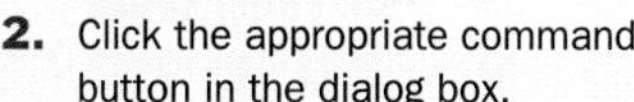
2. Click the appropriate command button in the dialog box.
3. Click **OK** when completed.

Print Preview
- Click the **Print Preview** button on the toolbar.
  or
- Click **File, Print Preview.**

Print
- Click the **Print** button on the toolbar. 
  or
- Click **File, Print.**

In Landscape Orientation
1. Click **File, Page Setup.**
2. Click the **Margins tab,** and choose **landscape orientation.**
3. Click **OK.**

TRYOUT
TASK 4

GOAL
To change the appearance of document text using following skill sets:

- Work with fonts
  - Change font face
  - Change font size
  - Change font style
  - Change font color
- Apply font effects
- Highlight text
- Change case
- Use symbols
- Format painter

WHAT YOU NEED TO KNOW

Work with Fonts

- A *font* is a complete set of characters designed in a specific face, style, and size.
- You can change font faces, styles, sizes, and colors before or after entering text. Remember to select existing text before applying a font format.

Change Font Face

- Each font design has a name and is intended to convey a specific feeling. The design is called a *font face.*
- There are basically three types of font faces—serif, sans serif, and script. A *serif* face has lines, curves, or edges extending from the ends of the letters (serif), whereas a *sans serif* face is straight-edged (sans serif), and *script* looks like handwriting (script). The default font in Word is Times New Roman, 12 point. Figure 1.33 illustrates a document that contains all three types of font faces.

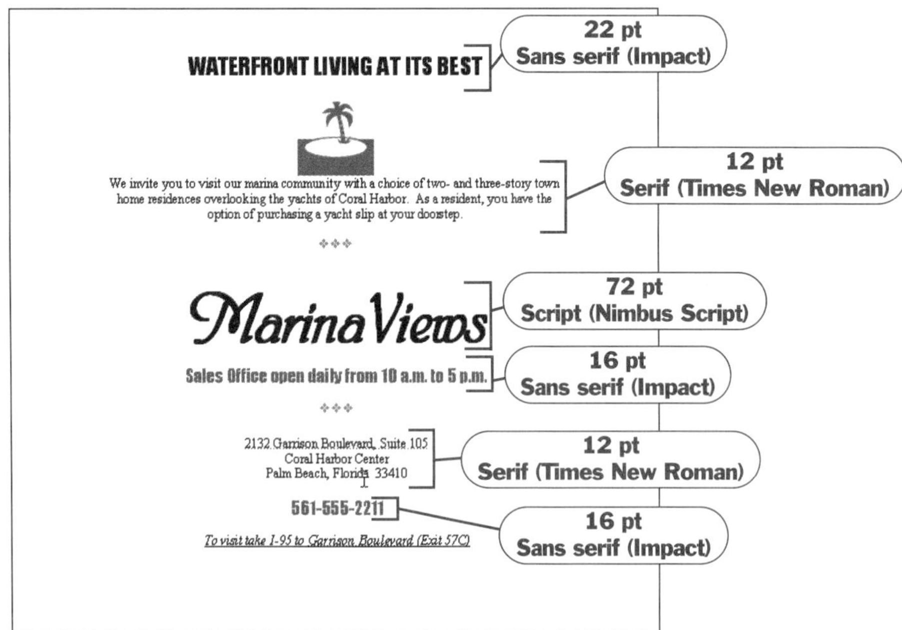
WATERFRONT LIVING AT ITS BEST
22 pt
Sans serif (Impact)
We invite you to visit our marina community with a choice of two- and three-story town home residences overlooking the yachts of Coral Harbor. As a resident, you have the option of purchasing a yacht slip at your doorstep.
12 pt
Serif (Times New Roman)
Marina Views
72 pt
Script (Nimbus Script)
Sales Office open daily from 10 a.m. to 5 p.m.
16 pt
Sans serif (Impact)
2132 Garrison Boulevard, Suite 105
Coral Harbor Center
Palm Beach, Florida 33410
12 pt
Serif (Times New Roman)
561-555-2211
To visit take I-95 to Garrison Boulevard (Exit 57C)
16 pt
Sans serif (Impact)

Figure 1.33 Document with varied font faces

▶ To change a font face quickly, click the Font list arrow on the Formatting toolbar and choose a font face, as shown in Figure 1.34.

Times New Roman

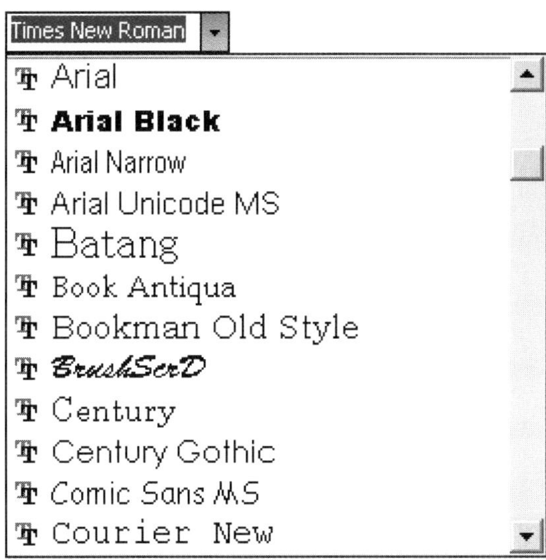

Figure 1.34 Font list

Font Size

▶ *Font size* refers to the height of the font, usually measured in points. There are 72 points to an inch. To change a font size quickly, click the Font size list arrow on the Formatting toolbar and choose a font size, as shown in Figure 1.35.

12

▶ *Font style* refers to the appearance of characters. Bold, italic, and underline are the most common examples of styles. Styles are generally used to emphasize text. To change a font style quickly, click the Bold, Italic, or Underline buttons on the Formatting toolbar. These buttons act as toggles to apply or remove the format. You can also use the following keyboard shortcuts to apply styles: Ctrl + B = bold; Ctrl + I = italic; Ctrl + U = underline.

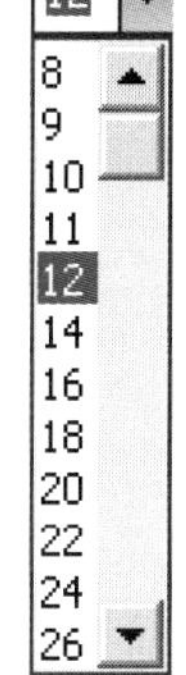

Figure 1.35 Font size list

Font Color

▶ To apply color to fonts, click the *Font color* list arrow on the toolbar and choose a color from the palette as shown in Figure 1.36.

Font Effects

In addition to emphasizing text using bold, italics, and underlining, Word provides other effects that you can apply to characters. These include small caps, all caps, strikethrough, double strikethrough, shadow, outline emboss, engrave, subscript, and superscript. *Superscripts* are characters that print slightly above the normal typing line; *subscripts* are characters that print slightly below the typing line. The *Hidden text* option allows you to hide text in your document. Because hidden text can easily be made visible by clicking the Show/Hide button on the toolbar, do not use hidden text formatting to keep sensitive data private. Figure 1.37 illustrates examples of each font effect.

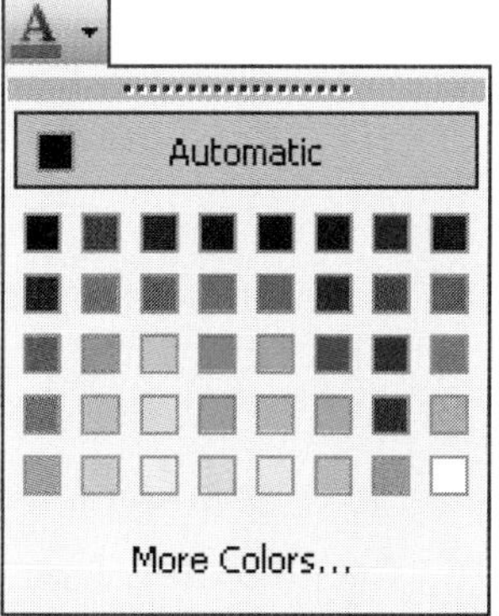

Figure 1.36 Font color palette

- To apply fonts, styles, sizes, and colors simultaneously, and/or to apply font effects, click Format, Font, then choose the options you want in the Font dialog box shown in Figure 1.38. You can also access the Font dialog box by right-clicking the document window and choosing Font from the Shortcut menu.

~~Strikethrough~~
~~Double strikethrough~~
SMALL CAPS
ALL CAPS
Shadow
Outline
Emboss
Engrave
Superscript: x^2
Subscript: $H_2 0$
Three words are hidden.

Figure 1.37 Font effects

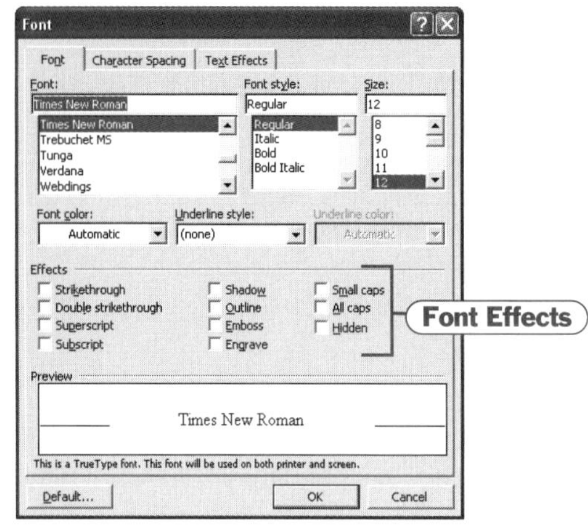

Figure 1.38 Font dialog box

- To remove character formatting from paragraphs in one step, select all the paragraphs that contain emphasis styles and click Edit, Clear Formats or press Ctrl + Spacebar.

Note: Return to your original settings after applying emphasis styles. Otherwise, the new format will remain in effect as you continue to work on your document.

TRY *it* OUT *w1-18*

1. Open **w1.18font practice** from the Data CD.
2. Select the word "blue."
3. Click the **Font** list arrow on the Formatting toolbar and click **Arial**. [Times New Roman ▾]
4. Click the **Font Size** list arrow on the toolbar and click **20.** [12 ▾]
5. Select the word "green."
6. Click the **Bold, Italic,** and **Underline** buttons on the Formatting toolbar.
7. Select the word "red."
8. Click the **Font color** list arrow, click **Red,** and press the **Ctrl** + **B** keys to make it bold.
9. Select the word "yellow."
10. Click **Format, Font.**
11. Click **Arial** as the font, **Bold** as the style, **24** as the size, and **Yellow** as the color and click **OK.**
12. Right-click the document window and click **Font** on the Shortcut menu.
13. Click **Times New Roman** as the font, **Regular** as the style, **12** as the size, and **Automatic** as the color, and click **OK.**
14. Select the word "strikethrough." Click **Format, Font,** click the **Strikethrough** check box, and click **OK.**
15. Select the "2" in $H_2 0$. Click **Format, Font,** click the **Subscript** check box, and click **OK.**
16. Select "in this sentence." Click **Format, Font,** click **Hidden,** and click **OK.**
17. Select all the text. Press the **Ctrl + spacebar** to remove the applied effects.
18. Close the file; do not save.

Use Symbols

- *Symbols* are ornamental font collections or special characters that you can use to separate items on a page, emphasize items on a list, or enhance a document. Figure 1.39 illustrates some ways to use symbols.
- To insert a symbol, click Insert, Symbol. In the Symbol dialog box that appears, as shown in Figure 1.40, click the Symbols tab and select a symbol collection from the Font list box. The symbol collection appears in the window. Click the symbol you want and click Insert. To insert multiple symbols, click Insert once for each symbol you want to insert. You can also copy a symbol and paste it as many times as you require.
- You can also access symbol collections through the Font dialog box or by clicking the Font list arrow on the Formatting toolbar. Symbols behave like fonts; therefore, you can change the point size, color, or emphasis style of a symbol just as you can with any other font face.

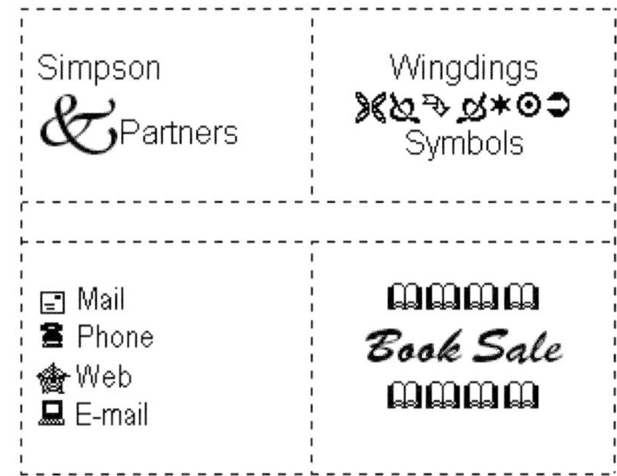

Figure 1.39 Ornamental font uses

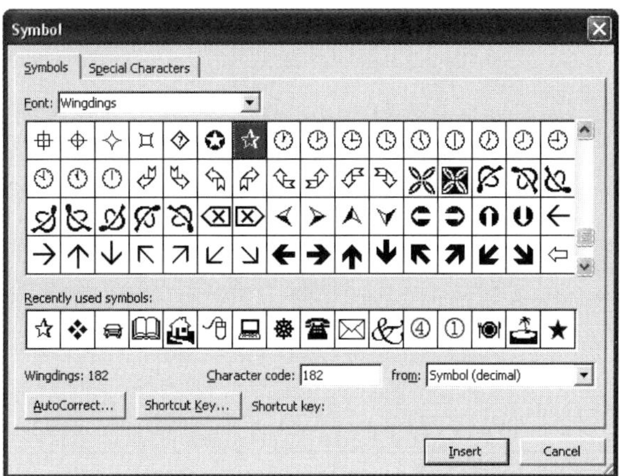

Figure 1.40 Symbol dialog box

TRY *it* OUT *w1-19*

1. Open a new blank document.
2. Type **THE READING CLUB** in all caps.
3. Position the insertion point before "The."
4. Click **Insert, Symbol.**
5. Click the **Font** list arrow and select **Wingdings.**
6. Click each symbol in the first row.
7. Click the **Book** symbol, click **Insert** three times, and click **Close.**
8. Copy the three book symbols.
9. Position the insertion point after the last word in the heading and click **Paste.**
10. Press the **Enter** key twice.
11. Change the font size to 10 point.
12. Click **Insert, Symbol.** Insert any four symbols, and click **Close.**
13. Select the symbols and click **Format, Font.**
14. Click the **Font Color** list arrow, select Red, and click **OK.** 
15. Print one copy.
16. Close the file; do not save.

Format Painter

- The *Format Painter* feature allows you to copy formatting such as font face, style, and size from one block of text to another.
- To copy formatting, select the text or data that contains the formatting you wish to copy, click the Format Painter button on the Formatting toolbar (the insertion point becomes a paintbrush), and select the text to receive the formatting. 
- To copy formatting from one location to several, select the text with the formatting you wish to copy and double-click the Format Painter button. You can now "paint" the formatting on several blocks of text or data by clicking a word or highlighting a block. To turn off this feature, click the Format Painter button again.

TRY *it* OUT *w1-20*

1. Open **w1.20pf painter** from the Data CD.
2. Double-click "Blue."
3. Click the **Format Painter** button on the Formatting toolbar. Note that the insertion point changes to a paintbrush.
4. Click "blueberries."
5. Copy the formatting from the word "Red" to "apples."
6. Double-click "Green."
7. Double-click the **Format Painter** button.
8. Click "lettuce," then click "grapes," then click "cabbage."
9. Click the **Format Painter** button to turn off the feature.
10. Close the file; do not save.

Highlight Text

- The Highlight feature allows you to emphasize a word, several words, a paragraph, parts of a document, symbols, or graphics using color.
- To highlight text, click the Highlight button on the Formatting toolbar. (When you hold your mouse pointer over a color, a ScreenTip displays the name of the color.) Select the text you wish to highlight (the mouse pointer changes to a pen), and Word automatically applies the highlighting color displayed on the highlight button. If it is not the color you want, click the list arrow to the right of the button, then select a color from the palette, shown in Figure 1.41.

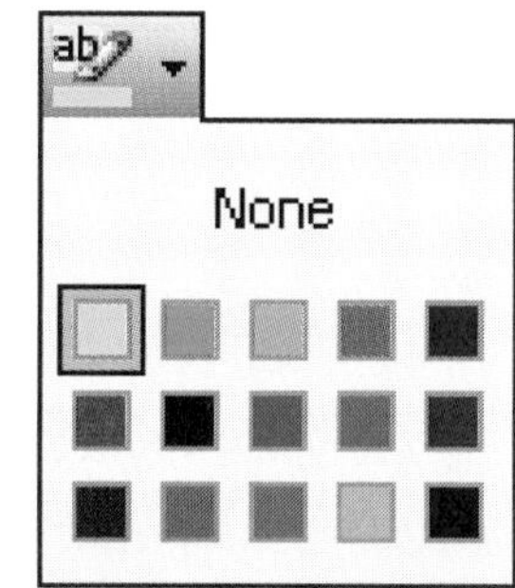

Figure 1.41 Highlight color palette

TRY *it* OUT *w1-21*

1. Open **w1.21pf highlight** from the Data CD.
2. Click the list arrow on the **Highlight** button.
3. Click **Bright Green** on the palette.
4. Select the first paragraph.
5. Click the **Highlight** list arrow.
6. Change the highlight color to **Turquoise.**
7. Select the second paragraph.
8. Click the **Highlight** list arrow and change the highlight color to **Yellow.**
9. Select the third paragraph.
10. Click the **Highlight** list arrow and change the highlight color to **Red.**
11. Close the file; do not save.

Change Case

- The change case feature allows you to easily convert one case (uppercase, lowercase, sentence case, title case) to another. To do so, select the text you wish to convert, and select Format, Change Case. Make the change you want in the Change Case dialog box that displays, shown in Figure 1.42.
- You can also use the shortcut method for changing case. Select the text you wish to change, then press Shift + F3 once to change to title case, twice to change to uppercase, and three times to change to lowercase.

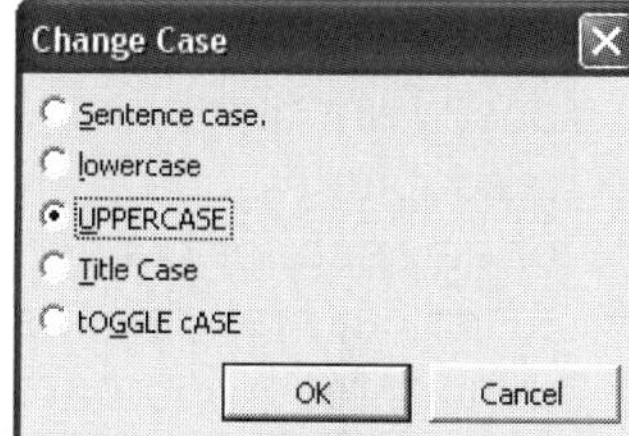

Figure 1.42 Change case dialog box

TRY *it* OUT *w1-22*

1. Open a new document.
2. Type the following. Enter each on a separate line.
   technology forum
   third annual summer conference
   embassy hotel, detroit, michigan
3. Select "technology forum." Press **Shift + F3** as many times as necessary to change it to uppercase.
4. Select "third annual summer conference." Click **Format, Change Case,** choose **Title Case,** and click **OK.**
5. Select the last line. Press **Shift + F3** as many times as necessary to change it to title case.
6. Close the file; do not save.

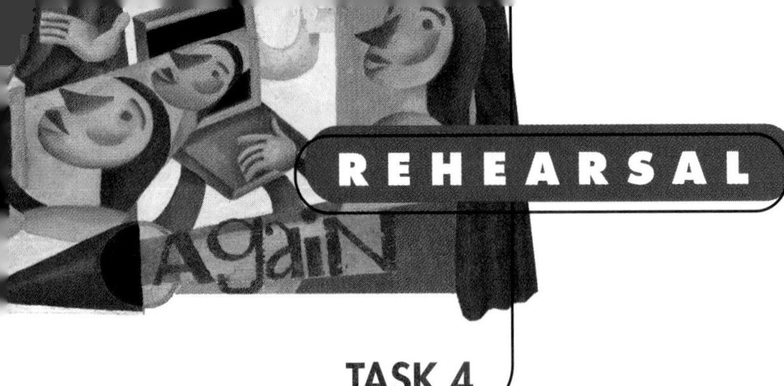

GOAL

To apply basic formatting (font, style, size, and color) to selected text; to print using print options and different orientations

SETTING THE STAGE/WRAPUP

Margins: Default
Start Line: At 1"
File names: **1.4ad**

WHAT YOU NEED TO KNOW

- It is important to remember to select existing text before you apply formatting.
- A serif font is typically used for document text because it is more readable. A sans serif font is often used for headlines or technical material. A script font is usually reserved for formal invitations and announcements.
- You should choose typefaces that will make your document attractive and communicate its particular message most effectively. As a rule, use no more than two or three font faces in any one document.
- In this Rehearsal activity, you will apply formatting to unformatted text so that it matches the advertisement in the illustration. You will use the Format Painter to copy formatting from one block of text to another and print using print options and landscape orientation.

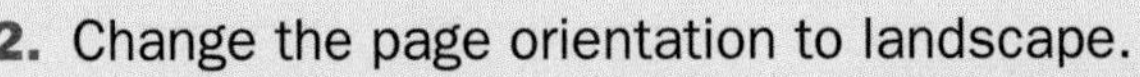

DIRECTIONS

1. Open **1.4ad** from the Data CD.
2. Change the page orientation to landscape.
3. Use the Change Case feature for all sections to match the text in the illustration on the facing page.
4. Change the first two sections of the text to match the font face, size, style, and color of those in the illustration.

Note: If you do not have the exact font faces indicated in the illustration, substitute others.

5. Use the Format Painter to copy the formatting from section 2 to section 5.
6. Use the Format Painter to copy the formatting from section 4 to section 6. Format section 7 to match the illustration on the facing page.
7. Delete "community" in the second section.
8. Undo the deletion.
9. Center a graphic symbol below the main heading and set it to 72 points. Insert any desired symbols between text as shown.
10. Highlight the phone number in yellow.
11. Set the magnification to **200%.**
12. Use Print preview.
13. Print one copy.
14. Set the magnification to **100%.**
15. Save and close the file.

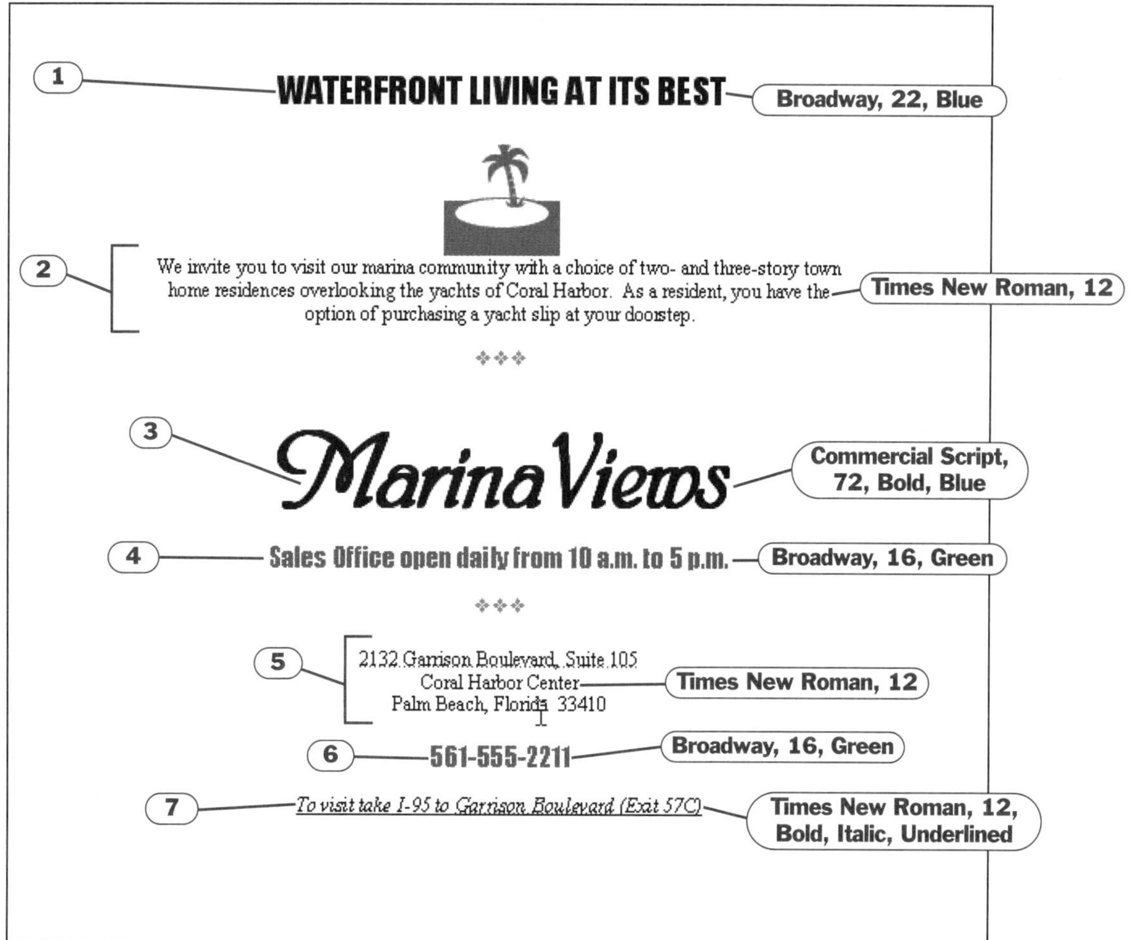
1
WATERFRONT LIVING AT ITS BEST
Broadway, 22, Blue
2
We invite you to visit our marina community with a choice of two- and three-story town home residences overlooking the yachts of Coral Harbor. As a resident, you have the option of purchasing a yacht slip at your doorstep.
Times New Roman, 12
3
Marina Views
Commercial Script, 72, Bold, Blue
4
Sales Office open daily from 10 a.m. to 5 p.m.
Broadway, 16, Green
5
2132 Garrison Boulevard, Suite 105
Coral Harbor Center
Palm Beach, Florida 33410
Times New Roman, 12
6
561-555-2211
Broadway, 16, Green
7
To visit take I-95 to Garrison Boulevard (Exit 57C)
Times New Roman, 12, Bold, Italic, Underlined

Cues for Reference

Change Font, Size, Style, and Color

1. Select the text to be formatted or position the insertion point where the new formatting is to begin.
2. Click **Format, Font,** or right-click the desktop and click **Font.**
3. Make the desired changes.
4. Click **OK.**

Or

- Click the **Font** list arrow on the toolbar and click the desired font. [Times New Roman]

Or

- Click the **Size** list arrow on the toolbar and click the desired size. [12]

Or

- Click the **Bold** button or press **Ctrl + B.**

Or

- Click the **Italic** button or press **Ctrl + I.**

Or

- Click the **Underline** button or press **Ctrl + U.**

Or

- Click the **Font Color** list arrow and click the desired color from the palette.

Format Painter

1. Select the text with the formatting you wish to copy.
2. Click the **Format Painter** button once to copy formatting from one location to another.
3. Select the text to receive the copied formatting.

Or

1. Select the text with the formatting you wish to copy.
2. Double-click the **Format Painter** button to copy formatting from one location to many.
3. Select text to receive the copied formatting.
4. Click the **Format Painter** button to turn the option off.

Apply Font Effects

1. Select the text you want to affect.
2. Click **Format, Font.**
3. Click a font effect.
4. Click **OK.**

Highlight Text

1. Select the text you want to affect.
2. Click the **Highlight** button on the Formatting toolbar.

Change Highlight Color

1. Click the **Highlight** list arrow.
2. Click to select a color from the palette.

Insert Symbols

1. Click **Insert, Symbol.**
2. Click the **Font** list arrow and choose a symbol font collection.
3. Click the symbol, and click **Insert.**

LESSON 2

Correspondence

In this lesson, you will learn to use features found in Word to format correspondence, create an envelope and labels, and send e-mail. Correspondence includes written communications such as letters, memos, and e-mails. You will complete the following projects:

- a business letter
- a personal letter and envelope
- a memorandum using a template
- a business letter using a Wizard

Upon completion of this lesson, you should have mastered the following skill sets:

- Set margins
- Insert the date and time
- Use Smart Tags
- Use AutoText
- Use horizontal text alignments
- Create envelopes and labels
- Use templates
- Open existing templates
- Create your own template
- Use wizards
- Send e-mail
- Create a new message
- Send a Word document as e-mail

Terms

Software-related

Portrait orientation
AutoText
Template
Placeholder
Wizard
E-mail

Document-related

Full-block business letter
Enclosure notation
Personal letter
Justified text
Delivery address
Letterhead
Logo
Memorandum

TRYOUT

TASK 1

GOAL

To create a full-block business letter by using the following skill sets:

- Set margins
- Date and time
- Smart Tags
- AutoText

WORD

WHAT YOU NEED TO KNOW

Set Margins

- The blank area at the edge of a page is the margin.
- The default margins for a page positioned in *portrait orientation* are 1" top, 1" bottom, 1.25" left, and 1.25" right.
- To change margins, select File, Page Setup. In the Page Setup dialog box that displays, shown in Figure 2.1, click the Margins tab, choose a page orientation, then enter the top, bottom, left, and right margins in the appropriate text boxes. A preview window displays a thumbnail showing the results of your selections.
- You can apply margin changes to the Whole document (the default) or from This point forward.

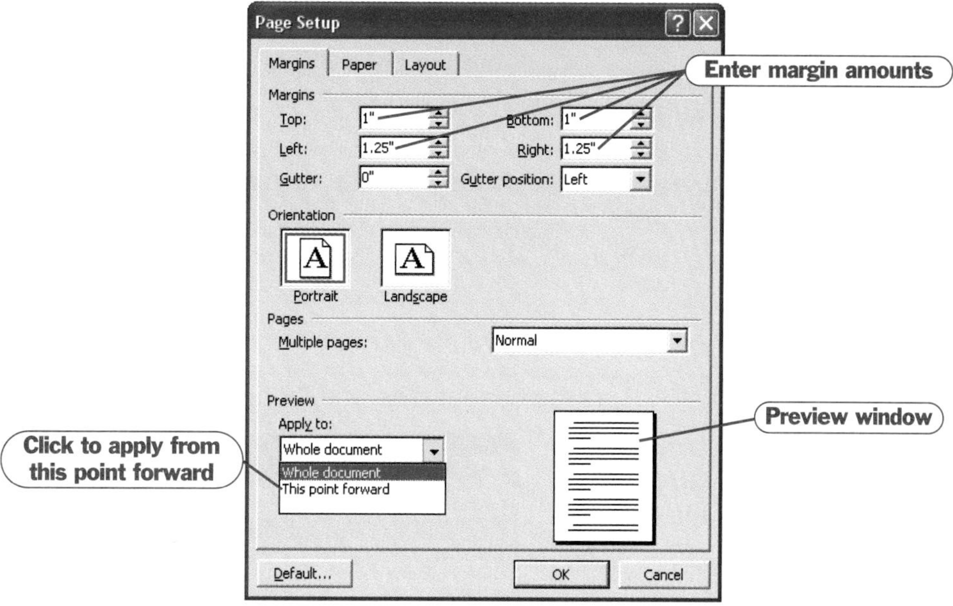

Figure 2.1 Page Setup dialog box

TRY *it* OUT *w2-1*

1. Open **w2.1pf letter** from the Data CD.
2. Click **File, Page Setup**.
3. Click the **Margins** tab.
4. Enter 1.5" in the Left and Right text boxes.
5. Click **OK**.
6. Do not close the file.

- You can also change margins by dragging the margin markers on the ruler. Use this method when you want to see the effect of the margin change on the document as you are doing it.
- To change margins using this method, position the mouse pointer on the marker; when it changes to a two-headed arrow (and displays a "Left Margin" ScreenTip as shown in Figure 2.2), drag the margin boundary to the position you want. Holding down Alt as you drag the margin marker displays the margin measurements on the ruler, as shown in Figure 2.2.

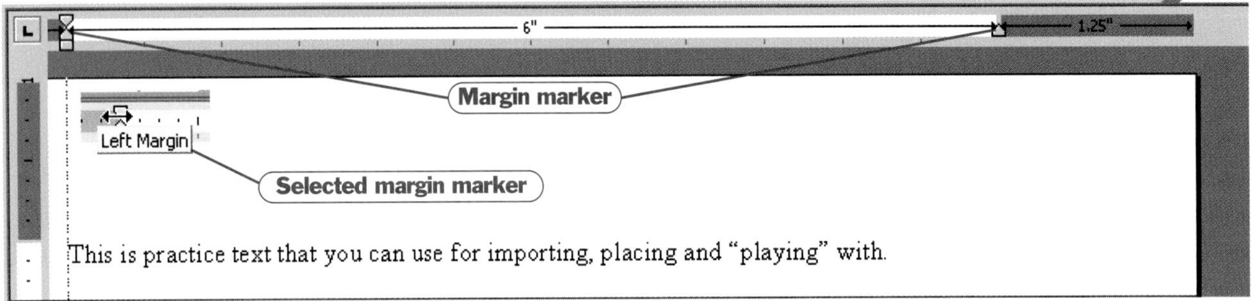

Figure 2.2 Margin markers on ruler

TRY *it* OUT *w2-2*

Note: ***w2.1pf letter*** *should be displayed on your screen.*

1. Position the mouse pointer on the left margin marker. When the pointer turns to a double-headed arrow, click and hold the **mouse button**, press and hold the **Alt** key, then drag the margin marker to 2".
2. Position the mouse pointer on the right margin marker. Click and hold the **mouse button**, press and hold the **Alt** key, then drag the margin marker to 2" from the right.
3. Close the file; do not save.

Insert Date and Time

- The Date and Time feature allows you to insert the current date and/or time into a document.
- To insert the date and/or time, select Insert, Date and Time, and choose a date and/or time format from the Available formats in the Date and Time dialog box, as shown in Figure 2.3. To set a default format, select the format you want, and click the Default button.
- To update the date each time the document is opened or printed, click the Update automatically check box.

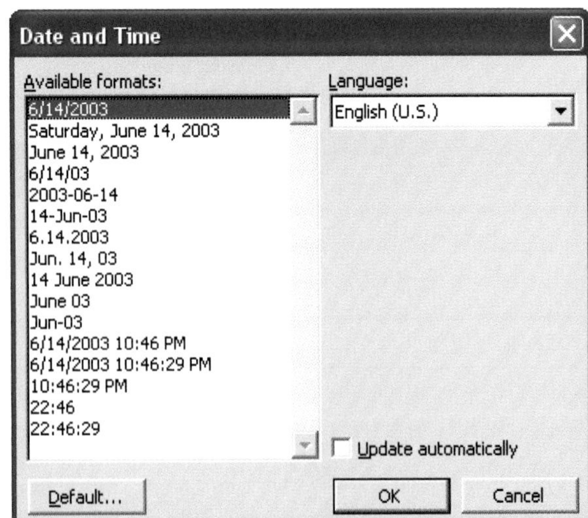

Figure 2.3 Date and Time dialog box

TRY it OUT *w2-3*

1. Click the **New Blank Document** button.
2. Click **Insert, Date and Time.**
3. Select the default date format.
4. Click **OK.**
5. Close the file; do not save.
6. Open a new blank document.
7. Click **Insert, Date and Time.**
8. Enter today's date again using this format: September 2, 200–.
9. Close the file; do not save.

Smart Tags

- When you type certain text in a document, Word labels it with a Smart Tag. Smart Tags appear as a purple dotted line beneath names, dates, addresses, and other text, as shown in Figure 2.4.
- When you move the insertion point over the purple underlined text, a Smart Tag Actions button appears, as shown in Figure 2.5.
- Click the button to see a menu of actions you can perform, shown in Figure 2.6. The action options displayed depend on the type of data that has been tagged. Names will display one set of actions, dates will display another, and phone numbers will display yet another. Many Smart Tag actions are performed with Outlook.

Kate Jackson

Figure 2.4 Smart Tag

Figure 2.5 Smart Tag Actions button

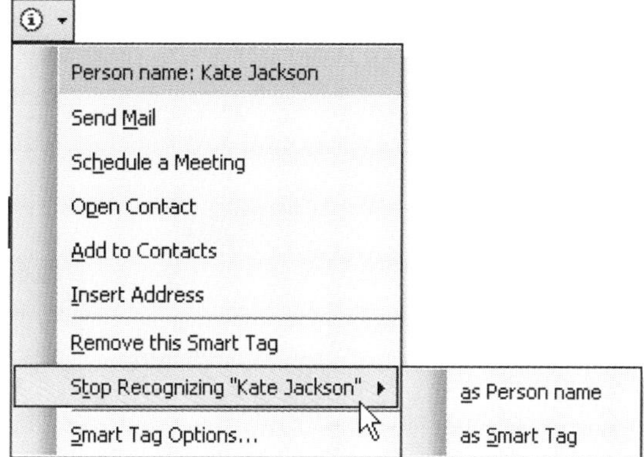

Figure 2.6 Smart Tag Actions menu

TRY it OUT *w2-4*

Note: Check to see that all Smart Tags options have been turned on. Click Tools, AutoCorrect Options. Click the Smart Tags tab and select all the check boxes below "Recognizers."

1. Click the **New Blank Document** button.
2. Enter your name and press the **Enter** key.
3. Position the insertion point over your name and click the **Smart Tag Actions** button.
4. View the actions.
5. Using the date and time feature, insert today's date, and press the **Enter** key.

Continued on next page

TRY *it* OUT *w2-4 Continued*

6. Position the insertion point over the date and click the **Smart Tag Actions** button.
7. View the actions.
8. Enter your address and press the **Enter** key.
9. Position the insertion point over the address and click the **Smart Tag Actions** button.
10. View the actions.
11. Close the file; do not save.

- To turn off Smart Tags, click Tools, AutoCorrect Options from the menu. Click the Smart Tags tab in the AutoCorrect dialog box shown in Figure 2.7, then deselect Show Smart Tag Actions buttons, and click OK.

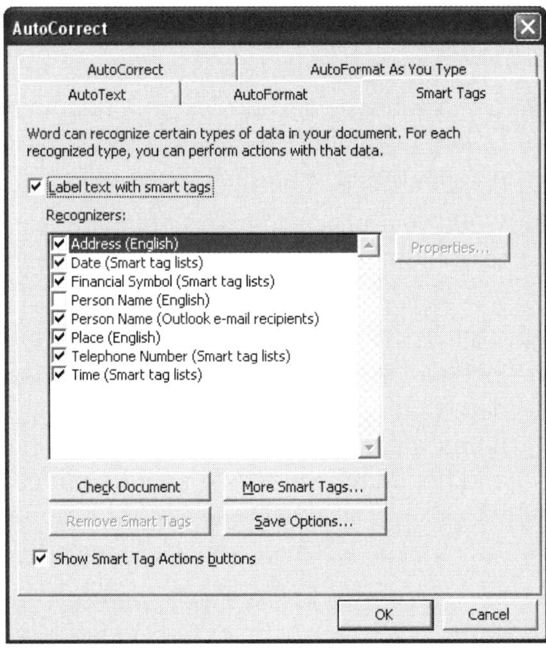

Figure 2.7 Smart Tags tab in AutoCorrect dialog box

AutoText

- The *AutoText* feature allows you to save and quickly insert frequently used text and graphics. You can easily create your own AutoText entries or use one of the numerous built-in entries that comes with Word.
- To create a *new* AutoText entry, select the text or graphic you want to store as an AutoText entry. Include the paragraph mark in your selection if you wish to store paragraph formatting with the entry. Click Insert, AutoText, New on the menu. In the Create AutoText dialog box that displays, shown in Figure 2.8, use the name Word suggests, or enter a new name for the entry, then click OK.

Figure 2.8 Create AutoText dialog box

- To insert an entry into a document, click where you want the entry to appear. Then, click Insert, AutoText on the menu. An AutoText menu, shown in Figure 2.9, will display the AutoText entries, which are arranged in categories. The Normal category contains the entries you have created. Click the name of the entry you want.
- You can also use a shortcut to insert an AutoText entry, but you must turn on AutoComplete. Click Insert, AutoText, click AutoText. In the AutoCorrect dialog box that displays, shown in Figure 2.10, click the AutoText tab, select Show AutoComplete suggestions, then click OK.
- To use the shortcut, type the first few characters in the AutoText entry's name. After typing the first four letters of the entry name, a ScreenTip will display, suggesting the entry. Press Enter or F3 to "autocomplete" (accept) the entry; continue typing to ignore the entry. You can also insert and delete as well as preview those AutoText entries listed on the AutoText tab of the AutoCorrect dialog box (see Figure 2.10).

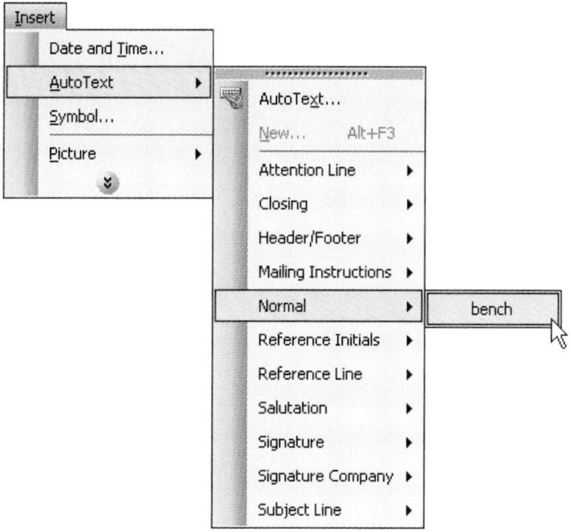

Figure 2.9 Insert AutoText menu

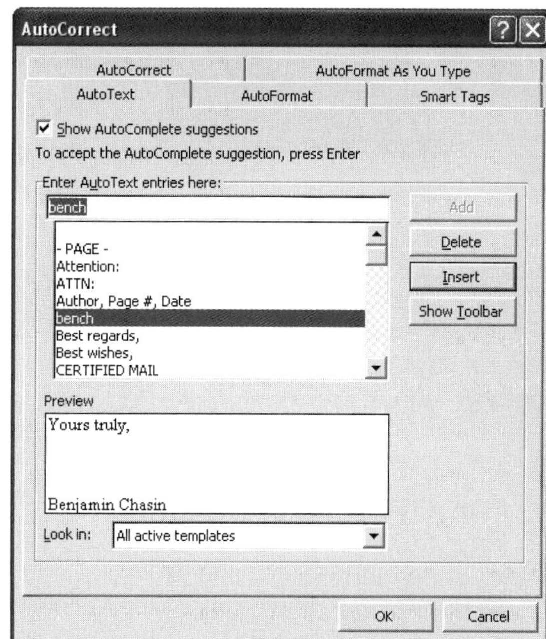

Figure 2.10 AutoText tab in AutoCorrect dialog box

TRY *it* OUT *w2-5*

1. Start a new blank document.
2. Click **Insert, AutoText, AutoText.** Select the **AutoText** tab and be sure Show AutoComplete suggestions has been selected. Then click **OK.**
3. Type the following at the top of the page. (See Figure 2.8.)

   Yours truly,

   ↓4x

   Benjamin Chasin

   President

   ↓2x

   bc/yo

4. Select all the text.
5. Click **Insert, AutoText, New.**
6. Enter **bench** as the AutoText name, and click **OK.**
7. Close the file; do not save.
8. Open a new blank document.
9. With your insertion point at the top of the page, type **benc**. AutoComplete will offer you an AutoText suggestion. Press **Enter** to accept the suggestion.
10. Close the file; do not save.

TASK 1

GOAL
To create a full-block business letter

SETTING THE STAGE/WRAPUP
Margins: 1.5" left and right
Start line: At 2.5"
File name: **2.1employment**

WHAT YOU NEED TO KNOW

- The layout of a letter is called a format. There are a variety of letter formats, but most have the following parts: date, inside address, salutation, body, closing, name and title of the writer, and reference initials of the writer and the person who prepares the document.
- In a *full-block business letter,* all parts begin at the left margin.
- The date generally begins 2.5" down from the top of the page. (The At indicator on the status bar displays 2.5".)
- The margins depend on the length of the letter. Short letters use wider left and right margins (more than 1"), whereas longer letters use narrower left and right margins (less than 1").
- "Sincerely" is generally used to close a letter. "Cordially," "Yours truly," and "Very truly yours" can also be used.
- An *enclosure notation* is indicated on a letter when something in addition to the letter is included in the envelope. The notation is generally placed at the left margin, two lines below the reference initials.
- In this Rehearsal activity, you will format a full-block business letter.

DIRECTIONS

1. Open a new blank document.
2. Turn on the AutoComplete feature, if it is not activated.
3. Create an AutoText entry for the word **enclosure**; name it **enclos.**
4. Close the file; do not save.
5. Open another new blank document.
6. Set **1.5"** left and right margins.
7. Press the **Enter** key to advance the insertion point to **2.5".**
8. Use the Date feature to insert the current date. Use this format: September 3, 200–.
9. Enter the letter as shown on the facing page. Press the **Enter** key between letter parts as shown.
10. Insert the AutoText entry named **bench** for the closing.
11. Insert the AutoText entry named **enclos** for the enclosure notation.
12. Correct spelling errors.
13. Preview the document.
14. Save the file; name it **2.1employment.**
15. Close the file.

Today's date

4

Mr. John Smith
34 West Street
New York, NY 10021 — inside address

2

Dear Mr. Smith: — salutation

2

Thank you for your inquiry regarding employment with our firm.

2

We have reviewed your qualifications with several members of our firm. We regret to report that we do not have an appropriate vacancy at this time.

2

We will retain your resume in our files in the event that an opening occurs in your field. Your interest in our organization is very much appreciated. We hope to be able to offer you a position at another time, and we are returning the portfolio you sent us. — body

2

Yours truly, — closing

4

Benjamin Chasin
Personnel Manager — Name and title of writer

2

bc/yo — Reference initials of writer and preparer

2

enclosure — Enclosure notation

Cues for Reference

Set Margins

1. Click **File.**
2. Click **Page Setup.**
3. Click the **Margins** tab.
4. Enter the measurements for the top, bottom, left, and/or right margins.
5. Choose a page orientation.
6. Click **OK.**

Insert Date and Time

1. Click **Insert.**
2. Click **Date and Time.**
3. Select a date and/or time format.
4. Click **OK.**

Create a New AutoText Entry

1. Select text/graphics to store as an AutoText entry.
2. Click **Insert.**
3. Click **AutoText.**
4. Click **New.**
5. Type name of AutoText entry.
6. Click **OK.**

Insert an AutoText Entry

1. Position the insertion point in the document where the AutoText entry will be inserted.
2. Type the AutoText entry's name.
3. When the ScreenTip displays, press **Enter** or **F3.**

or

1. Position the insertion point in the document where the AutoText entry will be inserted.
2. Click **Insert,** point to **AutoText.**
3. Select a category, then select an AutoText entry from the menu that displays.

GOAL
To create a full-block personal letter with an envelope by using the following skill sets:

- Horizontal text alignments
- Envelopes and labels

WHAT YOU NEED TO KNOW

Horizontal Text Alignments

- You can align text left (the default), right, and center. Text aligns between existing margins. You can also justify text. *Justified text* displays lines that are even at the left and right margins (except for the last line). Figure 2.11 shows the effect of different text alignments.

Left-Aligned Paragraph One. This is practice text that you can use for importing, placing and "playing" purposes. Practice text is useful when you are planning a layout. Using practice text rather than real text is a good way to concentrate on the form and design of your layout without reading the text itself.

Center-Aligned Paragraph Two. From now on, this file will be referred to as the "pf" (practice file) file. Have fun.!

Right-Aligned Paragraph Three. Practice text should have paragraphs so you can manipulate them and move them as you desire. Practice text should have paragraphs so you can manipulate them and move them as you desire. Practice text encourages you to experiment with alignments, typefaces, type styles, type sizes and leading.

Justified Paragraph Four. When working with practice text, you should have at least four paragraphs. This will enable you to move them and experiment with at least four different formats. The paragraphs should be long enough so that you can see the effects of a line spacing or paragraph spacing change, for example.

Figure 2.11 Text alignments

- You can change alignments before or after entering text.
- To align a paragraph or line of text after you enter it, position the insertion point anywhere in the paragraph or line and click an alignment button on the Formatting toolbar, as shown in Figure 2.12.

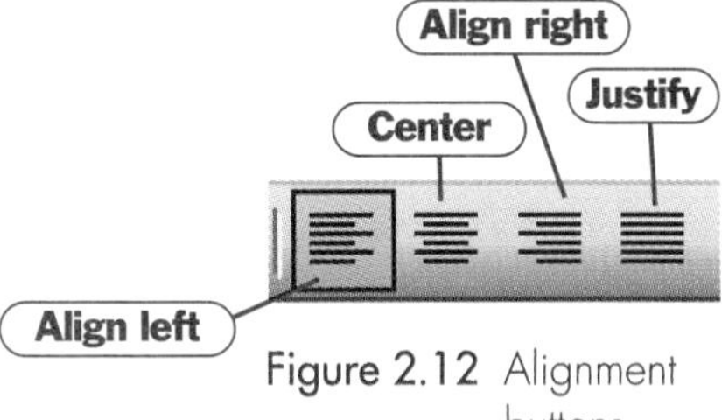

Figure 2.12 Alignment buttons

TRY *it* OUT *w2-6*

1. Open **w2.6alignments** from the Data CD. 
2. Position your insertion point anywhere in paragraph two. Click the **Center** button on the Formatting toolbar.
3. Position your insertion point anywhere in paragraph three. Click the **Align right** button on the Formatting toolbar. 
4. Position your insertion point anywhere in paragraph four. Click the **Justify** button on the Formatting toolbar. *Note: If the Justify button is not visible, click Toolbar Options.*
5. Position your insertion point anywhere in paragraph one. Click the **Center** button, then click the **Align Left** button.
6. Position your insertion point after the last word in paragraph four. Press the **Enter** key twice.
7. Enter your first and last names.
8. Click the **Center** button. 
9. Press the **Enter** key twice.
10. Enter today's date.
11. Click the **Align Right** button. 
12. Print one copy.
13. Close the file; do not save.

Envelopes and Labels

Envelopes

- To create an envelope, click Tools, Letters and Mailings, and Envelopes and Labels. Click the Envelopes tab, and in the Delivery address window enter the address of the person to whom the letter is to be sent. If a letter is on the screen, Word automatically places its mailing address into the Delivery address window, as shown in Figure 2.13.
- The *delivery address* on an envelope is the same as the inside address in a letter.
- Do not enter a return address if you are using envelopes that have a preprinted address.
- To complete the printing process, insert the envelope into your printer as shown in the Feed window and click Print.

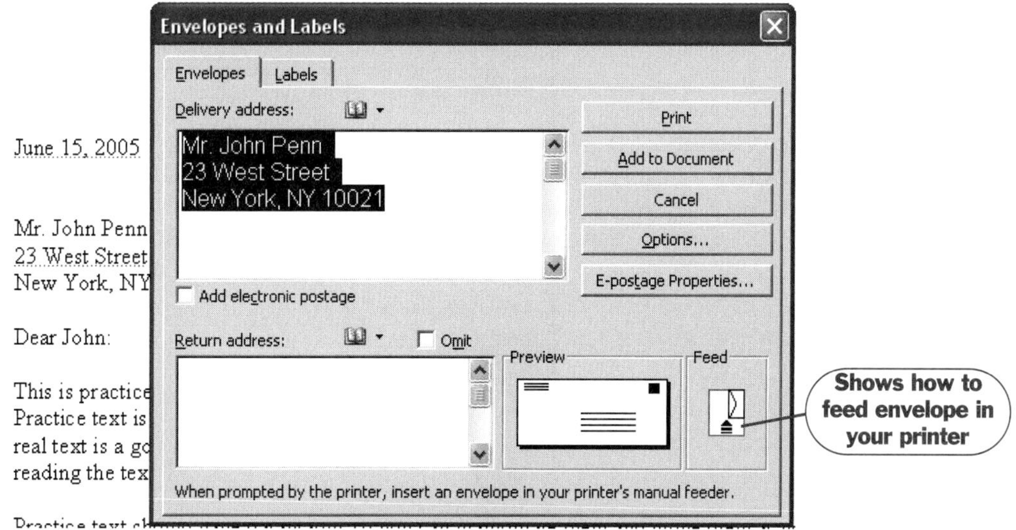

Figure 2.13 Envelopes and Labels dialog box

▶ Other envelope printing options are explained in the table below.

OPTION	EXPLANATION
Add to Document	Appends the envelope file to the beginning of the document, so the envelope prints along with the document. This makes it unnecessary to re-create the envelope the next time you print the document.
Options • *Envelope Options* tab • *Printing Options* tab	 Enables you to customize the size and format of an envelope. The default size is set for letter (No. 10), measuring 4⅛ × 9½ inches. Provides feed method options.
E-Postage Properties	Enables you to print U.S. Postal-Service approved postage and get feedback on incorrect addresses. Users must sign up with www.Stamps.com to use this service.

TRY *it* OUT *w2-7*

1. Open **w2.7pf letter** from the Data CD.
2. Click **Tools, Letters and Mailings.**
3. Click **Envelopes and Labels.**
4. Click the **Envelopes** tab. The address should automatically appear in the Delivery address window.
5. Click **Options.**
6. Click the **Printing Options** tab.
7. Select the feed method that is compatible with your printer.
8. Click **OK.**
9. Click **Add to Document.**
10. Insert an envelope into your printer. (It is not necessary to use an actual envelope for this tryout. You can print the address using plain paper.)
11. Click the **Print** button on the toolbar.
12. Close the file; do not save.

Labels

▶ The Labels feature allows you to create labels for mailings, file folders, business cards, name badges, or floppy disks.

▶ To create labels, click Tools, Letters and Mailings, and Envelopes and Labels. Click the Labels tab in the Envelopes and Labels dialog box, as shown in Figure 2.14.

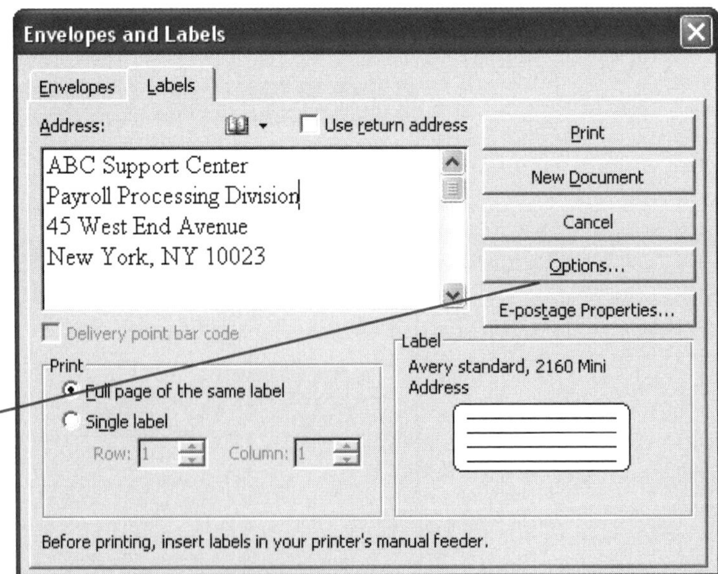

Figure 2.14 Labels tab in the Envelopes and Labels dialog box

WORD

- To specify the label type you want to use, click the Options button. In the Label Options dialog box that appears, as shown in Figure 2.15, choose the type of label you want from the predefined label products and product number lists. (Product numbers are typically indicated on the label box.)

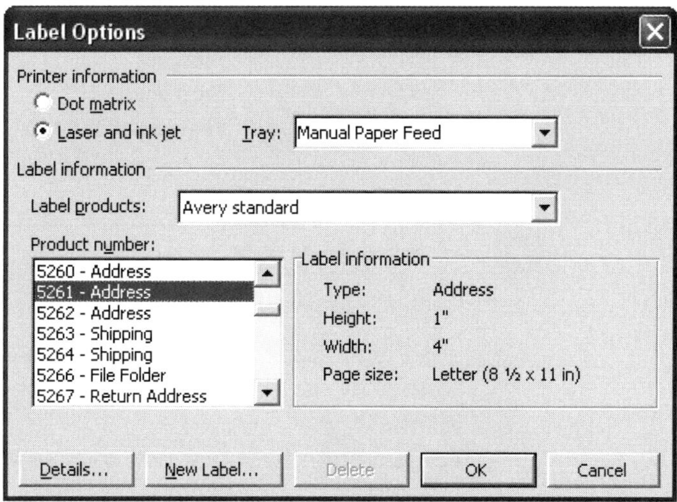

Figure 2.15 Label Options dialog box

- Once you specify the label format and click OK, you return to the previous dialog box. Click the New Document button and blank labels appear, ready for you to begin entering text.
- To print the labels, load the printer with the proper size and type of label paper you specified. When you print a single page, the entire physical page is printed.
- To print a sheet of labels with the same information, enter the information in the Address window of the Envelopes and Labels dialog box, and click the Full page of the same label option (see Figure 2.14).

TRY it OUT w2-8

1. Click the **New Blank Document** button. 
2. Click **Tools, Letters and Mailings.**
3. Click **Envelopes and Labels.**
4. Click the **Labels** tab.
5. Click **Options.**
6. Click **Avery standard** as the label product, if it has not already been selected.
7. Click **5261-Address** in the Product number list box.
8. Click **OK.**
9. Click **New Document.**
10. Enter the following address:

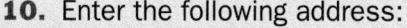

    Ms. Wendy Ng
    78 Jason Lane
    East Meadow, NY 11545
11. Press the **Tab** key twice to advance to the next label.
12. Enter the following address:

    Mr. Harmon Jones
    33 Pine Street
    Middletown, NJ 01154
13. If you have the specified label type, insert a sheet of labels and click **Print;** otherwise, print on letter-size paper.
14. Close the file; do not save.

GOAL
To create a full-block personal letter and envelope

SETTING THE STAGE/WRAPUP
Margins: 1.5" left and right
Start line: At 1"
File name: **2.2apply**

WHAT YOU NEED TO KNOW

- A *letterhead* is stationery used by an individual or a company that contains the name, address, phone number, and other contact information such as fax, e-mail, and Web address. Some company letterheads also contain a *logo,* which is a symbol, picture, or saying that creates an image of that company. Most companies use stationery with preprinted letterheads.
- Letterheads may appear at the top, sides, or bottom of a page, giving maximum space for the text of the letter.
- Individuals representing themselves, rather than a business firm, write a personal letter.
- In this Rehearsal activity, you will format a full-block personal letter.

Note: To add accent marks to the word "résumé," click Insert, Symbol, select (normal text) in the Font list, select the appropriate symbol, and click Insert.

DIRECTIONS

1. Click the **New Blank Document** button. 
2. Set the margins.
3. Format the letterhead, shown on the facing page, as follows:
   a. Center and set the individual's name to 16-point bold using any desired font color.
   b. Center and set the address information to 12-point italic using any desired font color.
   c. Right-align and set the communication information to 10-point italic using any desired font color.
   d. Insert any desired symbol before and after the individual's name.
4. Press the **Enter** key to advance the insertion point to approximately **2.5".**
5. Left-align and insert the current date.
6. Enter the remainder of the letter.
   a. Insert the AutoText entry **Sincerely** for the closing.
   b. Insert the AutoText entry **enclos** for the enclosure notation.
7. Justify the paragraph text.
8. Correct spelling errors.
9. Preview the document.
10. Prepare an envelope (size 10) with a return address (the name and address on the letterhead) and append the envelope to the letter.
11. Save the file; name it **2.2apply.**
12. Print the letter and envelope.
13. Prepare a full page of floppy diskette labels with the following information:
    `Marie Rose Weston`
    `Personal Correspondence`
    a. Center the text on the label.
    b. Print the label file (use plain paper for this Rehearsal); do not save.
14. Close all files.

★Marie Rose Weston★

230 West End Avenue
New York, NY 10025

PHONE: (212) 555-5555
FAX: (212) 666-6666
E-MAIL: fc@net.com

[Today's date]

Ms. Amelia Sutton, Vice President
Wise Financial Services, Inc.
60 Wall Street
New York, NY 10056

Dear Ms. Sutton:

Please consider me an applicant for the position of financial advisor that was advertised in the Sunday edition of *The Herald.*

As my enclosed résumé shows, I have been working for Sutton Investment Group for the past six years. I am particularly proud of one of my accomplishments. In 1997, I helped underwrite a $300 million offering for a foreign company.

I am confident that my experience will be an asset to your organization. If you would like to meet with me for an interview, I can be reached at the number indicated above.

Sincerely,

Marie Rose Weston

enclosure

Marie Rose Weston
230 West End Avenue
New York, NY 10025

Ms. Amelia Sutton, Vice President
Wise Financial Services, Inc.
60 Wall Street
New York, NY 10056

Cues for Reference

Envelopes and Labels

1. Click **Tools.**
2. Click **Letters and Mailings.**
3. Click **Envelopes and Labels.**
4. Click the desired tab.
5. Make the desired selections.
6. Click **OK.**

TRYOUT

TASK 3

GOAL
To create a memorandum using a template by using the following skill sets:

- Use templates
  - Open existing templates
  - Create your own template

WHAT YOU NEED TO KNOW

Use Templates

Open Existing Templates

- A *template* is a document that contains formatting, pictures, or text, which may be reused to create new documents.
- Word comes with numerous templates that you can use to create a variety of different documents. To access templates, select File, New. In the New Document task pane, click the *On my computer* link to open the Templates dialog box, and click a tab to display the template type you want, as shown in Figure 2.16.
- For each type of template, there are usually several styles from which to choose.

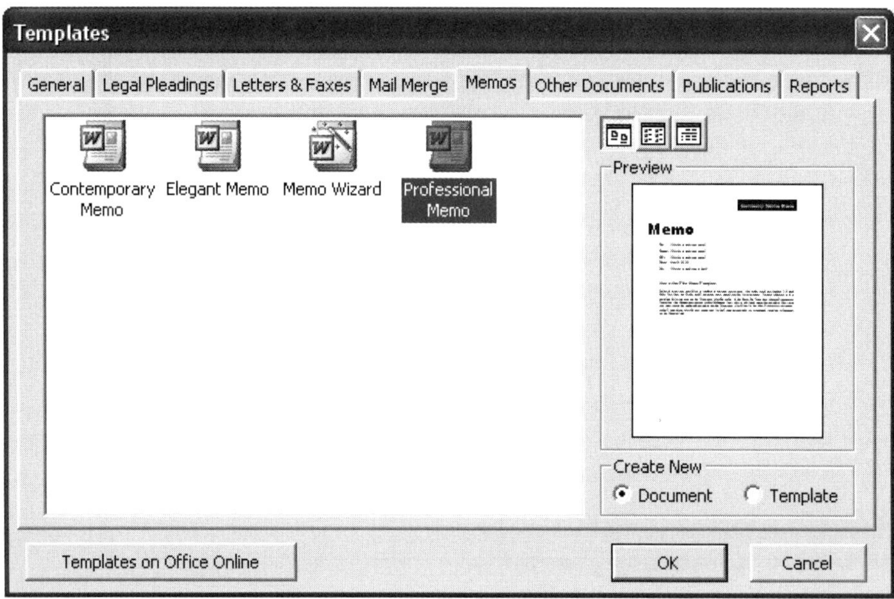

Figure 2.16 Templates dialog box

- Templates contain placeholders, which are boxes that identify the placement and location of text and contain preset text formats, as shown in Figure 2.17. Follow the directions in a placeholder to insert information. To replace sample text, highlight the existing text, then enter the new text. Word automatically inserts the date into date placeholders.

Note: To delete a placeholder, click to select it, then press the Delete key.

Company Name Here

Sample text

Memo

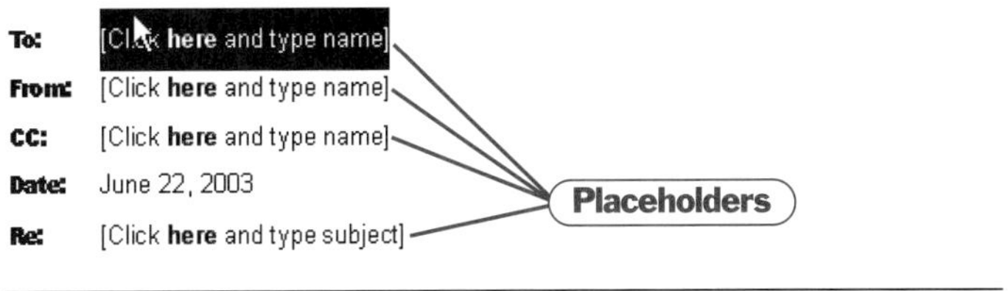

How to Use This Memo Template

Select the text you would like to replace, and type your memo. Use styles such as Heading 1-3 and Body Text from the Styles and Formatting work pane from the Format menu. To save changes to this template for future use, choose Save As from the File menu. In the Save As Type box, choose Document Template. Next time you want to use it, choose New from the File menu, select General Templates from the work pane, and then double-click your template.

Figure 2.17 Professional memo template sample

TRY *it* OUT *w2-9*

1. Click **File, New.**
2. Click **On my computer...** in the New Document task pane.
3. Click the **Letters & Faxes** tab.
4. Click **Contemporary Fax** and view the document format in the preview window.
5. Click **Contemporary Letter** and view the document format in the preview window.
6. Click the **Memos** tab.
7. Click **Professional Memo** to view the document format in the preview window.
8. Click **OK** to open the template or double-click the **Professional Memo** template.
9. Select **Company Name Here,** then enter: `AIS Travel Group`
10. Click in the placeholder to the right of "To:" and enter: `Ira Morre`
11. Click in the placeholder to the right of "From:" and enter your name.
12. Delete the "CC:" line.
13. Click in the placeholder to the right of "Re:" and enter: `Test`
14. Delete the text below the horizontal line, then enter: `This is a test`
15. Close the file; do not save.

Create Your Own Template

- You can create your own template by customizing an existing one or by creating a new one from scratch. For example, you can create your own letterhead and save it as a template. The template would then appear in the General tab of the Templates dialog box so that each time you want to send a letter, you can easily access your saved letterhead template.
- To save a document as a template, click File, Save As. In the Save As dialog box that appears, click the Save as type list arrow and choose Document Template. Enter a file name and click Save.

TRY *it* OUT *w2-10*

1. Click the **New Blank Document** button.
2. Create your own letterhead. Include your name, address, city, state, zip code, phone and fax numbers, and e-mail address. Use any desired font, font style, font colors, and alignments.
3. Click **File, Save As.**
4. Click the **Save as type** list arrow and click **Document Template.** (Notice that the template will automatically be saved in the Templates folder.)
5. In the File name text box, enter `My letterhead` as the name for the new template.
6. Click **Save.**
7. Click **File, Close.**
8. To access your newly created template, click **File, New.**
9. Click the **On my computer** link.
10. Click the **General** tab.
11. Scroll down and open **My letterhead.**

Note: You can now type a letter on your letterhead. When you save the letter, you are prompted to save it under a new file name, thus leaving your letterhead template intact for future use.

12. Close the file; do not save.

1
2
3

REHEARSAL

TASK 3

GOAL
To create a memorandum using a template

SETTING THE STAGE/WRAPUP
Margins: Default
Start line: At 1"
File name: **2.3memo**

WHAT YOU NEED TO KNOW

- A *memorandum,* or memo, is a written communication within a company.
- "Re" in the memo heading means "in reference to" or "subject."
- "CC" in the memo heading refers to "courtesy copy" or "copies." When a copy of the memo (or letter) is sent to other recipients, their names are indicated.

DIRECTIONS

1. Click **File, New.**
2. Use the **Contemporary Memo** template to create the memo, as shown on the facing page.
3. Delete the word "Confidential" at the bottom of the template.
4. Save the file as a Word document; name it **2.3memo.**
5. Print one copy.
6. Close the file.

Memorandum

To: Brenda Duffy

CC: Kevin Levale

From: Latifa Jones

Date: [Today's]

Re: San Francisco travel package

Please organize a San Francisco travel package for Mr. John Alan. As you know, Mr. Alan is president of Trilogy Productions, which uses our company for all its travel needs.

Mr. Alan would like a list of all hotels in the San Francisco area that have a business center, laptop computer rentals, and Internet access in guest rooms. He will need this information by Friday of this week.

CONFIDENTIAL 1

Cues for Reference

Use Templates

1. Click **File.**
2. Click **New.**
3. Click the **On my computer** link in the task pane.
4. Click the tab for desired template type.
5. Click the desired template.
6. Click **OK** or double-click the template.

Save a Document as a Template

1. Click **File.**
2. Click **Save.**
3. In the Save as type text box, click **Document Template.**
4. Click the **Templates** folder if it is not already selected.
5. Enter a file name.
6. Click **Save.**

TRYOUT

TASK 4

GOAL

To practice using the following skill sets:

- Wizards
- Send e-mail
  - Create a new message
  - Send a Word document as e-mail

WHAT YOU NEED TO KNOW

Use Wizards

- Word provides a wizard option within template groups, as shown in Figure 2.18. A *wizard* guides you through the steps for creating the template document.

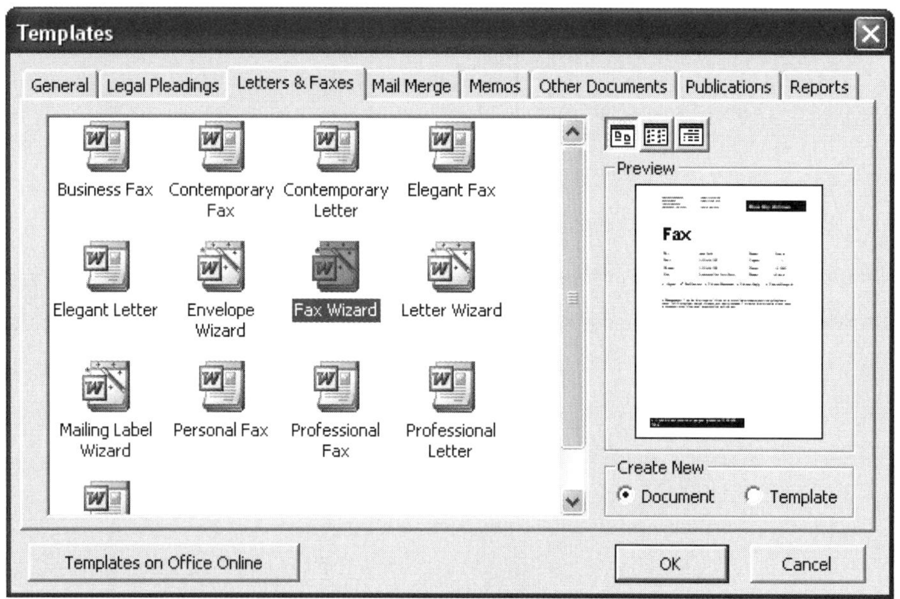

Figure 2.18 Templates dialog box with the Fax Wizard selected

TRY *it* OUT *w2-11*

1. Click **File, New.**
2. Click the **On my computer** link in the New Document task pane.
3. Click the **Letters & Faxes** tab.
4. Click **Fax Wizard.**
5. Click **OK.** The Fax Wizard dialog box opens.
6. Click **Next** twice.
7. Select **I want to print my document so I can send it from a separate fax machine** and click **Next.**
8. Enter `Pamela Watson` in the first Name box.
9. Enter `212-777-7777` in the first Fax Number box and click **Next.**
10. Click **Contemporary** as the style of the template and click **Next.**

Continued on next page

TRY it OUT *w2-11 Continued*

11. Enter the following information on the Who is the fax from? page.
    Name: `Your name`
    Company: `ABC Home, Inc.`
    Mailing Address: `2333 Gin Lane`
    `Boston, MA 02210`
    Phone: `1-800-555-6666`
    Fax: `1-800-555-7777`
12. Click **Next.**
13. Click **Finish.**

The completed fax cover sheet appears. You can enter any missing information at this time by selecting the bracketed text and entering new text.

14. Click **Print.**
15. Close the file; do not save.

Send E-mail

Create a New Message

- *E-mail*, which is an abbreviation for "electronic mail," refers to the transmission of messages over communication networks. You can send a message to a single person via e-mail or to an entire group simultaneously.
- To create a new e-mail message, you must display the e-mail message window. You can do this by:
  - clicking the E-mail message link in the New Document task pane, or
  - clicking the E-mail button on the Standard toolbar. Figure 2.19 illustrates the e-mail message links.

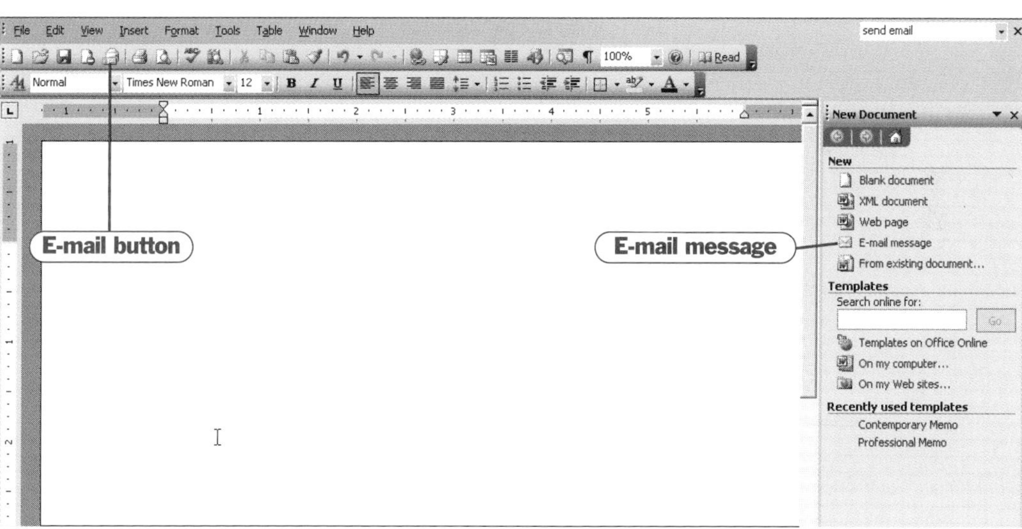

Figure 2.19 E-mail message links

▶ After displaying the e-mail message window, fill in recipient information and the message, as shown in Figure 2.20. Click the Send button to transmit your message.

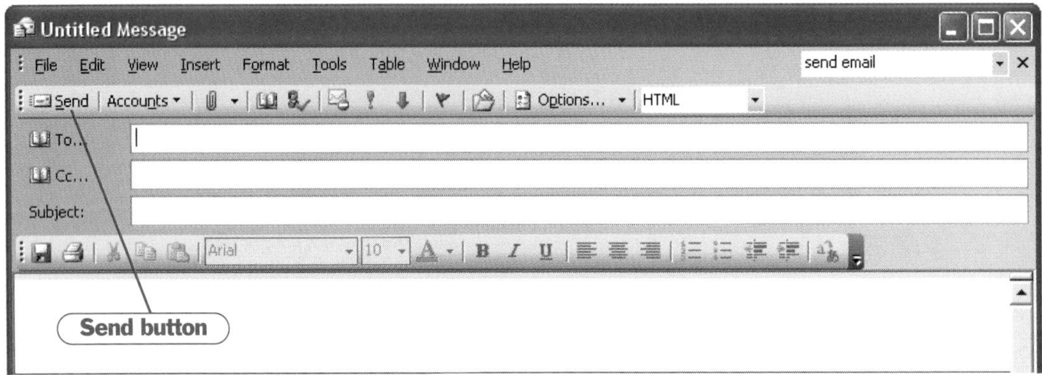

Figure 2.20 E-mail message window

TRY *it* OUT *w2-12*

1. Click **File, New.**
2. Click **E-mail message** in the task pane. Note that the Outlook window appears.
3. Click in the **To** box and enter the fictitious e-mail address: `jbond@bic.net`
4. Click in the **Subject** box and enter: `Test message`
5. Click in the message area and enter: `This is a test.`
6. Click the **Send** button.

Note: For the e-mail to be transmitted, Outlook must be your default e-mail program or must be configured to work with your default e-mail program.

Send a Word Document as E-mail

- You can also send a Word document that is on your screen as e-mail. After completing the document in Word, click the E-mail button on the toolbar, and the e-mail window appears, as shown in Figure 2.21. Notice that the file name automatically appears in the Subject box. You can insert instructions to the recipients in the introduction box.

- Complete the recipient information in the header and click the Send a Copy button. The document remains on screen so you can continue to work on it, while a copy of it is sent via e-mail. To hide the message window, click the E-mail button on the toolbar.

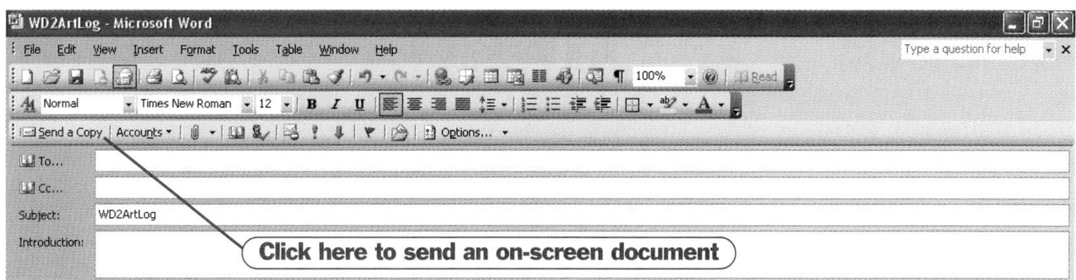

Figure 2.21 E-mail header window

TRY *it* OUT *w2-13*

1. Open **w2.13pf letter** from the Data CD.
2. Click the **E-mail** button on the toolbar. *Note: You may need to click the Toolbar Options button in order to see the Email-button.*
3. Click in the **To** box and enter the e-mail address: `jbond@bic.net`
4. Click in the **Introduction** box and enter: `Have a great conference.`
5. Click the **Send a Copy** button.
6. Close the file; do not save the changes.

GOAL
To create a letter using a wizard

SETTING THE STAGE/WRAPUP
Margins: Default
Start line: At 1"
File name: **2.4followup**

WHAT YOU NEED TO KNOW

- To send an e-mail message, you must have a connection to the Internet and you must know the e-mail address of the person to whom you are sending the message.
- With the Letter Wizard, pressing the Enter key once after a paragraph inserts two blank lines.
- In this Rehearsal activity, you will create a full-block letter as shown using the Letter Wizard. You will then make several editing changes. After the letter is complete, you will send it as an e-mail.

DIRECTIONS

1. Click **File, New.**
2. Click the **On my computer** link in the New Document task pane.
3. Use the Letter Wizard within the Letters and Faxes tab to create the letter shown in the illustration on the facing page. *Note: If you do not see the Letter Wizard in the Templates dialog box, you may need to install it.*

Note: The Letter Wizard uses a 10-point font size for the document text. Change the document font size to 12 point.

4. Respond to the wizard's prompts as necessary to format the letter as shown on the facing page.
5. Send one letter.
6. When the letter is completed, insert two additional blank lines between the date and the inside address.
7. Save the file; name it **2.4followup.**
8. Make the following changes to the document:
   a. Insert the following text as the first two sentences in the first paragraph.
      `It was a pleasure meeting you last week at the Business Financing Conference in Boston. I was very impressed with your new business idea.`
   b. Delete the last sentence in the third paragraph that reads, "The business plan plays a critical role when applying for a business loan."
   c. Insert the following as the last paragraph:
      `Please call my assistant, Pauline Jones, at (444) 555-5555 to schedule an appointment. We look forward to working with you.`
9. Print one copy of the letter.
10. E-mail the letter to: `qrk@net.com`
11. Close the file; save the changes.

[Today's date]

Ms. Wendy Olympus
10 Main Street
Harvard, MA 01451

Dear Ms. Olympus:

SUBJECT: BUSINESS FINANCING CONFERENCE FOLLOW-UP

I would be very interested in meeting with you in Boston to discuss the small-business loan options that the Bank of Boston has to offer. Our staff of small-business advisors is available to consult with you about your venture. Before we meet, however, you should provide us with a detailed business plan.

A business plan is a descriptive report of the business you want to open. It describes the products or services you want to sell and what makes your business unique.

A good business plan also includes a marketing plan, a management plan, a financial plan, and financial projections. The business plan plays a critical role when applying for a business loan.

If you need information about how to construct a business plan, you can go to the Small Business Administration's Web site at www.sba.org.

Sincerely,

[Your name]
Loan Officer

yo
cc: Mr. William Reed

2.4followup unedited

Cues for Reference

Start the Letter Wizard

1. Click **File, New.**
2. Click the **On my computer** link.
   Office XP: Click the **General Templates** link.
3. Click the **Letter and Faxes** tab and select **Letter Wizard.**
   or
   - Click **Tools.**
   - Click **Letters and Mailings.**
   - Click **Letter Wizard.**
4. Click each tab and fill in the appropriate information.
5. Click **OK.**

Send a New E-mail

1. Click **File, New.**
2. In the task pane under New, click the **E-mail message** link.
3. Enter the recipient information.
4. Enter the subject.
5. Enter the message.
6. Click **Send.**

Send a Word Document as E-mail

1. Create or open a Word document.
2. Click the **E-mail** button.

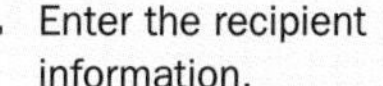

3. Enter the recipient information.

4. Click the **Send a Copy** button.

SETTING THE STAGE/WRAPUP
Act I File name: **2.p1dallas**
Act II File names: **2.p2alslet**
2.p2sanfran
Act III File name: **2.p3osha**

WHAT YOU NEED TO KNOW

In the Performance phase of each lesson, it is assumed that you work or correspond with one of the companies listed on pages xv–xvii of this textbook. A description of the company, its logo, and the company's communication information is indicated there. In subsequent exercises, only the logo will be presented, so if you need to review company information, you will have to refer to the front of this textbook. Your performance in preparing documents and projects typically used in business will apply the skills you developed in previous phases of this lesson.

Act I

You are interested in traveling to Dallas, Texas, in May. Write a personal letter to Ms. Robin Byron of the Air Land Sea Travel Group in New York. Request that they send you the famous *Travel Guide 2005*. Tell them you are particularly interested in visiting the Arts District, Civic Center, and the Farmer's Market and would like any additional information they might have about those areas.

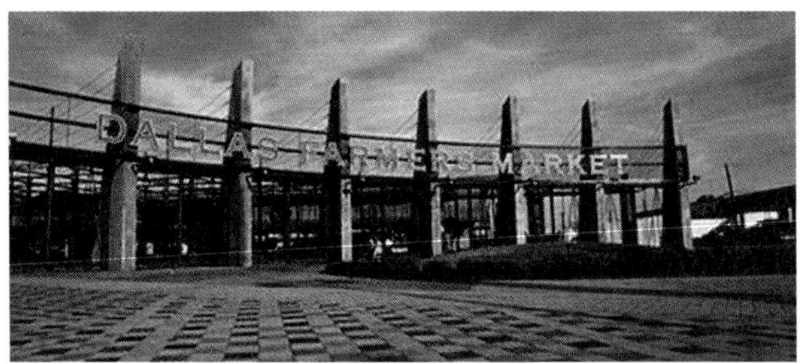

Follow these guidelines:

- Use your own name, address, and phone information for the letterhead.
- Use any desired margins, an appropriate letter style, and an appropriate closing.
- Save the file; name it **2.p1dallas.**
- Prepare an envelope.
- Print one copy of the letter and envelope.

travel group

Act II

You work for Wilson Jones, director of Corporate Travel. He has asked you to prepare a letter to Mr. John Alan, CEO and president of Trilogy Productions (the text of which is provided below). He has also asked you to design a new letterhead template, which you can use for this letter and future correspondence.

Follow these guidelines:

- Use the Professional Letter style to create a new letter template for the Air Land Sea Travel Group. After you have entered the company name and communication information as the letterhead (which you can find at the front of this textbook), save the document as a new template; name it **2.p2alslet.** Then, complete the text of the letter.
- Include an appropriate salutation and closing for the letter.
- Save the letter as **2.p2sanfran.**
- The text of the letter is as follows:

  Latifa Jones has referred your letter to me. You had asked her to provide you with a list of hotels in the San Francisco area that have a business center, laptop rentals, fax services, and teleconferencing capabilities.¶I have compiled a list of hotels that offer the services you requested. They appear below

  Regency Central
Surry Hotel
Fairmont Hotel
Renaissance Center
Marriott Mark
Grand Hyatt

  The Fairmont Hotel and Grand Hyatt are located nearest to where your meetings will take place. Please call our office when you have decided where to stay so we can finalize your bookings to San Francisco.

- Send the document as e-mail to Mr. Alan at Trilogy Productions (but actually send it to your teacher). In your e-mail to Mr. Alan, tell him that this letter outlines the hotel information he requested.

Act III

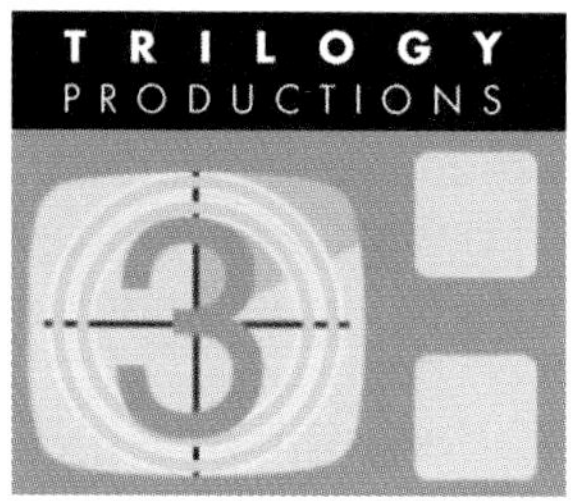

You work for the manager of the Human Resources Department. You have been asked to prepare a memo to all human resources personnel, reminding those working on Welcome Kits for new employees to include information on the *Occupational Safety and Health Act of 1970* on all printed material. You will need to search the Internet and copy and paste the information into your memo. You can find the information at: www.osha.gov/as/opa/worker/employer-responsibility.html.

Follow these guidelines:

- Use any memo template you prefer.
- Include an appropriate subject.
- Save the file; name it **2.p3osha.**
- The memo should read as follows:

  Please be sure that all Welcome Kits indicate that employers have certain responsibilities under the Occupational Safety and Health Act of 1970. Employees must be aware of these. The following list is a summary of the most important employer responsibilities.

  The Welcome Kits should refer employees to OSHA's Web site at http://www.osha.gov for more information about workers' rights and responsibilities.

- Copy from the Web site the bulleted information listed below "Employer responsibilities." Set the bulleted text to 10 point. Format the bulleted information so the font matches the other paragraph text.

Trilogy Productions

Welcome Kit
for
New Employees

A
b
c
1
2
3

LESSON 3

Reports and Long Documents

In this lesson, you will learn to use features found in Word to format and edit reports and long documents. You will complete the following projects:

- A one-page report with indented paragraphs
- A two-page report with headers and footers
- A bibliography
- A cover page for a report
- Five pages of a handbook

Upon completion of this lesson, you should have mastered the following skill sets:

- Insert page breaks
- Set line and paragraph spacing
  - Line spacing
  - Paragraph spacing
- Indent text
- Insert headers, footers, and page numbers
- Use bullets and numbering
- Set vertical centering
- Use borders and shading
- Create a section break
- Use columns
- Apply styles
- Use Research services
  - Dictionary
  - Thesaurus
  - Encyclopedia
  - Translation
  - Web search
- Find and replace text
- Insert a file
- Track Changes in a Document
- Insert, View, and Edit Comments
- Compare and Merge Documents
- Word Count and Document Summary

Terms

Software-related

Page break
Soft page break
Hard page break
Line spacing
Leading
Indent
First-line indent
Hanging indent
Header
Footer
Bullets and Numbering
Borders
Shading
Section break
Columns
Gutter space
Style
Research task pane
Dictionary
Thesaurus
Encyclopedia
Translation
Web search
Insert File
Comments
Track Changes
Compare and Merge Documents
Word Count

Document-related

Report
Manuscript
Internal citations
Title page
Bibliography
Manual
Handbook

GOAL

To practice using the following skill sets:

- Insert page breaks
- Set line and paragraph spacing
  - Line spacing
  - Paragraph spacing
- Indent text

WHAT YOU NEED TO KNOW

Insert Page Breaks

- A *page break* is the location on a page where that page ends and the next page begins. Word automatically inserts a page break when text goes beyond the bottom margin of a page. To end a page manually, press the Ctrl + Enter keys or select Insert, Break, Page Break. When Word enters a page break automatically, it is referred to as a *soft page break.* When you manually enter a page break, it is referred to as a *hard page break.*
- In Normal view, a hard page break appears as a dotted horizontal line across the screen, with the words Page Break in the center, as shown in Figure 3.1. In Print layout view, a hard page break appears as two pages.

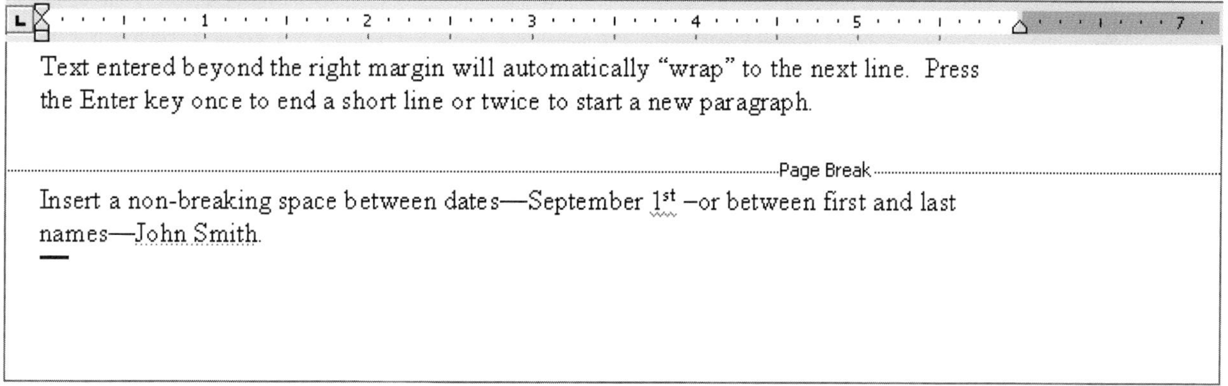

Figure 3.1 Page break in normal view

TRY*it* OUT *w3-1*

1. Open **w3.1pf2** from the Data CD.
2. Click **View, Normal.**
3. Position the insertion point after paragraph 2.
4. Press the **Ctrl + Enter** keys.
5. Scroll down and note the dotted horizontal line that indicates the page break.
6. Click **View, Print Layout.** The text should appear on two separate pages.
7. Close the file; do not save.

Set Line and Paragraph Spacing

Line Spacing

- Use *line spacing* to specify the spacing between lines of text. The default line spacing is set to single.
- Line spacing is measured in "lines" or "points." Line spacing measured in points (a more precise measurement) is referred to as *leading* (pronounced "ledding").
- To change spacing on existing text, position the insertion point in the paragraph, or select the paragraphs to receive the line-spacing change. Then, use one of the following methods to apply line spacing:
  - Click the Line Spacing button on the Formatting toolbar and choose a line-spacing amount, as shown in Figure 3.2.
  - Press the Ctrl + 1 keys for single spacing, the Ctrl + 2 keys for double spacing, or the Ctrl + 5 keys for 1.5 spacing.
  - Select Format, Paragraph. In the Paragraph dialog box that appears, shown in Figure 3.3, select the Indents and Spacing tab and choose a line-spacing option from the Line spacing list box. You can also access the Paragraph dialog box quickly by right-clicking and selecting Paragraph from the shortcut menu.
- To set leading, choose "Exactly" from the Line spacing list box and enter an amount in the At text box. (For 10-point type, 12-point leading is equivalent to single spacing.)
- To set spacing for new text, enter a spacing amount where the new text is to begin.

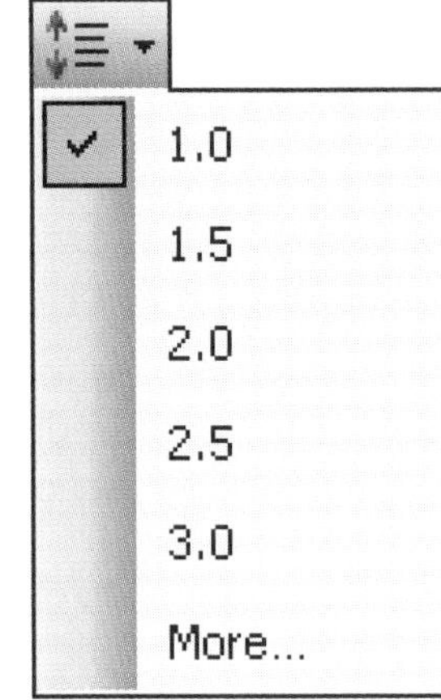

Figure 3.2 Line Spacing button

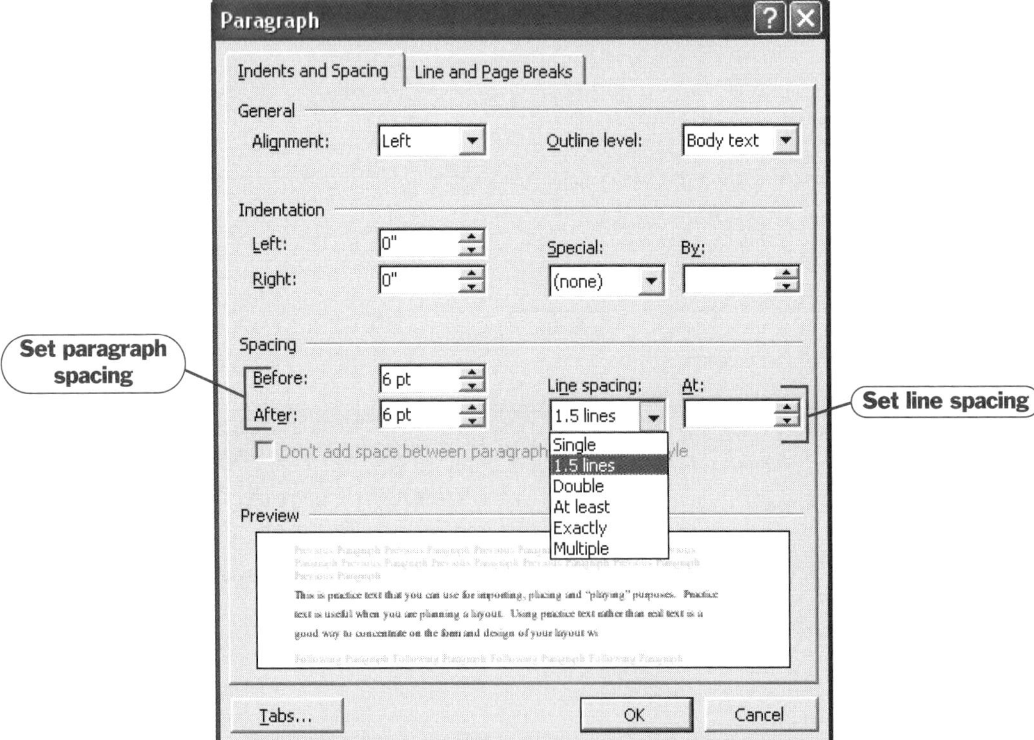

Figure 3.3 Paragraph dialog box

TRY it OUT *w3-2*

1. Open **w3.2pf** from the Data CD.
2. Position the insertion point in the first paragraph.
3. Click the **Line Spacing** button on the Formatting toolbar and select **2.5.**

Note: You may need to click Toolbar Options to display the Line Spacing button.

4. Position the insertion point in the second paragraph.
5. Click **Format, Paragraph.**
6. Click the **Line spacing** list arrow and click **Exactly.**
7. Enter 15 in the **At** text box.
8. Click **OK.**
9. Select the last two paragraphs.
10. Press the **Ctrl + 5** keys.
11. Close the file; do not save.

Paragraph Spacing

- The paragraph spacing feature allows you to set the amount of space before and after each paragraph.
- Paragraph spacing is set in the Paragraph dialog box (see Figure 3.3). Enter a spacing amount in the Before and/or After text box. Paragraph spacing is measured in points (there are 72 points in an inch).

TRY it OUT *w3-3*

1. Open **w3.3pf** from the Data CD.
2. Select all the paragraphs.
3. Click **Format, Paragraph.**
4. Click the **up** increment arrow once in the **Before** box, which will change the spacing amount to **6 pt.**
5. Click **OK.** Note the paragraph spacing change.
6. Close the file; do not save.

Indent Text

▶ The *Indent* feature allows you to set:

- Temporary left and/or right margins for paragraph text as shown in Figure 3.4.

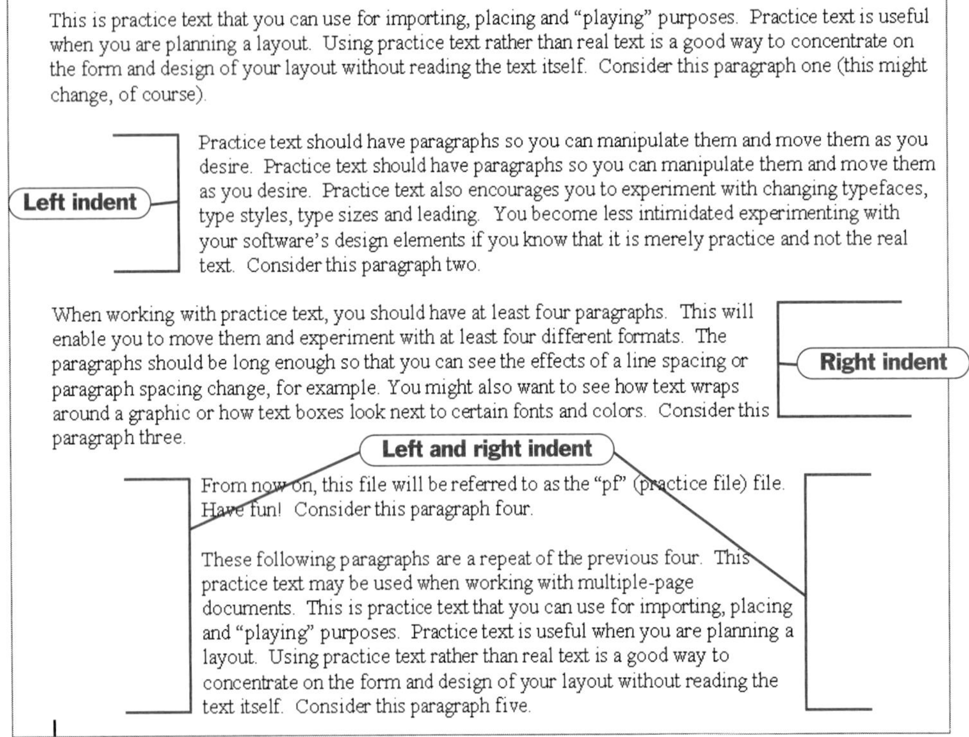

This is practice text that you can use for importing, placing and "playing" purposes. Practice text is useful when you are planning a layout. Using practice text rather than real text is a good way to concentrate on the form and design of your layout without reading the text itself. Consider this paragraph one (this might change, of course).

Practice text should have paragraphs so you can manipulate them and move them as you desire. Practice text should have paragraphs so you can manipulate them and move them as you desire. Practice text also encourages you to experiment with changing typefaces, type styles, type sizes and leading. You become less intimidated experimenting with your software's design elements if you know that it is merely practice and not the real text. Consider this paragraph two.

When working with practice text, you should have at least four paragraphs. This will enable you to move them and experiment with at least four different formats. The paragraphs should be long enough so that you can see the effects of a line spacing or paragraph spacing change, for example. You might also want to see how text wraps around a graphic or how text boxes look next to certain fonts and colors. Consider this paragraph three.

From now on, this file will be referred to as the "pf" (practice file) file. Have fun! Consider this paragraph four.

These following paragraphs are a repeat of the previous four. This practice text may be used when working with multiple-page documents. This is practice text that you can use for importing, placing and "playing" purposes. Practice text is useful when you are planning a layout. Using practice text rather than real text is a good way to concentrate on the form and design of your layout without reading the text itself. Consider this paragraph five.

Figure 3.4 Examples of left, right, and left/right indents

- A *first-line indent* for paragraphs. Once a first-line indent is set, each subsequent paragraph automatically begins at the indented setting.
- A *hanging indent*. A hanging indent is created when all lines in a paragraph are indented except the first line, as shown in Figure 3.5.

This is practice text that you can use for importing, placing and "playing" purposes. Practice text is useful when you are planning a layout. Using practice text rather than real text is a good way to concentrate on the form and design of your layout without reading the text itself.

Consider this paragraph one (this might change, of course). Practice text should have paragraphs so you can manipulate them and move them as you desire. Practice text should have paragraphs so you can manipulate them and move them as you desire.

Figure 3.5 Example of hanging indents

- To indent text, click Format, Paragraph. On the Indents and Spacing tab of the paragraph dialog box, as shown in Figure 3.6, enter the indent amounts in the Left and Right text boxes to set a left and/or right indent. Click the Special list to apply a First-line or Hanging indent, then enter the amount in the By text box.

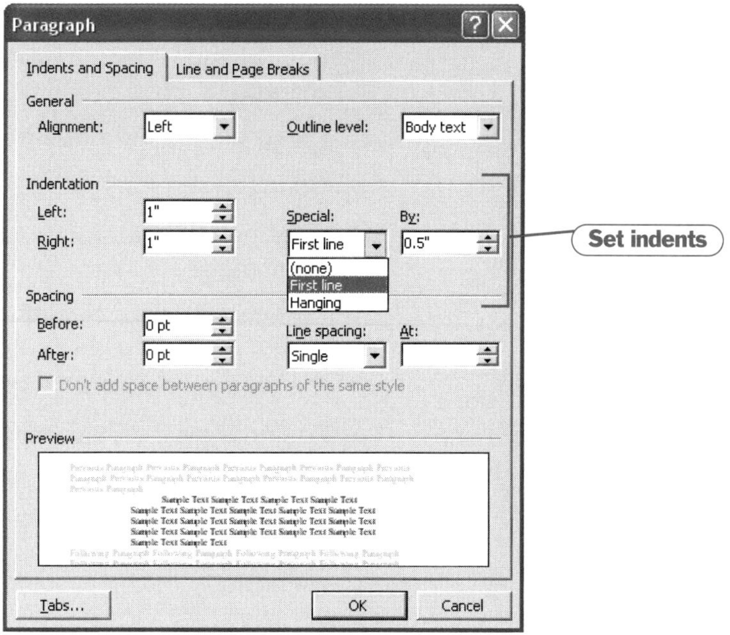

Figure 3.6 Paragraph dialog box with indent settings

- You can also set left and right indents in the following ways:
  - Click the Decrease Indent and/or Increase Indent buttons on the Formatting toolbar. Each click moves the text to the left (or right) 0.5".

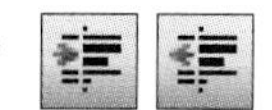

  - Drag the Indent markers on the ruler as shown in Figure 3.7.

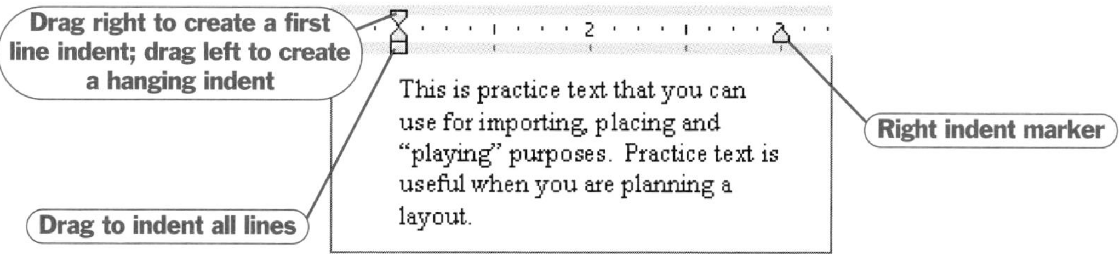

Figure 3.7 Indent markers on the ruler

- To return to your original settings, reset the indentation amounts in the Paragraph dialog box or drag the markers back to their original settings on the ruler.

TRY *it* OUT *w3-4*

1. Click the **New Blank Document** button.
2. Click **Format, Paragraph.**
3. Click the **Special** list arrow and click **First line.**
4. Click the increment arrow in the **By** text box and set value to **1.5".**
5. Click **OK.**
6. Enter these paragraphs:

   `We are happy to announce that we are expanding our services by building a second sports center, allowing us to offer several more fitness classes.¶When we open the second center this summer, we will finally be able to provide the advanced classes that our most loyal clients have requested, such as:`

7. Press the **Enter** key twice.
8. Click **Format, Paragraph.**
9. Enter `1.5` in the Left and Right text boxes.
10. Click **OK.**
11. Enter this paragraph:

    `Yoga Long and Lean combines the benefits of yoga and stretching and blends them together to create a total body/mind workout.`

12. Close the file; do not save.

13. Open **w3.4pf** from the Data CD.
14. Position the insertion point in the first paragraph.
15. Click the **Increase Indent** button twice on the toolbar. (You have just indented the paragraph 1" from the left margin.)

16. Position the insertion point in the second paragraph.
17. Click **Format, Paragraph.** Click the **Special** list arrow, select **Hanging**, and click **OK.**
18. Position the insertion point in the third paragraph.
19. Click **Format, Paragraph.** Enter `1"` in the **Left** and **Right** text boxes below Indentation, and click **OK.**
20. Close the file; do not save.

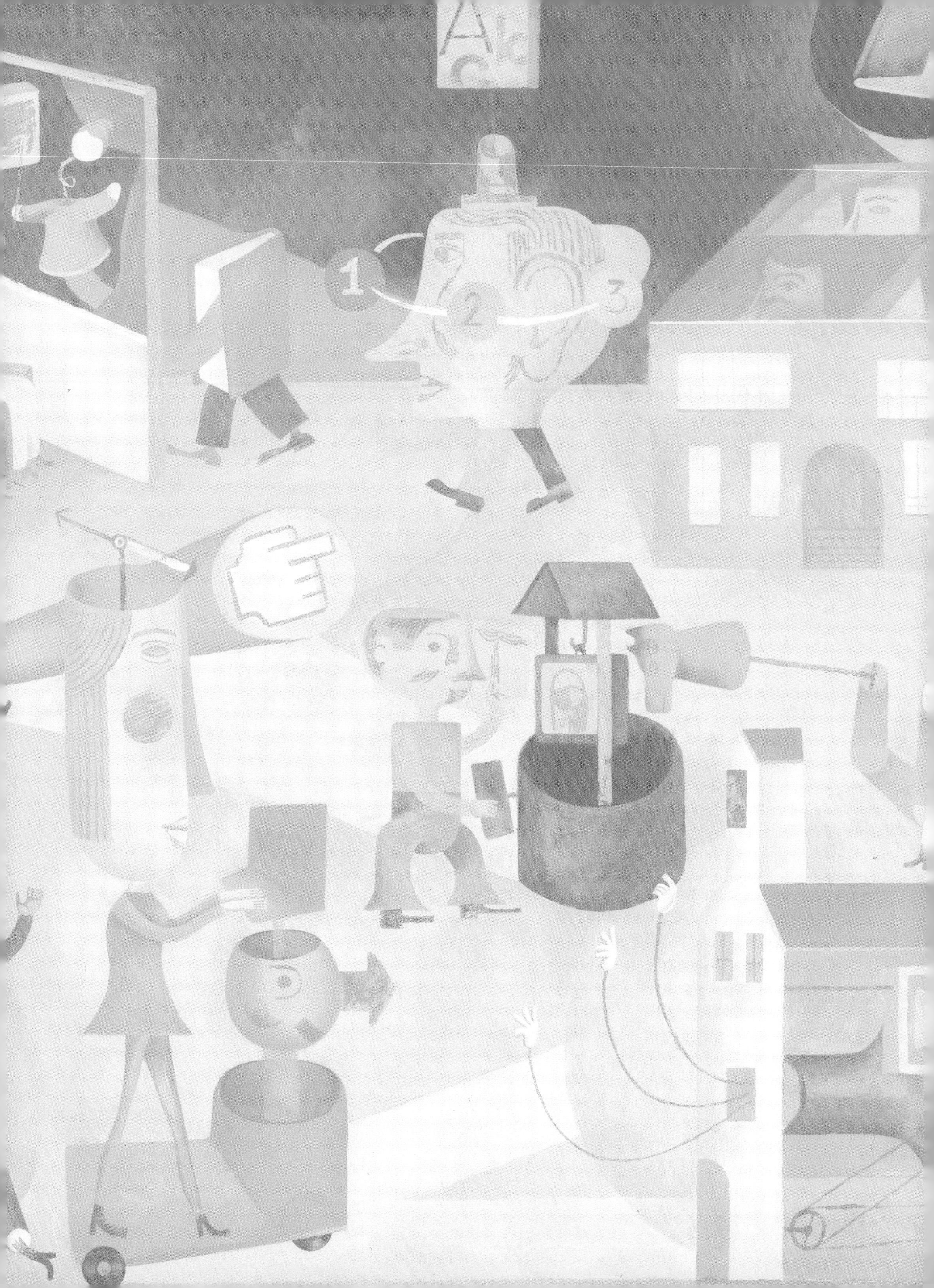
1
2
3

GOAL
To create a one-page report with indented text using the skill sets learned

SETTING THE STAGE/WRAPUP
Margins: Default
Start line: At 2.5"
File name: **3.1car**

WHAT YOU NEED TO KNOW

- A *report* or *manuscript* communicates information about a topic. The topic may be formal or informal. Although most reports require research, others include the writer's opinion or position on the topic.
- The margins for a report depend on how the report is bound. The recommended margin requirements for different bindings are as follows:
    - Unbound—1" or 1.25" left and right, 2" or 2.5" top, 1" bottom
    - Left-bound—1.5" left, 1" right, 2" or 2.5" top, 1" bottom
    - Top-bound—1" left and right, 2" or 2.5" top, 1" bottom
- The start line for the first page is generally 2" or 2.5".
- The title of the report is centered and in all caps.
- A report is generally double-spaced. Each paragraph starts 0.5" or 1" from the left margin.
- In this Rehearsal activity, you will create a one-page report with indented paragraphs.

DIRECTIONS

The illustration on the facing page is shown on one page; however, the final document will span two pages.

1. Click the **New Blank Document** button. Switch to Print Layout view if you are not already in that view mode.
2. Use the default margins.
3. Begin the document at **2"** (from the top edge of the page).
4. Key the report as shown or open **3.1car** from the Data CD. Format the title and the first two paragraphs as follows:
    a. Center the title and set it to a sans serif 14-point bold font.
    b. Insert any desired symbol before and after the title as shown.
    c. Set a **1"** first-line indent and line spacing to **Exactly 20 point.**
5. Format the side headings and paragraphs below the side headings as follows:
    a. Set side headings to a sans serif 10-point bold font. (Use **Format Painter** to copy the formatting from the first side heading to the second side heading.)
    b. Set a **0.5"** left and right indent on the paragraphs shown.
    c. Create a hanging indent and bold the first sentence on the paragraphs shown.
    d. Set paragraph spacing before and after each paragraph to **6 pt.** for the entire document. Note the soft page break; the document now spans two pages.
6. Spell check.
7. Save the file; name it **3.1buycar.**
8. Preview both pages.
9. Print.
10. Close.

❖❖❖ HOW TO PURCHASE A USED CAR ❖❖❖

For many people, the thought of purchasing a car is scary. Buying a car, whether new or used, is a huge investment. With new car prices at an all-time high, many are choosing to purchase used cars, but the unknowns in such a purchase are often intimidating.

The following are important questions to think about and some tips for the beginner who is in the early stages of buying a used car.

ASK YOURSELF THESE QUESTIONS

What is the condition of the car I currently own? Why do I want to replace it? If I do not presently own a car, what are my primary reasons for wanting to purchase one?

Do I want to buy a used car from a dealership or would I prefer to go through a private owner? What are the advantages and disadvantages of both?

How will I finance my purchase? How will my current transportation costs compare with owning my own vehicle?

What kind of car am I looking for? What functions does the car need to serve (i.e., daily transportation vs. weekend trips or both)?

0.5" left indent

0.5" right indent

THE FIRST FEW STEPS

Research, research, research. The most successful purchaser of a used car is one who is empowered with knowledge. Read consumer guides and books. Find the resources available to you online. Learn to speak "car talk." Look through the newspaper to get a sense of the used car market and to understand what car sellers are advertising.

Enlist the help and support of a friend or family member who knows about cars and is familiar with the process of purchasing a used car. Experience can be the best teacher.

Formulate a realistic budget so that you can arrive at a definite price range from which you will not waver when shopping and negotiating. Set up a meeting with a financial manager if necessary.

Dream a little. With knowledge, hard work, and a definite purpose, finding the used car of your dreams at the right price is possible.

Hanging indent

Cues for Reference

Line Spacing

1. Place insertion point where new line spacing is to begin or select paragraphs to receive line-spacing change.
2. Click **Format, Paragraph.**
3. Click the **Indents and Spacing** tab.
4. Click the **Line Spacing** list arrow.
5. Click the option you want.
   Or use a shortcut method:
   Press **Ctrl + 2** = double spacing;
   press **Ctrl + 1** = single spacing;
   press **Ctrl + 5** = 1.5 spacing.

Paragraph Spacing

1. Place the insertion point in paragraph or select paragraphs to format.
2. Click **Format, Paragraph.**
3. Click the **Indents and Spacing** tab.
4. Click **Before** and/or **After** text box.
5. Enter a spacing amount and click **OK.**

Indent Text

1. Click **Format, Paragraph.**
2. Click **Indents and Spacing** tab.
3. Make your selections and/or enter amount of the indent.
4. Click **OK.**

Hanging Indents

1. Place the insertion point in affected paragraph or select desired paragraphs.
2. Drag hanging indent marker on ruler to appropriate position, or press **Ctrl + T.**

or

1. Click **Format, Paragraph.**
2. Click the **Indents and Spacing** tab.
3. Click the **Special** list arrow and select **Hanging.**
4. Click increment arrow in the **By** text box to enter hanging indent amount.
5. Click **OK.**

GOAL

To practice using the following skill sets:

- Insert headers, footers, and page numbers
- Bullets and numbering
- Set vertical centering
- Borders and shading
- Word count

WHAT YOU NEED TO KNOW

Insert Headers and Footers and Page Numbers

- A *header* is the same text appearing at the top of every page or specified pages; a *footer* is the same text appearing at the bottom of every page or specified pages. A header or footer might include the name of the document, the page number, the current date or time, or any other text, graphic, or symbol.
- To view headers and footers (and page numbers) on screen, you must be in Print layout view. Headers and footers will not display in Normal or Outline views, but they will print.
- To insert a header or footer, click View, Header and Footer from the menu. A header box and the Header and Footer toolbar, as shown in Figure 3.8, appears on the screen.

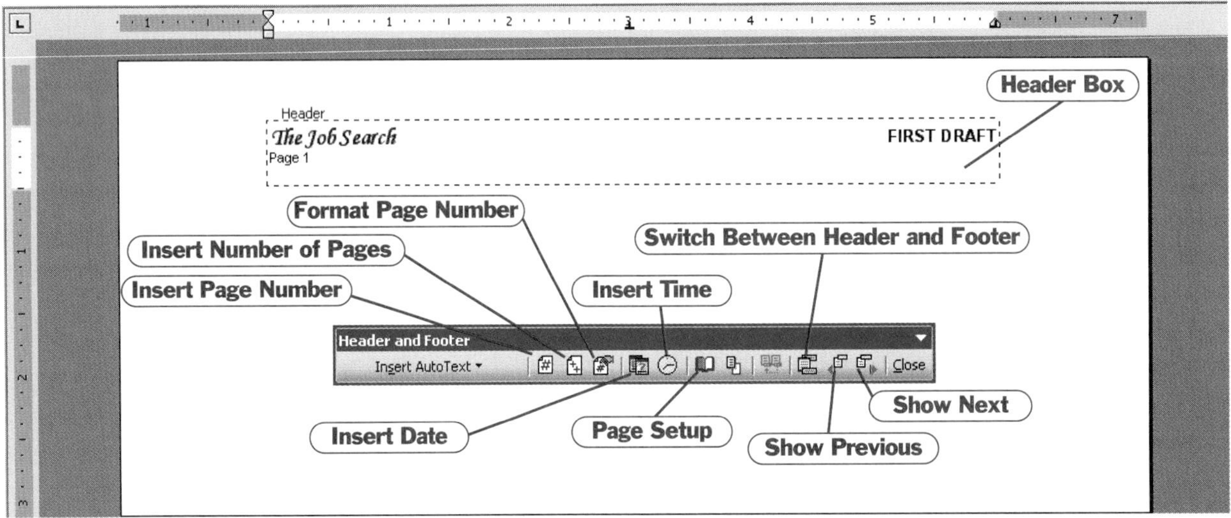

Figure 3.8 Header box and Header and Footer toolbar

- Insert the header text you want in the header box. To include a page number, date, and/or time as part of the header text, click the appropriate button on the Header and Footer toolbar. (To insert page numbers independent of headers and footers, see page 95.)
- As you enter header lines, the header box extends to accommodate the text.
- You can format header and footer text in the same way as any other text.
- To create a footer, click the Switch Between Header and Footer button on the Header and Footer toolbar and enter the footer text you want in the footer box.

TRY*it*OUT *w3-5*

1. Open **w3.5pf2** from the Data CD.
2. Be sure you are in Print layout view (**View, Print Layout**).
3. Select all the paragraphs and set the line spacing to **double.**
4. Click **View, Header and Footer.**
5. Enter `Practice Text` in the header box and press the **Enter** key once.
6. Enter: `Page` and press the **spacebar** once.
7. Click the **Insert Page Number** button, then press the **Enter** key.
8. Click the **Insert Date** button.

9. Click the **Switch Between Header and Footer** button.

10. Enter your name.

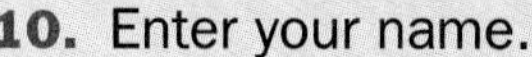

11. Click the **Page Setup** button.

12. On the layout tab, click the **Different first page** check box.

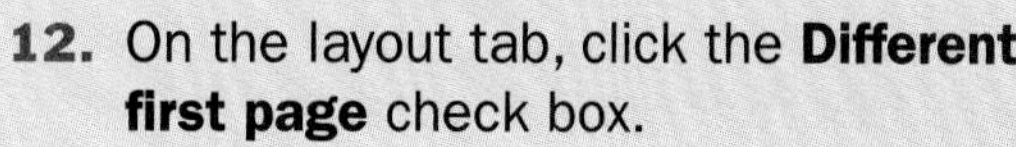

13. Click **OK.**
14. Click the **Close** button on the Header and Footer toolbar.
15. Print one copy.
16. Close the file; do not save.

Note: Headers, footers, and page numbers usually appear on the second and subsequent pages of a document; they generally do not appear on the first page. To suppress the header, footer, or page number on the first page, click the Page Setup button on the Header and Footer toolbar. In the Page Setup dialog box that appears, as shown in Figure 3.9, click the Layout tab, and click the Different first page check box.

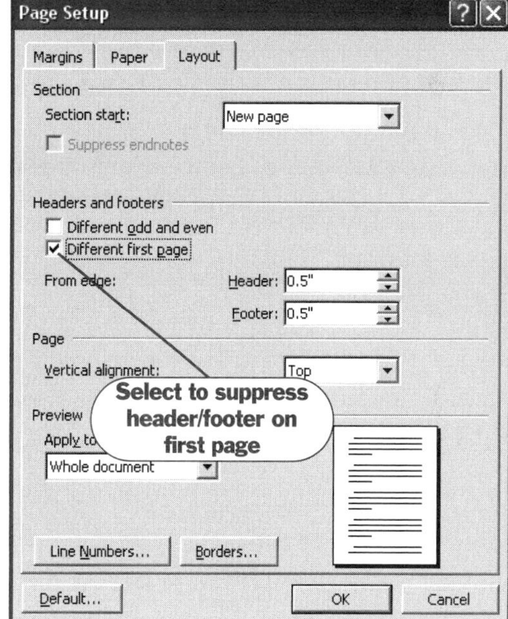

Figure 3.9 Layout tab on Page Setup dialog box

Insert Page Numbers (Independent of Headers and Footers)

▶ You can insert page numbers without using the Header and Footer feature. To do so, click Insert, Page Numbers from the menu. In the Page Numbers dialog box that displays, shown in Figure 3.10, enter the position of the page number and the alignment in the text boxes provided. To suppress the number on the first page, deselect the appropriate check box. Click the Format button if you wish to change the number format or to start numbering from a number other than one.

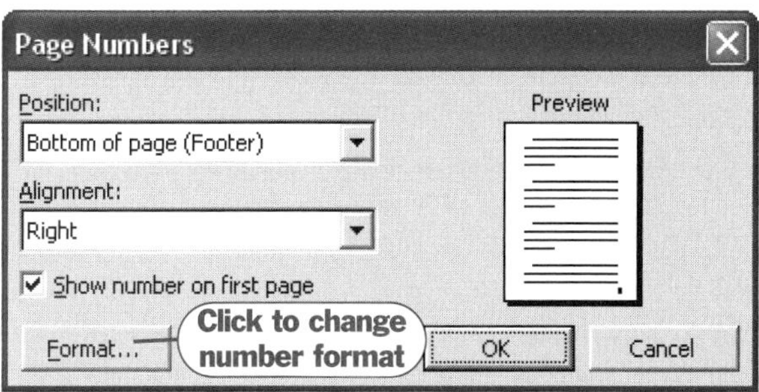

Figure 3.10 Page Numbers dialog box

TRY it OUT *w3-6*

1. Open **w3.6pf2** from the Data CD.
2. Be sure you are in Print layout view (**View, Print Layout**).
3. Set line spacing to **double** for the entire document.
4. Click **Insert, Page Numbers.**
5. Click the **Position** list arrow and select **Top of page (Header).**
6. Click the **Alignment** list arrow and select **Right.**
7. Click the **Format** button.
8. Click the **Number format** list arrow, select **I, II, III,** then click **OK.**
9. Click **OK.**
10. Scroll down and notice that Roman numeral II appears on the top of the second page.
11. Close the file; do not save.

Bullets and Numbering

- A bullet is a dot or symbol you use to highlight points of information or to itemize a list. Figure 3.11 shows how bullets and numbers can be used in a document.

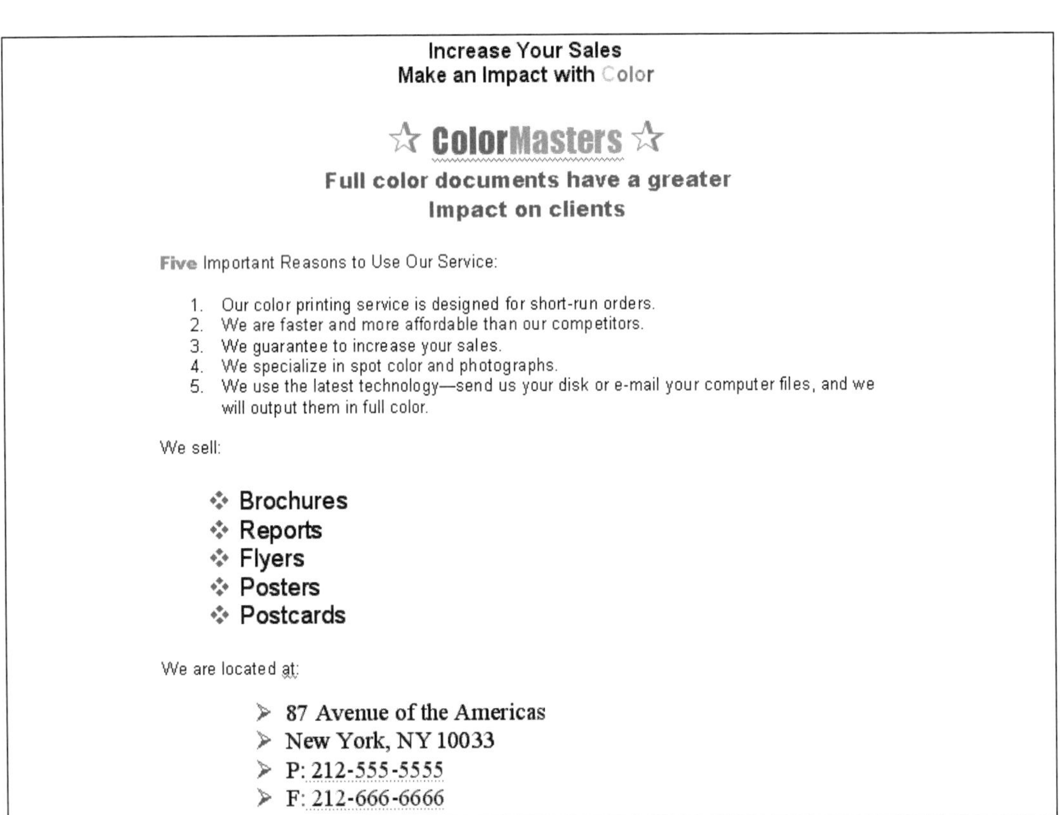
Increase Your Sales
Make an Impact with Color

☆ ColorMasters ☆

Full color documents have a greater
Impact on clients

Five Important Reasons to Use Our Service:

1. Our color printing service is designed for short-run orders.
2. We are faster and more affordable than our competitors.
3. We guarantee to increase your sales.
4. We specialize in spot color and photographs.
5. We use the latest technology—send us your disk or e-mail your computer files, and we will output them in full color.

We sell:

- Brochures
- Reports
- Flyers
- Posters
- Postcards

We are located at:

- 87 Avenue of the Americas
- New York, NY 10033
- P: 212-555-5555
- F: 212-666-6666

Figure 3.11 Bullets and numbering used in a document

- The *Bullets and Numbering* feature allows you to insert bullets and/or numbers automatically to create bulleted or numbered paragraphs.

- To bullet or number a paragraph, click the Bullets or the Numbering button on the Formatting toolbar and enter the text. Each time you press the Enter key, a new bullet or number appears automatically; numbers increase sequentially.
- To change the bullet symbol or numbering style, click Format, Bullets and Numbering, click the Bulleted or the Numbered tab on the Bullets and Numbering dialog box, and choose a style, as shown in Figure 3.12.
- To end bullets or numbering, click the Bullets or the Numbering button on the toolbar to deactivate the feature.
- To remove a single bullet or number, click between the number or bullet and the text that follows, then press the Backspace key.

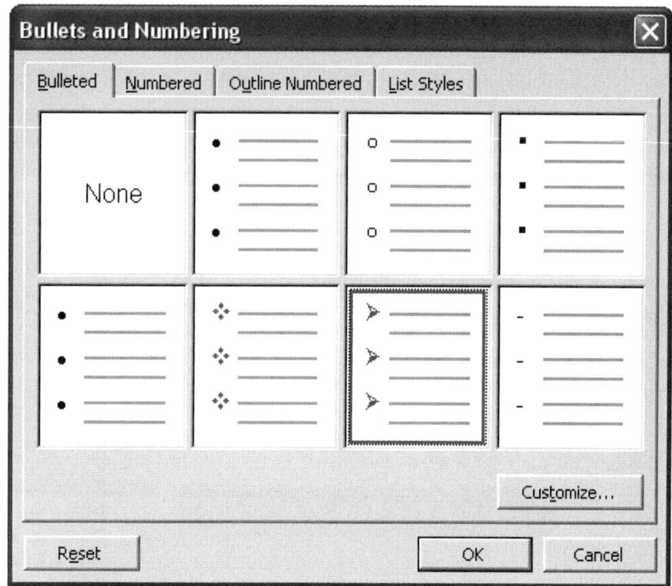

Figure 3.12 Bullets and Numbering dialog box

TRY *it* OUT *w3-7*

1. Click the **New Blank Document** button.
2. Click the **Bullets** button.
3. Enter the following words, pressing the **Enter** key after each word:

   `Red Green Purple`
4. Click the **Numbering** button
5. Enter the following words, pressing the **Enter** key after each word:

   `One Two Three`
6. Click **Format, Bullets and Numbering.**
7. Click the **Bulleted** tab.
8. Choose a different bullet style.
9. Click **OK.**
10. Enter the following words, pressing the **Enter** key after each word.

    `Monday Tuesday Wednesday`
11. Close the file; do not save.

Set Vertical Centering

▶ You can center text vertically between the top and bottom margins or between the top and bottom edges of the page. Figure 3.13 shows a report title that has been vertically centered on the page.

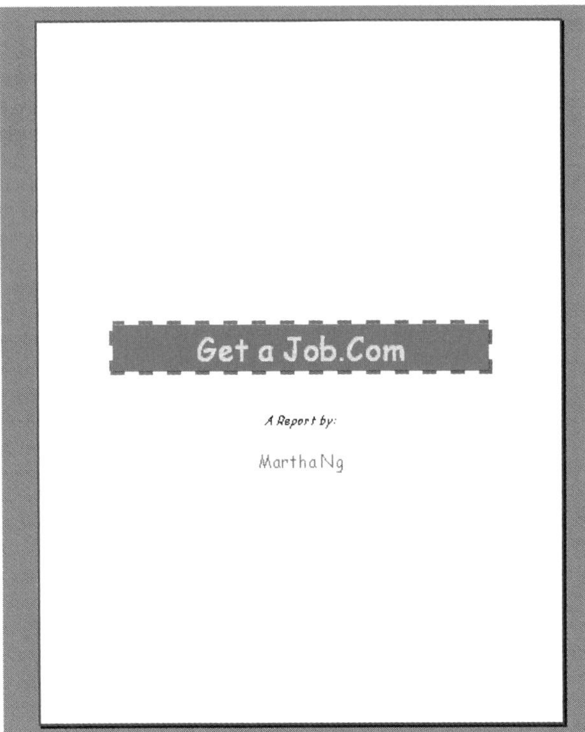

Figure 3.13 Text centered vertically on a page

▶ To center text vertically, click File, Page Setup. In the Page Setup dialog box that appears, shown in Figure 3.14, click the Layout tab, click the Vertical alignment list arrow, and click Center.

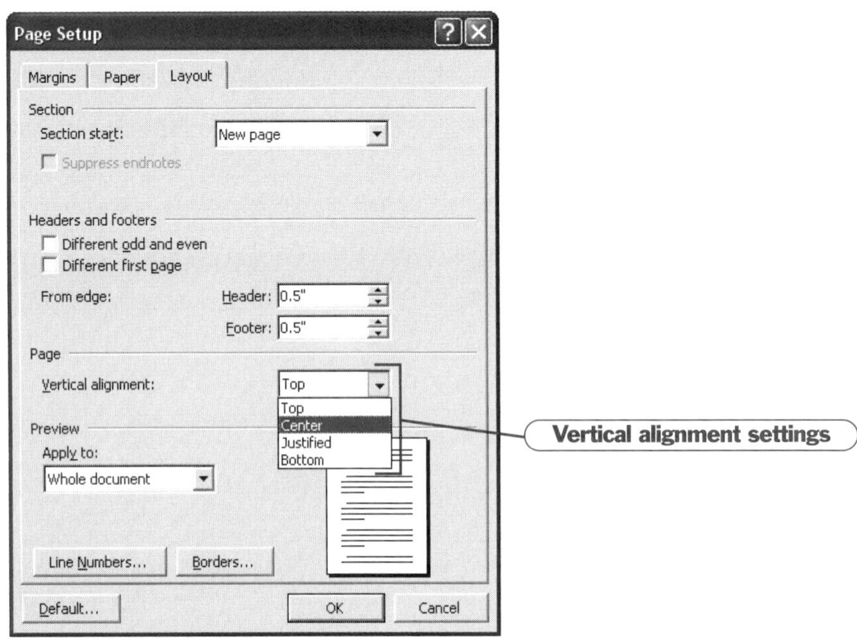

Figure 3.14 Page Setup dialog box

▶ To see how vertically centered text is positioned on the page, click the Print Preview button. 

TRY *it* OUT *w3-8*

1. Open **w3.8pf** from the Data CD.
2. Click **File, Page Setup.**
3. Click the **Layout** tab.
4. Click the **Vertical alignment** list arrow.
5. Click **Center.**
6. Click **OK.**
7. Click the **Print Preview** button. 
8.  Close the preview window.
9.  Close the file; do not save.

Borders and Shading

▶ *Borders* are lines or other graphical elements that appear around a paragraph, text, or a page to add emphasis. You can place single, double, thick, or dotted lines around one or more sides of a paragraph or selected text. You can also apply a border design around a page.

▶ *Shading* is a tint, color, or pattern that you can apply to a paragraph or text block. Figure 3.15 shows border and shading examples.

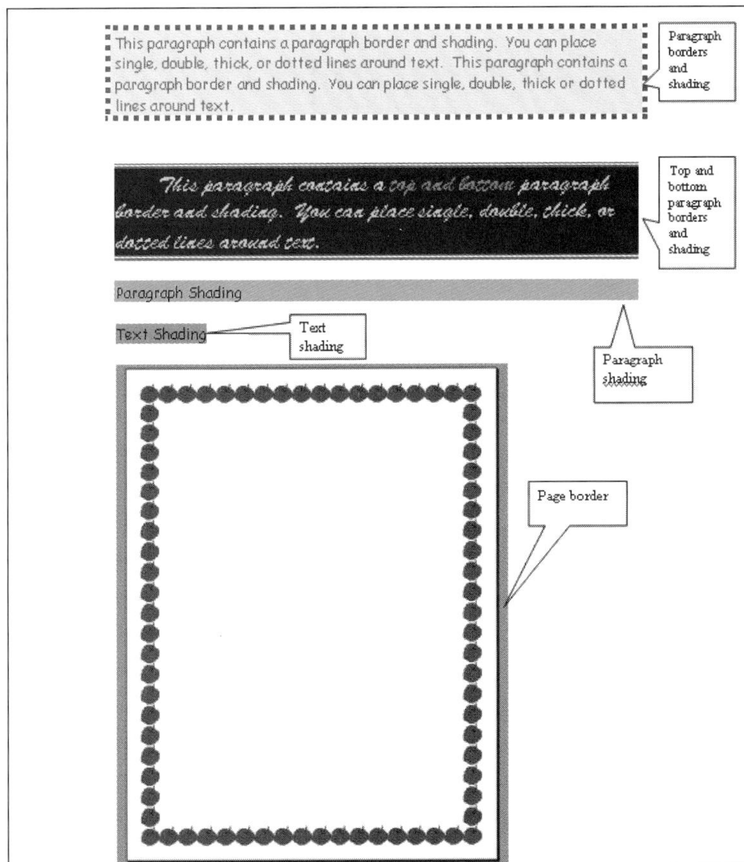

Figure 3.15 Border and shading examples

- To apply a border around a paragraph or selected text, select the paragraph or text then click Format, Borders and Shading. In the Borders and Shading dialog box that appears as shown in Figure 3.16, click the Borders tab, choose a line style from the Style list box, a line color from the Color list box, and a line width from the Width list box.
- To apply a border to one or more sides of a paragraph, click the Custom button in the Setting area and click the top, bottom, left, and/or right button in the Preview area to choose the sides on which to apply the line. Click the Apply to list arrow to indicate whether you are applying the selection(s) to a Paragraph or to Text.

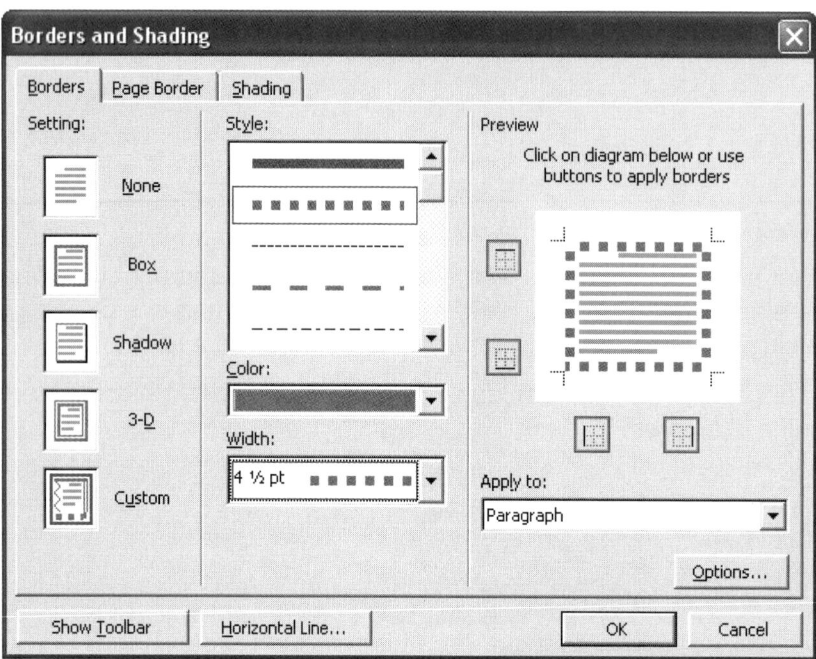

Figure 3.16 Borders tab on Borders and Shading dialog box

- To apply a border to an entire page, select the Page Border tab in the Borders and Shading dialog box, shown in Figure 3.17. Choose a line style from the Style list box, a line color from the Color list box, and a line width from the Width list box. Or, click the Art list arrow and select a page border design.

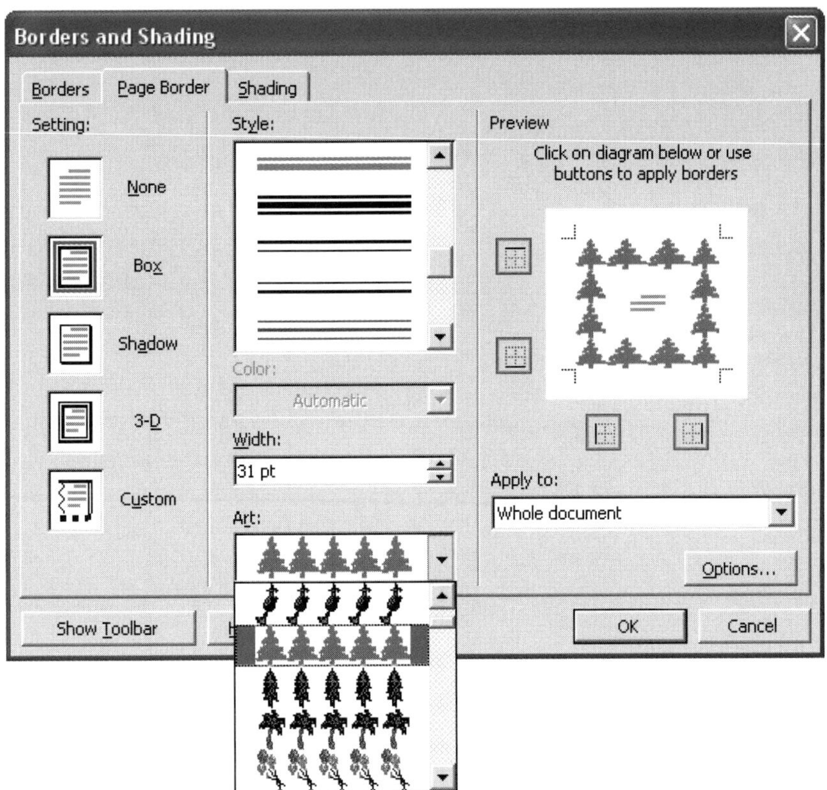

Figure 3.17 Page Border tab on Borders and Shading dialog box

▶ To apply paragraph shading, select the paragraph and click Format, Borders and Shading. Click the Shading tab, shown in Figure 3.18, and choose a color from the Fill palette and/or a style from the Patterns Style list box. Clicking the More Colors button displays the Colors dialog box, which provides additional colors, as shown in Figure 3.19.

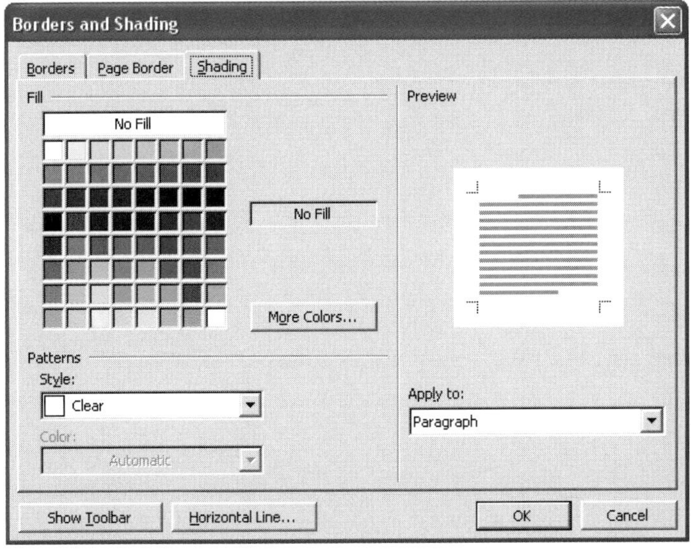

Figure 3.18 Shading tab on Borders and Shading dialog box

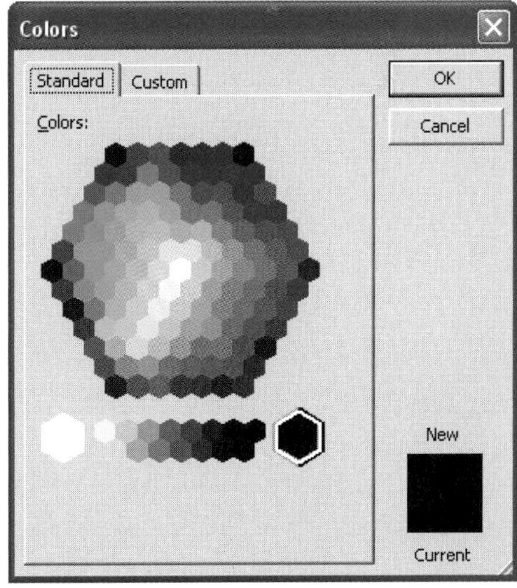

Figure 3.19 Colors dialog box

TRY *it* OUT *w3-9*

1. Open **w3.9pf** from the Data CD.
2. Select the first paragraph.
3. Click **Format, Borders and Shading.**
4. Click the **Borders** tab.
5. Select a dotted line from the Style list box.

Note: Be sure Paragraph is selected in the Apply to list box.

6. Click the **Color** list arrow, then click **Red.**
7. Click the **Width** list arrow, then click **2¼ pt.**
8. Click the **Shading** tab.
9. Click a **Light Yellow** fill.
10. Click the **Page Border** tab.
11. Click the **Art** list arrow and choose any page border. If this feature is not installed, choose a double line style page border.
12. Click **OK.**
13. Click the **Print Preview** button.
14. Close the file; do not save.

1
2
3

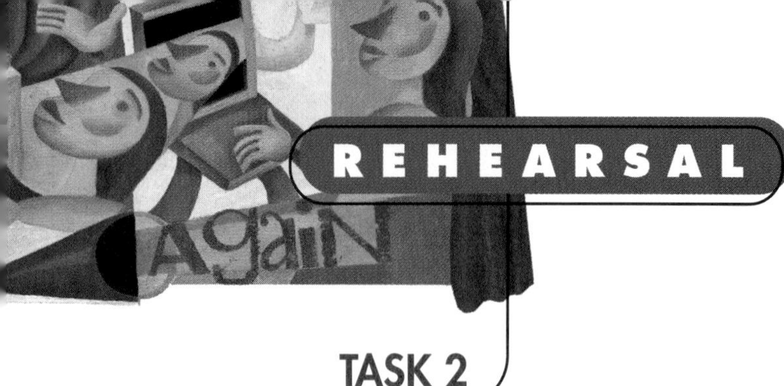

TASK 2

GOAL

To create a two-page report, bibliography, and cover page using the skill sets learned

SETTING THE STAGE/WRAPUP

Margins: Default
Start line: At 2.5" (3.2jobsearch)
At 1" (3.2jobsearch cover)
At 1" (3.2jobsearch biblio)
File names: **3.2jobsearch**
3.2jobsearch cover
3.2jobsearch biblio

WHAT YOU NEED TO KNOW

- Research reports usually contain quoted material from another source (a book, newspaper, magazine, encyclopedia, the Web, etc.). It is necessary to cite someone else's ideas, words, statistics, artwork, or lab results. Failing to do so constitutes plagiarism.
- Citations generally appear at the bottom of a page as footnotes or at the end of the report as endnotes. They may also appear as *internal citations,* that is, references that immediately follow the quoted or paraphrased material. In the internal citation, just the author's name and year of publication is listed. When using the internal citation for Web references, however, the author's last name, the Web site, and the date of Web posting (if available) are indicated.
- When quoted material is more than two lines, it is indented 0.5" or 1" from the left and right margins and single-spaced, and the quotation marks are omitted.
- A report should include a cover or title page and a bibliography. It may also include a table of contents.

DIRECTIONS

Report

1. Click the **New Blank Document** button.
2. Set the line spacing to **double.**
3. Advance the insertion point to approximately 2.5", then center and set the title GET AN EXCITING JOB.COM in **14-point bold.**
4. Set a 1" first-line indent.
5. Create a right-aligned header in **14-point** script that reads: `Searching for a Job`
6. Create a left-aligned footer that reads DRAFT and include a right-aligned page number.
7. Key the report as shown on pages 96-97.
   a. Single-space and indent the quoted material 0.5" from the left and right margins.
   b. Single-space the numbered list (shown on page 2).

Note: The completed report will be three pages if you begin the document 2.5" from the top of the page.

8. Correct any spelling errors.
9. Edit the header to read: `Get a Job.com.` Change the font to Arial italic.
10. Suppress the header and footer on the first page.
11. Save the file; name it **3.2jobsearch.**
12. Preview, print, and then close the file.

Continued on next page

- A *title page* typically contains the report title, the writer's name, and the date the report was submitted. It may also contain the school name, class, company name, or division.
- A *bibliography,* or references page, identifies sources used, quoted, or paraphrased within a document. The sources are generally listed in alphabetical order.
- Each bibliographical entry contains the author's last name and first name, the name of the article and the publication, the publisher, and the date of publication. If you used internal citations in the report, the bibliographical reference should include the exact page number of the quoted material.
- Generally, a bibliography is formatted with hanging indents.
- In this Rehearsal activity, you will create a two-page report with headers and footers, quoted material, and internal citations. You will also create a title page and bibliography for this report.

Title Page

1. Click the **New Blank Document** button. 
2. Create the title page as shown on the page 98.

Note: You may apply any spacing among the text blocks of the title page. The illustration is a guide.

   a. Center and set the title to 36-point bold; use any font or font color you want.
   b. Apply paragraph shading around the title and subtitles using any color(s) you want.
   c. Apply a dotted paragraph border around the last two subtitles using any color(s) you want.

3. Center the text vertically on the page.
4. Create a page border; use any desired border style.
5. Save the file; name it **3.2jobsearch cover.**
6. Preview, print, and then close the file.

Bibliography

1. Open **3.2jobsearch.**
2. Create a hard page break below the last paragraph of the document.
3. Create the bibliography as shown on page 99.
   a. Center and set the title to 16-point bold using the same font used on the title page.
   b. Create the same paragraph shading around the title that was used on the title page.
   c. Set the paragraph spacing after each entry to 10 points.
   d. Set the font for the bibliographical entries to 12-point Comic Sans MS.
   e. Set **0.5"** hanging indents for each paragraph.
4. Correct spelling errors.
5. Save the file; name it **3.2jobsearch biblio.**
6. Preview, print one copy of the page, and then close.

GET AN EXCITING JOB.COM

Finding a job is not an easy task. For some people, the process can seem overwhelming and, oftentimes, the rewards are few and far between. There are, however, several recommended methods that the job seeker should use in order to find his or her dream job in a relatively short amount of time. These techniques have been proven successful and can help the person seeking a job to focus on the task at hand.

It is important to begin a job search with a self-assessment. There are several books and tests available at the library, in career placement offices, at bookstores, and online that can help an individual begin to form a list of the kinds of jobs that she or he is seeking based on personal and professional goals. The job seeker should also begin by talking to a wide variety of individuals in several different fields to learn more about what types of jobs are available and at what level and salary range. This will help the seeker narrow her or his focus so that the search is more effective.

Some common methods of finding employment, such as using newspaper advertisements and employment agencies, are not as effective as was once thought. These resources can lead to jobs, but it is not smart to bet on them. Instead, employment experts explain that these resources should be seen as valuable research tools. John Noble, author of *The Elements of Job Hunting*, explains that "classified ads can provide names that will add measurably to your contact pool." (Nobel, 1999)

Forming this "contact pool" can be the most important step in finding employment. Who has not heard the saying "It's not what you know; it's whom you know?" Friends and family should be considered contacts. "It takes about seventy eyes and ears to find a job; if you tell everyone you know or meet that you are job hunting, and that you would appreciate their keeping their eyes and ears open and letting you know if they hear of anything, you acquire those seventy eyes and ears. (Allen, April 2000)

Searching for a Job

The traditional ways of finding a job—either through newspaper ads or employment agencies—have been replaced by the Internet. The Internet allows job seekers to find careers in their desired city and salary bracket faster than ever before, and it enables employers to fill their ranks by searching the Net for potential employees.

On most online job sites, you can both search and be sought out. You can search by entering the job title you are looking for. To be recruited, you can:

- fill out an online form, which asks you to provide details about yourself, or
- attach a copy of your resume.

> "Online job listings have a number of advantages, for both employers and employees, over traditional classified ads: The postings are free; and jobs can be pinpointed with greater specificity." (Lamorte, November 7, 2000)

There's another huge advantage of using online job hunting over classified ads. Most classified ads do not allow job seekers to know which company is doing the advertising or whether their resume has been read. Job sites such as Hotjobs com and Monster.com can let you know how many of their employers have looked at your resume.

There is a drawback to online job seeking. Remember, posting your resume to the Internet allows the world to see it—even your current boss. Also, your "private" information is no longer private. Here are four popular sites you might explore:

1. Careerbuilder.com
2. Monster.com
3. Headhunter.net
4. JobOptions.com

We know you will enjoy them!

DRAFT

GET AN EXCITING JOB.COM

"Your Newest Recruit May Be Just a Click Away"

A Report by:

Martha Ng

Presented to

Human Resources Personnel

Sutton Investment Group

Annual Conference

June 2005

BIBLIOGRAPHY

Allen, Joseph P. "Getting and Keeping a Job," *Entrepreneur*, April 2000, p.6.

Colson, David. "Effective Job Sites," www.zdimag.com, January 10, 2001.

Lamorte, Vicky G. "Classifieds on the Web," *PC Magazine,* November 7, 2000, p. 127.

Nobel, John. *The Elements of Job Hunting.* Boston: Houghton-Mifflin Company, 1999, p. 45.

Udall, Natasha C., and Hudson, Giles. "Smart E-employment," *Netpreneur,* September 15, 2001, p. 63.

Cues for Reference

Headers and Footers

1. Click **View, Header and Footer.**
2. Click the **Switch Between Header and Footer** button to view header or footer.
3. Enter and format header or footer text as you prefer:
   - Click **Insert Page Number** button to add a page number.
   - Click **Insert Date** button to add the date.
   - Click **Insert Time** button to add the time.
4. Click **OK.**

Suppress Header/Footer on First Page

5. Click **Page Setup** button. 
6. Click **Different first page.**
7. Click **OK.**
8. Click the **Close** button.

Insert Page Numbers (Independent of Headers and Footers)

1. Click **Insert.**
2. Click **Page Numbers.**
3. Select position and alignment of number.
4. Click **OK.**

Vertical Centering

1. Click **File, Page Setup.**
2. Click the **Layout** tab.
3. Click the **Vertical alignment** list arrow, then click **Center.**
4. Click **OK.**

Borders and Shading

1. Position insertion point in paragraph or select text to receive a border and/or shading.
2. Click **Format, Borders and Shading.**
3. Click the appropriate tab.
4. Click the desired options, and click **OK.**

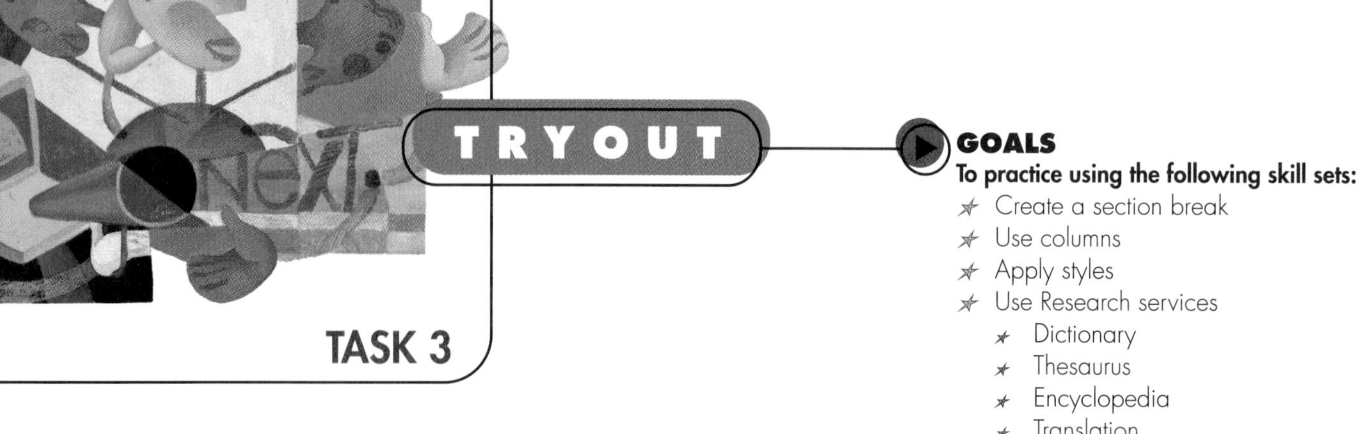

GOALS

To practice using the following skill sets:

- Create a section break
- Use columns
- Apply styles
- Use Research services
  - Dictionary
  - Thesaurus
  - Encyclopedia
  - Translation
  - Web search
- Find and replace text
- Insert a file

WHAT YOU NEED TO KNOW

Create a Section Break

- By default, a document contains one section. Word allows you to break your document into multiple sections, allowing you to format each one differently. Figure 3.20 shows a document that uses section breaks to format each section differently.

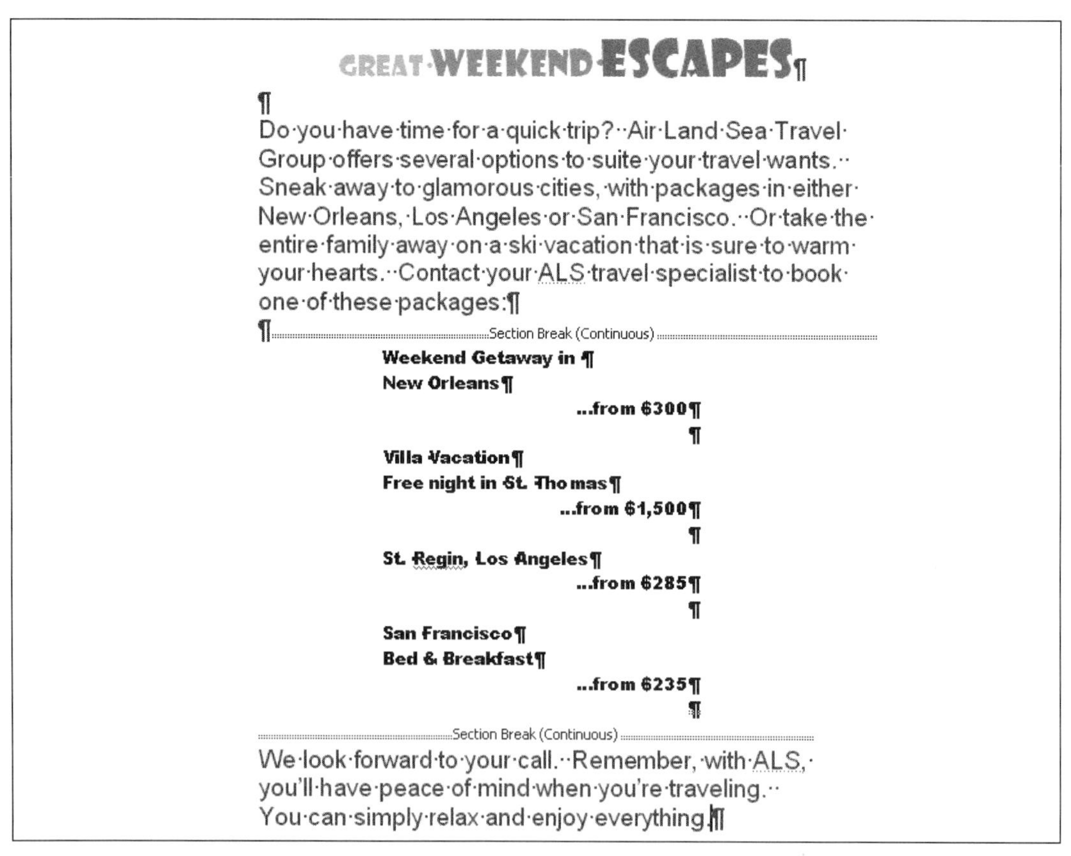

GREAT·WEEKEND·ESCAPES¶

¶
Do·you·have·time·for·a·quick·trip?··Air·Land·Sea·Travel·Group·offers·several·options·to·suite·your·travel·wants.··Sneak·away·to·glamorous·cities,·with·packages·in·either·New·Orleans,·Los·Angeles·or·San·Francisco.··Or·take·the·entire·family·away·on·a·ski·vacation·that·is·sure·to·warm·your·hearts.··Contact·your·ALS·travel·specialist·to·book·one·of·these·packages:¶

¶ ::::::::::Section Break (Continuous)::::::::::

Weekend Getaway in ¶
New Orleans¶
...from $300¶
¶
Villa Vacation¶
Free night in St. Thomas¶
...from $1,500¶
¶
St. Regin, Los Angeles¶
...from $285¶
¶
San Francisco¶
Bed & Breakfast¶
...from $235¶
¶

::::::::::Section Break (Continuous)::::::::::

We·look·forward·to·your·call.··Remember,·with·ALS,·you'll·have·peace·of·mind·when·you're·traveling.··You·can·simply·relax·and·enjoy·everything.¶

Figure 3.20 Sample document with section breaks inserted

- To create a *section break,* position the insertion point where you want the break. Then, click Insert, Break on the menu and choose the type of section break you want in the Break dialog box, as shown in Figure 3.21. Each section break option creates a break in a different location in the document.
  - Next page—creates a new section on the next page.
  - Continuous—creates a new section at the insertion point.
  - Even page—creates a new section on the next even-numbered page (usually a left-hand page).
  - Odd page—creates a new section on the next right-hand page.

Note: Section break marks store section formatting in the same way paragraph marks store paragraph formatting. Therefore, removing a section break may also delete all section formatting preceding the break.

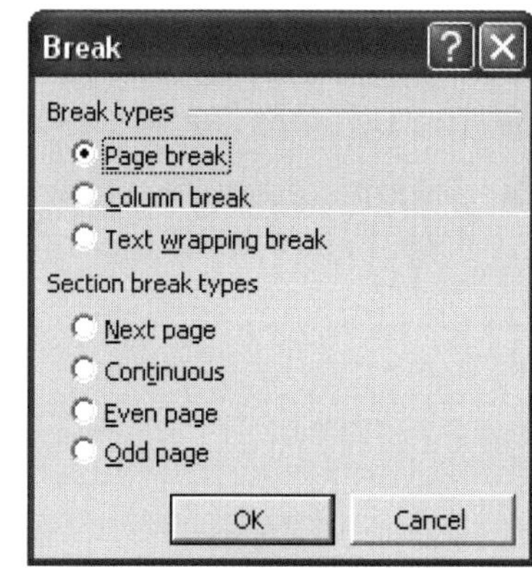

Figure 3.21 Break dialog box

TRY *it* OUT *w3-10*

1. Click the **New Blank Document** button.
2. Enter: `The Highland Grand Hotel is located on 17 acres in the historic Woodland Hills. Guests are offered a range of accommodations.`
3. Press the **Enter** key twice.
4. Click **Insert, Break, Continuous.** Click **OK.**
5. Change the left and right margins to **2".**
6. Enter these bulleted paragraphs:
   - `Rooms combine into family units to allow a small group or family to vacation in comfort within the privacy of their own spacious unit.`
   - `Five minute drive to beach.`
   - `Great value, well priced.`
7. Press the **Enter** key twice. Click **Insert, Break, Continuous.** Click **OK.**
8. Reset the left and right margins to **1.25"**.
9. Enter: `The Highland Grand Hotel also offers a newly created exercise gym and one of the most famous restaurants in the area.`
10. Print one copy (optional) and close the file; do not save.

Use Columns

- The *Columns* feature allows text to flow down one column and into the next column.
- Columns are particularly useful when creating manuals, newsletters, pamphlets, brochures, and lists. Figure 3.22 shows a document with columns.

Title of document

Subtitle of document

This is practice text that you can use for importing, placing and "playing" purposes. Practice text is useful when you are planning a layout. Using practice text rather than real text is a good way to concentrate on the form and design of your layout without reading the text itself. Consider this paragraph one (this might change, of course).

Practice text should have paragraphs so you can manipulate them and move them as you desire. Practice text should have paragraphs so you can manipulate them and move them as you desire.

Practice text also encourages you to experiment with changing typefaces, type styles, type sizes and leading.

When working with practice text, you should have at least four paragraphs. This will enable you to move them and experiment with at least four different formats.

Column breaks inserted

This is practice text that you can use for importing, placing and "playing" purposes. Practice text is useful when you are planning a layout. Using practice text rather than real text is a good way to concentrate on the form and design of your layout without reading the text itself. Consider this paragraph one (this might change, of course).

Practice text should have paragraphs so you can manipulate them and move them as you desire. Practice text should have paragraphs so you can manipulate them and move them as you desire. Practice text also encourages you to experiment with changing typefaces, type styles, type sizes and leading. You become less intimidated experimenting with your software's design elements if you know that it is merely practice and not the real text. Consider this paragraph two.

When working with practice text, you should have at least four paragraphs.

Section break inserted.
Two column format set.

Figure 3.22 Sample layout formatted with columns

- To create columns, click Format, Columns. In the Columns dialog box that appears, shown in Figure 3.23, you can choose the number of columns you want, set the width and spacing between columns, called *gutter space,* and add a vertical line between columns.
- You can also create columns by clicking the Columns button on the Standard toolbar, shown in Figure 3.24, and dragging the mouse to select the number of columns you require. However, the system will not display the Columns dialog box using this method.
- To force text to wrap to the next column before you reach the bottom of the current column, you must insert a column break. (See Figure 3.22.) To do so, click Insert, Break, Column break where you want the column to end.
- You can create columns in various parts of the same document as long as you insert a section break before and/or after each section. (See Figure 3.22.)
- To turn the Columns feature off and return to one column, click Format, Columns, and click One.

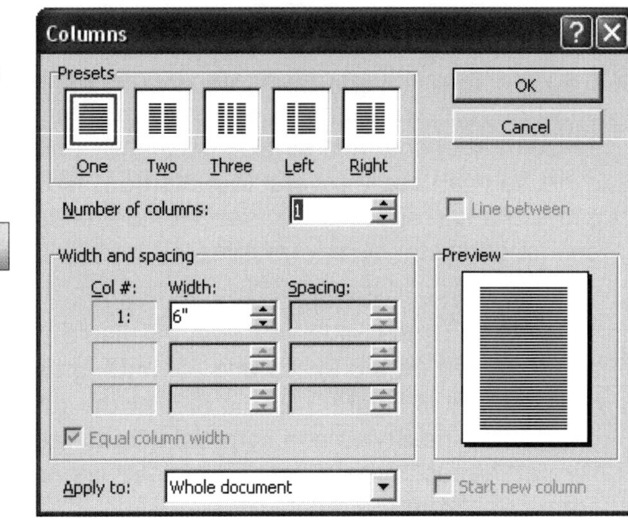

Figure 3.23 Columns dialog box

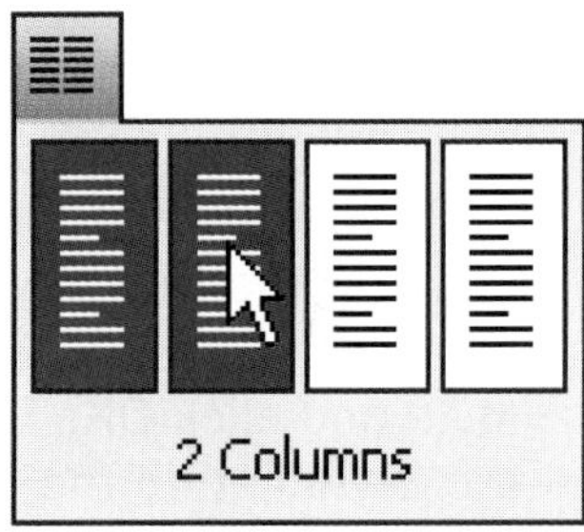

Figure 3.24 Columns button

TRY *it* OUT *w3-11*

1. Click the **New Blank Document** button.
2. Set the font size to **14 point.**
3. Click **Format, Columns.**
4. Select **Two** and click **OK.**
5. Enter: `E-mail, otherwise known as electronic mail, is the Internet's most used function. It is used to send messages, documents, and pictures, much as the post office is used to send a letter.`
6. Click **Insert, Break, Column break,** then click **OK** to force the text to the next column.
7. Continue entering: `However, e-mail does not require paper, stamps, or much travel time.`
8. Click **Insert, Break,** and **Continuous,** then click **OK** to create a section break.
9. Press the **Enter** key once. Then click **Format, Columns.**
10. Click **One** and click **OK.**
11. Enter: `To send e-mail, the sender and the receiver must each have an Internet account and an e-mail address.`
12. Print one copy (optional) and close the file; do not save.

Apply Styles

- A *style* is a collection of formats you can apply to selected text. For example, one style might specify 16-point Arial bold and single spacing. By using a style, you can apply several formats (font size, font style, and line spacing, for example) in one step and ensure consistency in formatting.
- You can use one of Word's numerous predefined styles or you can create your own. Available styles are displayed on the Styles and Formatting task pane, shown in Figure 3.25. To display the task pane, click the Styles and Formatting button on the Formatting toolbar, or select Format, Styles and Formatting from the menu.
- To display a style's characteristics, position the insertion point on a style name, which will display a pop-up box with the style information.
- To create a new style, format some text on which you want to base the style, select this text, and click New Style in the Styles and Formatting task pane. In the New Style dialog box that appears, shown in Figure 3.26, enter the name of the new style and click OK. The new style name appears in the Style list on the Formatting toolbar, as well as the Styles and Formatting task pane, as shown in Figure 3.27.
- To apply a style to new text, click a style, and enter the text. To apply a style to existing text, first select the text, then click the style you want to apply.

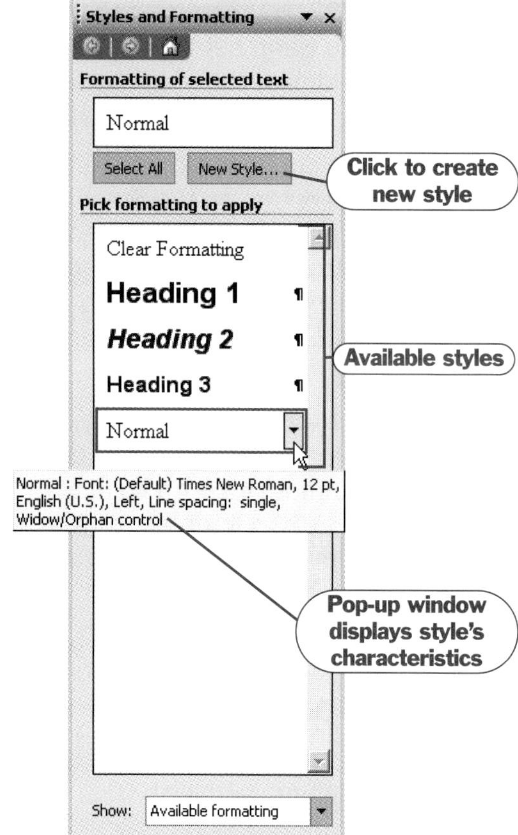

Figure 3.25 Styles and Formatting task pane

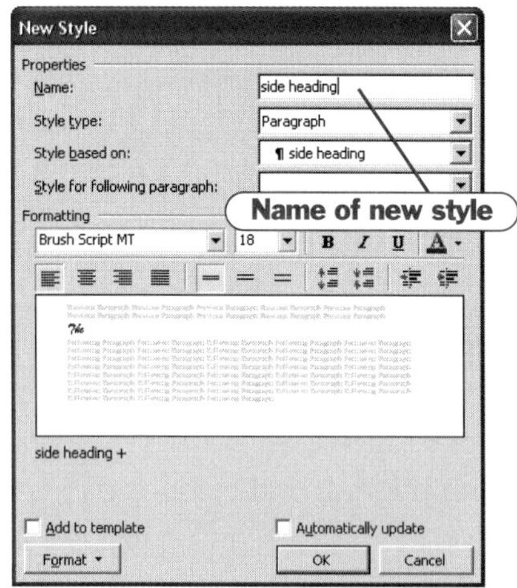

Figure 3.26 New Style dialog box

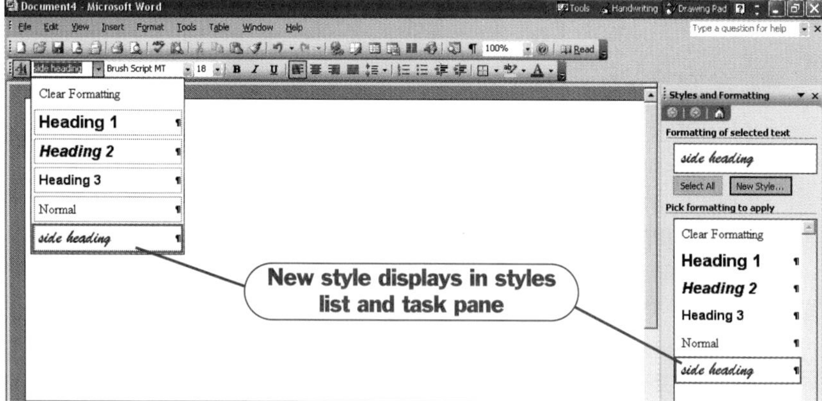

Figure 3.27 Styles List and Styles and Formatting task pane

TRY it OUT *w3-12*

Apply an Existing Style

1. Open **w3.12pf styles** from the Data CD.
2. Select the words "TOUR IN EGYPT."
3. Click **Format, Styles and Formatting.**
4. Click **Heading 1.**
5. Select the words "TOUR IN PERU."
6. Click the **Style** list arrow on the Formatting toolbar. *Note: You may have to click Toolbar Options to display the Style list arrow.*
7. Click **Heading 1.**

Create a New Style

8. Select the words "July 14-July 22."
9. Change the font to **10-point Comic Sans MS Italic;** change the font color to **Red.**
10. Click the **New Style** button in the Styles and Formatting task pane.
11. In the **New Style** dialog box, click in the **Name** text box and enter: `Date Head`
12. Click OK.
13. Select the words "June 14-June 22."
14. Click **Date Head** in the Style list.

▶ To modify or delete a style, click the list arrow next to the style name, as shown in Figure 3.28, and click Modify or Delete. Make the necessary modifications in the Modify Style dialog box that appears, as shown in Figure 3.29.

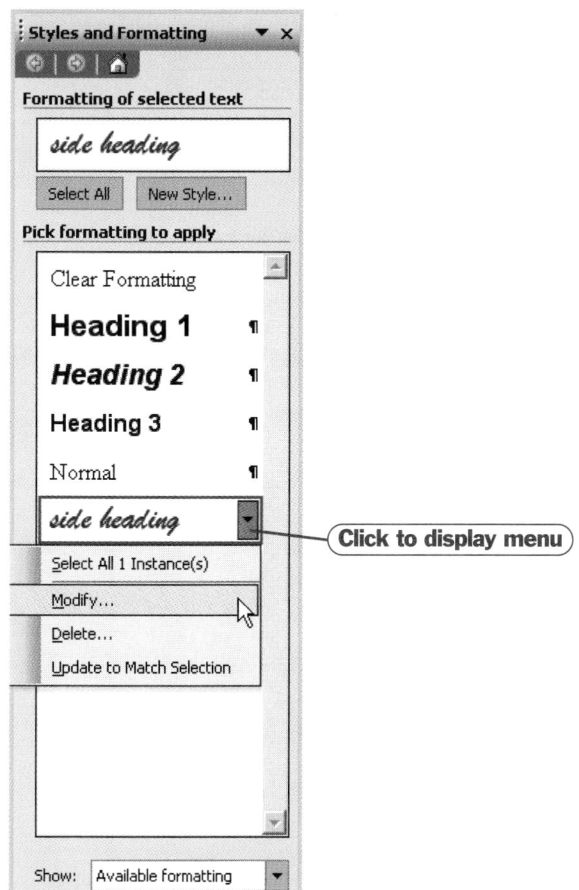

Figure 3.28 Modify styles on Styles and Formatting task pane

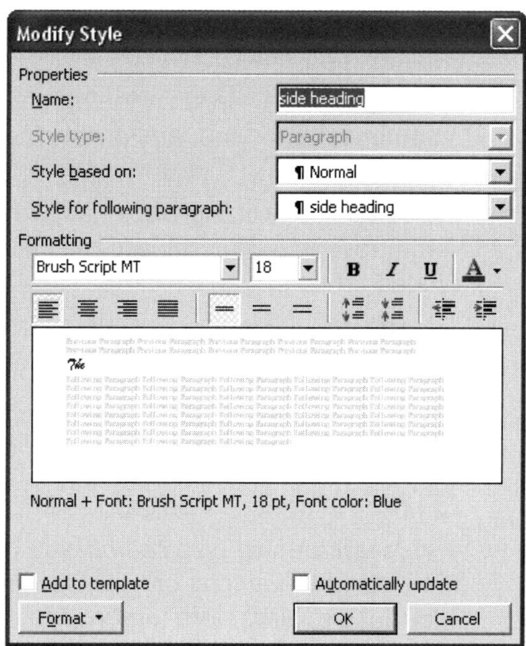

Figure 3.29 Modify Style dialog box

- If you make a change to a style, any text based on that style is updated automatically with the modified characteristics.
- To hide the Styles and Formatting task pane, click the Styles and Formatting button on the toolbar or click the Close button on the task pane. 

TRY *it* OUT *w3-13*

Modify an Existing Style

1. Position the Mouse pointer on Heading 1.
2. Click the list arrow.
3. Click **Modify.**
4. Change the font color to **Blue.**
5. Click **OK.** The two headings automatically change to blue.
6. Close the file; do not save.

Use Research Services

- The Research task pane, which can be displayed by clicking Tools, Research, provides you with the following services while you are working on your document. Once you have found what you are looking for, you can easily insert it into your document.
    - **Dictionary** The *Dictionary* feature provides you with definitions of words and phrases, which you can look up while you work.
    - **Thesaurus** The *Thesaurus* feature lists synonyms, sometimes antonyms, and parts of speech for a selected word.
    - **Encyclopedia** The *Encyclopedia* feature allows you to research your subject and click links to related articles.
    - **Translation** Using the *translation* feature, you can translate single words or short phrases into twelve different languages.
    - **Stock quotes and company information** This feature enables you to look up stock quotes and company information while you work.
    - **Web search** Using *Web search*, you can search the Web while working on your document, and click links to view more information on the Web.
- To use the features on the Research task pane, click the Search for list arrow, and choose a service you want to use, as shown in Figure 3.30. Enter what you are searching for in the Search for text box and click the Start Searching button.
- You can also use a method to select the Search for word or phrase as indicated in the table on the facing page.

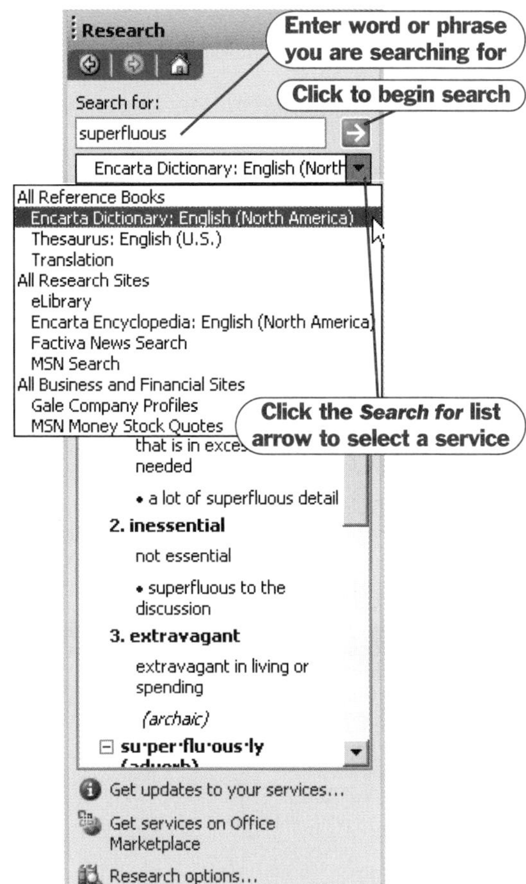

Figure 3.30 Research task pane

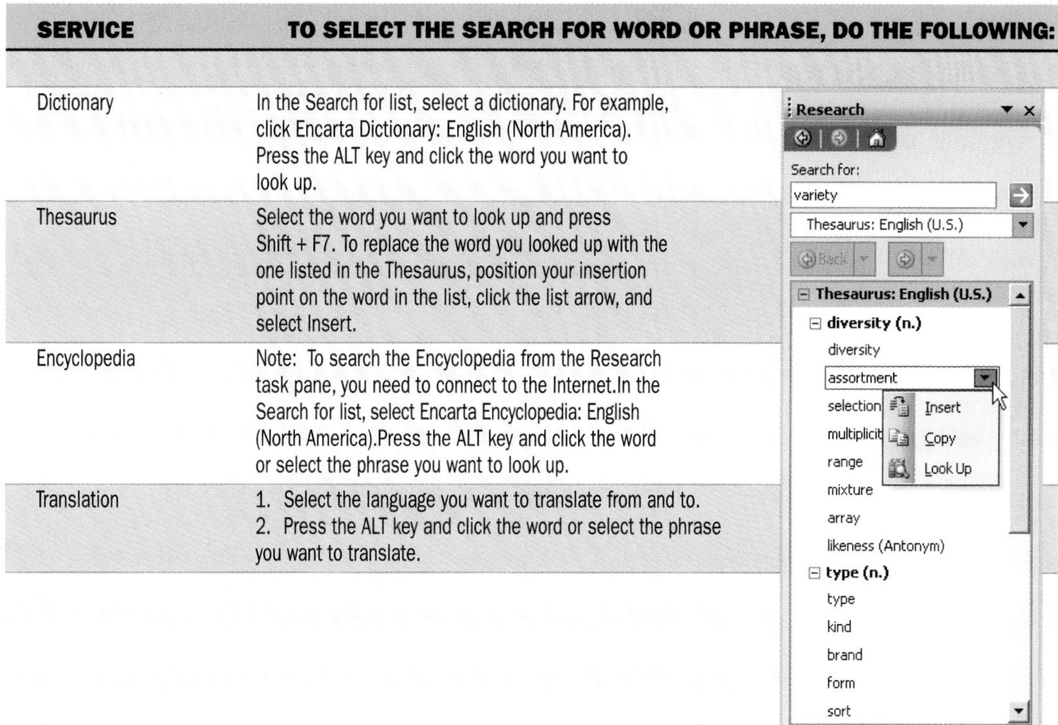

SERVICE	TO SELECT THE SEARCH FOR WORD OR PHRASE, DO THE FOLLOWING:
Dictionary	In the Search for list, select a dictionary. For example, click Encarta Dictionary: English (North America). Press the ALT key and click the word you want to look up.
Thesaurus	Select the word you want to look up and press Shift + F7. To replace the word you looked up with the one listed in the Thesaurus, position your insertion point on the word in the list, click the list arrow, and select Insert.
Encyclopedia	Note: To search the Encyclopedia from the Research task pane, you need to connect to the Internet.In the Search for list, select Encarta Encyclopedia: English (North America).Press the ALT key and click the word or select the phrase you want to look up.
Translation	1. Select the language you want to translate from and to. 2. Press the ALT key and click the word or select the phrase you want to translate.

TRY *it* OUT *w3-14*

1. Open **w3.14pf thesaurus** from the Data CD.
2. Position the insertion point on the first highlighted word.
3. Press the **Shift + F7** keys. (This will launch the Thesaurus feature on the Research task pane.)
4. Position your insertion point on an appropriate replacement word in the Research task pane and click its list arrow.
5. Click **Insert.**
6. Use the Thesaurus to substitute the remaining yellow highlighted words.
7. Print one copy.
8. Click the **Search for** list arrow to select the **Translation** service. *Note: If you do not have this feature installed or if you do not have online access, skip steps 8–11.*
9. Select to translate from **English** to **Italian.**
10. Press the **Alt** key and click on the first green highlighted word. Note the results in the Research task pane.
11. Use the Translation feature to translate the remaining green highlighted words.
12. Close the file; do not save.

Find and Replace Text

- The Find feature scans a document and searches for occurrences of specified text, symbols, or formatting.
- The Replace feature allows you to locate all occurrences of certain text and replace it with different text, special characters, or symbols.
- To find or replace text, click Edit, Find or Edit, Replace. In the Find and Replace dialog box that appears, as shown in Figure 3.31, click either the Find or the Replace tab and fill in the appropriate information.
- Clicking the More button will display a dialog box with additional search options, as shown in Figure 3.32.
- For example, if you were trying to locate the word "The," you would have to select "Match case" and "Find whole words only." Otherwise, your search will not only find "The" but also "the," "*the*rwise," "*the*sis," and any other word of which "the" is a part. If you are searching for a specific font, paragraph, tab, style, or other specialized mark, click Format or Special for other options.

Figure 3.31 Find and Replace dialog box

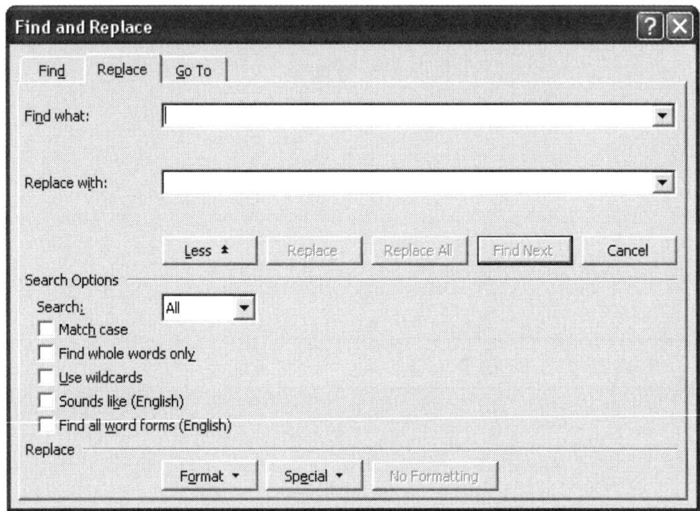

Figure 3.32 Find and Replace dialog box for advanced searches

TRY *it* OUT *w3-15*

1. Open **w3.15pf letter** from the Data CD.
2. Click **Edit, Find**. Find the word "intimidated." Use the Thesaurus to substitute another word.
3. Use **Edit, Replace** to find each occurrence of the words "practice text" and replace all with `exercise text` in **13-point bold.**
4. Find the abbreviation "pf" and replace it with: `ef.`
5. Use **Edit, Replace** to find the words "practice file" and replace all with `exercise file`
6. Close the file; do not save.

Insert a File

- The *Insert File* feature allows you to insert a file into the current document. The inserted file becomes part of the current document into which it is inserted. The file you insert remains intact, thus enabling you to use it again as needed.
- To insert a file, position the insertion point at the location in the document where you want the insert to appear, click Insert, File, choose the file to insert, and click Insert.

TRY *it* OUT *w3-16*

1. Open **w3.16pf realty** from the Data CD.
2. Position the insertion point at the start of the second paragraph (in front of "As").
3. Click **Insert, File.**
4. Click **3.16pf insert** from the Data CD.
5. Click **Insert.**
6. Print one copy.
7. Close the file; do not save.

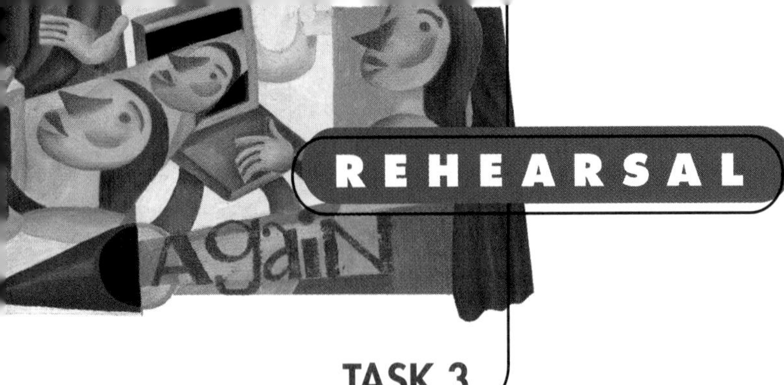

GOAL
To format the first six pages of a handbook

SETTING THE STAGE/WRAPUP
Margins: Default
Start line: At 1"
File names: **3.3benefits**
3.4education
3.4benefits.1

WHAT YOU NEED TO KNOW

- A *manual,* or *handbook,* is a booklet, catalog, or guidebook that provides instruction and/or information to a particular audience. For example, many companies provide new employees with an employee manual or handbook, which may contain information about company procedures, policies, and benefits.
- The pages of a manual should maintain a consistent format.
- When you create a long document, more than one person may work on it. The Insert File feature allows you to combine files from more than one source into a single document.
- In this Rehearsal activity, you will format the first four pages of a handbook. You will then work on a fifth page (which was created independently of the other pages), and insert it to become part of the larger file. The document will contain six pages after it has all been formatted.

DIRECTIONS

1. Open **3.3benefits text** from the Data CD.

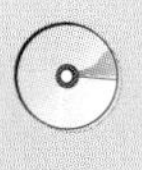

Note: This text is single-spaced and unformatted. You will apply styles that include paragraph spacing, as shown on the facing page.

2. Insert a hard page break before "Dental."
3. Select **Format, Styles and Formatting.**
4. Modify Heading 1 as follows:
   a. Change the font size to **48 point.**
   b. Click the **Format** button and click **Border.**
   c. Create a custom bottom border on the bottom using a **4½-point blue dotted line** and click **OK.**
   d. Click **OK.**
5. Modify Heading 2 by changing the font color to **Blue** and click **OK.**
6. Modify Heading 3 by changing the font size to **11 point.**
7. Apply Heading 1 to "Introduction" and "Dental."
8. Apply Heading 2 to all subheadings, as shown on the facing page.
9. Apply Heading 3 to all paragraph text.

Note: The bullets and numbering are removed when this style is applied. You will reinsert them using the traditional method.

10. Create a centered footer that reads: `Sutton Investment Group`
    a. Set the footer text to **18 point.** Use any desired font.
    b. Insert any symbol before and after the company name.
    c. Insert a centered page number below Sutton Investment Group in **10 point.**

Continued on next page

Introduction

THE SUTTON GROUP BENEFITS PROGRAM

YOUR ENROLLMENT KIT

This enrollment kit provides you with the information you will need to enroll for the Sutton Group Benefits Program. Here are all the pieces that make up your Benefits Enrollment Kit:

- ✓ Booklets about all the benefit plans available through this program
- ✓ Your personalized enrollment worksheet and
- ✓ This general information booklet describing how the Benefits program works, eligibility rules, tax information, and how to enroll over the telephone through the Sutton Group Benefits Enrollment Line.

Apply Heading 2 style

THE BENEFITS OF THE SUTTON GROUP BENEFITS PROGRAM

The Benefits program offers six major categories of benefits coverage. Within each category are several different benefit options. You select the option(s) from each category that you believe are right for you. The categories of coverage, discussed in detail in the booklets in the enrollment kit, are:

- ✓ Medical
- ✓ Dental
- ✓ Life Insurance
- ✓ Education Incentive Plan
- ✓ Vision Care
- ✓ Property and Casualty Insurance

WHO IS ELIGIBLE FOR BENEFITS?

Regular employees on the domestic payroll of Sutton Group who have completed at least one calendar month of service as a regular employee and who work at least 20 hours each week are eligible to participate in the benefit options available through Sutton Group Benefits.

❖ Sutton Investment Group ❖

Page 1

Page 1

You can also enroll your eligible dependents for Medical, Dental and Life Insurance coverage. For Sutton Group Benefits, your eligible dependents are your:

- ✓ Spouse, and
- ✓ Unmarried children who are under age 19 (or age 23 if they are full-time students).

Children include natural and legally adopted children, stepchildren living in your home, and any other child who is supported solely by you and living in your home. Coverage may be continued beyond age 23 under certain circumstances.

Dependents are not eligible for any benefits under the Benefits program if they are in military service and may not be eligible if they live permanently outside the United States or Canada.

Page 2

11. Enter new text on page 3, which is shown in red (Dental) as follows:

   a. Copy all the paragraphs below "WHO IS ELIGIBLE FOR BENEFITS?" on pages 1 and 2 and paste it below "WHO IS ELIGIBLE FOR DENTAL BENEFITS?" Enter the remaining paragraphs shown.

Note: Use a black font color for all new text. When entering new text, do not add extra space between paragraphs—the styles you apply will automatically insert paragraph spacing.

   a. Be sure to enter a continuous section break before and after creating columns.

   b. To resume entering text across the page, you must reset the number of columns to One.

   c. Apply appropriate styles to the newly inserted text to maintain formatting consistency.

12. Correct any spelling errors.

13. Save the file; name it **3.3benefits.**

14. Position the insertion point below the last paragraph of the last page.

Dental

As you read this booklet describing your dental coverage options through the Sutton Group Benefits Program, you should ask yourself what you want from your dental coverage:

1. **Do you want the freedom to choose any dentist regardless of cost?**
2. **Do you want to have lower costs in exchange for receiving dental care from a limited selection of dentists?**
3. **Would you rather have no dental coverage at all?**

WHO IS ELIGIBLE FOR DENTAL BENEFITS?

[Copy all paragraphs below "Who is Eligible for Benefits" on pages one and two and paste here.]

TRADITIONAL DENTAL PLAN
If you answered "yes" to the first question, you may want to elect the Traditional Dental Plan. Under the Traditional Dental Plan, you have the freedom to choose any licensed dentist. You also have the option of utilizing the Preferred Dentist Program offered with the Traditional Dental Plan to help control plan expenses and help lower your out-of-pocket costs.

PLEASE NOTE THE FOLLOWING:
This brochure is not a complete description of the dental plan offered through Sutton Group Benefits Program. This is only a summary and is not a substitute for the official plan documents.

The provisions of the official plan documents and of applicable law will govern in the event of any inconsistency between those provisions and the provisions of this brochure.

Enter new text

Insert a continuous section break; turn on column feature

Insert a continuous section break; reset to one column

Insert column break

❖ ***Sutton Investment Group*** ❖

Page 1

Page 3

Dental

As you read this booklet describing your dental coverage options through the Sutton Group Benefits Program, you should ask yourself what you want from your dental coverage:

1. Do you want the freedom to choose any dentist regardless of cost?
2. Do you want to have lower costs in exchange for receiving dental care from a limited selection of dentists?
3. Would you rather have no dental coverage at all?

copy

WHO IS ELIGIBLE FOR DENTAL BENEFITS?

Regular employees on the domestic payroll of Sutton Group who have completed at least one calendar month of service as a regular employee and who work at least 20 hours each week are eligible to participate in the benefit options available through Sutton Group Benefits.

You can also enroll your eligible dependents for Medical, Dental and Life Insurance coverage. For Sutton Group Benefits, your eligible dependents are your:

- ✓ Spouse, and
- ✓ Unmarried children who are under age 19 (or age 23 if they are full-time students).

Children include natural and legally adopted children, stepchildren living in your home, and any other child who is supported solely by you and living in your home. Coverage may be continued beyond age 23 under certain circumstances.

Dependents are not eligible for any benefits under the Benefits Program if they are in military service and may not be eligible if they live permanently outside the United States or Canada.

TRADITIONAL DENTAL PLAN

If you answered "yes" to the first question, you may want to elect the Traditional Dental Plan. Under the Traditional Dental Plan, you have the freedom to choose any licensed dentist. You also have the option of utilizing the Preferred Dentist Program offered with the Traditional Dental Plan to help control plan expenses and help lower your out-of-pocket costs.

❖ Sutton Investment Group ❖

Page 1

PLEASE NOTE THE FOLLOWING:

This brochure is not a complete description of the dental plan offered through Sutton Group Benefits Program. This is only a summary and is not a substitute for the official plan documents.

The provisions of the official plan documents and of applicable law will govern in the event of any inconsistency between those provisions and the provisions of this brochure.

Insert 3.3 education here.

❖ Sutto

15. Insert **3.3education** from the Data CD.
16. Insert a hard page break before "Education." (You should now have five pages.)
17. Apply the styles necessary to format the newly inserted file so it is consistent with the rest of the document. (After the styles are applied, you will have five pages.)
18. Reinsert the bullets.
19. Copy the first paragraph below "WHO IS ELIGIBLE FOR DENTAL BENEFITS?" and paste it as the first paragraph below "WHO IS ELIGIBLE FOR EDUCATION BENEFITS?"
20. Replace all occurrences of "Sutton Group" with "Sutton Investment Group."
21. Replace occurrences of "children" with "dependent children" in the paragraphs below "WHO IS ELIGIBLE FOR EDUCATION BENEFITS?"
22. Find the word "accumulate." Use the Thesaurus to substitute another word.
23. Determine the statistics for the document.
24. Save the file as **3.3benefits.1.**
25. Preview, print, and then close the file.

Education

EDUCATION INCENTIVE PLAN
The Sutton Group Benefits Program will help you pay for your children's education. The Education Incentive Plan helps you plan ahead for the day tuition bills begin to arrive.
WHO IS ELIGIBLE FOR EDUCATION BENEFITS?
The Education Incentive Plan is designed to help you save from $5,000 to $40,000 (over a 5- to 15-year period) toward the education costs you anticipate for each of your children. You may choose to set aside an amount needed to reach your savings goal for one or more children in the selected time period as follows:

Paste copied paragraph here.

- ✔ The maximum goal is $40,000 per child; the minimum is $5,000.
- ✔ You may have a maximum of four plan accounts per child.
- ✔ The company contributes 15% of the amount of your payroll toward Education Benefits.

The funds will accumulate over a period of 5 to 15 years, but not beyond your child's twenty-fifth birthday. When a plan reaches the level of money you want, the funds are paid to you. You can request that the account be canceled and paid out earlier.
HOW TO GET THE MOST OUT OF THE EDUCATION PLAN
The matching contributions from Sutton Group are reported as ordinary income on your W-2 tax form. That means that any money you earn through our investment is subject to taxes until all the proceeds are paid out to you.
Your savings and the company matching contributions are invested in stocks and bonds. The full amount of your account will automatically be paid to you upon cancellation of this plan.

Cues for Reference

Section Break

1. Position the insertion point where the break is to start.
2. Click **Insert, Break.**
3. Select the appropriate break.
4. Click **OK.**

Create Columns

1. Position the insertion point where the columns are to begin, or select text to format for columns.
2. Click **Format, Columns.**
3. Click to select the number of columns.
4. Click the **Apply to** list arrow to indicate the text to format in columns.

or

1. Position the insertion point where the columns are to begin, or select text to format for columns.
2. Click the Columns button on the Standard toolbar.
3. Move the mouse to select the number of columns.

To Set Space between Columns

1. Click **Format, Columns.**
2. Click in the **Spacing** text box.
3. Enter the value for the distance between columns.
4. Click **OK.**

To add a Vertical Line between Columns

1. Click **Format, Columns.**
2. Click the **Line between** check box.
3. Click **OK.**

To Force Text to the Next Column

1. Position the insertion point where the column is to end.
2. Click **Insert, Break, Column break.**
3. Click **OK.**

Create a New Style

1. Click the **Styles and Formatting** button to display the task pane.
2. Click **New Style.**
3. Click in the **Name** text box and enter the style's name.
4. Select style options from the Formatting toolbars. For additional options, click **Format** and make your selections.
5. Click **OK.**

Modify Existing Style

1. Click the **Styles and Formatting** button to display the task pane.
2. Point to a style and click its list arrow.
3. Click **Modify.**
4. Select style options.
5. Click **OK.**

Use Research Services

1. Display the Research task pane (**Tools, Research**).
2. Click the Search for list arrow to select a service.
3. Select the word or phrase to be looked up and click a shortcut method to activate the search.

or

1. Enter the word or phrase to be searched in the Search for text box.
2. Click the **Start searching** button.

Thesaurus

1. Position your insertion point on the word to replace.
2. Press **Shift + F7.**
3. Position your insertion point on the replacement word listed in the task pane.
4. Click the list arrow and select **Insert.**

Find and Replace Text

1. Position the insertion point at the top of the document.
2. Click **Edit, Find** or **Edit, Replace.**
3. Click the appropriate tab.
4. Enter text to find and/or replace.
5. To find text, click **Find Next.** To replace text, click **Replace** (to replace one occurrence at a time) or **Replace All** (to replace all occurrences at once).
6. Click **Cancel.**

Insert a File

1. Position the insertion point at the insert location.
2. Click **Insert, File.**
3. Click the file to insert.
4. Click **Insert.**

GOAL

To practice using the following skill sets to help you edit a document.

- Insert, View, and Edit Comments
- Track Changes in a Document
- Compare and Merge Documents
- Use Word Count and Document Summary

WHAT YOU NEED TO KNOW

Insert, View, and Edit Comments

- *Comments* are hidden notes or annotations that you or a reviewer can add to a document. The Comments feature is useful for facilitating the online review of documents.
- You can read comments on screen, hide them when the document is printed, or print them with the document. Figure 3.33 shows a document with comments inserted.

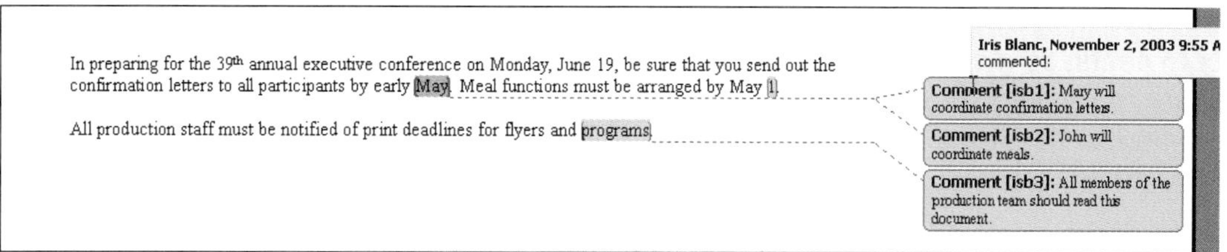

Figure 3.33 Document with comments

- To insert a comment, position the insertion point where you want to insert the comment, or select a block of text on which you want to make a comment, then click Insert, Comment. A comment balloon opens in Print and Web layout views for you to enter the comment text. *Note: If a balloon does not appear, display the Reviewing toolbar, click on Show, Balloons. Be sure "Always" or "Only for Comments/Formatting" is selected.*
- To see the author of the comment, as well as the date and time the comment was made, position the insertion point over the balloon, and a pop-up window displays this information, as illustrated in Figure 3.33.
- Display the Reviewing toolbar to make working with comments easier. The Reviewing toolbar is shown in Figure 3.34.

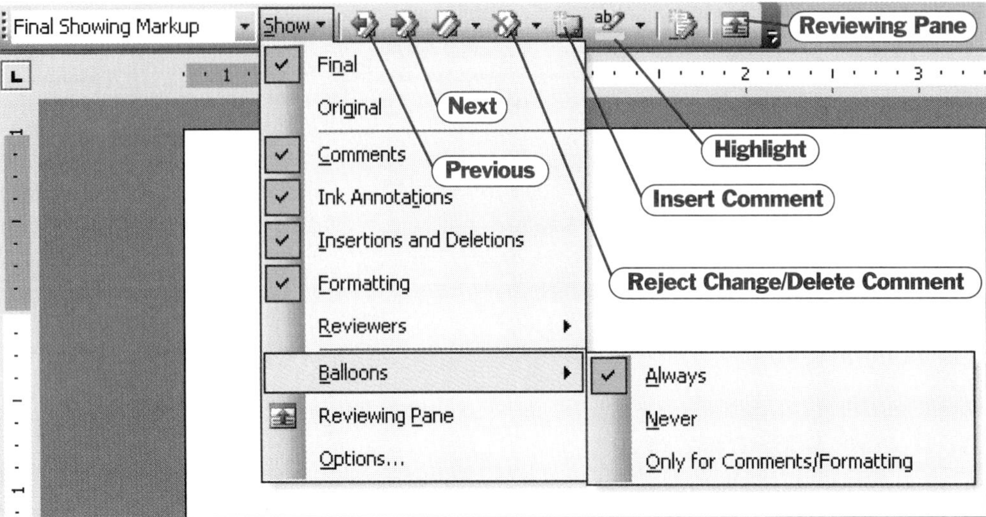

Figure 3.34 Reviewing toolbar

▶ To edit a comment, click in the comment balloon and make your change. You can view all the comments in a document by displaying the Reviewing pane, shown in Figure 3.35, and scrolling through the comments. To display this pane, click the Reviewing Pane button on the Reviewing toolbar. You can also edit a comment directly in the Reviewing pane. A change made to a comment in the Reviewing pane automatically changes the comment in the corresponding comment balloon.

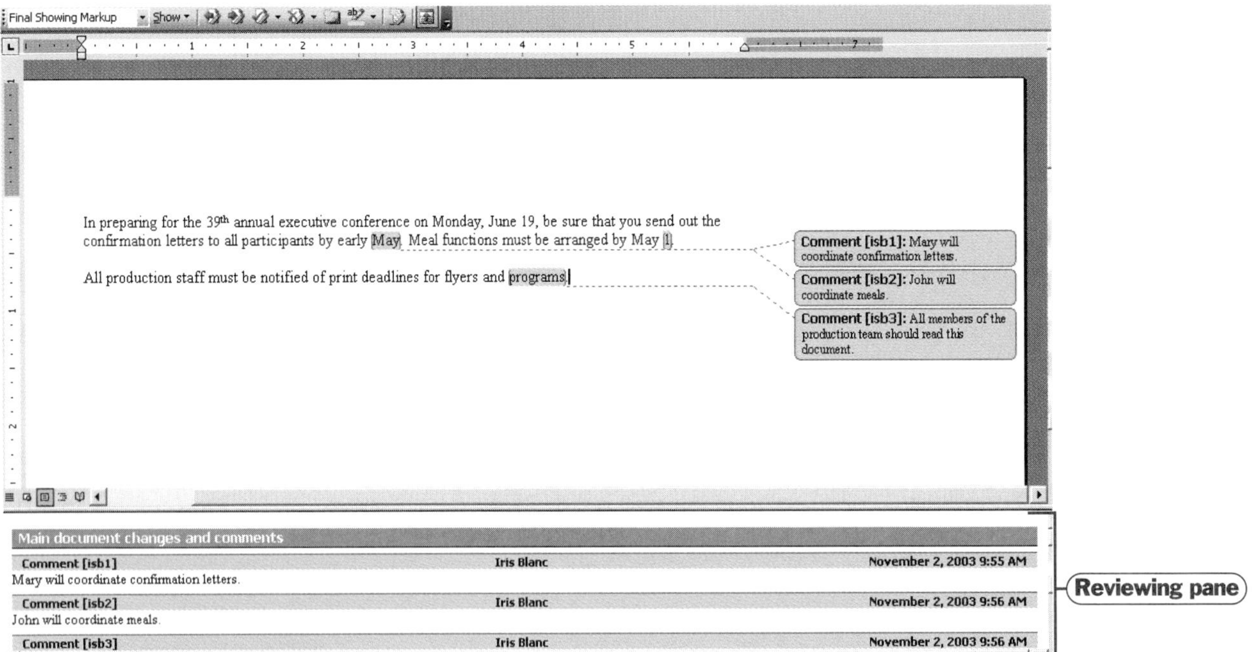

Figure 3.35 Reviewing pane

▶ To delete a comment, click the comment balloon, then click the Reject Change/Delete Comment button or right-click on the balloon and select Delete Comment from the shortcut menu. 

▶ To print a document with comments, click File, Print. In the Print dialog box, as shown in Figure 3.36, select Document showing markup from the Print what list box. To print without comments, select Document from the Print what list box.

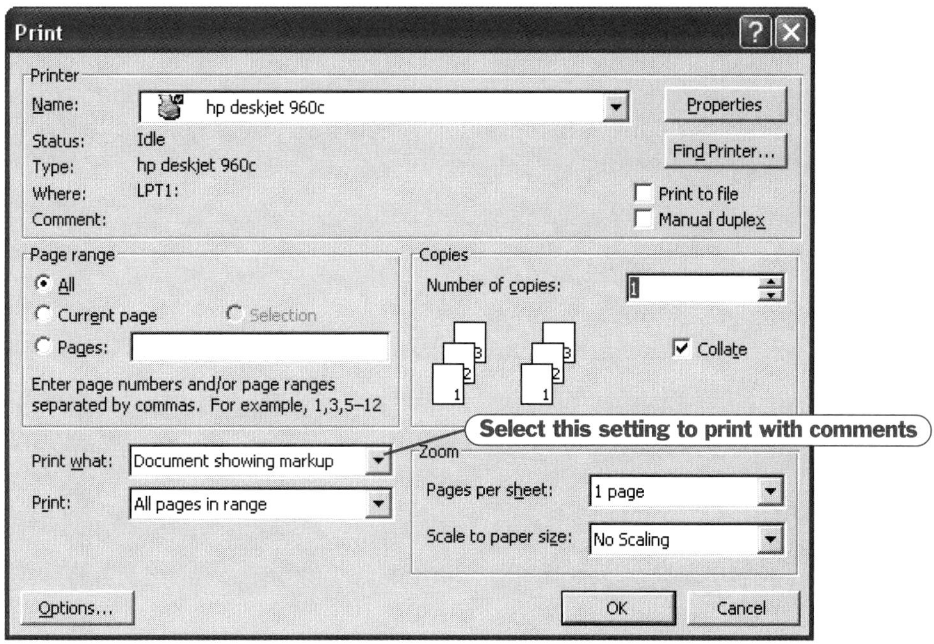

Figure 3.36 Printing with comments in the Print dialog box

TRY*it* OUT *w3-17*

1. Open **w3.17pf comments** from the Data CD. Display Print layout view.
2. Display the Reviewing toolbar.
3. Position the insertion point after the first sentence that ends with the word "May."
4. Click **Insert, Comment.**
5. Enter the following in the comment box: `Mary will coordinate confirmation letters.`
6. Position the insertion point after the second sentence that ends with "May 1."
7. Click the **Insert Comment** button on the Reviewing toolbar.
8. Enter the following in the comment box: `John will coordinate meals.`
9. Position the insertion point after the last sentence ending with the word "programs."
10. Click the **Insert Comment** button.
11. Enter the following in the comment balloon: `All members of the production team should read this document.`
12. Click the **Reviewing Pane** button on the Reviewing toolbar. 
13. Click in the second comment box and change the comment to: `John and Amy will coordinate meals.`
14. Click the third comment balloon, and click the **Reject Change/Delete Comment** button. 
15. Click **File, Print.** Be sure that **Document showing markup** is selected in the Print what list box and click **OK.**
16. Close the file; do not save.

Track Changes in a Document

- The *Track Changes* feature allows you to see where a deletion, insertion, or other formatting change has been made in a document. This feature is a useful tool when editing an online document.
- When you turn on the Track Changes feature, a balloon (like the one used for comments) displays deletions and formatting changes. Insertions are indicated as colored underlined text within the document. Figure 3.37 shows an edited document in which Track Changes has been turned on. This document also contains comments.

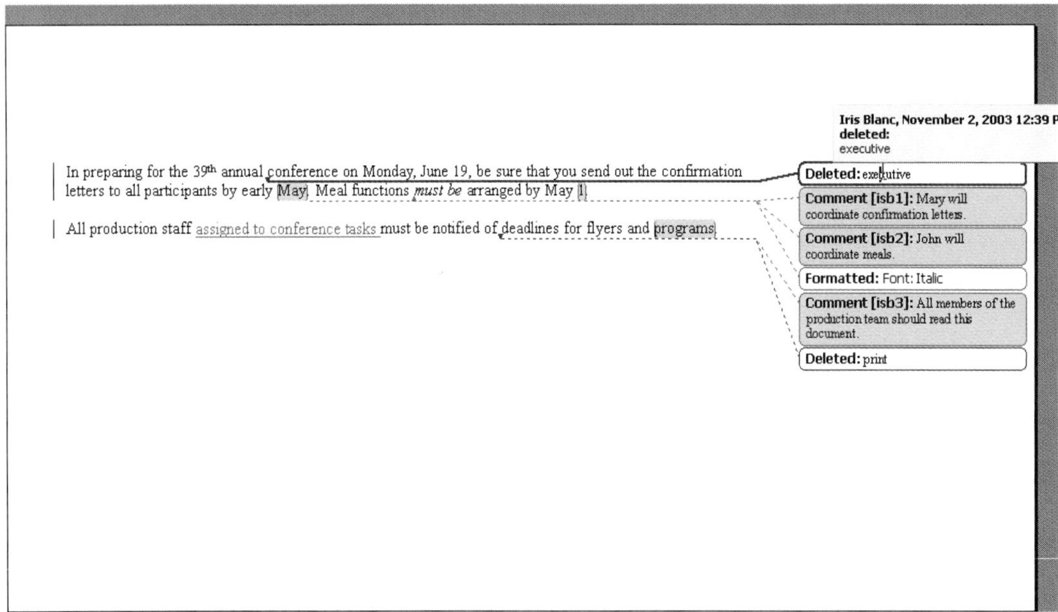

Figure 3.37 Document with tracked changes and comments

- By positioning your insertion point on the balloon, you can see the person and the date the change was made. (See Figure 3.37).
- To turn on the Track Changes feature, click Tools, Track Changes from the menu or click the Track Changes button on the Reviewing toolbar, as shown in Figure 3.38. The Reviewing toolbar contains other Track Changes feature buttons. When the Track Changes feature is enabled, TRK appears on the status bar at the bottom of your document. When you turn off change tracking, TRK is dimmed.

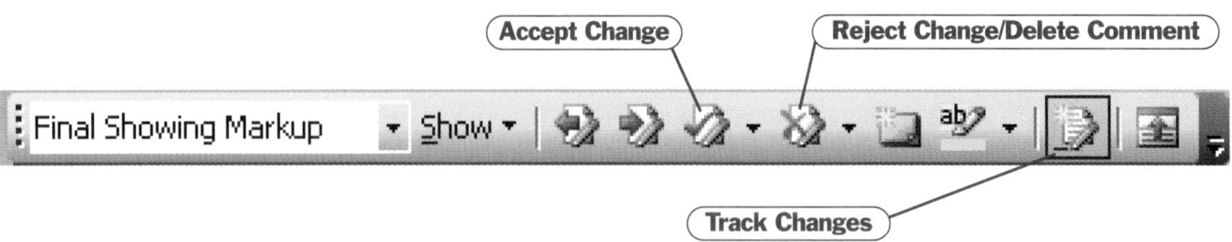

Figure 3.38 Reviewing toolbar

- You can review all changes to a document and decide which to accept or reject. To review changes to a document, display the Reviewing toolbar and select Original Showing Markup from the Display for Review drop-down list.
- You can accept or reject all changes to a document or review them one by one. To accept or reject changes to a document, click each balloon or each tracked insertion (to review one by one). Then, click the Accept Change or Reject Change list arrow on the toolbar, and choose a desired action from the menu. You can also right-click the change and choose an accept or reject change option from the shortcut menu.
- Accept Change Options are shown in Figure 3.39; Reject Change options are shown in Figure 3.40.
- Like comments, you can print the document showing the marked up changes by selecting Document showing markup from the Print what list box in the Print dialog box (see Figure 3.36). You can also print a list of changes as shown in Figure 3.41 by selecting List of markup from the Print what list box.

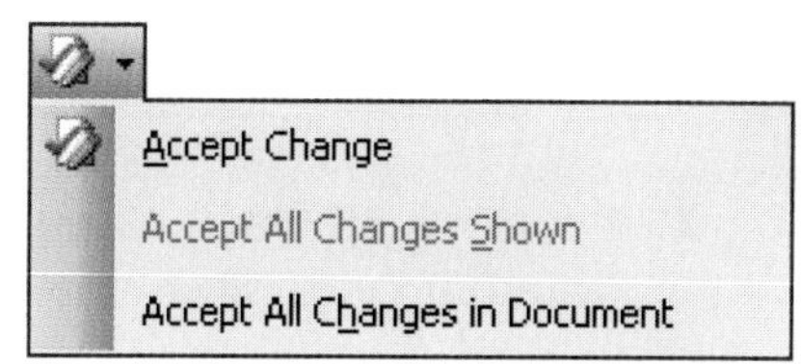

Figure 3.39 Accept Change options

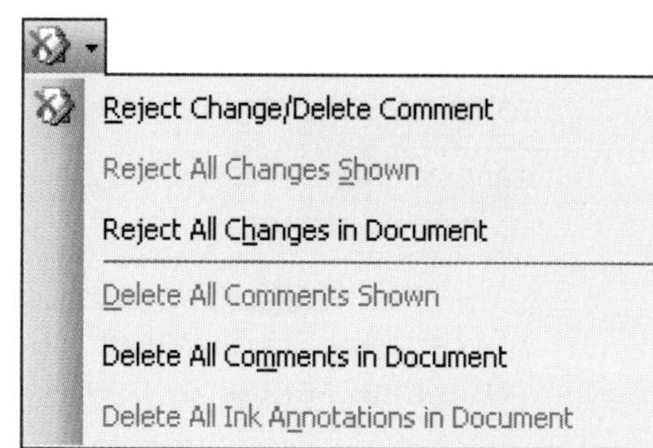

Figure 3.40 Reject Change options

Main document changes and comments		
Deleted executive	**Iris Blanc**	**November 2, 2003 6:26 PM**
Comment [isb1] Mary will coordinate confirmation letters.	**Iris Blanc**	**November 2, 2003 9:55 AM**
Comment [isb2] John will coordinate meals.	**Iris Blanc**	**November 2, 2003 9:56 AM**
Formatted Font: Italic	**Iris Blanc**	**November 2, 2003 6:26 PM**
Inserted assigned to conference tasks	**Iris Blanc**	**November 2, 2003 6:26 PM**
Deleted print	**Iris Blanc**	**November 2, 2003 6:26 PM**
Comment [isb3] All members of the production team should read this document.	**Iris Blanc**	**November 2, 2003 9:56 AM**
Header and footer changes (none)		
Text Box changes (none)		
Header and footer text box changes (none)		
Footnote changes (none)		
Endnote changes (none)		

Figure 3.41 Printed list of document edits

TRY *it* OUT *w3-18*

1. Open **w3.18 track changes** from the Data CD.
2. Display the Reviewing toolbar.
3. Click the **Track Changes** button on the toolbar to turn on the feature.
4. Delete the word "executive" in the first sentence.
5. Italicize the words "must be" in the second sentence.
6. Insert the words `assigned to conference tasks` after the word "staff" in the third sentence.
7. Delete the word "print" in the last sentence.
8. Click the first balloon (Deleted: executive). Click the **Accept Change** button to accept the revision. 
9. Click the last balloon (Deleted: print). Click the **Reject Change** button to reject the revision.
10. Right-click the insertion (assigned to conference tasks) and reject the insertion.
11. Print one copy showing markup.
12. Close the file; do not save.

Compare and Merge Documents

- The *Compare and Merge Documents* feature allows you to:
  - Compare any two documents. The differences between two documents are shown as tracked changes.
  - Merge the changes and/or comments from multiple reviewers into a single document. You can then review each change from the single document.
- To compare and merge documents, open the edited copy of the document and click Tools, Compare and Merge Documents. In the Compare and Merge Documents dialog box that appears, as shown in Figure 3.42, click the original document and click the Merge list arrow. Choose one of the following:
  - Merge—to display the results of the comparison in the original document.
  - Merge into current document—to display the results in the currently opened document.
  - Merge into new document—to display the results in a new document.

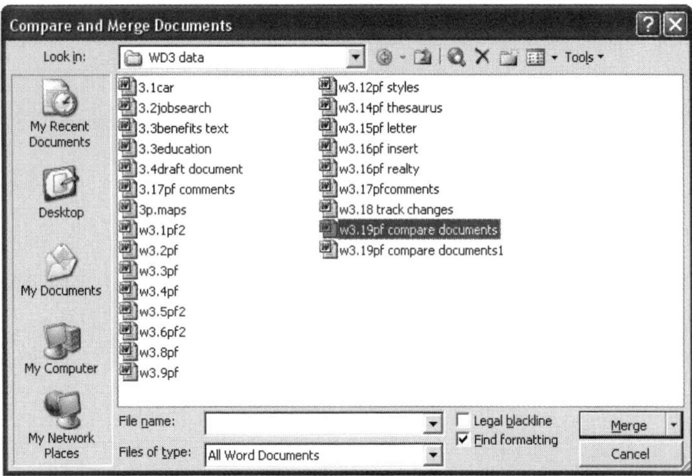

Figure 3.42 Compare and Merge Documents dialog box

- After you have completed the compare and merge process, Word displays the differences between the documents, as shown in Figure 3.43. A comment box to the right of the text indicates what deletions were made; insertions are noted as underlined text. The Reviewing toolbar also appears, to make working with edits easier. You can view the original document showing markups by clicking the Display for Review button on the Reviewing toolbar and then selecting Original Showing Markup.
- To accept or reject an edit, right-click the edit, and click Accept Insertion or Reject Insertion (or Deletion) from the shortcut menu that appears.

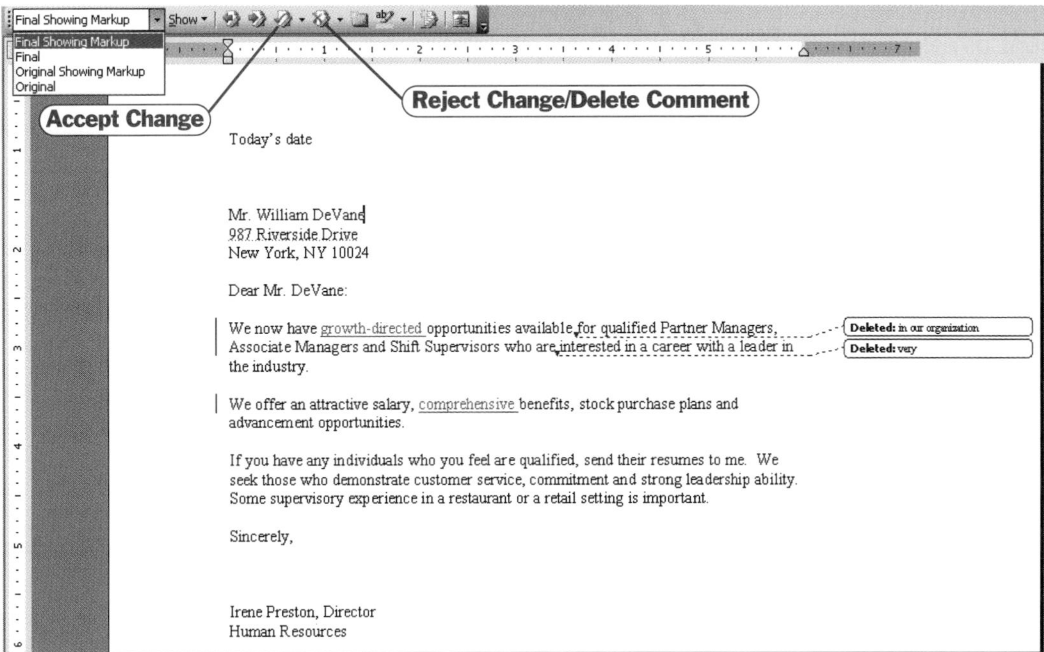

Figure 3.43 Results of comparing and merging documents

TRY *it* OUT *w3-19*

1. Open **w3.19pf compare documents** from the Data CD.
2. Save the file; name it **w3.19compare documents1.**
3. Make the following changes to the document:
   - Insert `growth-directed` before "opportunities" in the first sentence.
   - Delete "in our organization" in the first sentence.
   - Delete "very" in the first sentence.
   - Insert `comprehensive` before "benefits" in the second sentence.
4. Save the file; do not close.
5. Click **Tools, Compare and Merge Documents.**
6. Select the original document, **w3.19pf compare documents,** from the Data CD.
7. Click the Merge list arrow and choose **Merge into new document.** Notice the results of your compare and merge operation.
8. Right-click each edit and accept the change.
9. Close all files; do not save.

Word Count and Document Summary

- When working on a long document, you might want to know how many words, characters, paragraphs, and/or lines it contains—particularly if you have a page or word limit for the document. The *Word Count* feature calculates the pages, characters, paragraphs, and lines in a document or in the selected text. The insertion point can be anywhere in the document when you use this feature.
- To access this feature, position the insertion point anywhere in the document or select specifc text and click Tools, Word Count. The Word Count dialog box appears, as shown in Figure 3.44, displaying the statistics for the document.
- The Properties feature allows you to save summary information with each document. The information includes the document title, subject, author, keywords, and comments.

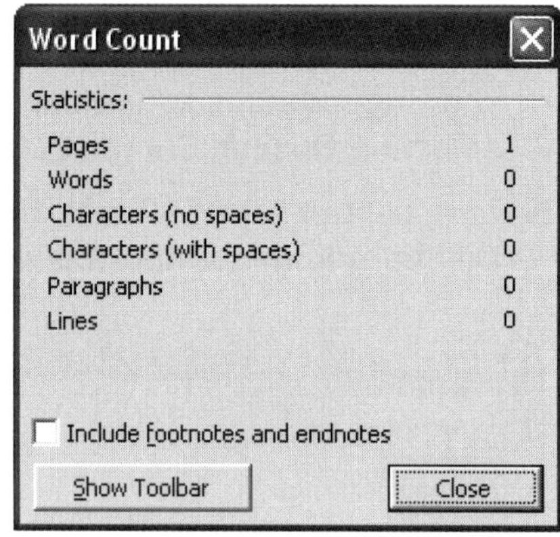

Figure 3.44 Word Count dialog box

- You can create, display, and edit summary information at any time by selecting File, Properties. In the Document Properties dialog box that displays, click the Summary tab, shown in Figure 3.45, and enter summary information about your document.
- Clicking the Statistics tab will give you statistics for your document—the same information that you received using the Word Count feature.

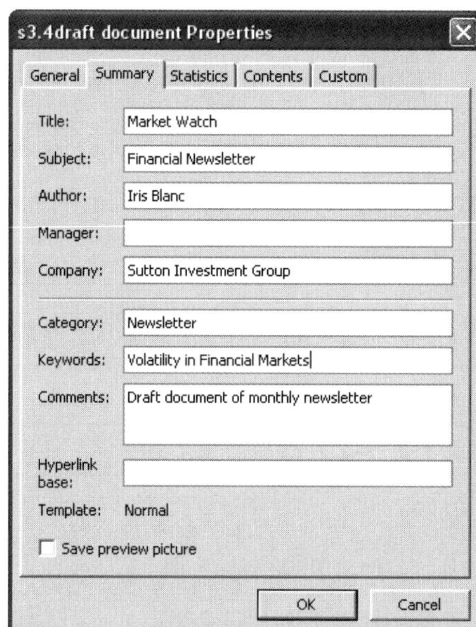

Figure 3.45 Document Properties dialog box

TRY *it* OUT *w3-20*

1. Open **w3.20pf compare documents** from the Data CD.
2. Click **File, Properties.**
3. Click the **Statistics** tab. Note the information contained on this page. Write down the number of words in the letter.
4. Click the **Summary** tab.
5. Enter the following summary information about this document:
   - Title: `Letter to Mr. DeVane`
   - Subject: `Employment Opportunities`
   - Author: `Your name`
   - Manager: `Your supervisor or teacher's name`
   - Company: `Your company or school name`
   - Category: `Human Resources`
   - Keywords: `Partner Managers, Associate Managers`
   - Comments: `We will send this letter to selected candidates.`
6. Click **OK.**
7. Click **Tools, Word Count.** Note that the statistics for the document are the same as those on the Statistics tab of the Document Properties dialog box.
8. Close the file; do not save.

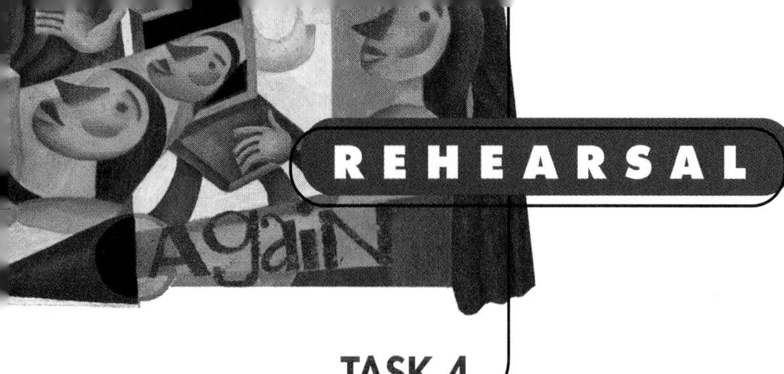

GOAL
To edit a document

SETTING THE STAGE/WRAPUP
Margins: Default
Start line: At 1"

WHAT YOU NEED TO KNOW

- In this Rehearsal activity, you will edit a document using Comments and the Track Changes and Compare and Merge Documents features. You will have another opportunity to apply the previous concepts learned to this document.

DIRECTIONS

1. Open **3.4draft document** from the Data CD.
2. Save the file as **3.4draft document1.**
3. Turn **Track Changes** on.
4. Edit the document as shown on the facing page by doing the following:
   a. Cut "Draft" from the document, and paste it as a header.
   b. Insert text shown as underlined; delete text shown as strikethrough.
   c. Change the font size of "Market Watch" to **26 point;** change the font color to **dark blue.**
   d. Change the font size of "Sutton Investment Group" and "Financial Newsletter" to **16 point.**
   e. Apply paragraph shading to each line of the title as shown using any shade of **blue.**
   f. Change the first side heading, "Volatility in Financial Markets…." to **14 point;** change the font color to **medium blue.** (This style will appear in your style list.)
   g. Apply the style you created for the first side heading to the remaining side headings.
   h. Set the line spacing for each paragraph to **double.**
   i. Set a **0.5"** first-line indent for the paragraph text.
   j. Set a **0.5"** left indent for the Year-to-Date information.
   k. Add a centered footer as shown; use any font size and style.
5. Insert a comment at the end of the first paragraph that reads, `"Rewrite the paragraph to more accurately reflect the time of this event."`
6. Save the file as **3.4edited draft.**
7. Compare and merge **3.4draft document1** with **3.4edited draft.**

Continued on next page

8. Print one copy of the merged document showing markups.
9. Accept all the changes.
10. Enter summary information for the document and determine the document statistics.
11. Print a final copy.
12. Close all files; do not save.

Draft

Market Watch
Sutton Investment Group
Financial Newsletter

Volatility in Financial Markets Seen as Opportunity by Many

Most people would agree that the U.S. economy was doing well, showing consistently high earnings, low interest rates, falling unemployment, and low inflation. Then in late October, the Down Jones Industrial Average plunged. For the first time the New York Stock Exchange used the "circuit breakers" it built after the 1987 crash, shutting trading twice during the course of the day and night. It was the largest single-day point-drop in history and the twelfth largest in percentage terms.

The market sell off resulted from the currency crisis in the Asian markets. This reprising has potentially far reaching effects for the world's emerging and developed markets. At Market Watch, we did not see any panic selling, nor did we receive any panicked inquiries from our clients.

Year-to-Date Investment Results of Profit Sharing

Fixed-Income Fund: 8.1%
Diversified Fund: 15.2%
Equity Fund: 26.5%
International Equity Fund: 1.6%
Money Market Fund: 4.7%

Latin American Real Estate Conference

In the largest Latin American real estate transaction this year, Market Watch advised Argentina's Desmo Company on the sale of its real estate subsidiary. Martin Walters and Diane Realto of the Real Estate Group discussed the deal and the globalization of the real estate industry with investors, developers, and real estate owners at the Latin American Real Estate Conference in Miami. Walters described a growing demand for office, retail, industrial, and residential space throughout Latin America.

Market Watch
Sutton Investment Group
Financial Newsletter

Volatility in Financial Markets Seen as Opportunity by Many

Most people would agree that the U.S. economy was doing very well, showing consistently high earnings, low interest rates, falling unemployment, and low inflation. Then in late October, the Dow~~n~~ Jones Industrial Average plunged. For the first time the New York Stock Exchange used the "circuit breakers" it built after the 1987 crash, shutting down trading twice during the course of the day and night. It was the largest single-day point-drop in history and the twelfth largest in percentage terms.

The market sell-off resulted from the currency crisis in the Asian markets~~.~~, which caused what many believe to be a fundamental reprising of global risk. This reprising has potentially far reaching effects for the world's emerging and developed markets. At Market Watch, we did not see any panic selling, nor did we receive any panicked inquiries from our clients. In fact, some of our clients were looking for buying opportunities.

Year-to-Date Investment Results of Profit Sharing

Fixed-Income Fund: 8.1%
Diversified Fund: 15.2%
Equity Fund: 26.5%
International ~~Equity~~ Fund: 1.6%
Money Market Fund: 4.7%

Sutton Investment Group
Financial Newsletter
Spring 2005

Latin American Real Estate Conference

In the largest Latin American real estate transaction this year, Market Watch advised Argentina's Desmo Company on the sale of its real estate subsidiary. Martin Walters and Diane Realto of the Real Estate Group discussed the deal ~~and the globalization~~ of the real estate industry with investors, developers, and real estate owners at the Latin American Real Estate Conference in Miami. Walters described a growing demand for office, retail, industrial, and residential space throughout Latin America. The conference proved to be a huge success.

Sutton Investment Group
Financial Newsletter
Spring 2005

Cues for Reference

Comments

Insert

1. Switch to Print layout view.
2. Click in the document where the comment will appear, or select the text on which you want to comment.
3. Click **Insert, Comment.**
4. Enter your comment in the comment balloon.

Delete

- Right-click the **comment balloon** and click **Delete Comment.**

Edit

- Click in the comment balloon or in the Reviewing pane and edit the text as appropriate.

Track Changes While Editing

1. Open the document you want to revise.
2. Click **Tools, Track Changes.**

or

1. Open the document you want to revise.
2. Click the **Track Changes** button 

Review Tracked Changes and Comments

1. Display Markup (click **View, Markup**).
2. Do one of the following:

Review each item in sequence:

1. On the Reviewing Toolbar, click the **Next** or **Previous** button.
2. Click the **Accept Change** or **Reject Change/Delete Comment** button. 

Accept all changes at once

- Click the arrow next to Accept Change, and then click **Accept All Changes in Document.**

Reject all changes or delete all comments at once

- Click the arrow next to Reject Change/Delete Comment. Do one of the following:
  - Click **Reject All Changes in Document.**
  - Click **Delete All Comments in Document.**

Compare and Merge Documents

1. Open the edited copy of the document.
2. Click **Tools, Compare and Merge Documents.**
3. Click the original document in the dialog box.
4. Click the **Merge list arrow** and choose a Merge to option.
5. Right-click each edit and either accept or reject the change.

Word Count

1. Click **Tools.**
2. Click **Word Count.**
3. Click the **Close** button. 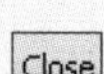

Document Summary

1. Open a document.
2. Click **File, Properties.**
3. Click the **Summary** tab.
4. Enter relevant summary information.
5. Click **OK.**

SETTING THE STAGE
Act I File name: **3p.travel guide**
Act II File names: **3p.travel guide1**
3p.guide cover

WHAT YOU NEED TO KNOW

Act I

You work in the Marketing Department at Air Land Sea Travel Group in New York. Your company is planning to update Travel Guide 2005, a handbook that contains practical information for the traveler. Your company plans to give this handbook to customers who use your company for their travel needs.

You have been asked to create and format the four pages of text shown on this page and the following pages. These pages will become part of the updated handbook. *Note: The text is shown unformatted. After applying formatting, the text may span five or six pages, depending on the font sizes and styles you choose.*

Follow these guidelines:

For the document

- The handbook is going to be bound on the left side, so set the margins accordingly.
- Create a header and/or footer that includes the name of the document and your company name. Format the header and/or footer using any font, color, alignment, and so on.
- Include page numbers and position them as you prefer. The page numbers may be part of the header/footer text.

For pages 1–3

- Create or modify styles to format the headings, short quotes, author's name, and body text, shown on pages 1, 2, and 3. You can design the styles for the headings, short quotes, and body text using any desired formatting.

PACKING: THE CHECKLIST OF ESSENTIALS

"We were very tired, we were very merry—
We had gone back and forth all night on the ferry."
Edna St. Vincent Millay

❑ adapter
❑ alarm
❑ binoculars
❑ camera with batteries and film
❑ credit cards
❑ driver's license
❑ earplugs
❑ flashlight
❑ guidebooks
❑ hanger
❑ itineraries
❑ laundry bag
❑ lock
❑ maps
❑ money belt
❑ passport
❑ pen
❑ plastic bags
❑ safety pins
❑ sewing kit
❑ sleeping bag
❑ sunglasses
❑ swimsuit
❑ traveler's checks
❑ travel iron
❑ umbrella
❑ walking shoes

You might consider taking other things with you such as a small photo album, chewing gum, picture postcards from home (to show other people you meet where you come from), a calling card, and small packaged snacks (in case you get hungry and are nowhere near food

PACKING TIPS

"She who travels lightest travels without shoulder pain."
Robin Mason

- Keep your color scheme simple.
- Select everything you think you should bring – then eliminate half.
- Fold delicate clothing in plastic bags to avoid wrinkles.
- Keep accessories to a bare minimum.
- Do not bring jewelry or other valuables.

DRESS

"Travel broadens the mind."
Elizabeth Winston

Be aware of dress standards in the countries you visit. In much of the world, women's dress codes are different from those in Western countries. For example, in Turkey short skirts are considered disrespectful. In Morocco, shorts are considered disrespectful. In Singapore, torn T-shirts are considered disrespectful. In many countries, you will not be able to enter places of worship if you are not dressed properly. This is particularly true in Muslim countries. In strict Muslim countries such as Iran, you may even be forced to cover up.

page 1

For page 1

- Use columns for the checklist shown.
- Use a square symbol preceding each checklist item.

For page 3

- Use columns for the Currencies and Languages of Popular Destinations information.
- Insert the missing currency and language information using the Internet. Go to www.infoplease.com, click on World, click Countries, then click the country name on which you need to gather the missing information.

For page 4

- Use hanging indents for the References listed.
- Save the file as **3p.travel guide.**
- Print one copy.

Optional: Create a page that contains a list of those words and phrases you think are important when traveling. Then, translate the words/phrases into French, German, and Spanish. Use any desired format to best display this list. Provide an appropriate page title and insert this page to become the fifth page of the travel guide.

ON THE PLANE

"It was a delightful visit—perfect, in being much too short."
Jane Austen

Dress in layers. Cabin temperature can change often on long flights. One minute you're cold; the next minute you're warm.

Dress comfortably. Wear loose-fitting clothing and comfortable shoes. Don't wear shoes that won't let your feet breathe – your feet tend to swell on a long flight.

Drink plenty of water. Cabin air is very dry and will cause dehydration. Avoid caffeine, because it can also cause dehydration.

Move around. Walk up and down the aisles periodically; flex your feet and stretch to keep your blood circulating. This will prevent cramping in your arms and legs.

Sleep before, during, and after the flight. Try to book a flight that gets in at bedtime to help you beat jet lag.

TRAVEL DO'S AND DON'TS

"Know before you go."
Alice Weston

- ***China*** – Avoid wearing blue and white. These are the colors of mourning.
- ***Columbia*** – It is impolite to yawn in public.
- ***Fiji*** – Folded arms are considered disrespectful.
- ***Greece and Bulgaria*** – A head nod means "no."
- ***Iceland*** – Giving a tip is considered insulting.
- ***Saudi Arabia*** – Tipping a taxi driver is expected.
- ***Taiwan*** – Blinking is considered impolite.
- ***New Zealand*** – Tipping is not customary; your tip may be refused.

SAFETY TIPS

"Travel is the most private of pleasures."
Latifa Roberts

- Travel light.
- Insure your belongings.
- Keep an eye on your luggage and lock it up.
- Keep your valuables and important documents with you at all times.
- Keep photocopies of important documents such as passport and visas in a separate bag from the original documents themselves. Leave a copy at home.
- Lock rental cars and hotel rooms.
- In crowds, carry your purse, camera, and other valuables in front of you and hold on to them securely.

page 2

CURRENCIES AND LANGUAGES OF POPULAR DESTINATIONS

"We all ended up with our pockets full of foreign coins."

Kate Emily

Country
Currency
Language

Australia
Dollar
English

Austria
?
German

Belgium
?
?

Brazil
Real
Portuguese

Bulgaria
Lev
Bulgarian

Canada
Dollar
English, French

Chile
?
?

China
Yuan
Chinese dialects

Colombia
Peso
Spanish

Cuba
Peso
Spanish

Czech Republic
Koruny
Czech

Denmark
Kroner
Danish

Egypt
Egyptian Pound
Arabic

Finland
Markka
Finnish, Swedish

France
?
French

Germany
Euro
German

Greece
?
Greek

Hungary
Forint
Hungarian

Ireland
Euro
Irish, English

Israel
Shekel
Hebrew, Arabi

Italy
Euro
Italian

Japan
Yen
Japanese

Luxembourg
Euro
French, Germa

Mexico
Peso
Spanish

Netherlands
Euro
Dutch, Frisian

Russia
Ruble
Russian

Sweden
Krona
Swedish

Switzerland
Franc
German, French, Italian

United Kingdom
Pound
English

page 3

REFERENCES

Axtell, Roger E. *Do's and Taboos Around the World.* John Wiley & Sons, 1993.

Brandenburger, Caroline. *The Traveler's Handbook: The Essential Guide for International Travelers,* 6th ed., Globe Pequot Press, 1994.

Fairechilde, Diana. *Jet Smart,* Celestial Arts, 1994.

Gilford, Judith. *The Packing Book,* Ten Speed Press, 1994.

White, Linda. *The Independent Woman's Guide to Europe,* Fulcrum Publishing, 1991.

Zepatos, Thalia. *Adventures in Good Company: The Complete Guide to Tours and Outdoor Trips,* Eighth Mountain Press, 1999.

page 4

Act II

Your boss is very pleased with the development of the *Travel Guide 2005* handbook so far. She has given you a file that contains maps of Europe, South America, and Asia and has asked you to insert them as the last three pages of the guide. She has also asked you to create a title page for the handbook.

Follow these guidelines:

- Open **3p.travel guide** that you completed in Act I.
- Insert the file **3p.maps** from the Data CD as the last three pages.
- Create a heading for each of the newly inserted pages.
- Format the headings on these pages to be consistent with the subheadings on the other pages.
- Save the file as **3p.travel guide1.**
- Print one copy.
- For the title page, include the following:

  Air Land Sea Travel Group
  505 Park Avenue
  New York, NY 10010
  Phone: 212-555-5555
  Fax: 212-666-6767
  Email: als@net.com

  - The name of the handbook.
  - A page border.
  - Borders and shading around the text as you prefer.

Note: Use the same fonts and colors on the title page that you used for the handbook. Set font sizes as you prefer.

- Vertically center the title page text.
- Save the file; name it **3p.guide cover.**
- Print one copy.

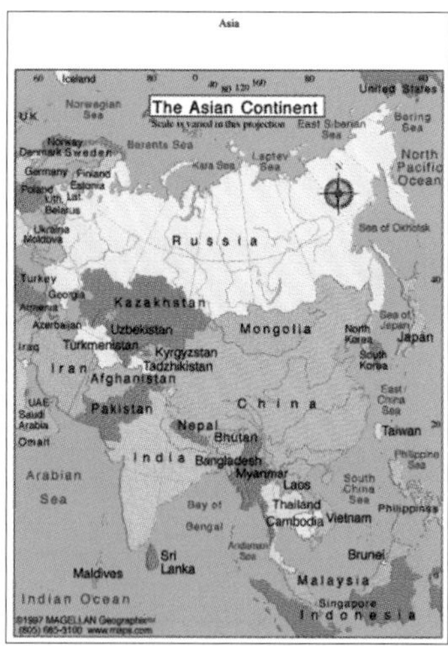

1
2
3

LESSON 4

Meeting Documents, Schedules, and Forms

In this lesson, you will learn to use the features found in Word to create meeting documents, schedules, and forms that typically organize information using an outline and/or table format.

Meeting documents include those that are used to prepare for a meeting, such as an agenda, a program, and minutes. Schedules include documents that list dates, times, and events. Forms are documents that contain fill-in blanks in which you enter information. (This lesson will focus on forms that are printed, then filled in on paper; creating online forms will be covered in Advanced Word, Lesson 10).

You will complete the following projects in this lesson:

- An outline of an agenda
- An agenda
- Minutes of a meeting
- An itinerary
- A schedule
- An employment form
- A letter with an inserted table

Upon completion of this lesson, you should have mastered the following skill sets:

- Create an outline
  - Edit an outline
  - Create an outlined numbered list
- Create a table and enter text
- Convert text to a table
- Modify a table
  - Change column width
  - Add/delete columns and rows
- Format a table
  - Align data within cells
  - Set row height
  - Apply borders and shading
  - Use AutoFormat
- Set and modify tabs
  - With leaders
  - Within table cells

Terms

Software-related

- Outline
- Table
- Rows
- Columns
- Cells
- Tabs
- Custom tabs
- Leader

Document-related

- Agenda
- Minutes
- Form
- Itinerary
- Schedule

GOAL
To practice using the following skill sets:

- Create an outline
- Edit an outline
- Create an outlined numbered list

WHAT YOU NEED TO KNOW

Create an Outline

- An *outline* is used to organize information in a hierarchical structure.
- Outlines are composed of levels and sublevels. Word's Outline feature automatically formats each level differently. You can create up to nine outline levels.
- To create an outline, click the Outline View button at the bottom of the document window or click View, Outline. When you switch to Outline view, the Outlining toolbar, shown in Figure 4.1, appears. The Outlining toolbar contains buttons to make working with outlines easier.

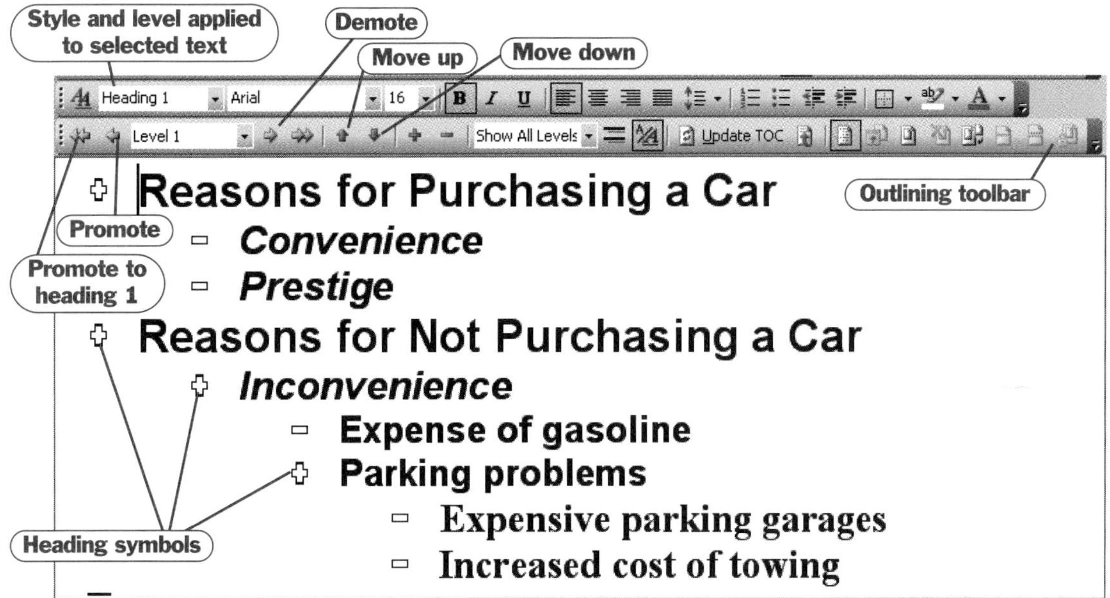

Figure 4.1 Text entered in Outline view

- When you enter text in Outline view, Word applies a style for each level. The Heading 1 style is applied to the first line of text you enter. When you press the Enter and Tab keys to advance to the next level, Word applies a Heading 2 style. The level is indicated on the Outlining toolbar, and the style is indicated on the Formatting toolbar (see Figure 4.1).
- Each level is preceded by a heading symbol. A plus sign (✚) indicates that subtext follows the heading; a minus sign (▭) indicates that no subtext follows the heading. Heading symbols do not print.

▶ Use the Tab key or click the Demote button on the Outlining toolbar to advance to the next-lower level. Click the Promote button to convert text to a higher-level heading (from Level 3 to Level 2, for example).

TRY *it* OUT *w4-1*

Note: See Figure 4.1 for the sample outline.

1. Start **Word.**
2. Click the **New Blank Document** button.

3. Click the **Outline View** button.

4. Enter the Level 1 heading:
   `Reasons for Purchasing a Car`
5. Press the **Enter** key and the **Tab** key.
6. Enter the Level 2 heading: `Convenience` and press the **Enter** key.
7. Enter the next Level 2 heading: `Prestige` and press the **Enter** key.
8. Click the **Promote to Heading 1** button.

9. Enter the next Level 1 heading:
   `Reasons for Not Purchasing a Car`
10. Press the **Enter** key and the **Tab** key.
11. Enter the Level 2 heading:
    `Inconvenience`
12. Press the **Enter** key and the **Tab** key.
13. Enter the Level 3 heading: `Expense of gasoline` and press the **Enter** key.
14. Enter the next Level 3 heading: `Parking problems` then press the **Enter** key.
15. Press the **Demote** button and enter: `Expensive parking garages.`

16. Press the **Enter** key.
17. Enter: `Increased cost of towing.`
18. Save the file; name it **4.1pf outline.**
19. Do not close the file.

Edit an Outline

- You can easily restructure or edit an outline in Outline view. To move a heading up or down without affecting the level, position the insertion point on the line you want to move and click the Move Up or Move Down button on the Outlining toolbar. When you use this procedure, only the heading itself moves up or down; any subtext below the heading remains in its original position.
- To move a heading as well as the subtext below it, select the heading symbol, then click the Move Up or Move Down button. You can also select and drag the heading symbol to its new location. When you drag text, the mouse pointer changes to a two-headed arrow, and a guideline moves with the mouse to assist you in positioning the heading, as shown in Figure 4.2.

Reasons for Purchasing a Car
- Convenience
- Prestige

Reasons for Not Purchasing a Car
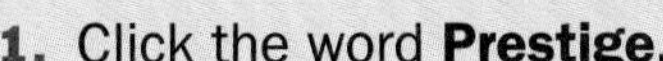
- *Inconvenience*
  - **Expense of gasoline**
  - **Parking problems**
    - **Expensive parking garages**
    - **Increased cost of towing**

Figure 4.2 Moving text in Outline view

TRY*it*OUT *w4-2*

Note: **4.1pf outline** *should be displayed on your screen.*

1. Click the word **Prestige.**
2. Click the **Move Up** button to move the heading up one line.
3. Position the insertion point on the plus heading symbol to the left of "Reasons for Not Purchasing a Car."
4. Drag the heading symbol (and the text below it) to become the first heading.
5. Print one copy.
6. Close the file; do not save.

Create an Outline Numbered List

▶ The outline you created in Outline view does not contain numbered or lettered topics and subtopics found in a traditional outline. You can create a traditional outline in Normal view or Print Layout view using the Outline Numbered List feature. This method displays numbered or lettered items at different levels, as shown in Figure 4.3.

1) Reasons for Purchasing a Car
    a) Convenience
    b) Prestige
2) Reasons for Not Purchasing a Car
    a) Inconvenience
        i) Expense of gasoline
        ii) Parking problems
            (1) Expensive parking garages
            (2) Increased cost of towing

Figure 4.3 Outline numbered list

▶ To create an outline numbered list, click Format, Bullets and Numbering. In the Bullets and Numbering dialog box that appears, shown in Figure 4.4, click the Outline Numbered tab, then select a numbering style that does not contain the text "heading." Click OK.

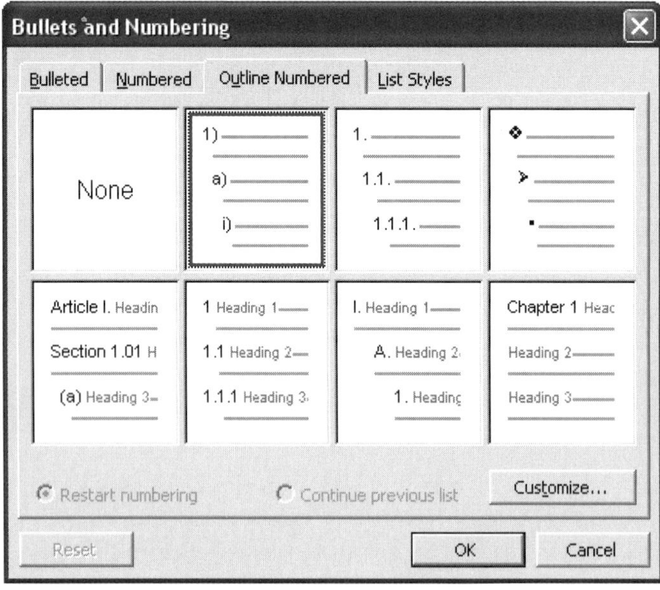

Figure 4.4 Outline Numbered tab on Bullets and Numbering dialog box

▶ Use the Tab key or the Increase Indent button on the Formatting toolbar to advance text to the next-lower level. Use the Decrease Indent button to return to a higher level.

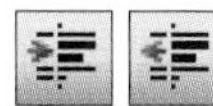

- You can also convert an Outline created in Outline view to an outline numbered list. This provides you with a traditional outline but also allows you to restructure the levels as you did when in Outline view. Figure 4.5 shows an outline created in Outline view that was converted into a numbered list.
- To convert an outline to a numbered list, display the outline in Outline view and select the entire outline. On the Outlined Numbered tab in the Bullets and Numbering dialog box, select a numbered list that contains the word "heading." *Note: In Print Layout or Normal views, the converted outline will display with paragraph spacing. To remove the spacing, change the Before and After paragraph settings in the Paragraph dialog box.*

I. Reasons for Purchasing a Car
- ***A. Convenience***
- ***B. Prestige***

II. Reasons for Not Purchasing a Car
- ***A. Inconvenience***
  - **1. Expense of gasoline**
  - **2. Parking problems**
    - **a) Expensive parking garages**
    - **b) Increased cost of towing**

Figure 4.5 Outline converted into a numbered list

TRY*it*OUT *w4-3*

1. Click the **New Blank Document** button.
2. Click the **Normal View** button.

3. Click **Format, Bullets and Numbering.**
4. Click the **Outline Numbered** tab.
5. Click the first outline on the left of the top row. *Note: This outline does not include numbers.*
   a. Create the outline shown in Figure 4.3.

   b. Press the **Enter** key, and click the **Increase Indent** button to enter the next lower level.

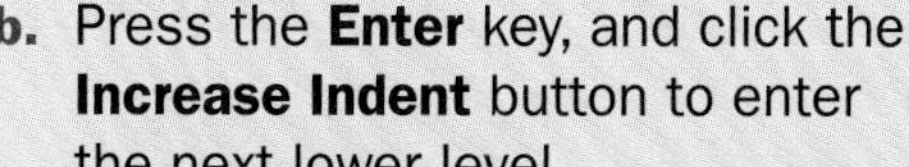

   c. Press the **Decrease Indent** button to enter a higher level.
6. Close the file; do not save.
7. Open **w4.3 outline** from the Data CD. (You should now be in Outline view.)

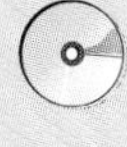

8. Select the entire outline.
9. Click **Format, Bullets and Numbering.**
10. Click the **Outline Numbered** tab.
11. Click the third outline on the bottom row (this should convert your outline to include outline numbers) and click **OK**.
12. Swtich to Print Layout view. Note that the Outline displays with paragraph spacing.
13. Close the file; do not save.

GOAL
To create and edit an agenda in an outline format

SETTING THE STAGE/WRAPUP
Margins: Default
Start line: At 1"
File names: **4.1inshape**
4.1inshape1

WHAT YOU NEED TO KNOW

- An *agenda* is a plan, or a list of things to be done, events to occur, or matters to bring before a committee, council, or board.
- The format of an agenda can vary, but is usually created as an outline. Regardless of the format used, an agenda always includes the date and time and sometimes the location of the planned activities.
- In this Rehearsal activity, you will create an agenda. You will format it in Outline view so you can modify it. You will then prepare it for distribution using the outline numbered list.

DIRECTIONS

1. Click the **New Blank Document** button. 
2. Switch to Outline view.
3. Create the agenda, as shown in Illustration A on the facing page.
4. Save the file; name it **4.1inshape.**
5. Move the "Company Mission" heading and its subtext after the subtext below "Overview."
6. Insert the following comment after the words "Employee Benefits": `Check to see if we are still offering GHI.`
7. Delete the comment. Delete **GHI** from the outline.
8. Save the changes; do not close the document.
9. Create the agenda as an outline numbered list, as shown in Illustration B on the facing page. Do the following:
   a. Select an Outline numbered format from the **Outlined Numbered** tab in the Bullets and Numbering dialog box. Use a traditional outline that contains the word "Heading."
   b. Switch to Print Layout view.
10. Remove the spacing between paragraphs. Do the following:
    a. Select the outline.
    b. Click **Format, Paragraph**, then select the Indents and Spacing tab.
    c. Change the Before and After paragraph spacing to "0."
11. Enter the following as a header using a 12-point sans serif font. Set "In-Shape Fitness Centers" and "Agenda" to bold.

Continued on next page

Illustration A

Welcome
Overview
- ***Company history***
  - **Started by Jonathan Treadmill**
  - **Began as a weight-training facility**
  - **Diversified into full-service fitness centers**
- ***Organizational structure***
- ***Company mission***
- ***Sales trends***
- ***Employee benefits***
- ***Questions and answers***

In-Shape Fitness Centers
- ***Robert Treadmill Jr., President***
- ***Wendy Loria, Vice President***
- ***Ben Chasin, Finance***
- ***Matt Asher, Customer Service***
- ***Pamela Young, Fitness Consultant***

Company Mission
- ***To design high-quality fitness centers throughout the United States***
- ***To maintain high-quality customer service at all centers***

Sales Trends
Employee Benefits
- ***Health benefits***
  - **Life insurance**
  - **Medical, dental, optical**
  - **GHI**
  - **Major medical**
- ***Commissions and Bonus***
- ***Vacation and Sick Leave***
  - **Vacation: 2 weeks after 12 months**
  - **Sick leave: 2.5 days earned each month**
  - **Extra provisions for employees who work winters**

Questions and Answers

In-Shape Fitness Centers
New Employee Orientation Meeting
January 5, 2005
Conference Room D

Agenda

12. Save the file; name it **4.1inshape1.**

13. Print one copy, then close the file.

Illustration B

In-Shape Fitness Centers
New Employee Orientation Meeting
January 5, 2005
Conference Room D

Agenda

I. Welcome
II. Overview
- ***A. Company history***
  - **1. Started by Jonathan Treadmill**
  - **2. Began as a weight-training facility**
  - **3. Diversified into full-service fitness centers**
- ***B. Organizational structure***
- ***C. Company mission***
- ***D. Sales trends***
- ***E. Employee benefits***
- ***F. Questions and answers***

III. Company Mission
- ***A. To design high-quality fitness centers throughout the United States***
- ***B. To maintain high-quality customer service at all centers***

IV. In-Shape Fitness Centers
- ***A. Robert Treadmill Jr., President***
- ***B. Wendy Loria, Vice President***
- ***C. Ben Chasin, Finance***
- ***D. Matt Asher, Customer Service***
- ***E. Pamela Young, Fitness Consultant***

V. Sales Trends
VI. Employee Benefits
- ***A. Health benefits***
  - **1. Life insurance**
  - **2. Medical, dental, optical**
  - **3. Major medical**
- ***B. Commissions and Bonus***
- ***C. Vacation and Sick Leave***
  - **1. Vacation: 2 weeks after 12 months**
  - **2. Sick leave: 2.5 days earned each month**
  - **3. Extra provisions for employees who work winters**

VII. Questions and Answers

Cues for Reference

Create an Outline

1. Click **View, Outline.**
2. Enter first heading, then press **Enter.**
3. Press **Enter** to keep the new heading at the same level as the previous heading.

or

Click the **Demote** button to create a lower-level heading or the **Promote** button to create a higher-level heading.

Create an Outline Numbered List

1. Click **Format**, **Bullets and Numbering**.
2. Click the **Outline Numbered** tab.
3. Select an outline numbered style.

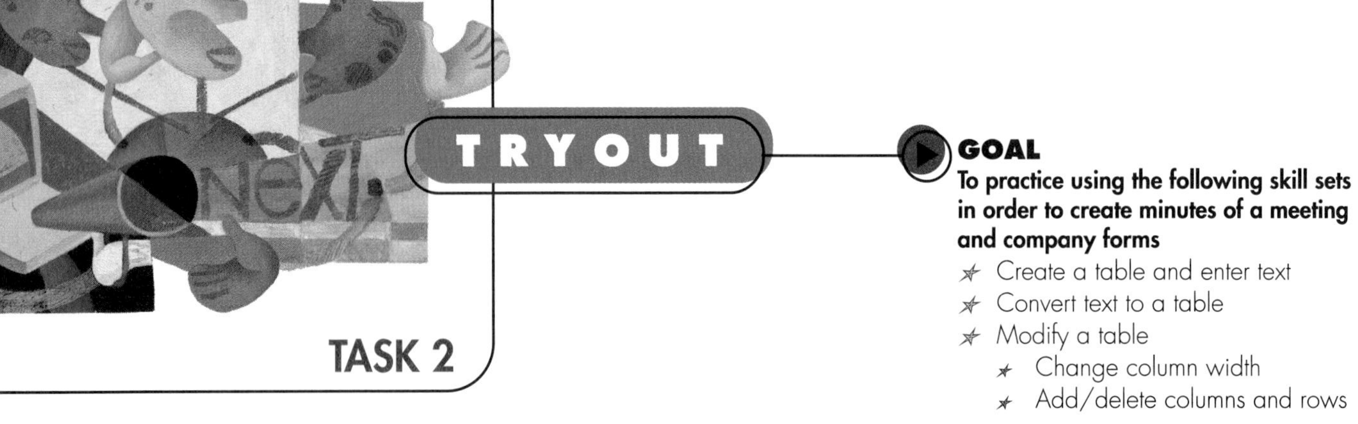

GOAL

To practice using the following skill sets in order to create minutes of a meeting and company forms

- Create a table and enter text
- Convert text to a table
- Modify a table
  - Change column width
  - Add/delete columns and rows

WHAT YOU NEED TO KNOW

Create a Table and Enter Text

- The *Table* feature lets you organize information into columns and rows. *Rows* run horizontally; *columns* run vertically. The rows and columns intersect to form a grid, made up of small boxes called *cells*. Figure 4.6 illustrates a table with three rows and three columns.

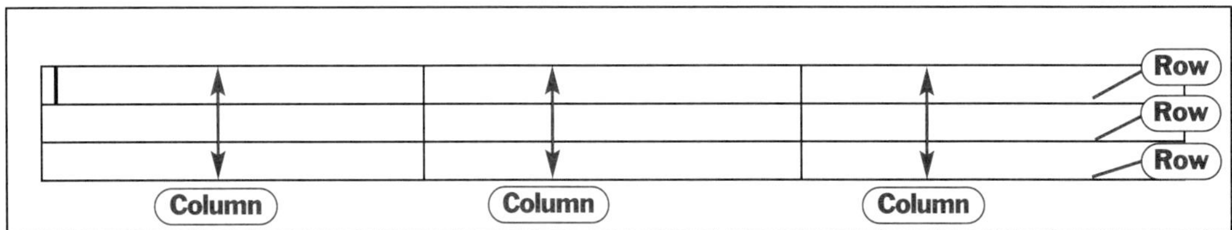

Figure 4.6 Table with three rows and three columns

- To create a table, click Table, Insert, Table. In the Insert Table dialog box that appears, shown in Figure 4.7, enter the number of columns and the number of rows in the appropriate text boxes.
- There is also a quick method to create a table. Click the Insert Table button on the Standard toolbar and drag the mouse to select the desired number of columns and rows, as shown in Figure 4.8.
- Columns automatically adjust to fit between the left and right margins.

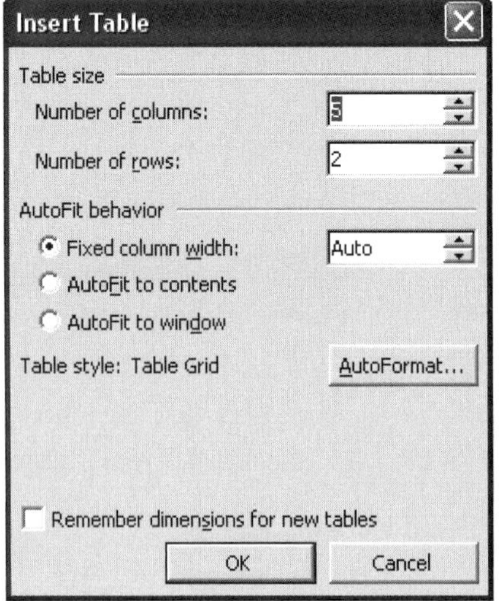

Figure 4.7 Insert Table dialog box

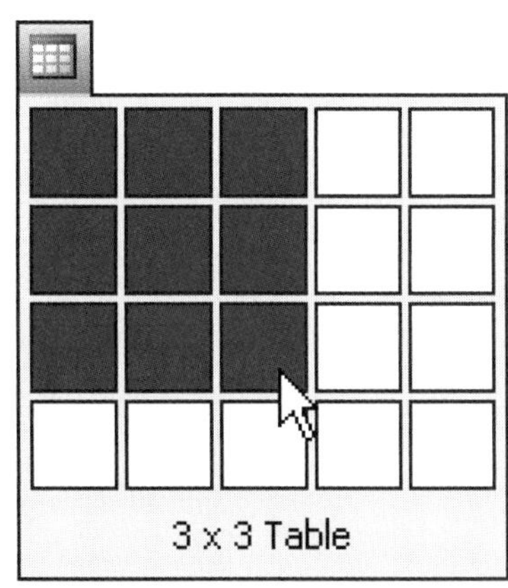

Figure 4.8 Insert Table drop down

- After you create the table, the ruler displays column markers that indicate the left and right boundaries of the table columns, as shown in Figure 4.9.

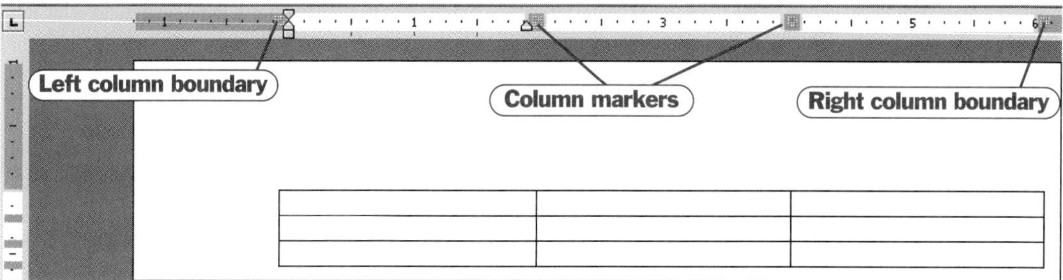

Figure 4.9 Ruler with column markers

- The insertion point moves within a table in the same way it moves within a document. You may use the mouse to click in the appropriate cell, or you may use the Tab key to move to the next cell.
- As you enter text in a table cell, the cell expands to accommodate the text. Pressing the Enter key in a cell expands the cell downward. It does not advance the insertion point to the next cell.

TRY *it* OUT *w4-4*

1. Click the **New Blank Document** button.
2. Click **Table, Insert, Table.**
3. Enter 3 in the Number of columns text box.
4. Use the default (2) for the Number of rows text box, and click **OK.**
5. Enter the following in the first, second, and third cells in the top row. Then, enter the text shown in the first, second, and third cells in the bottom row. Press the **Tab** key to advance from column to column.

First Term	Second Term	Third Term
Pass with Honors	Pass	Pass

6. Close the file; do not save.
7. Open a new blank document.
8. Click the **Insert Table** button on the Standard toolbar.

9. Drag to select three columns and two rows.
10. Enter the same text into the table as indicated in Step 5.
11. Close the file; do not save.

Convert Text to a Table

- You can convert text to a table so that the text is inserted into columns and rows. This is useful when you have typed text that you feel would be better presented in a more organized way.
- To convert text to a table, you must first separate the text with a comma, a tab, or other separator character you designate to indicate where a new column should begin. Use a paragraph mark to indicate where to begin a new row. Figure 4.10 shows text with separator characters, which will be converted into a table.

Debra, Jones, 205 West Street, New York, NY, 10021
Shameka, Roberts, 111 South Avenue, Brooklyn, NY, 11201
Valerie, Savoff, 90 East 18th Street, Bronx, NY, 10498
Steve, Mumolo, 108 West Mission Street, Santa Barbara, CA, 93101

Paragraph marks (invisible) indicate new rows

Commas indicate new columns

Figure 4.10 Text to be converted to a table

- After inserting the appropriate separators and paragraph marks, select the text to be converted and click Table, Convert, Text to Table. In the Convert Text to Table dialog box that displays, shown in Figure 4.11, enter the number of columns you want. Also indicate the separator character and click OK. Figure 4.12 illustrates the result of converting the text shown in Figure 4.10.

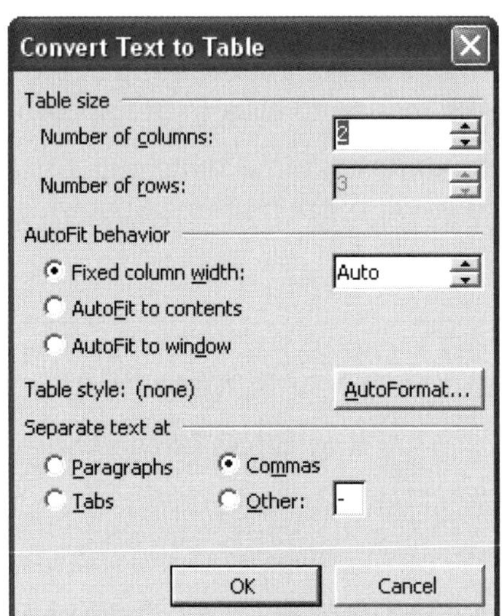

Figure 4.11 Convert Text to Table dialog box

Debra	Jones	205 West Street	New York	NY	10021
Shameka	Roberts	111 South Avenue	Brooklyn	NY	11201
Valerie	Savoff	90 East 18th Street	Bronx	NY	10498
Steve	Mumolo	108 West Mission Street	Santa Barbara	CA	93101

Figure 4.12 Text converted into a table

TRY it OUT *w4-5*

1. Click the **New Blank Document** button.
2. Enter the text shown in Figure 4.10.
3. Select the text.
4. Click **Table, Convert, Text to Table**. Select **Commas** below the *Separate text at* option.

Note the selections in the Convert Text to Table dialog box. The number of columns is automatically inserted based on the number of commas Word detects in your selected text.

5. Click **OK.**
6. Close the file; do not save.

Modify a Table

▶ You can modify a table by changing its column widths or by adding and/or deleting columns and/or rows. You can also modify a table's horizontal position on the page.

Change Column Width

▶ You can change column widths by a specific measurement or by dragging the vertical lines between columns to the desired width.

▶ To change column widths and see the immediate effect of the change on the table, you can:

- Drag a vertical table line left or right to the desired width of the column.
  - > To do this, position the mouse pointer on a vertical line bordering a column. When the pointer changes to the table-sizing arrow, press and hold the mouse button as you drag the dotted line left or right, as shown in Figure 4.13.

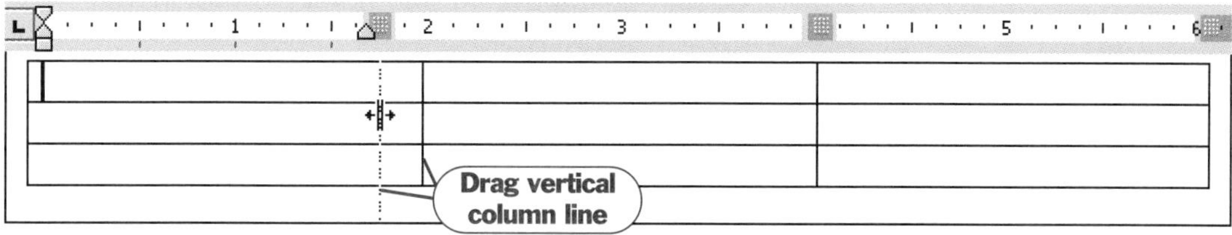

Figure 4.13 Drag vertical column line to change column width

- Drag the column markers on the ruler.
  - > To do this, position the insertion point on the column marker until you see a two-headed arrow. Click and drag the marker to the position you want, as shown in Figure 4.14.

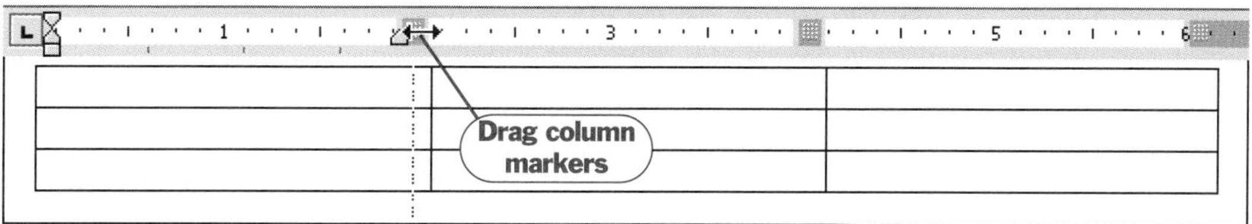

Figure 4.14 Drag column marker to change column width

▶ To adjust column widths using a specific measurement, click in the column or select the columns to affect. Then click Table, Table Properties. In the Table Properties dialog box that appears, shown in Figure 4.15, click the Column tab, and enter the width you want in the Preferred width text box. You can immediately open the Table Properties dialog box by double-clicking on the column markers.

▶ To make columns fit the cell contents, click Table, AutoFit, and AutoFit to Contents.

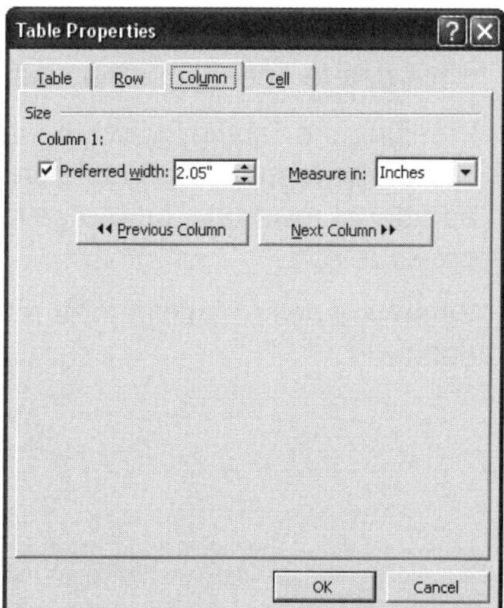

Figure 4.15 Table Properties dialog box

TRY*it*OUT *w4-6*

1. Click the **New Blank Document** button.
2. Click **Table, Insert, Table.**
3. Enter 2 in the Number of columns text box and 3 in the Number of rows text box and click **OK.**
4. Enter your first name in the first cell of the first column and your last name in the first cell of the second column.
5. Position the insertion point on the vertical line until the pointer becomes a two-headed arrow.
6. Drag the line to the left to create a narrow Column 1.
7. Position the insertion point anywhere in the second column.
8. Click **Table, Table Properties.**
9. Click the **Column** tab, enter 1" in the Preferred width text box, then click **OK.**
10. Position the insertion point anywhere in the table.
11. Click **Table, AutoFit,** and **AutoFit to Contents.** *Note that the columns adjusted to fit the longest entries in a column.*
12. Close the file; do not save the changes.

Insert/Delete Columns and/or Rows

- To insert a row, position the insertion point in the table, then click Table, Insert, Rows Above (or Rows Below). A new row is inserted above (or below) the insertion point.
- To insert a column, position the insertion point in a column, then click Table, Insert Columns to the Left (or Columns to the Right). A new column will be inserted to the left (or to the right) of the insertion point. Figure 4.16 shows table insert options on the menu.
- To delete a column, select the column and click Table, Delete Columns, or click the right mouse button and choose Delete Column from the shortcut menu.
- To delete a row, position the insertion point in the row to delete, and click Table, Delete, Rows. Figure 4.17 shows table delete options on the menu.
- Pressing the Tab key when the insertion point is in the last cell of the last row of a table creates additional rows. The additional rows take on the same formatting as the previous row.
- When you delete a column or row, its contents are also deleted.

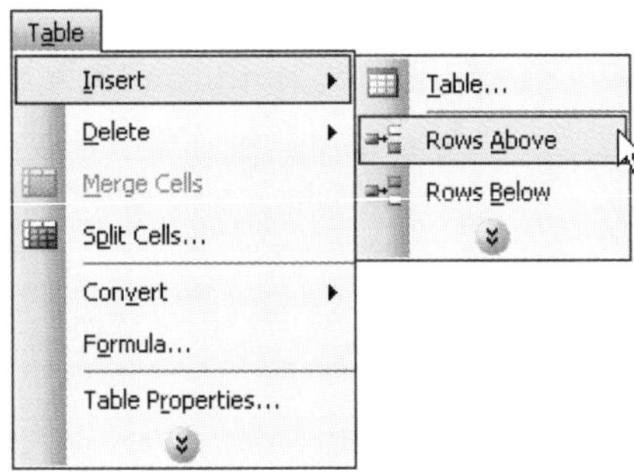

Figure 4.16 Table insert menu options

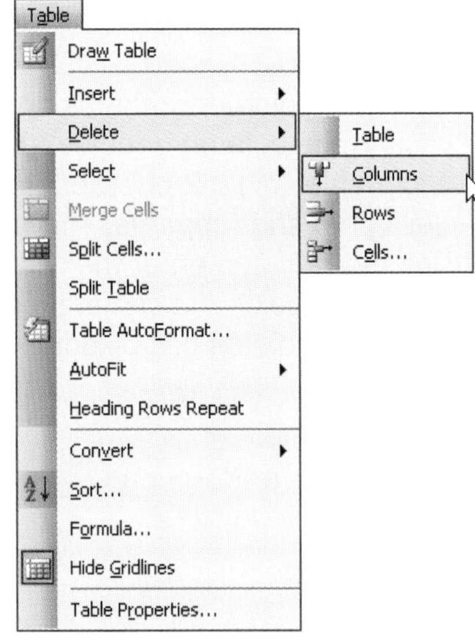

Figure 4.17 Table delete menu options

WORD

Position a Table on a Page

- Word sets columns in a table to spread out evenly between margins, whether the table contains two or ten columns. When you change column width or delete a column, Word keeps the same left margin. This means the table is no longer centered across the page.
- To center the table horizontally, click Table, Table Properties. In the Table Properties dialog box, shown in Figure 4.18, click the Table tab and choose Center alignment. You can also align the table to the left or right of the page by selecting the Left or Right alignment option.

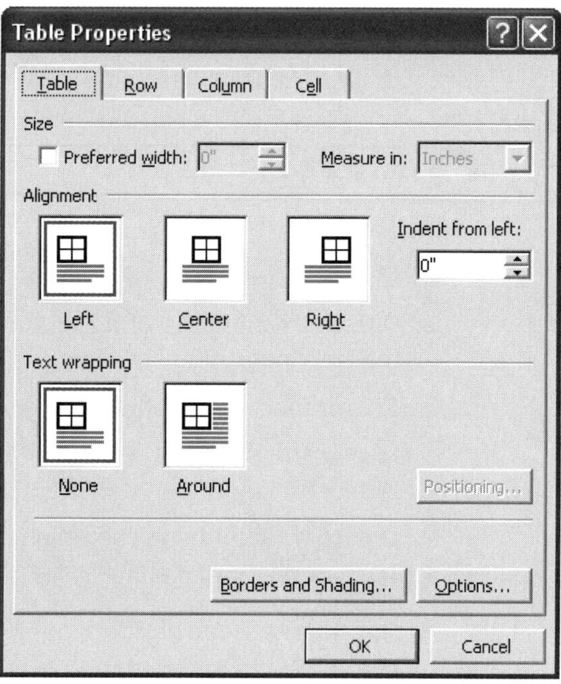

Figure 4.18 Table tab on Table Properties dialog box

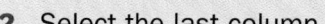

TRY *it* OUT *w4-7*

1. Open **w4.7pf table** from the Data CD.
2. Select the last column.
3. Right-click and select **Delete Columns.**
4. Position the insertion point in the second row ("Annual Appeal").
5. Click **Table, Insert,** and **Rows Above.**
6. Position the insertion point in the last cell of the last row ("107.0").
7. Press **Tab** to create a new row.
8. Position the insertion point in the row containing the word "Benefit."
9. Click **Table, Delete, Rows.**
10. Click **Table, Table Properties.**
11. Click the **Table** tab, click **Center,** and click **OK.** The table should now be horizontally recentered on the page.
12. Close the file; do not save the changes.

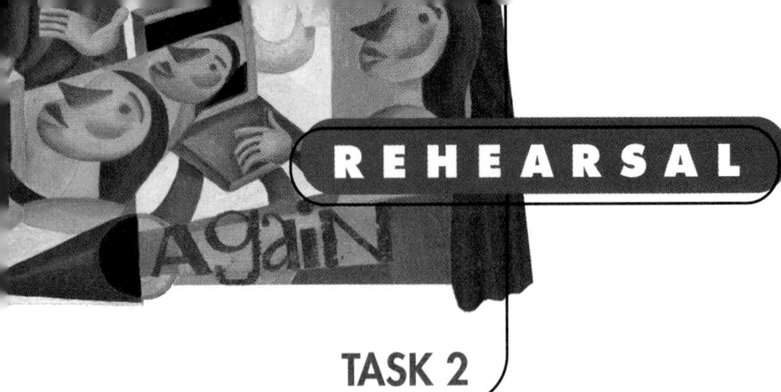

GOAL
To create minutes of a meeting and a company feedback form using a table format

SETTING THE STAGE/WRAPUP

Margins: Default
Start line: At 1"
File names: **4.2minutes**
4.2 feedback form
4.2 feedback form1

WHAT YOU NEED TO KNOW

- *Minutes* are summary points of a meeting. The summary points closely follow the agenda.
- You may use parallel columns to create a list, script, itinerary, minutes of a meeting, or any other document in which text in the left column relates to the text in the right column.

Monday	Meeting with John Smith at 9:00 a.m.
Tuesday	Lunch Appointment with Benjamin Chasin to discuss merger.

To create parallel columns, you must create a two-column table. After entering text in the left-column cell, press the Tab key, and then enter the necessary text in the right-column cell. Remember that the cell expands to accommodate the text.

- Many companies develop *forms* to collect information from their employees. Forms are often printed, filled out on paper, and collected. Some companies use online forms to collect information. This lesson will focus on developing printed forms only.
- In this Rehearsal activity, you will prepare minutes of a meeting and create a printed form. The minutes follow the agenda you prepared in Task 1.

DIRECTIONS

Minutes of a Meeting

1. Click the **New Blank Document** button.
2. Create the minutes of a meeting as shown on the next page.
3. Center the main heading using any 14-point bold font.
4. Center the subhead using any 10-point font. Press the **Enter** key twice after the subhead.
5. Create a table using two columns and 17 rows.
6. Enter the text as shown, using any 10-point font.
7. Set the column width for column 1 to 1.75". Set the column width for column 2 to 4.3".
8. Remove the table borders.
9. Save the file; name it **4.2minutes.**
10. Print one copy.
11. Close the file.

Continued on next page

In-Shape Fitness Centers

New Employee Orientation Meeting
January 5, 2005
Minutes of Meeting

Present	Laurie James, Brian Murphy, Jill Robinson, Chris Powell, Robert Johnson, and Adrian Monroe
Welcome	Laurie welcomed all the new employees and told those in attendance that there would be a follow-up meeting sometime next week.
Overview	Brian told the group what this meeting intended to cover. Among the topics to be included are a company history, organizational structure, company information, sales trends, and employee benefits. Brian explained that there would be ample time for questions and answers.
	Chris distributed a company organizational chart.
Company Mission	Jill explained that the company's mission was to design high-quality fitness centers throughout the United States, but most of all to maintain high-quality customer service at all centers.
In-Shape Fitness Centers	Adrienne introduced the officers of the company.
Sales Trends	Chris gave a detailed explanation of the sales trends and provided the group with a breakout of the most successful centers. Chris explained that the staffing was most critical in the effectiveness of the center.
Employee Benefits	Jill reviewed the company benefits, including health, life insurance, medical, dental, optical, and major medical.
	Robert talked about the commission and bonus structure and explained that for every new person who signed on for a one-year contract, there would be a 10% commission on the total yearly contract. A bonus would be added if five or more people signed on.
	Chris Powell talked about the vacation and sick leave benefits. Each employee would get two weeks after 12 months and 2.5 days earned each month.
	Extra provision would be made for employees who work winters.
Questions and Answers	Participants had 20 minutes for Q and A.
Adjournment	The meeting was adjourned at 11:00 a.m.

Form

1. Click the **New Blank Document** button.
2. Change the page orientation to landscape.
3. Create the company name and document name as shown in Illustration A on page 148.
   a. Use a sans serif 18-point font for the company name. Set the font to bold and the color to blue. Apply paragraph shading using a light blue.

Continued on next page

Illustration A

Delete column

Air Land Sea Travel Group

Supervisor Feedback Form

My Supervisor:	Disagree	Neither Agree Nor Disagree	Agree	No Comment
Treats me fairly	☐	☐	☐	☐
Brings out the best in employees	☐	☐	☐	☐
Treats me with respect	☐	☐	☐	☐
Takes initiative when solving problems	☐	☐	☐	☐
Develops new strategies	☐	☐	☐	☐
Applies policies and regulations fairly	☐	☐	☐	☐
Is skilled in conflict resolution	☐	☐	☐	☐
Develops appropriate solutions	☐	☐	☐	☐
Encourages my development	☐	☐	☐	☐
Communicates effectively	☐	☐	☐	☐

Insert row

   b. Use a sans serif 14-point font for the document name. Apply paragraph shading using a darker blue.

4. Create the feedback form shown using the appropriate number of columns and rows.
   a. Enter the text as shown using any font style; use a 12-point font size.
   b. Use a square symbol for the check boxes in the column (copy one and paste it in each cell).

5. Save the file; name it **4.2feedback form.**

6. Print one copy.

7. Delete the last column.

Continued on next page

4.2feedback form1

Air Land Sea Travel Group

Supervisor Feedback Form

Newly inserted row

Newly inserted row

My Supervisor:			
	Disagree	Neither Agree Nor Disagree	Agree
Treats me fairly	☐	☐	☐
Brings out the best in employees	☐	☐	☐
Treats me with respect	☐	☐	☐
Takes initiative when solving problems	☐	☐	☐
Develops new strategies	☐	☐	☐
Applies policies and regulations fairly	☐	☐	☐
Is skilled in conflict resolution	☐	☐	☐
My Manager:			
Develops appropriate solutions	☐	☐	☐
Encourages my development	☐	☐	☐
Communicates effectively	☐	☐	☐

WORD

8. Insert one row to become the first row as shown. Move "My Supervisor:" to the first column of the new row as shown in **4.2feedback form1.**
9. Insert another row where shown in Illustration A. Enter the text `My Manager` in the first column as shown in **4.2feedback form1.**
10. Apply grey shading to the newly inserted rows.
11. Center the table horizontally on the page.
12. Save the file as **4.2feedback form1.**
13. Print one copy.
14. Close the file.

Cues for Reference

Create a Table

1. Click the **Insert Table** button on the toolbar.
2. Drag to the right and down to indicate the number of columns and rows you want.

or

1. Click **Table.**
2. Click **Insert, Table.**
3. Click **Number of columns** and enter the number of columns.
4. Click **Number of rows** and enter the number of rows.
5. Click **Column width.** Enter the appropriate width.
6. Click **OK.**

Insert Rows/Columns

1. Place the insertion point in table where you wish to insert a row or column.
2. Click **Table.**
3. Click **Insert.**
4. Click **Rows Above/Rows Below** or **Columns to the Left/Columns to the Right.**

or

1. Select a column or row.
2. Right-click and choose **Insert Column** or **Row.**

Delete Rows/Columns

1. Select the columns or rows to delete.
2. Right-click and choose **Delete Column** or **Row.**

or

1. Click **Table.**
2. Click **Delete.**
3. Click **Rows/Columns.**

Change Column Width

1. Place the mouse pointer on a vertical line separating the column until it changes to the table-sizing arrow.
2. Drag the arrow left or right to adjust the column width.

or

1. Place the insertion point in the table.
2. Drag the column markers to change the table.
3. Drag the left- and right-indent markers to change table margins.

Change Column Width by a Specific Measurement

1. Position the insertion point in a column or select the columns to change.
2. Click **Table.**
3. Click **Table Properties.**
4. Click the **Column tab.**
5. Click the **Preferred width** text box and enter an amount.

or

1. Double-click on the column marker to open the Table Properties dialog box.
2. Make the desired changes.

TRYOUT

TASK 3

GOAL

To practice using the following skill sets in order to enhance the minutes of a meeting and form documents

- Format a table
  - Align data within cells
  - Set row height
  - Apply borders and shading
  - Use AutoFormat

WHAT YOU NEED TO KNOW

Format a Table

- You can format a table by changing the alignment and appearance of data in cells or by applying table borders and shading.

Align Data Within Table Cells

- You can align cell data in various ways during the table creation process or afterward. Figure 4.19 illustrates data alignment examples within table cells.
- To align data horizontally in a table cell, place the insertion point in any cell or select (highlight) several cells or columns in which you wish to align the data. Then, click an alignment button on the Formatting toolbar, as shown in Figure 4.20.
- To align data vertically in a table, select the cells to affect, click Table, Table Properties, and click the Cell tab. Choose a vertical alignment option, as shown in Figure 4.21.

Left (horizontal)	Right (horizontal)
Center (horizontal)	Justify Justified text needs more than one line to show its effect. The lines are even on the left and right.
Top (vertical)	Text rotated 90 degrees
Bottom (vertical)	
Center (vertical)	

Figure 4.19 Text alignment options in table cells

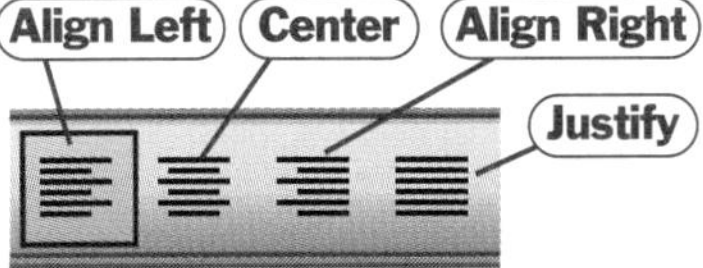

Figure 4.20 Alignment buttons on the Formatting toolbar

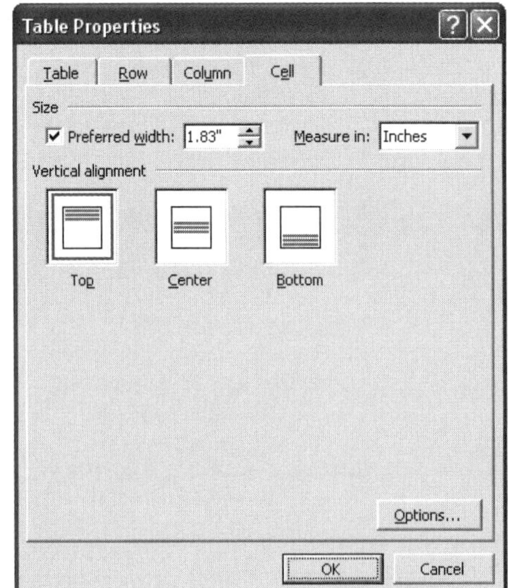

Figure 4.21 Cell tab on Table Properties dialog box

▶ To change the direction of text in 90-degree increments, click the cell containing the text you want to affect and click Format, Text Direction. In the Text Direction dialog box that appears, as shown in Figure 4.22, click the direction you want the text to appear. The Preview window displays the new direction. You can also click the Change Text Direction button on the Tables and Borders toolbar. (See Figure 4.25 later in this lesson.)

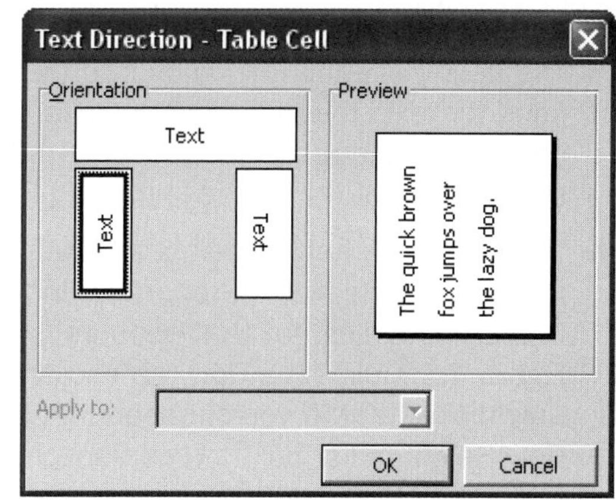

Figure 4.22 Text Direction dialog box

TRY *it* OUT *w4-8*

1. Open **w4.8pf table** from the Data CD.
2. Select the first row.
3. Click the **Center** button.
4. Click the **Bold** button.
5. Select the last column.
6. Click the **Center** button.
7. Click **View, Toolbars,** and **Tables and Borders.**
8. Click in the cell that contains the word "Campaign."
9. Click the **Change Text Direction** button twice.

10. Click in the cell that contains the word "Miscellaneous."
11. Click the **Change Text Direction** button twice. *Note that the word does not fit in the cell. (This will be fixed in Try it Out 4-9).*
12. Select all the headings except "Campaign."
13. Click **Table, Table Properties,** and click the **Cell** tab.
14. Click the **Center** vertical alignment option.
15. Click **OK.**
16. Do not close the file.

Row Height

- The height of each row adjusts to the font size used for text. You may, however, change the row height to make text more readable or to add special effects.
- To change row height, select the cells to affect, then click Table, Table Properties. In the Table Properties dialog box that appears, shown in Figure 4.23, click the Row tab and enter the row height you want. If you choose At least from the Row Height is list box, you can specify a minimum row height. If you select Exactly, you can specify a fixed row height.
- You can also drag a horizontal line separating the rows up or down to adjust the row height.

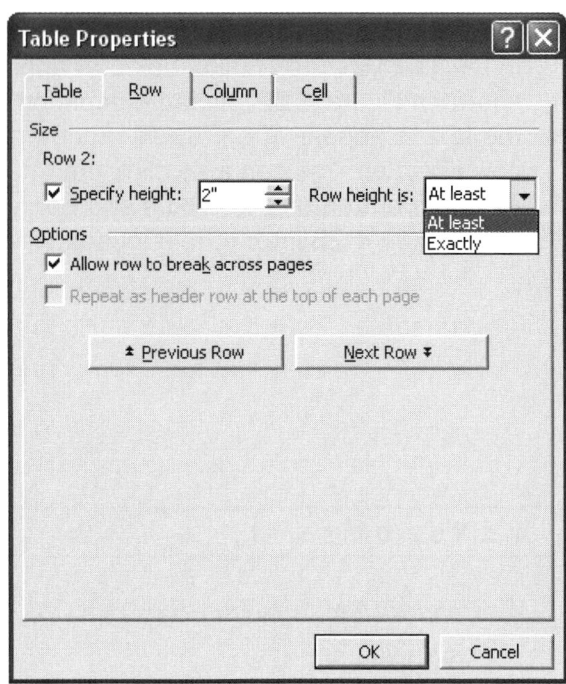

Figure 4.23 Row tab on Table Properties dialog box

TRY it OUT *w4-9*

Note: **w4.8pf table** *should be on screen. To allow "Miscellaneous" to fit in the cell, change the row height as follows:*

1. Click the cell containing the word "Miscellaneous."
2. Click **Table, Table Properties.**
3. Click the **Row** tab.
4. Enter `1.5` in the Specify height text box.
5. Click the **Row height is** list arrow and click **Exactly.**
6. Click **OK.**
7. Select the first row. Change the font size to 14-point.
8. Select all the cells containing numerical data.
9. Click the **Align Right** button on the toolbar. 
10. Close the file; do not save.

Table Borders and Shading

- By default, tables appear with ½-point gridlines, which are the inside and outside borders. If you remove the table border, you can still view the boundaries of the cells if the Gridline feature is turned on. To turn gridlines on and off, click Table, Show (or Hide) Gridlines. Gridlines do not print.
- Changing the line style of individual borders of a cell is an effective way to emphasize data. You can change the thickness, color, and other characteristics of borders in a table or lines around individual cells, as shown in Figure 4.24.
- Use the Tables and Borders toolbar, shown in Figure 4.25, to easily change borders and apply shading to a table (click View, Toolbar, Tables and Borders).
- To modify the table border, select the table, click the Line Style list arrow, choose a line style from the list and click the Line Weight list arrow and choose a line thickness from the list. To color the line, click the Border Color list arrow and choose a color from the drop-down palette. Finally, click the Outside Border button to apply the modifications to the table border.
- To modify lines surrounding a cell or cells, click in the cell or select the cells to affect. Then, choose a line style, a line thickness, and a line color using the Table and Borders toolbar buttons. To apply your choices to a line or lines surrounding a cell, click the Outside Border list arrow and click the cell border you want affected, as shown in Figure 4.26.
- To shade a cell, click the cell or select the cells to shade, click the Shading Color list arrow (see Figure 4.25), and choose a color from the menu that appears.

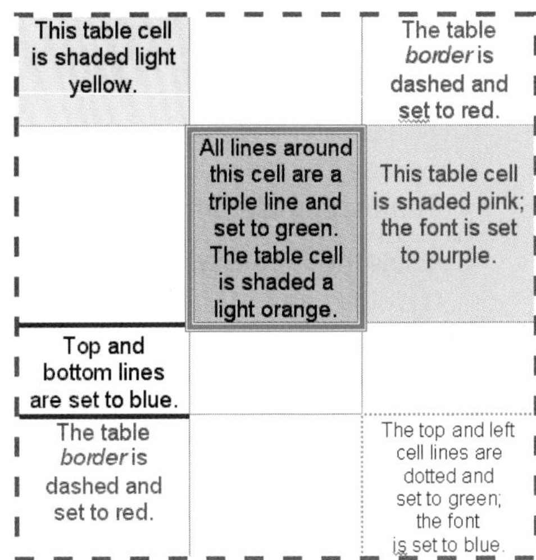

Figure 4.24 Table borders and shading examples

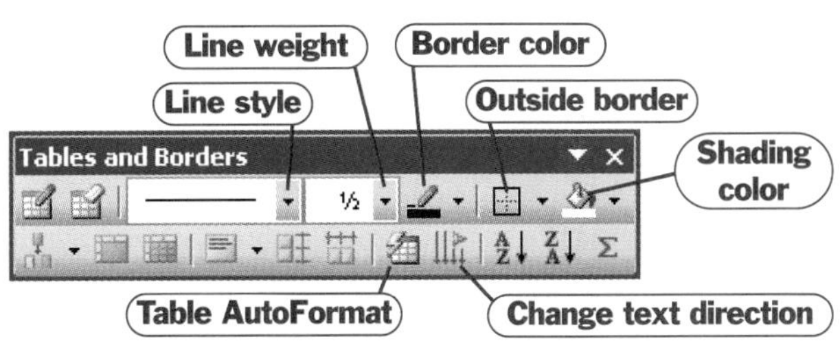

Figure 4.25 Tables and Borders toolbar

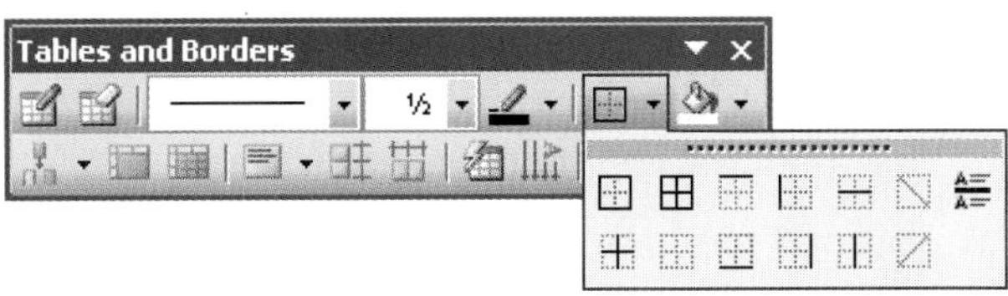

Figure 4.26 Outside Border menu

TRY *it* OUT *w4-10*

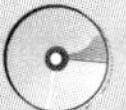

1. Open **w4.10pf table** from the Data CD.
2. Insert a new row to become the last row.
3. Select the table. Click **View, Toolbars, Tables and Borders**, if necessary.
4. Click the **Line Style** list arrow and select a dotted line style.
5. Click the **Line Weight** list arrow and select **4 ½ pt.**
6. Click the **Border Color** list arrow and select **Red.**
7. Click the **Outside Border** button.
8. Position the insertion point in the cell containing the number "107.0."
9. Click the **Shading Color** button and select **Yellow.**
10. Click the **Line Style** list arrow and select a double line.
11. Click the **Line Weight** list arrow and choose **1 ½ pt.**
12. Click the **Border Color** list arrow and select **Blue.**
13. Click the **Outside Border** list arrow and select the bottom line.
14. Select the first row.
15. Click the **Shading Color** button and select **Black.** (Notice that the text turns White.) 
16. Close the file; do not save.

AutoFormat

- The Table AutoFormat feature allows you to apply a professionally designed format to a table. Word provides numerous built-in styles from which you can choose.
- To apply a Table AutoFormat, select the table and click Table, Table AutoFormat, or click the Table AutoFormat button on the Tables and Borders toolbar. In the AutoFormat dialog box that appears, as shown in Figure 4.27, choose a format from the Table styles list box and click Apply. The Preview window displays the result of your choice.
- You can also apply an AutoFormat when you are creating a table from the Insert Table dialog box (see Figure 4.7).

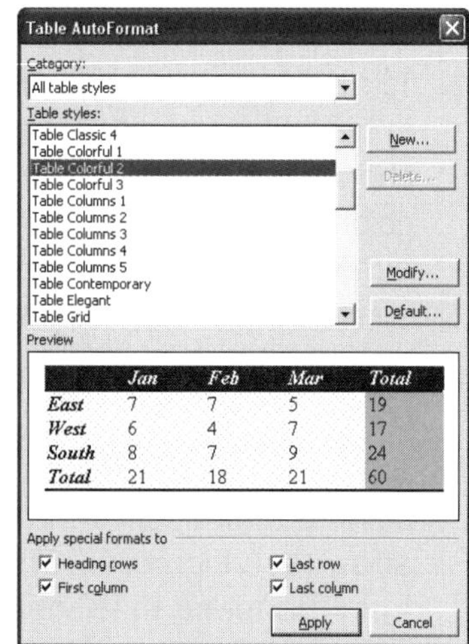

Figure 4.27 Table AutoFormat dialog box

TRY *it* OUT *w4-11*

1. Open **w4.11pf table** from the Data CD.
2. Click **Table, Table AutoFormat.**
3. Click on each table style to view them.
4. Choose any format from the Table styles list box.
5. Click **Apply.**
6. Close the file; do not save.

1
2
3

GOAL

To enhance the minutes of a meeting and company feedback form documents created in the previous Rehearsal

SETTING THE STAGE/WRAPUP

Margins: Default
Start line: At 1"
File names: **4.3minutes1**
4.3feedback form

WHAT YOU NEED TO KNOW

In this Rehearsal activity, you will add borders and shading and other enhancements to the documents you created in Task 2.

DIRECTIONS

Minutes

1. Open **4.2minutes,** if you completed it in Task 2, and save the file as **4.3minutes.** Or, open **4.3minutes** from the Data CD.
2. Enhance the document as shown on the facing page.
   a. Apply paragraph shading to the heading lines in any desired color.
   b. Add any table border.
   c. Set the font for the first column to sans serif 12-point.
   d. Rotate the text in the first cell as shown. Set the font size to 16 point.
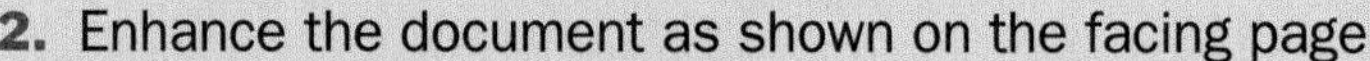
   e. Set the row height for the first cell to 1".
   f. Shade the first column and the rows shown in any desired light color; shade the first cell Dark Blue.
3. Save the file.
4. Print one copy.
5. Apply any Table AutoFormat you want. Change the paragraph shading for the heading to compliment the AutoFormat colors.
6. Save the file as **4.3minutes1.**
7. Print one copy.
8. Close the file.

Continued on next page

4.3minutes

In-Shape Fitness Centers
New Employee Orientation Meeting
January 5, 2005
Minutes of Meeting

Present	Laurie James, Brian Murphy, Jill Robinson, Chris Powell, Robert Johnson, and Adrian Monroe
Welcome	Laurie welcomed all the new employees and told those in attendance that there would be a follow-up meeting sometime next week.
Overview	Brian told the group what this meeting intended to cover. Among the topics to be included are a company history, organizational structure, company information, sales trends, and employee benefits. Brian explained that there would be ample time for questions and answers. Chris distributed a company organizational chart.
Company Mission	Jill explained that the company's mission was to design high-quality fitness centers throughout the United States, but most of all to maintain high-quality customer service at all centers.
In-Shape Fitness Centers	Adrienne introduced the officers of the company.
Sales Trends	Chris gave a detailed explanation of the sales trends and provided the group with a breakout of the most successful centers. Chris explained that the staffing was most critical in the effectiveness of the center.
Employee Benefits	Jill reviewed the company benefits, including health, life insurance, medical, dental, optical, and major medical. Robert talked about the commission and bonus structure and explained that for every new person who signed on for a one-year contract, there would be a 10% commission on the total yearly contract. A bonus would be added if five or more people signed on. Chris Powell talked about the vacation and sick leave benefits. Each employee would get two weeks after 12 months and 2.5 days earned each month. Extra provision would be made for employees who work winters.
Questions and Answers	Participants had 20 minutes for Q and A.
Adjournment	The meeting was adjourned at 11:00 a.m.

Form

1. Open **4.2feedback form1** if you completed it in Task 2. Or, open **4.3feedback form1** from the Data CD.
2. Save the file as **4.3feedback form.**
3. Change the page orientation to portrait.
4. Change the title of the form to read, `Supervisor and Manager Feedback Form,` as shown on the next page.
5. Change the text direction in the cells shown. Set the row height for these cells to 1.5".
6. Apply a dark blue shade to the cells shown.
7. Apply a light yellow shade to the cell shown.
8. Center align the data in columns 2, 3, and 4.
9. Apply a black top and bottom border to the cells shown.
10. Save the file.
11. Print one copy.
12. Close the file.

Continued on next page

4.3feedback form

Air Land Sea Travel Group

Supervisor and Manager Feedback Form

	Disagree	Neither Agree Nor Disagree	Agree
Treats me fairly	❐	❐	❐
Brings out the best in employees	❐	❐	❐
Treats me with respect	❐	❐	❐
Takes initiative when solving problems	❐	❐	❐
Develops new strategies	❐	❐	❐
Applies policies and regulations fairly	❐	❐	❐
Is skilled in conflict resolution			
Develops appropriate solutions	❐	❐	❐
Encourages my development	❐	❐	❐
Communicates effectively	❐	❐	❐

Cues for Reference

Row Height

1. Select a row or group of rows.
2. Click **Table, Table Properties.**
   or
   Double-click column marker to open Table Properties dialog box.
3. Click the **Row** tab.
4. Click the **Specify height** check box and enter the appropriate amount in the text box.
5. Click the **Row height is** list arrow and select an option.
6. Click **OK.**
   or

- Drag a horizontal line separating the rows to an appropriate height.

Vertical Alignment Within Table Cells

1. Select the cells to affect.
2. Click **Table, Table Properties.**
   or
   Double-click column marker to open Table Properties dialog box.
3. Click the **Cell** tab.
4. Click an alignment option.
5. Click **OK.**

Table Borders and Shading

Borders

1. Select the table or individual cells to receive borders.
2. Click the **Line style list arrow** on the Tables and Borders toolbar and choose a line style.
3. Click the **Line width list arrow** and choose a line width.
4. Click the **Border Color list arrow** and choose a border color.
5. Click the **Outside Border list arrow** and choose a cell border to receive your selections.

Shading

1. Select the cell or cells to receive shading.
2. Click the **Shading color list arrow** on the Tables and Borders toolbar, and choose a shading color.

Table AutoFormat

1. Position insertion point in a table cell.
2. Click **Table, Table AutoFormat**.
3. Choose a style option.
4. Click **Apply**.

GOAL

To practice using the following skill sets in order to create an itinerary, a schedule, and a letter with an inserted table

- Set and modify tabs
- Set tabs with leaders
- Set tabs within table cells

WORD

WHAT YOU NEED TO KNOW

Set and Modify Tabs

- *Tabs* are stopping points for the insertion point when the Tab key is pressed.
- In Task 2, you learned to use tables to organize information into columns. You can also align text into tabular columns by using the default tabs or by setting custom tabs. By default, tab stops are left-aligned and set every half-inch. Default tab markers are indicated on the ruler, as shown in Figure 4.28, by gray vertical tick marks. You can, however, change the distance between settings by clicking Format, Tabs. In the Tabs dialog box that appears, enter the distance between tabs in the Default tab stops text box, as shown in Figure 4.29. Tabs are applied to highlighted existing text or to text entered from that point forward.

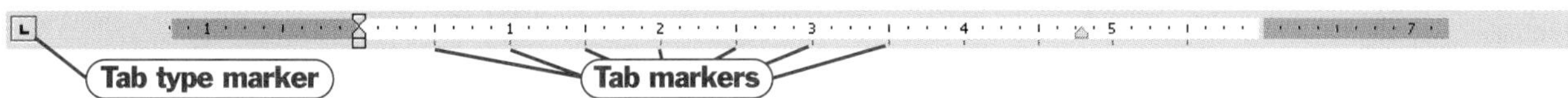

Figure 4.28 Tab markers on ruler

- *Custom tabs* are settings that you select, which affect the way text behaves once you begin entering text.
- Custom tabs are set in two steps:
  1. Click the Tab Type marker at the left side of the ruler (see Figure 4.28) until you see the symbol for the type of tab you wish to create (left, right, center, or decimal).
  2. Click the ruler at the position where you want a custom tab.
- When you set a custom tab, default tabs to the left of it are deleted.

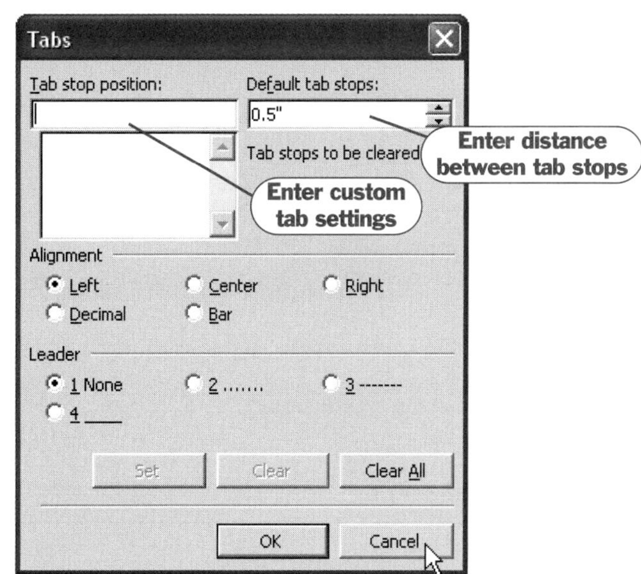

Figure 4.29 Tabs dialog box

▶ There are four different tab types: left, center, right, and decimal. Figure 4.30 illustrates text organized into tabular columns using custom tabs.

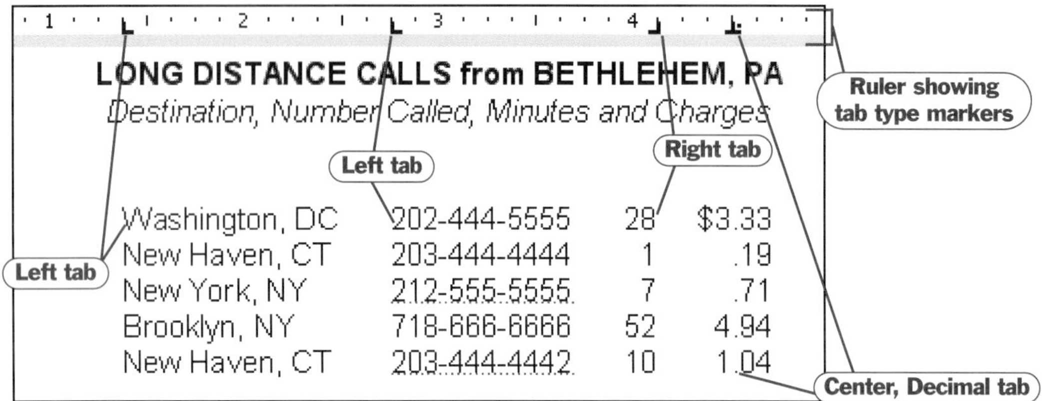

Figure 4.30 Tabular columns with custom tabs

▶ Each tab type is represented on the ruler by a different marker and has a different effect on text, as shown.

- The **Left Tab** moves text to the right of the tab as you enter text, as shown in Figure 4.31.

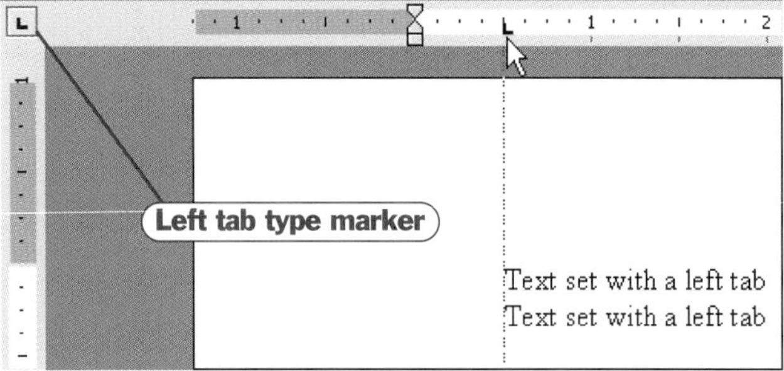

Figure 4.31 Text set with a left tab

- The **Center Tab** centers text at the tab stop, as shown in Figure 4.32.

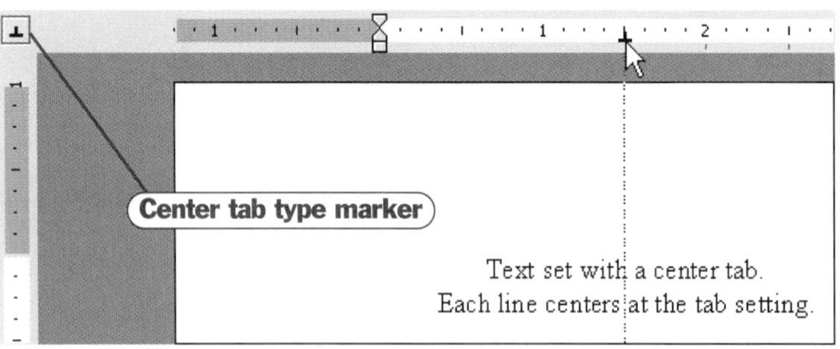

Figure 4.32 Text set with a center tab

- The **Right Tab** moves text to the left, or backward, from the tab as you enter text, as shown in Figure 4.33.

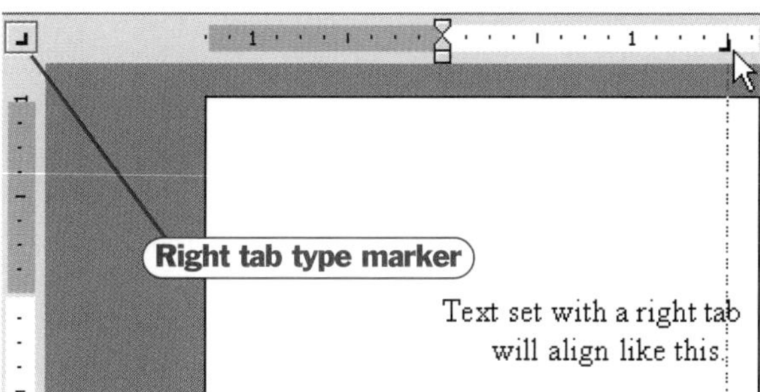

Figure 4.33 Text set with a right tab

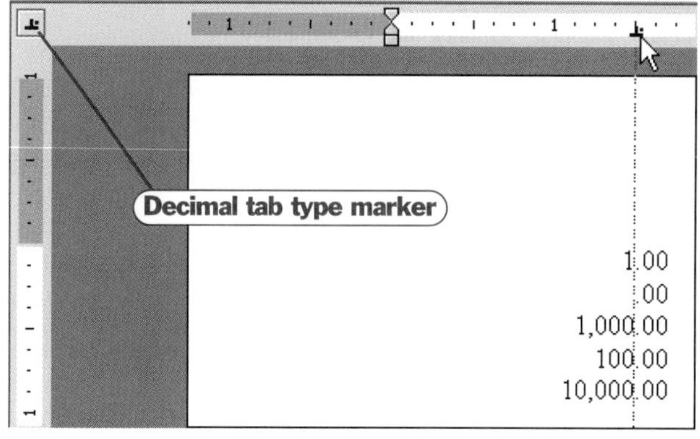

Figure 4.34 Text set with a decimal tab

- The **Decimal Tab** moves text before the decimal point to the left of the tab. Text entered after the decimal point moves to the right of the tab. The decimal points stay aligned, as shown in Figure 4.34.

▶ Tab settings become part of paragraph formatting, and all paragraph formatting is stored in the paragraph mark (¶) at the end of the paragraph. If you delete this mark, or if you move the insertion point to another paragraph, you might not have the tab settings you expect.

▶ You can delete a tab by dragging the tab marker off the ruler.

▶ You can move a tab by dragging the tab marker left or right on the ruler. You can also change the type of tab after it is set by clicking on it in the ruler and then clicking the tab marker on the left-hand side of the screen until the desired type of tab marker appears.

TRY *it* OUT *w4-12*

1. Click the **New Blank Document** button.
2. Click **View, Print Layout,** if necessary.

To create the four-column tabular table (not the heading) shown in Figure 4.30, do the following:

3. Click the **Tab Type** marker to the left of the ruler to display the **Left Tab,** if necessary.
4. Click the ruler at 1" (inserting a left tab).
5. Drag the Left Tab marker to 2".
6. Drag the Left Tab marker off the ruler.
7. Click the ruler at 1.5".
8. Click the ruler at 2.75" (inserting another left tab).
9. Click the **Tab Type** marker until a **Right Tab** marker displays.
10. Click the ruler at 4" (inserting a right tab).
11. Click the **Tab Type** marker until the **Decimal Tab** marker displays.
12. Click the ruler at 4.5" (inserting a decimal tab).
13. Press the **Tab** key and enter: `Washington, DC.`
14. Press the **Tab** key and enter: `202-444-5555.`
15. Press the **Tab** key and enter: `28.`
16. Press the **Tab** key, enter: `$3.33` and press the **Enter** key.
17. Enter each remaining line of text as shown.
18. Print one copy and close the file; do not save.

Set Tabs with Leaders

- You can set tabs that contain leaders. A *leader* is a series of dotted, dashed, or solid lines that connect one column to another to keep the reader's eye focused, as shown in Figure 4.35.
- To set tabs with leaders, click Format, Tabs. In the Tabs dialog box that appears, as shown in Figure 4.36, enter the tab position (1", 2", 2.5" for example) in the Tab stop position text box, and click Set. Click a tab type option below Alignment, click a leader type in the Leader section, and click OK. *Note: The settings shown in Figure 4.36 were used to create the table shown in Figure 4.35. The default tab stops remain in place to the right of the custom tab.*
- After you set all tabs, use the Tab key to advance to each column. The leaders automatically appear preceding those columns that contain a tab setting with a leader.

Meeting Dates and Minutes Recorders

April 15 .... Janice Risen
May 12 .... Paul Barry
June 14 .... Rose Benson
July 12 .... Ashanti Khan
August 5 .... Helene Santiago

Figure 4.35 Tabular columns with dot leaders

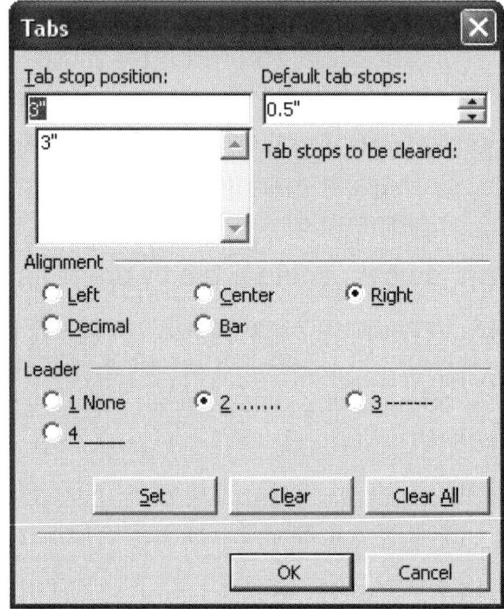

Figure 4.36 Leaders set in Tabs dialog box

TRY *it* OUT *w4-13*

Note: To create the two-column tabular table shown in Figure 4.35, do the following:

1. Click the **New Blank Document** button.
2. Center the title `Meeting Dates and Minutes Recorders` using a sans serif 12-point bold font. Press the **Enter** key twice.
3. Click **Format, Tabs**.
4. Enter `3"` in the Tab stop position text box, click **Right** as the Alignment option, and click `2` as the Leader option.
5. Click **Set,** then click **OK.**
6. Enter `April 15` at the left margin.
7. Press the **Tab** key, enter: `Janice Risen` and press the **Enter** key.
8. Enter the remaining text as shown in Figure 4.35.
9. Print one copy.
10. Close the file; do not save.

Set Tabs Within Table Cells

- You can create tabs within table cells using the same techniques used to create them in text paragraphs. Figure 4.37 shows an example of tabs within table cells.

Destination	Departs	No. of Days	Cost
Panama Canal	March 6	13	$2,092.00
Trans Pacific	March 19	11	$4,888.00
Left aligned	Left aligned	Center aligned	Right aligned

Figure 4.37 Tabs set within table cells

- To set a tab within a table cell, first place the insertion point in the cell or select the cells, and use the same procedures you learned to set a tab type.
- Once you create a tab in a table cell, press Ctrl + Tab to advance the insertion point to the tab stop for all tab enters except the decimal tab. Pressing just Tab will advance to a decimal tab setting.

TRY *it* OUT *w4-14*

Note: To create the table shown in Figure 4.37, do the following:

1. Open **w4.14pf table tabs** from the Data CD. 
2. Click the **Tab Type** marker to the left of the ruler until you display the **Left** Tab, if necessary.
3. Select the blank cells below "Destination," and then click at **.3**" on the ruler to set a left tab.
4. Select the blank cells below "Departs," and then click at **2**" on the ruler to set a left tab.
5. Click the **Tab Type** marker to the left of the ruler until you display the **Center** Tab.
6. Select the cells below "No. of Days" and click at **3.75**" on the ruler to set a center tab.
7. Click the **Tab Type** marker to the left of the ruler until you display the **Right** Tab.
8. Select the cells below "Cost" and click at **5.5**" on the ruler to set a right tab.
9. Click in the first row below "Destination."
10. Press the **Ctrl** + **Tab** keys and enter: `Panama Canal.`
11. Press the **Tab** key, the **Ctrl** + **Tab** keys, and enter: `March 6.`
12. Press the **Tab** key and the **Ctrl** + **Tab** keys, and enter: `13.`
13. Press the **Tab** key and the **Ctrl** + **Tab** keys, and enter: `$2,092.99.`
14. Click in the first column of the third row.
15. Enter the following in the proper columns, using the Tab and Ctrl + Tab keys as appropriate:

    `Trans Pacific March 19 11`
    `$4,888.00`
16. Enter your name in the last row.
17. Print one copy and close the file. Do not save.

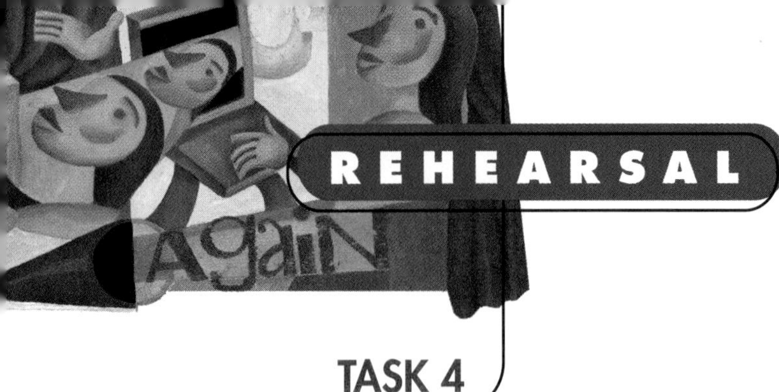

GOAL

To create a travel schedule (an itinerary) using tabular columns and leaders, and a fitness schedule that includes custom tabs within table cells. You will also create a letter with an inserted table.

SETTING THE STAGE/WRAPUP

Margins: 1" left and right for **4.4itinerary**
Default for **4.4fitness schedule**
1" left and right for **4.4hearings**

Start line: At 1"

File names: **4.4itinerary**
4.4fitness schedule
4.4hearings

WHAT YOU NEED TO KNOW

- An *itinerary* is a day-by-day travel *schedule* or timetable that includes times of arrival, meetings, departures, as well as contact information.
- You can use tables or tabular columns to create an itinerary.
- In the first Rehearsal activity, you will create an itinerary using tabular columns with leaders. This itinerary is being prepared for Ms. Robin Ashton, managing director of the Sutton Investment Group, who is traveling from London to New York.
- In the second Rehearsal activity, you will create a fitness schedule for In-Shape Fitness Centers, using a table with custom tabs and leaders.
- In the third Rehearsal activity, you will create a letter with an inserted table.

DIRECTIONS

Travel Itinerary

1. Click the **New Blank Document** button.
2. Switch to **Print Layout** view.
3. Set left and right margins to **1"**.
4. Create the itinerary as shown on the next page.
5. Right-align the headings; use any font and font size.
6. Set a 10-point font for the body of the itinerary.
7. Set a right tab at 1" from the left margin; set a left tab with a dot leader at 2" from the left margin.

Note: When you set a right tab at the 1" mark on the ruler, you are actually setting the tab 1" from the left margin, not from the left edge of the paper.

8. Enter the itinerary as shown.
9. Print one copy.
10. Save the file; name it **4.4itinerary.**
11. Close the file.

Continued on next page

SUTTON INVESTMENT GROUP
Private Placement Group – London

Itinerary for *Robin Ashton, Managing Director*
October 25-27, 2005

Tuesday, October 25

9:00 a.m. .... Depart London, Heathrow Airport, Sky Airlines, Flight 345 to NYC

10:25 a.m. .... Arrive New York, LaGuardia Airport

1:00 p.m. .... Check in, Plaza 50 Hotel, New York City

3:00 p.m. .... Meeting with Mike Hsu, 757 Fifth Avenue, 14th Floor

7:00 p.m. .... Dinner with Mike Hsu and Pat Parker at Tavern on the Green

Wednesday, October 26

8:00 a.m. .... Breakfast meeting with Dan Morris and Gretta Manning in hotel

1:00 p.m. .... Museum of Modern Art (4 tickets to be picked up at box office)

5:30 p.m. .... Dinner with Dan Morris at Merchants, 7th Avenue at 17th Street

8:00 p.m. .... Theater, 230 West 44th Street (4 tickets at box office)

Thursday, October 27

9:00 a.m. .... Depart New York City, LaGuardia Airport, Sky Airlines, Flight 33 to
.... London

9:21 p.m. .... Arrive London, Heathrow Airport

Continued on next page

Fitness Schedule

1. Click the **New Blank Document** button. 
2. Create the fitness schedule as shown on the next page.
3. Create a table using three columns and five rows.

Hint: After setting the tabs and entering the text for Row 5, you can press the Tab key to create additional rows. The new rows will contain the same tab settings as in Row 5.

4. Set the column widths as follows:
   a. Column 1: 1"
   b. Columns 2 and 3: 2.62"
5. Enter the text in Row 1. Format it as follows:
   a. Set the font size for Columns 1 and 2 to 18 point. Use any font style. Use any font size for Column 3.
   b. Rotate the text in Column 1. Set the row height to 2".
   c. Vertically and horizontally center the text in columns 2 and 3.
   d. Shade the cells in any color.
6. Enter the text in Row 3. Format it as follows:
   a. Set the font size for Column 1 to 10 point. Set the font size for Columns 2 and 3 to 14 point. Use any font style.
   b. Shade the cells in any color.
7. In row 5:
   a. Set the row height to 0.5".
   b. Enter the instructor's name in Column 1. Horizontally center and italicize the text. Set the font size to 11 point.
   c. In Columns 2 and 3, set a custom center tab in the middle of the column and a right tab with a dot leader at the end of the column.
   d. Enter the text in Columns 2 and 3. Set the font size to 11 point.

Note: Remember to use the Ctrl + Tab keys to advance to the custom tab stops. After entering the text in Column 3, press the Tab key to create the next row.

   e. Make the class titles ("Yoga," "Spin," etc.) bold.
   f. Shade the cells in any color.

8. Save the file; name it **4.4fitness schedule.**
9. Print one copy.
10. Close the file.

Continued on next page

WORD

In-Shape Fitness	**Weekend Schedule**	**Weekend Fitness Director** **Wendy Carroll** **Note:** **Classes will be held in either Studio 1, 2 or Studio Right (SR)**
Instructor	**Saturday**	**Sunday**
Ronnie	8:15-9:00 **Body Sculpt** 2	8:30-9:30 **Yoga** 2
John	9:00-10:00 **Yoga** 2	9:00-10:00 **Step** 2
Ronnie	10:00-11:00 **Spin** 1	9:30-10:30 **Body Sculpt** 1
Felicia	11:00-12:00 **Cardio** .... SR	11:00-12:00 **Step** .... SR
Forrest	12:00-1:00 **Stretch** 1	12:30-1:30 **Spin** 1
Jessica	3:30-5:30 **Ballet** .... SR	4:30-5:30 **Yoga** 2

Letter with Schedule

1. Click the **New Blank Document** button.
2. Create a letterhead for Four Corners Realty using any design you want. The illustration is a guide.
3. Create the letter as shown.
4. Create a table using four columns and three rows.
   a. Set the column widths as follows:
      Column 1: **1.1".**
      Columns 2–4: **1.45".**
   b. Enter the text as shown.
   c. Center the table.
   d. Apply any AutoFormat you want.
5. Save the file; name it **4.4hearings.**
6. Print one copy and then close the file.

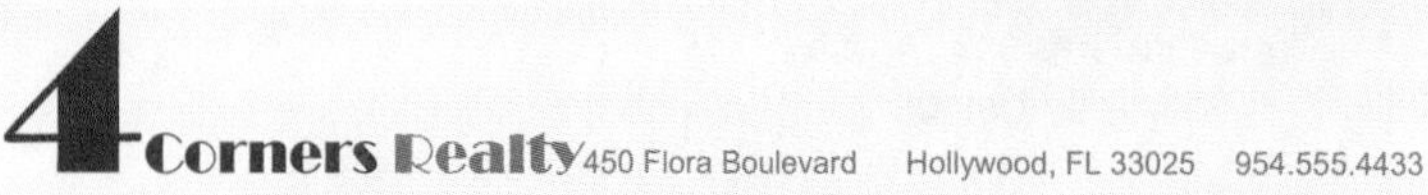

Today's date

Ms. Sara Mosler
768 Harbor Way
Hollywood, FL 33035

Dear Homeowner:

We wanted to inform all those who have purchased homes through our agency that the Hollywood Planning Commission will hold a series of public hearings on zoning and land uses throughout our county.

The hearings will be held on the dates and locations indicated below:

Date	August 1	August 2	August 3
Location	Hollywood High School	Hollywood Community Center	Hollywood College
Time	7-9:00 p.m.	7-8:30 p.m.	6-7:30 p.m.

We encourage you to attend these important hearings. While we feel that the proposals will have a major positive effect on homeowners, it is the homeowners themselves who must decide.

Cordially.

Dennis Halpern
President and CEO

dh

Cues for Reference

Change Default Tab Settings
1. Click **Format.**
2. Click **Tabs.**
3. Click the **Default tab stops** increment arrows and set a distance.
4. Click **OK.**

Set a Custom Tab on the Ruler
1. Position the insertion point in the paragraph or select the paragraphs in which to set the tab.
2. Click the **Tab Type** marker to the left of the ruler to set the tab.
3. Click the ruler where the tab is to be set.
4. Press the **Tab** key to advance to the next tab stop.

Set a Custom Tab with Leaders
1. Click **Format.**
2. Click **Tabs.**
3. Enter a tab stop for a new tab.
4. Click an Alignment option (Left, Center, Right, Decimal, Bar).
5. Click a Leader option.
6. Click **Set.**
7. Repeat Steps 3 through 6 for each tab to set.
8. Click **OK.**
9. Press the **Tab** key to advance to the next tab stop.

Remove a Custom Tab
- Drag the tab marker off the ruler.

Move a Tab
- Drag the tab marker left or right on the ruler to the appropriate location.

Set Tabs in Table Cells
1. Position the insertion point in the cell or select the columns.
2. Set tabs as outlined above (Set a Custom Tab on the Ruler, Set a Custom Tab with Leaders).
3. Press the **Ctrl** + **Tab** keys to advance to the next tab stop.

SETTING THE STAGE/WRAPUP

- Act I File name: **4.p1 expense form**
- Act II File name: **4.p2 agenda**
- Act III File name: **4.p3 brussels**
- Act IV File name: **4.p4 conference**

WHAT YOU NEED TO KNOW

Act I

Odyssey Travel Gear has asked you to prepare an expense report form for the company as shown on the next page.

Follow these guidelines:

- Create the company information and title of the form (Expense Report Form) using any desired font, font size, font color, and/or paragraph shading.
- Create two separate tables:
  - Create the first table to accommodate the Employee information using the appropriate number of columns and rows.
    - > Use any desired font, font size, and font color for the text.
    - > Remove table lines where necessary to create the form as shown.
    - > Apply text alignments and shading to cells as shown. Use any color shading you want.
    - > Adjust column widths to fit the heading text.
  - Create another table to accommodate the Expense information using the appropriate number of columns and rows.
  - Set the row height to Exactly **.3".** Vertically align the text in the cells.
  - Remove table lines where necessary to create the form as shown.
    - > Use any desired font and font color for the text. Use a 10-point font size for the heading text; use an 8-point font size for the "Total" information.
    - > Apply alignments and shading to cells as shown; use any color shading you want.
    - > Adjust column widths to fit the heading text.
- Enter the signature lines as shown.
- Horizontally center the tables.

- Print one copy of the form
- Save the file; name it **4.p1 expense form.**

OdysseyTravelGear

Expense Report Form

Employee ____________________
Department ____________________
From ____________________
To ____________________
Purpose of expense ____________________

Date	Description	Transportation/ Mileage	Air	Lodging	Meals	Other	Total
Totals							
						Subtotal	
						Less Cash Advanced	
						Total Owed To You	
						Total Due	

Employee Signature____________________ Date__________

Approved by ____________________ Date__________

Act II

Ms. Jane McBride of Odyssey Travel Gear is planning a meeting with her staff to discuss a new marketing idea. The Odyssey Travel Gear staff thinks that they can sell more of their products if they partner with various travel agencies. Jane has asked you to create an agenda of topics to be discussed at the meeting.

Once the members of the Marketing Department agree on the topics, it will form the basis for a presentation they plan to deliver at next year's travel convention.

Follow these guidelines:

- Using the outline feature, create the following topics and subtopics for an agenda:

```
Welcome
History of Odyssey Travel Gear
    Success Speaks for Itself
    Catalog and Internet Sales
    Retail Stores
         West Coast
         East Coast
New Market Strategy Proposal
  Linkage to Travel Agencies
  Benefits of the Partnership
Strategies for Making It Happen
The Partnership
  What We'll Offer
    Product Discounts
    Travel Specials Insert
    Client Referrals
Questions and Answers
```

- Insert a header that reads: `Draft Agenda for Staff Meeting.`
- After completing the outline, print one copy.
- Save the file; name it **4.p2agenda.**

Act III

Ms. Janice Pierce, President of the Air Land Sea Travel Group, is traveling from New York to Belgium for a three-day meeting, from June 14 to June 17, 2005. You have been asked to prepare an itinerary for her. Ms. Pierce wants the itinerary to include the name of the firm for whom the itinerary is being prepared, as well as the dates of travel.

The travel details are as follows:

Ms. Pierce is leaving on Tuesday, June 14, at 9:00 p.m. from New York's LaGuardia Airport, American Airlines, Flight 225, arriving in Brussels, Belgium, on Wednesday, June 15, at 8:00 a.m. She is staying at the Hotel Amigo, located at rue de l'Amigo, where she is scheduled to check in at 9:00 a.m. At 10:30 a.m. she is meeting with Mr. Ramone of the European Travel Society. At 6:30 p.m. she is having dinner with the Private Travel Group at Les Brigittines, 5 Place de la Chapelle. On Thursday, June 16, Ms. Pierce is scheduled to meet with Phillippe Haas of ARB SA Corporation at 8:30 a.m. The offices are located at Chaussee de La Hulpe 185. At 12:15 p.m. she is meeting Laurence Volpe for lunch at the ARB offices. She is returning to her hotel at 6:30 p.m. On Friday, June 17, she will be leaving Brussels at 8:00 a.m. American Airlines, Flight 225, and is scheduled to return to New York's LaGuardia Airport at 1:00 p.m.

Follow these guidelines:

- Organize the information above as an itinerary for Ms. Pierce, using a parallel-column table.
- Format the table using any desired table border, cell border, and shading.
- Adjust the column widths as desired.
- Print one copy.
- Save the file; name it **4.p3 brussels**.

Act IV

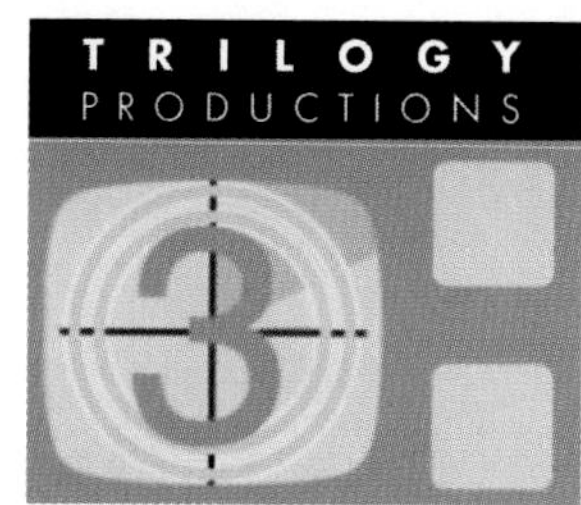

Each year, Trilogy Productions sponsors a major conference. This year's conference is scheduled for Monday, February 4 through Wednesday, February 6. As coordinator of special events at Trilogy Productions, one of your jobs is to coordinate the conferences, which includes notifying guest speakers of their topics and speaking times. You have been asked to prepare a letter to one of the speakers, Ms. Irene Quincy, director of sales, NVC Arts, 9145 Sunset Boulevard, Los Angeles, CA 90069. Use your name as the sender of the letter and include your title.

The body of the letter is as follows:

We are delighted that you are able to be a featured presenter at our upcoming conference on February 4, 5, and 6.¶You are scheduled to present "The History and Future of TV and the Internet" on Monday, February 4 at 2:00 p.m. We will be contacting you by phone very shortly to discuss the details of your presentation and to coordinate remarks among your fellow panelists.¶ Indicated below is a schedule of Monday's sessions:¶

1 p.m.......Webstation Lounge Box Lunch

2 p.m.......The History and Future of TV and the Internet

3:30 p.m.......How to Create Award-Winning Web Sites

Once again, thanks very much for your participation, and I look forward to meeting you in February.

Follow these guidelines:

- Use the default margins. Start the document at 1".
- Include today's date, an appropriate salutation, and a closing.
- Insert the schedule as tabular columns with leaders as shown below. Set a right tab for time of the session approximately 1" from the left margin (after p.m.) Set a right tab for the session titles 1" from the right margin.

1 p.m.	Webstation Lounge Box Lunch
2 p.m.	The History and Future of TV and the Internet
3:30 p.m.	How to Create Award Winning Web Sites

- Center the document vertically.
- Print one copy.
- Save the file; name it **4.p4 conference.**

LESSON 5

Sales and Marketing Documents

In this lesson, you will learn to use features found in Word to format sales and marketing documents. Sales and marketing documents include anything that helps sell or promote a product or service. Examples include press releases, flyers, advertisements, newsletters, brochures, and catalogs.

In this lesson, you will complete the following projects:

- A press release
- A flyer
- An advertisement
- A newsletter
- A catalog

Upon completion of this lesson, you should have mastered the following skill sets:

- Set character spacing
- Apply text effects
- Work with text boxes
  - Create a text box and enter text
  - Move and size a text box
  - Format a text box
  - Wrap text around a text box
- Work with images
- Work with objects
  - Shapes/AutoShapes
  - Lines
  - WordArt
  - Charts and diagrams
  - Wrap text around objects
- Group and layer objects

Terms

Software-related

Kern
Text box
Clip art
Inline graphic
Floating graphic
Objects
AutoShapes
WordArt
Organization chart
Layer
Group
Ungroup

Document-related

Press release
Flyer
Advertisement
Catalog
Newsletter

GOAL

To practice using the following skill sets:

- Set character spacing
- Apply text effects
- Work with text boxes
  - Create a text box and enter text
  - Move and size a text box
  - Format a text box
  - Wrap text around a text box

WHAT YOU NEED TO KNOW

Set Character Spacing

- Word sets a default for the amount of space it leaves between letters and words. You can adjust the relative space between characters using the character-spacing feature. Setting character spacing can affect the readability of text, particularly headlines.
- Word provides three character-spacing options. You can:
  1. Expand or condense space evenly among all selected characters. Character spacing is measured in points.
  2. Scale letters, that is, you can set their width. The width of characters is measured by a percentage.
  3. Kern characters. *Kerning* fits letters closer together and is used to refine letter spacing, particularly when working with large or decorative letters.

Joan	Normal
Mary	**Expanded** by **2** points
Paul	**Expanded** by **2** points & **scaled** by **150%.**
Fran	**Expanded** by **2** points & scaled by **80%.**
Alan	**Expanded 5** points.
Matt	**Condensed .5** points
Matt	**Condensed 1** point
Look	The "o" letters are kerned.
Look	Normal

Figure 5.1 Character-spacing and scaling examples

- To expand or condense character spacing, select the text and click Format, Font. On the Character Spacing tab of the Font dialog box, as shown in Figure 5.2, click the Spacing list arrow, select Expanded or Condensed, and specify how much space you want in the By text box.
- To set the width of characters, click the Scale list arrow, then select a scaling percentage.

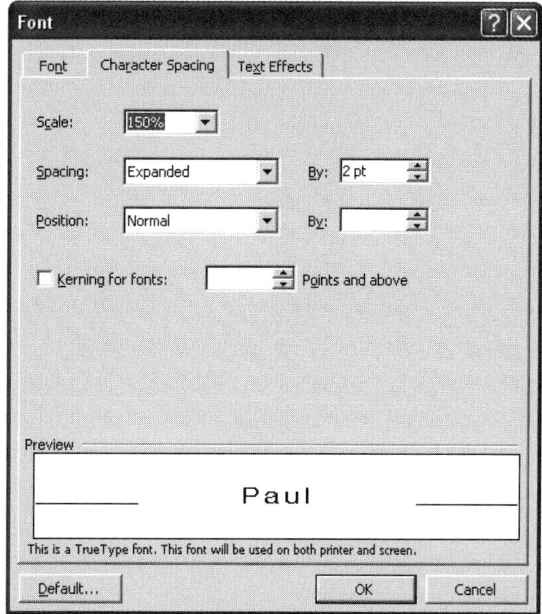

Figure 5.2 Character-spacing tab on Font dialog box

TRY *it* OUT *w5-1*

1. Open **w5.1pf letter spacing** from the Data CD.
2. Select **Joan.**
3. Click **Format, Font,** and the **Character Spacing** tab.
4. Click the **Spacing** list arrow and click **Expanded.**
5. Enter 2 in the **By** text box and click **OK.**
6. Select **Mary.**
7. Click **Format, Font.**
8. Click the **Spacing** list arrow and click **Condensed.**
9. Enter .5 in the **By** text box and click **OK.**
10. Select **Paul.**
11. Click **Format, Font.**
12. Click the **Spacing** list arrow and click **Expanded.**
13. Enter 2 in the **By** text box.
14. Click the **Scale** list arrow and click **200%.**
15. Click **OK.**
16. Select **Fran.**
17. Apply any letter spacing options.
18. Close the file; do not save.

Apply Text Effects

- Word allows you to create animation effects on selected text. Text animation is effective only when applied to e-documents, that is, documents that are e-mailed or viewed on the Web.
- To apply an animation to text, select the text, then click Format, Font, or right-click and choose Font from the shortcut menu. Click the Text Effects tab, then select an animation effect. The Preview window displays your choice, as shown in Figure 5.3.

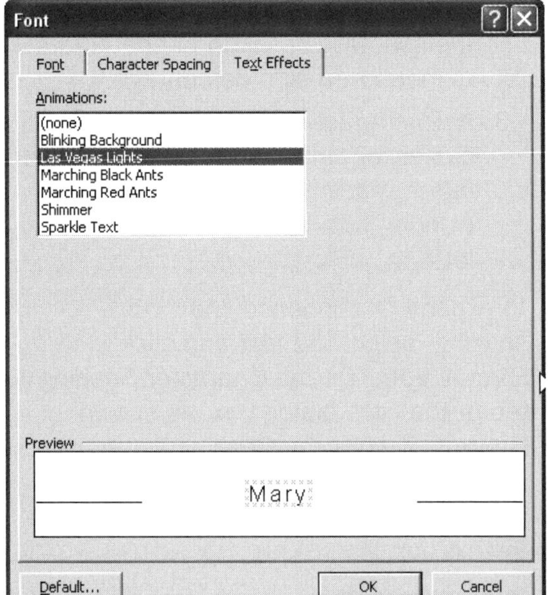

Figure 5.3 Text Effects tab on Font dialog box

TRY it OUT w5-2

1. Click the **New Blank Document** button.
2. Enter your first and last name.
3. Select your name.
4. Click **Format, Font.**
5. Click the **Text Effects** tab.
6. Click **Blinking Background** as the animation effect.
7. Click **Sparkle Text.**
8. Click **OK.**
9. Close the file; do not save.

Work with Text Boxes

- A *text box* allows you to set off text in a box, which you can then position anywhere on a page. A text box is considered an object. You will learn to work with other objects later in this lesson.
- Text that you enter inside a text box becomes part of the box and moves as you move the box. You can manipulate and format text boxes to create interesting effects. Figure 5.4 illustrates text box effects.

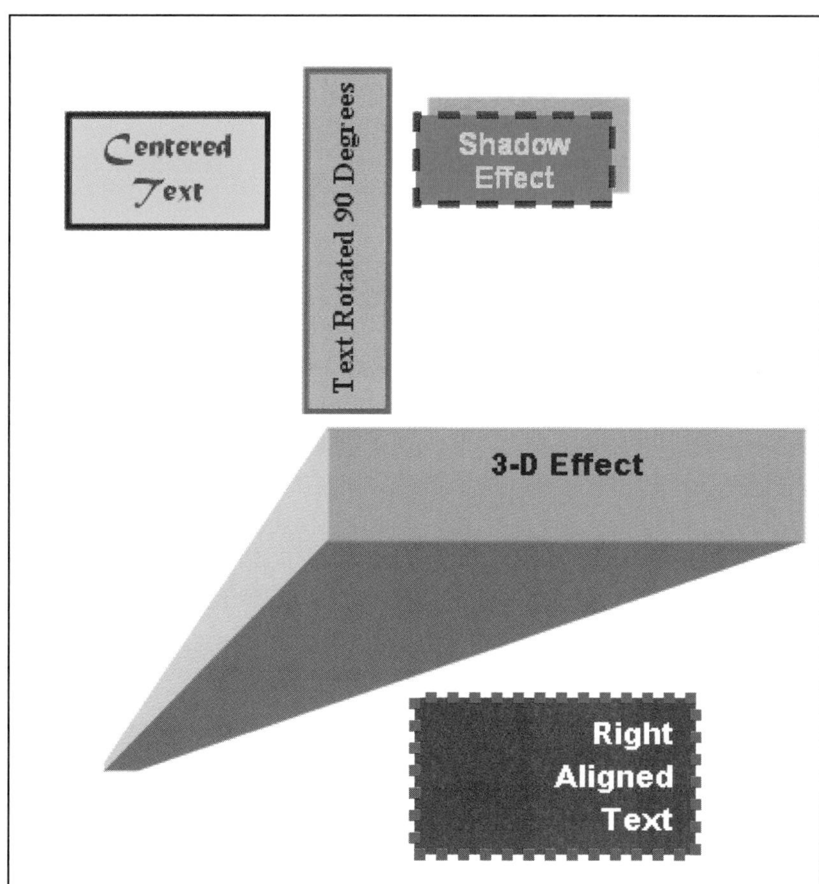

Figure 5.4 Text box examples

Create a Text Box and Enter Text

- To create a text box, click the Text Box button on the Drawing toolbar. Drag the Mouse pointer to the required box size and enter the text.

Note: When you insert a drawing in Word, a drawing canvas is placed around it. The drawing canvas helps you keep parts of your drawing together and is useful when working with multiple drawings. If you find this feature annoying, you can turn it off by clicking Tools, Options. On the General tab, deselect "Automatically create drawing canvas when inserting AutoShapes."

- The text box initially displays with sizing handles, small circles or squares that appear at the corners and sides of a selected box (see Figure 5.5).
  - Once you enter text in the box, you can align it to the left, center, right, or justify it by clicking an alignment button on the Formatting toolbar. You can also change the text direction by clicking the Text direction button on the Text box toolbar or clicking Format, Text Direction.

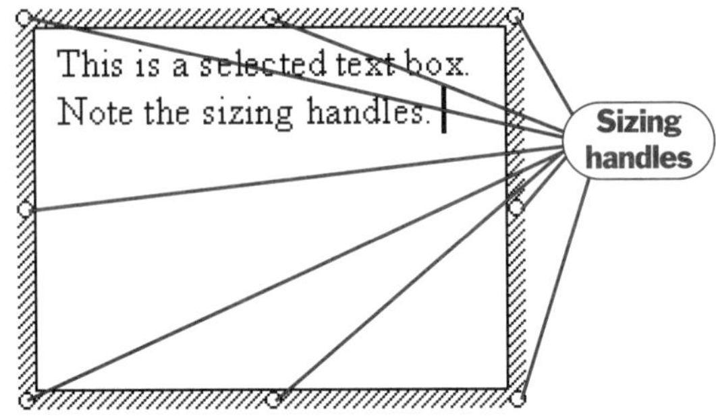

Figure 5.5 Selected text box

- After clicking outside the box, the handles disappear and Word automatically places a border around the text box. You will later learn to change border lines, add shading, and apply special effects to a text box.
- You can always activate a text box by clicking inside the box. You can then enter new text, edit existing text, and/or apply formatting.

TRY *it* OUT *w5-3*

1. Click the **New Blank Document** button.
2. Turn off the drawing canvas (click **Tools, Options, General Tab,** deselect **Automatically create drawing canvas when inserting AutoShapes** and click **OK**).
3. Display the Drawing toolbar, if necessary. Then, click the **Text Box** button on the Drawing toolbar.
4. Drag the insertion point diagonally to create the text box. Enter this word: `Communications.` (If the word does not fit, do not be concerned at this time.)
5. Create another text box and enter the word: `Effective.`
6. Create a third text box and enter the words: `is Essential.`
7. Click inside the text box containing the word "Effective" to activate it. Change the word to `Clear.`
8. For each text box, click inside the box to activate it, then click the Center alignment button.

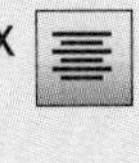

9. Save the file; name it **5.3 box.yi** (yi = your initials).
10. Do not close the file.

Move and Size a Text Box

▶ You can easily resize and/or reposition a text box. To do so, select the box so that the sizing handles appear. To resize the box, drag a sizing handle horizontally, vertically, or diagonally. You also have other sizing options:

- To size a text box by a specific amount, click Format, Text Box or right-click and select Format Text Box from the shortcut menu. Then, click the Size tab, and enter the amount you need in the Height and Width boxes, as shown in Figure 5.6.
- To set an internal margin within the text box, click the Text Box tab in the Format Text Box dialog box, and set the margins you want, as shown in Figure 5.7.
- To size the text box to fit the contents, click the Text Box tab in the Format Text Box dialog box, and select Resize AutoShape to fit text. (See Figure 5.7.)

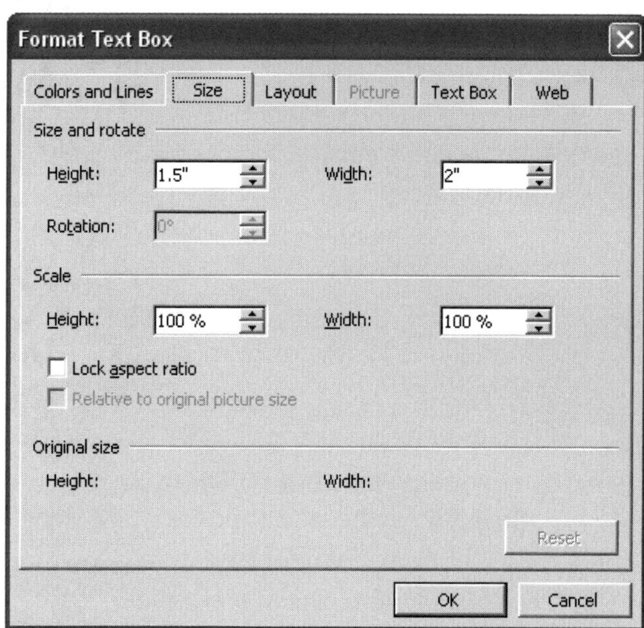

Figure 5.6 Size tab on Format Text Box dialog box

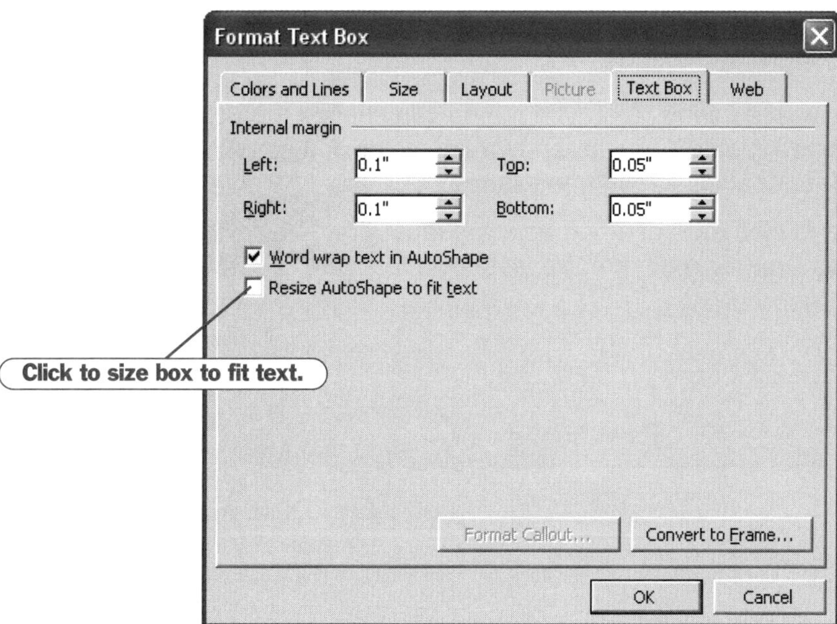

Figure 5.7 Text Box tab on Format Text Box dialog box.

- To reposition the box, select the box and position your mouse pointer over the box until it turns into a four-headed arrow. Click and drag the box to any location on the page.
- You can also apply the Copy, Cut, and Paste commands to copy, delete, and move a text box.

TRY*it* OUT *w5-4*

*Note: The file **5.3 box.yi** should be on your screen. If it is not, complete Try it Out 5-3 before starting this one.*

1. Click inside the box containing the word "Communications."
2. Click **Format, Text Box.** Click the **Size** tab; enter 2 in the Width box, and click **OK.**
3. Click **Format, Text Direction,** click a **90-degree** rotation, and click **OK.**
4. Click **Format, Text Box.** On the **Size** tab; enter **1.65"** in the Height box and **.47"** in the Width box, and click **OK.**
5. Click inside the box containing the word "Clear."
6. Click **Format, Text Box.** On the **Size** tab enter **.38"** in the Height box and **.65"** in the Width box, and click **OK.**
7. Click inside the box containing the words "is Essential." Repeat Step 6 and enter **.38"** in the Height box and **1.10"** in the Width box, and click **OK.**
8. Click and drag each box to move them into the order shown below .

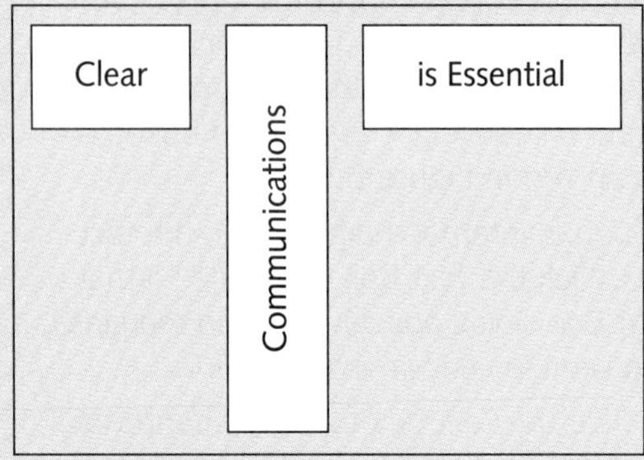

9. Save the file; do not close.

Format a Text Box

- By default, a text box appears with a solid line around it. You can change the border line around the box and also change the line style, line weight, and/or line color. You can fill the box with a color or pattern and add a 3-D or shadow effect (see Figure 5.4).
- Whenever you make a change to elements of a text box, you must first select it, which will display sizing handles. Use the Drawing toolbar buttons, shown in Figure 5.8, to easily apply formatting to a text box and other drawing objects.

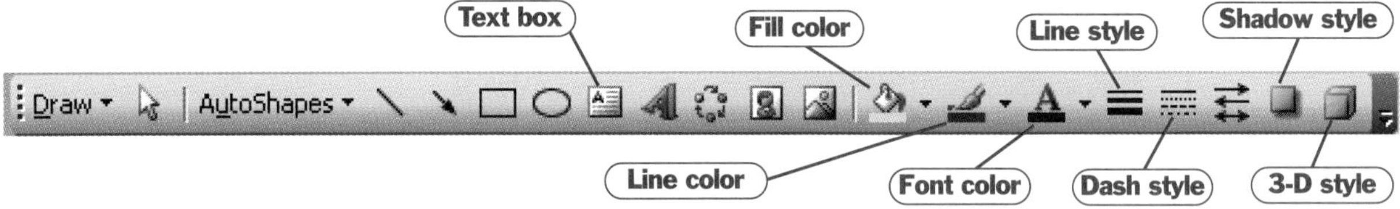

Figure 5.8 Drawing toolbar

- To change the border line around the text box, click the Line or Dash Style button and select a style from the menus shown in Figures 5.9 and 5.10. To change the line color, click the Line Color list arrow shown in Figure 5.11 and choose a color. To apply the color, click the button.

- To fill a text box with color, click the Fill Color list arrow shown in Figure 5.12 and choose a color. To apply the color, click the button.

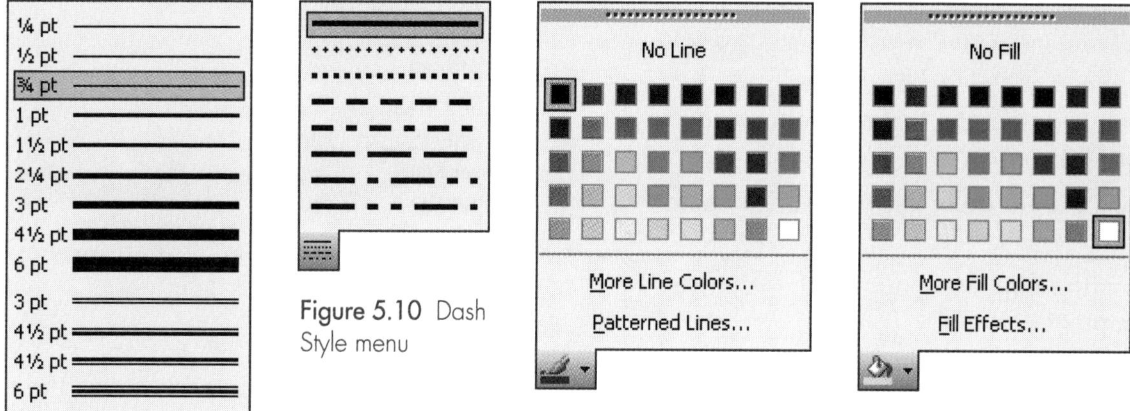

Figure 5.9 Line Style menu

Figure 5.10 Dash Style menu

Figure 5.11 Line color options

Figure 5.12 Fill Color menu

- You can apply multiple formats at once by selecting the text box, then clicking Format, Text Box. In the Format Text Box dialog box that opens, click the Colors and Lines Tab shown in Figure 5.13, and make the desired changes.

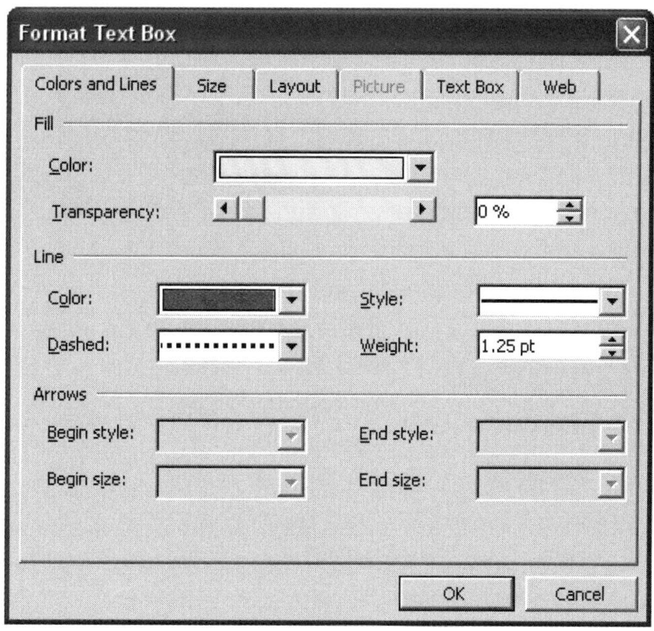

Figure 5.13 Colors and Lines tab in the Format Text Box dialog box

TRY it OUT w5-5

*Note: The file **5.3 box.yi** should be on your screen. If it is not, complete Try it Outs 5-3 and 5-4 before starting this one.*

1. Click to select the text box containing the word "Clear."
2. Click the **Fill Color** list arrow, then select a color.
3. Click the **Line Style** button, then select **2 ¼** point.
4. Click the **Line Color** list arrow, then select a color.
5. Click the **Shadow Style** button, then select a shadow effect.
6. For each word inside the box, do the following:
   - Select the word.
   - Click the Font Color list arrow. 
   - Apply a font color that complements the other colors you applied to the box.
7. Click to select the text box containing the word "Communications."
8. Repeat Steps 2–6.
9. Click to select the text box containing the words "is Essential."
10. Repeat Steps 2–6.
11. Save the file; print one copy, and then close the file.

Wrap Text Around a Text Box

▶ You can wrap text around text boxes and other objects to create interesting effects. Figure 5.14 shows text wrapped around a text box.

Happy New Year!

To celebrate the New Year, In-Shape is pleased to announce a new corporate fitness program. To find out how your company can provide you and your co-workers with significant savings on membership, please provide us with the name of the executive at your company who would make the decision on offering new employees benefit programs. When we get an appointment with the appropriate decision maker, you receive **ONE FREE MONTH**. If your company sponsors a corporate membership program, you receive up to ONE FULL YEAR FREE. Come be a part of one of the best fitness clubs in the U.S.A.

Corporate
Fitness
Sale

Figure 5.14 Text wrapped around a text box

- To wrap text, select the text box, and click Format, Text Box. In the Format Text Box dialog box that displays as shown in Figure 5.15, click the Layout tab and choose a wrapping style. You can also set the horizontal alignment of the text box in this dialog box.

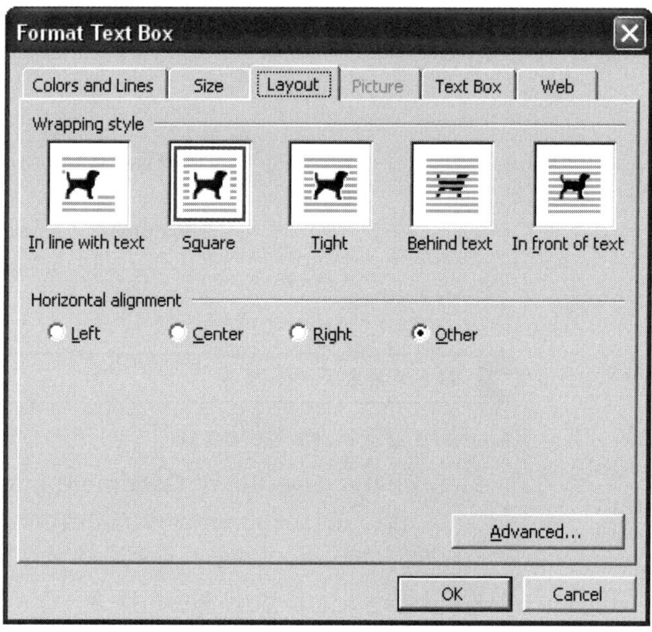

Figure 5.15 Layout tab on Format Text Box dialog box

TRY *it* OUT *w5-6*

1. Open **w5.6pf text wrap** from the Data CD.
2. Create a text box anywhere on the page.
   a. Enter the following words in the box. Press **Enter** after each word and center them: `Happy New Year to All.`
   b. Set the font size to **20 points.**
3. Click **Format, Text Box.** On the the **Size** tab, enter `1.75"` in the Height box and `1.25"` in the Width box, and click **OK.**
4. Drag to position the box in the middle of the paragraphs.
5. Click to select the text box, if necessary.
6. Click **Format, Text Box** and click the **Layout** tab.
   a. Click the **Square** wrapping style.
   b. Click the **Center Horizontal** alignment option, and click **OK.**
7. Close the file; do not save.

GOAL
To create a press release and a flyer using character spacing and text boxes

SETTING THE STAGE/WRAPUP

Margins: 1" left and right; .5" top and bottom for press release
Default for flyer

Start line: .5" for press release
Default for flyer

File names: 5.1press release
5.1flyer

WHAT YOU NEED TO KNOW

- A *press release* (also referred to as a news release) is a document that a business sends to various newspapers and magazines announcing a new product, a development, or an item of special interest. Multiple-page press releases traditionally have the word "more" keyed at the bottom of each page, except the last, which has ### symbols indicating "the end."
- A *flyer* is a communication that is posted in public or distributed. Its purpose is to attract immediate attention to inform the reader of a special event, service, or product. Think of a flyer as an informal advertisement.
- In this Rehearsal activity, you will create a press release announcing a new product for Green Brothers Gardening. You will also create a flyer that will be inserted into mailings and distributed to homeowners who are customers of Green Brothers.

DIRECTIONS

Create a Press Release

1. Click the **New Blank Document** button and create the press release shown on the facing page and as outlined in Steps 2 through 12. 
2. Create a text box. Size it **1.2"** high by **4.5"** wide. Enter the company name, address, and contact information using a sans serif font. Format the text as follows:
   a. Center the text.
   b. Set the company name to **14 point** and the font color to **Green.** Set the character spacing to Expanded by 2 points, and scale to **150%.**
   c. Set the address and contact information to **11 point.**
   d. Insert relevant symbols between parts of the address and contact information, as shown.
   e. Apply any desired text box border in any color. Fill the box with a light color.
3. Set double line spacing for the document.
4. Set the document font size to **11 point.** Use any font type.
5. Enter the remaining press release text using the alignments shown.
6. Set letter spacing for "Two New Software Products to Landscape Your Home" to Expanded by 1 point.
7. After entering the text, format it as follows:
   a. Apply the outline effect and any other text effect you want to "PRESS RELEASE." Change the font size to **14 point** and set the font color to **Green.**

Continued on next page

b. Set the words "GARDEN ADMINISTRATOR" and "LANDSCAPE HELPER" to **Arial Black.** Color each product name a different shade of Green. Copy the appropriate formatting to each occurrence of the product name.

8. Format the "Features include" list as follows:
   a. Set the line spacing to exactly 14 points.
   b. Insert an appropriate symbol before each featured item and set each symbol to 14 point.
   c. Apply the small caps effect to each feature ("Calendar," "Seed Sorter," "Shopping List," "Layout Manager," and "Vegetable Information"), as shown.

9. Center three hatch marks (###) to indicate the end of the document.

10. Save the file; name it **5.1press release.**

11. Print one copy.

12. Close the file.

Green Brothers Gardening
32 Braddock Road Fairfax, Virginia 22030
703-555-0005 703-555-0015 gbg@network.com
www.grenbros.com
1.2"
4.5"

Contact: Pete Moss

PRESS RELEASE

For Immediate Release

Two New Software Products to Landscape Your Home] Expanded by 1 pt.

Fairfax, Virginia, March 1, 2005 –

Green Brothers Gardening today introduced GARDEN ADMINISTRATOR and LANDSCAPE HELPER, two new software programs to help you landscape your home.

GARDEN ADMINISTRATOR is a unique product that will manage your square-foot garden.

Features include:

- A CALENDAR to help you plan what to plant and when
- A SEED SORTER to help you keep track of all your seeds
- A SHOPPING LIST to help you keep track of what to buy
- A LAYOUT MANAGER or help you lay out square-foot garden blocks
- A VEGETABLE INFORMATION database to help you keep track of the details of your crops

LANDSCAPE HELPER provides you with everything you need to design and build the ultimate landscape garden. Powerful software tools, helpful videos, and a library of professional designs make landscaping a pleasure.

Both products will be widely available the week of March 30. These products are available for the PC and require a Pentium 4 or higher with a minimum of 64 MB RAM, 100 MB free disk space, 8x CD-ROM, and a sound card.

The suggested retail price for GARDEN ADMINISTRATOR is $149.99, for LANDSCAPE HELPER, $69.99.

###

Create a Flyer

1. Create a flyer similar to one shown below by applying text box effects, alignments, fonts, sizes, colors, and character spacing. The text box and font sizes shown in the illustration are merely a guide.
2. Save the file as **5.1 flyer.**
3. Print one copy.
4. Close the file.

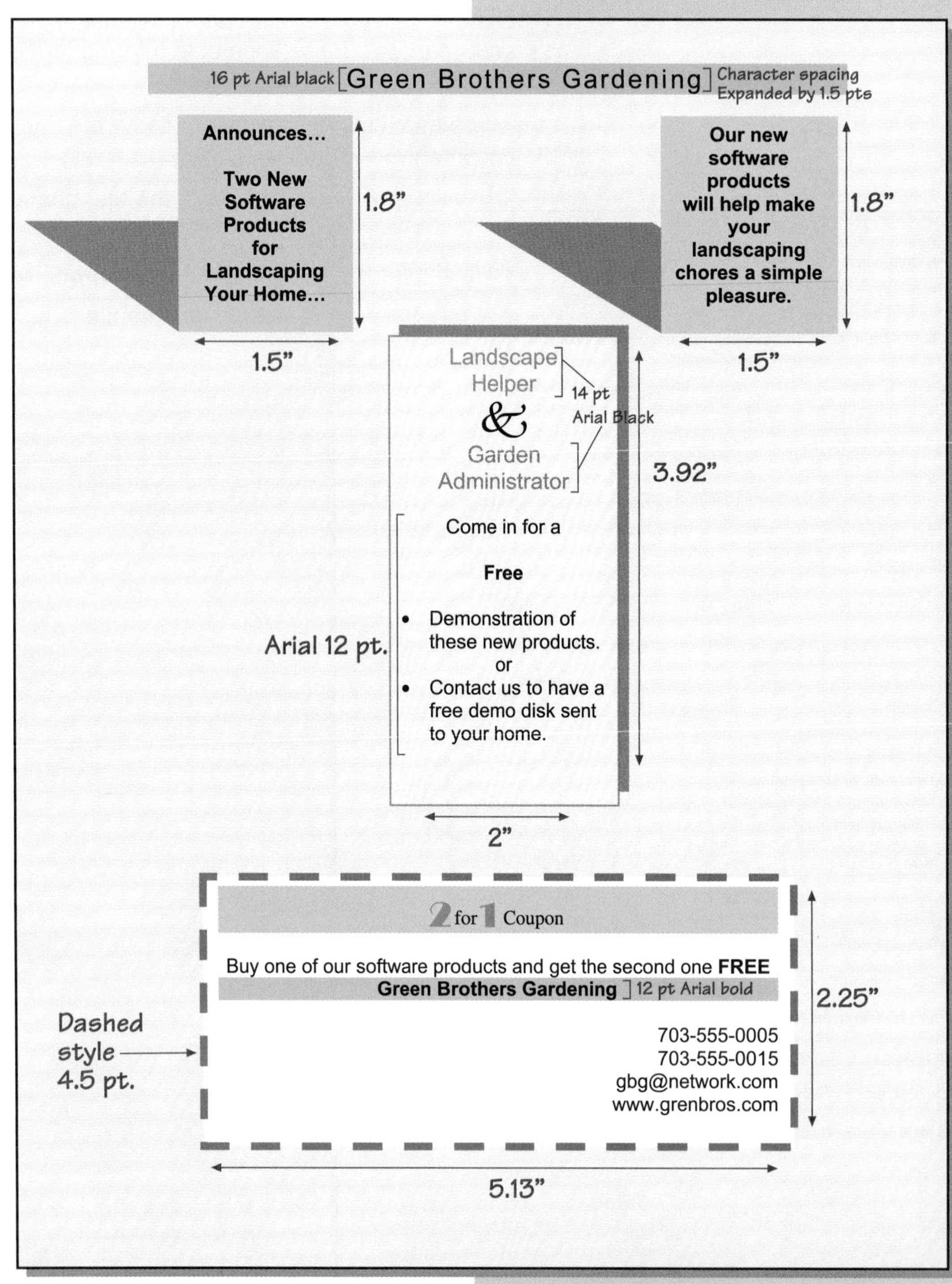

Cues for Reference

Set Character Spacing

1. Select the text you want to affect.
2. Click **Format, Font.**
   or
   Right-click and select **Font** from the list.
3. Click the **Character Spacing** tab.
4. Click the **Spacing** list arrow and select a spacing type.
5. Click the **By** list arrow, then enter a spacing amount.
6. Click **OK.**

Scale Text

1. Select the text you want to affect.
2. Click the **Scale** list arrow on the **Character Spacing** tab in the Font dialog box, and then select a scaling amount.
3. Click **OK.**

Apply Text Effects

1. Select the text you want to affect.
2. Click **Format, Font.**
3. Click the **Text Effects** tab.
4. Click an effect from the Animations list.
5. Click **OK.**

Create a Text Box

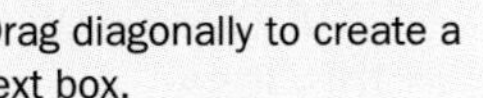

1. Click the **Text Box** button.
2. Drag diagonally to create a text box.
3. Enter text in box.

Move and Size a Text Box

1. Click to select the box.
2. Click **Format, Text Box.**
3. Click the **Size** tab and enter amounts in the Height and Width boxes.
4. Click **OK.**
   or
- Drag a corner handle to size the object proportionally, or drag a middle handle to size the height or width, or drag the object to the appropriate position on the page.

Format a Text Box

- Click to select the box.

Fill

1. Click the **Fill Color list arrow**.
2. Click a color.
3. Click the button to apply the fill.

Line Style

1. Click the **Line Style** button. or the **Dash Style** button.
2. Select a line or dash style.

Line Color

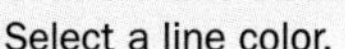

1. Click the **Line Color** list arrow.
2. Select a line color.
3. Click the button to apply the color.

Shadow/3-D Effect

1. Click the **Shadow Style** or the **3-D Style** button.
2. Select an effect.

Edit Fill Color, Line Color, Line Style, and Line Width in One Step

1. Click to select the box.
2. Click **Format, Text Box.**
   or
   Right-click and select **Format Text Box** from the list.
3. Click the **Colors and Lines** tab and select the options.
4. Click **OK.**

Wrap Text

1. Click to select the box.
2. Click **Format, Text Box.**
   or
   Right-click and select **Format Text Box** from the list.
3. Click the **Layout** tab and select a wrapping style.
4. Click **OK.**

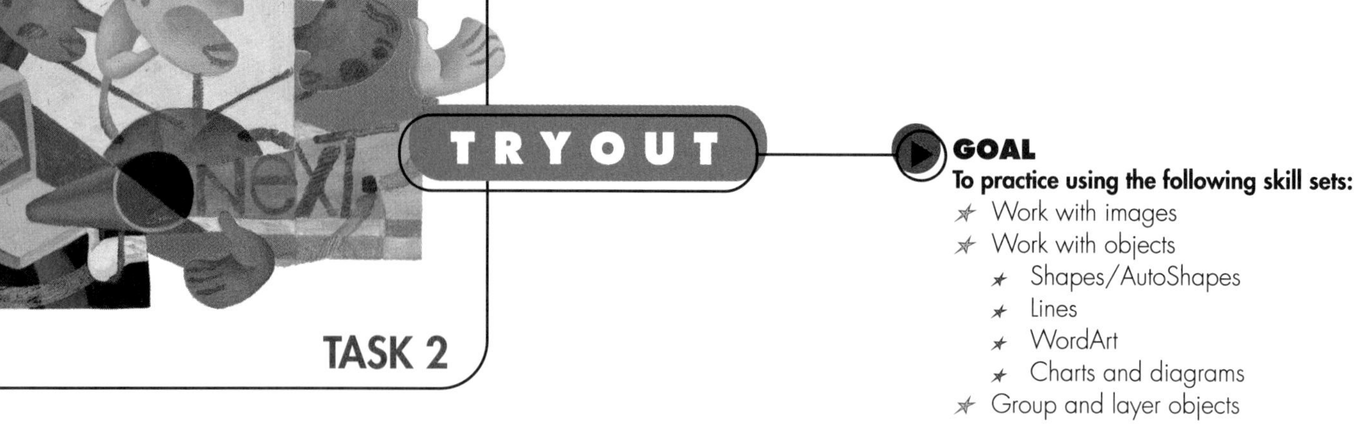

GOAL
To practice using the following skill sets:
- Work with images
- Work with objects
  - Shapes/AutoShapes
  - Lines
  - WordArt
  - Charts and diagrams
- Group and layer objects

WHAT YOU NEED TO KNOW

Work with Images

- To enhance the visual aspects of your document, you can insert images that include clip art, pictures, charts, diagrams, shapes, and drawn lines.
- *Clip art* is a collection of ready-made illustrations that are available when you install Word. You can also download images from the Internet or purchase them on a disk.
- You can save images in different formats that carry a file name extension identifying the image type. For example, you might see .bmp as a file name extension, which indicates that the image is a Windows bitmap, a format that almost all Windows applications recognize and use for photographs and illustrations. Other common image formats include .gif, .jpg, .wmp, and .tif.
- Most Web browsers support .gif and .jpg file formats, so these image types are popular for use on Web pages.

Insert an Image

- To insert clip art or a picture, click Insert, Picture, Clip Art from the menu, or click the Insert Clip Art button on the Drawing toolbar (see Figure 5.23 later in this lesson).
- In the Clip Art task pane that appears, as shown in Figure 5.16, enter a word or phrase in the Search for text box that describes the type of clip art you want to insert, then click Go. The default is to search All media file types, which includes Clip Art, Photographs, Movies, and Sounds. To search for clip art illustrations only, click the All media file types list arrow, then deselect the other media types.

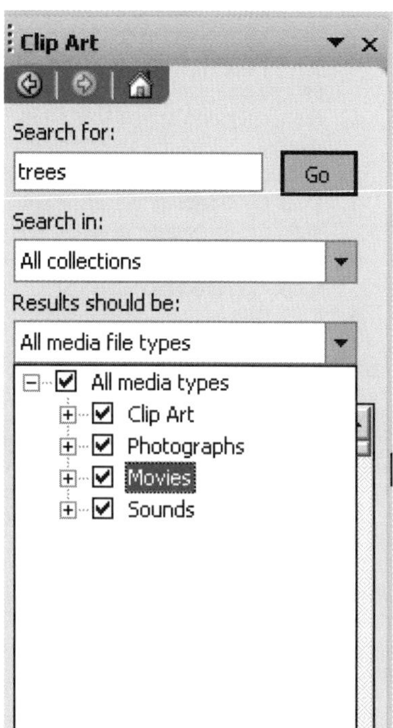

Figure 5.16 Clip Art task pane

- Word displays images in the task pane that match your search text, as shown in Figure 5.17. Click the image to insert it into your document.
- If Word does not have the images you want, you can find additional images on the Web. Click the Clip art on Office Online link in the Clip Art task pane, which displays Microsoft Office Online in your Web browser.
- The image appears in your document at the insertion point location. To edit the image (size, position, copy, or delete), you must select it. The selected image displays square sizing handles and a Picture toolbar. (If the Picture toolbar does not display, click View, Toolbars, Picture.) Figure 5.18 shows an image with handles displayed. Figure 5.19 shows the buttons on the Picture toolbar.

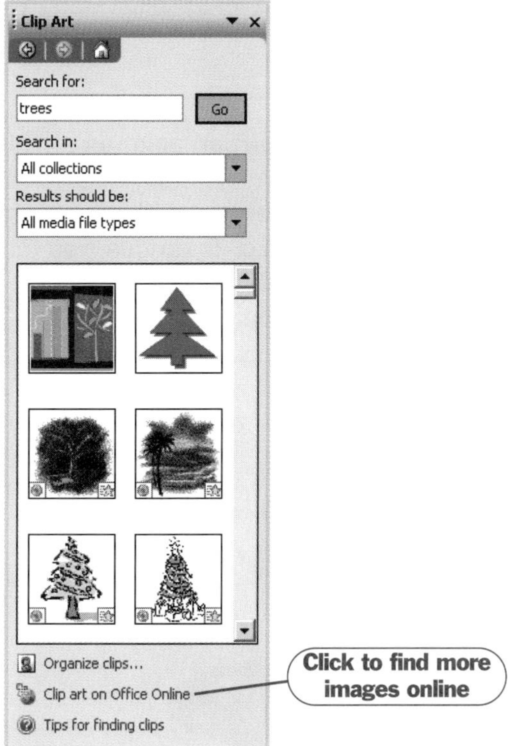

Figure 5.17 Insert Clip Art task pane with images displayed

Sizing handles

Figure 5.18 Selected clip art image

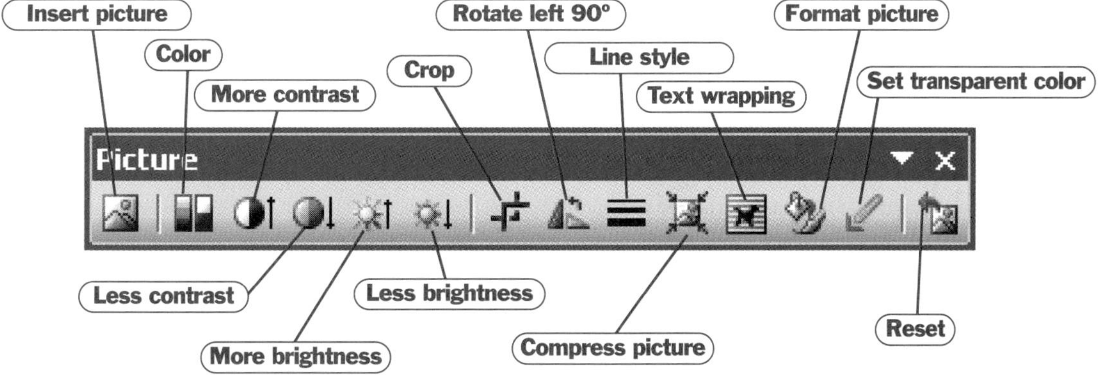

Figure 5.19 Picture toolbar

TRY*it* OUT w5-7

1. Click the **New Blank Document** button. 
2. Click **Insert, Picture,** and **Clip Art.**
3. Enter `people` in the Search for text box.
4. Click **Go.**
5. Click one of the images that display to insert it into your document.
6. Click to select the image. Note that square sizing handles and the Picture toolbar display. (If the Picture toolbar does not display, click **View, Toolbars, Picture.**)

Note: The image has been inserted into your document as an inline graphic.

7. Do not close the file.

Position an Image

- When you insert an image into your document, Word inserts it at the insertion point as an inline graphic. An inline graphic is positioned as part of a paragraph. You can horizontally align an inline graphic by using the alignment buttons on the Formatting toolbar. In order to position a graphic at a specific location in a document, you must change it to a floating graphic. To do this, you must change the graphic's wrapping style. Click to select the image, then click the Text Wrapping button on the Picture toolbar and choose either the Square or Tight wrapping style.
- When a text wrap option has been applied, the image will display with round sizing handles (as opposed to square) and a rotate handle as shown in Figure 5.20.
- To position an image, drag it to the required location on the page.

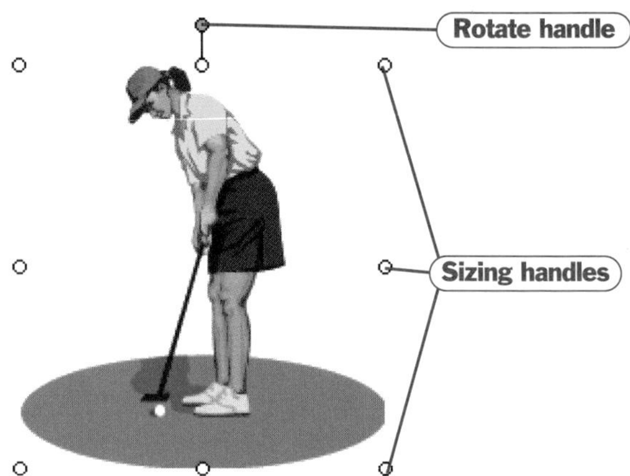

Figure 5.20 Clip art with sizing and rotate handles displayed

TRY*it* OUT w5-8

Note: The image from Try it Out 5-7 should be displayed on your screen. If it is not, complete Try it Out 5-7 before completing Try it Out 5-8.

1. Click to select the image. Click the **Text Wrapping** button on the Picture toolbar and select **Square.** *Note: You have created a floating image and now can easily move it.*
2. Drag the image to the upper-right corner of the page.
3. Do not close the file.

Size an Image

- To size an image proportionally, drag a corner handle. To change its height or width, drag a middle handle.
- Like text boxes, you can also set the size by a specific amount. Select the image, then click Format, Picture, or right click and select Format Picture from the shortcut menu. In the Format Picture dialog box, shown in Figure 5.21, click the Size tab and enter the measurements you want in the Height and Width text boxes.

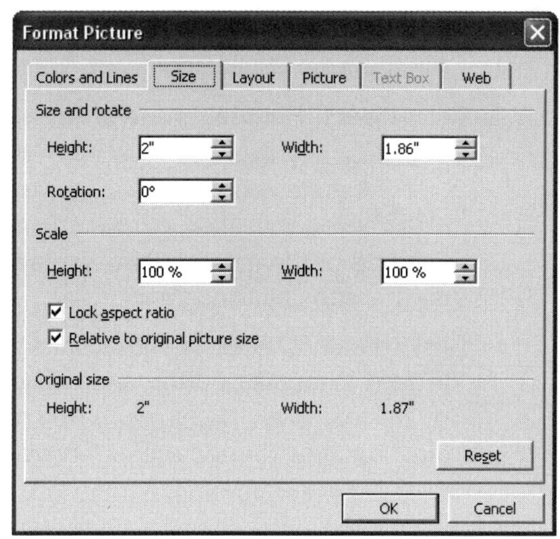

Figure 5.21 Size tab on Format Picture dialog box

TRY *it* OUT *w5-9*

Note: The image from Try it Out 5-8 should be displayed on your screen. If it is not, complete Try it Outs 5-7 and 5-8 before completing Try it Out 5-9.

1. Position the mouse pointer on a corner handle until it changes to a two-headed arrow.
2. Drag the handle diagonally to create a medium-sized image.
3. Click **Format, Picture.**
4. Click the **Size** tab. Enter 2 in the Height box and 2 in the Width box.
5. Click **OK.**
6. Drag the image to the bottom-right corner of the page.
7. Close the file; do not save.

Rotate an Image

- To rotate an image, click and drag the green rotate handle left or right to the appropriate angle. As you drag the handle, a dotted box indicates the placement, as shown in Figure 5.22. You can also set the rotation amount in the Rotation text box on the Size tab (see Figure 5.21).

Figure 5.22 Rotated image

TRY it OUT w5-10

1. Click the **New Blank Document** button.
2. Click **Insert, Picture,** and **Clip Art.**
3. Enter `trees` in the Search for text box.
4. Click **Go.**
5. Click one of the images that display to insert it into your document.
6. Click to select the image, then click the **Text Wrapping** button and apply a Square text wrap. *Note: you have created a floating image with a rotate handle.*
7. Drag the rotate handle and turn the image upside down.
8. Click off the image to hide the sizing and rotate handles.
9. Close the file; do not save.

Work with Objects

- In addition to clip art and text boxes, *objects* include photographs, charts, shapes, lines, video, and sound clips—items that visually (and audibly) enhance a document.
- Objects behave the same way. That is, you can size, position, and edit objects (change fill and border lines) using the same techniques you used with clip art and text boxes. You can also apply the Copy, Cut, and Paste commands to copy, delete, and move objects.

Shapes/AutoShapes

- You can draw a variety of shapes, using tools found on the Drawing toolbar, to create interesting effects, as shown in Figure 5.23.

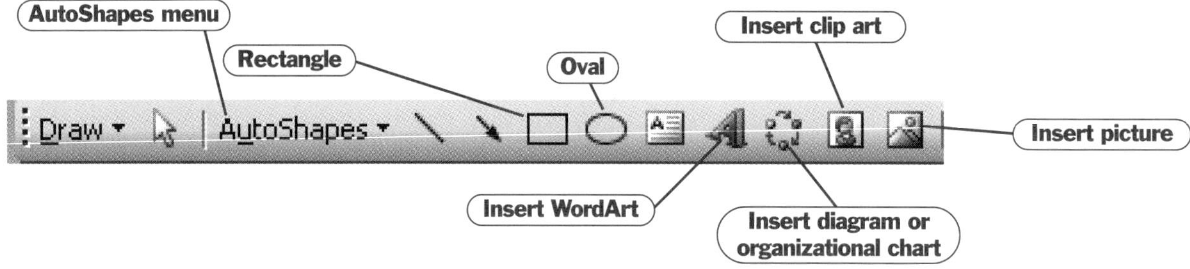

Figure 5.23 Shape and Image buttons on the Drawing toolbar

- To draw an oval or a rectangle, click the Oval or Rectangle button on the Drawing toolbar.

- Position the mouse pointer, which is now a crosshair (+), where you want to start the shape and drag diagonally. Release the Mouse button when you achieve the required size. To draw a perfect circle or square, hold down the Shift key as you drag the mouse. Figure 5.24 illustrates various shape examples.

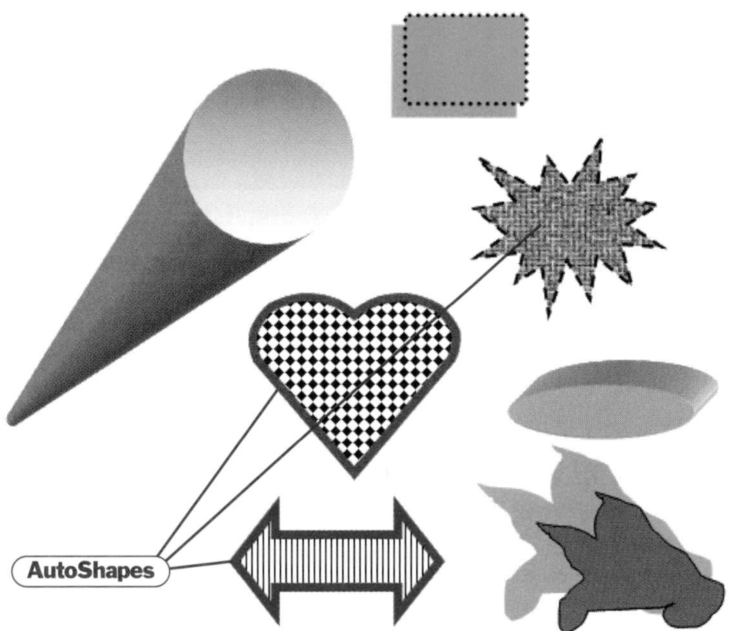

Figure 5.24 Shape samples

- You can select from a variety of predesigned shapes (lines, connectors, block arrows, stars and banners, flowchart elements, callouts, and basic shapes) by clicking the *AutoShapes* button on the Drawing toolbar and choosing from one of several menus, as shown in Figure 5.25. Each menu provides numerous shape options.
- As with floating images, shapes display size and rotate handles. Use the same procedures as you did with images and text boxes to format, position, size, and rotate shapes.

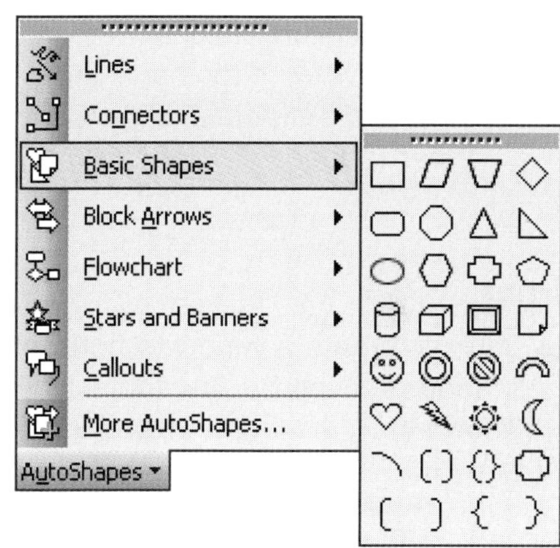

Figure 5.25 AutoShapes menu

TRY it OUT w5-11

Note: Be sure the handles are displayed each time you edit a shape.

1. Click the **New Blank Document** button.
2. Click the **Oval** button on the Drawing toolbar. (If the toolbar is not displayed, click **View, Toolbars,** and **Drawing** from the menu.)
3. Position the mouse pointer in a blank area of the page.
4. Hold down the **Shift** key, then click and drag the mouse diagonally until you create a small circle.
5. Select the circle and drag to move the circle to the upper-left corner of the page.
6. Click the **Fill Color** list arrow and choose **Yellow** from the palette.
7. Click the **Line Style** button and select **4½ point.**
8. Click the **Line Color** list arrow and choose **Red** from the palette.
9. Click the **AutoShapes** button on the Drawing toolbar, point to **Basic Shapes,** and click the **Heart** shape.
10. Position the mouse pointer in a blank area of the document and click and drag the mouse diagonally until you create a small heart.
11. Click the **Fill Color** list arrow and click **Red.** 
12. Click the **Fill Color** list arrow and click **Fill Effects.**
13. Click the **Pattern** tab.
14. Click any desired pattern and click **OK.**
15. Drag the heart so that it overlaps the circle.
16. Click the **Rectangle** button and draw a small rectangle in a blank area of the document.
17. Click the **3-D** button and select a 3-D effect. 
18. Click the **Shadow Style** button and select a shadow effect. 
19. Print one copy.
20. Close the file.

Lines

▶ You can create a variety of horizontal, vertical, and curved lines in a document or in headers and in footers using the line tools available on the Drawing toolbar and on the AutoShapes menu, as shown in Figure 5.26. Figure 5.27 illustrates lines you can create with the line tools in Word.

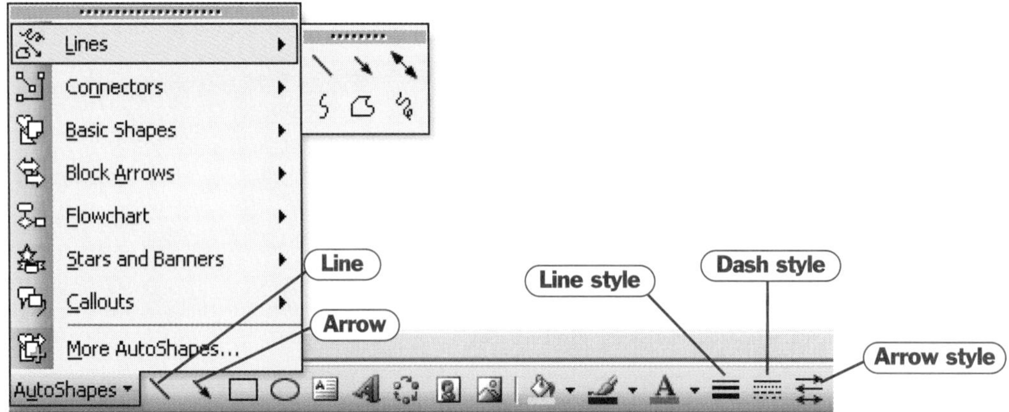

Figure 5.26 Line tools on Drawing toolbar and AutoShapes menu

- Click the Line button on the Drawing toolbar to create straight lines. Drag the insertion point (which becomes a crosshair) to the length you want. You can angle the line in any direction or adjust the size of the line when Word displays the handles.
- Use the the Lines menu in AutoShapes to create straight, curved, freeform, and scribble lines.
- Like other objects, you can use the same techniques to change a line style. Click the Line Style and/or Dash Style button to change the style of the selected line.
- When you click the Freeform or Scribble line style on the Lines menu, the insertion point becomes a crosshair. When you click to create the line, the crosshair becomes a pen. Use the mouse as a pen to draw the line as shown in Figure 5.28.
- When drawing a freeform line that does not result in a closed shape, you must double-click to end the line. When drawing a curve, you must click each time you create an angle, then click again to close the shape.
- You can also create lines with arrowheads. Click the Arrow button on the Drawing toolbar, then drag the insertion point to create the line. To change the arrow style, click the Arrow Style button and choose a style from the Arrow Style menu, as shown in Figure 5.29.
- Just like you can add color to border lines (on shapes, text boxes, or tables), you can add color to horizontal and vertical lines by clicking the Line Color button on the Drawing toolbar.

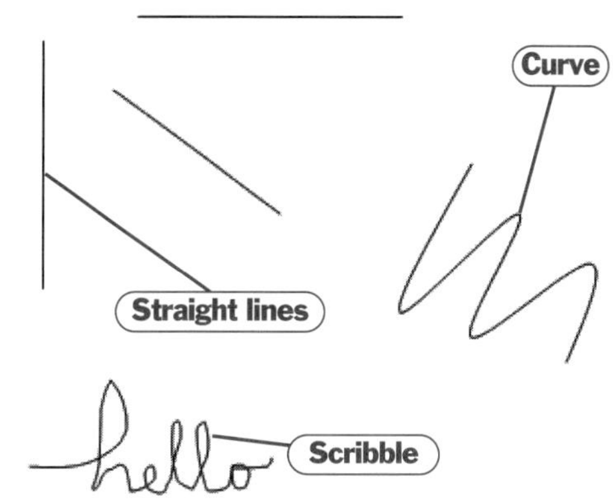

Figure 5.27 Line samples

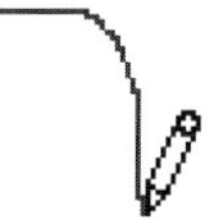

Figure 5.28 Drawing a freeform or scribble line

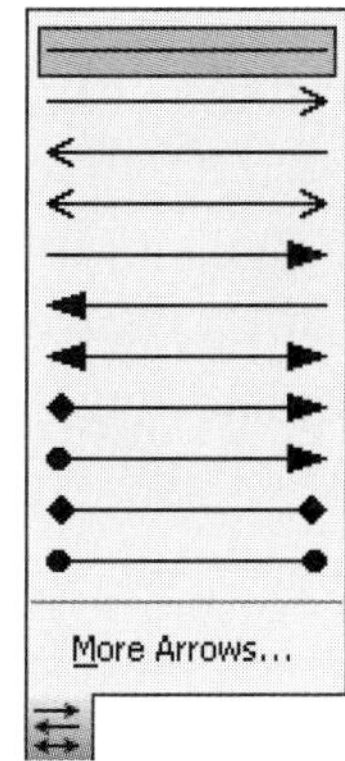

Figure 5.29 Arrow Styles menu

▶ To apply style and color options in one step, select the line and click Format, AutoFormat or right-click and choose Format AutoShape from the shortcut menu. On the Colors and Lines tab of the Format AutoShape dialog box, as shown in Figure 5.30, select the options you want. You can change the line size by clicking the Size tab and entering an amount in the Width box.

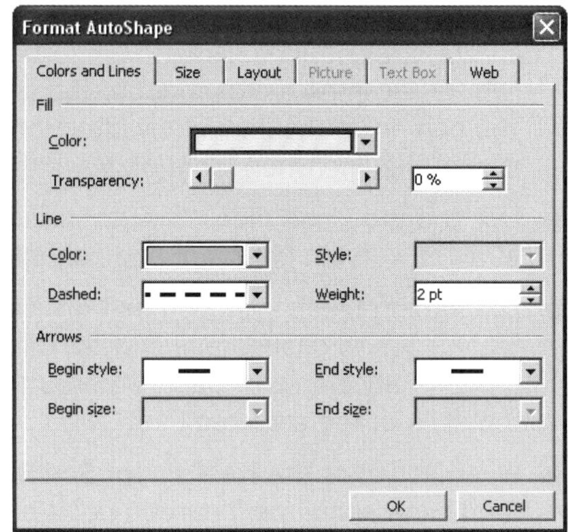

Figure 5.30 Colors and Lines tab in the Format AutoShape dialog box

TRY *it* OUT *w5-12*

1. Click the **New Blank Document** button.
2. Click the **Line** button on the Drawing toolbar.
3. Drag to create a small, straight horizontal line (before you release the mouse, be sure the line is straight).
4. Click **Format, AutoShape.**
5. On the **Size** tab, enter **4** in the Width box, and click **OK.**
6. Copy the line once, then paste it twice—one below the other.
7. Click to select the first line.
8. Click the **Line Style** button and select **4 ¼ point.**

9. Click the **Line Color** list arrow and select **Green.**

10. Click to select the second line.
11. Right-click and choose **Format AutoShape** from the shortcut menu.
12. Click the **Colors and Lines** tab.
13. Click the **Color** list arrow and select a color; click the **Dashed** list arrow and select a dashed style; click the **Line Style** button, click **3 point,** and click **OK.**
14. Click to select the third line.
15. Click the **Line Style** button and select **6 point.**

16. Click the **Arrow Style** button and select an arrow style.

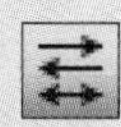

17. Click **AutoShapes, Lines,** and select the **Freeform** tool.
18. Create a diamond shape. Click to begin the line and click at each angle.
19. Click to select the first horizontal line and press the **Delete** key.
20. Close the file; do not save.

WordArt

- The *WordArt* feature lets you create a graphic object using text. Using Word's predesigned WordArt styles, you can create interesting text effects.
- To create WordArt, click the Insert WordArt button on the Drawing toolbar. In the WordArt Gallery dialog box that appears, as shown in Figure 5.31, click a WordArt style.

- After selecting a WordArt style, enter the text that you want to appear as WordArt in the Edit WordArt Text dialog box, as shown in Figure 5.32. Your text replaces the words "Your Text Here." Click OK to insert the WordArt into your document. As with clip art, WordArt is inserted into your document as an inline graphic. Apply a text wrap to it to create a floating graphic so that you can easily position it anywhere on the page.

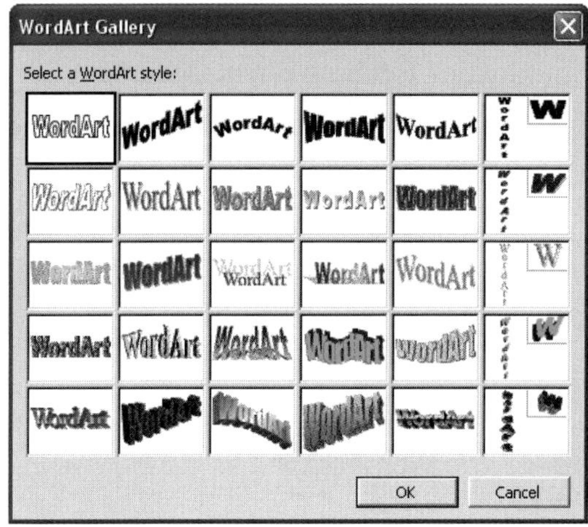

Figure 5.31 WordArt Gallery

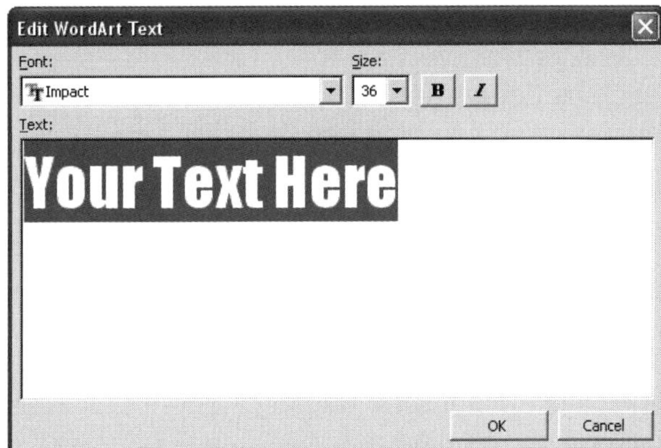

Figure 5.32 Edit WordArt Text dialog box

- When you select WordArt, the WordArt toolbar appears, as shown in Figure 5.33, so that you can change aspects of the WordArt shape.

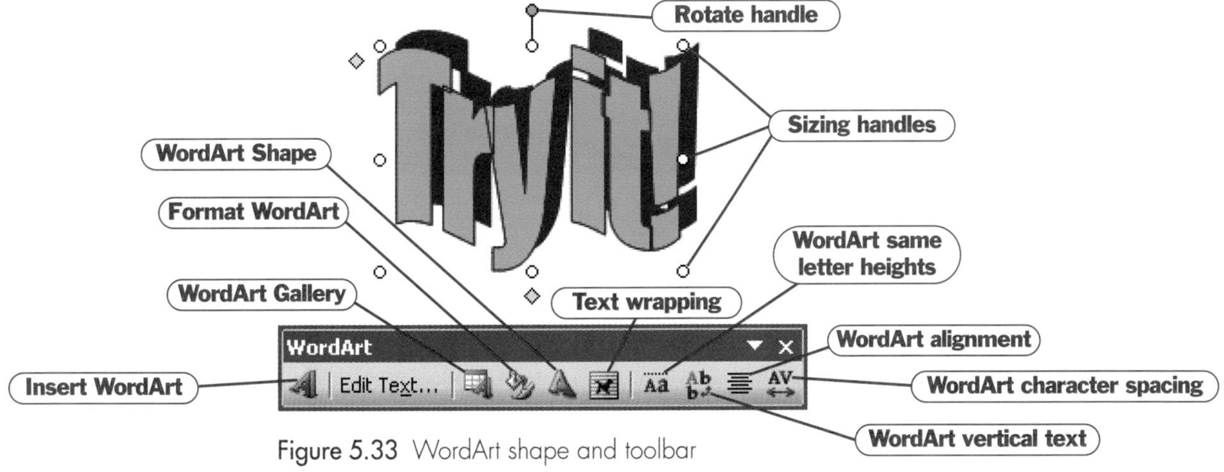

Figure 5.33 WordArt shape and toolbar

- You can size, position, copy, or delete WordArt graphics just as you can any other object.

TRY it OUT *w5-13*

1. Click the **New Blank Document** button.
2. Click the **Insert WordArt** button on the Drawing toolbar.
3. Click any WordArt style and click **OK.**
4. Enter: `Congratulations!` in the Text window and click **OK.**
5. Click to select the shape.
6. Click the **WordArt Shape** button on the WordArt toolbar.

7. Click the **Triangle Up** shape on the first row.
8. Click the **Format WordArt** button on the WordArt toolbar to open the Format WordArt dialog box.
9. On the **Colors and Lines** tab, click the **Fill Color** list arrow and select **Red;** click the **Line Color** list arrow and select **Yellow.**
10. Click **OK.**
11. Close the file; do not save.

Charts and Diagrams

- Word 2003 allows you to create, edit, and format conceptual diagrams and organization charts. These images help you to visualize information. You can use an *organization chart* to illustrate hierarchical structures, such as department reporting relationships within a company. You can also use it to show the flow of a project or family tree.
- To insert an organization chart or conceptual diagram, click the Insert Diagram or Organization Chart button on the Drawing toolbar.

- In the Diagram Gallery dialog box that appears, as shown in Figure 5.34, click a diagram type, which displays a short description indicating the context in which the diagram might be used.
- The Organization Chart toolbar also appears to assist you with chart formatting options, as shown in Figure 5.35.

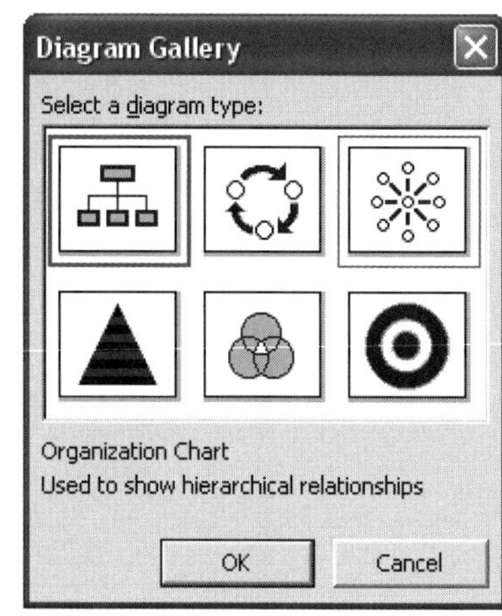

Figure 5.34 Diagram Gallery dialog box

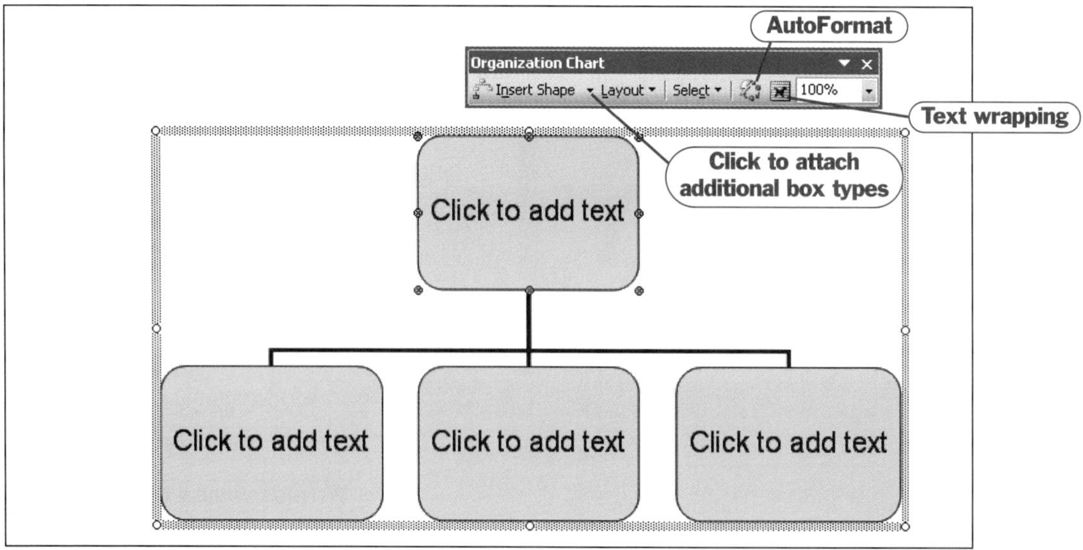

Figure 5.35 Organization Chart toolbar and organization chart

- An organization chart opens with four boxes, although you can attach additional box types—Subordinate, Coworker, or Assistant. To attach a box, click in the box to which you want to attach another box, click the Insert Shape list arrow on the Organization Chart toolbar (see Figure 5.35), and choose the box type to attach, as shown in Figure 5.36.

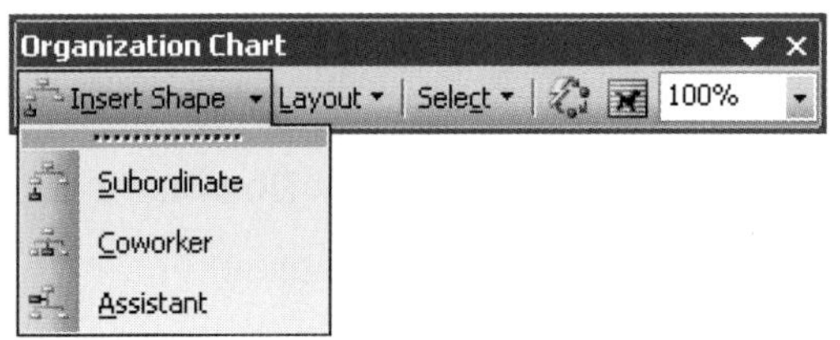

Figure 5.36 Organization chart box type options

- Each box type attaches to the existing boxes differently. A diagram next to the box type indicates how the box attaches. To enter text in the box, click in the box to display a box border (like other text boxes) and enter the text. Once text is in the box, you can align it using the buttons on the Formatting toolbar.
- You can format an organization chart or diagram with preset styles or you can format pieces of it as you would format shapes. That is, you can add color and text, change the line weight and style, and add fills, textures, and backgrounds, as shown in Figure 5.37.

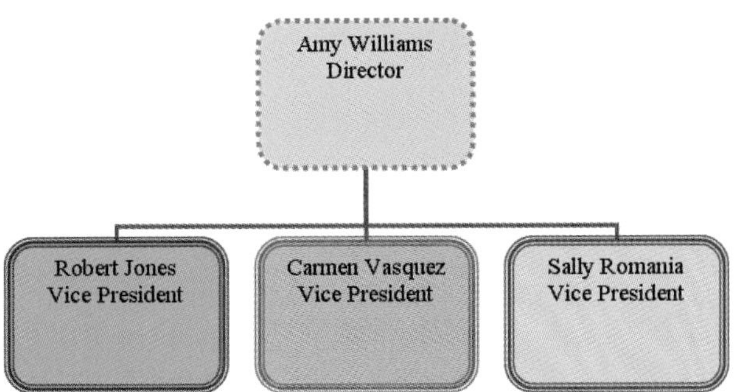

Figure 5.37 Organization chart with fill effects

- To apply a preset style, click the AutoFormat button on the Organization Chart toolbar and select a Diagram Style from those listed in the Organization Chart Style Gallery dialog box, as shown in Figure 5.38. You can also right-click a diagram part and choose a format option from the shortcut menu.

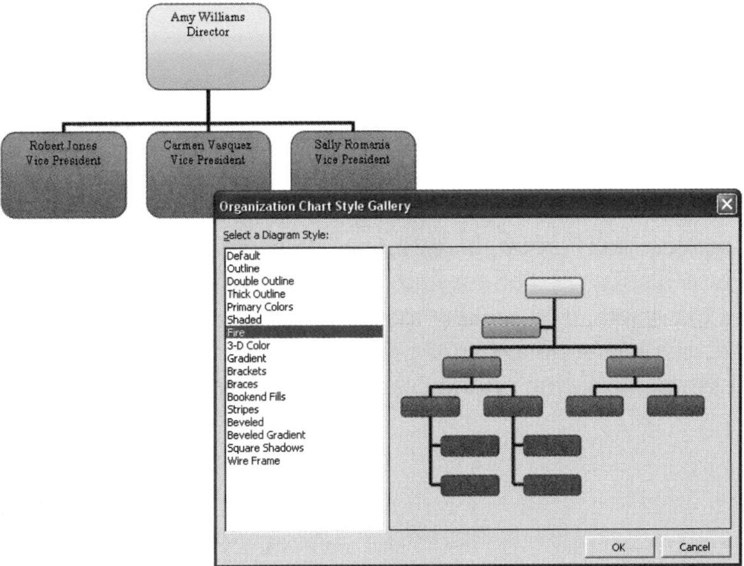

Figure 5.38 Organization Chart Style Gallery dialog box

TRY it OUT *w5-14*

1. Click the **New Blank Document** button. 
2. Click the **Insert Diagram or Organization Chart** button on the Drawing toolbar. Click **OK** to select the **Organization Chart,** which is the default selection.
3. Click in the top box and enter your name. Press the **Enter** key and enter: `Director.`
4. Click in the left box; enter: `Robert Jones.`
5. Press the **Enter** key and enter: `Vice President.`
6. Click in the middle box; enter: `Carmen Vasquez.`
7. Press the **Enter** key and enter: `Vice President.`
8. Click in the right box; enter: `Sally Romania.`
9. Press the **Enter** key and enter: `Vice President.`
10. Click in the box containing "Robert Jones."
11. Click the **Insert Shape** list arrow on the Organization Chart toolbar and click **Subordinate.**
12. Click in the newly inserted box; enter: `David Frome.`
13. Press the **Enter** key and enter: `Assistant.`
14. Click in the box containing your name.
    a. Position the insertion point at the edge of the box until a four-headed arrow appears. Right-click and choose **Format AutoShape.** Note that the Format AutoShape dialog box displays. On the Colors and Lines tab, click the **Fill Color** list arrow, and click **Light Blue.**
    b. Click the **Line Color** list arrow and click **Dark Blue.**
    c. Click the **Line Style** list arrow and click **3 point.**
    d. Click **OK.**
15. Click in the box containing the name "Robert Jones." Click the **Fill Color** list arrow and click **Light Green.**
16. Click in the box containing the name "Carmen Vasquez." Click the **Fill Color** list arrow and click **Light Orange.**
17. Click in the box containing the name "David Frome." Click the **Fill Color** list arrow and click **Lavender.**
18. Click in the box containing the name "Sally Romania." Click the **Fill Color** list arrow and click **Rose.**
19. Click on the edge of the box containing the name "David Frome." Press the **Delete** key to delete the box.
20. Print one copy.
21. Close the file; do not save.

Wrap Text Around Objects

- You can wrap text around images and other objects using the same techniques you used for wrapping text around text boxes. Click Format, (AutoShape, Organization Chart, Picture, or Text Box). Remember, you can also display the Format AutoShape, Organization Chart, Picture, or Text Box dialog box by selecting the object, right-clicking the mouse, and choosing the option from the shortcut menu. Choose a text-wrapping option on the Layout tab. You can also access the text wrap feature by clicking the Text Wrapping button on the Organization Chart or Picture toolbars.

TRY*it* OUT *w5-15*

1. Open **w5.15pf text wrap** from the Data CD.
2. Click the **Insert Diagram or Organization Chart** button. Choose the **Pyramid** diagram and click **OK.**
3. Click in the bottom box and enter: `Basic.` Set the font to 28-point bold.
4. Click in the middle box and enter: `Intermediate.` Set the font to 16-point bold.
5. Click in the top box and enter: `Expert.` Set the font to 10-point bold.
6. Click to select the diagram, click the **AutoFormat** button, select the **Primary Colors** diagram style, and click **OK.**
7. Click to select the diagram, right-click and choose **Format Diagram.**
8. Click the **Size** tab. Enter `2` in the Height box and `2` in the Width box, and click **OK.**
9. Click to select the diagram, click the **Text Wrapping** button, and click **Square** as the wrap option.
10. Click to select the diagram, position the insertion point on the border until it becomes a four-headed arrow, and drag the diagram to position it at the top and in the middle of the text. Click outside the diagram.
11. Click the **Oval** button.
12. Draw a small circle anywhere on the page. Fill it with any color or pattern.
13. Click **Format, AutoShape,** click the **Layout** tab, and click **Tight** as the wrap option. Click **Right** as the Horizontal alignment and click **OK.**
14. Close the file; do not save.

Group and Layer Objects

▶ When you *layer* or stack objects on top of each other, you create shadowing and other effects, as shown in Figure 5.39.

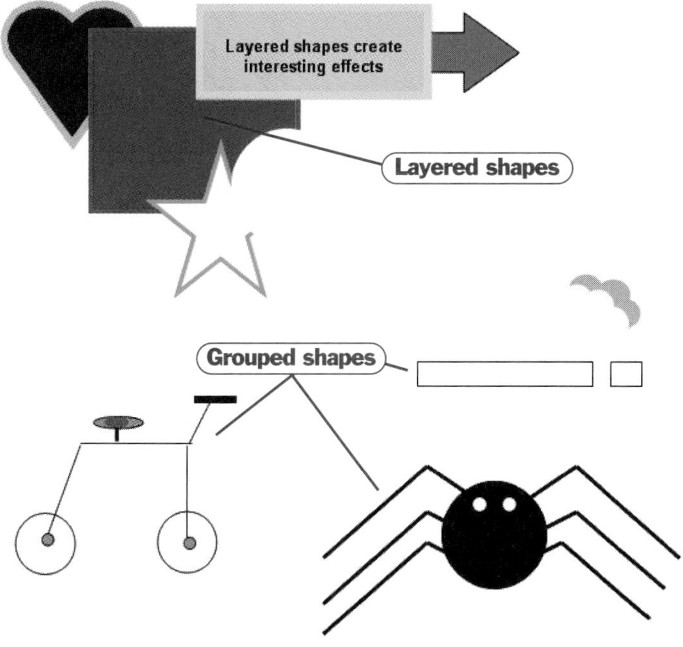

Figure 5.39 Layered and grouped objects

- You can rearrange the order of layered objects by selecting the object and clicking the Draw button on the Drawing toolbar. This opens the Draw menu, shown in Figure 5.40. Click Order, and Send to Back or Bring to Front. Send to Back moves an item to the bottom of all the other items in the stack; Bring to Front moves an item to the top of all other items in the stack. You can also display the Order options by right-clicking on the object and choosing Order from the shortcut menu.
- When you *group* objects, you create one object out of individual parts. Grouped objects behave like a single object (see grouped shapes in Figure 5.39). Grouping is particularly useful when you want to move or copy the objects as a single item. If you want to edit part of a grouped object, you must first *ungroup* it.
- To group objects, hold down the Shift key as you select the individual objects. You can select all individual objects at once by clicking the Select Objects button on the Drawing toolbar and dragging the pointer around all the objects, as shown in Figure 5.41. After selecting the individual parts, click Draw on the Drawing toolbar, and click Group. Figure 5.42 shows a grouped object. To ungroup, click the grouped object to select it, click Draw, and click Ungroup.

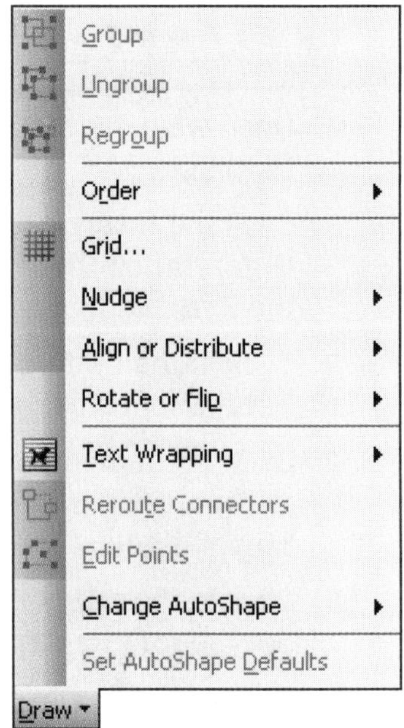

Figure 5.40 Draw menu options

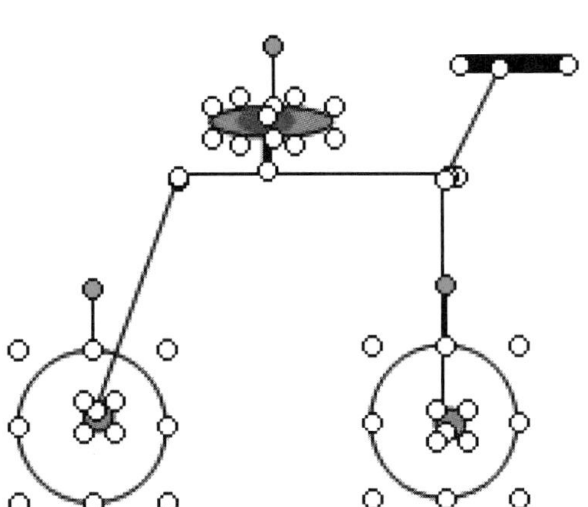

Figure 5.41 Selected parts of an object

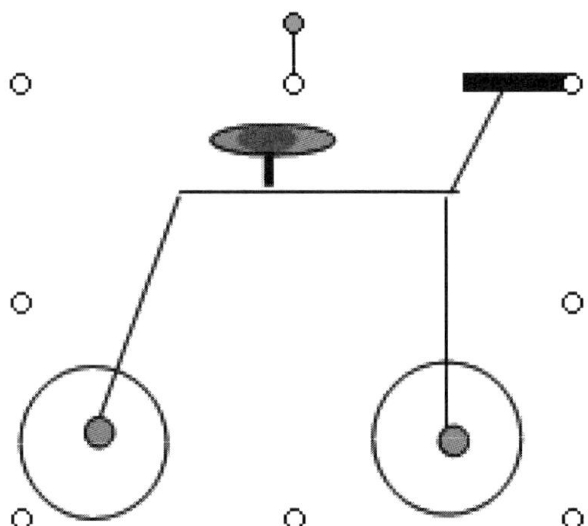

Figure 5.42 Grouped object

TRY*it*OUT *w5-16*

1. Open **w5.16pf shapes** from the Data CD.
2. Click to select the **text box.**
3. Click the **Draw** button and click **Order, Bring to Front.**

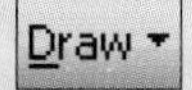

4. Click to select the **Star** shape.
5. Right-click, choose **Order,** and **Send to Back.**
6. Click to select the **Heart** shape.
7. Click **Draw, Order,** and **Send to Back.**
8. Click the **Select Objects** button.
9. Position the pointer at the top left of the bike. Drag to draw a box around the bike to select all bike parts.
10. Click **Draw, Group.**
11. Position the pointer at the top left of the cigarette. Drag to draw a box around all cigarette parts.
12. Click **Draw, Group.**
13. Click to select the **Bike.** Drag a corner handle to increase the size of the object.
14. Drag the bike to the lower-left corner of the page.
15. Click to select the **Bike.**
16. Click **Draw, Ungroup.**
17. Click to select the **Red Circle** on top of the bike seat. Press the **Delete** key.
18. Click the **Select Objects** button, select all bike parts, click **Draw, Regroup.**

19. Close the file; do not save.

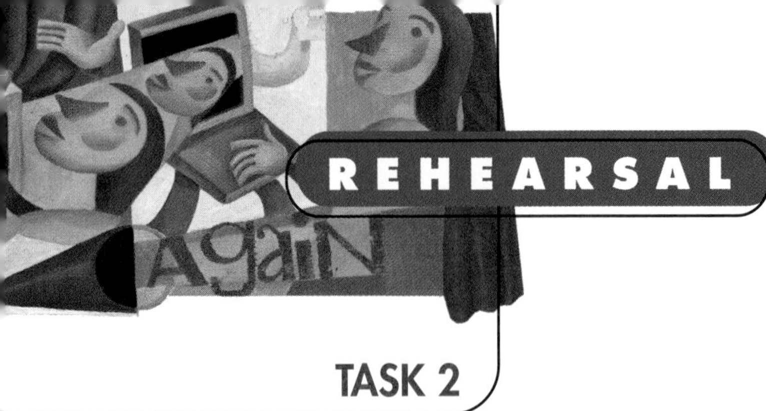

GOAL
To create an advertisement, a catalog page, and a newsletter using images and objects

SETTING THE STAGE/WRAPUP

Margins: 1" left and right for advertisement
1" default for catalog page
1" left and right, 0.5" bottom, for newsletter

Start line: 1" for all

File names: 5.2ad text
5.2advertisement
5.2catalog page
5.2newsletter text
5.2newsletter

WHAT YOU NEED TO KNOW

- An *advertisement* is a communication that conveys a message about a product or service and thus helps to market that product or service. An advertisement, therefore, is a sales tool.
- Advertisements may appear in magazines, newspapers, and billboards. The goal of a good advertisement is to have a clear, uncluttered presentation. Images should be relevant and relate to the subject or product advertised.
- In this Rehearsal activity, you will create an advertisement for Green Brothers Gardening.

DIRECTIONS

Create an Advertisement

1. Open **5.2ad text** from the Data CD. Enhance the text with images and objects as follows to create the advertisement shown on the following page.
2. Create a medium-sized text box and do the following:
   a. Enter `Green Brothers Gardening` in 48 point.
   b. Change the text direction as shown in the illustration.
   c. Size the text box height to 7.4" and the width to 1.12". Center the text.
   d. Apply a Square text-wrap option and horizontally align the box on the left.
   e. Apply a Light Yellow fill.
   f. Delete the "o" in "Brothers." Enter four spaces between the "r" and the "t."
   g. Use AutoShapes to create a star; fill it Green and position it between the "r" and "t" as shown on the next page.
   h. Group the text box and position it so that it is vertically centered on the page.
3. Create the tree as follows:
   a. Use the **Freeform** drawing tool to draw the tree trunk. (Delete the drawing canvas if it appears.) Color the trunk **Brown.**
   b. Use the **Oval** tool to draw one leaf. Color the leaf **Green.**
   c. Copy the leaf several times and position the copies around the tree trunk.

Continued on next page

d. Group the tree parts.
e. Size the image to **2"** high by **2"** wide.
f. Position the image in the middle of the text, as shown, and apply a **Tight** wrap option.

4. Center the featured plant text. Color the text as shown.

5. Create the design at the top of the page as follows:
   a. Draw a 10-point line from the left to the right margin at the top margin. Color it **Gray.**
   b. Copy the line five times and position each line below the other as shown.
   c. Color each line a different shade of **Gray.**
   d. Set the line width to 10 points for the first line; set the second line to 6 points, the third line to 3 points, the fourth line to 2.25 points, and the fifth and sixth lines to 1 point.
   e. Copy the tree image once. Size it to fit on one of the lines.
   f. Bring the graphic to the front (enabling the image to sit on top of the line).
   g. Copy the small tree five more times. Position and size each to resemble the illustration on the next page.

6. Create an organization chart.
   a. Center the text in each box and fill each box as shown.
   b. Apply a **Tight** wrap option and position the chart as shown.

7. Preview the document.

8. Print one copy.

9. Save the file; name it **5.2 advertisement.** Close the file.

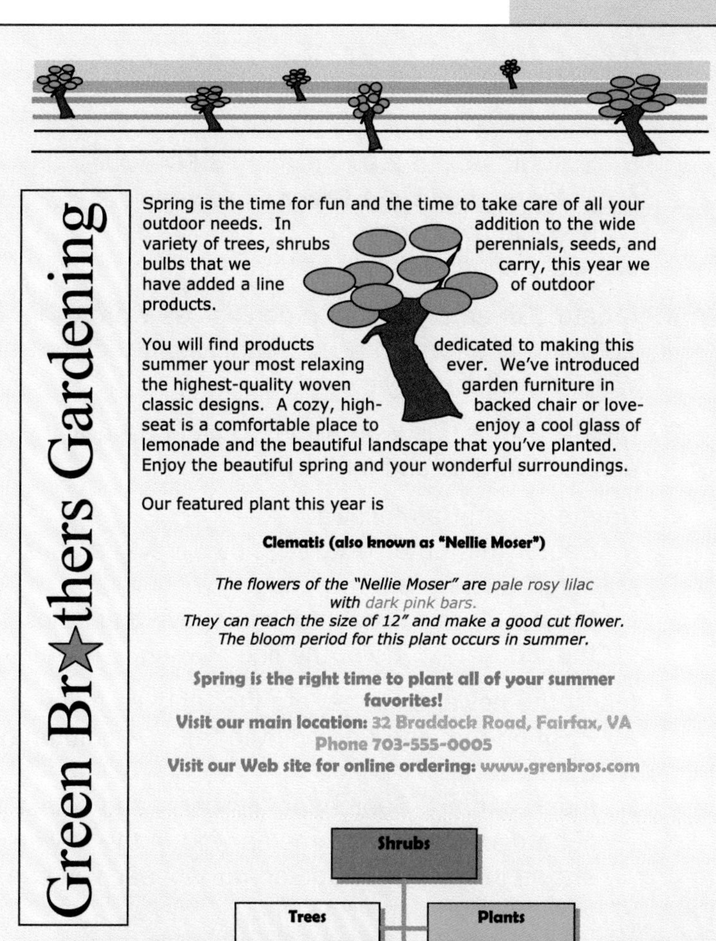

WHAT YOU NEED TO KNOW

- A *catalog* is a booklet that includes product photos, captions, prices, and an order form. A catalog is often sent to homes and businesses and is considered a direct-mail sales tool. Catalogs use a lot of color, which tends to increase their selling power. The inside page of a catalog usually describes the company. Sometimes there is a letter from the president explaining the company's philosophy.
- In this Rehearsal activity, you will create a sample catalog page for Green Brothers Gardening for a catalog they are developing.

DIRECTIONS

Create a Catalog Page

1. Click the **New Blank Document** button and create the catalog page shown on the next page as follows.

2. Begin the table approximately **3.3"** as noted by the At indictor on the Status bar. Create the table using two columns and seven rows.
3. Create a text box as follows:
   a. Enter the "Dear Gardener" text shown using a sans serif 10-point font.
   b. Size the box to **2.07"** high by **3.56"** wide.
   c. Color the box **Light Green.**
   d. Remove the border.
   e. Add a shadow effect and position it as shown.
4. Create "Green Brothers Gardening" as WordArt in 28 point, and rotated as shown. Use any desired WordArt and font style.
5. Create "Bulbs" as WordArt in 36 point. Use any desired WordArt and font style.
6. Create a footer as follows:
   a. Center the footer text, as shown, using a sans serif 12-point font.
   b. Draw a 3-point horizontal line above and below the footer text. Color the lines **Green.**
7. Insert the flower pictures into the table as follows:
   a. Position the insertion point in the first column of the first row.
   b. Insert clip art. Search for "Flowers" and select "Photographs" as the media type. If the flowers shown in the illustration do not appear, you can find them on Clip Art Online.
   c. Insert a photo of each flower type as shown. Size each photograph to approximately 1.25" high by 1.25" wide. (Some photos may require a different width to keep the photo in proportion. Adjust the width appropriately.)

Continued on next page

WORD

d. Apply a **Square** text-wrap and a **Right** alignment option.

e. Enter each flower name using a 12-point sans serif font, then apply a **Red** font color.

f. Enter the Price and Item No. information, as shown, using a 12-point font.

g. Position the insertion point in the second column of the first row and repeat Steps c. through f.

Hint: Copy the flower name and pricing information from one cell to another, then edit the information as necessary.

h. Apply a dashed border to the table, as shown.

8. Preview the document.

9. Print one copy.

10. Save the file; name it **5.2 catalog page.**

11. Close the file.

WHAT YOU NEED TO KNOW

- A *newsletter* is a communication that allows people who share a common interest to exchange ideas, developments, and information on a regular basis. Business organizations use newsletters to deliver a message about new products, promotions, achievements, and announcements.
- Although the format of newsletters varies, the following basic parts can be found on the first page of most newsletters:
  - Masthead—includes the newsletter title, the division or organization publishing the document, the volume or issue number, and the current date of the issue.
  - Contents—includes the articles or topics featured in the issue.
  - Headline—summarizes the contents of the articles that follow.
  - Body copy—includes the text of the articles.
- After applying a text-wrap option, adjust the position of objects to avoid awkward line breaks.
- In this Rehearsal activity, you will create a health-related newsletter, which In-Shape Fitness Centers will distribute to its clients.

DIRECTIONS

Create a Newsletter

1. Open **5.2 newsletter text** from the Data CD. You will format this text to become the newsletter shown on the facing page.
2. Position the insertion point before the first word, "In," and press the **Enter** key enough times so the At indicator on the status bar reads 2.7".
3. Create three columns (click **Format, Columns**).

Note: You must click the option "This point forward" in the Columns dialog box so that the column formatting is not applied to the entire document.

4. Format "In This Issue" in sans serif 10 point. Apply an **Orange** color to the text, as shown (apply a lighter shade of orange to "In This Issue").
5. Set the headlines to sans serif 12-point bold. Apply a **Blue** color to the headline text.
6. Set the body text to 11 point.
7. Draw a 3-point horizontal dashed line before and after "In This Issue," as shown.
8. To create the masthead, do the following:
   a. Create a text box and enter the text as shown. Right-align "Fall 2005."
   b. Format the text box text as sans serif.
   c. Set "Health" to 48 point, then set character spacing to condensed by 2 points. Apply a **Dark Orange** font color. Set "watch" to 36-point bold, set character spacing to condensed by **0.7** and scaled to **150%.** Apply a **Light Orange** font color.
   d. Position the masthead, as shown.
   e. Create a 12-point solid horizontal line below "Healthwatch."
   f. Set "A Newsletter from In-Shape Fitness Centers" to 12 point.
   g. Remove the border.

Continued on next page

9. Insert relevant images, where shown. Size them to keep the text on one page. Apply a **Square** text—wrap to each image.
10. Create the text box shown at the bottom of the newsletter as follows:
    a. Enter the text, as shown. Center and underline the heading using a sans serif 11-point font. Set the remaining text to 9 point.
    b. Apply a 4½ point dotted border and a **Light Yellow** fill color.
    c. Apply a **Tight** text-wrap.
    d. Stretch the text box to span two columns.
11. Preview the document.
12. Save the file; name it **5.2 newsletter.**
13. Print one copy.
14. Close the file.

Healthwatch

A Newsletter from In-Shape Fitness Centers

Fall 2005

In This Issue

Vitamin C Shown to Reduce Heart Disease

Beta-carotene Alert: It May Clear Your Arteries

Vitamin C Shown to Reduce Heart Disease

New studies have shown that high blood levels of vitamin C are associated with higher levels of "good" cholesterol in the blood and lower the risk of coronary heart disease. Research shows that vitamin C appears to prevent cholesterol from being oxidized in the blood; this may decrease the chance that the cholesterol circulating in the blood will end up in the arteries, increasing one's risk of acquiring heart disease.

Vitamin C can be found in one whole papaya, mango, orange, half of a cantaloupe, one cup strawberries, broccoli, orange or grapefruit juice, brussels sprouts, or cauliflower. Be sure to maintain your vitamin C intake—your life depends on it!

Beta-carotene Alert: It May Clear Your Arteries!

Beta-carotene, processed by the body to form vitamin A, has been noted as useful in treating fatty-cholesterol deposits in arteries that lead to heart attacks and strokes. Beta-carotene is found in yellow-orange or red foods, such as oranges, peaches, sweet potatoes, and carrots. It is also found in leafy, dark-green vegetables; the green color of chlorophyll masks the color of the beta-carotene.

For these reasons, it is important to consume fruits and vegetables as part of your regular diet. In fact, six servings of fruits and vegetables are recommended daily. If you choose one fruit and one vegetable high in vitamin C every day, your remaining portions should include some dark green vegetables, yellow vegetables, and fruit. Fresh fruit and vegetables provide more nutrients to the body than canned ones.

To maintain a healthy diet, one should eat moderately from the five basic food groups (fruits and vegetables, dairy, grains, meats, and fats) with low fats, simple sugars, low cholesterol, high carbohydrates, moderate protein, high fiber, and an adequate supply of vitamins, minerals and water. It's too bad we never followed our mothers' advice about eating vegetables. As more and more research is done, we are finding that Mom was smart to force us to eat that one last bite of broccoli at the dinner table. She was adding years to our lives.

Tips for Your Overall Diet

1. Always eat breakfast, even if you have only a piece of fruit and a glass of milk. Your blood sugar level is very low in the morning.
2. Eat five or six small meals during the day. This will help keep your energy levels high.
3. Avoid overeating. Large amounts of food require a lot of time to digest, thus draining the body of energy. Eat until you are satisfied and then stop.
4. Drink plenty of water throughout the day, especially after exercising.
5. Above all, listen to your body.

Cues for Reference

Insert an Image

1. Click the **Insert Clip Art** button.
2. Enter a word or phrase in the **Search for** text box to describe the clip art you want to insert.
3. Click **Go.**
4. Click the image to insert it. The image inserts as an inline graphic. To change it to a floating object, select the image, then click **Format, Picture, Layout** tab, and then click a **Wrapping style.**
   Or
   Right-click the image and choose **Format Picture** from the shortcut menu, then choose options from the dialog box.

Find Images on the Web

- Click **Clip art on Office Online** in the Clip Art task pane.

Create an Object

Shape

1. Click the **Rectangle** or **Oval** button. Press the **Delete** key to delete the drawing canvas (if necessary).
2. Drag diagonally to create a shape. (Hold down **Shift** as you drag to create a perfect circle or square.)

AutoShape

1. Click the **AutoShapes** button.
2. Select an **AutoShape** from the AutoShapes menu.
3. Drag diagonally to create a shape.

Line

1. Click the **Line** button. 
2. Drag vertically, horizontally, or diagonally to create the line.

WordArt

1. Click the **Insert WordArt** button. 
2. Click to select a WordArt style in the WordArt Gallery.
3. Enter the text to appear as WordArt and click **OK.**

Charts and Diagrams

1. Click the **Insert Diagram or Organizational Chart** button.
2. Click to select a diagram.
3. Edit the diagram or chart, and click **OK.**

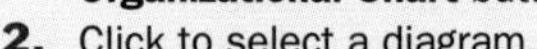

Group/Ungroup

1. Hold down **Shift** as you click each part to group, or click the **Select Objects** button and drag a box around all parts.
2. Click the **Draw** button.
3. Click **Group.**
4. To ungroup, click the object to select it and click **Draw, Ungroup.**
   Or
   Select the object(s), right-click and select, **Grouping, Group** or **Ungroup.**

SETTING THE STAGE

Act I Filename:	5.p1 barbeque
Act II Filename:	5.p2 airlines ad
	5.p2airlines
Act III Filename:	5.p3 als news
	5.p3als news text

WORD

WHAT YOU NEED TO KNOW

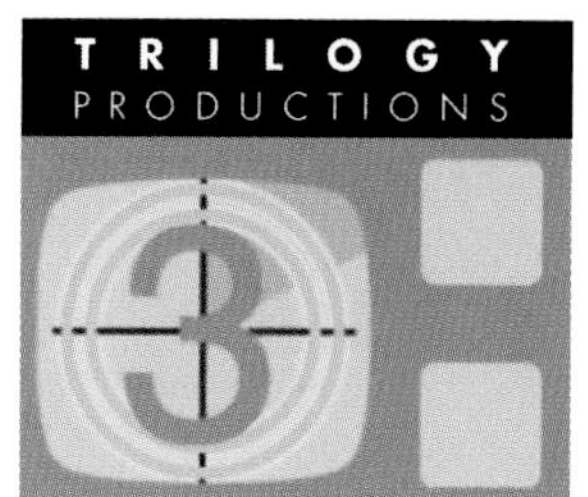

Act I

To boost company morale, John Alan, the CEO of Trilogy Productions, has invited the staff of the California office to a company barbeque that he is hosting at his home. It is scheduled for Saturday, June 17 at 1:00 p.m. John lives at 400 Beverly Glen in Beverly Hills, California. He would like people to R.S.V.P. to his assistant, Jim Bronson, at Extension 444.

You have been asked to create a flyer providing this information and encouraging all employees to attend.

Follow these guidelines:

- Use any font style(s), font color(s), and font size(s).
- Apply character spacing where applicable.
- Use at least one text box.
- Do not include clip art or pictures, but you may use shapes, lines, symbols, AutoShapes, and WordArt.
- Use any page border.
- Save the file; name it **5.p1 barbeque.**

Act II

Air Land Sea Travel Group has asked you to create the following advertisement, which will run in travel trade magazines and brochures that will be sent to clients. Your boss has sketched the following design, which she wants you to follow.

BON VOYAGE!

Cockpit

Luggage

Electronic Equipment

Smoking

We welcome your comments!

Beverage

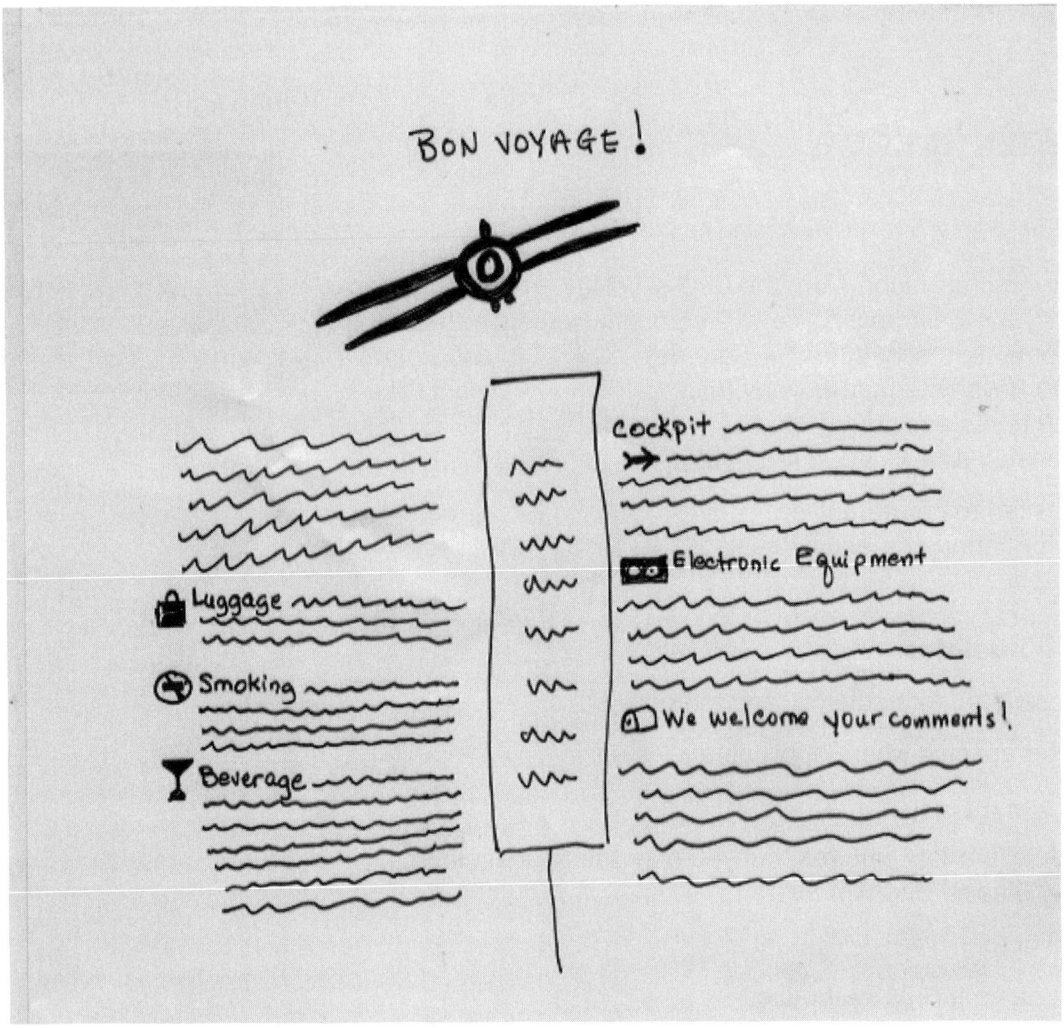

Follow these guidelines:

- The body text can be found on the Data CD under the file name **5.p2 airlines.**
- Draw the airplane using the drawing tools.
- Format the advertisement using two columns. Insert a vertical line between the columns.
- Draw the small illustrations or use clip art or symbols. Use a Square wrap option and left-align the images. Size them as you prefer.

- Create a text box and enter the following text:

  `On behalf of the ALS Travel Group and its affiliate offices, we offer you this important information to make your journey safe, comfortable, and enjoyable.`

- Position the text box, as shown, using a Tight wrap option. Use any font style, size, and fill color for the text box.
- Save the file as **5.p2 airlines ad.**

Act III

You have just landed a job as the public relations director and desktop publisher for the Air Land Sea Travel Group. The company would like to create a one-page newsletter that it will publish monthly. It will distribute the newsletter to employees of the firm as well as to ALS travel clients.

You have been asked to design a masthead for the newsletter, which the company wants to call *CLUB NEWS: A Newsletter of the ALS Travel Group.*

Follow these guidelines:

- The information to include this month is on the Data CD under the file name **5.p3 als newstext.**
- Format the newsletter using three or four columns. Set the column widths as you prefer.
- Include a Contents section.
- Use at least three images and place them where you choose. One of the images should be of Paris; another should be of Rome. (Search the Internet to find pictures of these cities.)
- Use at least one text box. Apply any font, font size, font colors, or fills to the text box. You can decide what text you would like to insert into the box.
- Emphasize headline text.
- Save the file; name it **5.p3 als news.**

LESSON 6

Integration/Word and the Web

In this lesson, you will learn to use features found in Word to integrate documents with other applications and with the Web. In addition, you will learn to merge documents and manage files. You will complete the following projects:

- Two merge letters, one with an imported table
- Two Web pages

Upon completion of this lesson, you should have mastered the following skill sets:

- Understand integration basics
- Import a table using Paste Special
- Use basic mail merge
- Create a hyperlink
- Save a document as a Web page
- Preview a Web page
- Create a Web page
  - using a template
  - using a blank page
- Use backgrounds and themes
- Save and retrieve files in specialized locations
- Create a new folder
- Rename or delete a file
- Move a file
- View files
- Work with Word and Outlook
  - Create a Contacts List and Address Book in Outlook
  - Use a Contacts List and Address Book in Word
  - Update a Contacts List through Smart Tags

Terms

Software-related

Embedded object
Linked object
Hyperlink
Hypertext
HTML
MHTML
Home page
Server
Contacts
Address Book

Document-related

Integration
Source
Destination
Main document
Variable information
Merge field
Data source document

GOAL
To practice using the following skill sets:
- Understand integration basics
- Import a table using Paste Special
- Use basic mail merge

WHAT YOU NEED TO KNOW

Understand Integration Basics

- *Integration* is the sharing or combining of data between files in the same application or between files in different applications. For example, you can import data you create in Excel into a Word document, or you can export a table you create in Word to PowerPoint (importing and exporting files in other applications are covered in their respective units). Figure 6.1 illustrates the integration of a table with a document.

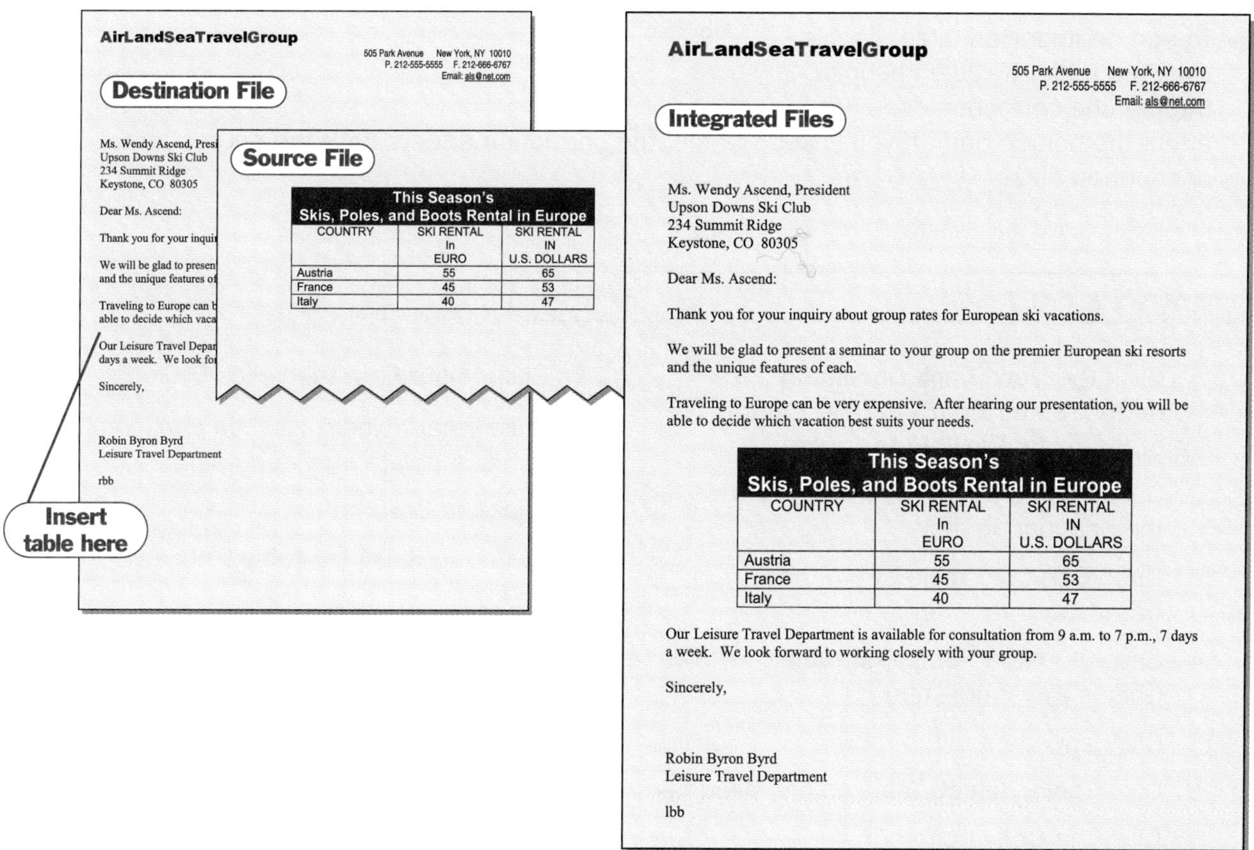

Figure 6.1 Integrating source and destination files

- When you share or combine data, it is important to know where the data is coming from and where it is going. The file where the data originates is called the *source* file. The file that receives the imported data is called the *destination* file.

Import a Table Using Paste Special

- To import a table from one document or file to another, select the table, click the Copy button on the Standard toolbar, then click Edit, Paste Special. In the Paste Special dialog box that displays, shown in Figure 6.2, choose Microsoft Office Word Document Object (to indicate how to paste the item) and click the Paste option. This creates an embedded object.
- With an *embedded object,* data in the destination file does not change if you modify the source file. Embedded objects become part of the destination file with no connection to the source file. Choosing the Paste link option in the dialog box creates a linked object. With a *linked object,* when you make any change to the source file, Word automatically updates the destination file. The source and destination files are connected by the link.

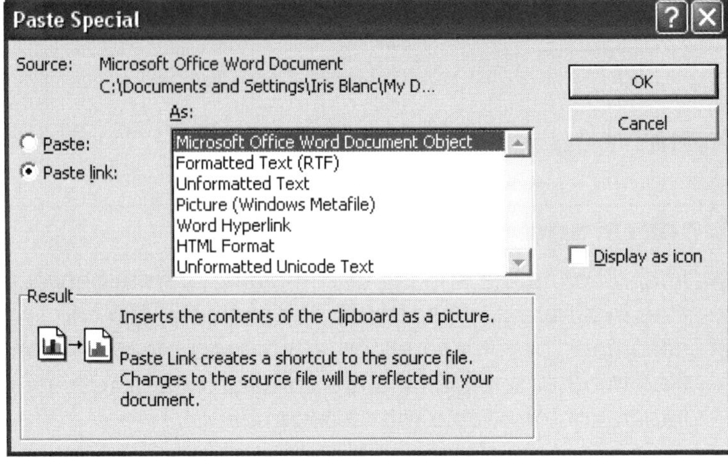

Figure 6.2 Paste Special dialog box

- To edit an imported table, double-click the table. If you embedded the file, the correction does not affect the source data. If you linked the file, the correction affects both the source and destination files.

TRY *it* OUT *w6-1*

1. Click the **New Blank Document** button. Enter today's date at the top of the page. Press **Enter** twice.

2. Save the file as **6.1paste special** (this is the destination file).
3. Open **6.1pf ski table1** from the Data CD.

4. Save the file as **6.1pf ski table1 my own** (this is the source file).
5. Click anywhere in the table.
6. Click **Table, Select, Table** on the menu bar.
7. Click the **Copy** button.

8. Switch to the **6.1paste special** document.
9. Click **Edit, Paste Special.**
10. Click **Microsoft Office Word Document Object** in the As list.
11. Click **Paste link**, then click **OK.**

Note: Like other objects, you can size, copy, move, edit, or delete a pasted table.

12. Click the **Save** button.
13. Switch to **6.1pf ski table1 my own** and close it.
14. In the **6.1paste special** document (which is still open), double-click the table. Notice, this opens the source file.
15. Change the Austrian Euro amount to 60 and the corresponding U.S. dollar amount to 70.
16. Click **Edit, Update Link**. Notice that the changes are reflected in the destination file.
17. Close the file, do not save.

Use Basic Mail Merge

- The mail merge process combines a letter with a list of information (such as names and addresses) so you can mass-produce a mailing to many people. The mail merge process starts with two documents:

Data Source Document

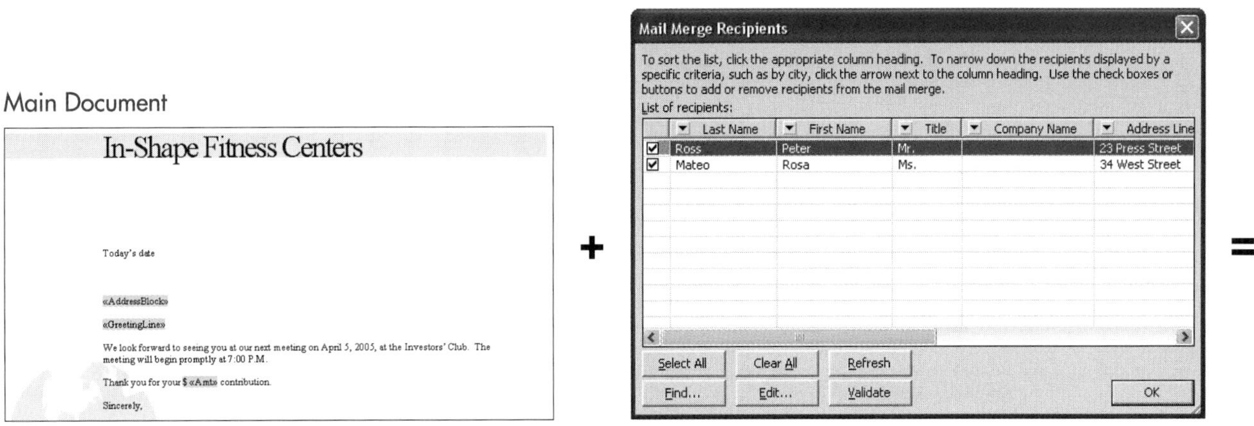

Merged Documents

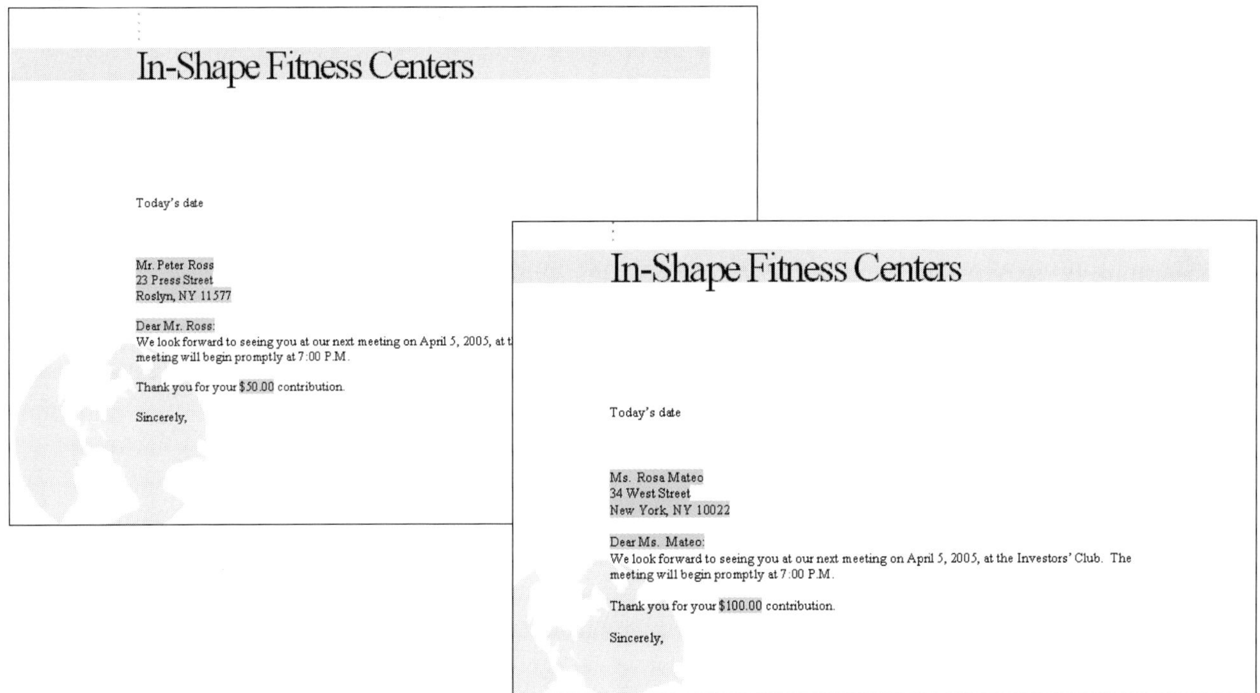

Figure 6.3 The Mail Merge process

1. The *main document* contains information that *does not* change, as well as merge fields where you insert variable information. *Variable information* is data that does change.
   - A *merge field* code acts as a placeholder for the variable information. Each field code is named for what will eventually be inserted into that location. A main document, as shown in Figure 6.4, must include all formatting, graphics, and paper size information. You must insert space between merge codes just as you would if actual information were there.

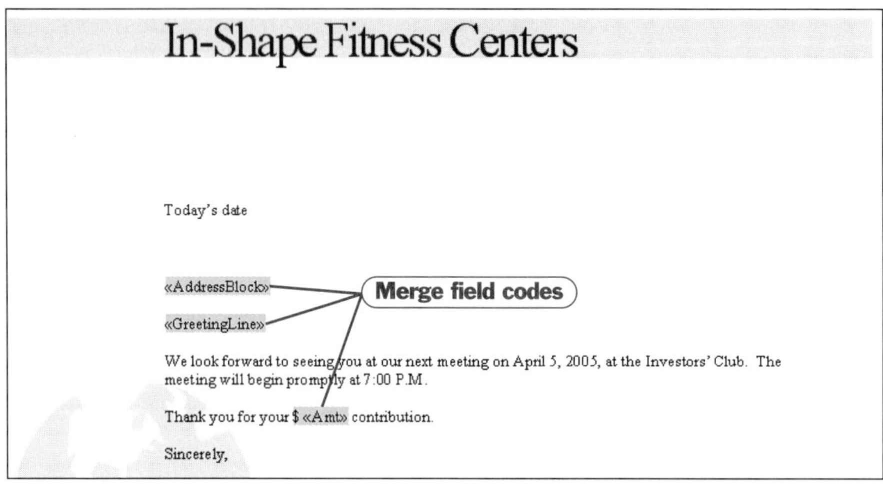
In-Shape Fitness Centers

Today's date

«AddressBlock»

«GreetingLine»

We look forward to seeing you at our next meeting on April 5, 2005, at the Investors' Club. The meeting will begin promptly at 7:00 P.M.

Thank you for your $ «Amt» contribution.

Sincerely,

Figure 6.4 Main document (letter) with merge codes

   - You can create a new blank document, use a template, or use an existing document as the main document.
2. The *data source document* contains variable information, that is, information that *does* change.

▶ A *data source document* contains many records. A record is a collection of related information about one person or one thing. After the data source creation process, Word displays the data in an Access table. (You can also use a Word table as a data source document.) Each row in the table is one record. Figure 6.5 shows an Access data source document, which contains names, addresses, and other variable information.

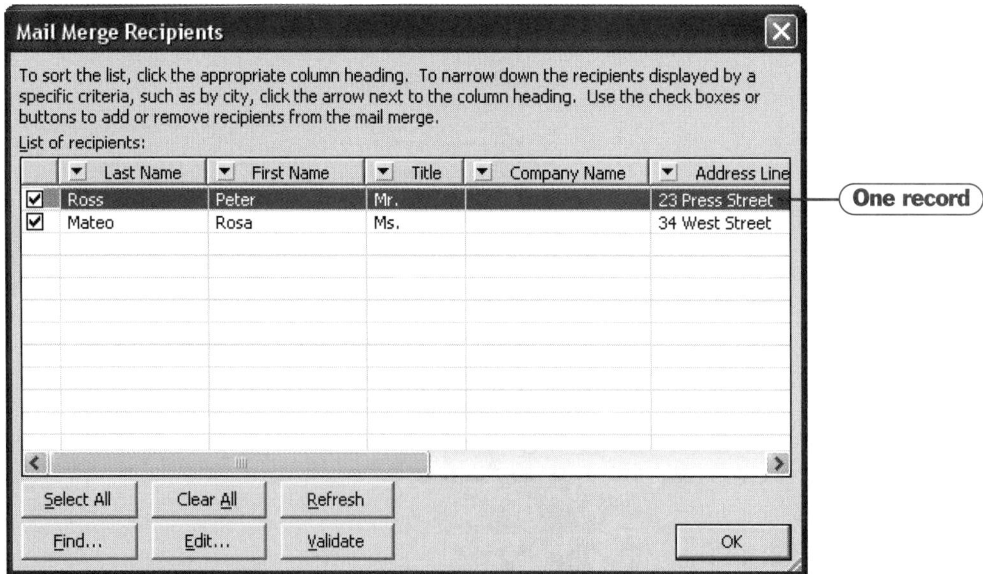

Figure 6.5 Data source document

- The main document (letter) and the data source document will be merged to produce individualized letters, one of which is shown in Figure 6.6.

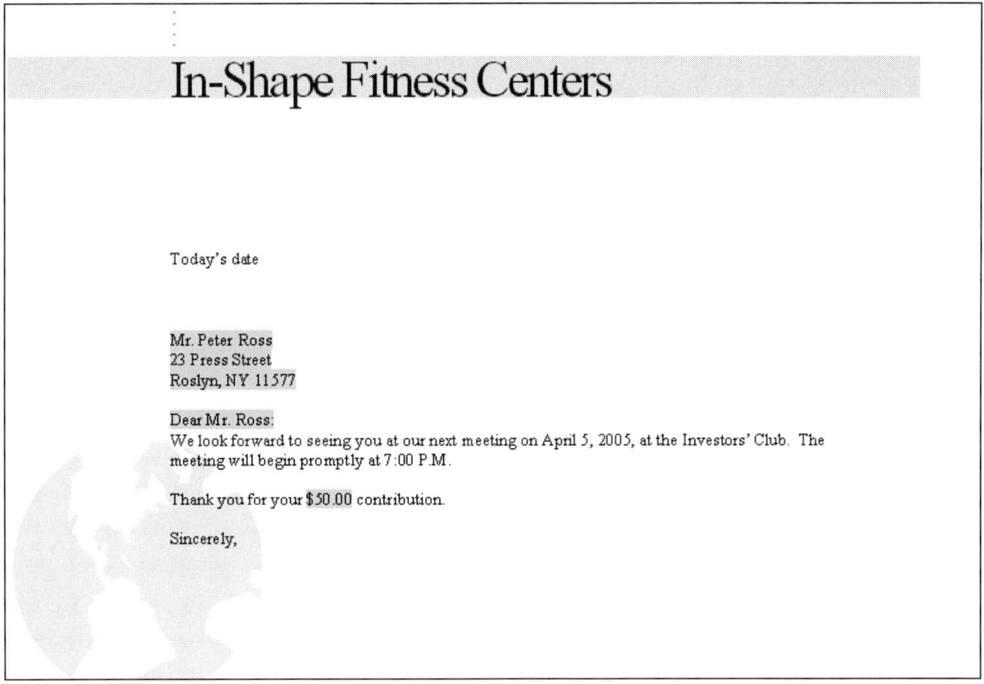

In-Shape Fitness Centers

Today's date

Mr. Peter Ross
23 Press Street
Roslyn, NY 11577

Dear Mr. Ross:
We look forward to seeing you at our next meeting on April 5, 2005, at the Investors' Club. The meeting will begin promptly at 7:00 P.M.

Thank you for your $50.00 contribution.

Sincerely,

Figure 6.6 Merged document

- Word provides a wizard to guide you through the mail merge process. To begin the process, click Tools, Letters and Mailings, and Mail Merge. The Mail Merge task pane appears, as shown in Figure 6.7. Follow the six steps to complete the merge process.

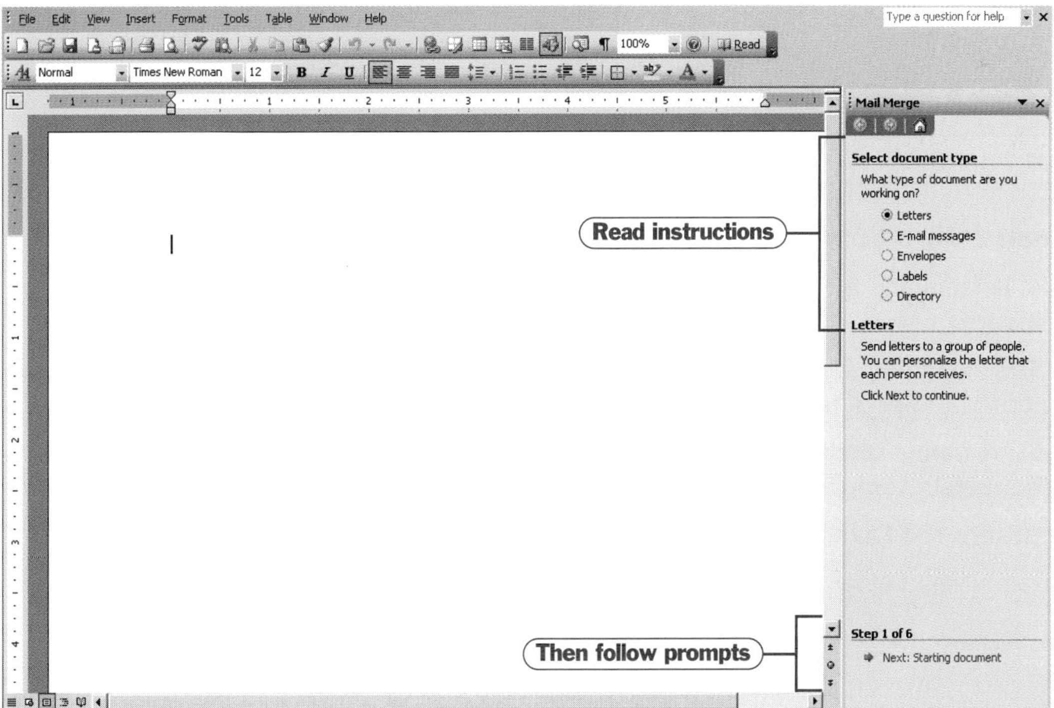

Figure 6.7 Merge Wizard in Mail Merge task pane

▶ In Step 3 of the merge process, Word prompts you to use either an existing mailing list or to create a new list. If you choose to create a new list, the New Address List dialog box opens, as shown in Figure 6.8. The dialog box includes blank fields in which to enter basic name and address contact information; however, you might want to include additional fields. To do so, click Customize and click Add on the next screen. Word prompts you to provide a name for the new field. This new field name appears in the New Address List dialog box.

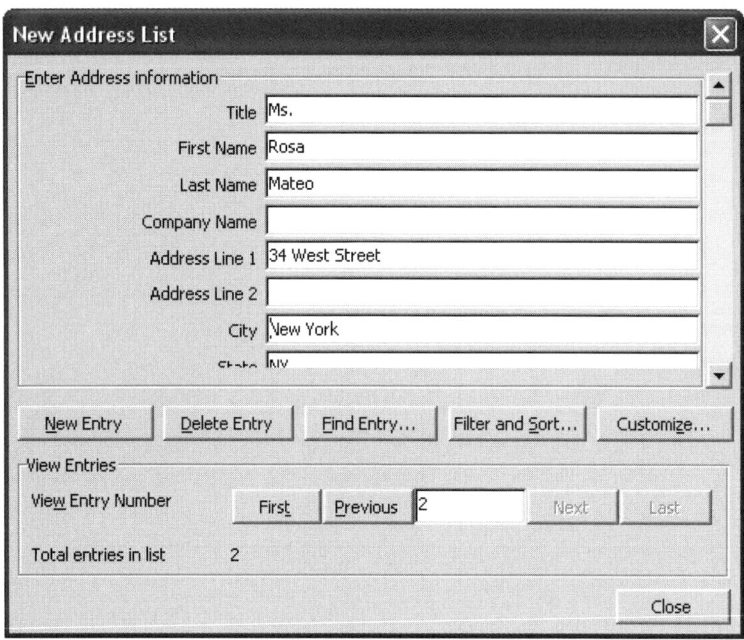

Figure 6.8 New Address List dialog box

▶ After completing the process, Word combines the main document and the data source document to form a new, third document. You can merge this third document to display it on the screen or send it directly to a printer.

TRY *it* OUT *w6-2*

1. Click the **New Blank Document** button.
2. Click **Tools, Letters and Mailings,** and **Mail Merge.**
3. Click the **Starting document** link at the bottom of the Mail Merge task pane.
4. Click the **Start from a template** option and click the **Select template** link.
5. Click the **Letters and Faxes** tab.
6. Click **Contemporary Letter** and click **OK.**
7. Click **Select recipients** from the Mail Merge task pane (Step 2).
8. Click the **Type a new list** option and click the **Create** link when prompted.
9. Click **Customize,** click **Add,** enter `Amt`, and click **OK.**
10. Click the **Move Down** button until "Amt" is the item below the ZIP code. Click **OK.**

Continued on next page

TRY it OUT *w6-2 Continued*

11. Enter the first record shown below, click **New Entry,** then enter the second record. When finished, click **Close.** Notice that you have now created your address list (data source document).

TITLE	FIRST NAME	LAST NAME	ADDRESS LINE	CITY	STATE	ZIP CODE	AMT
Mr.	Peter	Ross	23 Press Street	Roslyn	NY	11577	50.00

TITLE	FIRST NAME	LAST NAME	ADDRESS LINE	CITY	STATE	ZIP CODE	AMT
Ms.	Rosa	Mateo	34 West Street	New York	NY	10022	100.00

12. Save the file as **6.2members list,** click **Save,** then click **OK.**
13. Click **Write your letter** in the Mail Merge task pane (Step 3).
14. In the letter template, click **Click here and type recipient's address.** *Note: You will insert a merge code where variable information will appear.*
15. Click **Address block** in the Mail Merge task pane and click **OK.** Notice that Word inserts an Address Block merge field code.
16. In the letter template, select **Dear Sir or Madam.**
17. Click **Greeting line** in the Mail Merge task pane. In the Greeting Line dialog box, click to select the **colon** as the punctuation, and click **OK.**
18. Replace the sample body text with the following:

    `We look forward to seeing you at our next meeting on April 5, 2005, at the Investors' Club. The meeting will begin promptly at 7:00 p.m. Thank you for your $ contribution.`

19. Place the insertion point to the right of the dollar sign ($). Click **More items** in the Mail Merge task pane, click **Amt** in the Insert Merge Field box, and click **Insert.** Click **Close.**
20. In the letter template, click **Click here and type your name.** Enter your name. Click **Click here and type job title.** Enter `President` as your title.
21. Click **Preview your letters** in the Mail Merge task pane.
22. Click the forward arrows in the Mail Merge task pane to view the recipients.
23. Click **Complete the merge** in the Mail Merge task pane.
24. Save the file; name it **merged letters.**
25. Click **Print**, then close all files. Do not save.

Caution: After merging your documents, you might find that the address appears double-spaced. To correct this problem, select the address and click Format, Paragraph. In the Paragraph dialog box, set the Before and After spacing to 0 pt.

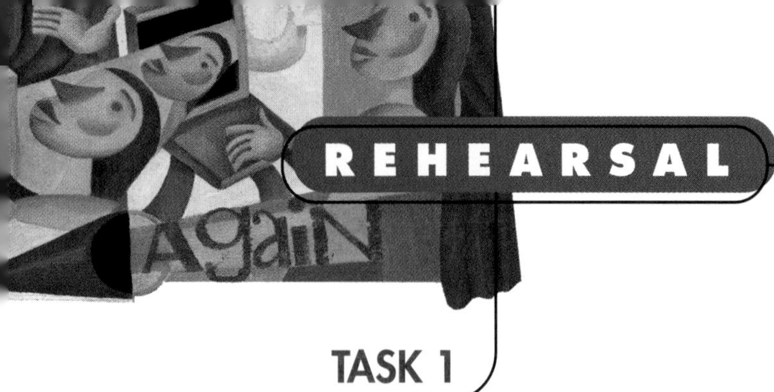

TASK 1

GOALS

To send personalized invitations to members of In-Shape Fitness Centers

To send personalized letters to vacation prospects who have inquired about ski vacations. This letter will contain an imported table.

SETTING THE STAGE/WRAPUP

Margins:	Default
Start line:	1" for both
File names:	6.1in-shape members list 6.1in-shape invite 6.1invite final 6.1ski vacation letter 6.1inquiry list 6.1table 6.1ski vacation letter final

WHAT YOU NEED TO KNOW

- In addition to letters, you can merge envelopes, fill-in forms, reports, and catalogs with an address list file (data source document).
- In this Rehearsal activity, you will create two merge letters. You will prepare the first letter for In-Shape Fitness Centers that will be sent to selected members, inviting them to attend a lecture. You will then prepare a letter for the Air Land Sea Travel Group that will be sent to people who have inquired about European ski vacations. This letter will include an imported table.

DIRECTIONS

In-Shape Fitness Centers

1. Click the **New Blank Document** button.
2. Use Mail Merge to create and merge the documents shown on the following page.
   a. Save the address list as **6.1in-shape members list.**
   b. Save the letter as **6.1in-shape invite.**
3. Use any letter template.
4. Print one copy of the merged letters.
5. Save the merged file as **6.1invite final.**

Continued on next page

54 Cactus Drive
Phoenix, AZ 85003
P: 602-555-1001
F: 602-555-1005

In-Shape Fitness Centers

Today's date

«AddressBlock»

«GreetingLine»

We cordially invite you to attend our first "Health is Wealth" lecture series. The first lecture will take place at the Boulders Conference Center in Phoenix on Thursday evening, June 22 at 7:00 p.m. We will be serving a light dinner.

We are confident that you will enjoy the first lecture of our series, for which you registered. We have several leading experts in the field of health and fitness, who will answer any questions and provide a wealth of information. A lecture series program is enclosed.

You have been assigned to Table No. «Table». Please confirm your attendance by calling our office and speaking with Janet.

Sincerely,

Jane Wilson
Events Coordinator

Jw/

Enclosure

Title	First Name	Last Name	Company Name	Address Line 1	City	State	Zip	Table
Mr.	John	Smith	ABC Company	456 Canyon Drive	Phoenix	AZ	85003	2
Ms.	Wendy	Blank		23 Winding Woods Way	Phoenix	AZ	85013	2
Ms.	Helen	Lane	Health & Fitness Magazine	123 Park Lane	Phoenix	AZ	85012	2
Ms.	Irene	Burns		98 Kildeer Court	Phoenix	AZ	85002	2
Ms.	Ashley	Badar		23 Kingsly Lane	Phoenix	AZ	85003	4
Mr.	Robert	Diaz		87 Trevor Street	Phoenix	AZ	85022	5

Continued on next page

Air Land Sea Travel Group

1. Open **6.1ALS letterhead** from the Data CD.
2. Save the file as **6.1ski vacation letter.**
3. Use Mail Merge to create and merge the documents shown below.
   a. Save the address list as **6.1inquiry list.**
   b. Open **6.1table** from the Data CD. Import the table as an embedded object into the letter where shown.
   c. Use the Research feature to search All Research Sites for "currency conversion." Select the MSN search results, then locate the Universal Currency Converter site (www.xe.net/ucc).
   d. Convert U.S. Dollar amounts to Euros, then enter each amount into the table.
4. Save the file.
5. Print one copy of the merged letters.
6. Saved the merged file as **6.1ski vacation letter**.

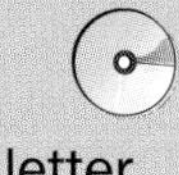

AirLandSeaTravelGroup

505 Park Avenue □New York, NY 10010
P. 212-555-5555□F. 212-666-6767
Email: ais@net.com

<<AddressBlock>>

<<Greeting Line>>

Thank you for your inquiry about group rates for European ski vacations.

We will be glad to present a seminar to your group on the premier European ski resorts and the unique features of each.

Traveling to Europe can be very expensive. After hearing our presentation, you will be able to decide which vacation best suits your needs.

Insert table here

Our Leisure Travel Department is available for consultation from 9 a.m. to 7 p.m., 7 days a week. We look forward to working closely with your group.

Sincerely,

Robin Byron Byrd
Leisure Travel Department

rbb

Title	First Name	Last Name	Company Name	Address Line 1	City	State	Zip
Ms.	Joan	King		56 Atlantic Avenue	Brooklyn	NY	11231
Ms.	Pamela	Blank		911 Park Avenue	New York	NY	10010
Mr.	Sam	Ashton	Rider, Inc.	4 West Street	Phoenix	AZ	85012
Ms.	Irene	Burns		98 Kildeer Court	Phoenix	AZ	85002
Ms.	Wendy	Ascend	Upson Downs Ski Club	234 Summit Ridge	Keystone	CO	80305

Cues for Reference

Import a Table Using Paste Special

1. Display the source file.
2. Select the table (click **Table, Select, Table).**
3. Click the **Copy** button.
4. Switch to the destination file.
5. Click **Edit, Paste Special.**
6. Click **Microsoft Word Document Object.**
7. Click the **Paste** option to embed the file.
   or
   Click the **Paste link** option to link the file.
8. Click **OK.**

Mail Merge

1. Click **Tools**, **Letters and Mailings**, and **Mail Merge**.
2. Click the **Starting document** link in the Mail Merge task pane.
3. Read the task pane directions and follow the prompts.

GOAL

To practice using the following skill sets:

- Create a hyperlink
- Save a document as a Web page
- Preview a Web page
- Create a Web page
  - using a template
  - using a blank page
- Use backgrounds and themes

WHAT YOU NEED TO KNOW

Create a Hyperlink

- You can connect two documents to each other or to another location by inserting a *hyperlink*.
- You can create a hyperlink on document text that links to an existing file, a Web page, another document, or an e-mail address. When you click the link, you go to that location. This is useful only if the document is on screen and you are connected to the Internet. Hyperlinks appear as underlined text, as colored text, or as a graphic. (If you use the Internet, you have clicked on hyperlinks to get from one page of information to another.)
- You can create a hyperlink on existing text or type new text on which to create the link.
- To create a hyperlink on existing text, select the word(s) or object on which you want to create the link, then click Insert, Hyperlink on the menu bar or click the Insert Hyperlink button on the Standard toolbar. In the Insert Hyperlink dialog box that displays, as shown in Figure 6.9, click a Link to button in the left pane that describes the location to which you want to link.

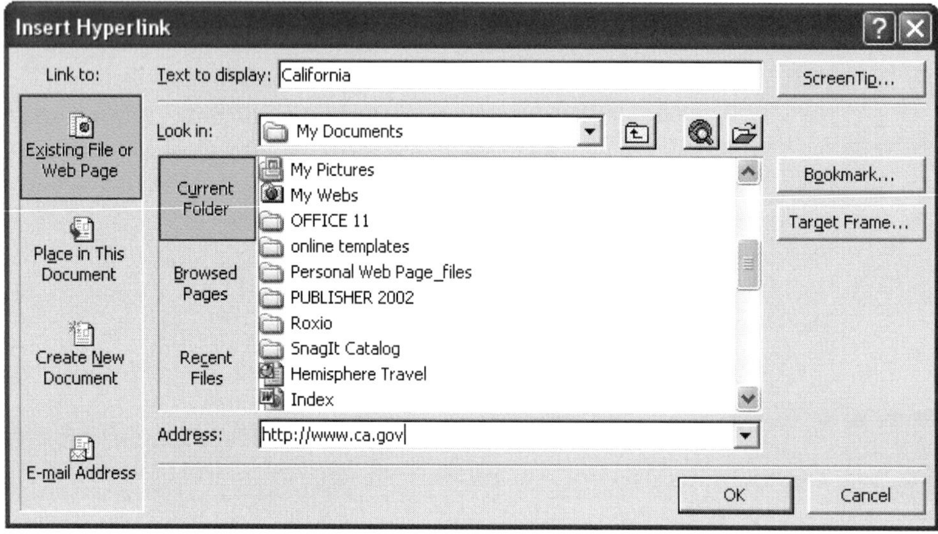

Figure 6.9 Insert Hyperlink dialog box

- Depending on the button you click, a window opens that requires you to enter either a file name, a Web address, or an e-mail address. In Figure 6.9, for example, the Existing File or Web Page button is selected to indicate where to link. Enter the file name or Web location in the Address text box. You can click the Look in list buttons to help you find the location.

- Notice that the selected text on which Word creates the hyperlink is indicated in the Text to display text box. After clicking OK, the selected word is underlined in blue. Text you format as a hyperlink is referred to as *hypertext*.
- If you type a Web or an e-mail address in a document, you automatically create a hyperlink, because the software recognizes the unique characters of these addresses.
- To launch a hyperlink, position the insertion point over the underlined text, then press Ctrl. When a hand symbol appears, click the left mouse button. Figure 6.10 illustrates a link ready to be launched and a ScreenTip, which describes the location to which you will link.
- To remove a link, right-click the link and click the Remove Hyperlink option from the shortcut menu shown in Figure 6.11.

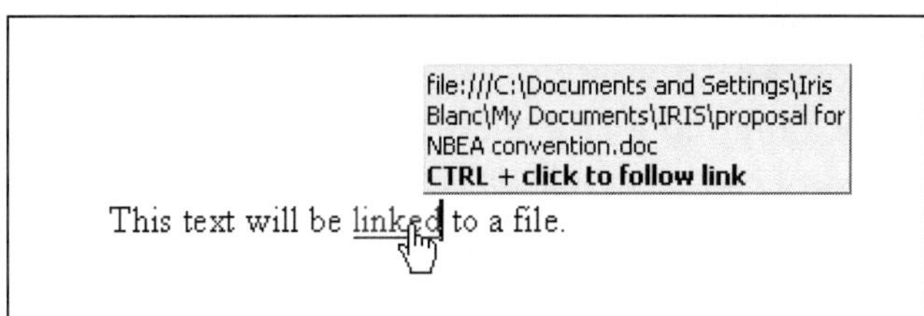

Figure 6.10 Launch a hyperlink

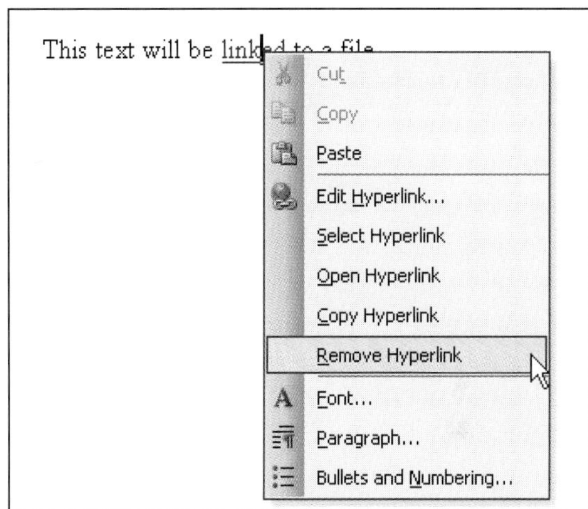

Figure 6.11 Hyperlink options on shortcut menu

TRY *it* OUT *w6-3*

1. Open **w6.3pf golf** from the Data CD.
2. Select **North America.**
3. Click **Insert, Hyperlink.**
4. Click the **Existing File or Web Page Link** button, if necessary.
5. Enter `www.golfdirect.com` in the Address text box.
6. Click **OK.**
7. Select **California.**
8. Click the **Insert Hyperlink** button.
9. Click the **Existing File or Web Page Link** button, if necessary.
10. Enter `www.ca.gov` in the Address text box and click **OK.**
11. Enter the following as the last sentence: **`You can also e-mail us at fun@vacations.com.`**

Notice that Word creates the link automatically.

12. Position the insertion point over "North America" and press the **Ctrl** key. When the insertion point changes to a hand, click the left mouse button. This opens the Web site (and works only if you are connected to the Internet).
13. Position the insertion point on **California**, right-click, and select **Remove Hyperink.**
14. Close the file; do not save.

Save a Document as a Web Page

- Pages you view on the Web must be in HTML format. *HTML* stands for Hypertext Markup Language and is the language or code used to create documents on the Web.
- To save an existing document as a Web page, click File, Save as Web Page. In the Save As dialog box that appears, shown in Figure 6.12, enter the document name in the File name text box. Word automatically enters the file type as Single File Web Page. This option saves all the elements of a Web site, including text and graphics, into a single file. Therefore, if you plan to send an entire Web site as an e-mail message or attachment, or move the folder, all the elements of the site will move together. This encapsulated aggregrate document is an *MHTML* file type, a format that is supported by Internet Explorer 4.0 and higher.
- After you click Save, the document automatically appears in Web layout view.

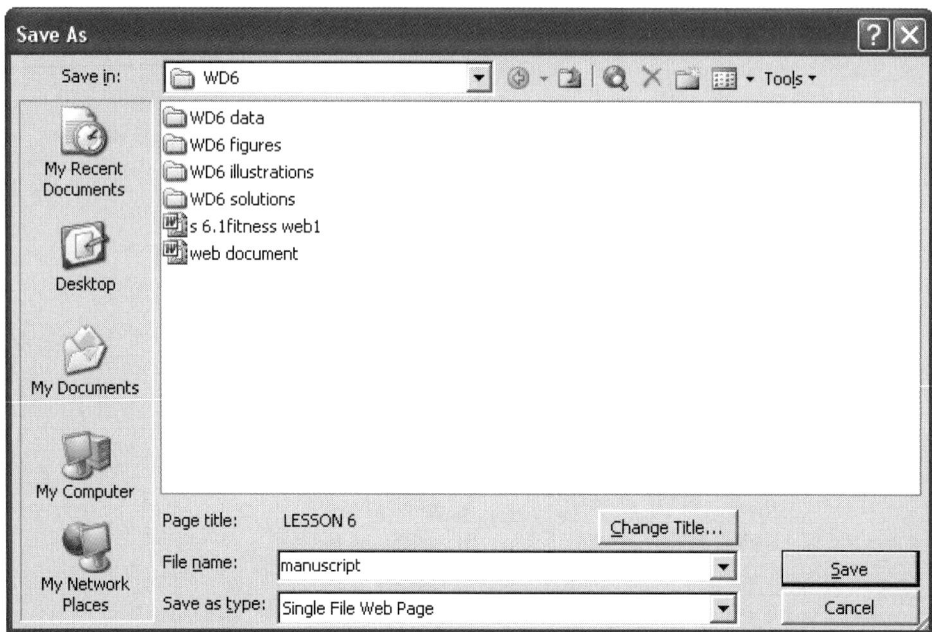

Figure 6.12 Save As dialog box

- Files saved as Web pages appear with a Word-Web icon to the left of the file name and MHTML document indicated as the file type in the Open and Insert File dialog boxes, as shown in Figure 6.13.

WORD

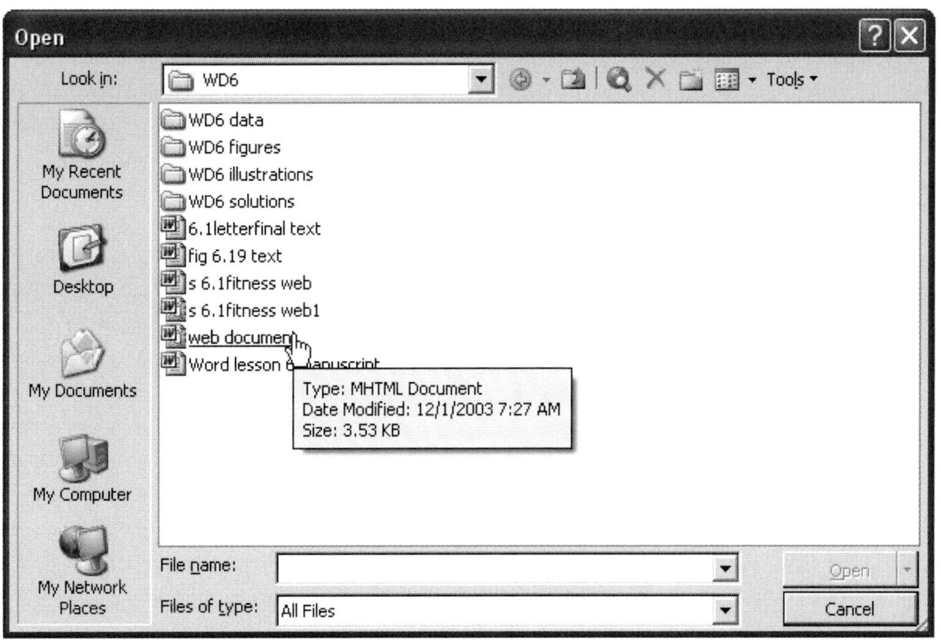

Figure 6.13 Open dialog box with saved Web files

TRY *it* OUT *w6-4*

1. Open **w6.4pf golf outing** from the Data CD. (See Figure 6.14.)
2. Select the words "Pebble Beach."
3. Click the **Insert Hyperlink** button.
4. Click the **Existing File or Web Page Link** button, if necessary.

5. Enter `www.pebble-beach.com/le.html` in the Address text box.
6. Click **OK.**
7. Select the word "e-mail."
8. Click the **Insert Hyperlink** button.

9. Click **E-mail Address.**
10. Enter `Sutton@net.net` in the E-mail address text box, `Golf Outing` in the Subject text box, and click **OK.**
11. Click **File, Save as Web Page.**
12. Enter `6.5pf golfoutingweb` as the file name, and click **Save.**
13. Make any necessary adjustments to the file.
14. Close the file; save the changes.

Preview a Web Page

▶ Once you save a document as a Web page, you will want to see how it will look when viewed in a browser. Word provides two options for previewing your document as a Web page.

1. **Web Layout View**. Once you save a document as a Web page, the document automatically appears in Web layout view. This view enables you to see how your document will look in a browser. You can see how Word positions backgrounds, text wraps, and graphics as a Web page. You can also edit the document in this view.

2. **Web Page Preview**. Clicking File, Web Page Preview will open your document in your default Web browser, as shown in Figure 6.14. (The browser opens, even if you are not connected to the Internet. This is referred to as "working offline.") You cannot edit the document in Web page preview.

Figure 6.14 Document displayed in Web page preview

TRY *it* OUT *w6-5*

1. Open **6.5pf golfouting web** that you saved in the previous Try it Out.
2. Click **File, Web Page Preview.**
3. If you are connected to the Internet, press the **Ctrl** key and click the link on **Pebble Beach** to test it.
4. Close the file; do not save.

Create a Web Page

Using a Template

- You can create your own Web page design from a blank page or use the Web page templates that are created for Word. These templates can be found online and include font formatting, bulleted lists, and tables to align text on a page, as shown in Figure 6.15.
- You can apply a background color, a theme, or a style to the template design. Templates sometimes include text that Word formats as hyperlinks. You can remove these hyperlinks or add your own.

Note: Word provides several basic Web page templates online; however, if you want more sophisticated template formats, it is recommended that you use Microsoft Publisher or FrontPage 2003 to develop your Web site.

WORD

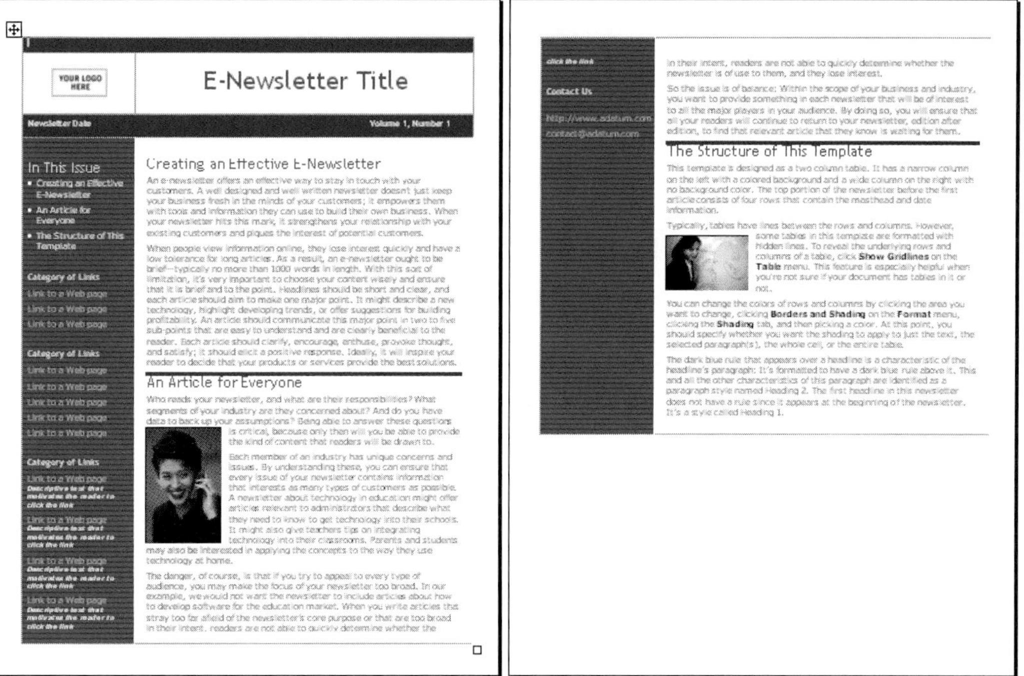

Figure 6.15 Word Web page template

▶ To use a Web page template, click File, New. In the New Document task pane, enter "Web site templates" in the Search online for box, and click Go. The results will display in the Search Results task pane, as shown in Figure 6.16. Click a Web template link, which will display a preview of the template in the Template Preview dialog box shown in Figure 6.17.

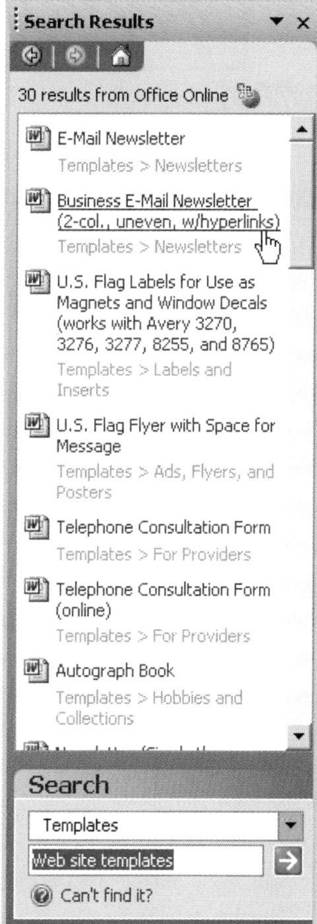

Figure 6.16 Search results on task pane

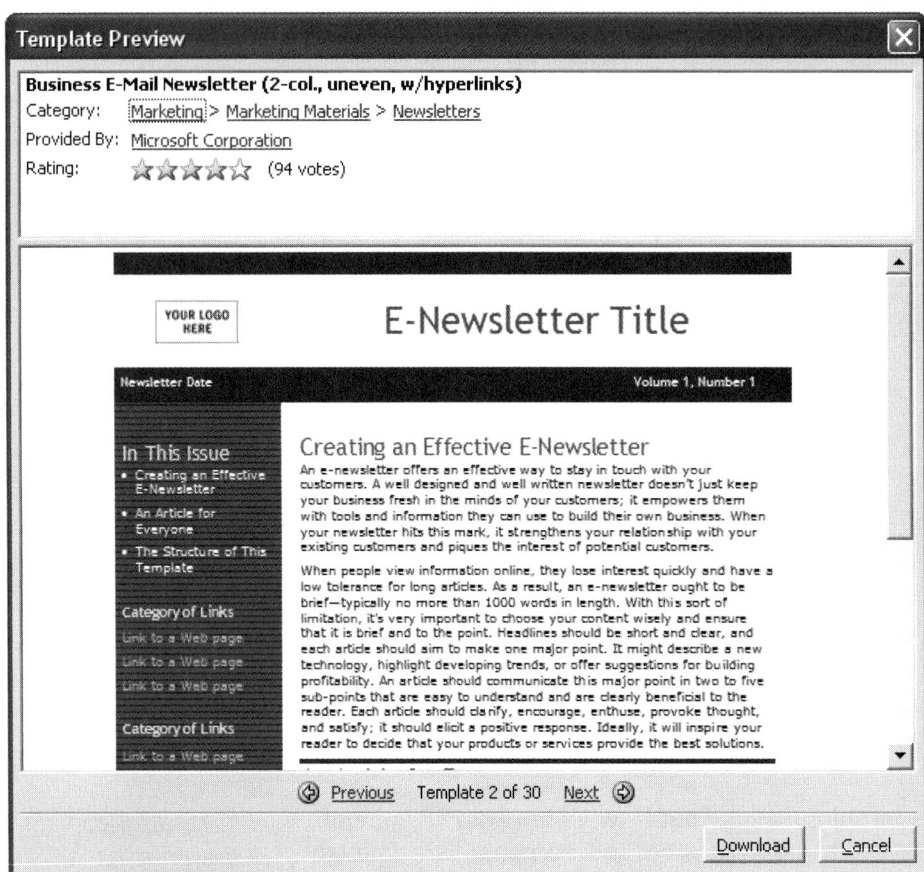

Figure 6.17 Template Preview dialog box

▶ If you like the template, click the Download button. The template will download to a new document window.

- You can change a template to suit your needs using the features you learned in the previous lessons. Create any hyperlinks you want, then save the document as a Web Page and view it in your browser using Web Page Preview. Figure 6.18 shows the template in Figure 6.15 after it was edited.

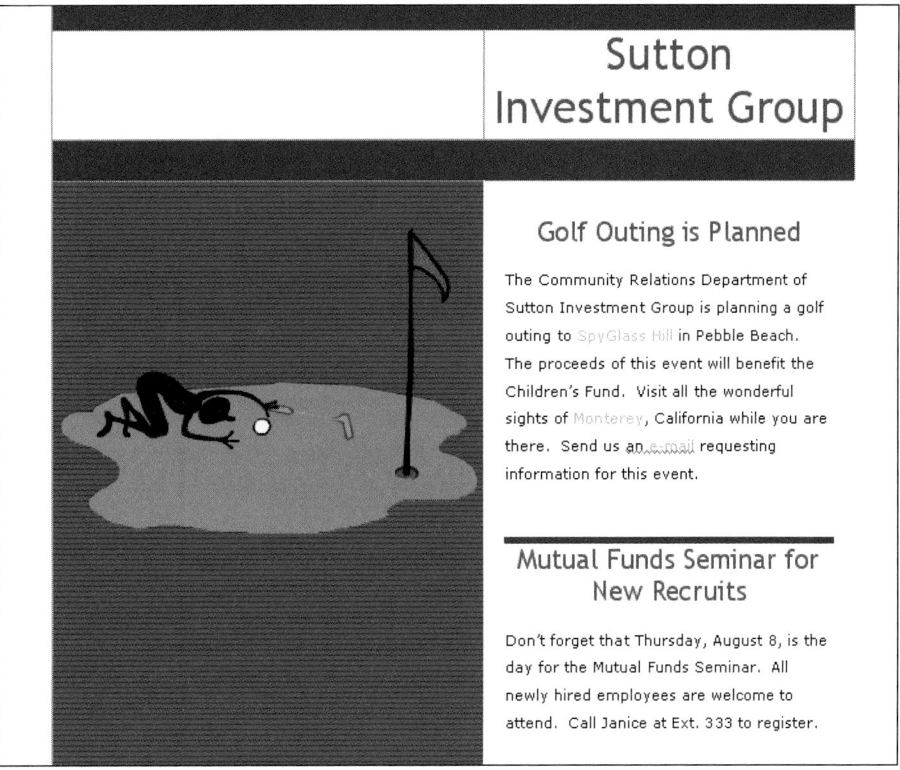

Figure 6.18 Edited template

- Creating a Web page does not mean that you have posted the page to the Web for the world to see—it means that you have prepared a page that you can view and test before you post it to the Web. Posting to the Web is an entirely separate procedure.

TRY *it* OUT *w6-6*

Note: The results of this Try it Out should resemble Figure 6.18.

1. Click **File, New.**
2. Enter `Web site templates` in the Search online for box, and click **Go.**
3. Select `Business E-mail Newsletter` from the Search Results task pane.
4. Click the **Download button.** The template will display as a new document in Word. If you are prompted to automatically download additional resources available with this document, click **Yes**.
5. Replace "E-Newsletter Title" with: `Sutton Investment Group.`
6. Replace "Creating an Effective E-Newsletter" with: `Golf Outing is Planned.` Apply a center alignment to the text.

Continued on next page

TRY it OUT *w6-6 Continued*

7. Set the line spacing to 1.5" for the document text. Then, replace the sample text below the first section heading with the following: **The Community Relations Department of Sutton Investment Group is planning a golf outing to SpyGlass Hill in Pebble Beach. The proceeds of this event will benefit the Children's Fund. Visit all the wonderful sights of Monterey, California while you are there. Send us an e-mail requesting information for this event.**
8. Replace the next section-heading with: **Mutual Funds Seminar for New Recruits.** Apply a center alignment to the text.
9. Replace the sample text below the second section heading with the following: **Don't forget that Thursday, August 8, is the day for the Mutual Funds Seminar. All newly hired employees are welcome to attend. Call Janice at Ext. 333 to register.**
10. Create a hyperlink on the words "SpyGlass Hill" to: www.pebble-beach.com/1e/html.
11. Create a hyperlink on the words "Monterey, California" to: www.monterey.com.
12. Create a hyperlink on the word "e-mail" to Sutton@net.net. Enter **Golf Outing** as the subject.
13. Delete the remaining text in the left and right columns.
14. Insert a graphic into the left column.
15. Save the file as a Web page; name it **6.6 Simple Web Page.**
16. Close the file;do not save.

Using a Blank Page

▶ You can design your own Web page using a blank document. However, you must place graphics and text into individual cells of a table to hold those elements into position on the page once you convert the file for viewing in a Web browser.

Use Backgrounds and Themes

▶ You can add visual appeal to Web page documents that have a white background by adding a background or theme.

- The Background feature allows you to apply a color, texture, pattern, or picture to the page. To apply a background, click Format, Background, select a color from the palette, or click Fill Effects. In the Fill Effects dialog box that appears, as shown in Figure 6.19, click the tab you want and choose a background effect.

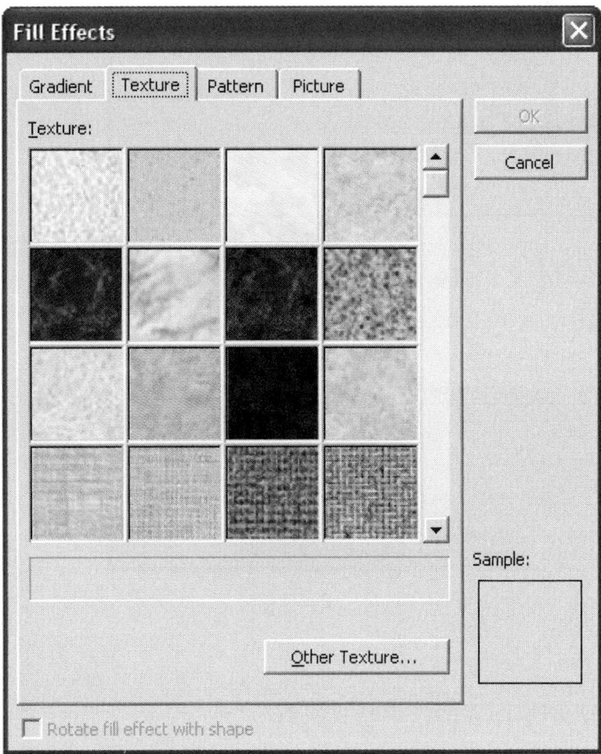

Figure 6.19 Fill Effects dialog box

- Themes include a background with coordinated font formatting and specialized Web bullets and lines. Word has numerous built-in themes that you can apply to a document.
- To apply a theme, click Format, Theme on the menu bar. In the Theme dialog box, shown in Figure 6.20, click a theme in the Choose a Theme list box and click OK.
- You can apply backgrounds and themes to any document, but they are particularly effective for formatting Web pages.

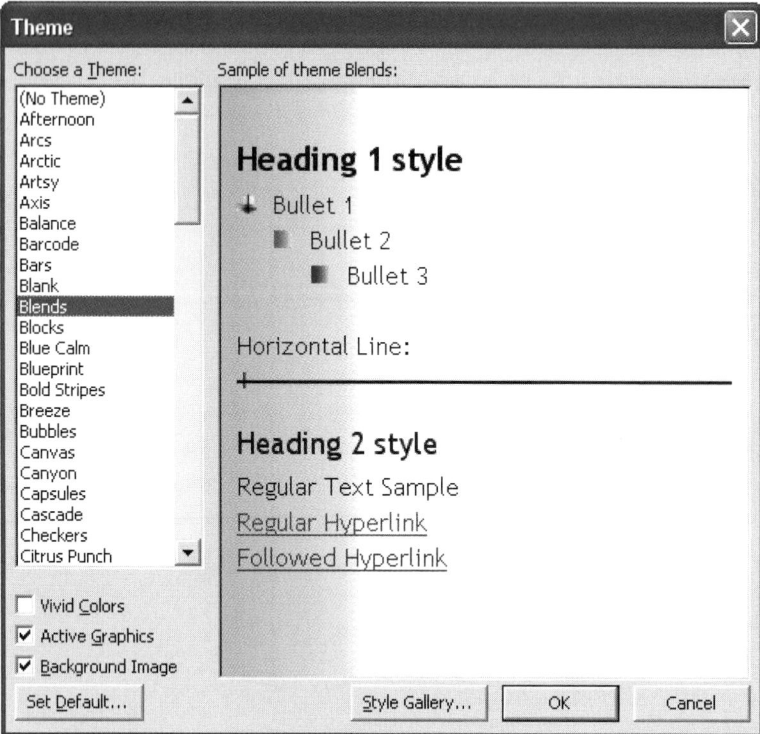

Figure 6.20 Theme dialog box

TRY *it* OUT *w6-7*

1. Open **w6.7fitness** from the Data CD.
2. Change to Web layout view, if necessary.
3. Click **Format, Background.**
4. Click **Fill Effects.**
5. Click the **Texture** tab.
6. Click the **Pink tissue paper** effect and click **OK.** Notice the effect of the background on your page.
7. Click **Format, Background.**
8. Click **Fill Effects.**
9. Click the **Picture** tab and click **Select Picture.**
10. Click any picture that is available to you. Then, click **Insert** and **OK.** Notice the effect of the background.
11. Click **Format, Theme.**
12. Press the **down arrow** key to view each theme.
13. Click **Industrial** from the Choose a Theme list box and click **OK.** Notice the effect. If Industrial is not available, substitute another theme.
14. Click **File, Web Page Preview.**
15. Click the first two links to test them.
16. Close the Web browser.
17. Close the file; do not save.

1
2
3

GOALS
To convert a document to a Web page
To create a Web page from a template

SETTING THE STAGE
File names: **6.2catalog**
6.2fitness web

WHAT YOU NEED TO KNOW

- Many companies consider the Web as another way to market their products.
- It is perfectly acceptable to include business contact information on a business Web page. On a personal Web page, you should not include your home phone number, home address, or Social Security number for privacy reasons. Do not include anything on a Web page that you do not want the world to see.
- A *home page* is the first page of a Web site and contains general information as well as links to related pages.
- Web sites that are attractive and easy to navigate engage the reader.
- In this Rehearsal activity, you will convert a catalog page you created previously for Green Brothers Gardening to a Web page. You will add links to it to make the site more engaging. You will also create a home page from a template for In-Shape Fitness Centers.

DIRECTIONS

Create a Web Page from a Document

Note: The Illustration shown on the next page is the printed solution of ***5.2 catalog page,*** *which you completed in Lesson 5. The file you are directed to open from the Data CD in this exercise* ***(6.2pf catalog)*** *has been modified so that all elements of the page can be viewed in a Web browser.*

1. Open **6.2 catalog page** from the Data CD.
2. Save the file as **6.2catalog.**
3. Link each of the following words on the catalog page to the Web site indicated in the illustration on the next page:
   Bulbs = www.bulb.com
   Lilies = www.bulb.com/summerguide98/lilium/index.asp
   Tulips = www.bulb.com/aboutspring/color.asp
   Irises = www.bulb.com/springguide98/iris.asp
   Orchids = www.bulb.com/summerguide98/roscoea.asp
   Daffodils = www.bulb.com/springguide98/narcissus/index.asp
4. Insert a hyperlink on the word “e-mail” in the footer to the address indicated.
5. Apply a Parchment background effect.
6. Save the document as a Web page.
7. Preview the Web page and test the links.
8. Make any necessary edits in Web Layout view.
9. Close the file; save the changes.

Continued on next page

Green Brothers Gardening

Dear Gardener: We take great pride in the reputation we have developed as the premier source of gardening and landscaping needs. We pride ourselves on this reputation and want you to know that we will continue to seek out and be the first catalog to offer unique landscape and garden products that you can order by mail, fax, or phone. Our new Web site will offer you the same ease of ordering.

Calvin Green, President

Bulbs

Lillies
Price: **$14.50** for **12 bulbs**
Item No. 112

Begonias
Price: **$14.50** for **12 bulbs**
Item No. 116

Gladiolus
Price: **$14.50** for **12 bulbs**
Item No. 113

Orchids
Price: **$6.95** for **2 bulbs**
Item No. 117

Tulips
Price: **$16.50** for **16 bulbs**
Item No. 114

Daffodils
Price **$ 6.95** for **2 bulbs**
Item No. 118

Irises
Price: **$16.50** for **16 bulbs**
Item No. 115

Arum Italicum
Price: **$8.25** for **4 bulbs**
Item No. 119

Green Brothers Gardening 32 Braddock Road, Fairfax, VA
Phone - 703-555-0005 Fax - 703-555-0015 E-mail - gbg@network.com

Continued on next page

Create a Web Page from a Template

Note: The Illustration shown on the next page is a printed version. Printed versions will differ from those viewed in a browser.

1. Create a new Web page using a Web newsletter template.
2. Replace the sample text with the text shown on the facing page.
3. Insert any images.
4. Use any font size and/or style for the heading. (You may use WordArt for the heading.)
5. Apply any background or theme, if you want.
6. Insert the **6.2fitness locations** file, located on the Data CD, where indicated. 
7. Create the following links below the underlined words in the right column to files found on the Data CD or other indicated locations. 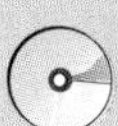
   e-mail us = inshape@net.com; the subject is "Information"
   weekend schedule = **6.2weekend schedule** on the Data CD
   newsletter = **6.2inshape newsletter** on the Data CD
   health tips = www.health-fitness-tips.com/features/10-essential-health-tips.htm
   employee orientation = **6.2new employee meeting** on the Data CD
8. View the Web page in your browser and test the links.
9. Save the file; name it **6.2fitness web.**
10. Close all files.

In-Shape Fitness Centers

About Us
Our Club
Locations

Classes/Schedules/Programs
Weekday Schedule
Weekend Schedule

Fitness, Health, and Other News
Our Newsletter
Employment Opportunities
Health Tips

Work Out with Us!

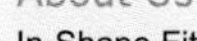

About Us

In-Shape Fitness Centers is a full-service health club with locations throughout Phoenix. In each of our locations, you find our immaculate, conveniently located facilities, each equipped with an inviting swimming pool, relaxing saunas, and steam rooms. Whether you are interested in yoga, martial arts, cardio fitness, conditioning, or just lounging in a whirlpool, we know you will find something exciting to make membership worthwhile.

Visit one of our convenient locations for a workout you will never forget.

Insert 6.2 fitness locations file here

You can e-mail us to request information of any kind. We look forward to your patronage.

Classes/Schedules/Programs

We offer the country's most unique classes, taught by the best fitness instructors. Our instructors are experts in their fields. Whether you choose kickboxing, fencing, yoga, or spinning or conditioning, you will begin to lose those pounds, build your strength, and have fun at the same time.

We have arranged weekday schedules to suit the busy executives and a full weekend schedule to meet the demand of classes.

Fitness, Health, and Other News

There is always something new and exciting happening at our centers. Check our newsletter for special events, lectures, and health tips. New employee orientation meetings are posted on our Web site. Come in and fill out an application – we offer full benefits and a wonderful environment in which to work.

Cues for Reference

Create a Hyperlink

1. Select the text on which you want to create a link.
2. Click **Insert, Hyperlink** or click the **Insert Hyperlink** button.
3. Click the appropriate Link to button.
4. Enter the link information in the appropriate text box.
5. Click **OK.**

Save a Document as a Web Page

1. Display the document you want to save as a Web page.
2. Click **File, Save as Web Page.**
3. Enter the file name in the File name text box.
4. Click **Save.** (Word converts the document to MHTML format.)

Preview a Web Page

1. Display the Web page you want to preview.
2. Click **File, Web Page Preview.**

Create a Web Page Using a Template

1. Click **File**, **New**.
2. Enter "Web site templates" into the Search online for text box and click **Go.**
3. Select an online template.
4. In the Template Preview dialog box, click **Download** if you want to use the template.
5. Make modifications to the template.
6. Save the file as a Web page.

Office XP

1. Click **File**, **New**.
2. Click **General Templates** in the New Document task pane.
3. Click the **Web Pages** tab and select a template.
4. Click **OK**.
5. Replace the sample text with your own text.
6. Save the file.

Use Backgrounds and Themes

1. Display the document on which you want to apply a background or theme.
2. Click **Format.**

To Apply a Background

1. Click **Background, Fill Effects.**
2. Click the necessary tab.
3. Select the appropriate effect.

To Apply a Theme

1. Click **Theme.**
2. Click a theme from the Choose a Theme list box.
3. Click **OK.**

GOAL

To practice using the following skill sets:

- Save and retrieve files in specialized locations
- Create a new folder
- Rename or delete a file
- Move a file
- View files

WHAT YOU NEED TO KNOW

Save and Retrieve Files in Specialized Locations

- It is important to manage the files you create. You might want or need to view, find, delete, rename, or reorganize your files and folders.
- Before manipulating files, you should understand how Windows organizes files and folders in your computer. You can manage your files through Office or through Windows Explorer, which is a Windows feature. See Appendix B for an explanation of file structure on a computer and how to use Windows Explorer.
- Office applications allow you to work with files and folders in the same way as Windows Explorer.
- The default location for saving files in Word is usually the My Documents folder. Remember that a folder can contain multiple files or other folders.
- You can manage files through the Save As, Open, or Insert File dialog boxes. When you use these commands, the Save As, Open, or Insert File dialog boxes appear with a Places bar and a toolbar, as shown in Figure 6.21. The Places bar contains buttons that link to dedicated folders or locations; the toolbar contains buttons to make working with files easier.

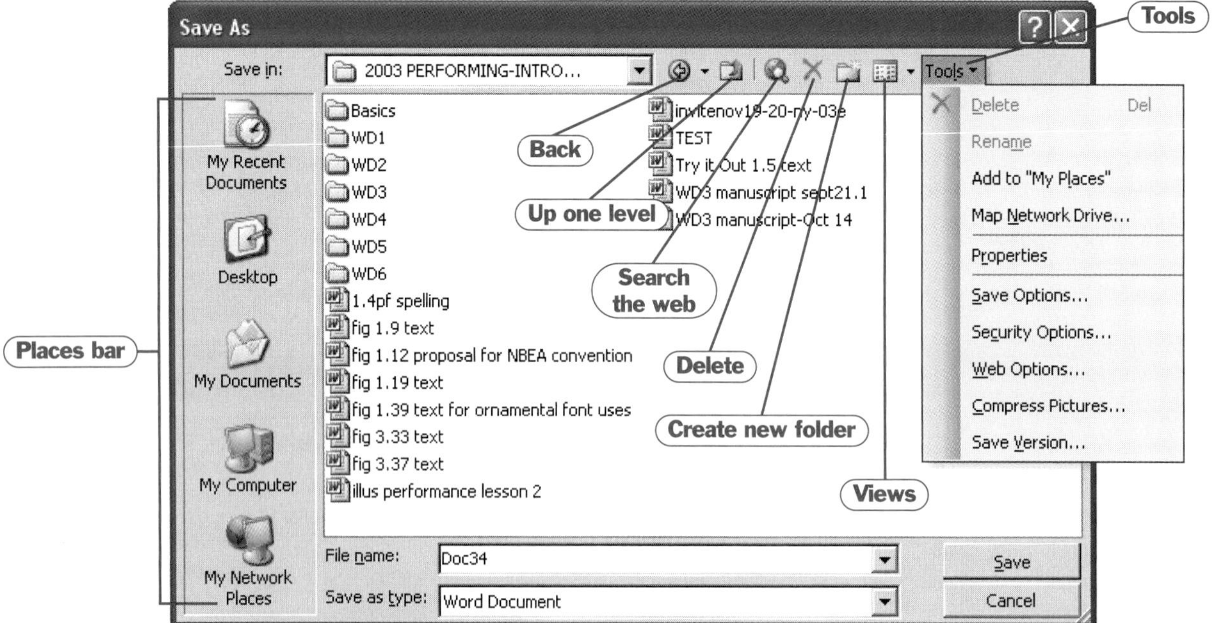

Figure 6.21 Save As dialog box

The following table explains each button on the Places bar:

BUTTON	ITS FUNCTION
My Recent Documents	Displays a Recent folder, which contains files and folders you worked on most recently.
Desktop	Saves files to your desktop.
My Documents	Saves files to a default location.
My Computer	Provides quick access to drive locations on your computer.
My Network Places	Saves (or retrieves) your files in folders that reside on a file server or other type of server. (A server is a computer dedicated to performing a particular task. For example, a Web server is a computer that manages Web sites, a print server is a computer that manages one or more printers, and a network server is a computer that manages network traffic.)

- You can also click the Save in (or Look in, in the Open and Insert File dialog boxes) list box and choose a save or retrieve location from the options that display.

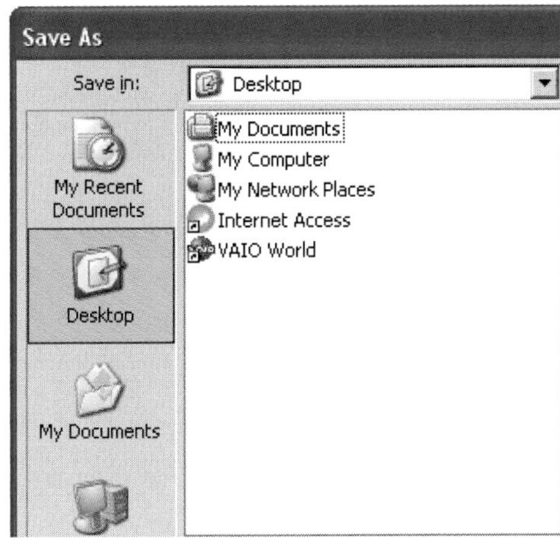

Figure 6.22 Save in options

TRY *it* OUT *w6-8*

1. Click the **New Blank Document** button.
2. Enter your name and today's date.
3. Click **File, Save As.**
4. Click the **My Documents** button (if My Documents is not already selected as the default folder).
5. Enter `myown` as the file name and click **Save.**
6. Click **File, Open.**
7. Click the **My Recent Documents** button. Notice the files and folders you worked on most recently; **myown** should be the first file listed.
8. Click the **My Documents** button. Notice the files and folders listed.
9. Click the **Desktop** button. Notice the items that are on your desktop.
10. Click the **My Computer** button.
11. Click **Cancel.** Close the file.

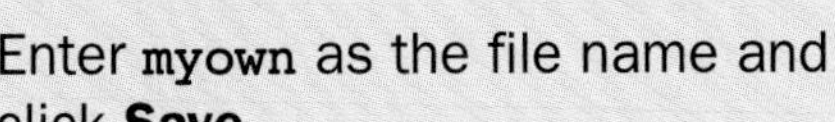

Create a New Folder

▶ To create a new folder, open the Save As, Open, or Insert File dialog box. In the dialog box that appears, click to select the drive or folder to receive the new folder. Then, click the Create New Folder button on the toolbar and enter the name of the new folder.

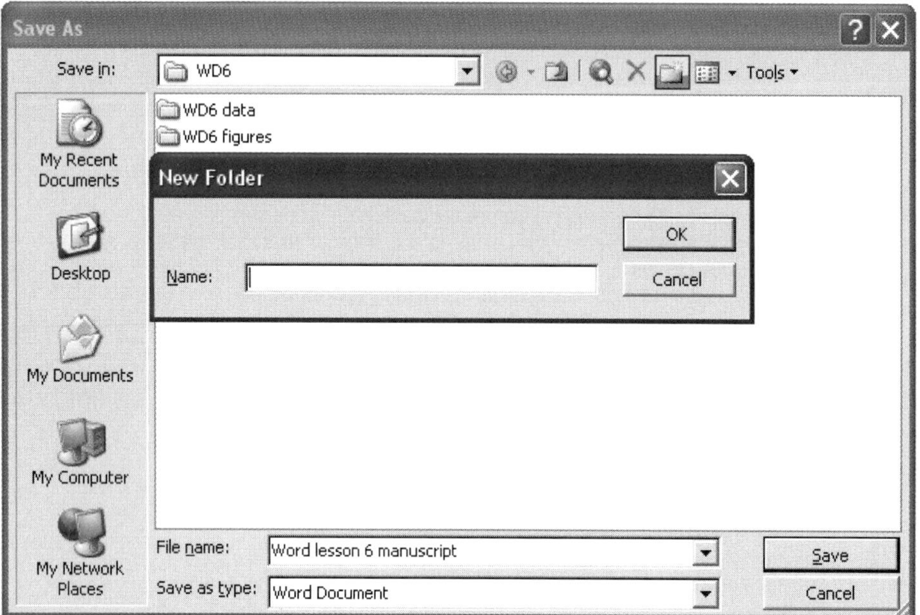

Figure 6.23 Create new folder

▶ Click the Back button to return to the My Documents folder. Click the Up One Level button to return to the next folder in the structure.

TRY *it* OUT *w6-9*

1. Click the **New Blank Document** button.

2. Enter your school name.

3. Click **File, Save As.**
4. Click the **My Documents** button on the Places bar.

5. Enter `Myschool` as the file name and click **Save.**
6. Click **File, Save As.**
7. Click the **Create New Folder** button.

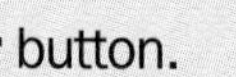

8. Enter your first and last name in the Name box and click **OK.**

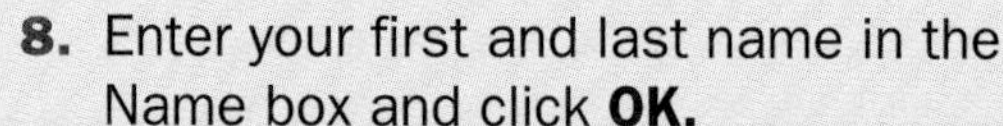

9. Click the **Back** button. Note the folder with your name.

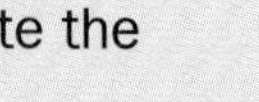

10. Click the **Up One Level** button.

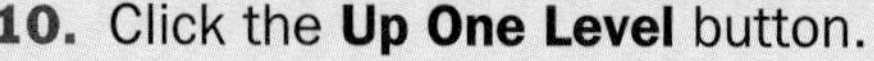

11. Click **Cancel.** Close the file.

Rename or Delete a File

- To rename or delete a file or folder, right-click the file or folder in the dialog box and click Rename or Delete on the shortcut menu that appears, as shown in Figure 6.24. You can also delete a file by selecting the file to delete and clicking the Delete button on the dialog box toolbar (see Figure 6.21).

Select
Open
Print
Upload using CuteFTP
Open With
PC-cillin
Send To
Cut
Copy
Create Shortcut
Delete
Rename
Properties

Figure 6.24 Shortcut menu

Move a File

- To move a file into a folder while in a dialog box, select the file to affect, then drag and drop it into the appropriate folder. It is more convenient, however, to use Windows Explorer to move and copy folders from one location to another.

TRY *it* OUT *w6-10*

1. Click **File**, **Open**.
2. Click the **My Documents** button.
3. Right-click the file **Myschool**.
4. Click **Rename** on the shortcut menu.
5. Enter: `About My School` and press the **Enter** key.
6. Click the file **myown**.
7. Click the **Delete** button on the toolbar. When prompted, click **Yes**.

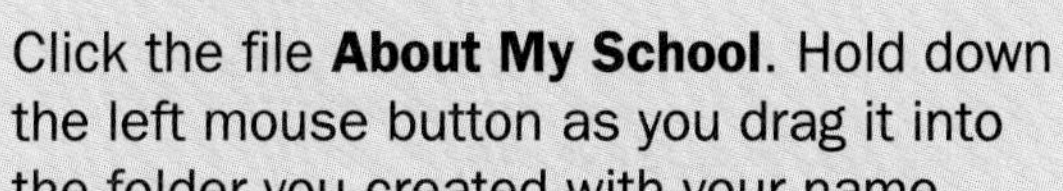

8. Click the file **About My School**. Hold down the left mouse button as you drag it into the folder you created with your name.
9. Double-click the folder with your name. Notice that the file **About My School** is in that folder.
10. Click **Cancel**.

View Files

- You can change the way you see files and folders in the dialog box by clicking the Views list arrow in the dialog box and selecting an option, as shown in Figure 6.25.

- The Details view, shown in Figure 6.26, allows you to view the name, size, and type of each file, as well as the date and time each was last modified. In this view, you can click the header to sort the files for that field in ascending or descending order.

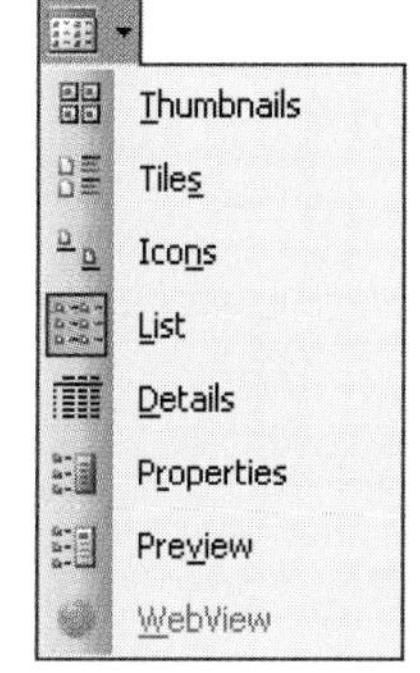

Figure 6.25 View options

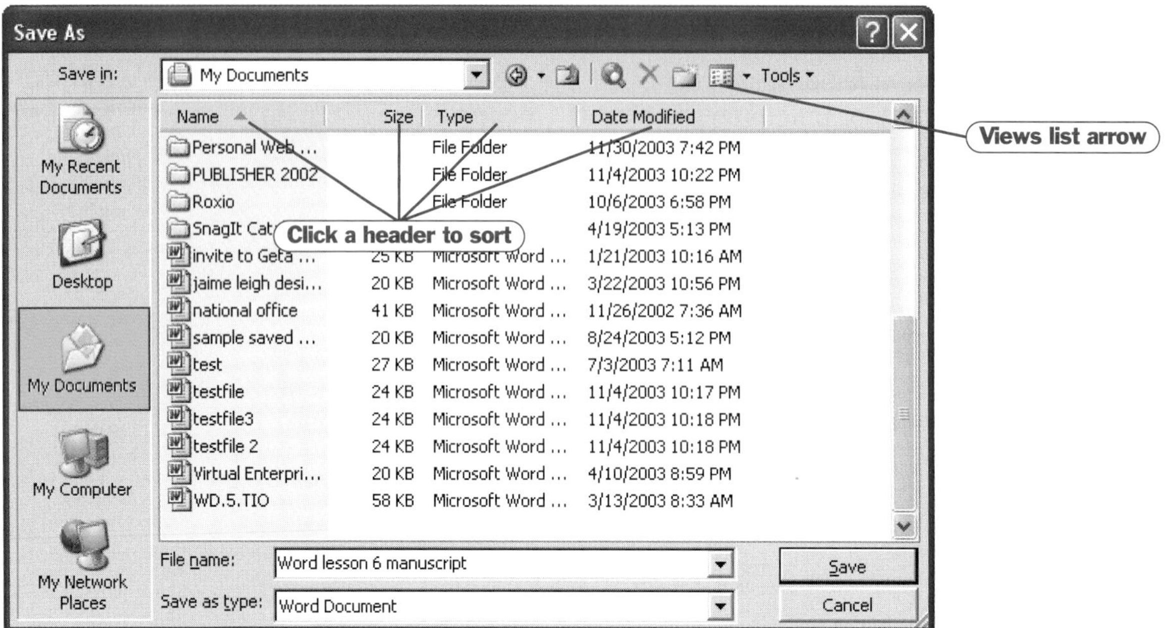

Figure 6.26 Details view

TRY *it* OUT *w6-11*

1. Click the **New Blank Document** button.
2. Click **File, Save As.**
3. Click the **Views** list arrow.
4. Click **Details.**
5. Click the **Name** header. Notice that the files are sorted in alphabetical order.
6. Click the **Date Modified** header. Notice that the files are now sorted in date order.
7. Click **Cancel.**

1
2
3

GOAL
To create another Web page from a template and save it in a specialized location.

SETTING THE STAGE
File name: 6.3occasions home page

WHAT YOU NEED TO KNOW

- All Office applications provide easy access for saving and retrieving files and folders in specialized locations.
- Organizing your files and folders before you begin working will save you time when you are looking for a file.
- A navigation bar is a set of links that is in the same place on every page of a Web site and provides the user with a consistent way to browse a Web site.
- In this Rehearsal activity, you will create a home page with navigation buttons for Occasions Event Planning. You will then save the file in a specialized location.

DIRECTIONS

1. Open a Web template from Templates on Office Online.
2. Create the home page shown on the facing page by replacing the template text with the text shown in the illustration. Use **6.3occasions web text**, which can be found on the Data CD.
   - Use any WordArt design for the heading
     Insert any desired graphics.
     You may apply a background or theme, if you want.
3. Create the navigation buttons using the oval and text box tools. Create a link on each navigation button as follows:
   Choose Theme = 6.3themes.xls on the Data CD.
   Price List = 6.3 occasions price list on the Data CD.
4. Save the file as a Web page as **6.3occasions home page.** Notice the default location where you saved the file.
5. View the page in your browser. Test the links and make any changes necessary.
6. Save the file.
7. Print one copy.
8. Create a new folder in the default location; name it: `Occasions Documents.`
9. Move **6.3occasions home page** into the Occasions Documents folder.
10. Rename the **6.3occasions documents** folder to `Occasions.`
11. Press the **Escape** key.
12. Close all files.

Continued on next page

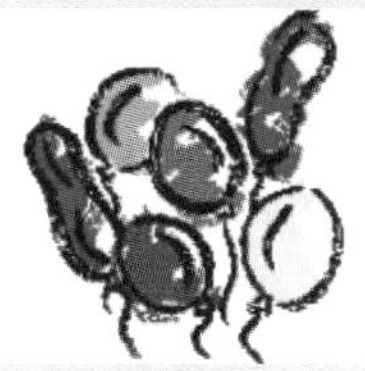

Occasions Event Planning

Home

Choose Theme

Menus

Price List

Party Planning and Rentals

"Whatever your party needs,

we can help!"

Occasions Event Planning offers customers a unique opportunity to plan all aspects of a party... with a little help from the experts.

Occasions takes the hassle out of using many different vendors for one event. We coordinate all aspects of party planning—from choosing a theme to decorating to equipment rentals to menu selection.

The first step in planning a successful event is choosing the theme. Then, we will work with you on decorations—this includes tables, chairs, dishes, balloons, flowers, candles, etc. Finally, we work with you on planning the menu. And then, any additional activities or services you desire, we will fulfill.

Explore our website and see how much you can do with us. Call us for a free consultation. We look forward to working with you.

Occasions Event Planning

Cues for Reference

Save Files in Specialized Locations

1. Click **File**, **Save As**.
2. In the dialog box that appears, click a button on the Places bar.
3. Click **OK**.

Create a New Folder

1. In the Save As, Open, or Insert File dialog box, click the **Create New Folder** button.
2. Enter the folder name and press **Enter.**

Rename/Delete a File or Folder

1. Right-click the file or folder.
2. Click **Rename,** enter the new file name, and press **Enter.**
   or
   Click **Delete,** then click **Yes** to confirm deletion when prompted.

TRYOUT

TASK 4

GOAL

To practice using the following skill sets:

- Work with Word and Outlook
  - Create a Contacts List and Address Book in Outlook
  - Use a Contacts List and Address Book in Word
  - Update a Contacts List through Smart Tags

WHAT YOU NEED TO KNOW

Work with Word and Outlook

- There are many features in Word that interface with Outlook. The most frequently used Outlook features that are used in Word are the Contacts List, the Address Book, and E-mail. Before starting this task, be sure that Outlook is configured on your computer to display the default views and toolbars.

Create a Contacts List and Address Book in Outlook

- When you click the Contacts view bar in Outlook, as shown in Figure 6.27, a Contacts folder as well as options for viewing your contacts displays in the Navigation pane. *Contacts* are the people and businesses with whom you want to communicate. The Contact feature stores, and allows you to retrieve, all types of information about your contacts, including street addresses, phone numbers, e-mail addresses, and Web page addresses. The Current View options sort the contacts according to the view you need to locate the desired information.

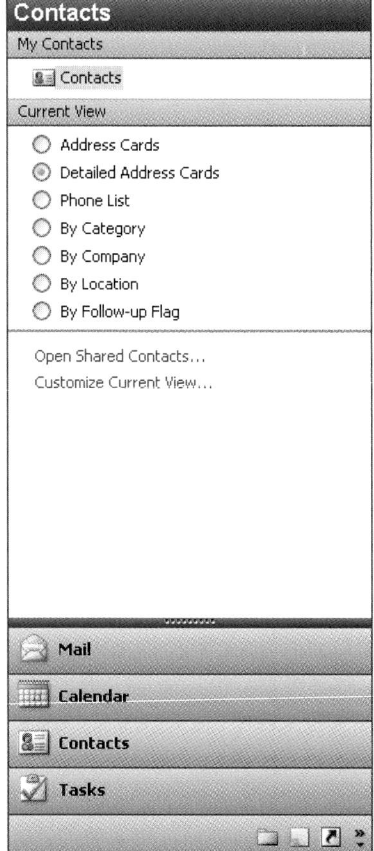

Figure 6.27 Contacts view bar

TRY *it* OUT *w6-12*

1. Start Outlook.
2. Click the **Contacts** view button.
3. Click **Address Cards** in the Current View list, if not already selected.
4. Click **Detailed Address Cards**.
5. Click **Phone List**.
6. Click the remaining views. All data in the Contacts folder are sorted by the view option.

Create a List of Contacts

▶ When you open the Contacts folder for the first time, *Address Cards* view opens, as shown in Figure 6.28.

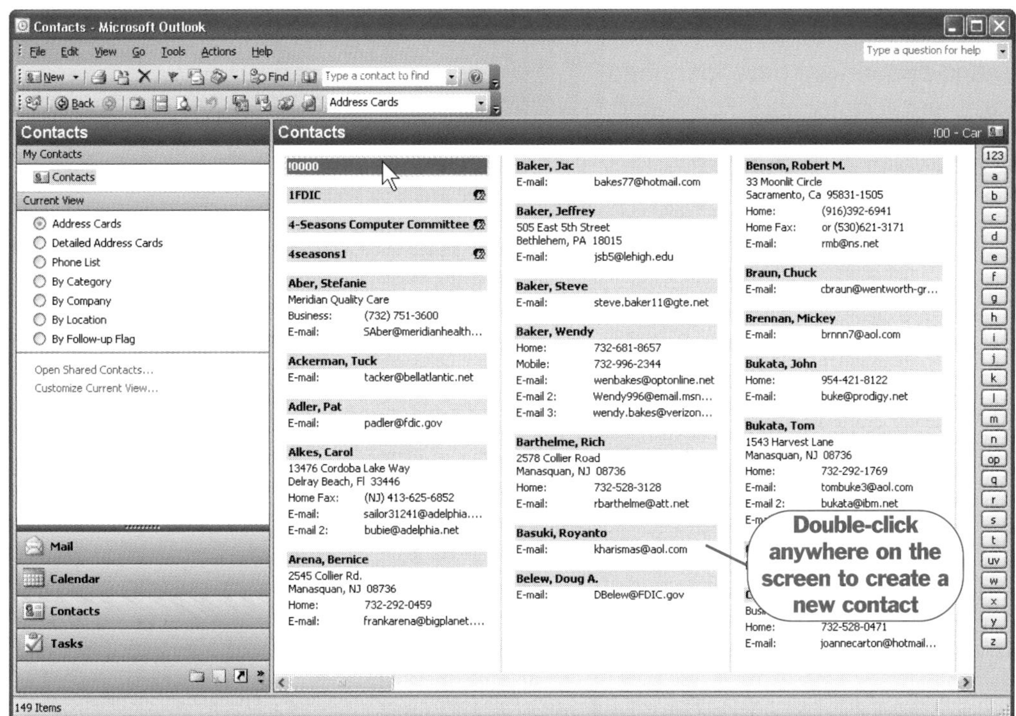

Figure 6.28 Contacts Address Cards view

▶ To add a new contact, double-click on a blank area in Address Cards view, or click the New button on the Standard toolbar. The Contact dialog box opens, as shown in Figure 6.29.

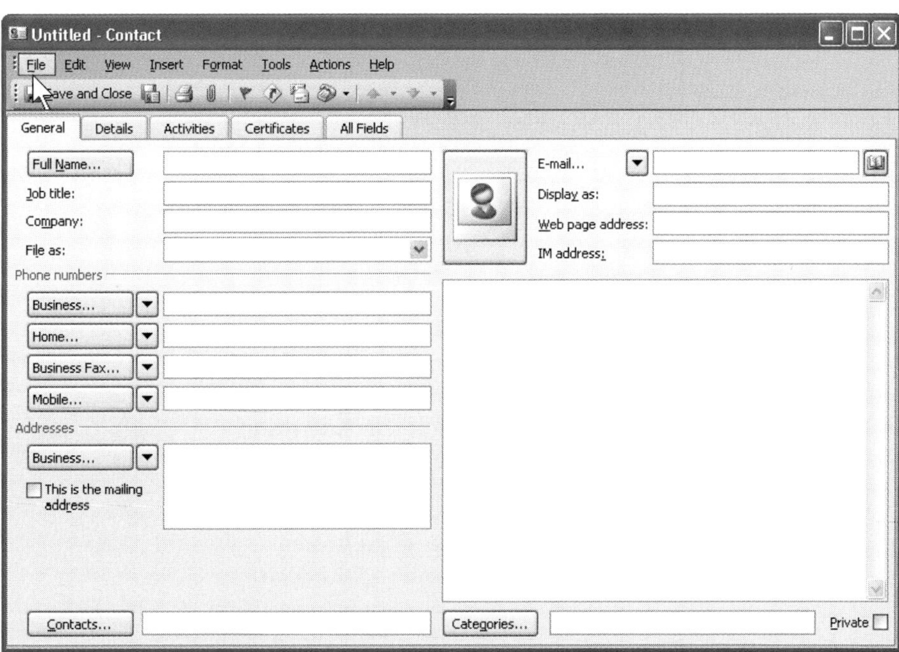

Figure 6.29 Contact dialog box

- The Contact feature automatically separates data for names, addresses, telephone numbers, etc. into separate *fields* that you can use for sorting. (Outlook will automatically insert the parentheses and dashes when you enter phone and fax numbers.)
- To display fields and ensure you have identified them correctly or to enter data, click Full Name, or the data you require, in the Contact dialog box. Figure 6.30 shows the Check Full Name dialog box.

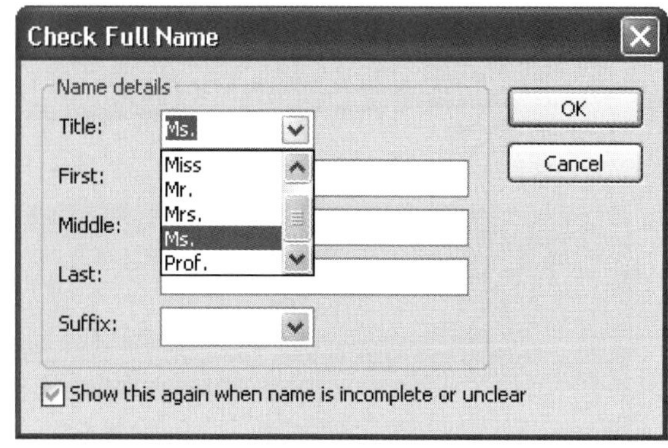

Figure 6.30 Check Full Name dialog box

Add New Contacts

- After entering the contact information in the Contact dialog box, click the Save and Close button to return to the Contacts window. To save information on one contact and immediately open another New Contact dialog box, click the Save and New button on the File menu.

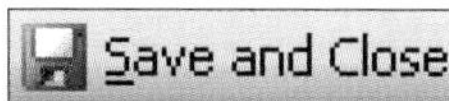

TRY *it* OUT *w6-13*

1. Click the **New** button on the Standard toolbar.
2. Click the **Full Name** button.
3. Enter `Ms. Marilyn Ellis` by using the list arrow to select the Ms. title and entering `Marilyn` (first name) and `Ellis` (last name). Click **OK**.
4. Enter the following in the **Job title** box: `Director of Leisure Travel.`
5. In the **Company** box, enter: `ALS Travel Group.`
6. Click **Business** in the first Phone numbers drop-down list, if not already selected.
7. In the **first phone number** box, enter: `212-555-5555.`
8. In the **Business Fax** area, enter: `212-555-6767`
9. Click **Business** in the Addresses drop-down list, if not already selected.
10. In the Address area, enter: `505 Park Avenue.`
11. Press the **Enter** key.
12. Enter: `New York, NY 10010.`
13. Click the **Business** button to display the Check address box. Click **OK**.
14. Click the **Close and Save** button. Repeat steps 1-13 to add the following contact:

```
Ms. Janice Pierce, Manager of
   Leisure Travel
ALS Travel Group
505 Park Avenue
New York, NY  10010
P: 212-555-5555
F: 212-555-6767
E-mail: mellis@msn.com
```

15. Click the **Save and Close** button.

Edit Contacts

- The Contact feature allows you to edit contact information easily so that if, for example, a phone number changes, you can simply record the new phone number for an existing contact.
- You can also save details about a contact, including information such as a nickname, a manager's name, or a birthday by clicking the Details tab on the Contact dialog box, as shown in Figure 6.31.

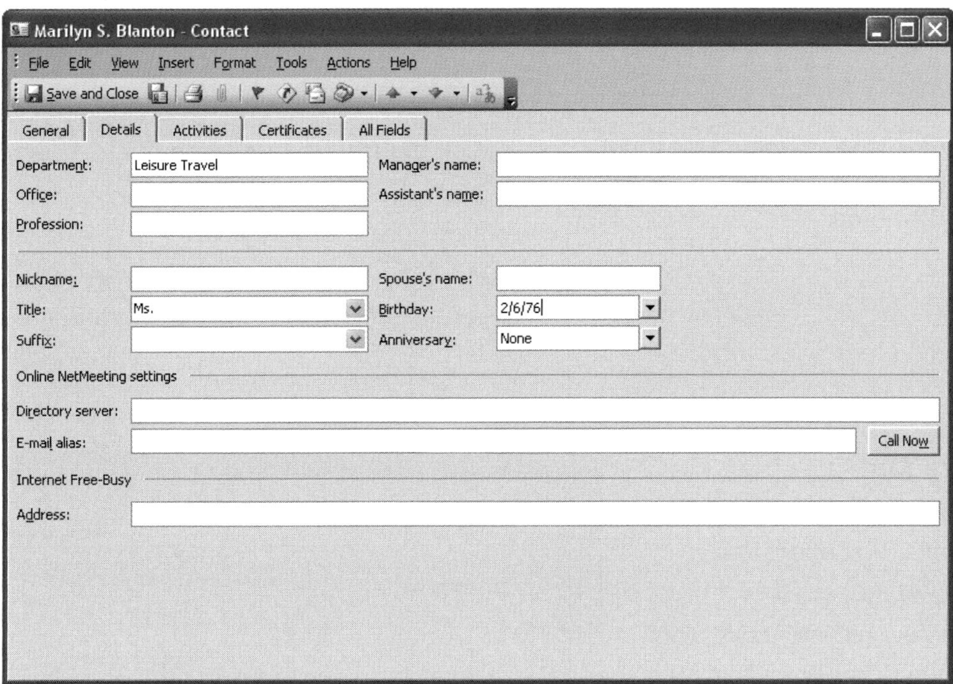

Figure 6.31 Contacts dialog box, Details tab

TRY *it* OUT *w6-14*

1. Double-click **Ellis, Marilyn** in the Address cards view list.
2. Click to place the insertion point in the **Address** box.
3. Delete the New York address and enter:

   `One Main Street, Boston, MA 11111`
4. Replace the business phone number with `617-555-6666.`
5. Replace the business fax number with `617-555-7777.`
6. Click the **Details** tab.
7. In the Department box, enter: `Leisure Travel.`
8. In the Manager's name box, enter: `Janice Pierce.`
9. Click the **Birthday** down arrow.
10. Click **June 7.**
11. Click the **Save and Close** button.

Delete Contacts

- To delete a contact, select it within Address Cards view and press Delete, or right-click and select Delete on the shortcut menu. You can also click the Delete button on the Standard toolbar.

- After you delete a contact, you can immediately retrieve it by clicking the Undo Delete button on the Advanced toolbar.

TRY *it* OUT *w6-15*

1. In Outlook, create a new address card with your own information, then click the **Save and Close** button.
2. Within **Address Cards** view, click your name.
3. Click the **Delete** button on the Standard toolbar.

4. Click **Edit, Undo Delete**.
5. With your name still selected, right-click and select **Delete** from the shortcut menu.

Print a Contacts List

- To print your Contacts list, click File, Print. The Print dialog box opens, as shown in Figure 6.32.
- Depending on the view you are using, you can print your Contacts list in a variety of styles: Card style, Small Booklet style, Medium Booklet style, Memo style, Table style, or Phone Directory style.

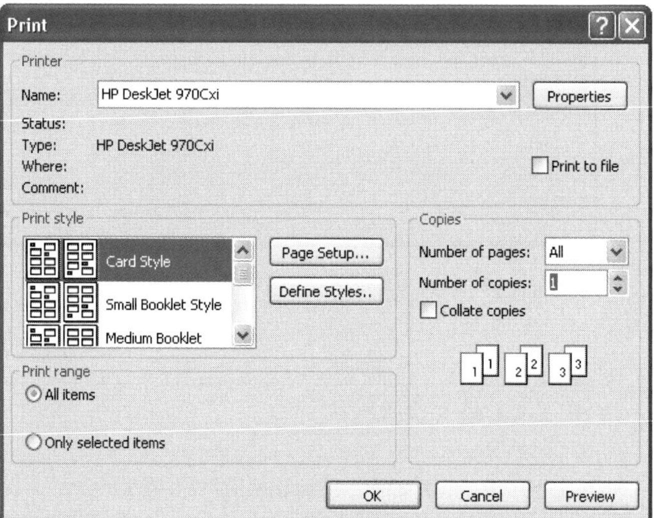

Figure 6.32 Print dialog box

TRY *it* OUT *w6-16*

1. In Outlook, click **Address Cards** in the Current view options.
2. Click the **Print** button on the Standard toolbar.
3. Click **Card Style** in the Print dialog box.
4. Click **Preview.** Close the Preview screen.
5. Click the **Print** button.
6. Click **Phone Directory Style** and click **Preview.** Close the Preview screen.
7. Click **Phone list** in the Current View options.
8. Click the **Print** button, then **Preview** the Table Style.
9. Click **Print** from the Preview screen and click **OK** on the Print dialog box.

Create and Use the Address Book

- Outlook automatically creates an *Address Book* from your Contacts list. You can use the Address Book to look up and select names, e-mail addresses, and distribution lists when you send messages. When you update your contacts, Outlook updates the Address Book as well.
- To display the Address Book, click Tools, Address Book. In the Address Book dialog box, shown in Figure 6.33, you can enter, edit, or delete names and/or create a distribution list. A distribution list is a collection of contacts. It provides an easy way to send messages to a group of people. You can create a category for the names in your list. For example, if you frequently send messages to the Human Resources department, you can create a distribution list called HR Department. Distribution lists are identified by a distribution list icon that appears in your Contacts folder.

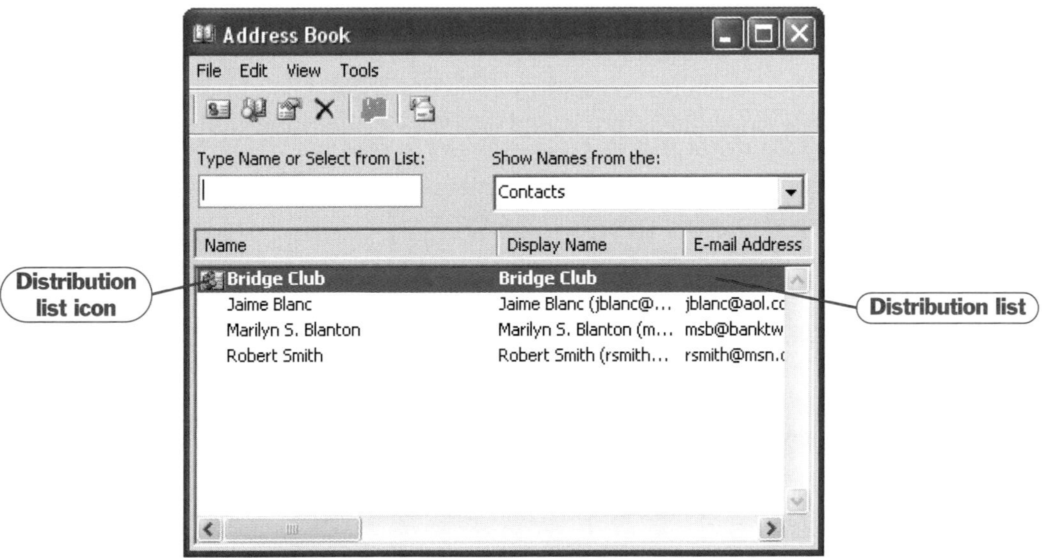

Figure 6.33 Address Book dialog box

TRY*it* OUT *w6-17*

1. In Outlook, click **Tools**, **Address Book**.
2. Click **File**, **New Entry** in the Address Book dialog box.
3. Select **New Distribution List** in the New Entry dialog box and click **OK**.
4. Enter `Bridge Club` in the **Name** box to identify your list.
5. Click the **Select Members** button to display the Contacts list.
6. Select **Marilyn Ellis**, and click **OK**.
7. Click the **Select Members** button to display the Contacts list.
8. Select **Janice Pierce**, and click **OK**. (Repeat steps 7 and 8 for each member you wish to add to your list.)
9. Click **Save and Close**. Notice that the Distribution List has been added to your Contacts List.

Use the Address Book in Word

For Correspondence

- You can use the Address Book to insert an inside address in a letter, address an envelope, or insert an e-mail address (or addresses in a distribution list) in an e-mail message. You can update your Contacts list (which updates your Address Book) while in Word.
- To use the Address Book when creating a letter, click the Insert Address button when you are ready to enter the inside address.

Note: The Address Book button is not part of the default Standard or Formatting toolbar buttons. You need to add the button to a toolbar if you use this feature frequently. To do so, Click View, Toolbars, Customize. On the Commands Tab, click Insert from the Categories list. Scroll down the Commands list until you see Address Book. Drag the Insert Address Book icon to the Standard or Formatting toolbar. Then, click Close to exit the Customize dialog box.

- In the Select Name dialog box that displays, as shown in Figure 6.34, click to select a name, then click OK. This will enter the individual's name and address at the insertion point location.

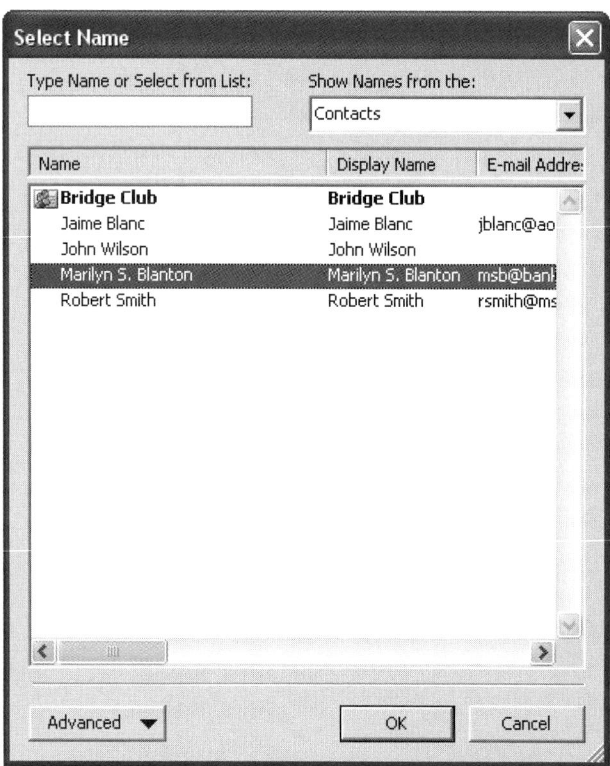

Figure 6.34 Select Name dialog box

- If you are using the Letter Wizard to create a letter, click the Address Book button on the Recipient Info tab of the Letter Wizard dialog box, shown Figure 6.35. This will open the Select Name dialog box (see figure 6.34). Click the name of the recipient, which will insert the appropriate information in the Recipient's name and Delivery address boxes.

Note: If the person's title does not appear along with the name in the recipient's name box, you may have to insert it.

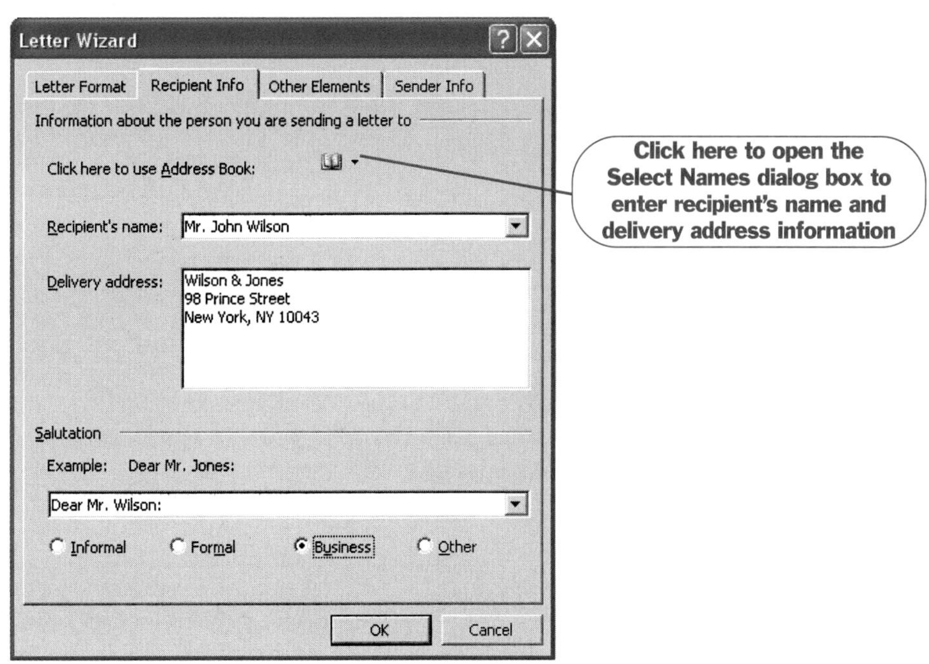

Figure 6.35 Letter Wizard dialog box

- The Other Elements tab and Sender Info tab on the Letter Wizard dialog box also displays the Address book button to help you access information from your contacts list.

For E-mail

- You can create and send an e-mail message in Outlook or in Word. To do so in Word, click File, New and select the Blank E-mail Message link in the task pane. You can also click the E-mail button on the Standard toolbar. This opens the e-mail message window shown in 6.36.

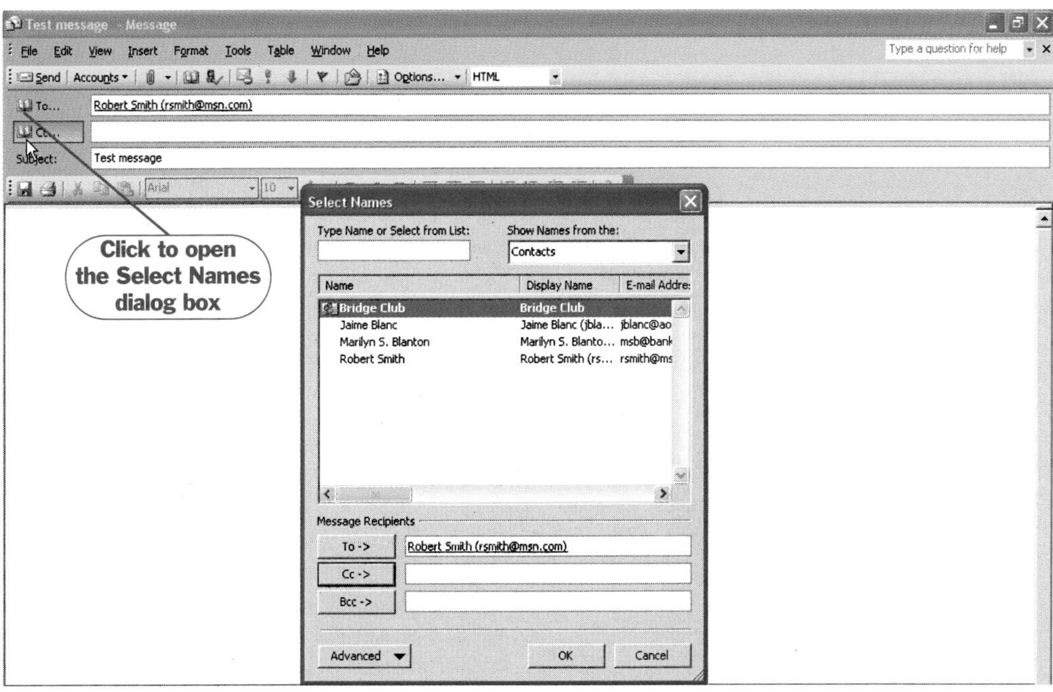

Figure 6.36 E-mail message window

▶ To enter an e-mail address from the Address Book, click the Address Book button in the message window and select a recipient from your contacts list. 

▶ To send a Word document as e-mail, click on the E-mail button on the toolbar while you have the document on the screen.

TRY *it* OUT *w6-18*

1. Open a new blank Word document.
2. Click **Tools**, **Letters and Mailings**, **Letter Wizard**.
3. On the **Letter Format** tab, select **Date line**.
4. Click the **Recipient Info** tab.
5. Click the **Address Book** button.

Note: To access the Address Book, Outlook must be set up as the default mail client for your system.

6. Select **Marilyn Ellis** and click **OK**.
7. Enter `Ms.` preceding her name in the Recipient's name box.
8. Click **Business** for the type of salutation
9. Click the **Other Elements** tab.
10. Click the **Address Book** button.
11. Select **Janice Pierce** to receive a courtesy copy and click **OK**.
12. Click the **Sender Info** tab.
13. Click the **Address Book**.
14. Select your name.
15. Click to Omit the return address.
16. Click to select a Complimentary closing.
17. Click **OK**.

Note: You now have the framework for the letter. To finalize it, you would have to add content and format the letter so that it is spaced properly. We will assume you have done that for the purpose of this exercise.

18. Click the **E-mail** button on the toolbar 
19. Click the **Address Book** button.
20. Click **Marilyn Ellis**, and click **OK**. Note that her e-mail address is automatically entered in the e-mail window.
21. Click the **E-mail** button on the toolbar to close the e-mail window.
22. Close the file.

Update a Contacts List through Smart Tags in Word

- As you learned previously, when you enter certain text in a document, Word labels it with a Smart Tag (a purple dotted line that appears below the text). You can use smart tags to perform actions in Outlook while you are in Word.

Note: You must enable Smart Tags by selecting Tools, AutoCorrect Options. Click the Smart Tags tab and select each Smart Tag recognizer option.

- Move your insertion point over the underlined text until the Smart Tag Actions button appears. You can then click the button to see a list of actions you can perform.
- The actions you can perform depend on the type of data that Word recognizes. Names will display one set of actions, whereas dates will display another. For example, when you enter an address and click on the Smart Tag Actions button, the smart tag actions that display, shown in Figure 6.37, will allow you to Add to Contacts. Clicking on this option will open the Contact dialog box in Outlook, where you can update the contact, if necessary. The actions shown in Figure 6.37 also allow you to display a map or driving directions (these actions require you to be connected to the Internet).

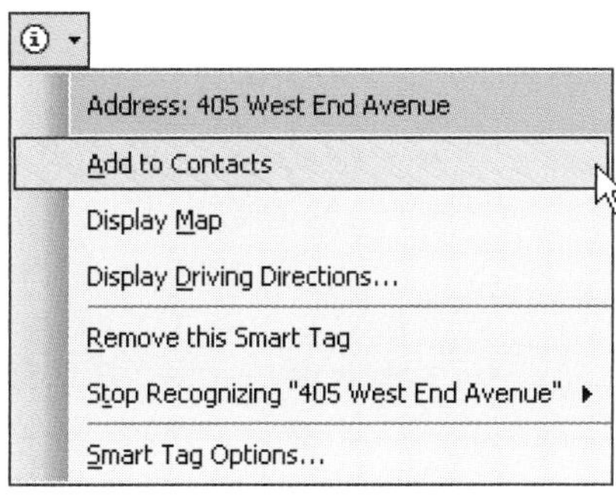

Figure 6.37 Smart Tag actions

- Word will label a name and/or phone number with a Smart Tag, which will provide actions that include updating your Contacts list.

TRY *it* OUT *w6-19*

1. Open a new document in Word.
2. Enter `405 West End Avenue` and press the **Enter** key.
3. Position your mouse pointer over the Smart Tag.
4. Click the **Smart Tag** actions button to display a menu of actions.
5. Click **Add to Contacts**.
6. Enter the following information in the appropriate text boxes in the Contact dialog box:
   Ms. Janet Mason, Manager
   Reeding & Company
   jm@aol.com
   212-555-5555 (business)
   212-666-6666 (business fax)
7. Click **Save and Close**.
8. Close the Word file; do not save.

GOAL
To create a list of contacts and edit some contact information

WHAT YOU NEED TO KNOW

- In this Rehearsal activity, you will create a list of contacts, edit contact information, and add details to a contact in Outlook. While in Outlook, you will print the list of contacts in the Card Style format. You will then create a letter in Word and use the address book to insert the inside address and other information.

DIRECTIONS

1. In Outlook, click the **Contact view** button.
2. Add the following contacts to the Contacts list:
   - `Mr. Tom Bukata, Director of Marketing and Sales Trilogy Productions 350 West 57 Street New York, NY 10106 business phone: 212-555-9999 business fax: 212-555-8900 e-mail: tb.tpny@world.com`
   - `John Alan, Chief Executive Officer Trilogy Productions 101 Sunset Boulevard Beverly Hills, CA 90210 business phone: 310-555-0000 business fax: 310-555-0000 e-mail: ja.tpca@world.com`
   - `Robert Banks, Chief Financial Officer Trilogy Productions 101 Sunset Boulevard Beverly Hills, CA 90210 business phone: 310-555-0000 business fax: 310-555-0000 e-mail: rbtpc@world.com`
   - `Air Land Sea Travel Group, 505 Park Avenue, New York, NY 10010, phone: 212-555-5555, fax: 212-555-6767, e-mail als@net.com, Web www.als.com.`
3. Display the Contacts list in Detailed Address Cards view.
4. Print the Contacts list in the Card Style format.
5. Switch to Word.
6. Open **6.4siglet** (Sutton Investment Group Letterhead) from the Data CD. 
7. Use Mail Merge to create the letter shown on the facing page.
   a. In Step 2 of the merge process, choose **use current document**.
   b. In Step 3 of the merge process, choose **Select from Outlook contacts**, then click to select only the following recipients from the Mail Merge Recipients dialog box: **Tom Bukata, John Alan** and **Robert Banks**.

Continued on next page

c. Use your name as the writer of the letter; give yourself the title of Benefit Coordinator.
d. Save the letter as **6.4support.**

8. Use any letter template.
9. Print one copy of the merged letters.
10. Save the merged file as **6.4support final.**

Today's date

«AddressBlock»

Dear «Title» «Last»:

Thank you for showing your support for the benefit reading of *Jacob's Room,* to be held at the Canby Theater on April 25.

Your tax-deductible donation of $500 includes admission to the reading, a banquet dinner, and two free raffle tickets.

Your support of our theater is most appreciated. We will be honored to have you at the benefit on April 25. You may pick up your tickets at the box office before the performance.

Sincerely,

Your Name
Benefit Coordinator

Cues for Reference

Add a New Contact in Outlook

1. Click the **Contacts view** button.
2. Click **New** on the Standard toolbar.
3. Click the **Full Name** button.
4. Enter the data. Click **OK**.
5. Enter the contact's title in the Job title box.
6. Enter the company name in the Company box.
7. Enter the business address in the Address box.
8. Click the first phone number down arrow and click **Business.**
9. Enter the phone numbers in the appropriate boxes using the down arrow to select a different phone option.
10. Enter other contact information.
11. Click the **Save and New** button on the toolbar to add another contact 
or
Click the **Save and Close** button to close the Contacts dialog box.

Edit Contacts in Outlook

1. Double-click the contact name in **Address Cards** view.
2. Delete any contact information you want to change.
3. Enter corrected contact information.
4. Click the **Save and Close** button. 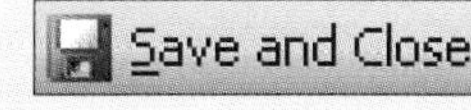

Print a Contacts List in the Card Style Format in Outlook

1. Click the **Print** button. 
2. Click **Card Style.**
3. Click **OK.**

PERFORMANCE

SETTING THE STAGE

Act I File names:

6.p1als radio

6.p1als clients

Act II File name:

6.p2als web

WHAT YOU NEED TO KNOW

Act I

You work in the Marketing Department of Air Land Sea (ALS) Travel Group in the New York office. Your company is considering advertising its services on a live radio Web site. Some members of your department are not sure that people will listen to a live radio Web site or even know that live radio sites exist.

Your boss has suggested that before deciding to advertise on a radio Web site, it would be a good idea to survey some of your clients. You have been asked to write a letter to some of your clients to get their feedback on this concept. You have also been asked to create a new letterhead that incorporates this concept.

Follow these guidelines:

- Design a new letterhead for Air Land Sea Travel Group. Include a tagline as a footer that reads: `The First to Be Heard...in Cyberspace!` Use the Address Book to insert the contact information for the letterhead:

  `505 Park Avenue, New York, NY 10010, phone 212-555-5555, fax 212-555-6767, e-mail als@net.com, Web www.als.com.`

- The content of the letter should contain the following:

  Explain the purpose of your letter (ALS is considering advertising on the Web and wants to know whether this form of marketing would appeal to them).

  Ask your clients to listen to the following existing radio Web sites and then provide feedback on what they liked or disliked about the sites by filling out the enclosed questionnaire (we will assume the questionnaire has been prepared) or by sending you an e-mail with this information.

  http://cd1019.com

  www.web-radio.fm

  Point out that as a thank-you for taking time to give feedback, ALS will provide a free weekend stay for two at the "W" Hotel in Manhattan.

Add the following individuals to your Contacts list in Outlook.

Mr. Seth Harris	Ms. Kadisha Pilgrim	Mr. Jose Diaz	Ms. Brenda Gretta
34 East 80 Street	789 Nostrand Avenue	876 Mercer Street	One Gracie Square
New York, NY 10022	Brooklyn, NY 11213	New York, NY 10001	New York, NY 10021

Use the Mail Merge feature to create and merge the main document (the letter to clients) with the Outlook contacts shown above.

- Print one copy of the merged letters.
- Save the letter as **6.p1als radio.**
- Save the data file as **6.p1als clients.**
- You might e-mail this letter to other clients who have e-mail addresses so they can access the Web sites directly from the letter, if they want. To test the links, send the letter to another member of your department (a friend in your class or your teacher). Have them test the links.

Act II

As part of its marketing strategy, ALS Travel Group plans to advertise on the Internet. You have been asked to create a home page for the company and have been given some guidelines, which are indicated below. To get ideas of what your page might look like and what information it should include, search the Internet and look at competitors' Web sites. Then, design your own.

Follow these guidelines:

- Use any Web template, or create one from scratch using a blank document. Save the file as a Web page.
- Apply any graphics, background, or theme.
- Format the following sections and information in any way that fits the template or design you choose.

Welcome to ALS Travel Group.

- At ALS, we offer professional services that suit the world's most demanding travelers. Our name guarantees value. Because of the personal relationships we have nurtured for over 40 years, we have connections with every luxury cruise line, reputable tour and adventure operators, and over 200 select hotels, resorts, spas, and ranches. Then, we'll add something extra—upgrades, special pricing, and/or complimentary excursions. All of our guests will receive a one-year complimentary subscription to our newsletter. We will always send you away with some interesting travel tips.

Land Vacations

- Some places demand your undivided attention—Europe, South America, India, Africa (Cape Town), and China, in particular. Explore the culture, encounter the unusual, and find the enlightenment that only a land journey provides. ALS Travel Group will arrange a trip to take you to the places of your dreams.

Skiing Vacations

- Enjoy some of the breathtaking scenes at the most famous ski resorts. Visit Whistler and Blackcomb Mountains in British Columbia, or ski down the magnificent slopes of Italy. Whatever your destination, our skiing vacations are second to none.

Cruises

- Alaska is spectacular and irresistible. Sail from Seward to Vancouver on the only all-suite, all-balcony luxury ship. There's plenty of time for great sightseeing in College Fjord, Hubbard Glacier, Tracy Arm, and the fabled Inside Passage. See St. Petersburg aboard the SS Rodder, which departs Dover, England, on June 14. This cruise will take you to Copenhagen and Stockholm for an exhilarating stay.

- Create links on the following words to the locations indicated.

SECTION:	WORD(S) ON WHICH TO CREATE THE LINK:	FILE/WEB SITE TO WHICH TO LINK:
First	newsletter	**5.p3als news** (a file you created in the previous lesson)
	interesting travel tips	**5.p2airlines ad** (a file you created in the previous lesson)
Second	Cape Town	www.cape-town.org
Third	skiing resorts	**6.2 ski week** (on the Data CD)
	Blackcomb Mountains	www.whistler-blackcomb.com/home.asp
	Italy	www.skiitaly.com/cortina/newpic/htm/pic4.htm
Fourth	Alaska	www.dced.state.ak.us/tourism
	St. Petersburg	www.interknowledge.com/russia/peter01.htm

- Be sure to include an e-mail link to your company's e-mail address at als@net.com (you will need to create the text in which to include this information).
- Copy **6.1pf ski table1** from the Data CD and paste it as an embedded object below the Skiing Vacations section.
- View the Web page in your browser and test all the links.
- Save the Web page as **6.p2als web.**
- Print one copy of the Web page.

PERFORMING WITH EXCEL
INTRODUCTORY UNIT

LESSON 1

Excel Basics

In this lesson, you will learn about the Excel screen, including the toolbars, menus, and view preferences. You will use navigation techniques, express movements, and learn some basic worksheet concepts while exploring the Excel screen. You will also learn about creating and renaming folders for file management.

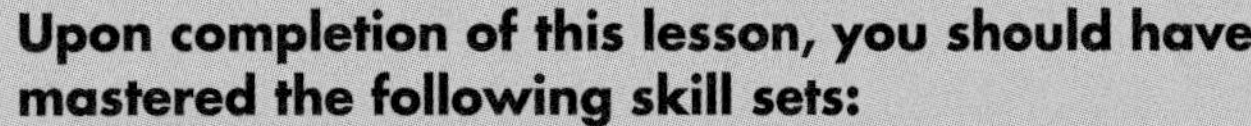

Upon completion of this lesson, you should have mastered the following skill sets:

- Start Excel
- Explore the Excel workbook
- Explore menus and toolbars
- Set view preferences
- Navigate the worksheet
- Use scroll bars
- Use the Go To command
- Create a folder for saving workbooks
- Rename a folder

Terms

- Worksheet
- Workbook
- Status bar
- Task pane
- Title bar
- Menu bar
- Toolbar
- Formula bar
- Active cell
- Name box
- Column
- Row
- Cell
- Cell address
- Active cell reference
- Scroll bars
- Working folder
- Folder

GOALS
To explore the Excel workbook
To practice using the following skill sets:
- Start Excel
- Explore the Excel workbook
- Explore menus and toolbars
- Set view preferences

EXCEL

WHAT YOU NEED TO KNOW

About Excel

- Excel is a powerful spreadsheet tool you can use to analyze, chart, and manage data for personal, business, and financial use. You can also use Excel to produce worksheets, charts, and databases, and to publish data to the Web.

Start Excel

- To start Excel, on the Windows taskbar, click Start, select All Programs, select Microsoft Office, and Microsoft Office Excel 2003. If you have customized your desktop or Start menu, just double-click the Excel icon.

TRY*it* OUT *E1-1*

1. Click **Start** on the Windows taskbar.
2. Select **All Programs.**
3. Select **Microsoft Office.**
4. Click **Microsoft Office Excel 2003.**

Explore the Excel Workbook

- When you start Excel, a new *workbook*, called Book1, appears containing three *worksheets* identified by the sheet tabs at the bottom of the workbook. The active sheet in Figure 1.1 is Sheet1, but you can click another sheet tab to make it the active sheet. You can increase the number of sheets in a workbook, as discussed in Lesson 4, to two hundred fifty-five.
- The bottom of the screen also contains the *status bar***,** which displays the condition of worksheet calculations and settings. This bar shows items such as the setting for caps or number lock.
- The *task pane* appears on startup on the right side of the screen and shows options for the task at hand. In the Getting Started task pane, the Microsoft Office Online section provides current links to online content and the Open section shows the last four files opened. You can close the task pane using the Close button on the top right corner of the pane. If the task pane does not display, use the View menu, as discussed on the next page.

TRY*it*OUT *E1-2*

1. Click **Sheet2.**
2. Click **Sheet3.**
3. Click **Sheet1.**
4. Click the **Close** button on the task pane to close the pane.

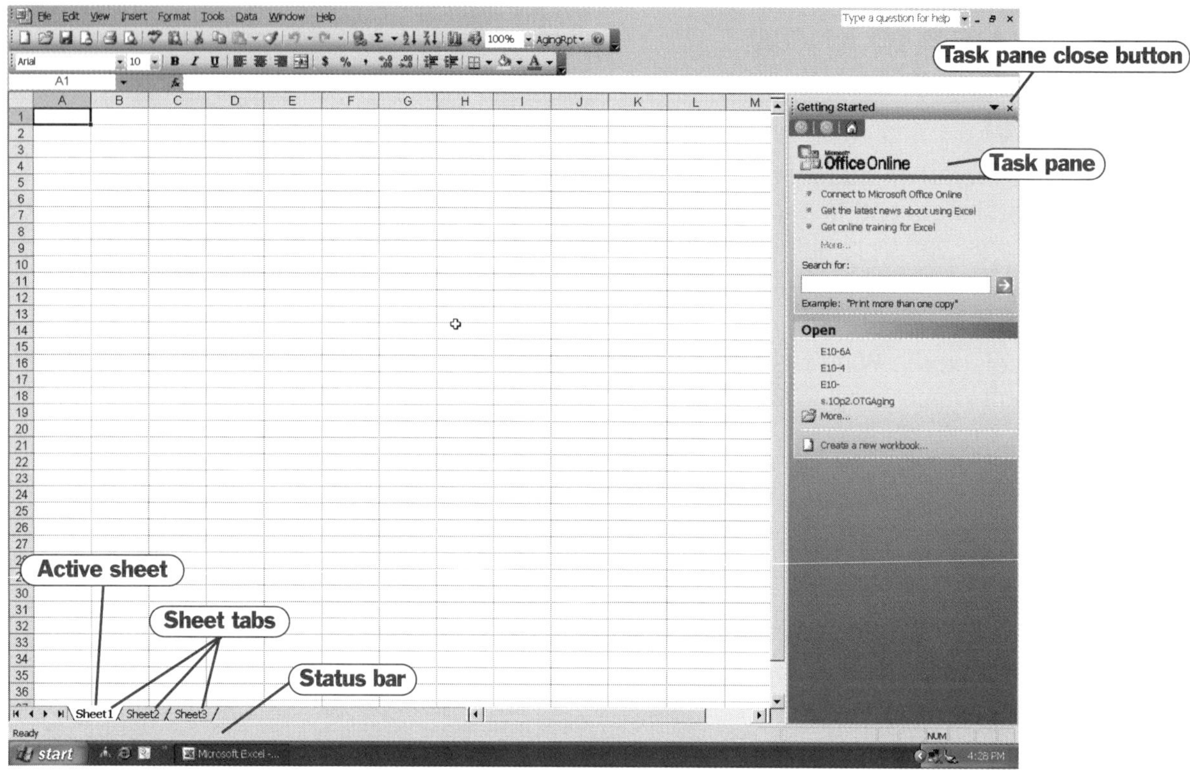

Figure 1.1 Excel workbook screen

Explore Menus and Toolbars

- The top portion of the screen contains the *title bar*, the *menu bar*, and two *toolbars*. The toolbars are the Standard and Formatting toolbars, as shown in Figure 1.2.
- Excel also has a *formula bar*, which contains the *Name box* on the left, the Insert Function button, and an area that displays the contents of the active cell. The *active cell* is the location of the worksheet insertion point, which shows where you are currently working. The name of the active cell appears in the *Name box.*
- Click the Toolbar Options arrow at the end of the toolbar to show the most frequently used buttons on one row or to add buttons that are not displayed.

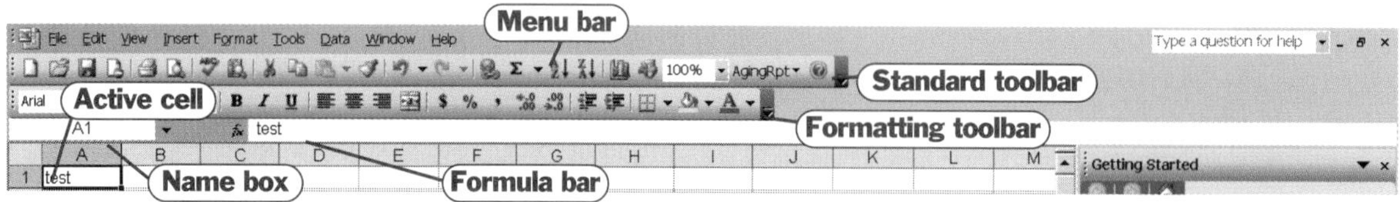

Figure 1.2 Excel title bar, menu bar, toolbar, and formula bar

TRY *it* OUT *E1-3*

1. In Cell A1, type `test`. Press Enter.
2. Click in Cell A1. Notice the text and the reference to A1, the active cell, in the Name box.
3. Click **File**.
4. Position the mouse pointer over all other menu headings to display the menu items.
5. Click the **Toolbar Options** arrow button on the Standard toolbar.
6. Click the **Show Buttons on One Row** option. Note that the Standard and Formatting toolbars are consolidated into one row.
7. Click the **Toolbar options** arrow button and click the **Show Buttons on Two Rows** option.
8. Position the mouse pointer over each button to view its function.

EXCEL

Set View Preferences

- Use the View menu to set display options for your Excel workbook. As shown in Figure 1.3, Task Pane, Formula Bar, and Status Bar are checked on the menu, which means they are displayed. Click the check marks to remove the features from the display.
- If you are working on a large worksheet or have difficulty seeing all the data, two View options will help:
  - The Full Screen option on the View menu expands the worksheet to fill the screen while closing the toolbars and the formula bar.
  - The Zoom option on the View menu lets you set the magnification of cells in a worksheet, as shown in Figure 1.4.
- To further customize view preferences, click Tools, Options, and then the View tab in the Options dialog box, as shown in Figure 1.5. Here, you can set display options for the Excel window, including showing formulas, gridlines, and setting gridline colors.

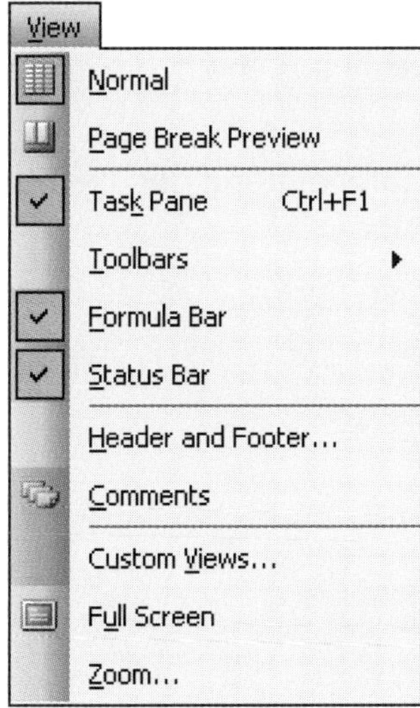

Figure 1.3 View menu

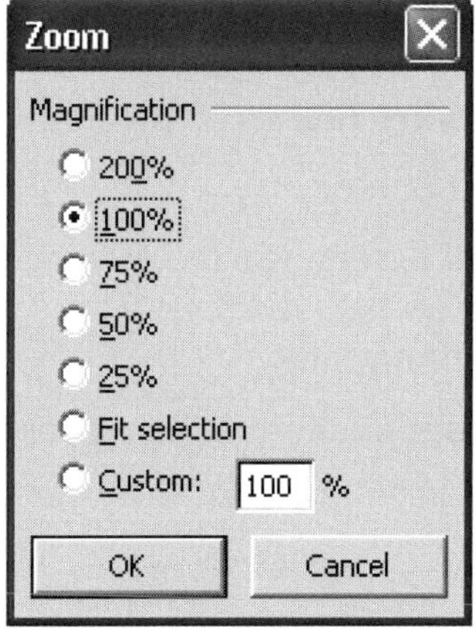

Figure 1.4 Zoom dialog box

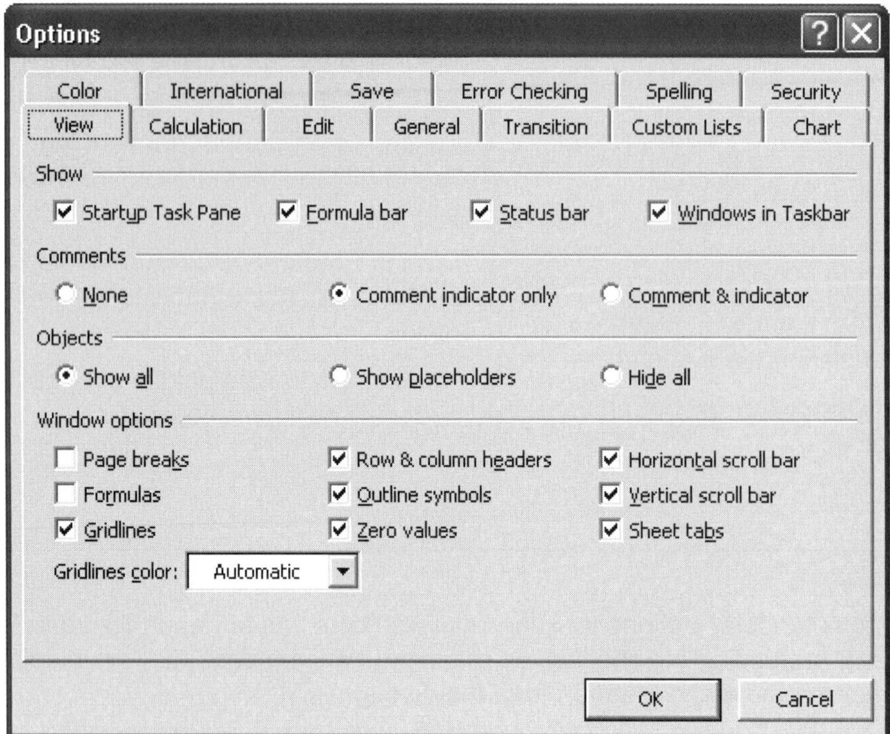

Figure 1.5 Options dialog box

TRY *it* OUT *E1-4*

1. Click the **View** menu and deselect the **Status bar**.
2. Click **View** and select the **Task Pane.**
3. Click **View, Toolbars**. Notice the checked and available toolbars.
4. Select the **Drawing Toolbar**.
5. Click **View, Full Screen.**
6. Click **Close Full Screen** (on the Full Screen toolbar on the worksheet) to return to the normal view.
7. Click **View, Zoom** to see the dialog box.
8. Select **200%** magnification and click **OK.**
9. Restore the magnification to **100%.**
10. Click **Tools, Options,** and then the **View** tab, if not already selected.
11. Click the **Status bar** check box to restore it. Click **OK**.
12. Click **View, Toolbars** and deselect the **Drawing Toolbar.**
13. Click the **Close** button to close Excel. Do not save the file. 

TASK 1

GOAL
To explore the Excel workbook

SETTING THE STAGE/WRAPUP
Start Excel

WHAT YOU NEED TO KNOW

- If you have a shortcut to Excel on your desktop, double-click it to start the application, or click Start, All Programs, Microsoft Office, and Microsoft Office Excel 2003.
- In this Rehearsal activity, you will explore the Excel workbook, toolbars, and menus. You will use the View menu to set and reset preferences.

DIRECTIONS

1. Click **File**. Notice the menu selections.
2. Click away from the File menu once to close it.
3. Select and view the commands on each menu.
4. Click **Sheet3**.
5. Click **Sheet1.**
6. Rest the mouse pointer on a toolbar button to display its name.
7. Find the toolbar buttons for **Bold, Print,** and **Save.**
8. Click **View**, **Toolbars**.
9. Deselect the **Formatting** and **Standard** toolbars.
10. Restore the toolbars.
11. Click **View, Zoom.**
12. Select other magnifications to view the effect.
13. Return to **100%** magnification.
14. Use the View menu to deselect the **Task Pane, Formula Bar,** and **Status Bar.**
15. Use the View menu to reselect the **Formula Bar,** the **Task Pane,** and the **Status Bar.**
16. Click **Tools, Options** to open the dialog box and make the following changes. In the View tab:
    a. Deselect the vertical and horizontal scroll bars.
    b. Set the gridline color to **Red**.
17. Restore the vertical and horizontal scroll bars and set the color back to **Automatic.**

Cues for Reference

Start Excel
- Double-click the **Microsoft Excel** icon on the desktop or Shortcut Bar.
  or
- Click **Start, All Programs, Microsoft Office, Microsoft Office Excel 2003.**

Office XP Click **Start, Programs, Microsoft Excel.**

Set Zoom
1. Click **View**, **Zoom**.
2. Select percentage of magnification.
3. Click **OK**.

Select Toolbars
1. Click **View**, **Toolbars**.
2. Select or deselect toolbars.

Set Options
1. Click **Tools**, **Options**.
2. Select appropriate tab.
3. Select or deselect options.
4. Click **OK**.

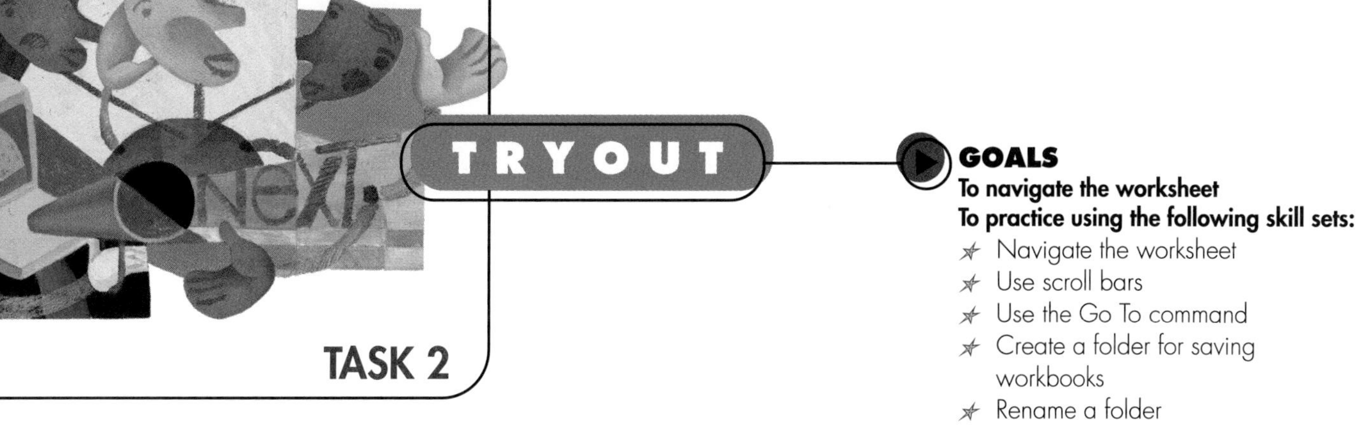

GOALS
To navigate the worksheet
To practice using the following skill sets:
- Navigate the worksheet
- Use scroll bars
- Use the Go To command
- Create a folder for saving workbooks
- Rename a folder

EXCEL

WHAT YOU NEED TO KNOW

Navigate the Worksheet

- A worksheet has alphabetical *column* headings and numbered *rows*. The intersection of a column and row is called a *cell*. A worksheet contains 256 columns and 65,536 rows, which means that over 16 million cells are available for data. As you will see after the tryout, only a small part of the worksheet is visible on the screen at one time.
- A cell is referenced (referred to) by its unique *cell address*, which is made up of the column and row number. Cell B2, as shown in Figure 1.6, has a heavy border indicating that it is the active cell. The *active cell* is also identified in the *Name box* on the formula bar, which always displays the *active cell reference*, and by the highlighted column and row of the active cell. The mouse pointer is a plus sign when on the worksheet, as shown below.

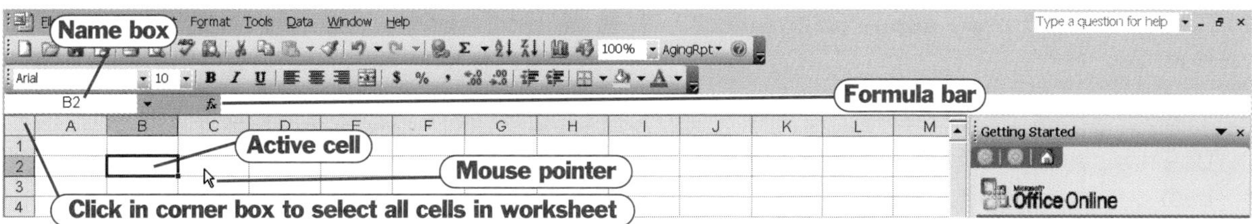

Figure 1.6 Worksheet with active Cell B2 in Name box

TRY*it* OUT *E1-5*

1. Click **Cell D5** to make it active.
2. Press the left arrow key until **Cell B5** is selected.
3. Press the arrow keys to select **Cell H20**.

▶ To move around the worksheet, press the arrow keys or press both an arrow key and the Ctrl key for express (fast) movements. As you move through the worksheet, the active cell changes, as does the active cell reference in the Name box. A table of keystrokes to select cells and to navigate the worksheet is shown below.

SELECT WORKSHEET CELLS	
Select a cell	Click the cell
Select the worksheet	Ctrl+A, or click corner box
Select a row	Shift+Space
Select a column	Ctrl+Space
NAVIGATE THE WORKSHEET	
Move one cell	Use the left, right, up, or down arrow
Move one screen up or down	Page Up or Page Down
First cell in worksheet	Ctrl+Home
First cell in current row	Home
First cell in current column	Ctrl+↑
Last cell in current row	Ctrl+→
Last cell in current column	Ctrl+↓

TRY it OUT *E1-6*

Note: H20 should be the active cell.

1. Press the **Shift** key + **spacebar** to select **Row 20.**
2. Press the **Ctrl+Home** keys.
3. Use navigation express shortcuts to go to:
   Last cell in current row: **Ctrl+→**
   First cell in current row: **Home**
   Last cell in current column: **Ctrl+↓**
4. Return to the first cell in the worksheet.
5. Click the corner box to the left of the Column A heading, as shown in Figure 1.6, to select the entire worksheet.
6. Click any cell to deselect it.

Use Scroll Bars

▶ To scroll to different areas in a worksheet, use the mouse pointer and the *scroll bars* at the right and bottom of the worksheet window, as shown in Figure 1.7, and summarized in the table below. Scrolling does not change the active cell.

USE SCROLL BARS	
One column left or right	Click left or right scroll arrows
One row up or down	Click up or down scroll arrows
Scroll quickly	Click and drag scroll bar, press and hold Shift

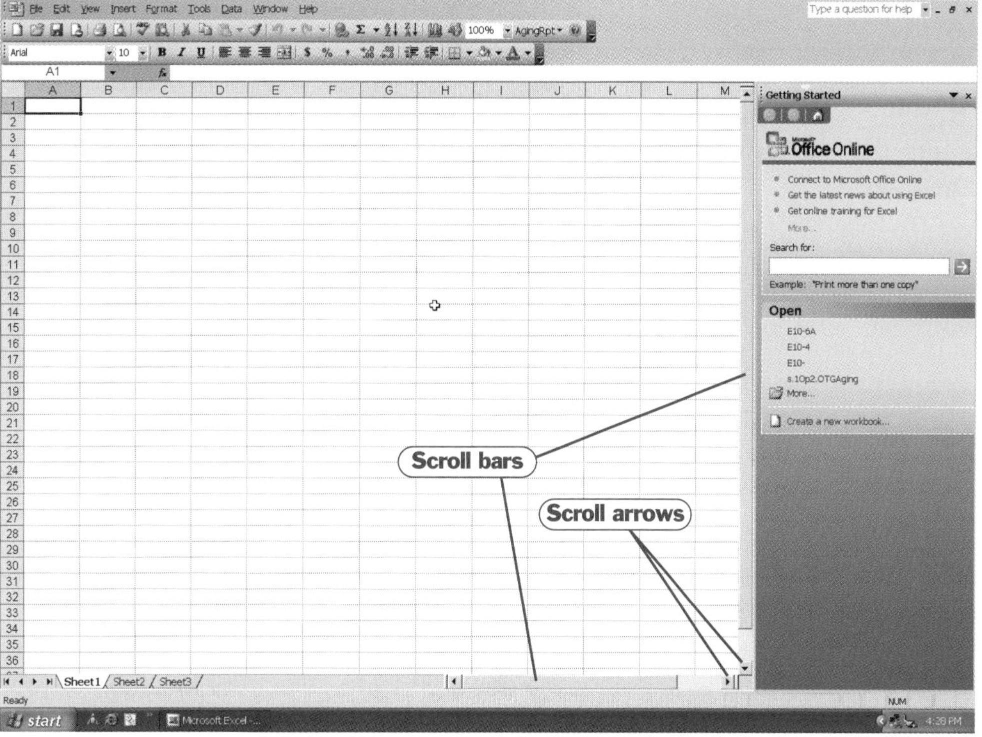

Figure 1.7 Scroll bars

TRY*it* OUT *E1-7*

1. Click the **down** scroll arrow on the vertical scroll bar.
2. Click the **right** scroll arrow on the horizontal scroll bar.
3. Click the **horizontal** scroll bar, press the **Shift** key, and drag to the right.
4. Click and drag the **horizontal** scroll bar to the left, back to Column A.
5. Click the **up** scroll arrow on the vertical scroll bar.

Use the Go To Command

- You can move directly to a specific cell by entering the cell address in the Name box or by using the Go To command.
- Click Edit, Go To or press the F5 key to display the Go To dialog box, as shown in Figure 1.8. You can enter the desired cell address, or select a location from your list of previously selected locations. The dollar signs displayed with the cell addresses indicate that the address is an absolute reference (see Lesson 4) to that specific location.

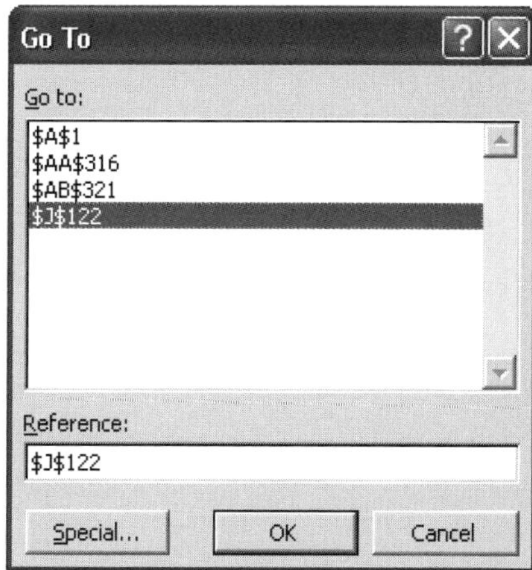

Figure 1.8 Go To dialog box

TRY *it* OUT *E1-8*

1. Click **Edit**, **Go To**.
2. In the Reference text box, enter **J122** and press the **Enter** key.
3. Press the **F5** key and go to **Cell AB321.** Click **OK**.
4. Click the **Name box** on the left side of the formula bar.
5. Enter **E15** and press the **Enter** key.
6. Press the **F5** key and double-click to select **Cell J122** from the Go To list.
7. To return to Cell A1 press the **Ctrl+Home** keys.

Create a Folder for Saving Workbooks

- The *working folder,* or default location for saving your files, is usually the My Documents folder. A *folder* is a location on a drive that you create to hold files that are related to each other. See Appendix B for more file management procedures.
- Use the Open dialog box to create folders or subfolders to organize your workbook files. Click the Open button on the Standard toolbar and click the down arrow to select the location for your new folder. Click the Create New Folder button on the Open dialog box toolbar, as shown in Figure 1.9, and name the folder. You will then be able to select this folder so that it is in the Look in box. Use the same procedure to create subfolders within the new folder.
- Once you have selected a folder for opening and saving, it remains in the Look in box until you turn off the computer.

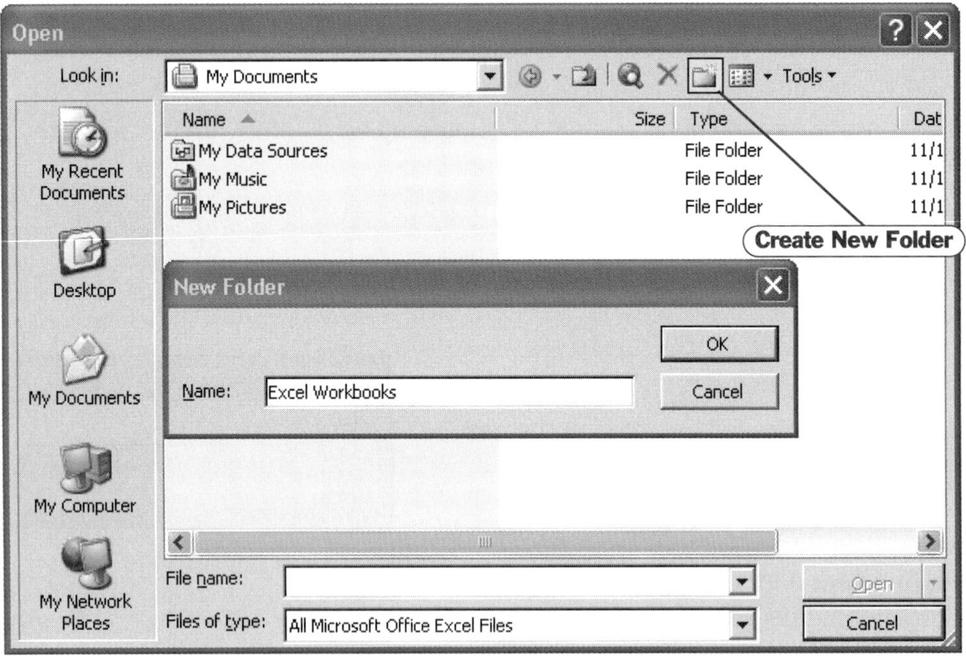

Figure 1.9 Open dialog box, opening a new folder

Renaming Folders

▶ To rename any folder, right-click the folder and select Rename from the shortcut menu as shown in Figure 1.10. Type the new folder name and press Enter.

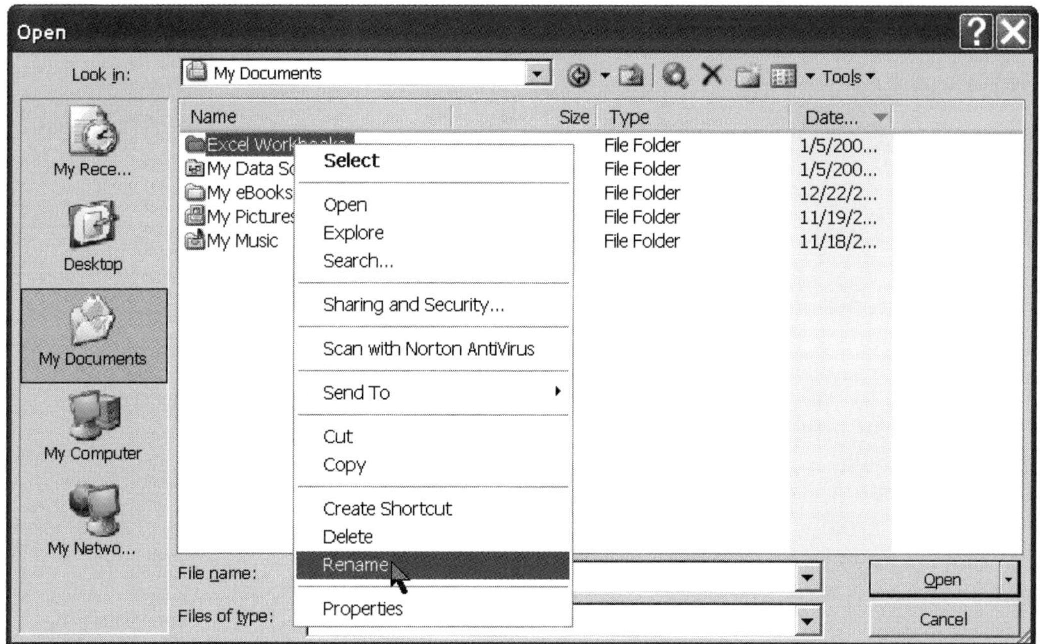

Figure 1.10 Open dialog box, shortcut menu for folders

TRY it OUT *E1-9*

1. Click the **Open** button on the Standard toolbar.
2. Click the **Create New Folder** button on the Open dialog box toolbar.
3. Type the name of the folder: `Excel Workbooks`. Click **OK.** (Notice that the folder is empty and the folder name is in the Look in box.)
4. Click the **Up One Level** button to return to the main folder.
5. Right-click the **Excel Workbooks** folder.
6. Select **Rename** from the shortcut menu.
7. Type `Excel Solutions`, and press **Enter**.
8. Click the **Cancel** button on the Open dialog box.
9. Click the **Save** button on the Standard toolbar. Notice your new working folder. 
10. Click **Cancel**.

REHEARSAL

AGAIN

TASK 2

GOAL
To navigate the worksheet

SETTING THE STAGE/WRAPUP
Start Excel

WHAT YOU NEED TO KNOW

- Notice the active cell reference in the Name box as you move through the worksheet.
- In this Rehearsal activity, you will navigate the worksheet using shortcut keys and express movements. You will also create and rename a subfolder in your Excel Solutions folder.

DIRECTIONS

1. Click **Cell E5** to make it active.
2. Press the arrow keys to select **Cell AA45.**
3. Use express keystrokes to go to the following locations:
   a. Last cell in current row
   b. Last cell in current column
   c. First cell in current row
   d. First cell in worksheet
4. Click the **horizontal** scroll bar, press the **Shift** key, and drag to the right.
5. Click the **horizontal** scroll bar and press the **Shift** key until you can see **Column BZ.**
6. Drag the **horizontal** scroll bar to the left, back to **Column A.**
7. Press the **F5** key to go to **Cell J33.**
8. Repeat Step 7 to go to **Cell BB159** and **Cell J33** again.
9. In the Name box, enter **G5.** Press **Enter.**
10. Press the **Ctrl** key + **spacebar** to select **Column G.**
11. Select the entire worksheet.
12. Select any cell.
13. Move one screen down.
14. Press the **Ctrl+Home** keys to return to **Cell A1.**
15. Click the **Open** button on the Standard toolbar; then, if Excel Solutions is not in the Look in box, select it from the list of folders and double-click the folder.
16. Create a new folder and name it **Lesson 1**.
17. Move up one level in the Open dialog box and rename the new folder **Lesson 2.**
18. Click **Cancel**.

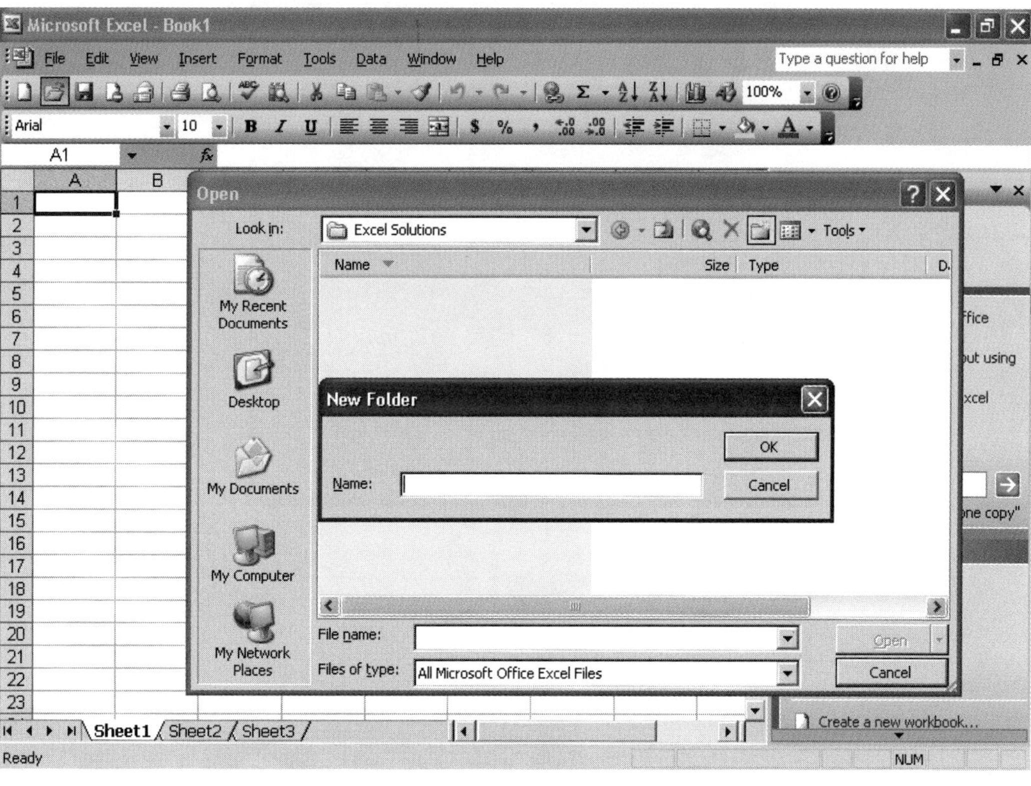

EXCEL

Cues for Reference

Scroll Through a Worksheet

- Click **scroll bar arrow** to move worksheet view.
  or
- Click **Shift+scroll bar arrow** to quickly scroll through worksheet.

Use Go To (Express Navigation)

1. Click F5.
2. Enter cell address.
3. Click **OK**.

Use Navigation Express Shortcuts

Select a row	**Shift+spacebar**
Select a column	**Ctrl+spacebar**
Move one cell	Use the **left, right, up,** or **down arrow**
Move one screen up or down	**Page Up** or **Page Down**
First cell in worksheet	**Ctrl+Home**
First cell in current row	**Home**
First cell in current column	**Ctrl+↑**
Last cell in current row	**Ctrl+→**
Last cell in current column	**Ctrl+↓**

Create New Folder

1. Click the **Open** button.
2. If necessary, click the list arrow in Look in box, or double-click a listed folder to select location.
3. Click the **Create New Folder** button.
4. Enter the folder name.
5. Click **OK.**

Rename a Folder

1. Right-click the folder.
2. Enter the new folder name.
3. Press **Enter.**

LESSON 2

Business Forms

In this lesson, you will learn to use Excel to design business forms and to customize both software and online templates. You will use the Internet to e-mail a form and to access Microsoft Office Online.

Upon completion of this lesson, you should have mastered the following skill sets:

- Enter text, dates, and numbers
- Use Smart Tags
- Format cell data
  - Format dates
  - Format for currency
  - Format text
- Use Save and Save As
- Edit cell data
  - Edit cell contents
  - Align cell data
  - Clear cell contents
  - Check spelling
  - Use the Thesaurus
- Use AutoComplete
- Use Print Preview
- Select a range of cells
- Print
  - Set Print Area
  - Change print settings
- Work with templates
- Save a file as a template
- View Web templates

Terms

Software-related

Label
Left-aligned
Value
Right-aligned
Edit mode
Thesaurus
AutoComplete
Range
Template

Document-related

Business form
Transaction
Professional invoice
Purchase order
Vendor
Sales invoice

GOALS

To create an invoice for services

To practice using the following skill sets:

- Enter text, dates, and numbers
- Use Smart Tags
- Format cell data
  - Format dates
  - Format for currency
  - Format text
- Use Save and Save As

EXCEL

WHAT YOU NEED TO KNOW

Enter Text, Dates, and Numbers

- When you enter an alphabetic character or symbol (text) as the first character in a cell, the cell contains a *label.* Labels are *left-aligned* in the cell by default.
- When you enter a number or date as the first character in a cell, the cell contains a *value.* Values are *right-aligned* in the cell by default.
- After you enter a label or value in a cell, press the Enter key or the arrow key that points to the location of the next data entry to enter the data. Notice the following in Figure 2.1:
  - Labels are left-aligned.
  - Dates and values are right-aligned.
- The default cell width displays approximately nine characters, depending on the font, but you can enter over 32,000 characters in each cell. If you enter text beyond the default cell width, it appears in the next cell's space as long as no other data is there. Notice in Figure 2.1 that the label AV Equipment in Cell A4 would be truncated if there were data in the next cell. However, the formula bar would show that the full label is stored in the cell.

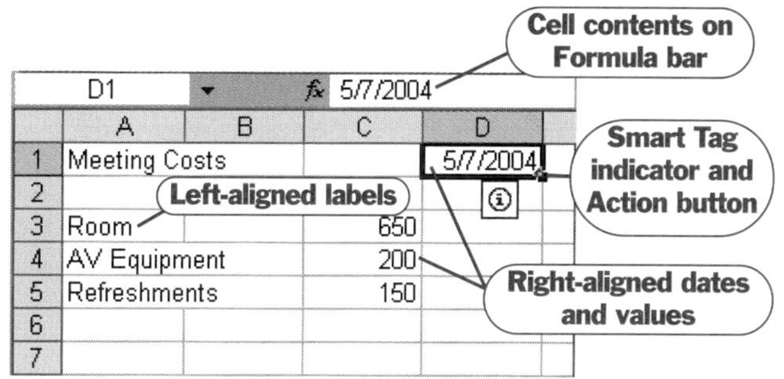

Figure 2.1 Label and value entries

TRY *it* OUT E2-1

1. Start Excel.
2. Enter the label in **Cell A1,** as shown in Figure 2.1.
3. Press the **right arrow** key to enter the data and move to cell D1.
4. Enter the date in **Cell D1,** as shown on the formula bar.
5. Enter the data in **Row 3** of the illustration. Notice the alignment of data.
6. Enter the data in **Row 4** of the illustration.
7. Click **Cell A4** and **Cell B4**. Notice that the label is stored only in Cell A4.
8. Enter data for **Row 5.**
9. Do not close or save the file.

Use Smart Tags

- As shown in Figure 2.1, Excel labels certain types of data with Smart Tags. The Smart Tag indicator, a purple triangle, displays in the cell and the Actions button displays nearby on the worksheet. Click the list arrow on the button to display custom actions associated with that data element, as shown in Figure 2.2. If Smart Tags do not display on your screen, click Tools, AutoCorrect options, and then click the Smart Tags tab, select Label data with smart tags, and click OK.
- In Excel, you can activate a Smart Tag when you enter dates, stock symbols, Outlook e-mail recipients, and numeric labels.

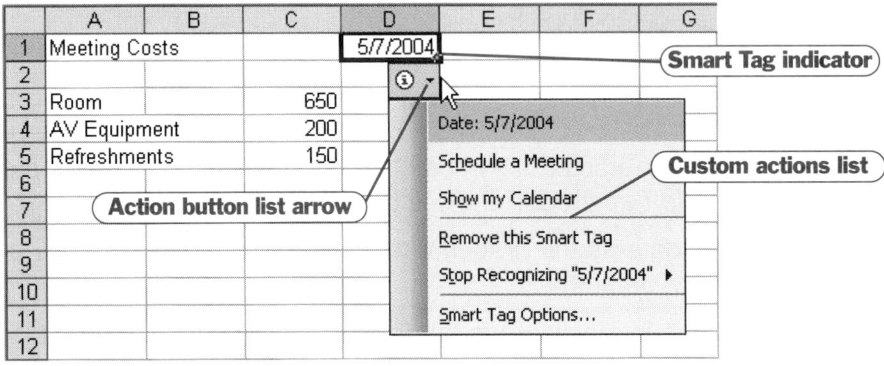

Figure 2.2 Smart Tag actions for dates

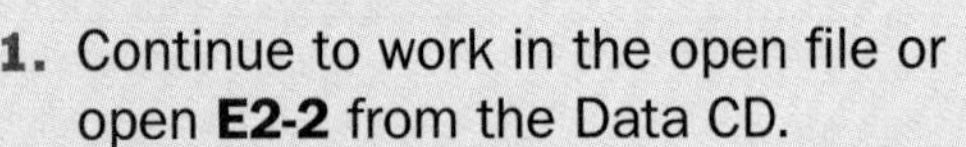

TRY it OUT *E2-2*

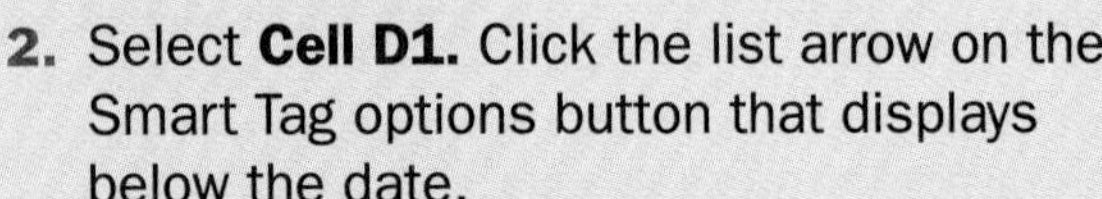

1. Continue to work in the open file or open **E2-2** from the Data CD.
2. Select **Cell D1.** Click the list arrow on the Smart Tag options button that displays below the date.
3. Click **Show my Calendar.** Your calendar in Outlook will display.
4. Close the calendar.
5. Enter **MSFT** in **Cell E1.** Press **Enter** and then move the mouse over the cell.
6. View the Smart Tag options for the stock symbol.
7. Do not close or save the file.

Format Cell Data

Format Dates

- You can enter a date in any format and reformat it in one of 17 date formats. For example, if you enter the date in the mm/dd/yyyy format, you can change it to mm/dd/yy.
- To format dates, select the date and click Format, Cells. In the Format Cells dialog box, click the Number tab, click Date from the Category list, and click a date format from the Type list, as shown in Figure 2.3.

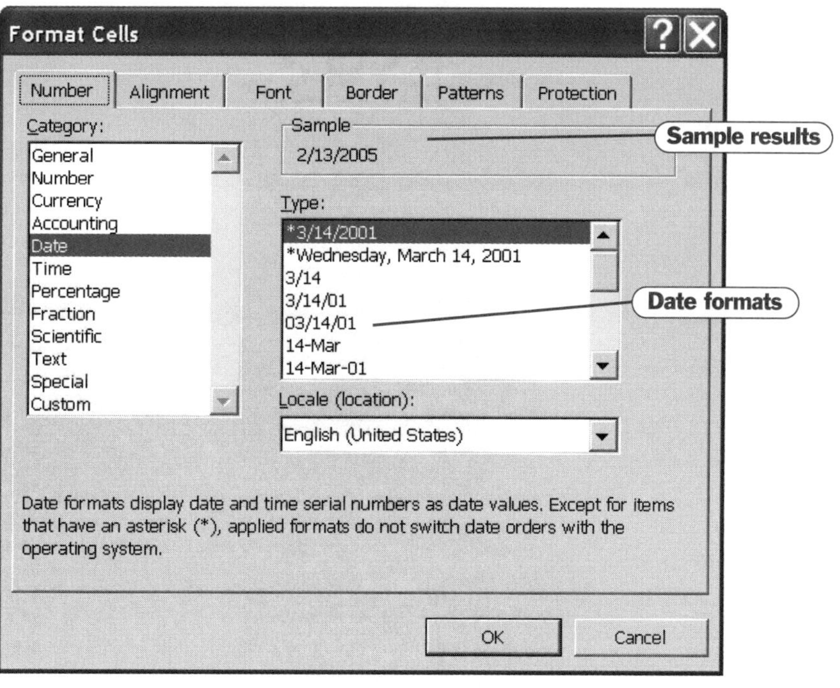

Figure 2.3 Format Cells dialog box

TRY *it* OUT *E2-3*

1. Continue to work in the open file or open **E2-3** from the Data CD.
2. Click **Cell D1.**
3. Click **Format, Cells.**
4. On the Number tab, click **Date,** if necessary.
5. Scroll down and select the **March 14, 2001,** or full date format.
6. Click **OK.**
7. Do not close or save the file.

Format for Currency

▶ When you enter numbers or values, they are in the General format, which means that decimal places are only shown if there are decimal values. To add a dollar sign and two decimal places (Currency format) for the selected cell, click the Currency Style button on the Formatting toolbar, as shown in Figure 2.4.

$

Format Text

▶ The default font is Arial, 10 point. To change font and font size, select the cell(s) and click the Font and Font Size list arrows on the Formatting toolbar and choose the desired settings. Bold, Italic, and Underline styles may also be set.

B I U

EXCEL

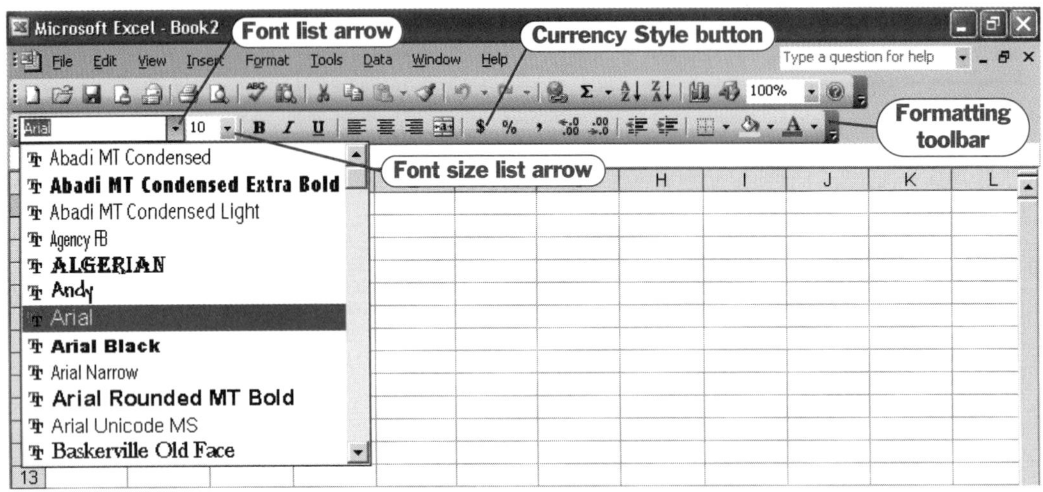

Figure 2.4 Formatting toolbar – font list

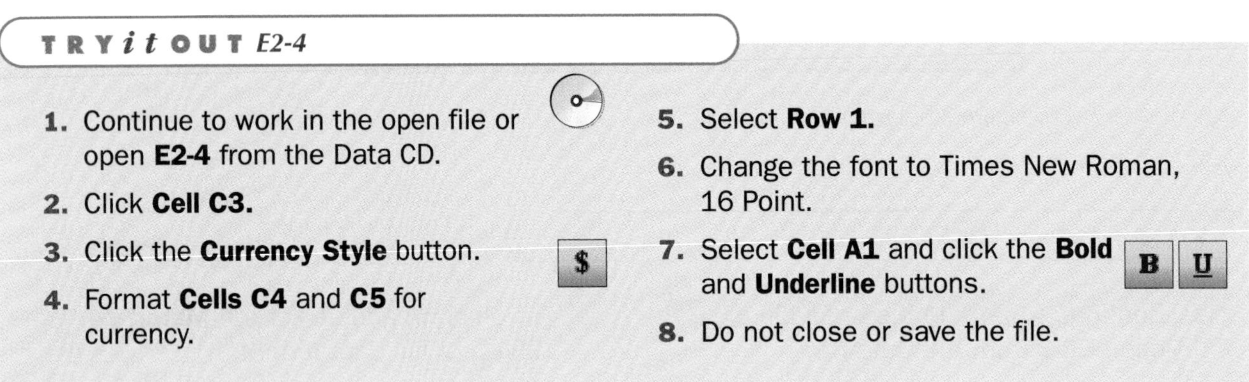

TRY *it* OUT *E2-4*

1. Continue to work in the open file or open **E2-4** from the Data CD.
2. Click **Cell C3.**
3. Click the **Currency Style** button.
4. Format **Cells C4** and **C5** for currency.
5. Select **Row 1.**
6. Change the font to Times New Roman, 16 Point.
7. Select **Cell A1** and click the **Bold** and **Underline** buttons.
8. Do not close or save the file.

Use Save and Save As

- Excel workbooks are named Book1, Book2, and so forth, until you save them with your own file names. Click the Save button on the Standard toolbar to save a new file or to overwrite an existing file.

- When you click the Save button to save a new file, the Save As dialog box opens. Naming a file in the Save As dialog box creates an Excel Worksheet file with an .xls extension.
- You can save Excel files with different names, in different locations, and in different file formats using the settings in the Save As dialog box. To save a file with any of these changes, click File, Save As, and select the appropriate settings. Notice the Save as type list, as shown in Figure 2.5.

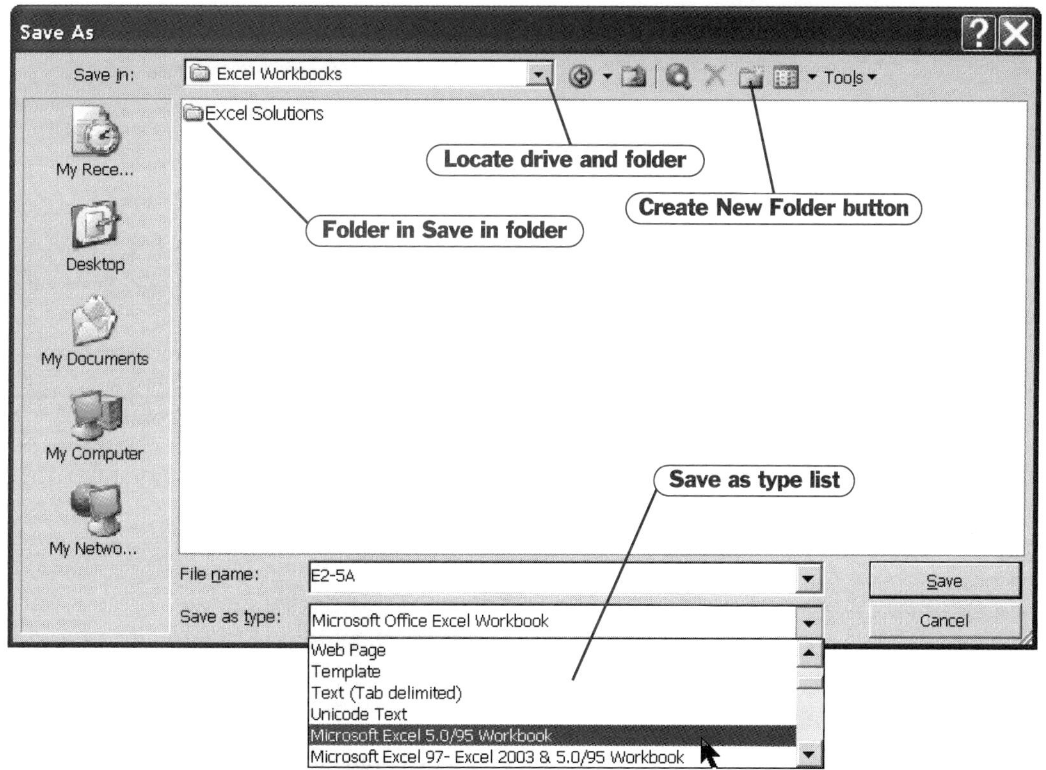

Figure 2.5 Save As dialog box with Save as type list

EXCEL

TRY *it* OUT *E2-5*

1. Continue to work in the open file or open **E2-5** from the Data CD.
2. Click the **Save** button.
3. Double-click the name of your working folder, **Lesson 2,** if it is listed, or locate your folder using the list arrow in the Save in box.
4. Enter **E2-5** as the file name.
5. Click **Save.** Notice the file name on the title bar.
6. Enter `Total` in **Cell A6.**
7. Click the **Save** button. The new data is saved in that file.
8. Click **File, Save As.**
9. Enter **E2-5A** as the file name, to save the file under a new name.
10. In the Save as type box, click **Microsoft Excel 97-Excel 2003 & 5.0/95 Workbook,** for use with the earlier version of the software.
11. Click **Save.** Click **File, Close.**

GOAL
To create an invoice for services

SETTING THE STAGE/WRAPUP
File names: **2.1proinv**
2.1solution

WHAT YOU NEED TO KNOW

- A *business form* is a document format that you develop for a business activity that occurs often. Once you create the form, you always use it to record that particular *transaction*, or business event, in a uniform manner. Many business forms are numbered consecutively for reference in records or communications.
- Consultants and professionals in fee-based businesses use a *professional invoice* to bill their clients for the services provided.
- You can use preprinted forms or predesigned Excel worksheets for business forms or you can create your own forms with Excel.
- In this Rehearsal activity, you will use the model illustration to create an invoice for planning services for Occasions Event Planning.

DIRECTIONS

1. Open a new blank worksheet. In **Cell C1,** enter the label as illustrated on the facing page. (Press the arrow keys to move to **Cell A3.**)
2. Enter the long label in **Cell A3.**
3. Enter the label in **Cell E3** and the date with the current year in **Cell F3.**
4. Click **Cell F3** to make it the active cell.
5. Click the Smart Tag button to view the list of actions. Click **Remove this Smart Tag.**
6. Click **Format, Cells,** to set the date format, as illustrated.
7. Enter the remaining data in the exact locations illustrated.
8. Format the date in **Cell B14** using the same date format.
9. In **Cell F16,** enter the value and format for currency.
10. Save the file in your **Lesson 2** folder; name it **2.1proinv.**
11. Resave the file as **2.1solution,** as an Excel 97 file type.
12. Close the file.

	A	B	C	D	E	F
1			INVOICE			
2						
3	Occasions Event Planning				Date:	5-Mar-04
4	675 Third Avenue					
5	New York, NY 10017				212-555-1234	
6						
7						
8	Bill to:		Mr. Martin Meyers			
9			1050 Greenway Street			
10			Brooklyn, NY 12015			
11						
12	Description					Amount
13	Event:	Training Seminar				
14	Date:	5-Mar-04				
15						
16		Professional event planning services				$ 525.00

EXCEL

Cues for Reference

Enter a Label or Value

1. Click cell to receive data.
2. Enter the label or value.
3. Press **Enter** or press an **arrow** key to move to next cell.

Format Dates

1. Select the date.
2. Click **Format, Cells.**
3. In the Number tab, click **Date.**
4. Select a date format.
5. Click **OK.**

Format Currency

1. Select the value to format.
2. Click the **Currency Style** button.

Use Smart Tag

1. Click the **Smart Tag** button list arrow.
2. Select the action.

Save

- For a new file, click the **Save** button; see Save As, Steps 2 through 5, at right.

or

- To resave an existing file, click the **Save** button.

Save As

1. Click **File, Save As.**
2. In Save in box, select location.

   or

   Double-click folder in current folder.
3. Enter file name in File name box.
4. Click **Save as type** down arrow, and click file type, if necessary.
5. Click **Save.**

GOALS

To create a purchase order

To practice using the following skill sets:

- Edit cell data
  - Edit cell contents
  - Align cell data
  - Clear cell contents
  - Check spelling
  - Use the Thesaurus
- Use AutoComplete
- Use Print Preview
- Select a range of cells
- Print
  - Set Print Area
  - Change print settings

WHAT YOU NEED TO KNOW

Edit Cell Data

Edit Cell Contents

- If you notice an error *before* you complete an entry, press the Backspace key to edit data before you press the Enter key. Once you press the Enter key, the data is entered in the cell.
- If you notice an error *after* you enter the data, you can redo the entry so that the new data overwrites the original data. To correct an entry in *Edit mode*, press the F2 key, which places the insertion point at the end of the incorrect label. Or, double-click in the cell at the edit location. Note the items to be edited in Figure 2.6.

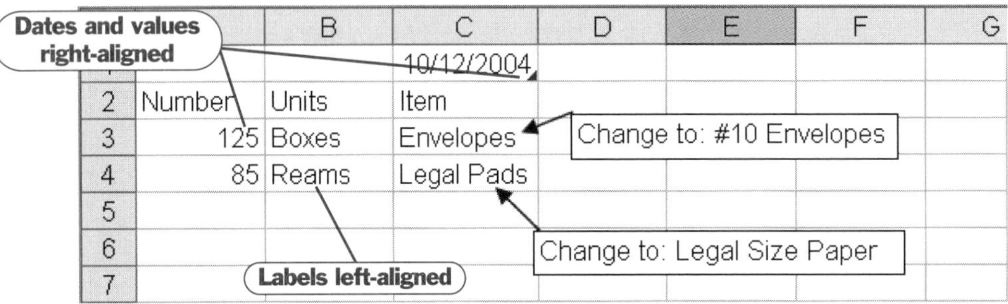

Figure 2.6 Default alignments with items for edit

TRY*it* OUT *E2-6*

1. Open **E2-6** from the Data CD.
2. Change "Legal Pads" to "Legal Size Paper":
   a. Click **Cell C4.**
   b. Press the **F2** key. The insertion point is at the end of the label.
   c. Press the **Backspace** key to delete "Pads" and enter `Size Paper.`

Continued on next page

TRY it OUT *E2-6 Continued*

3. Change "Envelopes" to "#10 Envelopes":
   a. Place the mouse pointer at the beginning of **Cell C3** and double-click the cell. You should be in Edit mode with the insertion point at the beginning of the cell.
   b. Enter `#10` and a space.
4. In **Cell A6,** enter `130`. Before it is entered, press the **Backspace** key once and enter `5` to make it `135`. Then press the **Enter** key.
5. In **Cell A7,** enter `182` and then press the **Enter** key.
6. In **Cell A7,** enter `185` to overwrite. Then, press the **Enter** key.
7. Do not close or save the file.

Align Data

- As discussed in Task 1, by default, label text is left-aligned, whereas values and dates are right-aligned in the cell, as shown in Figure 2.6.
- However, you can change the alignment of data to improve the appearance of the worksheet by using the alignment buttons on the Formatting toolbar, shown in Figure 2.7. Select the cell and click the appropriate alignment button to left-align, center, or right-align data.

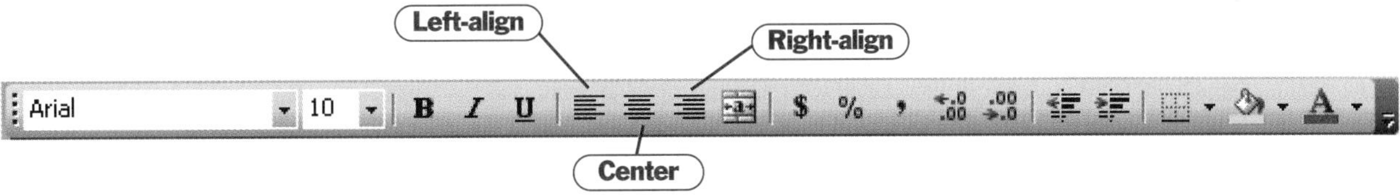

Figure 2.7 Alignment buttons on Formatting toolbar

TRY it OUT *E2-7*

1. Continue working in the open file or open **E2-7** from the Data CD.
2. Click **Cell A2** and click the **Center** alignment button.
3. Center the label in **Cell B2.**
4. Center the label in **Cell C2.**
5. Left-align the data in **Cell A6.**
6. Right-align the data in **Cell A6.**

7. Do not close the file.

Clear Cell Contents

- If you want to remove data you enter in a cell, select the cell and press the Delete key.
- You can also remove data by clicking Edit, Clear, and Contents.

TRY it OUT *E2-8*

1. Continue working in the open file or open **E2-8** from the Data CD.
2. Click **Cell A6.**
3. Press the **Delete** key.
4. Click **Cell A7.**
5. Click **Edit, Clear,** and **Contents.**
6. Do not close the file.

Check Spelling

- The Spelling feature compares the words in your file to the words in the application's dictionary. In Excel, there is no indication of a spelling error until you use the Spelling feature. Click the Spelling button on the Standard toolbar to check the spelling of worksheet labels.

TRY it OUT *E2-9*

1. Continue working in the open file or open **E2-9** from the Data CD.
2. In **Cell B6,** type the word `reem` and then press the Enter key.
3. Click the **Spelling** button.

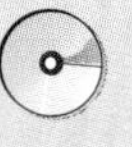

4. Click **Yes** to start at the beginning of the worksheet.
5. Select **ream** in the Suggestions box, if necessary, and click **Change.** Click **OK.**
6. Delete the text in **Cell B6.**
7. Do not save or close the file.

Use the Thesaurus

- Excel has a new Research tool that includes thesaurus references in English, French, and Spanish. A *thesaurus* provides synonyms for the selected word that may better express the intended meaning. Type the word to be researched, click the Research button on the Standard toolbar, and select the appropriate reference book from the Research task pane, as shown in Figure 2.8. Click the green arrow to start the search and view the results of your research. Replace the word, if you wish, by overwriting it with the appropriate synonym.
- You can change or update the list of reference books that display using the Research options hyperlink.

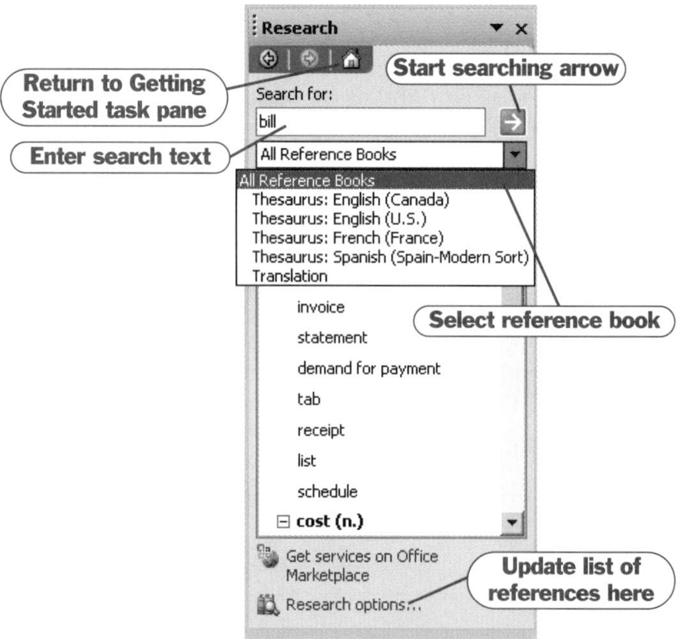

Figure 2.8 Research task pane.

TRY it OUT E2-10

1. Continue working in the open file or open **E2-10** from the Data CD.
2. In **Cell A1,** enter the word `bill` and then select **Cell A1.**
3. Click the **Research** button. The Research task pane appears.
4. Click the list arrow and select **Thesaurus: English (U.S.).** Click the green Go arrow and notice the synonyms.
5. Click the list arrow and check the results in the **French Thesaurus** and in the **Translation** reference. *Note: If you do not have these references, check others available to you.*
6. Close the Research task pane.
7. In **Cell A1,** enter the word `Invoice.`
8. Do not save or close the file.

Use AutoComplete

- The *AutoComplete* feature lets you enter labels automatically if you have previously entered them in the same column.
- When you enter the first letter or letters of repeated data, Excel AutoCompletes the label from your previously entered data. If the label is correct, press the Enter key to confirm the entry. If it is not correct, continue entering the new label.

TRY it OUT E2-11

1. Continue working in the open file or open **E2-11** from the Data CD.
2. Follow the steps below to add 10 Boxes Pencils in **Row 5.**
   a. In **Cell A5,** enter `10.`
   b. In **Cell B5,** start to enter `Boxes.` TheAutoComplete feature will complete the label.
   c. Press the **Enter** key to accept the completed label.
3. In **Cell C5,** enter `Pencils.`
4. Do not save or close the file.

Use Print Preview

- Before printing, it is advisable to preview the worksheet because worksheets can become too large for one page. Click the Print Preview button on the Standard toolbar to open Print Preview.
- If the preview is satisfactory, you can print the worksheet using the Print button on the Preview screen as shown in Figure 2.9.

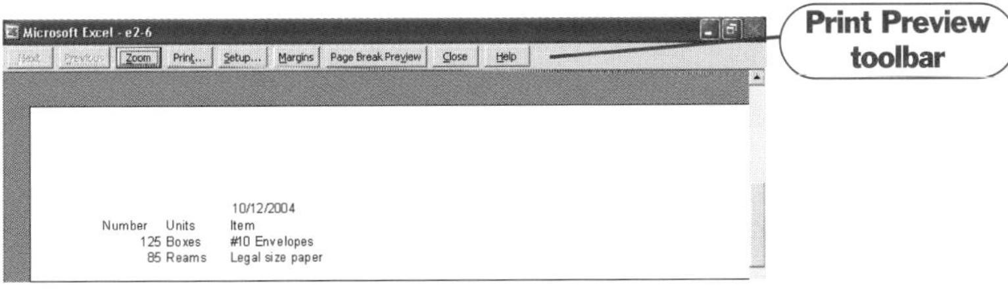

Figure 2.9 Print Preview screen

TRY *it* OUT *E2-12*

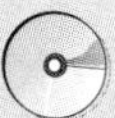

1. Continue working in the open file or open **E2-12** from the Data CD.
2. Click the **Print Preview** button.
3. Click the data to get a better view.
4. Click the **Print** button on the Preview toolbar.
5. Click **OK** in the Print dialog box. The worksheet prints as previewed.

Select a Range of Cells

▶ A *range* is a group of cells in a row, column, or block. The beginning and ending cell addresses identify a range. For example, A2:C5 is selected in Figure 2.10. To select a range, click the first cell in the range, hold down the mouse, and drag the selection until all the cells in the range are selected. Notice that a dark border outlines the range and, except for the first cell, all cells are shaded.

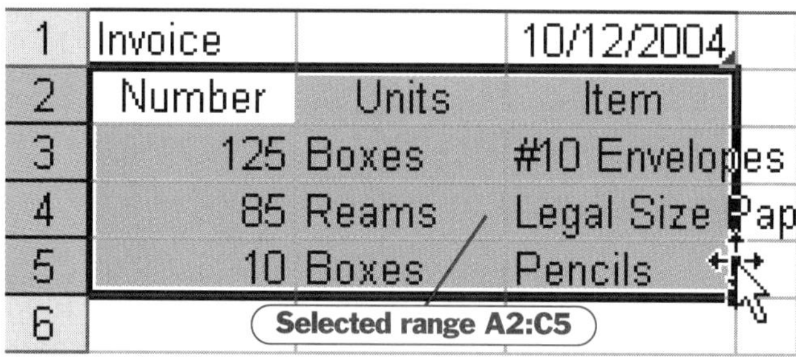

Figure 2.10 Selected cells in a range

TRY *it* OUT *E2-13*

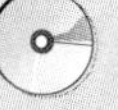

1. Continue working in the open file or open **E2-13** from the Data CD.
2. Select the cells in the range **A2:C5.**
3. Click on any cell to deselect the range.

Print

▶ Use the Print button on the Standard toolbar to print a worksheet. Printing with the toolbar button prints the worksheet with default settings. The entire worksheet prints in portrait orientation without gridlines or row and column headings. If this is satisfactory, the Print button is the most efficient way to print.

Set Print Area

▶ To print only part of a worksheet, you must define the print area. With the mouse, select the block of cells you want to print, and click File, Print Area, and Set Print Area. You must clear this setting if you wish to print any other selection. You can clear the print area by clicking File, Print Area, and Clear Print Area.

Change Print Settings

▶ Click File, Page Setup to customize print settings. The Page Setup dialog box contains tabs for setting Page, Margins, Header/Footer, and Sheet options. For example, to set up gridline printing click File, Page Setup, click the Sheet tab, and select Gridlines in the Print section, as shown in Figure 2.11.

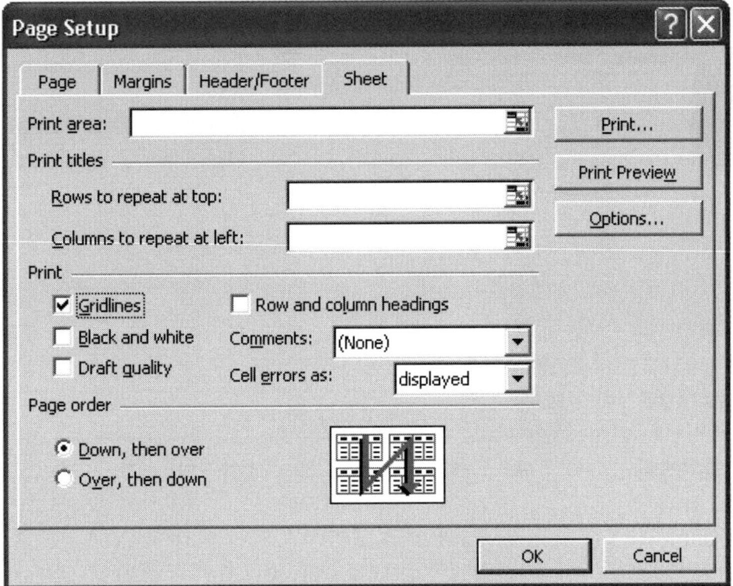

Figure 2.11 Page Setup dialog box with Sheet tab and Gridlines selected

TRY *it* OUT *E2-14*

1. Continue working in the open file or open **E2-14** from the Data CD.
2. Click the **Print** button on the toolbar. The worksheet prints with default settings.
3. Click in **Cell A2,** select the block of cells from **A2** to **D5.**
4. Click **File, Print Area,** and **Set Print Area.** The area is outlined.
5. Click **File, Page Setup,** and click the **Sheet** tab.
6. Click the **Gridlines** check box in the Print section, and click **OK.**
7. Click the **Print Preview** button.
8. Click the **Print** button on the Preview toolbar.
9. Click **OK.** The worksheet prints as previewed with area and gridline settings.
10. Save the file as **E2-14** in the **Lesson 2** folder you created in Lesson 1; close the file.

REHEARSAL

Again

TASK 2

GOAL
To create a purchase order

SETTING THE STAGE/WRAPUP
File name: 2.2purord

WHAT YOU NEED TO KNOW

- A *purchase order* is a business form that a firm completes and sends to a *vendor*, or supplier, when merchandise or supplies are needed.
- The Received column is left blank, because it is used to check the order when it is received. The terms of the purchase define the agreement for payment. You can obtain the stock or item numbers and descriptions for the purchase order from the vendor's catalog, quotations, or Web site.
- When you enter data in a cell containing both values and text, such as an address, Excel formats the entry as a label.
- In this Rehearsal activity, you will create a purchase order for supplies for Time Out Sporting Goods. You must enter formulas to calculate the purchase order amounts and total. Therefore, you will not complete the purchase order until the next lesson.

DIRECTIONS

1. Open a new blank worksheet. Create the purchase order illustrated on the facing page by entering the values, date with the current year, and labels in the appropriate cell locations. Press the arrow keys to enter the data and move to the cell you need for the next data item.
2. In **Cell B15,** notice the AutoComplete effect as you begin to enter the label.
3. Go to **Cell A13.**
4. Double-click the cell to switch to Edit mode and change the value to `3`.
5. Center and bold the labels in the range **A12:C12.**
6. Right-align the labels in the range **G12:H12.**
7. Select **Cell D15.** Press the **F2** key to go into Edit mode. Change the cell data to `#2345 Folders - Green.`
8. Overwrite data in **Cell H5;** Change "30 days" to `Check.`
9. Remove the Smart Tag that appears in **Cell H4** for UPS.
10. Place your cursor in **Cell A1** and use Spell Check. Ignore any errors that arise for proper names.
11. Bold column headings and text in **Cells F2** to **F6, A8,** and **D1.**
12. Change the font size in **Cell D1** to **12.**
13. Set the print area for the range **A1:H6** to print the heading.
14. Check the Print Preview screen.
15. Clear the print area.
16. Use Page Setup to set and print the entire purchase order with gridlines.
17. Save the file and name it **2.2purord.** Close the file.

	A	B	C	D	E	F	G	H	I	J
1				PURCHASE ORDER						
2	Time Out Sporting Goods					Date:		10/15/04		
3	1412 Barkely Street					Order #:		1000		
4	Chicago, IL 60064					Ship Via:		UPS		
5						Terms:		30 days		
6	Phone:	847-555-1200				Ordered by:		Bill		
7										
8	TO:	Supplies Unlimited								
9		545 Industrial Way								
10		Chicago, IL 60064								
11										
12	Quantity	Unit	Received	Description			Price	Amount		
13	5	Boxes		#2343 Folders			10.55			
14	4	Cartons		#654 Copy Paper			23.85			
15	2	Boxes		#2345 Folders			11.95			
16										
17										
18										
19										
20										

Remove SmartTag (H3)

Change to: Check (H5)

Change to: 3 (A13)

Change to: #2345 Folders - Green (D15)

EXCEL

Cues for Reference

Enter a Label or Value

1. Click cell to receive data.
2. Enter data.
3. Press **Enter** or press appropriate arrow to move to next cell.

Align Labels

1. Select the cell to align.
2. Click the appropriate alignment button:
   Align Left
   Center

   Align Right

Format Text Font

1. Select the cell(s) to format.
2. Click the **Font List** arrow.
3. Select the font.
4. Click the **Font Size** arrow.
5. Select the size.

Format Text Style

1. Select the cell to align.
2. Click the appropriate style button(s):
   Bold B
   Italic I
   Underline U

Edit Data

1. Double-click cell at edit location or press **F2.**
2. Edit data using Backspace, arrows, or other edit keys.

Clear Cell Contents

- Click **Edit, Clear, Contents.**

or

1. Click the cell.
2. Press **Delete.**

Select a Range

1. Click the first cell in the range.
2. Hold down the mouse.
3. Drag to the last cell in the range.

or

1. Click the first cell in the range.
2. Hold down the Shift key.
3. Click the last cell in the range.

Set Print Area

1. Select area to print.
2. Click **File, Print Area, Set Print Area.**

Clear Print Area

- Click **File, Print Area, Clear Print Area.**

Print with Gridlines

1. Click **File, Page Setup,** and **Sheet** tab.
2. Click **Gridlines** check box.
3. Click **Print** in the dialog box.
4. Click **OK.**

GOALS

To create a sales invoice from a customized template

To practice using the following skill sets:

- Work with templates
- Save a file as a template
- View Web templates

WHAT YOU NEED TO KNOW

Work with Templates

- Excel provides model worksheet designs, or *templates,* for common business forms. A template contains worksheet settings, such as fonts, formatting, styles, and formulas, that are not changed or overwritten.
- You can open Excel templates using the New Workbook task pane in the Templates section, as shown in Figure 2.12. Click File, New, if the task pane is not displayed. Click On my computer to open the Templates dialog box and click the Spreadsheet Solutions tab, as shown in Figure 2.13.

Figure 2.12 New Workbook task pane

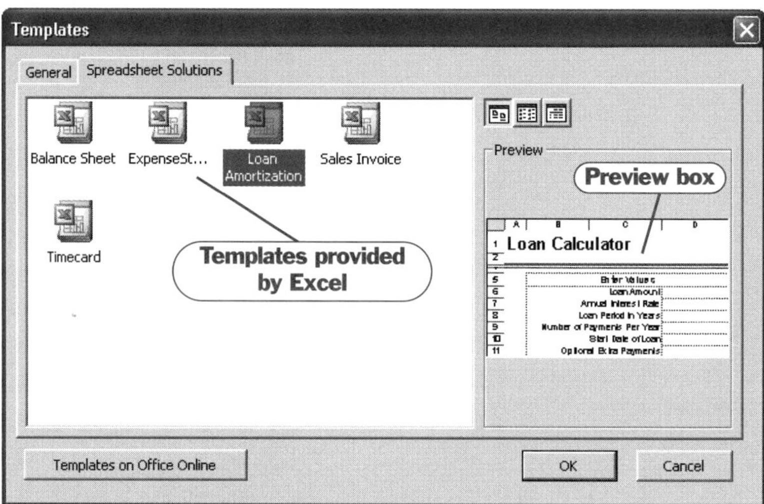

Figure 2.13 Templates dialog box, Spreadsheet Solutions tab

TRY *it* OUT *E2-15*

1. If the New task pane is not displayed, click **File, New.**
2. Click **On my computer** on the New Workbook task pane to open the Templates dialog box.
3. Click the **Spreadsheet Solutions** tab.
4. Click each icon and view a sample in the Preview box.
5. Double-click the **ExpenseStatement** template.
6. Double-click the **Name** box, then enter your name on the expense statement. Press the **Enter** key.
7. Do not save or close the file.

Save a File as a Template

- If you customize a template, save it as a template file so that it will remain intact after each use.
- Save a file as a template in the Save As dialog box by clicking Template in the Save as type drop-down list, as shown in Figure 2.14. The new template file, with an .xlt extension, is automatically saved in the Templates folder. Your template can be found in the General tab in the Templates dialog box.

EXCEL

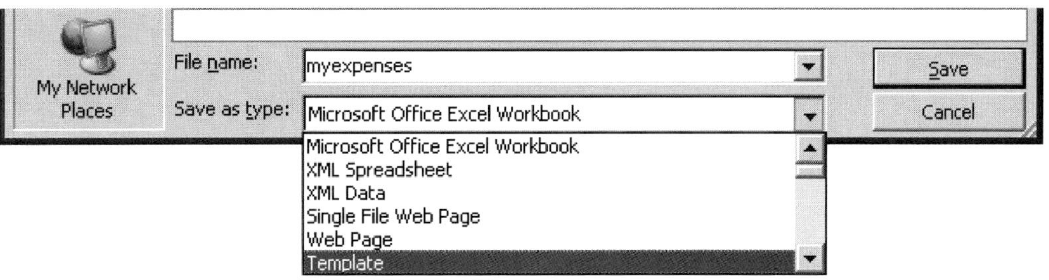

Figure 2.14 Saving a file as a template

TRY it OUT E2-16

1. Continue to work in the open file or open **E2-16** from the Data CD.
2. Click **File, Save As.**
3. Name the file **myexpenses.**
4. Click the **Save as type** list arrow and click **Template.**
5. Click **Save.** Close the file.
6. Click **On my computer** in the New Workbook task pane.
7. Click the **General** tab in the Templates dialog box. Notice the location of your template.
8. Right-click your template's icon and click **Delete.** Click **Yes** to send the template to the Recycle Bin.
9. Close the Templates dialog box.

View Web Templates

- Additional templates are available at Microsoft Office Online or at Web sites you have personally located. You can view, customize, and save them to your computer. If you are online, you can select Templates on Office Online from the New Workbook task pane, which will directly link you through Internet Explorer to the appropriate Web site, as shown in Figure 2.15.
- To save time searching for the appropriate Web template on the site, you should use the **Search online for:** box in the Task pane, as shown in Figure 2.12. Enter the name of the template you wish to find and click Go. This will connect you to the site and display the results of the search.

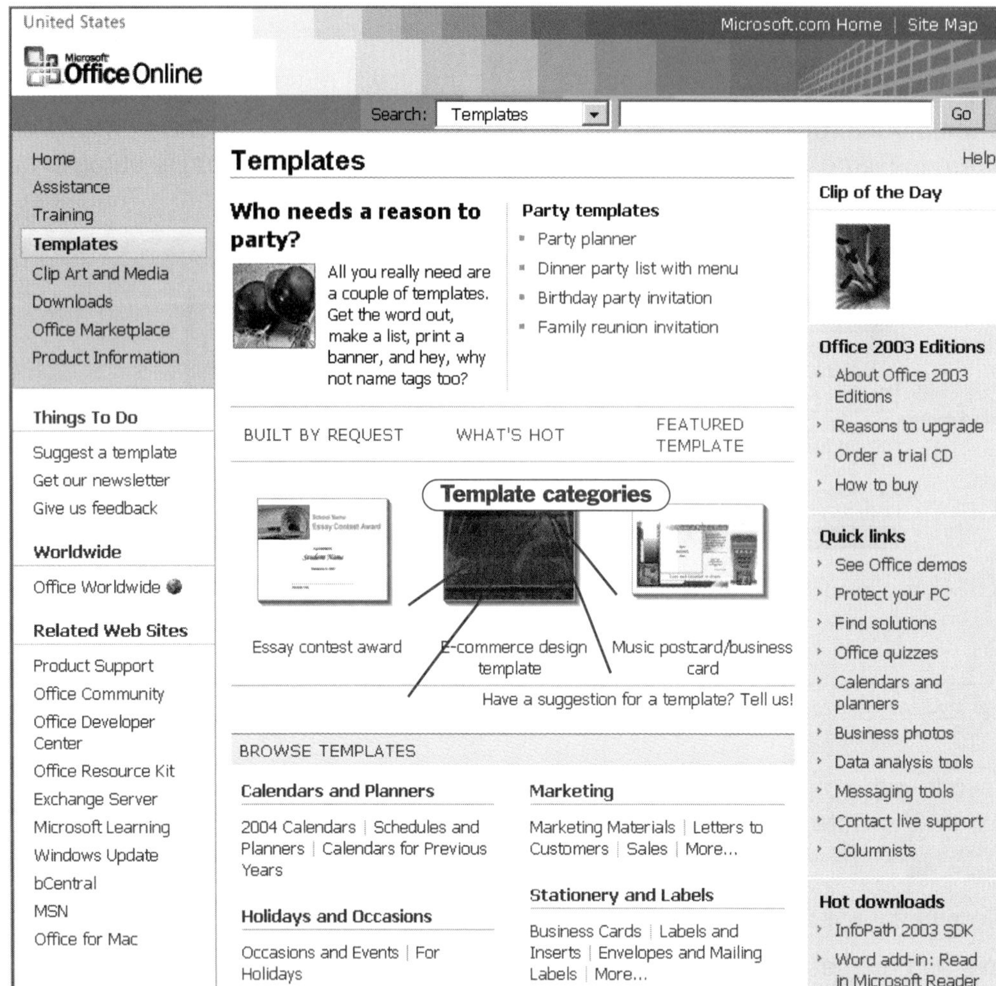

Figure 2.15 Office Online Templates page

TRY *it* OUT *E2-17*

Note: You need Internet capabilities for this Try it Out.

1. Click **File, New** to display the task pane.
2. Click **Templates on Office Online.**
3. Click **Orders and Inventory,** and under Order Management, click **Invoices and Purchase Orders.**
4. Select and view the template **Invoice that Calculates Total.**
5. Exit the browser.
6. Place cursor in the **Search online for** box.
7. Enter `Invoice.` Click **Go**. Notice the results.
8. Exit the browser and close Excel.

1
2
3

TASK 3

GOAL
To create a sales invoice from a customized template

SETTING THE STAGE/WRAPUP
File names: **2.3invoice**
2.3timeout

WHAT YOU NEED TO KNOW

- A *sales invoice* is a bill that a seller prepares and sends to a customer for goods supplied by the seller. It usually contains an itemized list of items sold, as well as shipping and payment information, and may contain the customer's purchase order number.
- After you customize a sales invoice Excel template for your company and save it as a template, you can use it to prepare all company invoices in the future. Because the template contains formulas, it automatically calculates the total bill.
- In this Rehearsal activity, you will customize the invoice template, as shown in Figure 2.16, for Supplies Unlimited. The company will ship office supplies ordered by Time Out Sporting Goods and needs to prepare the invoice for the sale.

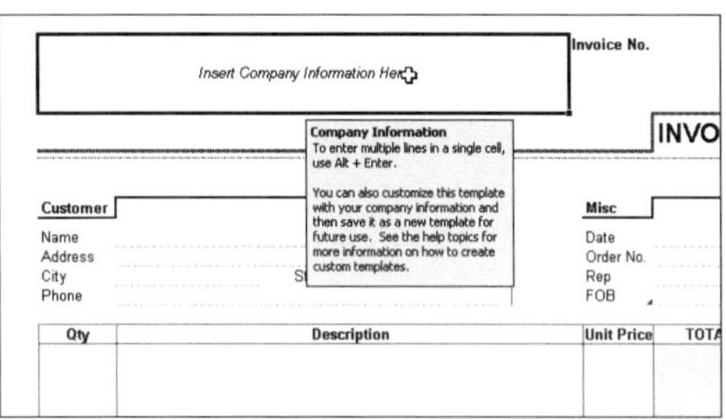

Figure 2.16 Sales Invoice template, company information

DIRECTIONS

1. Open the **Sales Invoice** template in the Spreadsheet Solutions tab of the Templates dialog box.
2. Click in the **Company Information** box at the top of the invoice and enter the company information as illustrated on the facing page. As indicated in the comment box, use **Alt+Enter** to move to a new line in the company letterhead.
3. Scroll to the bottom of the invoice to the **Insert Fine Print Here** section.
4. Select the box and use the **Edit** menu to clear the contents of this box.
5. Click in the **Insert Farewell Statement Here** box and enter the slogan, as illustrated.
6. Save the file as a template; name it **2.3invoice.**
7. Close the file.
8. Open the new **2.3invoice** template file in the General tab of the Templates dialog box.
9. Complete the invoice, as illustrated. Notice that the totals are automatically calculated.
10. Enter shipping charges of `$10.` Click the **Undo** button and change the amount by entering `$15.`
11. Enter the tax rate of `6.25%` in Cell L38, the white box closest to the **Tax Rate** label.
12. Print the invoice.
13. Save the file as an Excel workbook file in your solutions folder and name it **2.3timeout.**

EXCEL

Supplies Unlimited
545 Industrial Way
Chicago, IL 60064
847-555-6545

Invoice No.

INVOICE

Customer

Name	Time Out Sporting Goods		
Address	1412 Barkely Street		
City	Chicago	State IL	ZIP 60064
Phone	847-555-1200		

Misc

Date	10/20/XX
Order No.	1000
Rep	Joe
FOB	

Qty	Description	Unit Price	TOTAL
3	Boxes #2543 Folders	$ 10.55	$ 31.65
4	Cartons #654 Copy Paper	$ 23.85	$ 95.40
2	Boxes #2545 Folders	$ 11.95	$ 23.90

Enter shipping charges as directed

	SubTotal	$ 150.95
	Shipping	
Tax Rate(s)	6.25%	$ 9.43
	TOTAL	$ 160.38

Payment Select One...

Comments
Name
CC #
Expires

Office Use Only

This value will change when shipping charges are added

Your unlimited resource for supplies!

Enter farewell statement here

Cues for Reference

Open Templates Dialog Box

1. Click **File, New** to display the New Workbook task pane.
2. Click **On my computer** in the New Workbook task pane template section.

- **Office XP:** Click **General Templates** in the New Workbook task pane.

Customize Template

1. Select area to customize.
2. Double-click on placeholder text, and drag mouse to select it.
3. Enter the custom information.

or

1. Click placeholder.
2. Enter the custom information.

Save File as Template

1. Click **Save.**
2. Enter the file name.
3. Click **Template** in the Save as type box.
4. Click **Save.**

PERFORMANCE

SETTING THE STAGE/WRAPUP

- Act I File names: **2p1proinv**, **2p1.bill**
- Act II File names: **2p2.otginv**, **2p2.bertle**
- Act III File name: **2p3.quote**

WHAT YOU NEED TO KNOW

Act I

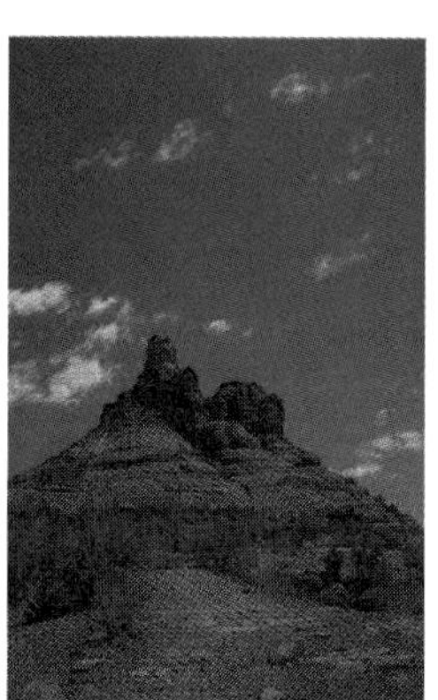

Wilson Jones, the director of the Corporate Travel Group at Air Land Sea Travel Group, has just completed arrangements and travel bookings for a corporate conference in Scottsdale, Arizona. The conference is planned for February 10–13 for Garrison Games, Inc, 342 Third Avenue, New York, NY 10017. You are to prepare a bill for $2200 using a Professional Invoice form to bill for conference-planning services.

- In the New Workbook task pane, click **From existing workbook,** and open the file **2p1proinv** from the Data CD. This opens the Professional Invoice file from Task 1 as a new file.
- Edit the file using the current information. Use today's date on the invoice.
- Save the file; name it **2p1.bill.**

Act II

You work for Marilyn Healy in the Marketing Department at Odyssey Travel Gear. Odyssey has started to use a catalog to market its merchandise wholesale to hotel gift shops. You are asked to prepare a customized invoice template for wholesale catalog sales and an invoice for a sale made today.

- Use the Sales Invoice template to create a new invoice template for Odyssey Travel Gear. Enter the company name and address, and the "Fine Print" and "Farewell Statement" as listed below:

  Fine Print: For questions, call Customer Service at 630-555-8888, Extension 15.

  Farewell Statement: Thank you for choosing Odyssey Travel Gear.

  Save the file as a new template; name it **2p2.otginv.**

- Use the new template to create an invoice for the sale made today:

  Use today's date.

  The sale was made to the Bertleson Hotel, 2356 Lakeshore Drive, Chicago, IL 60611, 800-555-8787.

Invoice No. 2000, Order No. BH543, Rep. Marilyn

Qty	Description	Unit Price
12	Leather waist packs #432	12.35
6	Collapsible luggage carts #1654	18.50
12	Travel Alarm Clock #211	14.50

Shipping is $18.50.

There is no sales tax, because this is a wholesale transaction.

Payment method is Credit. Select it from drop-down list.

Save the document; name it **2p2.bertle.**

- Attach the invoice to an e-mail to Mr. Mark at the Bertleson Hotel (but send it to your teacher). Tell Mr. Mark that his order is being shipped, that the invoice is attached, and that the invoice will also be included with the shipment.

Act III

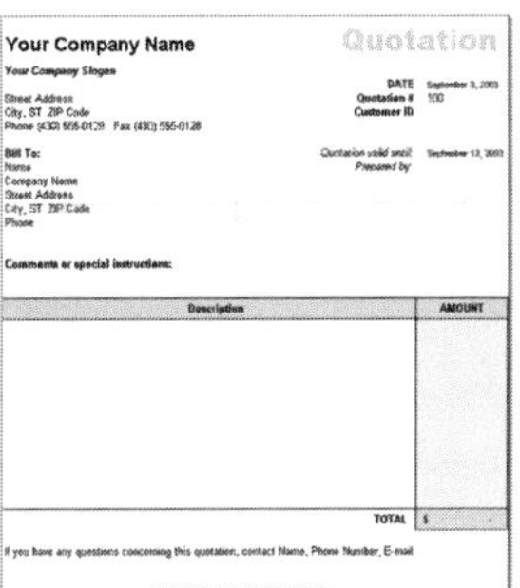

You work for the sales manager, Kiley Thompson, in the New York office of Trilogy Productions. A small independent film company has requested a quotation of rates for use of the studios and editing facilities. Locate a template for a price quotation using the Template Home Page on Microsoft Office Online or the Search online feature. *If you are using Office XP, click Templates on Microsoft.com in the New Workbook task pane.*

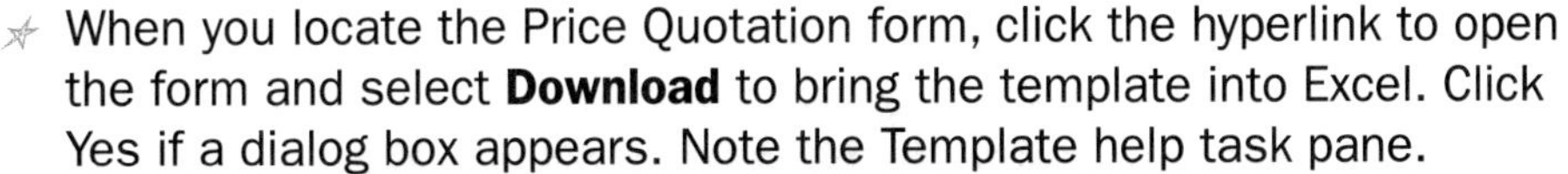

- When you locate the Price Quotation form, click the hyperlink to open the form and select **Download** to bring the template into Excel. Click Yes if a dialog box appears. Note the Template help task pane.

  Enter the name and address for Trilogy Productions. Delete the company slogan line. Save the file as a template; name it **2p3.quote** and disconnect from the Internet.

- Use the template to create a quotation for Mr. Thompson using the following information:

  Date: 8/10/2004, Quotation valid until: 9/10/2004, Quotation: 100, Customer ID: 346

  Prepared by: Your name

  Bill to: Jamal Carson, Carson Films, Inc 432 Christopher Street NY, NY 10012, 212-555-4388

2 days	Use of studio for filming short subject	$4200.00
1 day	Use of editing facilities	$1000.00

  Customer will provide personnel.

- Use Edit mode to edit the line below the total to read: **`If you have any questions concerning this quotation, contact Kiley Thompson, Extension 420.`**

- Save the worksheet as **2p3.quotecarson.**

LESSON 3

Accounting Records

In this lesson, you will learn to use Excel to create accounting records and statements. You will use formulas, functions, and formatting to complete the tasks. You will use the Internet to locate tax forms and rates.

Upon completion of this lesson, you should have mastered the following skill sets:

- Change row or column size
- Cut, copy, and paste
- Apply and clear number formats
- Use the Office Clipboard to cut, copy, and paste
- Use formula basics
- Enter functions
  - AutoSum
  - Enter the range in a formula
  - AutoSum List
  - Formula bar
- Use the Fill Handle tool
- Modify page setup options
  - Orientation
  - Set page margins and centering
- Edit formulas using the Formula bar
- Move selected cells
- Insert, view, and edit cell comments
- Apply and modify cell formats with the Format Cells dialog box
- Use the Format Painter

Terms

Software-related

AutoFit
Office Clipboard
Formulas
Order of mathematical operations
Function
AutoSum
Insert Function button
Function arguments
AutoFill
Fill handle
Series
Drag-and-drop
Cell comment
Format Painter
Research tools

Document-related

Account
General ledger
Accounts receivable
Accounts payable
Account statement
Journal
Sales journal
Tax status
Payroll register
Reimburse
Expense report

GOAL

To create an account and account statement

To practice using the following skill sets:

- Change row or column size
- Cut, Copy, and Paste
- Apply and clear number formats
- Use the Office Clipboard to cut, copy, and paste
- Use formula basics

EXCEL

WHAT YOU NEED TO KNOW

Change Row or Column Size and Alignment

- Columns are set for a standard column width of 8.43, the number of characters displayed using the standard font. When you enter long labels, they appear in the next cell, if it is empty. When you enter long values, Excel fills the cell with number signs (#), or displays the number in scientific notation to indicate the need to widen the column.
- To change the width of a column, place the mouse pointer on the line between the column letter headings and, when the mouse pointer changes to a double-headed arrow, drag the column to size. The width is displayed as you make this adjustment, as shown in Figure 3.1. However, the most efficient way is to double-click the column header line, and the column will *AutoFit,* or widen to fit the data in that column.

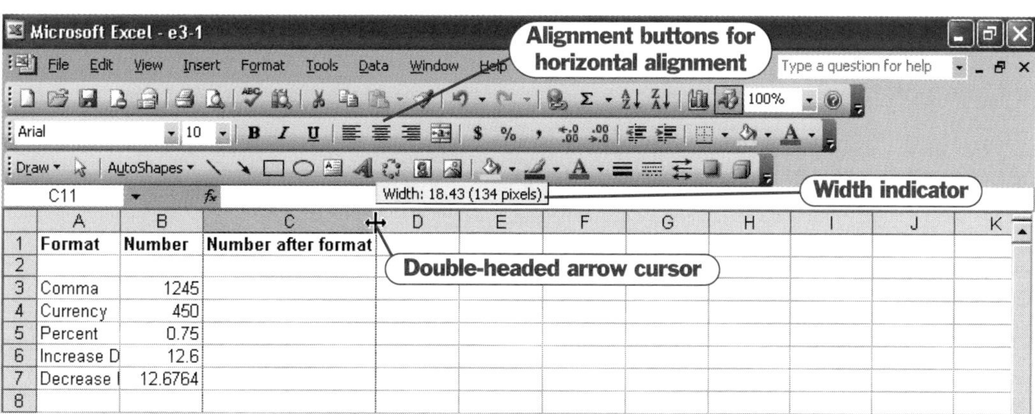

Figure 3.1 Column width indicator display

- By default, row height is automatically determined by the font point size and cell data is vertically aligned at the bottom of the row. However, you may change row height by dragging the row to the desired size.
- Use the alignment buttons to align data horizontally. Data in a row can be aligned vertically to the top, middle, or bottom of a row by clicking Format, Cells, and setting the vertical alignment on the Alignment tab.

TRY*it* OUT *E3-1*

1. Open **E3-1** from the Data CD. Notice the cells with errors due to column width.
2. Double-click the line between **Columns A** and **B** to AutoFit the text in **Column A.**
3. Place the insertion point between **Columns C** and **D**.
4. When you see the double-headed arrow, drag to increase the column width to **18.43**.
5. Select **Cell C1** and change the font size to **14.** Notice the change in the row height.
6. Select **Cells A1 to C1.**
7. Click **Format, Cells, Alignment** tab and set the Vertical alignment to **Center.** Click **OK.**
8. Select **Cell C1** and change the font size back to **10**.
9. Select **Rows 1** and **2,** place the insertion point between **Rows 2** and **3,** and drag to set both row heights to **18.00.**
10. Do not close the file.

Cut, Copy, and Paste Data

- Cut and Paste are tools to move text or data from one location and place it in another. To remove data, select it and click the Cut button on the Standard toolbar. The data is placed temporarily on the Office Clipboard, a temporary storage area.

- Copy and Paste are tools to copy data from one location and place it in another. To copy data, select it and click the Copy button on the Standard toolbar.

- In both cases, to place the data in a new location, select the first cell of the range and click the Paste button on the Standard toolbar.

- Because Cut, Copy, and Paste commands are used frequently, you can use shortcut methods for performing these tasks: Ctrl+X = cut; Ctrl+C = copy; Ctrl+V = paste.

TRY*it* OUT *E3-2*

1. Use the open file or open **E3-2** from the Data CD.
2. Select **Cells A3** to **A7** and click the **Cut** button on the toolbar.

3. Select **Cell A10** and click the **Paste** button on the toolbar to move the data.
4. Click the **Undo** button to restore the data.

5. Select **Cells B3** to **B7** and click the **Copy** button on the toolbar.
6. Select **Cell C3** and click the **Paste** button on the toolbar to copy the data.
7. Do not close the file.

Apply and Clear Number Formats

- You can format numbers with the Formatting toolbar buttons. Select the data to format and then click the appropriate button, as shown in Figure 3.2 and demonstrated in Figure 3.3.

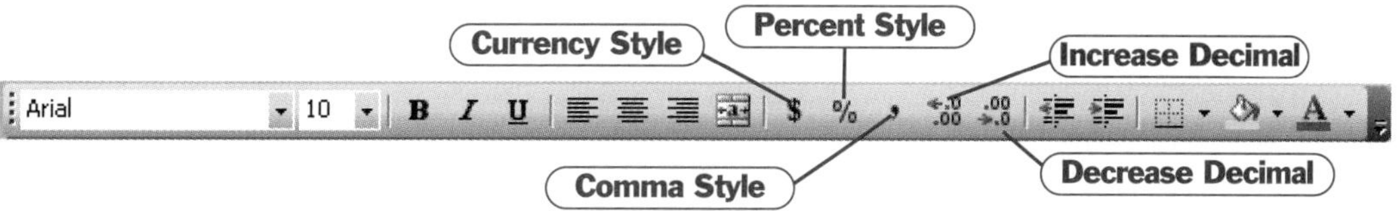

Figure 3.2 Formatting toolbar, number format buttons

EXCEL

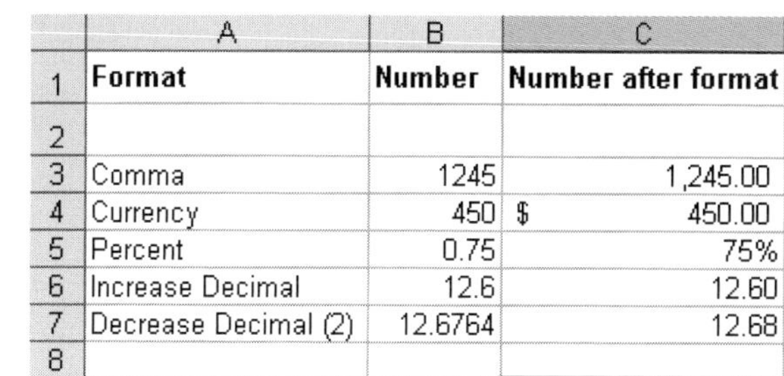

	A	B	C
1	**Format**	**Number**	**Number after format**
2			
3	Comma	1245	1,245.00
4	Currency	450	$ 450.00
5	Percent	0.75	75%
6	Increase Decimal	12.6	12.60
7	Decrease Decimal (2)	12.6764	12.68
8			

Figure 3.3 Sample number formats

- The number format buttons on the Formatting toolbar are listed and illustrated below:
  - Currency Style adds two decimal places and a dollar sign.
  - Percent Style changes the value to a percentage.
  - Comma Style adds commas and two decimal places.
  - Increase Decimal adds one decimal place.
  - Decrease Decimal decreases one decimal place.

  Note: Decreasing decimals causes the values to be rounded.
- To clear number formats without deleting the values, click Edit, Clear, and Formats.

TRY*it* OUT *E3-3*

1. Use the open file or open **E3-3** from the Data CD.
2. Format the cells in **Column C** to match the illustration in Figure 3.3.
3. Select **Cells C3** to **C7** and clear all formats by clicking **Edit, Clear,** and **Formats.**
4. Click the **Undo** button to reverse the Clear Formats command.

5. Deselect the range by clicking another cell.
6. Do not close the file.

Use the Office Clipboard to Cut, Copy, and Paste

- When you copy data in Excel, it is stored in a memory location called the *Office Clipboard.* If you plan to copy more than one group of data, you can display the Office Clipboard task pane by clicking Edit, Office Clipboard. This is useful if you are reordering or reassigning locations for several items of data, or if you want to paste items several times. As shown in Figure 3.4, after each row is copied the sample appears on the Clipboard, with the last selection shown on top.

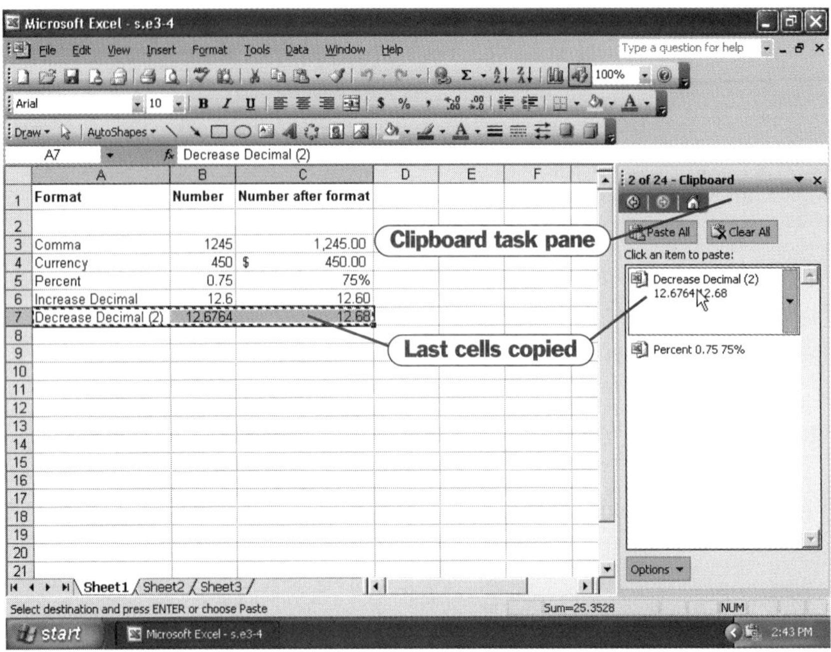

Figure 3.4 Office Clipboard task pane

TRY it OUT *E3-4*

1. Use the open file or open **E3-4** from the Data CD.
2. Click **Edit, Office Clipboard** and click **Clear All,** if necessary.
3. Cut the data in the range **A5:C5.**
4. Cut the data in the range **A7:C7.**
5. Copy the data in the range **A1:C1.**
6. Select **Cell A5** and click the **Decrease Decimal** data on the Clipboard. The data is pasted.
7. Select **Cell A7** and click the **Percent** data on the Clipboard.
8. Save the file; name it **E3-4.** Close the file.

Use Formula Basics

- *Formulas* are equations or instructions to calculate values on the worksheet. All formulas start with an equal sign (=), contain no spaces, and include the cell addresses and mathematical operators necessary to complete the formula. For example, =B5+B6 adds the values in B5 and B6.
- The standard mathematical operators used in formulas are:

  + Addition   – Subtraction   * Multiplication

  / Division   ^ Exponentiation

- To enter formulas correctly, you should understand the way the computer processes an equation. The computer executes all operations from left to right, in order of appearance and mathematical priority. The *order of mathematical operations*, or *priority*, is listed below:

  1. Parentheses ( )
  2. Exponents ^
  3. Multiplication * Division /
  4. Addition + Subtraction –

- For example, in the formula =A1*(B1+C1), B1+C1, the values in parentheses are calculated first, before the multiplication is performed. If the parentheses were omitted, A1*B1 would be calculated first and C1 would be added to that answer. This would result in a different outcome.
- You can enter a formula directly by keying the symbols and cell addresses. You can also enter the symbols and select the cell addresses as they appear in the formula. Selecting the cell addresses minimizes the possibility of entry errors. As you enter the formula, it appears in the Formula bar. After the formula is entered into the cell, the answer appears in the cell and you can see the formula in the Formula bar, as shown in Figure 3.5.

EXCEL

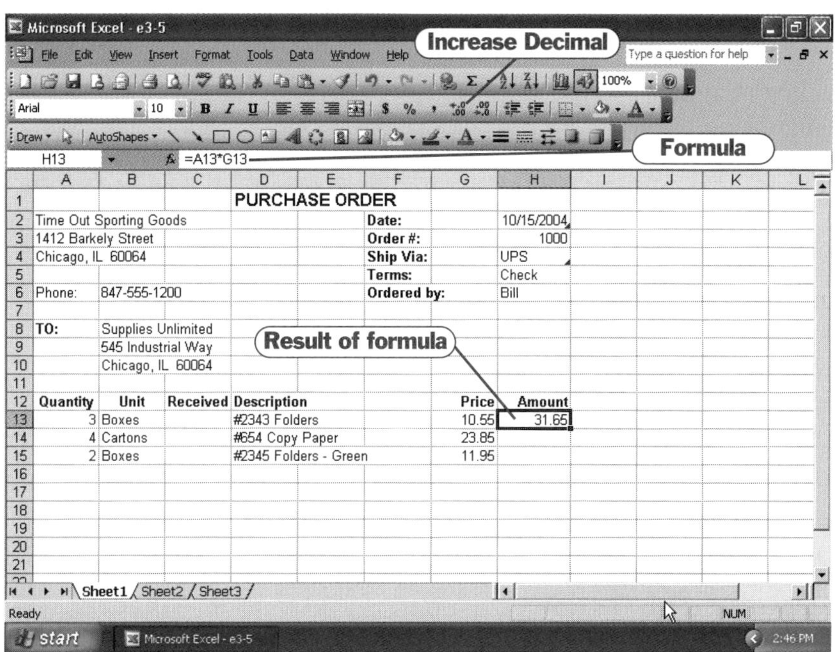

Figure 3.5 Answer appears in cell and formula appears on Formula Bar

TRY *it* OUT *E3-5*

1. Open **2.2purord** from your files or **E3-5** from the Data CD.
2. In **Cell H13,** enter a formula to multiply the quantity by the price:
   a. Enter = (equal sign).
   b. Click **Cell A13.**
   c. Enter * (asterisk).
   d. Click **Cell G13.**
   e. Press the **Enter** key.
3. Click **Cell H13** and notice the formula in the Formula bar.
4. Enter the appropriate formula in **Cell H14.** *(Hint: =A14**G14)*
5. Click **Cell H14,** copy the formula, and paste it to **Cell H15.** Notice that the formula in **Cell H15** copies relative to the new location.
6. Select the range **H14:H15** and click the **Increase Decimal** button to add one decimal place.
7. Enter a formula in **Cell H17** to add the three values in Column H. *(Hint: =H13+H14+H15)*
8. Format the total for currency.
9. Save the file; name it **E3-5.** Close the file.

TASK 1

GOAL

To create an acount and account statement

SETTING THE STAGE/WRAPUP

File names: 3.1account
3.1statement

WHAT YOU NEED TO KNOW

- An *account* is an accounting record that keeps track of the increases and decreases in the value of an item in a business. It is set up in a bankbook-style arrangement that contains columns for increases, decreases, and balances. Accounts are used to record transactions from journals, as you will learn in Task 2.
- The *general ledger* contains all the accounts of a business. In addition, there are supplemental ledgers; the *accounts receivable (AR)* ledger containing records of customers, the people who owe the business money, and the *accounts payable (AP)* ledger containing records of creditors, the people to whom the business owes money.
- Customers' accounts are used to create the *account statements* or bills that are sent out each month.
- In this Rehearsal activity, you will create an account and an account statement for a Time Out Sporting Goods customer. On accounts receivable accounts, invoices (which increase the account) and credits and returns (which decrease the account) are used to tabulate the account balance. The account statement or bill is sent out at the end of the month to every customer, based on the activity in the account.

DIRECTIONS

1. Open **3.1account** from the Data CD.
2. Adjust column width as necessary.
3. As shown in Illustration A below, in **Cell F8,** calculate the balance on 5/3. Because the first invoice is also the balance on 5/3, enter **=D8** in **Cell F8.**

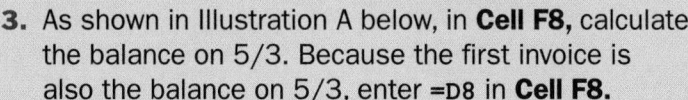

	A	B	C	D	E	F	G
1	Accounts Receivable Ledger						
2							
3	Customer:		Central High School - Health Ed. Dept.				
4			2382 Margate Avenue				
5	No: C15		Chicago, IL 60064				
6							
7	Date	Explanation	Reference	Charges	Credits	Balance	
8	5/3/2004	Invoice #2325	S5	434.56			
9	5/15/2004	Return - #CM450	J9		65.35		
10	5/22/2004	Invoice #2336	S5	1045.32			
11	5/25/2004	Damaged #CM501	J9		150		
12							
13		Adjust column width			Enter formulas here to calculate daily balance		
14							
15							

Illustration A

4. Calculate the balance on 5/15 in **Cell F9.** The formula should subtract the return in **Cell E9** from the previous balance in **Cell F8.** *(Hint: =F8-E9)*
5. Enter a formula in **Cell F10** that can be used for any balance calculation in this account. *(Hint: Previous balance+charges–credits =F9+D10-E10)*
6. Format the credit in **Cell E11** by adding two decimal places.
7. Clear all formats in **Cell E11.** Click **Undo** to keep the format.
8. Copy the formula from **Cell F10,** and paste it to **Cell F11.**
9. Select and format the values in **Column F** for commas.
10. Save the file as **3.1 account.**

Continued on next page

11. As shown in Illustration B below, copy the following ranges to the clipboard to create the account statement:
    a. **C3:C5** Name and address of customer
    b. **A7:F7** Column headings
    c. **A8:F11** Account data
12. Open **3.1statement** from the Data CD. 
13. Paste the following data to the locations listed below:
    a. Name and address to **Cell A9**
    b. Column headings to **Cell A13**
    c. Account data to **Cell A15**

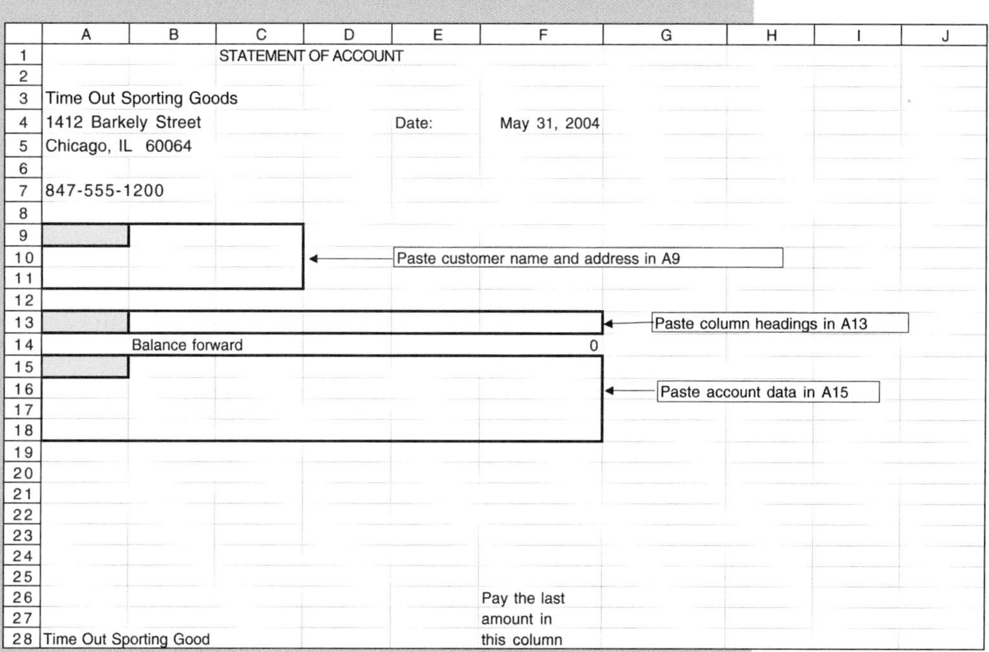

STATEMENT OF ACCOUNT
Time Out Sporting Goods
1412 Barkely Street
Chicago, IL 60064
Date:
May 31, 2004
847-555-1200
Paste customer name and address in A9
Paste column headings in A13
Balance forward
0
Paste account data in A15
Pay the last amount in this column
Time Out Sporting Good

Illustration B

14. Adjust column width as necessary.
15. Format the final balance in **Cell F18** for currency.
16. Print the account statement without gridlines.
17. Save the file as **3.1 statement.** Close both files.

Cues for Reference

Apply Number Formats
1. Select cell or range of cells.
2. Click format button:
   - **Percentage Style** %
   - **Currency Style** $
   - **Comma Style** ,
   - **Increase Decimal**
   - **Decrease Decimal**

Clear Number Formats
1. Select cell or range of cells.
2. Click **Edit, Clear, Formats.**

Use Office Clipboard Task Pane
1. Click **Edit, Office Clipboard.**
2. Cut or copy data.
3. Select location for pasted data.
4. Click data sample on Office Clipboard.

Enter Formulas
1. Enter = (equal sign)
2. Select formula data.
3. Enter a mathematical operator.
4. Select formula data.
5. Repeat Steps 3 and 4 until formula is complete.
6. Press **Enter.**

GOAL
To create a Sales Journal
To practice using the following skill sets:

- Enter functions
  - AutoSum
  - Enter the range in a formula
  - AutoSum List
  - Formula bar

WHAT YOU NEED TO KNOW

Enter Functions

- A *function* is a built-in formula that performs a special calculation automatically. Function formulas, for example, =SUM(B4:B7), add all the values, or arguments, in the range specified. A function contains an equal sign, function name, open parenthesis, range or arguments, and then close parenthesis.

AutoSum

- The *AutoSum* feature automatically enters a function to find the total of a group of cells. To add a column of data, make the location of the total the active cell and click the AutoSum button on the Standard toolbar. Excel selects the cells it thinks you want to add and surrounds them with a moving dotted line, as shown in Figure 3.6.
- In the cell where the total is to appear, you see the automatic sum formula to add the cells, =SUM(B4:B47). If the cells selected are the ones you want to add, just press the Enter key; if not, revise the selected range of data.

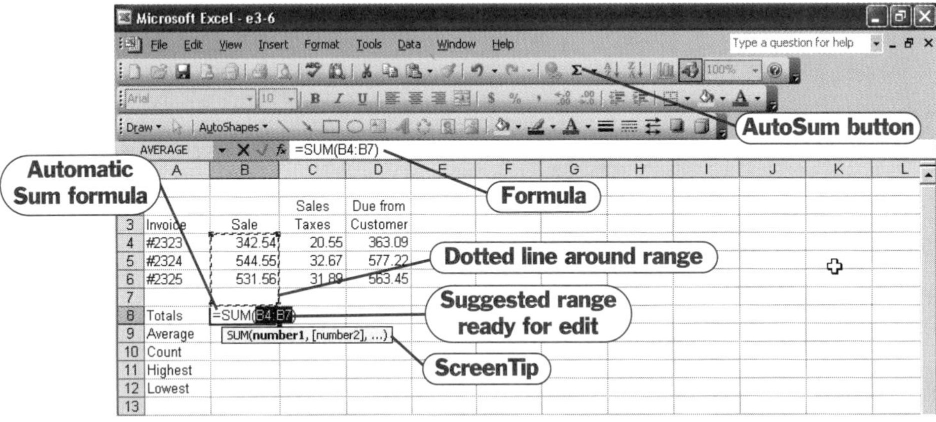

Figure 3.6 AutoSum feature

Enter the Range in a Formula

- If the range suggested by AutoSum is not correct, you must enter the correct range. An accurate way to enter a range address in any formula is to drag through the range with the mouse pointer.

TRY*it* OUT *E3-6*

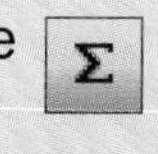

1. Open **E3-6** from the Data CD.
2. Go to **Cell B8.**
3. Click the **AutoSum** button. Notice the formula in the cell and on the Formula bar.
4. Press the **Enter** key.
5. Repeat steps 3 and 4 for Cells C8 and D8. If the range is incorrect, then correct it by dragging the dotted line to the appropriate location.
6. Select Cells **B8** to **D8** and format for commas.
7. Add the Sales Taxes and Sales totals horizontally to see if they equal the "Due from Customer" total. Go to **Cell E8.**
   a. Click the **AutoSum** button. Notice that the range is incorrect.
   b. Drag to select the range **B8:C8,** the correct range.
   c. Press the **Enter** key.
8. Do not close the file.

EXCEL

AutoSum List

▶ At the right of the AutoSum button is a list arrow, as shown in Figure 3.7, that provides other commonly used functions you can select for the range of data. The functions available are listed below:

Sum	Calculates the total of numbers in a range
Average	Calculates the average, or mean, of numbers in a range
Count	Counts the number of values in a range
Max	Calculates the highest value in a range
Min	Calculates the lowest value in a range

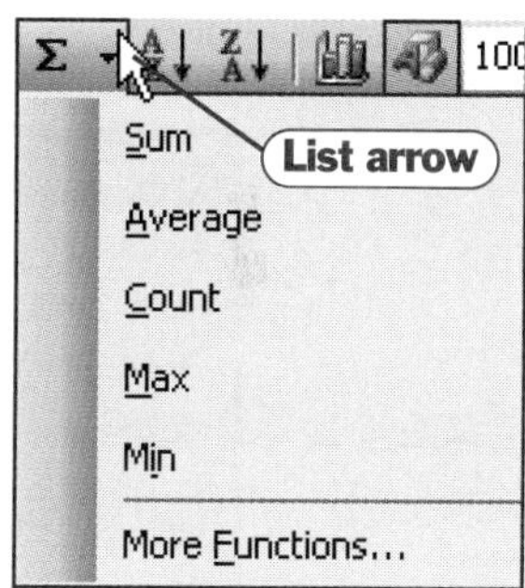

Figure 3.7 AutoSum options list

TRY*it* OUT *E3-7*

1. Use the open file or open **E3-7** from the Data CD.
2. Go to **Cell B9.**
3. Click the **AutoSum** list arrow.
4. Click **Average.**
5. Drag through to correct the range to **B4:B6** and press the **Enter** key.
6. For the following, be sure to correct the range to **B4:B6** before pressing the **Enter** key:
   a. In **Cell B10,** find the COUNT, or number of values.
   b. In **Cell B11,** find the MAX, or highest value.
   c. In **Cell B12,** find the MIN, or lowest value.
7. Do not close the file.

Formula Bar

- Formulas may be entered using the Formula bar. When you press the equal sign, the Formula bar provides a drop-down list of commonly used functions, Cancel and Enter buttons, and the *Insert Function button*, as shown in Figure 3.8. The ***fx*** button will be discussed in Lesson 4.

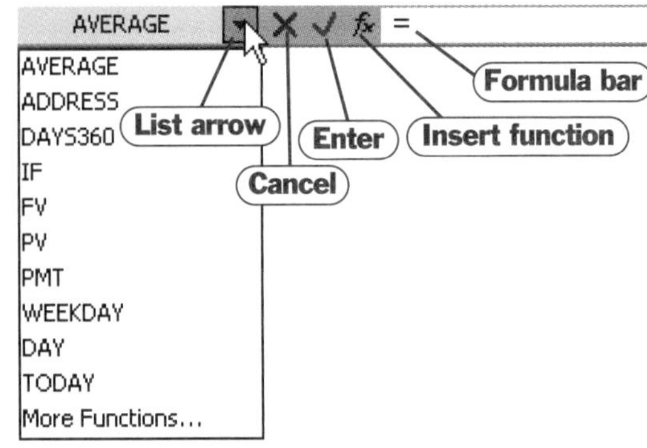

Figure 3.8 Formula bar function list

- When you select a function from the list, Excel enters the function name automatically in the formula and prompts you for the *function arguments*, the cell ranges that supply the data for the formula. The Function Arguments dialog box, shown in Figure 3.9, displays the arguments or range, explains the function, the result of the formula, and provides Help features.
- The Collapse Dialog Box button, at the right of the range, collapses the dialog box to help you select the correct range. When the dialog box is collapsed, it still may obstruct the range, but you can move it away by dragging its title bar with the mouse pointer. After you make your selection, you can click the Expand Dialog Box button to redisplay the dialog box.

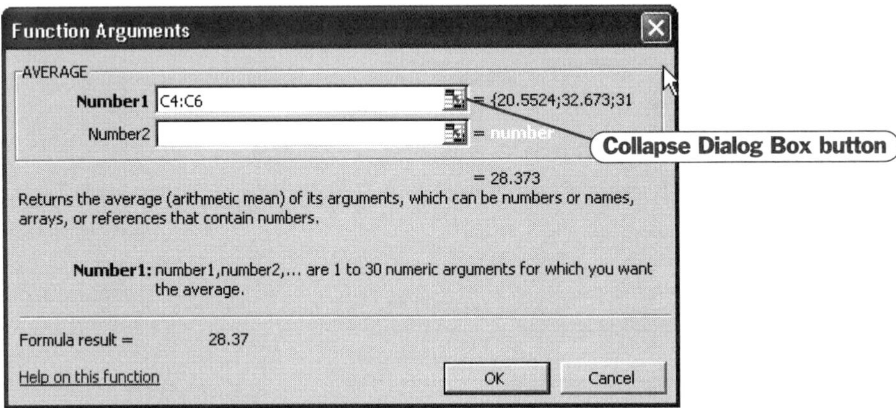

Figure 3.9 Function Arguments dialog box

TRY *it* OUT *E3-8*

1. Use the open file or open **E3-8** from the Data CD. 
2. Enter the equal sign (=) in **Cell C9.**
3. Click **Average** from the drop-down list of functions.
4. Click the **Collapse Dialog Box** button.
5. Drag the dialog box title bar out of the way, if necessary.
6. Select the range **C4:C6.**
7. Click the **Expand Dialog Box** button.
8. Click **OK.**
9. Use the same method to complete the formulas for **Cells C10, C11,** and **C12.** *Note:* If the Count, Max, and Min functions are not visible, click more functions to locate them.
10. Format the values in **Cells B11** to **C12** for two decimal places.
11. Copy the formulas from Cells **C9:C12** to **D9.**
12. Save the file **E3-8.** Close the file.

TASK 2

GOAL
To create a Sales Journal

SETTING THE STAGE/WRAPUP
File name: 3.2journal

WHAT YOU NEED TO KNOW

- Accounting records, such as *journals*, keep track of financial events or transactions for money management and decision-making purposes. One type of journal, a *sales journal*, is a record of the sales made to customers on credit.
- The sales invoice, created when a sale is made on credit, is the basis for the entry in the journal. Entries from the journal are then transferred to each customer's account, as discussed in Task 1. In some businesses, the journal and ledger accounts are generated from the preparation of the invoice, using accounting system software.
- The final (retail) consumer of merchandise pays sales tax while wholesale customers who are resellers and nonprofit organizations are tax exempt.
- In this Rehearsal activity, you will prepare a sales journal for Time Out Sporting Goods to record sales for its credit business, which is a small part of its sales.

DIRECTIONS

1. Open **3.2journal** from the Data CD.
2. Adjust column width for **Column C**.
3. Select the range **A3:F4**. Center and italicize the column headings.
4. Format **Cell C2** to Arial, 14 point, bold, and format the date column to mm/dd/yy.
5. Enter the additional invoices as follows:
   a. Enter data in columns A, B, C, and F as shown in the illustration on the facing page. Note that AutoComplete will help you enter the customers' names.
   b. Copy the formulas from **Columns E and D** down for the new invoices. Notice that the Sales Tax formula is applied only to the Kelly Klinger invoice.
6. Select the range **D5:F18** and format for two decimal places using the Comma format.
7. Use the AutoSum feature to find the total in **Cell D20.**
8. Use the AutoSum feature to find the average of the range **D5:D18** in **Cell D22.** Use the mouse to correct the range in the function.
9. Enter the **equal sign** in **Cell D23** and use the function list on the Formula bar to find the highest value (Max). Click the **Collapse Dialog Box** button to select the range **D5:D18.**
10. Use the method you prefer to find the remaining data.
11. Select the range **D20:D25** and format for two decimal places using the Comma format.
12. Copy the range of summary data in **D20:D25.**
13. As illustrated on the facing page, paste the range twice to **Cells E20** and **F20.**
14. Print the journal with gridlines.
15. Save the file **3.2journal.** Close the file.

	A	B	C	D	E	F
1	Arial, 14 point, bold				Centered and italicized	
2			**SALES JOURNAL**			Page 5
3				*Accounts*	*Sales*	*Sales*
4	*Date*	*Invoice #*	*Customer*	*Receivable*	*Taxes*	*Income*
5	5/3/04	2325	Central H.S. Health Ed Dept	434.56		434.56
6	5/4/04	2326	Jason Gym	550.00		550.00
7	5/7/04	2327	Eastern H.S. - Gym	515.00		515.00
8	5/9/04	2328	Fitness King	1,255.00		1,255.00
9	5/11/04	2329	Harry Putter	185.94	10.94	175.00
10	5/14/04	2330	Eastern H.S. - Gym	325.00		325.00
11	5/14/04	2331	Jason Gym	385.00		385.00
12	5/16/04	2332	Fitness King	155.00		155.00
13	5/17/04	2333	Harry Putter	313.44	18.44	295.00
14	5/18/04	2334	Eastern H.S. - Gym	660.00		660.00
15	5/21/04	2335	Kelly Klinger	143.44	8.44	135.00
16	5/22/04	2336	Central H.S. Health Ed Dept	1,045.32		1,045.32
17	5/24/04	2337	Jason Gym	451.56		451.56
18	5/31/04	2338	Kelly Klinger	90.31	5.31	85.00
19						
20	Enter new sales		Totals			
21						
22			Averages			
23			Highest			
24			Lowest			
25			Count			
26					Copy D20:D25 to E20 and F20	
27						
28						

EXCEL

Cues for Reference

Use Auto Sum

1. Select cell to display answer.
2. Click the **AutoSum** button. Σ
3. If range is correct, press **Enter.**
4. If not, use mouse pointer to reselect the correct range and press **Enter.**

Enter Range in a Formula

1. Place mouse pointer on first cell in range.
2. Click, hold, and drag to last cell in range.

Use Functions on AutoSum List

1. Select cell to display answer.
2. Click **AutoSum** list arrow.
3. Select function.
4. Correct the range.
5. Press **Enter.**

Use Functions from the Formula bar

1. Select cell to display answer.
2. Enter **Equals (=).**
3. Select function from drop-down list.
4. Click the **Collapse Dialog Box** button.
5. Drag the dialog box title bar out of the way, if necessary.
6. Select the range.
7. Click the **Expand Dialog Box** button. 
8. Press **OK.**

GOAL
To create a payroll
To practice using the following skill sets:
- Use the Fill Handle tool
- Modify page setup options
  - Orientation
  - Set page margins and centering
- Edit formulas using the Formula bar

WHAT YOU NEED TO KNOW

Use the Fill Handle Tool

- You can use the *AutoFill* tool to copy labels, values, or formulas or to create sequential lists of values or labels.
- To use AutoFill as a copy tool, select the cell to be copied and place your insertion point on the *fill handle*, the small square at the bottom right of the cell to copy, as shown in Figure 3.10. When the mouse pointer changes to a thin black plus sign, click and drag the cell border to fill the appropriate range. You will find this to be an easy way to copy formulas. You can also click Edit, Fill to access this feature.

	A	B	C	D	E
1					
2		Gross	Taxes	Union	Net
3	Employee	Pay		Dues	Pay
4					
5	1000	280	67	10	203
6	1001	300	79	10	211
7	1002	295	72		
8	1003	655	146		
9	1004	432	96		
10	1005	425	89		
11					

Fill handle

Figure 3.10 AutoFill activated

Create a Series

- To create a *series* of values or labels, such as check numbers, days of the week, months, years, etc., enter the first two items in the series and then use the fill handle to complete the column.

TRY *it* OUT *E3-9*

1. Open **E3-9** from the Data CD.
2. AutoFill a value:
   a. Click **Cell D6** and place your mouse pointer on the fill handle.
   b. When the insertion point changes to a black plus sign, click and drag the border down to **Cell D10.**
3. AutoFill a formula: In **Cell E6,** use the fill handle to fill the formula down to **Cell E10.**
4. Fill a formula from **Cells B12** to **E12:**
   a. Select the range **B12:E12.**
   b. Click **Edit, Fill,** and **Right.**

Continued on next page

TRY it OUT *E3-9 Continued*

5. Enter `1000` in **Cell A5** and `1001` **in Cell A6.**
6. Select both values and use the fill handle to create a sequential list to **Cell A10**.
7. Enter `January` in **Cell F1** and `February` in **Cell G1.**
8. Select **both values** and use the fill handle to fill to **Cell K1.**
9. Do not close the file.

EXCEL

Modify Page Setup Options

Orientation

- If you Print Preview your worksheet and note that it is wider than the page width, use landscape orientation to print the worksheet horizontally on the page. Or, you can scale the data to fit on one page, which reduces the font size.
- In the Page Setup dialog box with the Page tab selected, shown in Figure 3.11, you can set page orientation and scaling.

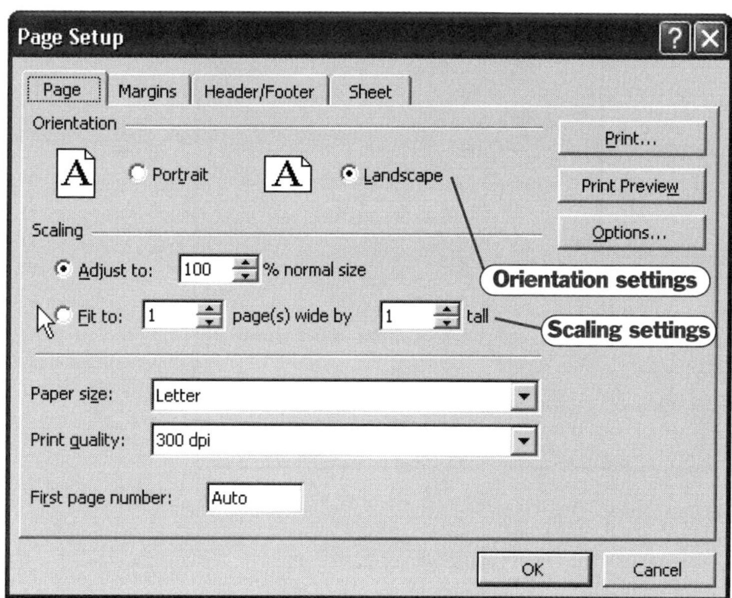

Figure 3.11 File Page Setup, Page tab selected

TRY it OUT *E3-10*

1. Continue working in the open file or open **E3-10** from the Data CD.
2. Click **File, Page Setup,** and click the **Page** tab, if not already displayed.
3. Click the **Print Preview** button. Notice that the worksheet is not completely visible. Click **Setup** on the Print Preview toolbar.
4. Click **Fit to 1 page wide by 1 tall** in the Page tab of the Page Setup dialog box.

Continued on next page

TRY *it* OUT *E3-10 Continued*

5. Click **OK.** Notice that the full worksheet displays with a smaller font.
6. Click **Setup** on the Print Preview toolbar.
7. Select **Adjust to 100% normal size** and click **Landscape** orientation in the Page tab of the Page Setup dialog box.
8. Click **OK.**
9. Click **Close** on the Print Preview toolbar.
10. Do not close the file.

Set Page Margins and Centering

▶ On the Margins tab, as shown in Figure 3.12, you can center the worksheet on the page and set margins. You can also set Margins manually, in Print Preview mode, by clicking the Margins button on the Print Preview toolbar.

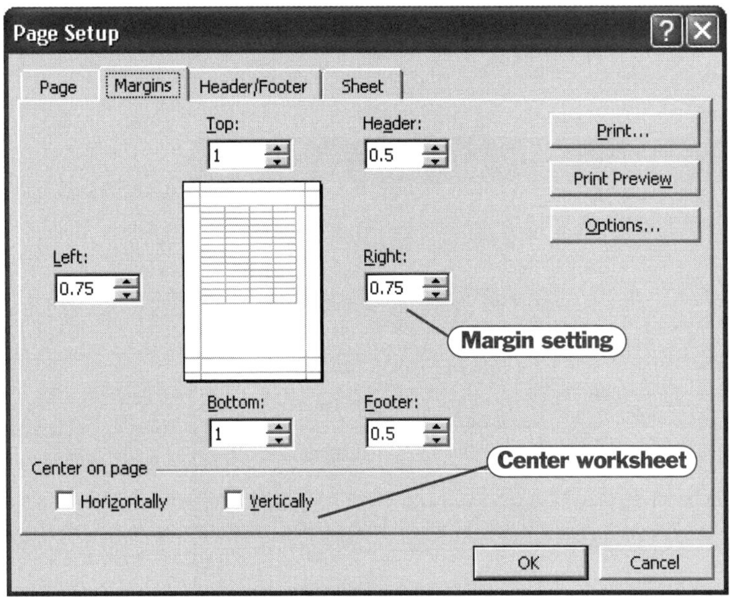

Figure 3.12 Page Setup dialog box, Margins tab

TRY *it* OUT *E3-11*

1. Continue working in the open file or open **E3-11** from the Data CD.
2. Click **File, Page Setup,** and click the **Margins** tab.
3. Under **Center on page,** click **Horizontally** and **Vertically.**
4. Click the **Print Preview** button.
5. Click the **Margins** button on the Print Preview toolbar.
6. Drag the margin grids to move the margins closer to the data.
7. Click **Close** on the Print Preview toolbar.
8. Do not close the file.

Edit Formulas Using the Formula Bar

- To edit or revise a formula in Edit mode, press the F2 key or double-click the formula. Excel then color codes the arguments in the cell formula and on the Formula bar to match a box around the actual arguments. This clearly identifies each part of the formula and may clarify the errors that need correction.
- Once you are in Edit mode, you can drag the border of the range or cell, or backspace to correct errors. Figures 3.13 and 3.14 show how formula arguments and a range appear in Edit mode.

	A	B	C	D	E	
1						Jan
2		Gross	Taxes	Union	Net	
3	Employee	Pay		Dues	Pay	
4						
5	1000	280	67	10	=B5+C5-D5	
6	1001	300	79	10		
7	1002	295	72	10		
8	1003	655	146	10		
9	1004	432	96	10		
10	1005	425	89	10		

Cursor in edit location

Color-coded formula arguments

Figure 3.13 Edit mode for formula arguments

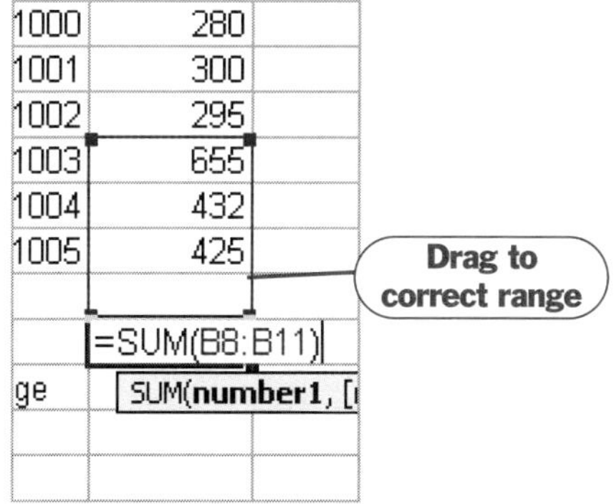

Figure 3.14 Edit mode for arguments in a range

TRY it OUT *E3-12*

1. Continue working in the open file or open **E3-12** from the Data CD.
2. Double-click **Cell E5** to edit the formula.
3. Revise the formula to read =B5-C5-D5 because both the taxes and dues should be subtracted. Use the **left arrow** and the **backspace** keys to make the change from plus to minus.
4. Press the **Enter** key.
5. In **Cell E5,** click the **fill handle** to AutoFill the revised formula from **Cell E5** down to **E10.**
6. Double-click **Cell B12** and notice the range.
7. Drag the range border to correct it so that it adds the range **B5:B10.**
8. In **Cell B12,** click the **fill handle** to AutoFill the revised formula across from **Cells B12** to **E12.**
9. Find the Averages in **Row 13** and format the data for no decimal places.
10. Save the file as **E3-12.** Close the file.

TASK 3

GOAL
To create a payroll

SETTING THE STAGE/WRAPUP
File name: **3.3payroll**

WHAT YOU NEED TO KNOW

- To complete payroll calculations, you need to know the employee's *tax status* data, i.e., marital status and the number of dependents claimed. Use the tax status and the salary to look up the federal withholding tax on tax tables. State tax rates vary with each state having different tables and rules. Social Security and Medicare taxes are deducted from all payrolls at the rates of 6.2% and 1.45%, respectively. You can use a percent in an Excel formula.
- Payrolls may be completed by outside services or by the Accounting Department in a large firm. A *payroll register* is a form used to calculate the salaries, taxes, and net pay due each employee for the pay period. You will calculate gross pay (the salary before taxes), the taxes on gross pay, and the net pay (the salary less all the deductions). Once you complete a payroll register, you can save the worksheet as a template to use for each week's payroll. Internet sites also provide paycheck calculators for small businesses.
- In this Rehearsal activity, you will prepare a weekly payroll for WorkOut Centers, located in Austin, Texas. There is no state or local withholding tax in this state.

DIRECTIONS

1. Open **3.3payroll** from the Data CD. Adjust **Column C's** column width.

2. *Employee Number:* Select the range **A7:A8** and use the fill handle to drag the series of numbers to every employee.
3. *Gross Pay:* In **Cell F7,** enter a formula to find gross pay.

   (Hint: =Regular Earnings+Overtime – use cell addresses in the formula)
4. Use the fill handle in **Cell F7** to copy the formula down to each employee's payroll.
5. *Social Security:* In **Cell H7,** enter a formula to find the Social Security tax, which is 6.2% of the gross pay. *(Hint: =Gross Pay*6.2%)*
6. *Medicare:* In **Cell I7,** enter a formula to find the Medicare tax, which is 1.45% of the gross pay.
7. *Total Deductions:* In **Cell J7,** use AutoSum to enter a formula to find the total of all the payroll deductions from the range **G7:I7.**
8. *Net Pay:* In **Cell K7,** enter a formula to find net pay, which is the gross pay less the total deductions.
9. As shown in the illustration on the facing page, select the range **H7:K7,** and use the fill handle to fill all the formulas for the payroll.
10. In **Cell D15,** use AutoSum to find the total of the column.
11. In **Cell D17,** press **equal (=)** and use the Formula bar drop-down function list to enter the formula for the column average. Be sure to select the correct range.
12. In **Cell D18,** use the AutoSum drop-down list to find the count. Be sure to correct the range.

Continued on next page

13. Double-click each formula just completed in Steps 10, 11, and 12 to check the ranges in Edit mode.
14. Select the range **D15:D18** and use the fill handle to copy the formulas across to all columns.
15. Format payroll data in the range **D7:K17** in comma format.
16. Center column headings for the range **D5:K6.**
17. Format the worksheet: Italicize and bold all column headings. Bold text in Cells A3, F3, and C15 to C18. Change the font for the title in Cell E1 as illustrated or to a similar font, and increase the font size to 14.
18. Use Page Setup to print the payroll in landscape orientation, centered horizontally. Print one copy.
19. Save the file **3.3payroll.** Close the file.

EXCEL

	A	B	C	D	E	F	G	H	I	J	K
1			Lucida Sans, 14 point →		PAYROLL REGISTER						
2										Bold and Italics	
3	**For Pay Period Ended:**			15-Jun-04		**Date of Payment:**		20-Jun-04			
4											
5	***Employee***			***Regular***		***Gross***	***Federal***	***Social***		***Total***	***Net***
6	***Number***	***Status***	***Name***	***Earnings***	***Overtime***	***Pay***	***W.T.***	***Security***	***Medicare***	***Deductions***	***Pay***
7	225	S1	Bosco, Vince	280.00	85.00		32.63				
8	226	M2	Ingram, Sally	800.00	200.00		102.26				
9		S2	Josephs, Ted	250.00			8.17				
10		M2	Lee, Gina	435.00			19.37				
11		M4	Montez, Maria	475.00			11.63				
12		S0	Pasternak, Joan	250.00			24.18				
13		S1	Thompson, John	450.00	100.00		60.38				
14											
15			**Totals**								
16											
17			**Average**								
18			**Count**								

Cues for Reference

Edit Formulas
1. Select formula.
2. Press **F2.**
3. Edit range by dragging border, or Edit operators in formula.

Use AutoFill
1. For series, select first two cells in series. For formulas, values, and text, select a cell.
2. Point cursor to fill handle in bottom right corner.
3. Drag to fill series.

Modify Page Orientation
1. Click **File, Page Setup,** and click **Page** tab.
2. Click **Landscape.**
3. Click **OK.**

Set Page Margins and Centering
1. Click **Print Preview** button.
2. Click **Margins** button on the Print Preview toolbar.
3. Drag margins to appropriate location.
4. Click **Close** on the Print Preview toolbar.

or

1. Click **File, Page Setup,** and click **Margins** tab.
2. Set margins or centering.
3. Click **OK.**

GOAL

To create an expense report

To practice using the following skill sets:

- Moving selected cells
- Insert, view, and edit cell comments
- Apply and modify cell formats with the Format Cells dialog box
- Use the Format Painter

WHAT YOU NEED TO KNOW

Moving Selected Cells

- You can move data by using the Cut and Paste buttons on the Standard toolbar, or by selecting the range and dragging it to the paste location (known as *drag-and-drop*). Moving data removes it from the first location and pastes it to the new location. This will overwrite any data in the new location.
- To drag-and-drop data, select the data to move and place the mouse pointer on the edge of the range until it changes to a four-headed arrow. Drag the outline of the range to the first cell in the new location's range. As shown in Figure 3.15, as you drag the data, the new range or location appears. Data formats move with the data, but you must check that formulas are correct after a move operation.

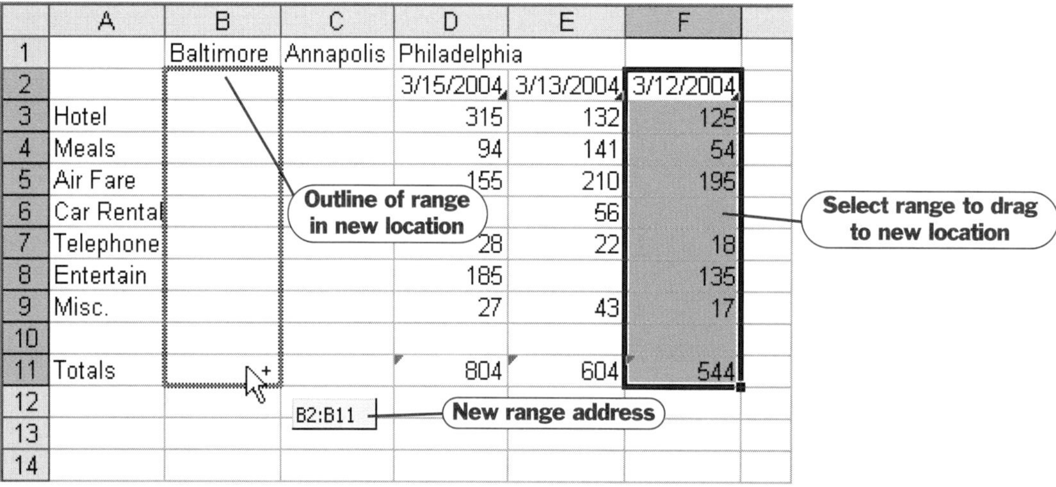

Figure 3.15 Selected range moved to new location

TRY*it* OUT *E3-13*

1. Open **E3-13** from the Data CD.
2. Select the range **E2:E11.**
3. Click the **Cut** button.
4. Select **Cell C2,** and then click the **Paste** button.
5. Select the range **F2:F11.**
6. Place the mouse pointer at the edge of the range until the pointer becomes a four-headed arrow.
7. Click, hold, and drag-and-drop the range to **B2:B11.**
8. Do not close the file.

Insert, View, and Edit Cell Comments

- You can attach a text comment in a cell to document formulas or assumptions built into the worksheet, or to comment on data sent to you by someone else. Because this feature is used when sharing workbooks, the user's name will also be on the comment.
- Insert a comment in the cell by clicking Insert, Comment and entering the comment in the comment box. A red triangle appears in the top corner of the cell to indicate the presence of a *cell comment,* as shown in Figure 3.16.
- When the mouse moves over a cell with a comment indicator, you can view the comment. If this does not occur, click Comment indicator only on the Tools, Options, View tab.

Cell comment

	A	B	C	D
1	Comment indicator	Baltimor	A	
2		3/12/2004	3/	
3	Hotel	125.00		
4	Meals	54.00	141.00	94.00
5	Air Fare	195.00	210.00	155.00
6	Car Rental		56.00	
7	Telephone	18.00	22.00	28.00
8	Entertain	135.00		185.00
9	Misc.	17.00	43.00	27.00
10				
11	**Totals**	544.00	604.00	804.00

Your Name:
Meeting with J & R
Equipment Supply

Figure 3.16 Cell comment

- To edit or delete a comment, right-click the comment cell and select the desired action.
- To print comments, select one of the Comments drop-down list print options on the Sheet tab of the Page Setup dialog box, as shown in Figure 3.17.

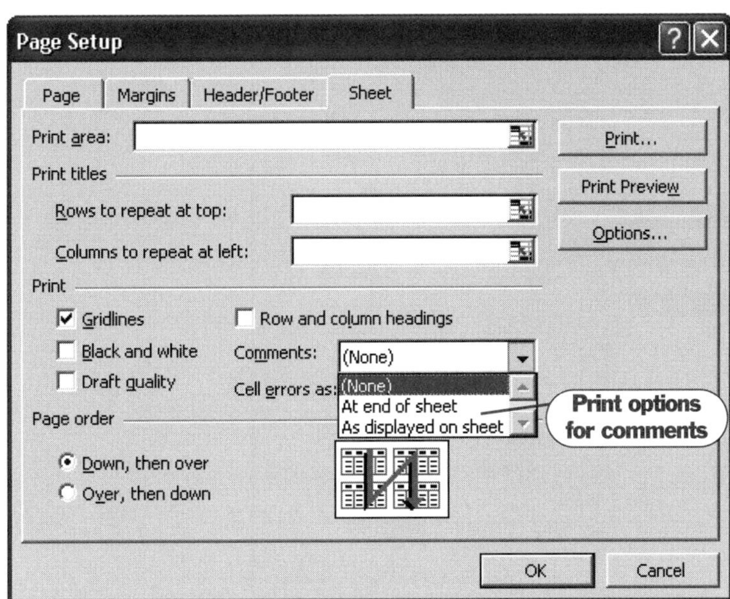

Figure 3.17 Page Setup, Sheet tab

TRY *it* OUT *E3-14*

1. Continue working in the open file or open **E3-14** from the Data CD.
2. In **Cell B1,** click **Insert, Comment.**
3. Enter this text:

   J&R Equipment Supply

4. Click on any cell to come out of Comment mode.

Continued on next page

TRY it OUT *E3-14 Continued*

5. Right-click **Cell C1,** select **Insert Comment,** and enter:

   `Sailboat Show and Conference`

6. Right-click **Cell B1,** select **Edit Comment.**
7. Edit the comment to read: `Meeting with J&R Equipment Supply.`
8. Click on any cell to come out of Comment mode.
9. Enter a comment in **Cell D1:** `Meeting with Michael Collins.`
10. Right-click **Cell D1** and select **Delete Comment**.
11. Use the Page Setup dialog box to print the worksheet. Select **Comments: At end of sheet.**
12. Do not close the file.

Apply and Modify Cell Formats with the Format Cells Dialog Box

▶ You have been using the Formatting toolbar buttons to format cells. You can set all formats at once and have additional formatting options if you use the Format Cells dialog box as shown in Figure 3.18. Click Format, Cells, or the Ctrl+1 keys and notice the six cell formatting tabs that appear. Format a cell by selecting the appropriate options from any or all tabs and click OK.

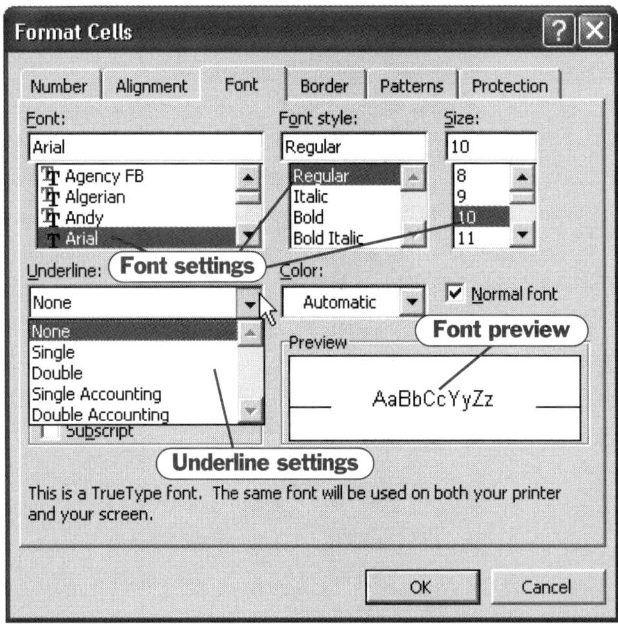

Figure 3.18 Format Cells dialog box, Font tab

TRY it OUT *E3-15*

1. Continue working in the open file or open **E3-15** from the Data CD.
2. Select the range **B1:D1.**
3. Click **Format, Cells,** and click the **Font** tab in the Format Cells dialog box.
4. Format for the Book Antiqua font, bold, Single Accounting Underline. Note the Preview box.
5. Click **OK.**

Continued on next page

TRY it OUT *E3-15 Continued*

6. Select the range **B3:D9** and press the **Ctrl+1** keys.
7. In the **Number** tab, select a number format with two decimals.
8. Click **OK.**
9. Do not close the file.

Use the Format Painter

- Once you have set formats for text or values, you can copy formats from one cell to another by using the *Format Painter* button on the Formatting toolbar. When you are in Format Painter mode, the mouse pointer includes a paintbrush icon, as shown in Figure 3.19.
- To format more than one area of the worksheet with the Format Painter option, double-click the button. After formatting is complete, click the Format Painter button again to exit Format Painter mode.

	A	B	C	D
1		**Baltimore**	**Annapolis**	**Philadelphia**
2		3/12/2004	3/13/2004	3/15/2004
3	Hotel	125.00	132.00	315.00
4	Meals	54.00	141.00	94.00
5	Air Fare	195.00	210.00	155.00
6	Car Rental		56.00	
7	Telephone	18.00	22.00	28.00
8	Entertain	135.00		185.00
9	Misc.	17.00	43.00	27.00
10				
11	**Totals**	544.00	604.00	804.00
12				

Cursor in Format Painter mode

Figure 3.19 Format Painter

TRY it OUT *E3-16*

1. Continue working in the open file or open **E3-16** from the Data CD.
2. Select **Cell B9.**
3. Click the **Format Painter** button.
4. Select and apply the format to the range **B11:D11.**
5. Select **B1** and click **Format Painter.**
6. Select and apply the format to **Cell A11.**
7. Save the file **E3-16.** Close the file.

GOAL
To create an expense report

SETTING THE STAGE/WRAPUP
File name: **3.4expense**

WHAT YOU NEED TO KNOW

- When employees travel on company business, the company usually *reimburses,* or refunds, their expenses. They may get a cash advance before the trip, which reduces the reimbursement amount.
- After the trip, they must submit all expenses and receipts for reimbursement with an *expense report.* The tax laws require detailed records for business entertainment because business travel expenses are part of the costs of doing business.
- In this Rehearsal activity, you will prepare an expense report for Sara Vikers, an employee of Occasions Event Planning. She is applying for reimbursement of expenses for her business trip to Rochester, N.Y., to meet with the hotels, vendors, and co-sponsor of the photography conference she is planning.

DIRECTIONS

1. Open **3.4expense** from the Data CD. Adjust column width as necessary.
2. Select the range **A1:A3** and use the Format Cells dialog box to format for Tahoma, bold, 12 point.
3. Move the letterhead, using drag-and-drop, to **Cell C1.**
4. Use **Format Painter** to apply the font format from **Cell C1** to the EXPENSE REPORT title.
5. Select the labels in the range **A6:A8** and format them for bold.
6. Double-click the **Format Painter** button and apply bold format to the column headings in **Rows 10, 24,** and **25**, as shown on the facing page.
7. Click **Format Painter** to turn off multiple cell format.
8. Center the column headings in the range **C10:H10.**
9. Format the dates as shown in the illustration on the facing page.
10. Select the range **A23:H31** and move the range to **Cell A18.**
11. As illustrated on the facing page, in **Cell C18,** use AutoSum to find the total of the column.
12. Use the fill handle to extend the formula to **Cell H18.**
13. In **Cell H21,** enter a formula to find the amount due Sara Vikers. *(Hint: =Total-Advance)*
14. Select the range **C11:H21** and format for two decimals.
15. Use **Format Painter** to apply the same format to **Cell G26.**
16. Click **Cell H20,** click **Insert, Comment,** and enter the comment `Receipt #86 9/10.`
17. Click **Cell H21,** click **Format, Cells,** and click the **Font** tab to add a Double Accounting underline.

Continued on next page

18. Edit the comment to add the current year.
19. Print the expense report with the comment displayed at the end of the sheet.
20. Save the file **3.4expense**. Close the file.

	A	B	C	D	E	F	G	H
1			**Occasions Event Planning**					
2			**675 Third Avenue**					
3			**New York, NY 10017**					
4	**EXPENSE REPORT**							
5								
6	**Employee:**		Sara Vikers					
7	**Purpose:**		Trip to Rochester, NY to plan Photography Conference					
8	**Date (s):**		September 12 and 13, 2004					
9								
10	**Date**	**Description**	**Meals**	**Travel**	**Lodging**	**Telephone**	**Other**	**Total**
11	9/12	Employee	35		96	23	15	169
12	9/12	Entertainment*	137					137
13	9/13	Car Rental Charges		75				75
14	9/13	Fuel		35				35
15	9/13	Tolls		8.5				8.5
16	9/13	Employee	52			21	22	95
17								
18		Totals		→	→	→	→	→
19								
20						Less: Advance		250
21						Net due		
22								
23								
24	**Entertainment Expenses Detail***							
25	**Date**	**Client/Company Entertained**	**Purpose**		**Restaurant**		**Amount**	
26	9/12/04	R. Frank, Vision Camera Co.	Conference planning		Blue Hill Restaurant		137	

EXCEL

Cues for Reference

Move Data
1. Select data to move.
2. Place mouse pointer at edge of selection, click, hold, and drag to new location.

Insert Cell Comment
1. Select cell.
2. Click **Insert, Comment.**
3. Enter comment.
4. Click on any cell to exit Comment mode.

Edit Cell Comment
1. Right-click cell with comment to edit.
2. Click **Edit Comment**.
3. Edit comment.
4. Click on any cell to exit Comment mode.

Use Format Cells Dialog Box
1. Select range to format.
2. Click **Format, Cells** or **Ctrl+1.**
3. Select appropriate tab.
4. Set format.
5. Click **OK.**

Use Format Painter
1. Select cell with format to copy.
2. Click the **Format Painter** button.
3. Select cell to receive format.

Use Format Painter for Multiple Formats
1. Select cell with format to copy.
2. Double-click **Format Painter.** 
3. Apply formats to cells.
4. Click **Format Painter** to release Format Mode.

PERFORMANCE

SETTING THE STAGE/WRAPUP

Act I: File name: **3p1.salejour**
Act II: File name: **3p2.payroll**
Act III: File names: **3p3.expense.xlt**
3p3.exp1012

Act I

Ralph Green, the CFO of Green Brothers Gardening, has asked you to work on the sales journal to record credit sales. This sales journal for Green Brothers' smallest nursery divides sales into the services provided at that location, i.e., nursery, maintenance contracts, and landscaping. Use 4.5% for the sales tax rate for Virginia and apply it only to nursery sales. Although the sales journal normally provides totals at the end of the month, Mr. Green wants data on June 15 to help with business decisions.

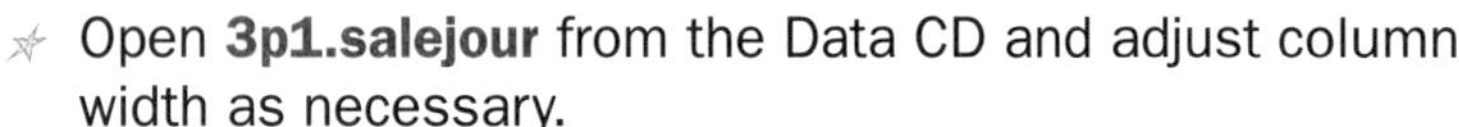

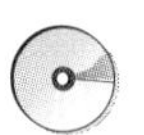

- Open **3p1.salejour** from the Data CD and adjust column width as necessary.
- Sales Income column: Enter formula to add all services.
- Sales Tax column: Enter formula to calculate taxes on nursery sales only. Zero should appear if there is no tax.
- Accounts Receivable column: Enter formula to add tax to sales.
- Fill the formulas down the columns.
- Invoice number column: Use AutoFill.
- Find totals and statistics for all columns.
- Format numbers for commas, except for the Count row, and set alignments, column widths, and text formats to improve the appearance of the worksheet.
- Print the journal using landscape orientation.
- Save and close the file **3p1.salejour.**

Act II

Odyssey Travel Gear has asked you to complete the weekly payroll for the Chicago store for the week ending July 20. Store employees are paid based on an hourly rate.

The deductions for federal and state income taxes are based on the salary and tax status of the employee and are obtained from tax tables or from online services. The tax status M2, for example, is made up of the marital staus (M = married, S = single) and the number of federal exemptions. Social Security (6.2%) and Medicare (1.45%) taxes are calculated using the current tax rate.

Odyssey Travel Gear									Chicago Store #01	
Payroll Register								For the week ended:		20-Jul-04
				Gross	Federal	State	Social	Medicare	Total	Net
Name	Status	Hours	Rate	Pay	W.T.	W.T.	Security Tax	Tax	Deductions	Pay
Miller, Carson	M 2	40	14.50		39.26	17.40				
Vaughn, Tamika	M 1	40	10.95		26.76	13.14				
Sanchez, Linda	S 0	35	9.00		33.93	9.45				
Frommel, Sam	S 2	38	9.00							
Witnaur, Mary	M 0	40	8.25							
	Total									
	Average									
	Highest									
	Lowest									

EXCEL

- Open **3p2.payroll** from the Data CD and adjust column widths as necessary.

- The employees' hours for the week are shown below:

Name	Status	Hours	Rate
Miller, Carson	M 2	40	14.50
Vaughn, Tamika	M 1	40	10.95
Sanchez, Linda	S 0	35	9.00
Frommel, Sam	S 2	38	9.00
Witnaur, Mary	M 0	40	8.25

- The federal and state taxes are included for the first three employees. Use the Paycheck Calculator on the Personal Calculator link on www.paycheckcity.com to look up the federal and state taxes for the last two employees. On the Web site, you will have to enter the State (Illinois), Gross Pay, Pay Frequency (weekly), Married or Single for federal filing status and enter the number of federal exemptions. When you click Calculate, the detailed paycheck will appear. Copy the state and federal taxes and enter them on your worksheet.
- Enter formulas for Gross Pay *(Hint: Hours*Rate)*, Social Security Tax, Medicare Tax, Total Deductions, and Net Pay. Fill the formulas for all employees and format values.
- Find summary values for the payroll, including Totals, Averages, Highest, and Lowest. Format all values for commas.
- Print Preview, change the orientation to print the worksheet on one page, print, save, and close the file **3p2.payroll.**

Act III

Carl Westfield, from the Television Division in the California office of Trilogy Productions, has just returned from a business trip to San Diego, California where he met with local stations and writers. He needs an expense report for the trip made October 12 to October 15, 2004. The company reimburses him for mileage driven at $.36 per mile.

Trilogy Productions

101 Sunset Boulevard

Beverly Hills, CA 90211

EXPENSE REPORT

Employee:

Purpose:

Date (s):

Date	**Description**	**Transport**	**Fuel**	**Meals**	**Lodging**	**Phone**	**Other**	**Total**
						Total		
						Less: Advance		
						Net due		

(Mileage reimbursed at $.36 per mile.)

Entertainment Expenses Detail"

Date	**Client/Company Entertained**	**Purpose**	**Restaurant/Event**	**Amount**

- Open **3p3.expense** from the Data CD, and format font, font size and style, as you want, for the Trilogy Productions heading and report title. Center the column headings and save the file as a template.

- Mr. Westfield provides you with the following receipts and list of expenses. Enter and place the expense amounts in the appropriate columns.

  10/12 Fuel $20.76

  10/13 Entertainment: $325.64 - Dinner meeting - Ocean View Restaurant, SDTV Marketing Team

10/14 Entertainment: $114.95 - Luncheon, XY Project - Carson Willers, screenwriter, at LaTavola

10/15 Other expenses: $72.89, Hotel $389.85, Meals $412.65, Telephone $45.89, Fuel $23.54

10/15 Mileage: 300 miles @ $.36 per mile (Enter a formula to multiply the mileage by $.36 in the Transport column to find the expense.)

- Mr. Westfield drove from Sunset Boulevard in Beverly Hills, CA 90210 to Federal Boulevard in San Diego, CA 92102. Mr. Westfield just estimated the mileage. You have been asked to check the distance of this trip on the Internet by going to www.mappoint.msn.com. Use the Directions tab to determine the one-way mileage for this trip. Then, on an unused area of the worksheet, calculate the mileage by doubling the one-way mileage and adding 50 miles for in-town driving. (Edit the formula and the label to show the new mileage figure.)
- Enter a comment in the Transport calculation cell to note the number of trip miles and the number of in-town miles.
- Mr. Westfield received an advance of $300 before the trip and would like to be reimbursed for the balance.
- Complete formulas to add values across and down and format as necessary.
- Print the expense report, changing the print settings if necessary. Save the file as an Excel workbook file; name it **3p3.exp1012.**

LESSON 4

Data Analysis

In this lesson, you will learn to use Excel features, functions, and multiple worksheet workbooks to create and complete analyses of business data. Completed worksheets and workbooks will be saved as a Web page.

Upon completion of this lesson, you should have mastered the following skill sets:

- Apply and modify cell formats
  - Cell borders
  - Decimal place and negative number format
- Insert a page break
- Lists
  - Sort lists
  - Filter lists using AutoFilter
- Use numeric labels
- Indent text
- Insert and delete rows and columns
- Use formulas with absolute and relative reference
- Convert workbooks into Web pages
  - Add a Background Pattern
  - Use Web Page Preview
  - Save a workbook as a Web page
- Apply and modify worksheet formats
  - AutoFormat
  - Fill color and font color
- Modify workbooks
  - Insert and delete worksheets
  - Move and copy worksheets
  - Rename and format worksheet tabs
  - Group worksheets
- Use date formats and functions
- Use financial functions
  - The PMT function
  - The FV function
  - The PV function
- Use Paste Special, Values

Terms

Software-related

Border
Negative numbers
Page break
Sort
AutoFilter
Numeric label
Label prefix
Relative reference
Absolute reference
Web page
Interactivity
AutoFormat
Tab Scrolling buttons
Group sheets
Serial value
Date function
Financial functions
PMT
Principal
Rate
Annual interest rate
Nper
FV
PV
Paste values

Document-related

Budget
Quarterly
Income statement
Revenue
Credit terms
Reciprocal

GOALS

To create a budget analysis

To practice using the following skill sets:

- Apply and modify cell formats
  - Cell borders
  - Decimal place and negative number format
  - Background color
- Insert a page break
- Lists
  - Filter lists using AutoFilter
  - Sort lists

WHAT YOU NEED TO KNOW

Apply and Modify Cell Formats

- Excel provides several ways for you to format the cells in a worksheet to create professional-looking documents. You can add a variety of borders and format numeric values appropriately.

Cell Borders

- To outline or separate data, you can include a variety of line styles that *border* the edge of a cell or range of cells. You add borders by selecting the range, clicking the Borders button on the Formatting toolbar, as shown in Figure 4.1, and selecting the border style.
- Click the last Border button option to open the Draw Borders toolbar, as shown in Figure 4.2. To draw your borders, select the line style, use the pencil cursor to draw the border, and use the eraser button to make corrections.

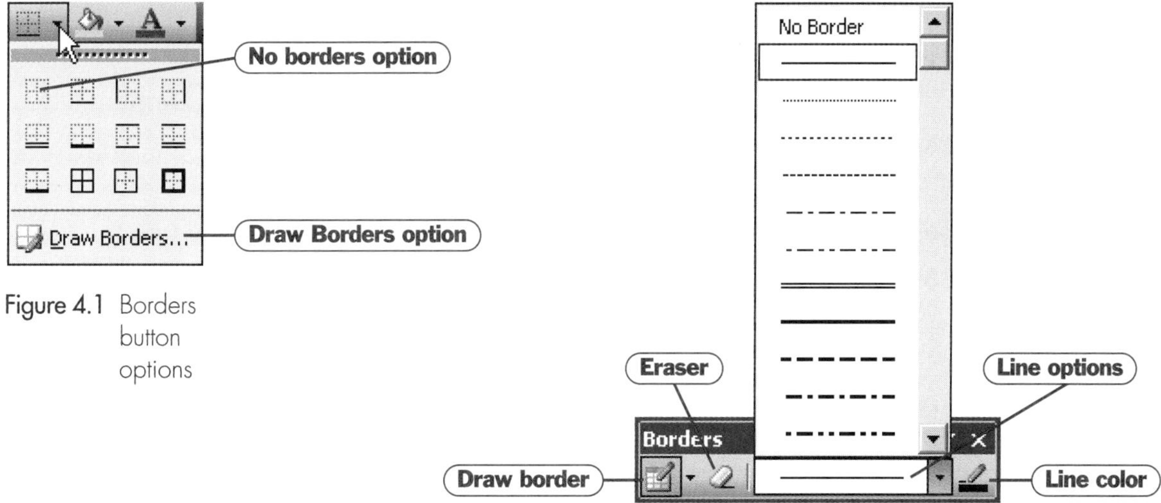

Figure 4.1 Borders button options

Figure 4.2 Draw Borders toolbar and line options

- Borders can also be set and previewed using the Border tab in the Format Cells dialog box, as shown in Figure 4.3. The dialog box contains three preset border formats and other border styles illustrated around the preview box. Line Style and Color boxes allow you to set these features for the selected border style.

▶ Border formats remain when you clear cell contents. Therefore, you must clear border settings separately. To clear borders, select the No Border option from the Borders button drop-down list, or the None style in the Border tab of the Format Cells dialog box.

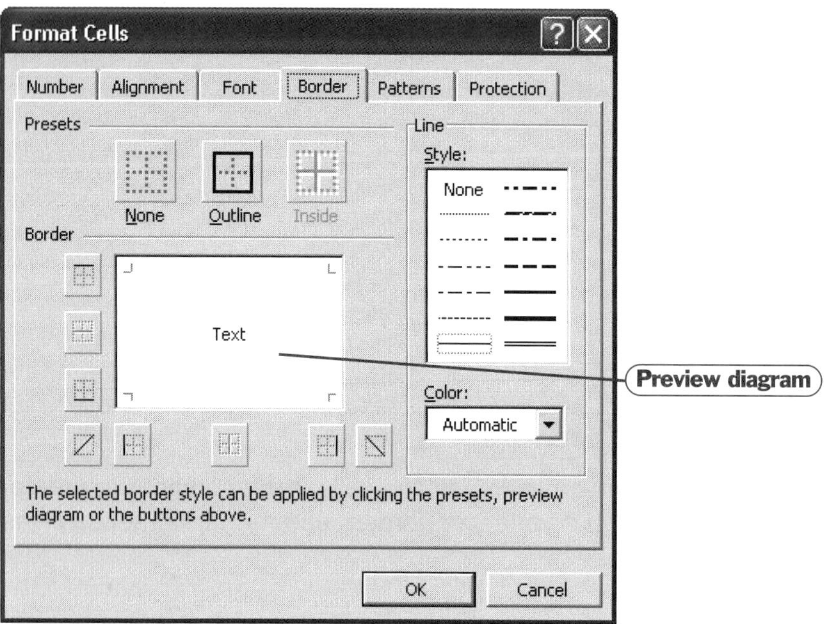

Figure 4.3 Format Cells dialog box, Border tab

TRY*it* OUT *E4-1*

1. Open **E4-1** from the Data CD.
2. Select columns **B:F** and double-click between columns **F** and **G** to AutoFit the data.
3. Select the range **A4:F4** and click the **Borders** button list arrow.
4. Select the **Thick Bottom Border** style.
5. Select the range **C36:F36.**
6. Click **Format, Cells,** and click the **Border** tab.
7. Select the **Double Line** style and click the preset **Outline** style. Notice the preview box. Click **OK.**
8. With the range **C36:F36** still selected, click the **No Border** style on the Borders button menu to clear the borders.
9. Click **Undo** to reverse the **No Border** style.
10. Click the **Borders** button and the **Draw Borders** option.
11. Select the thick line style and use the pencil cursor to outline the range **A5:F7.**
12. Click the **Erase** button on the Borders toolbar and erase the border in the ranges **A5:A7** and **F5:F7.**
13. Close the Borders toolbar but do not close the file.

Decimal Place and Negative Number Format

▶ Make settings for decimal places and commas with the toolbar buttons discussed earlier. However, formats for decimal places, commas, and for negative numbers, may be set by clicking the Number tab in the Format Cells dialog box, as shown in Figure 4.4.

- When *negative numbers* are the result of a calculation, the default format displays the value with parentheses. However, you can set negative values to display with a minus sign, in red with parentheses, or both. You need a color printer to print red numbers.

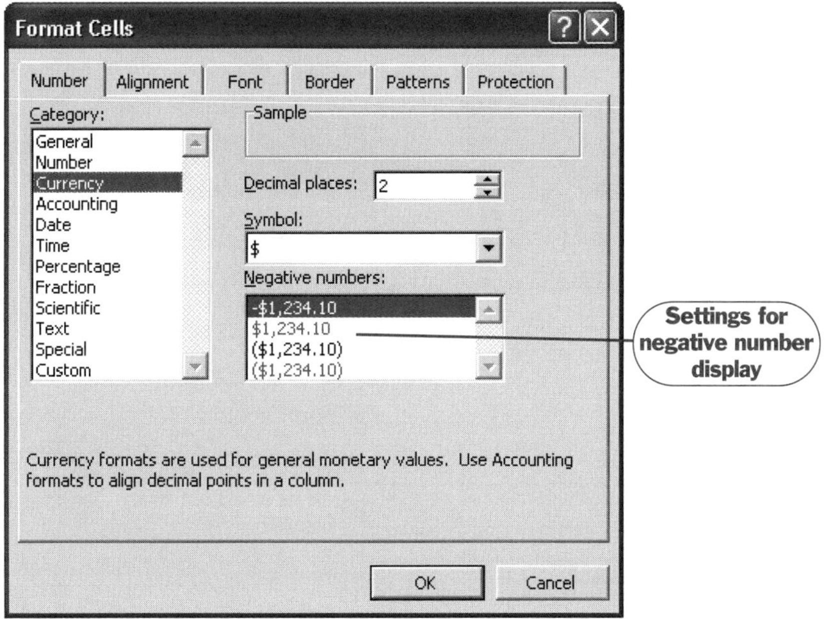

Figure 4.4 Format Cells dialog box, Number tab

TRY *it* OUT *E4-2*

1. Continue to work in the open file, or open **E4-2** from the Data CD.
2. Select **Cell E36.**
3. Click **Format, Cells,** and click the **Number** tab.
4. Click **Currency** in the Category list.
5. Select red negative numbers with parentheses.
6. Click **OK.**
7. Do not close the file.

Insert a Page Break

- A *page break* is the location on the page where one page ends and another begins. Excel automatically inserts a page break when data goes beyond the bottom and right margins of a page.
- Use the View, Page Break Preview commands to go into Page Break Preview, as shown in Figure 4.5, to view the existing page breaks to see if your worksheet will fit on one page. You can adjust the page breaks by dragging the dotted lines that represent the breaks. If you move the page breaks to include more rows, the cell size decreases to fit all rows on the page. Use the View menu to return to normal view.

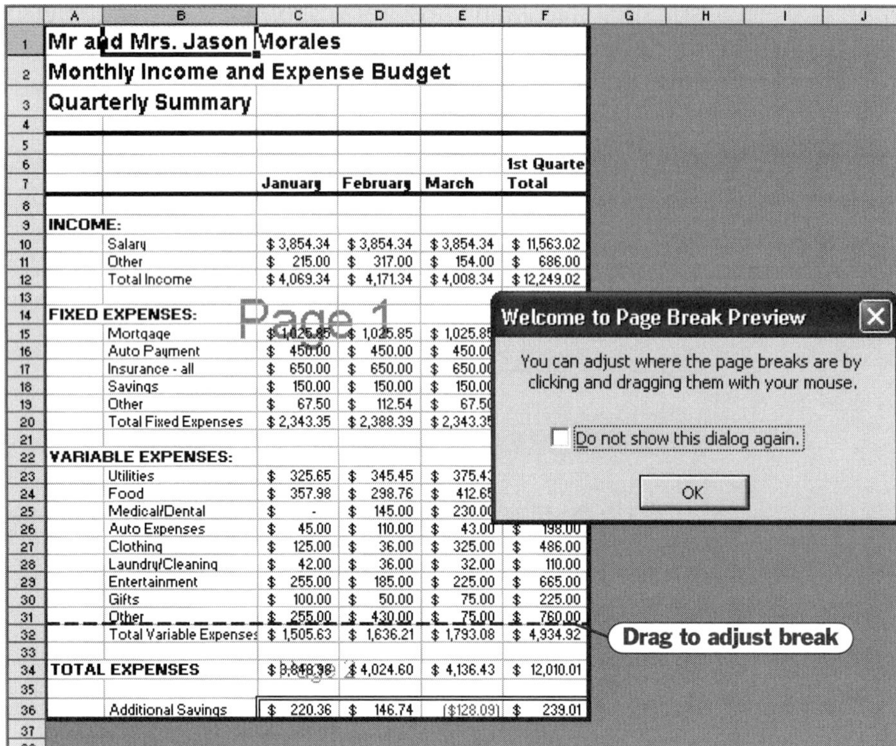

Figure 4.5 Page Break Preview

TRY it OUT *E4-3*

1. Continue to work in the open file, or open **E4-3** from the Data CD.
2. Click **File, Page Setup,** and click **Landscape** on the Page tab. Click **OK.**
3. Click **View, Page Break Preview** and close the Welcome to Page Break Preview dialog box.
4. Scroll down, if necessary, and notice the blue dotted line that breaks page 1 from page 2.
5. Drag the line down so that all the data appears on page 1.
6. Click **File, Page Setup,** and notice that the worksheet has been scaled to 84%. Note: The scaling percentage may vary depending on your system.
7. Print Preview the file and return to **Normal** on the View menu. Note that Portrait orientation would be a better choice for this worksheet.
8. Save the file **E4-3.** Close the file.

Lists

- Data arranged in columns with headers or in a table is called a list. You can sort or filter lists to arrange or find data.

Sort Lists

- You can use the Sort Ascending or Sort Descending buttons on the toolbar for quick sorts or use the Sort dialog box for additional features.

▶ To sort tables, select the entire table without the column headings and click Data, Sort. The Sort dialog box displays, as shown in Figure 4.6. Select the first-, second-, and third-level sort data and select ascending or descending sorts. The header row becomes the column names as long as the Header row option is selected and the headers are in the row above the table. You can re-sort or use the Undo and/or Redo buttons to return to the original settings.

EXCEL

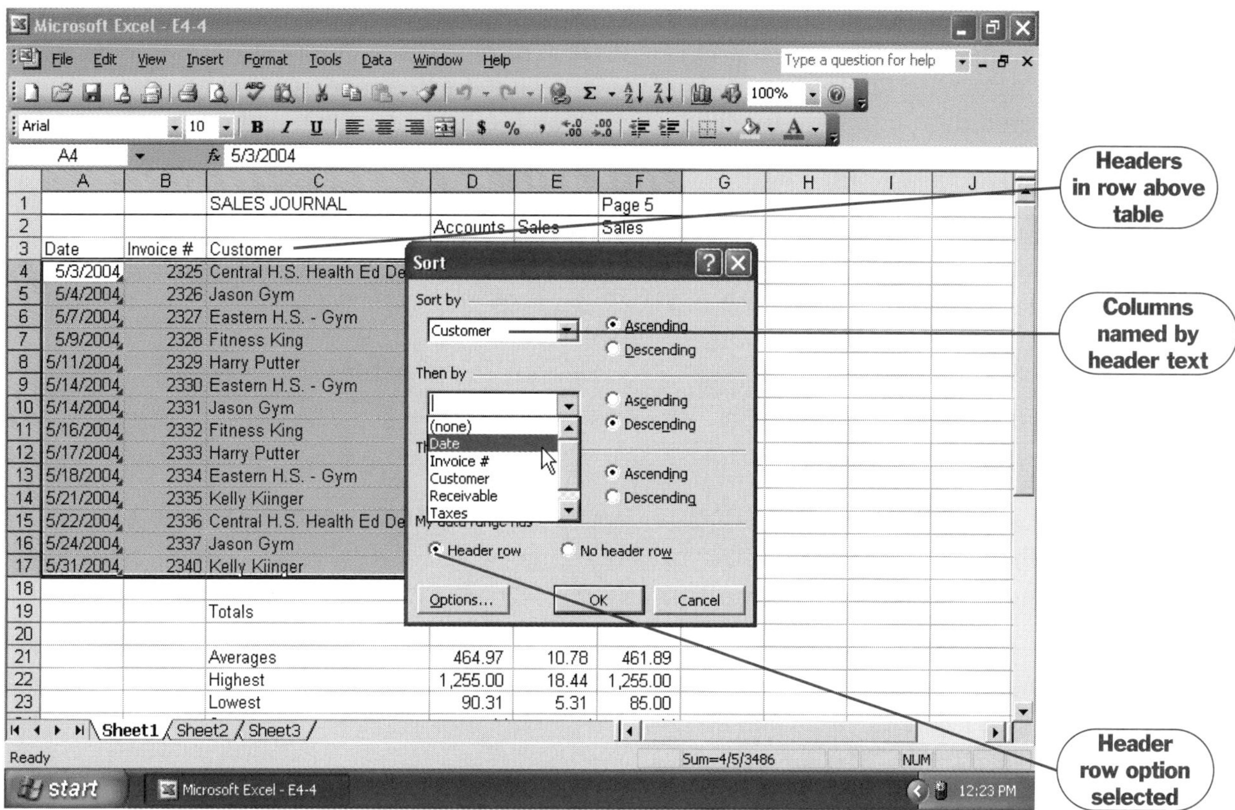

Figure 4.6 Sort data dialog box

TRY *it* OUT *E4-4*

1. Open **E4-4** from the Data CD.
2. Select the range **B26:B29.**
3. Click the **Sort Descending** button. Click the **Sort Ascending** button.
4. Select the range **A4:F17.**
5. Click **Data, Sort** to display the Sort dialog box.
6. Use the list arrows to Sort by **Customer** (ascending), and then by **Date** (descending).
7. Click **OK.** Note that the customers are in alphabetical order and the dates are in reverse chronological order by customer.
8. Click **Data, Sort** and Sort by **Invoice #** (ascending), and then by **(none).**
9. Click **Undo** and then click **Redo**.
10. Do not close the file.

Filter Lists Using AutoFilter

- *AutoFilter* is an Excel data list feature that applies a filter that hides all items that do not meet the criteria you set. To apply AutoFilter, select any cell in a list or the entire list and click Data, Filter, AutoFilter. A series of arrows appears at the top of each column. When you select a column and an item from the drop-down list, you are setting a criterion, which will filter the list and show only the items you select.
- For example, in the sales journal shown in Figure 4.7, after you select a customer's name from the drop-down list in the Customers column, you see all the sales made to that customer. All others are filtered out. To remove the filter, click All on the drop-down list, and deselect AutoFilter on the Data, Filter menu.

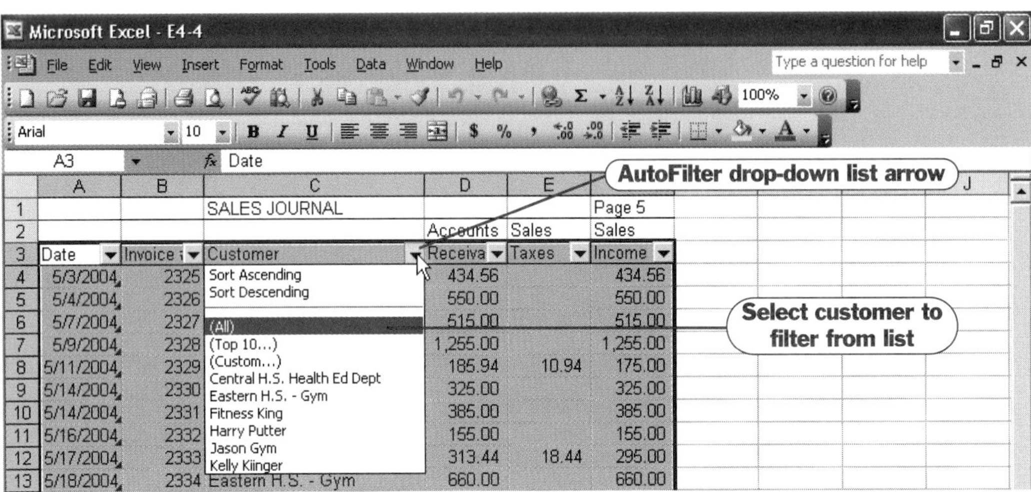

Figure 4.7 AutoFilter and drop-down filter list

TRY *it* OUT *E4-5*

1. Continue to work in the open file, or open **E4-5** from the Data CD.
2. Select the range **A3:F17** and click **Data, Filter,** and **AutoFilter.**
3. Click the list arrow in the **Customer** column, and select **Fitness King.** Sales to Fitness King appear.
4. Click the same **list arrow,** and select **Eastern H.S. - Gym.**
5. Click the **list arrow** again and select **All** to remove the filter.
6. Click **Data, Filter** and **AutoFilter** to remove the filter arrows.
7. Open your solution to E4-3 or open **E4-5a** from the Data CD.
8. Apply **AutoFilter** in the **VARIABLE EXPENSES** section.
9. Filter to find the amount of Medical/Dental expenses.
10. Remove the filter and deselect **AutoFilter.**
11. Close both files. Do not save.

A
1
2
3

GOAL
To create a budget analysis

SETTING THE STAGE/WRAPUP
File name: **4.1budget**

WHAT YOU NEED TO KNOW

- A *budget* is an analysis of the projected income and expenses for a future period. Companies create budgets based on past history and projections of future trends. Budgets are the basis for management decisions and plans for expenditures.
- Businesses analyze data *quarterly,* which is every three months, or four times a year, using percentages for ease of comparison.
- In this Rehearsal activity, you will create a budget analysis for the quarter ending September 30, 2004, for Time Out Sporting Goods. This company is comparing its budget for the third quarter, prepared earlier, with the actual expenditures to note the items that created the change in expected profits.

DIRECTIONS

1. Open **4.1budget** from the Data CD.
2. Drag column borders to make width changes as follows: **Column A** to **23.00**, **Columns B:E** to **12.00.**
3. Set the following formats as illustrated on the facing page:
   a. Select **Cell B1** and format for 18 point, Arial.
   b. Select the range **A3:F3** and apply a Thick Bottom Border for the row.
   c. Use the Draw Borders tool to add a Thick Bottom Border to the range **A7:F7.**
   d. Format **Columns B** and **C** for commas with no decimal places.
4. Enter a formula in **Cell D9** to find the Increase/Decrease from Budget. *(Hint: Actual-Budget)*
5. Click **Format, Cells,** and click the **Number** tab in the Format Cells dialog box. Click Number and format **Cell D9** for red negative numbers with parentheses and for commas with no decimal places. (Set the decimal places, and check the comma separator.)
6. Copy the formula down to **Cell D33.** Delete dashes or zeros where there are no entries in **Columns B** and **C.**
7. Enter a formula in **Cell E9** to find the % Increase/Decrease from Budget. *(Hint: D9/Budget)*
8. Format **Cell E9** for percent with two decimal places. (Click the **Percent** and **Increase or Decrease Decimal** buttons.)
9. Copy the formula down to **Cell E33.** Delete error messages as necessary.
10. Use the Draw border tool or the **Border** button to:
    - Add a Bottom Border under the values for **Rows 12** and **28.**
    - Add a single Top and Double Bottom border under the values for **Row 33.**

Continued on next page

11. Select the expenses in the range **A17:E28** and sort in ascending order by **Column A.**

12. Use AutoFilter on the Expenses list to find the Supplies data.

13. Display all the data and remove the AutoFilter.

14. In Page Setup, set to print in landscape mode and set Margins to horizontally and vertically center the worksheet. Click **OK.**

15. In Page Break Preview, extend the margins to fit the worksheet on one page.

16. Return to Normal view, Print Preview, and print the worksheet.

17. Save the file **4.1budget.** Close the file.

	A	B	C	D	E	F	G	H
1		Time Out Sporting Goods				18 point Arial		
2	Comparison of Budgeted Income Statement with Actual Income Statement							
3		For Quarter Ended September 30, 2004						
4					% of			
5				Increase/	Increase/	Thick bottom borders		
6		Budget	Actual	Decrease	Decrease			
7		3rd Qtr	3rd Qtr	from Budget	from Budget			
8	Revenue:							
9	Net Sales	442,500	443,780					
10								
11	Cost of Goods Sold:							
12	Cost of Goods Sold	287,625	291,456			Bottom border		
13								
14	Gross Profit	154,875	152,324					
15								
16	Expenses:							
17	Advertising/promotions	3,750	3,795					
18	Depreciation	5,625	5,625					
19	Insurance	4,500	4,500					
20	Legal/accounting	4,125	4,075					
21	Loan interest payments	6,375	6,375					
22	Miscellaneous expenses	2,850	2,815					
23	Payroll expenses	3,150	3,165					
24	Rent	56,250	56,250					
25	Repairs/maintenance	1,350	1,858					
26	Salaries/wages	20,738	20,805					
27	Supplies	1,988	1,850					
28	Utilities	1,935	1,925					
29	Total Expenses	112,635	113,038					
30								
31	Net Income before Taxes	42,240	39,286					
32	Taxes	12,672	11,786			Top and bottom double border		
33	Net Income after Taxes	29,568	27,500					
34								

Cues for Reference

Apply Borders

1. Select area to receive border.
2. Click **Border** button list arrow.
3. Click border style.

or

1. Click **Format, Cells,** and click the **Border** tab.
2. Select line, color, and style.
3. Click **OK.**

or

1. Click **Border** button list arrow.
2. Click **Draw Borders.**
3. Click the list arrow to set the line style.
4. Draw the border.

Format Decimals and Negative Numbers

1. Select data to format.
2. Click **Format, Cells,** and click the **Number** tab.
3. Click the **Number** category.
4. Use list arrows to select decimal settings.
5. Use list arrows to select negative number setting.
6. Select comma indicator, if appropriate.

Correct Page Break

1. Click **View, Page Break Preview.**
2. Drag margin line(s) to correct page break.
3. Click **View, Normal** to leave Page Break Preview.

Sort

1. Select the table data without the column headings.
2. Click **Data, Sort.**
3. Select the first, second, and third sort columns and sort order.
4. Click **OK.**

or

1. Select column to sort.
2. Click the **Sort Ascending** or **Sort Descending** button.

Apply AutoFilter

1. Select any cell in the list to filter or select the data.
2. Click **Data, Filter, AutoFilter.**
3. Click the list arrow in column to filter.

Show All Data in Filtered List

1. Click the list arrow in filtered column.
2. Select **All.**

End AutoFilter

- Click **Data, Filter,** and **AutoFilter** to deselect the feature.

GOALS

To create an income statement analysis and publish it to the Web

To practice using the following skill sets:

- Use numeric labels
- Indent text
- Insert and delete rows and columns
- Use formulas with absolute and relative reference
- Convert workbooks into Web pages
  - Add a background pattern
  - Use Web Page Preview
  - Save a workbook as a Web page
  - Publish to the Web

WHAT YOU NEED TO KNOW

Use Numeric Labels

- A *numeric label* is a value or number that is not used for calculations and is treated as a label or text. It is wise to enter numeric column headings as numeric labels so the values are not included in the total by mistake.
- To enter a number as a numeric label, begin the entry with an apostrophe ('), which serves as the *label prefix*. For example, to enter the year 2005, you would enter '2005. The label prefix appears only on the formula bar, and the number is formatted as left-aligned text, as shown in Figure 4.8. Note the Smart Tag indicator and message.

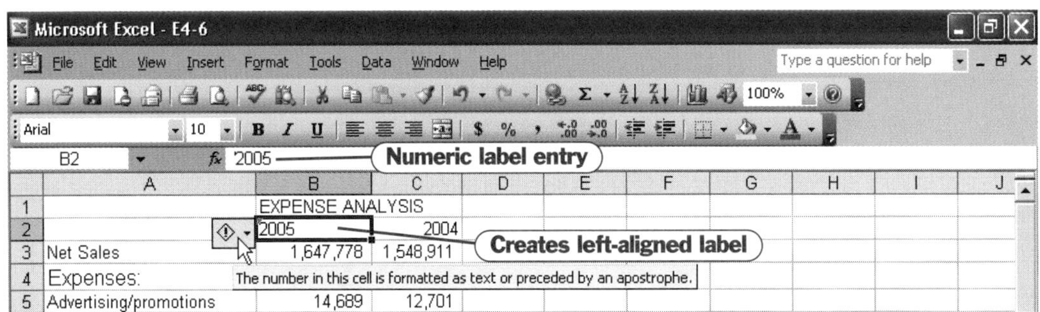

Figure 4.8 Numeric label and related smart tag

TRY*it* OUT *E4-6*

1. Open **E4-6** from the Data CD.
2. In **Cell B2,** overtype the value with a numeric label: **'2005.**
3. Enter a numeric label in **Cell C2** for 2004: **'2004.**
4. Center the labels.
5. Do not close the file.

Indent Text

▶ The indent text feature allows you to align text away from the left edge of the cell. Indent text quickly by clicking the Increase Indent button on the Formatting toolbar, and adjust or undo indentation by clicking the Decrease Indent button. Use indentations to set off lists of text from heading labels.

EXCEL

TRY *it* OUT *E4-7*

1. Continue to work in the open file, or open **E4-7** from the Data CD.
2. Select the range **A5:A16.**
3. Click the **Increase Indent button.**
4. Do not close the file.

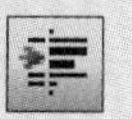

Insert and Delete Rows and Columns

▶ You can insert or delete columns or rows to change the structure of a worksheet. Always save a workbook before doing this to avoid deleting data in error.

▶ When you insert a column or row, existing data shifts to allow for the new space. Select the column or row where you want the new space to be and click Insert, Columns or Rows, or you can right-click to use the shortcut menu. If you want to insert more than one column or row, select that number of rows or columns, starting with the location where the new column or row begins. An Insert Options Smart Tag will appear with format options when columns or rows are inserted.

▶ When you delete a column or row, all data in that space is eliminated and existing data shifts to fill in the space. If you attempt to delete data by selecting cells, and not the entire row or column, the Delete dialog box opens, as shown in Figure 4.9, to provide options to clarify the request.

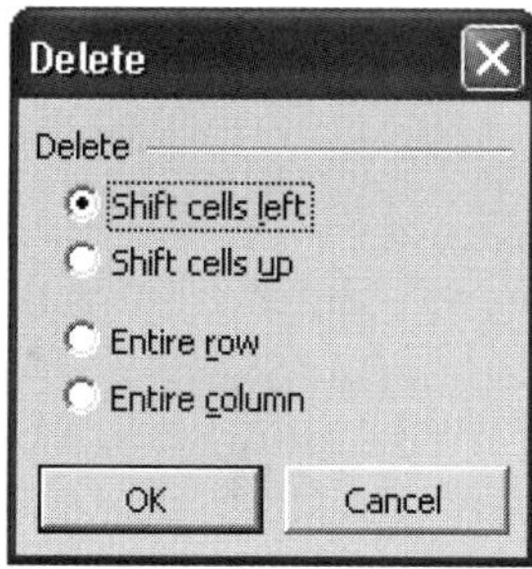

Figure 4.9 Delete dialog box

TRY *it* OUT *E4-8*

1. Continue to work in the open file, or open **E4-8** from the Data CD.
2. Select **Column C.**
3. Click **Insert, Columns** and note the Insert Options Smart Tag.
4. Select **Clear Formatting** on the Insert Options Smart Tag.
5. Select **Row 3,** right-click, and select **Delete** on the shortcut menu. The row and the data are deleted.
6. Select **Row 2** and insert a row.
7. Select the range **B5:C5** and click **Edit, Delete.** (Notice the Delete dialog box.)
8. Click **Cancel.**
9. Do not close the file.

Use Formulas with Absolute and Relative Reference

- When you copy formulas from one cell to another, the cell references change, relative to their new location. This is called *relative reference,* the most commonly used technique of entering and copying formulas.
- However, in some cases a value in a formula must remain constant when copied to other locations. This is called an *absolute reference.* To identify a value as an absolute reference, or constant, a dollar sign ($) must precede the column and row references for that cell.
- For example, you need an absolute reference to find the percentage each value in a list represents of the total, because the total must be the constant in each formula. Therefore, in the formula =B5/$B$17, B17 represents the total and is an absolute reference. When this formula is copied, B17 remains constant in the formula but B5, with no absolute reference code, changes relative to the formula location. You can enter the dollar signs ($) in the formula by keying them in or by pressing the F4 key.

TRY *it* OUT *E4-9*

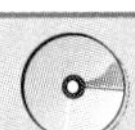

1. Continue to work in the open file, or open **E4-9** from the Data CD.
2. In **Cell B17,** check the formula on the formula bar.
3. Copy the formula to **Cell D17** and check the formula (copied with relative reference).
4. Enter a label in **Cells C3** and **E3:** `% of Total.`
5. Enter a formula in **Cell C5** to find the percentage each expense is of the total. (Hint: **=B5/$B$17:** press the equal sign, click **B5,** press **/,** click **B17,** press the **F4** key to enter the dollar signs.)
6. Format the value for percent with no decimal places.
7. Use the fill handle to copy the formula down to **Cell C16** for all expenses.
8. Check the formulas for each expense (copied with absolute reference).
9. Find the total in **Cell C17** and format for percent (100%).
10. Complete the formulas for Column E.
11. Save the file as **E4-9.** Do not close the file.

Convert a Workbook into a Web Page

- You can make workbooks available to employees or stockholders who may be in various locations by saving all or part of a workbook as a Web page. A *Web page* is a location on an Internet server, part of the World Wide Web, which can be reached and identified by a Web address. Web pages have an .mht or .html file extension.

Add a Background Pattern

- A background may be added to a worksheet to enhance its display. The background pattern does not print, but will be retained if the worksheet is published as a Web page. Click Format, Sheet, Background and select a graphic to use for the pattern. The graphic will fill the sheet. Remove the background by clicking Format, Sheet, Delete Background.

Use Web Page Preview

▶ Before you save an Excel workbook as a Web page, carefully edit and check the content, then save the file. You can preview your worksheet without publishing it, as shown in Figure 4.10, by clicking File, Web Page Preview. Close the Web Page Preview window to edit the worksheet as necessary.

EXCEL

EXPENSE ANALYSIS				
	2005	% of Total	2004	% of Total
Expenses:				
Advertising/promotions	14,689	3%	12,701	3%
Depreciation	21,544	5%	21,544	5%
Insurance	18,000	4%	18,000	4%
Legal/accounting	15,965	4%	13,165	3%
Loan interest payments	25,500	6%	25,500	6%
Miscellaneous expenses	10,644	2%	8,576	2%
Payroll expenses	11,434	3%	10,322	2%
Rent	225,000	50%	204,000	49%
Repairs/maintenance	6,547	1%	5,439	1%
Salaries/wages	82,434	18%	81,342	20%
Supplies	6,805	2%	5,765	1%
Utilities	7,487	2%	6,987	2%
Total Expenses	446,049	100%	413,341	100%

Figure 4.10 Worksheet with background in Web page preview

TRY it OUT E4-10

1. Continue to work in the open file, or open **E4-10** from the Data CD.
2. Click **Format, Sheet, Background** and open the Sample Pictures folder.
3. Select the **Blue hills** picture file and click **Insert.**
4. Click the **Print Preview** button and note that the background does not print. Close the Print Preview window.
5. Click **File, Web Page Preview.** (The worksheet with its background is displayed as a Web page.) Close the Web Page Preview window.
6. Save the file as **E4-10.**

Save a Workbook as a Web Page

▶ To save your workbook as a Web page, click File, Save As Web Page to open the Save As dialog box with Web page settings. You can save the entire workbook or the selected sheet, and add interactivity. The *Interactivity* setting allows users to make changes to the workbook on the Web site.

▶ To create a title for your Web page, click the Change Title button. The Set Page Title dialog box opens, as shown in Figure 4.11, and the title you enter appears centered over your worksheet on the Web page.

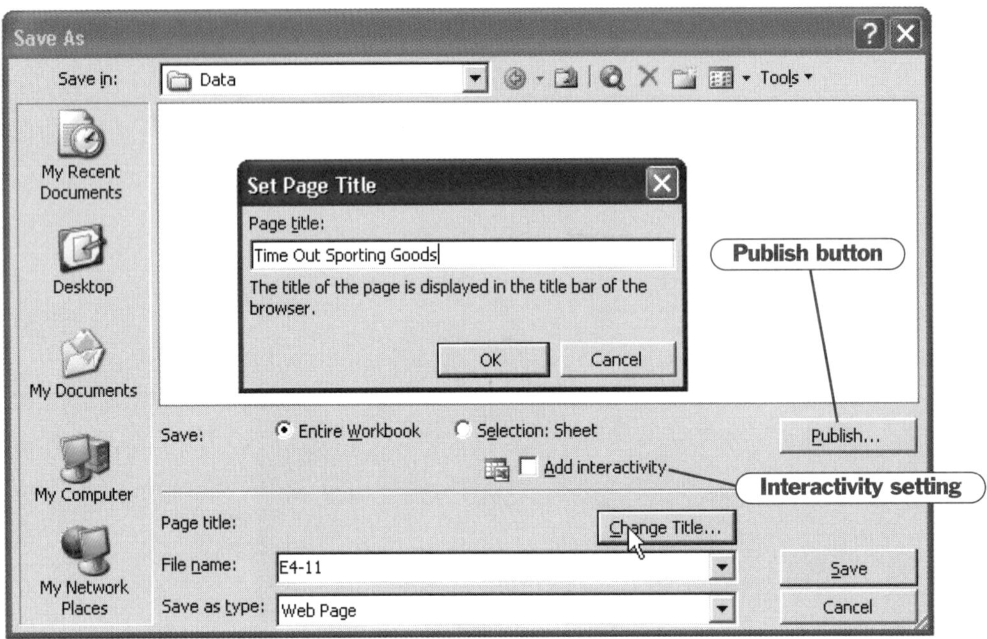

Figure 4.11 Save As Web Page and Set Title dialog box

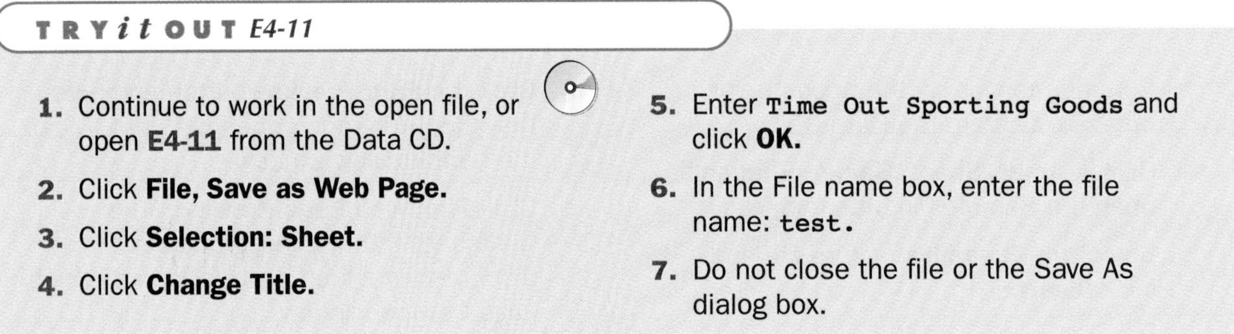

TRY *it* OUT *E4-11*

1. Continue to work in the open file, or open **E4-11** from the Data CD.
2. Click **File, Save as Web Page.**
3. Click **Selection: Sheet.**
4. Click **Change Title.**
5. Enter `Time Out Sporting Goods` and click **OK.**
6. In the File name box, enter the file name: `test.`
7. Do not close the file or the Save As dialog box.

Publish to the Web

▶ After you name the file and choose the save settings, click Publish, and click Browse to select a local disk folder as the publish location. On the Publish as Web Page dialog box, as shown in Figure 4.12, check Open published web page in browser, and click Publish. The published page is saved to your local drive and the Web page opens in Internet Explorer or your Web browser for you to preview.

▶ If you added interactivity, you can now make changes to the workbook in the browser; otherwise, you need to go back to the Excel file to make any changes. When your edits are complete, you can republish the Web page to your public location.

- Some Web site hosting companies let you publish Web pages directly to the Internet, but you or your facility must sign up for an account. Some accounts are free if you accept advertisements that automatically appear on your site.

EXCEL

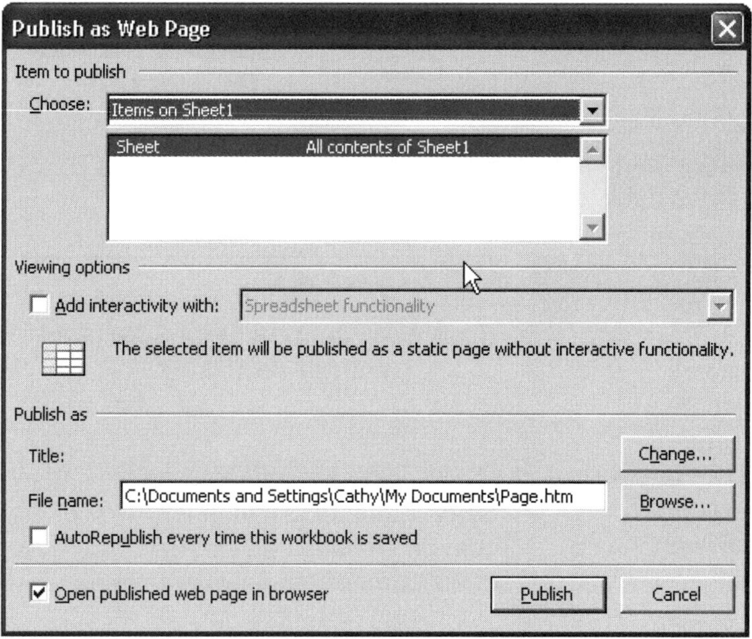

Figure 4.12 Publish as Web Page dialog box

TRY *it* OUT *E4-12*

1. Continue to work in the open file.
2. Click **Publish.**
3. Click **Browse** and select location for the file. Click **OK.**
4. Check **Open published web page in browser.** Click **Publish.** (The file will open in Internet Explorer or your default browser.)
5. Review the data, and then click the **Close** button.
6. In the worksheet, bold the title in **Cell B1.**
7. Format the totals in **Cells B17** and **D17** for currency with no decimal places, adjusting column width as necessary.
8. Republish the worksheet:
   a. Click **File, Save as Web Page.**
   b. Click **test.**
   c. Check **Republish:Sheet.**
   d. Click **Publish** on the Save As dialog box.
   e. Click **Publish** on the Publish as Web Page dialog box.
9. Note the edits and close the browser.
10. Save the file as **E4-12.** Close the file.

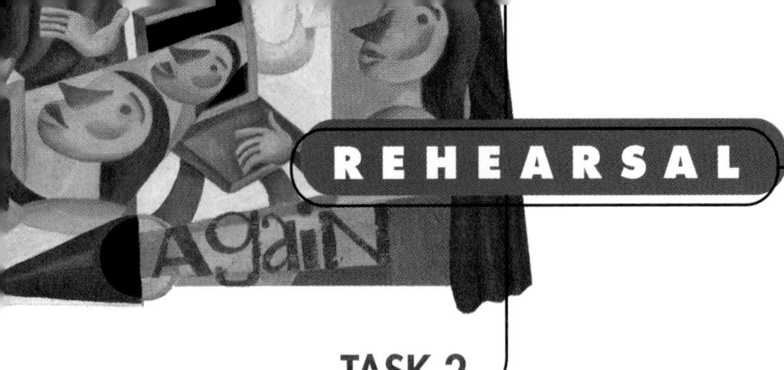

GOAL
To create an income statement analysis with absolute reference formulas and to save the file as a Web page

SETTING THE STAGE/WRAPUP
File name: 4.2is

WHAT YOU NEED TO KNOW

- At the end of the year companies prepare an *income statement* to show the income, expenses, and profits for the year. The current income statement data is compared to the statement for the previous year to determine trends.
- To analyze the data, we compare the percentage each item is of net sales for each period. Because net sales are used as a constant in every formula for this analysis, it is necessary to use an absolute reference.
- In this Rehearsal activity, you will prepare a comparison of summary income statements for Time Out Sporting Goods for two years, and save it as a Web page.

DIRECTIONS

1. Open **4.2is** from the Data CD and adjust column width as necessary.
2. Insert two rows at **Row 5.**
3. Indent text in the range **A8:A9.**
4. Select **Column C** and insert two columns. Create column headings as illustrated on the facing page, using numeric labels where necessary.
5. Enter a formula in **Cell C8,** using an absolute reference, to find the percentage each line is of net sales.
6. Format the result for Percent style. (The answer in **Cell C8** should be 100%, because this is the net sales value.)
7. Copy the formula down for each item.
8. Delete unnecessary formula results.
9. Delete **Row 12.**
10. Enter a formula in **Cell F8** to find the percentage of net sales.
11. Format the result for percent, copy the formula, and clear unwanted results.
12. Add borders as shown in the illustration on the facing page.
13. Check your formats and results.
14. Save the file as **4.2is.**
15. Add a background pattern. Preview the worksheet as a Web page. Close the preview.
16. Save the file as a Web page with the same file name. Change the title to: `Financial Data.`
17. Publish the file to your directory and open the published Web site in your browser.
18. Close the browser and the file.

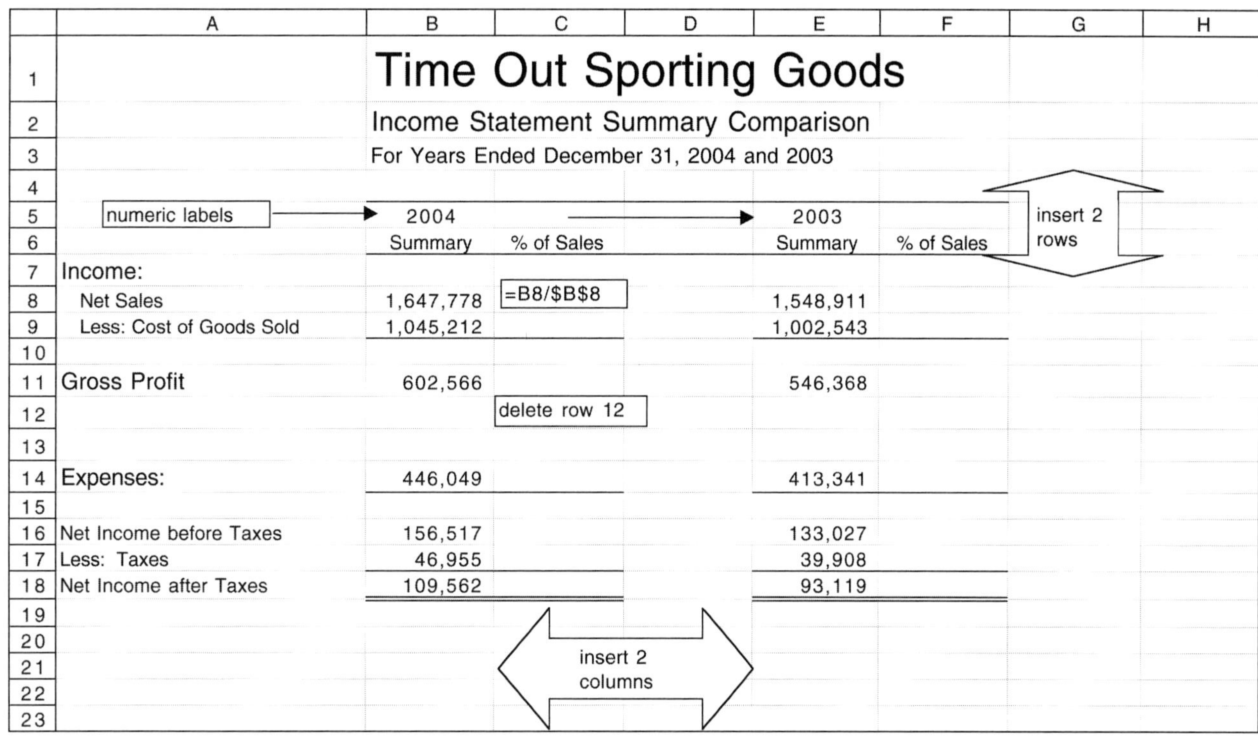

	A	B	C	D	E	F	G	H
1		Time Out Sporting Goods						
2		Income Statement Summary Comparison						
3		For Years Ended December 31, 2004 and 2003						
4								
5	numeric labels	2004			2003		insert 2	
6		Summary	% of Sales		Summary	% of Sales	rows	
7	Income:							
8	Net Sales	1,647,778	=B8/$B$8		1,548,911			
9	Less: Cost of Goods Sold	1,045,212			1,002,543			
10								
11	Gross Profit	602,566			546,368			
12			delete row 12					
13								
14	Expenses:	446,049			413,341			
15								
16	Net Income before Taxes	156,517			133,027			
17	Less: Taxes	46,955			39,908			
18	Net Income after Taxes	109,562			93,119			
19								
20								
21			insert 2 columns					
22								
23								

Cues for Reference

Indent Text
1. Select cells with data to indent.
2. Click **Increase Indent** button.

Insert Rows or Columns
1. Select row(s) or column(s) at the insertion point.
2. Click **Insert, Column** or **Insert, Row.**

Enter Numeric Label
1. Enter apostrophe (').
2. Enter a value.
3. Press **Enter.**

Delete Rows or Columns
1. Select row(s) or column(s) to delete.
2. Click **Edit, Delete.**

Use Absolute Reference Formulas
1. Enter formula, including absolute reference cell.
2. Press **F4** to insert dollar signs.

Add Background Pattern
1. Click **Format, Sheet, Background.**
2. Select the graphic.
3. Click **Insert.**

Save as Web Page and View in Browser
1. Click **File, Save as Web Page.**
2. Click **Change Title.**
3. Enter Web page title.
4. Click **OK.**
5. Name file.
6. Click selection: **Worksheet.**
7. Click **Publish.**
8. Click **Open published web page in browser.**
9. Click **Publish.**

TRYOUT

TASK 3

GOALS

To create a revenue analysis on multiple worksheets

To practice using the following skill sets:

- Apply and modify worksheet formats
  - AutoFormat
  - Fill Color and Font Color
- Modify workbooks
  - Insert and delete worksheets
  - Move and copy worksheets
  - Rename and format worksheet tabs
  - Group worksheets

WHAT YOU NEED TO KNOW

Apply and Modify Worksheet Formats

- Excel provides built-in formats that you can apply to a range of data.

AutoFormat

- The *AutoFormat* feature includes automatic formats for numbers, fonts, borders, patterns, colors, alignments, row heights, and column widths.
- When you select a range and click Format, AutoFormat, you find a selection of 16 table formats on the AutoFormat dialog box. As shown in Figure 4.13, all formats include only column headings and data. When you use AutoFormat, you must format title rows separately.

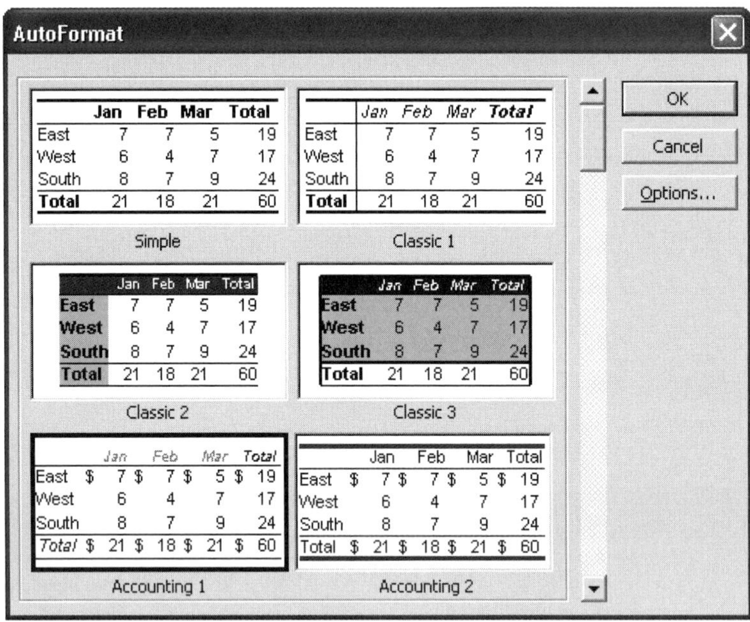

Figure 4.13 AutoFormat dialog box

TRY*it* OUT *E4-13*

1. Open **E4-13** from the Data CD.
2. Select the range **A4:F17.**
3. Click **Format, AutoFormat.**
4. View the AutoFormat selections.
5. Select the **Classic 3** AutoFormat.
6. Click **OK.**
7. Do not close the file.

EXCEL

Fill Color and Font Color

- The Fill Color and Font Color buttons on the Formatting toolbar provide a palette of colors to format a selected cell or range of cells. You can use them to format sections of an entire worksheet or titles on an AutoFormat worksheet.
- You can also apply shading or patterns to a selected range by clicking Format, Cells, and the Patterns tab. Select a color from the Cell shading color palette or a pattern from the Pattern palette, as shown in Figure 4.14. If you place your mouse pointer over a pattern or color in the Patterns tab, or over a color on the toolbar palettes, the name of the pattern or color will appear.

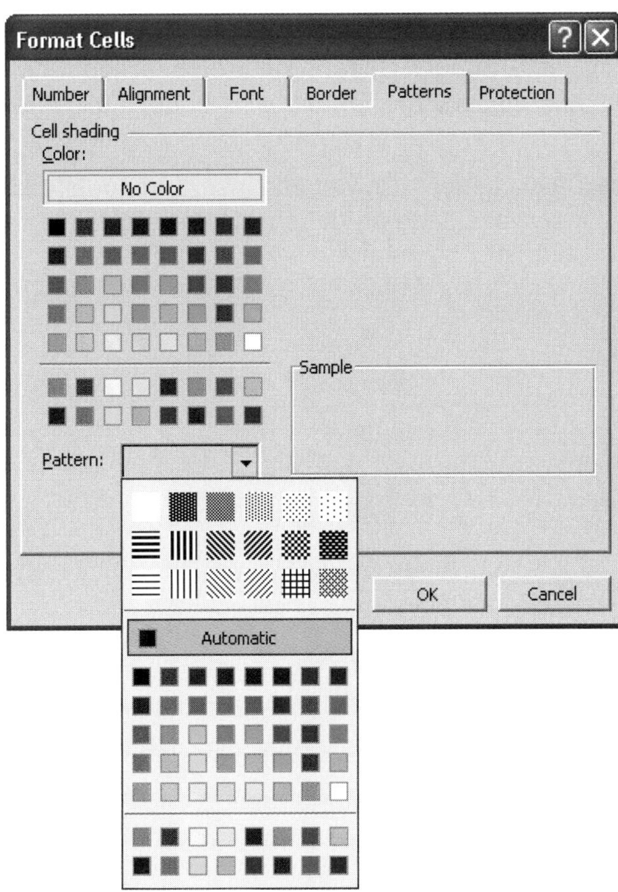

Figure 4.14 Format, Cells dialog box, Patterns tab

TRY *it* OUT *E4-14*

1. Continue to work in the open file, or open **E4-14** from the Data CD. 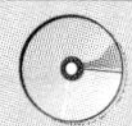
2. Select the range **A1:F3.**
3. Click the **Format, Cells, Patterns** tab, and click the **Pattern** list arrow to select the **12.5% Gray** pattern. Click **OK.**
4. Click elsewhere to view the setting. Click **Undo**.
5. Re-select the range **A1:F3.**
6. Click the **Fill Color** button list arrow and select **Gray 25%.** 
7. Click the **Font Color** button list arrow and select **Dark Blue.** 
8. Save the file **E4-14**. Close the file.

Modify Workbooks

- You can create the same worksheet for several months or for several divisions of the same company by using multiple worksheets in the same workbook. Excel lets you work with sheets in many ways. For example, you can delete, insert, rename, move, copy, and hide sheets.

Insert and Delete Worksheets

- There are three sheets, labeled Sheet1 through Sheet3, on the sheet tabs. The active sheet tab is white, and the inactive sheets are shaded. The *Tab Scrolling buttons* allow you to scroll hidden sheets into view.
- Select Insert, Worksheet to insert a worksheet. Or, you can insert and delete sheets by right-clicking a sheet tab and clicking Insert or Delete on the shortcut menu, as shown in Figure 4.15.

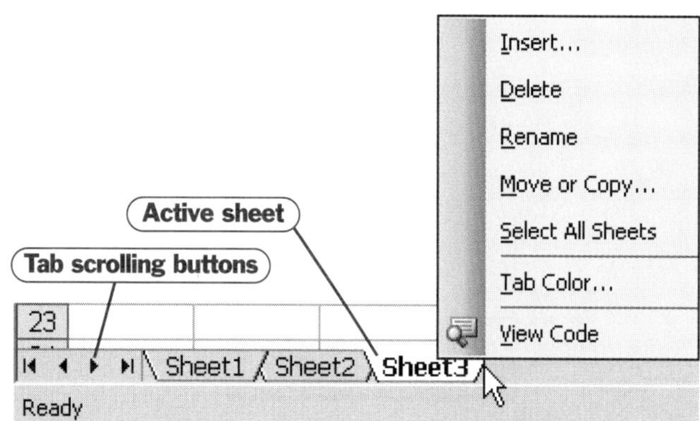

Figure 4.15 Sheet tabs and worksheet shortcut menu

TRY*it* OUT E4-15

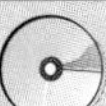

1. Open **E4-15** from the Data CD.
2. Click **Insert, Worksheet.** A new sheet appears.
3. Right-click any sheet tab.
4. Click **Insert** and click **OK** in the Insert dialog box. A new sheet appears.
5. Right-click **Sheet4.** Click **Delete.**
6. Delete **Sheet1.**
7. Do not close the file.

EXCEL

Move and Copy Worksheets

- You can move sheets by using the drag-and-drop method. When you drag the sheet tab, the mouse pointer displays a sheet that you can drop in any location.
- To move or copy a sheet, right-click the sheet tab and select Move or Copy. When the Move or Copy dialog box opens, as shown in Figure 4.16, notice that you have the option of moving or copying the sheet to another workbook, or to a location in the current workbook. When you copy a sheet, it will copy with the same sheet name, identified with a (2) to show it is a second copy.

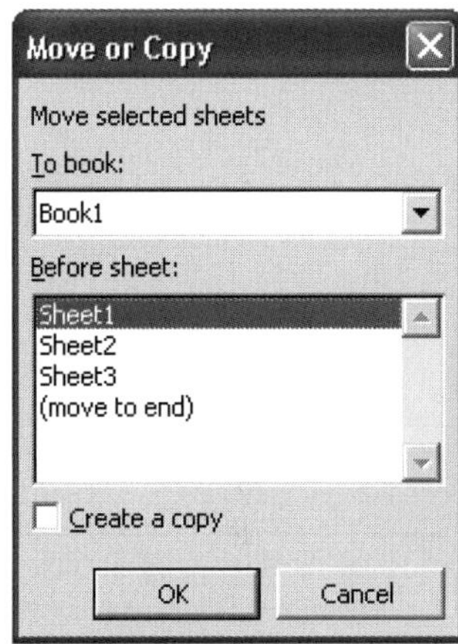

Figure 4.16 Move or Copy dialog box

TRY*it* OUT E4-16

1. Continue to work in the open file, or open **E4-16** from the Data CD.
2. Make a copy of the January sheet, and move it to the end:
   a. Right-click the **JANUARY** tab.
   b. Select **Move or Copy.**
   c. Click **Create a copy.**
   d. Select **(move to end).**
   e. Click **OK.**
3. On Sheet2, which shows February data, copy the sales in range **D7:D12,** then paste them into the **JANUARY (2)** sheet in **Cell D7.**
4. Click the **Match Destination Formatting** option on the Paste Options Smart Tag button.
5. Select and drag the **JANUARY (2)** sheet to the second worksheet position.
6. Do not close the file.

Rename and Format Worksheet Tabs

- To rename a sheet, you can select Rename on the shortcut menu, as shown in Figure 4.15, or double-click the sheet tab and enter the new name.

- You can format the color of the sheet tab by clicking Format, Sheet, Tab Color, or clicking Tab Color on the shortcut menu. Then, select the color from the Format Tab Color dialog box, as shown in Figure 4.17. The color will display at the bottom of the tab if it is active; otherwise, the color will fill the tab.

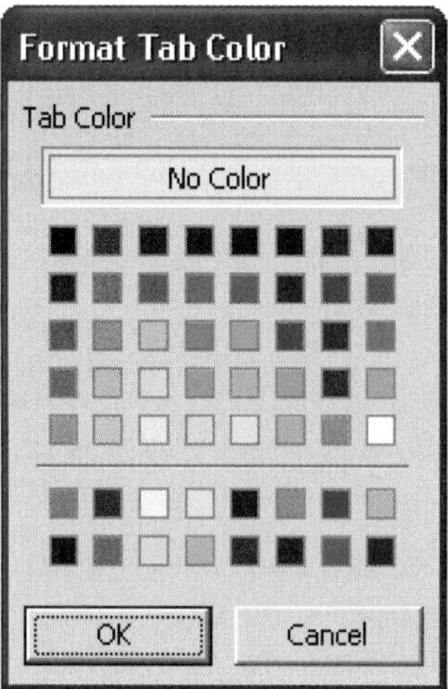

Figure 4.17 Format Tab Color dialog box

TRY *it* OUT *E4-17*

1. Continue to work in the open file, or open **E4-17** from the Data CD.
2. Double-click the **JANUARY(2)** sheet and rename it: **`FEBRUARY`**.
3. In **Cell F4,** enter **`FEBRUARY`** and widen the column.
4. Click **Sheet2,** right-click, and delete the sheet. Click **Delete** again to confirm deletion.
5. Click the **JANUARY** sheet, then click **Format, Sheet, Tab Color, Blue.** Click **OK.**
6. Right-click the **FEBRUARY** sheet, and click **Tab Color, Red.** Click **OK.**
7. Do not close the file.

Group and Print Worksheets

- If you are creating a worksheet that you want to copy to one or more worksheets, you can group the sheets and make the entries on all sheets simultaneously. To *group sheets,* click the first sheet, press and hold the Ctrl key, and select all other sheets. Or, if the sheets you want to select are next to one another, you can click the first sheet, press and hold the Shift key, and click the last sheet.
- To print a multiple worksheet file or to make print settings for the entire workbook, first group all sheets. Make print settings with sheets grouped, and click Entire workbook in the Print what section in the Print dialog box, as shown in Figure 4.18.

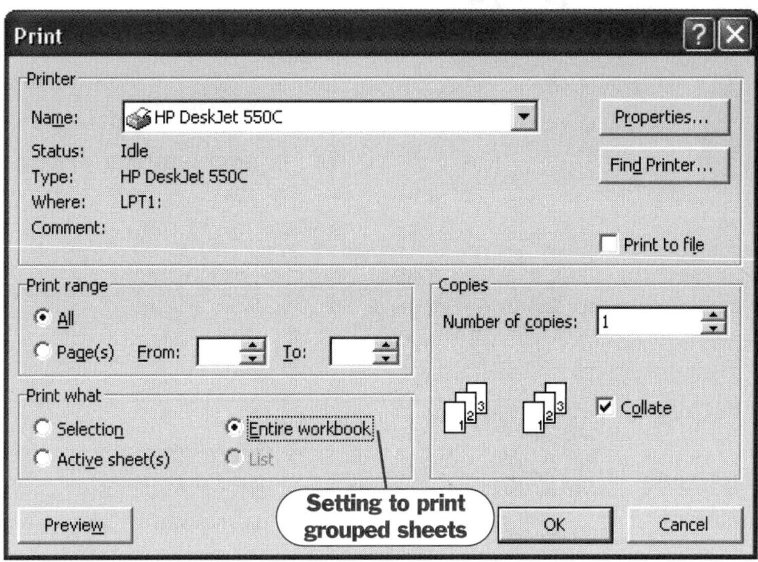

Figure 4.18 Print dialog box

TRY *it* OUT *E4-18*

1. Continue to work in the open file, or open **E4-18** from the Data CD.
2. Select the **JANUARY** tab, press and hold the **Shift** key, and click **FEBRUARY.** Notice that both sheets are active.
3. In **B3,** enter: `Boston Store.` Check both sheets.
4. With sheets still grouped, click **File, Page Setup.**
5. Deselect the **Gridlines** and the **Row and column** settings on the Sheet tab.
6. Click **OK.**
7. Click **File, Print.**
8. Click **Entire workbook, OK.**
9. Click **Sheet3** to clear grouping and check the **January** and **February** sheets.
10. Save the file **E4-18.** Close the file.

GOAL
To create a revenue analysis on multiple worksheets

SETTING THE STAGE
File name: **4.3revenue**

WHAT YOU NEED TO KNOW

- Income or revenue for a business will vary depending on seasonal or economic factors. Business owners analyze revenue figures to note trends, warning signs, and to make management decisions.
- Occasions Event Planning plans conferences, parties, seminars, meetings, etc. The company makes arrangements with vendors such as hotels, food caterers, printers, etc., to plan clients' events. Its revenues come from charges for consultation hours and a charge of 18% of all contract vendor bills.
- In this Rehearsal activity, you will create a revenue analysis workbook using a quarterly analysis on multiple worksheets.

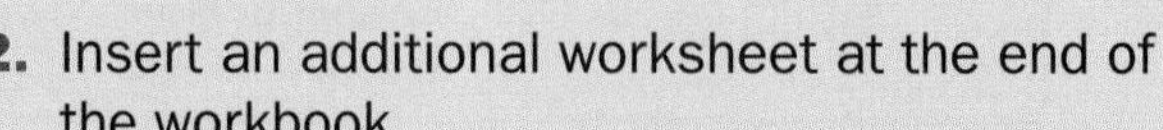

DIRECTIONS

1. Open **4.3revenue** from the Data CD.
2. Insert an additional worksheet at the end of the workbook.
3. Copy Column A from Sheet1 to remaining sheets:
   a. Copy **Column A** on Sheet 1.
   b. Group Sheets 2–4 by clicking **Sheet2,** pressing and holding the **Shift** key, and clicking **Sheet4.**
   c. Paste data to **Cell A1** on Sheet2. (Column A data will be on all sheets.)
   d. Widen **Column A** by double-clicking the column edge, if necessary.
4. Rename Sheets 1–4: 1st Qtr., 2nd Qtr., 3rd Qtr., and 4th Qtr.
5. Cut and paste **April, May,** and **June** data as illustrated on the facing page, from 1st Qtr. sheet to 2nd Qtr. sheet in **Cell B3.**
6. Group all sheets. (Select **1st Qtr.,** press and hold the **Shift** key, and click **4th Qtr.**)
7. Enter the following labels, formats, and formulas on all grouped sheets:
   a. In **Cell E3,** enter a column heading: `Total.`
   b. In **Cell E5,** enter a formula to add the values for the three months.
   c. AutoFill the formula down to Cell **E12.**
   d. In **Cell B13,** enter a formula to add the values for the month.
   e. AutoFill the formula for all months and the Total column.
   f. In **Cell B16,** enter a formula to find Fees on Contracts. (Hint: 18% of total billings for the month: =Total*18%.) AutoFill across for all months.
   g. In **Cell B18,** enter a formula to find Total Revenue by adding Fees and Consultation Revenues. AutoFill across for all months.
   h. Format all values for commas with no decimal places.

Continued on next page

i. Select the range **A3:E18** and AutoFormat the sheets using the List 1 format.
j. Select the range and **A1:E2,** and Fill Color the range using a light turquoise.

8. Ungroup sheets by clicking the **3rd Qtr.** sheet tab.
9. Group 3rd and 4th Qtr. sheets and widen **Columns B:E** to **8.00.** (These sheets have no data yet.)
10. Color sheet tabs as you prefer.
11. Group all sheets and print workbook by clicking **Entire workbook** in the Print dialog box in the Print what section.
12. Save the file **4.3revenue.** Close the workbook.

EXCEL

	A	B	C	D	E	F	G
1	OCCASIONS EVENT PLANNING						
2	Revenue and Billings Analysis						
3		January	February	March	April	May	June
4	Billings for Contract Vendors:						
5	Food/Catering	53445	43766	33232	56433	49876	65876
6	Hotels/Venues	87543	65888	73455	98665	82565	98665
7	Printing/Advertising	13232	10533	8564	11654	10112	14323
8	Music/Entertainment	45865	45865	45865	45865	45865	45865
9	Personnel/Speakers/Security	56454	43566	44345	53888	48975	57645
10	Audio/Visual	17654	15433	13245	16543	14987	17909
11	Computers/Special Equipment	54333	54678	32122	50323	42945	44567
12	Miscellaneous	11342	9453	6590	7645	6588	9856
13	Total						
14							
15	Revenue:						
16	Fees on Contracts						
17	Consultation Revenues	10540	11450	11340	12500	12600	11800
18	Total						
19							
20							
21							

1st Qtr. / 2nd Qtr. / 3rd Qtr. / 4th Qtr.

Cues for Reference

AutoFormat Data
1. Select worksheet data beginning with column headers.
2. Click **Format, AutoFormat.**
3. Click **AutoFormat style.**
4. Click **OK.**

Group Consecutive Sheets
1. Click the first sheet to group.
2. Press and hold **Shift.**
3. Click last sheet to group.

Group Nonconsecutive Sheets
1. Click the first sheet to group.
2. Press and hold **Ctrl.**
3. Click the second sheet to group.
4. Repeat as necessary.

Delete Sheet
1. Right-click sheet tab of sheet to delete.
2. Click **Delete.**
3. Click **OK.**

Insert Sheet
1. Right-click any sheet tab.
2. Click **Insert.**
3. Click **OK.**

Rename Sheet
- Double-click sheet and type new name

or

1. Right-click sheet tab of sheet to rename.
2. Click **Rename.**
3. Enter new name.

Format Tab Color
1. Right-click sheet tab to format.
2. Click **Tab Color.**
3. Click color.
4. Click **OK.**

TRYOUT

TASK 4

GOALS

To analyze purchase options using financial and date functions

To practice using the following skill sets:

- Use date formats and functions
  - Use the Insert Function button
  - Use financial functions
    - The PMT function
    - The FV function
    - The PV function
  - Use Paste Special, Values

WHAT YOU NEED TO KNOW

Use Date Format and Functions

- When you enter a date, Excel automatically creates a *serial value,* or you can use the date function, =DATE(year, month, day), to do so. The serial, or numeric, value allows you to use dates in formulas and represents the number of days from January 1, 1900, to the date entered. To view a date's serial value, format the date as a number using the General format, as shown in Figure 4.19.

	A	B	C	D	E
1	**Date Functions:**	Test dates:	1/1/1900	1/30/1900	1/30/2005
2	Serial or numeric values when dates formatted as General numbers		1	30	38382
3					

Figure 4.19 Dates formatted to show serial values

- Once you enter a date, you can change the format, as discussed in Lesson 1, by clicking Format, Cells, the Number tab, and then clicking Date from the Category list. The format of the date does not affect or change its serial value.
- You can enter the current date, based on the computer's clock, by pressing the Ctrl + ; (semicolon) keys. This method will retain the date entered today in the file. Or you can enter the current date and time by using =NOW(). This will change to the current date whenever the file is reopened.

TRY*it* OUT *E4-19*

1. Open **E4-19** from the Data CD.
2. Notice the test dates and select the range **C1:E1.**
3. Click **Format, Cells,** and the **Number** tab. Select **General** to format the dates as numbers. (These are the serial values.)
4. Reformat the range **C1:E1** as dates in a format that shows a four-digit year.
5. In **Cell C2,** press the **Ctrl** + **;** keys, to get today's date.
6. In **Cell D2**, enter `=Now()`, to get today's date and time.
7. In **Cell B7,** enter a formula to calculate 15 days after the date in **Cell B5.** *(Hint: =B5+15.)*

Continued on next page

TRY *it* OUT *E4-19 Continued*

8. In **Cells B8, B9,** and **B10,** enter formulas to calculate the dates for 30, 45, and 90 days after the purchase date in B5.
9. If dates did not appear as the answers in the range B7:B10, format the serial values in a date format.
10. Do not close the file.

EXCEL

Use the Insert Function button

- If you want to view all the functions available in Excel, you can click the AutoSum list arrow and click More Functions or use the Insert Function button on the formula bar.
- When you click the Insert Function button, an equal sign appears and the Insert Function dialog box opens, as shown in Figure 4.20. You can state what you want to accomplish in the Search for a function box, or find the function you need in the Or select a category box. The Function Arguments dialog box, shown in Figure 4.21 on the next page, appears after you select the function.

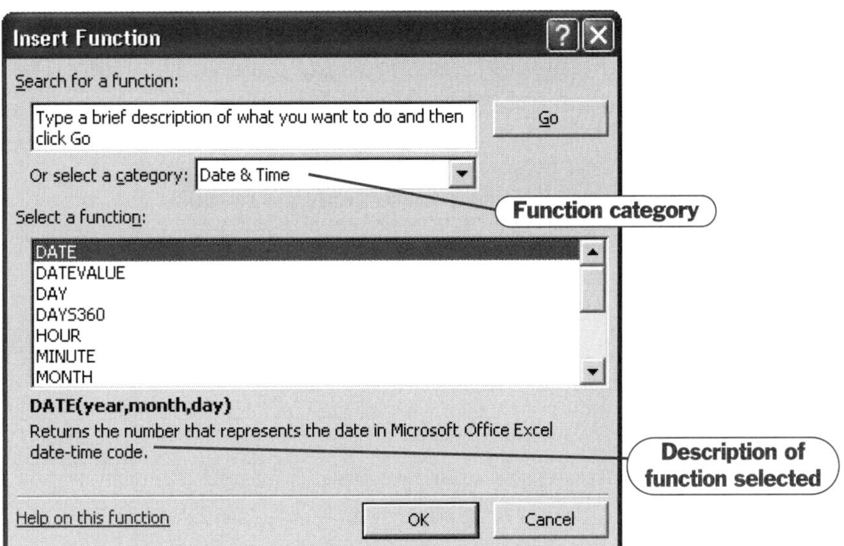

Figure 4.20 Insert Function dialog box

TRY *it* OUT *E4-20*

1. Continue working in the open file or open **E4-20** from the Data CD.
2. In **Cell E2,** click the **Insert Function** button on the formula bar to open the Insert Function dialog box.
3. In the Or select a category box, click the list arrow and select **All.** Scroll to view the functions.
4. Select the **Date & Time** category.
5. Scroll and double-click the **TODAY** function from the Select a function box and click **OK.**
6. Save the file as **E4-20.** Close the file.

Financial Functions

- *Financial functions* are used to analyze loans, calculate payments, and compute depreciation on assets. The financial functions most frequently used for analyzing loans are the PMT, FV, and PV functions.

The PMT Function

- The *PMT* (payment) function is used to calculate a loan payment when you know the principal (present value of loan), interest rate, and number of payments. The function and required arguments are =PMT(Rate, Nper, Pv).
  - *Rate* =interest rate per period. Because rates are generally stated as *annual interest* rates, you must divide the annual interest rate by 12 when calculating a monthly payment. For example, you would enter 7% annual interest rate as 7%/12.
  - *Nper* =number of payments.
  - *Pv* =present value or principal of loan.
- To enter financial functions, click the Insert Function button on the Standard toolbar, select the Financial category and the function. Once you select the function, the Function Argument box appears where you use the Collapse Dialog Box buttons to select function arguments. You may have to enter absolute reference codes or divide the annual interest rate after you select the appropriate argument, as shown in Figure 4.21. (Note: The last two arguments are optional here and in the other financial functions in this lesson.)

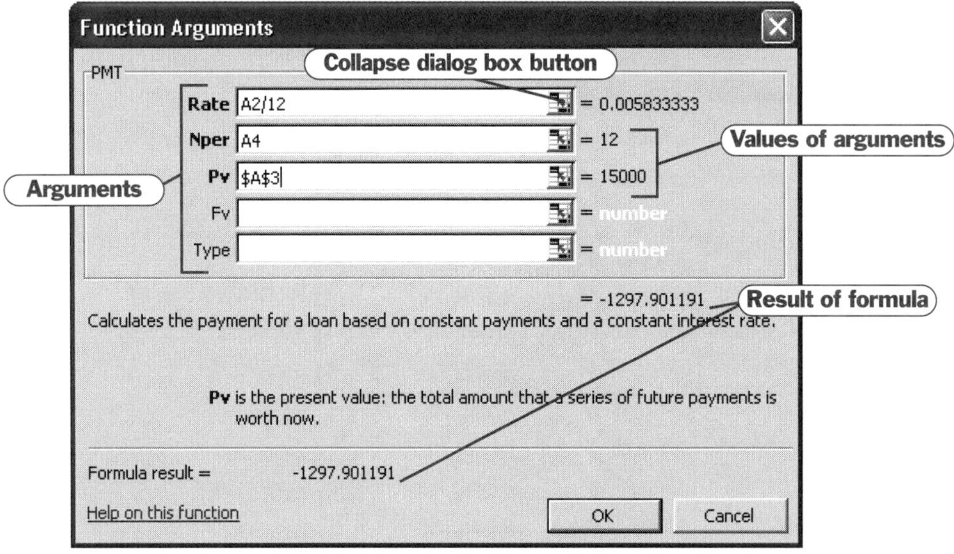

Figure 4.21 PMT Function Arguments dialog box

TRY it OUT *E4-21*

Note: You will find the monthly payment to repay $15000 over 12 months at 7% interest.

1. Open **E4-21** from the Data CD.
2. In **Cell E2,** click the **Insert Function** button on the formula bar, and select the **Financial** category in the Insert Function dialog box.

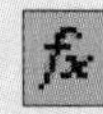

3. Click **PMT,** under Select a function, and click **OK.**

Continued on next page

TRY it OUT *E4-21 Continued*

4. In the Rate box, click the **Collapse dialog box** button and select **Cell A2.** Click the **Restore dialog box** button.
5. Next to **A2** in the Rate box, enter `/12` to divide the annual rate into a monthly rate.
6. In the Nper box, for number of payments, select **A4.**
7. In the Pv box, the principal, select **Cell A3,** and click **F4** to make it absolute. (For practice, not necessary here. Note the result.)
8. Click **OK.** (The payment is stated as a negative number that reduces the loan.)
9. Do not close the file.

EXCEL

The FV Function

- The *FV* (future value) function is used to calculate the future value of a series of equal payments, at a fixed interest rate, for a specific number of payments. You can use this function to calculate the value of equal savings deposits at the end of a period. The function and required arguments are =FV(Rate,Nper,Pmt), as shown in Figure 4.22.

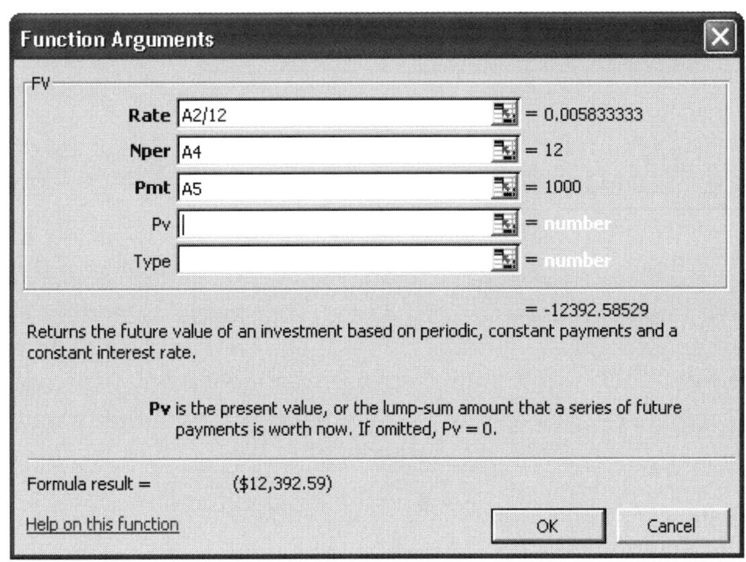

Figure 4.22 FV Function Arguments dialog box

TRY it OUT *E4-22*

Note: You will find the future value of 12 payments of $1000 earning 7% interest.

1. Continue to work in the open file or open **E4-22** from the Data CD.
2. In **Cell E3,** enter the FV function as follows:
   a. Click the **Insert Function** button and in the **Financial** category select **FV** function.
   b. For Rate, select **Cell A2,** an annual rate, which should be divided by 12.
   c. For Nper, select **Cell A4,** for 12 payments.
   d. For Pmt, select **Cell A5,** for $1000.
3. Click **OK.**
4. Do not close the file.

The PV Function

- The *PV* (present value) function is used to calculate the present value of a series of equal payments, at a fixed interest rate, for a specific number of payments. Therefore, you can calculate the principal, or money needed now, to generate equal payments in the future. The function and arguments are =PV(Rate,Nper,Pmt), as shown in Figure 4.23.

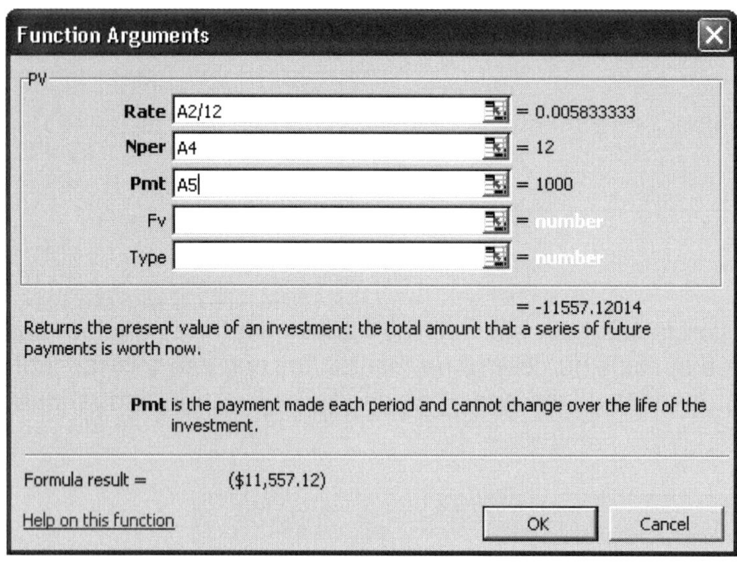

Figure 4.23 PV Function Arguments dialog box

TRY it OUT *E4-23*

Note: You will find the present value or money needed now at a 7% rate, to generate equal payments of $1000 in the future.

1. Continue to work in the open file or open **E4-23** from the Data CD.
2. In **Cell E4,** enter the PV function to find the present value of 12, $1000 payments, at 7%. (Divide the annual rate by 12.)
3. Check your formulas and answers against the Check column. (Absolute references, as shown in Figure 4.21, would be necessary if the formulas were to be copied.)
4. Do not close the file.

Use Paste Special, Values

- When you used the Copy and Paste functions in previous tasks, you copied the entire contents of a cell. If you want to copy and paste specific cell contents, use the Paste Options button, the Smart Tag that appears on the worksheet, or use the Paste button options list on the Formatting toolbar, as shown in Figure 4.24.

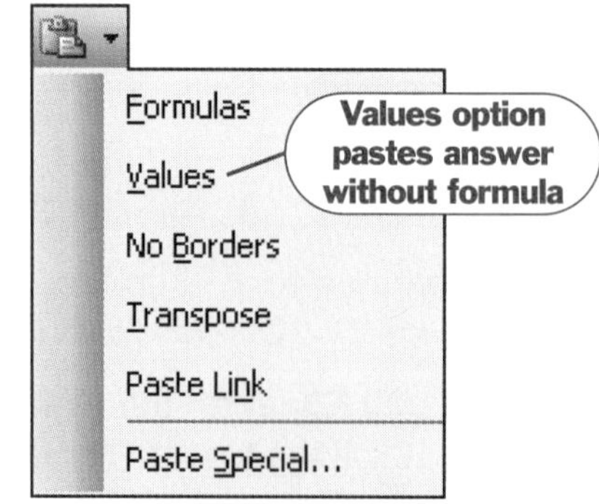

Figure 4.24 Paste button options list on the Formatting toolbar

▶ The Values option will paste the numeric value or answer without including the formula in cases where the formula will not work in the new location. You can also paste values and formats by selecting Paste Special on the Paste button options list shown in Figure 4.24, and then select Values and number formats. Or, it is faster to use the Paste Options button list on the worksheet, as shown in Figure 4.25, and select Values and Number Formatting.

EXCEL

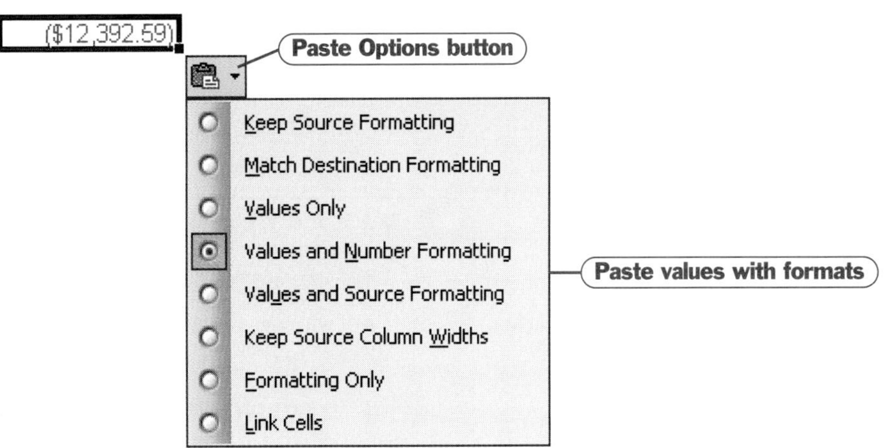

Figure 4.25 Paste Options button, options list

TRY *it* OUT *E4-24*

1. Continue to work in the open file or open **E4-24** on the Data CD.
2. Click **Cell E2,** which includes a formula and answer, and click **Copy.**
3. Click **Cell B8** and click **Paste.** (Zeros or a #REF error appears.)

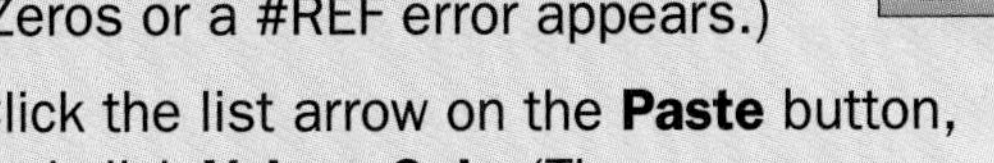

4. Click the list arrow on the **Paste** button, and click **Values Only.** (The answer appears.)
5. Check the formula bar for **Cells B8** and **E2.** Notice the difference.
6. Click **Cell E3,** which includes a formula and an answer, and click **Copy.**
7. Click **Cell B9,** click the **Paste** list arrow on the Standard toolbar, and click **Paste Special, Values and number formats** and click **OK.**
8. Copy the answer from **Cell E4** and paste it into **Cell B10**. Use the Paste Options button on the worksheet and select **Values and Number Formatting.**
9. Save the file **E4-24**. Close the file.

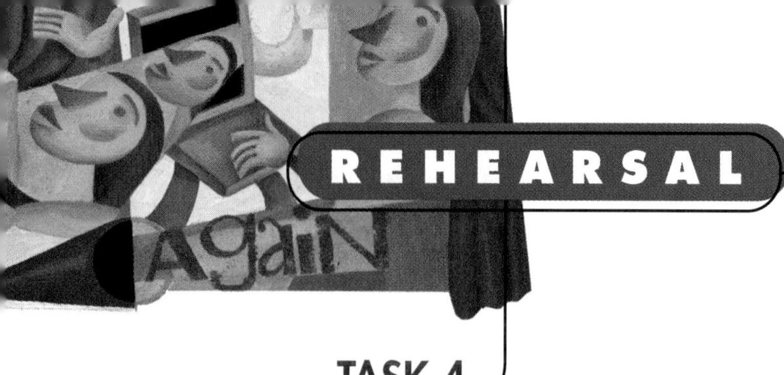

GOAL
To use financial and date functions to analyze the options for the purchase of equipment

SETTING THE STAGE/WRAPUP
File name: 4.4loan

WHAT YOU NEED TO KNOW

- When making a large purchase, individuals and businesses should analyze all the options for payment. Use financial functions to calculate the costs of the money over the time of the loan at the prevailing interest rates.
- Sellers often give buyers credit *terms* that involve discounts for early payment. Thus, the notation 2/30, 1/60, n/90 means that the buyer will get 2% off the bill if paid in 30 days, 1% if paid in 60 days, or the full amount is due in 90 days.
- When calculating the amount due after a 2% discount is taken, you can multiply by the *reciprocal,* the difference from 100%, or 98%, to calculate the discounted payment.
- In this Rehearsal activity, you will prepare a multiple sheet analysis to help In-Shape Fitness Centers consider payment options for additional equipment for the gym. The options include paying cash, taking a loan, or saving for the purchase.

DIRECTIONS

1. Open **4.4options** from the Data CD.
2. First view each sheet, select the **Purchase** sheet, and then group all sheets.
3. On the **Purchase** sheet, adjust column width and format the titles as illustrated on the facing page using **Blue** fill color and **White** font color. Note: Use another font if Eurostyle is not available.
4. In **Cell B9,** find the total amount of the purchase and format the row as illustrated in **Pale blue.**
5. Click any sheet to ungroup the sheets.
6. On the **Cash Options** sheet:
   a. In **Cell B15, B16,** and **B17,** enter formulas to calculate the dates for each discount and for full payment, using the Purchase Date plus the appropriate number of days.
   b. In **Cell C15,** enter a formula to find the purchase price after a 2% discount. *(Hint: Total Loan Principal*98%.)*
   c. In **Cell C16,** enter a formula to find the purchase price after a 1% discount.
   d. In **Cell C17,** enter the full payment amount.
   e. Copy **Cells B15:C17** and switch to the Loan Options sheet.
7. On the **Loan Options** sheet:
   a. In **Cell A13,** click **Paste**, then click the **Paste Options** button and select **Values and Number Formatting**.
   b. All loan calculations are for 12 months. In **Cell C13,** enter a financial function to find the monthly payment (PMT), using the annual interest rate in **Cell C12** divided by 12, 12 payments, and the principal in **Cell B13** with an absolute reference.

Continued on next page

c. Copy the formula across for all interest rate choices to **Cell G13.**

d. Enter formulas in Cells **C14** and **C15** and fill each formula across. *Note: Use absolute reference for the principal amounts in B14 and B15, and divide the annual rate by 12.*

8. On the **Fund Options** sheet: (saving for the purchase):

   a. In **Cell B14,** enter a formula to calculate the Total Payments if you make 12 payments of $1125.

   b. In **Cell B16,** enter a financial function to calculate the future value (FV) of the annual interest in **Cell A16** divided by 12, for 12 payments (absolute reference), for the payment in **Cell B12** (absolute reference).

   c. Copy the formula down for all interest rates.

9. Color the worksheet tabs in shades of blue.

10. Group all sheets and print the workbook.

11. Save the file **4.4options.** Close the file.

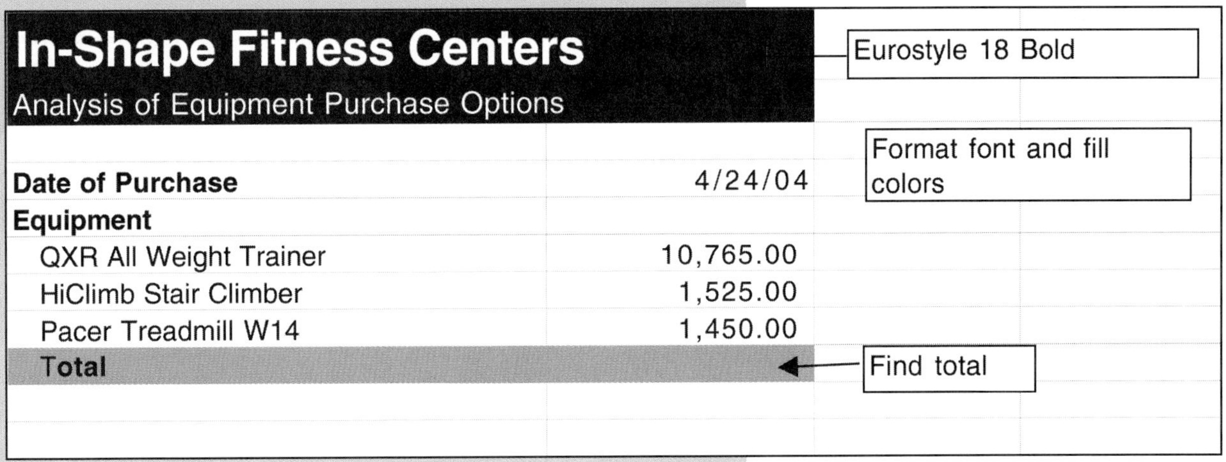

In-Shape Fitness Centers Analysis of Equipment Purchase Options		Eurostyle 18 Bold
		Format font and fill colors
Date of Purchase	4/24/04	
Equipment		
QXR All Weight Trainer	10,765.00	
HiClimb Stair Climber	1,525.00	
Pacer Treadmill W14	1,450.00	
Total	←	Find total

Purchase Sheet

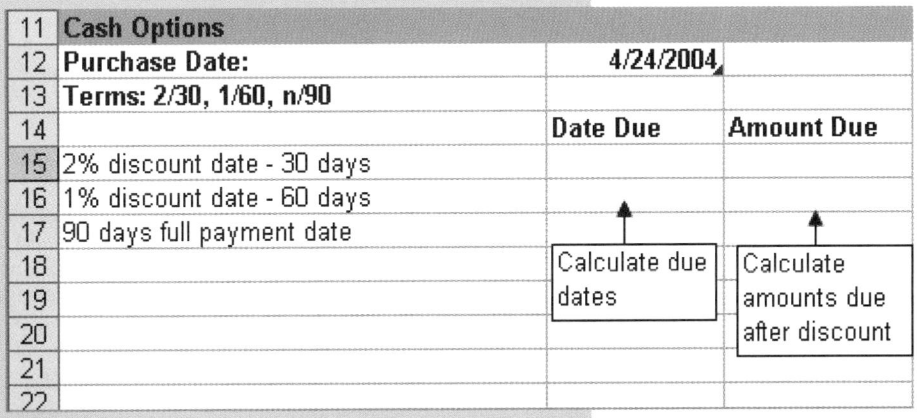

11	**Cash Options**		
12	**Purchase Date:**	**4/24/2004**	
13	**Terms: 2/30, 1/60, n/90**		
14		**Date Due**	**Amount Due**
15	2% discount date - 30 days		
16	1% discount date - 60 days		
17	90 days full payment date	↑	↑
18		Calculate due dates	Calculate amounts due after discount
19			
20			
21			
22			

Cash Options Sheet

EXCEL

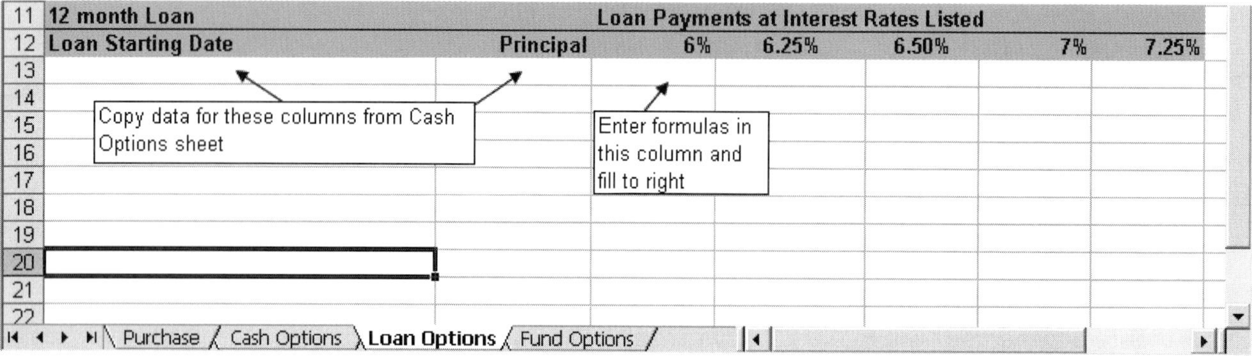

Loan Options Sheet

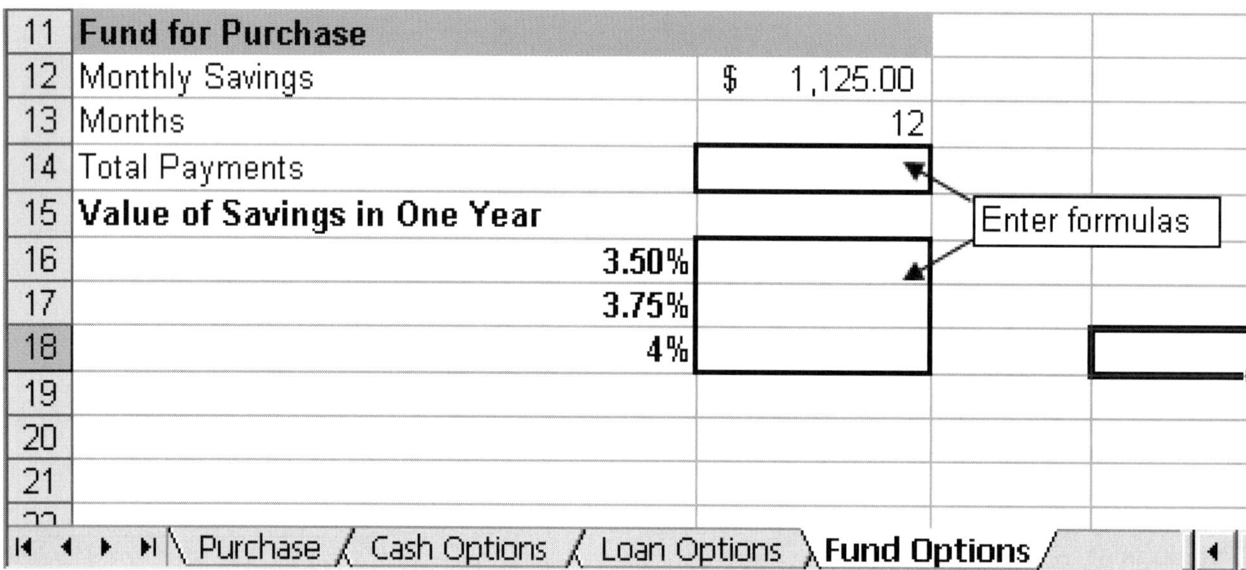

Fund Options Sheet

Cues for Reference

Paste Special, Values and Formatting

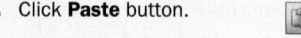

1. Select item to copy.
2. Click **Copy** button.
3. Select paste location.
4. Click **Paste** button. 

For Paste button on Toolbar

5. Click list arrow on **Paste** button.
6. Select **Values and Number Formatting** option and click **OK**.

For Paste Options button on worksheet

5. Click the **Paste Options** button.
6. Select the **Values and Number Formatting** option.

Insert a Financial Function

1. Click **Insert Function** button on formula bar.
2. Click list arrow to select **Financial** category.
3. Select **Function.**
4. Click **OK.**
5. Click the **Collapse Dialog Box** button to select each argument from the worksheet.
6. Add any additional formula items, as necessary (absolute reference or division of annual interest rates by 12).
7. Click **OK.**

SETTING THE STAGE/WRAPUP

Act I File name: **4p1.budget**
Act II File name: **4p2.incomebk**
Act III File name: **4p3.loanoptions**

EXCEL

Act I

You prepare accounting data for the Boston office of the Air Land Sea Travel Group. The office manager has asked you to develop an analysis of expenses for the last two years and has provided his estimate of expenses for the year 2005. This report will be e-mailed to the other offices in California and New York, so that they can complete similar analyses for consolidation into one report.

	A	B	C	D	E	F
1		Air Land Sea Travel Group				
2	Boston Office	Expense Budget Analysis				
3						
4		2003	2004	2005	Projected	
5	Expense	Actual	Actual	Budget	Change	% Change
6	Advertising	36,736	39,055	42,450		
7	Depreciation	10,200	10,790	10,790		
8	Insurance	5,640	5,855	6,140		
9	Miscellaneous	5,500	6,050	6,660		
10	Payroll	175,450	193,100	223,997		
11	Rent	39,500	41,500	41,500		
12	Supplies	8,800	9,350	9,900		
13	Utilities	6,820	7,015	7,535		
14	Total	288,646	312,715	348,972		

Follow these guidelines:

- Open **4p1.budget** from the Data CD.
- Create title lines for the report that include the company name, report name "Expense Budget Analysis," and "Boston Office." Insert rows if necessary, and format text using any desired font and font size.
- Reenter year column headings as numeric labels.
- Adjust column widths as necessary.
- Enter and fill formulas to complete Projected Change and % Change columns, and Totals row.
    - The Projected Change column shows the change the 2005 budget is from the 2004 actual numbers.
    - The % Change is the percentage the Projected Change is of the 2004 Actual data. Include the Totals line when you copy down the formula in Cell F5, to get the % Change for the Totals line.
- Total Cells B14:E14.
- Format numbers and percentages as appropriate.
- AutoFormat the column headings and data in one of the styles provided.
- Use color buttons to format the area above the column headings to match the AutoFormat selected.
- Check your work and save the file.

- Attach the worksheet to an e-mail to the other offices (using an address provided by your instructor). Write a note to accounting personnel requesting that they complete a similar analysis for their office so that all the reports can be consolidated.
- Save the file **4p1.budget.** Close the file.

Act II

You work in the company headquarters of Odyssey Travel Gear. All the retail stores have sent in income statement data over the last year. You have been asked to format the existing raw data and to create an analysis for each store on a separate worksheet. The resulting workbook will be saved as a Web page to provide corporate information.

	A	B	C	D	E	F	G
1		Odyssey Travel Gear					
2		Income Statement					
3		For the six months ended December 31, 2004					
4							
5		*Boston*	*Chicago*	*Dallas*	*Miami*	*San Diego*	*Totals*
6	*Income*						
7	**Net Sales Income**	625,206	743,036	350,510	362,232	499,854	2,580,838
8	**Less: Cost of Goods Sold**	393,822	467,307	228,765	231,575	315,752	1,637,221
9	**Gross Profit on Sales**	231,383	275,729	121,745	130,657	184,102	943,617
10							
11	*Expenses*						
12	**Selling**	79,978	92,019	45,323	45,403	62,852	325,575
13	**Administrative**	44,343	53,456	24,324	27,564	34,567	184,254
14	**Miscellaneous**	9,980	10,936	7,104	5,425	5,942	39,387
15	**Total**	134,301	156,411	76,751	78,392	103,361	549,216
16							
17	**Net Income Before Taxes**	97,083	119,318	44,993	52,265	80,741	394,401

Follow these guidelines:

- Use the file **4p2.incomebk** from the Data CD.

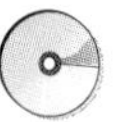

- Group the June 30 and December 31 worksheets, add a "Totals" heading in Column G, and calculate the totals.
- Add additional worksheets to create one for each store; rename and color the tabs accordingly.
- Group the store worksheets and paste Rows 1:3 and Column A data to all the store worksheets. On the store worksheets create columns named "June 30," "December 31," "Totals," and "% of Sales."
- Copy the data from the June and December sheets to the appropriate columns on each sheet.
- Group store worksheets and complete the Totals and % of Sales columns. You will need to use an absolute reference formula to find % of Sales.
- Format all store worksheets as a group. Use the AutoFormat and color and fill buttons to format the worksheet. Print a copy of the entire workbook.
- Save the file **4p2.incomebk** and save the workbook as a Web page with an appropriate title. Preview the workbook on your browser.

Act III

Trilogy Productions is contemplating the purchase or lease of warehouse space in Brooklyn, New York, to service its New York distribution center. The price of the building has been negotiated at $550,000. The company has researched loan costs and has determined that for 10-year loans, the interest rate decreases as the amount of the down payment increases. As an alternative, Trilogy could also sign a 10-year lease for the property. The company has asked you to develop an analysis of the options to help it make this decision.

	A	B	C	D	E	F
1		Trilogy Productions				
2		Property Purchase or Lease Options				
3						
4	Property Purchase					
5		Down	Down	Net		FV of Down
6	Price	Payment %	Payment	Principal		Payment @ 8%
7	550,000	20%				
8	550,000	25%				
9	550,000	30%				
10						
11				Monthly		
12	Net Principal	Interest	Payments	Payment		
13		8%	120			
14		7.75%	120			
15		7.5%	120			

EXCEL

Follow these guidelines:

- Use the file **4p3.warehouse** from the Data CD.
- Group both sheets and format the headings in Rows 1 and 2 using any color and/or font settings of your choice.
- On the Purchase sheet:
  - Calculate the Down Payment and Net Principal columns. (Hint: Down Payment %*Principal=Downpayment.)
  - Use Paste Options to copy the range D7:D9 to Cell A13.
  - Calculate the monthly payments beginning in Cell D13 for each set of loan terms using the PMT function.
  - Optional: Find the future value (FV) of each down payment in Column C, beginning in Cell F7, to show what the funds could do if they were invested in the business and not spent on the building. Use 8% as the growth Rate, 10 (years) for Nper, omit the Pmt argument, and use the down payment as the Pv.
- On the Lease sheet:
  - In Cell A7 find the total cost of the lease. (Hint: Payments*Monthly payment.)
  - To analyze the real cost of the lease payments, calculate the present and future value of the lease payments at a rate of 8%. The interest rate must be divided by 12 since these are monthly payments.
- Format both worksheet column headings using color, border, and/or font settings.
- Preview and print a copy of the workbook.
- Save the file **4p3.warehouse.**

LESSON 5

Financial Reports

In this lesson, you will learn to use logical functions, 3-D formulas, print settings, and the linking and formatting features in Excel to prepare financial reports.

Upon completion of this lesson, you should have mastered the following skill sets:

- Merge, center, and split cells
- Workbook layout and links
  - Split and arrange multiple workbooks
  - Paste link between workbooks
  - Hide workbooks
- Work with hyperlinks
  - Insert a hyperlink
  - Use a hyperlink
  - Edit a hyperlink
- Modify row and column layout
  - Hide and unhide rows and columns
  - Freeze and unfreeze rows and columns
- Modify page set up options
  - Print nonadjacent sections of a worksheet
  - Print titles
- Use logical functions in formulas
- Add headers and footers to worksheets
  - Add customized headers and footers
- Enter 3-D references
- Use styles
  - Apply a style
  - Define a new style
  - Modify a style
  - Remove a style
- Find and replace cell data and formats
  - Find cell data
  - Find and replace data and formats

Terms

Software-related

Merge and Center button
Splitting cells
Paste Link option
Hyperlink
Freeze Panes
Print Titles
IF statement
Headers and footers
3-D references
Styles
Find and Replace

Document-related

Schedule of accounts receivable
Schedule of accounts payable
Trial balance
Worksheet
Consolidated income statement
Balance sheet

TRYOUT

TASK 1

GOALS

To create a trial balance with linked accounts receivable and payable schedules

To practice using the following skill sets:

- Merge, center, and split cells
- Workbook layout and links
  - Split and arrange multiple workbooks
  - Paste link between workbooks
  - Hide workbooks
- Work with hyperlinks
  - Insert a hyperlink
  - Use a hyperlink
  - Edit a hyperlink

EXCEL

WHAT YOU NEED TO KNOW

Merge, Center, and Split Cells

- The *Merge and Center* button on the Formatting toolbar centers text over a selected range by merging the cells. To center a title across the top of a worksheet, enter the title in Column A, select the title and the range over which to center it, and click the Merge and Center button. The title is still in Column A, but it is centered in one large cell you created by merging the cells across the range. You can merge only one line at a time.
- Returning the cells to their normal width is called *splitting* the cells. You can set or remove these features in the Alignment tab of the Format Cells dialog box, as shown in Figure 5.1. Or, reselect the range and click the Merge and Center button to split the cells.

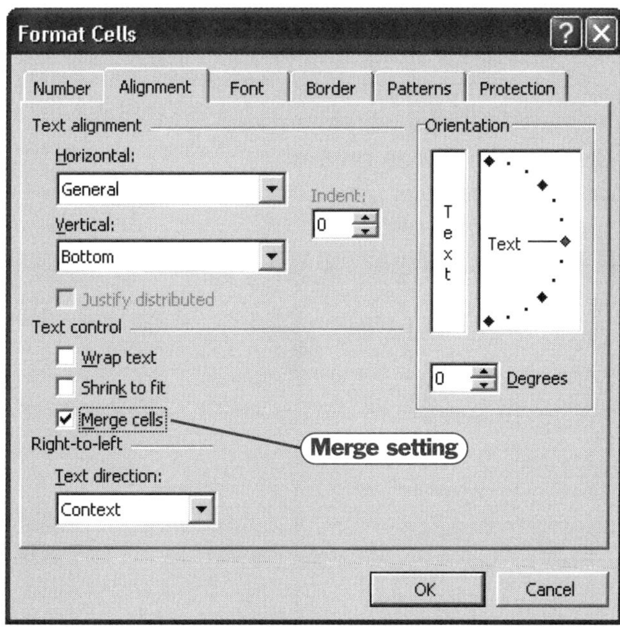

Figure 5.1 Format Cells dialog box, Alignment tab, Merge setting

TRY it OUT *E5-1*

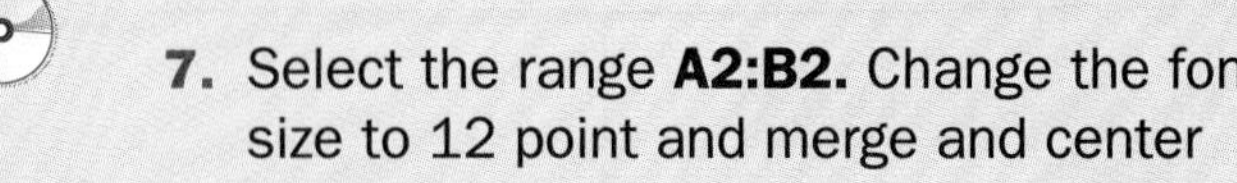

1. Open **E5-1** from the Data CD.
2. Group the AR and AP worksheets.
3. Select the range **A1:B1** and change the font size to 14 point.
4. Click the **Merge and Center** button to merge the cells and center the text.
5. Click the **Merge and Center** button again to split the cells.
6. Click the **Undo** button to keep the merge and center setting.
7. Select the range **A2:B2.** Change the font size to 12 point and merge and center the text.
8. Select Cell **A2** and click **Format, Cells** and the **Alignment** tab.
9. Deselect Merge cells and click **OK.**
10. Click the **Undo** button to keep the center setting.

11. Do not close the file.

Workbook Layout and Links

Split and Arrange Multiple Workbooks

- When working with more than one workbook, you can switch between workbooks using the file buttons on the taskbar or by selecting the file name from the list of open files on the Window menu, as shown in Figure 5.2.
- To view multiple workbooks, you can click Window, Compare Side by Side. Or click Window, Arrange to display the Arrange Windows dialog box, shown in Figure 5.3, which provides other options for arranging multiple files as well as for viewing windows of the active workbook.
- When you click Compare Side by Side, the files are arranged on the screen, as shown in Figure 5.4. The active file is indicated by the blue title bar. Click any cell in a worksheet to make that the active file. Click Close Side by Side on the Window menu to return to your previous view.

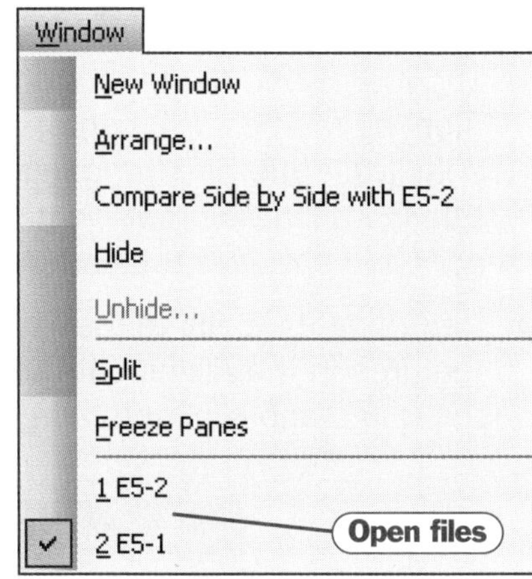

Figure 5.2 Window menu with list of open files

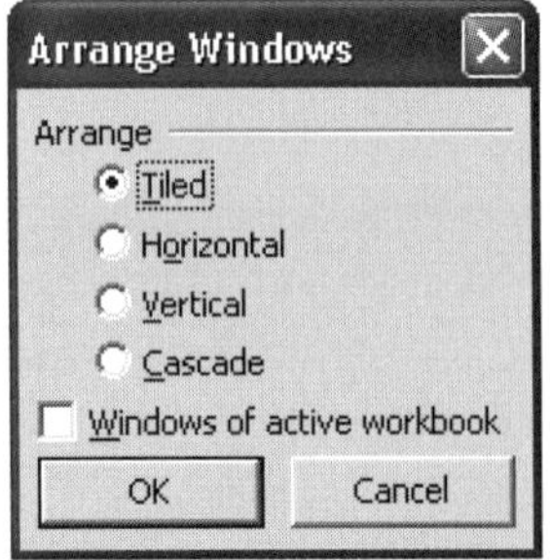

Figure 5.3 Arrange Windows dialog box

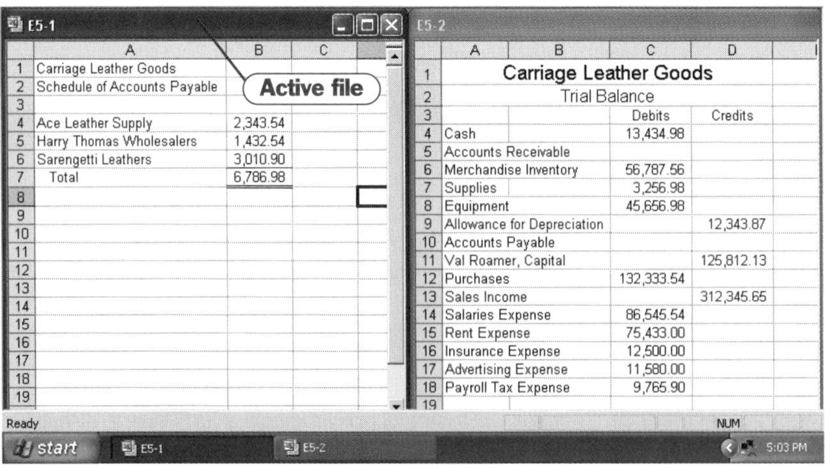

Figure 5.4 Files arranged vertically

TRY it OUT E5-2

1. Continue to work in the open file or open **E5-2A** from the Data CD.
2. Open **E5-2** from the Data CD and notice the totals. They should be in balance, but are not at this time.
3. Switch to the original file using the Window menu.
4. To arrange both files on the screen, click **Window, Compare Side by Side with E5-2.xls.**
5. To change the arrangement option, click **Window, Arrange,** and **Horizontal**. Click **OK**.
6. On any worksheet, click the scroll bar and notice the synchronous scroll.
7. Close the files without saving them.

EXCEL

Paste Link Between Workbooks

- In the last lesson, you used the Paste Special, Values feature to copy and paste the values or answer in a formula cell. Another Paste Special feature is the *Paste Link* option. This option links cells to another worksheet or workbook so that if you change the original data, it changes in the linked location as well.
- This feature is invaluable when combining schedules or data from various workbooks into a summary workbook, because any corrections you make to the source data will be reflected in the summary worksheet.
- To link a cell or cells, copy the cell(s), go to the location to link (which may be in another workbook), and click the Paste button list arrow on the Standard toolbar and click Paste Link from the drop-down list.

- On the formula bar of a linked cell you will see a reference to the original file. For example, =[E5-3A.xls]AR!$B$10, means that the cell is linked to Cell B10 on the AR sheet of the E5-3A file.
- Links between files are saved when you save and close the files. When you open a linked file, a prompt appears, as shown in Figure 5.5, requesting permission to update the file by activating the link. The file updates automatically, without a prompt, if you select that option in the Tools, Options menu.

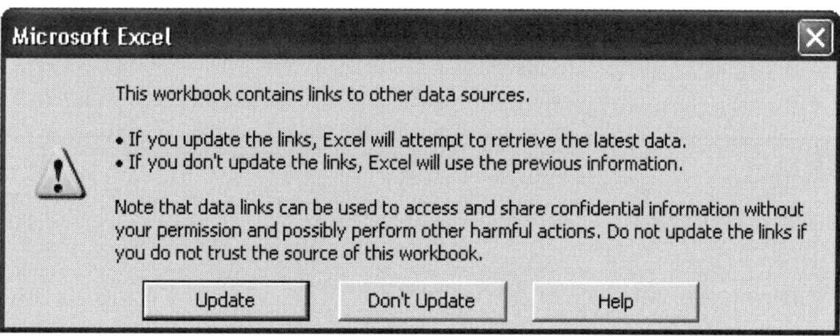

Figure 5.5 Prompt to update linked files

TRY it OUT *E5-3*

1. Open **E5-3** and **E5-3A** from the Data CD. Make sure they are both arranged vertically on the screen.
2. In **E5-3A** on the **AR** sheet, copy the total in **Cell B10.**
3. In **E5-3** in **Cell C5,** click the list arrow on the **Paste** button and click **Paste Link** to link the data.
4. Click **Cell C5** and notice the paste link reference on the formula bar.
5. In **E5-3A,** select the **AP** sheet and copy **Cell B7.**
6. In **E5-3** in **Cell D10,** click the list arrow on the **Paste** button and click **Paste Link** to link the data. Notice the totals now.
7. In **E5-3A,** select the **AR** sheet and correct Mary Cainter's balance (**Cell B5**) to: `$1311.55.`
8. Notice the updated Accounts Receivable total on both worksheets and the grand totals in **E5-3.**
9. Save both files **E5-3** and **E5-3A.** Do not close the files.

Hide Workbooks or Worksheets

- You may wish to hide a workbook or worksheet for presentation purposes. To hide a worksheet, select the sheet and click Format, Sheet, Hide. To redisplay a sheet, click Format, Sheet, Unhide and select the sheet to unhide. To hide a workbook, click Window, Hide and click Window, Unhide to redisplay the workbook.

TRY it OUT *E5-4*

1. Use the open files or open **E5-4** and **E5-4A** from the Data CD. If you open the files, select the Update option and make sure they are both arranged vertically on the screen.
2. Click anywhere in the AR worksheet and click **Format, Sheet, Hide.** The AR sheet is hidden.
3. In the same file, click **Window, Hide.** The workbook is hidden.
4. Click **Window, Unhide** and click **OK** to accept the file name.
5. Click **Format, Sheet, Unhide** and click **OK** to accept the sheet name.
6. Close both files without saving them.

Work with Hyperlinks

Insert a Hyperlink

- A *hyperlink* is a shortcut that allows you to jump to another location that provides additional or related information. When you click a hyperlink, it can open another workbook, a file on your hard drive or network, or an Internet address.
- To insert a hyperlink, first enter the text that will lead to the link. Then, click the Insert Hyperlink button on the Standard toolbar to open the Insert Hyperlink dialog box. As you can see in Figure 5.6, in the Link to pane on the left side of the dialog box you can select the location to hyperlink to, then select the file or location in the Look in box.

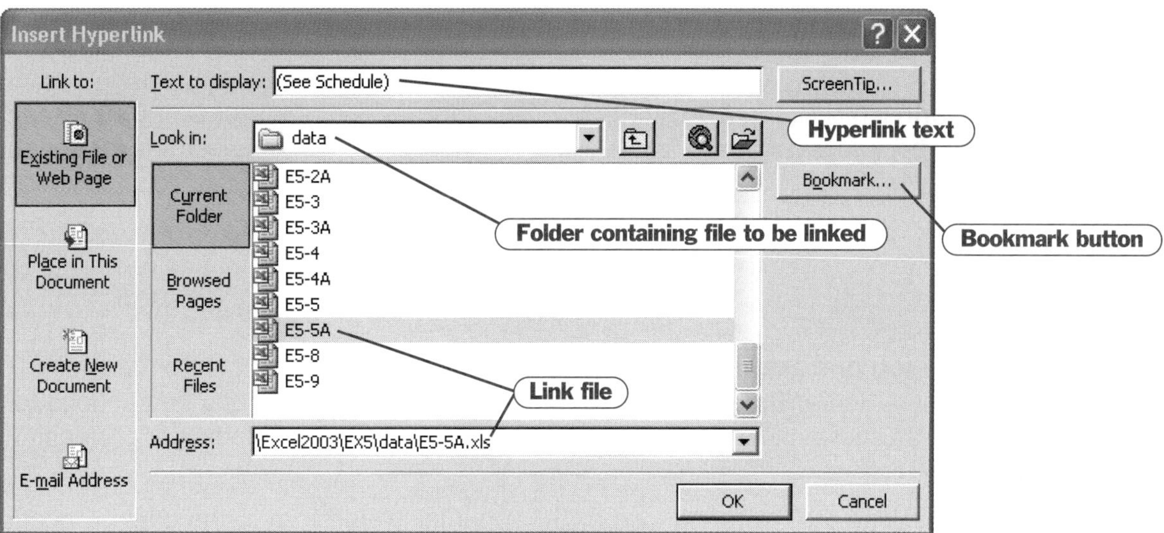

Figure 5.6 Insert Hyperlink dialog box

- To link to a specific location in a workbook, click the Bookmark button on the Insert Hyperlink dialog box to open the Select Place in Document dialog box. Figure 5.7 shows the dialog box and the sheet names in the file, as well as any other defined names.

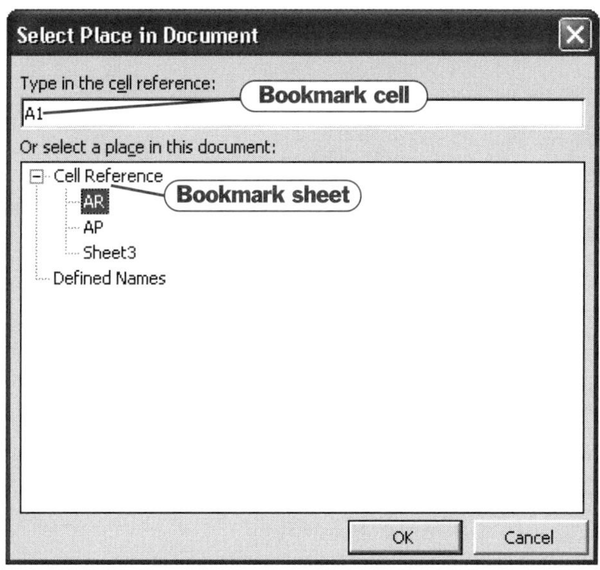

Figure 5.7 Bookmark dialog box

TRY *it* OUT *E5-5*

1. Open **E5-5** and **E5-5A** from the Data CD, select **Update** and arrange them on the screen vertically.
2. In **Cells B5** and **B10** of **E5-5**, enter: **`(See Schedule).`**
3. Widen **Columns A** and **B** to fit the widest entry.
4. In **Cell B5,** click the **Insert Hyperlink** button. 
5. In the Insert Hyperlink box, click **E5-5A** in the current folder.

Continued on next page

EXCEL

TRY*it* OUT *E5-5 Continued*

6. Click **Bookmark** and click the **AR** sheet. *(A specific cell is not necessary in this case.)*
7. Click **OK** twice.
8. Repeat Steps 4–7 for **Cell B10,** except change Step 6 to select the **AP** sheet.
9. Do not close the files.

Use a Hyperlink

- When you point to text or a graphic that contains a hyperlink, the mouse pointer becomes a hand to indicate the link. A ScreenTip also appears, stating the link reference and instructions for using a hyperlink, as shown in Figure 5.8. You can click once to follow the link or click and hold to select and edit the cell.
- After you view and close the file referenced by the hyperlink, you return to the original location.

4	Cash		13,434.98		
5	Accounts Receivable	(See Schedule)	9,994.15		
6	Merchandise Inventory				
7	Supplies				
8	Equipment				
9	Allowance for Depreciation				
10					
11					

file:///C:\Documents and Settings\Cathy\My Documents\Excel Solutions\Excel2003\EX5\solutions\s.E5-5A.xls - AR!A1 - Click once to follow. Click and hold to select this cell.

Figure 5.8 ScreenTip display for a hyperlink

TRY*it* OUT *E5-6*

1. Continue to work in the open files.
2. In **E5-5,** move your mouse pointer near **Cell B5** to view the ScreenTip.
3. Click **Cell B5** to jump to the AR sheet in **E5-5A.**
4. Close the file **E5-5A.**
5. In **E5-5,** click **Cell B10** to jump to the AP sheet in **E5-5A.**
6. Close the file **E5-5A.**
7. Do not close **E5-5.**

Edit a Hyperlink

- To edit only the hyperlink text, click the hyperlink, hold the mouse button down until the hand pointer changes to a plus sign, as shown in Figure 5.9, then edit the text on the formula bar.

Figure 5.9 Hold mouse pointer down for edit mode

▶ To edit any part of the hyperlink, right-click the hyperlink and click Edit Hyperlink from the shortcut menu. Use the Edit Hyperlink dialog box, shown in Figure 5.10, to edit any part of the hyperlink. It looks like the Insert Hyperlink dialog box, except that it has a Remove Link button.

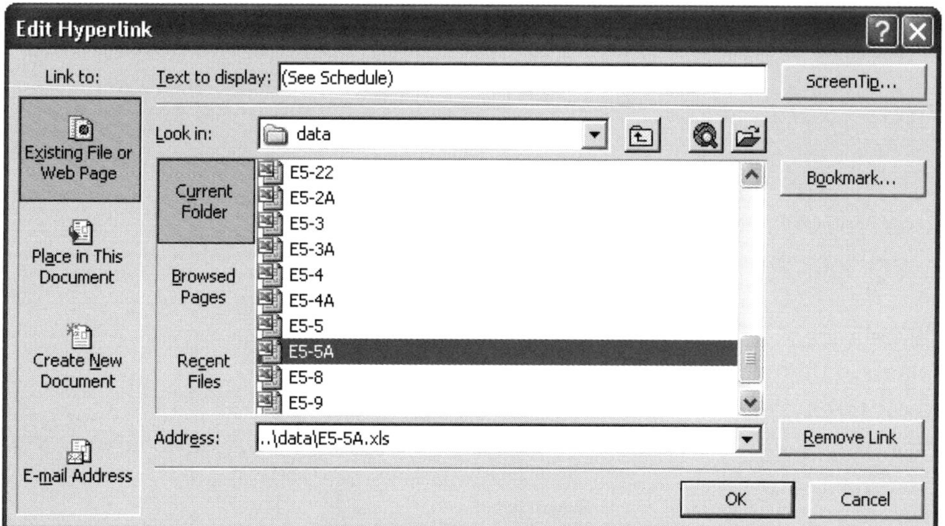

Figure 5.10 Edit Hyperlink dialog box

EXCEL

TRY *it* OUT *E5-7*

1. Continue to work in the open file.
2. Click and hold the mouse pointer on the hyperlink text in **Cell B5** until it changes to a plus sign.
3. In the formula bar, edit the hyperlink text to read: `(See AR Schedule).`
4. Right-click the hyperlink text in **Cell B10** and click **Edit Hyperlink.**
5. In the Text to display box, edit the text to read: `(See AP Schedule).`
6. Click **OK.** Adjust column width.
7. Save the **E5-5** file. Close the file.

GOAL
To create a trial balance with linked accounts receivable and payable schedules

SETTING THE STAGE/WRAPUP
File names: **5.1sched**
5.1tb

WHAT YOU NEED TO KNOW

- Schedules and trial balances are lists of account balances that a business prepares at the end of each month to check the accuracy of its accounts.
- The *schedule of accounts receivable* (AR) is a list of all the customers that owe the business money. The *schedule of accounts payable* (AP) is a list of all the business's creditors, or vendors, that it must pay.
- The *trial balance* is a list of all the accounts in a business ledger and their balances for the end of the month. Accounts either have debit (left side) or credit (right side) balances, depending on the type of account. For example, Accounts Receivable and Cash have debit balances and Accounts Payable and Sales have credit balances. In a trial balance, the debit and credit balances must be equal to prove the accuracy of the ledger, or book of accounts.
- In this rehearsal activity, Green Brothers Gardening wants to check its schedules and trial balance for the year ended December 31, 2004. You will merge and center the headings, paste link the schedule totals, correct the schedules, and create and edit hyperlinks on the trial balance.

DIRECTIONS

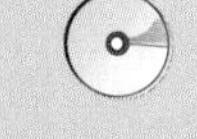

1. Open **5.1sched** from the Data CD.
2. Group both the Schedule of AR and the Schedule of AP sheets (Illustrations A and B).
3. Merge and center each of the three title rows over **Columns A** to **E.**
4. Bold titles in **Rows 1** and **2.**
5. Click **Sheet3** to ungroup the sheets and check the titles on both sheets.
6. Use AutoSum to find the totals on each schedule and format for currency.
7. Open **5.1tb** from the Data CD (Illustration C).
8. Merge and center each of the three title rows over **Columns A** to **E.**
9. Practice splitting the cells for **Row1** to return to the original settings.
10. Merge and center **Row1** again.
11. Use AutoSum to find the total of all the debits in **Column D** and all the credits in **Column E.**
12. Arrange both worksheets on the screen side by side.
13. Copy the total of the Schedule of AR (**5.1sched, Cell D22**) and paste link it to **Cell D7** on the trial balance, as illustrated on the facing page.
14. Copy the total of the Schedule of AP (**5.1sched, Cell D14**) and paste link it to **Cell E15** on the trial balance, as illustrated on the facing page.
15. Check to see if the trial balance actually balances; debits should equal credits.

Continued on next page

16. To find the error, the bookkeeper first checked the schedule accounts and found an error in the Miller Plant Supply AP account. The business owes $950, not $1950. Make the correction on the Schedule of AP sheet as illustrated and notice the automatic update to the trial balance.

17. Save the **5.1sched** and **5.1tb** files. Hide the **5.1sched** file.

18. Enter hyperlink text in **Column C** of the Trial Balance to refer users to the schedules, as illustrated.
    a. In **Cell C7,** enter: `(see Schedule of AR).`
    b. In **Cell C15,** enter: `(see Schedule of AP).`

19. Create hyperlinks for each text string, using bookmarks to send the user to the correct sheet.

20. Check the hyperlinks.

21. Edit the hyperlink text to delete the word "see" on both hyperlinks.

22. Print a copy of the Trial Balance.

23. Save the **5.1tb** file. Unhide the **5.1sched** file and save the file. Close both files.

	A	B	C	D	E	F	G
1		**Green Brothers Gardening**					
2		**Schedule of Accounts Receivable**					
3		For the Year Ended December 31, 2004					
4							
5		Abermarle, Kelly		2144.65			
6		Capital Bank		5434.54			
7		Drury, David		1232.87			
8		Engle, Dr. Carrie		346.87			
9		Fairfax Water Co		1124.75			
10		Grinder, Sam		769.76			
11		Harrison Tools Co		2212.77			
12		Johnson, Linda		435.87			
13		Logan, Harry		909.56			
14		Loomis, Bart		212.87			
15		Samson, Peter		543.98			
16		Samuels, Larry		634.87			
17		Souten, Willem G.		540.00			
18		Toomey, Martin		563.55			
19		United Cars		2389.00			
20		Whiticomb, Roger		1876.98			
21					Copy total and paste link to Trial Balance		
22				21372.89			
23							

Schedule of AR / Schedule of AP / Sheet3

Illustration A

	A	B	C	D	E	F	G
1		**Green Brothers Gardening**					
2		**Schedule of Accounts Payable**					
3		For the Year Ended December 31, 2004					
4							
5		Bulbs Unlimited		1439.55			
6		Nursery Supply Inc		976.65			
7		Varsity Nurseries		3426.98			
8		Grollier Farms		1549.75			
9		KCG Supply Co		549.45			
10		Pride Farms		1290.67			
11		Miller Plant Supply		950.00	correct value		
12		Jay's Perrenials		1540.00			
13					Copy total and paste link to Trial Balance		
14				11723.05			
15							

Illustration B

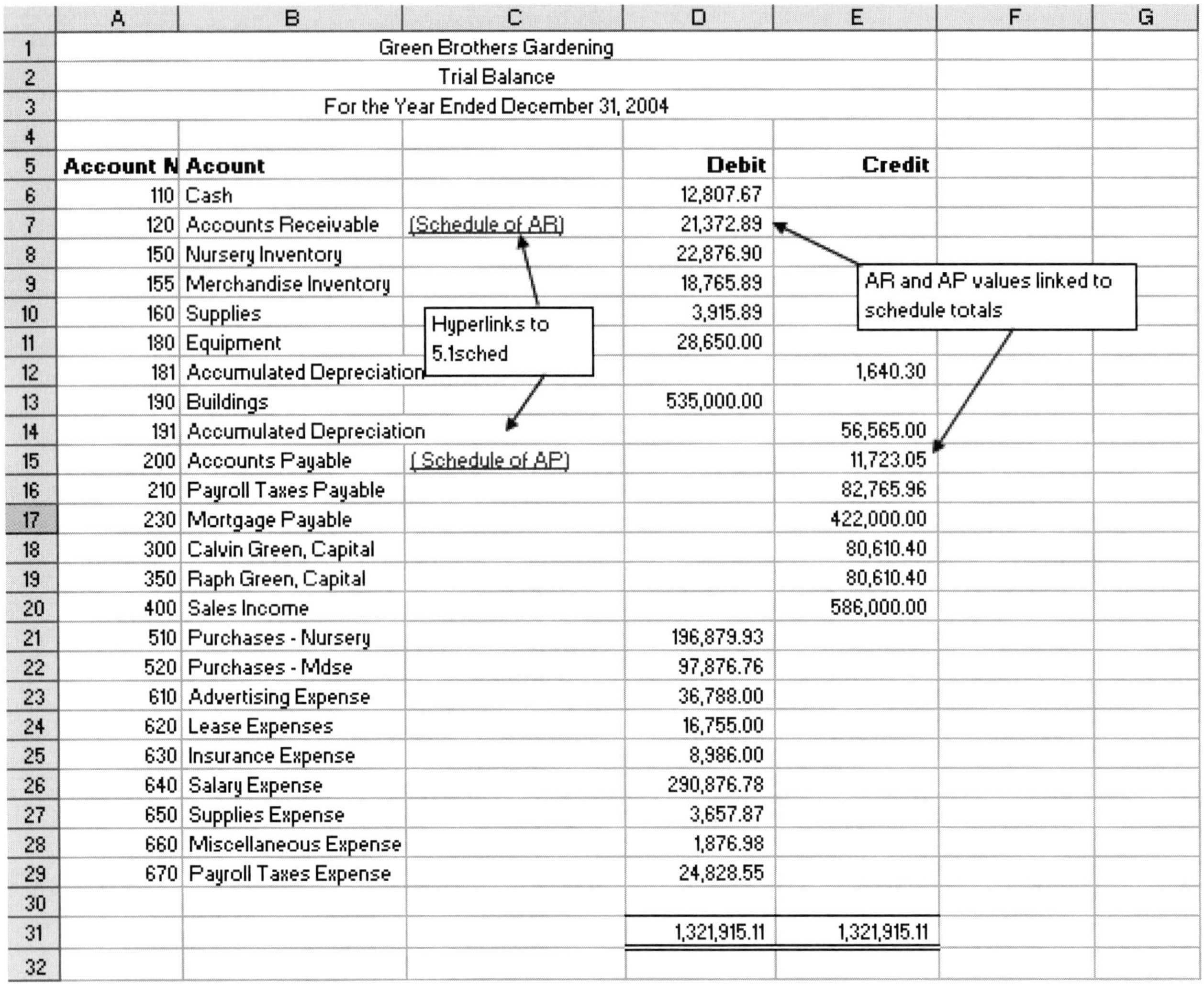

	A	B	C	D	E	F	G
1	Green Brothers Gardening						
2	Trial Balance						
3	For the Year Ended December 31, 2004						
4							
5	**Account N**	**Acount**		**Debit**	**Credit**		
6	110	Cash		12,807.67			
7	120	Accounts Receivable	(Schedule of AR)	21,372.89			
8	150	Nursery Inventory		22,876.90			
9	155	Merchandise Inventory		18,765.89			
10	160	Supplies		3,915.89			
11	180	Equipment		28,650.00			
12	181	Accumulated Depreciation			1,640.30		
13	190	Buildings		535,000.00			
14	191	Accumulated Depreciation			56,565.00		
15	200	Accounts Payable	(Schedule of AP)		11,723.05		
16	210	Payroll Taxes Payable			82,765.96		
17	230	Mortgage Payable			422,000.00		
18	300	Calvin Green, Capital			80,610.40		
19	350	Raph Green, Capital			80,610.40		
20	400	Sales Income			586,000.00		
21	510	Purchases - Nursery		196,879.93			
22	520	Purchases - Mdse		97,876.76			
23	610	Advertising Expense		36,788.00			
24	620	Lease Expenses		16,755.00			
25	630	Insurance Expense		8,986.00			
26	640	Salary Expense		290,876.78			
27	650	Supplies Expense		3,657.87			
28	660	Miscellaneous Expense		1,876.98			
29	670	Payroll Taxes Expense		24,828.55			
30							
31				1,321,915.11	1,321,915.11		
32							

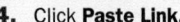

Illustration C

Cues for Reference

Merge and Center Cells
1. Select cells to merge.
2. Click **Merge and Center** button.

Split Cells
1. Select merged cells to split.
2. Click **Merge and Center** button. 

Compare Workbooks
1. Open workbooks.
2. Click **Windows**, **Compare Side by Side with [another file].**

Paste Link Cells
1. Copy the cell to link.
2. Select link location.
3. Click **Paste** button list arrow.
4. Click **Paste Link.**

Insert a Hyperlink
1. Enter hyperlink text.
2. Select the cell and click **Hyperlink** button.
3. Select location in the Look in box.
4. Click **Bookmark,** if a specific location is necessary.
5. Select a bookmark.
6. Click **OK.**
7. Click **OK.**

Hide Workbooks
- In the workbook to hide, click **Window, Hide.**

Unhide Workbooks
1. Click Window, Unhide.
2. Select the file to unhide.
3. Click OK.

Edit a Hyperlink
1. Right-click hyperlink text and click **Edit Hyperlink.**
   or
   Hold down mouse over hyperlink.
2. Make corrections as necessary.
3. Press **Enter.**

GOALS

To create a sales and commissions analysis and link the data to a worksheet
To complete a quarterly worksheet
To practice using the following skill sets:

- Modify row and column layout
  - Hide and unhide rows and columns
  - Freeze and unfreeze rows and columns
- Modify page setup options
  - Print nonadjacent sections of a worksheet
  - Print titles
- Use logical functions in formulas

EXCEL

WHAT YOU NEED TO KNOW

Modify Row and Column Layout

Hide and Unhide Rows and Columns

- You can hide detail columns and rows on the screen display to simplify a complicated worksheet, or for security purposes. Hidden columns and rows do not print.
- To hide columns or rows, select the rows or columns to hide, click Format, Column or Row, and click Hide. You can also drag the border of the row or column to hide it. When you hide a column or row, the worksheet border does not display the column letter or row number.
- You can display hidden columns by selecting the columns or rows before and after the hidden area and dragging right for columns or down for rows, as shown in Figure 5.11. You can also click Format, Columns or Rows, and select Unhide.

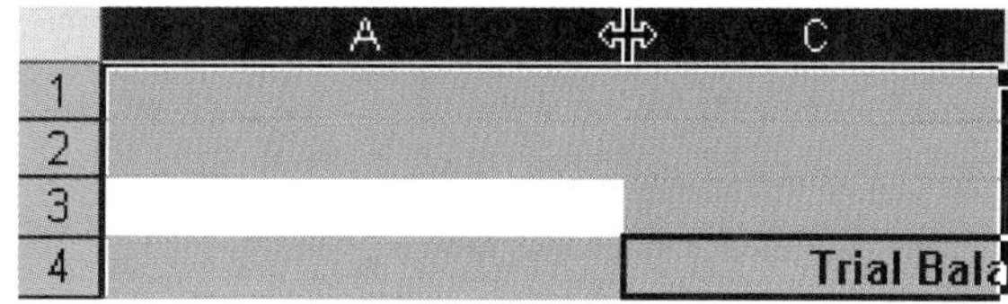

Figure 5.11 Display hidden column – drag to right

TRY*it* OUT *E5-8*

1. Open **E5-8** from the Data CD.
2. Click **Don't Update** at the update prompt.
3. Select **Column B.**
4. Click **Format**, **Column**, and **Hide.**
5. Click **Format**, **Column**, and **Unhide.**
6. Select **Rows 23:28.**
7. Click **Format**, **Row**, and **Hide.**
8. Select **Rows 22** and **29,** and drag down to unhide the rows.

Note: Be sure to return rows to normal height.

9. Click at the right edge of **Column B** and drag to the left to hide the column.
10. Do not close the file.

Freeze and Unfreeze Rows and Columns

- When you work with a large worksheet, you may find that the column headings or row labels that identify the data scroll out of view. You can keep them in view by freezing them. Select the row below or the column to the right of the data to freeze, and click Window, Freeze Panes.
- The *Freeze Panes* command locks the pane, a group of rows or columns above or to the left of the cell you select, so that area does not move during scrolling. To remove the freeze, click Windows, Unfreeze.

TRY*it* OUT *E5-9*

1. Continue to work in the open file or open **E5-9** from the Data CD. *Click Don't Update if you open E5-9.*
2. Click in **Cell A6** and click **Window, Freeze Panes.**
3. Use the vertical scroll bar to scroll down the page and notice the frozen rows at the top of the screen.
4. Click **Window**, **Unfreeze Panes.**
5. Click in **Cell E6** and freeze the panes.
6. Use the horizontal scroll bar to scroll to the right to view the entire worksheet in comparison to the Trial Balance columns.
7. Clear the freeze.
8. Do not close the file.

Modify Page Setup Options

Print Nonadjacent Sections of a Worksheet

- To print sections of a worksheet that are not adjacent, you can hide the columns or rows that are not needed and print the data as displayed.
- If a worksheet is wider or longer than the width of the page, you can adjust the page break lines, or you can use the Page Setup dialog box and click the Page tab, to select the Fit to 1 page wide by 1 page tall scaling option, as shown in Figure 5.12.

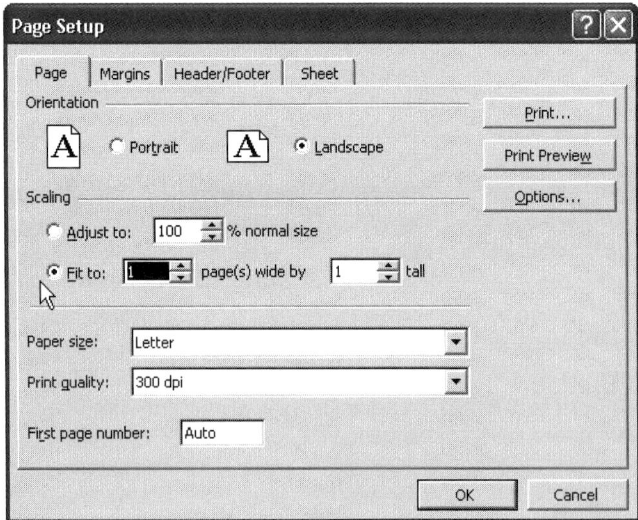

Figure 5.12 Scaling options in Page Setup dialog box

TRY it OUT *E5-10*

1. Continue to work in the open file or open **E5-10** from the Data CD. Click **Don't Update** if you open **E5-10.**
2. Hide Columns **C:F.**
3. Click **View, Page Break Preview.** (Notice that the worksheet is wider than the page.)
4. Click **OK** to the Welcome to Page Break Preview dialog box.
5. Click **View, Normal.**
6. Click **File, Page Setup.**
7. On the **Page** tab, with the Scaling option displayed, click **Fit to 1 page wide.** Click **OK.**
8. Print the worksheet as displayed. Only Columns A, G, H, I, J, K, and L will print.
9. Select Columns **A** and **G** and unhide the columns. (Keep Column B hidden.)
10. Click **File, Page Setup.** Click **Adjust to,** and change the size back to 100% normal size. Click **OK.**
11. Do not close the file.

EXCEL

Print Titles

- The *Print Titles* feature allows you to print column or row titles on subsequent pages of a multiple page worksheet. For example, if the worksheet in E5-9 were fully displayed, it would require two pages to print. You can set column titles to repeat at the left of the second page so that you can identify the values on each page.
- To print titles, click File, Page Setup, select the Sheet tab, and use the Collapse Dialog Box button to select the rows or columns to repeat in the Print titles section, as shown in Figure 5.13. If you have merged cells for the title rows, you must undo the merge first.

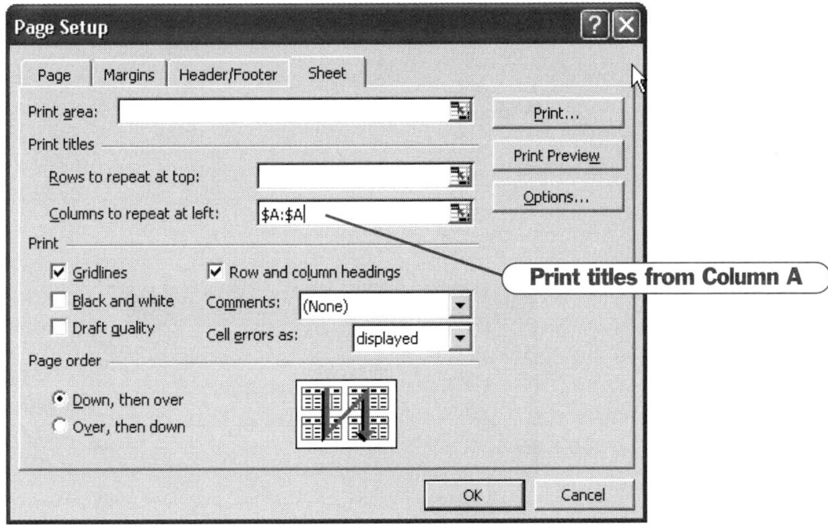

Figure 5.13 Page Setup dialog box, Sheet tab, Print titles setting

TRY it OUT *E5-11*

1. Continue to work in the open file or open **E5-11** from the Data CD. *Click Don't Update if you open E5-11.*
2. Click each merged title row and click the **Merge and Center** button to undo the merge.

Continued on next page

TRY it OUT *E5-11 Continued*

3. Click **File**, **Page Setup**, and click the **Sheet** tab.
4. Click the **Collapse Dialog Box** button for columns to repeat at left.
5. Click **Column A** and click the **Restore Dialog Box** button.
6. Click **OK.**
7. Click the **Print Preview** button.
8. Click **Next** on the preview screen to see Page 2.
9. Click **Close** to close the preview.
10. Save the file **E5.11.** Close the file.

Use Logical Functions in Formulas

- You can use an *IF statement* in a formula to test a situation and determine a value based on the outcome of the test. An IF statement is a function in the Logical Functions category. The format for an IF statement is:

  =IF(CONDITION,X,Y) If a condition you are testing for is true, then the result is X. If the condition is false, then the result is Y. Notice that the parts of the function are separated by commas.

- For example, we will calculate the bonus for salespeople who get a 1% bonus on sales when they make sales over $30,000. In other words, if sales are greater than $30,000, then their bonus equals their sales multiplied by 1%, otherwise their bonus equals zero. The IF statement would read as follows if the sales amount resides in Cell B2:

  =IF(B2>30000,B2*1%,0)

- The following table shows how to translate this statement:

FORMULA	FUNCTION	CONDITION	X	Y
English	If	Sales are greater than $30,000	Then multiply sales by 1% to calculate the bonus	Else the bonus equals 0
Excel	=IF	(B2>30000,	B2*1%,	0)

- IF statements use the following conditional operators to state the conditional question:

  = Equal

  > Greater than

  < Less than

  <> Not equal to

  <= Less than or equal to

  >= Greater than or equal to

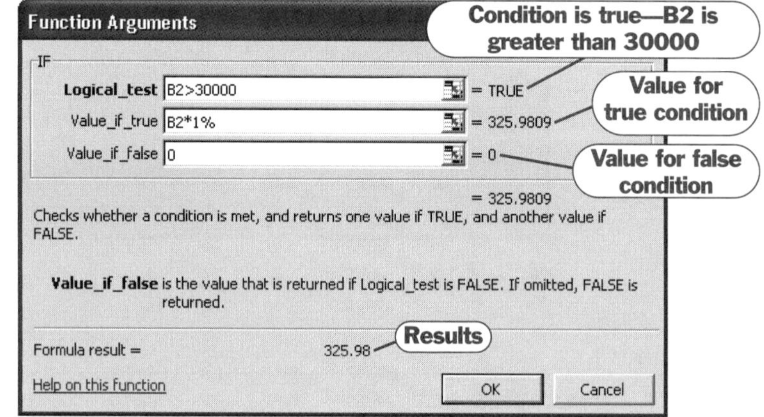

Figure 5.14 IF statement function arguments

- To enter an IF statement, click the Insert Function button on the formula bar and select IF from the Logical category. There are Collapse Dialog Box buttons to select cells from the worksheet, or you can enter the function directly into the cell. Notice the entries in the dialog box in Figure 5.14.

TRY *it* OUT *E5-12*

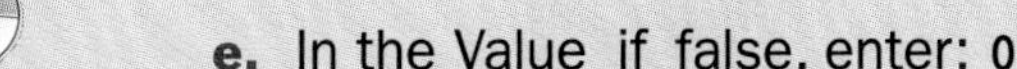

1. Open **E5-12** from the Data CD. Notice the sales in Column B.
2. In **Cell D2,** enter an IF statement to calculate the bonus.
   a. Click the **fx (Insert Function) button.**
   b. Select the **Logical** category and the **IF** function. Click **OK.**
   c. In Logical test, enter: `B2>30000`.
   d. In the Value_if_ true, enter: `B2*1%`.
   e. In the Value_if_false, enter: `0`.
   f. Click **OK.**
3. In **Cell D2,** view the resulting formula on the formula bar.
4. Use the fill handle to copy the formula for all salespeople. Notice how the bonuses were applied.
5. Do not close the file.

EXCEL

► You can use an IF statement to insert text depending on a condition. For example, if the sales are greater than a certain amount, you can insert "Great work"; if not, you can insert "Sales seminar on Thursday." When you use an IF statement to enter text, the text must be placed within quotation marks. Excel automatically inserts quotation marks if you use the Insert Function dialog box; however, you must enter them if you enter the formula directly into the cell. Notice the formula bar and the Sales and Note columns in Figure 5.15.

G2 fx =IF(B2>30000,"Great work!","Sales seminar on Thursday")

	A	B	C	D	E	F	G	H
1	SALES STAFF	SALES	COMMISSION	BONUS	SALARY	EARNINGS	NOTE	
2	Acosta, Sam	32,598.09	651.96	325.98	1,500.00	2,477.94	Great work!	
3	Billings, Mary	28,321.32	566.43	-	1,500.00	2,066.43	Sales seminar on Thursday	
4	Camino, Juan	18,545.77	370.92	-	1,500.00	1,870.92	Sales seminar on Thursday	
5	Kelly, Joe	51,567.54	1,031.35	515.68	1,500.00	3,047.03	Great work!	
6	Lincoln, Terry	29,921.22	598.42	-	1,500.00	2,098.42	Sales seminar on Thursday	
7	Parson, Alice	35,325.78	706.52	353.26	1,500.00	2,559.77	Great work!	
8	Sulfa, Sally	55,896.95	1,117.94	558.97	1,500.00	3,176.91	Great work!	
9								

Figure 5.15 IF statement to enter text

TRY *it* OUT *E5-13*

1. Continue to work in the open file or open **E5-13.**
2. In **Cell G2,** enter an **IF** statement to generate the notes.
   a. Click the **fx (Insert Function)** button.
   b. Select the **Logical** category and **IF** function. Click **OK.**
   c. In the Logical_test box, enter: `B2>30000`.
   d. In the Value_if_true box, enter: `Great work!`
   e. In the Value_if_false box, enter: `Sales seminar on Thursday`.
   f. Click **OK.**
3. In **Cell G2,** view the resulting formula on the formula bar.
4. Use the fill handle to copy the formula for all salespeople.
5. Save the **E5-13** file. Close the file.

GOALS

To create a sales and commissions schedule and to link the data into a worksheet

To complete a quarterly worksheet

SETTING THE STAGE/WRAPUP

File names: **5.2bonus**
5.2worksheet

Format: All values should be formatted for commas with no decimal places

WHAT YOU NEED TO KNOW

- In Excel, spreadsheets are called worksheets. In accounting terminology, however, a *worksheet* is a form used to gather trial balance and adjustments information at the end of an accounting period to plan the preparation of the income statement and balance sheet. It is for the accountant's use.
- The worksheet adjustments, usually prepared by the accountant, are corrections that are made at the end of the period so that the accounts will reflect their true balances. The net income is calculated and the income statement and balance sheet are planned on the worksheet using the adjusted trial balance data. Many corporations round numbers on financial reports, as noted in the Setting the Stage directions above.
- The sales and commission schedule calculates the sales, commissions, and bonuses for the period. IF statements are used to calculate the commissions and bonus for each salesperson. The commission expense for the period is linked to the appropriate location on the worksheet.
- In this Rehearsal activity, Sutton Investment Group wants you to prepare and format the quarterly Sales and Commissions Schedule (Illustration A) and link the data to the worksheet (Illustration B). On the worksheet, you will format and complete totals, modify the columns and rows, and print part of the worksheet.

DIRECTIONS

1. Open **5.2bonus** from the Data CD.
2. Set font sizes for titles, as indicated in Illustration A on the next page, and merge and center the title rows.
3. Bold all column headings, center headings in **Columns B:F**, and adjust column width, as illustrated.
4. Enter a formula in **Cell C6** to calculate a 1.5% commission on sales. (Hint: Sales*1.5%.)
5. Enter an IF statement in **Cell D6** to calculate a .5% bonus on sales greater than $2,000,000.

   (Hint: Condition: Sales>2000000 If True: Sales*.5% If False: 0.)
6. Enter a formula in **Cell E6** to calculate the total paid to the employee. (Hint: Commission + Bonus.)
7. Enter an IF statement in **Cell F6** to enter an asterisk (*) if the sales were over $2,500,000 and nothing if they were not. (Hint: Use quotation marks around the asterisk and around the blank, i.e., "*" or " ")
8. Copy formulas down for all salespersons and total the columns.
9. Save the file **5.2bonus.**
10. Copy the total in **Cell E19.**
11. Open **5.2worksheet** from the Data CD.
12. Paste link the total of Column E to the Commissions Expense location in **Cell B22.**
13. Format titles and column headings, as shown in Illustration B on page 128.
14. Insert a column after Column A.
15. In **Cell B22,** enter a hyperlink to **5.2bonus** using "(See Schedule)" as the hyperlink text.

Continued on next page

16. Freeze panes in **Cell B7** and find totals for **Columns C:L.**

    Note: Columns C and D, E and F, and G and H should match or balance with each other.

17. In a blank area below the worksheet, subtract the Income Statement totals, Column I from Column J (J-I). This value, the net income, should be placed in **Cells I31** and **L31.**

18. In **Cell I32,** add **Cells I30** and **I31.** Copy this formula to **Columns J:L.**

    Note: Columns I and J and K and L should balance with each other.

19. Include borders and lines, as shown in Illustration B.

20. Unfreeze panes, hide **Columns B:F,** and print the worksheet to fit on one page.

21. Unhide the columns and print the worksheet on two pages with column titles.

22. Save the file **5.2worksheet.** Close both files.

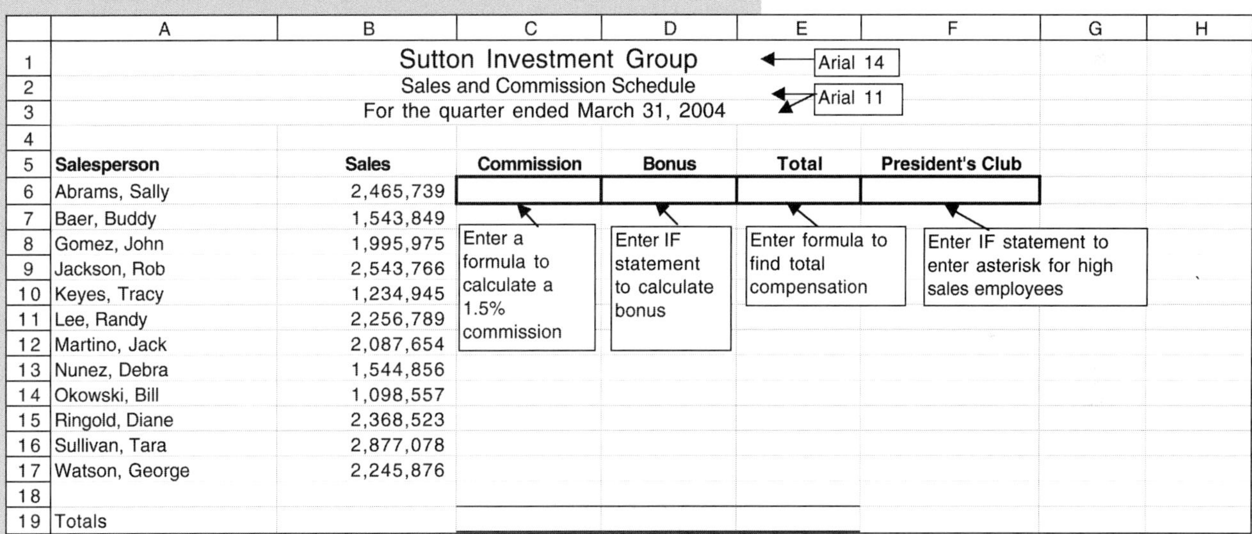

	A	B	C	D	E	F	G	H
1			Sutton Investment Group					
2			Sales and Commission Schedule					
3			For the quarter ended March 31, 2004					
4								
5	**Salesperson**	**Sales**	**Commission**	**Bonus**	**Total**	**President's Club**		
6	Abrams, Sally	2,465,739						
7	Baer, Buddy	1,543,849						
8	Gomez, John	1,995,975						
9	Jackson, Rob	2,543,766						
10	Keyes, Tracy	1,234,945						
11	Lee, Randy	2,256,789						
12	Martino, Jack	2,087,654						
13	Nunez, Debra	1,544,856						
14	Okowski, Bill	1,098,557						
15	Ringold, Diane	2,368,523						
16	Sullivan, Tara	2,877,078						
17	Watson, George	2,245,876						
18								
19	Totals							

Illustration A

EXCEL

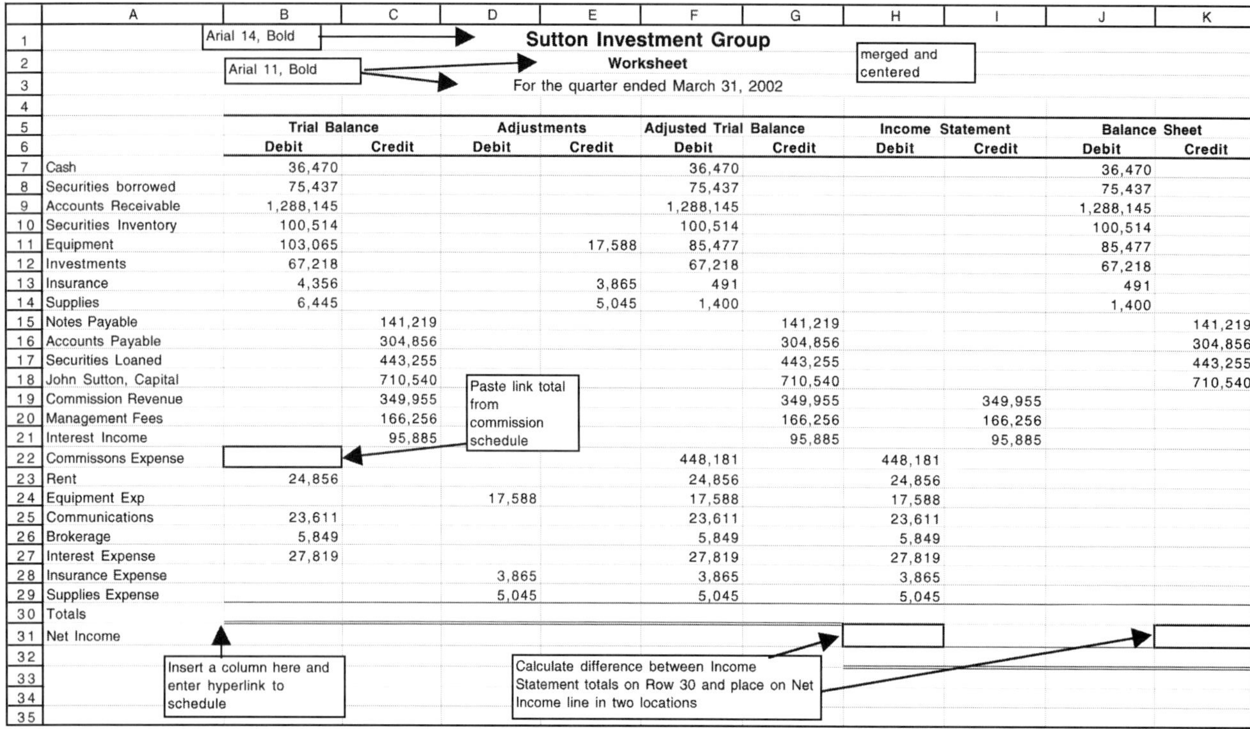

	A	B	C	D	E	F	G	H	I	J	K
1						Sutton Investment Group					
2						Worksheet					
3						For the quarter ended March 31, 2002					
4											
5		Trial Balance		Adjustments		Adjusted Trial Balance		Income Statement		Balance Sheet	
6		Debit	Credit	Debit	Credit	Debit	Credit	Debit	Credit	Debit	Credit
7	Cash	36,470				36,470				36,470	
8	Securities borrowed	75,437				75,437				75,437	
9	Accounts Receivable	1,288,145				1,288,145				1,288,145	
10	Securities Inventory	100,514				100,514				100,514	
11	Equipment	103,065			17,588	85,477				85,477	
12	Investments	67,218				67,218				67,218	
13	Insurance	4,356			3,865	491				491	
14	Supplies	6,445			5,045	1,400				1,400	
15	Notes Payable		141,219				141,219				141,219
16	Accounts Payable		304,856				304,856				304,856
17	Securities Loaned		443,255				443,255				443,255
18	John Sutton, Capital		710,540				710,540				710,540
19	Commission Revenue		349,955				349,955		349,955		
20	Management Fees		166,256				166,256		166,256		
21	Interest Income		95,885				95,885		95,885		
22	Commissons Expense					448,181		448,181			
23	Rent	24,856				24,856		24,856			
24	Equipment Exp			17,588		17,588		17,588			
25	Communications	23,611				23,611		23,611			
26	Brokerage	5,849				5,849		5,849			
27	Interest Expense	27,819				27,819		27,819			
28	Insurance Expense			3,865		3,865		3,865			
29	Supplies Expense			5,045		5,045		5,045			
30	Totals										
31	Net Income										
32											
33											
34											
35											

Illustration B

Cues for Reference

Hide Columns or Rows

1. Select row(s) or column(s) to hide.
2. Click **Format, Row** or **Column,** and **Hide.**

Unhide Columns or Rows

1. Select rows or columns on either side of hidden area.
2. Click **Format**, **Row** or **Column**, and **Unhide.**

Freeze Columns or Rows

1. Place insertion point after column(s) or row(s) to freeze.
2. Click **Window**, **Freeze Panes.**

Unfreeze Columns or Rows

- Click **Window, Unfreeze Panes.**

Enter IF Statement

1. Click **fx (Insert Function)** button.
2. Click **Logical** category and **IF** function.
3. In Logical test, enter or select condition.
4. In Value_if_true, enter or select data or formula.
5. In Value_if_false, enter or select data or formula.
6. Click **OK.**

Print Nonadjacent Sections of a Worksheet

1. Hide columns or rows that are not needed.
2. Click **Print** button.

Fit Worksheet to One Page

1. Click **File, Page Setup.**
2. On Page tab, click **Fit to one page wide.**
3. Click **OK.**

Print Titles

1. Clear merged cells, if necessary.
2. Click **File**, **Page Setup**, and click the **Sheet** tab.
3. Select row or column titles to repeat.
4. Click **OK.**

TRYOUT

TASK 3

GOALS

To create a consolidated income statement using 3-D references and a custom footer

To practice using the following skill sets:

- Add headers and footers to worksheets
  - Add customized headers and footers
- Enter 3-D references

EXCEL

WHAT YOU NEED TO KNOW

Add Headers and Footers to Worksheets

- *Headers and footers* allow you to repeat the same information at the top (header) or bottom (footer) of every page. You use this feature to enter a company name, date, file name, sheet name, etc. You can select from built-in headers or footers, or you can customize your own.
- To add a header or footer, click View, Header and Footer to display the Header/Footer tab of the Page Setup dialog box. You can select built-in header and footer text from the drop-down lists in each section. In Figure 5.16, notice the built-in footers that are displayed.

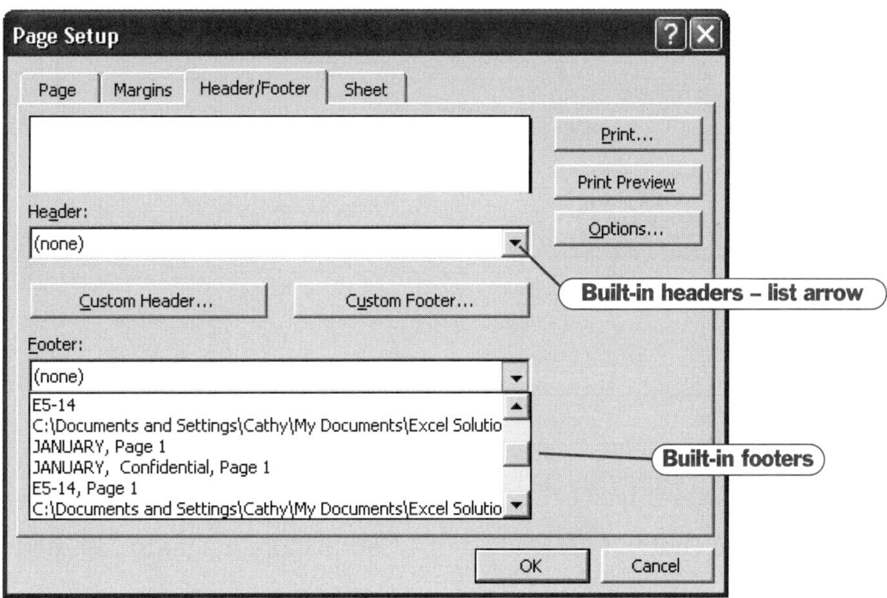

Figure 5.16 Header and Footer dialog box displaying built-in footers

TRY*it*OUT *E5-14*

1. Open **E5-14** from the Data CD and verify that the January tab is selected.
2. Click **View**, **Header and Footer.**
3. Click the list arrow in the Header section, and select the **JANUARY, Page 1** header.
4. Click the list arrow in the Footer section and select the file name or the **E5-14** footer.
5. Click **OK.**

Continued on next page

TRY *it* OUT *E5-14 Continued*

6. Click the **Print Preview** button. Notice the headers and footers.
7. Click **Close** to close the preview screen.
8. Close the file. Do not save.

Add Customized Headers and Footers

- To enter a customized header or footer, click the Custom Header or Custom Footer button on the Header/Footer page, (see Figure 5.16), and the Header or Footer custom dialog box opens.
- As shown in Figure 5.17, text entered into the left, center, and right sections is aligned in that section. You may click the appropriate button to include the date, time, page number, tab name, file name, or picture. You can use the picture option to insert a logo or graphic and the Format Picture button to customize settings once the picture is in place.

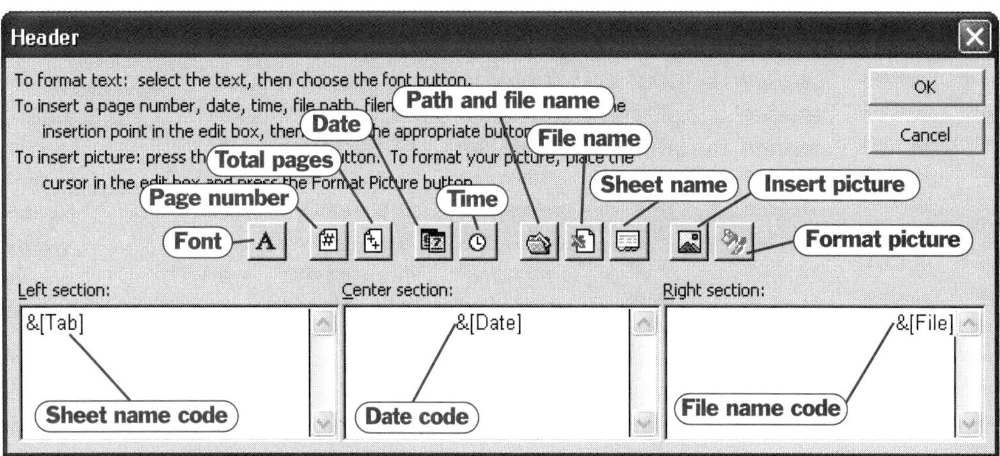

Figure 5.17 Custom Header dialog box

TRY *it* OUT *E5-15*

1. Open **E5-15** from the Data CD.
2. Click **View, Header and Footer.** Click **Custom Header.**
3. In the left section, click the **Sheet Name** button; in the center section, click the **Date** button; in the right section, click the **File Name** button. Click **OK.**
4. Click **Custom Footer**, and in the left section, click the **Insert Picture** button.
5. From your data folder, select the **E5-13logo** and click **Insert.**
6. Click the **Format Picture** button.
7. Set picture height to *.79"* and click **OK.**
8. Enter `Trainor's Department Store` in the left section after the picture code. Click **OK.**
9. Click the **Print Preview** button.
10. Click **Close** to close the preview screen.
11. Do not close the file.

Enter 3-D References

- If you want to summarize data from several sheets onto a totals sheet within a workbook, you can use a formula in the *3-D reference* style. The style is called three dimensional because it calculates values through the sheets of a workbook to a summary worksheet at the end of the workbook.
- A 3-D reference includes the range of sheet names, an exclamation point, and the cell or range reference.

EXAMPLE OF 3-D REFERENCES	EXPLANATIONS
=SUM(Sheet1:Sheet3!D7)	Adds the values in D7 from sheets 1 to 3.
=AVERAGE(Sheet3:Sheet5!D7:D12)	Averages values in D7:D12 from sheets 3 to 5.
=January!D8+February!D8	Adds the values in D8 from the January and February sheets.

EXCEL

- To enter a 3-D reference, either enter the reference in the formula, or select the sheets and cells involved, and enter the mathematical operators, as necessary. Notice the formula in Figure 5.18, which was entered by selection. When 3-D references are copied, the cell references change, relative to the new location, but the sheet names remain constant.

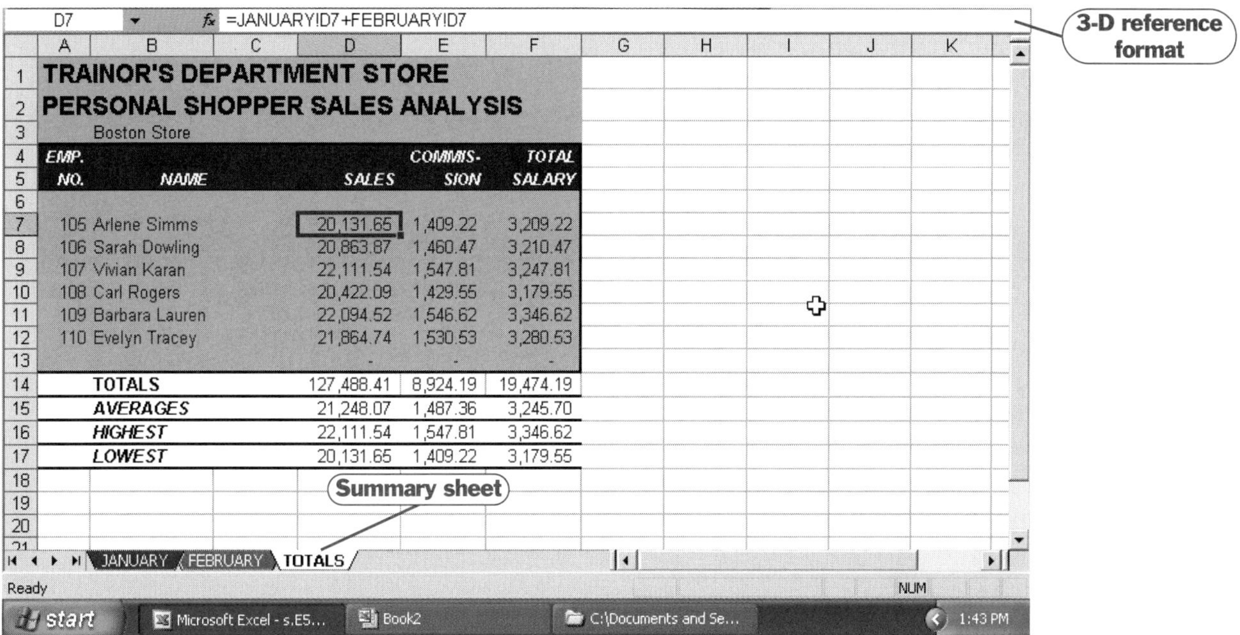

Figure 5.18 3-D formula entered by selection

TRY *it* OUT *E5-16*

1. Continue to work in the open file or open **E5-16** from the Data CD.
2. Rename Sheet3: **TOTALS.**
3. Use the selection method to enter a 3-D reference in **Cell D7** to add the values from the JANUARY and FEBRUARY sheets:
   a. In **Cell D7** on the Totals sheet, enter: = **.**
   b. Click **Cell D7** on the JANUARY sheet.
   c. Enter: + .
   d. Click **Cell D7** on the FEBRUARY sheet.
   e. Press the **Enter** key and go to **Cell D7** to view the formula.
4. In **Cell E7,** enter in a 3-D reference to add the values in **Cell E7** from the JANUARY and FEBRUARY sheets. (Hint: =Sum(January:February!E7.)
5. Use AutoFill to copy **Cell E7** to **Cell F7,** and copy all three formulas down to, and including the Totals, **Row 14.**
6. Adjust color and line formats.
7. Save the **E5-16** file. Close the file.

1
2
3

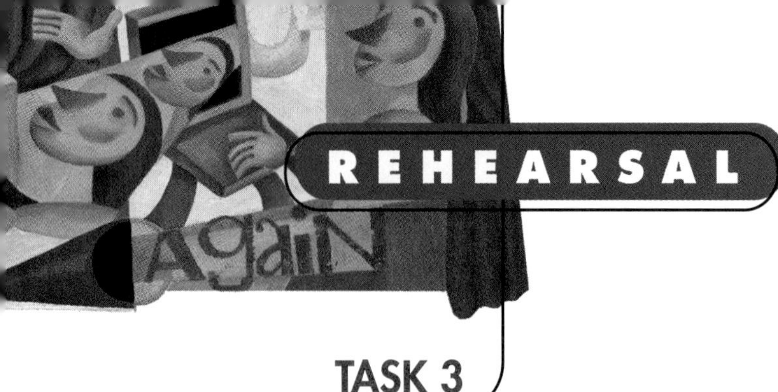

GOAL

To create a consolidated income statement using 3-D references and a custom footer

SETTING THE STAGE/WRAPUP

File name: **5.3income**

Format: All values should be formatted for commas with no decimal places

WHAT YOU NEED TO KNOW

- Corporations must report their financial data to their stockholders quarterly and annually. If a company has branches or divisions in various parts of the country, they need to combine income statement data into one financial report called a *consolidated income statement.*
- An income statement is prepared at the end of a financial period using income, cost, and expense accounts from the trial balance. It calculates gross profit, the markup on your product or service, and net profit, which is the final profit for the period after deducting expenses. It is a valuable source of information for stockholders or owners and for potential investors or lenders.
- In this Rehearsal activity, you will create a consolidated income statement for Time Out Sporting Goods. You will combine the numbers from the Barkely and Montrose stores into one income statement using 3-D references, and add a custom footer to the report.

DIRECTIONS

1. Open **5.3income** from the Data CD.
2. Group the Barkely and Montrose sheets and format as shown in the illustration on the facing page. (Font and bold settings, borders and lines, fill color, and values in comma format with no decimals.)
3. With the sheets still grouped, enter formulas in the cells listed below to calculate the following income statement items. (Hints are listed for some formulas.)
   C9: Net Sales (Hint: Sales - Sales Returns)
   C13: Gross Profit (Hint: Net Sales - Cost of Goods Sold)
   C25: Total Expenses
   C27: Net Income before Taxes (Hint: Gross Profit - Total Expenses)
   C29: Net Income after Taxes
4. Ungroup the sheets using the worksheet tab shortcut menu.
5. Copy the entire Barkely worksheet.
6. Use the worksheet tab shortcut menu to insert a new sheet.
7. Paste the Barkely worksheet to **Cell A1** on the new sheet.
8. Move the new sheet to the last position; rename it: `Consolidated Income Statement.`
9. Adjust column widths as necessary and change the second title to read: `Consolidated Income Statement.`
10. Delete the values in **Column B** on the Consolidated Income Statement sheet.

Continued on next page

11. Group the sheets and freeze panes in **Cell A4** so that you can view the length of the report without losing the title. Ungroup the sheets using the shortcut menu.
12. In **Cell B7,** on the Consolidated Income Statement sheet, enter a 3-D formula to add the values from the Barkely sheet and the Montrose sheet in **Cell B7.** (Hint: =Barkely!B7+Montrose!B7.)
13. Use AutoFill to copy the formula down to **Cell B28.** Delete all zeros or dashes where the formula did not find values.
14. Check your work by looking at a value on the consolidated sheet to see if it totals the two sheets correctly.
15. Format the worksheet tabs with colors, as appropriate.
16. Group the sheets and set a custom footer to print the sheet name, date, and file name.
17. Save the file **5.3income** and print a copy of all worksheets.
18. Close the file.

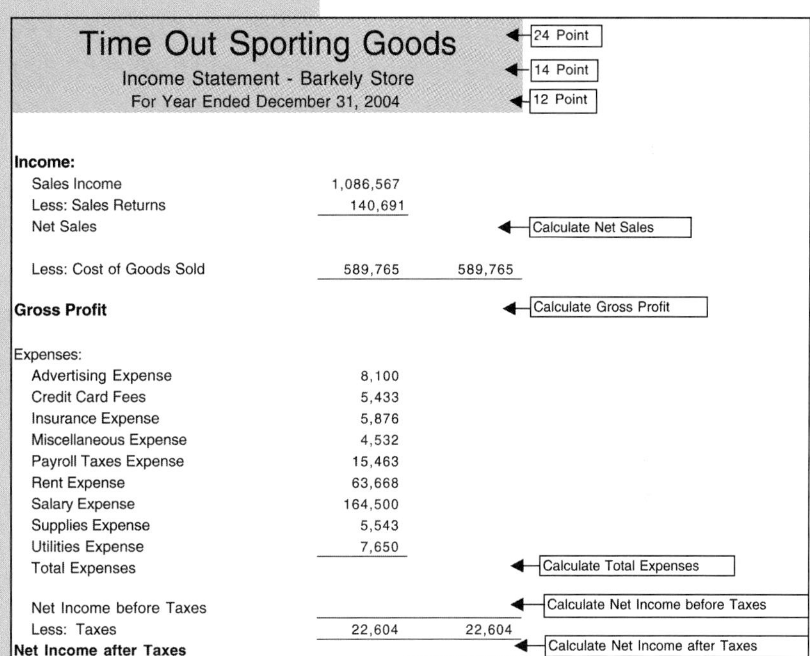

Cues for Reference

Add Headers and Footers

1. Click **View, Header and Footer.**
2. To select a built-in header or footer:
   - Click **Header** or **Footer** drop-down list.
   - Select header/footer.

Add Customized Headers and Footers

1. Click **View, Header and Footer.**
2. Click **Custom Header** or **Custom Footer.**
3. Click in section.
4. Enter text or insert header or footer code.
5. Repeat as necessary.
6. Click **OK.**
7. Click **OK.**

Enter 3-D References

- Enter the reference.

or

Use the mouse:

1. Enter equal sign, function, and parentheses, if necessary.
2. Select sheet and cell to reference.
3. Enter mathematical operator.
4. Repeat Steps 2 and 3 and close parentheses, if necessary.
5. Press **Enter.**

GOALS
To create a balance sheet using styles and the Find and Replace features
To practice using the following skill sets:

- Use styles
  - Apply a style
  - Define a new style
  - Modify a style
  - Remove a style
- Find and replace cell data and formats
  - Find cell data
  - Find and replace data and formats

WHAT YOU NEED TO KNOW

Use Styles

Apply a Style

- A *style* is a defined collection of data formats, such as font, font size, indentation, number formats, alignments, etc., that you name and store so that you can apply all those formats at once.
- Excel provides basic styles for numbers, as listed in the Style dialog box. To apply a basic style, select the cells to format, click Format, Style, and click the style from the Style name list. When you apply a style, you apply all the defined formats. Notice the Normal, or default, style formats for data, as shown in Figure 5.19.

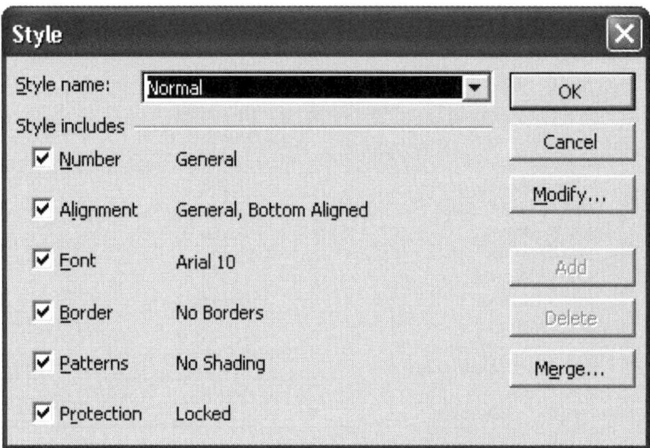

Figure 5.19 Style dialog box, Normal style

TRY *it* OUT *E5-17*

1. Open **E5-17** from the Data CD.
2. Select the range **C6:C10** and click **Format**, **Style.** Notice the settings for Comma style.
3. Click the **Style name** list arrow and select the **Normal** style. Notice the settings for Normal style.
4. Click **OK**. Notice the changes in the numbers.

Continued on next page

TRY it OUT *E5-17 Continued*

5. Click **Format**, **Style,** and apply the **Comma [0]** style (commas with no decimal places).
6. Click **OK.**
7. Use the Format Painter feature to copy the style to **Cell D11.**
8. Do not close the file.

EXCEL

Define a New Style

- If you find that you need a combination of formats in your work, you can define a new style. You can specify the formats in the Style dialog box or select a cell with the formats you want and name it in the Style dialog box. Once you name the style, the cell formats appear in the dialog box. Notice the "title" style in the Style dialog box in Figure 5.20.

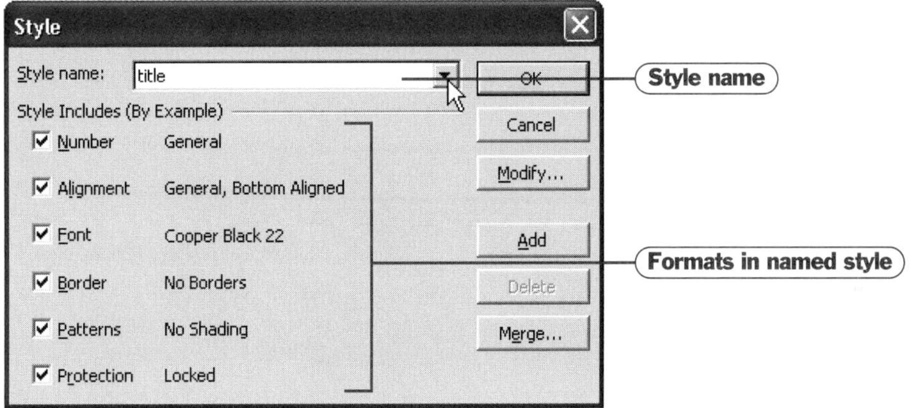

Figure 5.20 Style dialog box, Title style

TRY it OUT *E5-18*

1. Continue to work in the open file or open **E5-18** from the Data CD.
2. In **Cell A1,** change the font to **Cooper Black, 22 point.** (If this font is not installed, use another heavy, dark font.)
3. Click **Format**, **Style.**
4. Enter `Title` in the Style name box, and notice the settings.
5. Click **OK.**
6. Click **Cell A2** and apply the **Title** style setting.
7. Do not close the file.

Modify a Style

- Use the Style dialog box to modify existing formats by clicking the format to change and then clicking Modify. In the Format cells dialog box that opens, click a tab to select the format you want and click OK. Repeat this procedure as necessary, and click OK to return to the Style dialog box. Click OK to apply the style or, if you just want to add the style to your styles list without applying it, click Add.
- If you modify a style, all the data using that style automatically changes. The Style feature provides consistency and saves reformatting the entire worksheet for a format modification.

TRY *it* OUT *E5-19*

1. Continue to work in the open file or open **E5-19** from the Data CD.
2. In **Cell A2,** click **Format**, **Style.**
3. Change "Title" to read `Title2` in the Style name box.
4. Click **Modify.**
5. In the Format Cells dialog box, with the **Font** tab selected, click **16 point.**
6. Click **OK** to set the format.
7. Click **OK** to apply.
8. Do not close the file.

Remove a Style

- You can remove a style from selected cells by clicking Format, Style, and click Normal style.
- You can remove a style from the Style name list by clicking the style and clicking the Delete button. Any cells set with that style revert to the Normal style setting.

TRY *it* OUT *E5-20*

1. Continue to work in the open file or open **E5-20** from the Data CD.
2. In **Cell D11,** click **Format**, **Style**, and **Normal.**
3. Click **OK.**
4. Click the **Undo** button.

5. Click **Format**, **Style**, and **Title2.**
6. Click **Delete.**
7. Click **OK.**
8. Apply the **Title** style to **Cell A2.**
9. Save the **E5-20** file. Close the file.

Find and Replace Cell Data and Formats

- If you want to review or edit specific text or numbers, you can search for the data and replace it, if necessary. This is called the *Find and Replace* feature. You can also find cells that match a format of a cell you specify. This feature is helpful if you want to change a format, because you can replace all occurrences as you find them.

Find Cell Data

- To find data, click Edit, Find and the Find and Replace dialog box opens in the Find tab. If you click the Options button, you notice, as shown in Figure 5.21, that you can define your search by looking in the sheet, in the workbook, searching by columns or rows, and looking for formulas, values, or comments. In addition, you can select options to match the case or the contents of the entire cell, and you can search for specific formats.
- Once you set your options, you can click Find All or Find Next. When you click Find All, you get a list of all the cell addresses that contain a match. When you click Find Next, you go to each location as it appears in the worksheet.

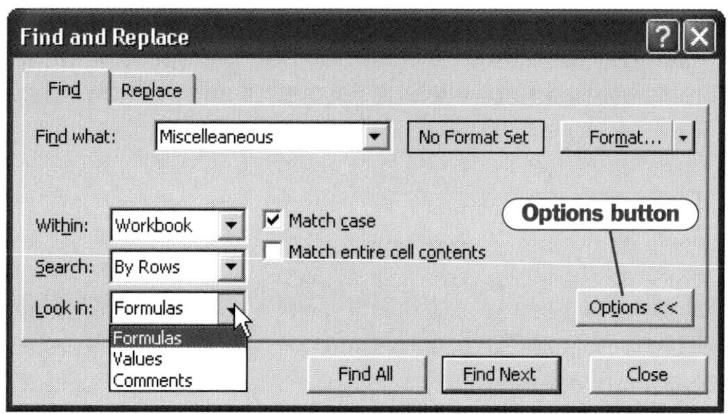

Figure 5.21 Find and Replace dialog box, Find tab, Look in list

TRY*it* OUT *E5-21*

1. Open **E5-21** from the Data CD.
2. Click **Edit**, **Find**, and the **Options** button.
3. Enter `Miscellaneous` in the Find what box.
4. Set the search **Within** the Workbook and click the **Match case** check box.
5. Click **Find Next** and keep clicking it until you find all occurrences.
6. Click **Find All** to see a list of all the locations.
7. Click the **Close** button in the dialog box.
8. Do not close the file.

Find and Replace Data and Formats

- To find specific data and replace it, click Edit, Replace, and the Find and Replace dialog box opens in the Replace tab as shown in Figure 5.22.
- After entering the Find and Replace information, you can click Replace All or just Replace. Clicking Replace All replaces all occurrences without giving you a chance to view each change. Clicking Replace lets you view each replacement before it is made, so you can be sure you want to replace it. You can undo a Find and Replace operation.

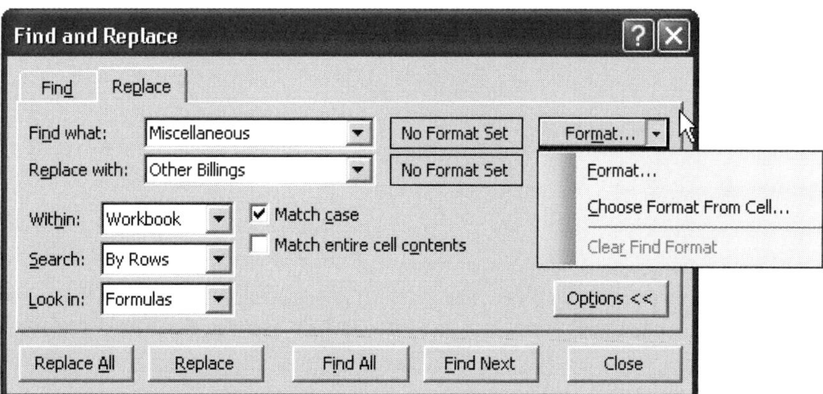

Figure 5.22 Find and Replace dialog box, Replace tab

EXCEL

▶ To search for a certain format, you can select a cell with the format you want, click the Format list arrow, click Choose Format From Cell, and that format becomes the search criteria. You can then change the format on the Replace with line by clicking Format to set the new format.

TRY *it* OUT *E5-22*

1. Continue to work in the open file or open **E5-22** from the Data CD.
2. Click **Edit**, **Replace**, and **Options** to display the Options buttons if they are not displayed.
3. Enter the information as shown in Figure 5.22, but do not press the Format button.
4. Click **Replace All** and notice the changes. Click **OK.**
5. Click the **Undo** button and click the **Redo** button.
6. Select and delete the text in the Find what and Replace with boxes.
7. Click the **Format** button list arrow on the Find what line and click **Choose Format From Cell.**
8. With the Choose cell pointer, click **Cell B3.**
9. Click the **Format** button list arrow on the Replace with line and click **Format.**
10. In the **Font** tab, set the format for **Arial, 10 point, bold, Dark Blue** color, and click **OK.** Notice the preview.
11. Click **Replace** each time to view the corrections.
12. Click the **Format** button list arrow on the Find what line and click **Clear Find Format.**
13. Click the **Format** button list arrow on the Replace with line and click **Clear Replace Format.**
14. Click the **Close button.**
15. Save the **E5-22** file. Close the file.

1
2
3

REHEARSAL

Again

TASK 4

GOAL

To create a balance sheet using styles and the Find and Replace features

SETTING THE STAGE/WRAPUP

File name: **5.4balsheet**

WHAT YOU NEED TO KNOW

- A business prepares a *balance sheet*, which is a financial report that shows the value of the firm's assets and liabilities, owner's worth, or stockholder's equity on a certain date. The balance sheet is based on the basic accounting equation: assets = liabilities + capital (owner's worth).
- The figures for the balance sheet come from the accounts and the worksheet. The owner's worth includes the profit for the period and shows the owner's share of the business. According to the formula, the creditors, or liabilities listed, and the owner share in the ownership of the assets. The proportion of ownership and the types of assets and liabilities listed are valuable information for a stockholder or owner, and for potential investors or lenders.
- In this Rehearsal activity, you will complete a balance sheet for Sutton Investment Group, set styles for enhancing the report, and find and replace data and formats.

DIRECTIONS

1. Open **5.4balsheet** from the Data CD.
2. Using the illustration on the facing page as a guide, enter the formulas to complete the balance sheet. The values in Total Assets, **Cell E21,** and in Total Liabilities and Owner's Equity, **Cell E38,** should balance or be equal.
3. Include lines under the numbers to indicate the additions, as illustrated.
4. In **Cell A1,** merge and center the title, and set the font for **Photina Casual Black, 16 point, bold.** (If this font is not installed, select a font similar to that shown in the illustration.)
5. Use Format Painter to format **Cell A2** with the same formats.
6. In **Cell A2,** change the font size to **14 point.**
7. Click **Cell A2** and define a style using that format; name it: `header2`.
8. Apply the **header2** format to **Cells A3, A6, A23,** and **A33.** (Hint: You can select each of these cells while pressing and holding the **Ctrl** key so that you can apply the style all at once.)
9. Format **Cell B7** for **Arial, 12 point, bold,** and define it as a style named: `header3`.
10. Apply the **header3** format to **Cells B16, B21, B24, B29,** and **B38.**
11. As shown in the illustration, indent labels that have not been formatted.
12. Select all the values in **Columns C, D,** and **E,** and format for commas with no decimal places.
13. Modify the **header2** style so that it includes a double-accounting underline. (All cells formatted with the header2 style will change.)

Continued on next page

14. Use the Find and Replace feature to find the word "Capital" and replace it with the word `Equity` in all occurrences.
15. Select **Cell E21** and format the cell for Currency with no decimals and a bold font. Define the style as **Totals.**
16. Apply the Totals style to **Cell E38.**
17. Select the entire report, the range **A1:E38,** and use Fill Color to shade it a light green.
18. Enter a footer that contains the file name and date.
19. Center the report vertically and horizontally using the Page Setup dialog box.
20. Print one copy.
21. Save the **5.4balsheet** file. Close the file.

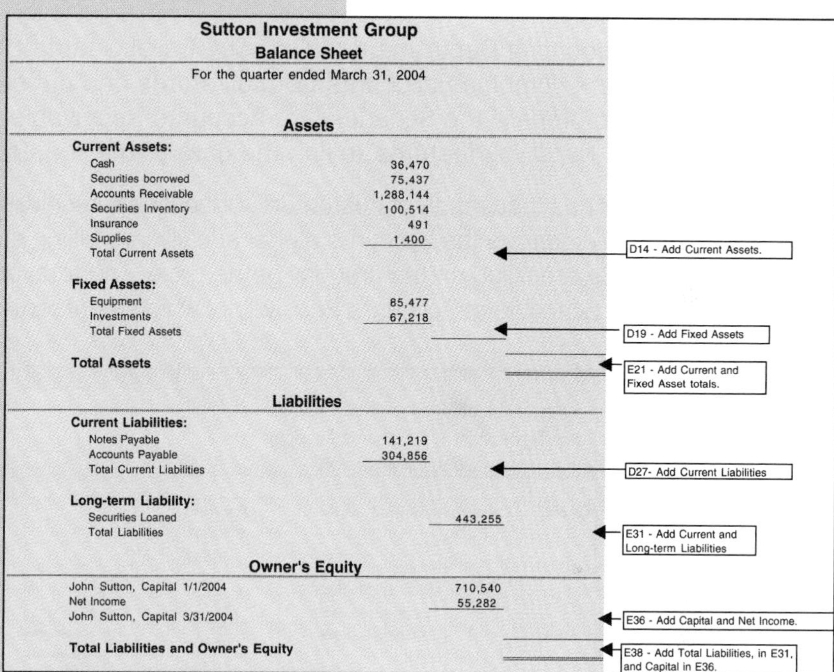

Sutton Investment Group
Balance Sheet
For the quarter ended March 31, 2004

Assets			
Current Assets:			
Cash	36,470		
Securities borrowed	75,437		
Accounts Receivable	1,288,144		
Securities Inventory	100,514		
Insurance	491		
Supplies	1,400		
Total Current Assets			D14 - Add Current Assets.
Fixed Assets:			
Equipment	85,477		
Investments	67,218		
Total Fixed Assets			D19 - Add Fixed Assets
Total Assets			E21 - Add Current and Fixed Asset totals.
Liabilities			
Current Liabilities:			
Notes Payable	141,219		
Accounts Payable	304,856		
Total Current Liabilities			D27- Add Current Liabilities
Long-term Liability:			
Securities Loaned		443,255	
Total Liabilities			E31 - Add Current and Long-term Liabilities
Owner's Equity			
John Sutton, Capital 1/1/2004		710,540	
Net Income		55,282	
John Sutton, Capital 3/31/2004			E36 - Add Capital and Net Income.
Total Liabilities and Owner's Equity			E38 - Add Total Liabilities, in E31, and Capital in E36.

Cues for Reference

Define a New Style
1. Click a cell that contains the style you want.
2. Click **Format**, **Style.**
3. Enter a name for the style in the Style name box.
4. Click **Add.**
5. Click **OK.**

Apply a Style
1. Select cell(s) to receive style.
2. Click **Format**, **Style.**
3. Click the **Style** list arrow and click style to apply.
4. Click **OK.**

Modify a Style
1. Click **Format, Style.**
2. Click the **Style** list arrow and click style to modify.
3. Click **Modify.**
4. In the Format Cells dialog box, set the format.
5. Click **OK** twice.

Find and Replace Data
1. Click **Edit, Replace.**
2. Enter data in Find what box.
3. Enter data in Replace with box.
4. Click Options and set, if appropriate.
5. Click **Replace** to do one at a time.

or

- Click **Replace All** to replace all occurrences.

Find and Replace Formats
1. Click **Edit, Replace.**
2. Clear text in Find and Replace boxes.
3. On the Find what line, click **Format, Choose Format From Cell.**
4. Select cell with format to find.
5. On Replace with line, click **Format** and select **Format.**
6. Set the new format.
7. Click **Replace** or **Replace All.**

PERFORMANCE

SETTING THE STAGE/WRAPUP

Act I File names:	**5p1.sched**
	5p1.trialbal
Act II File name:	**5p2.cis3d**
Act III File names:	**5p3.worksheet**
	5p3.balsheet

WHAT YOU NEED TO KNOW

Act I

You work in the Accounting Department of Odyssey Travel Gear in Chicago, and at the end of the year your department combines accounts from all stores and outlets into one Trial Balance. You have been asked to prepare the Schedules of Accounts Receivable and Accounts Payable and use the Paste Link and Hyperlink features to link the data to the Trial Balance.

Odyssey Travel Gear has thousands of customers, or accounts receivable, that are billed on a 20-day cycle. The business organizes the accounts alphabetically into billing groups; for example, customers with names from Aa to Be are billed on the first day of the cycle. The total due from each billing group is summarized on the Schedule of Accounts Receivable, which represents the total due from all customers.

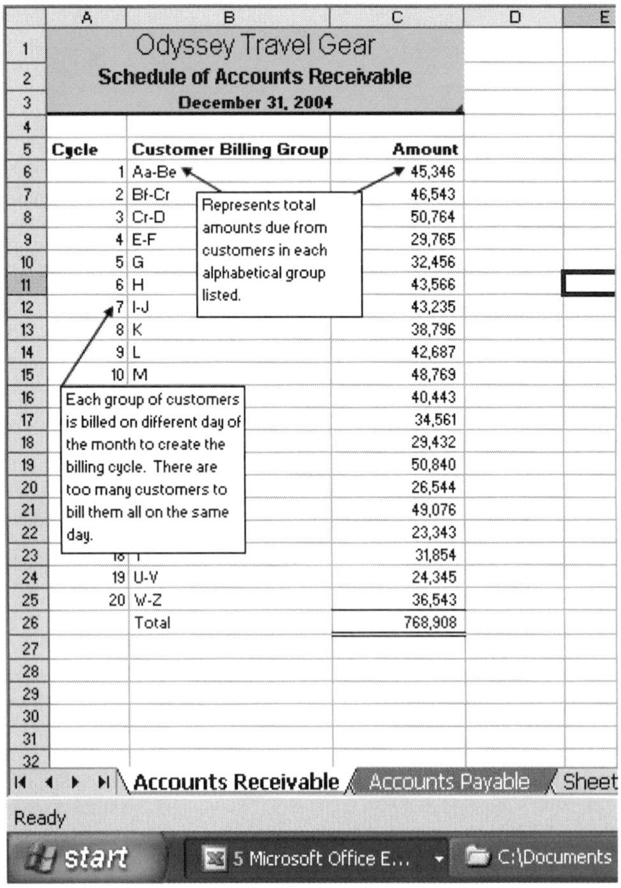

Odyssey Travel Gear
Schedule of Accounts Receivable
December 31, 2004

Cycle	Customer Billing Group	Amount
1	Aa-Be	45,346
2	Bf-Cr	46,543
3	Cr-D	50,764
4	E-F	29,765
5	G	32,456
6	H	43,566
7	I-J	43,235
8	K	38,796
9	L	42,687
10	M	48,769
		40,443
		34,561
		29,432
		50,840
		26,544
		49,076
		23,343
18	T	31,854
19	U-V	24,345
20	W-Z	36,543
	Total	768,908

Represents total amounts due from customers in each alphabetical group listed.

Each group of customers is billed on different day of the month to create the billing cycle. There are too many customers to bill them all on the same day.

Accounts Receivable | Accounts Payable | Sheet

Ready

start | 5 Microsoft Office E... | C:\Documents

Follow these guidelines:

- Open the files **5p1.sched** and **5p1.trialbal** from the Data CD. In both files, group sheets where possible, and format the titles and column headings using Merge and Center, bold and font formats, lines, colors, or borders. Format workbook values for commas with no decimal places.
- In the schedules file, rename and color the tabs. Find the total for each schedule, and add single and double lines.
- Copy the Accounts Receivable and Accounts Payable totals from the schedules and paste link them to the proper location on the Trial Balance. Link the totals next to the account title, in the Debit column for Accounts Receivable and in the Credit column for Accounts Payable.
- Total the Trial Balance and include a single line for adding and double lines under totals. The Debits and Credits should balance. Add a column to the right of the account titles. Insert hyperlinks to the correct schedule sheet in the file **5p1.sched,** using appropriate hyperlink text.
- Enter appropriate footers, save both files, print a copy of the Trial Balance and both schedules, and close the files.
- Attach both files to an e-mail to the managers of the five retail stores. (You can use the Internet addresses of other students in your class or addresses provided by your instructor.) Inform them that you are sending the trial balance and schedule data for the year ending December 31, 2004, for their records.

Act II

The Air Land Sea Travel Group has agencies in Boston, New York, Los Angeles, and San Francisco. Each agency has sent its quarterly income statement data, which has been copied into one worksheet. Ms. Janice Pierce, the president of the company, would like a consolidated report along with the supporting agency reports.

Follow these guidelines:

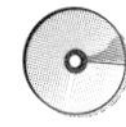

- Open the file **5p2.cis** from the Data CD.
- Copy any sheet and place it at the end of the worksheets. Rename and color-format each tab using the city name, and name the last tab: `Consolidated Income Statement.`

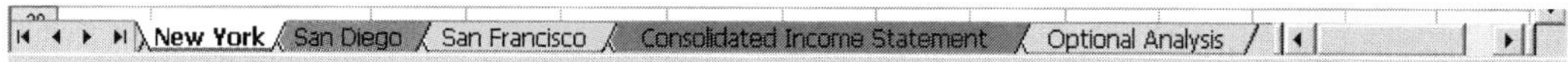

- Group sheets to enter formulas for calculating Total Income (D11), Total Expenses (D25), and Net Income (D27). Include lines for adding and double lines for totals, where necesasary.
- Ungroup the sheets, and on the last sheet, clear the data from Column C, which belonged to one of the agencies, leaving the formulas in Column D. Correct the title to read: `Consolidated Income Statement.` Use 3-D references in Column C to combine all the data from the four agencies onto the Consolidated Income Statement sheet. Clear any unnecessary formulas, and check to make sure the existing formulas in Column D are working correctly.
- Group the sheets to format values for commas with no decimals, use color buttons to format the Income Statements as desired, format the Net Income value for currency with no decimals, include headers and/or footers, and include the sheet name, date, file name, and company logo.
- Save the workbook, print copies of all sheets, and close the file.
- *Optional:* Insert another sheet and create an Income Analysis comparing the total and net income from the agency in each city. Calculate what percentage the net income is of total income so you can compare the results.

Act III

Green Brothers Gardening's chief financial officer, Ralph Green, has started to prepare the worksheet and Balance Sheet for the year. He has asked you to complete and format the reports. Ralph Green needs the Balance Sheet for meetings with bankers and the president, Calvin Green, because Green Brothers is contemplating an expansion and requires additional funding.

Follow these guidelines:

- Open the files **5p3.worksheet** and **5.p3balsheet** from the Data CD.
- Format worksheet titles and column headings using fonts, merge and center, and bold settings. Format worksheet values for commas with no decimal places.
- In Cell B5 of the worksheet, freeze panes to be able to work in the worksheet. The yellow areas show where you should place formulas. Find totals in cells B30:C30 and in cells D32:K32. In Cell H33, find Net Income by subtracting the total in Cell H32 from Cell I32. Enter the Net Income value in Cell K33 and find the totals in the range H34:K34. The values in each set of debit and credit columns, beginning with Columns B and C, should be equal. After formulas are completed, remove the color.

	A	B	C	D	E	F	G	H	I	J	K
1	Green Brothers Gardening										
2	Worksheet										
3	For the year ended December 31, 2004										
4											
5		Trial Balance		Adjustments		Adjusted Trial Balance		Income Statement		Balance Sheet	
6		Debit	Credit	Debit	Credit	Debit	Credit	Debit	Credit	Debit	Credit
7	Cash	34565				34565				34565	
8	Accounts Receivable	145765				145765				145765	
9	Nursery Inventory	257654		205444	257654	205444				205444	
10	Supplies	5456			3234	2222				2222	
11	Equipment	568433				568433				568433	
12	Allowance for Depreciation		181900		54678		236578				236578
13	Accounts Payable		142789				142789				142789
14	Loan Payable		25000				25000				25000
15	Ralph Green, Capital		386944				386944				386944
16	Calvin Green, Capital										
17	Purchases	865789				865789		865789			
18	Contracts Income		345765				345765		345765		
19	Nursery Sales Income		739872				739872		739872		
20	Landscaping Fees Income		673657				673657		673657		
21	Advertising Expense	36543				36543		36543			
22	Depreciation Expense			54678		54678		54678			
23	Equipment Maintenance	8745				8745		8745			
24	Interest Expense	2309				2309		2309			
25	Insurance Expense	11574				11574		11574			
26	Payroll Tax Expense	36546				36546		36546			
27	Rent Expense	89759				89759		89759			
28	Salary Expense	432789				432789		432789			
29	Supplies Expense			3234		3234		3234			
30	Totals										
31	Income Summary			257654	205444	257654	205444	257654	205444		
32	Totals										
33	Net Income										
34	Totals										
35											
36											
37											
38											
39											

Enter formulas in yellow areas

EXCEL

- On the Balance Sheet, format the titles and values and establish styles for the headings in Cells A6, A21, and A29, and for the section headings in Cells B7, B14, B19, B22, B25, B27, B37, and B39.
- Subtract the Allowance for Depreciation from the Equipment account balance. Divide the Net Income (H33) from the worksheet in half, and place it under each partner's equity to calculate their new equity. Enter all formulas necessary to complete the Balance Sheet.
- Find and replace all occurrences of the word "Equity" with "Capital."
- Ralph Green needs the following printouts:

  Balance sheet.

  Partial worksheet with the Trial Balance and Adjustments columns hidden.

  Full worksheet on two pages using the Print Titles feature.
- Save and close all files.
- Search the www.entrepreneurmag.com site to develop a list of the "best banks for small businesses" for the state of Virginia.
- *Group Project:* Use the same Web site to research the characteristics, problems, and advantages of organizing a business as a partnership (as in this family business) or as a corporation. The Green brothers are discussing incorporation and would like more information about this type of business organization. Write an essay that summarizes the aspects of organizing a business as a partnership, as compared to a corporate form of organization. (Hint: You can use "advantages of incorporation" as keywords.)

LESSON 6

Charts and Diagrams

In this lesson, you will learn to use features in Excel to create, modify, print, and position charts, diagrams, and graphics.

Upon completion of this lesson, you should have mastered the following skill sets:

- Create, modify, and position charts
- About charts
- Create charts
- Apply chart options
- Create pie chart
- Position a chart
- Chart types and subtypes
- Modify charts
- Copy and paste charts
- Format charts
- Print charts
- Create, position, and modify graphics
- Insert and download graphics and clip art
- Create, modify, and position diagrams
- Create stock charts

Terms

Software-related

Charts
Nonadjacent selection
Series labels
Legend
Y-axis or value axis
X-axis or category axis
Category labels
Data series
Chart Wizard
Embedded chart
Chart sheet
Pie chart
Column chart
Line chart
Graphics
AutoShapes
Diagrams

Document-related

Portfolio
S&P 500

TRYOUT

TASK 1

GOALS

To use charts to analyze sales and income data

To create charts to compare expense data for several years

To practice using the following skill sets:

- Create, modify, and position charts
- About charts
- Create charts
- Apply chart options
- Create pie chart
- Position a chart
- Chart types and subtypes
- Modify charts
- Copy and paste charts
- Format charts
- Print charts

EXCEL

WHAT YOU NEED TO KNOW

Create, Modify, and Position Charts

About Charts

- *Charts* present and compare data in a graphic format so that you can compare information visually.
- To create a chart, you must first select the data to plot. Figure 6.1 shows two selections of data; each selection produces the chart shown in Figure 6.2. The list of guidelines below refer to the selection of chart data:
    - The selection should be rectangular.
    - The selection should not contain blank or unrelated columns or rows. (See Selection A in Figure 6.1.)
    - Use a *nonadjacent selection* when data is not contiguous (see Selection B in Figure 6.1). Select data while pressing and holding the Ctrl key to eliminate blanks or unrelated data. You can also hide columns you do not want to select.
    - The blank cell in the upper left corner of a selection indicates that the data to the right are *series labels* and the data below are category labels for the values.

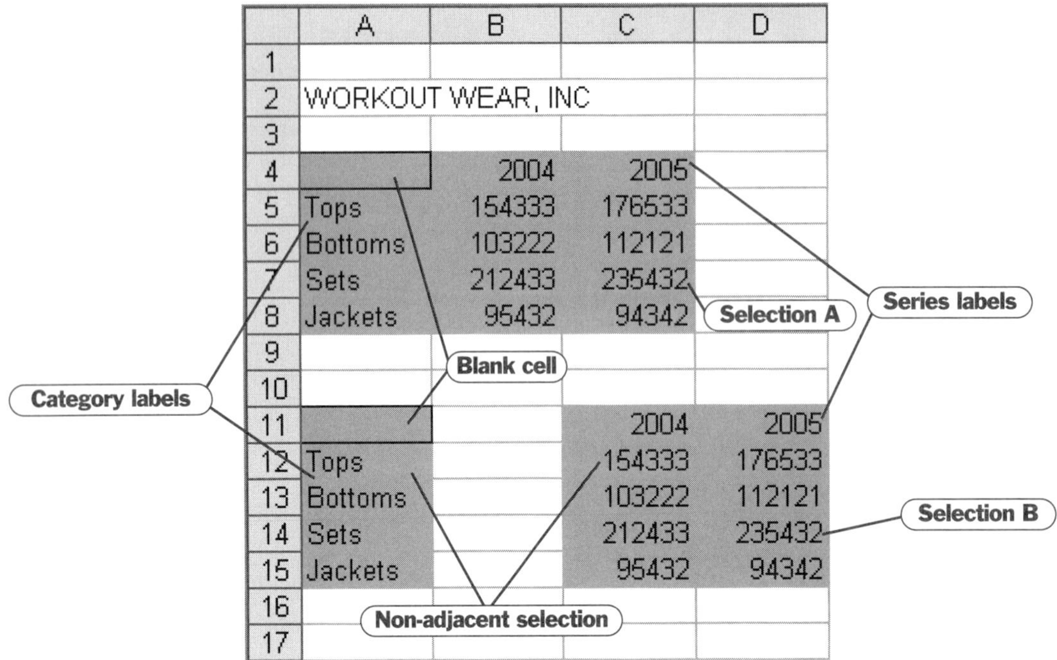

Figure 6.1 Data selections for a chart

▶ The chart in Figure 6.2 is a column chart produced from either selection in Figure 6.1 (because the same data is selected). Move the mouse pointer over the parts of a chart to view the ScreenTip that displays the name of the chart object. The objects in the column chart are labeled on Figure 6.2 and defined below:

- The chart title—identifies the data in the chart and is entered using the Chart Wizard.
- The *y-axis* or *value axis*—typically represents the vertical scale. The scale values are entered automatically by Excel.
- The y-axis or value axis title—identifies the values and is entered using the Chart Wizard.
- The *x-axis* or *category axis*—typically represents the horizontal scale and the data series categories.
- The *category labels*—identify each category and are obtained from the selected data (see Figure 6.1).
- The x-axis or category axis title—identifies the category and is entered using the Chart Wizard.
- The series labels-legend—identifies each data series and is obtained from the selected data (see Figure 6.1).
- The *data series*—groups of values identified by a label, such as 2004 data in the illustration.
- The plot area—the space where the values are charted.

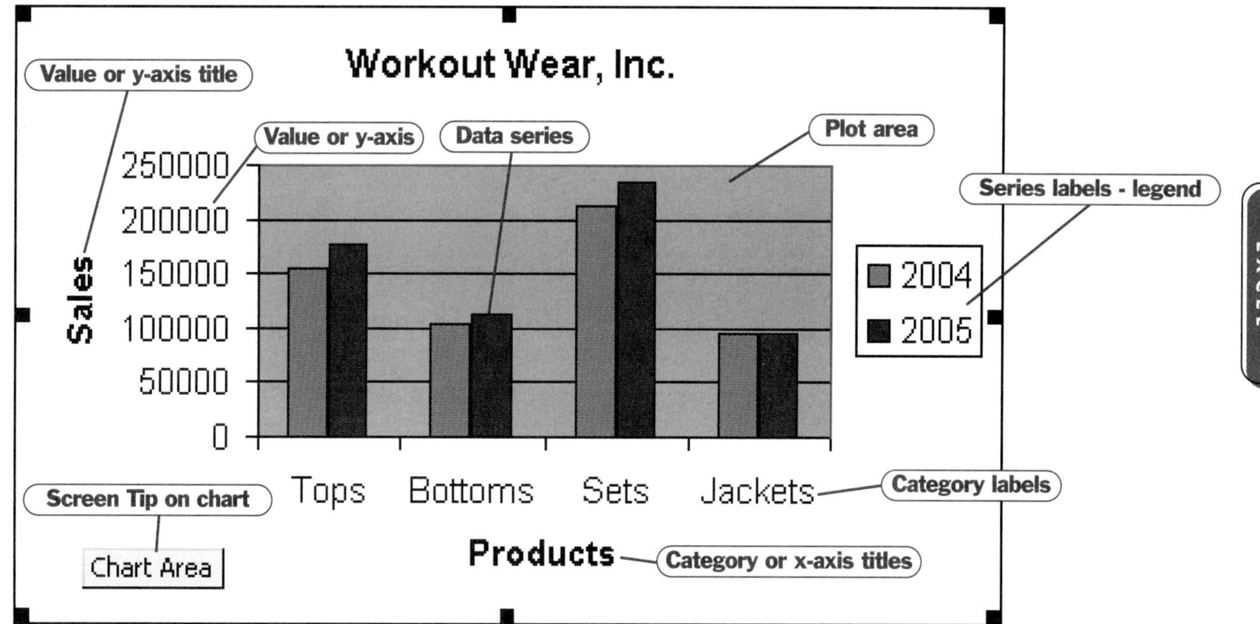

Figure 6.2 Column chart objects

EXCEL

TRY *it* OUT *E6-1*

1. Open **E6-1** from the Data CD.
2. Select the range **A4:C8.** This is the charted data.
3. Select the range **A11:A15,** press and hold the **Ctrl** key, and select the range **C11:D15.** This is also the charted data, using a nonadjacent selection.
4. Move the mouse pointer over all the chart objects to locate each ScreenTip, one of which is shown in Figure 6.2.
5. Close the file. Do not save.

Create Charts

- The *Chart Wizard* makes creating charts easy by providing step-by-step instructions.
- The basic steps to create a chart are:
  - Select the worksheet data to chart.
  - Click the Chart Wizard button.
  - Follow the Chart Wizard prompts on four screens:

    Screen 1. Select chart type.

    Screen 2. Check chart source data range.

    Screen 3. Select chart options.

    Screen 4. Select chart location.

- The Chart Wizard takes you through the four screens to create a chart. Each screen consists of tabbed dialog boxes that allow you to select and format all the objects in your chart. As you make selections, the Chart Wizard shows you exactly how the chart looks so you can select the format that is best for presenting your data.

- On Screen 4, when you select the chart location, you create either an *embedded chart,* which exists as an object on your worksheet, or a *chart sheet,* which exists on a separate sheet within the workbook. Figure 6.3 shows Screen 4 displaying the chart placement options. Excel names chart sheets as Chart1, Chart2, etc, however, when you select As new sheet you can name the chart sheet to describe the chart better.

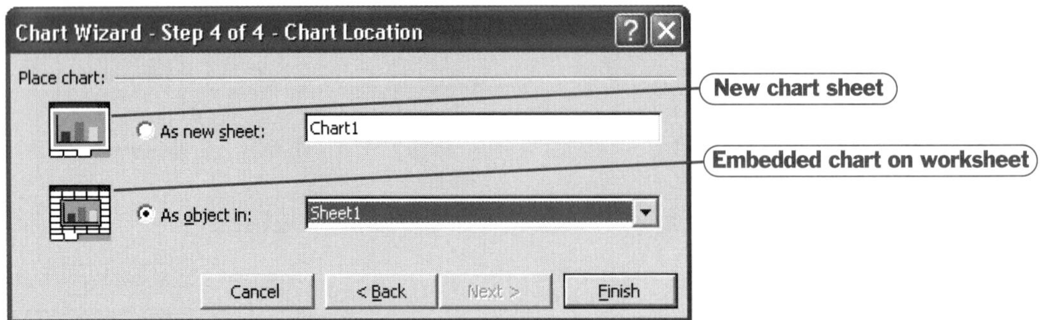

Figure 6.3 Chart Wizard, Screen 4

TRY it OUT *E6-2*

1. Open **E6-2** from the Data CD.
2. Select the range **A4:C7.** This is the data range to chart.
3. Click the **Chart Wizard** button. 
4. Click **Next** to accept the Column chart type.
5. Click **Next** to accept the data range.
6. In the Step 3 dialog box on the Titles tab, enter `Art 'n Stuff - Sales by Store` as the chart title.
7. Click **Next** to accept the title.
8. Select **As new sheet** for the chart location.
9. Enter `Column Chart` as the sheet name.
10. Click **Finish** to complete the chart. The chart appears on Column Chart, a new sheet.
11. Do not close the file.

Apply Chart Options

- Screen 3 of the Chart Wizard allows you to set chart options on six options tabs. You can change or enter chart titles, axes, gridlines, legends, data labels, and a data table for most charts. The number of tabs and options vary with the type of chart selected. For example, pie charts have only three option tabs.
- In Figure 6.4, you can see Screen 3 on the Titles tab for the column chart in E6-2. You can set and view each option on your chart in the preview window as you add the option.

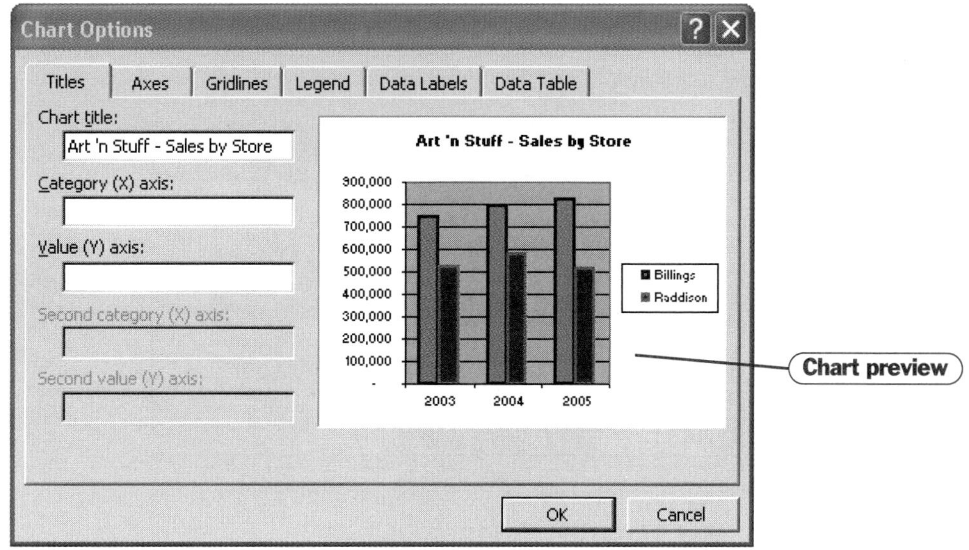

Figure 6.4 Chart Wizard, Screen 3, Chart Options, Titles tab

Create Pie Chart

▶ The *pie chart,* shown in Figure 6.5, is a circular graph you can use to show the relationship of each value in a data range to the entire range. The size of each slice of the pie represents the percentage each value contributes to the total. Select only one numeric data range for a pie chart.

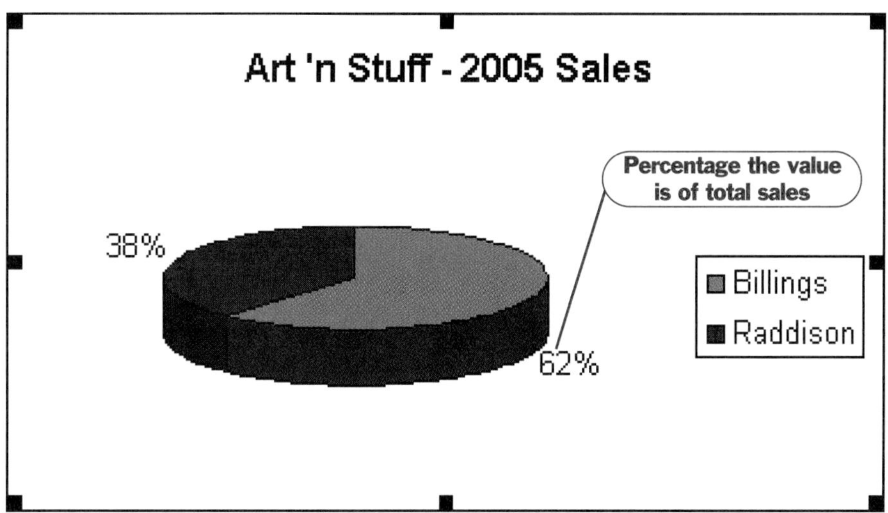

Figure 6.5 Pie chart

Position a Chart

▶ You have placed a chart on a new sheet. However, on the last screen of the Chart Wizard, you can also elect to embed the chart on the worksheet, which requires you to size and position the chart.

▶ To position, size, edit, move, and copy a chart on a worksheet, click the chart once to select it. As shown in Figure 6.6, handles appear around the chart border to indicate that the chart is selected and in Edit mode. Notice that Excel highlights the charted data as well.

▶ To move a chart, you must select the chart, click it, and drag it to its new location. The mouse pointer changes to a four-headed arrow during the move. You can size the chart by dragging the handles to the desired size.

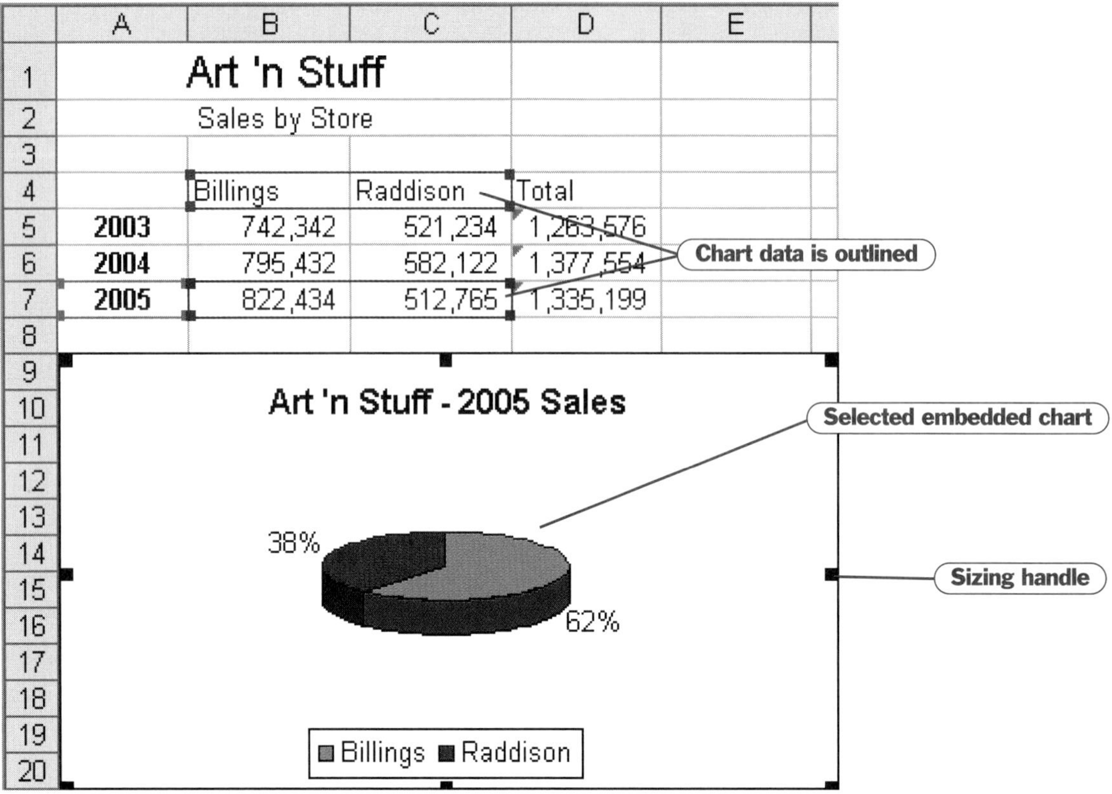

Figure 6.6 Selected embedded chart

TRY it OUT *E6-3*

1. Continue to work in the open file on Sheet1 or open **E6-3** from the Data CD.
2. Select the range **A4:C4,** press and hold the **Ctrl** key, and select the range **A7:C7.**
3. Click the **Chart Wizard** button.
4. Select **Pie** chart, **second** sub-type, **3-D visual effect,** and click **Next.**
5. Click **Next** to accept the data range.
6. On the Titles tab, enter: `Art 'n Stuff – 2005 Sales`
7. On the Legend tab, select **Bottom placement** for the legend.
8. On the Data Labels tab, select **Percentage.**
9. Click **Finish.** The pie chart appears on the worksheet, as shown in Figure 6.6
10. Click and drag the chart to **A9,** a blank location on the worksheet.
11. Do not close the file.

Chart Types and Subtypes

- The *column chart* (see Figure 6.2) compares individual or sets of values. The height of each bar is proportional to its corresponding value in the worksheet.
- Fourteen standard chart types are available in the Chart Wizard. Each of these types offers at least two subtypes. The subtypes for the Column chart are shown in Figure 6.7.

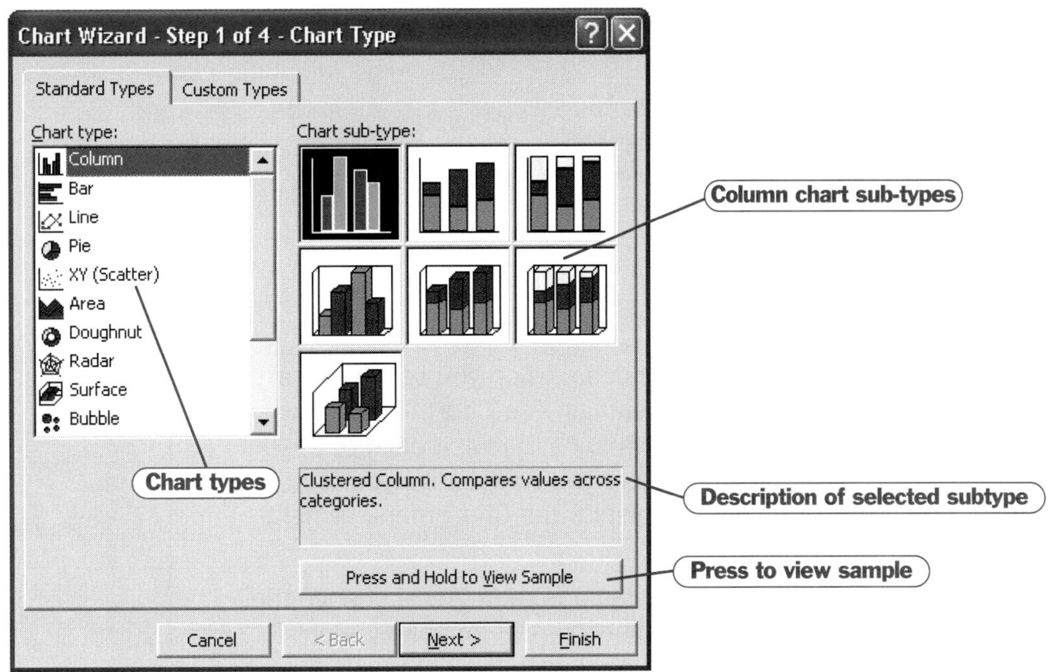

Figure 6.7 Chart Wizard, Screen 1, Chart Type

- A *line chart,* shown in Figure 6.8, is like a column chart because it compares individual sets of values, but lines connect the points of data. This is useful if you want to show a progression over time.

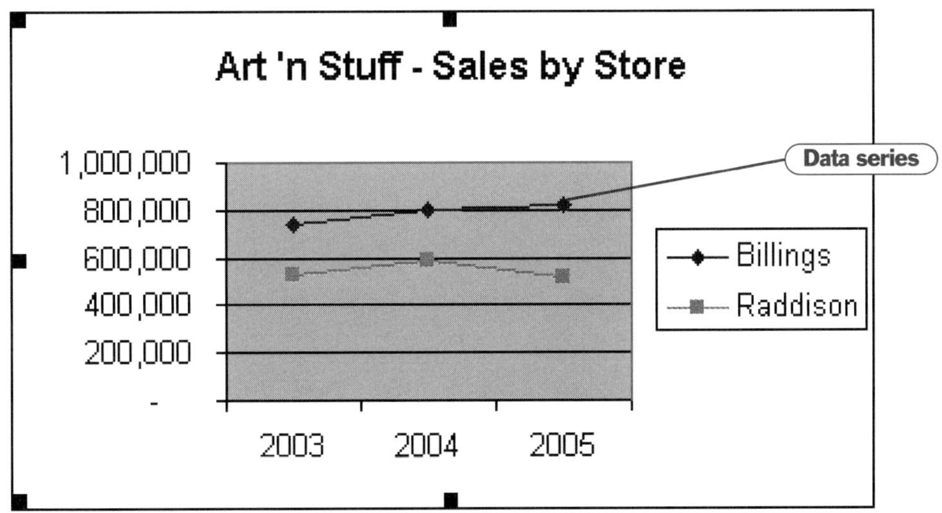

Figure 6.8 Line chart

TRY it OUT *E6-4*

1. Continue to work in the open file on Sheet1 or open **E6-4** from the Data CD.
2. Select the range **A4:C7** and click the **Chart Wizard** button.
3. Select each of the Column chart subtypes, and click and hold the **Press and Hold to View Sample** button.
4. Switch to Bar charts and test the subtypes as described in Step 3 above.
5. Switch to Line charts and select the **Line with Markers** subtype. Click **Next**.
6. Click **Next** to accept the data range.
7. Enter the title: `Art 'n Stuff - Sales by Store.` Click **Next.**
8. Place the chart as an embedded object on the sheet and position it in Cell F9 or next to the pie chart.
9. Do not close the file.

Modify Charts

- Use the Chart menu, which appears when you select a chart, to modify or edit your chart settings. The Chart menu, as shown in Figure 6.9, lists commands to revisit each of the steps in the Chart Wizard, where you can change your settings as necessary. You can also display the Chart menu by right-clicking the chart.
- You can modify the Source Data on Screen 2 and change the orientation of the data. By selecting rows or columns on the Source Data screen, you will change the emphasis of the charted data.

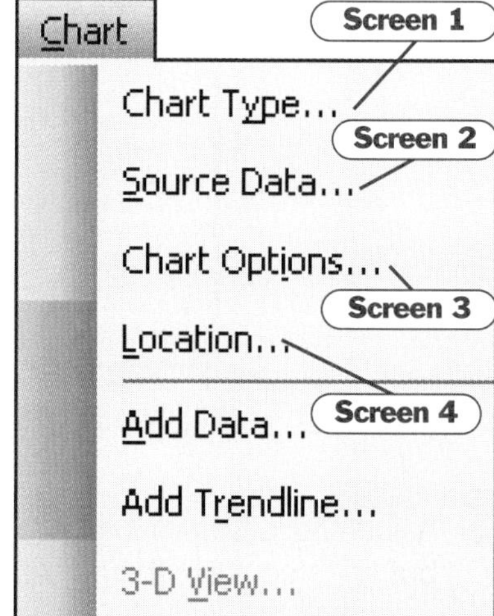

Figure 6.9 Chart menu

Copy and Paste Charts

- Once you select a chart, you can copy and paste it. Use the Copy and Paste buttons as you do with any other data.

TRY it OUT *E6-5*

1. Continue to work in the open file or open **E6-5** from the Data CD.
2. Select and copy the line chart and paste it in **Cell A22** or to a location under the chart in Column A. A second chart, selected, appears.
3. Click **Chart, Chart Type,** and change the type to **Bar.** Click **OK.**
4. Right-click the chart and select **Source Data.**
5. In the **Series in** option area, change the orientation from columns to rows. Click **OK.**
6. Do not close the file.

Format Charts

- You can format every object on a chart using the Format Chart dialog box. You can open the dialog box, as shown in Figure 6.10, by double-clicking a chart or any object in a chart. When you double-click a chart object, Excel marks it with a border and handles and displays the name of the object in the name box.
- The Format Chart dialog box varies, depending on which chart object you want to format. Figure 6.10 shows the Format Chart Area dialog box.

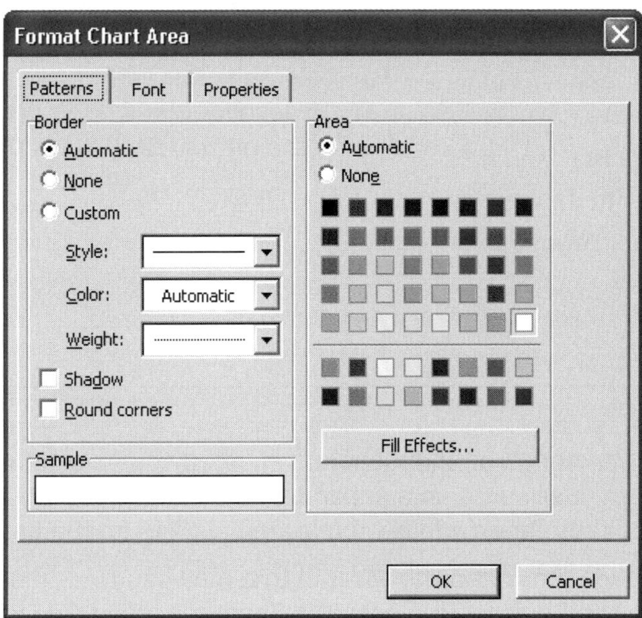

Figure 6.10 Format Chart Area dialog box

- In addition, every object in a chart has a shortcut menu that lets you change the chart type and the source data, format the object, or use other commands relevant to the object. Figure 6.11 shows the shortcut menu for the data series in a pie chart.

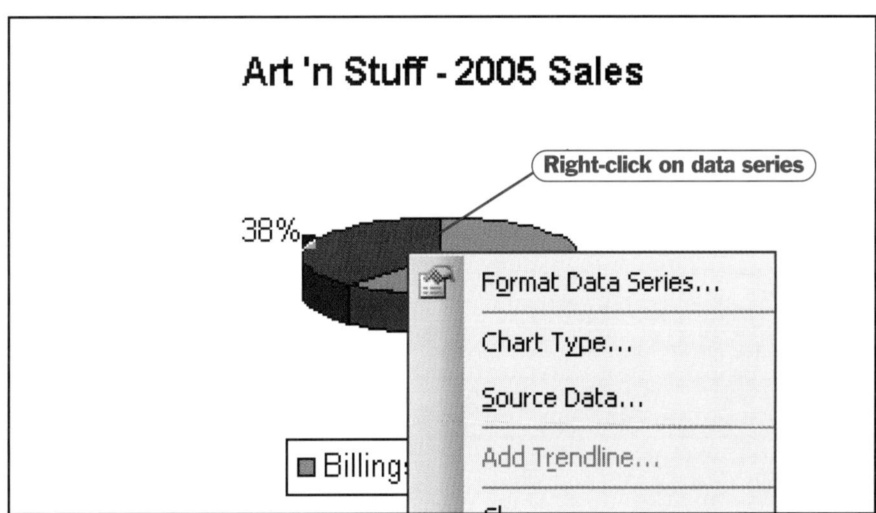

Figure 6.11 Data series shortcut menu

TRY *it* OUT E6-6

1. Continue to work in the open file or open **E6-6** from the Data CD.
2. Double-click the chart title of the pie chart. The title is bordered and the Format Chart Title dialog box appears.
3. In the Font tab, change the font to **Century, 16 point, bold, blue.** *Note:* Use another font if Century is not available.
4. Click **OK.**
5. Select the **embedded line chart** and right-click the **value axis** labels on the left.
6. On the shortcut menu, click **Format Axis** and click the **Alignment** tab.
7. Set the text alignment to **16 degrees** rotation. Click **OK.**
8. Return the Value Axis alignment to **0 degrees** rotation.
9. Double-click the Plot area and change the area color to **White** in the Format Plot Area dialog box. Click **OK.**
10. Select the Bar chart and double-click on the legend. Change the background color of the area to **Grey.** Click **OK.**
11. Do not close the file.

Print Charts

- You can print charts with the worksheet, or on a separate sheet. If you select an embedded chart on a worksheet or a chart sheet, it will print on a separate sheet to fit one page. If you print charts with the worksheet, use Print Preview to be sure everything fits on the page.
- Excel selects the page orientation (portrait or landscape) that matches the shape of the chart. On the Page Setup dialog box, the Chart tab replaces the Sheet tab, as shown in Figure 6.12. Chart setup options include chart size and printing quality.

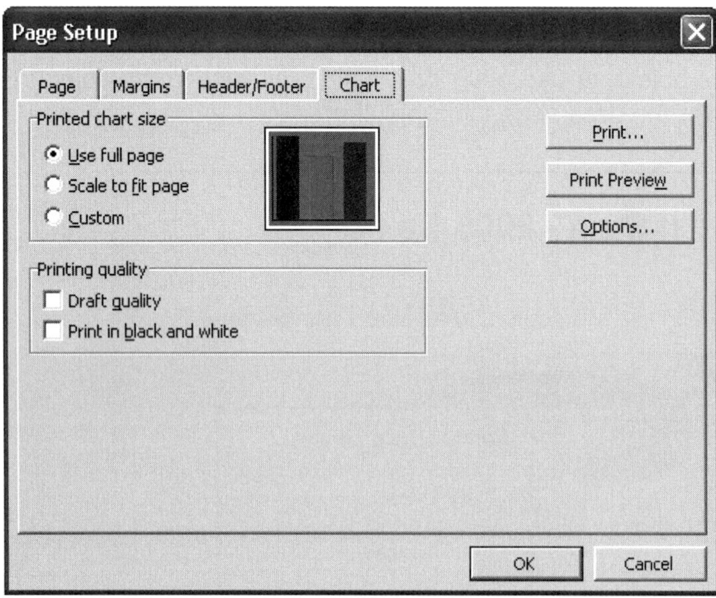

Figure 6.12 Page Setup dialog box, Chart tab

TRY *it* OUT *E6-7*

1. Continue to work in the open file or open **E6-7** from the Data CD.
2. Select the **Column Chart** sheet.
3. Click the **Print Preview** button.
4. Click **Print** and **OK.**
5. On Sheet1, select the pie chart.
6. Click the **Print Preview** button.
7. Click **Setup** and click the **Chart** tab.
8. Click **Print in black and white** and click **OK.**
9. Click **Print, OK.**
10. Select the range **A1:L34,** and click the **Print Preview** button.
11. Click **Setup** and change the orientation to **Landscape.** Close the preview screen.
12. Save the file as **E6-7.** Close the file.

TASK 1A

GOAL
To use charts to analyze sales and income data

SETTING THE STAGE/WRAPUP
File name: **6.1salechart**

WHAT YOU NEED TO KNOW

- Although detailed data is found on financial reports and analysis worksheets, businesses frequently use charts to summarize data for meetings, presentations, and annual reports. The chart type you select often determines the impression the data makes.
- Column and bar charts are similar, except that the data markers are vertical in column charts and horizontal in bar charts. You can copy and paste a chart and change the chart type to provide a different display.
- In this Rehearsal activity, you will create and modify charts using various chart types on chart sheets, and in the workbook for Time Out Sporting Goods. They are testing chart types to determine which chart makes the best impression.

DIRECTIONS

1. Open **6.1salechart** from the Data CD.
2. On the Chart data sheet, use a nonadjacent selection to select the ranges **A3:A6** and **C3:D6.**
3. Create a column chart with the following options on the Chart Wizard screens:
   Screen 1: In the **Column** chart type, select the Clustered column with a 3-D visual effect subtype (Row 2, Column 1); click **Next.**
   Screen 2: Setting should be for **Series in: Columns,** check the data range and, if correct, click **Next.**
   Screen 3: In the Titles tab, enter `Time Out Sporting Goods` for the Chart title. Enter `Stores` for the x-axis title. On the Legend tab, place the legend at the bottom of the chart. Click **Next.**
   Screen 4: Place the chart as a new sheet and enter `Column Chart` as the chart name. Click **Finish.**
4. Select the chart title and format it for Arial Black, Regular style, 24 point.
5. Format the text in the legend and both axes for bold. Expand the legend box as necessary.
6. Select the **Chart data** sheet. Using the same data, create a bar chart with the following options on the Chart Wizard screens:
   Screen 1: Click **Bar** chart. Use the Clustered bar with a 3-D visual effect subtype (Row 2, Column 1); click **Next.**
   Screen 2: Check the data range and, if correct, click **Next.**
   Screen 3: In the Titles tab, enter `Time Out Sporting Goods` for the chart title. On the Legend tab, place the legend at the bottom of the chart. Click **Next.**

Continued on next page

Screen 4. Place the chart as a new sheet and enter `Bar Chart` as the chart name. Click **Finish.**

7. Format title, legend, and axes as you did in steps 4 and 5.
8. Insert a new worksheet and copy the bar chart to the new sheet.
9. Select the new chart and use the Chart menu to modify the type of chart to a line chart. Name the sheet `Line Chart.`
10. Select the **Chart Data** sheet. Use a nonadjacent selection to select ranges **A3:D3** and **A6:D6.**
11. Create a pie chart with the following options on the Chart Wizard screens:
    - Screen 1: Click **Pie** chart. Use the Pie with a 3-D visual effect subtype (Row 1, Column 2); click **Next.**
    - Screen 2: Check the data range and, if correct, click **Next.**
    - Screen 3: In the Titles tab enter `Time Out Sporting Goods – Net Income` for the chart title. On the Legend tab, place the legend at the bottom of the chart. Set data labels to show percentage and category name; click **Next.**
    - Screen 4: Place the chart as an object in Chart Data. Click **Finish.**
12. Drag the pie chart to **Cell A11.**
13. Select and print Column Chart, Bar Chart, and Chart Data sheets.
14. Delete the line chart sheet, because it was not the best way to present the data.
15. Save the file **6.1salechart.** Close the file.

EXCEL

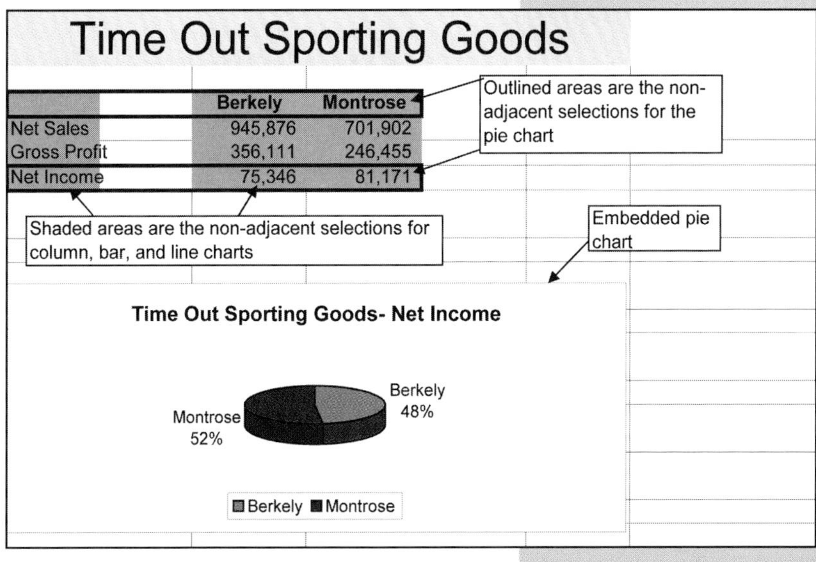

Cues for Reference

Select Chart Data

1. Always keep a blank cell in top-left corner.
2. Select rectangular data to chart.
   or
   Press and hold **Ctrl** while selecting nonadjacent data.

Create a Chart

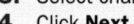

1. Select chart data.
2. Click **Chart Wizard** button.
3. Select chart type and subtype.
4. Click **Next.**
5. Check data range and reenter if incorrect.
6. Click **Next.**
7. Click appropriate tab and set chart options.
8. Click **Next.**
9. Select placement: Click **As new sheet** and enter sheet name in text box.
   or
   Click **As object in**, accept option offered, or enter sheet name.
10. Click **Finish.**

Select Chart

Embedded Chart

- Click chart. (A border with handles surrounds the chart.)

Chart Sheet

- Select sheet

Position Chart

1. Select the embedded chart.
2. Drag to new location. (Mouse pointer changes to four-headed arrow.)

Size Embedded Charts

1. Select chart.
2. Place mouse pointer on the handle on side of border to size. Use corner to size proportionally. The mouse pointer becomes a double-headed arrow when positioned correctly.
3. Drag border outline until you reach the required size.

Format Charts

1. Double-click the chart object to format.
2. Click the appropriate Format dialog box tab.
3. Set the format.
4. Click **OK.**

Modify Charts

1. Select chart.
2. Click **Chart** and chart option to modify.
   or
   Right-click chart and select chart option to modify.
3. Make modification.
4. Click **OK.**

Print Charts

Chart Sheet

1. Select sheet.
2. Click the **Print** button.

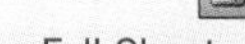

Embedded Chart on a Full Sheet

1. Select chart.
2. Click the **Print** button.

Embedded Chart on the Worksheet

1. Select worksheet range including chart.
2. Click **Print** button.

1
2
3

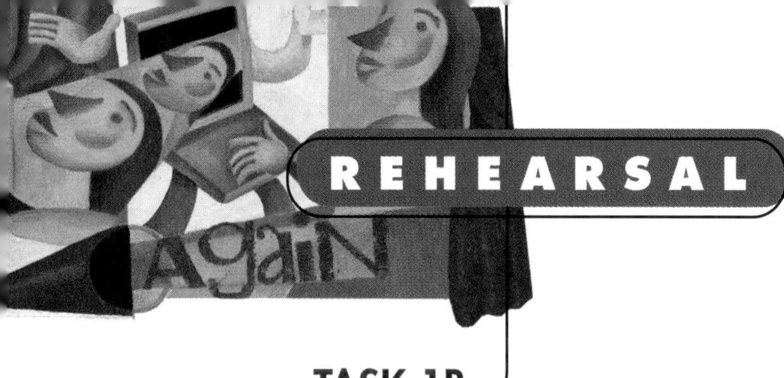

GOAL
To create charts to compare expense data for several years

SETTING THE STAGE/WRAPUP
File name: **6.1expchart**

WHAT YOU NEED TO KNOW

- In this Rehearsal activity, you will create, format, and modify charts using various chart types on chart sheets and embedded in the worksheet for the Sutton Investment Group. This company is comparing expenses for the past three years to see the developing trends and to determine where it can make changes.

DIRECTIONS

1. Open **6.1expchart** from the Data CD.
2. Use nonadjacent selection to select the labels and data in the ranges **C4:C11** and **E4:G11,** as shown in Illustration C on page 164.
3. Create a column chart, as shown in Illustration A. Include the following:
   a. 3-D visual effect (clustered column) subtype
   b. Enter the chart title: `Sutton Investment Group`
   c. X-axis title: `Expenses`
   d. Legend: Place at the top of the chart
   e. Place the chart on a chart sheet named: `Expense Column Chart`
4. Modify the x-axis data series labels to an **8 point** font.
5. Modify the chart title to a **16 point** font. Select the title area and add `– Expense Analysis` so that the title reads: `Sutton Investment Group – Expense Analysis`
6. Use the shortcut menu on the Expense Column Chart Sheet tab to create a copy of the chart sheet and move it to the end.
7. Select the chart copy and change the chart type to an Area chart with 3-D visual effect, as shown in Illustration B.
8. Select **Chart, Chart Options** and on the Gridlines tab, add major and minor gridlines to the x-axis.
9. Rename the Expense Column Chart(2) sheet to `Expense Area Chart.`
10. Delete Sheet2 and Sheet3.
11. On Sheet1, select the data labels in the range **C4:C11** and the data in **Column G** to create a pie chart for 2005 data. Use the following options:
    a. Apply the 3-D Visual Effect subtype.
    b. Enter the chart title: `Sutton Investment Group 2005 Expense Dollar.`

Continued on next page

c. Place the legend at the bottom of the chart.
d. Set data labels to show percentages.
e. Place the chart as an object on Sheet1.

12. Drag and size the chart so it fits in the range **A13:I41.**
13. Select the chart title, click after "Group," and press the **Enter** key so that the title is arranged on two lines, as shown in Illustration C.
14. Modify the legend so that it has a light yellow background.
15. Use the Patterns tab of the Format Chart Area dialog box to modify the color of the chart background and the border color to a light green.
16. Select the range **A1:I41** and change the background to a light green.
17. Rename Sheet1 as `Expense Data and Pie Chart.`
18. Group all the sheets and print the entire workbook.
19. Ungroup the sheets.
20. Save the file **6.1expchart** and close the file.

EXCEL

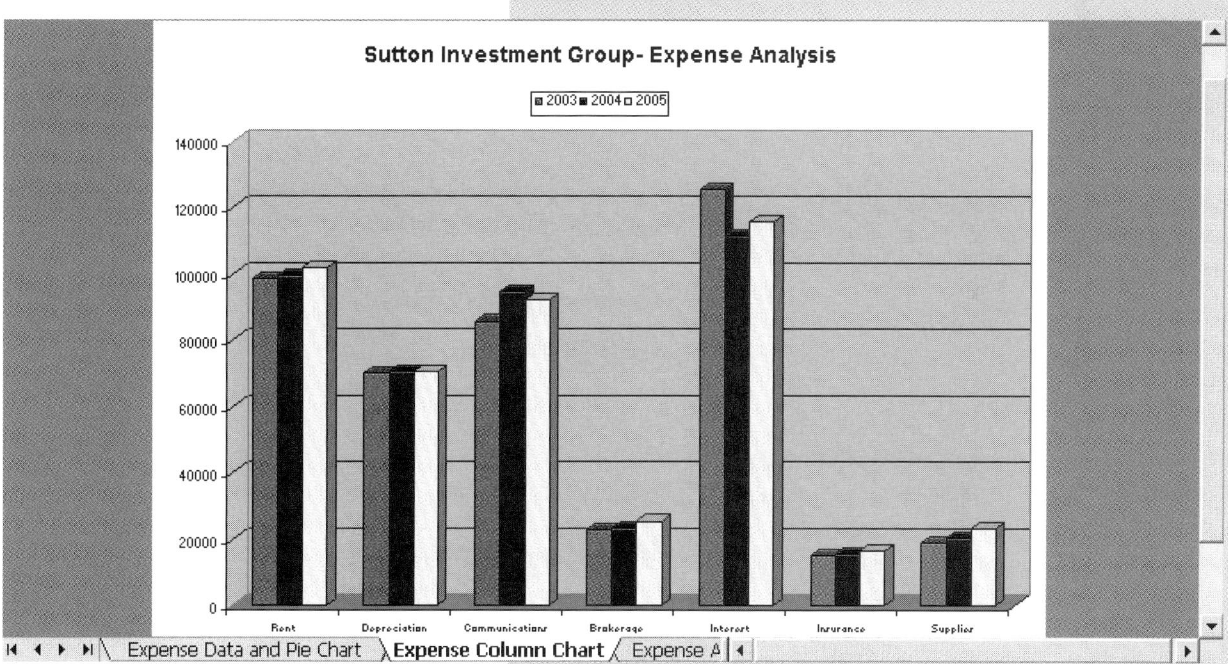

Illustration A

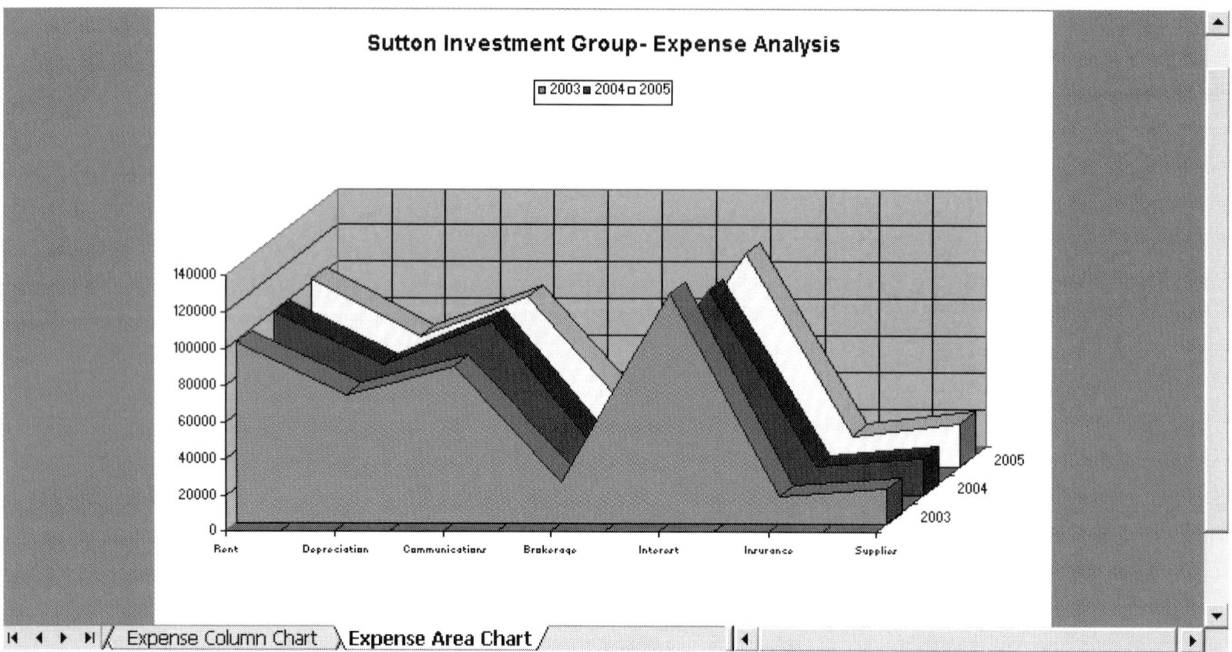

Illustration B

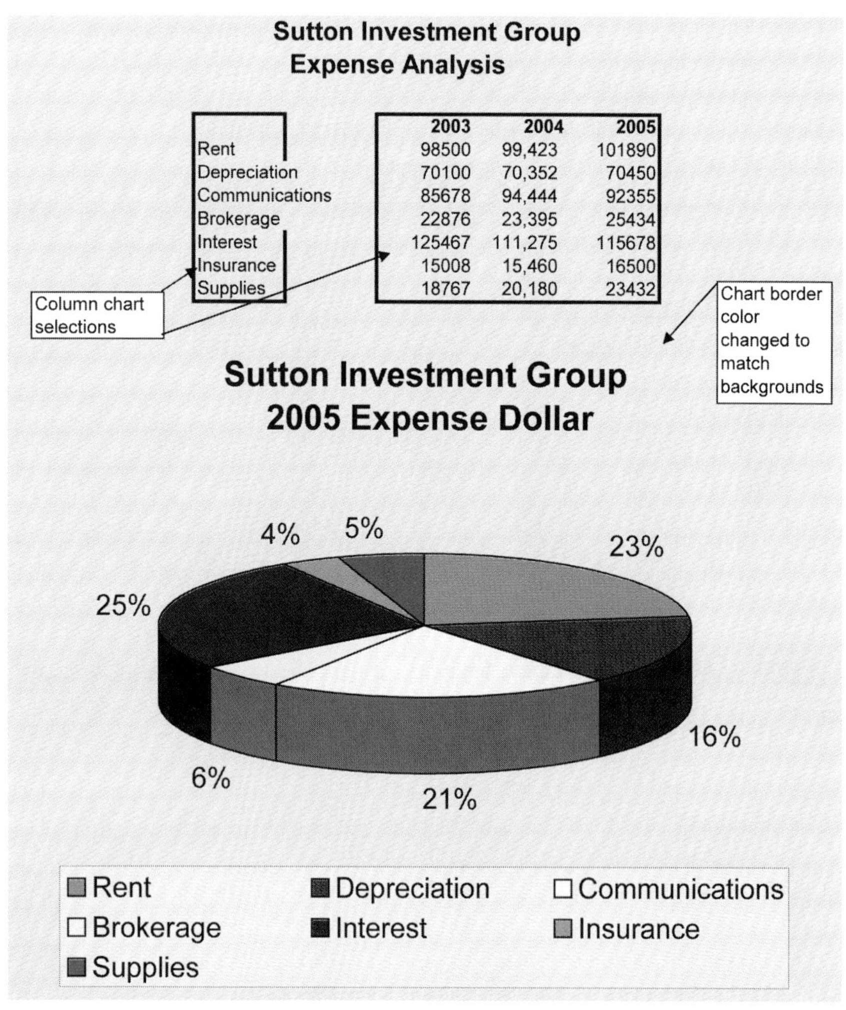

Illustration C

GOALS

To create graphics, diagrams, and stock charts for a presentation

To practice using the following skill sets:

- Create, position, and modify graphics
  - Position graphics
  - Modify graphics
- Insert and download graphics and clip art
- Create, modify, and position diagrams
- Create stock charts

EXCEL

WHAT YOU NEED TO KNOW

Create, Position, and Modify Graphics

- Drawing objects or pictures are *graphics*, or graphical images, that you can create or insert into your worksheets. If you want to add drawing objects to a worksheet or to a chart, you can create a customized object by using the tools available on the Drawing toolbar.
- Click View, Toolbars, and Drawing to display the Drawing toolbar, as shown in Figure 6.13. You can draw lines, arcs, arrows, rectangles, polygons, and a selection of shapes or freehand graphics on any area of a worksheet or chart. You can also add text boxes and shadows or three-dimensional enhancements to shapes.

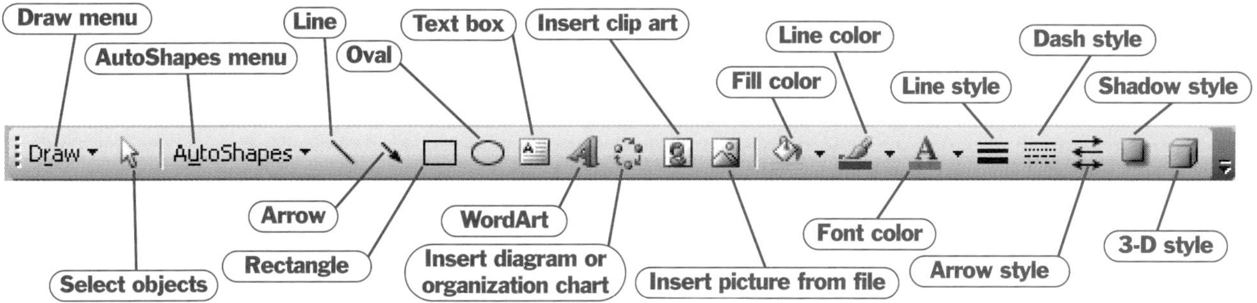

Figure 6.13 Drawing toolbar

- *AutoShapes* are predefined graphical images that you can place and size. When you place your mouse pointer over an AutoShape, the name of the shape appears as a ScreenTip, as shown in Figure 6.14.

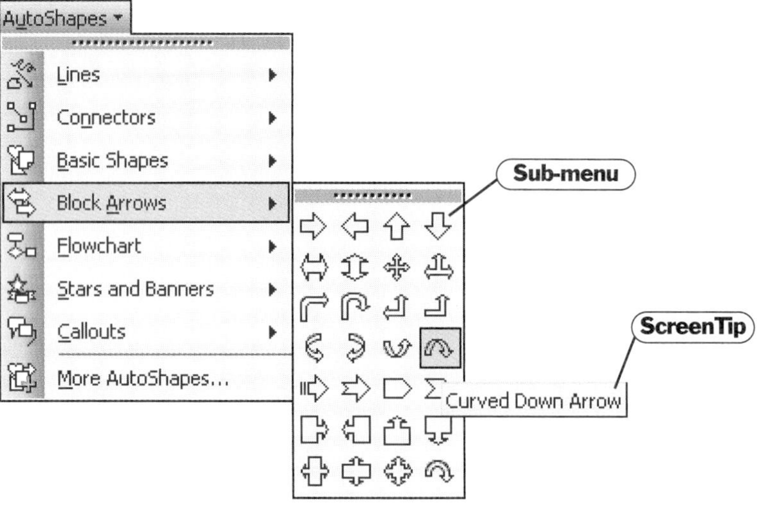

Figure 6.14 AutoShapes menu

- Select a Drawing Toolbar button to draw or format an object. The Line, Arrow, Rectangle, Text Box, and Oval buttons enable the mouse pointer to draw those objects as you drag them to the appropriate size. Figure 6.15 shows some of the graphic objects you can create with the Drawing toolbar.
- You can place graphics or drawing objects anywhere on a worksheet, as well as on charts. However, you must display, create, and modify graphics with charts deselected because they disappear when the chart is selected.

Position Graphics

- A selected graphic has small, white circles at the ends or on the border of the graphic, as seen in the text box graphic selected in Figure 6.15. Click a graphic to select it. However, notice that to select a graphic you do not select the chart.
- To move a selected graphic, place the mouse pointer over the graphic until you see a four-headed arrow, then click and drag to the new position. As with handles on charts, you can use the white circles to size the object.

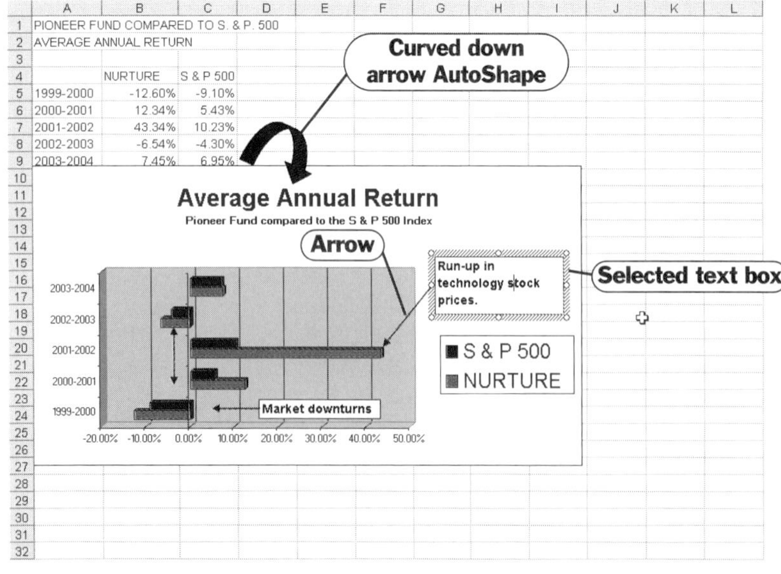

Figure 6.15 Chart with drawing objects

TRY*it* OUT E6-8

1. Open **E6-8** from the Data CD.
2. If necessary, click **View, Toolbars**, and **Drawing.**
3. On the Drawing toolbar, click the **Text Box** button.
4. Draw a text box on the chart above the legend box, as shown in Figure 6.15, and enter the text shown. (Do not select the chart.)
5. On the Drawing toolbar, click the **Arrow** button.
6. Draw a single arrow as shown, starting at the text box and dragging to the area where the arrow should point.
7. Repeat steps 3-6 and create the "Market downturns" text box and arrow.
8. On the Drawing toolbar, click the **AutoShapes** button, select **Lines,** and click the **Double Arrow.** Place as shown.
9. On the Drawing toolbar, click the **AutoShapes** button, select **Block Arrows,** and click the **Curved Down Arrow.** Place it starting in **Cell D7,** as shown in Figure 6.15.
10. Do not close the file.

EXCEL

Modify Graphics

▶ To modify or change a graphic, select it and press the Ctrl + 1 keys, or right-click and select the Format option. The Format dialog box, appropriate to the type of graphic selected, appears. For example, Figure 6.16 shows the Format AutoShape dialog box. You can modify all the items indicated in the tabs, including properties, where you can set the object to move and size proportionally with the chart.

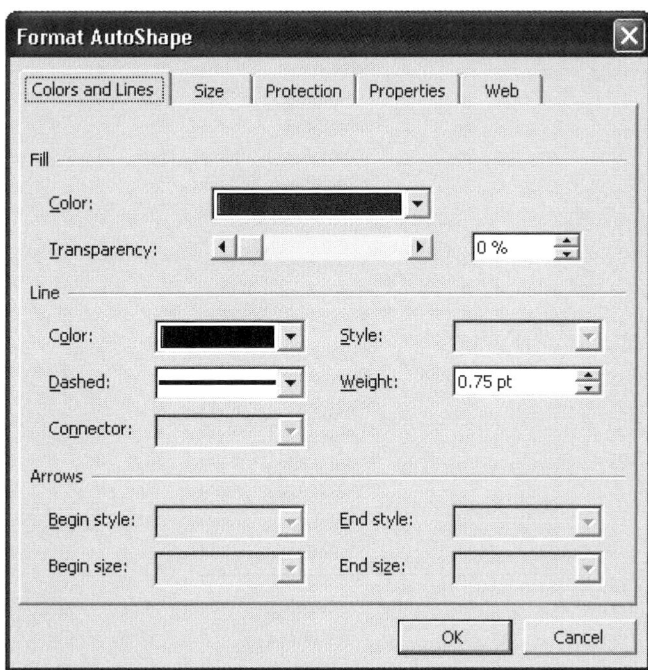

Figure 6.16 Format AutoShape dialog box

TRY *it* OUT *E6-9*

1. Continue to work in the open file or open **E6-9** from the Data CD.
2. Click the **Curved Down Arrow** to select it.
3. Press the **Ctrl** + **1** keys and make the following changes:
   a. Change Fill Color to **Plum.**
   b. Change Line Color to **Navy.**
   c. In the Size tab, change Rotation to **30 degrees.**
   d. Click **OK.**
4. Position the graphic by dragging it so that the graphic starts in **Cell D9** and the arrow is on the chart.
5. Right-click each graphic arrow on the chart, select **Format Autoshape**, and change the Line Color to **Plum.**
6. Right-click each text box and change the font to bold and the color to **Plum.**
7. Resize the text boxes, if necessary.
8. Save the file as **E6-9.** Close the file.

Insert and Download Graphics and Clip Art

- You can use the Insert menu to insert pictures from various sources. Notice the Picture options on the Insert menu, as shown in Figure 6.17, and refer to Figure 6.13 to see the corresponding buttons on the Drawing toolbar. You can use the Insert Picture From File button to insert a company logo, or any picture file.

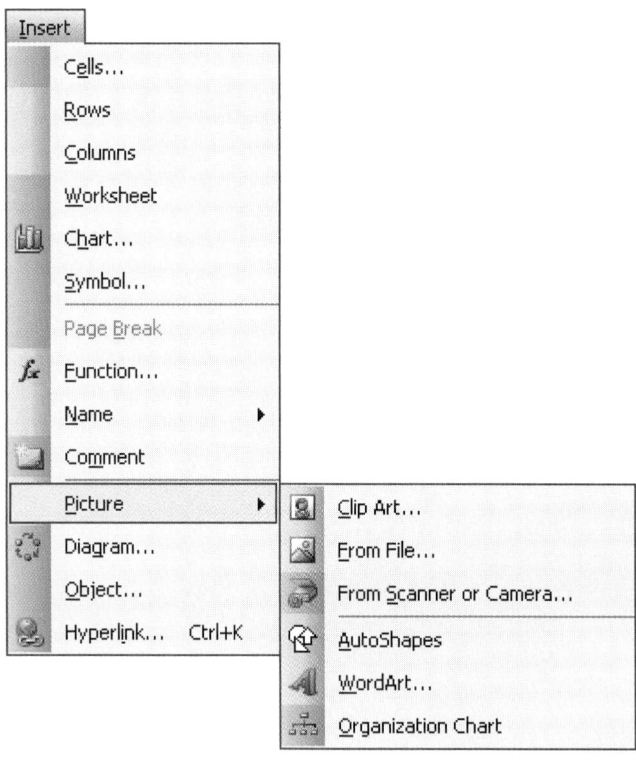

Figure 6.17 Insert menu

- When you click the Insert Clip Art button or the Clip Art option on the Insert, Picture menu, the Insert Clip Art task pane appears with search options for clip art, as shown in Figure 6.18.

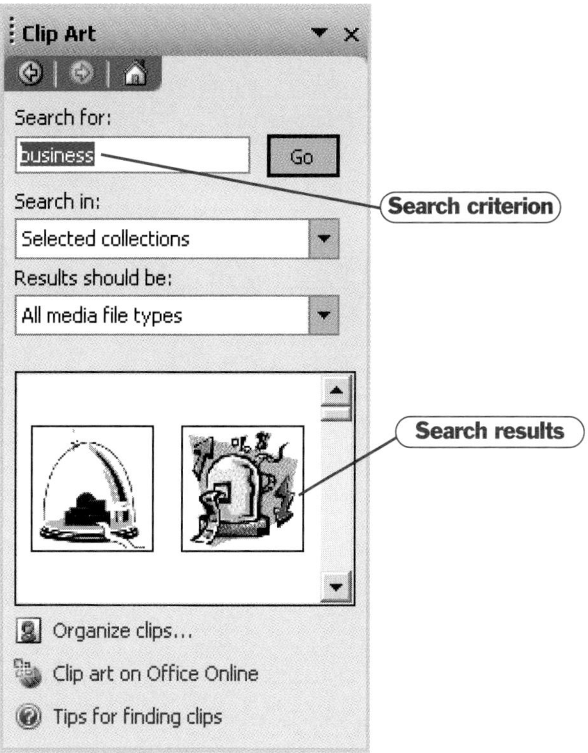

Figure 6.18 Insert Clip Art task pane

- Each clip art graphic that appears in the task pane contains an arrow that displays a menu of options. Insert is the first option, and you must click it to place the clip art on your worksheet. Notice the Clip Art list arrow menu in Figure 6.19.
- You can view clip art collections directly by clicking Organize clips or, if you have an Internet connection, click Clip art on Office Online. You can select graphics to download from the Web, in Microsoft Clip Art and Media.
- Once you select a picture from the collections and insert it, use the set of handles that appear to position and size the object. The Picture toolbar, as shown in Figure 6.20, appears when you select a picture with buttons to modify all aspects of the picture.

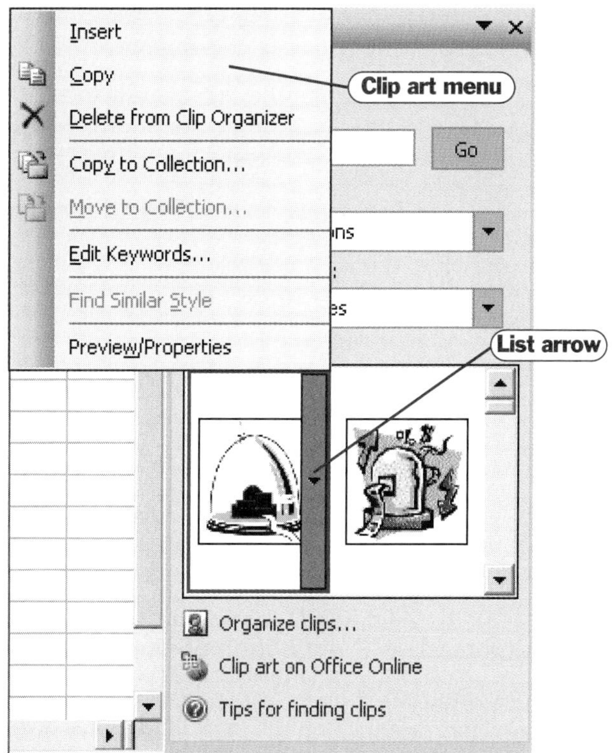

Figure 6.19 Clip Art list arrow menu

EXCEL

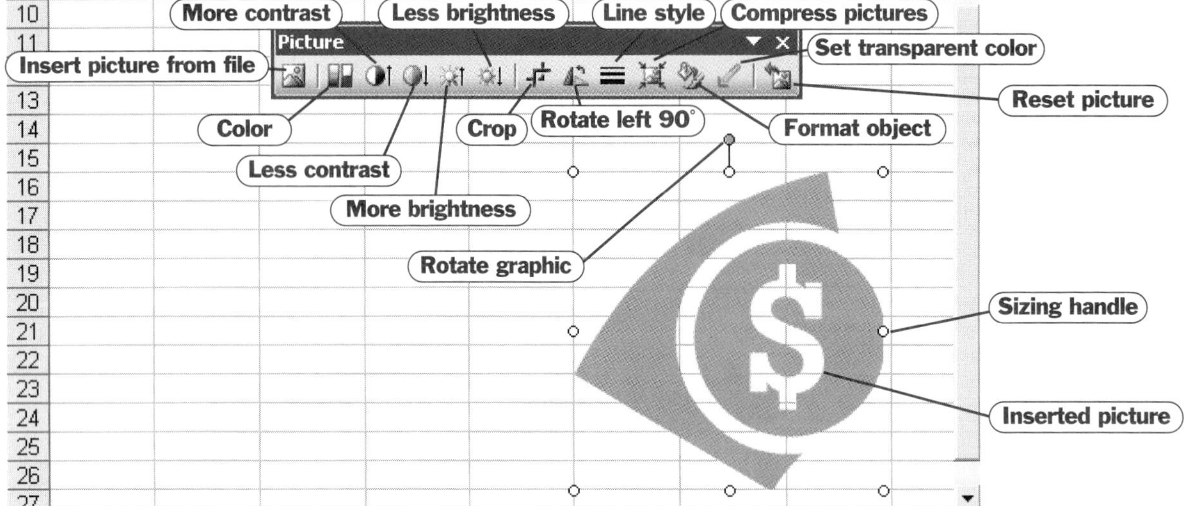

Figure 6.20 Picture toolbar

TRY *it* OUT *E6-10*

1. Open **E6-10** from the Data CD.
2. Click **Insert, Picture,** and **Clip Art.**
3. In the Insert Clip Art task pane, enter `Business` as the search text. Be sure that **All collections** is the Search in value.
4. Click **Go** and locate the clip art, as shown in Figure 6.20. *Note:* If you do not have this graphic, use another appropriate clip art.
5. Click **the list arrow** on the Clip Art menu and click **Insert.**
6. Place the clip art to the right of the data in the range G1:I12.
7. On the Picture toolbar, click the **Less Brightness** button several times to darken the graphic.
8. If you have an Internet connection, view graphics on Office Online:
   a. Click **Insert, Picture,** and **Clip Art.** In the task pane; click **Clip art on Office Online.**
   b. Enter a search criterion for Business and view available clip art.
   c. Close Office Online.
9. Save the file **E6-10.** Close the file.

Create, Modify, and Position Diagrams

- *Diagrams* can be added to spreadsheet reports to illustrate materials. They are not based on number values, but can clarify concepts or organization. To add a diagram to a worksheet, click Insert, Diagram, or click the Insert Diagram or Organization Chart button on the Drawing toolbar.
- In the Diagram Gallery dialog box that appears, the name and description of each diagram appears as it is selected, as shown in Figure 6.21. The diagram types are organization chart, cycle, radial, pyramid, Venn (showing areas of overlap), and target.

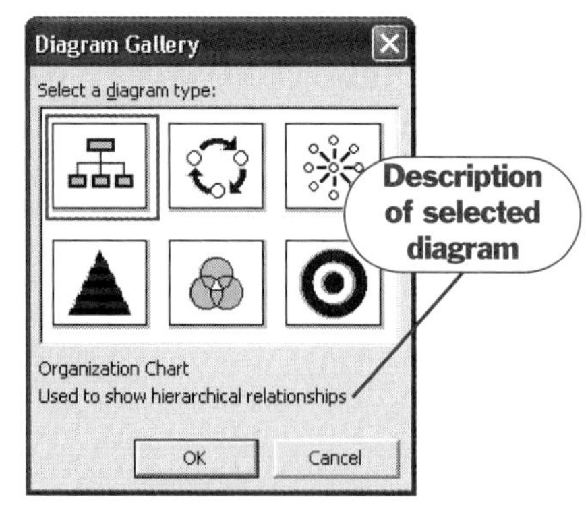

Figure 6.21 Diagram Gallery dialog box

- When you select a diagram and click OK, the Diagram toolbar appears and the diagram is displayed in a frame. You can add text to complete the diagram. Diagrams can be moved, sized, and positioned using the handles and mouse as discussed for charts and graphics.
- To format elements of a diagram, select the element(s) and right-click to open the format dialog box. Or, on the Diagram or Organization Chart toolbar that displays, as shown in Figure 6.22, you can select the AutoFormat button to view and select a series of preset formats.

Figure 6.22 Organization chart and Diagram toolbar

TRY *it* OUT *E6-11*

1. Open **E6-11** from the Data CD.
2. If necessary, display the Drawing toolbar by clicking **View, Toolbars, Drawing.**
3. Switch to the Company sheet and click the **Insert Diagram or Organization Chart** button.
4. With the Organization Chart selected, click **OK.**
5. Size and move the chart so that it is placed within the range **A3:G17.**
6. Click the **Autoformat** button on the Organization Chart toolbar.
7. Select the **Beveled Gradient** style. Click **OK.**
8. Enter the text as shown in Figure 6.22.
9. Create the Target diagram using the Text tool, as illustrated in Figure 6.22, and place it within the range **A19:G32.**
10. AutoFormat the diagram using the **Square Shadows** style.
11. Save the **E6-11** file. Do not close the file.

Create Stock Charts

- Excel provides four chart subtypes for stock market and price analysis, as shown in Figure 6.23. The High-Low-Close, Open-High-Low-Close, Volume-High-Low-Close, and Volume-Open-High-Low-Close charts can track the changes in stock data during a specific period. The terms used in stock charts are:

  Volume: sales volume for the stock for the day

  Open: opening price of the stock

  High: the highest price for the day

  Low: the lowest price for the day

  Close: closing price of the stock

- In the Open-High-Low-Close chart shown in Figure 6.24, white bars indicate a close that is up in price and black bars indicate a close that is down in price. The data table is a chart option that you can add to show the charted data. To display the table, click the Data Table tab on the Step 3 Chart Options screen and select the Show data table option.

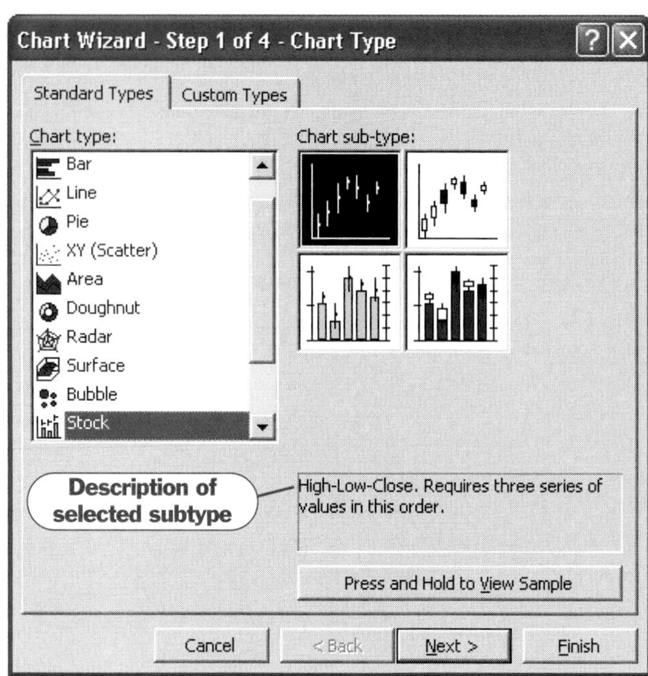

Figure 6.23 Stock chart subtypes

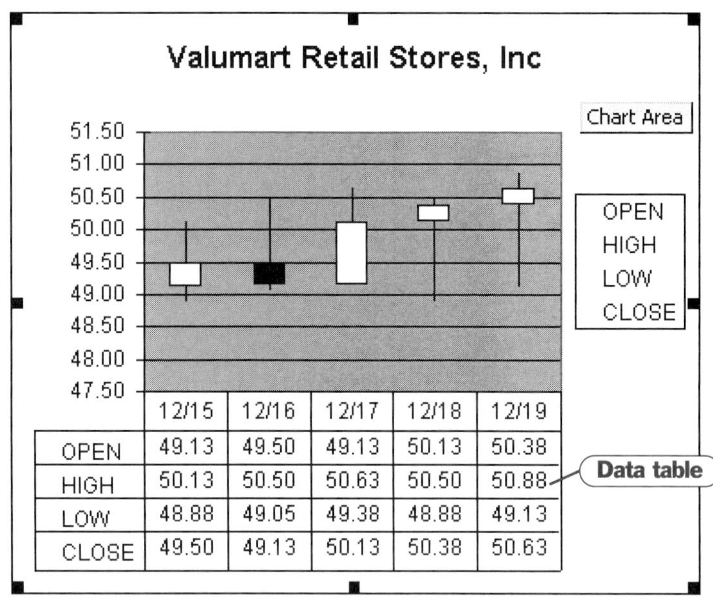

	12/15	12/16	12/17	12/18	12/19
OPEN	49.13	49.50	49.13	50.13	50.38
HIGH	50.13	50.50	50.63	50.50	50.88
LOW	48.88	49.05	49.38	48.88	49.13
CLOSE	49.50	49.13	50.13	50.38	50.63

Figure 6.24 Open-High-Low-Close chart subtype

TRY *it* OUT E6-12

1. Continue to work in the open file or open **E6-12** from the Data CD.
2. Switch to the Stock Prices sheet.
3. Use nonadjacent selection to select the ranges **A5:A10** and **C5:F10.**
4. Click the **Chart Wizard** button and create a stock chart as follows:
   Screen 1: Click **Stock** Chart Type and **Open-High-Low-Close** as the chart subtype; click **Next**.
   Screen 2: Check data series; click **Next.**
   Screen 3: Enter: `Valumart Retail Stores, Inc` as the chart title. On the Data Table tab, click **Show data table**; click **Next**.
   Screen 4: Locate the chart as an object on the Stock Prices sheet; click **Finish.**
5. Place the chart in the range **A12:H35.**
6. Create a Volume-Open-High-Low-Close chart using all the data in the range **A5:F10.** In Step 2, change the data so that the series is arranged by columns. Enter an appropriate chart title and place it on a new chart sheet.
7. Move the Chart1 sheet so that it is the third sheet.
8. Save the file **E6-12.** Close the file.

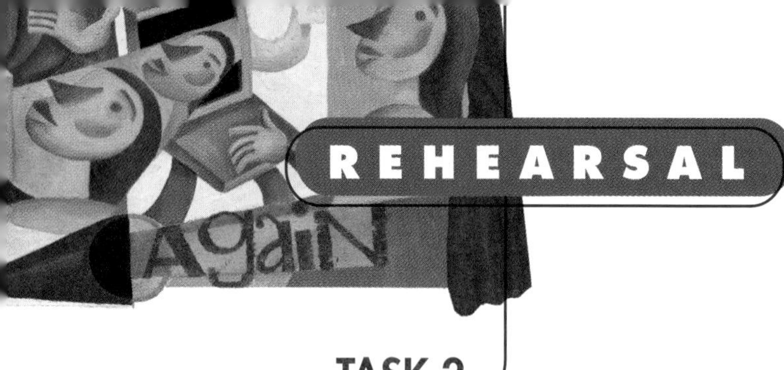

GOAL
To create diagrams and charts to demonstrate and analyze investment portfolio performance for stocks and fund investments

SETTING THE STAGE/WRAPUP
File name: **6.2portfolio**

WHAT YOU NEED TO KNOW

- Individuals who invest in stocks and mutual funds, and businesses whose stocks are traded publicly, are interested in tracking the performance of their stocks. The stocks or investments that people or businesses own are said to be in an investment *portfolio*.
- The performance of a stock can be compared to the Standard & Poor's (S&P) 500 index and/or to the performance of other stocks in the same industry or sector. The sector average shows the growth of the stocks in that industry. The *S&P 500* is a market index, made up of 500 blue-chip stocks, that is used to predict the general trend of U.S. stocks. If the S&P 500 index increases, it is generally a sign that the market is in a positive mode.
- In this Rehearsal activity, you will create and format charts and diagrams to present investment options to Alivea James, the president of In-Shape Fitness Centers. The workbook will consist of a diagram to show the company's investment goals, an analysis of stock funds in the health sector, and a chart to track the prices for a specific stock she is interested in purchasing.

DIRECTIONS

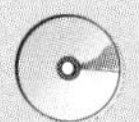

1. Open **6.2portfolio** from the Data CD.
2. On the **Portfolio** sheet, create a pyramid diagram to display the company's investment objectives.
   a. Enter the text in the diagram as shown in Illustration A.
   b. Use the AutoFormat button on the diagram bar to select the **3-D color diagram** style.
   c. On the Page Setup dialog box on the Margins tab, center the worksheet vertically and horizontally.
3. On the **Fund Analysis** sheet, create a bar chart to show the comparison between both health funds, the sector average, and the S&P 500 average.
   a. Use a bar chart and select the clustered bar with a **3-D visual effect** style.
   b. In Step 2, select **columns** as the orientation for the data series.
   c. Chart title: `Investment Returns for Health Funds`
   d. X-axis title: `Years Held`
   e. Place on the Fund Analysis sheet.
4. Place the chart under the worksheet and size it appropriately.
5. Format both axis labels and the legend to **8 point** font.
6. Create the following graphics as shown in Illustration B on page 176:
   a. Arrow to point to TR Health value. Format color to match TR Health bar.
   b. Text box with text as shown.
   c. Establish an Internet connection and find a stock market graphic from Office Online.
7. Format the worksheet and place and size the graphics.

Continued on next page

8. On the **Stock Analysis** sheet for Jackson Laboratories, create a Volume-Open-High-Low-Close chart with a data table. Be sure to plot the data by columns.
9. Place and modify the chart as needed to view data clearly, including formatting the data table and axis labels for **8 point** font.
10. Search for clip art in Medical, Health, or Science categories, and enter the graphics, as shown in Illustration C on page 177.
11. Use fill color to shade the background of all sheets, charts, and chart borders. Format titles and headings to improve their appearance.
12. Print one copy of each worksheet.
13. Save the file **6.2portfolio.** Close the file.

EXCEL

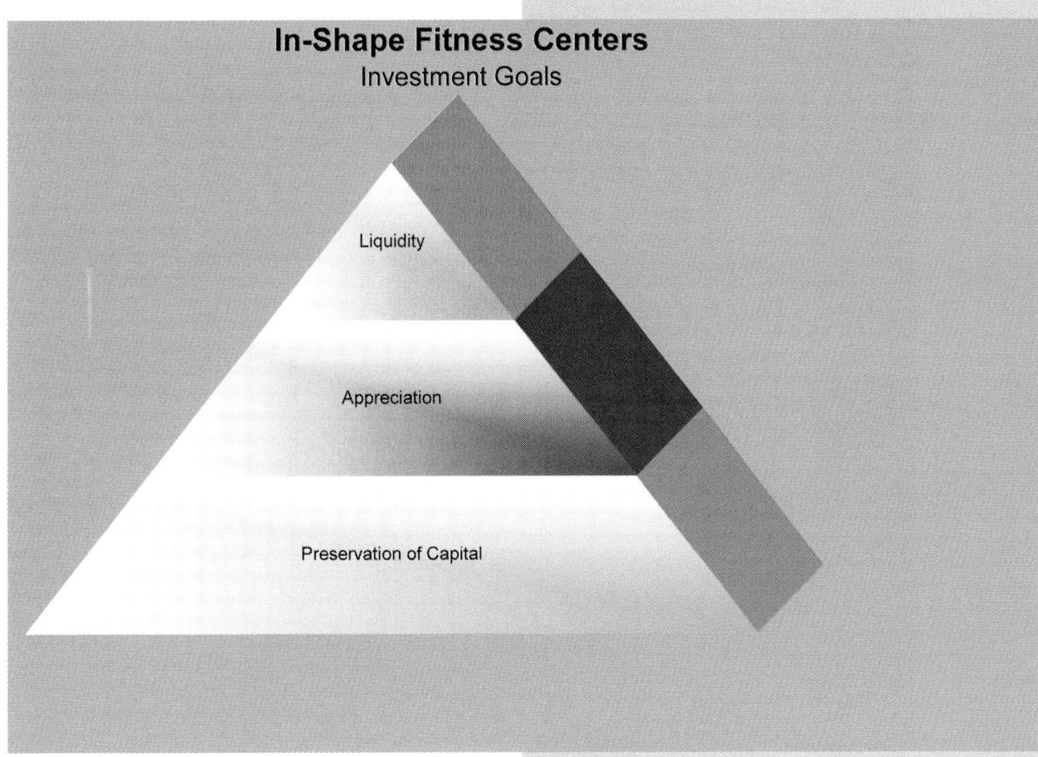

Illustration A

Investment Returns over Years Held

Health Funds compared to Health Sector and S & P 500

Years	TR Health	FD Health	Sector	S & P 500
One	21.88%	10.24%	20.27%	-0.90%
Three	17.97%	12.20%	17.89%	13.15%
Five	16.92%	14.53%	12.42%	18.36%
Ten	19.97%	15.75%	14.62%	17.37%

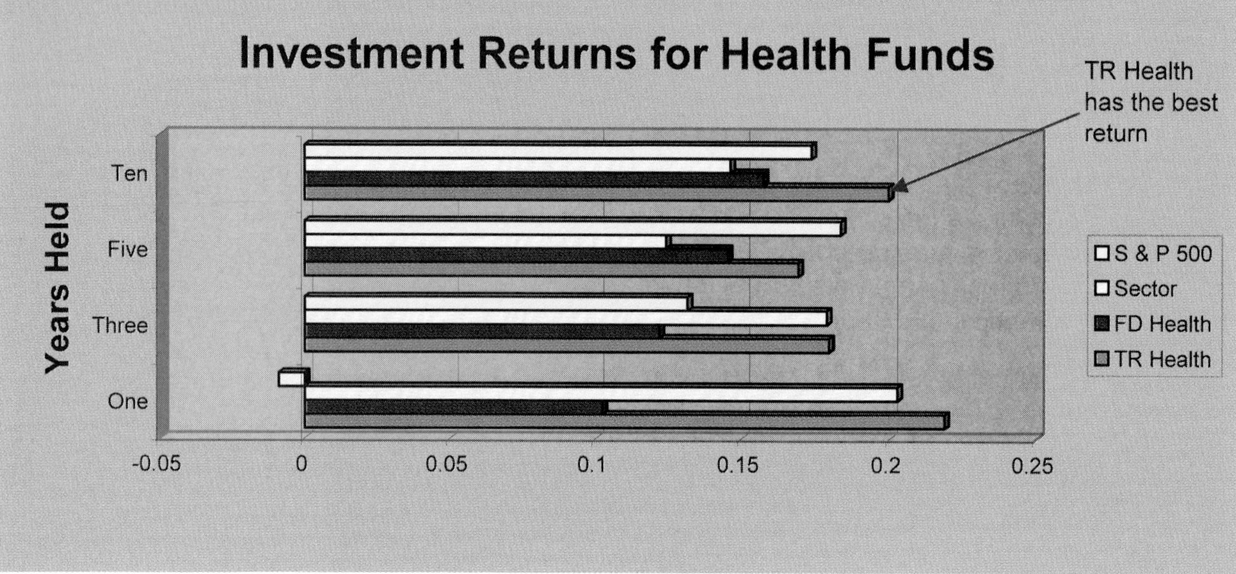

Illustration B

JACKSON LABORATORIES

Stock Prices for the week of June 12

DATES	VOLUME	OPEN	HIGH	LOW	CLOSE
6/12	143567	56.25	58.75	55.85	57.67
6/13	158764	57.67	59.60	57.25	59.60
6/14	149870	59.60	59.60	57.65	57.80
6/15	154334	58.20	60.00	58.20	59.75
6/16	153235	59.75	60.75	59.25	60.25

market-wide downturn

JACKSON LABORATORIES

160000
155000
150000
145000
140000
135000

62.00
61.00
60.00
59.00
58.00
57.00
56.00
55.00
54.00
53.00

VOLUME
OPEN
HIGH
LOW
CLOSE

	6/12	6/13	6/14	6/15	6/16
VOLUME	143567	158764	149870	154334	153235
OPEN	56.25	57.67	59.6	58.2	59.75
HIGH	58.75	59.6	59.6	60	60.75
LOW	55.85	57.25	57.65	58.2	59.25
CLOSE	57.67	59.6	57.8	59.75	60.25

Illustration C

Cues for Reference

Create Diagrams

1. Click **View, Toolbars,** and **Drawing.**
2. Click **Insert Diagram** or **Organization Chart** button.
3. Select diagram type.
4. Click **OK.**
5. Add appropriate text.
6. Drag to size.

Modify Diagrams

- Right-click diagram element, select Format Diagram or Format Autoshape, and use the dialog box to make settings.

or

1. Click the **AutoFormat** button on the Diagram or Organization Chart toolbar.
2. Select the diagram style.
3. Click **OK.**

Create Graphics

1. Click **View, Toolbars,** and **Drawing.**
2. Click desired graphic button.
3. Drag to size.

Modify Graphics

1. Right-click graphic.
2. Click **Format** (graphic name).
3. Select formatting changes.
4. Click **OK.**

Size and Place Graphics

1. Click graphic.
2. Use handles to drag to size.
3. Place mouse pointer on graphic until it becomes a four-headed arrow, and drag to location.

Insert Pictures

1. Click **Insert, Pictures, Clip Art.**
2. In task pane, enter search criteria.
3. Click **Go.**
4. Locate required graphic.
5. Click down arrow and click **Insert.**
6. Size and place graphic.

Download Pictures

1. Establish your Internet connection, if necessary.
2. Click **Insert, Pictures, Clip Art.**
3. In task pane, click **Clip art on Office Online.**
Office XP: In task pane, click **Clips Online.**
4. Enter search criteria. Click **Go.**
5. Click selection box on desired clip.
6. Click **Download 1 item, Download Now.**
7. Right-click clip art in your task pane and click **Insert.**

SETTING THE STAGE/WRAPUP

Act I File name: **6p1.income**
Act II File name: **6p2.expense**
Act III File name: **6p3.stock**

WHAT YOU NEED TO KNOW

Act I

You work in the Finance Department of the Air Land Sea Travel Group. Your department has been asked to create charts for a branch manager meeting about the income and profit figures for the quarter.

Follow these guidelines:

- Open **6p1.income,** and use the Optional Analysis sheet for the chart data.
- Create a column chart on a chart sheet to compare Total Income and Net Income. Format the chart titles, axis labels, and tab name so that the data is easy to read.
- Copy the column chart sheet and do the following:
  - Change the type to a bar chart and the sheet name to `Bar Chart.`
  - On the Source Data step, change the orientation of data from columns to rows to get a different perspective for the bar chart, as shown in the illustration on the next page.
  - Format the data series to display data labels for values.
- Create a pie chart for Total Income and one for Net Income data and place both on the Optional Analysis sheet. Use percentages as labels on the pie sections, and color the charts and chart borders to match the worksheet.
- Add graphics, if necessary, to point out important information, or add the company logo to the charts or worksheet. Download a travel graphic, if possible, to add to the blank area on the bar chart.

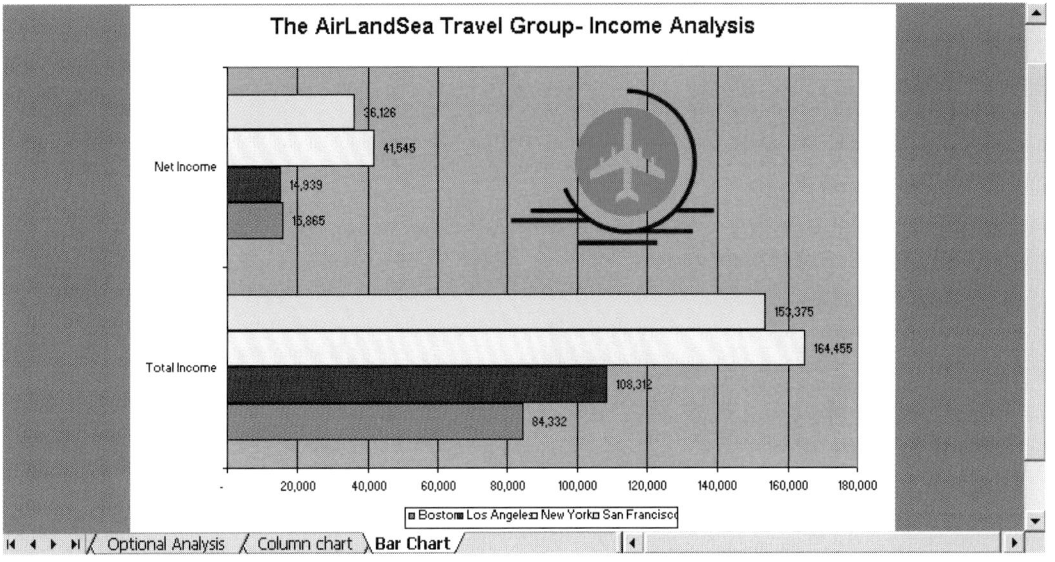

- Print the charts and the Optional Analysis sheet.
- Save your work.

Act II

Odyssey Travel Gear has prepared income statements for June 30 and December 31, 2004, by combining data from all its stores. The president is interested in reducing expenses and has asked you to prepare charts to analyze and compare the expenses for the stores for each semiannual report.

Follow these guidelines:

- Open **6p2.expense.** You will use the December 31 and June 30 sheets for your chart data.
- On the December 31 sheet: Create a line chart of the December 31 expense data and place it on the sheet. Use a nonadjacent selection of data, including titles in the range A5:F5 and expense data in the range A12:F14. Format the axis label and legend fonts. Add a travel graphic or logo to the chart. Copy the line chart and place it below the original chart. Change the type to a bar chart, so that there are two charts on the worksheet.
- Repeat this analysis for the June 30 sheet.
- Insert a new sheet and name it: `Expense Dollar`. Create two pie charts to show the total expense dollar for December 31 and June 30, as shown in the illustration on the next page. For each pie chart, select the Expenses labels in Column A and the Totals in Column G and place the pie charts on the Expense Dollar sheet. Be sure to indicate the date in the chart title and add percentage labels.
- Use drawing objects to point out the area of increased expenses and add other graphics, if necessary. Color the background and borders of the pie charts.

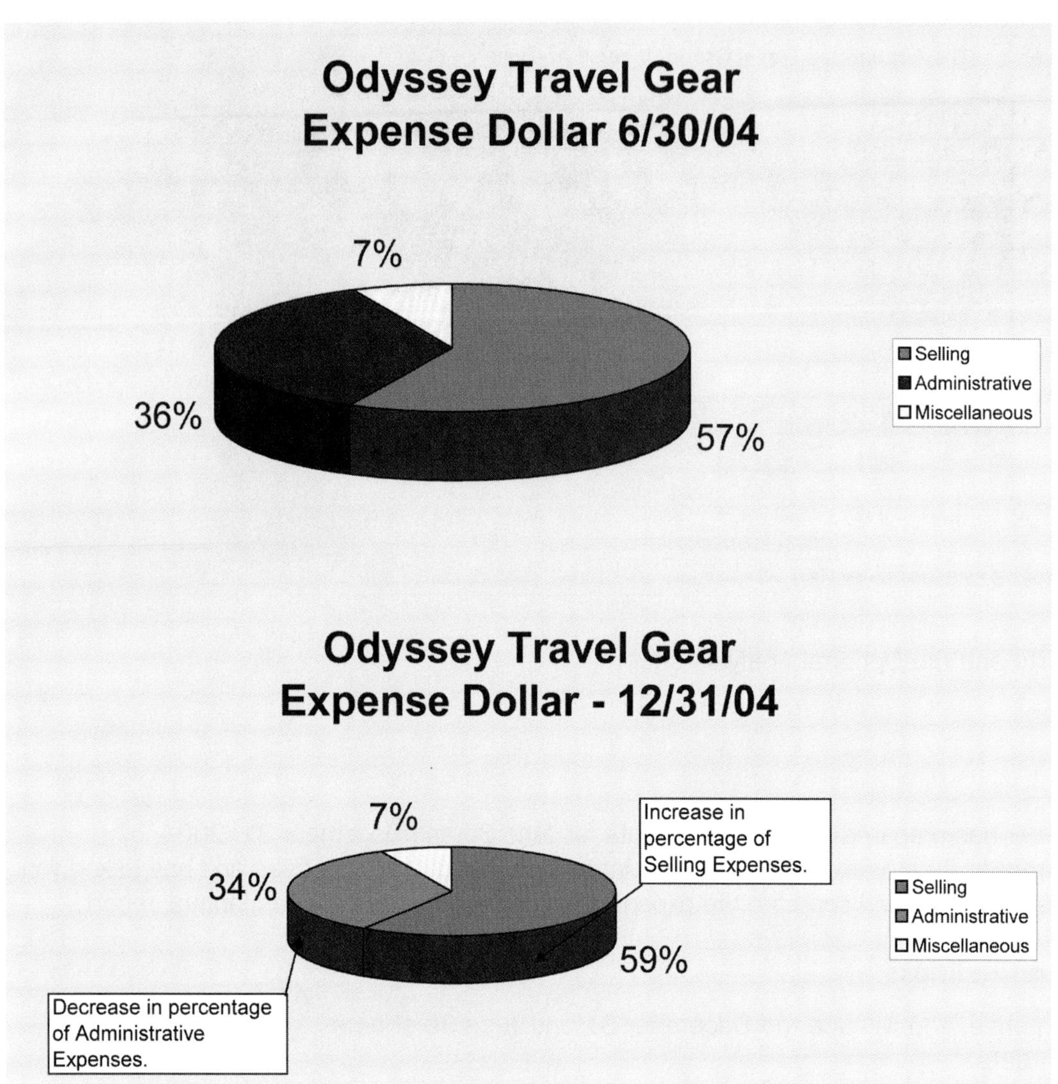

Print the sheets that contain charts and save and close the file.

Act III

Trilogy Productions is a public corporation whose stock is traded daily on the stock exchange. The management of the company tracks the open, high, low, and close prices of the stock and the volume of shares traded each day. Management also wants to compare the investment value of owning a share in the company to the average return of other companies in their sector, and to the general market or to the S&P 500. The company is in the Media or Entertainment sector.

You have been asked to prepare charts from the stock data provided for the next meeting of the board of directors. Also, you will research the Media sector on the Internet.

Follow these guidelines:

- Use the file **6p3.stock.**
- On the Investment Analysis sheet, create a column chart to compare the investment growth of Trilogy stock as compared to that of the S&P 500 and the Media sector. Begin your data selection in Cell A6.
- Create a line chart of the prices for 2000–2004 and place it on a separate chart sheet named Price History Chart. Use a data table to show the stock prices.

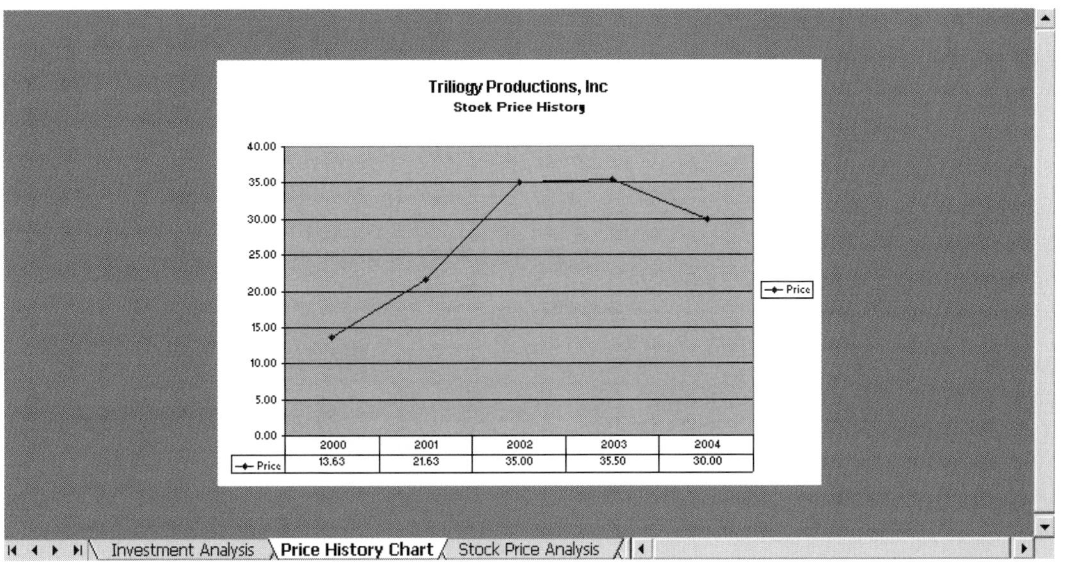

- On the Stock Price Analysis sheet, create an Open-High-Low-Close chart. Also use the data to create a Volume-Open-High-Low-Close chart on a separate sheet named Stock Price Chart 11-15.
- Format charts and font sizes on titles and axis labels so that they present well. Add a company logo to the charts and/or worksheets. Add drawing objects to point out the increase in the stock price on 11/17 because of a favorable announcement about a new production.
- Research the Media, or Media and Entertainment, sector and print a company capsule on one or more media companies, such as Dreamworks, Disney, or Pixar. Also, compare the annual revenue of several such companies on a worksheet or in a report.
- You can use a search engine to look up the sector or find it on the www.hooversonline.com Web site. Their home page provides links to the most frequently viewed companies by industry or sector. Select the sector and complete your research.
- Print a copy of all worksheets in the file. Save your work.

LESSON 7

Integration/Excel and the Web

In this lesson, you will learn to use Excel features to integrate worksheets, charts, and Internet elements into Word documents. You will create a benefit statement, a letter, a travel guide, a quarterly report, and use Outlook features to make apointments and meeting arrangements.

Upon completion of this lesson, you should have mastered the following skill sets:

- Understand integration basics
- Copy and paste data between applications
- Embed worksheets or charts
  - Edit an embedded object
- Insert a worksheet in Word
- Link data between applications
  - Edit a linked object
- Display and use the Web toolbar
  - Paste Web data
- Use Smart Tags to find stock information
- Convert files to alternative file types
- Use Outlook features with Excel
- Create and modify appointments in Outlook
- Create and respond to meeting requests.

Terms

Software-related

Integration
Source file
Destination file
Embedded file
Linked file
Appointments
Events
Meetings

Document-related

Benefits

GOALS

To create documents containing worksheets and charts

To practice using the following skill sets:

- Understand integration basics
- Copy and paste data between applications
- Drag and drop between applications
- Embed worksheets and charts
  - Edit an embedded object
- Insert a worksheet in Word

EXCEL

WHAT YOU NEED TO KNOW

Understand Integration Basics

- *Integration* is the sharing or combining of data between Office applications. The source file provides the data, and the destination file receives the data. For example, an Excel chart or worksheet (the *source file*) can provide supporting or visual documentation of materials for a Word document (the *destination file*), as shown in Figure 7.1. You can paste, embed, or link data into the destination file; the choice depends on the features you require for the file.

	A	B	C	D	E	F	G
1	Four Corners Realty Company						
2	Multiple Listing Service						
3	Type	Sq. Ft.	Bedrooms	Baths	View	Maintenance	Price
4	Condo	1200	2	2	Intracoastal	325	145,999
5	Condo	1050	2	1 1/2	Ocean	390	142,900
6	Condo	1400	2	2	No	285	139,900
7	Condo	1000	2	1 1/2	Ocean	385	143,999
8	Condo	1350	2	2	Intracoastal	325	146,545
9							

Source file

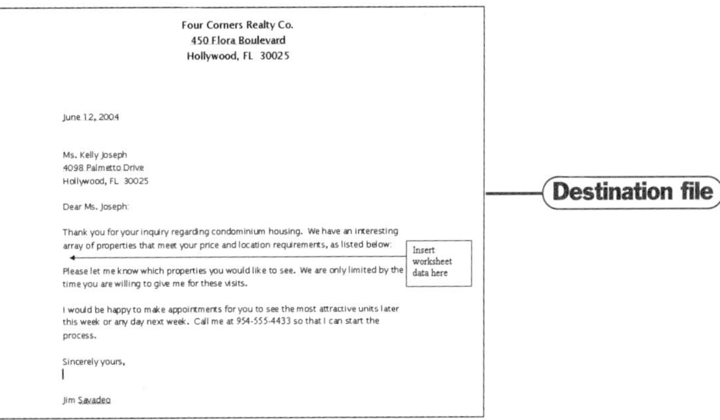
Four Corners Realty Co.
450 Flora Boulevard
Hollywood, FL 30025

June 12, 2004

Ms. Kelly Joseph
4098 Palmetto Drive
Hollywood, FL 30025

Dear Ms. Joseph:

Thank you for your inquiry regarding condominium housing. We have an interesting array of properties that meet your price and location requirements, as listed below:

Insert worksheet data here

Please let me know which properties you would like to see. We are only limited by the time you are willing to give me for these visits.

I would be happy to make appointments for you to see the most attractive units later this week or any day next week. Call me at 954-555-4433 so that I can start the process.

Sincerely yours,

Jim Savadeo

Destination file

Figure 7.1 Source and destination files

Copy and Paste Data Between Applications

- To copy and paste data between applications, the source and destination files should both be open. You can open either file in its application and then click Start to open the second application. Use the taskbar buttons to switch between applications, as shown in Figure 7.2.

Figure 7.2 Taskbar application buttons

- To paste Excel data into a Word document, go to the Excel file and copy the data you need from the worksheet. Then, switch to the Word document and paste it to the location you want in the document.
- You can edit a worksheet that you paste into a Word document. However, there is no connection to the original worksheet or to Excel, and you cannot view or change the formulas. Use this method only when updated or linked data is not necessary or when formulas do not need editing.

TRY*it* OUT *E7-1*

1. In Excel, open **E7-1.xls** from the Data CD.
2. Click **Start, All Programs, Microsoft Office, Microsoft Office Word 2003,** and open **E7-1WD.doc** from the Data CD.
3. Switch to the Excel source file using the taskbar button.
4. Select the worksheet data in the Excel file, **A1:G8.**
5. Click the **Copy** button.
6. Switch to the Word destination file using the taskbar button.

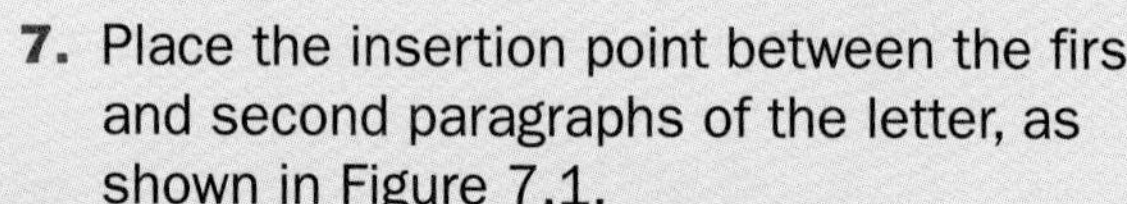

7. Place the insertion point between the first and second paragraphs of the letter, as shown in Figure 7.1.
8. Click the **Paste** button. The worksheet is integrated into the Word document.

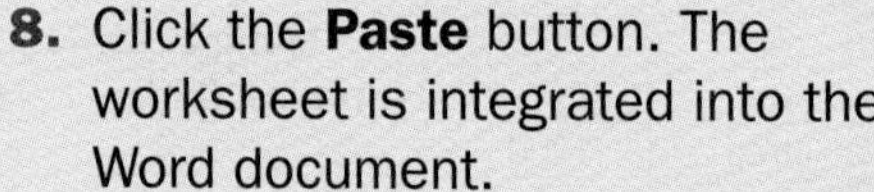

9. Change the price of the first condo to: `144,999`.
10. Switch back to the Excel file and notice that the change did not affect the worksheet.
11. Close the files without saving them.

Drag-and-Drop Data Between Applications

- You can also use the drag-and-drop technique to copy and paste the data if you make both the source and destination documents visible using Window options.
- To see both files, right-click the taskbar to display the shortcut menu, as shown in Figure 7.3. Click Tile Windows Vertically; both files become visible on the screen, arranged vertically.
- To drag-and-drop the data between files, select the data, point the mouse at the selection until you see the four-headed selection arrow, and press and hold the Ctrl key to copy (rather than move) the data.

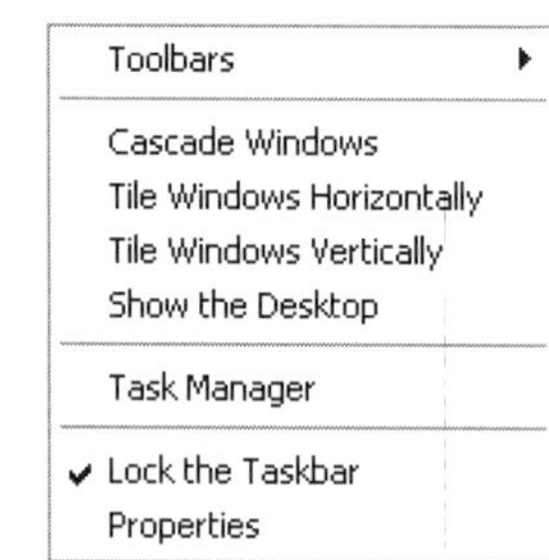

Figure 7.3 Taskbar shortcut menu

TRY it OUT *E7-2*

1. Open **E7-2.xls** and **E7-2WD.doc** from the Data CD.
2. Right-click the **taskbar** and click **Tile Windows Vertically** from the shortcut menu.
3. In the Excel source file, select the worksheet data.
4. Point the mouse at the edge of the selection until the pointer becomes a four-headed selection arrow, and press and hold the **Ctrl** key.
5. Drag-and-drop the worksheet data in the space between the first and second paragraphs of the Word document.
6. If necessary, insert a blank line above and below the worksheet in the document.
7. Double-click on the worksheet in the Word document to change the price of the first condo to `144,999`.
8. Notice that the change did not affect the worksheet.
9. Save and close the files.

EXCEL

Embed Worksheets or Charts

- An *embedded file* is pasted in a destination file as an object that becomes part of the file and that can be edited in its source application. Therefore, when you double-click an embedded Excel file, you can edit it in Excel mode.
- To embed a worksheet, copy the worksheet in Excel, and in the Word application, click Edit, Paste Special, and click Microsoft Office Excel Worksheet Object. Notice the source file name in the Paste Special dialog box, shown in Figure 7.4, and the Result text in both Figures 7.4 and 7.5.

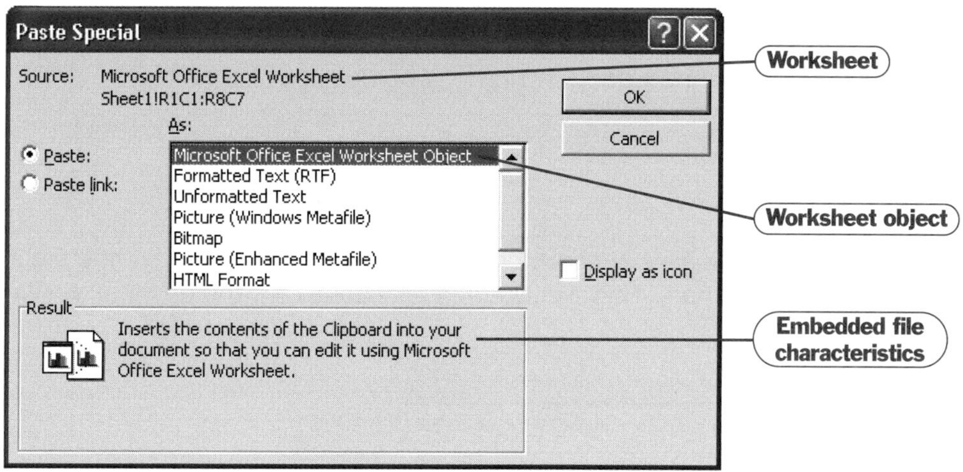

Figure 7.4 Paste Special dialog box for worksheet

- To embed a chart, first copy the chart in Excel, then insert the chart in the desired Word document by clicking Edit, Paste Special in the Word application. When the Paste Special dialog box opens, as shown in Figure 7.5, select Microsoft Office Excel Chart Object and click OK.

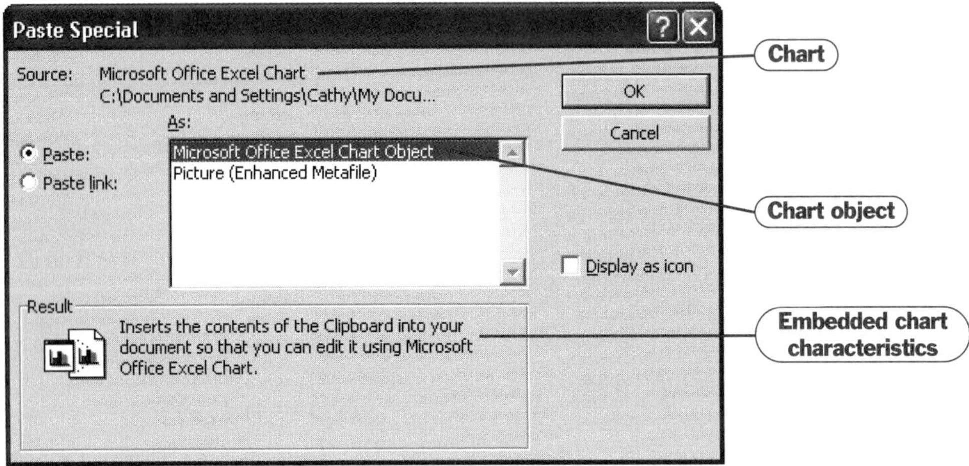

Figure 7.5 Paste Special dialog box for chart

TRY*it* OUT *E7-3*

1. Open **E7-3WD.doc** and **E7-3.xls** from the Data CD in the appropriate applications.
2. On the Excel worksheet, copy the worksheet in the range **B1:D10.**
3. Switch to the Word document and place the insertion point below the last line of text.
4. Click **Edit, Paste Special**, and select **Microsoft Office Excel Worksheet Object.**
5. Click **OK** and the file is embedded.
6. Switch to the Excel worksheet and copy the chart.
7. Switch to the Word document and place the insertion point below the embedded worksheet.
8. Click **Edit, Paste Special,** and check that **Microsoft Office Excel Chart Object** is selected.
9. Click **OK** and the chart is embedded.
10. Do not close the files.

Edit an Embedded Object

▶ To edit an embedded worksheet or chart, double-click it. You can then edit the file in Excel mode with Excel menus and toolbars. However, your edits change only the destination (Word) file, not the source (Excel) file.

TRY*it* OUT *E7-4*

1. Continue to work in the open files or open **E7-4.xls** and **E7-4WD.doc** in the appropriate application.
2. Double-click the embedded worksheet.
3. Format the values in the ranges **B4:B5** and **C8:C10** for currency.
4. Click on the document page to leave **Excel** Edit mode. (Notice the edits.)
5. Switch to the Excel file and notice that the source file did not change.
6. Save the files. Close both files.

Insert a Worksheet in Word

▶ On the Standard toolbar in Word, there is an Insert Microsoft Excel Worksheet button that allows you to create a new embedded Excel worksheet. When you click this button, you can select the number of cells for the width and length of the new worksheet, as shown in Figure 7.6. You will be in Excel mode, with Excel menus, and can then create a worksheet with the number of rows and columns you specified.

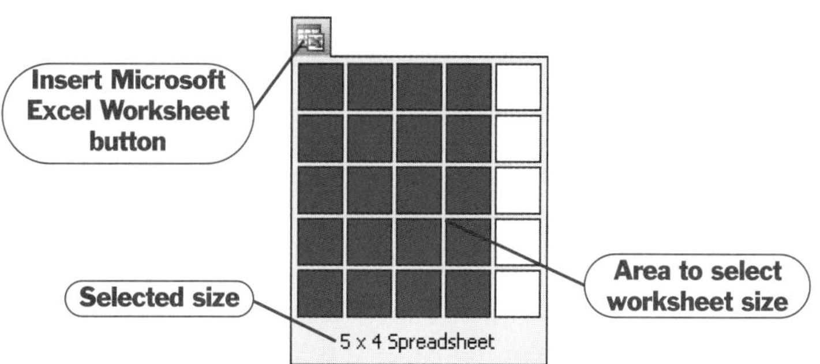

Figure 7.6 Insert Microsoft Excel Worksheet button

TRY it OUT *E7-5*

1. In Word, open **E7-5WD.doc** from the Data CD.
2. In the space under the first paragraph, click the **Insert Microsoft Excel Worksheet** button.
3. Select an Excel worksheet that is four cells wide by four cells high. Use sizing handles to expand it to 5 rows.
4. Enter the following data:

REIMBURSEMENT CALCULATION			
Dental bill	$350		
First	$100	100%	$100
100–500	$250	80%	
Reimbursement			

5. Enter a formula in **Cell D4** to calculate 80% of 250.
6. Enter a formula in **Cell D5** to add the contents of the range **D3:D4.**
7. Format cells D4 and D5 for currency with no decimals.
8. Adjust column width as necessary.
9. Click the Word document page.
10. Save and close the file.

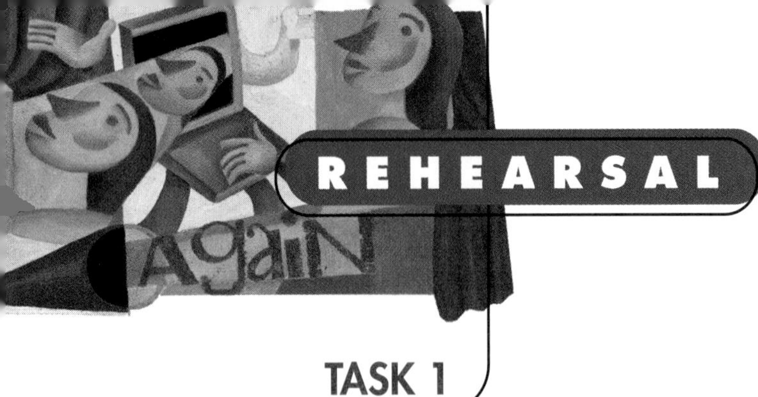

GOAL
To create correspondence and a benefits program document that includes worksheets and a chart

SETTING THE STAGE/WRAPUP

Margins: 1" left and right
Start line: At 2.5"
File names: **7.1benefits.doc**
7.1rates.xls
7.1calcmemo.doc

WHAT YOU NEED TO KNOW

- New employees are often given an employee manual containing company procedures, policies, and benefits. *Benefits* are medical, dental, life insurance, and other plans that the employer makes available to employees. The employer may provide the benefits or the employee may pay a group rate premium for the policies.
- When you integrate Excel worksheets and charts into a Word document, you can size the data and move the margins to align worksheets to the center of the page.
- In this Rehearsal activity, you will integrate worksheets and charts from an Excel workbook to enhance the Sutton Investment Group Benefits Program, which is contained in a Word document.

DIRECTIONS

1. Open **7.1benefits.doc** and **7.1rates.xls** from the Data CD in the appropriate application. 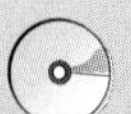
2. On Page 4 of the Benefits Program, at the end of the Dental section, enter the following text, as illustrated on page 190: **DENTAL PLAN RATES AND BENEFITS.**
3. Use Format Painter to copy the format from the paragraph headers to the new text. Format the new text in **Heading 2** style.
4. Switch to the Excel worksheet to copy the data on the Dental sheet and paste it to the Benefits Program.
5. Move the margin manually so that the worksheet is centered horizontally.
6. On the worksheet, use Find and Replace to change the word "Covered" to: **100%.**
7. Switch to the Education sheet in the Excel workbook.
8. Copy the worksheet in the range **A1:F22** and use Paste Special to embed the data on Page 6 of the Benefits Program, the last page.
9. Double-click the worksheet in the Word document and edit the title as illustrated; using the **Forte** font, **18 point.** Format the subtitle as **Forte 10pt.**
10. Change the annual contribution by employee to **$1,200**, as illustrated. (Notice the changes in the growth data.)
11. Switch to the Education sheet in the Excel workbook.
12. Select the chart, and use Copy and Paste Special to embed the chart under the worksheet on the last page of the Benefits Program; center the chart on the page.
13. Print a copy of the Benefits Program.

Continued on next page

14. Save both files. Close both files.

15. Open **7.1calcmemo.doc** from the Data CD, as shown on page 191. 

16. Insert a worksheet that is 4 cells wide by 4 cells long two lines below the last line of the memo. Expand it to five rows, enter the following data, and expand columns as necessary:

	BILLED	COVERAGE	PAYMENT
Exam	$80	100%	
X-Rays	$120	100%	
Oral Surgeon	$950	75%	
Reimbursement			

17. Calculate the payment for each item and the total reimbursement.

18. Print a copy of the memorandum.

19. Save the file **7.1calcmemo.doc.** Close the file.

Introduction

THE SUTTON INVESTMENT GROUP BENEFITS PROGRAM

YOUR ENROLLMENT KIT

This enrollment kit provides you with the information you will need to enroll for the Sutton Investment Group Benefits Program. Here are all the pieces that make up your Benefits enrollment kit:

- ✓ Booklets about all the benefit plans available through this program;
- ✓ Your personalized enrollment worksheet; and

This general information booklet describing how Benefits works, eligibility rules, tax information, and how to enroll over the telephone through the Sutton Investment Group Benefits Enrollment Line.

THE BENEFITS OF THE SUTTON INVESTMENT GROUP BENEFITS PROGRAM

The Benefits program offers six major categories of benefits coverage. Within each category are several different benefit options. You select the option(s) from each category that you believe are right for you. The categories of coverage, discussed in detail in the booklets in the enrollment kit are:

- ✓ Medical
- ✓ Dental
- ✓ Life Insurance
- ✓ Education Incentive Plan
- ✓ Vision Care
- ✓ Property and Casualty Insurance

WHO IS ELIGIBLE FOR BENEFITS?

Regular employees on the domestic payroll of Sutton Investment Group, who have completed at least one calendar month of service as a regular employee and

Page 1

who work at least 20 hours each week are eligible to participate in the benefit options available through Sutton Investment Group Benefits.

You can also enroll your eligible dependents for Medical, Dental and Life Insurance coverage. For Sutton Investment Group Benefits, your eligible dependents are your:

- ✓ Spouse, and
- ✓ Unmarried children who are under age 19 (or age 23 if they are full-time students).

Children include natural and legally adopted children, stepchildren living in your home and any other child who is supported solely by you and living in your home. Coverage may be continued beyond age 23 under certain circumstances.

Dependents are not eligible for any benefits under the Benefits Program if they are in military service and may not be eligible if they live permanently outside the United States and Canada.

Page 2

Dental

As you read this booklet describing your dental coverage options through the Sutton Investment Group Benefits Program, you should ask yourself when you want from your dental coverage:

1. Do you want the freedom to choose any dentist regardless of cost?
2. Do you want to have lower costs in exchange for receiving dental care from a limited selection of dentists?
3. Would you rather have no dental coverage at all?

WHO IS ELIGIBLE FOR DENTAL BENEFITS?

Regular employees on the domestic payroll of Sutton Investment Group, who have completed at least one calendar month of service as a regular employee and who work at least 20 hours each week are eligible to participate in the benefit options available through Sutton Investment Group Benefits.

You can also enroll your eligible dependents for Medical, Dental and Life Insurance coverage. For Sutton Investment Group Benefits, your eligible dependents are your:

- ✓ Spouse, and
- ✓ Unmarried children who are under age 19 (or age 23 if they are full-time students).

Children include natural and legally adopted children, stepchildren living in your home and any other child who is supported solely by you and living in your home. Coverage may be continued beyond age 23 under certain circumstances.

Dependents are not eligible for any benefits under the Benefits Program if they are in military service and may not be eligible if they live permanently outside the United States and Canada.

TRADITIONAL DENTAL PLAN

If you answered, "yes" to the first question, you may want to elect the Traditional Dental Plan. Under the Traditional Dental Plan, you have the freedom to choose any licensed dentist. You also have the option of utilizing the Preferred Dentist Program offered with the Traditional Dental Plan to help control Plan expenses and help lower your out-of-pocket costs.

Page 3

PLEASE NOTE THE FOLLOWING:

This brochure is not a complete description of the Dental Plan offered through Sutton Investment Group Benefits Program. This is only a summary and is not a substitute for the official Plan documents.

The provisions of the official Plan documents and of applicable law will govern in the event of any inconsistency between those provisions and the provisions of this brochure.

Dental Plan Rates and Benefits

Sutton Investment Group
Dental Plan Monthly Premium

Type of Coverage	Employee	Each Dependent
Traditional Dental Plan	27	22
Preferred Dentist Plan	20	15

Dental Plan Benefits

Service	
Examination	100%
X-Rays	100%
Cleaning	100%
Restorative	80%
Endodontists	75%
Oral surgeons	75%
Periodontics	60%
Orthodontics	50%

Page 4

Education

EDUCATION INCENTIVE PLAN

The Sutton Investment Group's Benefits Program will help you pay for your children's education. The Education Incentive Plan helps you plan ahead for the day tuition bills begin to arrive.

WHO IS ELIGIBLE FOR EDUCATION BENEFITS?

Regular employees on the domestic payroll of Sutton Investment Group, who have completed at least one calendar month of service as a regular employee and who work at least 20 hours each week are eligible to participate in the benefit options available through Sutton Investment Group Benefits.

The Education Incentive Plan is designed to help you save from $5,000 to $40,000 (over a five-to-fifteen year period) toward the education costs you anticipate for each of your dependent children. You may choose to set aside an amount needed to reach your savings goal for one or more dependent children in the selected time period as follows:

- ✓ The maximum goal is $40,000 per child; the minimum is $5,000.
- ✓ You may have a maximum of four plan accounts per child.
- ✓ The Company contributes 15% of the amount of your payroll toward Education Benefits.

The funds will accumulate over a period of five to fifteen years, but not beyond your child's 25th birthday. When a plan reaches the level of money you desire, the funds are paid to you. You can request that the account be cancelled and paid out earlier.

HOW TO GET THE MOST OUT OF THE EDUCATION PLAN

The matching contributions from Sutton Investment Group are reported as ordinary income on your W-2 tax form. That means that any money you earn through our investment, are subject to taxes until all the proceeds are paid out to you.

Your savings and the company matching contributions are invested in stocks and bonds. The full amount of your account will automatically be paid to you upon cancellation of this plan.

Page 5

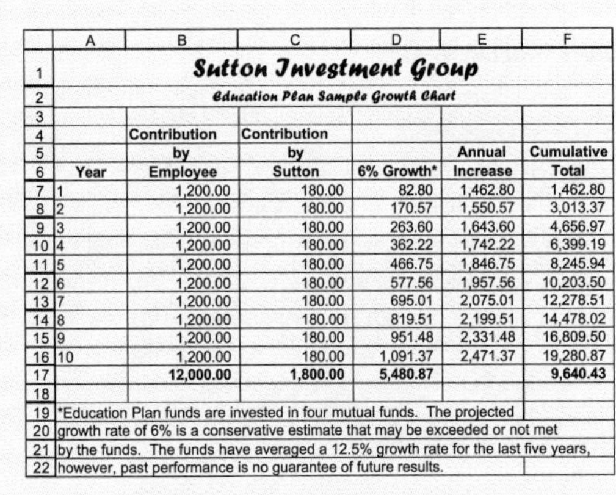

Sutton Investment Group
Education Plan Sample Growth Chart

Year	Contribution by Employee	Contribution by Sutton	6% Growth*	Annual Increase	Cumulative Total
1	1,200.00	180.00	82.80	1,462.80	1,462.80
2	1,200.00	180.00	170.57	1,550.57	3,013.37
3	1,200.00	180.00	263.60	1,643.60	4,656.97
4	1,200.00	180.00	362.22	1,742.22	6,399.19
5	1,200.00	180.00	466.75	1,846.75	8,245.94
6	1,200.00	180.00	577.56	1,957.56	10,203.50
7	1,200.00	180.00	695.01	2,075.01	12,278.51
8	1,200.00	180.00	819.51	2,199.51	14,478.02
9	1,200.00	180.00	951.48	2,331.48	16,809.50
10	1,200.00	180.00	1,091.37	2,471.37	19,280.87
	12,000.00	**1,800.00**	**5,480.87**		**9,640.43**

*Education Plan funds are invested in four mutual funds. The projected growth rate of 6% is a conservative estimate that may be exceeded or not met by the funds. The funds have averaged a 12.5% growth rate for the last five years, however, past performance is no guarantee of future results.

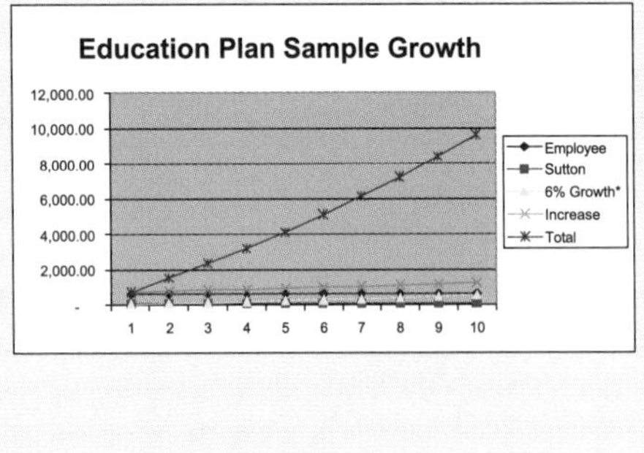

Page 6

Sutton Investment Group

MEMORANDUM

To: Michael Jasko, Brokerage Department

From: Lynn Goodwin, Human Resources

Date: November 15, 2004

Re: Dental coverage

In response to your call regarding the coverage for your dental bills listed below, please note the calculations that will be applied by our Dental Plan administrators. You should be receiving a check shortly.

Dental Bill as per your telephone call:

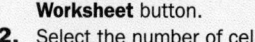

Exam	$ 80
X-Rays	$120
Oral Surgeon	$950

Insert worksheet here

Cues for Reference

Open Office Files from Multiple Applications

1. Start the first application.
2. Open the file.
3. Click **Start, All Programs, Microsoft Office** and the name of the second application.
4. Open the file.

Office XP:

1. Click Start, Open Office Document.
2. Click the file to open. The second application opens automatically.

Switch Between Applications and Files

- Click the **File** button on the Taskbar.

Copy Files Between Applications

1. In the first application, select the data you want to copy.
2. Click the **Copy** button.

3. Click the **File** button on the taskbar to switch between files and applications.
4. Place the insertion point in the location you want.
5. Click the **Paste** button.

Embed a Worksheet/Chart in a Word Document

1. In Excel, select the worksheet/chart you want to embed.
2. Click the **Copy** button.
3. Click the **File** button on the taskbar to switch between files and applications.
4. Place the insertion point in the location you want.
5. Click **Edit, Paste Special.**
6. Click **Microsoft Office Excel Worksheet Object** or **Microsoft Office Excel Chart Object.**
7. Click **OK.**

Edit an Embedded Worksheet/Chart

- Double-click worksheet/chart to work in Excel mode.

Insert a Worksheet in Word

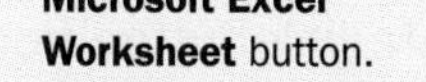

1. In Word, click the **Insert Microsoft Excel Worksheet** button.
2. Select the number of cells for the width and length of the worksheet.
3. Release the mouse and make worksheet entries in the worksheet.

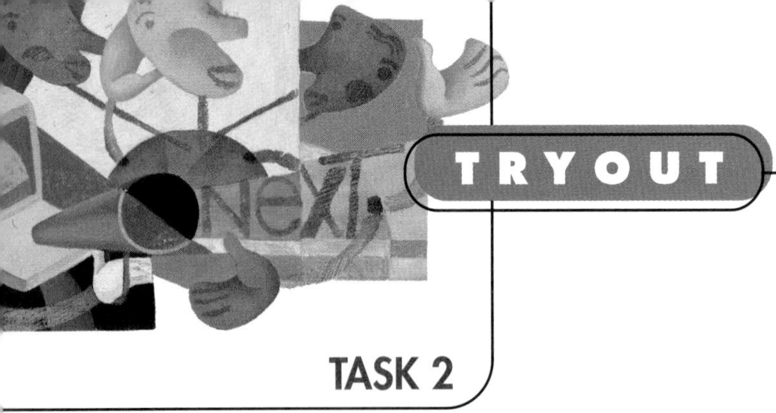

GOALS

To create a letter with a linked worksheet with Internet updates

To practice using the following skill sets:

- Link data between applications
  - Edit or format a linked object
- Display and use the Web toolbar
  - Paste Web data
- Use Smart Tags to find stock information
- Convert files to alternative file types
- Use Outlook features with Excel
- Create and modify appointments in Outlook
- Create and respond to meeting requests.

WHAT YOU NEED TO KNOW

Link Data Between Applications

- In Lesson 5, you used the Paste Link feature to link data between different workbooks or worksheets. You can also use paste link between different applications to create a *linked file,* so that if the source data changes, it will change in the destination document as well. The Link feature differs from embedding and copying, because a link is a shortcut to the source file; therefore, the data is not actually located in the destination file.
- There are three advantages to linking integrated data:
  - When you double-click a linked Excel worksheet in a Word destination file, you are brought into Excel to make edits and view formulas.
  - Any change you make to the worksheet in either the source or destination documents will appear in both places.
  - The destination file is smaller in size than a copied or embedded file because the data remains stored in the source file.
- To paste link data between applications, copy the data from the source file, switch to the destination file, click Edit, Paste Special, select the object type, and the Paste link button from the dialog box, as shown in Figure 7.7. You can use this method to link worksheet or chart data to another application.

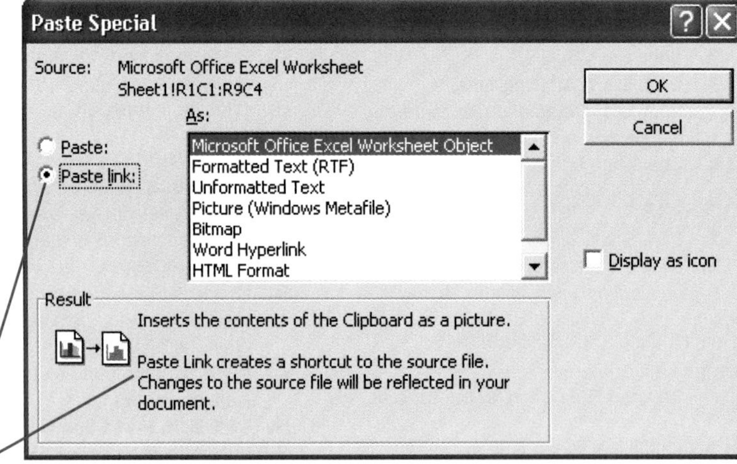

Figure 7.7 Paste Special dialog box with Paste link selected

TRY *it* OUT *E7-6*

1. Open **E7-6WD.doc** and **E7-6.xls** from the Data CD in the appropriate applications.
2. On **E7-6,** the worksheet, select and copy the data in the range **A1:D9.**
3. Switch to **E7-6WD,** the document, and place the insertion point below the last line of text.
4. Click **Edit, Paste Special,** and click **Microsoft Office Excel Worksheet Object.**
5. Click **Paste link** and **OK.** (The worksheet is linked to the document.)
6. Switch to the worksheet and select and copy the chart.
7. Place the insertion point below the linked worksheet.
8. Click **Edit, Paste Special,** and click **Microsoft Office Excel Chart Object.**
9. Click **Paste Link** and **OK.** (The chart is linked to the document.)
10. Size the chart so that it fits on the page.
11. Do not close the files.

EXCEL

Edit or Format a Linked Object

- To edit a linked Excel object in a destination file, double-click the object. You will be in Excel, in the source file, and able to use Excel menus to make changes. All changes you make are saved to the original source file and, therefore, automatically update in both locations. If you edit information in the source file, it also automatically updates in the linked location.
- You can format an object by selecting it and using the appropriate format buttons on the toolbar, or by right-clicking it and using the Format Object dialog box.

TRY *it* OUT *E7-7*

1. Continue to work in the open files or open **E7-7WD.doc** and **E7-7.xls** in the appropriate applications.
2. In the Word file double-click the worksheet data.
3. In Excel mode, select the graphic and delete it.
4. Switch to the Word document, using the taskbar button.
5. Right-click the worksheet and click the **Update link** option, if necessary, to view the edit.
6. Switch to the Excel workbook and change the value in **Cell B9** to `33.54%.` Notice the change in the chart.
7. Switch to the Word document, repeat Step 5, and notice the updates.
8. Center the worksheet and chart horizontally. Select each and click the **Center** alignment button. 
9. Save both files as **E7-7WD.doc** and **E7-7.xls**. Close both files.

Display and Use the Web Toolbar

- The Internet provides access to countless Web sites, many of which contain information you can use to enhance your presentation, provide documentation, or provide current data for worksheets and other Office applications.

Every Office application has a Web toolbar that allows you to use Internet features seamlessly with your application. Click View, Toolbars, and Web to display the toolbar, as shown in Figure 7.8. You must have an Internet Service Provider (ISP) to use the Web toolbar.

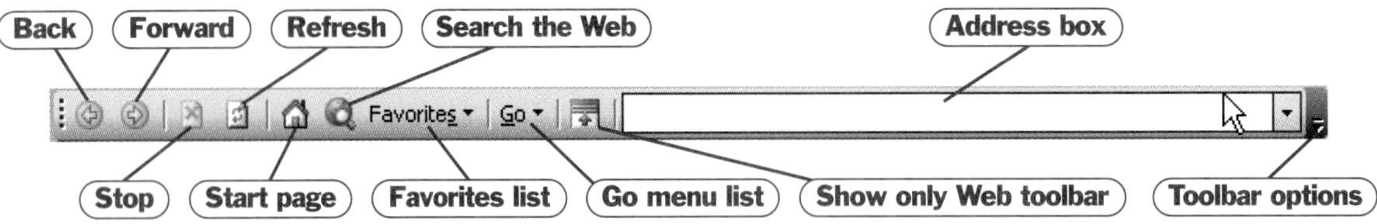

Figure 7.8 Web toolbar

To locate information on the Web, you may use the Search button and search engines on the Web or enter the address of a known site. When you are online and click the Search button, a screen displays, similar to that shown in Figure 7.9. You can select an area to search or enter a text string in the Search box.

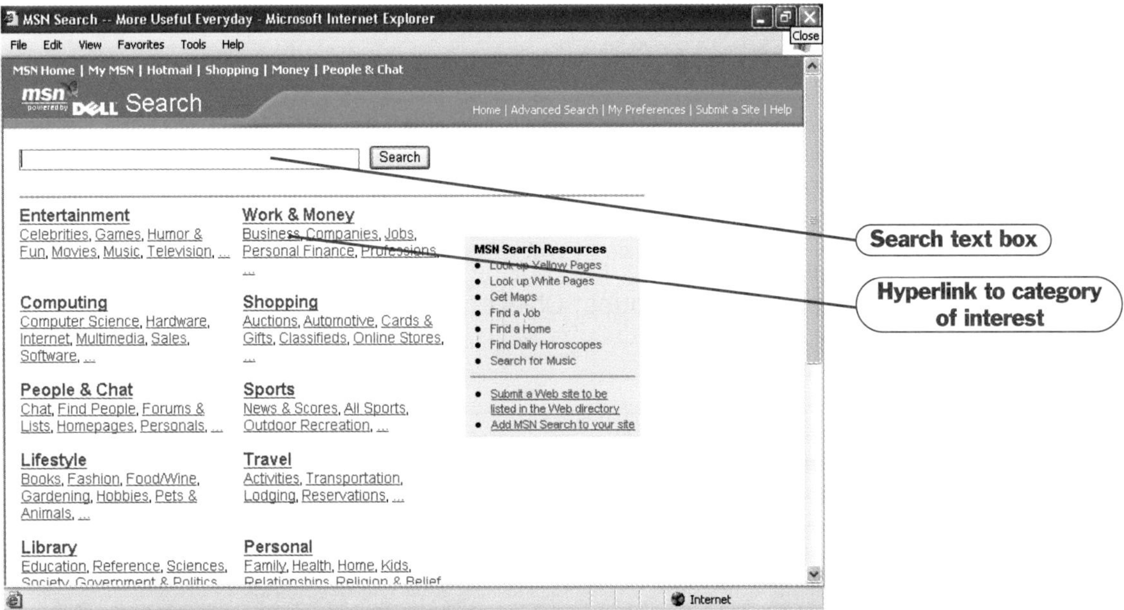

Figure 7.9 Sample of an Internet search window

TRY*it*OUT *E7-8*

1. Open **E7-8** from the Data CD.
2. Click **View, Toolbars,** and **Web.**
3. Click the **Search the Web** button on the Web toolbar. (Your Internet connection is established, and a search window displays.)
4. Enter "currency rates" in the Search box. Click **Search.**
5. Select the **moneycentral.msn.com** site titled World Currency Rates.

   Note: If you knew this address, you would enter it in the address box on the Web toolbar to go there directly.
6. View the currency rates Web site.
7. Continue to work on this Web site in the next Try*it*Out.

Paste Web Data

▶ You can copy Web data using Edit, Copy while in the Web browser. Sometimes you must copy an entire block of data even though you only need a portion of it. When you switch back to Excel, you can click Paste and use the Paste Options button to select one of three options: Keep Source Formatting, Match Destination Formatting, or Create Refreshable Web Query, as shown in Figure 7.10. You can delete any unnecessary data once it is in Excel.

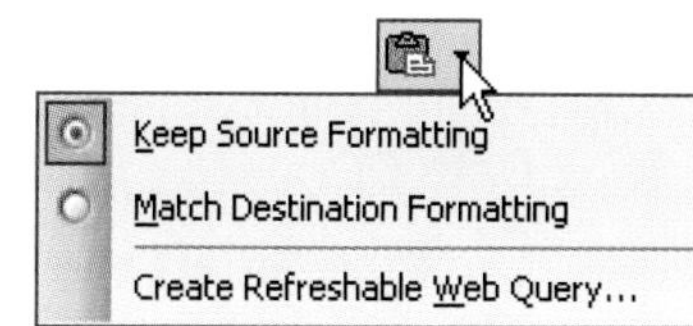

Figure 7.10 Paste options for Web paste

EXCEL

TRY it OUT *E7-9*

1. Continue to work in **E7-8** and on a currency rate Web site or on moneycentral.msn.com.
2. On the Web site, select the table of currency rates provided, click **Edit, Copy,** or right-click and click **Copy.**
3. Switch to Excel and paste the table to the bottom of E7-8.
4. Click the **Paste Options** button on the screen and click **Match Destination Formatting.**
5. Move the data from the Per US$ column to the appropriate currency listed on the worksheet.
6. Replace the contents of Cell D4 with today's date (press Ctrl+;).
7. Delete the currency table from the bottom of the worksheet.
8. Save the file as **E7-9.** Close the file. *Note:* Solution file will vary since rates change daily.

Use Smart Tags with the Internet

▶ Smart tags for financial symbols utilize the Internet to provide updated information to your worksheet. As noted in Lesson 2, if Smart Tags do not display on your computer, click Tools, AutoCorrect options, and then on the Smart Tags tab, click Label data with smart tags and check Financial Symbol, if it is not already selected.

▶ When you enter a stock symbol, the Smart tag options button provides Internet research options for that company, as shown in Figure 7.11. You can use this feature just to view stock quotes, company reports, or recent news, or you can insert a refreshable stock price. This price will update in the file as long as you are online. The refreshable stock price provides a considerable amount of information and should be placed on a separate sheet.

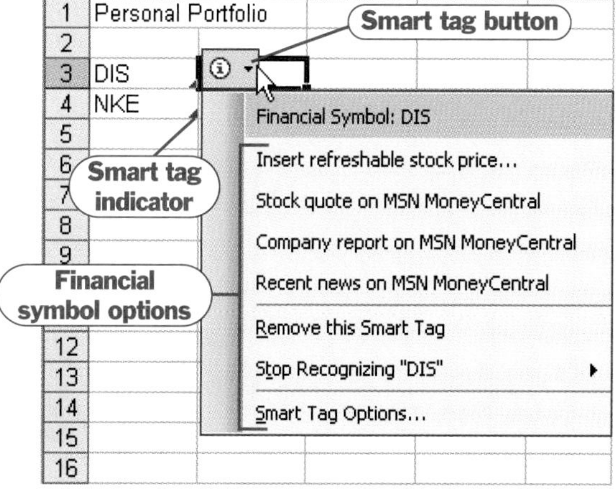

Figure 7.11 Smart tag options for financial symbols

TRY it OUT *E7-10*

1. While online, open **E7-10** from the Data CD.
2. Click the **Smart tag options** arrow for the **DIS** (Disney) financial symbol.
3. Select **Stock quote on MSN MoneyCentral.**
4. View the current quote and close the window.
5. Click the **Smart tag options** arrow for the **NKE** (Nike) financial symbol.
6. Select **Company report on MSN MoneyCentral.**
7. View the report and close the window.
8. Click the **Smart tag options** arrow for **DIS.**
9. Select **Insert refreshable stock price** and click **OK** to place data on a new sheet.
10. Rename the sheet `Disney.`
11. Repeat the procedure for the **NKE** symbol.
12. Save the file as **E7-10.** Close the file. You may wish to open the file on another day, and click the **Refresh Data** button on the External Data toolbar, to view the refreshed data.

Convert Files to Alternative File Types

- Excel generally saves files using the .xls format. However, you can save worksheets using other file formats for data transportability, including various versions of Excel, Lotus and Quattro Pro, and text formats, by selecting the file type in the Save As dialog box.
- When you save a file in a text format, you will be warned that Excel formats and features will not be preserved and that only the active sheet is saved. You can save in text formats such as .txt (tab separated values) or .csv (comma separated values), as shown in Figure 7.12. Columnar data will be separated either by tabs or commas, depending on your choice. Each row of data will end in a carriage return.

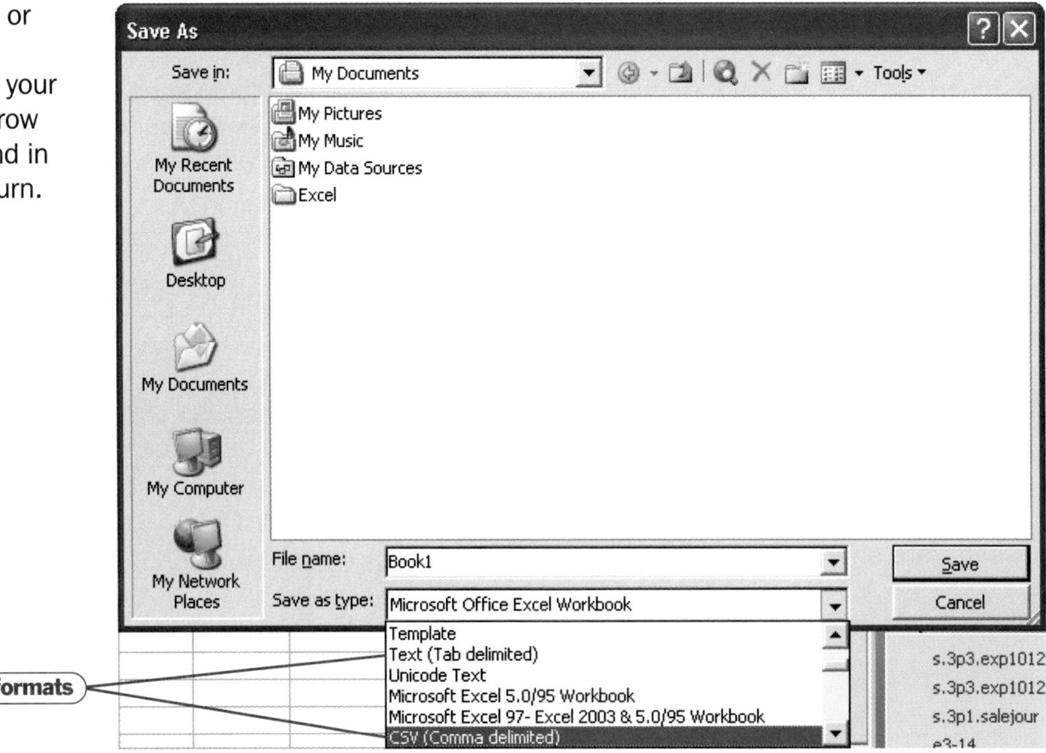

Figure 7.12 Save As dialog box

TRY*it*OUT *E7-11*

1. Open **E7-11** from the Data CD.
2. Save the file as a Text (Tab delimited) file, **E7-11txt.**
3. Click **OK** at the warning that only the active sheet will be saved.
4. Click **Yes** to acknowledge that Excel formats will be lost.
5. Save the file as a CSV (Comma delimited) file, **E7-11csv.**
6. Click **OK** and **Yes** to bypass the two warning messages.
7. Close the file.
8. In Word, open **E7-11txt.** Note the tab separated values.
9. In Word, open **E7-11csv.** Note the comma separated values.
10. Close the Word files.

EXCEL

Use Outlook Features with Excel

- If you are using Outlook as your communications software, you can use its features to help you work with Excel. Refer to Appendix I for an introduction to Outlook.
- There are many ways to use Outlook with Excel worksheets or tasks, such as:
  - Send worksheets via e-mail to anyone in your Contacts list.
  - Use the calendar or task feature to schedule preparation or review of financial reports.
  - Use the journal to document decisions or record interactions made with someone on your contacts list.
  - Distribute reports to members of your committee or staff via e-mail.
  - Use the calendar and/or journal to document dates and times for billing clients for your time.
- If you wish to send a file from Excel, click File, Send to, and Mail Recipient. Then, you can click the To button to select the recipient from your contacts list, as shown in Figure 7.13.

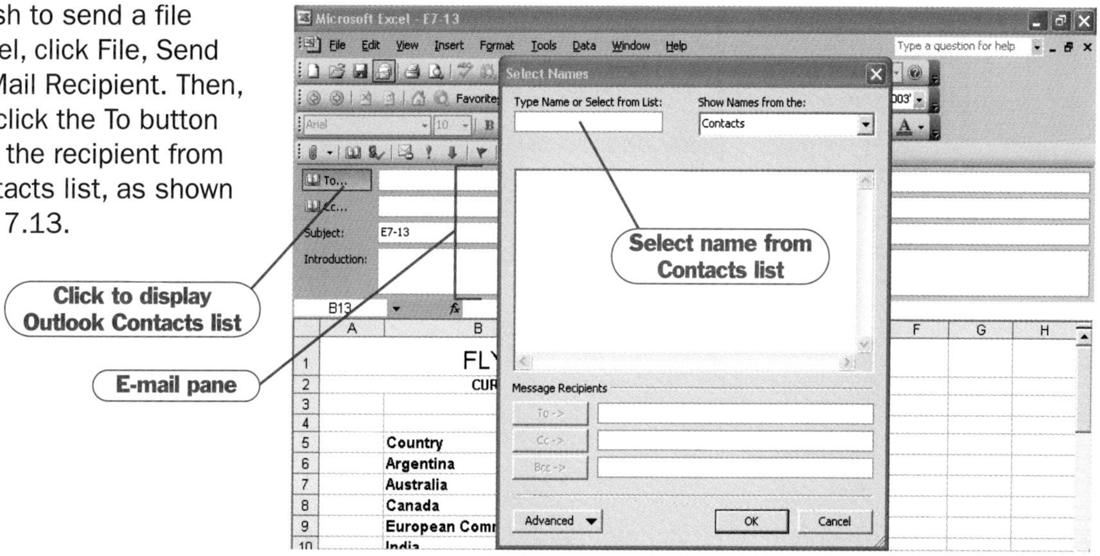

Figure 7.13 Select Names dialog box and e-mail screen in Excel

TRY it OUT *E7-12*

1. Open Outlook and your Internet connection. In Excel, open **E7-12**
2. Click **File, Send to,** then **Mail Recipient.**
3. Click the **To** button and select a contact from your Outlook address book. (If you have no contact entries, click **Cancel** and enter an e-mail address in the To box.)
4. Note that the file name is the Subject.
5. In the Introduction box enter `These are the current currency rates.` *Note: Outlook Express users will not get an Introduction box.*
6. Click the **Send this Sheet** button. 
7. Switch to Outlook.

Create and Modify Appointments and Events in Outlook

Create New Appointments and Events

▶ *Appointments* are activities that you schedule in your calendar that do not involve inviting other people or reserving resources. *Events* are activities that last 24 hours or longer such as trade shows, seminars, or vacations. In Calendar view, to add an appointment or an event, click New on the Standard toolbar, as shown in Figure 7.14, or double-click the day (or hour) on the calendar, as shown in Figure 7.15.

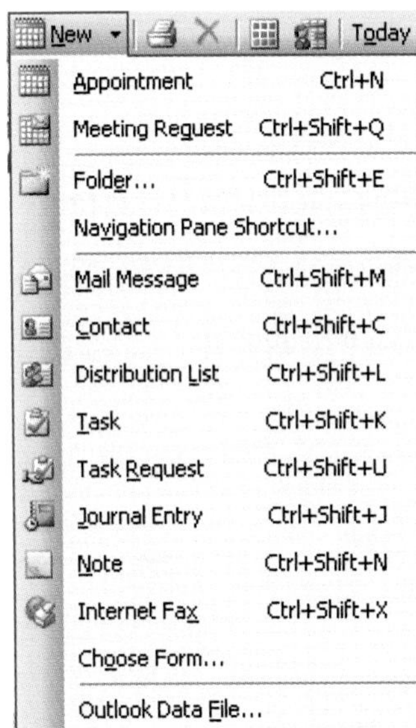

Figure 7.14 New button options in Outlook

Figure 7.15 Calendar view

▶ Input the information into the Appointment dialog window that displays, as shown in Figure 7.16. You can set a reminder to occur at a specified interval before an appointment or event. Reminders pop up on your screen at the designated time when Outlook is running, even if it is not your active application. When a calendar item has a reminder setting, a bell symbol appears in the daily and weekly calendar views.

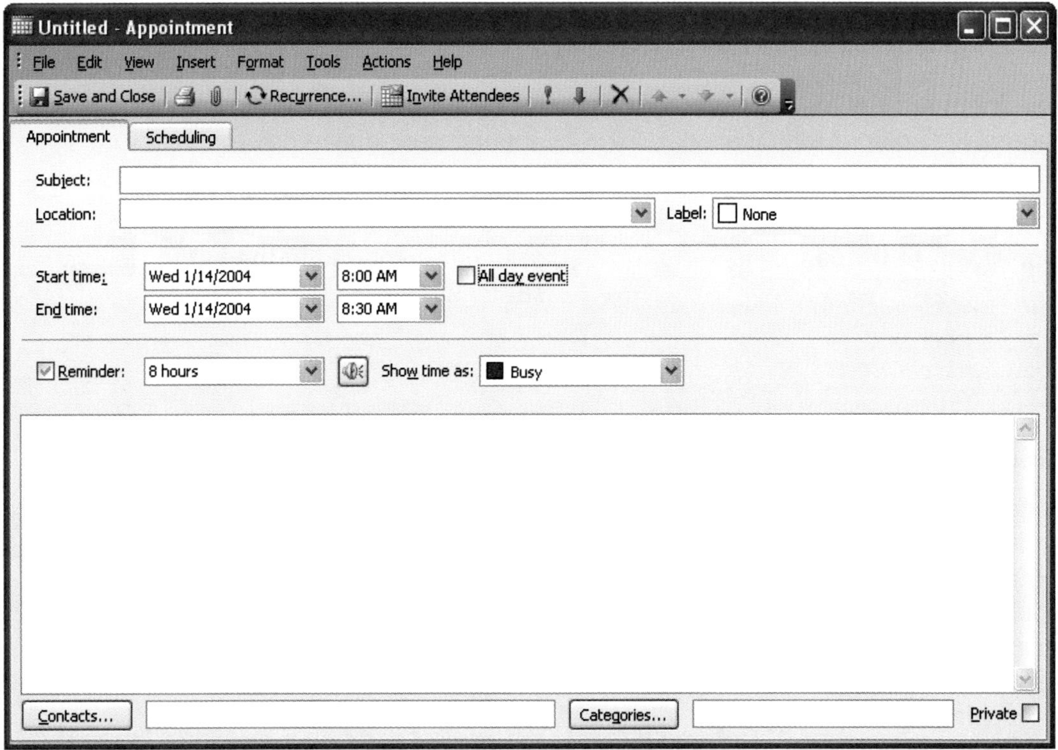

Figure 7.16 Appointment dialog window

- The Show time as window is used to insert an identifying colored bar on the left side of an appointment or event in the 1-day and 5-days views: Busy–blue, Free–clear, Tentative–blue/white striped, Out of Office–purple.
- You can make an appointment or event private so that it is hidden from others who may share your calendar from their own networked computers by clicking the Private box in the lower-right corner of the screen. The sharing computers will only see that the time has been blocked out but you will have the details. A key symbol appears next to private appointments or events in the daily and weekly calendar views on your computer.

EXCEL

TRY *it* OUT *E7-13*

1. In Outlook, click the **Calendar View** button.
2. Click the **New** button on the Standard toolbar.
3. Enter: `Lunch with Marilyn Ellis` in the Subject box in the Appointment Window.
4. In the Location box, enter: `ALS Travel Group executive dining room.`
5. Select next Thursday's date, using the **Start Time** down arrow to display the Calendar.
6. Set **12:00 PM** for a Start time. If the Start Time and End Time Hour boxes are not visible, click on **All day event** to deselect that option.
7. In the End Time location, set the same date and select **1:00 PM** for the time.
8. In the Notes section (the large text box) in the lower portion of the Appointment Dialog Box, enter: `Bring employee list.`

Continued on next page

TRY*it* OUT *E7-13 Continued*

9. Click **Reminder** to set the feature and select 2 hours. A reminder will display at 10 a.m. that day.
10. Click the list arrrow for the **Show time as** setting. Select **Out of Office.**
11. Click on the **Private** box in the lower right corner of the screen.
12. Click on **Save and Close** on the Appointment dialog box toolbar.
13. Click on the **5 Work Week** button and select the appropriate week from the calendar displayed at the left to view your settings.

Create Recurring Appointments with Labels

- If the appointment or event will be one of a recurring series, click the Recurrence button on the tool bar of the Appointment dialog window. Settings for pattern and range of the appointment can then be set on the Appointment Recurrence dialog box, as shown in Figure 7.17. The recurring symbol will appear next to any recurring appointments or events.
- In the Appointment dialog box you can label an appointment according to several categories, including Business, Personal, Must Attend, Vacation, and Travel Required, by selecting from the items on the drop-down list, as shown in Figure 7.18. This feature displays the appointment in a distinct color; for example, the Business label displays your appointment with a blue highlight; the Personal label appears in green.

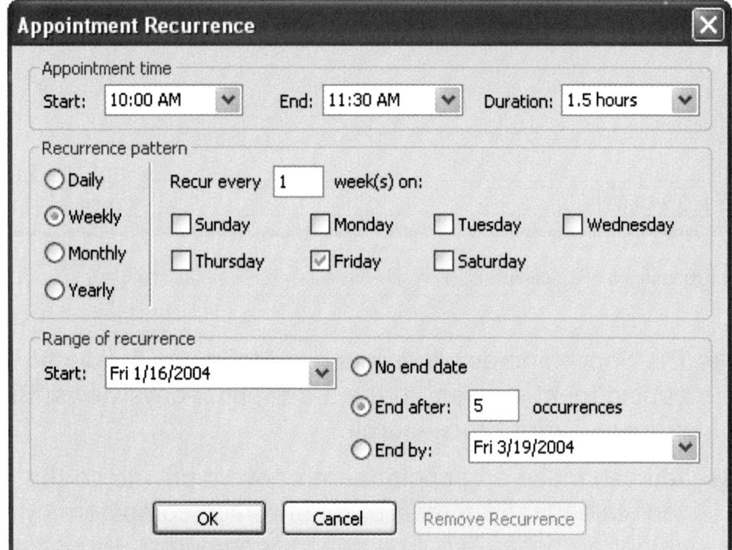

Figure 7.17 Appointment Recurrence dialog box

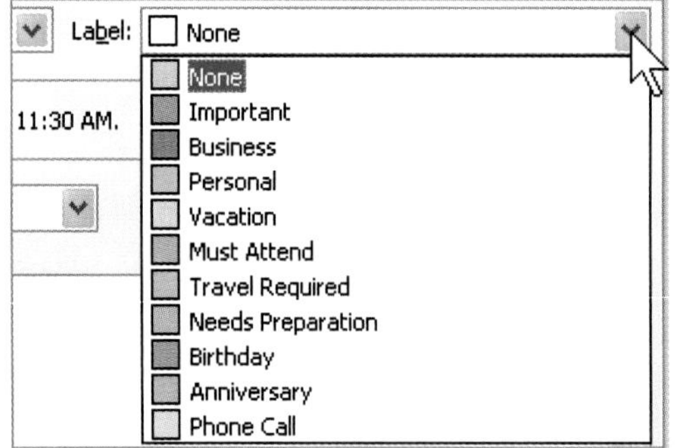

Figure 7.18 Label settings on Appointment window

TRY*it*OUT *E7-14*

You should be in Calendar View in Outlook.

1. On the Calendar, double-click on next Friday's date, or click **New, Appointment.**
2. Enter: `Training Session` in the Subject box in the Appointment Window.
3. In the Location box, enter: `Conference room`.
4. Note that the Start time date is set. Set **10:00 AM** as the Start time. *Note: Click on* **All day event** *to deselect that option if the time options are not available.*
5. In the End time location, select **11:30 PM** for the time.
6. In the Notes section in the lower portion of the Appointment dialog box, enter: `Salesmanship Course`.
7. Click **Reminder** to set the feature and select **1 hour**.
8. Click the **Recurrence** button on the toolbar. 
9. Make settings for a weekly pattern on Friday that ends after 5 occurrences, as shown in Figure 7.17. Click **OK.**
10. Click the list arrow for Label on the Appointment window and select **Must Attend.**
11. Click on **Save and Close** on the Appointment dialog box toolbar.
12. Click on the **5 Work Week** and the **31 Month** buttons, changing the selected weeks as necessary to view your settings. 

Modify or Delete Appointments and Events and Set Level of Importance

- You can double-click an appointment or event in any Calendar view to open its Appointment dialog window for purposes of viewing details or changing information. Edit the appointment or event information as desired. To delete a calendar item, right-click it and select Delete from the shortcut menu.
- When an appointment is created, it has a neutral level of importance. Use the Appointment window toolbar to change the level of importance of an appointment or event to either High or Low.

TRY*it*OUT *E7-15*

You should be in Calendar View in Outlook.

1. Click on the Thursday luncheon date on the Calendar.
2. Double click **Lunch with Marilyn Ellis** on the Calendar.
3. Select the text **ALS Travel Group executive dining room** in the Location box and enter: `The Trolley Restaurant`.
4. Use the drop-down list in the Start time box to change the appointment to **12:30,** ending at **1:30.**
5. Click the **Importance: High** button on the toolbar. 
6. Click **Business** in the Label box.
7. Click **Save and Close** on the toolbar.
8. Click Thursday's date in the Calendar window to display the rescheduled appointment.

Create and Respond to Meeting Requests

- *Meetings* are appointments to which you invite others and/or reserve resources. To add a meeting to your calendar and send requests to others to attend, click the list arrow to the right of the New button and select Meeting Request from the options that display. (See Figure 7.19.)
- The Meeting dialog window that displays, as shown in Figure 7.20, is very similar in appearance to the Appointment dialog window. However, the Meeting dialog window has a To... box for listing the e-mail addresses of persons you are inviting. When you click the To button, the Contacts in your Address book display so that you can select participants. When you click the Send button on the toolbar, the completed meeting request is sent to the invitees.

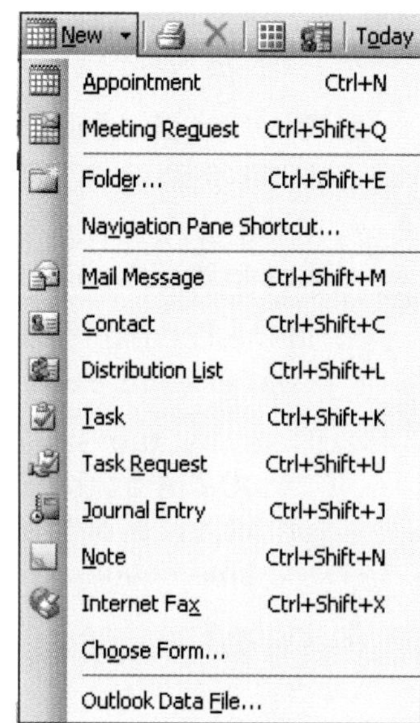

Figure 7.19 New button list options

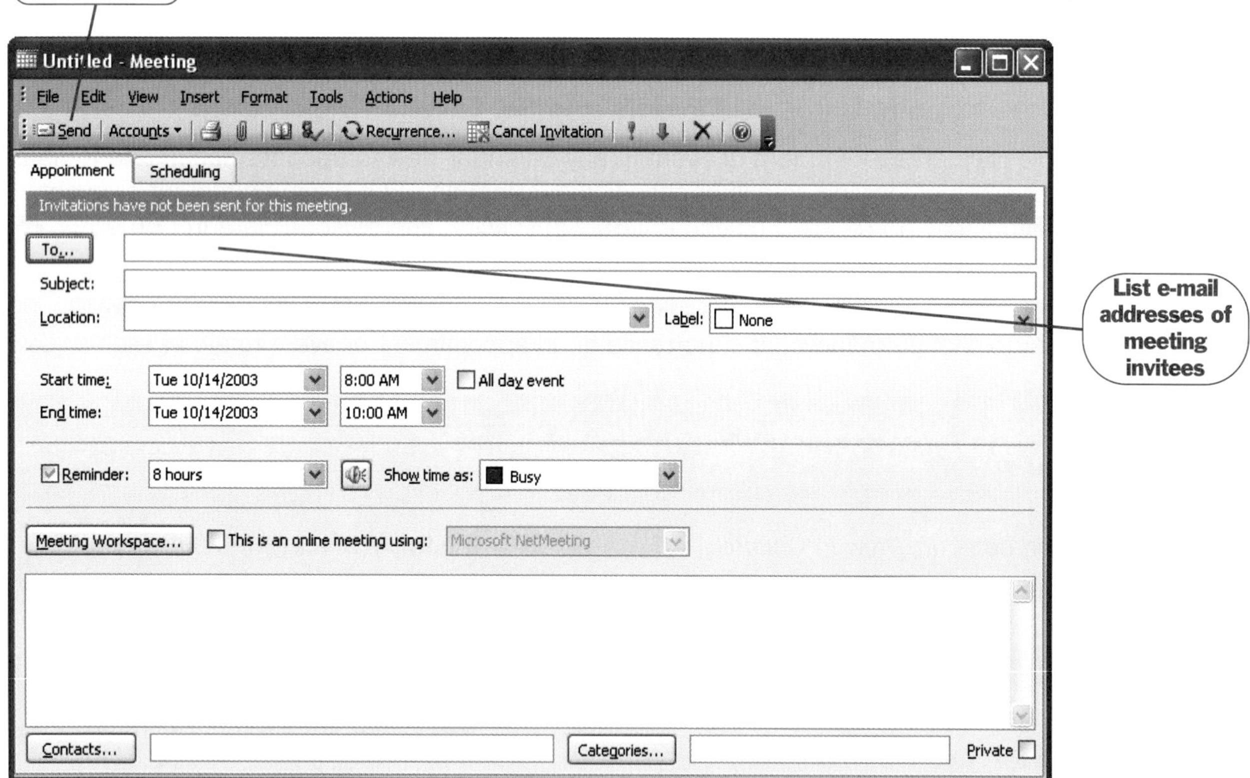

Figure 7.20 Meeting dialog window

TRY *it* OUT *E7-16*

You should be in Calendar View in Outlook.

1. Click the list arrow to the right of the **New** button and select **Meeting Request.**
2. Click the **To...** button.
3. Select a participant from your Contacts list and click **Required.**
4. Select a second participant from your Contacts list and click **Required.** Click **OK**.
5. In the Subject box, enter: `Meet with Tom Bukata`.
6. In the Location box, enter: `Trilogy Productions, New York Office`.
7. Click tomorrow's date and **2:30 PM** for the Start time.
8. Click tomorrow's date and **3:30 PM** for the End time.
9. Set a three-hour reminder.
10. In the Notes section, enter `Presentation of communications proposal.`
11. Click **File, Close;** click **Yes** when asked if you want to save changes. The meeting request is saved in the calendar.
12. Click **No** when asked if you want to send.

EXCEL

Respond to Meeting Requests

▶ When one of your invitees receives a meeting request from you, it will appear as an e-mail, as shown in Figure 7.21. He or she can Accept, Tentatively accept, Decline, or Propose a new Time using the buttons on the Meeting toolbar. The response will be sent back to your e-mail address.

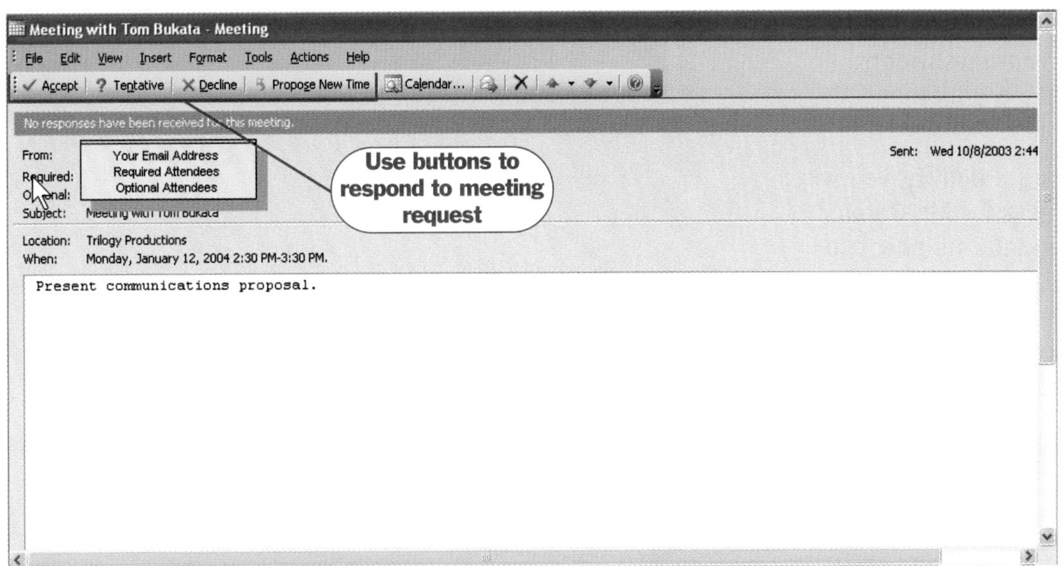

Figure 7.21 Meeting Request response dialog window

GOALS
To create a letter with a linked worksheet with Internet updates
To schedule an appointment and to e-mail a worksheet

SETTING THE STAGE/WRAPUP
Margins: Default
Start line: At 1"
File names: **7.2stocks.xls**
7.2broker.doc

WHAT YOU NEED TO KNOW

- Investment or brokerage firms can manage your stock or equity holdings. Most brokerage firms now also have online brokerage Web sites so that you can buy or sell stocks directly in your account.
- Stocks represent your ownership certificates in publicly traded companies. The current prices of stocks vary with the economy and market conditions, and can be obtained on your investment firm's Web site or on other "quote" sites.
- In this Rehearsal activity, you will work on projects for Mr. Calarco, as follows: update his portfolio worksheet with current stock prices from the Internet, integrate the worksheet into a letter to the Sutton Investment Group, save the worksheet as a text file, use the information in an e-mail, and schedule a meeting with Mr. Roxbury.

DIRECTIONS

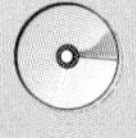

1. Open **7.2stocks.xls** from the Data CD and view the names and symbols of the stocks in the portfolio.
2. Verify that the Web toolbar is displayed and search for a site that shows stock quotes, or go to www.stockquotes.com or www.moneycentral.msn.com.
3. Use the stock symbol from the worksheet and look up each current market price. Copy and paste each price to the Excel worksheet, matching the destination format.
4. Enter a formula, multiplying market price by shares owned, to find the market value of the shares in **Column G,** as shown in Illustration A.
5. Find the total market value and correct number formats, if necessary.
6. Open **7.2broker.doc** from the Data CD.
7. Copy and paste link the Excel worksheet from **7.2stocks.xls** to the Word letter after the second paragraph, as shown in Illustration B.
8. Switch back to the Excel worksheet and check the formula for the cost total in **Column E.**
9. Edit and correct the formula.
10. Switch back to the Word document to check if the changes updated to the linked file. Right-click the linked file and update, if necessary.
11. Print a copy of the letter.
12. Save both files. Close **7.2broker.doc**.
13. Save the Excel file as a .csv (comma separated values) file and name it **7.2stockcsv.** Close the file and Excel.
14. In Word, open the **7.2stockcsv** file.

Continued on next page

15. Delete the rows of text above and below the names of the stocks and the values to the right of the number of shares, and insert the text as shown in Illustration C.

16. Send the document by e-mail to Mr. Calarco's original stock broker. Use an address provided by your instructor or from your Contacts list. Change the subject to `Account transfer.`

17. Close and save the Word file.

18. In Outlook, create an appointment with Mr. Roxbury of Sutton Investment Group for one week from today at 4:30 p.m. in his office.

19. Close all files.

EXCEL

JAMES CALARCO
Investment Record

COMPANY NAME	SYMBOL	SHARES	DATE BOUGHT	COST	MARKET PRICE	MARKET VALUE
Nike Inc	NKE	300	09/30/02	12,345.32		
MicroSoft	MSFT	200	06/04/02	5,342.54		
Bank of America	BAC	200	10/14/03	16,342.32		
J P Morgan Chase	JPM	100	11/25/03	3,632.98		
Intel	INTC	100	07/07/04	3,132.89		
TOTALS				28,450.73		

Find current market prices for stocks on the Internet

Enter formulas to find total market value for each stock

Check formula

Find totals

Illustration A

James Calarco
460 West End Avenue
New York, NY 10023
Phone: 212-555-3432

March 5, 2005

Mr. Marcus Roxbury
Sutton Investment Group
34562 Corona Street
Los Angeles, CA 90001

Dear Mr. Roxbury:

I am interested in transferring my portfolio of investments to your firm as I am dissatisfied with my current brokerage firm. After our telephone conversation and my visit, I feel that your company can provide me with the service I require.

A list of my investments with the current market value is provided below:

Please send me the necessary forms. I look forward to hearing from you.

Sincerely yours,

James Calarco

Paste link worksheet here

Illustration B

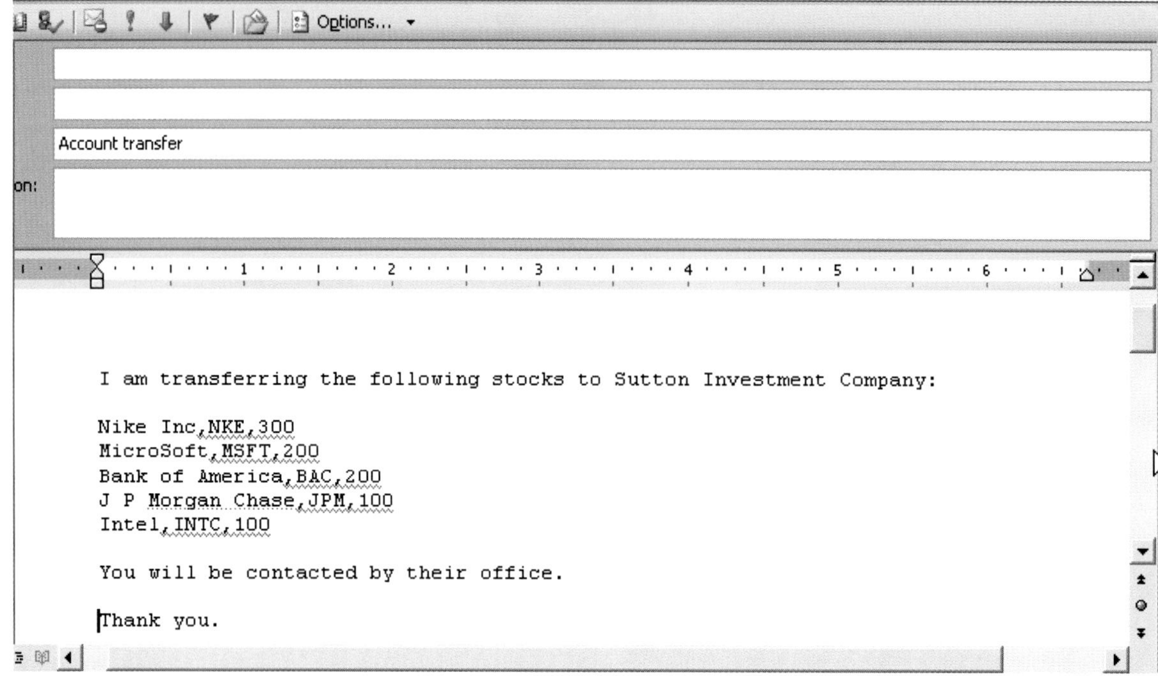

Options...
Account transfer
on:
I am transferring the following stocks to Sutton Investment Company:
Nike Inc,NKE,300
MicroSoft,MSFT,200
Bank of America,BAC,200
J P Morgan Chase,JPM,100
Intel,INTC,100
You will be contacted by their office.
Thank you.

Illustration C

Cues for Reference

View Web Toolbar

- Click **View, Toolbars,** and **Web.**

Paste Link Between Applications

1. Open files you want to link.
2. In source file, select data to link.
3. Click the **Copy** button.
4. Switch to desination file.
5. Click **Edit, Paste Special.**
6. Click **Paste Link** and select object to link.
7. Click **OK.**

Edit a Linked File

- Edit data in either the source or destination files. (The data will change in both locations.)

Copy and Paste from the Web

1. Locate data you need from Web site.
2. Select data.
3. Click **Edit, Copy,** or right-click and choose **Copy** option, or click **Copy** button.
4. Switch back to Excel.
5. Click **Paste** button.

   or
5. Click **Paste Options** list arrow.
6. Select appropriate Paste option.

Save Excel File as a Text File

1. Click **File, Save As.**
2. Click the list arrow in the Save as type box.
3. Select the .txt or .csv format.
4. Click **Save.**

E-mail Word or Excel files

1. Click **File, Send to, Mail Recipient.**
2. Select a contact from the Address book in the To box or enter an address.
3. Change the subject line, if necessary.
4. Type introductory comments, if necessary.
5. Click the **Send** button.

Schedule an Appointment

1. Click **File, New,** and **Appointment.**

   or

   Click **Actions, New Appointment.**
2. Enter subject in Subject box.
3. Enter location in Location box.
4. Click the arrow to open the Start time calendar.
5. Set Date.
6. Set Start time.
7. Set End time.
8. Set Categories, Notes, or Recurrence as necessary.
9. Click the **Save and Close** button.

SETTING THE STAGE/WRAPUP

Act I File names: **7p1.travel guide.doc**
7p1.tips.doc

Act II File names: **7p2.income.xls**
7p2.quarterly.doc

WHAT YOU NEED TO KNOW

Act I

You work in the Marketing Department of the Air Land Sea Travel Group. Your company has developed Travel Guide 2005, a handbook that contains practical information for the traveler. Your supervisor would like to add several pages on currency conversion tips, including information about the euro and the latest exchange rates for a list of currencies.

Follow these guidelines:

- Open **7p1.tips.doc, 7p1.currency.xls,** and **7p1.travel guide.doc** from the Data CD. 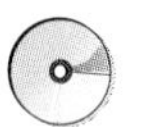 
- In **7p1.currency.xls**:
  - Enter today's date in Cell B2.
  - Find what one unit of the currency in Column A is in U.S. dollars for each item. You may find currency converters using a search engine or you can go to www.moneycentral.msn.com and use their conversion feature. Enter the information in Column B.
- In **7p1.tips.doc:**
  - Use Office Online to insert a clip art object in the second paragraph representing "foreign currency."
  - Integrate the worksheet data from **7p1.currency.xls** into the location above the "What is the EURO" paragraph.
  - Select the entire document and copy and paste it to **7p1.travel guide.doc,** immediately before the References page. Center the linked sheet.
- In **7p1.travel guide.doc,** check that the new information copied correctly and that the pagination is appropriate. (The References material can be placed at the bottom of the 7p1.tips text.)
- Save all files and print a copy of the new guide.

Act II

You work in the Accounting Department of the Air Land Sea Travel Group. Your department has developed an income workbook for the second quarter consisting of income statements for all offices, a consolidated income statement, an income analysis, and two charts.

The chief financial officer, Tyler Willem, has prepared a document explaining the quarterly results and would like the worksheet data integrated into one report. The report will be sent electronically to all managers, officers, and interested parties, and a printed copy will be kept on file. Tasks will be entered into Outlook and a meeting will be scheduled to review these reports.

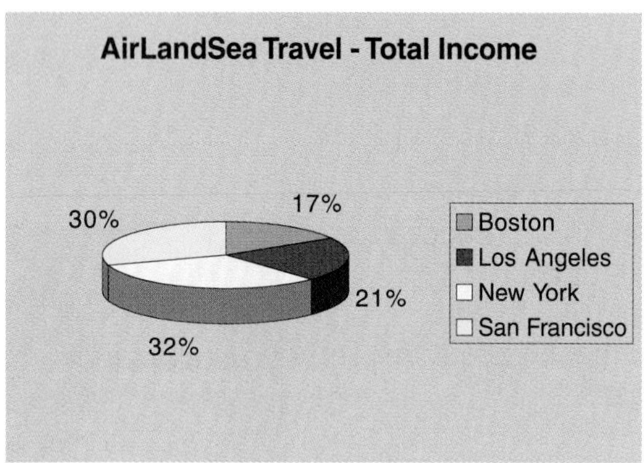

Follow these guidelines:

- Open **7p2.income.xls** and **7p2.quarterly.doc** from the Data CD. 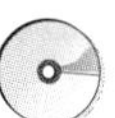
- Link the worksheets and chart data where appropriate, as indicated in the document.
    - Remove the parenthetical insert instructions from the document.
    - Remove the text box and arrow from the Net Income pie chart.
    - Create a hyperlink with appropriate text to the worksheet.
    - Adjust the size of the objects so that the pages do not have large blank areas, and center the objects horizontally on the page.
- Research the current outlook for the travel industry on the Internet. Summarize your findings in several sentences. (If you quote or copy data from a Web site, be sure to indicate your source.)
- Write an e-mail, addressed to managers and officers, that includes the following:
    - Announce that the quarterly report and income data are attached.
    - Report on the current outlook for the travel industry, as per your research.
    - Attach the quarterly report and income files to the e-mail.
- In Outlook, schedule a conference call with the staff in the store for 4:00 p.m. EST two days from today. Send an e-mail to the store informing them of the conference call meeting.
- Print a copy of the quarterly report. Save and close all files.

PERFORMING WITH ACCES
INTRODUCTORY UNI

LESSON 1

Access Basics

In this lesson, you will be introduced to Access and its basic features.

Upon completion of this lesson, you should have mastered the following skill sets:

- About Access
- About database concepts
- About database management systems
- Start Access
- Explore the Access window
- About database objects
- Explore the Database window
- Understand database design
- Understand database views

Terms

Software-related

- Access window
- Wizard
- View
- Design view
- Datasheet view
- PivotTable view
- PivotChart view

Database-related

- Database
- Database management system
- Relational database management system
- Database objects
- Table
- Record
- Fields
- Field name
- Field content
- Datasheets
- Primary key
- Forms
- Queries
- Reports

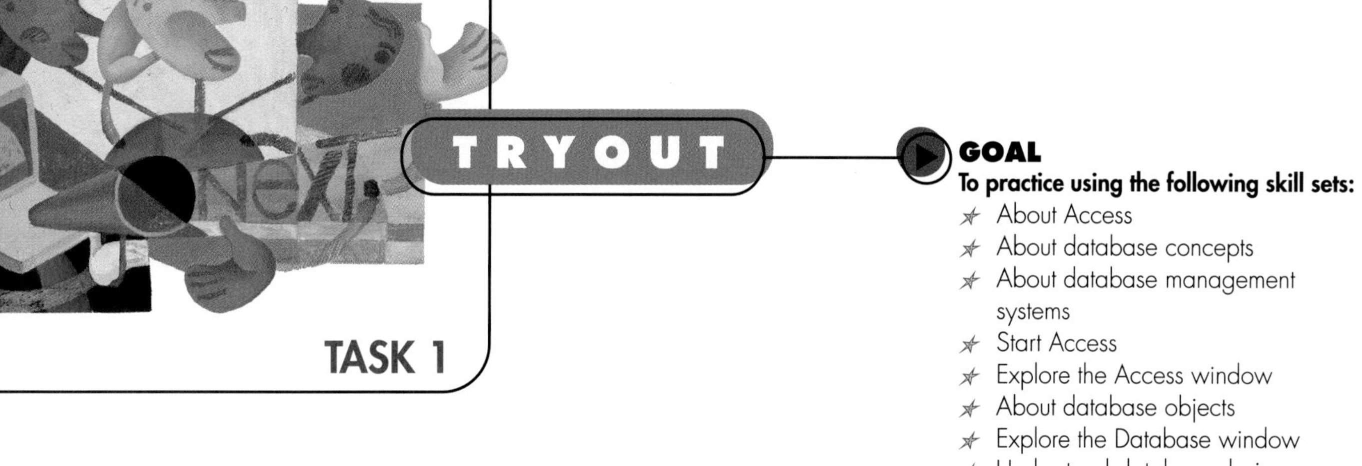

GOAL
To practice using the following skill sets:

- About Access
- About database concepts
- About database management systems
- Start Access
- Explore the Access window
- About database objects
- Explore the Database window
- Understand database design
- Understand database views

ACCESS

WHAT YOU NEED TO KNOW

About Access

- Access is a database management system that you can use independently or as part of the Office suite.

About Database Concepts

- A *database* is an organized collection of facts about a particular subject. For example, databases provide the information about your account when you call your telephone company, your bank, or your credit card company for information. A database is a way to organize vast amounts of data so that you can access, analyze, or update it easily.
- A database that is maintained manually, such as an index card file of all of the books in a library, requires physically locating and revising records.
- An Access database is the equivalent of an electronic file cabinet. It lets you organize facts and provides a way for you to maintain the data electronically.

About Database Management Systems

- A *database management system* provides functions to store, search, filter, query, and report on the data in a database. For example, to identify all the books in the library that were published 10 years ago, you would have to review each card in a card catalog and write down the name and call number of every book that meets the search criterion. With an automated database management system, once the information is in the database, you can locate the books with a few keystrokes.
- Access provides many additional functions besides data maintenance and storage. Access is a *relational database management system* with tools to link databases that contain related information. For example, you can use the information from two databases that contain customers' account numbers. One database might contain customer names and addresses, and the other database might contain sales information. By using the customer number to link the data between the two databases, you can generate invoices and reports, as shown in Figure 1.1.

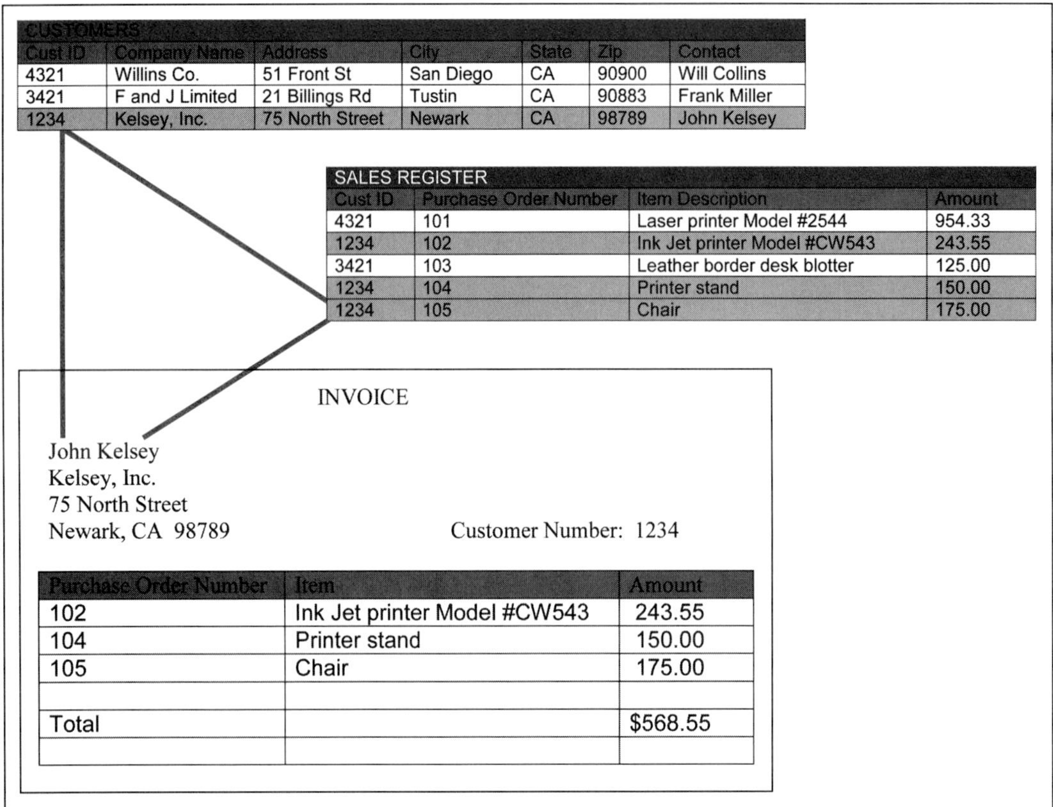

CUSTOMERS						
Cust ID	Company Name	Address	City	State	Zip	Contact
4321	Willins Co.	51 Front St	San Diego	CA	90900	Will Collins
3421	F and J Limited	21 Billings Rd	Tustin	CA	90883	Frank Miller
1234	Kelsey, Inc.	75 North Street	Newark	CA	98789	John Kelsey

SALES REGISTER			
Cust ID	Purchase Order Number	Item Description	Amount
4321	101	Laser printer Model #2544	954.33
1234	102	Ink Jet printer Model #CW543	243.55
3421	103	Leather border desk blotter	125.00
1234	104	Printer stand	150.00
1234	105	Chair	175.00

INVOICE

John Kelsey
Kelsey, Inc.
75 North Street
Newark, CA 98789

Customer Number: 1234

Purchase Order Number	Item	Amount
102	Ink Jet printer Model #CW543	243.55
104	Printer stand	150.00
105	Chair	175.00
Total		$568.55

Figure 1.1 Linking databases to produce an invoice

Start Access

▶ To start Access, click Start on the taskbar, select All Programs, Microsoft Office, and then Microsoft Office Access 2003, as shown in Figure 1.2. If you have placed Access on your Quick Start menu, you can click Microsoft Office Access 2003 to start Access.

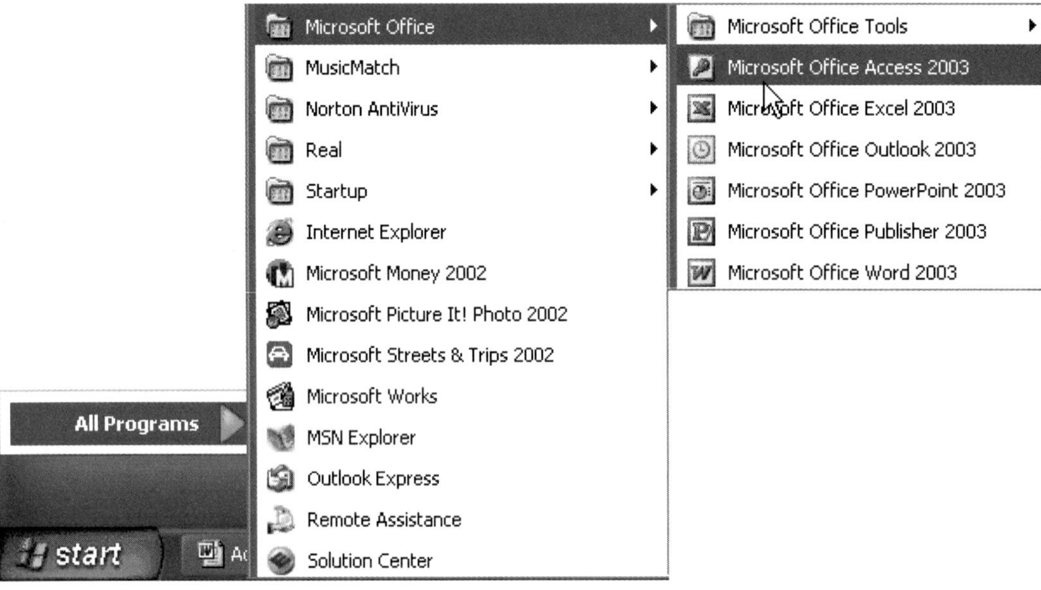

Figure 1.2 Start Access

TRY *it* OUT *A1-1*

1. Click **Start.**
2. Select **All Programs.**
3. Select **Microsoft Office.**
4. Click **Microsoft Office Access 2003.**
5. Do not close the program.

Explore the Access Window

- The *Access window* is similar to those of other Office applications. The top portion of the screen contains the title bar, menu bar, and toolbar. The Access toolbar contains buttons to accomplish many common database tasks and commands. The Getting Started task pane appears on the right of the window, as shown in Figure 1.3, containing links to help, training, to create a new database, or to open saved databases.
- To display more of the Access window, you can close the task pane by clicking the Close button on its title bar or by clicking View and deselecting Task Pane.
- You can also hide the toolbars by clicking View, Toolbars and deselecting those you want to hide.

ACCESS

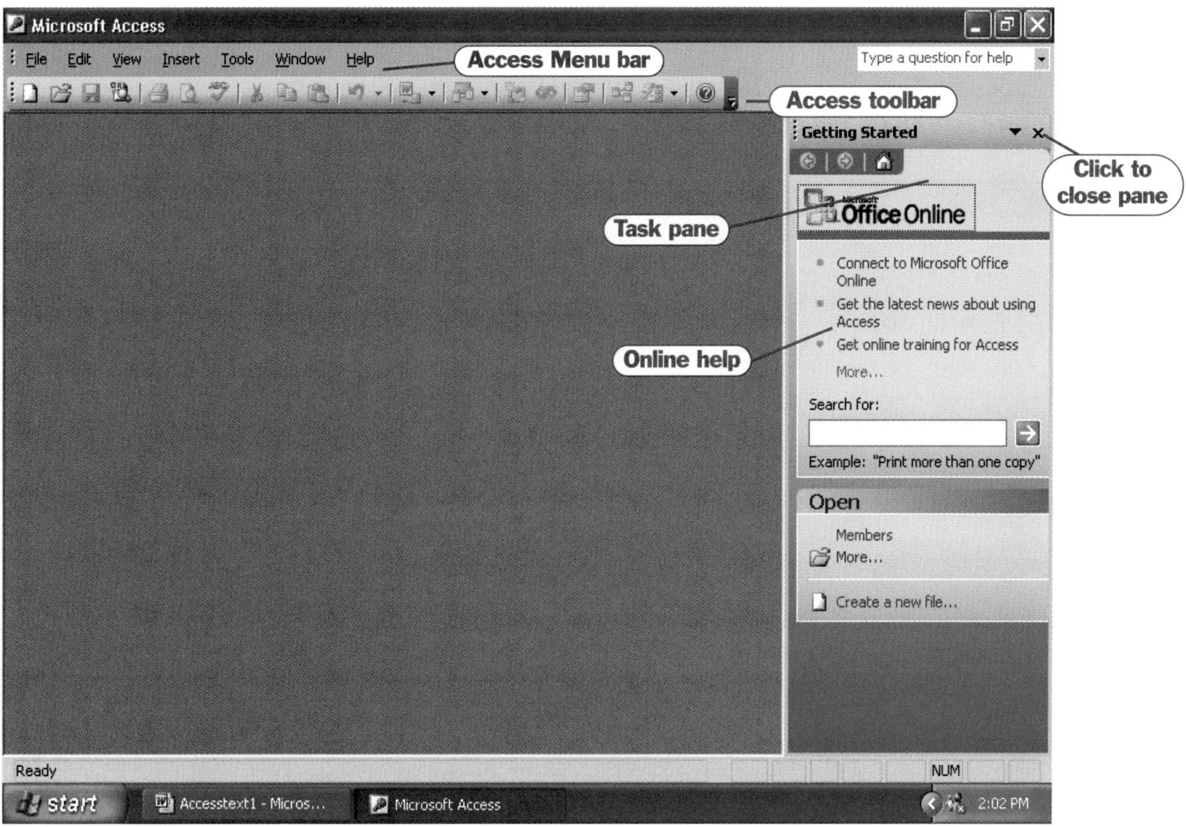

Figure 1.3 Access window and task pane

TRY*it* OUT *A1-2*

Note: Access should be open with the task pane displayed.

1. Click on each menu item and notice the options under each.
2. Move the mouse over each toolbar button to view the name of the button.
3. Click the **Close** button on the task pane title bar.
4. Click **View, Toolbars, Task Pane**. Do not close Access.

About Database Objects

- *Database objects* are tools that you need to store, maintain, search, analyze, and report on data in a database program such as Access. In this lesson you will learn about four database objects: tables, forms, queries, and reports, as indicated by the button displayed to the right of each database object's explanatory text.
- In a *table* or spreadsheet format, each row in a table represents one *record* in a database. The table shown in Figure 1.4 contains the membership list of a swim and golf club, and each member's data is a record. The items of data that make up each record, such as the Member ID, Name, Address, etc., are called *fields*. Each field is identified by a *field name*. A table can have up to 255 fields. Specific data in a field is called the *field content*. Tables are sometimes referred to as *datasheets*.

Tables

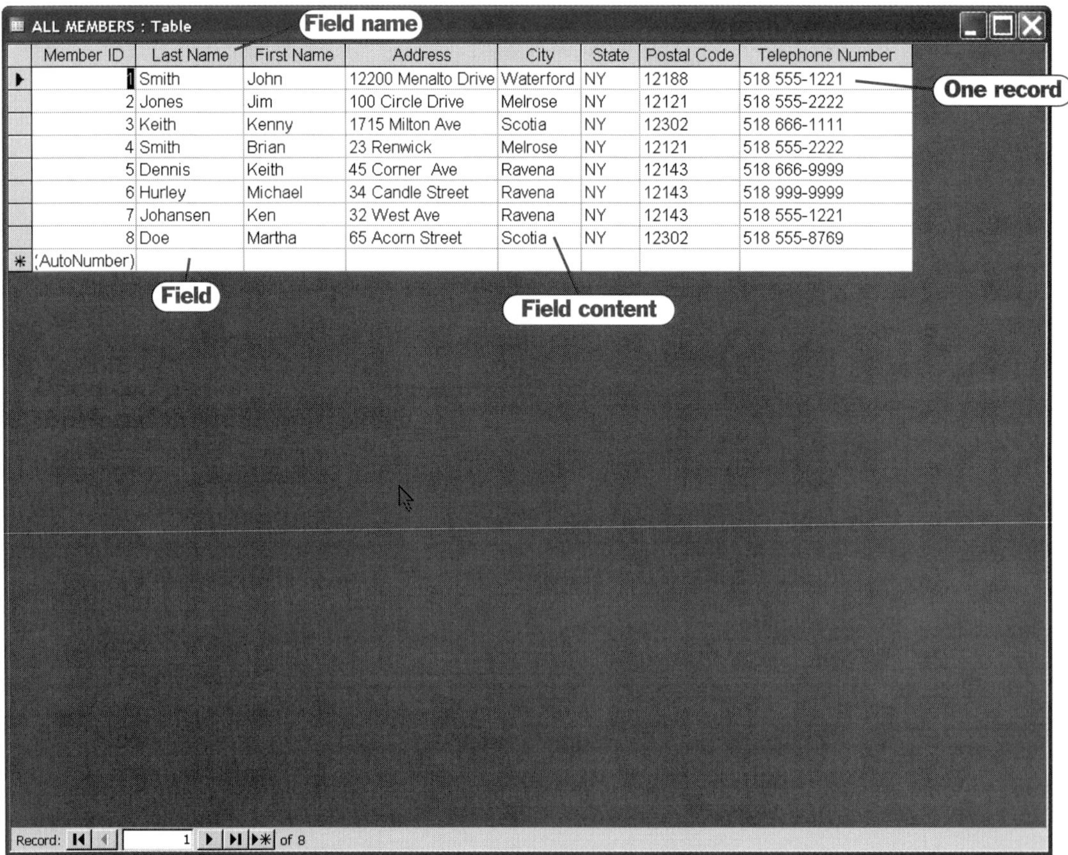

ALL MEMBERS : Table

Member ID	Last Name	First Name	Address	City	State	Postal Code	Telephone Number
1	Smith	John	12200 Menalto Drive	Waterford	NY	12188	518 555-1221
2	Jones	Jim	100 Circle Drive	Melrose	NY	12121	518 555-2222
3	Keith	Kenny	1715 Milton Ave	Scotia	NY	12302	518 666-1111
4	Smith	Brian	23 Renwick	Melrose	NY	12121	518 555-2222
5	Dennis	Keith	45 Corner Ave	Ravena	NY	12143	518 666-9999
6	Hurley	Michael	34 Candle Street	Ravena	NY	12143	518 999-9999
7	Johansen	Ken	32 West Ave	Ravena	NY	12143	518 555-1221
8	Doe	Martha	65 Acorn Street	Scotia	NY	12302	518 555-8769
(AutoNumber)							

Figure 1.4 Access table

▶ When designing a database, you should provide at least one field in each table that provides a unique code or number to identify each record. This field, called a *primary key*, may be used in other tables to identify data. In Figure 1.4, the primary key is the Member ID. This field also exists in another table containing golf members, as shown in Figure 1.5. The Member ID primary key in the GOLF MEMBERS table provides the key to the identifying information in the ALL MEMBERS table.

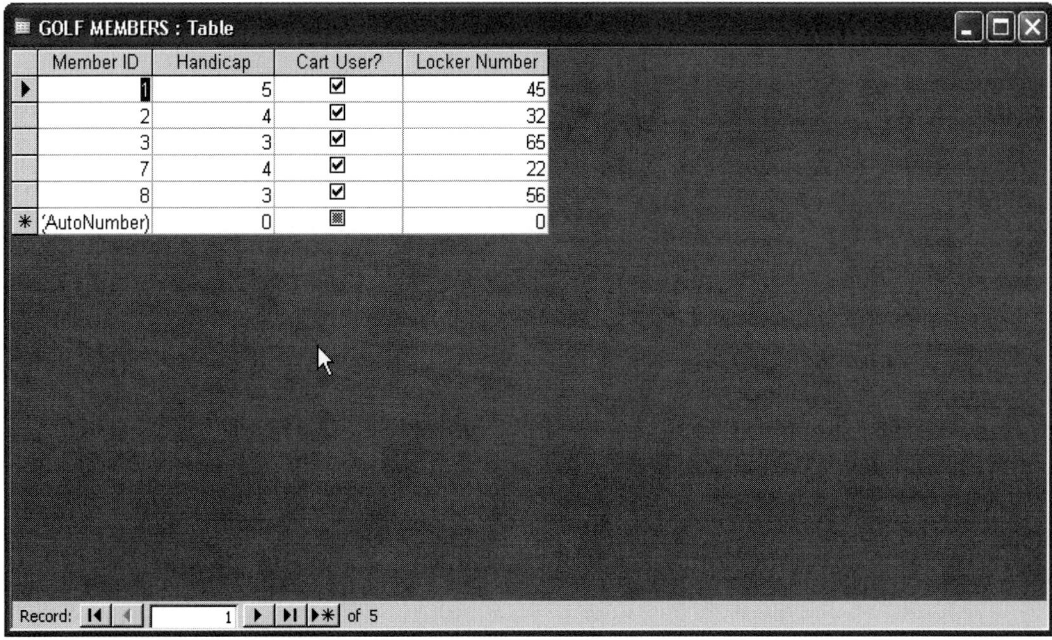

GOLF MEMBERS : Table

Member ID	Handicap	Cart User?	Locker Number
1	5	☑	45
2	4	☑	32
3	3	☑	65
7	4	☑	22
8	3	☑	56
(AutoNumber)	0	▩	0

Record: 1 of 5

Figure 1.5 Access: linked table

▶ *Forms* are used to display one record at a time. It is easier to enter or update data with a form than on the row of a table where records may be changed in error. The form illustrated in Figure 1.6 shows data from the first record in the ALL MEMBERS table (see Figure 1.4).

Forms

ALL MEMBERS

Member ID	1
Last Name	Smith
First Name	John
Address	12200 Menalto Drive
City	Waterford
State	NY
Postal Code	12188
Telephone Number	518 555-1221

Record: 1 of 8

Figure 1.6 Access form

ACCESS

- *Queries* are a structured way to tell Access to search the records and retrieve data that meets certain criteria from one or more database tables. For example, a query may request that Access retrieve data from the ALL MEMBERS table for all members who live in Ravena, NY. The data is displayed in a table format, as shown in Figure 1.7.

Queries

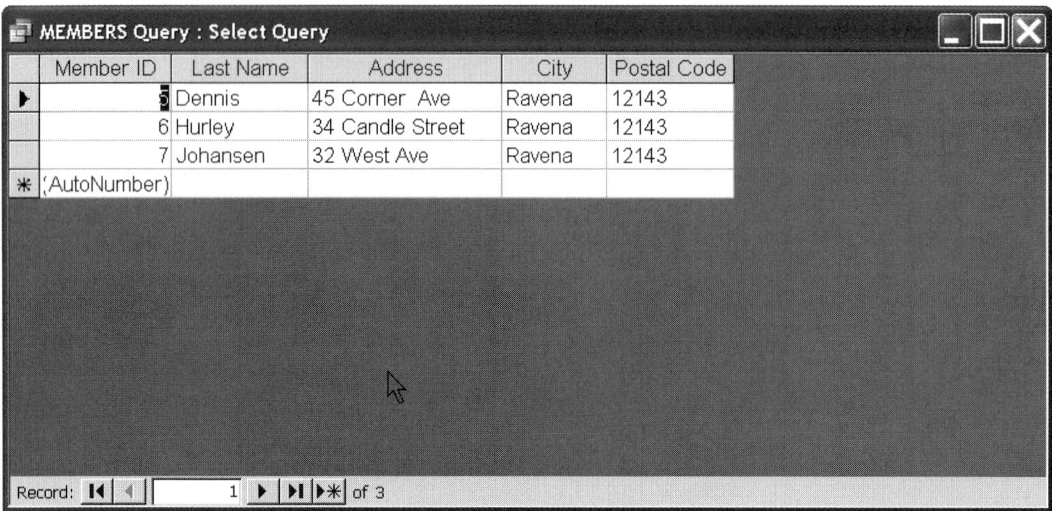

MEMBERS Query : Select Query

Member ID	Last Name	Address	City	Postal Code
5	Dennis	45 Corner Ave	Ravena	12143
6	Hurley	34 Candle Street	Ravena	12143
7	Johansen	32 West Ave	Ravena	12143
(AutoNumber)				

Record: 1 of 3

Figure 1.7 Access query

- *Reports* display information retrieved from the database. A report analyzes the data you specify. Notice that in the report shown in Figure 1.8, the data from the ALL MEMBERS table is displayed, formatted, and grouped by City.

Reports

ALL MEMBERS

City	*FirstName*	*LastName*
Melrose		
	Brian	Smith
	Jim	Jones
Ravena		
	Ken	Johansen
	Michael	Hurley
	Keith	Dennis
Scotia		
	Martha	Doe
	Henry	Keith
Waterford		
	John	Smith

Figure 1.8 Access report

- There are other database objects (pages, macros, and modules) that are not covered at the core skills level.

Explore the Database Window-View Objects

- When you create or open a database, the Database window appears, as shown in Figure 1.9. This window represents everything in your database file and is the place where you can create, organize, maintain, and open all database objects.
- To open an existing database, click File, Open, select the folder and file to open, and click Open.
- At the left side of the window, the Objects pane lists the database objects. As you click each object button, you are presented with options for creating the object as well as a list of saved objects of that type. You can also click the View menu and select the Object name from the Database Objects submenu. Notice that you can use a wizard to create each object. A wizard is a tool that asks you questions, then automatically designs an object based upon your answers.
- You can open a saved object by double-clicking the object. You can delete an object by selecting the object and clicking the Delete button in the database window.

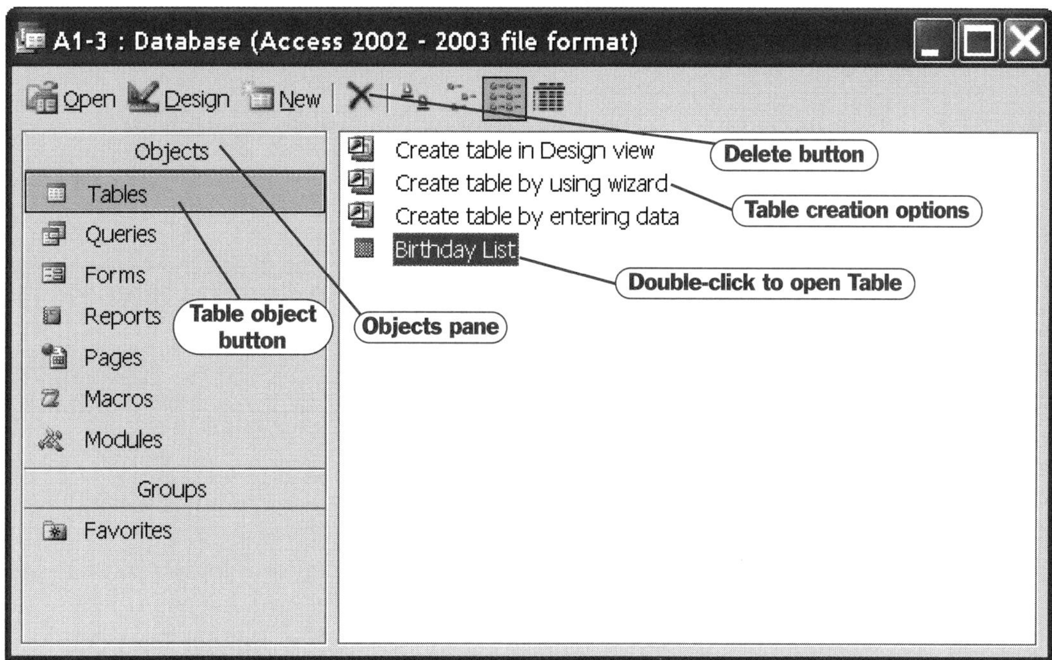

Figure 1.9 Database window

TRY *it* OUT *A1-3*

1. Click **File, Open** and select **A1-3** from the Data CD.
2. Notice that the Tables object is selected in the Objects pane at the left.
3. Notice that all of the object types are listed.
4. Click **View, Database Objects** and **Forms** to view the Forms object.
5. Click each of the objects either from the menu or on the database window to see what tools are available.
6. Close the Database window.

Understand Database Design

- Before creating a database, you must determine what type of information the database will contain, and how you will organize it. Plan your database on paper first by listing the fields that best identify the information you plan to enter as field contents. For example, if you want to create a mailing list, you should include first name, last name, address, etc.
- Identify the tables you need. Tables should contain information about one subject. With the exception of primary key fields, a table should not contain information duplicated in another table.
- Define the fields you need in each table. Each field should relate to the subject of the table. Break information down into small segments (for example, first name and last name, rather than name).
- Determine unique fields with unique values. Each record must have a field that links it to another record. This is the primary key.
- Detail the links between tables. Determine if and how the tables you are designing relate. In order to relate, they must share a primary key field.
- When you are satisfied that the table structures meet your goals, add your data and create any queries, forms, reports, macros, and modules required.

TRY *it* OUT *A1-4*

1. Open the **A1-4** database from the Data CD and select the Tables object.
2. Notice that two tables are displayed: **Friends** and **Birthday.**
3. Open **Friends.**
4. Notice that there are two fields for the name: First and Last.
5. Notice that there are four fields for the address: Address, City, State, and Zip.
6. Close **Friends.**
7. Open **Birthday.**
8. Notice that the only field duplicated from the **Friends** table is Idno.
9. Close **Birthday.**
10. Close the Database window.

- The planning process can be illustrated using the A1-4 database viewed in the last Try it Out. Before the database was developed, the information was kept manually.
- In the database planning phase, it was decided that there was a need for two tables and that the data would be stored in the tables as follows:

FRIENDS	BIRTHDAY
Idno	Idno
First	Month
Last	MonthNO
Address	Day
City	
State	
Zip	
Telephone	

Understand Database Views

- A database *view* is a way to look at data or the structure of a table, form, query, or report. Some views are common to all database objects, and some are unique. Click the down arrow on the View button on the toolbar to determine the views available for each object.
- In a table window, the views are Design, Datasheet, PivotTable, and PivotChart, as shown in Figure 1.10. The View button will display icons for all views other than the one you are in. This allows you to switch to that view without using the arrow list.
- You can open a table in Design or Datasheet view. To switch between views, click the View button, which will display the icon for the other view. In *Design view* you can create and modify table structures. In *Datasheet view* you can add, edit, delete, and view data.
- Tables also have *PivotTable view* and *PivotChart view*. A PivotTable interactively summarizes and analyzes data from tables. A PivotChart graphically represents the information in a PivotTable.

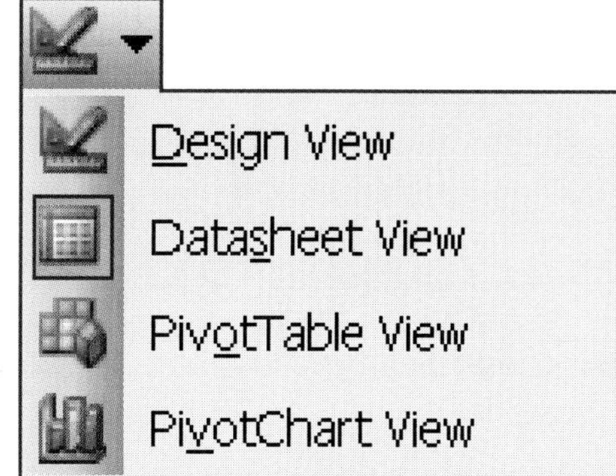

Figure 1.10 Table views

ACCESS

TRY *it* OUT *A1-5*

1. Open the **A1-5** database from the Data CD.
2. Double-click to open the **Friends** table in the Tables object list.
3. Click the list arrow at the right of the View button. Note the icons for each view.
4. Click the **Design** button to change to Design view.
5. Click the **Datasheet** view button, which should be displayed.

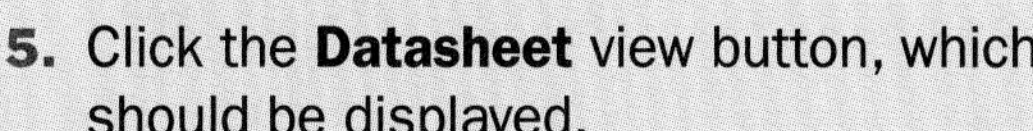

6. Close the **Friends** table window.
7. For each of the objects in the Database window listed below, notice the options for creating the object.
   a. Click the **Queries** button. Double-click to open the **Friends Query** and note the view list on the View button.
   b. Click the **Forms** button. Open the **Friends** form and note the view list on the View button.

   c. Click the **Reports** button. Open the **Birthday List** report and note the view list on the View button.

8. Close the Database window.

REHEARSAL

TASK 1

GOAL:
To start Access and to explore the database window and database objects

SETTING THE STAGE/WRAPUP

Database: **Members**
Tables: **ALL MEMBERS**
GOLF MEMBERS
SWIM MEMBERS

WHAT YOU NEED TO KNOW

- Access files have an .mdb extension.
- A table is also called a datasheet. You establish a primary key to link tables.
- In this Rehearsal activity, you will familiarize yourself with different elements of an Access database, as shown in the illustration on the facing page.

DIRECTIONS

1. Start Access.
2. Open **Members.mdb** from the Data CD.
3. Check that **Tables** is selected in the Objects list.

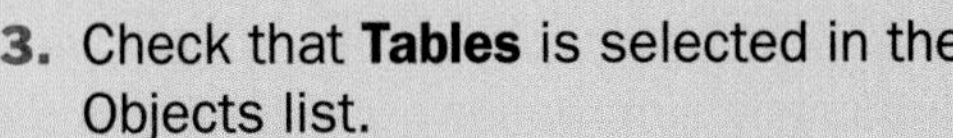

4. Open **ALL MEMBERS.**
5. Notice that there are eight fields.The field named "Member ID" is the primary key.
6. Close the window.
7. Open **GOLF MEMBERS.** Notice the field named "Member ID."
8. Close the window.
9. Open **SWIM MEMBERS.** Notice the field named "Member ID." The three tables are linked by this common field.
10. Close the window.
11. Click **Queries** in the Objects list and open the **MEMBERS Query.**This query answers the question, "What members live in the city of Ravena?"
12. Close the query.
13. Click **Forms** in the Objects list and open **ALL MEMBERS.** This form displays one record of the **ALL MEMBERS** table.
14. Close the window.
15. Click **Reports** and open the **ALL MEMBERS** report. This report lists all members by City.
16. Close the window and the file.
17. Close Access.

ALL MEMBERS : Table

	Member ID	Last Name	First Name	Address	City	State	Postal Code	Telephone Number
▶	1	Smith	John	12200 Menalto Drive	Waterford	NY	12188	518 555-1221
	2	Jones	Jim	100 Circle Drive	Melrose	NY	12121	518 555-2222
	3	Keith	Kenny	1715 Milton Ave	Scotia	NY	12302	518 666-1111
	4	Smith	Brian	23 Renwick	Melrose	NY	12121	518 555-2222
	5	Dennis	Keith	45 Corner Ave	Ravena	NY	12143	518 666-9999
	6	Hurley	Michael	34 Candle Street	Ravena	NY	12143	518 999-9999
	7	Johansen	Ken	32 West Ave	Ravena	NY	12143	518 555-1221
	8	Doe	Martha	65 Acorn Street	Scotia	NY	12302	518 555-8769
*	(AutoNumber)							

All Members table

GOLF MEMBERS : Table

	Member ID	Handicap	Cart User?	Locker Number
▶	1	5	☑	45
	2	4	☑	32
	3	3	☑	65
	7	4	☑	22
	8	3	☑	56
*	(AutoNumber)	0		0

Golf Members table

ACCESS

SWIM MEMBERS : Table

	Member ID	Swim Team	Locker Number	Sauna User	Whirlpool User
▶	1	☑	23	☑	☑
	2	☑	22	☐	☑
	4	☑	21	☐	☐
	5	☑	12	☑	☑
	6	☐	13	☐	☐
	8	☑	20	☑	☐
*	(AutoNumber)		0		

Swim Members table

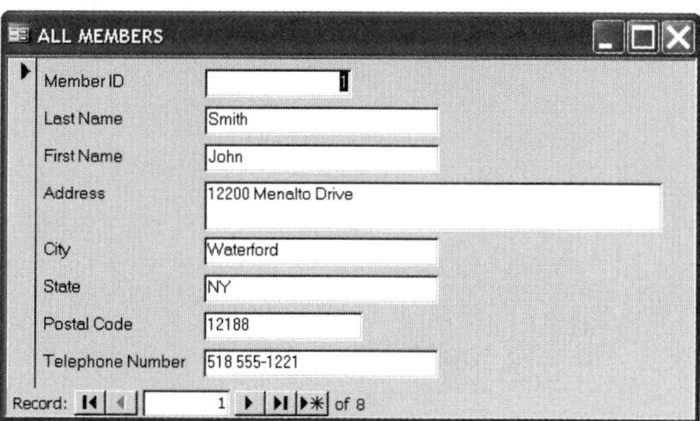

ALL MEMBERS

Member ID: 1
Last Name: Smith
First Name: John
Address: 12200 Menalto Drive
City: Waterford
State: NY
Postal Code: 12188
Telephone Number: 518 555-1221

Record: 1 of 8

All Members form

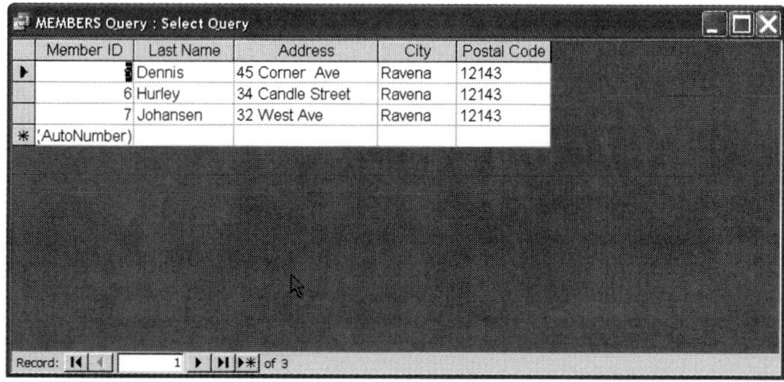

MEMBERS Query : Select Query

	Member ID	Last Name	Address	City	Postal Code
▶	5	Dennis	45 Corner Ave	Ravena	12143
	6	Hurley	34 Candle Street	Ravena	12143
	7	Johansen	32 West Ave	Ravena	12143
*	(AutoNumber)				

Record: 1 of 3

Members query

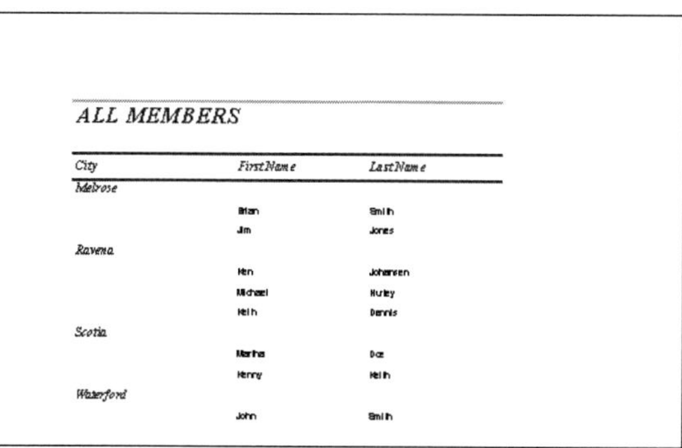

ALL MEMBERS

City	FirstName	LastName
Melrose		
	Brian	Smith
	Jim	Jones
Ravena		
	Ken	Johansen
	Michael	Hurley
	Keith	Dennis
Scotia		
	Martha	Doe
	Kenny	Keith
Waterford		
	John	Smith

All Members report

TASK 1A

GOAL
To use different database views

SETTING THE STAGE/WRAPUP
Database: Members
Table: ALL MEMBERS
Query: MEMBERS
Form: ALL MEMBERS
Report: ALL MEMBERS

WHAT YOU NEED TO KNOW

- Database objects have multiple views.
- In this Rehearsal activity, you will familiarize yourself with the different views Access provides. You will work with objects in Design view, as shown in the illustrations on the facing page.

DIRECTIONS

1. Start Access.
2. Open the **Members** database from the Data CD.

3. Click the **Tables** object.
4. Click **ALL MEMBERS**.
5. Click **Design** view.
6. Click on any line in each of the following columns and read the definition in the bottom right pane of the window:

   Field Name

   Data Type

   Description
7. Click the **View** button to change to Datasheet view.
8. Close the window.
9. Click **Queries**, and double-click the **MEMBERS Query**.
10. Change to Design view.
11. Close the query.
12. Click **Forms**, and double-click **ALL MEMBERS**.
13. Change to Design view.
14. Close the window.
15. Click **Reports**, and double-click **ALL MEMBERS**.
16. Change to Design view.
17. Close the window.

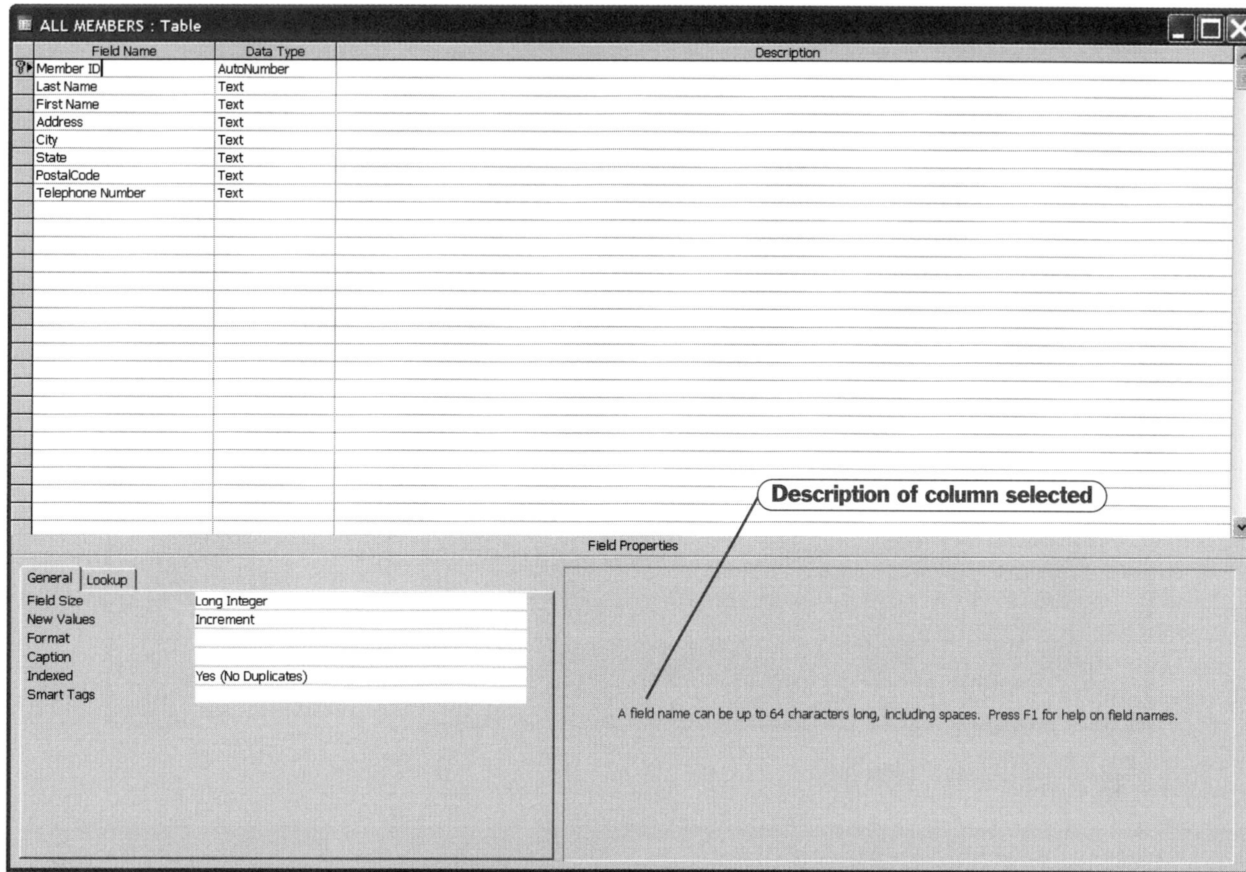

All Members table in Design view

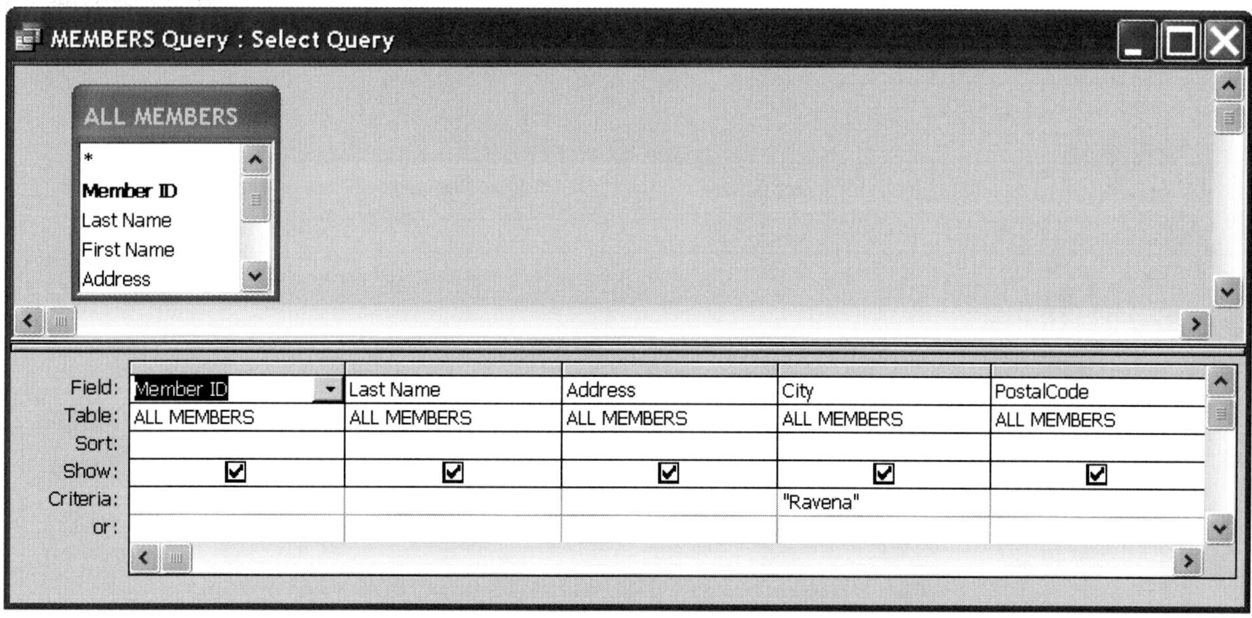

Members query in Design view

ACCESS

ALL MEMBERS : Form
Form Header
Detail
Member ID
Member ID
Last Name
Last Name
First Name
First Name
Address
Address
City
City
State
State
Postal Code
PostalCode
Telephone Number
Telephone Number
Form Footer

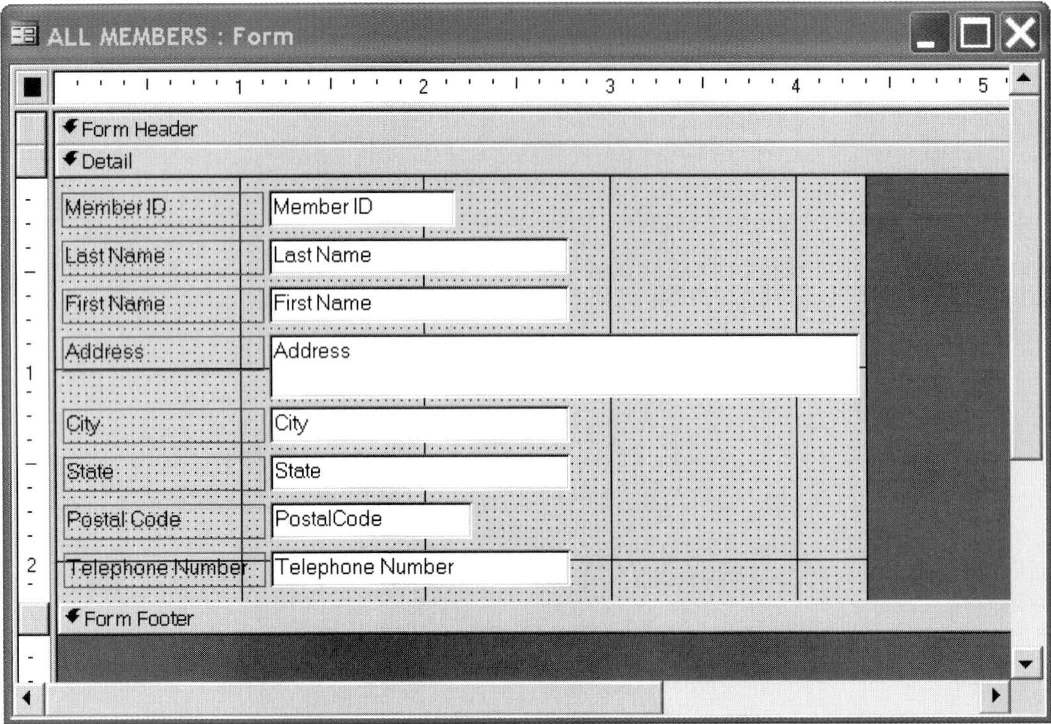

All Members form in Design view

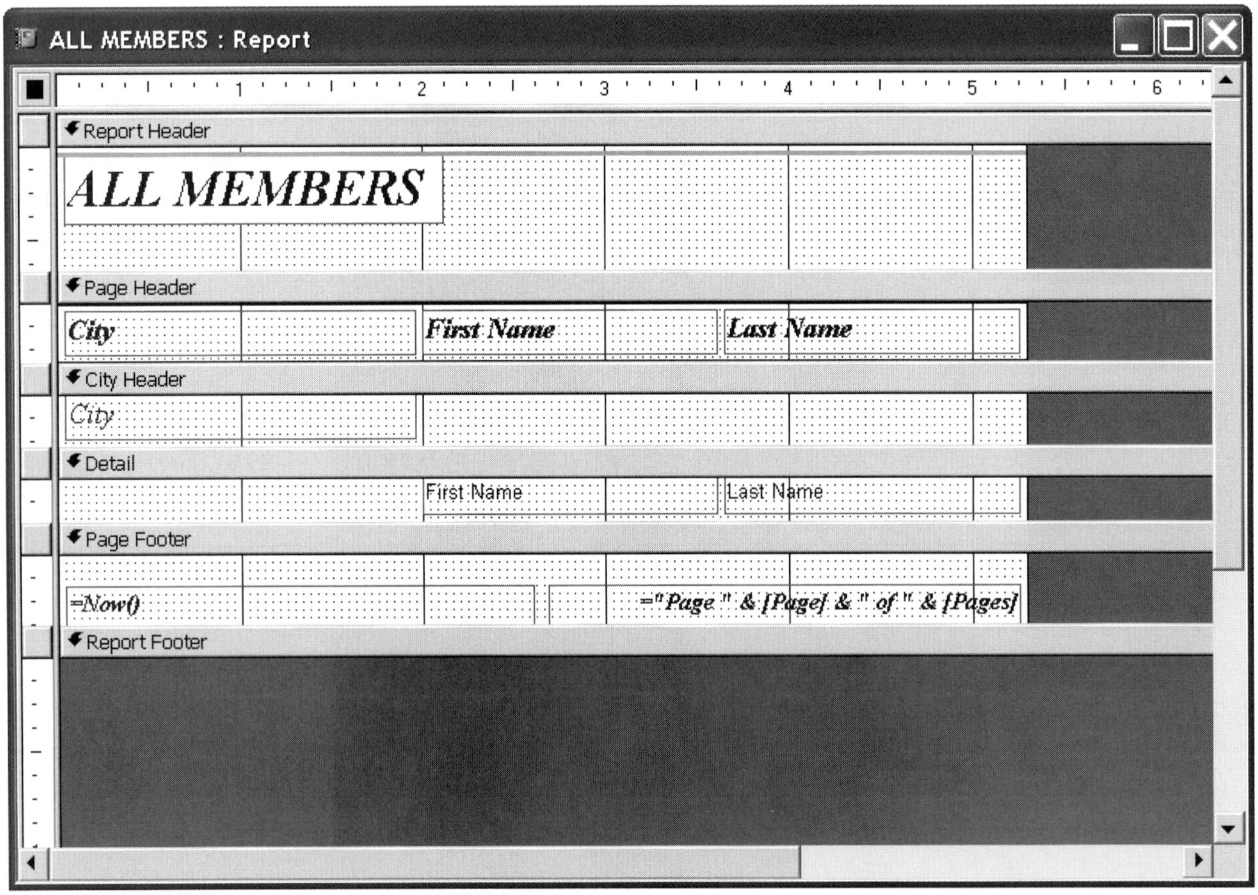

ALL MEMBERS : Report
Report Header
ALL MEMBERS
Page Header
City
First Name
Last Name
City Header
City
Detail
First Name
Last Name
Page Footer
=Now()
="Page " & [Page] & " of " & [Pages]
Report Footer

All Members report in Design view

ACCESS

Cues for Reference

Start Access

- Click **Start, All Programs, Microsoft Office, Microsoft Office Access 2003.**

Office XP

- Click **Start, All Programs,** and **Access.**

Design a Database

1. Plan database on paper.
2. Identify tables.
3. Define fields in each table.
4. Determine unique fields with unique values.
5. Define relationships between tables.
6. Add data.
7. Create any queries, forms, reports, macros, and modules required.

View Objects

- Click **View** on menu bar, click **Database Objects,** and click object type.

or

- Click object type in Database window.

Open Table/Form/Query/Report

1. Click object in Objects list.
2. Double-click an object.

Open Table/Form/Query/Report in Design View

1. Click object in Objects list.
2. Click an object.
3. Click the **Design** button.

Change View

- Click the **View** button.

LESSON 2

Access Tables and Datasheets

In this lesson, you will learn to use features in Access to create and modify tables. You will learn about field data types and properties. You will also learn to enter and edit data.

Upon completion of this lesson, you should have mastered the following skill sets:

- Create tables with the Table Wizard
  - Set the primary key with the Table Wizard
- Set data types
- Enter data using a datasheet
- Use navigation controls to move through records in datasheets
- Edit and delete records from a table
- Modify field and table properties
- Create tables in Design view
  - Set primary keys in Design view
- Use the Lookup Wizard
- Use the Input Mask Wizard
- Format a table datasheet for display

Terms

- Table Wizard
- Data type
  - Text
  - Memo
  - Number
  - Date/Time
  - Currency
  - AutoNumber
  - Yes/No
  - OLE Object
  - Hyperlink
  - Lookup Wizard
- Record selector
- Field properties
- Caption
- Lookup Wizard
- Table properties
- Row Source type
- Lookup field
- Input mask
- Input Mask Wizard

GOALS

To create an Employee table with two data types and a primary key

To practice using the following skill sets:

- Create a new file using a blank database
- Create tables with the Table Wizard
- Set the primary key with the Table Wizard
- Set data types
- Enter data using a datasheet
- Use navigation controls to move through records in datasheets
- Edit and delete records from a table
- Modify field and table properties

WHAT YOU NEED TO KNOW

ACCESS

Create a New File with a Blank Database

- Tables are created first in a database because all the other objects rely on their data. You can create a table in Design view, using the Table Wizard, or by entering data in a table and then modifying the design. We will practice the first two options in this lesson.
- To create a new file, click Create a new file on the Getting Started task pane; then select Blank database on the New File task pane, as shown in Figure 2.1.

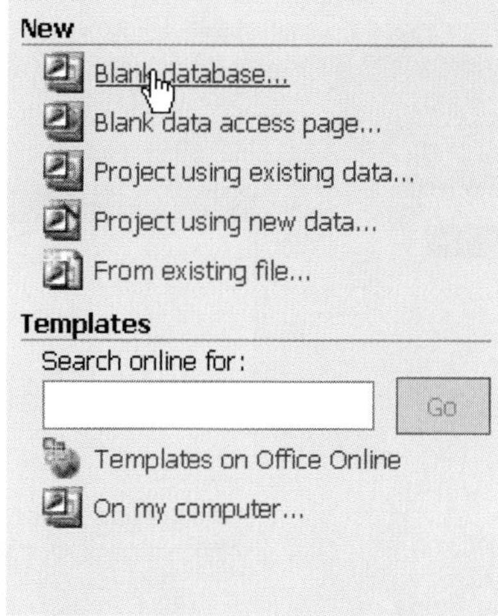

Figure 2.1 New File task pane

Create Tables with the Table Wizard

- Access provides a *Table Wizard* to assist you in building new tables. The Wizard is available in the Database window when you select Tables, as shown in Figure 2.2.

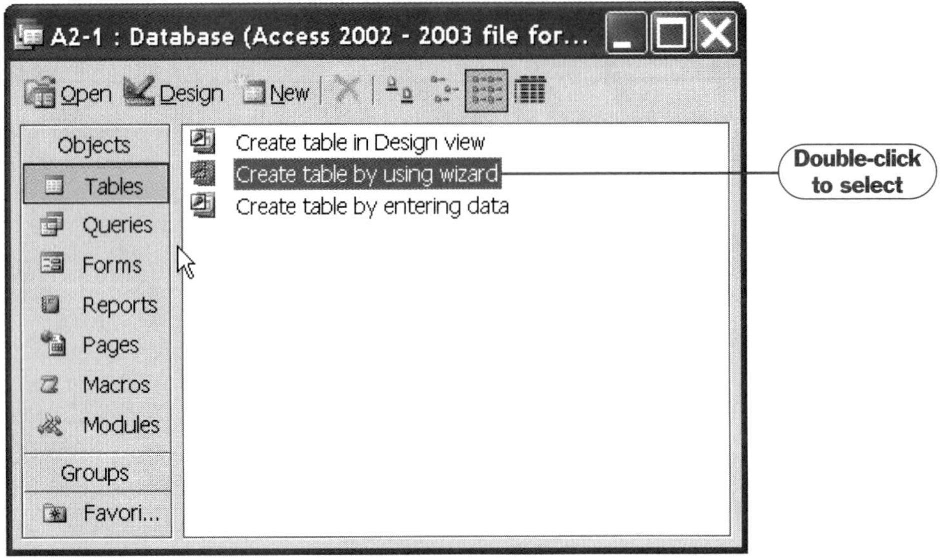

Figure 2.2 Table Wizard selection on Table Object screen

- The Table Wizard provides 25 business and 20 personal sample tables from which you can choose. Each sample table contains predetermined fields you can select to build a table to meet your specific needs, as shown in Figure 2.3.

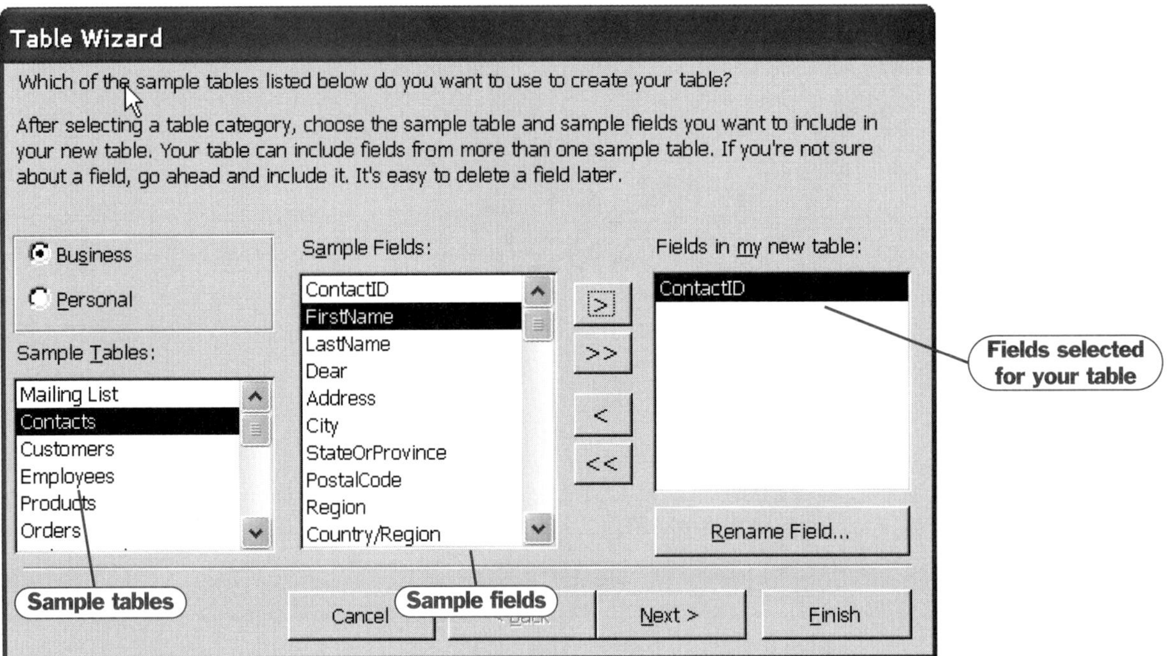

Figure 2.3 Table Wizard—sample tables

- First, choose the sample table that best meets your requirements, and then select the appropriate fields. You have the option of selecting fields one at a time, or selecting all the fields and later removing the ones you do not need. You can also choose fields from different sample tables to build your table, and you may rename the fields as you choose them. To continue, click Finish or Next.
- If you click Finish, the Wizard ends and a table appears without a primary key. Access names the datasheet with the name of the sample you have chosen. You can then enter data in the datasheet.

▶ If you click Next, the Table Wizard opens a dialog box, as shown in Figure 2.4, that prompts you to rename the table and to choose how you want to set the primary key.

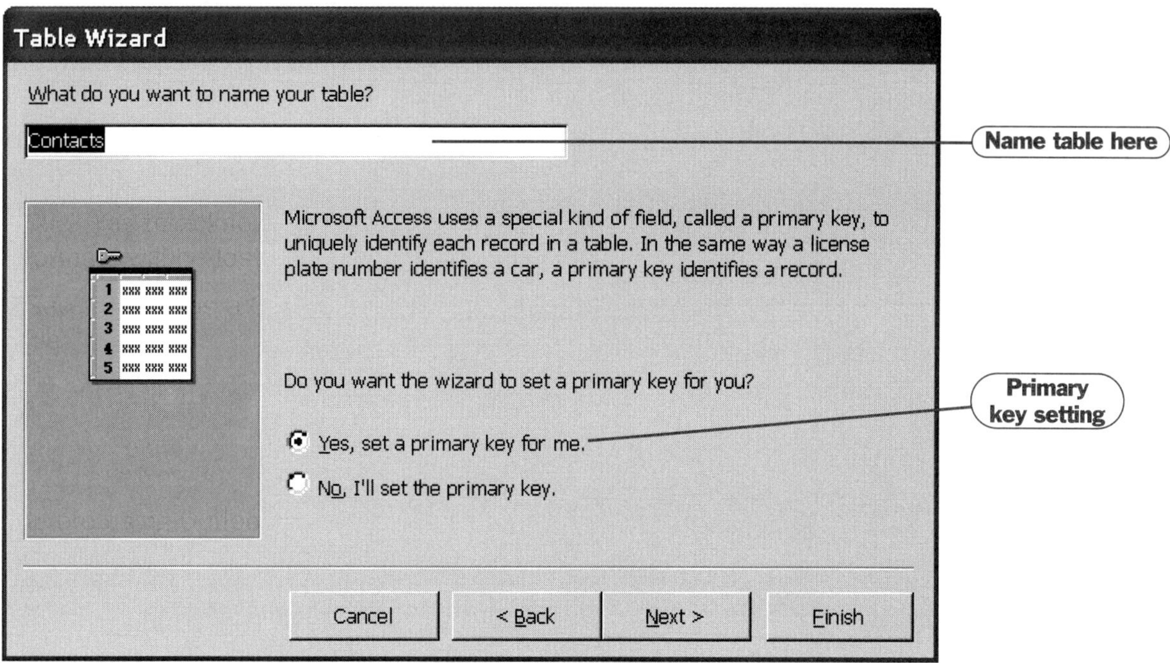

Figure 2.4 Table Wizard—name your table

ACCESS

TRY *it* OUT *A2-1*

1. Start Access.
2. Click **Create a new file** on the Getting Started task pane.
3. Click **Blank database** on the New File task pane.
4. Name it **A2-1** and click **Create.**
5. Notice that **Tables** is selected.
6. Double-click **Create table by using wizard.**
7. Read the instructions. You are going to build a Contacts table.
8. Under Sample Tables, click **Contacts.**
9. Under Sample Fields, double-click each of the following fields or use the single arrow to move them to your table in the right column one at a time:

   ContactID

   LastName

   Address

   City

   StateOrProvince

   WorkPhone

   Birthdate
10. Select the **StateOrProvince** field and click **Rename Field.**
11. Rename the field: `State.` Click **OK.** Click **Next.**
12. The Table Wizard names the table **Contacts,** and asks if you want to set the primary key.
13. Stop at this point; do not close the table.

Set the Primary Key with the Table Wizard

- When you use the Table Wizard, you can have Access assign the primary key, or you can designate the primary key. The primary key identifies each record in a table in a unique way.
- If you choose to set the primary key field, the Wizard asks you, "What field will hold data that is unique for each record?" and "What type of data do you want the primary key field to contain?" as shown in Figure 2.5.

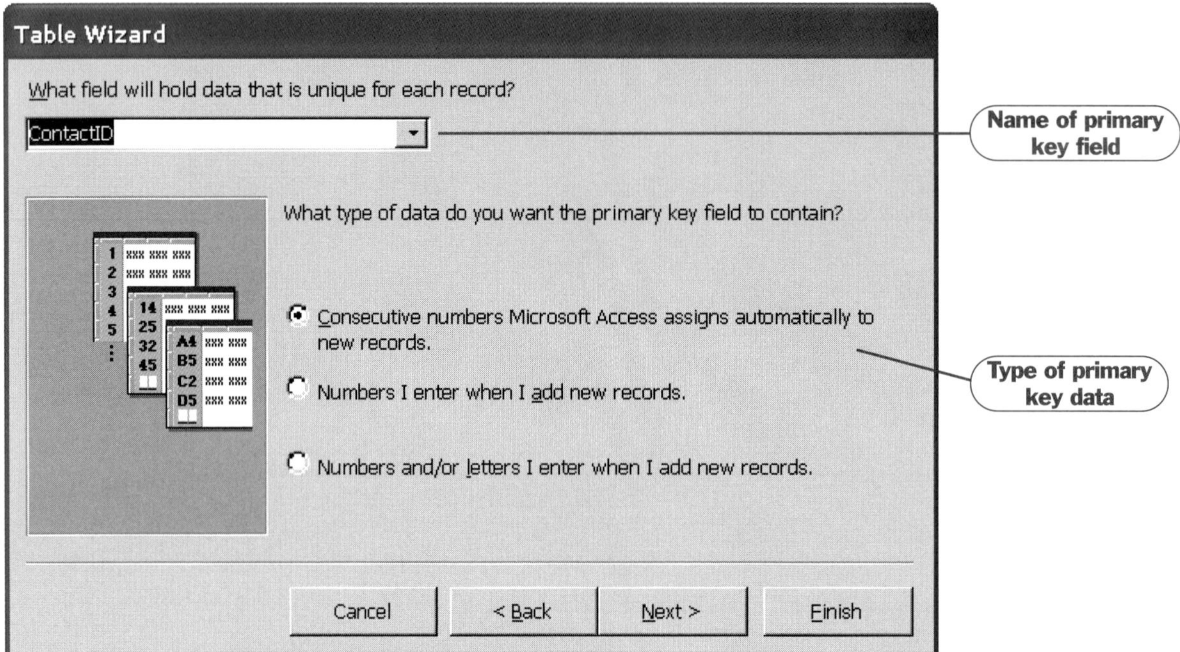

Figure 2.5 Table Wizard—identifying the primary key

- After choosing the primary key field and the type of data, Access displays the screen shown in Figure 2.6, which asks what you would like to do next. If the Table Wizard assigned the primary key, the same screen would now be displayed. The primary key field is identified by the Primary Key icon, which is seen only in Design view.

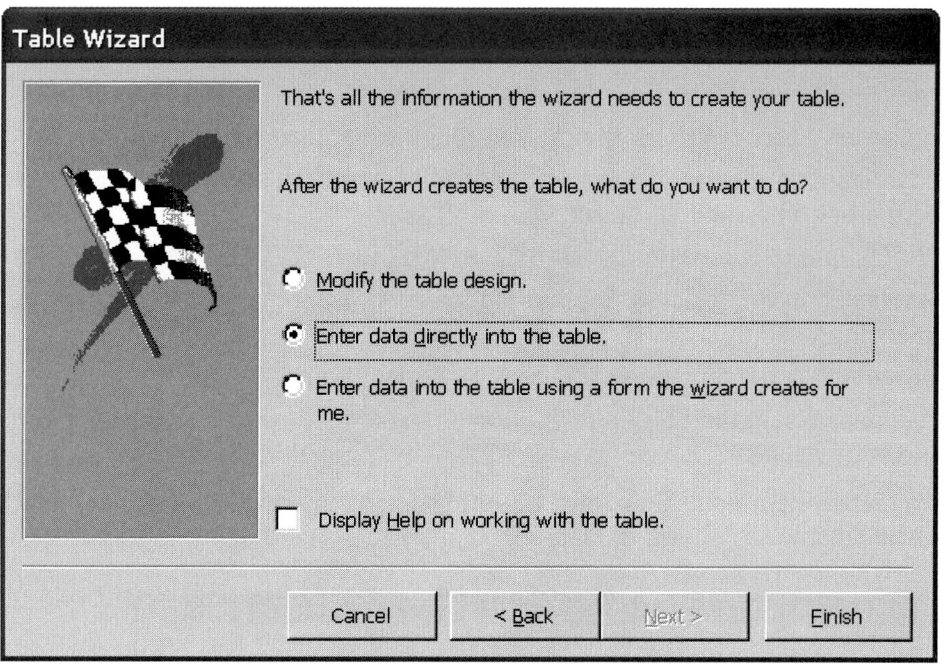
Table Wizard
That's all the information the wizard needs to create your table.
After the wizard creates the table, what do you want to do?
Modify the table design.
Enter data directly into the table.
Enter data into the table using a form the wizard creates for me.
Display Help on working with the table.
Cancel
< Back
Next >
Finish

Figure 2.6 Table Wizard—What do you want to do?

TRY *it* OUT *A2-2*

Note: The screen in Figure 2.4 should be displayed.

1. The Wizard has asked if you want to set the primary key. Review the definition of primary key in the Table Wizard dialog box. You will set a primary key in this exercise.
2. Click **No, I'll set the primary key.**
3. Click **Next.**
4. Notice that ContactID is the suggested field in the list box below the question "What field will hold data that is unique for each record?"
5. Click the down arrow to see the other fields you have selected for the table, but leave ContactID selected.
6. Click **Consecutive numbers Microsoft Access assigns automatically to new records,** if necessary, in answer to the question: "What type of data do you want the primary key field to contain?"
7. Click **Next.**
8. After reading the options, leave Enter data directly into the table selected.
9. Click **Finish.** Do not close the table.

Set Data Types

- All fields, including those you choose when using the Table Wizard, have a specific data type. A *data type* is an attribute that determines what type of information a field can contain.
- The following 10 data types are available to you:
  - *Text*—text, or a mix of text and numbers (street addresses), or numbers that are not calculated (zip codes). The field size is up to 255 characters, and the default size is 50.
  - *Memo*—long text, such as notes or descriptions. Field limit is 65,536 characters.

- *Number*—numeric data you can use in mathematical calculations, except calculations involving money (use Currency type).
- *Date/Time*—dates and times.
- *Currency*—monetary or currency values that do not round off during calculations.
- *AutoNumber*—identification number Access automatically enters, in sequential (incrementing by one) or random order, when you add a record.
- *Yes/No*—data that is one of two values, such as Yes/No, True/False, On/Off.
- *OLE Object*—data linked to an object in another file, created using the OLE (object linking and embedding) protocol (procedure).
- *Hyperlink*—a path to a file on a hard drive, a UNC (LAN Server) path, or a URL (Internet address).
- *Lookup Wizard*—a data type option that assists in defining a field that looks up values from another table or list of values.

▶ Field data types are displayed in table Design view. A drop-down list appears when you click the arrow in the Data Type column, as shown in Figure 2.7.

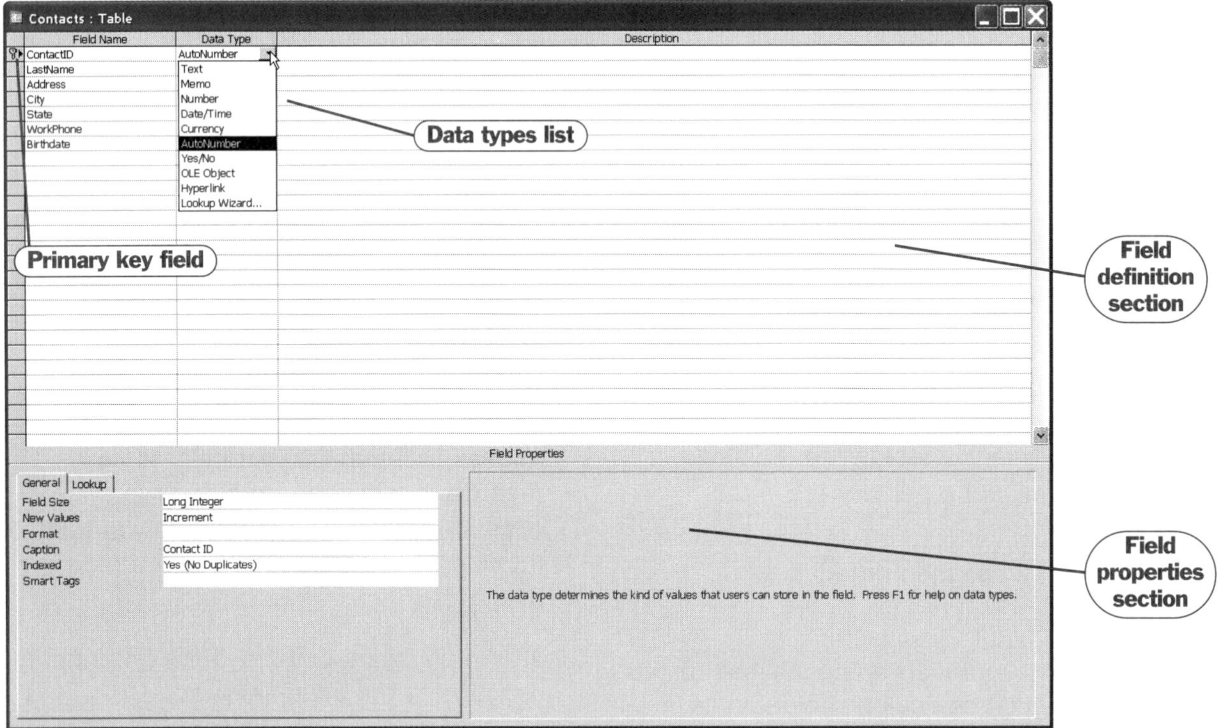

Figure 2.7 Design view—data types

TRY *it* OUT *A2-3*

1. The **Contacts** table in **A2-1** should be displayed, or open **A2-3** from the Data CD and double-click the **Contacts** table.
2. Click **View, Design View** and notice the **Primary Key** icon next to the ContactID field.
3. Click **ContactID** in the Field Name column.
4. Notice that this field is an AutoNumber field.
5. Click the **LastName** field in the Data Type column.

Continued on next page

TRY it OUT *A2-3 Continued*

6. Notice that this field is a Text field.
7. Click the down arrow in the **Data Type** column. Notice the 10 data type options.
8. Click **Birthdate** in the Field Name column.
9. Notice that this field is a Date/Time field. Do not close the table.

Enter Data Using a Datasheet

- Use a datasheet, in datasheet view, to enter data (i.e., records) in your database.
- To enter records in a datasheet, enter the data below each field name as you would in a spreadsheet. Use the Tab key to advance from column to column. To advance to the next row, press the Enter key, press the Tab key, or use the arrow keys. When you leave a record, Access automatically saves it in the table.
- As shown in Figure 2.8, it is not necessary to enter data in an AutoNumber field; Access automatically assigns a consecutive number. Also, when you enter data in a field with an input mask, such as the slash format for a date, Access displays the format as you enter the data in the field. Creating input masks will be discussed later in this lesson.

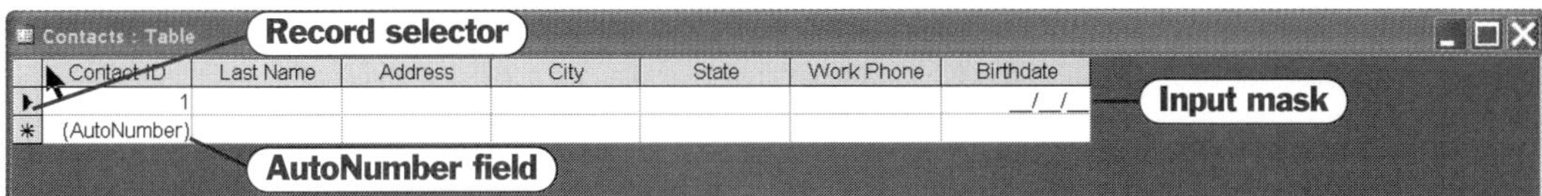

Figure 2.8 Entering data—AutoNumber and input mask fields

- If you make a mistake in data entry, press the ESC key to empty the contents of the field. If you enter invalid data in a field, such as a letter in a number field, Access displays an error message indicating that the value is not valid for the field. To proceed, click OK, and correct the entry.

TRY it OUT *A2-4*

1. The **Contacts** table in **A2-1** should be displayed, or open **A2-4** from the Data CD and double-click the **Contacts** table.
2. Click **Datasheet** view.
3. Enter the information from the chart below. Do not enter anything in the Contact ID field; Access automatically assigns a number to each record. Do not enter slashes in the date; Access automatically adds them.

CONTACT ID	LAST NAME	ADDRESS	CITY	STATE	WORK PHONE	BIRTHDATE
	Trainor	47 Menalto Drive	Berwyn	PA	610-555-6543	091278
	Grenaldi	543 Euclid Street	Paoli	PA	610-555-3213	100582
	Cardowski	65 Warren Road	Radnor	PA	610-555-2546	042580

4. Save the table; do not close it.

Edit or Delete Records in a Table

- To edit an entry in a table, click in the edit location and make the edit or press F2 to select the data and retype the entry. When you move to the next record, the edits are saved.
- To delete a record, select the row by clicking the *record selector*, the small box to the left of the first field in a record, as shown in Figure 2.8. When you click the record selector, you select the entire record. You can delete the record by using the Edit menu or pressing the Delete key. You can also use the Delete Record button on the toolbar.
- There is no Undo option within Access. Therefore, you will be asked to confirm the deletion.

Use Navigation Controls to Move through Records in Datasheets

- Access provides buttons on the bottom of the Datasheet window that allow you to move efficiently through a datasheet or table. The Navigation toolbar also indicates which record is active and how many records are in the table.
- Use the arrow buttons on the table scroll bar to scroll through records. Buttons are provided to bring up the location of the first record, last record, next record, previous record, current record, and new record quickly. Notice the location of the buttons, as shown in Figure 2.9.

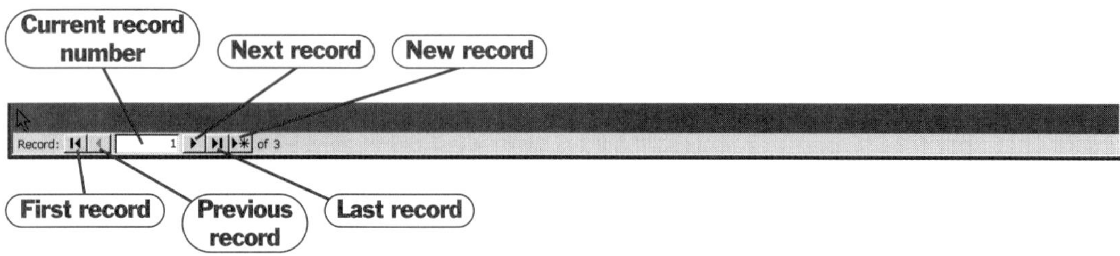

Figure 2.9 Navigation toolbar

TRY *it* OUT *A2-5*

1. The **Contacts** table in **A2-1** should be displayed, or open **A2-5** from the Data CD and double-click the **Contacts** table.
2. Click the Navigation buttons to view each record.
3. Edit Grenaldi's telephone number to read `610-555-3215` either by retyping the number or by placing the cursor at the end of the number and replacing the last number.
4. Click the **record selector,** the box to the left of the third record.
5. Press the **Delete** key.
6. Click **Yes** to confirm deletion.
7. Close the table.

Modify Table and Field Properties

Table Properties

- You can modify *table properties* or any object's properties by right-clicking the object and selecting Properties. The table properties dialog box, shown in Figure 2.10, is used to document table information.

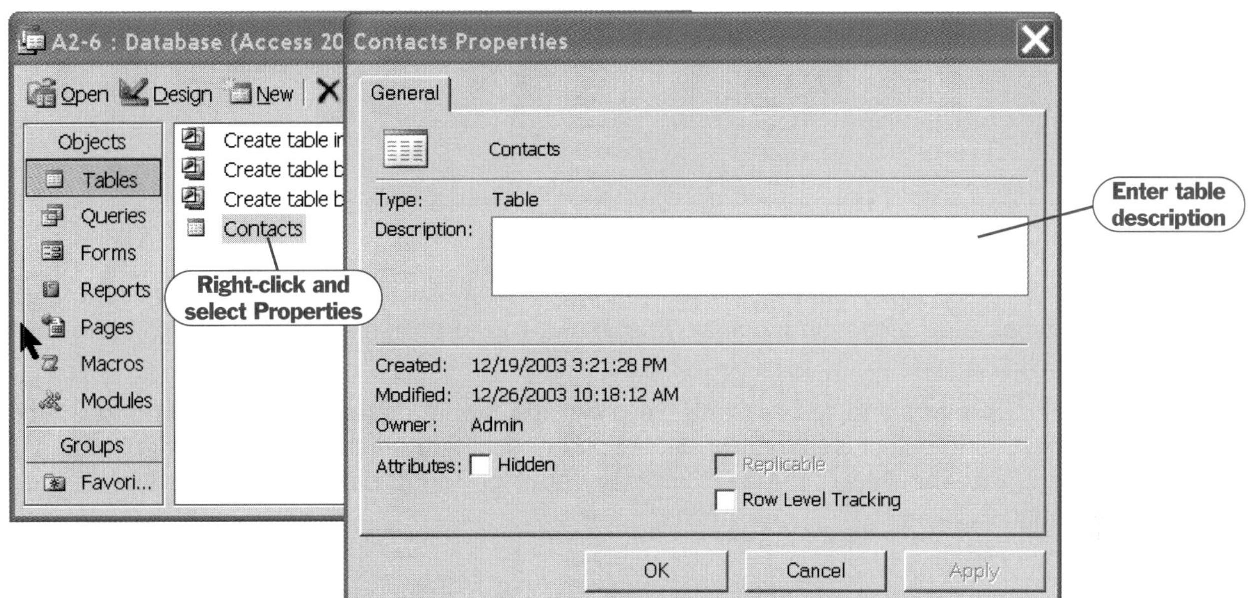

Figure 2.10 Table properties dialog box

Field Properties

- You can set or modify *field properties* to define how Access stores, manipulates, and displays data in Design view by selecting the field in the upper pane, and then selecting the property you want in the lower pane. You can move from the top pane, for field definition, to the bottom pane, for setting field properties, by pressing F6.
- The choice of field properties depends on the data type you select for the field. For example, Text data type fields have a field size property, and AutoNumber data type fields do not. Notice the difference between text data type field properties, shown in Figure 2.11, and AutoNumber data type properties, shown in Figure 2.12.

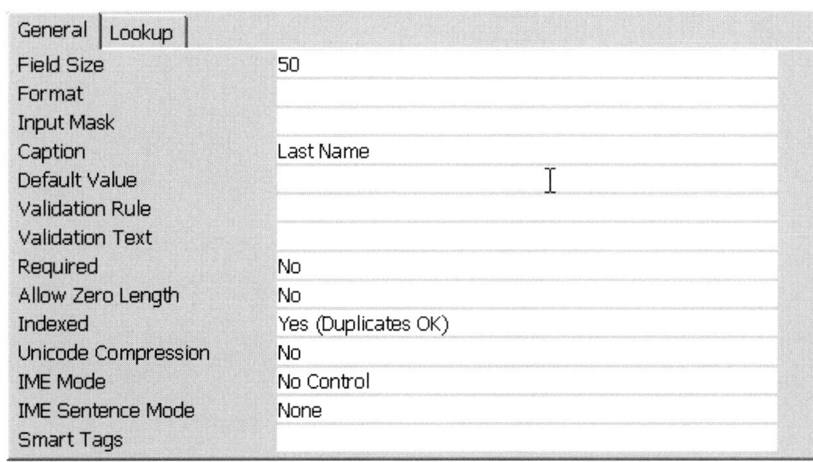

Figure 2.11 Design view—text properties

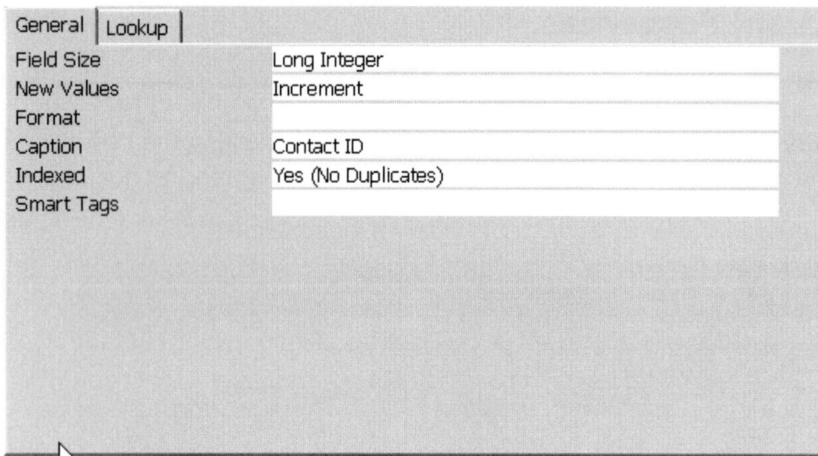

Figure 2.12 Design view—AutoNumber properties

- All field data types have a *caption* property. This allows you to assign a name to a field other than its field name.
- The Date/Time, Currency, and Yes/No data types provide format instead of field size options. You use field properties to select a format for each type by clicking the list arrow on the right side of the Format box. Note the Date/Time and Currency data type formatting options, as shown in Figures 2.13 and 2.14.

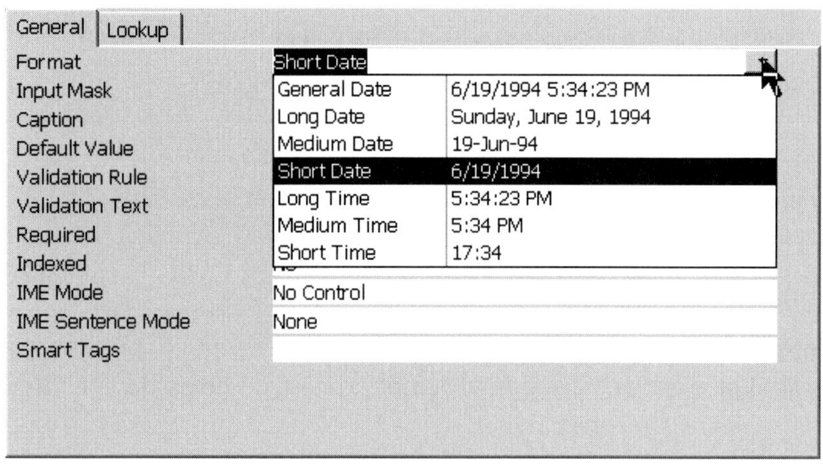

Figure 2.13 Design view—Date/Time format options

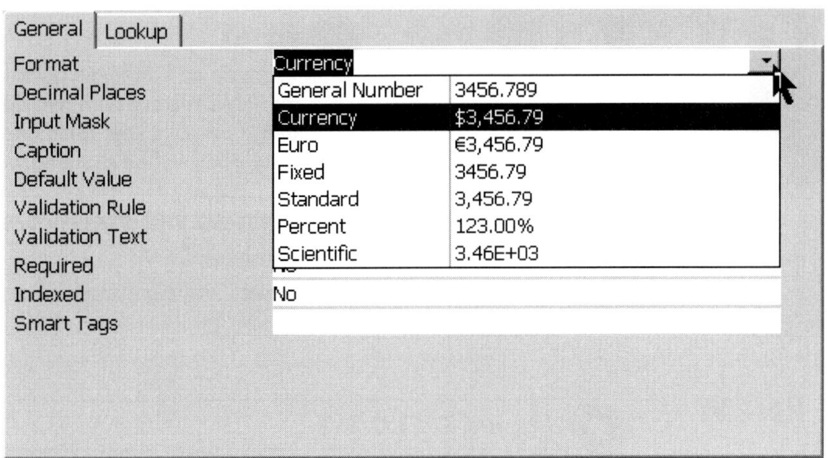

Figure 2.14 Design view—Currency format options

- To change a field property, click the field name in the top pane of Design view, press F6 or the box next to the property you want to change, and replace what is there with the new setting. For example, to change the field size of a Text data type field, select the field, delete the current field size, and enter the size you want.
- You must save a table each time you make a property change to a field.

ACCESS

TRY *it* OUT *A2-6*

1. The **Contacts** table in **A2-1** should be displayed, or open **A2-6** from the Data CD.
2. Right-click the **Contacts** table and click **Properties.**
3. Enter the following in the Table Description box: `The table includes business and personal contacts.` Click **OK.**
4. Click the **Design View** button.
5. Click **Contact ID,** if necessary, in the Field Name column. Notice that the data type is AutoNumber and that there are six options under the General tab in Field Properties.
6. Click the **LastName** field. Notice that this field is a Text field and that there are 14 options in the General tab in Field Properties.
7. Notice that the Field Size is set at the default (50 characters).
8. Change the Field Size to 25.
   a. Click the **Field Size** property box.
   b. Select **50.**
   c. Enter: `25.`
9. Click **Birthdate** in the Field Name column. Notice that this field is a Date/Time field and that this field has a Short Date format and an input mask (see Task 2) set to restrict how a date can be entered.
10. Click the **Format** property box in the Field Properties pane.
    a. Click the **Format** drop-down list arrow to display other formatting options available for the Date/Time data type.
11. Save the table and close the database. Note: You may get a warning that you shortened a field. Click **Yes** to accept the change.

REHEARSAL

Again

TASK 1

GOAL

To create an Employee List table using the Table Wizard with two data types and a primary key. Table and field properties will be changed.

SETTING THE STAGE/WRAPUP

Database: 2EMP
Table: EmployeesList

WHAT YOU NEED TO KNOW

- Businesses create database tables to provide information for various reasons. For example, companies need employee contact information and may need additional data as well.
- In this Rehearsal activity, you will use the Table Wizard to create a table that provides information for the president of a company to call employees on the anniversary of their start dates. The table you create will contain employee contact information, their start dates, and will contain four records.

DIRECTIONS

1. Open a blank database.
2. Name it `2EMP` and click **Create.**
3. Create a table using the Table Wizard, and click the **Business** category and the **Employees** sample table, as shown on the facing page.
4. There are 32 sample fields available. Select the following fields:

   EmployeeID

   FirstName

   LastName

   Address

   City

   StateorProvince (Rename the field State)

   PostalCode (Rename the field Zip)

   DateHired
5. Name the table `Employees.`
6. Let Access asssign the primary key.
7. Enter the following information in the table:

EmployeeID	1	2	3	4
FirstName	Charles	Karen	Terry	Michael
LastName	Williams	Popper	Carlyle	Thompson
Address	43 Voight Street	92 Carson Drive	451 Bard Avenue	543 Ray Road
City	Phoenix	Tempe	Phoenix	Phoenix
State	AZ	AZ	AZ	AZ
Zip	85006	85281	85003	85017
DateHired	10/08/01	05/25/02	12/10/03	6/30/03

8. Edit the record for Terry Carlyle. His new address is **490 Bard Avenue,** with the same zip code.

Continued on next page

9. Delete the record for Michael Thompson. He left the company.
10. Switch to Design view and change the FirstName and LastName field size properties to 25 characters. Change the field size property for State to 2 characters.
11. Save the table and click **Yes** to accept the warning that the fields are being shortened.
12. Close the table.
13. Right-click the **Employees** table in the Database window and select **Properties** to add the following description of the table:

    `This table will be used to locate employees and their anniversary dates.`
14. Save and close the database.

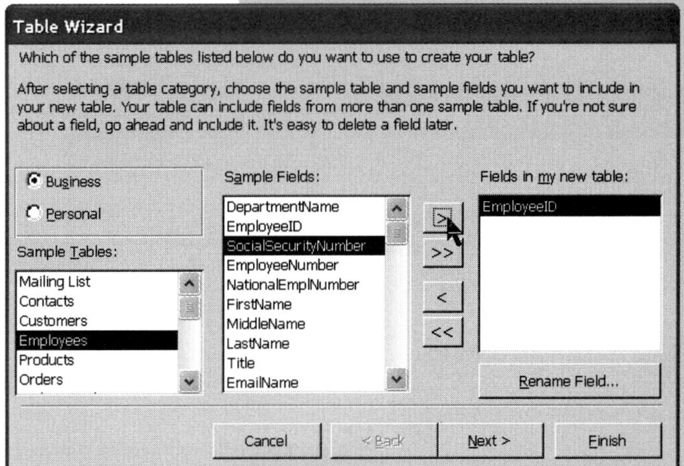

ACCESS

Cues for Reference

Create a Table with the Table Wizard
1. Create a blank database, or open an existing database file.
2. Click **Tables.**
3. Double-click **Create table by using wizard.**
4. Click a sample table.
5. Double-click fields to select them.
6. Name the table.
7. Set the primary key.
8. Choose data types.

Rename Fields
1. While creating the table, select the field to be changed.
2. Click **Rename field.**
3. Enter the new name.
4. Click **OK.**

View Field Data Type
1. Open table in Design view.
2. Click **Field Name** in top pane of Design window, and look at data type.

Change Field Properties
1. Open table in Design view.
2. Click **Field Name** in top pane of Design window.
3. Click **F6.**
4. Make changes as desired.

Enter Data Using a Datasheet
1. Open table in Datasheet view.
2. Press **Tab,** press **Enter,** or use the arrow keys to proceed from field to field.

Delete a Record
1. Click **Record Selector.**
2. Click **Delete.**
3. Click **Yes** to confirm deletion.

Edit a Record
- Overtype or correct data.

Add Table Properties
1. Right-click **Table** in the Database window.
2. Select **Properties.**
3. Enter table description.
4. Click **OK.**

GOALS

To create a formatted table in Design view with a primary key field, three data types, an input mask, and one lookup field

To practice using the following skill sets:

- Create tables in Design view
- Set primary keys in Design view
- Use the Lookup Wizard
- Use the Input Mask Wizard
- Format a table datasheet for display

WHAT YOU NEED TO KNOW

Create Tables in Design View

- You have created tables using the Table Wizard. You can also create a table in Design view from the Database window, using one of the following options:
  - Click Tables and click Create table in Design view, as shown in Figure 2.15.

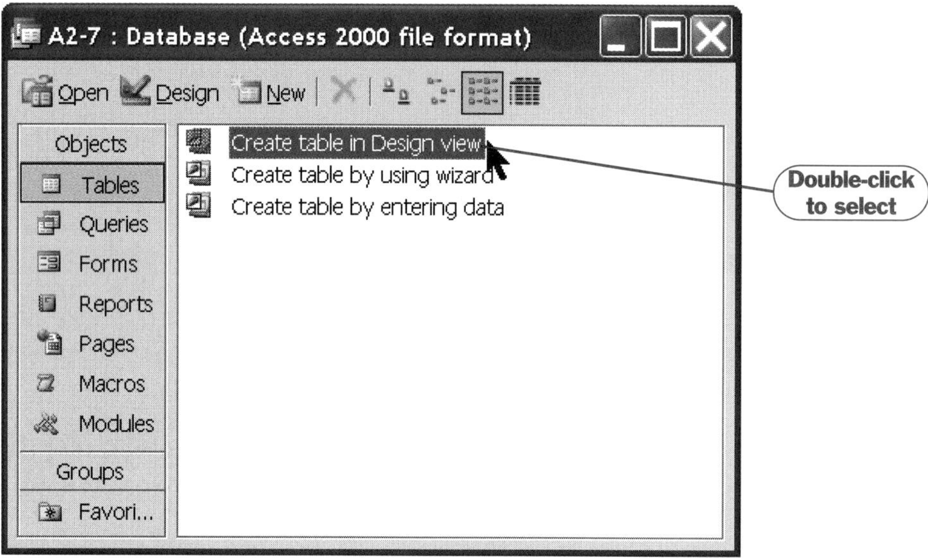

Figure 2.15 Create table in Design view

- Click Tables, click the New button, and select Design view, as shown in Figure 2.16.

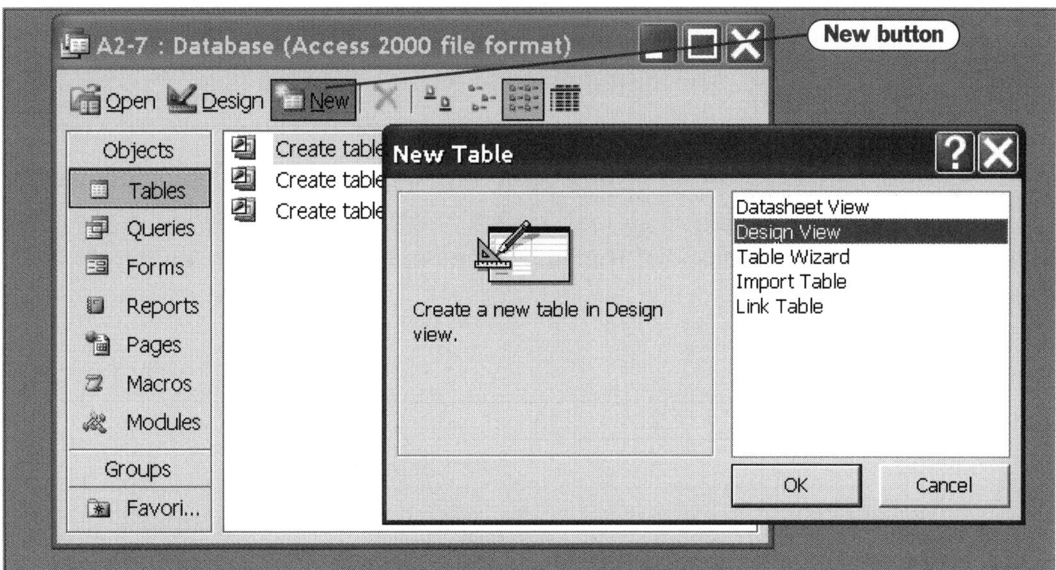

Figure 2.16 Create a table in Design view—New Table button

▶ A table in Design view is shown in Figure 2.17.

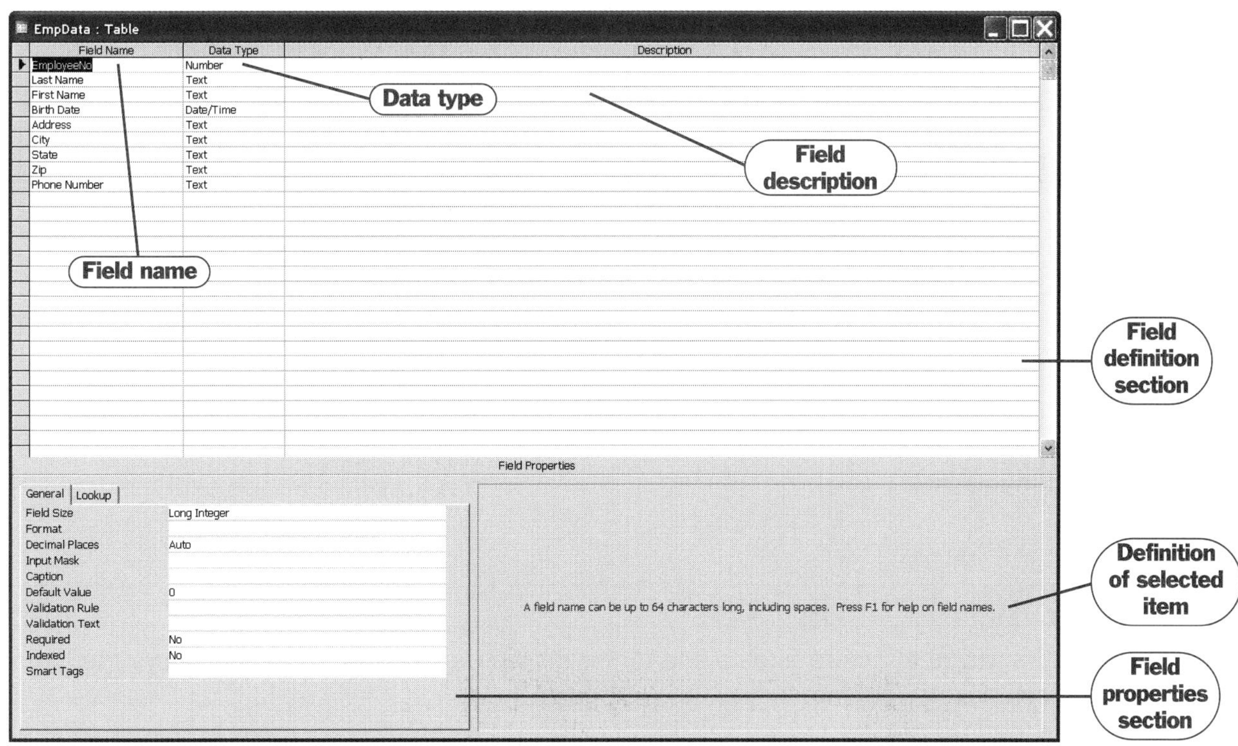

Figure 2.17 Table in Design view

▶ Enter the field name first. It can contain up to 64 characters. Valid characters include letters, numbers, nonleading spaces, and special characters, except the period (.), exclamation point (!), accent grave (`), and brackets ([ ]). Each field name must be unique.

- Set the data type next. The default data type is Text. To change it, click the list arrow and select the data type you want. You learned about the 10 data types earlier in this lesson.
- The Description field is optional. You can identify a field with a description of up to 255 characters.
- After entering the field name and data type, next define the properties of the data.
- To switch between panes, press the F6 key or move the insertion point.
- After designing a table, name it, and save it. If you do not save the table, Access prompts you to do so.
- Access also prompts you to set a primary key. This is not required, but is recommended if you want to link the table to another table.
- To enter data, change to Datasheet view.

TRY *it* OUT *A2-7*

1. Open a blank database and name it **A2-7.**
2. Double-click **Create table in Design view.** Notice that the insertion point is at the top of the screen under Field Name.
3. Create the following fields and set the indicated data types.

FIELD NAME	DATA TYPE
EmployeeNo	Number
Last Name	Text
First Name	Text
Birth Date	Date/Time
Address	Text
City	Text
State	Text
Zip	Text
Phone Number	Text

4. Save the table; name it **EmpData.** Click **No** when you are asked if you want to create a primary key.
5. Leave the table open in Design View.

Set Primary Keys in Design View

- When you use a wizard to create a table and to assign the primary key, Access displays the Primary Key icon next to the primary key field in Design view.
- To set the primary key without using a wizard, or to change the primary key field, select the table in Design view, click the field to be the primary key, and click the Primary Key button on the toolbar, as shown in Figure 2.18. The primary key is then displayed to the left of the field name.

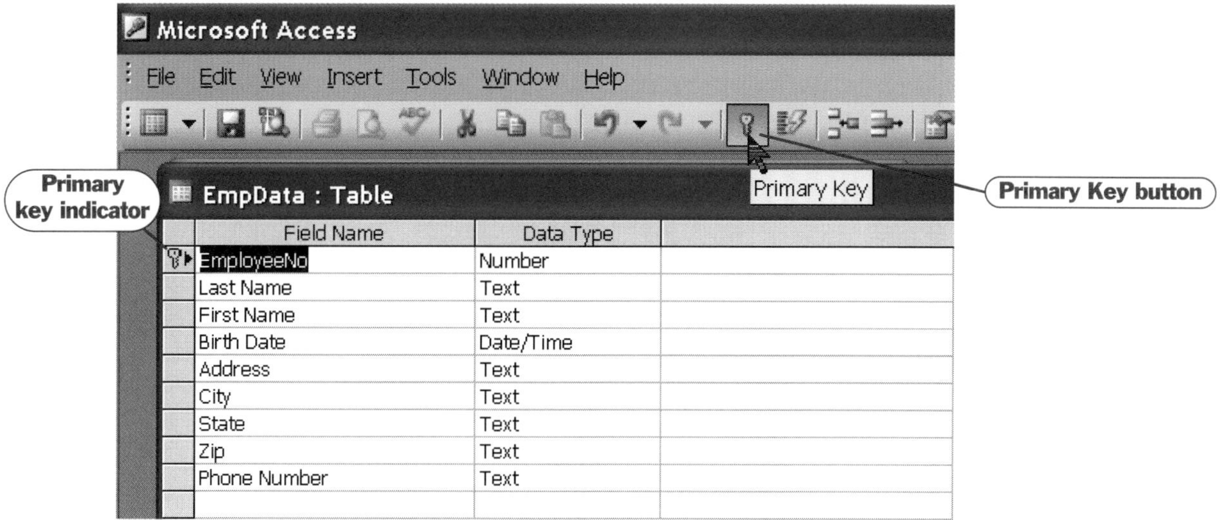

Figure 2.18 Design view—setting the primary key

TRY *it* OUT *A2-8*

1. The **EmpData** table in **A2-7** should be displayed in Design view; or, open **A2-8** from the Data CD and open the **EmpData** table in Design view.
2. To establish the Employee Number field as the primary key, click the **Employee Number** field, if necessary.
3. Click the **Primary Key** button on the Database toolbar.

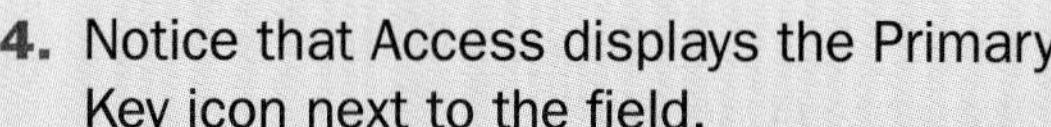

4. Notice that Access displays the Primary Key icon next to the field.
5. Close and save the table. Do not close the database.

ACCESS

Use the Lookup Wizard

- One of the data types is Lookup Wizard, which automates the process of creating a lookup field. A lookup field is useful when there are a limited number of values for the field. For example, if you have employees who work in certain states, you can create a list or table of those states. When you use the Tab key to move to the State field, Access displays a list, as shown in Figure 2.19, from which you can choose one entry, eliminating the need to enter it each time.

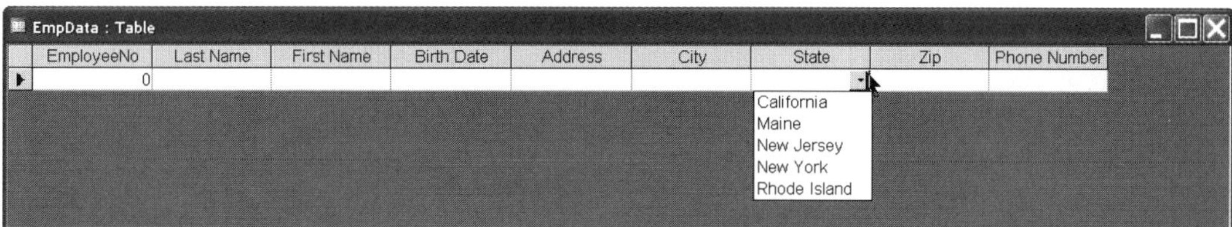

Figure 2.19 Table with Lookup Field

- The *Lookup Wizard* guides you through the process of identifying where to obtain the values to create a lookup column. It can reference a column in an existing table, or you can enter the values you need, as shown in Figure 2.20. To enter the values, select **I will type in the values that I want,** and click Next.

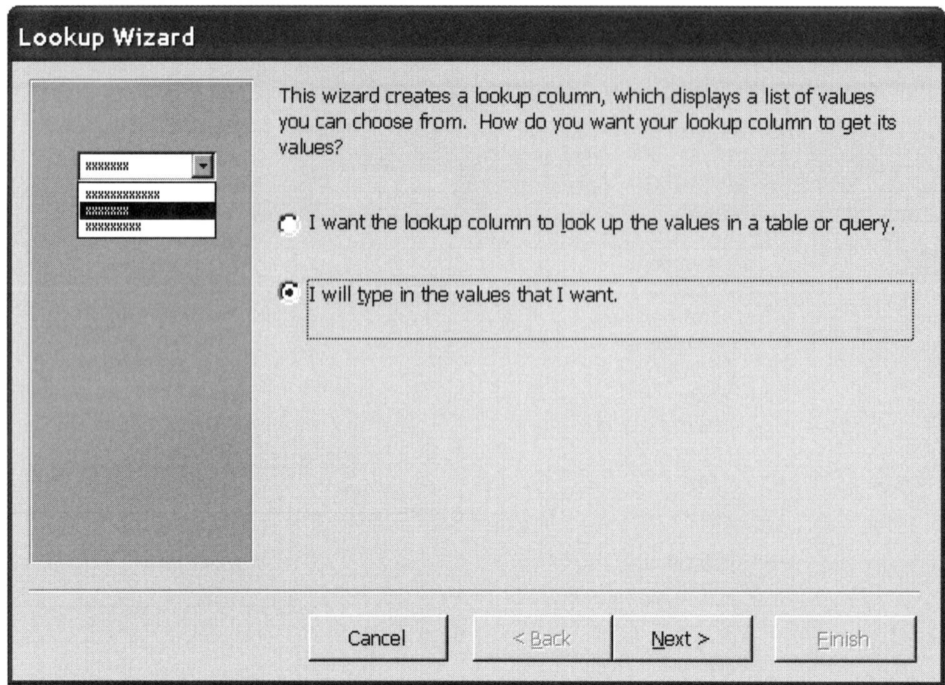

Figure 2.20 Data types—Lookup Wizard

- The Lookup Wizard displays a dialog box that lets you set up one or more columns, as shown in Figure 2.21. The Wizard will then ask you for the field name; the name you provided in the design is the default setting.

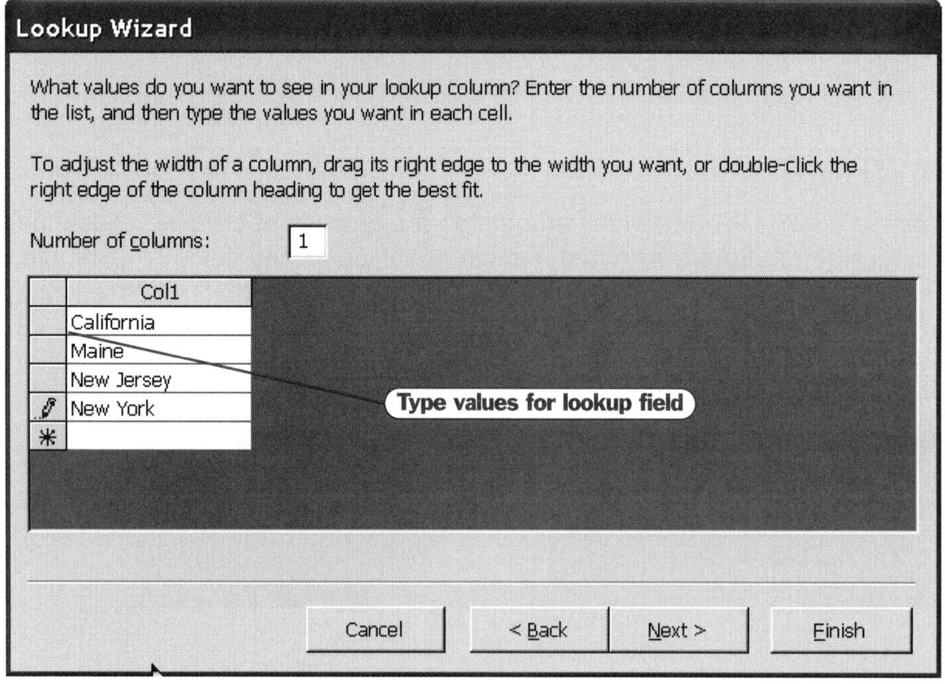

Figure 2.21 Data types—Lookup Wizard column

▶ To view or edit the lookup value list that you created, click the field and then click the Lookup tab in the Field Properties pane of Design view. The list is stored in, and can be edited in, the Row Source property, as shown in Figure 2.22. The *Row source type*, located above Row Source, is the property that specifies the source Access will use for *a lookup field.*

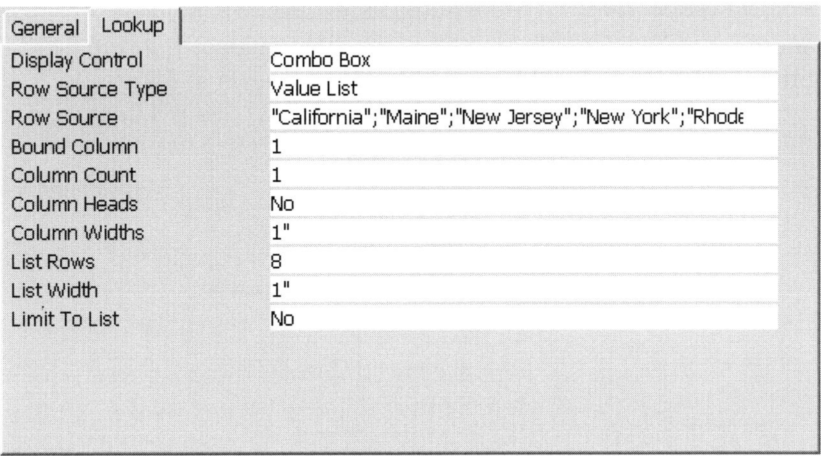

Figure 2.22 Field Properties—Lookup, Row Source Type

TRY *it* OUT *A2-9*

1. The **EmpData** table in **A2-7** should be displayed in Design view, or open **A2-9** from the Data CD and open the **EmpData** table in Design view.
2. Click the **State** field.
3. Click the down arrow in the **Data Type** column.
4. Click **Lookup Wizard.**
5. Click **I will type in the values that I want.** Click **Next.**
6. Leave the number of columns at 1 and click the cell under Col 1.
7. Enter the following states, pressing the **Tab** key after each:

   `California`

   `Maine`

   `New Jersey`

   `New York`
8. Click **Next.**
9. Accept State as the field label and click **Finish.**
10. Click the **Lookup** tab in the Field Properties pane.
11. Notice that the states you entered are listed in the Row Source property setting. Add `Rhode Island` to the list.
12. Save the table. Switch to Datasheet view and click in the **State** field to view the lookup list, as shown in Figure 2.19. Your list will include Rhode Island.
13. Close the table. Do not close the database.

Use the Input Mask Wizard

▶ Another data type setting is the *input mask,* which controls how Access enters data in a field. An input mask provides a pattern, or template, to which data must conform. This ensures that data is entered in a field in a consistent format.

- For example, you can set a Date/Time format that automatically requires two digits each for the month and day, requires four digits for the year, and uses slashes as separators (02/09/2005). This reduces data entry keystrokes and errors.
- To assist you in defining input masks, Access provides an *Input Mask Wizard*. The Input Mask Wizard works with the Text or Date/Time data types only.
- To use the Wizard you must be in Design view and have the field selected. In the Field Properties pane, click the Build button in the Input Mask property field, as shown in Figure 2.23.

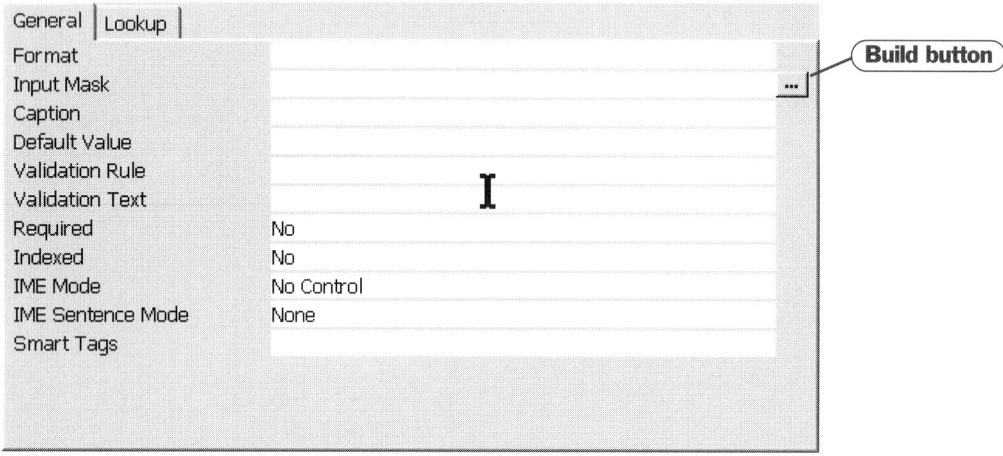

Figure 2.23 Field Properties, Input Mask—Build button

- First, the Wizard may prompt you to save the table. The Input Wizard then opens a dialog box with available formats. If you are working with a Date/Time field, the dialog box appears as shown in Figure 2.24.

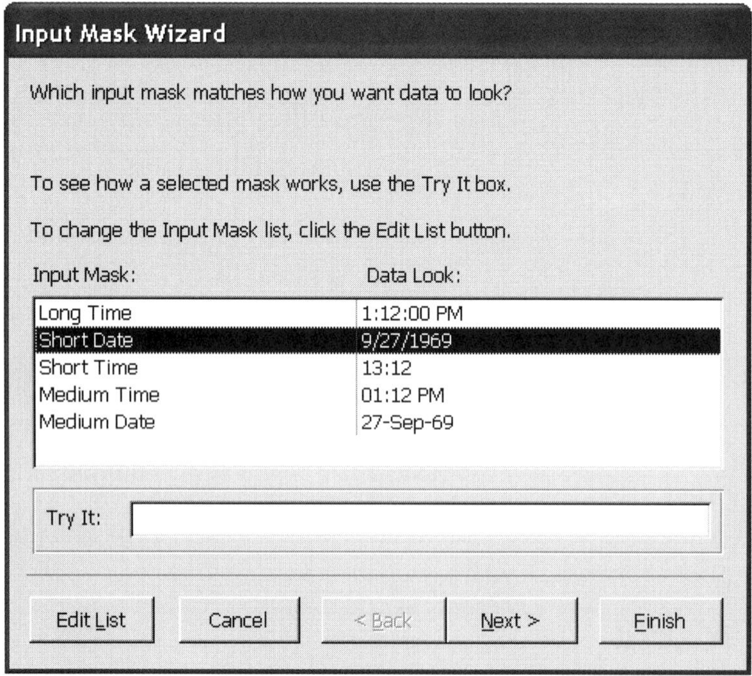

Figure 2.24 Date/Time field properties—Input Mask Wizard

▶ If you are working with a Text field, the dialog box appears as shown in Figure 2.25.

Figure 2.25 Text field properties—Input Mask Wizard

▶ The Wizard allows you to customize the mask and choose the placeholder characters, which disappear as you enter data in the field. In Text fields, you also have the option of deciding if you want to store the symbols with the data.

TRY *it* OUT *A2-10*

1. The **EmpData** table in **A2-7** should be displayed in Design view, or open **A2-10** from the Data CD and open the table in Design view.
2. Click the **Birthdate** field. Notice that the BirthDate field is a Date/Time field.
3. In the Field Properties pane, click the **General** tab, if necessary.
4. Click the **Input Mask** property field.
5. Click the **Build** button in the Input Mask property field.
6. Click **Yes** when the Input Mask Wizard prompts you to save the table.
7. Click **Short Date.**
8. Click **Next.** Notice that you can change the input mask, and you can choose the placeholder character. The placeholder character is an underscore.
9. Click **Next.**
10. Click **Finish.**
11. Repeat the procedures from Step 2 for the **Phone Number** field to set a Phone Number input mask. Elect to store the symbols with the data.
12. Click **Datasheet View.**
13. Save the table when prompted.

Continued on next page

14. Enter the data in the table below into the datasheet. In the State field, click the list arrow to view the values and click the correct one. Enter the dates and telephone numbers without the symbols since they are provided by the input mask.

FIELD NAMES	RECORD 1	RECORD 2	RECORD 3
Employee No	1	2	3
Last Name	LiBecci	Peterson	Perry
First Name	Barbara	Charles	Michael
Birth date	7/9/1987	9/8/1986	3/11/1990
Address	12 Carling Lane	654 East Drive	60 Main Street
City	Providence	San Jose	Fair Haven
State	Rhode Island	California	New Jersey
Zip	02903	95110	07704
Phone Number	401-555-7853	408-555-7853	908-555-7637

15. Close the table. Do not close the database.

Format a Table Datasheet

- If you are familiar with the formatting concepts in Word and Excel, then you already know the formatting options available in Access.
- Access establishes default settings for a datasheet. You can change these settings. In Datasheet view, click Format on the menu bar to display a Format menu, as shown in Figure 2.26.

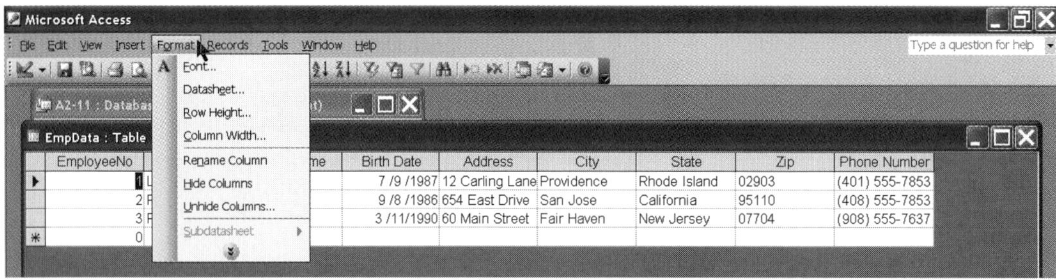

Figure 2.26 Datasheet Format menu

- Click Format, Font, to open the Font dialog box that lists available fonts, font sizes, style options, and effects. There is a sample box for you to preview your choices, as shown in Figure 2.27.

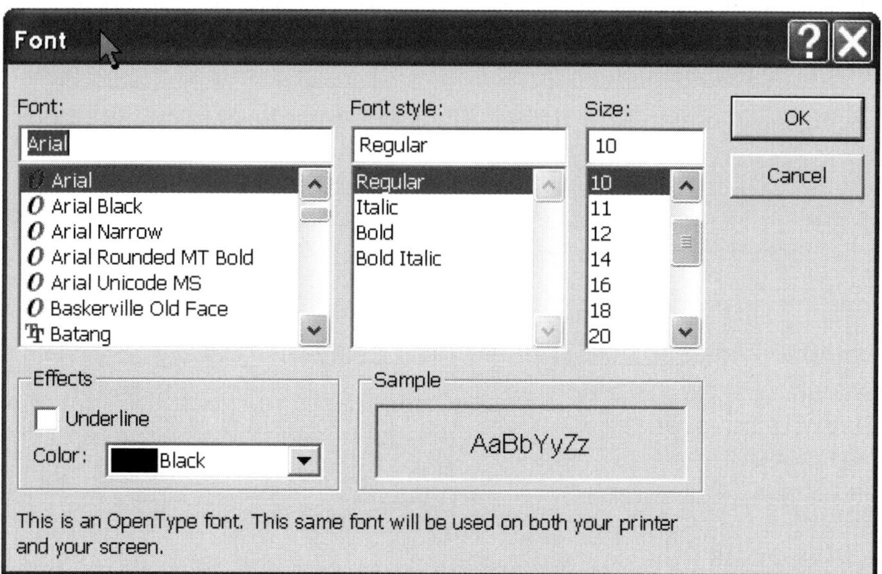

Figure 2.27 Format—font options

- Click Format, Datasheet to open the dialog box that lists cell and gridline effects and color options. You can choose border and line styles and set the direction for entering data in a datasheet, as shown in Figure 2.28.

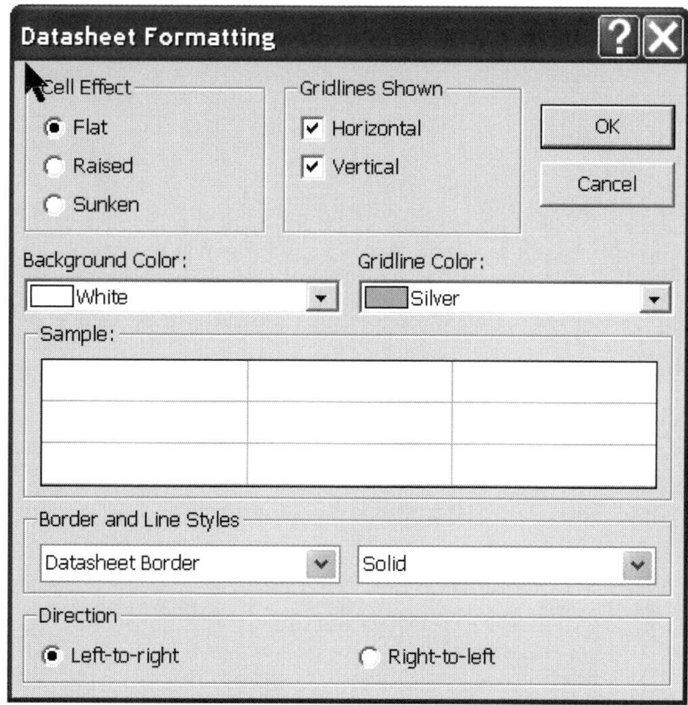

Figure 2.28 Format—datasheet options

- You can change a column width without affecting the field size specified in the table design. You can use the Format menu, or drag the right edge of the field name cell to the width you want.
- If you change the font size of a table, you might need to adjust the size of some columns. As in Excel, when you double-click the line between two column headers, the column width adjusts to accommodate the size of the longest field entry.
- To change the row height, click Format, Row Height. Then, enter the height you want in the Row Height dialog box.

TRY *it* OUT *A2-11*

1. The **EmpData** table in **A2-7** should be displayed in Datasheet view, or open **A2-11** from the Data CD and open the **EmpData** table in Datasheet view.
2. Click **Format, Font.**
3. Under Size, click **14** and click **OK.**
4. Notice that the data in the Address, State, and Phone Number columns cannot be fully displayed.
5. Click the **Address** column.
6. Click **Format, Column Width.**
7. Click **Best Fit.**
8. Double-click the line at the right of the column header for the State and Phone Number fields to widen those columns.
9. Click **Format, Datasheet.**
10. In the Background Color drop-down list, select **Blue.**
11. In the Gridline Color drop-down list, select **Fuchsia.** Click **OK.**
12. Save the table.
13. Close the table and the database.

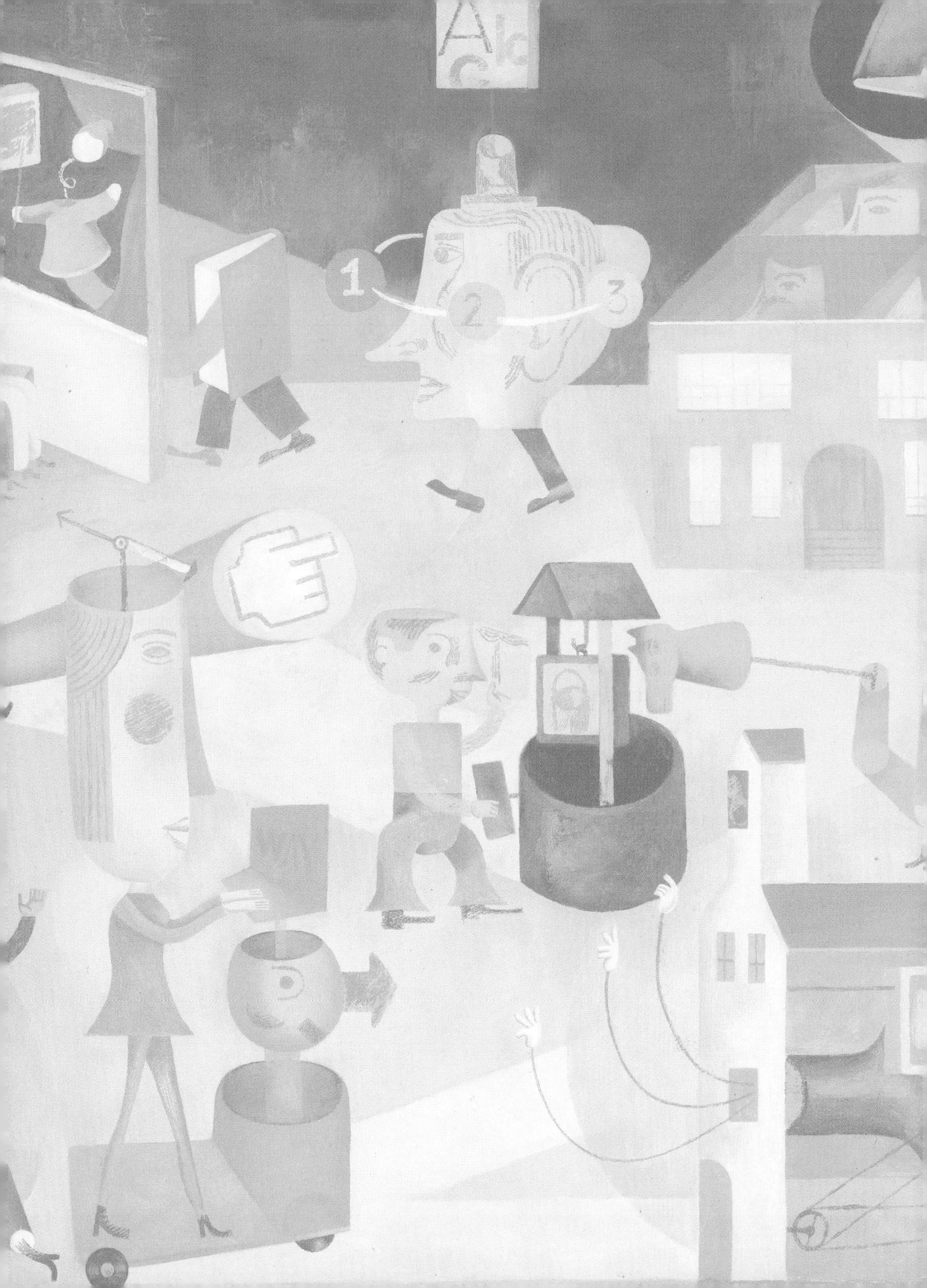
1
2
3

GOAL:
To create a formatted table in Design view with a primary key field, three data types, an input mask, and one lookup field

SETTING THE STAGE/WRAPUP
Database: 2EMP2
Table: Table1

WHAT YOU NEED TO KNOW

- A business depends on the accuracy of its data. Data in databases must be reliable so that the business can make decisions with confidence. For this reason, Access provides tools to restrict data formats and limit mistakes made when data is entered.
- The presentation of data is also important. The business must present data in a format that others can read and understand.
- In this Rehearsal activity, you will use Design view to create a table, with a primary key, to add to an existing database. You will use the Input Mask Wizard to restrict the format of a field, and you will use the Lookup Wizard to create a lookup field that will improve the accuracy of data entry. You will also use datasheet format options to create a table that looks attractive and that can be read easily.

DIRECTIONS

1. Open **2EMP2** from the Data CD or use your solution to Task1, **2EMP.**
2. Create a new table in Design view to store the information shown in Illustration A on the facing page with the data types indicated in Illustration B.
3. Set the Employee ID field as the primary key.
4. Save the table as **EmpData.** You will be prompted to save the table after you make the structure changes in Steps 5-8.
5. Set the data type for the Department field to Lookup Wizard. Create a list of departments as follows:

   `Administration`

   `Maintenance`

   `Teaching Staff`
6. Use an input mask to format the Work Phone field using the Phone number format. Store the symbols with the data.
7. Use an input mask to format the Home Phone field using the Phone number format. Store the symbols with the data.
8. Use an input mask to format the Birth Date field using the Short Date format.
9. Save the table and switch to Datasheet view.
10. Enter the data shown in Illustration A in the table.
11. Format the table with a font size of **14.**
12. Select the **Arial Narrow** font.
13. Select a background color of **Silver.**
14. Select a gridline color of **Red.**
15. Be sure all information is displayed.
16. Save and close the table.
17. Close the database.

EMPLOYEE ID	DEPARTMENT	WORK PHONE	HOME PHONE	BIRTH DATE
1	Administration	480-555-5002	480-555-8765	10/03/1980
2	Maintenance	480-555-5003	480-555-9845	05/01/1986
3	Teaching Staff	480-555-5005	480-555-2654	09/30/1990

Illustration A

FIELD	DATA TYPE
Employee ID	AutoNumber (Primary Key)
Department	Text (Lookup Field)
Work Phone	Text (Input mask)
Home Phone	Text (Input mask)
Birth Date	Text (Input mask)

Illustration B

ACCESS

Cues for Reference

Create a Table in Design View

1. Create a blank database, or open an existing database file.
2. Do one of the following:
   - Click **Create table in Design view.**

   or

   - Click **Tables** in Objects list and click the **Design** button.

Set the Primary Key in Design View

1. Click field to designate as primary key.
2. Click the **Primary Key** button.

Create a Lookup Field

1. Click field.
2. Click down arrow in **Data Type** column.
3. Click **Lookup Wizard.**
4. Click **I will type in the values that I want.**
5. Enter values.
6. Click **Next.**
7. Assign label to values.
8. Click **Finish.**

Use the Input Mask Wizard

1. Click **Design view.**
2. Click the field you want to mask.
3. Click the **Build** button in the Input Mask property field.

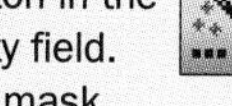

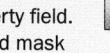

4. Select the desired mask style; click **Next.**
5. Set any storage options. Click **Finish.**

Format a Datasheet

1. Click **Datasheet.**
2. Click **Format.**
3. Select options.

SETTING THE STAGE/WRAPUP
Database: Trilogy Employees
Table: Emp Contact

WHAT YOU NEED TO KNOW

Act I

You work for Trilogy Productions, a motion picture and television production company. They have released 50 feature films and numerous Emmy-winning television programs. The Motion Picture and Television Divisions are located in Beverly Hills, California.

You work for Trilogy in New York City, where Trilogy maintains a small office that primarily handles all marketing and sales distribution. Your supervisor is Ms. Cindy Napster, the manager of the Human Resources Department. The company is preparing to expand and is planning to hire 20 people over the next two months.

Cindy has asked you to develop a database to store all the contact information for Trilogy employees. Cindy has mentioned that she wants to have office phone numbers and e-mail addresses at her fingertips. She also wants home numbers and emergency contacts, in case she needs to get in touch with someone while he or she is traveling.

Cindy has given you the following data:

Employee # 6
John Alan - CEO (chief executive officer) and president
101 Sunset Boulevard
Beverly Hills, CA 90211
Office Phone: (310) 555-0000
E-mail: jatpc@world.com
Home Phone: (310) 555-1111
Emergency Contact: Jamie Lang
Emergency Contact Telephone Number: (310) 555-9876

Employee # 14
Andrew Martin - CFO (chief financial officer)
101 Sunset Boulevard
Beverly Hills, CA 90211
Office Phone: (310) 555-0000
E-mail: amtpc@world.com
Home Phone: (310) 555-1234
Emergency Contact: Jane Smith
Emergency Contact Telephone Number: (310) 555-1322

Employee # 12
Christopher Manning - director of Marketing and Sales
350 West 57 Street
New York, NY 10106
Office Phone: (212) 555-7777
E-mail: cmtpny@world.com
Home Phone: (212) 555-1234
Emergency Contact: Joe Schwartz
Emergency Contact Telephone Number: (212) 555-1000

Employee # 9
Cindy Napster - manager of Human Resources
350 West 57 Street
New York, NY 10106
Office Phone: (212) 555-7777
E-mail: cntpny@world.com
Home Phone: (212) 555-4321
Emergency Contact: Jena Jones
Emergency Contact Telephone Number: (212) 555-9876

Follow these guidelines:

- Review the existing data.
- Make a list of all the fields you think you should include in this database.
- Review each field in terms of data type, input mask, and lookup field requirements. You should use an input mask setting for telephone fields and lookup fields for the State and Office Phone fields.
- Review the Table Wizard samples to see if there is a sample table that comes close to meeting your needs.
- Create the table using the Table Wizard.
- Name the database: `Trilogy Employees.`
- Name the table: `Emp Contact.`
- If necessary, modify the field data types. Add input masks and lookup fields.
- Select one field for the primary key.

Act II

Cindy is very pleased with your database design and the speed with which you delivered it! She would like you to enter the data that she has provided you with thus far, while she collects additional information. You also know that the company colors are blue and green, and that the corporate font is Verdana.

Follow these guidelines:

- Enter information in one record.
- Make any necessary changes to the design of the database before entering additional records.
  - Change field properties to reduce the size of the text fields where possible.
  - Create a description for the table in the table properties dialog box.
- Add formatting to the datasheet, including color and font.
- Complete the data entry.
- Make sure all of the data is displayed.
- Save and close the database.

1
2
3

LESSON 3

Access Forms

In this lesson, you will learn how to create, use, and modify forms. You will learn about field controls, including calculated controls. You will also learn how to enter records using a form.

Upon completion of this lesson, you should have mastered the following skill sets:

- Create a form with AutoForm
- Create forms using the Form Wizard
  - Use the Form Wizard to Apply Layout and Style
- Enter, edit, and delete records using a form
- Print database objects
- Use Form Design view
- Show/Hide form headers and footers
- Add, align, and space controls
- Modify the properties of specific controls on a form
- Modify the properties of a form
- Add a calculated control to a form

Terms

Software-related

AutoForm
Form Wizard
Controls
Bound control
Form Design toolbox
Form header
Form footer
Page header
Page footer
Label control
Unbound control
Form selector
Calculated control
Text box

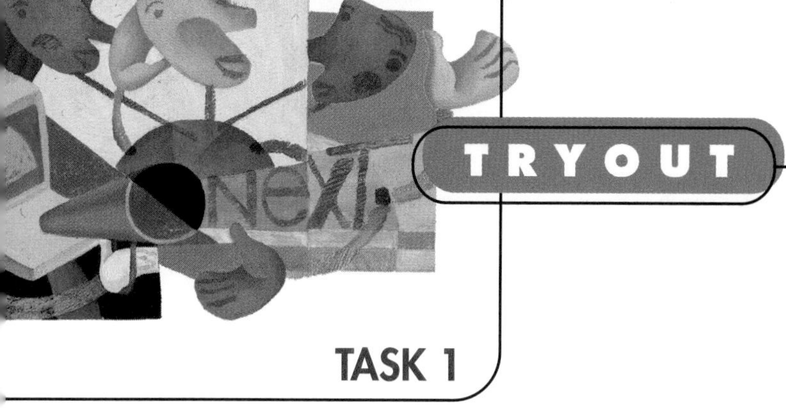

GOALS

To create a form that a real estate office can use to enter new home listings, update current listings, and delete listings that have sold

To practice using the following skill sets:

- Create a form with AutoForm
  - Use AutoForm Wizards
- Create forms using the Form Wizard
  - Use the Form Wizard to Apply Layout and Style
- Enter, edit, and delete records using a form
- Print database objects

WHAT YOU NEED TO KNOW

Create a Form with AutoForm

- You have been entering database data directly into the datasheet table. Access provides a Form object to assist you in entering data in a database. As you would fill out a paper form, you fill out an electronic form to enter, edit, or delete records.
- There are three ways to create forms: AutoForm, Form Wizard, and Form Design view. You will learn about AutoForm and the Form Wizard in this lesson.
- *AutoForm* automatically creates a form to display all the fields in a table, one record at a time. When a table is open, click the New Object button, and click AutoForm. A form appears, as shown in Figure 3.1, displaying the first record, and the table remains open.

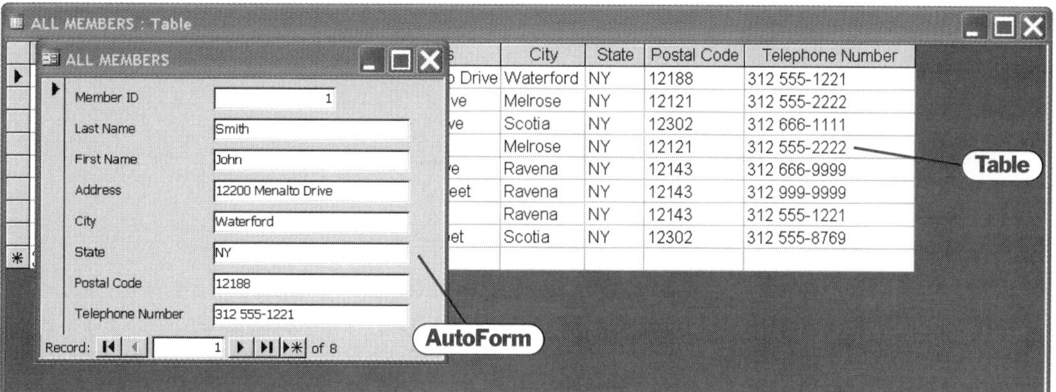

Figure 3.1 Create AutoForm—table is open

TRY it OUT *A3-1*

1. Start Access.
2. Open the **Members** database from the Data CD.

3. Click the **Tables** object.
4. Double-click **ALL MEMBERS.**
5. Click the down-arrow list on the **New Object** button.

6. Choose **AutoForm.**
7. Notice the form displays the first record.
8. Close the form. Do not name or save the form.
9. Close the table.

Use AutoForm Wizards

- You can also access the AutoForm feature from the Database window. Click Forms and click the New button. This opens the New Form dialog box, as shown in Figure 3.2.

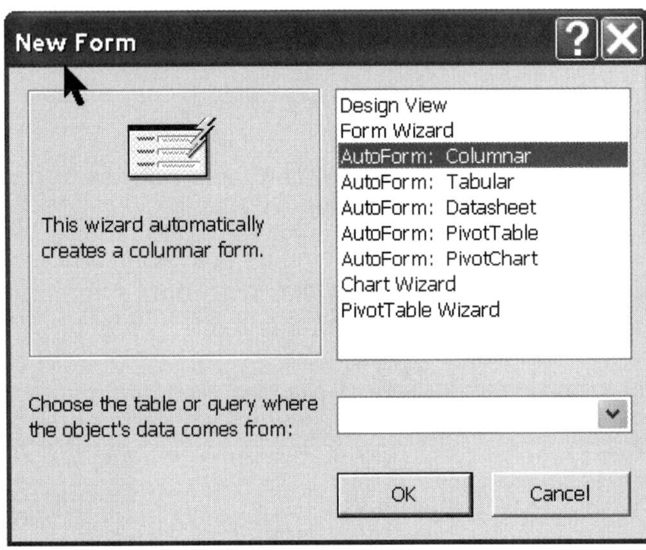

Figure 3.2 New Form dialog box

- The New Form dialog box offers options for creating forms with different layouts. Each layout is associated with an AutoForm Wizard. Each wizard builds a form with a different layout. There are five AutoForm Wizards, AutoForm: Columnar, AutoForm: Tabular, AutoForm: Datasheet, AutoForm: PivotTable, and AutoForm: PivotChart.
- You can click each wizard to preview its layout and an example of the layout appears in the left portion of the window.
- After you select an AutoForm Wizard, click the name of the data source table, and click OK. A form appears in the format you chose with the same name as the data source table.

TRY *it* OUT *A3-2*

Note: The Members database should be open.

1. Click **Forms** in the Objects list.
2. Click the **New** button and the New Form window appears.
3. Click each AutoForm Wizard to preview the layout.
4. Click **AutoForm: Tabular.**
5. Click the down arrow to the right of "Choose the table or query where the object's data comes from."
6. Click **ALL MEMBERS.**
7. Click **OK.**
8. Close the form; do not name or save it.

Create Forms Using the Form Wizard

- Using the *Form Wizard* to create forms is useful when:
  - All the fields in a table are not required.
  - Layout and style are required.
  - A form contains fields from more than one table.
- In the Database window, click Forms, and double-click Create form by using wizard, as shown in Figure 3.3. (The Wizard is also available in the New Form dialog box shown in Figure 3.2.)

ACCESS

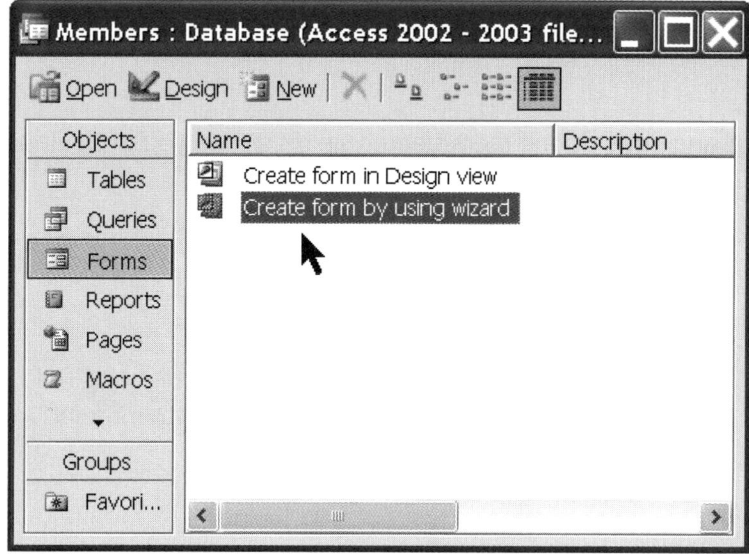

Figure 3.3 Create a form with wizard

▶ The Form Wizard asks you to select the data source table and the fields to include, as shown in Figure 3.4.

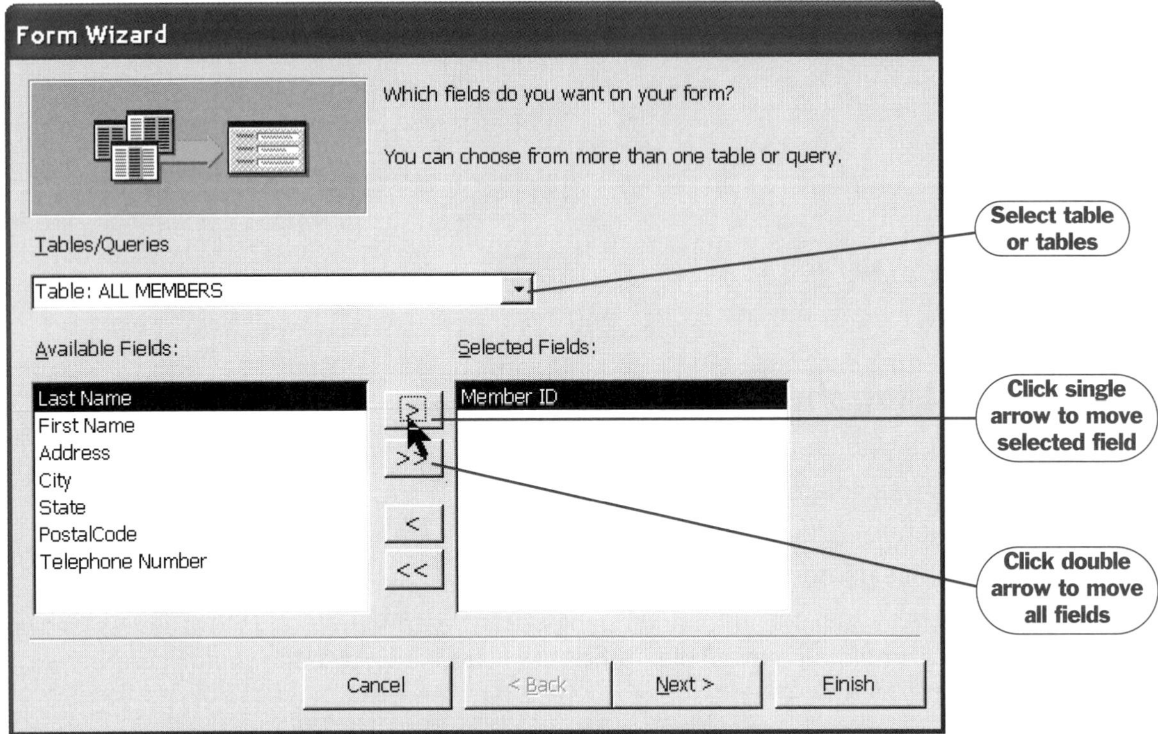

Figure 3.4 Form Wizard—selecting tables and fields

▶ Click the data source table and double-click the selected fields. When you click Finish, Access displays a basic form.

TRY it OUT *A3-3*

Note: You should be in the Members database in the Forms object.

1. Double-click **Create form by using wizard.**
2. Notice that ALL MEMBERS appears selected under Tables/Queries.
3. Click the list arrow, and notice the other tables' names; leave ALL MEMBERS selected.
4. Double-click the following fields to move them to the Selected Fields box:
   a. **MemberID**
   b. **First Name**
   c. **Last Name**
   d. **Telephone Number**
5. Click **Finish**.
6. Close the form, then select the form and click the **Delete** button to delete it. Click **Yes** to confirm.

Use the Form Wizard to Apply Layout and Style

- The Form Wizard provides preset layouts and styles you can apply to a form. In the Database window, click Forms, and then double-click Create form by using wizard. Double-click the fields you want and click Next.The Form Wizard asks you to select a layout, as shown in Figure 3.5.

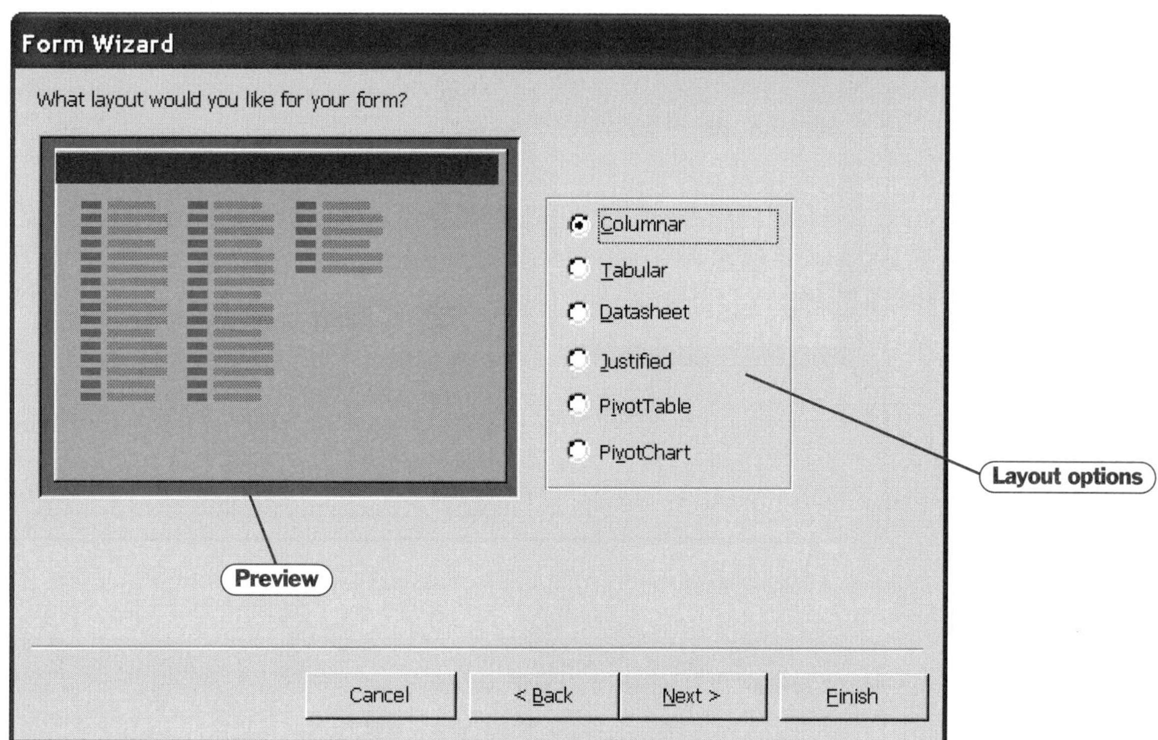

Figure 3.5 Form Wizard—What layout would you like for your form?

- The layout options are the same as in AutoForm: Columnar, Tabular, Datasheet, Justified, PivotTable, or PivotChart. When you click to preview each option, an example appears in the left portion of the window.
- When you click the layout option you want and click Next, the Wizard asks, "What style would you like?", as shown in Figure 3.6.

ACCESS

- Click to preview each style; an example appears in the left portion of the window. When you click Finish, a form appears, containing the first record from the data table in the format and style you chose. The Wizard names the form with the same name as the table.
- Click Next to name the form and choose how to open it, as shown in Figure 3.7. Enter a name and choose a method for opening the form and click Finish.

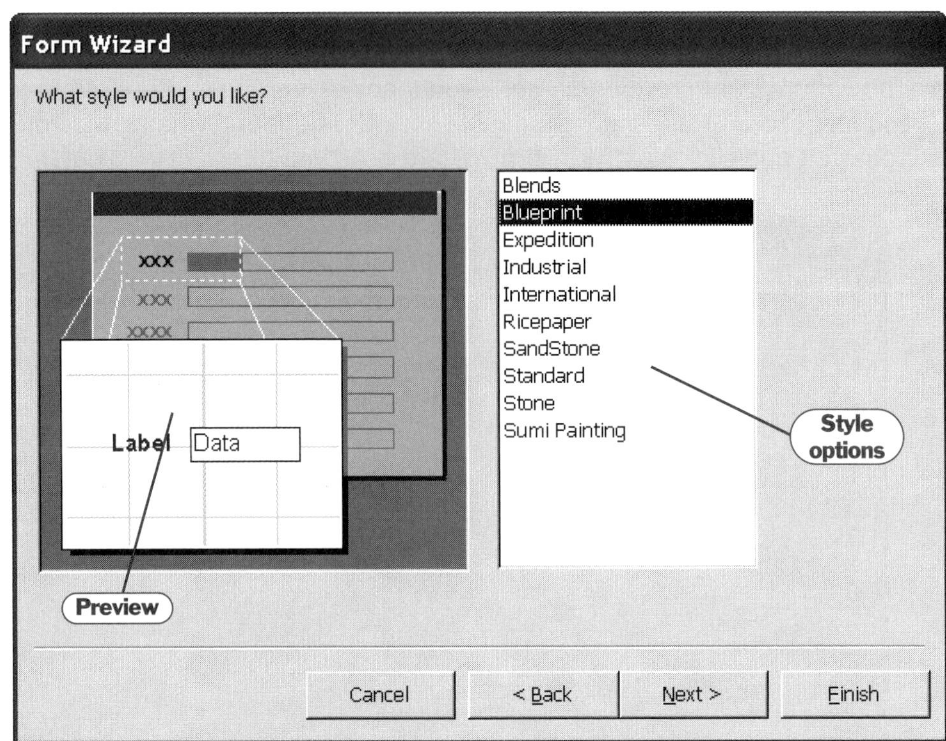

Figure 3.6 Form Wizard—What style would you like?

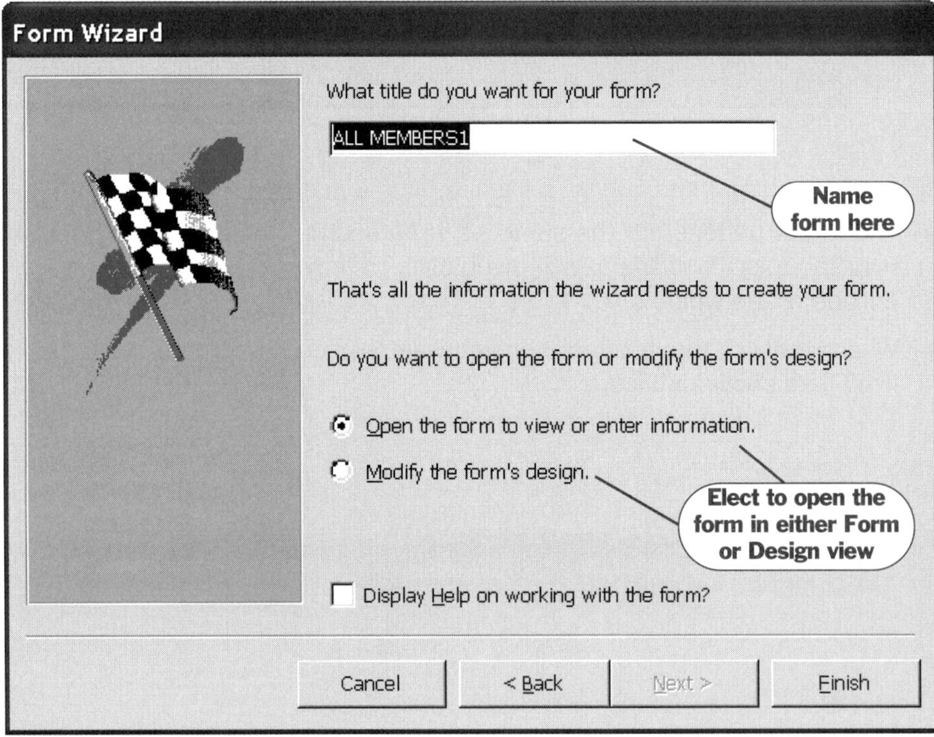

Figure 3.7 Form Wizard—last step

TRY *it* OUT *A3-4*

Note: You should be in the Members database in the Forms object.

1. Double-click **Create form by using wizard**.
2. Notice that ALL MEMBERS appears selected under Tables/Queries.
3. Double-click the following fields to move them to the Selected Fields box:
   a. **MemberID**
   b. **First Name**
   c. **Last Name**
   d. **Address**
   e. **City**
   f. **Telephone Number**
4. Click **Next**.
5. Click each layout option to preview available formats.
6. Click **Columnar**.
7. Click **Next**.
8. Click each style option to preview available styles.
9. Click **Blueprint**.
10. Click **Next**.
11. Notice that the Wizard has named the form **ALL MEMBERS.**
12. Notice that you have two options: "Open the form to view or enter information" and "Modify the form's design."
13. Leave **Open the form to view or enter information** selected.
14. Click **Finish**.
15. Close the form.

ACCESS

Enter, Edit, and Delete Records Using a Form

Enter Records Using a Form

▶ Now that you have created a form, you can use it to enter data. To use a form to enter records, click the Forms object in the Database window. Double-click the form you want to use. The form appears, as shown in Figure 3.8.

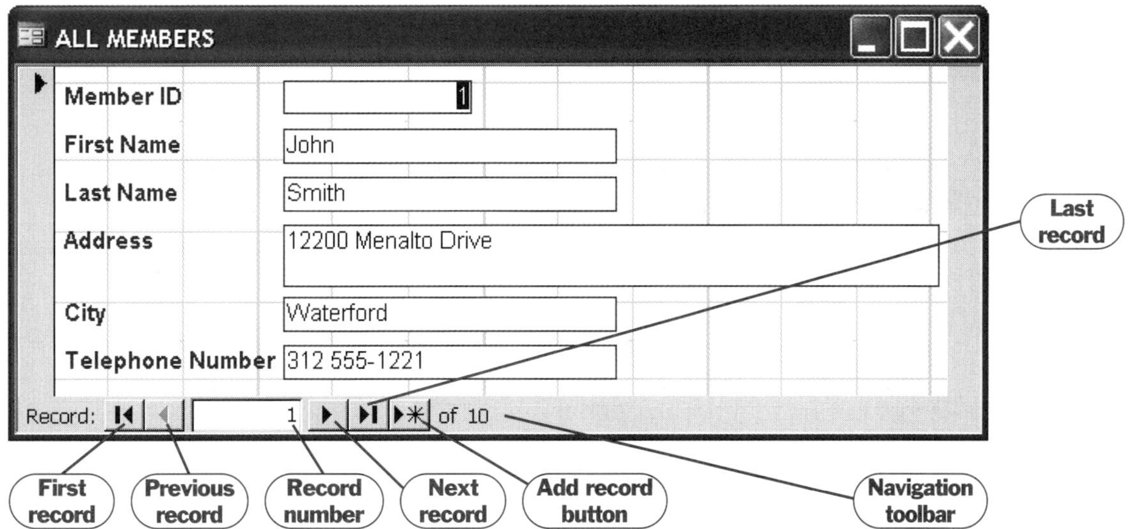

Figure 3.8 Enter records using a form

- Click the Add Record button, on the Navigation toolbar, to add a record. Enter records in a form the same way you would in Datasheet view. Press the Tab key to move from field to field. Press the Tab key to move to the next record, or click the Add Record button on the Navigation toolbar.

- Access saves data automatically as you enter it. If you add a record using a form, it is automatically visible in the datasheet. Click View, Datasheet View to see new records and click View, Form View to return to the form. Data entered into a form is stored in the datasheet. Therefore, if the form is deleted, the data you entered through the form is still in the datasheet.

TRY *it* OUT *A3-5*

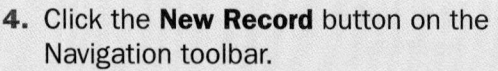

1. The **Members** database should be open from the last Try it Out, or open **A3-5** from the Data CD.
2. Click **Forms** in the Objects list.
3. Double-click **ALL MEMBERS.**
4. Click the **New Record** button on the Navigation toolbar.
5. Add records shown in the table below:
   - **a.** Press the **Tab** key to move from field to field.
   - **b.** Click the **New Record** button to display a new record form.

MemberID	9 (AutoNumber – no entry)	10 (AutoNumber – no entry)
FirstName	James	Tracey
LastName	Deer	Pappas
Address	23 Still River Road	78 Shaker Road
City	Melrose	Scotia
Telephone	312-555-0476	312-555-1054

6. Click **View.**
7. Click **Datasheet View.**
8. Notice that the records have been added to the datasheet.
9. Click **View.**
10. Click **Form View.**

Edit Records Using a Form

- To use a form to edit records, click the Forms object in the Database window. Double-click the form you want to edit.
- There are several methods to locate the record you want to edit:
  - Click the Next Record button to move through the records consecutively.
  - Click the Last Record button to move through the records in reverse order.
  - Click Edit, Find to use the Find feature, as shown in Figure 3.9.

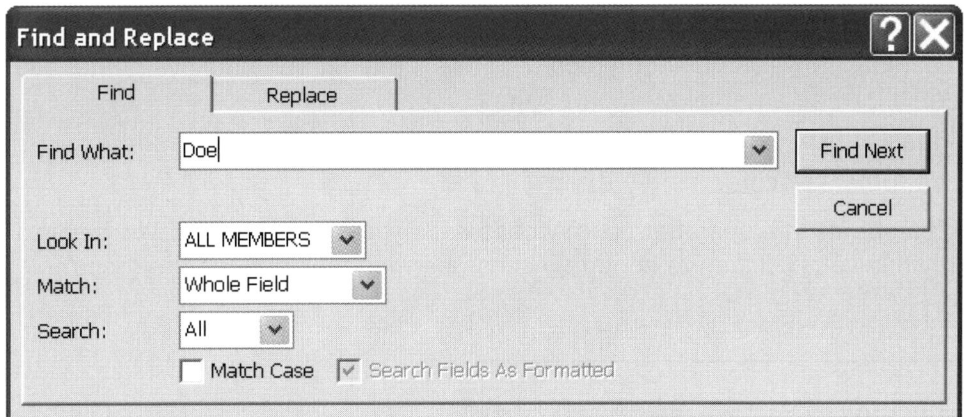

Figure 3.9 Find and Replace dialog box

- The method you use depends on the information you have to locate the record. If you have the record number, you can use the Navigation toolbar. If you do not have a record number, or if there are a large number of records, use the Find feature to search for data to edit. Be certain that you have located the correct record, because different records may contain similar information.
- When you click the name of the field to edit, Access selects its contents. Delete the field contents and enter the new data. Access saves changes to a field when you move to the next record.

ACCESS

TRY *it* OUT *A3-6*

1. The **ALL MEMBERS** form in the Members database should be open from the last Try it Out; or open **A3-6** from the Data CD, click **Forms** on the Objects list, and double-click on **All Members.**
2. Click the **Previous Record** button, if necessary, on the Navigation toolbar until you find the record containing information about Kenny Keith.
3. Click the **Address** field name.
4. Delete the field contents and enter: `54 Scott Lane.`

   Note: Now you will change Martha Doe's name to Martha Howard. You do not have the record number.
5. Click **Edit, Find.**
6. Enter `Doe` in the Find What box.
7. Select **ALL MEMBERS** in the Look In list.
8. If necessary, move the Find and Replace dialog box so you can see the ALL MEMBERS form.
9. Click **Find Next.**
10. Check to see that this is a record containing information about Martha Doe. If not, click **Find Next** again.
11. Click **Cancel** to close the Find and Replace dialog box.
12. Highlight Doe in the **Last Name** field if necessary, delete the contents and enter: `Howard.`

Delete Records Using a Form

- Often, updating a database involves deleting records. For example, in an employee database, a record might be deleted when an employee leaves the company.
- To delete a record using a form, locate and display the record and click the Delete Record button. Or, click Edit, Delete Record.

- There is no undo feature for this operation, and Access asks you to confirm that you want to delete the record. When you click Yes to confirm, Access permanently deletes the record.

TRY *it* OUT *A3-7*

Note: In this Try it Out you will delete Records 9 and 10.

1. The ALL MEMBERS form should still be displayed from the last Try it Out; or open **A3-7** from the Data CD, click **Forms** on the Objects list, and double-click on **ALL MEMBERS.**
2. Click the **Next Record** button twice, if necessary, on the Navigation toolbar to locate Record 10.
3. Click **Edit**, **Delete Record.**
4. Click **Yes** in answer to the question, "Are you sure you want to delete these records?" Access deletes the record.
5. Display Record 9.
6. Click the **Delete Record** button.

7. Click **Yes**.
8. Close the form.

Print Database Objects

- You can easily print datasheets, forms, or selected records of either object. To view how an object will print, click Print Preview. You can then select Setup from the Preview pane to change settings. To print a datasheet or a displayed form with the default print settings, click the Print button. To change print settings, click File, Page Setup.

- If you wish to print selected table records, use the record selector in Datasheet view and click File, Print and click Selected Record(s), as shown in Figure 3.10.

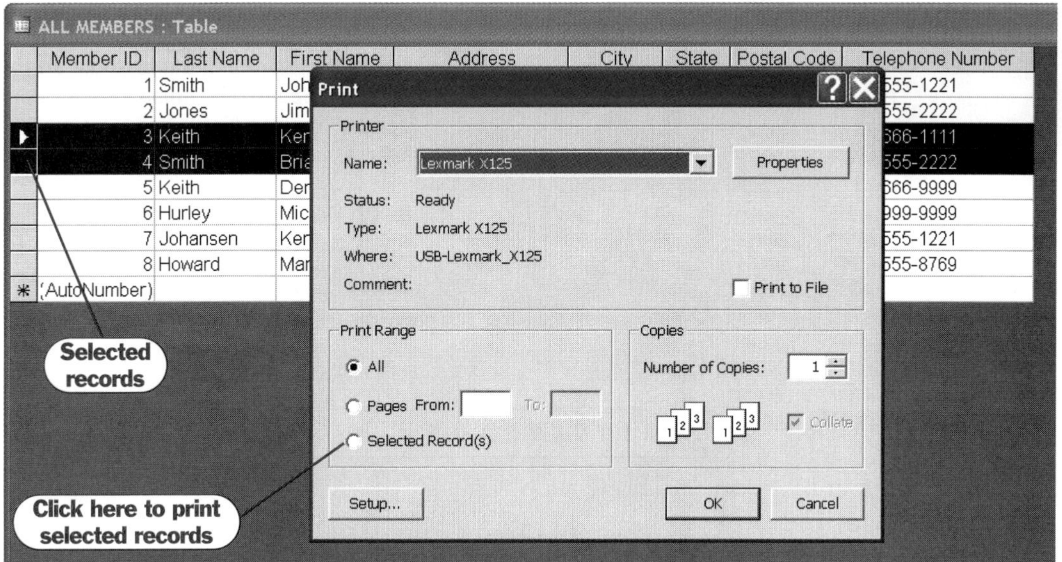

Figure 3.10 Printing selected records from a datasheet

TRY *it* OUT *A3-8*

Note: If you are unable to print, just preview each print operation.

1. You should be in the MEMBERS database window; or open **A3-8** from the Data CD.
2. Open the **ALL MEMBERS** Table object.
3. Click **Print Preview.**
4. Click **Setup** on the Print Preview toolbar and select the Page tab.
5. Click **Landscape** and **OK.**
6. Click the **Print** button on the Print Preview toolbar.
7. Open the **ALL MEMBERS** Forms object and select the last record, Martha Howard.
8. Click the **Print** button. 
9. Open the **ALL MEMBERS** table and select the record selectors for records 3 and 4.
10. Click **File, Print** and click the **Selected Record(s)** setting. Click **OK.**
11. Close the database.

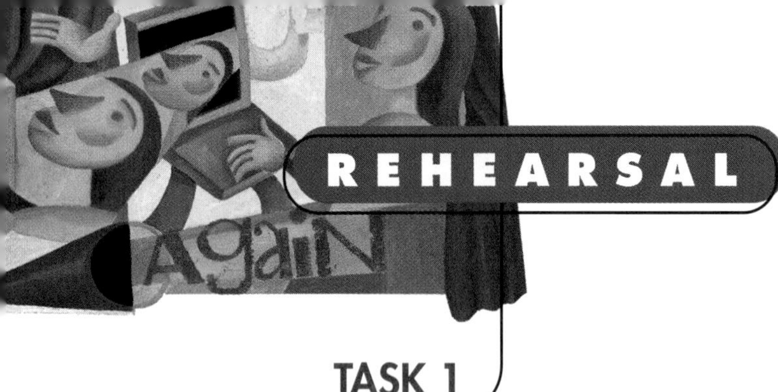

GOAL

To create a form that a real estate office can use to enter new home listings, to update current listings, and to delete listings that have sold

SETTING THE STAGE/WRAPUP

Database: **Four Corners Realty**
Table: **Listings**
Form: **Listings**

WHAT YOU NEED TO KNOW

- One of the key requirements in a business is that its databases be current and accurate. In a real estate office, agents are paid on commission only, which means they are paid only when a home is sold. It is, therefore, imperative that they know about new properties as soon as they come on the market and when properties are sold by other agents. They must also be constantly aware of any reductions in the price of a home.
- In this Rehearsal activity, you will create a form for the Four Corners Realty Company of Hollywood, Florida. The purpose of the form is to allow agents to enter new property listings, edit existing listings, and delete listings that have sold.

DIRECTIONS

1. Start Access.
2. Open the **Four Corners Realty** database file from the Data CD.

3. Open the **Listings** table.
4. Review the fields in the table.
5. Close the table.
6. Click **Forms.**
7. Double-click **Create form by using wizard.**
8. Click the double arrow to move all fields to the Selected Fields box, then select **Next.**
9. Click the **Columnar** layout, then select **Next.**
10. Click the **Ricepaper** style, then select **Next.**
11. Name the form: `Listings`. Click **Open the form to view or enter information,** then select **Finish.**
12. Click the **New Record** button on the Navigation toolbar.
13. Add the two new listings, as shown in the table on the facing page.
14. The price of ListingID 3 has been reduced to $175,000.
    a. Click the **Previous Record** button until ListingID 3 is displayed.
    b. Update the price to **$175,000.**
    c. Print a copy of the ListingID 3 form.
15. ListingID 1 has sold. Select, print, and then delete the record.
16. Close the form and close the database.

NEW LISTING FOR FOUR CORNERS REALTY		
FirstName	Margie	Katy
LastName	Kelley	Vargas
Address	101 East Avenue	21 Green Street
City	Hollywood	East Hollywood
Listing Agent	Olsen	Moran
Date Built	12/12/90	10/10/75
Price	175,000	100,000
Appraised Value	150,000	75,000
Property Description	3 bedroom 2 bath ranch, .25 acres	2 bedroom 1 bath cottage, .25 acres

ACCESS

Cues for Reference

Create a Form Using the Form Wizard

1. Double-click **Create form by using wizard.**
2. Double-click the fields you want. Click **Next.**
3. Choose a layout and click **Next.**
4. Choose a style and click **Next.**
5. Enter a title, select how to open the form, and click **Finish.**

Enter Records Using a Form

1. Click **Forms.**
2. Double-click the form title.
3. Click the **Add Record** button.
4. Press **Tab** to move from field to field.

Edit Records Using a Form

1. Click **Forms.**
2. Double-click the form title.
3. Locate the record.
4. Delete the field contents.
5. Enter new data.

Delete Records Using a Form

1. Click **Forms.**
2. Double-click the form title.
3. Locate the record.
4. Click **Edit.**
5. Click **Delete Record.**
6. Click **Yes.**

or

1. Click **Forms.**
2. Double-click the form title.
3. Locate the record.
4. Click the **Delete Record** button.
5. Click **Yes.**

Print Database Objects

1. Select the record, form, or datasheet.
2. Click the **Print** button.
   or
   Click the **Print Preview** button.
   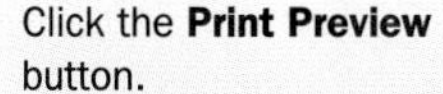

   Click **Setup** to change settings. Click **OK** then click **Print** to print from Preview screen.

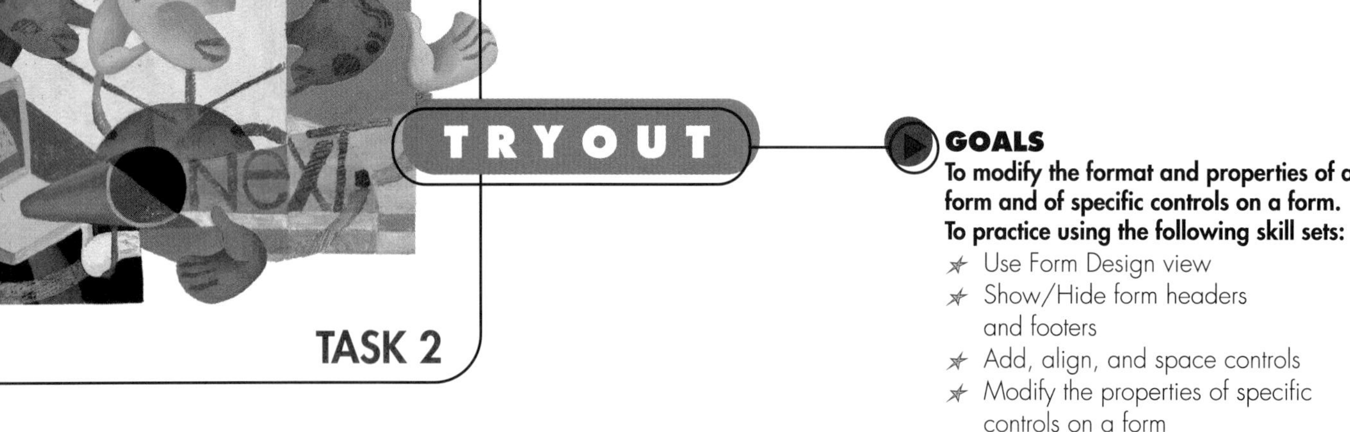

GOALS

To modify the format and properties of a form and of specific controls on a form.
To practice using the following skill sets:

- Use Form Design view
- Show/Hide form headers and footers
- Add, align, and space controls
- Modify the properties of specific controls on a form
- Modify the properties of a form
- Add a calculated control to a form

WHAT YOU NEED TO KNOW

Use Form Design View

- Form objects have three views: Form view, Design view, and Datasheet view. You learned about Form view and saw that records entered using the form were stored in the Datasheet view. However, you can also create or modify a form in Design view. To work in Design view, select the form and click View, Design View.
- In the Detail section of Design view you see *controls*, which are the objects that display or organize data on a form. Controls can be bound, unbound, or calculated. A *bound control* is connected to a field in a table. The text box controls, with an attached label, shown in Figure 3.11, are bound controls because they represent fields in the database. You will learn about unbound and calculated controls later in this lesson.

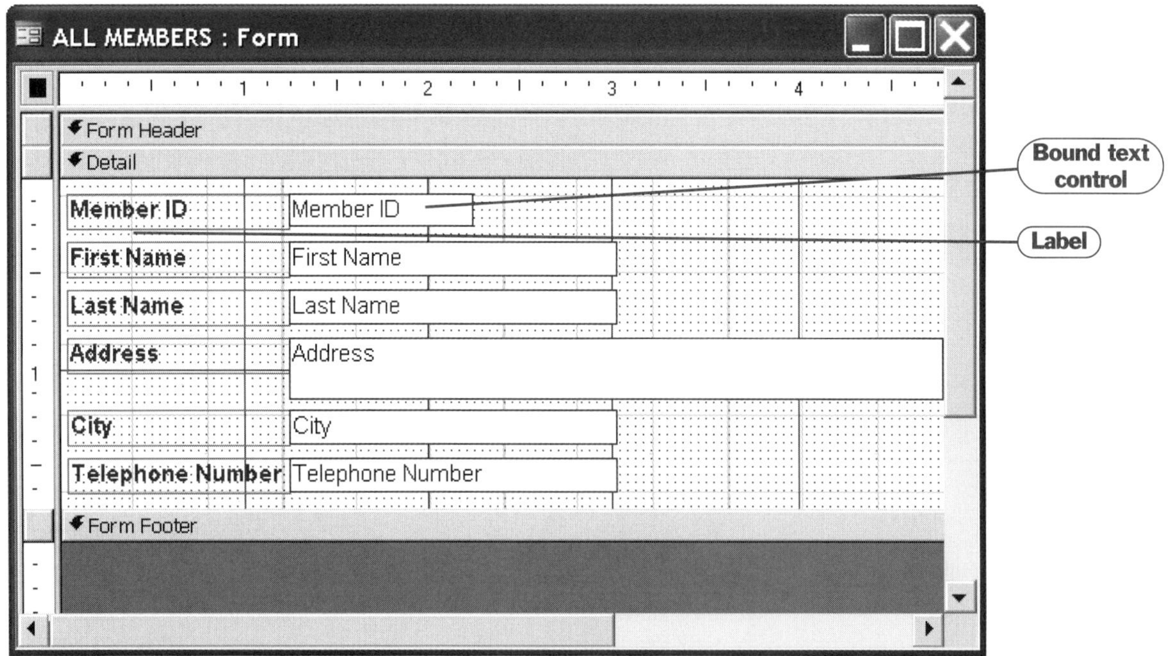

Figure 3.11 Use Form view—Design view

▶ Design view also displays the *Form Design toolbox*, which contains 18 objects to design a form, such as Text Box, Check Box, Toggle Button, Combo Box, List Box, and Command Button, as shown in Figure 3.12. You can click each tool and press the F1 key to display a description of each tool. When Access displays the description of a tool, the toolbox disappears. To display or hide the toolbox, click View, Toolbox.

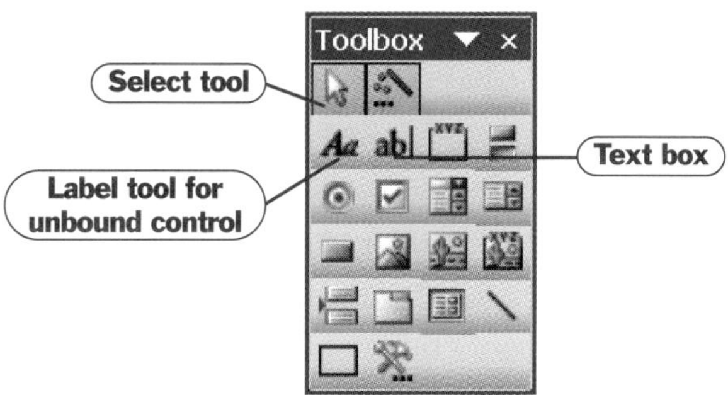

Figure 3.12 Use Form view—Form Design toolbox

1. Start Access.
2. Open the **Members2** database from the Data CD.
3. Click the **Forms** object.
4. Double-click **ALL MEMBERS.**
5. Click **View**.
6. Click **Design View**.
7. Notice how the fields appear in Design view.
8. Notice the toolbox. Click **View, Toolbox** if it is not displayed.
9. Place the mouse pointer over each tool to display what each tool does.
10. Click each tool, and press the **F1** key to display a description of each tool.
11. Press the **ESC** key to close each description and to redisplay the toolbox.
12. Click the **Select Objects** tool and do not close the form.

ACCESS

Show/Hide Headers and Footers

▶ A form has form and page header and footer sections, as shown in Figure 3.13. Click View, Form Header/Footer or View, Page Header/Footer to display or hide these sections.

▶ The *form header* displays information you want to show for every record, such as the form title. The header appears at the top of the screen in Form view and at the top of the first page when it is printed.

▶ The *form footer* displays information that you want to show for every record. It appears at the bottom of the screen in Form view and after the last detail section on the last page when it is printed.

▶ Page headers and page footers appear only on printed forms. A *page header* displays information you want at the top of every printed page. A *page footer* displays information you want at the bottom of every printed page.

- You can change the height of a form section by placing the mouse pointer on the bottom edge of the section. Drag the pointer up or down to the desired height. If you change the width of a section, the entire form is changed.

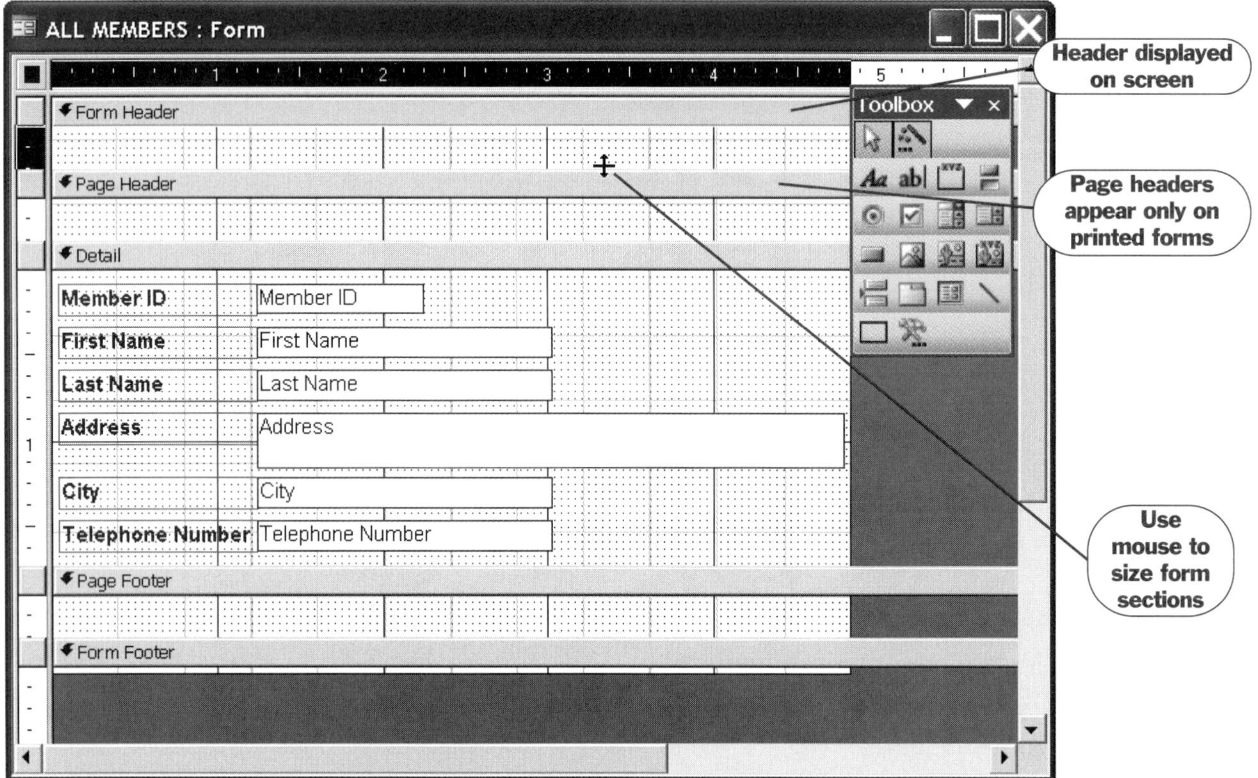

Figure 3.13 Use form sections—page header/footer

TRY *it* OUT *A3-10*

Note: The ALL MEMBERS form should be displayed in Design view.

1. Notice the location of the form header.
2. Notice that the detail section contains the fields of the form.
3. Notice the location of the form footer.
4. Click **View.**
5. Click **Page Header/Footer**.
6. Notice the location of the page header and footer.
7. Click **View, Page Header/Footer** to deselect and hide the section.
8. Place the mouse pointer on the bottom edge of the Form Header section.
9. Drag it down to expand the section to approximately ¾ of an inch.
10. Size the Form footer section in the same manner.
11. Do not close the form.

Add, Align, and Space Controls

Add a Label Control

- You may customize forms by adding a title or a date to every form. To accomplish this, add a label control to the header or footer section of a form in Form Design view. A *label control* displays a title or caption and is an *unbound* control, which is not connected to a data source. Unbound controls are used to display information such as text, lines, rectangles, and pictures.
- To add a label control, click the Label tool in the Form Design toolbox. Click the location where you want the upper-left corner of the control to be. A small box appears, as shown in Figure 3.14. When you enter the information you want to display, the box expands as necessary. Change to Form view to see the label.

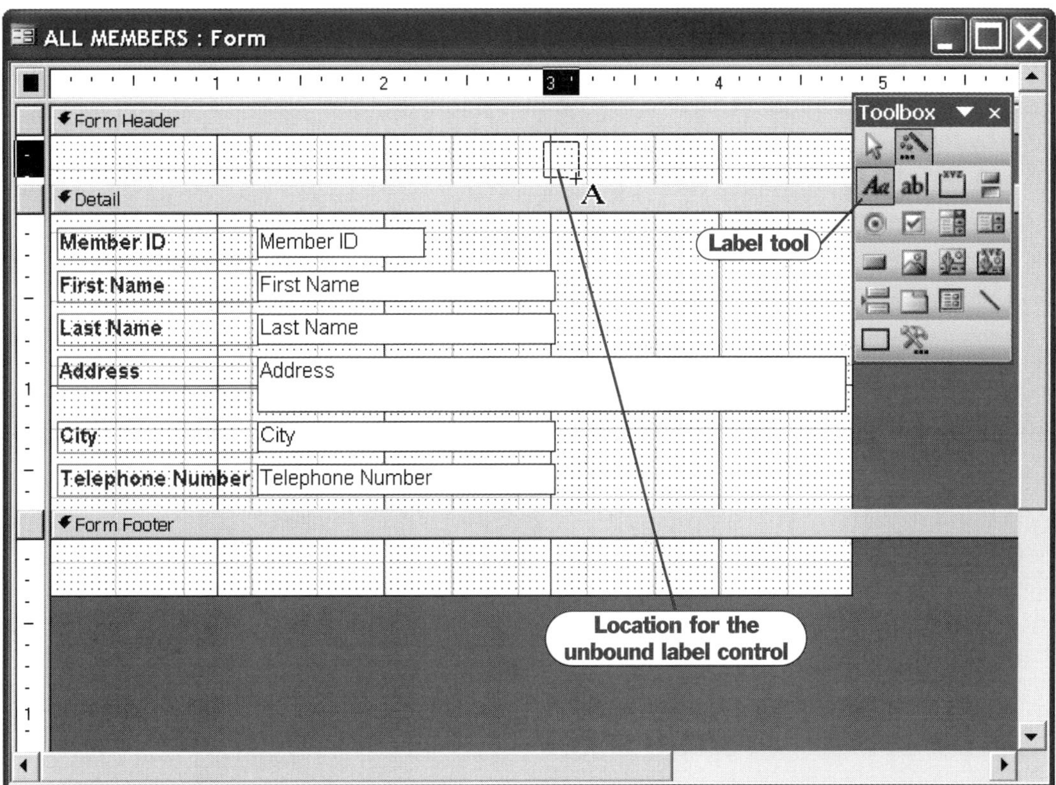

Figure 3.14 Add a label control

TRY it OUT *A3-11*

Note: You will add a label containing the date to the Form Header section and a label containing the name of the table to the Footer section.

1. The ALL MEMBERS form should be displayed in Design view, or open **A3-11** from the Data CD and go to the form in Design view.
2. Click the **Label** tool on the Form Design toolbox.
3. In the Form Header section, click the location where you want the upper left-hand corner of the control to be.
4. Enter today's date in the small box.

Continued on next page

TRY it OUT *A3-11 Continued*

5. Click the **Label** tool on the Form Design toolbox.
6. In the Form Footer section, click the location where you want the upper left-hand corner of the control to be.
7. Enter **ALL MEMBERS.**
8. Click **Form View.**
9. Notice that the Form Header and Footer sections are displayed.
10. Scroll through the records. Notice that the Form Header and Footer appear on every form.
11. Switch to Design view.

Align and Space Controls

- When you select a control in Design view, handles appear, as shown in Figure 3.15, and a mouse pointer in the shape of a hand appears. When the pointer changes to an open hand, you can move the control by moving the mouse and releasing the button at the correct position. Use the grid lines in Design view for manual placement of a control.
- Or, if you wish to align a control to the others in a column, select all the controls using the Select tool, click Format, Align, then select the desired alignment setting, as shown in Figure 3.15.

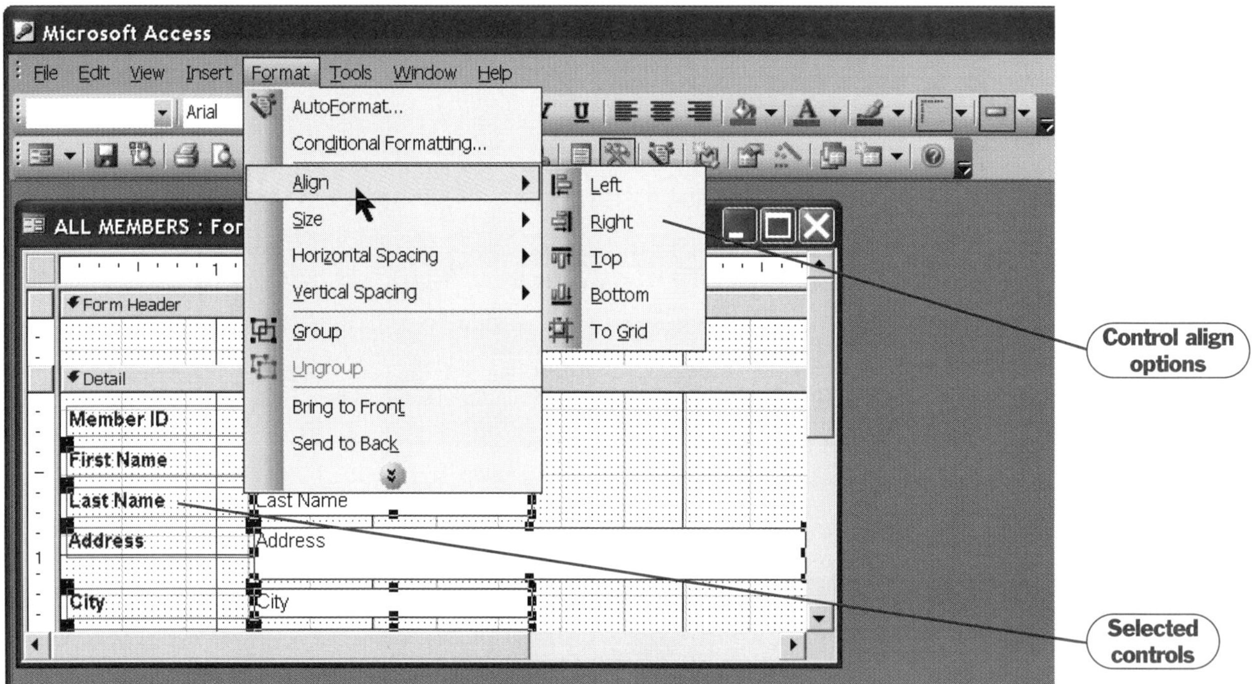

Figure 3.15 Format, Align submenu

- Space controls by selecting the controls and then clicking Format, Vertical Spacing or Horizontal Spacing, and then selecting the spacing settings, as shown in Figure 3.16. You can also select controls by clicking the controls while holding down the Shift key.

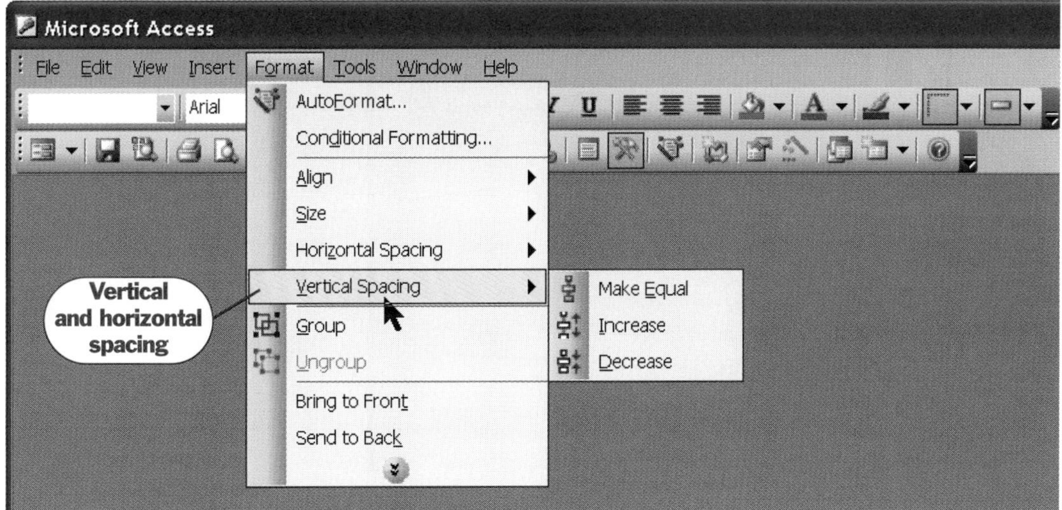

Figure 3.16 Format, Vertical Spacing submenu

TRY *it* OUT *A3-12*

Note: You will align and space the label controls added in the previous TryitOut.

1. The ALL MEMBERS form should be displayed in Design view, or open **A3-12** from the Data CD and go to the form in Design view.
2. Click the **Select** tool button from the toolbar and select all the controls on the form. (A box will be drawn around the controls.)
3. Click **Format, Align, Left.** Click a blank area to deselect the controls.
4. Select the Date label control in the Form header. Note the selection handles.
5. Drag the selected label control with the open hand pointer so that it is in line with the data controls, at approximately 1 ¼".
6. Repeat this with the label control in the Form footer.
7. Hold down the Shift key and select all the controls.
8. Click **Format, Horizontal Spacing, Make Equal.**
9. Switch to Form view to view the changes.
10. Save the form design.
11. Switch to Form Design view.

ACCESS

Modify the Properties of Specific Controls on a Form

- Every control on a form has properties. These properties determine a control's format, appearance, and behavior. They also detail the characteristics of the text or data contained in the control.
- You modify the properties of a control in Design view by making changes to its property sheet. Click the control you want to change. Click View, Properties or right-click the control and click Properties. A property sheet appears, as shown in Figure 3.17. You can change a label by entering the new caption on the Format property sheet. Changes appear in Design, Form, and Datasheet views. To change the width of a control, double-click Width, delete the existing value, and enter the new value.
- Close the property sheet to view the change.

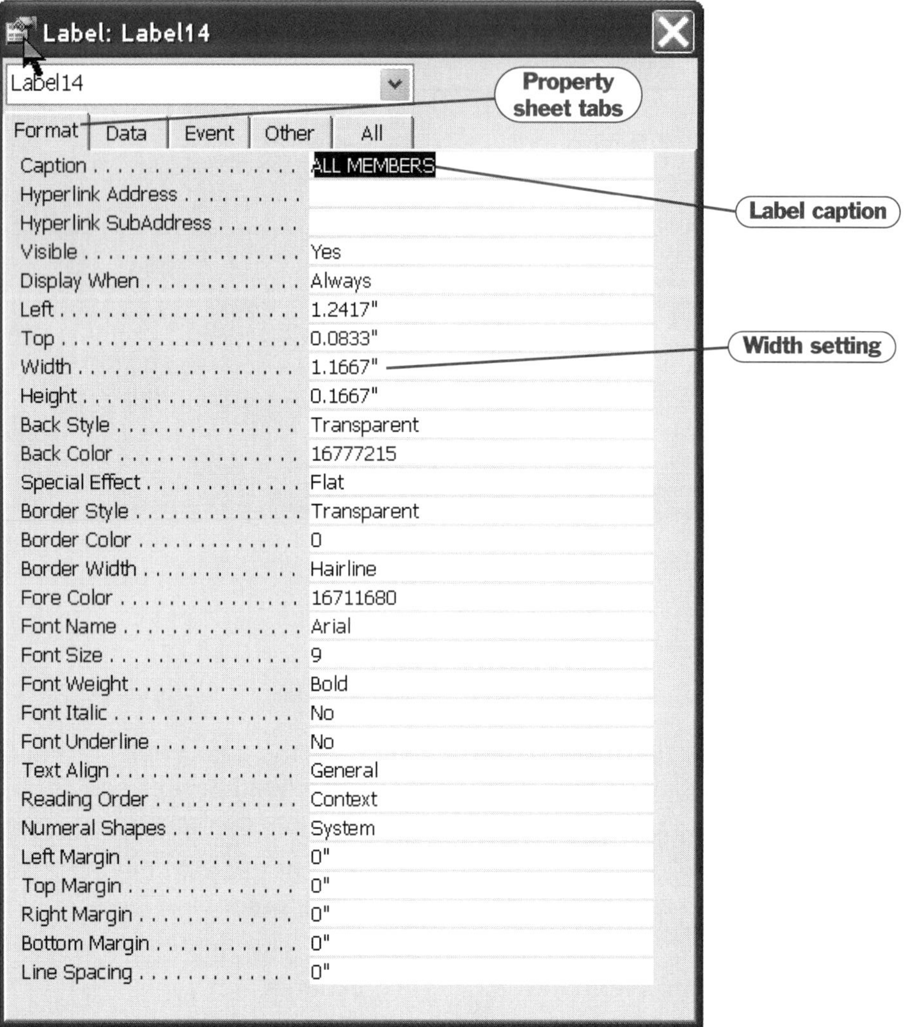

Figure 3.17 Modify properties of controls on a form

TRY *it* OUT *A3-13*

Note: You will change a caption on a label control and change the width of the Address control.

1. The ALL MEMBERS form should be displayed in Design view, or open **A3-13** from the Data CD and go to the form in Design view.
2. Right-click the label of the label control in the Form Footer. Click **Properties.**
3. Click the **Format** tab.
4. Click **Caption**, if necessary.
5. Delete the ALL MEMBERS caption and enter **`CLUB MEMBERS.`**
6. Close the property sheet.
7. Check the new label in Design view and Form view.
8. Click the bound control for Address (on the right).
9. Click **View, Properties.**
10. Click **Format** tab and double-click **Width**.
11. Change the width to 3".
12. Close the property sheet and notice the size of the control.
13. Close the form and save your changes.

Modifying the Properties of a Form

- We have already set control properties, but the form itself has properties that define the form's characteristics. Use the *form selector,* which is the box where the rulers meet in a form in Design view, to view the properties of a form, as shown in Figure 3.18.

Figure 3.18 Form selector

- Double-click the form selector and the form's property sheet appears, as shown in Figure 3.19. The properties fall into four categories: Format, Data, Event, and Other; to view all the properties, click All. Use the scroll bar on the right side of the property window to view property sheet options. Double-click the name of the property to select and then change the setting. When you make a change to the form, you do not make a change to the underlying data source or table.

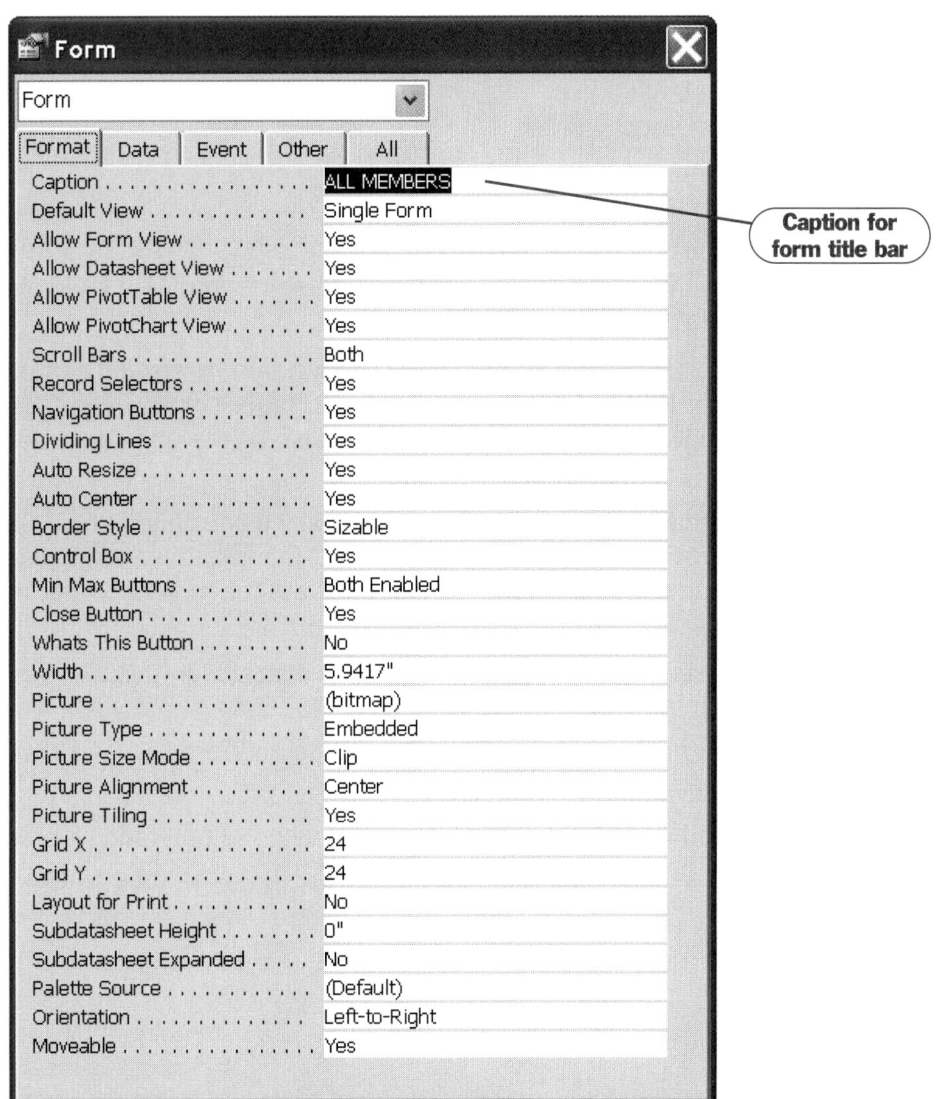

Figure 3.19 Modify the properties of a form

TRY *it* OUT *A3-14*

1. The **ALL MEMBERS** form should be displayed in Form view, or open **A3-14** from the Data CD and open the form.
2. Click **Design View**.
3. Double-click the form selector. Notice the five tabs of the Form property sheet.
4. Click each tab and scroll through the property settings.
5. Click **Format** and double-click **Caption**.
6. Enter: `NEW ALL MEMBERS.`
7. Close the property sheet.
8. Click **View, Form View**.
9. Notice that the caption in the title bar of the form has changed to: NEW ALL MEMBERS.
10. Click the **Design View** button. Notice that the caption has not been changed in Design view. 
11. Double-click the form selector.
12. Click **Format** and double-click **Caption**.
13. Enter: `ALL MEMBERS.`
14. Close the property sheet.
15. Close the database.

Use a Calculated Control in a Form

- There are times when you want to display a calculated value on a form. For example, a retail store may need to know the value of merchandise on order.
- A *calculated control* uses an expression as its source of data. An expression can use data from a field in an underlying table or from another control on the form. For example, you can create a calculated control that multiplies the price of the merchandise by the units on order and displays the value of the outstanding orders.
- A *text box* is the most common type of control used to display a calculated value. To add a text box, click the Text Box tool in the Form Design toolbox. To make this field a calculated field, modify the Control Source property, found under the Data tab in field properties, as shown in Figure 3.20. 
- In a calculated control, preface each expression with the = operator. In this expression: =[UnitsOnOrder]*[UnitPrice].
  - [UnitsOnOrder] and [UnitPrice] represent the values in the controls.
  - * is the multiplication operator.
  - UnitsOnOrder is multiplied by UnitPrice to calculate the value of outstanding orders.
- The formula appears in a calculated control in Design view. Click Form View to see the contents of calculated controls.

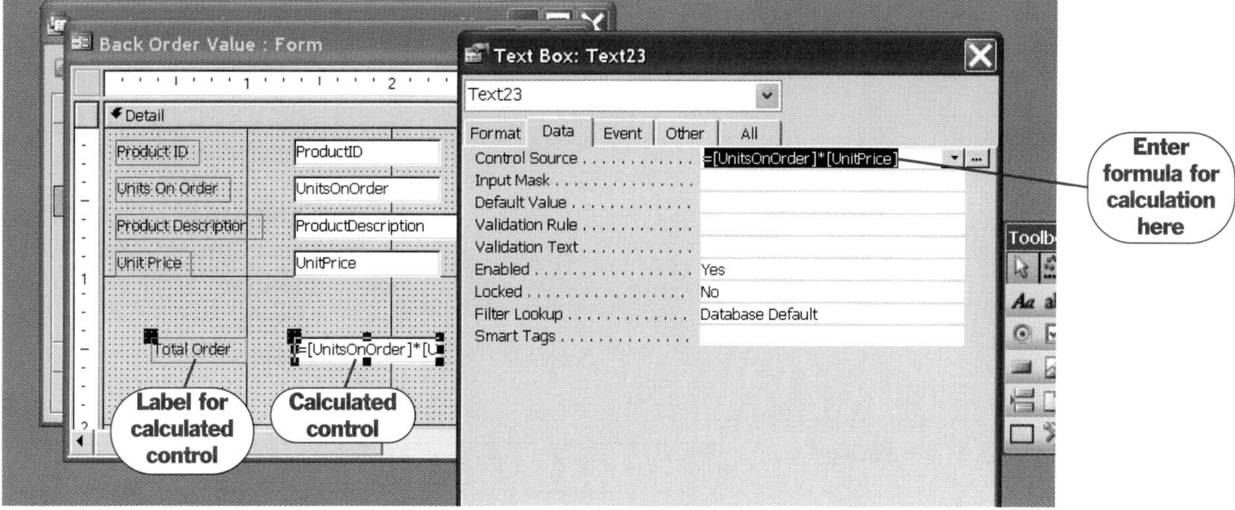

Figure 3.20 Use a calculated control in forms—Design view

TRY *it* OUT *A3-15*

1. Open the **Product** database from the Data CD.
2. Click the **Forms** object.
3. Double-click **Back Order Value.**
4. Click the **Design View** button on the toolbar.

Note: If the Form Design toolbox does not appear, click View, Toolbox.

5. Click the **Text Box** tool in the Form Design toolbox.
6. Click a location under the last field.
7. The text box appears with a label Access assigns.
8. Click the text box.
9. Click **View, Properties.**
10. Click **Data** and **Control Source.**
    a. Enter: `=[UnitsOnOrder]*[UnitPrice]` in the Control Source Property box.
11. Click **Format** and change the number format to **Currency.**
12. Close the property sheet.
13. Right-click the Label box and select **Properties.**
14. Change the Caption property to read: `Total Order.`
15. Close the property sheet.
16. Click the **Form View** button.

17. Use the navigation controls to view each form and the value in the calculated control.
18. Save and close the form and the database.

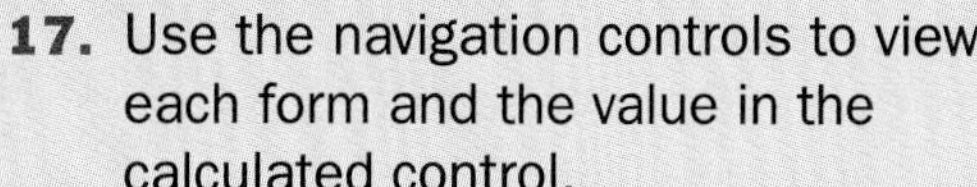

ACCESS

TASK 2

GOAL

To modify the format and properties of a form and of specific controls on a form. You will add a form header and footer and a calculated control to the form

SETTING THE STAGE/WRAPUP

Database: Four Corners Realty2
Table: Listings
Forms: Listings
Listings1

WHAT YOU NEED TO KNOW

- In the last Rehearsal, you created the listings form for the Four Corners Realty Company of Hollywood, Florida. The form is used to enter new property listings, edit existing listings, and delete listings that have sold, as shown on the facing page.
- In this Rehearsal activity, you will modify that form as follows:
  - You will add a date to the header so that the date that you updated the data will appear in the form. This will tell the agents how current the information is.
  - You will also add the name of the company in the form footer.
  - The agents have requested that you display the annual taxes on the form for each house. To meet this requirement, you will add a calculated control to the form. Taxes in the three towns that Four Corners Realty covers are based on the appraised value of the houses in the towns. The tax rate for the three towns is .02% of the Appraised Value.

DIRECTIONS

1. Start Access.
2. Open the **Four Corners Realty2** database file from the Data CD. 
3. Open the Listings form in Design view.
4. Resize the Form Header section so that it is approximately one inch high.
5. Display the toolbox, if necessary, and click the **Label** tool in the Form Design toolbox.
6. Select a location and enter today's date in the Form Header section.
7. Resize the Form Footer section to approximately one inch high.
8. Click the **Label** tool in the Form Design toolbox.
9. In the Form Footer section, place a label for the name of the company. Enter: `Four Corners Realty Company of Hollywood, Florida.`
10. View the form and notice the top and bottom sections of the form.
11. In Design view, click the **Text Box** tool in the Form Design toolbox.
12. Click in a location where you want to place a calculated control for the taxes.
13. Click **View, Properties,** and click the **Data** tab.
14. In the Control Source property box enter: `=[Appraised Value]*.02.`
15. On the **Format** tab, in the Format property, set the format to **Currency.** Modify the label caption properties to read: `Tax.`

Continued on next page

16. To improve the readability of the labels and the forms, change the width of the labels and the width of the form by dragging to size. Compare your design to that in Illustration A below.
17. Many Florida real estate clients are from other countries; therefore, the company wishes to change their form format. Use the Form selector to select the Form.
18. Click **Format, AutoFormat** and change the form format to International.
19. Switch to Form View. Compare your form to that in Illustration B.
20. Use the Navigation controls to view each record and the value in the calculated control.
21. Save the form as **Listings1.**
22. Print a copy of the form for Listing ID 2. Change the Print Setup to **Landscape** mode.
23. Close the form and close the database.

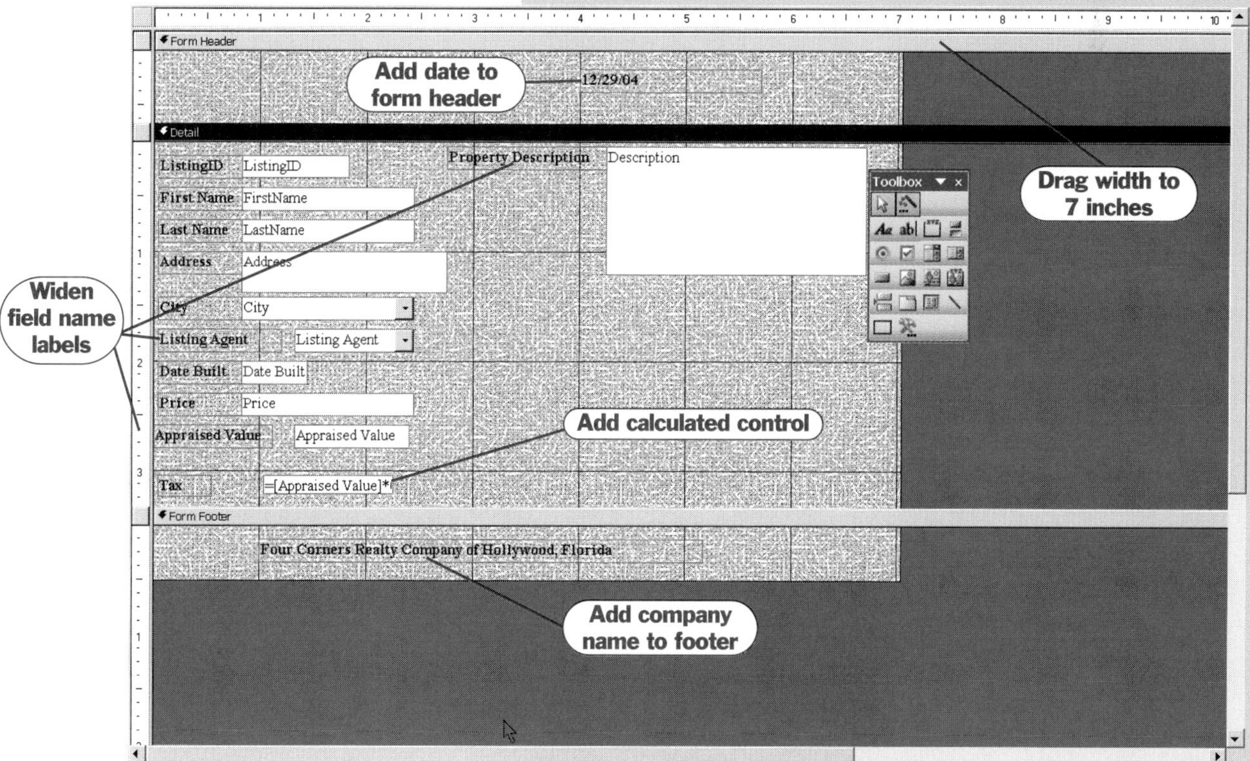

Illustration A

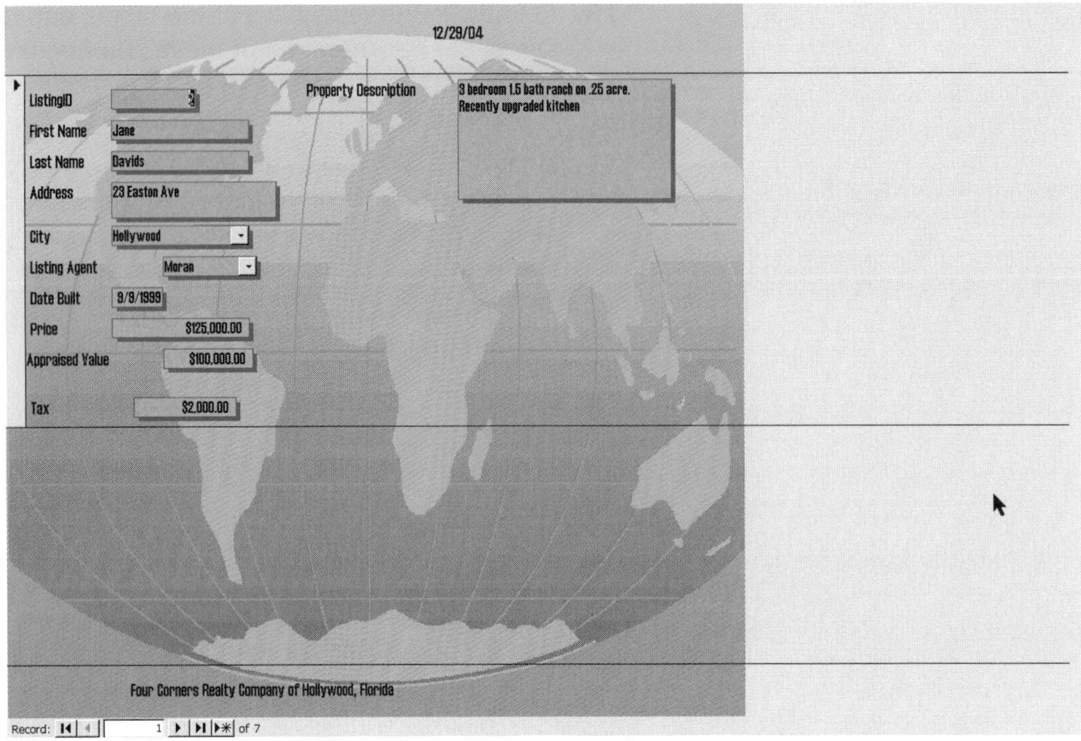

Illustration B

Cues for Reference

Use Design View

1. Click **Forms.**
2. Double-click the name of the form you want.
3. Click **Design View.**

Use Datasheet View

1. Click **Forms.**
2. Double-click the name of the form you want.
3. Click **Datasheet View.**

Change the Size of Form Sections

1. Click **Design View.**
2. Place mouse pointer on edge of section.
3. Drag the pointer.

   or

- Double-click **section selector.**
- Click **Format Tab**, set **Height**.

Add a Label Control

1. Click **Design View.**
2. Click the **Label** tool in the Form Design toolbox.
3. Click the location where you want to place the upper-left corner of the control.
4. Enter the information.

Modify the Properties of a Form

1. Select the form.
2. Click **Design View.**
3. Double-click **form selector.**

Modify the Properties of Controls

1. Right-click the **control.**
2. Click **Properties.**

Use a Calculated Control in a Form

1. Click **Design View.**
2. Click the **Text Box** tool in the Form Design toolbox.
3. Click the location you want.
4. Click the **Text Box** control.
5. Click **View, Properties.**
6. Click **Data.**
7. Click **Control Source.**
8. Enter the expression.

Change the Label Caption of a Text Box

1. Click **Design View.**
2. Right-click the **Label.**
3. Click **Properties.**
4. Click the **Format** tab.
5. Double-click **Caption.**
6. Replace the contents of the property box.

Change Form Format

1. Click the Form selector.
2. Click **Format, AutoFormat.**
3. Select the desired format.

SETTING THE STAGE/WRAPUP
Database: Green Brothers Gardening
Table: Homeowners
Form: Homeowners

WHAT YOU NEED TO KNOW

Act I

You work for Green Brothers Gardening, a full-service landscape contractor. There are two locations in Fairfax, VA.

The company is interested in keeping accurate information on each of their homeowner clients. You have been asked to build a form they can use to enter data as well as to update the homeowner database.

ACCESS

Follow these guidelines:

- The data is contained in the **Green Brothers Gardening** database in the **Homeowners** table on the Data CD. 
- All the fields in the table must be included in the form.
- Calvin Green, the president and CEO, prefers a justified layout.
- You should choose a style that reflects the company's business.
- Name the form: `Homeowners.`
- Add the following information to the table:

Customer ID	12	34
Contact First Name	James	Michael
Contact Last Name	Ericson	Sullivan
Billing Address	23 Stone Hill Drive	73 Kingsley Road
City	Fairfax	Fairfax
Zip Code	22030	22030
Phone Number	703-555-4324	703-555-6342
Service Description	Lawn Maintenance	Pruning
Monthly Rate	$200	$120

- Make the following changes to the data:
  - Change Customer ID 1 to a monthly rate of: $250.
  - Change David Cotter's service to Pruning and change his monthly rate to: $200.
  - Change the first name at 56 Renwick Road to: Alexia.

Act II

The homeowner form has been working very well. You have been asked to modify the form to include the name of the company, the main address, the phone, fax, and e-mail address on every form.

The main nursery and office are located at 32 Braddock Road, Fairfax, VA 22030. The phone number is 703-555-0005, the fax is 703-555-0015, and the e-mail is: gbg@network.com. Use separate labels as illustrated below.

Ralph Green, the chief financial officer, has requested that you add the yearly rate to the form.

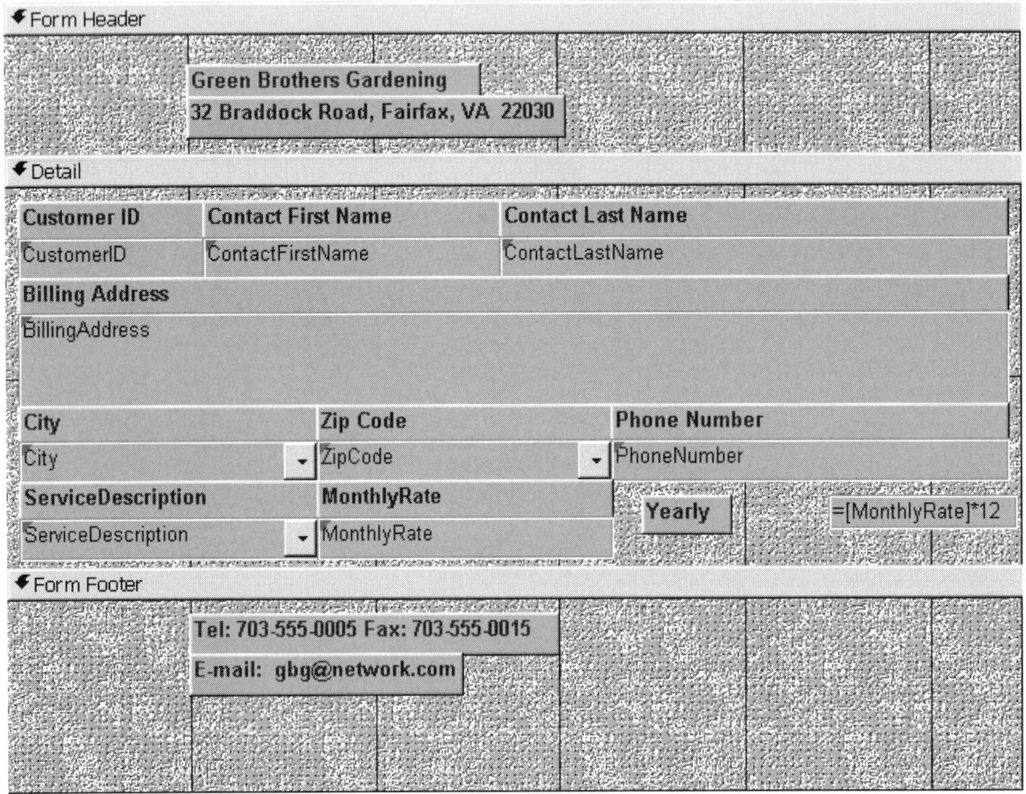

Follow these guidelines:

- Make the form header and footer at least one inch high.
- Add the company name and address to the form header.
- Add the company phone number, fax number, and e-mail address to the form footer.
- Add a calculated control to the form that multiples the monthly rates by 12 to display a yearly rate. Format the yearly rate for currency.
- Change the label name to: Yearly.
- The company received a call from David Cotter, who wants a record of his change in service. Print a copy of his form.
- Save and close the database.

1
2
3

LESSON 4

Getting Information

In this lesson, you will learn how to obtain the information you need from a database. You will learn more about finding and sorting records, and you will learn to create and edit queries. You will also learn to establish table relationships and enforce referential integrity.

Upon completion of this lesson, you should have mastered the following skill sets:

- Find and replace a record
- Sort records in a datasheet
- Apply and remove filters
  - Filter datasheets by form
  - Filter datasheets by selection
- Create a query object
- Create select queries using the Simple Query Wizard
- Create select queries with calculations
- Create crosstab, unmatched, and duplicate queries
- Modify queries in Design view
- Use aggregate functions
- Add a calculated field to queries in Query Design view
- Format query results
- Create and modify a one-to-many relationship
- Enforce referential integrity in a one-to-many relationship
- Create a multi-table query

Terms

Software-related

Match box
Match case
Fields as Formatted
Find and Replace
Sort
Filters
Filter By Form
Filter By Selection
Query
Query wizards
Simple Query wizard
Select query
Crosstab query
Duplicates query
Unmatched query
Query Design view
Criteria
Specify criteria
Aggregate functions
Query design grid
Total row
Calculated field
Relationships
One-to-many relationship
Foreign key
Referential integrity
Multi-table select query

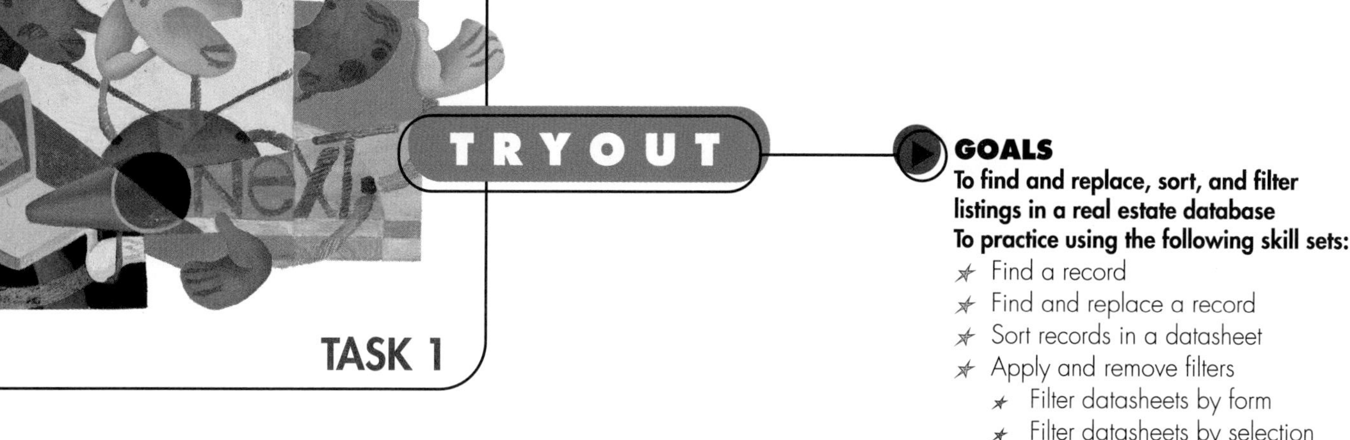

GOALS

To find and replace, sort, and filter listings in a real estate database

To practice using the following skill sets:

- Find a record
- Find and replace a record
- Sort records in a datasheet
- Apply and remove filters
  - Filter datasheets by form
  - Filter datasheets by selection

WHAT YOU NEED TO KNOW

Find a Record

- You are familiar with the Find and Replace dialog box from the last lesson; you used it to search a datasheet to locate data. You can also use this feature to search for contents of specific fields or to speed up a search.
- To search for data in a specific field, with a datasheet displayed, click the column representing the field to search. Click Edit, Find or click the Find button to open the Find and Replace dialog box, as shown in Figure 4.1.

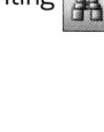

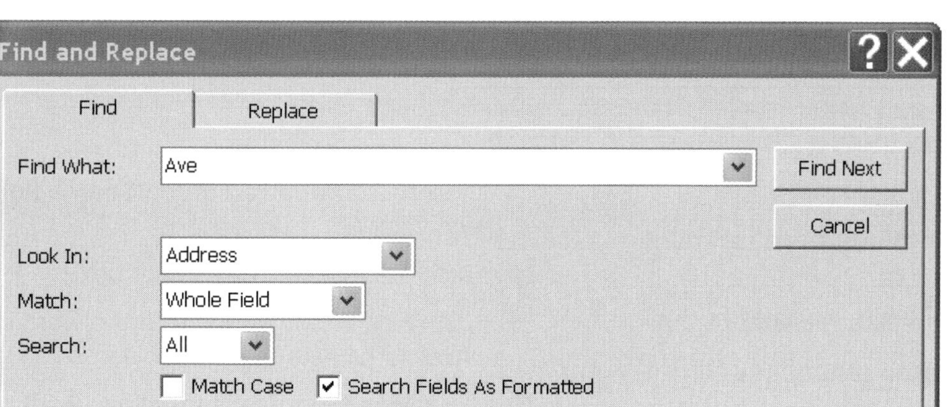

Figure 4.1 Find and Replace dialog box—Find tab

- In the Find tab, enter the data or criteria for the search in the Find What box. The selected column appears in the Look In box. Decide if you want an exact match, or if you want the field to include the data. Click the down arrow in the *Match box* to choose to match any part of the field, the whole field, or the start of the field, as shown in Figure 4.2. Click the down arrow in the Search box to choose to search Up, Down, or All of the records.

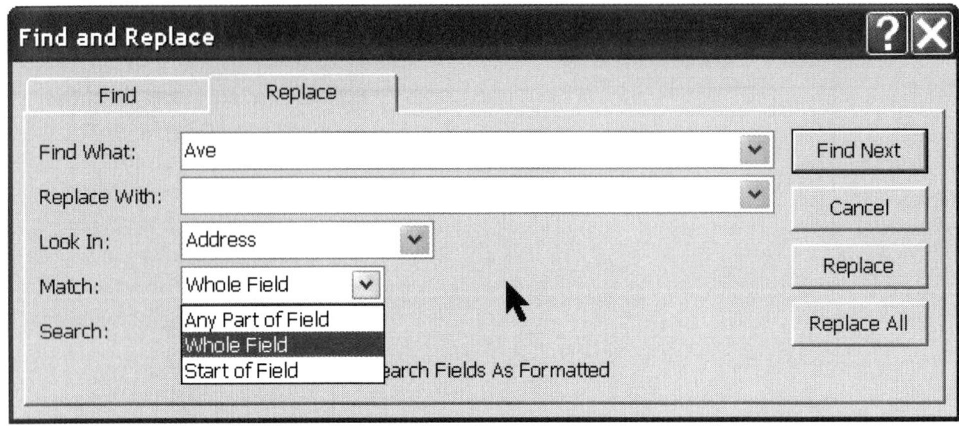

Figure 4.2 Find and Replace dialog box—Match

- Click *Match Case* to match uppercase and lowercase entries; if Match Case is not selected, Find ignores case. Click *Search Fields As Formatted* if the data format in the view is different from the defined format.
- Click Find Next to start the search. Access displays the first record that meets your criteria and selects the data. Click Find Next to go to the next record meeting your criteria. Access displays a message that it is finished searching when no more records meet your criteria. Click Cancel to close the Find and Replace dialog box.

TRY *it* OUT *A4-1*

1. Start Access.
2. Open the **MEMBERS** database from the Data CD.
3. Double-click the **ALL MEMBERS** table.
4. Click the **Address** column to select it.
5. Click **Edit, Find.**
6. Enter `Ave` in the Find What box. Notice that "Address" is displayed in the Look In box.
7. Click the down arrow of the **Match** box.
8. Click **Any Part of Field.**
9. Click the down arrow of the **Search** box and click **All,** if necessary.
10. Click the **Match Case** check box.
11. Click **Find Next.** Notice that the word "Ave" is selected in the table.
12. Click **Find Next.** Notice that the word "Ave" is selected.
13. Click **Find Next.** Notice that Access displays a message that the search is complete.
14. Click **OK.**
15. Click **Cancel.** Do not close the datasheet.

Find and Replace a Record

- Sometimes you need to update field contents in many records. For example, the telephone company may decide to change an area code. This means that you need to find each record containing a field with that area code and update it. There are also times when you need to replace some, but not all, of the information. To assist in these situations, Access provides a *Find and Replace* feature.

- Click Edit, Replace to open the Find and Replace dialog box on the Replace tab, as shown in Figure 4.3. Within the Replace tab are many of the same features found in the Find tab. However, in this tab you enter information in both the Find What box and the Replace With box.

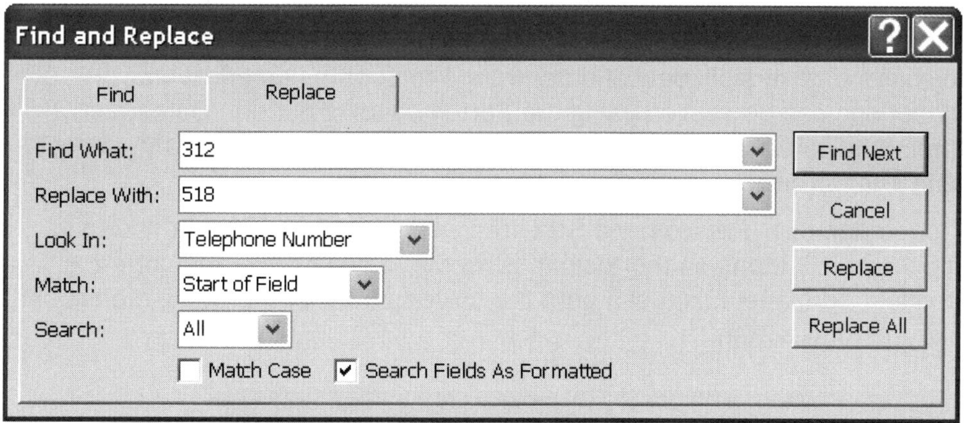

Figure 4.3 Find and Replace dialog box—Replace tab

- After you select your criteria, you have three options: Find Next, Replace, and Replace All. Click Find Next to go to the next occurrence. Click Replace to replace one occurrence at a time. Click Replace All to change all occurrences automatically. Access will ask you to confirm all replacement choices because there is no Undo feature.

ACCESS

TRY *it* OUT *A4-2*

*Note: The **ALL MEMBERS** table should be open from the last exercise.*

1. Click the **Telephone Number** column to select it.
2. Click the **Find** button.
3. Click the **Replace** tab in the Find and Replace dialog box.
4. Enter `312` in the Find What box. Notice that **Telephone Number** appears in the Look In box.
5. Enter `518` in the Replace With box.
6. Click the list arrow of the **Match** box and click **Start of Field.**
7. Click the list arrow of the Search box and click **All,** if necessary.
8. Click the **Match Case** check box.
9. Click **Replace.** Notice that Access replaces the first instance.
10. Click **Replace All.** Access will ask you to confirm replacements.
11. Click **Yes.**
12. Click **Cancel**.
13. Do not close the ALL MEMBERS table.

Sort Records in a Datasheet

- You often enter records into a datasheet in random order. There are times when you need to sort or rearrange the sequence in which records are displayed. This might be the case, for example, if you were asked to present a membership list in alphabetical order.

- Sorting records is also useful when you need to arrange data into groups. For example, you might want to group the records of all the people who live in a specific town.
- Access provides a *Sort* feature with which you can sort a column in a table in ascending or descending order. This feature is available in Form or Datasheet view, but you can see all the sorted records in Datasheet view.
- Ascending order displays data in alphabetical order from A to Z, or in numerical order from lowest to highest and can be applied using the Sort Ascending button. Dates and times are sorted from earliest to latest in ascending order. Descending order is the opposite of ascending order and it is applied using the Sort Descending button.
- Click the column to reorder. Click Records and Sort. The Sort options appear, as shown in Figure 4.4. Or, click the sort buttons on the toolbar. Save the table to make the sorted version of the datasheet permanent. You can print the sorted datasheet by using the File, Print menu commands or the Print button.

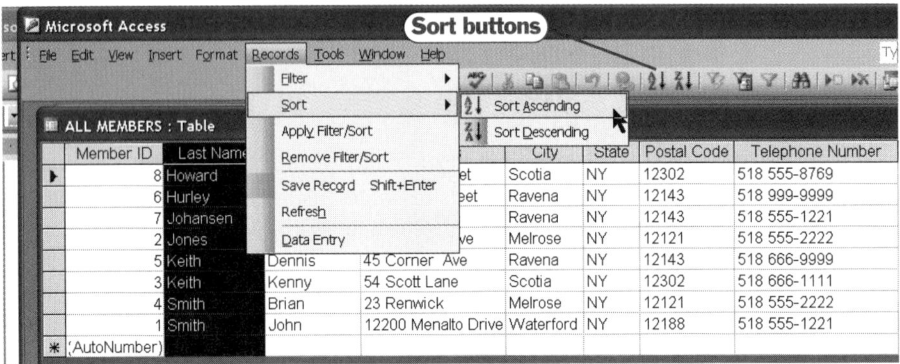

Figure 4.4 Sort records in a datasheet

TRY*it*OUT *A4-3*

1. The ALL MEMBERS table should be displayed, or open **A4-3** and open the **ALL MEMBERS** table. 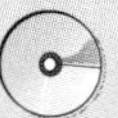
2. Click the **Last Name** column to select it.
3. Click **Records, Sort,** and **Sort Ascending.**
4. Notice that the Last Name column is now in alphabetical order.
5. Click the **Print** button to print the datasheet. 
6. Click the **City** column to select it.
7. Click the **Sort Descending** button. 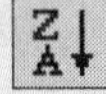
8. Notice that the cities are grouped in reverse alphabetical order.
9. Notice the Last Name column is no longer in alphabetical order. Do not close the table.

Apply and Remove Filters

- Occasionally, you want to view only records that satisfy a specific set of conditions. For example, you may be asked to provide a list of members from two towns. Access provides *filters,* which isolate records meeting a certain set of conditions. These filtering features are available in Form and Datasheet views. Click Records and click Filter to select the appropriate filter, as shown in Figure 4.5.

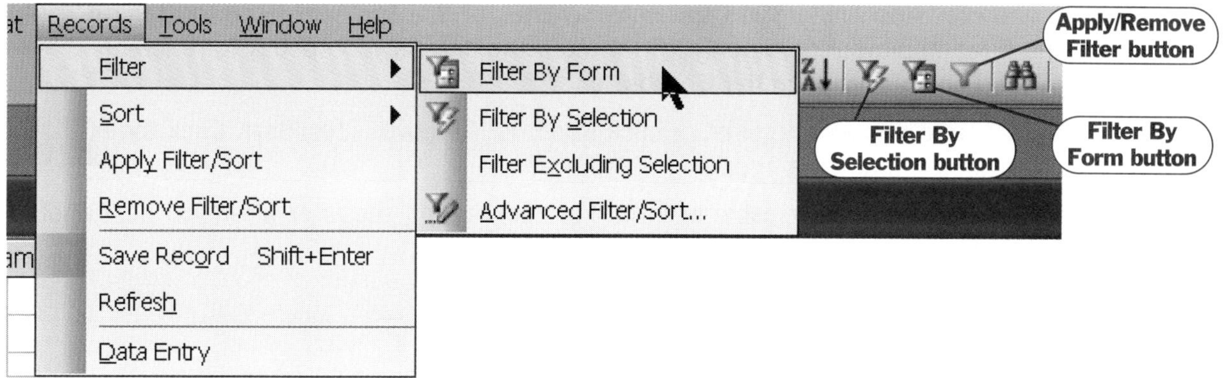

Figure 4.5 Apply and remove filters

▶ You can also use buttons on the Standard toolbar to apply filters. You will learn about Filter By Form and Filter By Selection buttons in this lesson.

TRY*it*OUT *A4-4*

1. The ALL MEMBERS table should be displayed from the last Try*it*Out or open **A4-4** from the Data CD and open the **ALL MEMBERS** table in Table objects.
2. Click **Records** on the menu bar.
3. Click **Filter.**
4. Notice the Filter options. Press Esc twice.
5. Locate the Filter By Form button on the toolbar.
6. Locate the Filter By Selection button on the toolbar. Do not close the table.

ACCESS

Filter Datasheets by Form

▶ *Filter By Form* is a method that allows you to use a sample of the form or datasheet to indicate your selection criteria. In a datasheet or form, click Filter, Filter By Form or click the Filter By Form button to use this feature. A version of the datasheet or form you are working with appears, as shown in Figure 4.6.

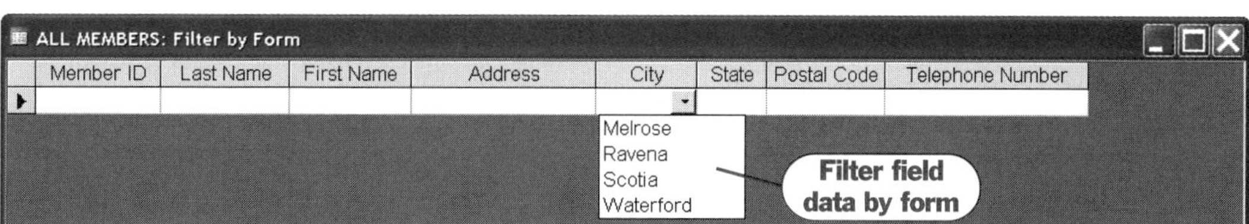

Figure 4.6 Filter datasheets by form

▶ Click the down arrow of each field to see the list you may use to filter the datasheet. Click on the value, or enter it into the field, to select the filtering criteria. To specify multiple values, click the Or tab at the bottom of the window and enter another criteria. You can specify values for more than one field.

- Click Records and click Apply Filter/Sort to apply the filter, or use the Apply Filter button on the toolbar. The filter displays records only if they meet the criteria you specify for each of those fields in the Look for tab or in the Or tabs.

- Click the Filter button to remove the filter, or click Records, Remove Filter/Sort. Click the Filter By Form button to modify the filter.

- The filter is saved when you save a table or form. You can reapply the filter when you next open the object. The datasheet and underlying data are not changed.

TRY it OUT *A4-5*

1. The ALL MEMBERS table should be displayed, or open **A4-5** from the Data CD and open the **ALL MEMBERS** table.
2. Click **Records, Filter,** and **Filter By Form.**
3. Click the **City** field.
4. Click the list arrow.
5. Click **Ravena.**
6. Click **Filter, Apply Filter/Sort.**
7. Notice that Access displays three records.
8. Click the **Remove Filter** button to remove the filter.
9. Click the **Filter By Form** button.

10. Click the **Or** tab at the bottom of the page.
11. Click the **City** field and click **Melrose.**
12. Click the **Apply Filter** button. Notice that Access displays records from the towns of Ravena and Melrose.

13. Click **Records, Remove Filter/Sort.** Do not close.

Filter Datasheets by Selection

- Another method of filtering datasheets and forms is *Filter By Selection.* This feature allows you to filter only one value at a time. You select all or part of a value and filter records to obtain those that contain the value.
- Click a field containing the value you want. Click Record, Filter, and Filter By Selection, or click the Filter By Selection button on the toolbar to find all records with the selected value. Click the Remove Filter button to remove the filter.

TRY it OUT *A4-6*

1. The ALL MEMBERS table should be displayed or open **A4-6** from the Data CD and open the **ALL MEMBERS** table in the Tables object.
2. Locate the third record.
3. Double-click **Scotia** to select it in the City field.
4. Click the **Filter By Selection** button.

5. Notice that two records appear.
6. Click the **Remove Filter** button to remove the filter.
7. Save the changes to the table and close it.
8. Close the database.

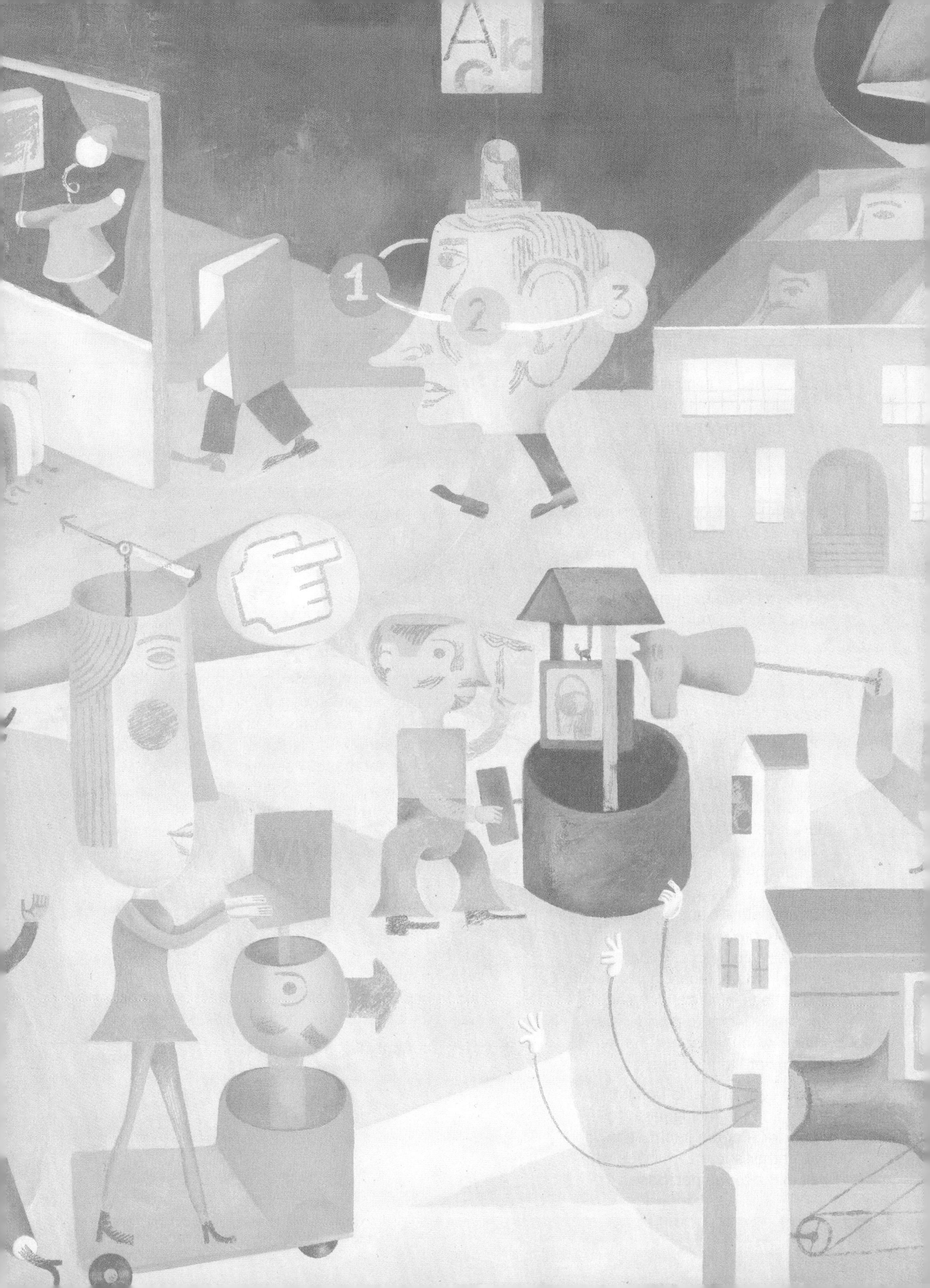
1
2
3

GOAL

To find and replace listings in the Four Corners Realty Company's database of homes for sale. You will sort the listings by price and use filters to identify listings in specific cities and price ranges

SETTING THE STAGE/WRAPUP

Database: **Four Corners Realty**
Table: **Listings**

WHAT YOU NEED TO KNOW

- In a real estate company, it is very important to identify houses that meet the requirements of prospective buyers. Often buyers have a specific town they are interested in, as well as an acceptable price range. Sometimes the most important requirement is the size of the home or the number of bedrooms in the house. Some clients require new homes, while others want older homes.
- A real estate agent must be able to search listings quickly to identify the ideal properties to present to his or her clients. An agent must also be able to update the listings when they change.
- In this Rehearsal activity, you will search and update the listing database of the Four Corners Realty Company. You have a number of prospective client inquiries to answer concerning current listings, and because one of the homeowners has recently married, you need to update a last name in the database.You will sort the listings, print the datasheets, and apply filters to provide your clients with the listings that are appropriate to their needs.
- Use a copy of the To Do List, shown on the facing page, to keep track of the information you will gather and the changes you will make to the database.

DIRECTIONS

1. Start Access.
2. Open the **Four Corners Realty** database file from the Data CD. 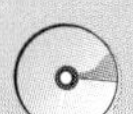
3. Open the **Listings** table.
4. One of your prospective clients is interested in a home he saw on Overlook Drive. He is not sure of the street number, but he saw a Four Corners Realty Company sign in the front yard. He has called you to find out the price of the home. Click **Edit, Find** to find the record that matches.
5. Notice that the house is located at 8 Overlook Drive and the price is $150,000. Make note of this on your copy of the form, as shown on the facing page.
6. Agnes Taylor, a homeowner in the database, has remarried and her last name is now Taylor-Smith. You are not sure if she is the only person named Taylor in the database. Use Find and Replace to replace Taylor with Taylor-Smith. Before replacing it, confirm that the replacement will be made in the record of the Agnes Taylor who owns the house at 1 Somers Road.
7. One client wants a list of all the houses that Four Corners has listed in order of price. Use the Sort feature to create this list and print a copy.
8. Another client wants to know about all of the homes in Hollywood that are listed. Use the Filter By Form option and the City field to locate those records. Make a note of the four homes listed in Hollywood.
9. Click the **Apply Filter** button to remove the filter.

Continued on next page

10. Your last client request is to see your listings for houses that have list prices of $200,000. Click the **Price field of ListingID 3,** and use the $200,000 price and the Filter By Selection feature to find these listings. Make a note of the two listings that appear.

11. You have answered all of your client inquiries; be sure you have noted all the answers in your copy of the form shown below.

12. Close the table, but do not save the changes to the design. Close the database.

QUESTIONS/REQUESTS	ANSWERS/ACTION
Price of home on Overlook Drive	
Change Agnes Taylor's name to Agnes Taylor-Smith. Check when complete.	
Homes that Four Corners has listed in price order. Print a copy of the list.	
All listed homes in Hollywood. Make a note of addresses and prices.	
Listings for homes that have list prices of $200,000. Make a note of addresses and number of bedrooms in each home.	

Cues for Reference

Find a Record

With a table open:

1. Click **Edit, Find.**
2. Enter value in the Find What box.
3. Choose a Look In option.
4. Choose a Match option.
5. Choose a Search list box option.
6. Click **Match Case** to restrict search.
7. Click **Search Fields As Formatted** to restrict search.
8. Click **Find Next.**

Find and Replace a Record

With a table open:

1. Click **Edit, Replace.**
2. Enter the find value in Find What box.
3. Enter the replacement value in Replace With box.
4. Choose a Look In option.
5. Choose a Match option.
6. Choose a Search option.
7. Click **Match Case** to restrict search.
8. Click **Search Fields As Formatted** to restrict search.
9. To replace next field, click **Find Next.**
10. Click **Replace.**
11. To replace all matching fields at once, click **Replace All.**
12. Click **OK** to confirm changes.

Sort Records

With a table open:

1. Click the column to sort.
2. Click **Records.**
3. Click the **Sort Ascending** button. 

or

- Click the **Sort Descending** button. 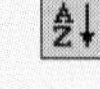

Filter Records By Form

With a table open:

1. Click the **Filter By Form** button. 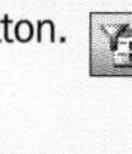
2. Enter items required in appropriate fields.

   or

   Click on the appropriate field list box arrow.
3. Click the data item.
4. Click **Filter.**
5. Click the **Apply Filter** button.

Filter Records By Selection

With a table open:

1. Click selected item in a field location.
2. Click **Filter By Selection** button. 

Remove a Filter from Records

1. Click **Records.**
2. Click **Remove Filter button.**

GOALS
To build queries to search a property listings database to answer questions
To practice using the following skill sets:

- Create a query object
- Create select queries using the Simple Query Wizard
  - Create select queries with calculations
- Create crosstab, unmatched, and duplicate queries
- Modify queries in Design view

WHAT YOU NEED TO KNOW

Create a Query Object

- In addition to the search tools you have used, Access provides a more powerful tool called a *query*. A query is a database object that you create to answer questions and to view, modify, and analyze data in a database. A saved query can be run any time and will include new data added to the database.

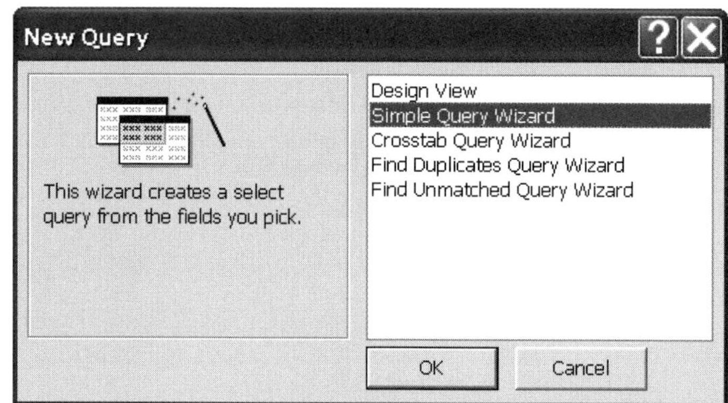

Figure 4.7 New Query dialog box—create queries using wizards

- Access provides four *query wizards* to help you develop different types of queries that retrieve and analyze data from the fields you specify within one or more tables or queries. Click the Queries object in the Database window and click the New button. The New Query dialog box opens, as shown in Figure 4.7.

TRY*it* OUT *A4-7*

1. Open the **Members** database by opening **A4-7** from the Data CD.
2. Click **Queries.**
3. Click the **New** button.
4. Notice the four query wizards.
5. Click each wizard:
   - **Simple Query Wizard**
   - **Crosstab Query Wizard**
   - **Find Duplicates Query Wizard**
   - **Find Unmatched Query Wizard**
6. Review the descriptions that Access displays.
7. Click **Cancel.**

Create Select Queries Using the Simple Query Wizard

- The *Simple Query Wizard* creates a *select query,* which asks a question about the data stored in one or more tables. It returns a result set in the form of a datasheet and does not change the original data. Once the results appear, you can view and, in some cases, modify the data in the underlying tables.
- To use the Simple Query Wizard, click the Queries object in the Database window and click New. The New Query dialog box opens (see Figure 4.7). Double-click the Simple Query Wizard and a dialog box opens, as shown in Figure 4.8.

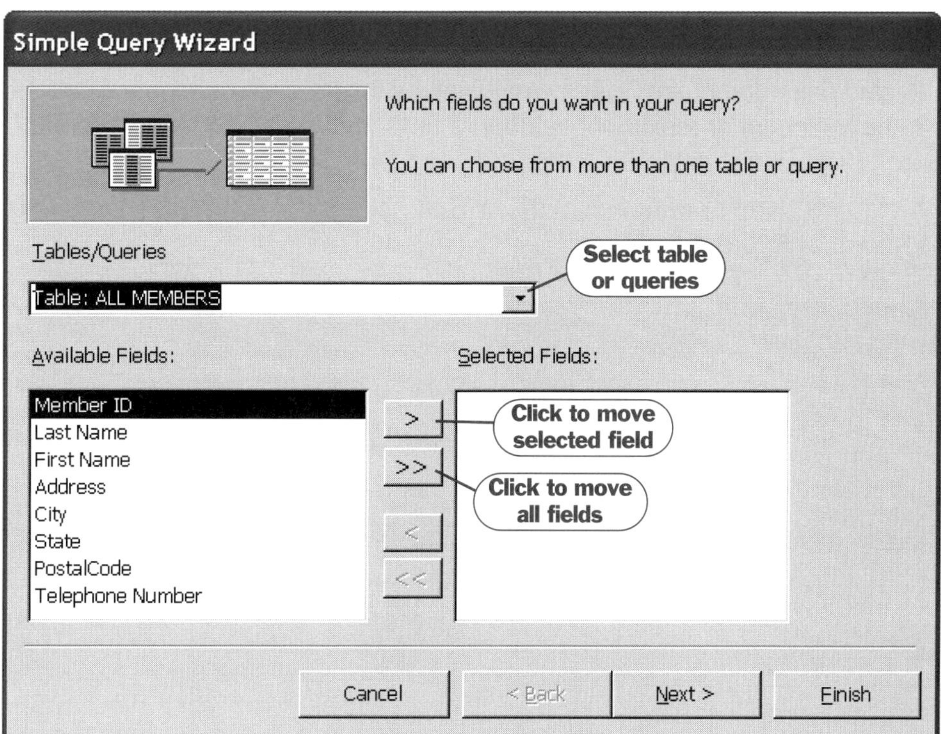

Figure 4.8 Create select queries using the Simple Query Wizard

- Click the table and double-click the fields for the query. To choose fields from more than one table or query, click each table and double-click the fields to include. Repeat this step until you have selected all the fields you want. Click Next, then Finish to view the select query.
- Queries can be printed by using the File, Print menu commands or the Print button.

ACCESS

TRY *it* OUT *A4-8*

Note: The Members database should be open from the last Try it Out.

1. Click **Queries,** if not already selected.
2. Click the **New** button and then double-click **Simple Query Wizard.**
3. Click the list arrow under **Tables/Queries.**
4. Click **Table: GOLF MEMBERS.**
5. Double-click **Member ID** and **Handicap** to move them from Available Fields to Selected Fields.
6. Click **Next.**
7. Click **Detail,** if necessary.

Continued on next page

TRY*it* OUT *A4-8 Continued*

8. Click **Next.** Notice that the name of the query is GOLF MEMBERS Query.
9. Click **Finish.**
10. A query appears showing the golf handicap for each golf member ID.
11. Click the **Print** button to print the query. 
12. Close the query.

Create Select Queries with Calculations

- The Simple Query Wizard can sum, count, and average values for groups of records or all records, and it can calculate the minimum or maximum value in a field. It can build queries in one or more tables or queries.
- If you choose fields that are Number data types, the Wizard asks you if you would like a detail or summary query, as shown in Figure 4.9.

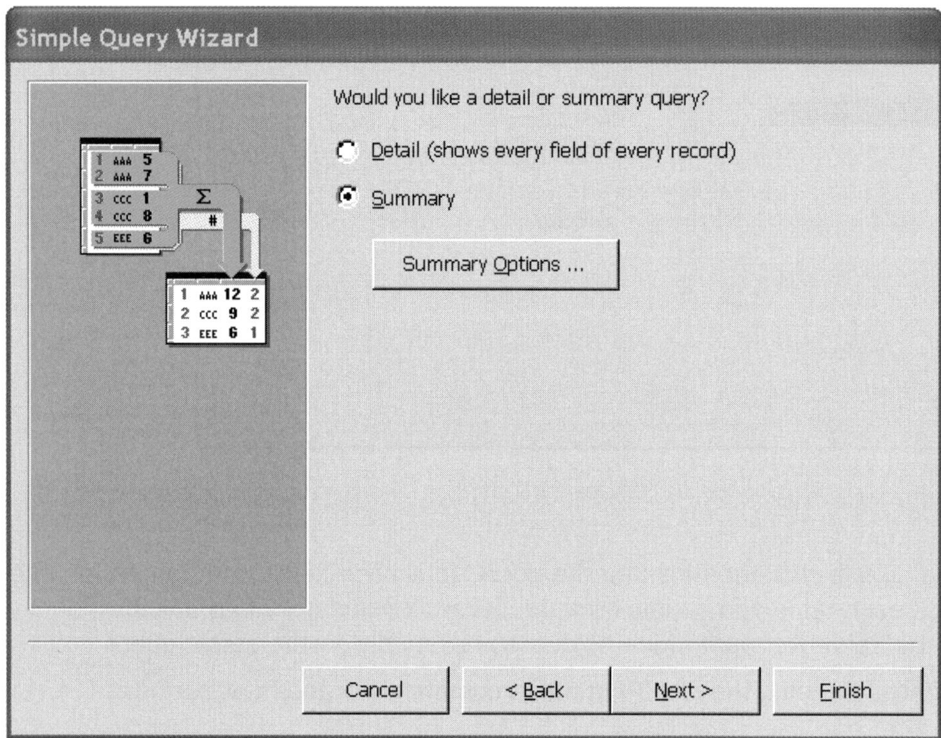

Figure 4.9 Simple Query Wizard—Would you like a detail or summary query?

- Click Detail to show every record. Click Summary and click Summary Options to have the Wizard sum, count, average, or calculate minimum or maximum values, as shown in Figure 4.10.

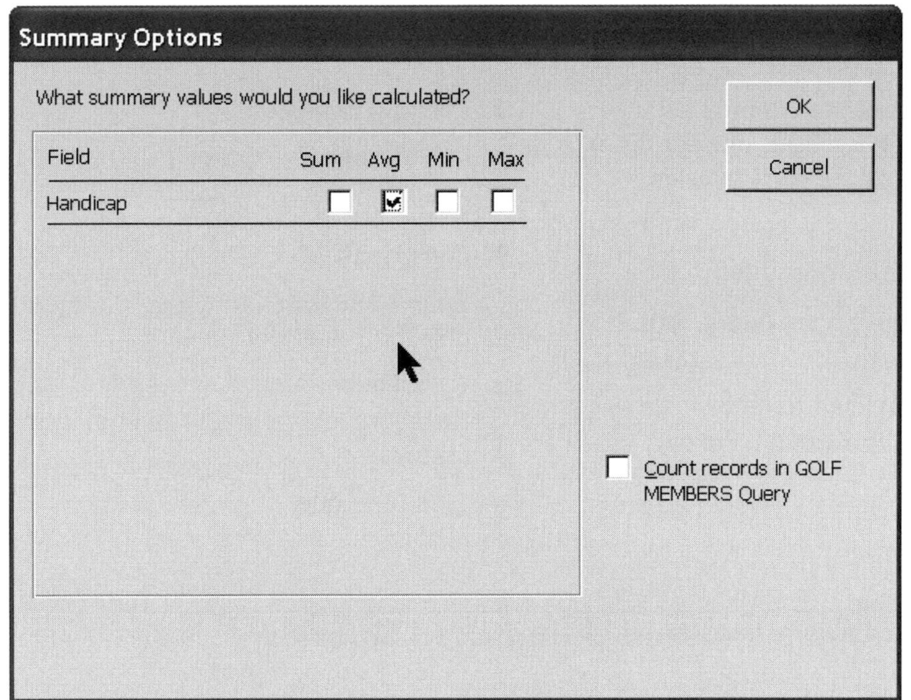

Figure 4.10 Summary Options—What summary values would you like calculated?

▶ Click your choice and click OK. The last steps are to name the query and decide how to open the query, as shown in Figure 4.11.

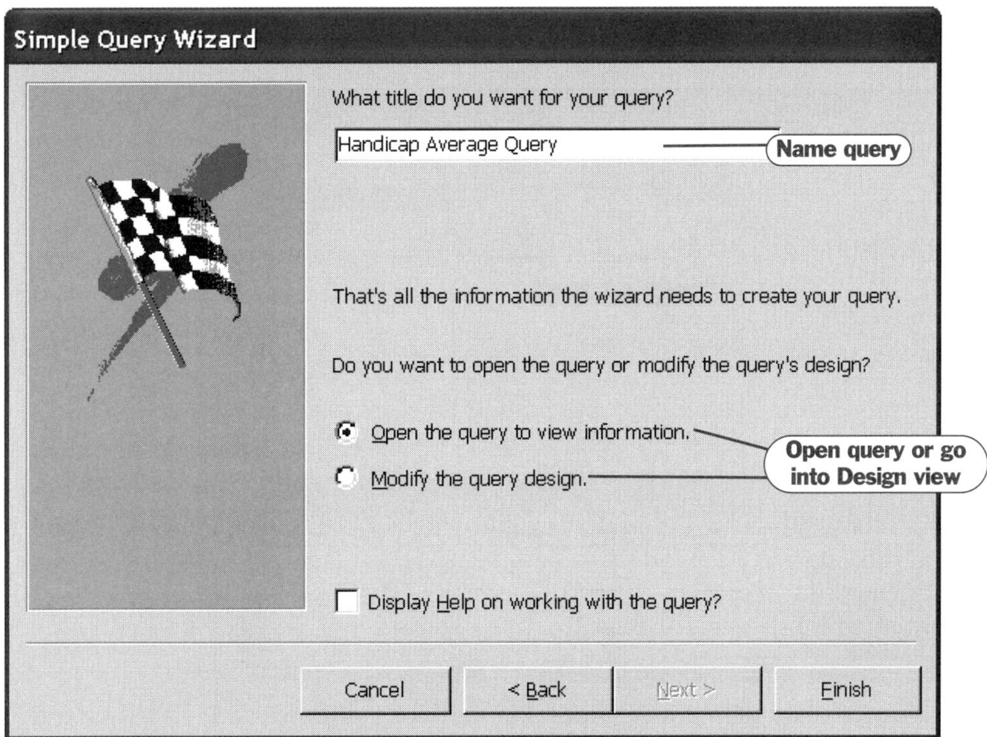

Figure 4.11 Simple Query Wizard—last step

ACCESS

TRY it OUT *A4-9*

1. The Members database should be open in the Queries object or open **A4-9** from the Data CD and click **Queries.**
2. Click **New.**
3. Double-click **Simple Query Wizard.**
4. If it is not selected, click **Query: GOLF MEMBERS Query** under Tables/Queries.
5. Double-click **Handicap** to move it from Available Fields to Selected Fields.
6. Click **Next.**
7. Click **Summary.**
8. Click **Summary Options.**
9. Click **Avg** and click **OK.**
10. Click **Next.**
11. Enter `Handicap Average Query` as the title for this query.
12. Click **Finish.** A query appears, showing the average golf handicap of all golf members.
13. Close the query.

Create Crosstab, Duplicate, and Unmatched Queries

Crosstab Query

- A *crosstab query* arranges fields in a spreadsheet format and provides summary options. In the Queries object, click New, Crosstab Query Wizard. The Crosstab Wizard dialog box displays, where you select the table, query, or both to use for the query.
- After making your selection and clicking Next, the next screen asks you to select up to three fields to be row headers, as shown in Figure 4.12. The row headers depend on what question you are asking in the query.

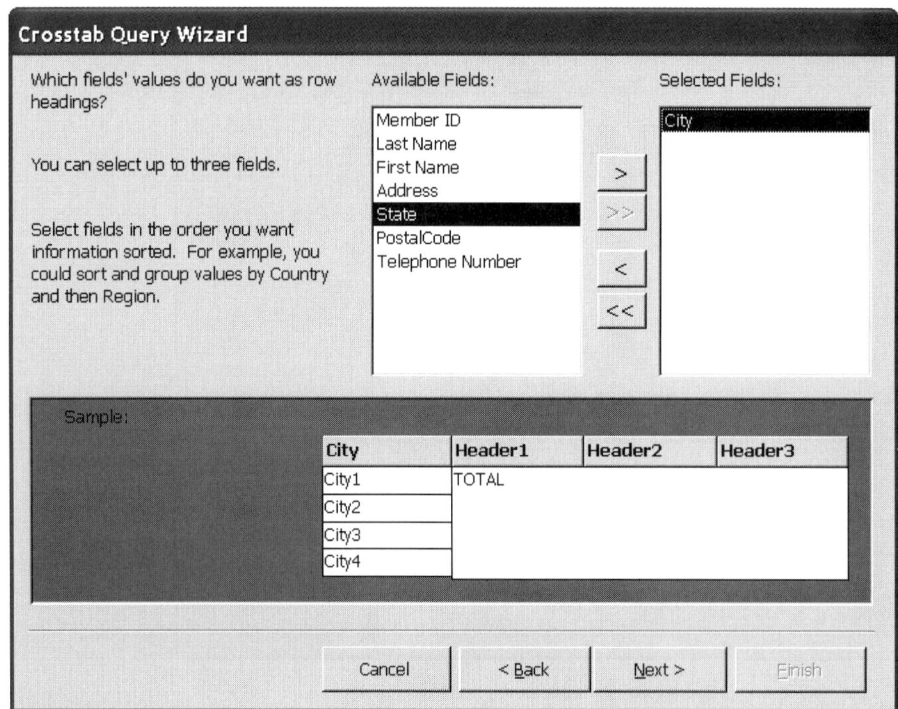

Figure 4.12 Crosstab Wizard Query, row headers

▶ The next screen asks you to select column headings, as shown in Figure 4.13. This could be a field related to the row headers, such as City or Postal Code, where there are a limited number of different entries.

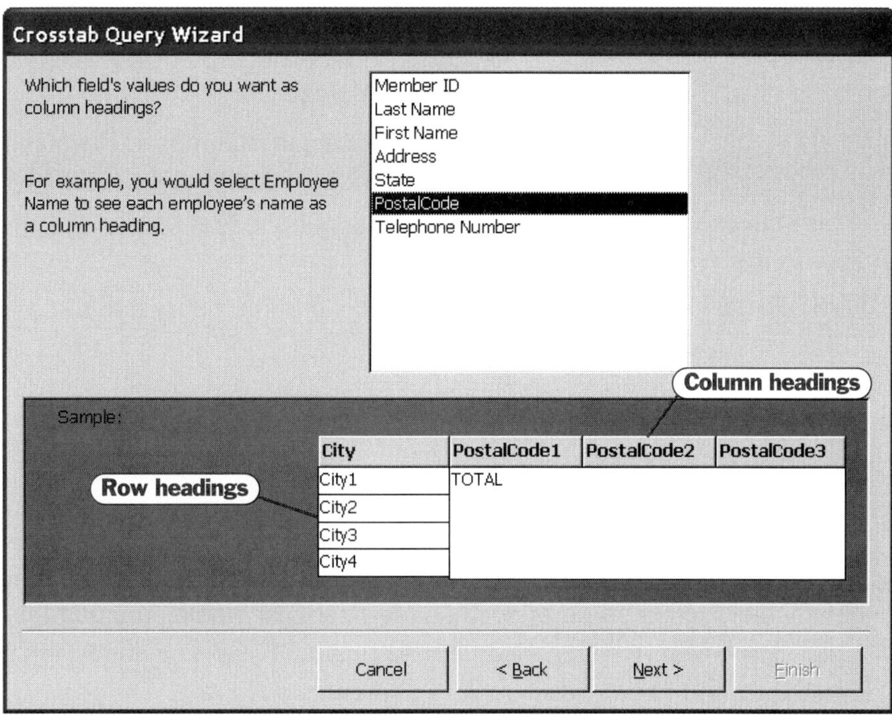

Figure 4.13 Crosstab Wizard Query, column headers

▶ The last screen allows you to request calculation options, as shown in Figure 4.14.

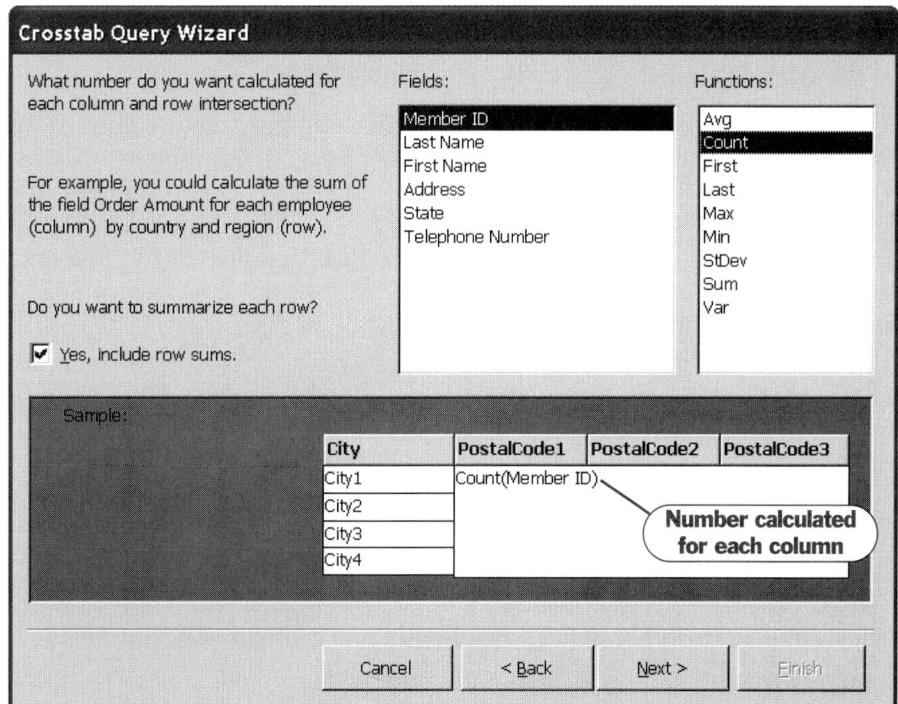

Figure 4.14 Crosstab Wizard Query, calculation options

TRY it OUT *A4-10*

Note: A crosstab query will be created to find the number of members in various cities and postal codes.

1. The Members database should be open in the Queries object or open **A4-10** from the Data CD and click **Queries.**
2. Click **New.**
3. Double-click **Crosstab Query Wizard.**
4. Select the **ALL MEMBERS** table and click **Next**.
5. Select **City** as the row header and click **Next**.
6. Select **Postal Code** as the column header and click **Next**.
7. Select **Count** to summarize the number of members in each category. Click **Next**.
8. Name the query `CITY QUERY` and click **Finish**.
9. View and close the query and the database.

Duplicates Query

▶ The *duplicates query* can be used to detect duplicate entries in a field, if that presents an error. In the Query object, click New, Find Duplicates Query Wizard. On the screens that follow, you will select the table, queries, or reports to use, select the field where duplicates might be found, and then select fields to identify the duplicates data, such as MemberID or Name. You can then name and view the query.

TRY it OUT *A4-11*

Note: The club is having a problem with swim lockers and needs a duplicates query to see if the same locker was assigned twice.

1. Open **A4-11** from the Data CD and click the **Queries** object.
2. Click **New** and double-click **Find Duplicates Query Wizard**.
3. Select the **SWIM MEMBERS** table and click **Next**.
4. Select the **Locker Number** field to search for duplicates. Click **Next**.
5. Select the **MemberID** field to identify the data. Click **Next**.
6. Name the query `Locker Duplicates` and click **Finish**.
7. After checking the original records, we find that MemberID 8 should have locker 20.
8. Change the locker number in the query.
9. Close the query, switch to the **Tables** object.
10. Double-click **SWIM MEMBERS** and check that the update has been recorded.
11. Close the table and the database.

Unmatched Query

▶ The *unmatched query* finds records in one table that do not match records in another. This query can be used to find records that you may wish to solicit for additional services.

▶ In the Query object, click New, Find Unmatched Query Wizard. On the screens that follow:

- Select the table or query that should have Unmatched records.
- Select the table or query that contains the related records.

- Select the field that is the same in both tables, as shown in Figure 4.15.
- Select the fields you need to see in the results table.
- Name the table.

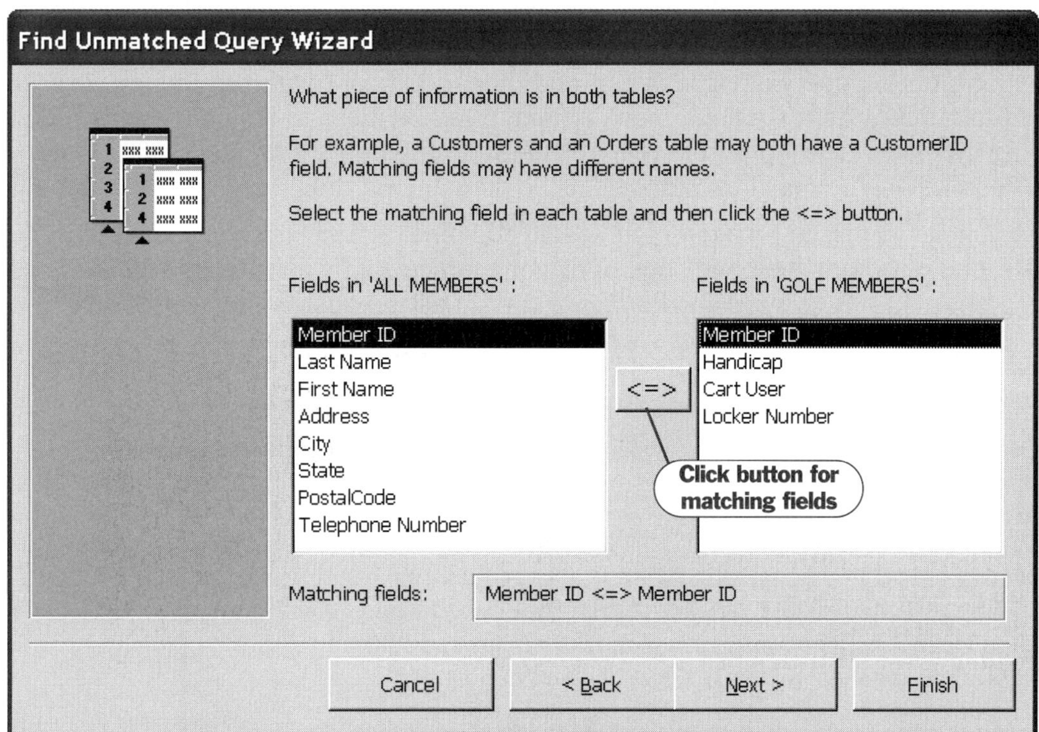

Figure 4.15 Find Unmatched Query Wizard — select fields to match

ACCESS

TRY *it* OUT *A4-12*

Note: The club wants a telephone list for non-golf members to be able to call them to promote golf membership.

1. Open **A4-12** from the Data CD and click the **Queries** object.
2. Click **New** and double-click **Find Unmatched Query Wizard**.
3. Select the **ALL MEMBERS** table and click **Next**.
4. Select the **GOLF MEMBERS** table to match with first table. Click **Next.**
5. Select the **MemberID** field to relate the tables. Click the <=> button. Click **Next.**
6. Select the following fields necessary for the telephone promotion: **MemberID**, **LastName**, **FirstName**, **Telephone Number**. Click **Next.**
7. Name the query: `Non-golf members-telephone list.` Click **Finish**.
8. Print a copy of the query, if a printer is available.
9. Close the query and the database.

Modify Queries in Design View

- You can create and modify queries in *Query Design view,* which shows the structure of a query. To open a query in Design view, in the Database window, click the Queries object, click the query you want to open, and click Design. If the query is already open, just click the Design View button.
- It is convenient to create a query using a wizard and then modify or tailor it in Design view. You may add a field to a query, delete a field, move a field, or add criteria to limit your search. To add a field, drag the field name from the table at the top to the query grid. To delete a field, select it and press Delete. To move a field, select the column and drag it to the new location.
- *Criteria* are restrictions you place on a query to specify the records with which you want to work. For example, instead of viewing the handicaps of all golf members, you can view members whose handicaps are greater than 3. To *specify criteria* in a query, use the design grid, as shown in Figure 4.16.

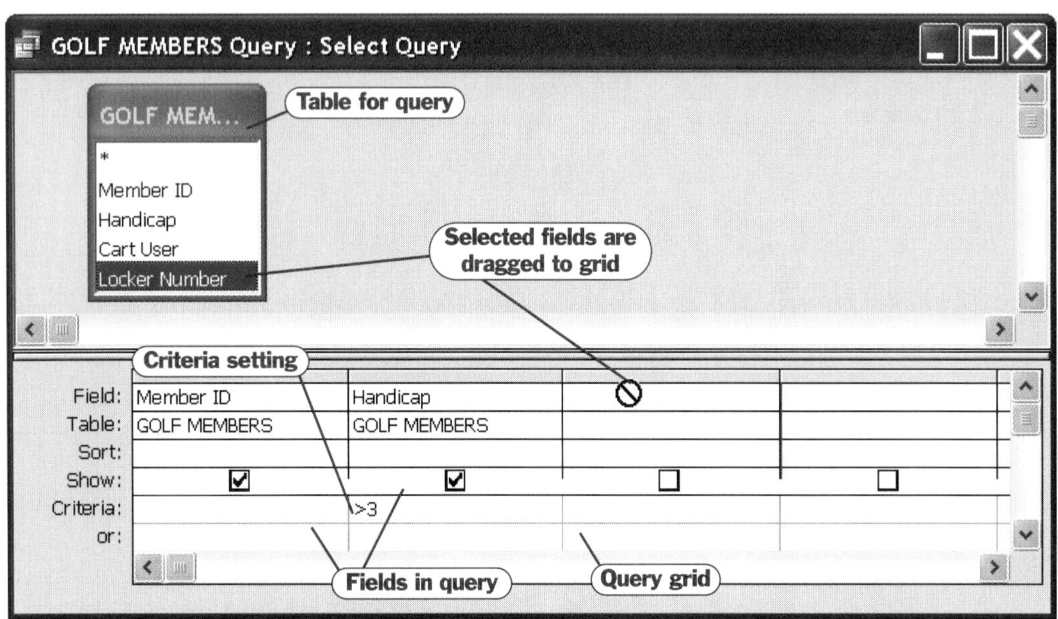

Figure 4.16 Query Design view

- In the example shown in Figure 4.16, the table is GOLF MEMBERS, and the fields are Member ID and Handicap. The Locker Number field is being added to the query for informational purposes. A criteria is set, in the Criteria row of the Handicap field, to view members whose handicaps are greater than 3. You can add additional criteria for the same field or different fields. Click the Datasheet View button or the Run button to see the query results.

TRY *it* OUT *A4-13*

1. Open **A4-13** from the Data CD and click the **Queries** object.
2. Double-click **GOLF MEMBERS Query.** Notice that Access displays handicaps ranging from 3 through 5.
3. Click the **Design View** button.
4. Select the **Locker Number** field from the table list and drag it to the third column position on the grid.
5. Click the **Criteria** cell in the Handicap column.
6. Enter: **>3.**
7. Click the **Datasheet View** button. Notice that Access displays handicaps ranging from 4 through 5.
8. Click the **Design View** button.
9. Click the **Criteria** cell in the Handicap column and delete the cell contents.
10. Enter **=4** and click the **Datasheet View** button. Notice that members with handicaps of 4 are displayed.
11. Close the query. Do not save the changes.
12. Close the database.

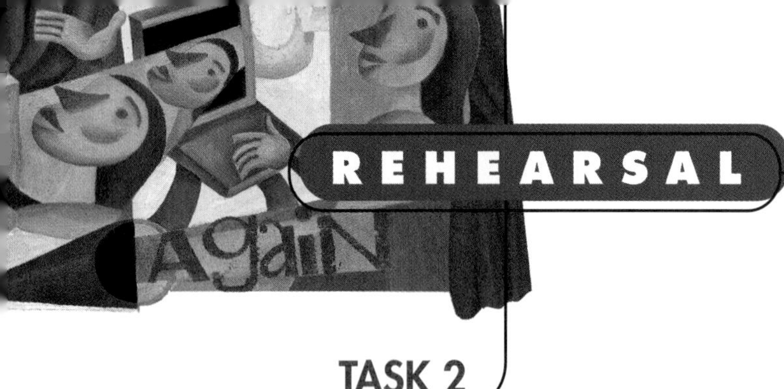

GOAL

To build queries to search the property listings in the Four Corners Realty Company's database to answer questions

SETTING THE STAGE/WRAPUP

Database: **Four Corners Realty**
Table: **Listings**
Queries: **Pricing Statistics**
Agents without matching listings
Agents – total listings by city
Listings query

WHAT YOU NEED TO KNOW

- Property listings change on a daily basis. New properties are added, properties are sold, and the prices of listings change. What does not change is the information that real estate agents and customers want from a property listing database. Building queries allows you to answer quickly the standard questions that agents and customers have. You can run these queries repeatedly, and any new or updated data will be included.
- In this Rehearsal activity, you will build queries that agents can use on a daily basis. Use a copy of the table shown in Illustration A on the facing page as an outline and a place to record answers.

DIRECTIONS

1. Start Access.
2. Open the **Four Corners Realty** database from the Data CD. 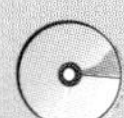
3. You have been asked to provide a query to calculate pricing statistics for the homes in the database by city. Use the **Simple Query Wizard** with the **Listings** table.
4. Move the **City** and **Price** fields to the Selected Fields box.
5. Select the **Summary** query and the **Sum, Avg, Max,** and **Min** summary options.
6. Name the query: `Pricing Statistics.`
7. Print a copy of the query.
8. The owner of the agency would like to be able to quickly check to see which agents have no listings. Use the **Find Unmatched Query Wizard** with the **Agents** and **Listings** tables.
9. The results of the query should show all the information about the agent.
10. Name the query: `Agents without matching listings.`
11. Write the name(s) of the agent(s) with no listings on a copy of the table in Illustration A.
12. The owner needs a list of agents with their total listings broken down by city. Use the **Crosstab Query Wizard** with the **Listings** table.
13. Use Illustration B as a guide to prepare the query. Find the total of the Price field.

Continued on next page

14. Name the query: `Agents – total listings by city.`

15. Compare your query to the illustration. Modify your query or delete and prepare a new query if yours is not correct.

16. Create a Listings query that agents can use to search for properties with specific criteria. Use the **Simple Query Wizard** and the **Listings** table.

17. Include the fields in the order listed: **Price, City, Description, Address, Date Built, Appraised Value.**

18. Name the query: `Listings query.`

19. Switch to **Design view.** Modify the query by moving the Description column to the right of the Address column so that it is the fourth column. Save the query.

20. On the Criteria line, set criteria to find homes for less than $130,000 in Hollywood. Hint: Enter `<130000` under Price and `Hollywood` under City.

21. Run the query and record the address(es) on your table. Do not save the criteria to the query so that agents can enter their own criteria as necessary.

22. Close the database.

ACCESS

QUERIES TO BE PREPARED:		
Name of Query	***Type of Query***	***Action***
Pricing Statistics	Simple query with summary options	Print
Agents without matching listings	Unmatched query with all fields of Agent table	Name(s)?
Agents – total listings by city	Crosstab query (see illustration)	Compare to Illustration
Listings query	Simple query	Save query
Listing query –Step 20	Add criteria to query as specified	Address(es)?

Illustration A

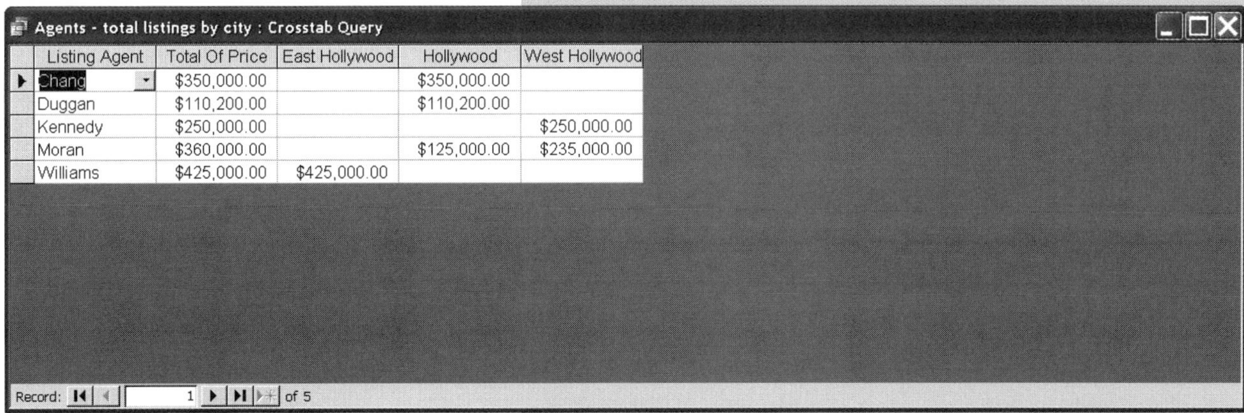

Agents - total listings by city : Crosstab Query

Listing Agent	Total Of Price	East Hollywood	Hollywood	West Hollywood
Chang	$350,000.00		$350,000.00	
Duggan	$110,200.00		$110,200.00	
Kennedy	$250,000.00			$250,000.00
Moran	$360,000.00		$125,000.00	$235,000.00
Williams	$425,000.00	$425,000.00		

Record: 1 of 5

Illustration B

Cues for Reference

Use the Simple Query Wizard
1. Click the **Queries** object.
2. Click the **New** button.
3. Click **Simple Query Wizard.** Click **OK.**
4. Choose a table or query.
5. Double-click fields to move from Available Fields to Selected Fields.
6. Click **Next.**
7. Name the query. Click **Finish.**

Use the Simple Query Wizard with Summary Options
1. Click the **Queries** object.
2. Click the **New** button.
3. Click **Simple Query Wizard.** Click **OK.**
4. Choose a table or query.
5. Double-click fields to move them from the Available Fields to the Selected Fields.
6. Click **Next.**
7. Click **Summary.**
8. Click **Summary Options.**
9. Click **Calculation Option.**
10. Click **OK.**
11. Click **Next.**
12. Name the query. Click **Finish.**

Use the Find Unmatched Query Wizard
1. Click the **Queries** object.
2. Click the **New** button.
3. Click **Find Unmatched Query Wizard.** Click **OK.**
4. Choose a table or query that contains unmatched records. Clilck **Next.**
5. Choose a table or query that contains the search records. Click **Next.**
6. Click the arrows to select matching fields between tables. Click **Next.**
7. Select fields to appear in results table. Click **Next.**
8. Name the query. Click **Finish.**

Use the Crosstab Query Wizard
1. Click the **Queries** object.
2. Click the **New** button.
3. Click **Crosstab Query Wizard.** Click **OK.**
4. Select the table or query containing the data to search. Click **Next.**
5. Select the field(s) for row headers. Click **Next.**
6. Select the field for column headers. Click **Next.**
7. Select the field and function for calculations. Click **Next.**
8. Name the query. Click **Finish.**

Modify a Query
1. Drag fields from table to grid to add to query.
2. Select field column and press **Del** key to remove from query.
3. Select field column and drag to change location of data.

Specify Criteria in a Query
1. Click the **Queries** object.
2. Double-click **Query.**
3. Click **Design view.**
4. Set field criteria.
5. Click the **Run** button. 

GOALS

To add a calculated field to a query, to create a relationship between tables, and to build a multi-table based query.

To practice using the following skill sets:

- Use aggregate functions
- Add a calculated field to queries in Query Design view
- Format query results
- Create and modify a one-to-many relationship
- Enforce referential integrity in a one-to-many relationship
- Create a multi-table query

WHAT YOU NEED TO KNOW

Use Aggregate Functions

- You can calculate functions for grouped data, which are called *aggregate functions,* in Query Design view. In a query where you are using an aggregate function, you need to display a field to group the data by and a numeric field that you want calculated within the groups specified.
- Click the Total button to display the Total row in the *query design grid*, as shown in Figure 4.17. The *Total row* is a row in the design grid used to perform calculations on the values in a field. Click the down arrow of the Total list box to view and set the available calculations. Click the Run button or click the Datasheet View button to display the results. Access will rename the calculated field.
- For example, if you want to count or total the number of units on order for each department in a Products database, you can set up a query displaying the Department and Units On Order fields. To group department data, click the Totals button on the Access toolbar, and click Group By in the Total box under Department. Then select Sum in the Total box under the Units Ordered field.

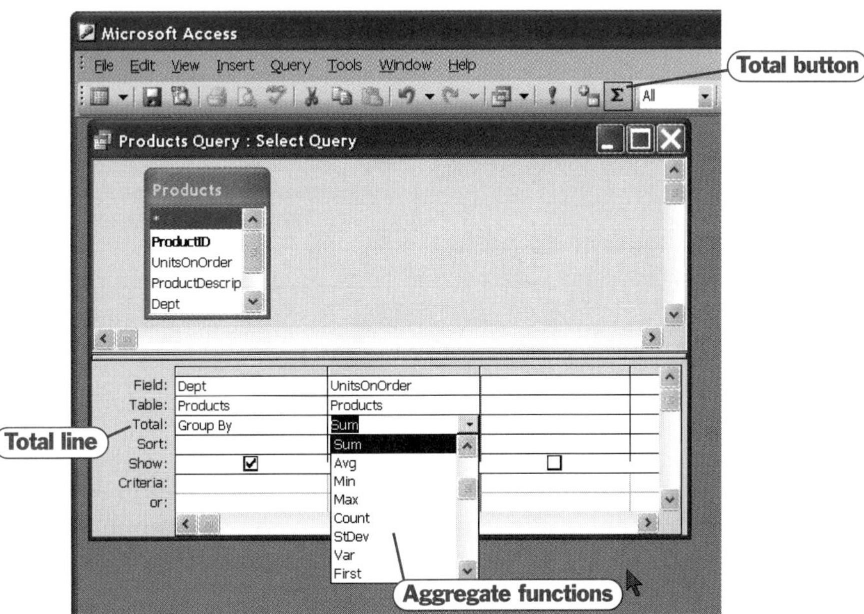

Figure 4.17 Total row in query design grid

TRY*it*OUT *A4-14*

1. Open **A4-14** from the Data CD and click the **Queries** object.
2. Click the **New** button and double-click **Simple Query Wizard.**
3. In the Products table, double-click the **Dept** and **Units on Order** fields to move them from the Available Fields box to the Selected Fields box.
4. Click **Next.**
5. Click **Finish.** Notice that Access displays each record in the table.
6. Click the **Design View** button.
7. Click the **Totals** button.

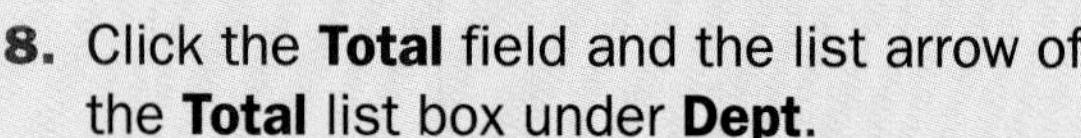

8. Click the **Total** field and the list arrow of the **Total** list box under **Dept.**
9. Click the list arrow of the **Total** list box under **Units on Order**.
10. Click **Sum**.
11. Click the **Run** button. Notice that the department groups are summarized.

12. Close and save the **Products Query**. Close the database.

Add a Calculated Field to Queries in Query Design View

- You can develop queries to total, average, or multiply the value of fields. You can perform calculations as part of a query on the entire database, on selected groups of data, or on data that meet specific criteria.
- A *calculated field* is a field defined in a query that displays the result of an expression. An expression contains field names in brackets with mathematical operators between items, as shown in illustration 4.18. They are entered on the FIELD line of the grid. If you wish to name the column of answers, precede the expression with the column name and a colon. The figure illustrates adding a calculated field, TOTAL, by multiplying the Units on Order by the Unit Price and adding the Shipping Costs.

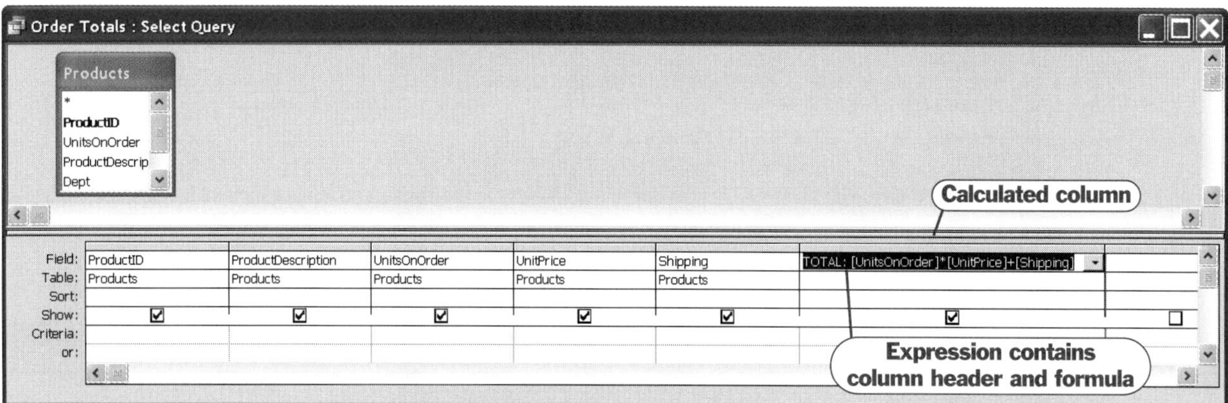

Figure 4.18 Adding a calculated field, Design view

- Access does not store the results of the calculation in the underlying table. It recalculates the value each time a value in the expression changes, and each time you open the query.

TRY *it* OUT *A4-15*

1. Open **A4-15** from the Data CD and click the **Queries** object.
2. Open the **Order Totals** query in Design view.
3. Click the first empty field in the top cell.
4. Enter the expression and column title as follows:
   TOTAL: `[UnitsOnOrder]*[UnitPrice]`
   `+[Shipping]`
5. Click the **Run** button.
6. Notice the total order amounts at the right.
7. Save the query. Keep the database open.

Format Query Results

- A field in a query inherits its properties from the underlying table or query. In the case of calculated fields, or for display purposes, you may wish to change the format of field data. You can change field format settings on the field property sheet. In Query Design view, right-click the field and click Properties. A field property sheet appears, as shown in Figure 4.19. Change the properties to meet the formatting requirements by editing the existing settings, and close the property sheet when done.
- You may also change font, font size, shading and other display options before printing a query result. Use all the same formatting features used for tables and in other applications to enhance the result list.

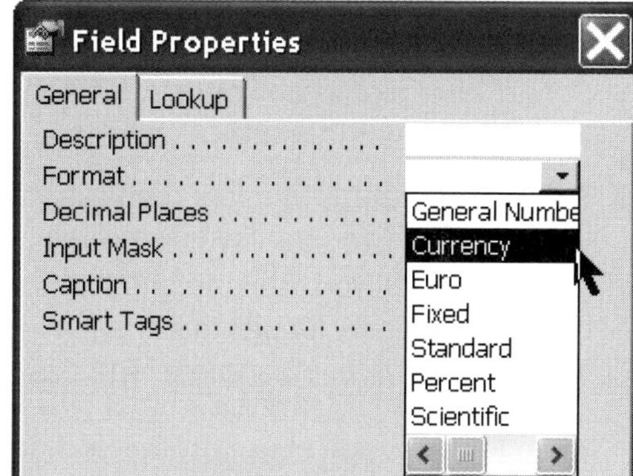

Figure 4.19 Field property sheet

ACCESS

TRY *it* OUT *A4-16*

1. You should be in the Products database (A4-15) or open **A4-16** from the Data CD.
2. Open the **Order Totals** query in **Datasheet View** and note the number formats.
3. Click the **Design View** button.
4. Right-click the grid column for the calculated field. Click **Properties**.
5. In the Field property sheet that displays, change the format to **General Number**.
6. Close the property sheet.
7. Click the **Datasheet View** button. Note the change in format.
8. Click the **Design View** button. Right-click the calculated field and click **Properties**.
9. In the Field property sheet that displays, change the format to **Currrency**. Close.
10. Click the **Datasheet View** button. Note the change in format.
11. Click **Format**, **Datasheet** and select the raised effect. Click **OK**.
12. Close and save the query and the database.

Create and Modify a One-to-Many Relationship

- To create queries, forms, and reports that display information from several tables, you must first establish how the tables relate. You accomplish this by using the Relationships window.
- A *relationship* is a correlation established between shared fields or columns in two tables. There are three kinds of relationships you can build in the Relationships window (one-to-one, one-to-many, many-to-many). We will create a one-to-many relationship in this lesson.
  - *One-to-many relationship*—a record in one table can match many records in a second table. However, each record in the second table can only have one match in the first table.

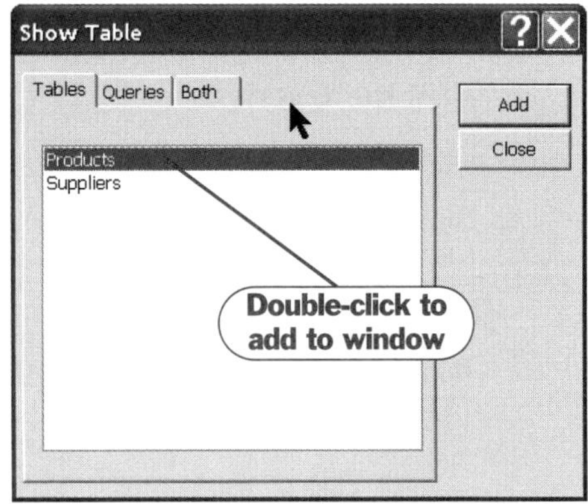

Figure 4.20 Show Table dialog box

- If the database toolbar containing the Relationships button is not displayed on your system, click View, Toolbars, and Database. Click the Relationships button on the toolbar and the Show Table dialog box opens, as shown in Figure 4.20. Double-click the names of the tables you want to connect and close the Show Tables dialog box.
- The Relationships window displays the tables you selected with a list of fields, as shown in Figure 4.21. Drag the field that you want to relate from one table to the related field in the other table. In most cases, you drag the primary key field from one table to a similar field, called the foreign key, in the other table. A *foreign key* is a field in one or more tables that refers and relates to the primary key field or fields in another table. The data in the foreign key and primary key fields must match.

Figure 4.21 Create relationships—Relationships window

- The Edit Relationships dialog box opens allowing you to make settings for the relationship, as shown in Figure 4.22. Notice that it is set as a one-to-many relationship.

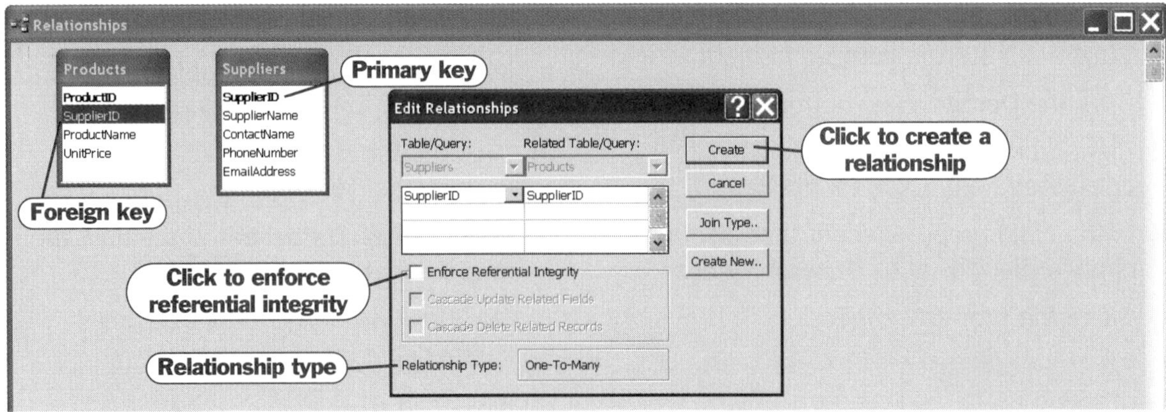

Figure 4.22 Edit Relationships box

TRY*it*OUT A4-17

1. Open **A4-17**, the Suppliers database, from the Data CD.
2. Click the **Relationships** button.
3. Double-click **Products.**
4. Double-click **Suppliers.**
5. Close the **Show Table** dialog box.
6. Click **SupplierID** in the Suppliers field list.
7. Drag to **Supplier ID** in the Products field list. Notice that the Edit Relationships dialog box opens with both fields listed. Also, notice the option Enforce Referential Integrity. Do not close the dialog box.

Enforce Referential Integrity in a One-to-Many Relationship

- *Referential integrity* is an option you set to enforce rules to maintain the relationship between tables when you enter or delete records.
- If you enforce referential integrity, it prevents you from adding records to a related table if there is no relating record in the primary table. For example, you could not add a supplier to the Products table unless it was listed in the Supplier table. This ensures that detailed information is available for suppliers listed in the Products table.
- To enforce referential integrity, click the check box preceding the option Enforce Referential Integrity in the Edit Relationships dialog box (see Figure 4.22).
- Click the Create button to create the relationship. Access draws a join line connecting the two related fields. A "1" above the join line shows which table is on the "one" side of a one-to-many relationship and an infinity symbol indicates which table is on the "many" side, as shown in Figure 4.23.

ACCESS

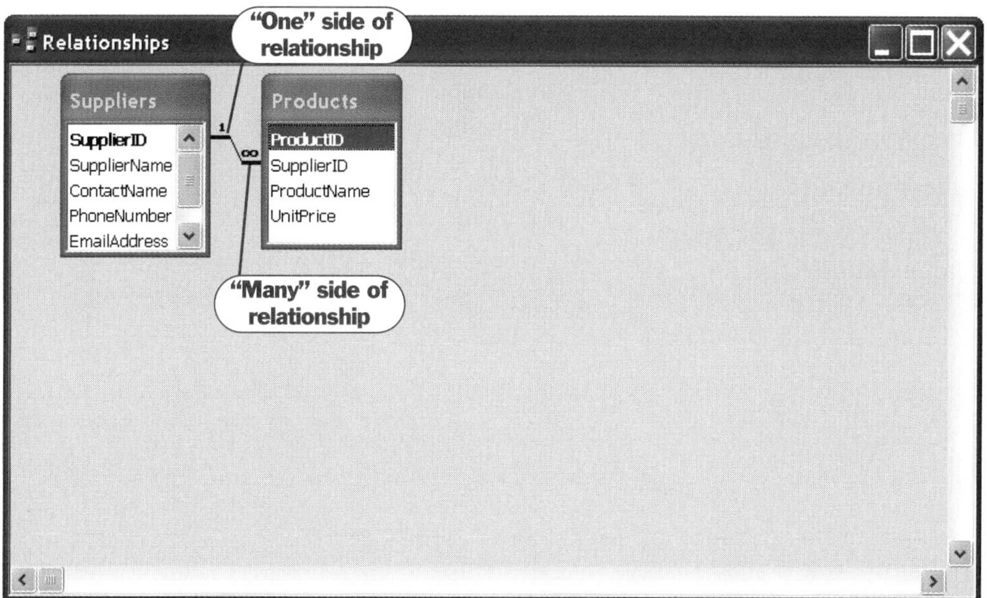

Figure 4.23 Relationships

- You repeat the same steps for each pair of tables you want to relate. When you close the Relationships window, Access asks if you want to save the layout. Whether you save the layout or not, it saves the relationships you create in the database. You can now create queries, forms, or reports using both tables.

TRY*it* OUT *A4-18*

Note: The Edit Relationships dialog box should be displayed.

1. Click the **Enforce Referential Integrity** check box.
2. Click **Create.**
3. Notice the line connecting the two tables.
4. Notice the "1" on the side of the **Suppliers** table, indicating it is the "one" side.
5. Notice the infinity symbol above the **Products** table line, indicating it is on the "many" side.
6. Close the Relationships window.
7. Click **Yes** to save the window.

Create a Multi-Table Query

- The query feature is especially powerful when you build queries based on more than one table. When the tables are related, you can create a *multi-table select query,* by using a wizard the same way you did to create a single table query.
- With the Queries object selected, click New, Simple Query Wizard or click Create a query using a wizard. Click the first table to include in the query and double-click each field to add to the query. When you are done, click the down arrow in the Tables/Queries list box and click the next table to include. Double-click each field to include. Then complete the process in the normal way.

TRY*it* OUT *A4-19*

1. Continue in the Suppliers database or open **A4-19** from the Data CD.
2. Click the **Queries** object.
3. Click **Create query by using wizard**.
4. Click the **Products** table.
5. Double-click the following fields: **Product ID**, **Product Name**, **Unit Price**.
6. Click the down arrow within Tables/Queries and click the **Suppliers** table.
7. Double-click the following fields: **Supplier Name**, **Contact Name**, **Phone Number.**
8. Click **Next** twice. Name the query `Order Information.` Click **Finish**.
9. Close the query and the database.

1
2
3

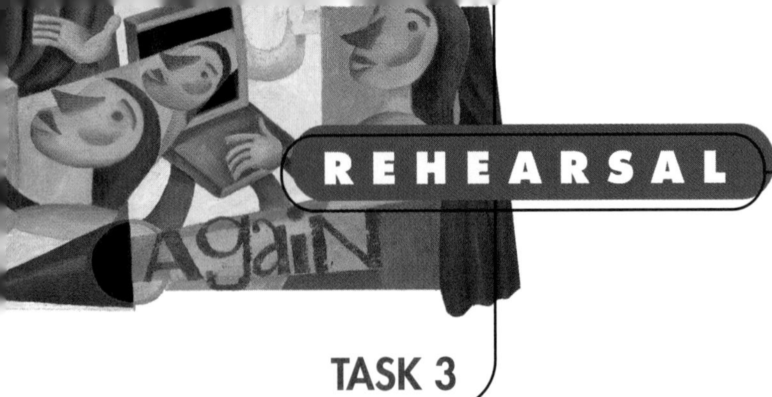

GOAL
To add a calculated field to a query and to create a relationship between tables and to build a multi-table–based query.

SETTING THE STAGE/WRAPUP

Database: **Four Corners Realty3**
Tables: **Listings**
Agents
Query: **Agents and Listings**
Listings–Approximate Tax

WHAT YOU NEED TO KNOW

- Every agent is concerned with selling homes and acquiring new listings. This is because commissions are split between the listing firm and the selling firm. If the listing firm sells the property, it earns the entire commission.
- You have been asked to link the existing agent database to the listing agent database. This will enable you to build a multi-table query that shows which agents have which listings. You will create another query with a calculated field to provide agents with approximate real estate taxes for their buyers.
- In this Rehearsal activity, you will use the chart shown on the facing page to keep track of the information you will gather using the queries you build.

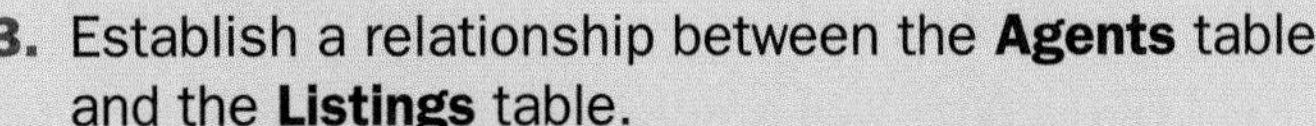

DIRECTIONS

1. Start Access.
2. Open the **Four Corners Realty3** database from the Data CD.
3. Establish a relationship between the **Agents** table and the **Listings** table.
   a. With the **Tables** object selected, click the **Relationships** button to display the Show Table dialog box.
   b. Click the **Agents** and **Listings** tables and add them to the Show Table list.
   c. In the **Listings** table, locate the Listing Agent field, and drag it to the Listing Agent field in the Agents field list.
   d. Do not establish referential integrity. Click **Create.** Notice the join lines between the fields. Close and save the relationships.
4. Create a query that produces listings by agent. In the **Queries** object, click **Create a query using wizard.**
5. From the **Agents** table, double-click the **Listing Agent** and **Telephone** fields.
6. From the **Listings** table, double-click the **Listing ID, Last Name, Address,** and **Price** fields.
7. Name the query: `Agents and Listings.`
8. Close the query.
9. Create a query that produces a table of listings information to calculate approximate real estate taxes. In the **Queries** object, click **Create a query using a wizard.**
10. From the Listings table, double-click the **Listing ID, Address, City, Price,** and **Appraised Value** fields.

Continued on next page

11. Name the query: `Listings-Approximate Tax.`

12. In Design view, add a calculated field to calculate the approximate tax.

    Enter an expression that includes a field name (Approximate Tax) and a formula that multiplies Appraised Value by the county tax rate of .0237. Hint: Approximate Tax: `[Appraised Value]*.0237.`

13. Click the **Run** button to see the change.

14. In Design view, format the properties of the Approximate Tax data for **Currency**.

15. In Datasheet view, format the query datasheet using the raised cell style and print a copy of the query.

16. Close the query; save the changes.

17. Answer the questions on the table below using any one of the queries in this database.

18. Close the database.

ACCESS

ANSWER THESE QUESTIONS USING ANY ONE OF THE QUERIES CREATED IN THE FOUR CORNERS REALTY DATABASE.
1. What are the approximate taxes on the house at 12 Gale Way?
2. Mr. Davids, the homeowner, called and wants the telephone number of his listing agent. Provide the name and telephone number.
3. Any agents without listings are being asked to come in this Saturday for telephone duty. Who will be called to come in to work?
4. Which agent has the highest value in listings? Provide the agent's name and value of listings.
5. What is the average price of the homes we have listed in West Hollywood?

Cues for Reference

Add a Calculated Field to Queries

1. Click **Design View** button for the selected query.
2. Enter the expression in the first blank column.
3. Click the **Run** button to view the results.

Format Results Displayed in a Calculated Field

1. The query should be open.
2. Right-click the **calculated field.**
3. Click **Properties.**
4. Click the property to change.
5. Delete any contents and replace with the necessary value or format.
6. Close field properties.
7. Click the **Run** button to view the change in format.

Create One-to-Many Relationships

1. Click the **Relationships** button.
2. Double-click each table and/or query to include.
3. Click **Close.**
4. Drag the primary key field in the one table to the foreign key field in the many table.
5. Click **Create.**

Create a Multi-Table Select Query

1. Click the **Queries** object.
2. Double-click **Create a query using a wizard.**
3. Click the first table to include in the Tables/Queries box.
4. Double-click the fields required in the Available Fields box to move them to the Selected Fields box.
5. Click the list arrow in the Tables/Queries list box.
6. Click the next table to include.
7. Double-click the fields required in the Available Fields box to move them to the Selected Fields box.
8. Click **Finish.**

Act I Database: ALS
Table: Customers
Queries: Travel Partner Trip Count
Travel Preferences Count
Most Recent Travel Count
Next Travel Interest Count

Act II Tables: Customers
Travel Partners
Queries: Travel Partners Query
Travel Partners Query1

WHAT YOU NEED TO KNOW

Act I

Air Land Sea Travel Group, also known as ALS Travel Group, has offices in Boston, New York, and California. ALS specializes in both corporate and leisure travel packages. The director of the Corporate Travel Department in New York is Mr. Wilson Jones and the director of the Leisure Travel Department is Ms. Robin Byron.

- You are working for Robin in the Leisure Travel Department. She would like to begin a direct mail campaign in conjunction with a cruise company. Before investing in the campaign, Robin would like a better understanding of the interests of the current customer base.
- Robin has listed some questions about existing customers that she would like you to answer by using information stored in the customer database. She has also recommended a method of obtaining the information from the database.
- These questions and recommendations are shown in the chart on the next page. Use a copy of the chart to keep track of the information you gather using the sorts, filters, and queries you build.

Follow these guidelines:

- The data is contained in the **ALS** database, in the **Customers** table on the Data CD.

- A worksheet has been included for you to use. It provides Robin's questions, and the suggested method for obtaining the answer.

- Use Find and Filter tools to answer the questions as listed. To answer the questions that have a Query indication, create four queries and name them as listed below. Each query should contain only the one field indicated in the query name. In Design view, add another copy of the field and use the Total line to set the Group By and Count functions for the fields.
    - Travel Partner Trip Count
    - Travel Preferences Count
    - Most Recent Travel Count
    - Next Travel Interest Count

Question	One-Time Search	Filter	Query	Answer
Where does Richard McCarthy live?	x			
How many customers are satisfied?		x		
How many customers are not satisfied?		x		
How many customers are from New York?		x		
How many customers are from Florida?		x		
How many customers are from Texas?		x		
How many customers are from California?		x		
How many customers prefer to travel by cruise ship?			x	
What is the most popular travel preference?			x	
Which Travel Partner have most customers used? How many customers used the services of that Travel Partner?			x	
How many customers have used Travel Partner "2"?			x	
Which is the most popular travel destination indicated as the next travel interest?			x	
Which is the second most popular destination indicated as the next travel interest?			x	
How many customers recently took cruises?			x	

Act II

Based on your analysis of the customer database, Robin is moving forward with a Travel Partners Cruise Promotion, targeted to the customer base. An important corporate account has asked Wilson Jones, the director of the Corporate Travel Department, to arrange a cruise for one of its key executives. Wilson has asked Robin for some information about customer satisfaction with specific travel partners. He has also asked Robin to provide him with contact information for the partners with the highest levels of satisfaction.

- Robin has asked you to provide the information to her in the form shown below.

TRAVEL PARTNER CUSTOMER SATISFACTION FORM	
Name of the company with the highest number of Very Satisfied customers	
Names of companies with a Not Satisfied rating.	
Name of contact for the company with the highest number of Very Satisfied customers	

Follow these guidelines:

- The travel partner information is found in the **Travel Partners** table in the **ALS2** database.
- Establish the relationship between the **Customers** and **Travel Partners** tables. Use the Travel Partner ID field in the **Travel Partners** table and the Travel Partner Latest Trip field in the **Customers** table to establish the relationship. You do not need to establish referential integrity for this exercise.
- Use the Simple Query Wizard to create a multi-table query that contains the following fields from the **Customers** and **Travel Partners** tables:

TRAVEL PARTNERS	CUSTOMERS
Travel Partner ID	Satisfaction with latest trip
Company Name	

- Name the query: `Travel Partners Query`
- Modify the query, using a criteria setting, to view partners who were given a rating of "Very Satisfied." Fill in the name of the company that has the highest number of "Very Satisfied" rankings in the Travel Partner Customer Satisfaction form.
- Modify the query to view partners who were given a rating of "Not Satisfied." Fill in the name of those companies in the Travel Partner Customer Satisfaction form.
- Close the query; save the modifications you made.
- Create another query that contains the following fields from the **Customers** and **Travel Partners** tables:

TRAVEL PARTNERS	CUSTOMERS
Travel Partner ID	Satisfaction with latest trip
Company Name	
FirstName	
LastName	
Phone	
E-mail	

- Name the query: `Travel Partners—Satisfaction Count.`
- Modify the query to add a column to count the satisfaction ratings for each firm.
- Fill in the name, telephone number, and e-mail address of the contact person in the firm with the highest ratings in the Travel Partner Customer Satisfaction form.
- Save the changes you made to the query.
- Close the database.
- Exit Access.

ACCESS

LESSON 5

Access Reports

In this lesson, you will learn how to create reports based on a database; to use AutoReports and the Report Wizard to create a report; to preview and print a report; to use the Report Design Toolbox to add controls; and to add a calculated field to a report. You will also learn to modify report controls and modify report sections and properties.

Upon completion of this lesson, you should have mastered the following skill sets:

- Create a report using AutoReport
- Create a report using the LabelWizard
- Create and format reports using the Report Wizard
  - Preview a report
  - Modify page settings and print a report
- Use report sections
- Modify report layout
- Use the Report Design Toolbox to add controls
- Add calculated controls to a report section
  - Modify controls

Terms

Software-related

Reports
AutoReport
AutoFormat
Label Wizard
Report Wizard
Design view
Print Preview
Layout Preview
Report sections
Report header
Report footer
Report detail
Group header
Group footer
Report selector
Section selector
Aggregate function
Running Sum
Over All

GOALS

To create and print reports from a real estate database

To practice using the following skill sets:

- Create a report using AutoReport
- Create a report using the Label Wizard
- Create and format reports using the Report Wizard
  - Preview a report
  - Modify page settings and print a report

ACCESS

WHAT YOU NEED TO KNOW

- *Reports* are database objects that use data from tables and queries to create a presentation-quality printout. You can build reports from more than one table or query. Additional information, such as headings or logos, can be part of the design of the report.
- Report objects are extremely valuable business tools because once they are created and saved, you can reuse them to present data with new or updated information.
- Access provides AutoReports and the Report Wizard to help you create various types of reports. In addition, the Label Wizard is a report tool that produces labels.

Create a Report Using AutoReport

- *AutoReport* automatically creates a basic report to display all the fields in a table or a query. In the Database window, with the Table object selected, double-click the data source table. Then, click the New Object button and click AutoReport, as shown in Figure 5.1.

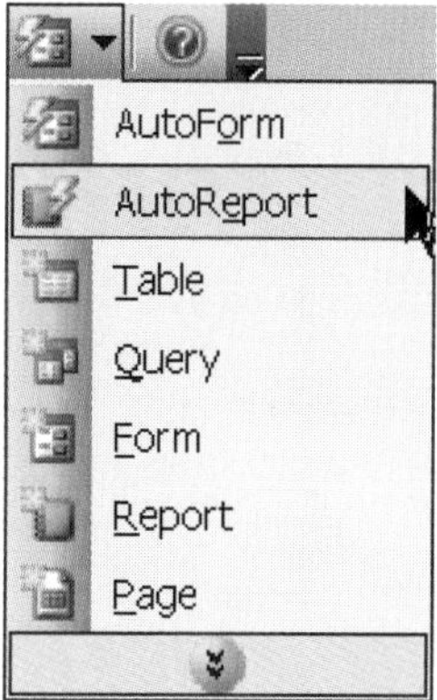

Figure 5.1 New Object list

- Access applies a standard *AutoFormat* and a report appears without report or page headers and footers and arranged in columnar fashion. Unless this is satisfactory, a better choice is to use the AutoReport:Tabular layout.
- In the tabular layout, the fields in each record appear on one line and the labels print once at the top of each page. In the Database window, click the Reports tab and click New. The New Report dialog box opens, as shown in Figure 5.2.

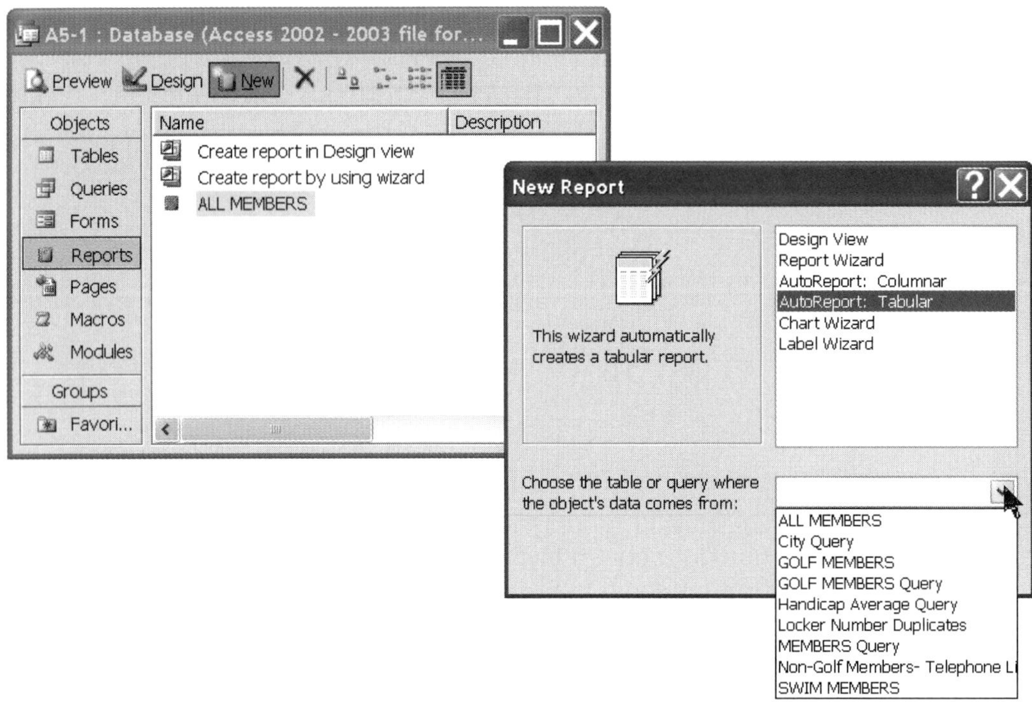

Figure 5.2 New Report dialog box

▶ Click AutoReport: Tabular. Click the list arrow in the lower box to select the data source table or query. Click OK, and a tabular report appears, as shown in Figure 5.3. Access applies a standard AutoFormat unless another AutoFormat is set.

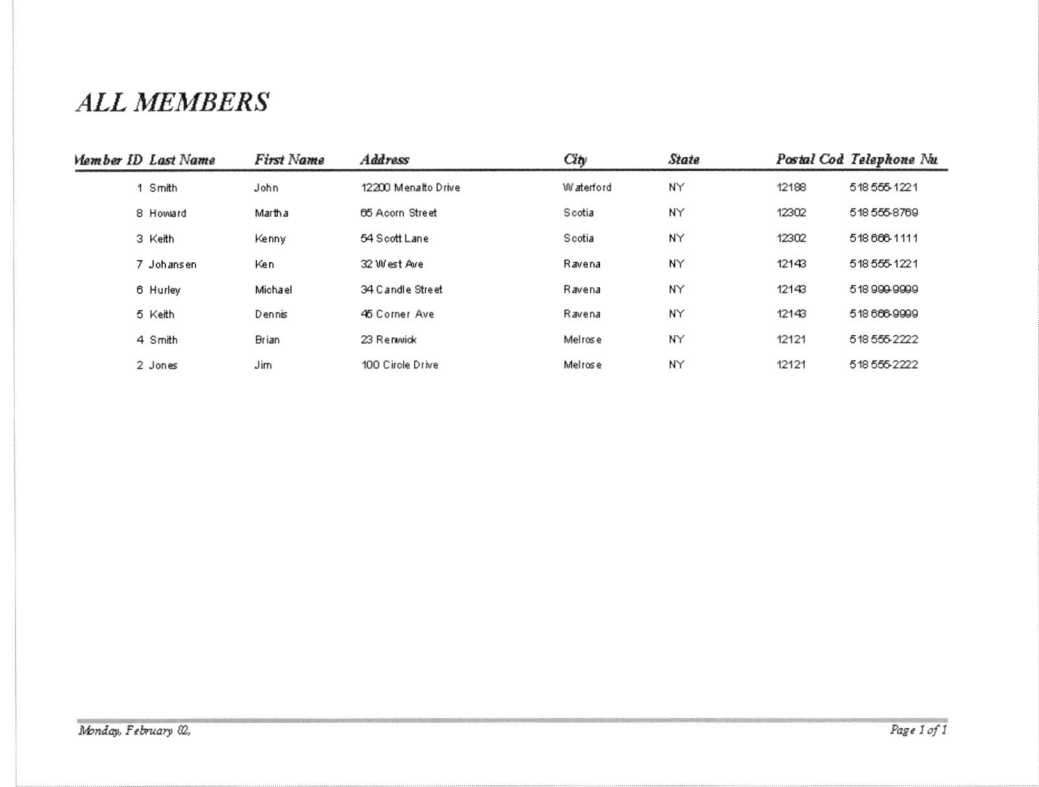

ALL MEMBERS

Member ID	*Last Name*	*First Name*	*Address*	*City*	*State*	*Postal Cod*	*Telephone Nu*
1	Smith	John	12200 Menalto Drive	Waterford	NY	12188	518 555-1221
8	Howard	Martha	65 Acorn Street	Scotia	NY	12302	518 555-8769
3	Keith	Kenny	54 Scott Lane	Scotia	NY	12302	518 666-1111
7	Johansen	Ken	32 West Ave	Ravena	NY	12143	518 555-1221
6	Hurley	Michael	34 Candle Street	Ravena	NY	12143	518 999-9999
5	Keith	Dennis	45 Corner Ave	Ravena	NY	12143	518 666-9999
4	Smith	Brian	23 Renwick	Melrose	NY	12121	518 555-2222
2	Jones	Jim	100 Circle Drive	Melrose	NY	12121	518 555-2222

Monday, February 02, *Page 1 of 1*

Figure 5.3 AutoReport: Tabular

TRY it OUT *A5-1*

1. Start **Access.**
2. Open the **Members** database in **A5-1** from the Data CD.
3. Click the **Tables** object and double-click **ALL MEMBERS.**
4. Click the list arrow on the **New Object** button.

5. Click **AutoReport.** Notice that this is a multi-page columnar report.
6. Close the report. Do not name or save the report.
7. Close the ALL MEMBERS table.
8. In the Report object, click the **New** button.

9. Click **AutoReport:Tabular.**
10. Click the list arrow in the lower box. Click **ALL MEMBERS.** Click **OK.**
11. Notice that this is a single-page report with header and footer information.
12. Close the report. Do not name or save it.

Create a Report Using the Label Wizard

- Access provides a *Label Wizard* that allows you to create mailing and other label types in standard and custom sizes, based on the data in a database.
- To create labels, in the Database window click the Reports object. Click New to open the New Report dialog box, and click Label Wizard. Click the data source table or query and click OK. The Label Wizard opens, as shown in Figure 5.4.

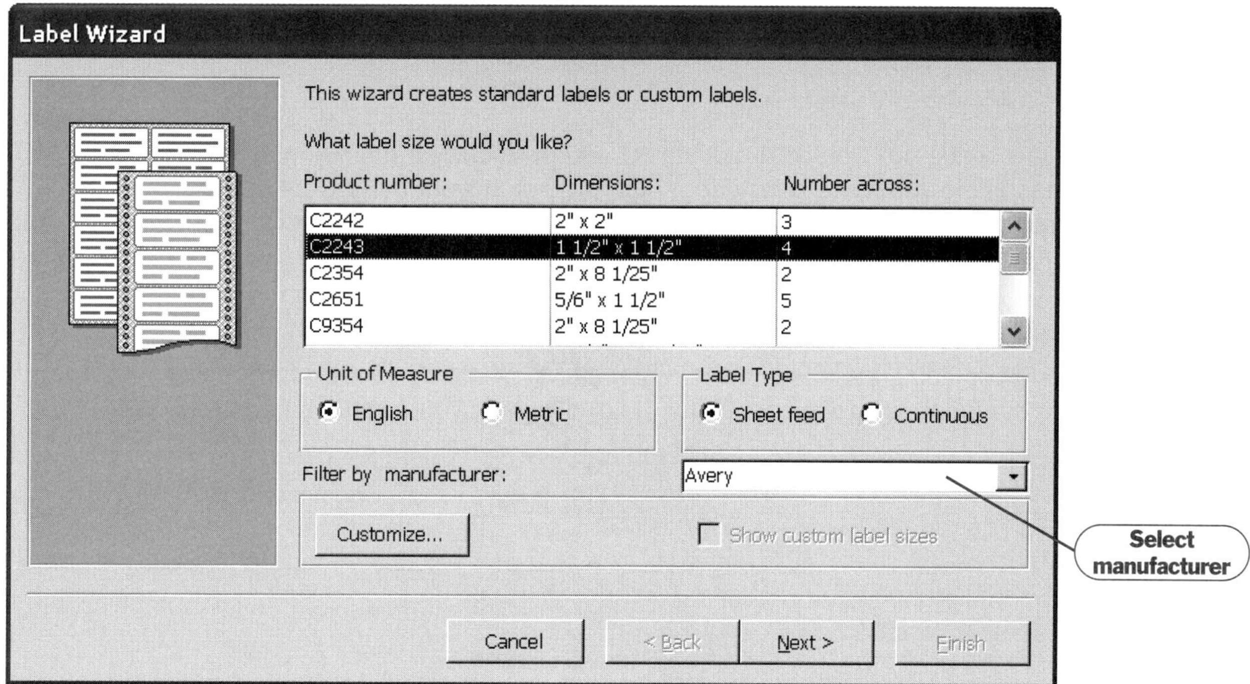

Figure 5.4 Label Wizard

- The Wizard lists the most popular product numbers for the leading label manufacturers. Click the manufacturer and then click the product number of the labels you are using. Also, click the appropriate Unit of Measure and Label Type.
- Click Next to open a dialog box where you can set the font, font size, and font weight. You can also set text color and italic and underline formats. You can preview the formatting changes in the left portion of the Wizard, as shown in Figure 5.5.

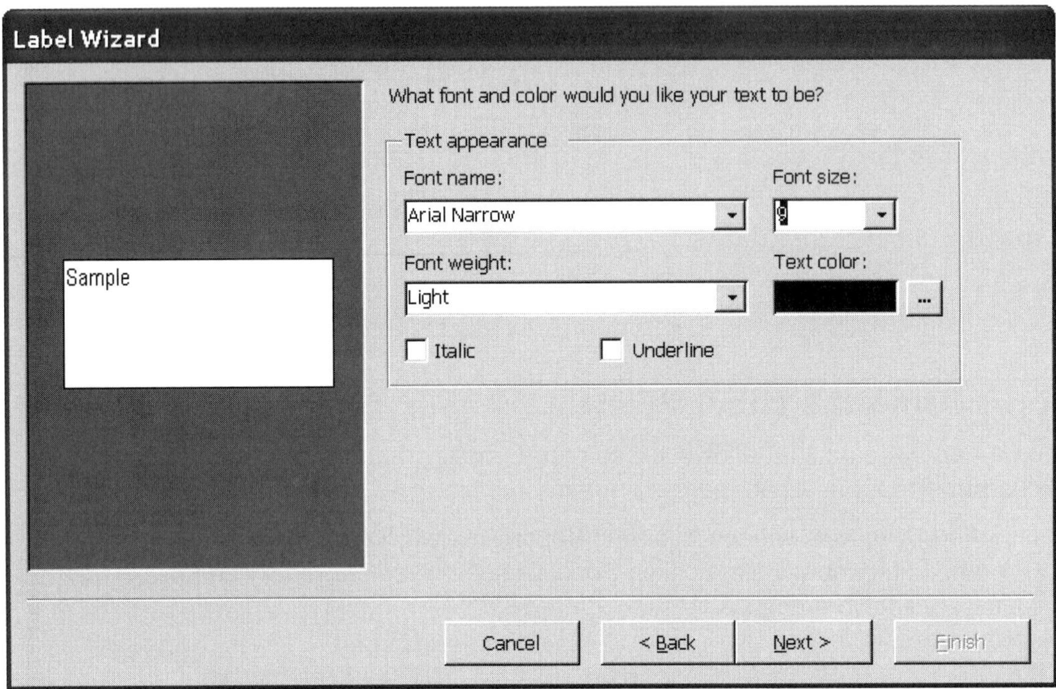

Figure 5.5 Label Wizard—text format

- Click Next, and a dialog box opens to assist you in constructing the label, as shown in Figure 5.6. Double-click each field you want to include, in the order you want them to print. Add spaces, returns, and punctuation between fields. Be certain that the field layout represents how you want the label to print. As you complete each line in the address, use the Enter or Tab key to move to the next line.
- You can enter text that you would like to appear on every label in the Prototype label box. For example, if you were doing a mailing to the membership of a club about a family event, you might want to create the label using the Last Name field followed by the word Family, as shown in Figure 5.6.

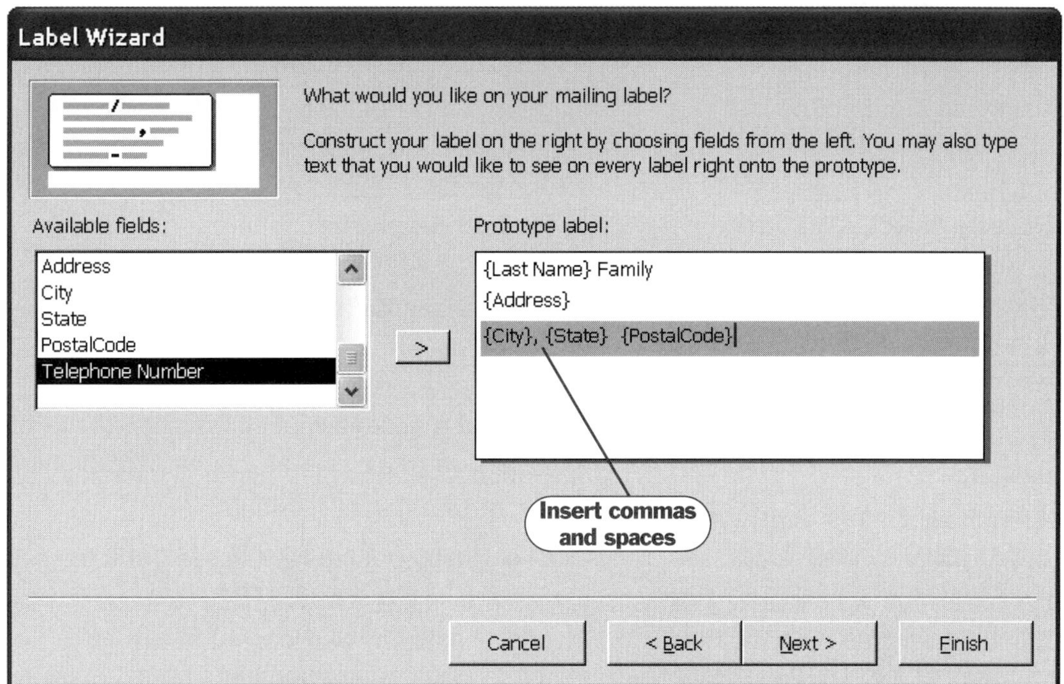

Figure 5.6 Label Wizard—construct label

▶ Click Next, and a dialog box opens, prompting you to choose sort order, as shown in Figure 5.7. You may choose to sort your mailing by zip code to take advantage of the post office's special mailing rates. You can also sort by more than one field. Double-click the Sort by choice or choices, and click Next to display the Wizard's last step. Title the report and click Finish to open the label report.

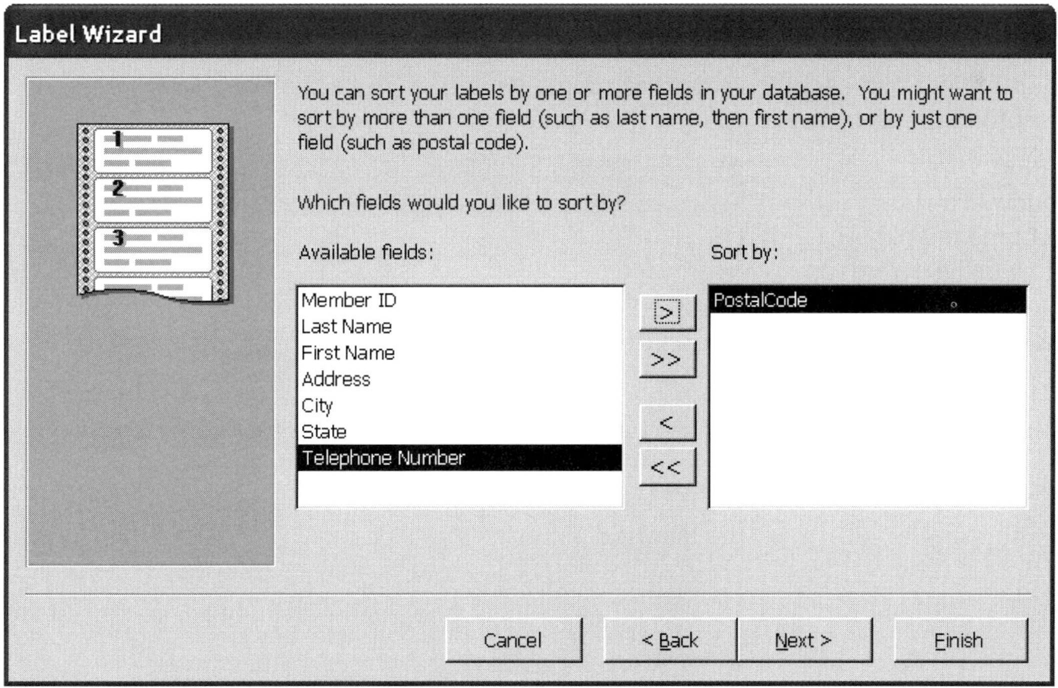

Figure 5.7 Label Wizard—sort

TRY *it* OUT *A5-2*

1. Continue using the file from the last Try it Out or open **A5-2** from the Data CD.
2. Click the **Reports** object. Click **New.**
3. Click **Label Wizard.** Click the list arrow in the lower box.
4. Click **ALL MEMBERS.** Click **OK.**
5. If necessary, click **Avery** in the Filter by manufacturer box, and click **English** under Unit of Measure.
6. Click Product number **C2243** in the What label size would you like? box. Notice that this choice prints four labels across a page.
7. Click **Next.** Click the list arrow in the **Font name** box. Click **Arial Narrow,** if necessary.
8. Click the list arrow in the **Font size** box. Click **9,** if necessary.
9. Click **Next.** Double-click the **Last Name** field to move it from the Available fields box to the Prototype label box.
10. Press the **spacebar.** Enter `Family` and press the **Enter** key.
11. Double-click **Address.** Press the **Enter** key.
12. Double-click **City.** Enter a comma and press the **spacebar.**
13. Double-click **State.** Press the **spacebar** twice. Double-click **PostalCode.**
14. Click **Next.** Double-click **PostalCode** to move it to the Sort by box.
15. Click **Next, Finish.** Notice that the information appears in label format.
16. Close the report. Notice that it is saved as a Report object.

Create and Format Reports Using the Report Wizard

- You can build a report using the *Report Wizard*. Similar to other wizards, the Report Wizard asks you questions about what information you want to include in a report and how you want to present and format it. You can modify the resulting report, if changes are necessary.
- You should use the Report Wizard to create reports when you do not require all the fields in a table, you require layout and style, the report contains fields from more than one table or query, or if AutoReport formats do not meet your requirements.
- To use the Report Wizard, in the Database window click the Reports object, and double-click Create report by using wizard, as shown in Figure 5.8. (The Wizard is also available in the New Report dialog box shown in Figure 5.2.)

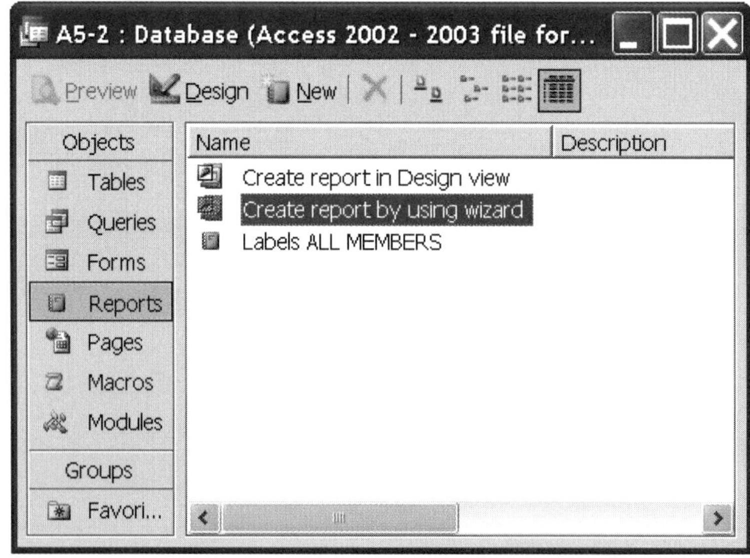

Figure 5.8 Report Wizard

- The Report Wizard asks you to select the data source table or query and select the fields to include, as shown in Figure 5.9. Click the data source table or query and double-click the selected fields. If the report is based on more than one table or query, click the additional data source and double-click the fields to add. Tables must have established relationships before you can include them, or a related query, in a report.

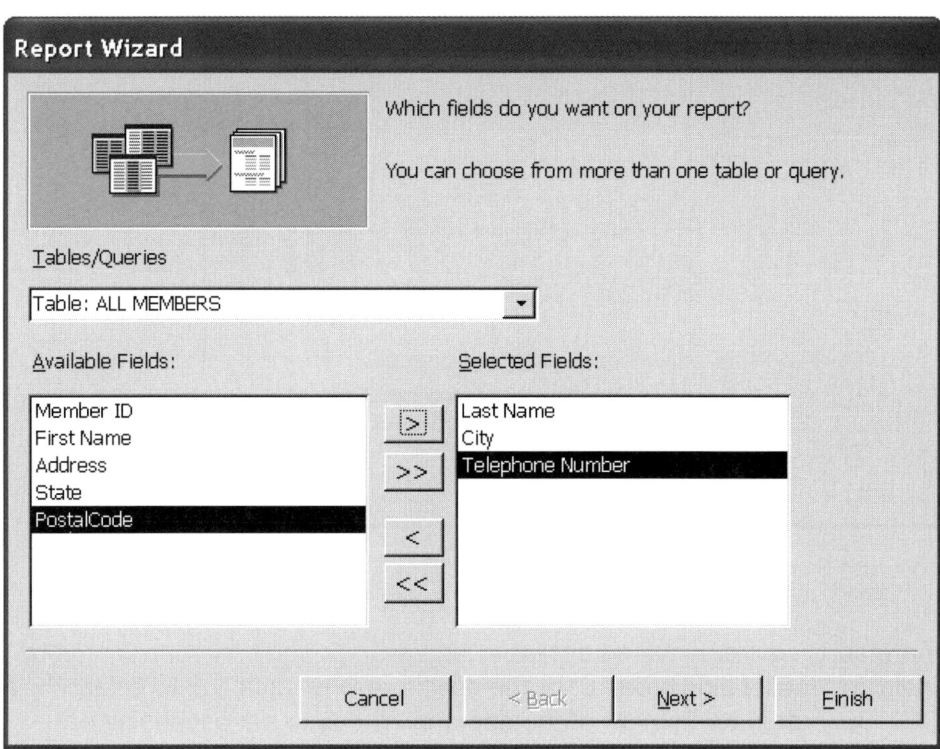

Figure 5.9 Report Wizard—selecting tables and fields

- Click Next to display the grouping options, as shown in Figure 5.10. You can group records in a report based on the values of more than one field; the Wizard allows you to choose up to four fields by which to group. For example, you may want to present a report on the membership of an organization by city and zip code. The first field you group by is the first and most significant group level; the second field you group by is the next most significant group level, etc.

ACCESS

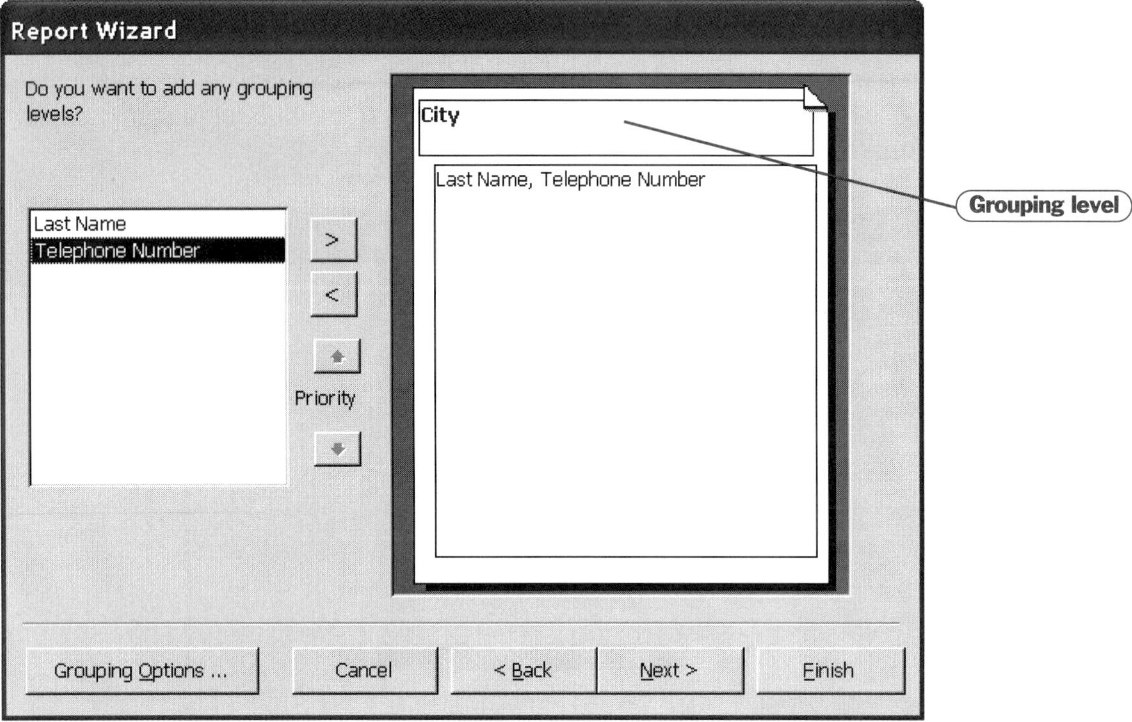

Figure 5.10 Report Wizard—grouping

▶ Click Next to enter any sort requirements, as shown in Figure 5.11. You can sort records by up to four fields in ascending or descending order. Click the down arrow in each box to select the fields by which to sort. Click the button to the right of the appropriate box to set ascending or descending order.

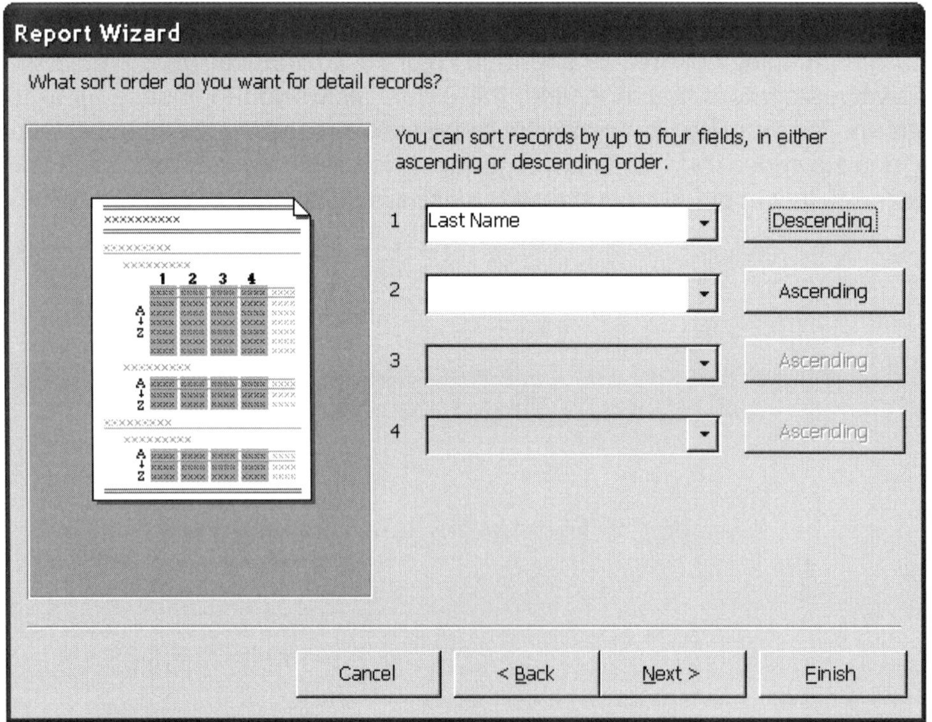

Figure 5.11 Report Wizard—sort

▶ Click Next and layout options appear, as shown in Figure 5.12. The Wizard provides six layout options, and the choice of a portrait or landscape page orientation. Click each layout to see a preview of the format and then select the layout and orientation you want.

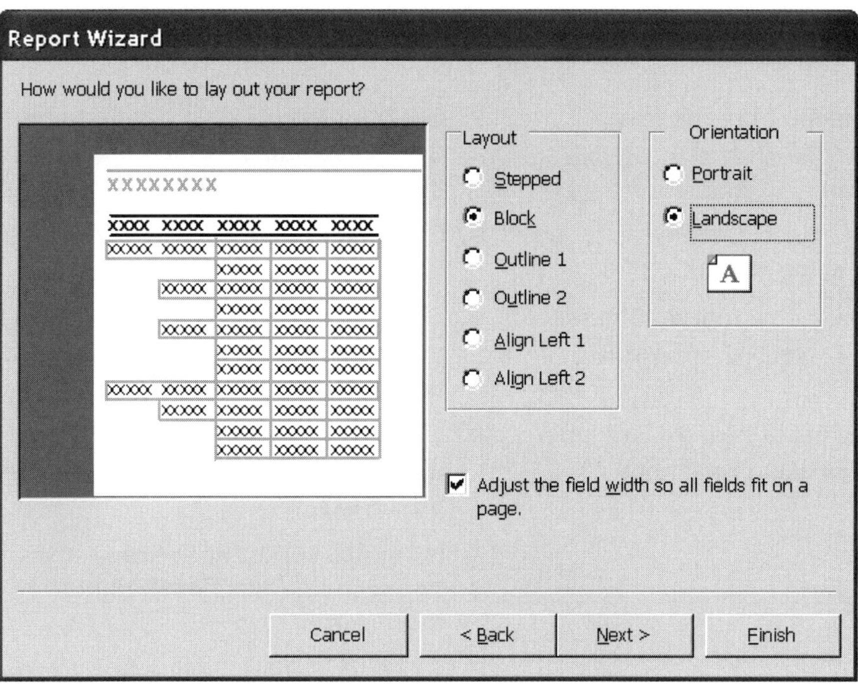

Figure 5.12 Report Wizard—layout

▶ Click Next to select a style for the report, as shown in Figure 5.13. Click each style to preview. Click the style you want, and click Next to provide a title for the report. Click Finish, and Access presents a zoomed-in version of the Print Preview screen.

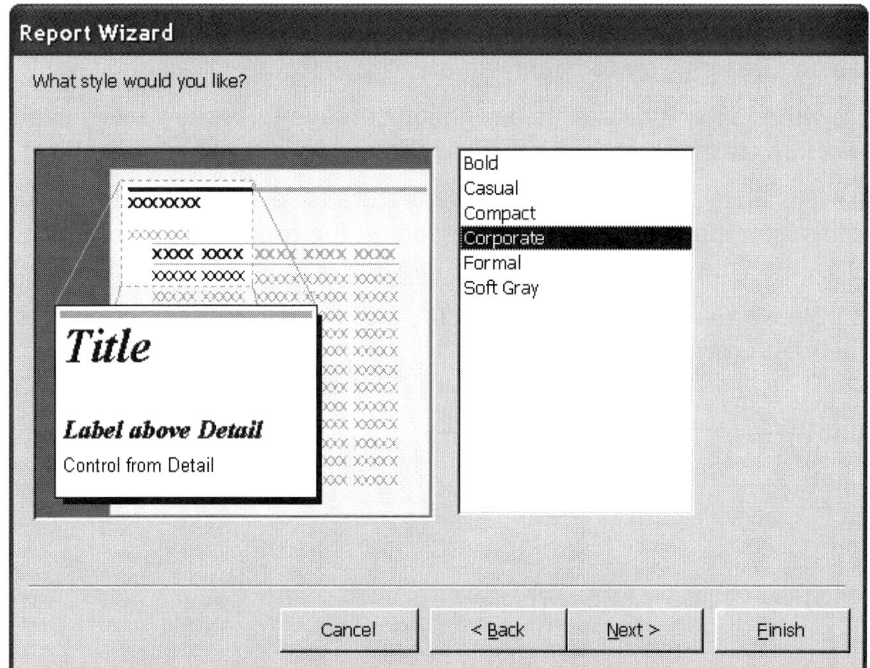

Figure 5.13 Report Wizard—style

▶ The Report Wizard adds the date, the page number, and the number of pages in a footer to the bottom of the report.

TRY *it* OUT *A5-3*

1. Continue using the file from the last Try it Out or open **A5-3** from the Data CD.
2. Click the **Reports** object. Double-click **Create report by using wizard.**
3. Click the list arrow in the **Tables/Queries** list box and click **Table: ALL MEMBERS**, if not already selected.
4. Move the following fields from the Available Fields box to the Selected Fields box:

   Last Name

   City

   Telephone Number
5. Click **Next.**
6. Double-click **City** to group by city. Click **Next.**
7. Click the list arrow in the first sort box. Click **Last Name.** Notice that Ascending is displayed to the right of the box.
8. Click **Ascending.** Notice that Descending is now displayed. Click **Next.**
9. Click each layout option to preview the available layouts. Click **Block, Landscape orientation,** and **Next.**
10. Click each style option to preview available styles. Click **Corporate,** and then **Next.**
11. Name the report `Members - City and Telephone`. Click **Finish** to preview the report.
12. Close the report. Notice that the name of this report is saved as a report object.

Preview a Report

▶ Reports have three views: Design view, Print Preview, and Layout Preview.

▶ Use *Design view* to create a report if the Report Wizard or AutoReport tools do not meet your requirements. You also use Design view to modify an existing report.

▶ Use *Print Preview* to view the report's data. Use navigation controls to preview every page in the report. Use the Print Preview toolbar buttons to preview the report in different magnifications.

▶ The *Layout Preview* is available in Design view. Use this feature to review a report's layout, but not its data, because this view may not include all the data in the report. If your database has a small number of records, the Print Preview and Layout Preview windows may be identical.

▶ To view a report in Print Preview as shown in Figure 5.14, with the Reports object selected, click the report and click the Print Preview button.

Members-City and Telephone

City	Last Name	Telephone Number
Melrose	Smith	518 555-2222
	Jones	518 555-2222
Ravena	Keith	518 666-9999
	Johansen	518 555-1221
	Hurley	518 999-9999
Scotia	Keith	518 666-1111
	Howard	518 555-8769
Waterford	Smith	518 555-1221

Figure 5.14 Open report in Print Preview

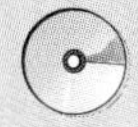

- Access displays a preview of the report. To view the report in Design view, click the Design View button and the report appears in Design view. (You will be working with Design view in the second part of this lesson.) Click the list arrow of the View button and click Layout Preview to view the report layout.

TRY *it* OUT *A5-4*

1. Continue using the file from the last Try it Out or open **A5-4** from the Data CD and click the **Reports** object.
2. Click the **Members – City and Telephone** report.
3. Click the **Preview** button. Notice that the report you created in the last Try it Out appears in Print Preview view.
4. Click **Design View** to change to Design view.
5. Click the list arrow of the **View** button.
6. Click **Layout Preview.**
7. Notice that, in this report, the Print Preview and Layout Preview views are the same.
8. Close the report.

Modify Page Settings and Print a Report

- To print a report, click the report in the Database window, or open the report, and click the Print button on the toolbar.
- If you need to change any print or formatting options, click File, Page Setup to open the Page Setup dialog box, as shown in Figure 5.15. Change the margins by deleting the box contents and entering the content you want. Click Print Data Only to omit labels, control borders, gridlines, and graphics.

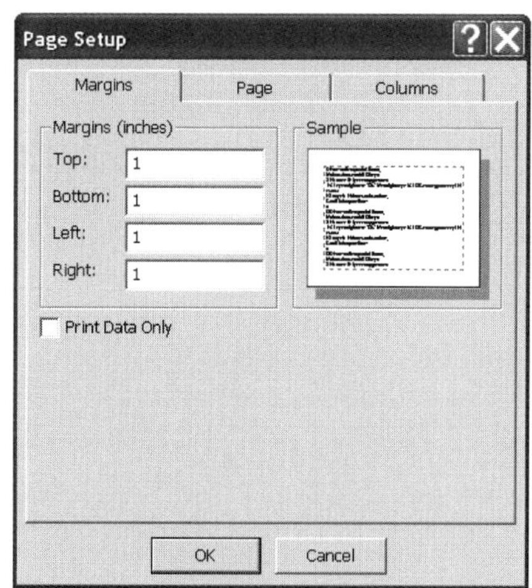

Figure 5.15 Page Setup—margins tab

▶ Click the Page tab to select the orientation, the paper size and source, and the printer, as shown in Figure 5.16. Click the Columns tab to change grid settings, column size, and column layout, as shown in Figure 5.17. Access displays an error message if you select options it cannot print on a page. Click OK and click the Print button to print the report.

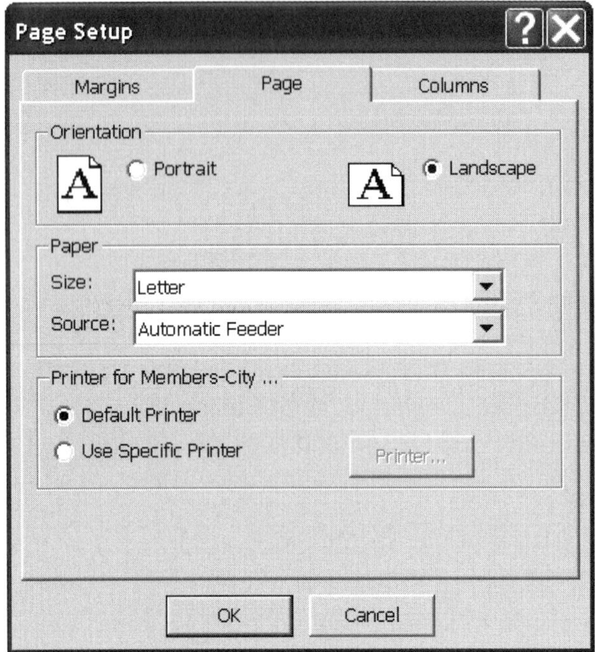

Figure 5.16 Page Setup—page tab

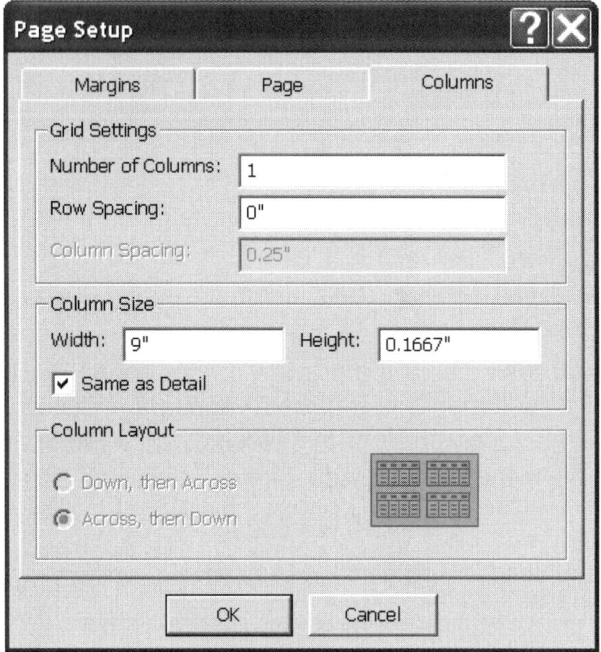

Figure 5.17 Page Setup—columns tab

TRY *it* OUT *A5-5*

1. Continue using the file from the last Try it Out or open **A5-5** from the Data CD and click the **Reports** object.

2. Double-click the **Members – City and Telephone** report.
3. Click **File, Page Setup.**
4. Review the Margins options, but do not make any changes.
5. Click the **Page** tab and click **Landscape,** if not already selected.
6. Click the **Columns** tab.
7. Change Number of Columns to **2** and Column Size Width to **4"**.
8. Click **OK.** Notice the change in format.
9. Click the **Print** button.

10. Close the report; do not save changes. Close the database.

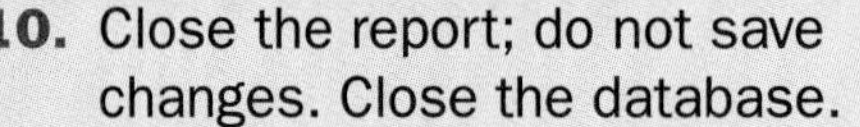

1
2
3

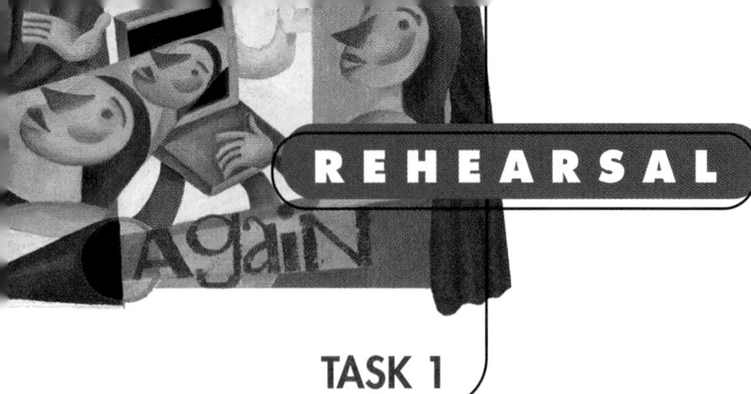

GOALS

To create standard reports based on Four Corners Realty Company's database of homes for sale; to create a report that presents listings by town, in order of price; to prepare a mailing label report to use for a company family outing; and to print the reports you create.

SETTING THE STAGE/WRAPUP

Database: Four Corners Realty
Tables: Listings
Agents
Report: Weekly Listing report
Employee Picnic Labels

WHAT YOU NEED TO KNOW

- Real estate agents are often out of the office showing properties and are unable to interface with their company's database. For this reason, many rely on printed material that they carry with them at all times.
- You have been asked to produce a report that presents all of the property listings by town, in order of price. This report will be printed weekly.
- Every year Four Corners Realty has a company picnic; each agent's family is invited. You have been asked to prepare mailing labels to use to send invitations to each family.
- In this Rehearsal activity, you will create two reports using the Report Wizard and the Label Wizard to do so. You will preview and print both reports.

DIRECTIONS

1. Open the **Four Corners Realty** database from the Data CD.
2. Click **Reports** and double-click **Create report by using wizard** to create a report from the Listings table that includes the following fields:
   Address
   City
   Price
   Description
3. Group by **City** and sort by **Price** in Ascending order.
4. Use the **Align Left 1** layout, **landscape** orientation, and **Formal** style.
5. Rename the report **Weekly Listing Report** and print it. Compare your printout with the report shown on the facing page.
6. Close the report.
7. Use the **Label Wizard** and the **Agents** table to create labels for the agents.

Note: Set the Unit of Measure to English and the Avery Product Number to C2242.

8. Use the Comic Sans MS font with a 10 point font size and format the label as shown in the sample report on the facing page.
9. Move the following fields from the Available fields box to the Prototype label box:
   Listing Agent
   Home Address
   City
   State
   Zip Code
10. Remember to add the word `Family` after the Listing Agent field.

Continued on next page

11. Sort by **Listing Agent.**
12. Rename the report: **Employee Picnic Labels.**
13. Compare your report to Illustration B.
14. Print and close the report. Close the database.

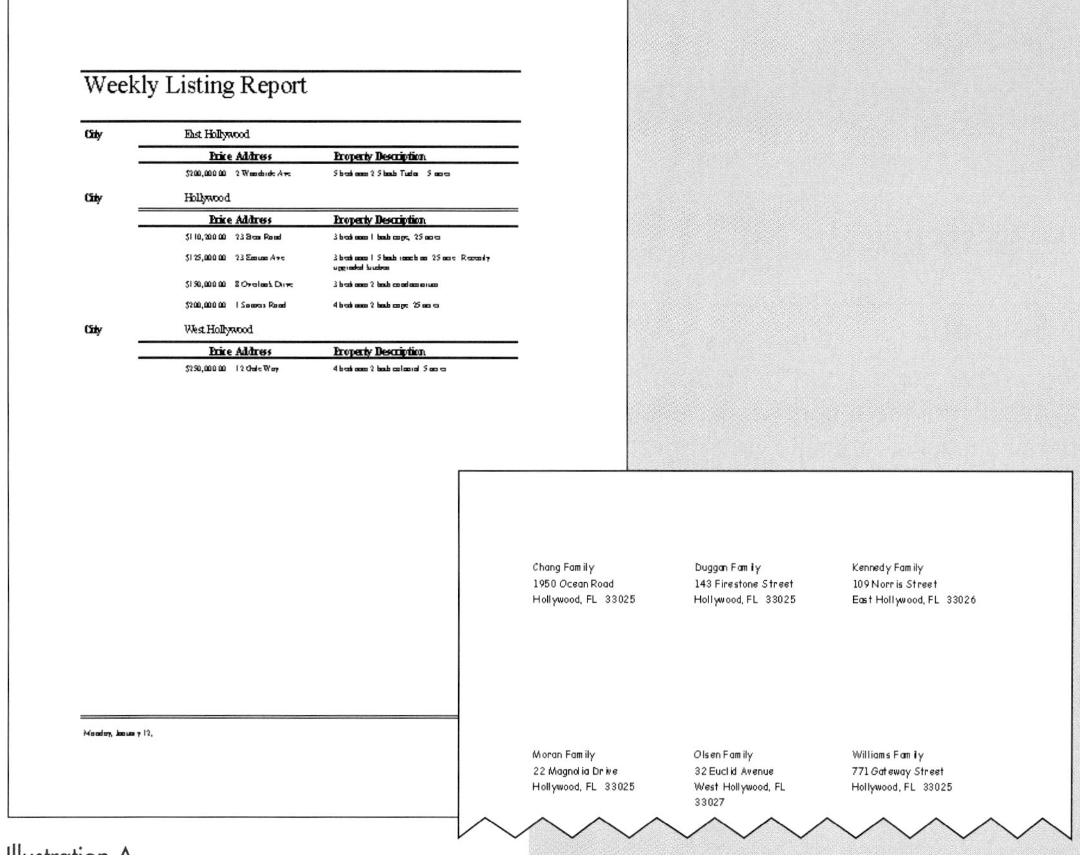

Weekly Listing Report

City East Hollywood

Price Address Property Description

City Hollywood

Price Address Property Description

City West Hollywood

Price Address Property Description

Chang Family
1950 Ocean Road
Hollywood, FL 33025

Duggan Family
143 Firestone Street
Hollywood, FL 33025

Kennedy Family
109 Norris Street
East Hollywood, FL 33026

Moran Family
22 Magnolia Drive
Hollywood, FL 33025

Olsen Family
32 Euclid Avenue
West Hollywood, FL
33027

Williams Family
771 Gateway Street
Hollywood, FL 33025

Illustration A

Illustration B

Cues for Reference

Create a Report using AutoReport
With a table open:
1. Click the **New Object** button list arrow.
2. Click **AutoReport.**

Create a Report Using AutoReport: Tabular
1. Click the **Reports** object.
2. Click **New.**
3. Click **AutoReport: Tabular.**
4. Click the **list arrow**, and click table or query.
5. Click **OK.**

Create a Report Using the Label Wizard
1. Click the **Reports** object.
2. Click **New.**
3. Click **Label Wizard**, click the **list arrow**, click table or query, and click **OK.**
4. Double-click the product number and click **Next.**
5. Select the font and color, and click **Next.**
6. Select the design layout and click **Next.**
7. Select the sort option and click **Next.**
8. Name the report and click **Finish.**

Create and Format Reports Using the Report Wizard
1. Click the **Reports** object.
2. Click **Create report by using wizard**. Click the **list arrow**, and click table or query.
3. Double-click the fields to include.
4. Click additional tables/queries and double-click the fields to include.
5. Click **Next.**
6. Double-click grouping fields and click **Next.**
7. Click the **sort box** list arrow. Select the sort order and click **Next.**
8. Select the layout and orientation, and click **Next.**
9. Select the style and click **Next.**
10. Name the report and click **Finish.**

Preview a Report
1. Click the report.
2. Click **Preview.**

Print a Report
1. Double-click the report.
2. Click the **Print** button.

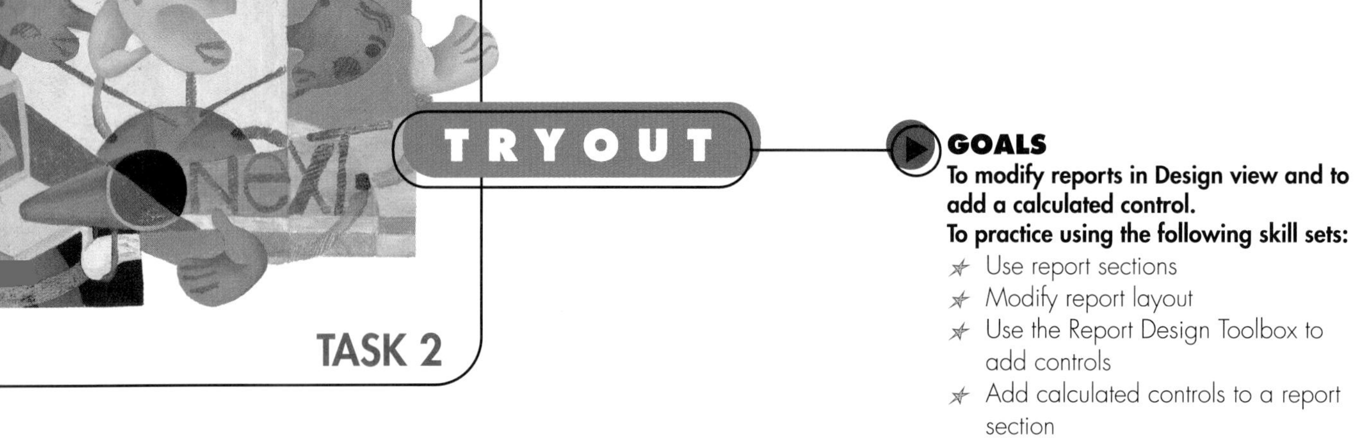

TRYOUT

TASK 2

GOALS

To modify reports in Design view and to add a calculated control.

To practice using the following skill sets:

- Use report sections
- Modify report layout
- Use the Report Design Toolbox to add controls
- Add calculated controls to a report section
  - Modify controls

WHAT YOU NEED TO KNOW

Use Report Sections

- You add *report sections* to a report to improve its design and usefulness. The sections of a report that you can include are the report header and footer, group header and footer, page header and footer, and detail sections. You can view report sections in report Design view. When a report is in Print Preview, click the Design View button to view the sections of a report, as shown in Figure 5.18.

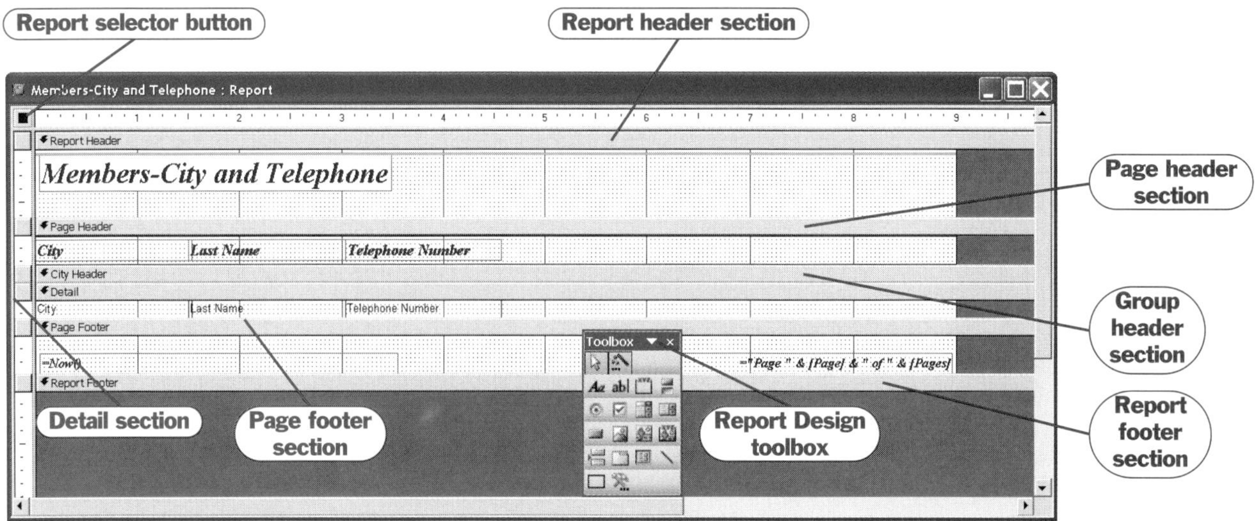

Figure 5.18 Report Design View

- The *report header* displays information that you want to show for every record, such as the form title. The header appears at the top of the first page when it is printed or previewed. The *report footer* appears once at the end of the report. You can use it to display data such as report totals. It prints, and previews, after the last detail section on the last page. Notice the Report Design toolbox that displays.
- The *report detail* section displays the main body of the report. A report also has page header and footer sections. Page headers and page footers appear in Print Preview, Layout Preview, and on printed forms. A page header displays information you want at the top of every printed page. A page footer displays information you want at the bottom of every printed page. Page headers and footers can contain controls for page numbers and dates.

- Use the *group header* to present information, such as a group title or total, at the beginning of a group of records. Use the *group footer* to present information at the end of a group of records. Notice that Access does not display the group footer automatically, as illustrated in Figure 5.18.
- To display the group footer, click View, Sorting and Grouping, and the Sorting and Grouping dialog box opens, as shown in Figure 5.19. Group properties appear in the bottom pane of the dialog box. Click Group Footer, click the list arrow, and click Yes to display the group footer. The group header and footer take on the name of the field that you are grouping, City Header and City Footer in this example.

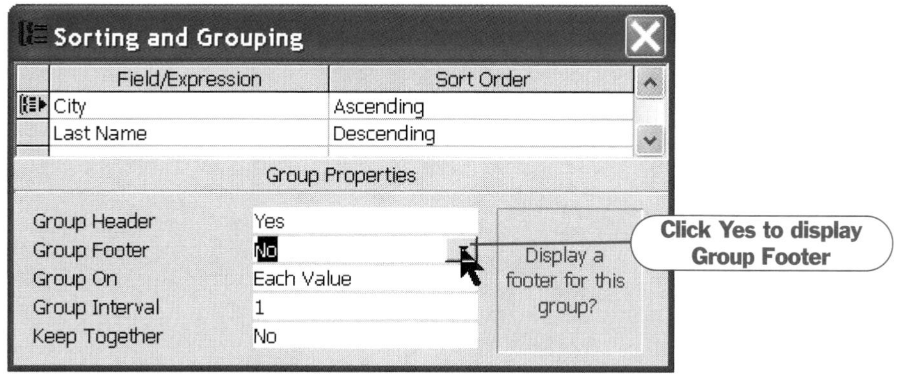

Figure 5.19 Sorting and Grouping properties

ACCESS

TRY *it* OUT *A5-6*

1. Open the **A5-6** file from the Data CD.
2. Click the **Reports** object. Double-click **Members – City and Telephone.**
3. Click **View, Design View.**
4. Notice the location of the Report Header and Footer. Notice that the Detail section contains the fields of the report. Notice the location of the Group Header and that the Group Footer is not displayed.
5. Click **View, Sorting and Grouping.**
6. Click **Group Footer,** click the list arrow, and click **Yes.**
7. Close the **Sorting and Grouping** dialog box. Notice that the Group Header section is titled "City Header" and the Group Footer is titled "City Footer."
8. Notice the location of the Report Footer. Notice the location of the Page Header and Footer.
9. Notice also that the Report Wizard adds two controls to the Page Footer section:

=Now()	*Contains the date the report is printed.*
="Page" &[Page] & "of" & [Pages]	*Contains the printed page number and how many pages are in the report.*

10. Do not close the report.

Modify Report Format Properties

- A report has properties, which Access stores in a property sheet that defines the report's characteristics. Use the report selector to view the properties of a report. The *report selector* is the box where the rulers meet in the upper-left corner of a report in Design view (see Figure 5.18). Double-click the report selector and the report's property sheet appears, as shown in Figure 5.20.

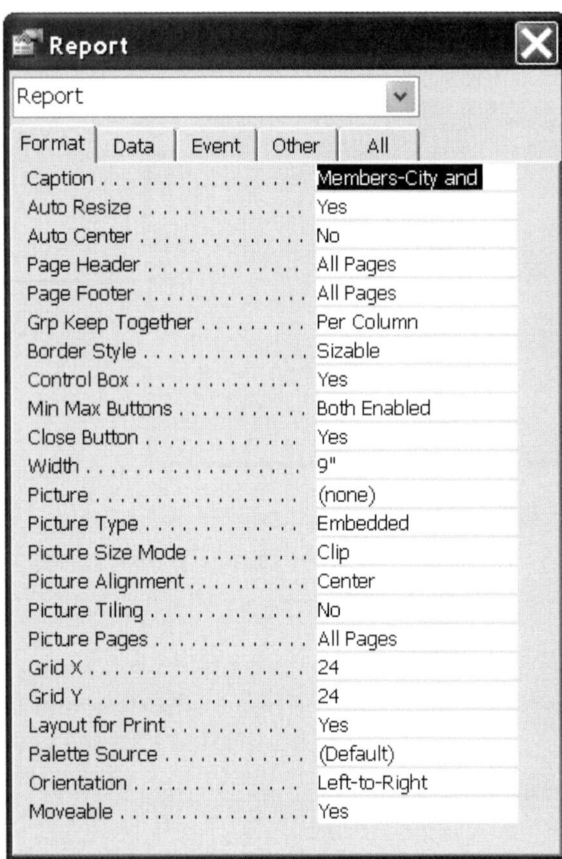

Figure 5.20 Modify the properties of a report

- The properties fall into five categories: *Format*, *Data*, *Event*, and *Other*; to view *All* the properties, click the All tab. Use the scroll bar on the right side of the property window to view property sheet options. Click the name of the property to change it. Delete what is in the box. Enter the new setting. When you make a change to the report, you do not make a change to the underlying data source or table.

- Each section of a report also has properties. To view the properties of a section, click the *section selector*, which is the box to the left of a section bar. Double-click this box to select the section and to open the section's property sheet. The property sheet for a page header section is shown in Figure 5.21.

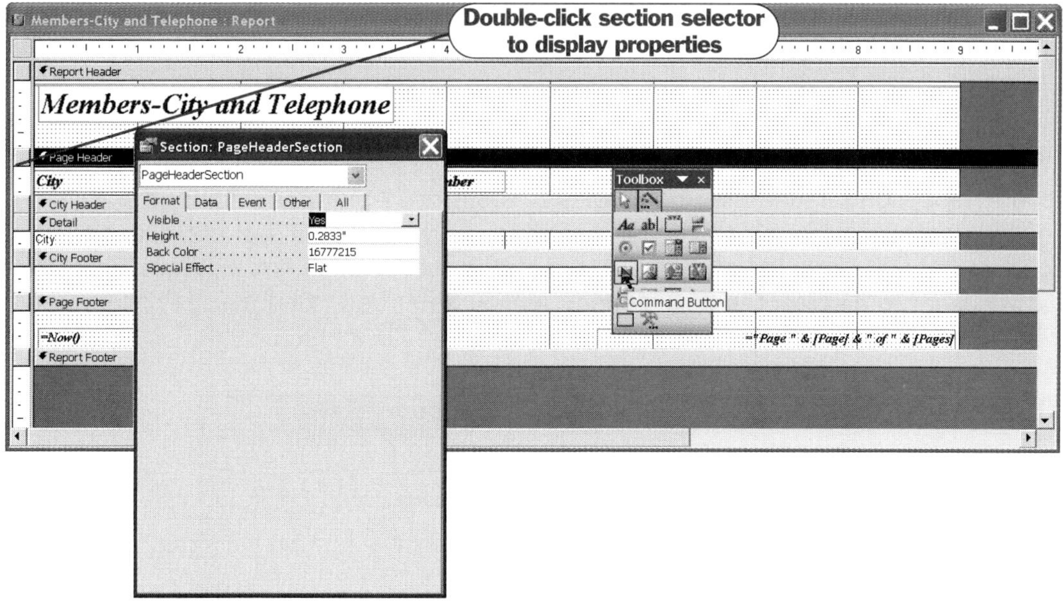

Figure 5.21 Modify the properties of a report—sections

- To change the height of a report section, in the Format tab, click Height. Delete the existing value and replace it with the height you want. You can also change the size of report header/footer, group header/footer, or page header/footer sections using the mouse. To change the height of a section, place the mouse pointer on the bottom edge of the section. Drag the pointer up or down to change the height of the section.
- You can change the width of a section by placing the mouse pointer on the right edge of the section and dragging the pointer to the left or right.
- Report sections can have different heights; however, the report has one width. When you change the width of one section, you change the width of the entire report.

ACCESS

TRY *it* OUT *A5-7*

1. Continue using the file from the last Try it Out or open **A5-7** from the Data CD. You should be in Design view of the **Members – City and Telephone** report.
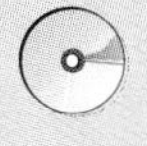
2. Place the mouse pointer on the bottom edge of the Report Header section.
3. Drag the pointer down approximately one inch.
4. Double-click the **Report Footer section selector.**
5. Click the **Height** property on the Format tab of the section property sheet.
6. Replace the contents with: `1.`
7. Close the section property sheet.
8. Click the **View** button.
9. Notice the top and bottom sections of the report.
10. Click the **Design View** button to change to Design view. Do not close the report.

Use the Report Design Toolbox to Add Controls

- To customize a report, you may want to have a title or a date appear on every report. To accomplish this, add a label control to the header or footer section of a report to display a title or caption. It is unbound and remains the same for each record.
- To add an unbound label control, use the Report Design toolbox, as shown in Figure 5.22. Click View and click Toolbox, if the toolbox is not displayed. Click the Label tool and click the location where you want the upper-left corner of the control to be. A small box appears. Enter the information you want to display. The box expands as you enter data. Change to Print Preview view to see the label as it will print.

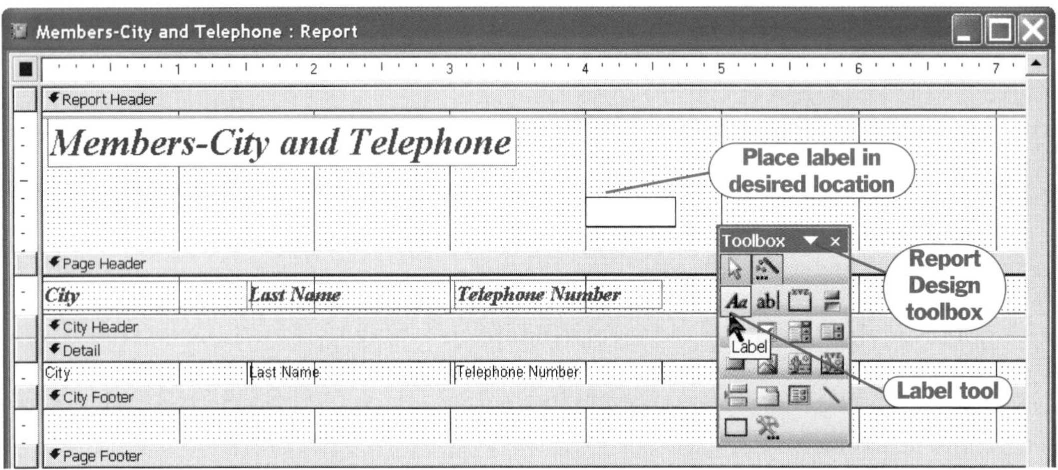

Figure 5.22 Report Design toolbox

TRY *it* OUT *A5-8*

1. Continue using the file from the last Try it Out or open **A5-8** from the Data CD. You should be in Design view of the **Members – City and Telephone** report.
2. Click **View, Toolbox** to show the Report Design toolbox if it is not displayed. Click the **Label** tool.
3. In the Report Header section, click a location on the 4" ruler line where you want the upper-left corner of the control to appear. Enter your last name in the small box.
4. Click the **Label** tool in the Report Design toolbox.
5. In the Report Footer section, click the location where you want the upper-left corner of the control to be. Enter:

   `ALL MEMBERS`
6. Click the **View** button to change to Print Preview.
7. Notice that the Report Header and Footer sections appear.
8. Close and save the report. Close the database.

Add Calculated Controls to a Report Section

- At times you will want to calculate and display data on a report. For example, you may want to total the value of the inventory shown on a report. To do so, you add a calculated control to the report.
- As you learned in the Forms lesson, a calculated control uses an expression as its source of data. An expression can use data from a field in an underlying table or from another control on the report. A text box is the most common type of control to display a calculated value.
- To add a text box that is a calculated control, click the Text Box tool in the Report Design toolbox. You can place controls in all sections of a report; however, if you want to total the value of all the records in a report, place the control in the report footer section.

- Click the location where you want the upper-left corner of the control to be. The text box appears with a label that Access assigns, as shown in Figure 5.23.

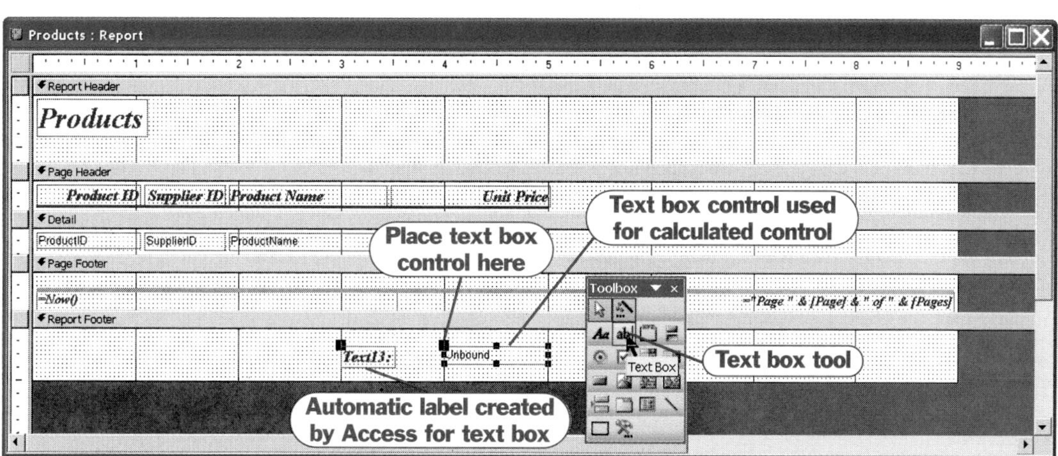

Figure 5.23 Adding a calculated control with the Text Box tool

- To make this field a calculated field, as in forms, you modify the Control Source, found in the Data tab of field properties, by entering the expression (as shown in Figure 5.24). Expressions begin with the = operator, as in the expression =Sum([UnitPrice]):
  - *=Sum* is the aggregate function that totals the values in a control. An *aggregate function* is used to calculate totals and includes functions such as Sum, Count, Average, or Variance.
  - *[UnitPrice]* represents the field name of the value in the control.
- Click Over All in the Running Sum property box to total the entire list. You use the *Running Sum* property to calculate record-by-record or group-by-group totals in a report. *Over All* displays a running sum of values in the same group level; the values accumulate until the end of the report.
- Close the property sheet and the expression appears in a calculated control in Design view. Click View to see the contents of calculated controls in Print Preview.

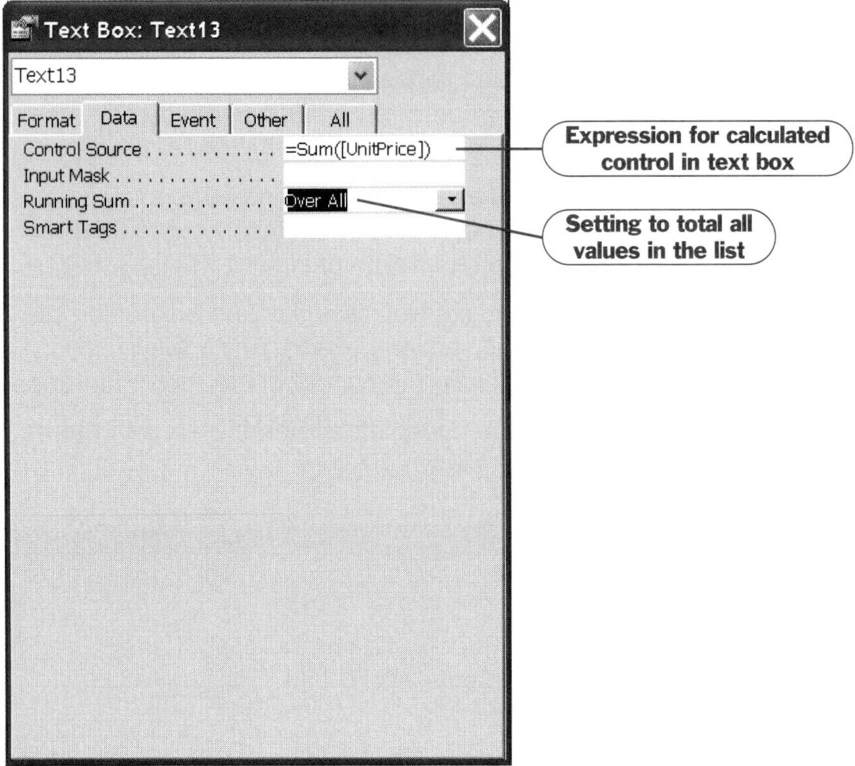

Figure 5.24 Expression for calculated control

TRY it OUT *A5-9*

1. Open **A5-9** from the Data CD for the Suppliers database and click the **Reports** object.
2. Click **New, AutoReport: Tabular** to create a report using the **Products** table.
3. Save the report as **Products.**
4. Click **Design View.**
5. Double-click the **Report Footer section selector.** Change the height setting to **.5".**
6. Click the **Text Box** tool in the Report Design toolbox.
7. In the Report Footer section, at the 4" vertical rule, click to place the control. The text box appears with a label that Access assigns.
8. Click the **text box.** Click the **View** menu.
9. Click **Properties, Data,** and **Control Source.**
10. Enter: `=Sum([UnitPrice])` in the Control Source property box.
11. Click **Running Sum,** the list arrow of the box, and **Over All.**
12. Close the property sheet.
13. Click **View.** Notice that the total is 69 and that the format does not include decimal places. Notice, also, that the text label for the calculated control has been assigned by Access.
14. Switch to Design view. Do not close the form.

Modify Controls

▶ Every control on a report has properties. These properties determine a control's format, appearance, and behavior. They also detail the attributes of the text or data contained in the control.

- You modify the properties of a control in Design view by making changes to its property sheet. Right-click the control you want to change, and click Properties. A property sheet appears, as shown in Figure 5.25. To change a caption assigned by Access, in the Caption property, delete the contents of the property box, and enter the new caption.

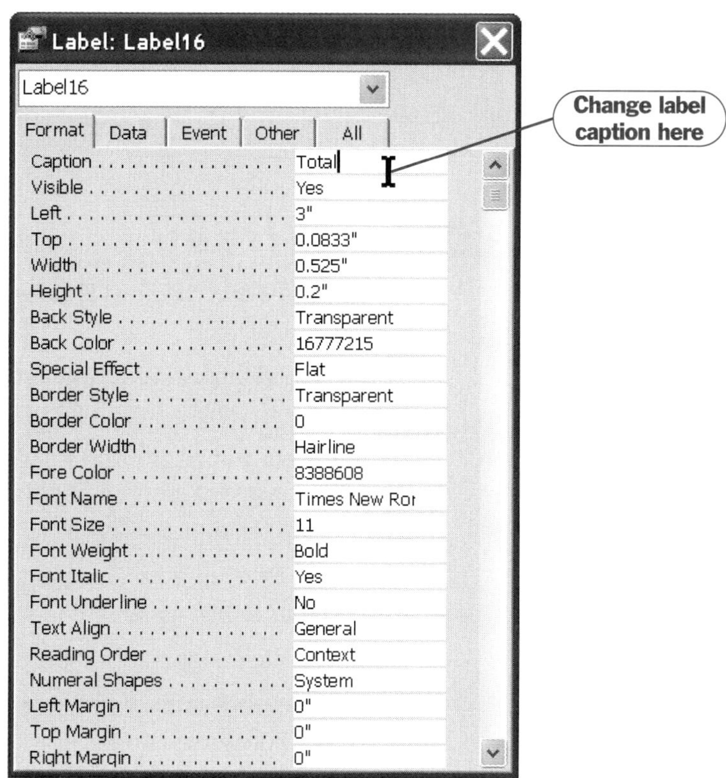

Figure 5.25 Modify the properties of controls on a report

- To change the format of a calculated control to Currency, right-click the control and click Properties, then click the Format tab, and in the Format box, select Currency.
- Click View to see the changes to the report in Print Preview.

TRY *it* OUT *A5-10*

1. Use the file from the last Try it Out or open **A5-10** from the Data CD. The **Products** report should be open in Design view.
2. Right-click the **calculated control text box** that you added in the last exercise. Click **Properties.**
3. Click the **Format** tab, if not already displayed.
4. Click **Format,** click the **list arrow** in the box, and **Currency.**
5. Close the property sheet.
6. Right-click the **Label** of the text box and click **Properties.**
7. Click **Format, Caption.**
8. Delete the contents of the caption box and enter: `Total.`
9. Click **View** to review the changes in Print Preview.
10. Close the report and save the changes.
11. Close the database.

ACCESS

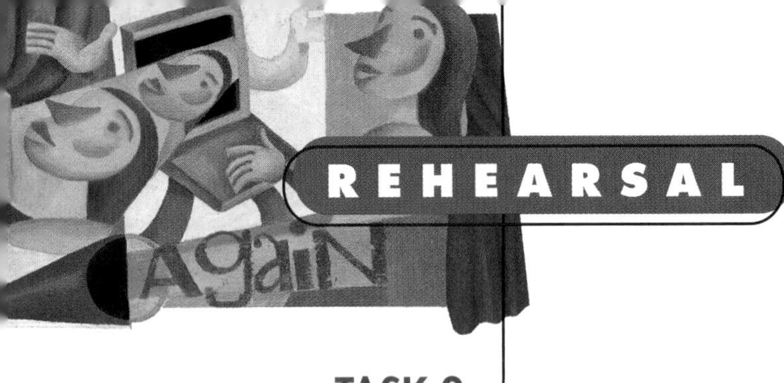

GOAL
To modify existing reports by adding calculated controls and changing the properties of the report format

SETTING THE STAGE/WRAPUP
Database: Four Corners Realty1
Table: Listings
Report: Weekly Listing Report

WHAT YOU NEED TO KNOW

- There has been significant activity in the office, and Four Corners Realty has added many listings to its database. You have been asked to print out the Weekly Listing Report you created in the last Rehearsal.
- The agents have requested that "Average Price of Homes" be added to each City section of the report. Now that there are more listings, it will be useful to have this information. You have been asked to make the change to next week's report.
- In this Rehearsal activity, you will modify a report. You will use report sections, and you will add a calculated control to a report section. You will also modify a report control and preview and print the report.

DIRECTIONS

1. Open the **Four Corners Realty1** database from the Data CD. 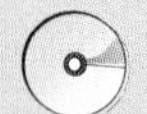
2. Find and print the **Weekly Listing Report.** Notice that this is now a two-page report.
3. Click **View** to change to Design view. To meet the agents' request, you will add a calculated control to the Group Footer section.
4. Use the Sorting and Grouping dialog box to display the group footer.
5. Change the height of the **City Footer** section to **1.**
6. Use the Text Box tool to place a calculated control in the City Footer section.
   a. Right-click the **text box,** and click **Properties.**
   b. Click **Data, Control Source.**
   c. Enter: `=AVG([Price])` in the Control Source property box.
   d. Click **Running Sum,** the list arrow of the box, and **No.**
   e. In the Format tab click **Format,** the list arrow, and **Currency.**
   f. Close the property sheet.
   g. Name the label associated with the calculated control: **Average Price.**
   h. Change the label width to **1.**
7. Click the **View** button and compare your report to the report shown in the Illustration.
8. Use the navigation controls to review the average price of homes in each city.
9. Print the report, close it, and close the database.

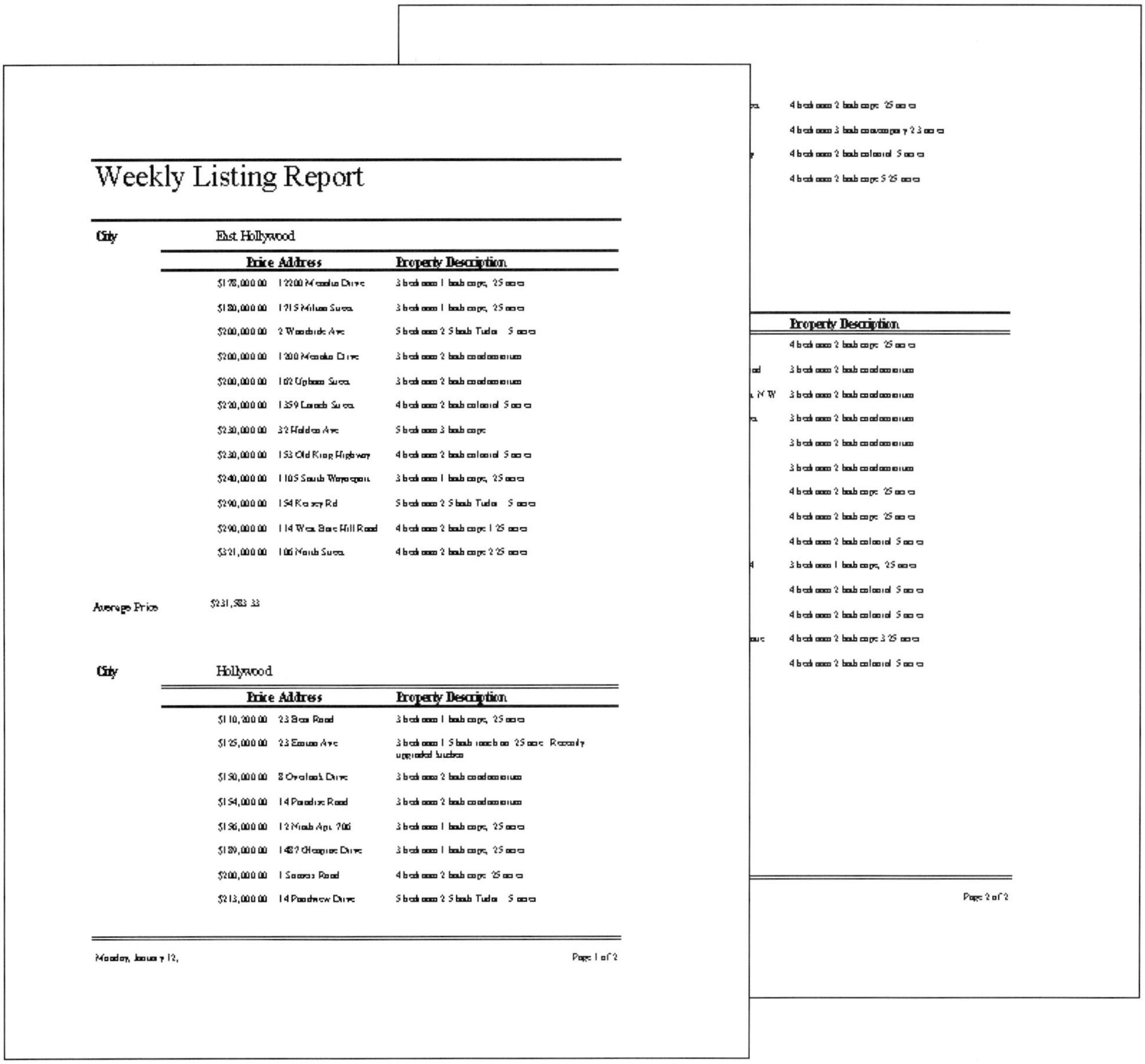

Weekly Listing Report

City East Hollywood

Price	Address	Property Description
$178,000.00	12200 Meadow Drive	3 bedroom 1 bath cape, .25 acre
$180,000.00	1215 Milton Street	3 bedroom 1 bath cape, .25 acre
$200,000.00	2 Woodside Ave	5 bedroom 2.5 bath Tudor .5 acre
$200,000.00	1200 Meadow Drive	3 bedroom 2 bath condominium
$200,000.00	102 Uptown Street	3 bedroom 2 bath condominium
$220,000.00	1359 Lynch Street	4 bedroom 2 bath colonial .5 acre
$230,000.00	32 Holden Ave	5 bedroom 3 bath cape
$230,000.00	153 Old King Highway	4 bedroom 2 bath colonial .5 acre
$240,000.00	1105 South Waypoint	3 bedroom 1 bath cape, .25 acre
$290,000.00	154 Kearsey Rd	5 bedroom 2.5 bath Tudor .5 acre
$290,000.00	114 West Bear Hill Road	4 bedroom 2 bath cape 1.25 acre
$321,000.00	106 North Street	4 bedroom 2 bath cape 2.25 acre

Average Price $231,583.33

City Hollywood

Price	Address	Property Description
$110,200.00	23 Bear Road	3 bedroom 1 bath cape, .25 acre
$125,000.00	23 Easton Ave	3 bedroom 1.5 bath ranch on .25 acre. Recently upgraded kitchen
$150,000.00	8 Overlook Drive	3 bedroom 2 bath condominium
$154,000.00	14 Paradise Road	3 bedroom 2 bath condominium
$156,000.00	12 North Apt. 706	3 bedroom 1 bath cape, .25 acre
$189,000.00	1487 Glasgow Drive	3 bedroom 1 bath cape, .25 acre
$200,000.00	1 Sunset Road	4 bedroom 2 bath cape .25 acre
$213,000.00	14 Parkview Drive	5 bedroom 2.5 bath Tudor .5 acre

Monday, January 12, Page 1 of 2

Page 2 of 2

ACCESS

Cues for Reference

Display a Group Footer

1. Click **Design View.**
2. Click the **View** menu.
3. Click **Sorting and Grouping.**
4. Click **Group Footer.**
5. Click the **list arrow** and click **Yes.**
6. Close the **Sorting and Grouping** dialog box.

Modify Report Format Properties — Height

1. Place mouse pointer on bottom edge of report section.
2. Click and drag the pointer down or up.

or

1. Double-click the section selector.
2. Click **Height property** in the section property sheet.
3. Replace contents of Height Property box and close section property sheet.

Use the Report Design Toolbox to Add Controls

1. In Design view, click the **View** menu.
2. Click **Toolbox** to display the Report Design toolbox.
3. Click a tool.
4. Click the location for the upper-left corner of the control.

Add Calculated Controls to a Report Section

1. In report Design view, click the **Text Box** tool.
2. Click the location where you want to place the control.
3. Click the **text box.**
4. Click **View**, **Properties**, and **Data.**
5. Click **Control Source.** Enter an expression.
6. Close the property sheet.
7. Click **View.**

Modify Controls

1. Right-click the control.
2. Click **Properties.**
3. Modify the property sheet.

SETTING THE STAGE/WRAPUP

Database: **ALS**

Tables: Customers
Travel Partners

Reports: Travel Preferences–Geographic Breakdown
Customer Preference
Campaign Mailing Labels

WHAT YOU NEED TO KNOW

Act I

The president of Air Land Sea Travel Group, Ms. Janice Pierce, has signed a strategic agreement with Clark's Cruise Company. The director of the Leisure Travel Department, Robin Byron, has been charged with managing this relationship for the Leisure Travel Department.

Robin anticipates the need for more standard reporting to support pending marketing campaigns and has asked you to create reports that she can provide to Janice on a weekly basis.

Follow these guidelines:

- The data is contained in the **ALS** database in the **Customers** table on the Data CD. 
- Robin prefers the Corporate style, Outline 1 layout, and portrait format.
- Robin would like to see the following:
  - A report showing the travel preferences of customers, grouped by state. Sort the data in ascending order by travel preference. Name the report **Travel Preferences-Geographic Breakdown**, as illustrated on the next page.

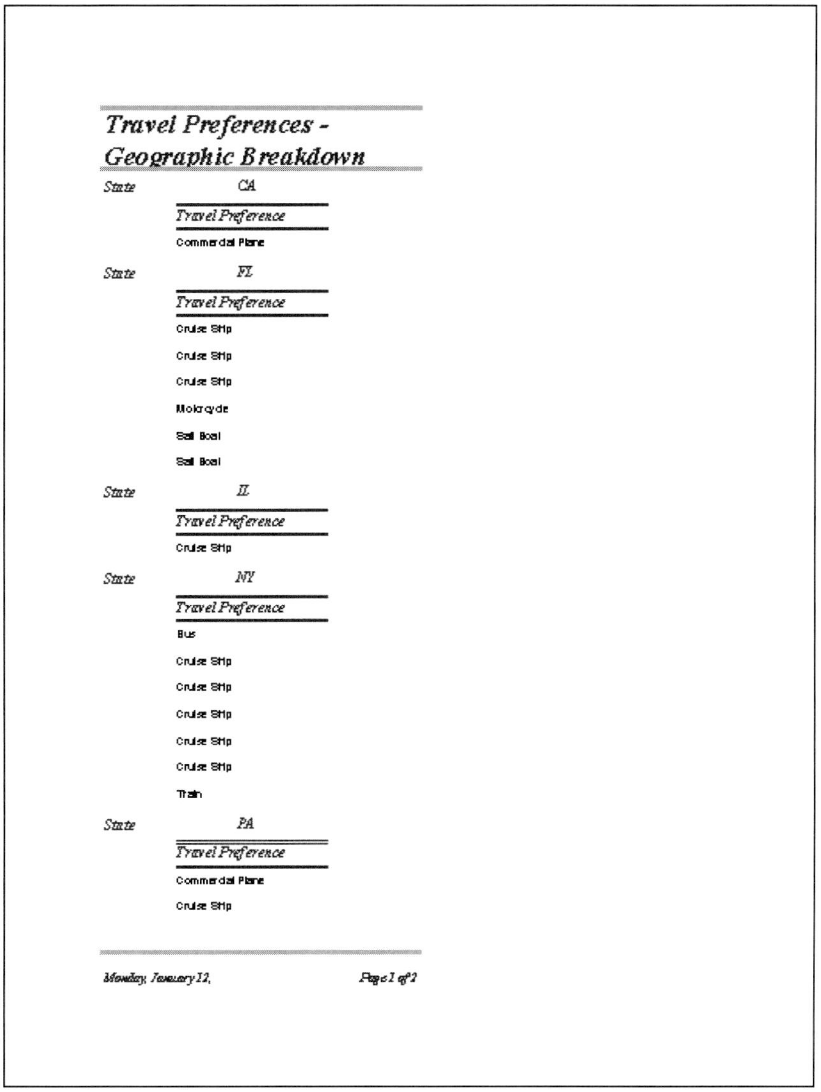

Travel Preferences - Geographic Breakdown

State CA

Travel Preference

Commercial Plane

State FL

Travel Preference

Cruise Ship

Cruise Ship

Cruise Ship

Motorcycle

Sail Boat

Sail Boat

State IL

Travel Preference

Cruise Ship

State NY

Travel Preference

Bus

Cruise Ship

Cruise Ship

Cruise Ship

Cruise Ship

Cruise Ship

Train

State PA

Travel Preference

Commercial Plane

Cruise Ship

Monday, January 12, *Page 1 of 2*

- A report showing all customers grouped by travel preference. The report should contain no more than four fields, but must include last name and state. Name the report **Customer Preference.**

Act II

The marketing plans are moving forward rapidly. Robin has asked you to prepare a label report, so that she can quickly respond to a request she anticipates receiving. She has also asked you to modify the Customer Preference report. Use the **ALS** database or open **ALS2** from the Data CD.

ACCESS

Follow these guidelines:

- Robin would like you to make these specific changes to the Customer Preference report, part of which is shown in the illustration:

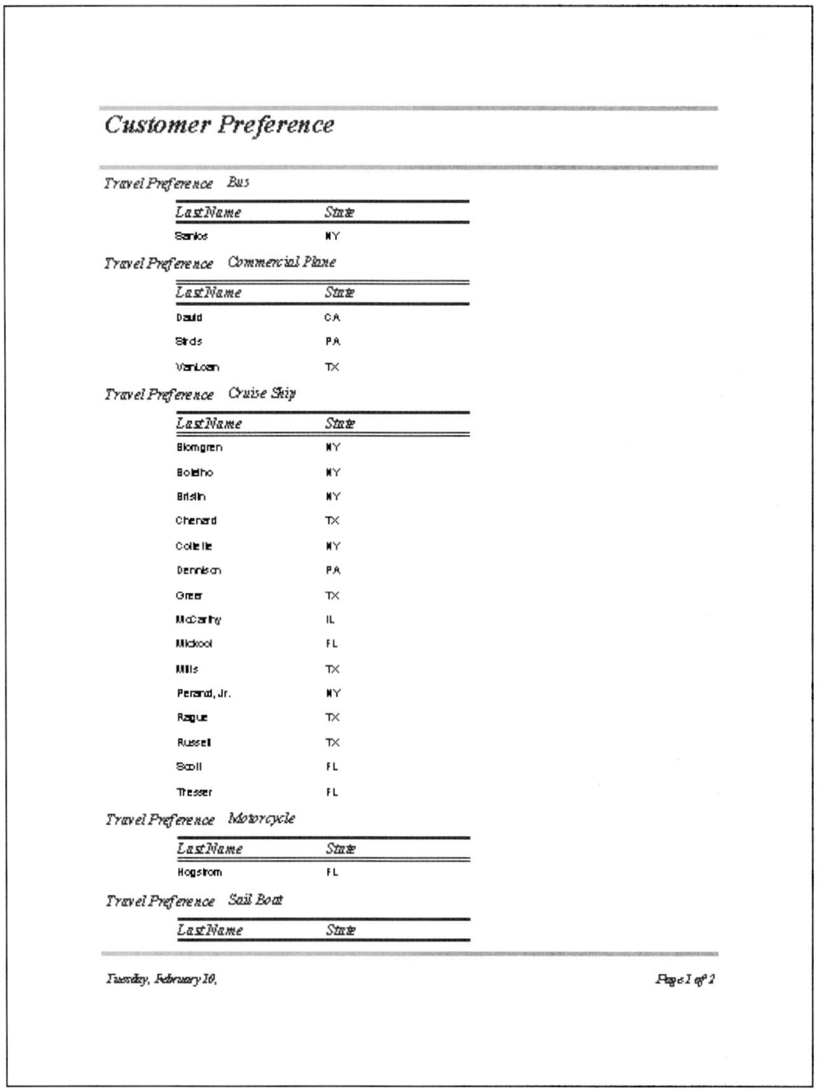

Customer Preference

Travel Preference Bus

LastName	State
Santos	NY

Travel Preference Commercial Plane

LastName	State
David	CA
Sirds	PA
VanLoan	TX

Travel Preference Cruise Ship

LastName	State
Blomgren	NY
Botelho	NY
Bristin	NY
Chenard	TX
Collette	NY
Dennison	PA
Greer	TX
McCarthy	IL
Mickool	FL
Mills	TX
Perand, Jr.	NY
Rague	TX
Russell	TX
Scott	FL
Tresser	FL

Travel Preference Motorcycle

LastName	State
Hogstrom	FL

Travel Preference Sail Boat

LastName	State

Tuesday, February 10, *Page 1 of 2*

Existing Report

- Display the group footer and add a calculated control to the Travel Preference footer that counts the number of customers. Use the Count aggregate function to do so. The calculated control label caption should be Count.
- She would like you to add the word "Transportation" to the report header, under the title Customer Preference. Compare your report to the sample report shown.

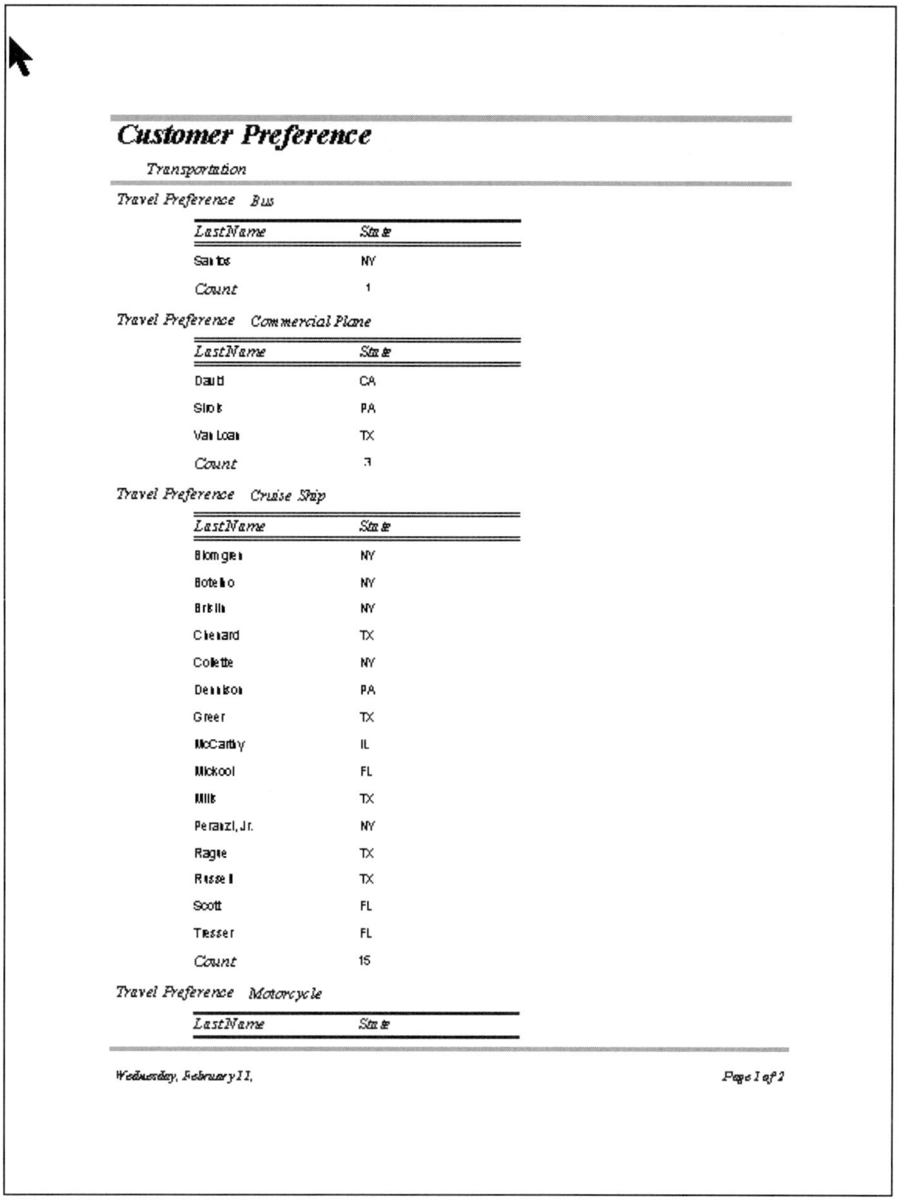

Customer Preference

Transportation

Travel Preference *Bus*

LastName	*State*
Santos	NY
Count	1

Travel Preference *Commercial Plane*

LastName	*State*
David	CA
Sirok	PA
Van Loan	TX
Count	3

Travel Preference *Cruise Ship*

LastName	*State*
Blomgren	NY
Botelho	NY
Brislin	NY
Chenard	TX
Colette	NY
Dennison	PA
Greer	TX
McCarthy	IL
Mickool	FL
Mills	TX
Peranzi, Jr.	NY
Rague	TX
Russell	TX
Scott	FL
Tesser	FL
Count	15

Travel Preference *Motorcycle*

LastName	*State*

Wednesday, February 11, *Page 1 of 2*

Modified Report

- Although the customer database does not contain zip code information as yet, Robin would like you to prepare a mailing label report. The company font is Arial Narrow, and the label product used is an Avery, English Unit of Measure, C2241.
- She would like the label to be addressed to the family, not to a specific person, because most customers travel with their partners. The labels should be sorted by Last Name. Name this report **Campaign Mailing Labels.**
- Save your work.

ACCESS

LESSON 6

Integration

In this lesson, you will learn how to import structured data into Access tables and to export data from tables and queries. You will also learn how to maintain your database and to create data access pages using the Page Wizard.

Upon completion of this lesson, you should have mastered the following skill sets:

- Import structured data into Access tables
  - Import Access table objects
  - Import Excel spreadsheet data to append a table
  - Import Excel spreadsheet data into a new table
- Export data from Access tables or queries
  - Export an Access object to another Access database
  - Export Access data to an Excel spreadsheet
  - Export Access data to Word
- Back up a database
- Compact and repair a database
- Identify and modify object dependencies
- Create a data access page using the Page Wizard
  - Create a data access page using the Page Wizard with a theme
- Use Web Page Preview

Terms

Software-related

Import
Link
Structured data
Append
Export
Backup
Fragmentation
Compact
Object dependencies
Pages object
Data access page
AutoPage: Columnar
Page Wizard
Navigation controls
Theme
Web Page Preview

GOALS

To import and export data to and from an Access database to other Office applications

To practice using the following skill sets:

- Import structured data into Access tables
  - Import Access table objects
  - Import Excel spreadsheet data to append a table
  - Import Excel spreadsheet data into a new table
- Export data from Access tables or queries
  - Export an Access object to another Access database
  - Export Access data to an Excel spreadsheet
  - Export Access data to Word

ACCESS

WHAT YOU NEED TO KNOW

Import Structured Data into Access Tables

- There are times when you want to use data from other Access databases, or from a source other than Access, in a database you are building. Access provides two choices for working with data from an outside source: importing and linking.
- *Importing* copies data from a text file, spreadsheet, or database table to an Access table. You can import data to create a new table or add the data to an existing table. The source of the data is not modified.
- *Linking* establishes a connection to data from another application. You can view and edit the data in both the original application and in Access. The data stays in its current location and format.
- *Structured data* is data that adheres to a format. Access can import or link structured data from other Access databases, as well as data from other applications and file formats, such as Microsoft Excel, dBASE, Microsoft FoxPro, or Paradox.
- If you want to use the data only in Access, you should import it. If you plan to use an application other than Access to update the data, you should link it. You will learn about importing data into a new table, as well as into an existing table.

Import Access Table Objects

- To import data, you first create or open the Access database that will contain the imported table. You can also import database objects other than tables, such as queries, forms, or reports, from another Access database. To import data, click File, Get External Data. Click Import, and the Import dialog box opens, as shown in Figure 6.1.

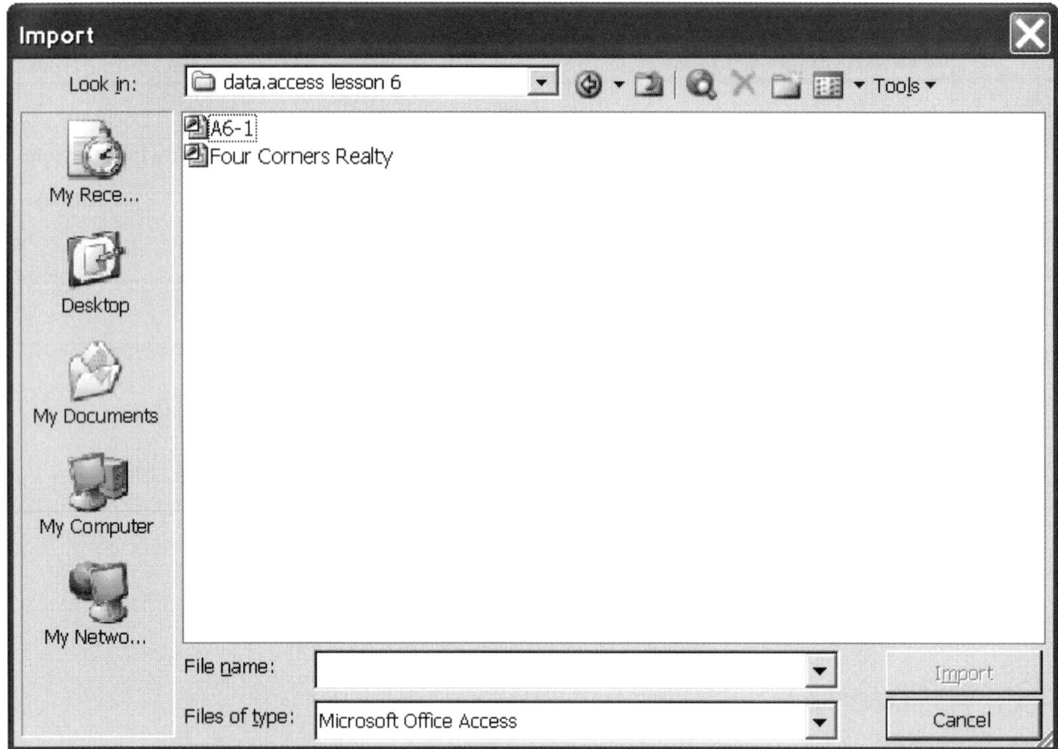

Figure 6.1 Import dialog box

- Double-click the name of the database containing the table you want to import and click Import. The Import Objects dialog box opens, as shown in Figure 6.2. Click the desired object tab, and click the specific object to import. Click Select All to import all objects that Access displays.

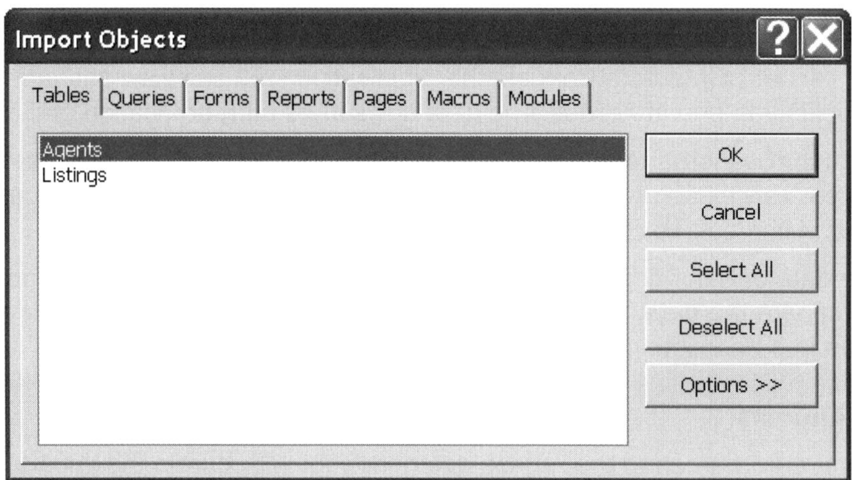

Figure 6.2 Import Objects dialog box

- Click Options to specify additional import characteristics, as shown in Figure 6.3. To import a table, click the Tables tab, click the table to import, and click OK. Access imports the table into the database.

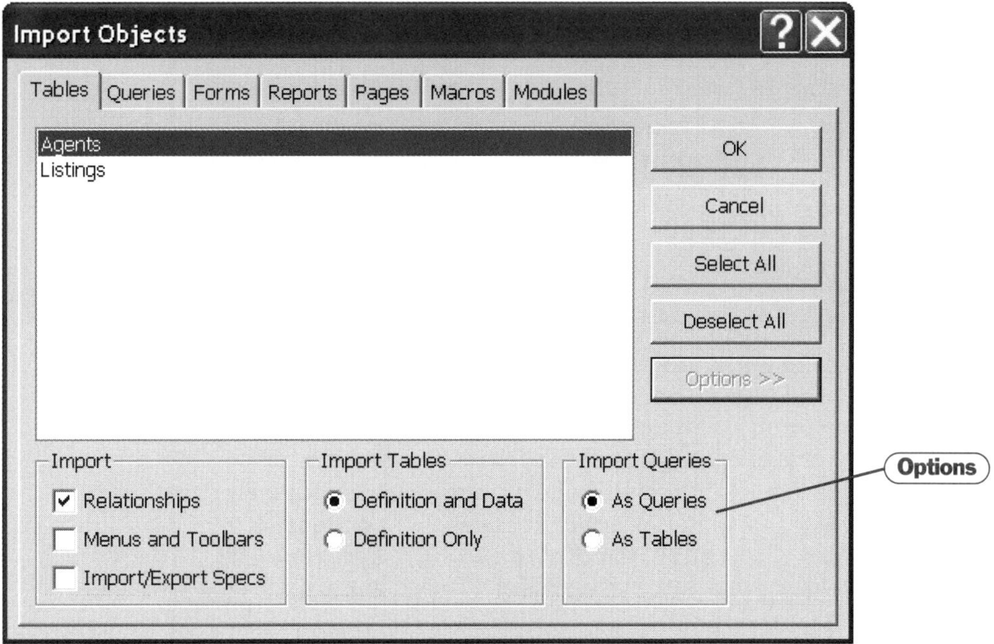

Figure 6.3 Import Objects options

ACCESS

Note: Before performing the Try it Outs in Lesson 6, create a top-level directory on your hard drive (C:\) and name it C:\Access Lesson 6. You will copy the Lesson 6 data files from the Data CD to this directory. The Lesson 6 data files are on the Data CD in \Access Lesson 6.

TRY *it* OUT *A6-1*

1. Open **A6-1** from the Access Lesson 6 Directory you have created.
2. Click **File.**
3. Point to **Get External Data.**
4. Click **Import.**
5. Double-click **Four Corners Realty** from your directory.
6. In the Tables tab, click the **Agents** table and click **OK.**
7. Notice that Access now lists the **Agents** table in the Database window of the original file. Keep the database open.

Import Excel Spreadsheet Data to Append a Table

▶ To import data from a source other than Access, such as an Excel spreadsheet, click File, Get External Data. Click Import and when the Import dialog box opens (see Figure 6.1), click the folder containing the data, and click Microsoft Excel in the Files of type box. Click the name of the spreadsheet containing the data to import, and click Import. The Import Spreadsheet Wizard opens, as shown in Figure 6.4.

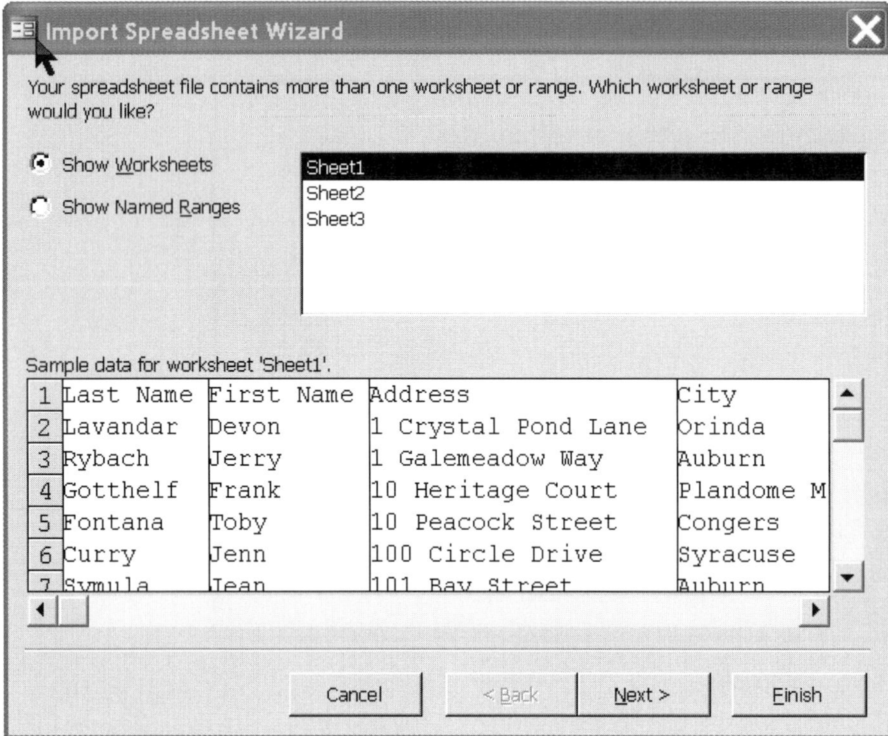

Figure 6.4 Import Spreadsheet Wizard

▶ Click Show Worksheets, and click the specific sheet to import. Click First Row Contains Column Headings, and click Next to use column headings as field names for the table, as shown in Figure 6.5.

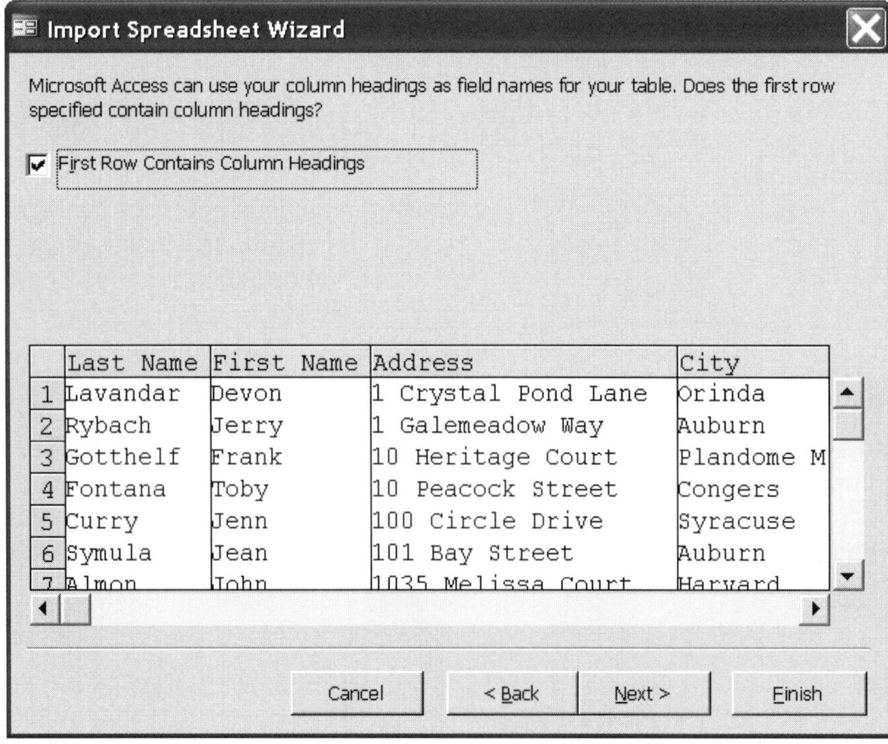

Figure 6.5 Import Spreadsheet Wizard—column headings

▶ Click Next to choose where to store your table, In a New Table or In an Existing Table, as shown in Figure 6.6. To *append,* or add, the data from a spreadsheet to an existing table, click In an Existing Table, click the list arrow, and click the table to which you want to add the data. Click Next, and click Finish to complete the import. Open the table to which you appended the data, and the new records appear. The fields in the spreadsheet should match those in the table to which it is appended.

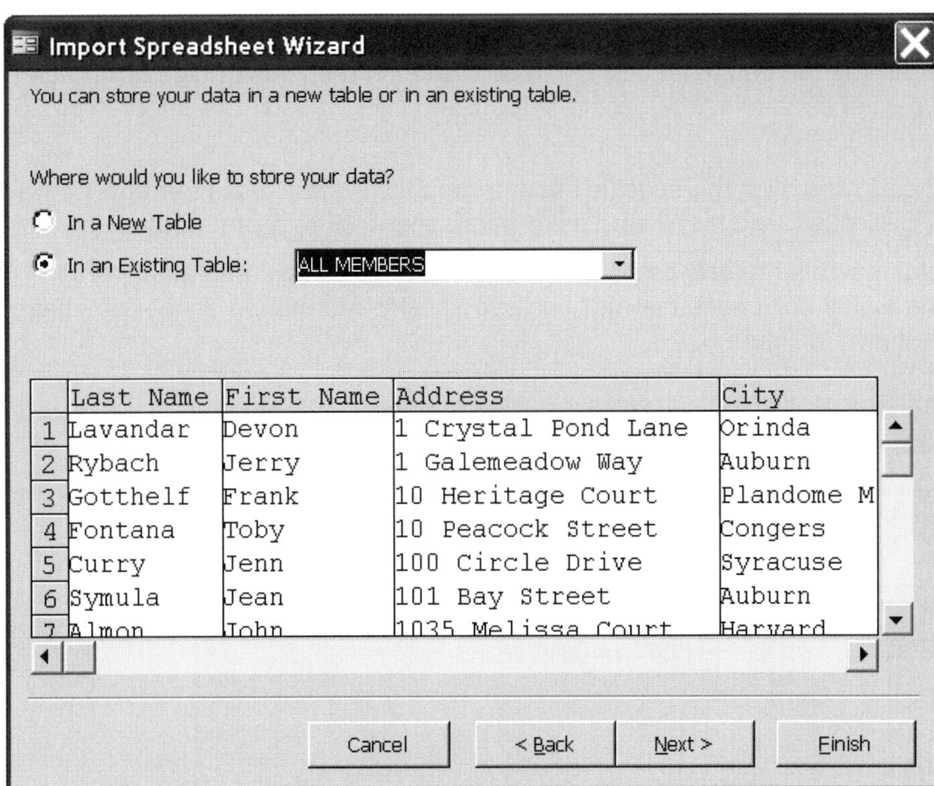

Figure 6.6 Import Spreadsheet Wizard—store table

TRY *it* OUT *A6-2*

1. Use the open file or open **A6-2** from the Access Lesson 6 directory you have created.
2. Click **File, Get External Data,** and **Import.**
3. Click the folder containing the data files.
4. Click **Microsoft Excel** in the Files of type box.
5. Double-click **Members.xls.**
6. Click **Show Worksheets,** if necessary, and click **Next.**
7. Notice that the first row contains column headings.
8. Click **First Row Contains Column Headings,** and click **Next.**
9. Click **In an Existing Table,** the list arrow, and **ALL MEMBERS.**
10. Click **Next** and click **Finish.**
11. Click **OK.**
12. Double-click the **ALL MEMBERS** table to view the new records.
13. Close the table.

ACCESS

Import Excel Spreadsheet Data into a New Table

- You can append the data from spreadsheet or text files to an existing table that has a matching data structure—that is, if the first row of the file matches the table's field names, as in the last Try it Out. However, in most cases, you cannot store or append data to an existing table.
- To import data that does not match the data structure of an existing table, such as an Excel file with no headings, click File and click Get External Data. Click Import and the Import dialog box opens.
- Click the folder containing the data, and click Microsoft Excel in the Files of type box. Click the name of the spreadsheet containing the data to import and click Import. The Import Spreadsheet Wizard opens.
- Click Show Worksheets, and click the specific sheet to import. Do not click First Row Contains Column Headings. Click Next, and the Wizard asks where you want to store the data.
- Click In a New Table, which is the only other option available. Click Next, and an Import Spreadsheet Wizard dialog box opens in which you can specify information about each field you want to import, as shown in Figure 6.7.

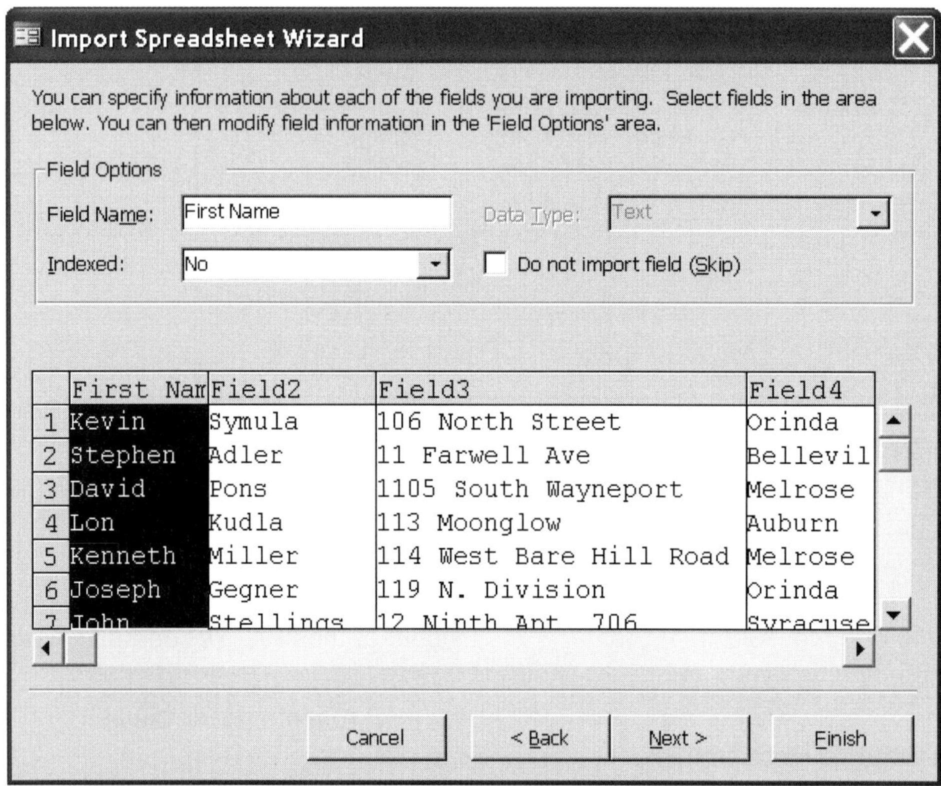

Figure 6.7 Import Spreadsheet Wizard—specify fields

- You can rename Field 1 by deleting the current contents and entering a new name. You can skip fields so that you do not import them. Click Next to add, or allow Access to add, the primary key, as shown in Figure 6.8. Click Next to name the table and click Finish to complete the import. Access lists the new table in the Database window. You can rename fields in the Design view of the new table.

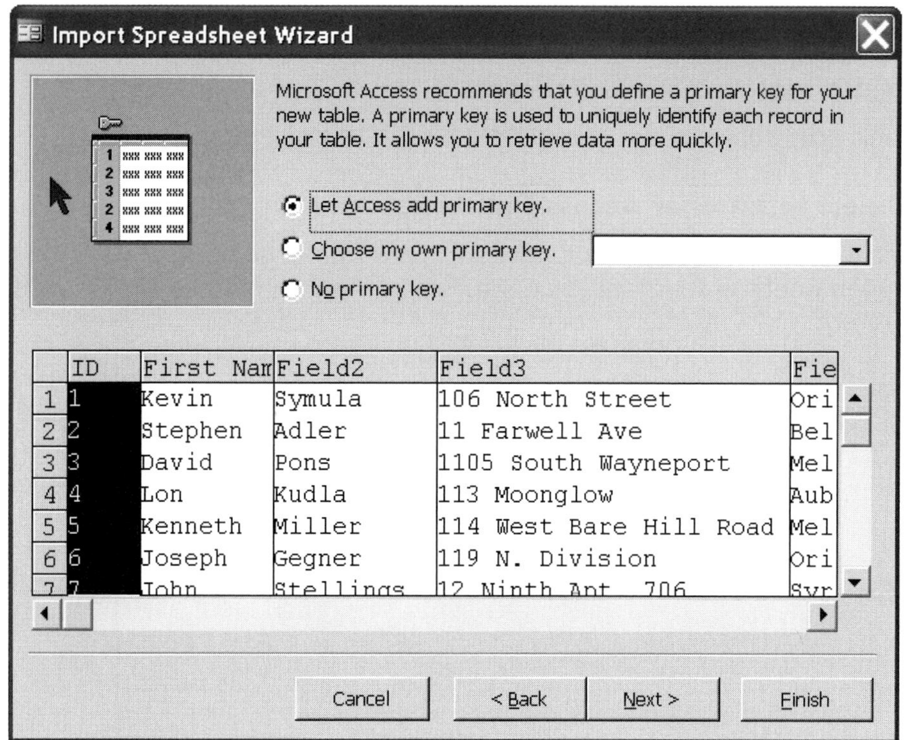

Figure 6.8 Import Spreadsheet Wizard—set primary key

ACCESS

TRY *it* OUT *A6-3*

1. Use the open file or open **A6-3** from the Access Lesson 6 directory you have created.
2. Click **File, Get External Data,** and **Import.**
3. Click the folder on the Data CD containing the data files.
4. Click **Microsoft Excel** in the Files of type box.
5. Double-click **New Members.xls.**
6. Click **Show Worksheets** and click **Next.**
7. Do not click First Row Contains Column Headings. Click **Next.**
8. Click **In A New Table,** if not already selected, and click **Next.**
9. Delete the contents of the Field Name box.
10. Enter: `First Name` and click **Next.**
11. Click **Let Access add primary key** and click **Next.**
12. Name the table:

    `NEW MEMBERS`
13. Click **Finish.**
14. Click **OK.**
15. Double-click the **NEW MEMBERS** table to view the table. You can edit field names in Design view.
16. Close the table and the database.

Export Data from Access Tables or Queries

▶ To copy data and database objects from Access to another database, spreadsheet, or file, you use the *export* feature. You can export data from Access tables or queries to many different formats. You can also export most database objects to another Access database.

- When you export a table, Access exports its data, data definitions, and primary key, but not the table's other properties. When exporting an object to another database, you should consider exporting related objects, such as tables and queries.
- You will learn about exporting objects and data from tables in this lesson.

Export an Access Object to Another Access Database

- To export a table or query to another Access database, in the Database window, click the name of the table or query you want to export and click File, Export. An Export Table dialog box opens, as shown in Figure 6.9.

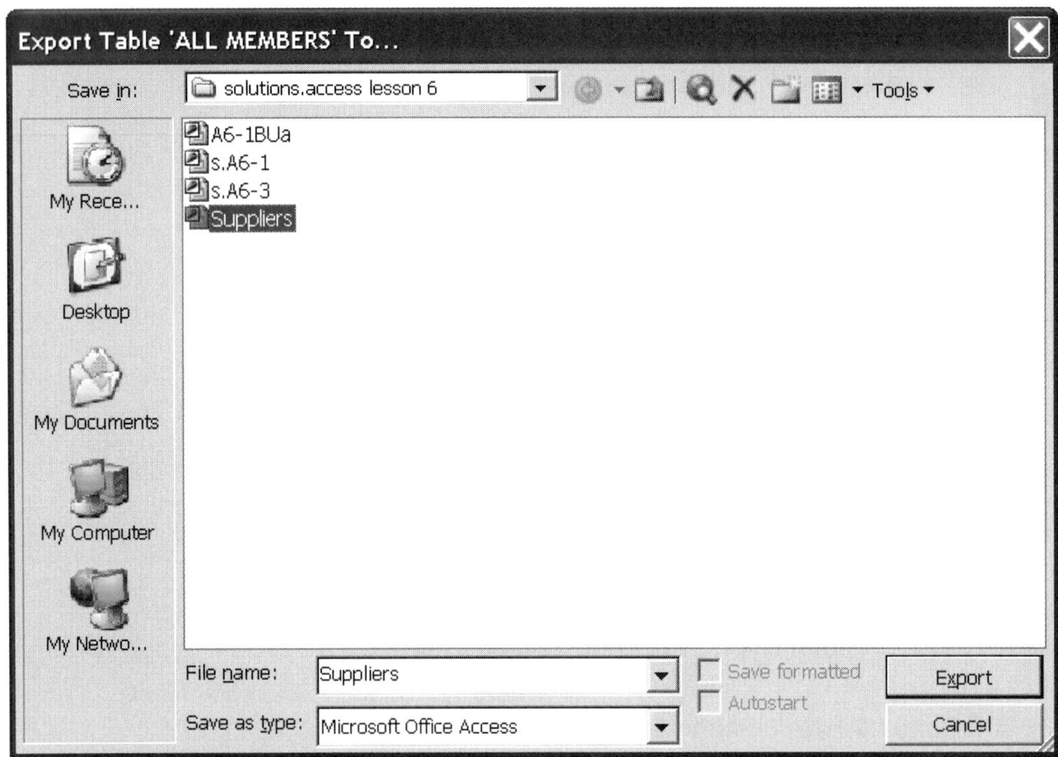

Figure 6.9 Export Table dialog box

- Click the name of the file to which you want to export the table or query, and click Export. An Export dialog box opens, as shown in Figure 6.10.

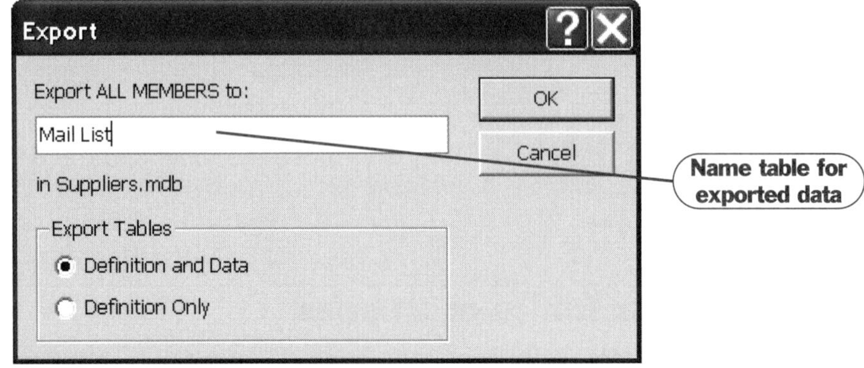

Figure 6.10 Export dialog box

- You can choose to export the table definition and data, or the definition only. If you need to create a new table with a very similar design to an existing table, but do not need the data in the existing table, you might want to export only the definition. You can then modify the table to meet your requirements.
- Click Definition and Data and click OK. Access exports the table or query.

TRY *it* OUT *A6-4*

1. Open **A6-4** from the Access Lesson 6 directory you have created.
2. Click **ALL MEMBERS** in the Members database.
3. Click **File.**
4. Click **Export.**
5. You will export the **ALL MEMBERS** table to the **Suppliers** database. Click **Suppliers**, then click **Export.**
6. Change the table name to **Mail List** in the Suppliers database.
7. Click **Definition and Data** and click **OK.**
8. Open the **Suppliers** database.
9. Click **Tables.**
10. Notice that Access has added **Mail List** with the data from the ALL MEMBERS table.
11. Close both open databases.

ACCESS

Export Access Data to an Excel Spreadsheet

- To export data from a table or query to an Excel spreadsheet, in the Database window, click the name of the table or query you want to export and click File, Export. The Export Table dialog box opens (see Figure 6.9).
- Click the list arrow in the Save as type box to select the Microsoft Excel 2003 format and, if necessary, edit the information in the File name box. Click Export and Access exports the data to a new Excel file.

TRY *it* OUT *A6-5*

1. Open **A6-5** from the Access Lesson 6 directory you created.
2. Click **ALL MEMBERS.**
3. Click **File, Export.**
4. Click the list arrow in the **Save as type** box and click **Microsoft Excel 97-2003** and then **Export.**
5. Access exports the data to an Excel file called **ALL MEMBERS.**
6. In Excel, open **ALL MEMBERS.xls.**
7. Notice that the headings are the same as they are in the **ALL MEMBERS** Access table.
8. Close the spreadsheet and close Excel.

Export Access Data to Word

- You can also export Access data to a Word document. In the Database window, click the name of the table or query you want to export, and click File, Export. The Export Table dialog box opens.
- Click the list arrow in the Save as type box to select Rich Text Format, and edit the contents of the File name box, if necessary. Click Export and Access exports the data to a new Word file.

TRY *it* OUT *A6-6*

1. Use the file from the last Try it Out or open **A6-6** from the Access Lesson 6 directory you created.
2. Click **ALL MEMBERS.**
3. Click **File, Export.**
4. Click the list arrow in the **Save as type** box and click **Rich Text Format.**
5. Click **Export.**
6. Access exports the data to a Word file called **ALL MEMBERS.**
7. In Word, open **ALL MEMBERS.rtf.**
8. Notice that the headings are the same as they are in the **ALL MEMBERS** Access table.
9. Close the document and close Word.
10. Close the database.

1
2
3

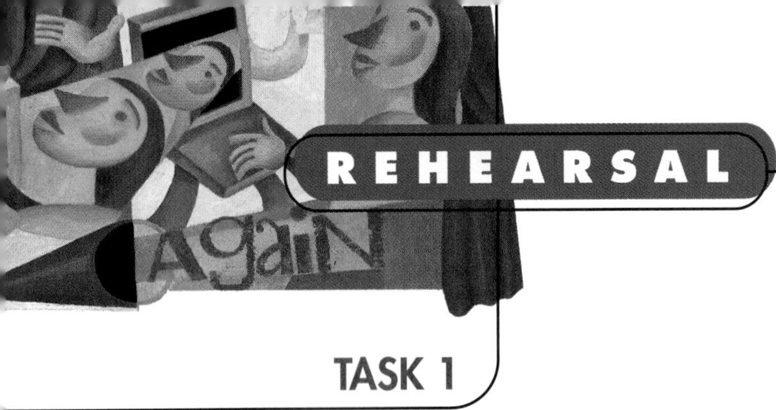

GOALS

You will import an Excel file of new rental listings into the Four Corners Realty1 database, and export the Agents database to a Word file. You will also export data from the Listings database to Excel, so that the agency can conduct a financial analysis

SETTING THE STAGE/WRAPUP

Database:	Four Corners Realty1
Tables:	Listings
	Agents
	Rental Listings
Excel Files:	Rental Listings
	New Listings
	Listings
Word File:	Agents

WHAT YOU NEED TO KNOW

- Real estate offices deal with homes for rent as well as for sale. Up until now, Four Corners Realty has kept rental listings in an Excel spreadsheet. Recently, the company decided to focus on the rental business, and the Excel spreadsheet is no longer efficient. You have been asked to import this data into the **Four Corners Realty1** database in a separate table.
- The chief financial officer of the company wants to conduct an analysis of the pricing trends in the Hollywood area. He has asked you to export the **Listings** database to Excel for this purpose.
- You have been asked to provide a Word document that contains a table with data exported from the **Agents** database. This table will be distributed to the agents for review.
- In this Rehearsal activity, you will import and export data using the **Four Corners Realty1** database as required by the various requests listed above. Notice that Excel and Word are two of the many file formats to which Access can export data, as shown in the Illustrations on the facing page.

DIRECTIONS

1. Open the **Four Corners Realty1** database from C:\Access Lesson 6.
2. Import the **Rental Listings** Excel file into a new table within the database.
   a. Click **First Row Contains Column Headings.**
   b. Store the data in a new table and let Access add the primary key.
   c. Name the table: **Rental Listings.**
   d. View the data and close the table. (See Illustration A.)
3. Export the **Listings** table to Excel.
   a. Name the spreadsheet **Listings,** select a **Microsoft Excel 97-2003 format,** and click **Export.**
   b. Open the **Listings** spreadsheet to view the exported data.
   c. Close the spreadsheet; close Excel.
4. Export the **Agents** table to Word.
   a. Name the file **Agents,** select **Rich Text Format,** and click **Export.**
   b. Open the **Agents** Word document to view the exported data.
5. Change the page setup to Landscape mode and adjust column widths as necessary. (See Illustration B.)
6. Close and save the document and close Word.
7. Close the database.

Rental Listings : Table

ID	Last Name	First Name	Address	City	Telephone	Monthly Price
1	MCGLONE	Jason	182 W. 82nd Street #3	Hollywood	555-475-2900	2000
2	WENNING	David M.	11 Housatonic Street	East Hollywood	555 546-2582	4000
3	Auslander	Marc	20 Landau Rd	West Hollywood	555-389-6233	3000
4	Denner	Selma	555 WODBURY RD	Hollywood	555-705-6294	2500
5	Al-Abbas	Sarah	1461 Creekside Dr	East Hollywood	555-472-4221	6000
6	ARABACK	Bob	1454 Pacific Beach Dr.	West Hollywood	555 253-6620	1000
7	Barthelmes	Barry	PO BOX 459	Hollywood	555-765-9876	2500
8	Beganny	Patrick	12101 HUCKLEBERRY LN.	East Hollywood	555-895-2580	2000
9	Boyle	Sue	4931 ALSACE ST.	West Hollywood	555-895-1317	4000
10	BROWN	Jim	60 West 84th street	Hollywood	555 962-5956	3000
11	CALAHAN	Andrea	10520 Wilshire Blvd, #303	East Hollywood	555 493-2043	2500
12	Carkhum	Dave	1333 Madison Street #5	West Hollywood	555-498-9154	6000
13	CHISHOLM	Sharrieff	206 Siskiyou Ct	Hollywood	555 866-5466	1000
14	CHRISTMAS	Royce	7362 SW 38th St.	East Hollywood	555-835-7644	2500
15	CLARK	Elise	35B Windle Park	West Hollywood	555 823-6708	2000
16	COHEN	Kevin F.	333 East 89th Street	Hollywood	555-238-5710	4000
17	Conley	Kathy	41 Park St. #105	East Hollywood	555-276-5355	3000
18	CONRAD	Charles R.	4543 South Lavergne	West Hollywood	555-895-2045	2500
19	COOK	Mary	1122 E. Pike, #581	Hollywood	555 895-1428	6000
20	Cooper	Denyse	6402 Swift Ave S	East Hollywood	555 487-6283	1000
21	Cromwell	Mike	917 Louisiana	West Hollywood	555 487-6567	2500
22	CULLEN	Trisha	2142 South Victor St. #A	Hollywood	555 848-0561	2000
23	Curry	Davida	10405 Snapdragon St.	East Hollywood	555 486-5335	4000
24	D'Abate	Vincent	575 Main St.	West Hollywood	555-895-2648	3000
25	DALLESANDRO	Lesley	5983 Norway Pine 19.65 lane	Hollywood	555 276-5286	2500
26	Delaney	Vin	631 Fir Park Ln	East Hollywood	555-276-5326	6000
27	Dellesendro	Wayne	19411 Gagelake Lane	West Hollywood	555-276-5286	1000
28	DERRY	Rolf H.	97 Atlantic Avenue	Hollywood	555 280-2242	2500
29	DRUSKAT	Buel	7370 Sea Island Road	East Hollywood	555-276-5353	2000
30	Duncan	Susan	3598 Sth Ocean Blvd	West Hollywood	555-642-3415	4000
31	Elias	Eric K.	9522 Lakeshore Blvd NE	Hollywood	555-895-1462	3000
32	FICHTEL	Robert P.	1132 First Street	East Hollywood	555-895-2728	2500
33	Finnecy	Jim	365 Blaine Ave.	West Hollywood	555-642-5397	6000
34	Fitch	Ellen	15 Patricia Lane	Hollywood	[illegible]	[illegible]

Record: 87 of 101

Illustration A

Employee Number	Listing Agent	Telephone	Email address	Home Address	City	State	Zipcode
1	Duggam	555 456-0987	Duggan@fcr.com	34 West Ave	Hollywood	Florida	09090
11	Daniels	555 654-0981	Daniels@fcr.com	43 Ash Street	Hollywood	Florida	09090
3	Moran	555 234-3456	Moran@fcr.com	33 Elm Street	Hollywood	Florida	09090
6	Williams	555 432-5555	Williams@fcr.com	12 Slough Road	Hollywood	Florida	09090
8	Kennedy	555 345-1234	Kennedy@fcr.com	21 Main Street	Hollywood	Florida	09090
9	Olsen	555 876-0933	Olsen@fcr.com	25 Gain Street	Hollywood	Florida	09090

Illustration B

ACCESS

Cues for Reference

Import Access Table Objects

1. Open a database.
2. Click **File, Get External Data.**
3. Click **Import.**
4. Double-click the database containing the table.
5. Click the table and click **OK.**

Import Excel Spreadsheet Data to Append a Table

1. Open a database.
2. Click **File, Get External Data.**
3. Click **Import.**
4. Click the folder containing the spreadsheet.
5. Click **Microsoft Excel** in the Files of type box.
6. Double-click the spreadsheet.
7. Click **Show Worksheets.**
8. Click **Next.**
9. Click **First Row Contains Column Headings.**
10. Click **Next.**
11. Click **In an Existing Table.**
12. Click the **list arrow** and click table to append.
13. Click **Next, Finish.**
14. Click **OK.**

Import Excel Spreadsheet Data into a New Table

1. Open a database.
2. Click **File, Get External Data.**
3. Click **Import.**
4. Click the folder containing the spreadsheet.
5. Click **Microsoft Excel** in the Files of type box.
6. Double-click the spreadsheet.
7. Click **Show Worksheets.**
8. Click **Next.**
9. Click **First Row Contains Column Headings.**
10. Click **Next.**
11. Click **In a New Table.**
12. Click **Finish.**

Export Data from Tables or Queries

1. Open a database.
2. Click the table/query to export.
3. Click **File, Export.**
4. Enter the file name.
5. Click the **list arrow** and click the type of file.
6. Click **Export.**

GOALS

To backup, compact, and repair the database; to view object dependencies; to create two data access pages; and to preview the data access page on the Web

To practice using the following skill sets:

- Back up a database
- Compact and repair a database
- Identify and modify object dependencies
- Create a data access page using the Page Wizard
  - Create a data access page using the Page Wizard with a theme
- Use Web Page Preview

WHAT YOU NEED TO KNOW

Back Up a Database

- Databases contain data that is difficult to replace quickly. To prevent loss of data due to file corruption, virus attack, computer problems, etc., it is advisable to *back up*, or copy, the database to another location. Your company should develop daily or weekly backup procedures to ensure database safety.
- To back up your database, open the database, click File, Back Up Database, and name the backup file. If this is repeated weekly or daily, the backup file will contain most of the latest information in the database. You can open and use the backup file if the original file is contaminated.

ACCESS

TRY *it* OUT *A6-7*

1. Open **A6-7** from the Access Lesson 6 directory you have created.
2. Click **File, Back Up Database.**
3. On a floppy disk or in another directory, save the backup to **A6-7BU**. Click **Save.**
4. Close the database.

Compact and Repair a Database

- When you use a database regularly, especially when you add or delete database objects, a database becomes fragmented. *Fragmentation* occurs when data from a database is located in different areas on the disk where it is stored. The result is that the database runs slowly. Also, if Access is shut down improperly errors can develop in the files.
- To improve the performance of a database, Access provides a Compact and Repair feature. *Compacting,* or defragmenting, is a process by which Access eliminates unnecessary space within a database. To compact a database, click Tools, select Database Utilities, and click Compact and Repair Database, as shown in Figure 6.11.

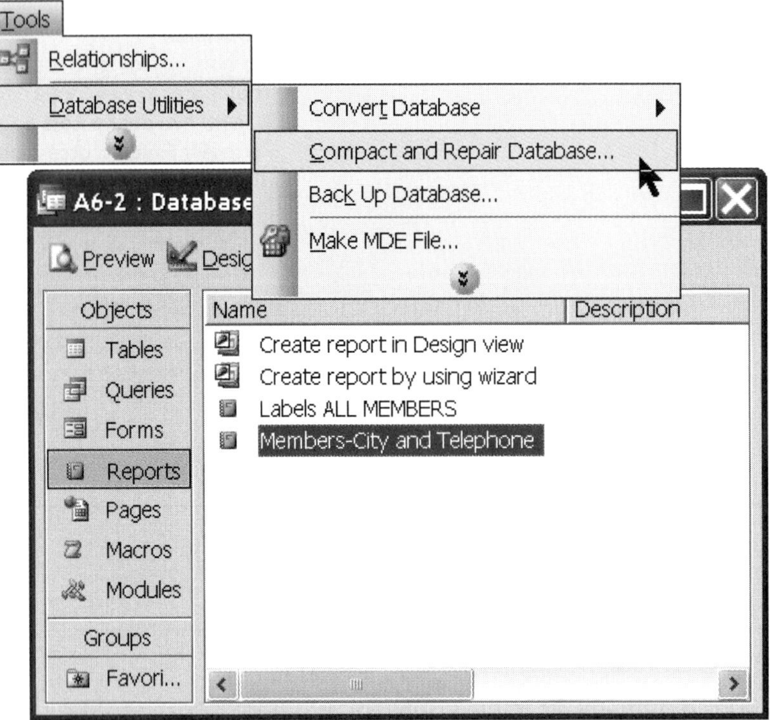

Figure 6.11 Compact and Repair Database

- It is recommended that you compact a database on a regular basis.

TRY *it* OUT *A6-8*

1. Open **A6-8** from the Access Lesson 6 directory you have created.
2. Click **Tools.**
3. Select **Database Utilities.**
4. Click **Compact and Repair Database.**
5. Close the database, do not close Access.

Identify Object Dependencies

- As you develop relationships between tables and use multiple tables in queries, reports, or forms, *object dependencies* are developed between database objects. If later you decide to delete a query or table that is no longer useful, it is helpful to be able to see what other objects in the database use the query. Then, you could either modify the dependent objects to remove dependencies, or delete the dependent objects, before deleting the query. Viewing a complete list of dependent objects helps you save time and minimize errors.
- To view object dependencies, select the object, click View, Object Dependencies and the Object Dependencies task pane displays. Before the task pane displays, you may get a message to enable the track name AutoCorrect. As shown on the task pane in Figure 6.12, you can select Objects that depend on me or Objects that I depend on to view all the connections this object has with the others in the database.

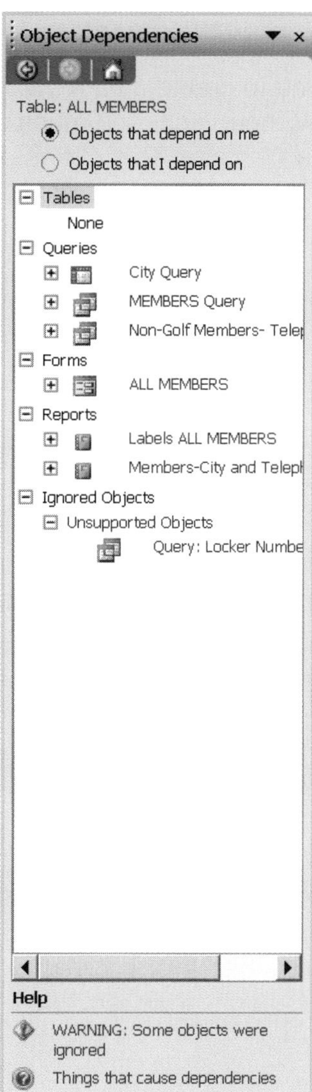

Figure 6.12 Object Dependencies task pane

ACCESS

TRY *it* OUT *A6-9*

1. Open **A6-9** from the Access Lesson 6 directory you have created.
2. Select the **ALL MEMBERS** table in the Table object.
3. Click **View, Object Dependencies.** Click **Yes** to enable name AutoCorrect to continue if the error message displays.
4. In the task pane that displays, note the objects that depend on this table.
5. Click **Objects that I depend on.** Note that there are none.
6. In the **Queries** object, click the **Locker Number Duplicates** query.
7. Click **View, Object Dependencies.** Click **Objects that depend on me.** Note that the query itself is listed as an unsupported dependency but there are no other dependencies.
8. Click the **Delete** key to delete the query. Click **Yes** to confirm the deletion.
9. Close and save the database.

Create a Data Access Page Using the Page Wizard

- Access provides a *Pages object* to enable you to create a *data access page,* which is a Web page linked to an Access database. You can view, input, edit, and manipulate data stored in a database by using a data access page on a Web site. This allows employees to use the database while away from the office.
- Access provides two shortcuts to help you create data access pages: *AutoPage: Columnar* and the *Page Wizard*. You can also create a data access page in Design view or by using an existing Web page. You will learn about the Page Wizard in this task.

Caution: When you create a data access page, you create an HTML file. The page object you see in Access is actually a link to this HTML file.

Important: For a link to a data access page to be valid, you must not move or rename the linked HTML file or the database after you create the data access page.

- When you build a data access page using the Page Wizard, it asks you questions about what information you want to include in a data access page and how you want to present and format it. If changes are necessary, you can modify the resulting data access page.
- To use the Page Wizard, in the Database window, click the Pages object, and double-click Create data access page by using wizard. The Page Wizard opens, as shown in Figure 6.13.

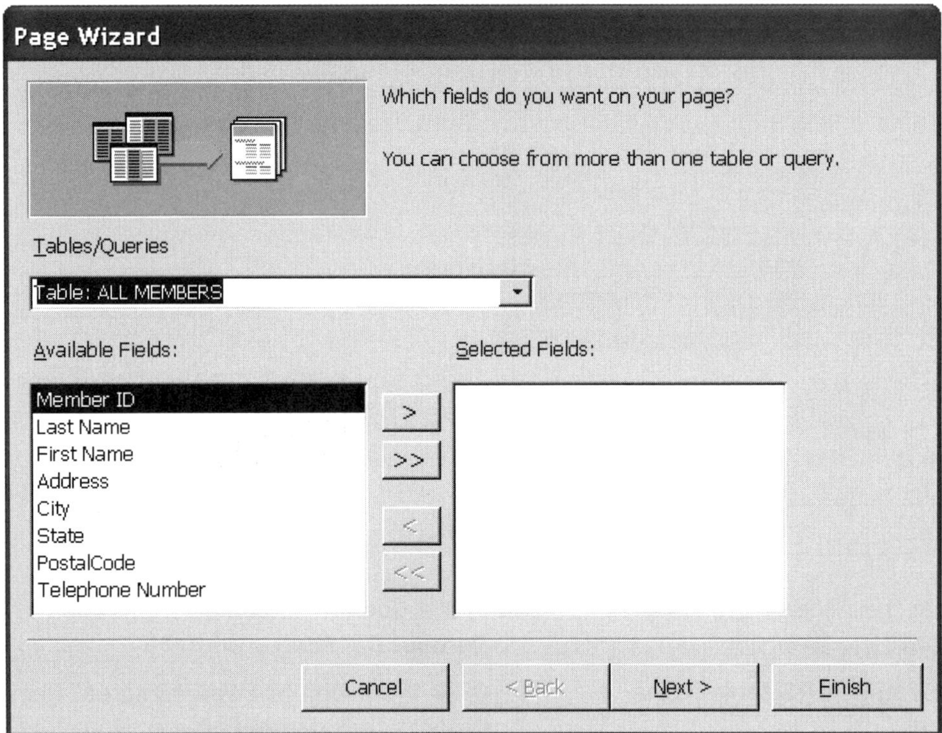

Figure 6.13 Page Wizard

- The Page Wizard asks you to select the data source table or query, and select the fields to include. Click the data source table or query, and double-click the selected fields. If the page is based on more than one table or query, click the additional data source, and double-click the fields to add. Tables must have established relationships before you can include them, or a related query, in a data access page.

▶ When you have completed the design of the Page object, it appears in Design view, as shown in Figure 6.14. When you switch to Page view, the *navigation controls* become active, as shown in Figure 6.15.

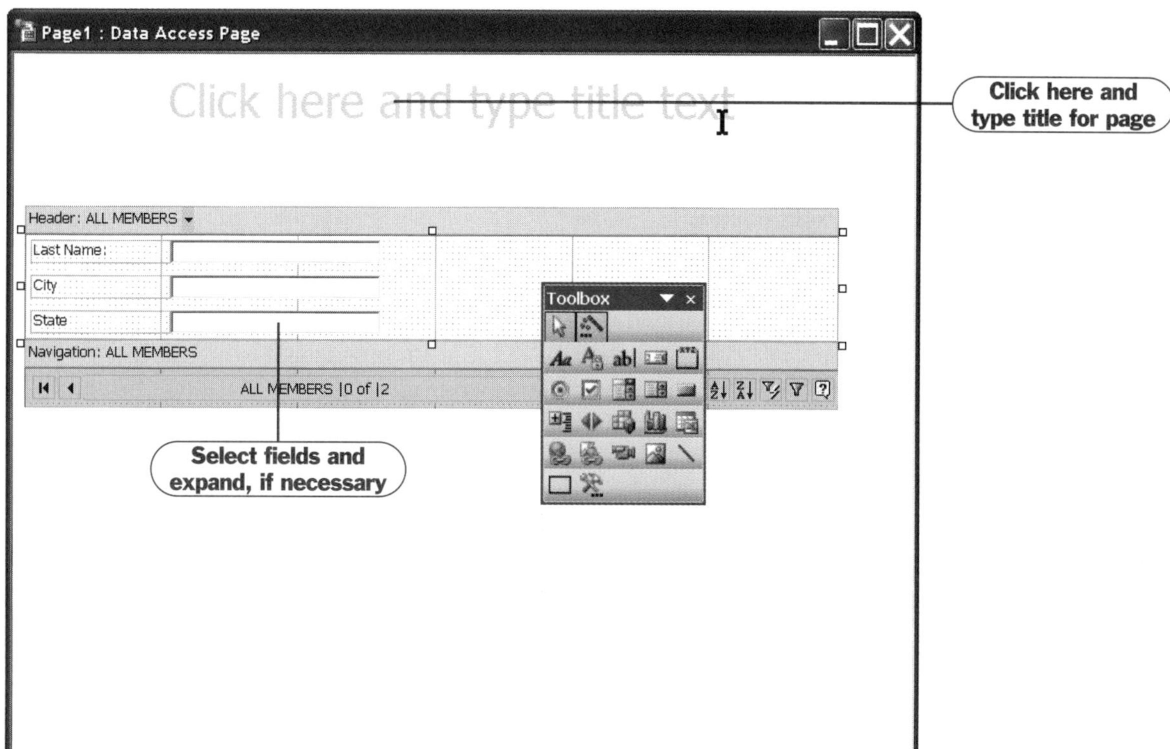

Figure 6.14 Page object in Design view

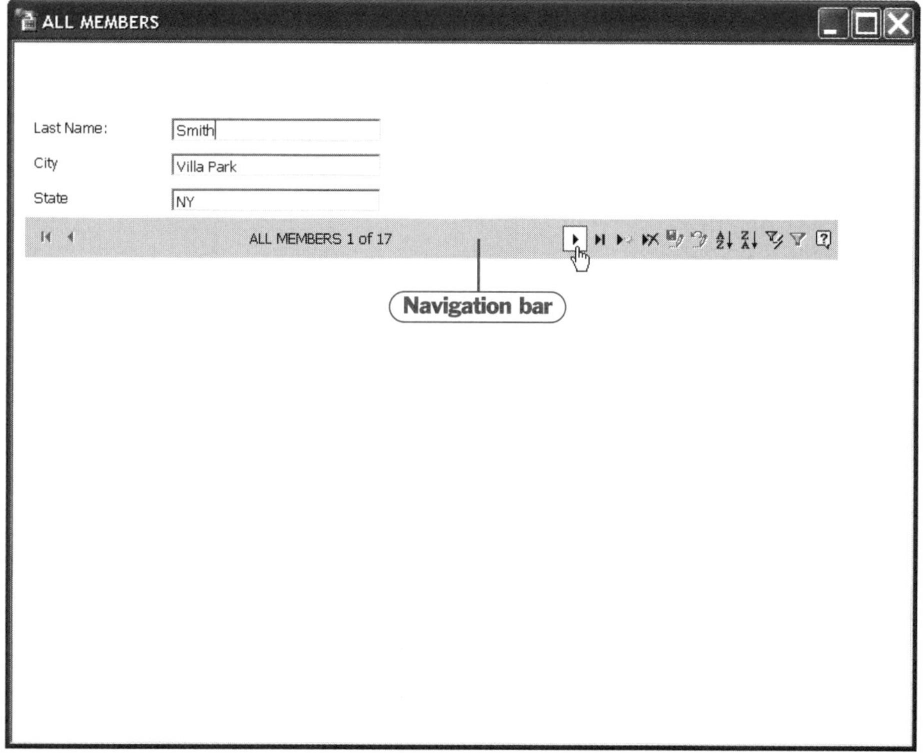

Figure 6.15 Page object in Page view

ACCESS

TRY it OUT *A6-10*

1. Open **A6-10** from the Access Lesson 6 directory you created.
2. Click the **Pages** object.
3. Double-click **Create data access page by using wizard.**
4. Click the list arrow in the **Tables/Queries** box. Click **Table: ALL MEMBERS.**
5. Move the following fields from the Available Fields box to the Selected Fields box:

   Last Name

   City

   State
6. Click **Finish.**
7. Notice that the page opens in Design view.
8. Notice that the page has a header and navigation controls that are not accessible.
9. Click **View** to change to Page view.
10. Notice that the navigation controls are active. Use the navigation controls to move through the records.
11. Close, but do not save the page. Close the database.

Create a Data Access Page Using the Page Wizard with a Theme

- A *theme* is a format or design template for creating Web pages. You can use the Page Wizard to select a theme that creates a data access page with customized body and heading styles, background color or graphics, table border color, horizontal lines, bullets, hyperlink colors, and controls. You can also select options to brighten colors for text and graphics.
- To apply a theme using the Page Wizard, click the Do you want to apply a theme to your page? box on the last page of the Wizard, as shown in Figure 6.16. Click Finish and the Theme dialog box opens, as shown in Figure 6.17.

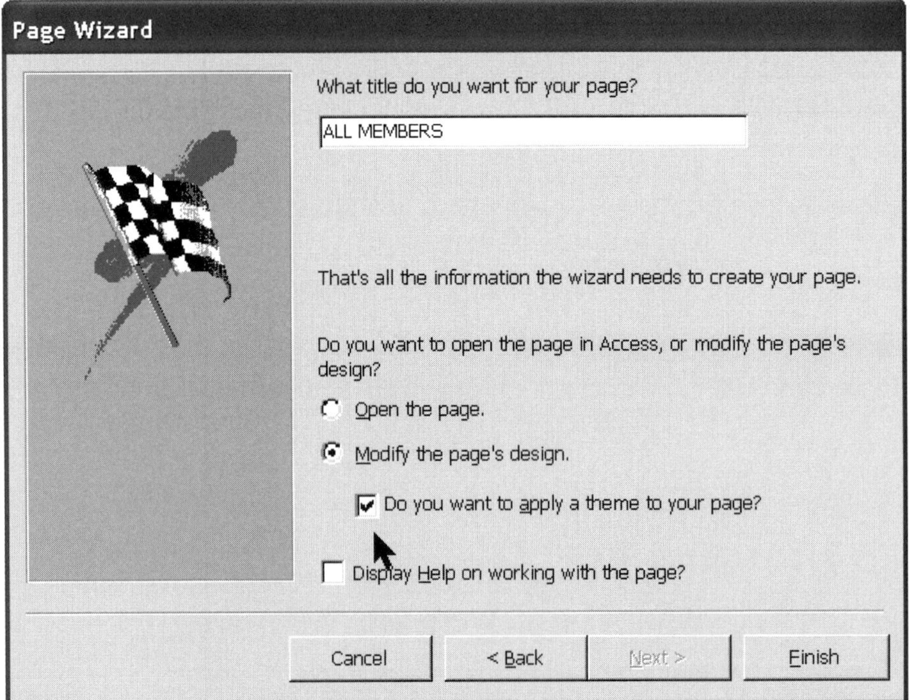

Figure 6.16 Page Wizard—last step

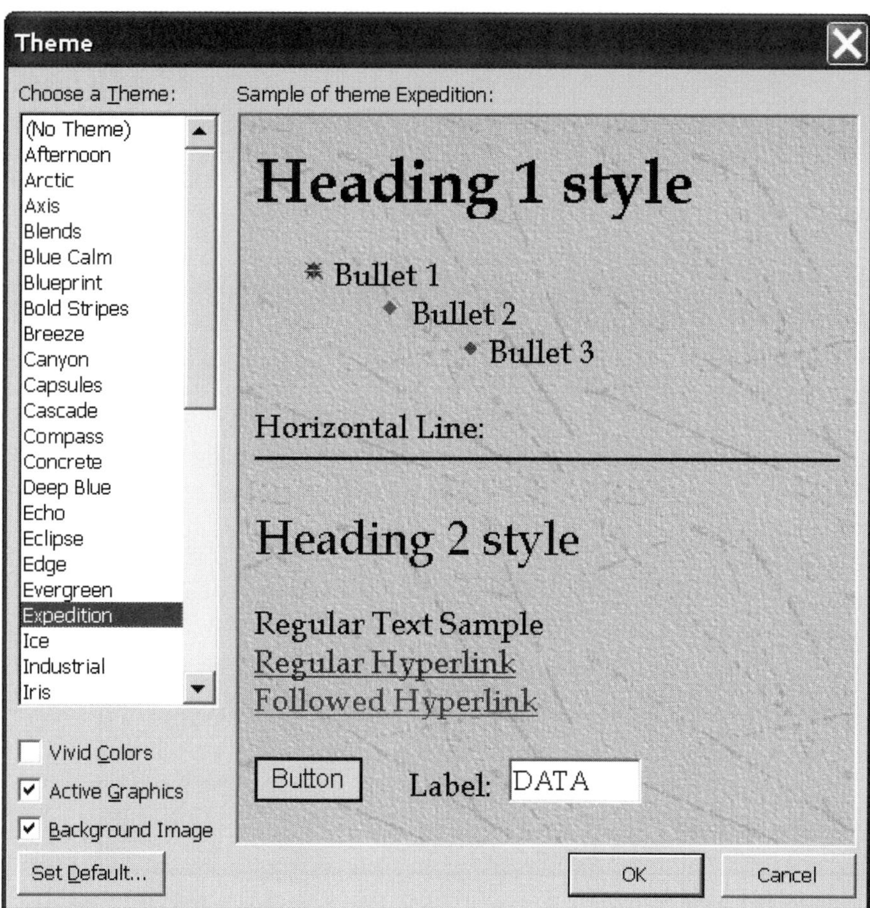

Figure 6.17 Theme dialog box

ACCESS

- Click each theme to preview the formats, select your choice, and click OK. The data access page appears in Design view with the theme applied, as shown in Figure 6.18. Click Page View to review the form. If the theme applied causes the text to be truncated in the field control, in Page Design view, click each field while holding down the Control key, and expand the size of all the field controls.

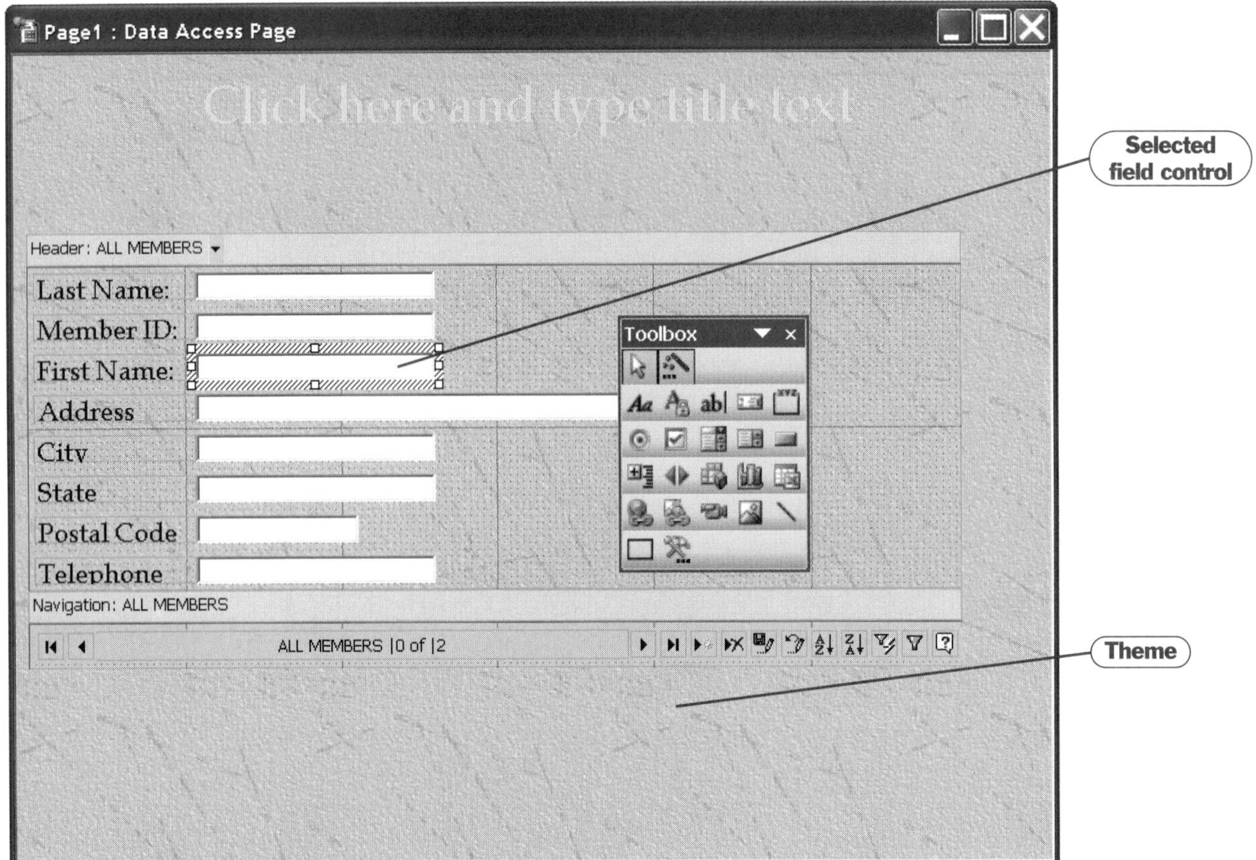

Figure 6.18 Page Design view with a theme

TRY *it* OUT *A6-11*

1. Open **A6-11** from the Access Lesson 6 directory you created.
2. Click the **Pages Object.**
3. Double-click **Create data access page by using wizard.**
4. Click the list arrow in the **Tables/Queries** box. Click **Table: ALL MEMBERS.**
5. Move all the fields from the Available Fields box to the Selected Fields box.
6. Click **Next.**
7. Click **Next** without selecting grouping levels.
8. Select **Last Name, Ascending** as the sort order. Click **Next.**
9. Click **Do you want to apply a theme to your page?** and click **Finish.**
10. Click **Expedition** as a theme and click **OK.**
11. In Page Design view, click the header area titled "Click here and type title text." Enter: `Club Members` as the title.
12. Click the **Page View** button. 
13. Click **File, Save** and name the page **ALL MEMBERS.** Click **OK** when the warning message appears.
14. Do not close the database.

Use Web Page Preview

▶ You can preview a data access page if you have Internet Explorer version 5.5 or later on your computer. To do so, click the arrow next to the Page View button, and click Web Page Preview, as shown in Figure 6.19.

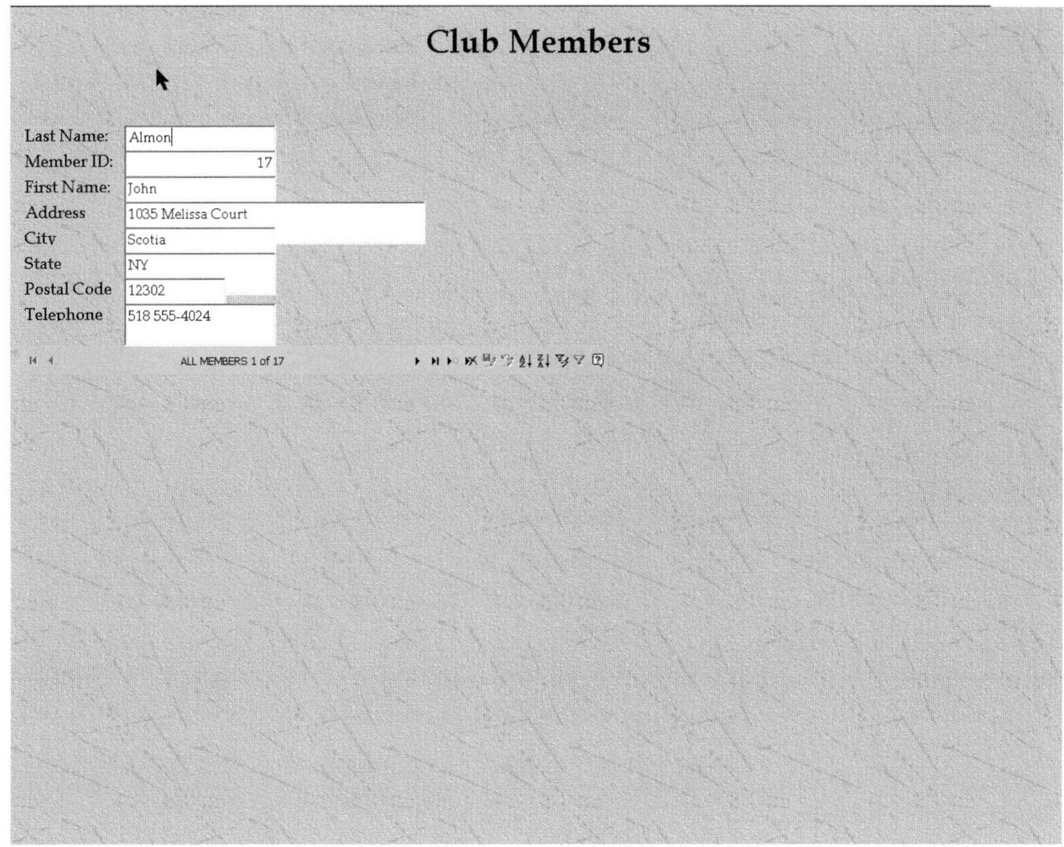

Figure 6.19 Web Page Preview

▶ *Web Page Preview* enables you to see how the data access page will appear as a Web page. The data access page must be saved before you can preview it as a Web page.

TRY *it* OUT *A6-12*

1. Use the file from the last Try it Out or open **A6-12** from the Access Lesson 6 directory and click the **Pages** object.
2. Double-click the **ALL MEMBERS** data access page.
3. Click the arrow next to the **Page View** button. 
4. Click **Web Page Preview.**
5. A preview of the Web page appears.
6. Click the **Next Record** control to view each record.
7. Close Internet Explorer.
8. Close the page, the database, and Access.

ACCESS

TASK 2

GOALS
To backup, compact, and repair the database; to view object dependencies; to create two data access pages; and to view the data access pages on the Web

SETTING THE STAGE/WRAPUP

Database: Four Corners Realty2
Table: Listings
Data Access Pages: Listings
Rental Listings

WHAT YOU NEED TO KNOW

- Four Corners Realty has recently made a major technology investment. The company has given laptop computers to each of the agents. As part of this initiative, management has instituted database maintenance procedures and will provide data access pages.
- To maintain the database, the company will back up the database daily at the end of each day. They will also run the Compact and Repair utility weekly to eliminate any data fragmentation. The dependencies for the queries will be viewed and one of the queries will be deleted.
- Management would like you to build data access pages that will allow agents to view and update their listings using Internet Explorer. In this Rehearsal activity, you will create:
  - A simple data access page, sorted by city and price.
  - A data access page grouped by agent, using the Watermark theme.

DIRECTIONS

1. Start **Access.**
2. Open the **Four Corners Realty2** database in your Access Lesson 6 directory.
3. Backup the database and name the back up copy **FCRBackup.**
4. Compact and repair the database using the **Tools, Database Utilities, Compact and Repair Database** feature.
5. Select the **Queries object** and the **Agents without matching listings** query.
6. View the **Object Dependencies.** Click **OK** to enable the AutoCorrect track name if you get an error message.
7. If there are no objects that depend on this query, delete the query.
8. Use the **Page Wizard** to create a data access page using all the fields in the **Listings** table.
9. Sort the list first by **City** in **Ascending order** and second by **Price** in **Descending order.**
10. Name the page **Listings** and use the **Watermark Theme.**
11. In Page Design view, change the title to read: `Four Corners Realty Listings.`
12. Save the data access page. Click **OK** when the warning message appears. (See Illustration A.)
13. Use the **Page Wizard** to create a data access page using all the fields in the **Rental Listings** table.
14. Sort the list first by **City** in **Ascending order** and second by **Monthly Price** in **Descending order.**

Continued on next page

15. Save the page and name it **Rental Listings** and use the **Watermark Theme.**
16. In Page Design view, change the title to read: `Four Corners Realty, Rental Listings.` Expand the Monthly Price label control to display the entire label.
17. Save the data access page. Click **OK** when the warning message appears. (See Illustration B.)
18. Use Web Page preview to view the Rental Listings data access page. What is the highest price rental in East Hollywood?
19. Close the database.

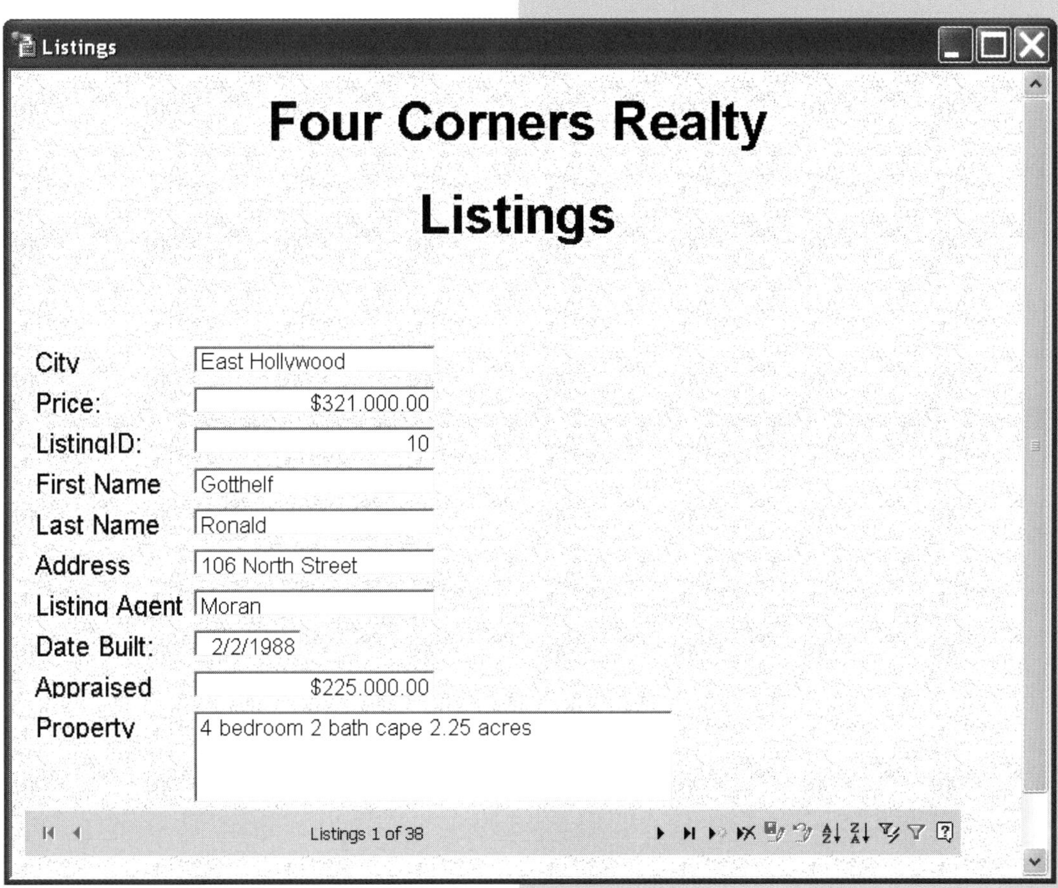

Illustration A

ACCESS

Rental Listings

Four Corners Realty

Rental Listings

City: East Hollywood

Monthly 6000

ID: 5

Last Name: Al-Abbas

First Name: Sarah

Address: 1461 Creekside Dr

Telephone: 555-472-4221

Rental Listings 2 of 101

Illustration B

Cues for Reference

Back Up a Database

1. Open database.
2. Click **File, Back Up Database.**
3. Select location and name backup file.
4. Click **Save.**

Compact and Repair a Database

1. Open database.
2. Click **Tools, Database Utilities, Compact and Repair Database.**

View Object Dependencies

1. Select database object.
2. Click **View, Object Dependencies.**
3. Click **OK** to enable AutoCorrect track option, if prompted.
4. Select **Objects that depend on me** or **Objects that I depend on.**

Create a Data Access Page Using Page Wizard

1. Click the **Pages** object.
2. Double-click **Create data access page by using wizard.**
3. Click the list arrow in the **Tables/Queries** box.
4. Click a data source.
5. Move fields from the Available Fields box to the Selected Fields box.
6. Click **Next.**
7. Click **Next** and click a sort order.
8. Name the page and click **Do you want to add a theme to this page?**
9. Click **Finish.**

Preview Data Access Page on the Web

1. Select data access page.
2. On the View button, click list arrow and click **Web Page Preview.**

SETTING THE STAGE/WRAPUP

Act I	**Database:**	ALS
	Tables:	Customers
		Prospects
	Excel File:	**Prospects**
	Word Files:	**Customers**
		Prospects
Act II	**Database:**	ALS2
	Tables:	Customers
		Prospects
	Data Access Pages:	
		Customers
		Prospects

WHAT YOU NEED TO KNOW

Act I

The director of the Leisure Travel Department at Air Land Sea Travel, Robin Byron, has been charged with developing lists to support a direct marketing campaign targeted to current customers, as well as to prospective customers. She is comfortable with the **Customers** table, but not with the **Prospects** list, because it is in the form of an Excel spreadsheet and is not part of the **ALS** database.

ACCESS

Robin has asked you to import the prospects information into the existing **ALS** database. She wants it to be in a separate table named **Prospects.** She has also asked that you export the data from the existing **Customers** table and the **Prospects** table (which you will create) to Word.

Follow these guidelines:

- The prospects data is stored in **Prospects.xls.** Import it into the database as a new table. There are no column headings and you will need to assign field names. Name the first field in the Wizard screens and assign other field names in Table Design view. Notice that one field contains travel preferences, and one contains customers' future travel interests.
- Export the Prospects table to Word; name the Word file: **Prospects.** Format the Word table in landscape mode, as illustrated.
- Export the Customers table to Word; name the Word file: **Customers.** Format the Word table so that it is easy to read.

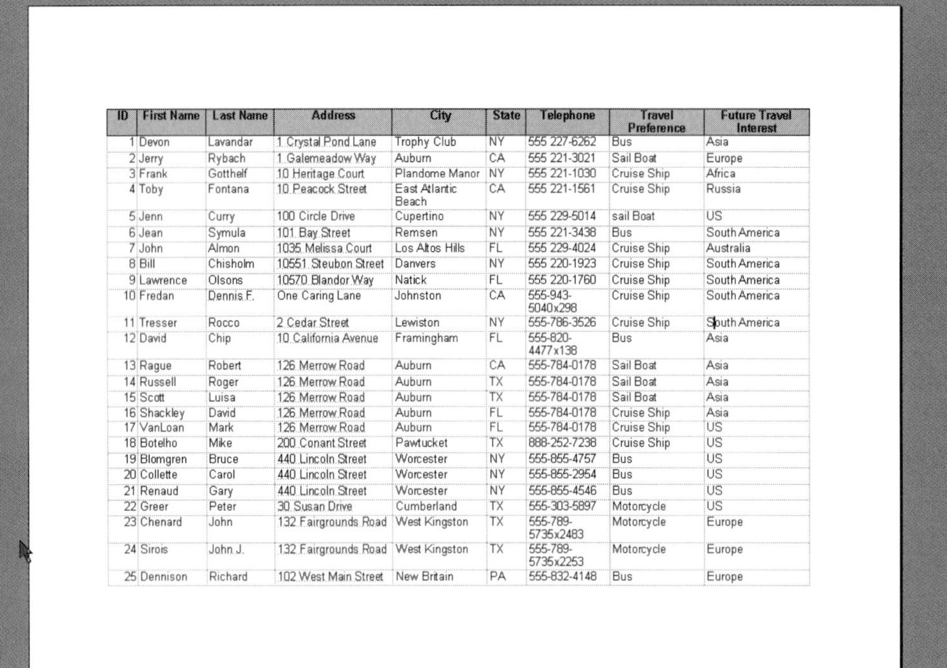

ID	First Name	Last Name	Address	City	State	Telephone	Travel Preference	Future Travel Interest
1	Devon	Lavandar	1 Crystal Pond Lane	Trophy Club	NY	555 227-6262	Bus	Asia
2	Jerry	Rybach	1 Galemeadow Way	Auburn	CA	555 221-3021	Sail Boat	Europe
3	Frank	Gotthelf	10 Heritage Court	Plandome Manor	NY	555 221-1030	Cruise Ship	Africa
4	Toby	Fontana	10 Peacock Street	East Atlantic Beach	CA	555 221-1561	Cruise Ship	Russia
5	Jenn	Curry	100 Circle Drive	Cupertino	NY	555 229-5014	sail Boat	US
6	Jean	Symula	101 Bay Street	Remsen	NY	555 221-3438	Bus	South America
7	John	Almon	1035 Melissa Court	Los Altos Hills	FL	555 229-4024	Cruise Ship	Australia
8	Bill	Chisholm	10551 Steubon Street	Danvers	NY	555 220-1923	Cruise Ship	South America
9	Lawrence	Olsons	10570 Blandor Way	Natick	FL	555 220-1760	Cruise Ship	South America
10	Fredan	Dennis F.	One Caring Lane	Johnston	CA	555-943-5040x298	Cruise Ship	South America
11	Tresser	Rocco	2 Cedar Street	Lewiston	NY	555-786-3526	Cruise Ship	South America
12	David	Chip	10 California Avenue	Framingham	FL	555-820-4477x138	Bus	Asia
13	Rague	Robert	126 Merrow Road	Auburn	CA	555-784-0178	Sail Boat	Asia
14	Russell	Roger	126 Merrow Road	Auburn	TX	555-784-0178	Sail Boat	Asia
15	Scott	Luisa	126 Merrow Road	Auburn	TX	555-784-0178	Sail Boat	Asia
16	Shackley	David	126 Merrow Road	Auburn	FL	555-784-0178	Cruise Ship	Asia
17	VanLoan	Mark	126 Merrow Road	Auburn	FL	555-784-0178	Cruise Ship	US
18	Botelho	Mike	200 Conant Street	Pawtucket	TX	888-252-7238	Cruise Ship	US
19	Blomgren	Bruce	440 Lincoln Street	Worcester	NY	555-855-4757	Bus	US
20	Collette	Carol	440 Lincoln Street	Worcester	NY	555-855-2954	Bus	US
21	Renaud	Gary	440 Lincoln Street	Worcester	NY	555-855-4546	Bus	US
22	Greer	Peter	30 Susan Drive	Cumberland	TX	555-303-5897	Motorcycle	US
23	Chenard	John	132 Fairgrounds Road	West Kingston	TX	555-789-5735x2483	Motorcycle	Europe
24	Sirois	John J.	132 Fairgrounds Road	West Kingston	TX	555-789-5735x2253	Motorcycle	Europe
25	Dennison	Richard	102 West Main Street	New Britain	PA	555-832-4148	Bus	Europe

Prospects table in Word

Act II

Robin is concerned about the maintenance of the company database. She has asked you to back up the file, run the compact and repair utility, and to delete a query that is no longer necesssary.

She has also asked you to prepare data access pages based on the data in the **ALS** database, as an interactive way to view a large database of prospects and the growing database of customers. You will create two data access pages, one using the **Customers** table as its data source and one using the **Prospects** table for its data source. Use the **ALS** file from Act 1 or open **ALS2** from the Data CD.

Follow these guidelines:

- Back up the database to a file named **ALS2BU.** Compact and repair the database. View the Object Dependencies for the Travel Partner Trip Count Query. If no objects depend on the query, delete it.
- Create two data access pages using the **Compass theme.** Your pages should be similar to the Prospects data page illustrated on the next page and should contain the company name.
- Create a data access page for prospects data sorted by future travel interests and by last name in alphabetical order. Name this data access page: **Prospects.**
- Robin also needs a data access page built on the **Customers** table, using all but the Most Recent Trip and Travel Partner latest trip fields. She would like this page sorted by state and next travel interest. Name this data access page: **Customers.**
- If necessary, in Page Design view, select all the fields using the Control key and expand the size to accommodate the theme font size. Print a copy of each data access page.

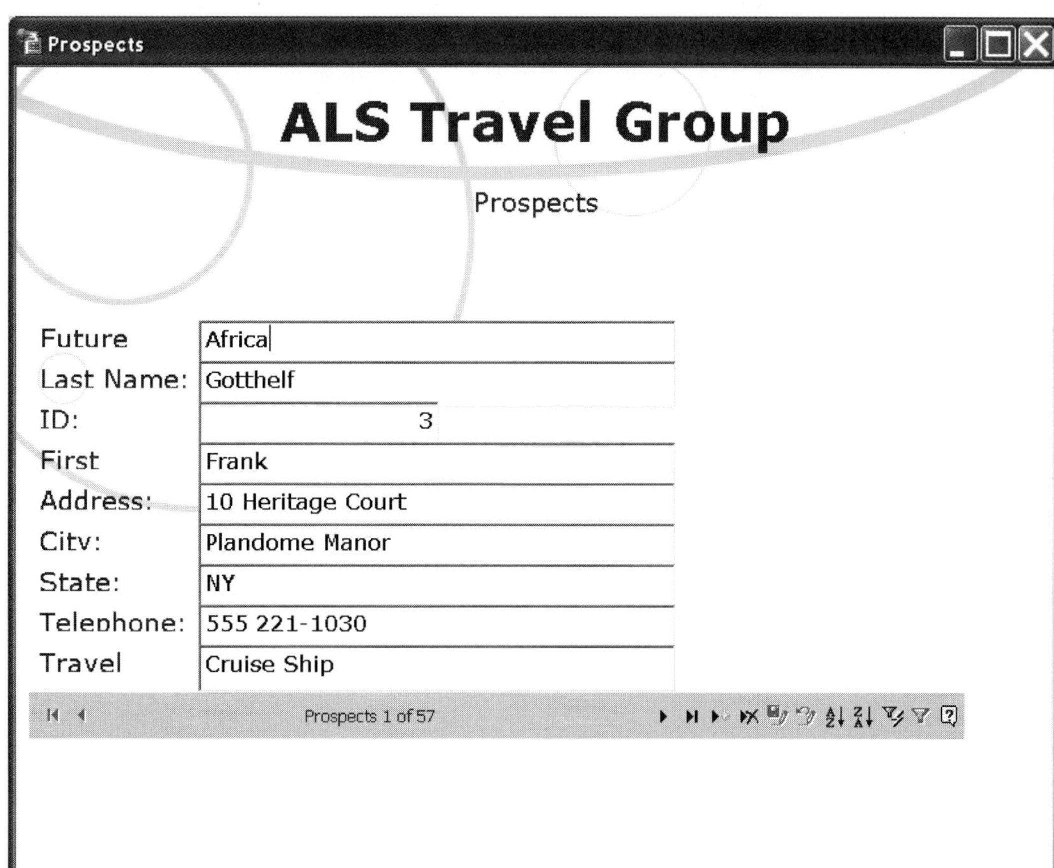
Prospects
ALS Travel Group
Prospects
Future
Africa
Last Name:
Gotthelf
ID:
3
First
Frank
Address:
10 Heritage Court
City:
Plandome Manor
State:
NY
Telephone:
555 221-1030
Travel
Cruise Ship
Prospects 1 of 57

1
2
3

PERFORMING WITH POWERPOINT
INTRODUCTORY UNIT

LESSON 1

PowerPoint Basics

In this lesson, you will be introduced to PowerPoint and its basic features.

Upon completion of this lesson, you should have mastered the following skill sets:

- Start PowerPoint
- Explore the PowerPoint window
- Open a presentation
- Navigate through a presentation
- Change views
- Run a slide show
- Select page setup options
- View a presentation in grayscale or black and white
- Print a presentation

Terms

Software-related

Presentation
Slide pane
Outline and Slides tab pane
Task pane
Normal view
Slide sorter view
Slide show view
Portrait orientation
Landscape orientation
Grayscale

TRYOUT

TASK 1

GOAL

To practice using the following skill sets:

- Start PowerPoint
- Explore the PowerPoint window
- Open a presentation
- Navigate through a presentation

WHAT YOU NEED TO KNOW

About PowerPoint

- PowerPoint is the *presentation* program within Office that lets you create and save on-screen slide shows, slides for transparencies, 35-mm slides, and handouts.
- The features found in PowerPoint allow you to enhance the slides in your presentation with graphics, charts, animation, sound, and video to create exciting visuals that support and complement an oral report. You can even record and time your oral report so that it is automatically delivered when you run the slide show.
- PowerPoint also allows you to publish your presentation to the Web so that others can view it.

Start PowerPoint

- There are two basic ways to start PowerPoint:
  1. Click the Start button on the taskbar, point to All Programs, Microsoft Office, and then click Microsoft Office PowerPoint 2003, as shown in Figure 1.1.
  2. Click the PowerPoint program icon on the desktop, as shown in Figure 1.2.

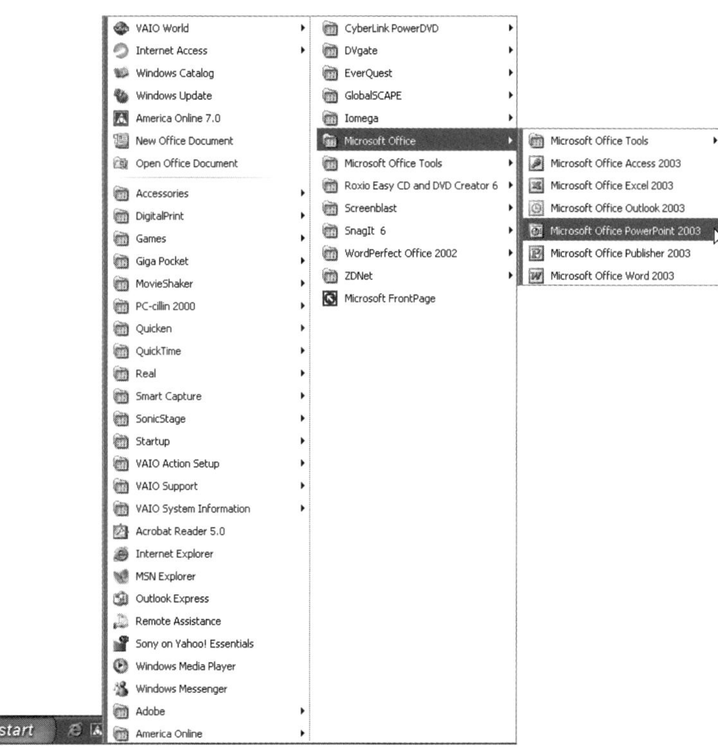

Figure 1.1 Start PowerPoint from taskbar

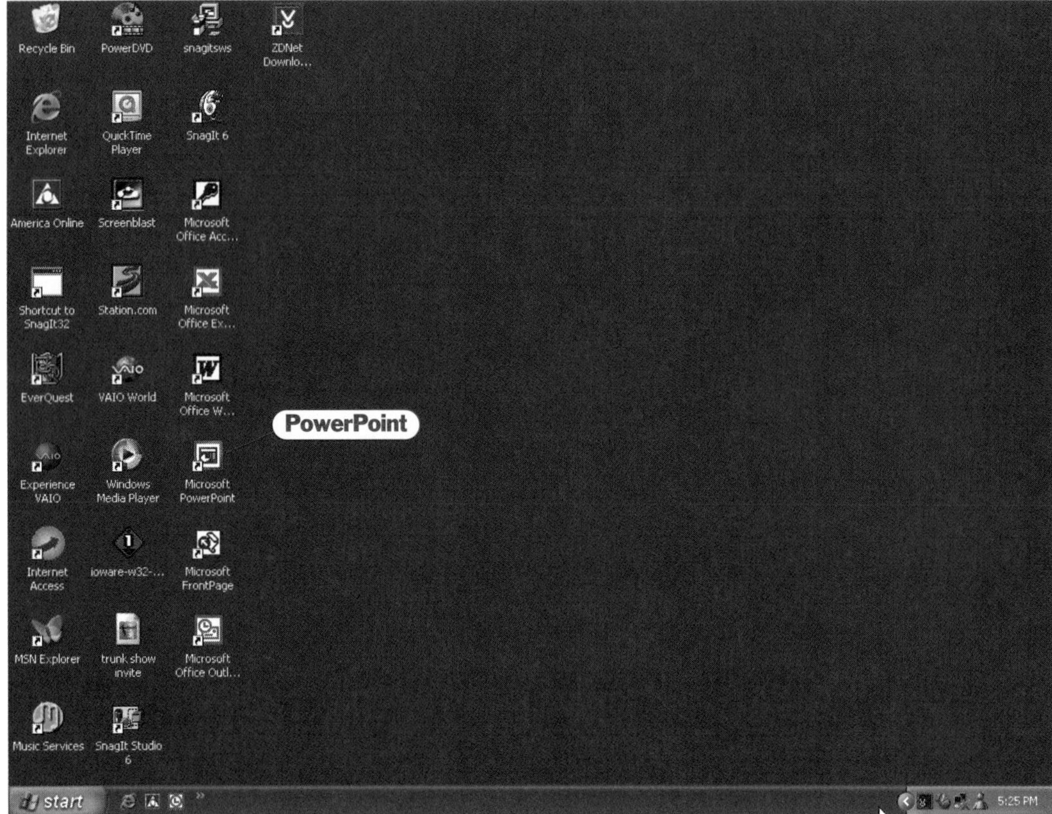

Figure 1.2 Start PowerPoint from desktop

TRY *it* OUT *p1-1*

1. Click **Start.**
2. Select **All Programs.**
3. Select **Microsoft Office.**
4. Click **Microsoft Office PowerPoint 2003.**
5. Click the **Close** button on the Program window. 

Explore the PowerPoint Window

- After PowerPoint starts, the PowerPoint window appears, as shown in Figure 1.3.
- The main window contains three panes unique to PowerPoint:
  1. The *Slide pane* contains a new blank slide for you to begin creating a presentation.
  2. The *Outline and Slides tab pane* is to the left of the slide.
  3. The *task pane* is to the right of the slide.
- Parts of the window are described below.
  - The **title bar** displays the program and presentation names.
  - The **menu bar** displays items to execute commands.
  - The **Standard toolbar** contains buttons to accomplish many common Office tasks, such as printing and saving a document, but also contains buttons unique to PowerPoint.

- The **Formatting toolbar** contains buttons to change the appearance of text on slides. It also contains two buttons for commonly used tasks: a New Slide button for adding additional slides, and a Design button for applying a design template.

- The **Rulers** display the horizontal and vertical measurements of a slide and allow you to quickly change margins, text indentations, and tabs.
- The **Slide pane** displays the current slide.

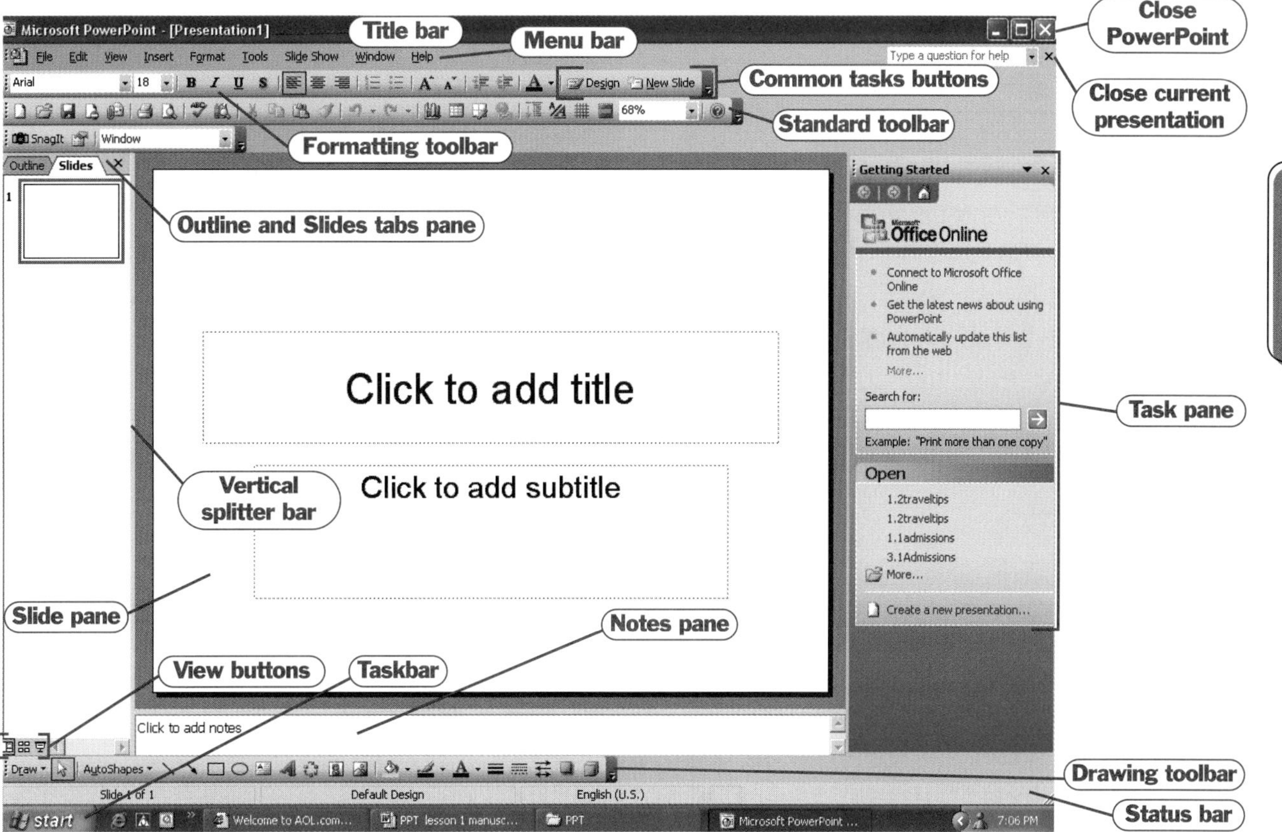

Figure 1.3 PowerPoint window

- The **Outline and Slides tab pane** contains the Outline and Slides tabs. When selected, the Slides tab displays miniatures, called thumbnails, of all the slides in a presentation; the Outline tab displays an outline of the text on each slide.
- The **vertical splitter bar** divides the Slide pane from the Outline and Slides tab pane.
- The **Notes pane** allows you to add speaking notes to accompany the current slide.
- The **Drawing toolbar** contains buttons to enhance a slide with shapes, special effects, and colors.
- The **task pane** provides quick access for opening, creating, formatting, and communicating presentations.
- The **view buttons** allow you to change presentation views.
- The **Status bar** displays the current slide number and the total number of slides in the presentation (Slide 1 of 1), as well as the name of the current template design. It also contains a spelling check icon.
- The **task bar** displays the Start button, as well as open documents and programs.

- To display more of the Slide pane, you can do the following:
  a. Close the task pane and/or the Outline and Slides tab pane: Click the Close buttons on the appropriate pane.
  b. Reduce the size of the Outline and Slides tab pane: Drag the vertical splitter bar to the left.
  c. Hide toolbars and rulers: Click View, Toolbars and deselect those toolbars you wish to hide. To hide the ruler, click View and deselect Ruler.

TRY *it* OUT *p1-2*

1. Start Powerpoint, if necessary.
2. Click each menu bar item. Notice the submenu commands.
3. Move the mouse pointer over each toolbar button to display its ScreenTip.
4. Click **View, Ruler** to hide or display the rulers, depending on whether or not they are already showing.
5. Click **View, Ruler** to redisplay or rehide the rulers.
6. Click the **Close** button on the task pane.
7. Click **View, Task Pane** to redisplay the task pane.
8. Click the **Close** button on the Outline and Slides tab pane.
9. Click **View, Normal** to redisplay the Outline and Slides tab pane.

Open a Presentation

- As with other Office applications, presentations can be opened by selecting File, Open or by clicking the Open button on the Standard toolbar. 
- The Getting Started task pane displays links to recently opened presentations, as shown in Figure 1.4. To open a presentation displayed on the task pane, click its link. To open a presentation not displayed, click the More link, then select the presentation you wish to open.

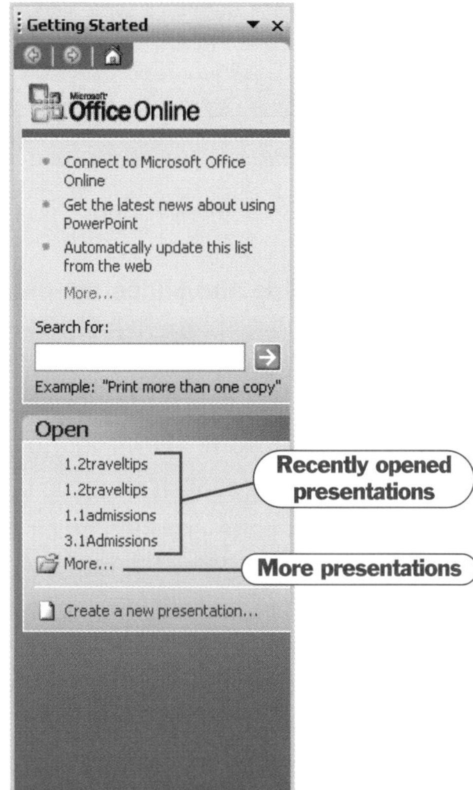

Figure 1.4 Getting Started task pane

TRY *it* OUT p1-3

1. Click the **More** link in the Getting Started task pane.
   - Click the **Look in** list arrow.
   - Select the Data CD.
2. Open **1.1latte** from the Data CD.
3. Click the **Outline tab** in the Outline and Slides tab pane.
4. Click the **Slides tab** in the Outline and Slides tab pane.
5. Click and drag the **vertical splitter bar** to the left to enlarge the Slide pane.
6. Do not close the presentation.

POWERPOINT

Navigate through a Presentation

- You can move from slide to slide using one of the following methods:
  a. Press the Page Down key to display the next slide or the Page Up key to display the previous slide.
  b. Click the scroll up arrow to scroll up one slide or the scroll down arrow to scroll down one slide.
  c. Click the Next Slide button or the Previous Slide button on the vertical scroll bar. These buttons appear on the scroll bar when a presentation contains multiple slides.
  d. Drag the vertical scroll box up or down until the desired slide appears. As you drag the scroll box, a slide label displays indicating the slide number and slide name, as shown in Figure 1.5.
  e. Click above the scroll box to scroll up one slide or below the scroll box to scroll down one slide.
  f. Click the slide thumbnail displayed on the Slides tab.

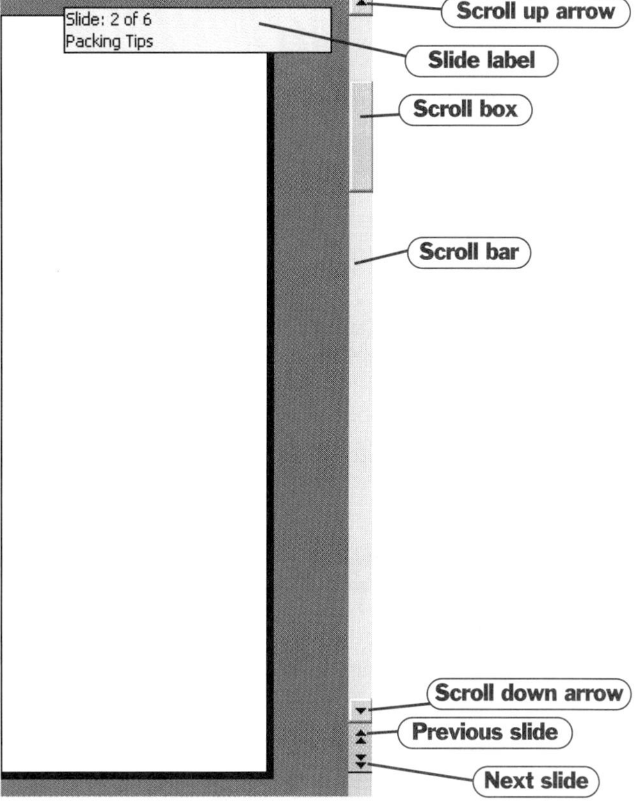

Figure 1.5 Scrolling through slides

TRY *it* OUT p1-4

*Note: The **1.1latte presentation** should be displayed. If it is not, open the file from the Data CD.*

1. Press the **Page Down** key twice.
2. Press the **Page Up** key once.
3. Drag the scroll box to display Slide 5.
4. Click the **Previous Slide** button on the scroll bar twice. 
5. Click the **Next Slide** button once. 
6. Click **Slide 1** on the Slides tab.
7. Close the file; do not save.

GOAL
To open a presentation and navigate through slides

SETTING THE STAGE/WRAPUP
File name: **1.1losangelestv**

WHAT YOU NEED TO KNOW

- When moving from slide to slide, use the navigation techniques with which you are most comfortable.
- In this Rehearsal activity, you will open a presentation, explore the PowerPoint window, and use slide navigation methods to move from slide to slide.

DIRECTIONS

1. Open **1.1losangelestv** from the Data CD.

2. Close the **task pane,** if it is displayed.
3. Click the **Outline tab.**
4. Widen the **Slide pane.**
5. Click the **Slides tab.**
6. Close the **Outline and Slides tab pane.**
7. Use any method to display Slide 2.
8. Use another method to display Slide 4.
9. Use another method to display Slide 1.
10. Close the file; do not save.

Cues for Reference

Start PowerPoint
1. Click **Start.**
2. Select **All Programs.**
3. Select **Microsoft Office.**
4. Click **Microsoft PowerPoint 2003.**

or
- Click the Microsoft PowerPoint icon on the desktop.

Office XP
1. Click **Start.**
2. Select **Programs.**
3. Click **PowerPoint.**

or
1. Click **New Office Document.**
2. Click the **General** tab.
3. Double-click **Blank Presentation.**

Hide/Show Screen Elements

Hide
- Click the **Close** button on the task panes.

or
1. Click **View.**
2. Click item to hide.

Show
1. Click **View.**
2. Click item to appear.

Navigate through a Presentation
- Click **Page Up** and **Page Down** keys.

or
- Click the **scroll up arrow** and the **scroll down arrow** on the scroll bar.

or
- Click the **Next Slide** or the **Previous Slide** button on the scroll bar.

or
- Drag the vertical scroll box up or down.

or
- Click above the scroll box to move up one slide or below the scroll box to move down one slide.

or
- Click the slide thumbnail displayed on the Slides tab.

Open a Presentation
- Click the **Open** button on the standard toolbar.

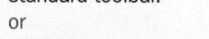

or
1. Click **File.**
2. Click **Open.**

or
1. Click **View, Task pane** (if not already displayed).
2. Click the **More** link.
3. Click the **Look in** list arrow.
4. Select the desired drive or folder.
5. Click the file name to open.
6. Click **Open.**

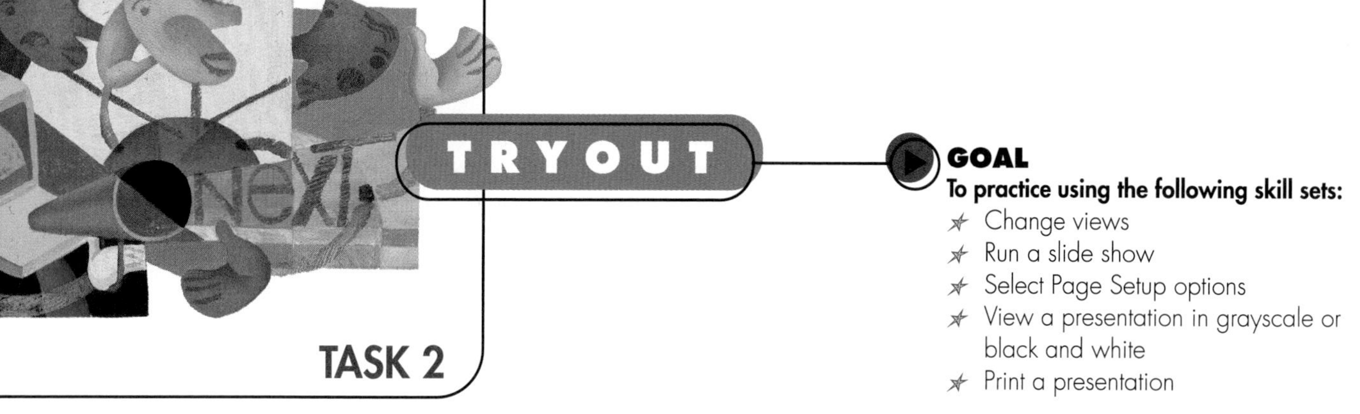

GOAL
To practice using the following skill sets:
- Change views
- Run a slide show
- Select Page Setup options
- View a presentation in grayscale or black and white
- Print a presentation

POWERPOINT

WHAT YOU NEED TO KNOW

Change Views

- PowerPoint lets you view your presentation in several different ways. To access these view options, click the appropriate button at the bottom left of the screen, as shown in Figure 1.6, or click View on the menu and choose a view option.

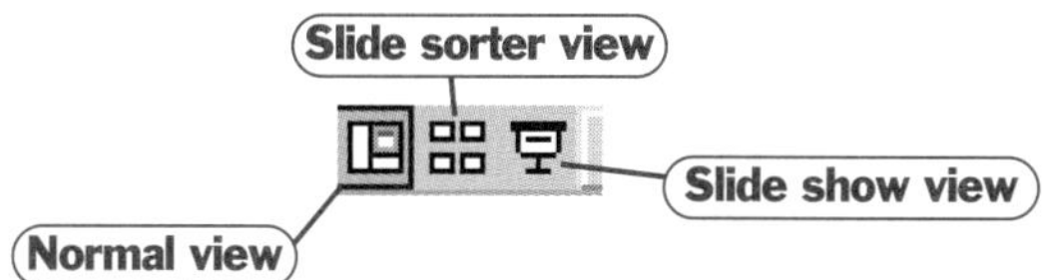

Figure 1.6 Slide view buttons

- *Normal view,* the default, displays three panes: the Slide pane, the Outline and Slides tab pane, and the Notes pane, as shown in Figure 1.7. Use this view to enter and edit text on a slide.

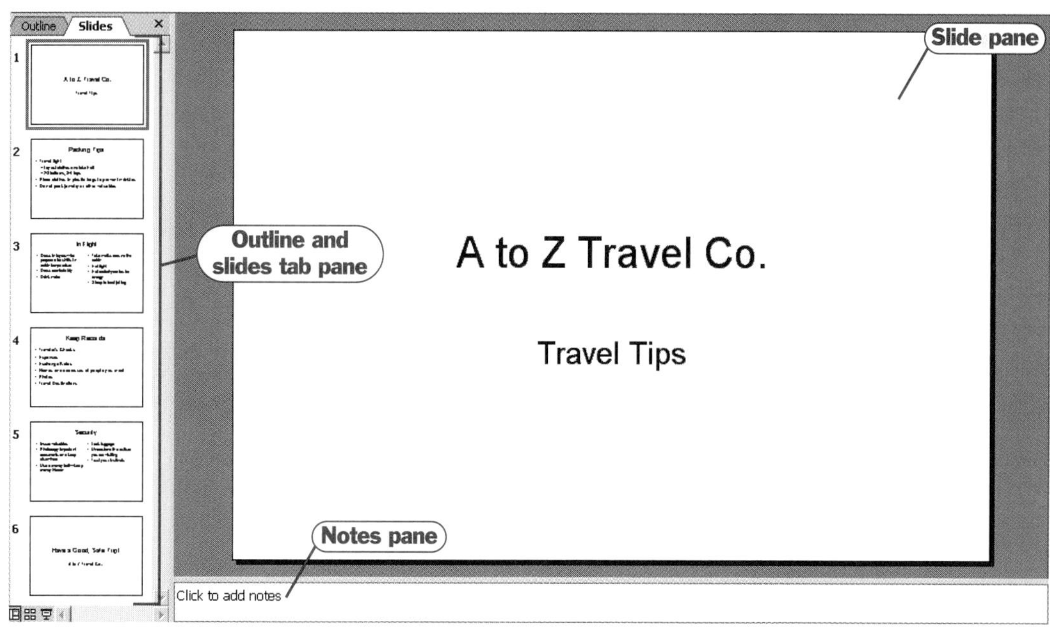

Figure 1.7 Normal view

▶ *Slide sorter view* displays slides as thumbnails so that you can see the flow of the presentation, as shown in Figure 1.8. Use this view to move, copy, and delete slides. (Moving, copying, and deleting slides are explored in Lesson 2.) Double-clicking on a slide will display that slide in Normal view.

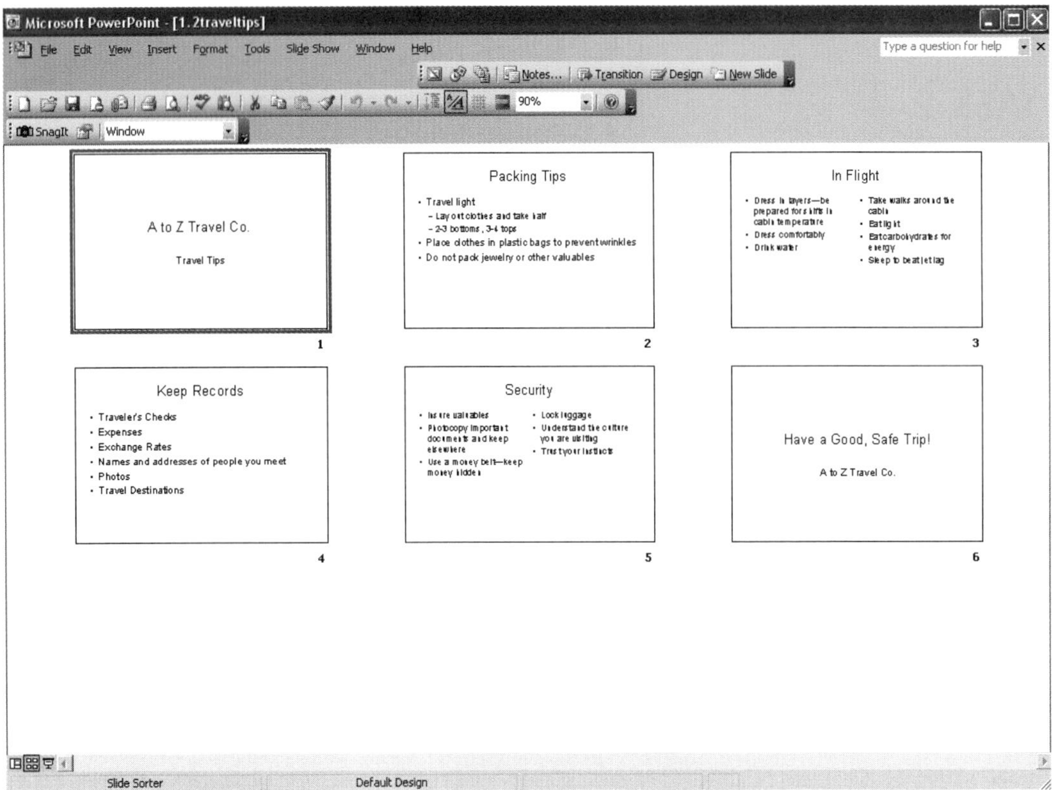

Figure 1.8 Slide Sorter view

▶ *Slide show view* lets you see your slides as an on-screen presentation.

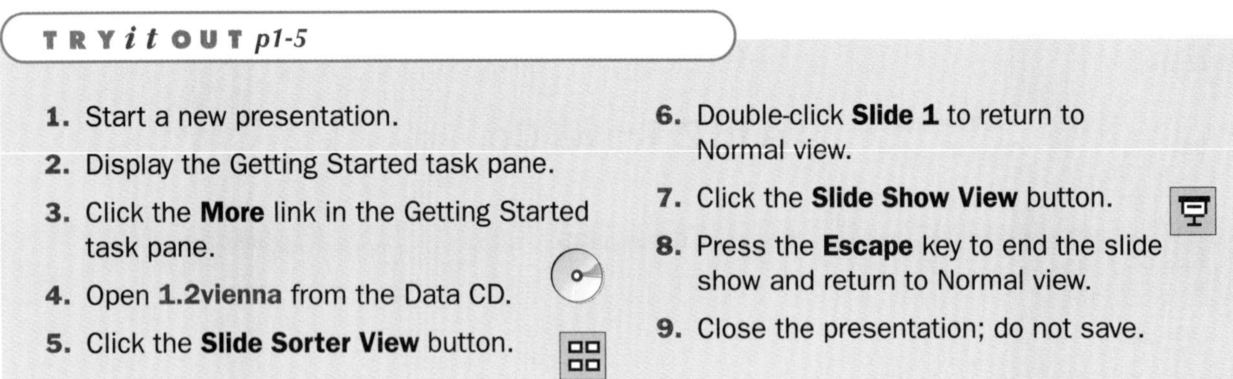

TRY *it* OUT *p1-5*

1. Start a new presentation.
2. Display the Getting Started task pane.
3. Click the **More** link in the Getting Started task pane.
4. Open **1.2vienna** from the Data CD.
5. Click the **Slide Sorter View** button.
6. Double-click **Slide 1** to return to Normal view.
7. Click the **Slide Show View** button.
8. Press the **Escape** key to end the slide show and return to Normal view.
9. Close the presentation; do not save.

Run a Slide Show

- When you run a slide show, each slide appears on the entire screen without showing the toolbars and menus.
- As you learned previously, you can activate a slide show by displaying the first slide to be shown and clicking the Slide Show View button or clicking View, Slide Show.

- You can navigate through a slide show using the following techniques:
  1. Click the left mouse button each time you want to advance to the next slide.
  2. Press the Page Up or Page Down keys to move forward and back through the slides.
  3. Click the forward and/or back navigation buttons, which appear at the bottom of the slide as shown in Figure 1.9.
  4. Press the Enter key each time you want to advance to the next slide.

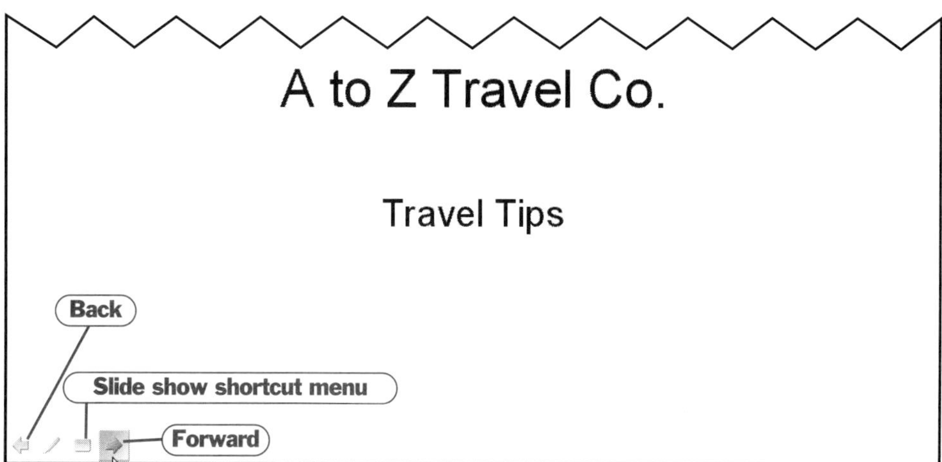

Figure 1.9 Slide show forward and back navigation buttons

- To return to a specific slide during a slide show, click the shortcut menu button on the slide (see Figure 1.9), select Go to Slide on the menu, then click the slide you want to display, as shown in Figure 1.10. The buttons appear only when the mouse is moved.

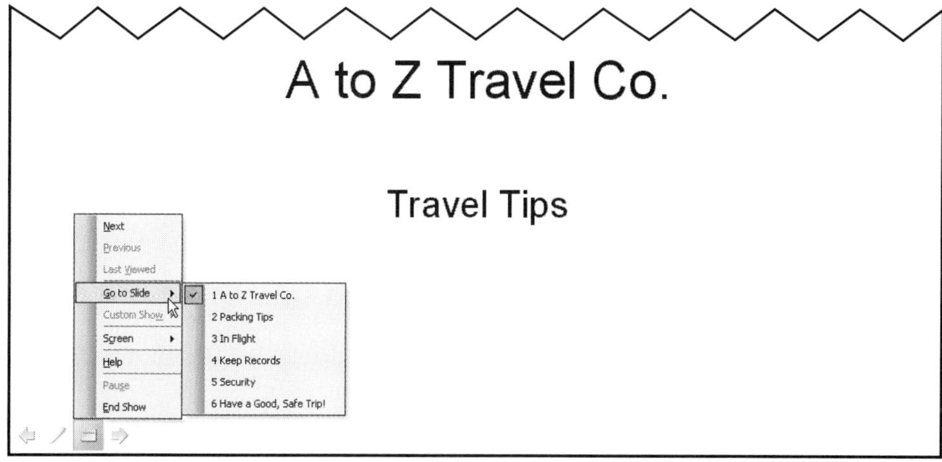

Figure 1.10 Slide show shortcut menu

- Press the Escape key to end the show.

T R Y *it* O U T *p1-6*

1. Open **1.1admissions** from the Data CD.
2. Click the **Slide Show View** button.
3. Click the **left mouse button** to advance one slide.
4. Move the mouse to the lower left of the slide and click the **shortcut menu** button on the slide. Then click **Go to Slide,** and select **1.**
5. Press the **Escape** key.
6. Click **View, Slide Show.**
7. Press the **Page Down** key to advance to each slide in the presentation.
8. At the end of the slide show, press the **Escape** key.
9. Close the presentation; do not save.

Select Page Setup Options

- Before creating a presentation, you must think about how you will deliver it. You can deliver a presentation using handouts, overhead transparencies, 35-mm slides, or as an on-screen slide show.
- The delivery method you choose will determine the output format (it may also require that you get additional viewing equipment).

Figure 1.11 Page Setup dialog box

- You can set the orientation of your slides, notes pages, handouts, and/or outline. *Portrait orientation* positions the page so that it is taller than it is wide; *landscape orientation* positions the page so that it is wider than it is tall.
- The default orientation for slides is landscape.
- To change the output format and/or orientation, select File, Page Setup. In the Page Setup dialog box, shown in Figure 1.11, select the Slides sized for list box and choose an output option or select a desired orientation for slides, notes pages, handouts, or outlines.

T R Y *it* O U T *p1-7*

1. Open **1.2vienna** from the Data CD.
2. Click **File, Page Setup.**
3. Click **Portrait** to change the slide orientation.
4. Click the **Slides sized for** list box and change the output to **35-mm Slides.** Note the width and height sizes.
5. Click **OK.**
6. Click **File, Page Setup.**
7. Click the **Slides sized for** list box and change the output to **On-screen Show.** Note the width and height sizes.
8. Click **OK.**
9. Close the file; do not save.

View a Presentation in Grayscale or Black and White

- You can preview your presentation to see what it will look like when printed in black and white, or *grayscale,* which uses tones of gray to show the effects of color. Or, you might choose to work in black and white if you find color distracting while creating a presentation.
- There are several ways to preview a slide in black and white or grayscale. The quickest way is to click the Color/Grayscale button on the Standard toolbar and choose Color/Grayscale or Pure Black and White as shown in Figure 1.12.

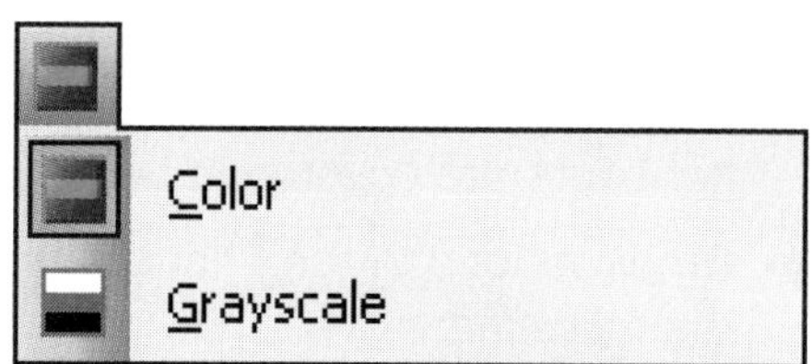

Figure 1.12 Color/Grayscale options

- To redisplay your presentation in color, click the Close Grayscale View or close Black and White View button on the Standard toolbar.

POWERPOINT

TRY *it* OUT *p1-8*

1. Open **1.2vienna** from the Data CD.
2. Click the **Color/Grayscale** button on the Standard toolbar and select **Grayscale.** Note: The Color/Grayscale button is visible when Show Buttons on Two Rows is selected.
3. Click **Close Grayscale View.**
4. Click the **Color/Grayscale** button on the Standard toolbar and select **Pure Black and White.**
5. Click the **Close Black and White View** button.
6. Close the presentation; do not save.

Print a Presentation

- To print a presentation, click File, Print. The Print dialog box appears, in which you can choose to print All slides, the Current slide, or a Selection of slides that you specify. The default selection, as shown in Figure 1.13, prints All slides.

- The Print what option lets you indicate whether you want your presentation printed as slides, notes pages, handouts (with 1, 2, 3, 4, 6, or 9 slides per page), or as an outline. (Outlines, notes pages, and handouts are covered in Lesson 4.)
- Other options in the Print dialog box include the following:
  - Properties changes elements specific to the printer, such as paper size and type, orientation, and print quality.
  - Print to file prints the presentation to a disk file so that it may be sent to a service bureau for printing in an alternate format, such as 35-mm slides.
  - Black and White prints in pure black and white without grayscale. Selecting this option will minimize the amount of toner used when printing.

Figure 1.13 Print dialog box

  - Grayscale prints color using various shades of gray.
  - Collate prints multiple copies in their proper order.
  - Scale to fit paper scales presentation slides proportionally to fit a custom or different-sized page.
  - Frame slides adds a frame to slides when printed.
- You can also print slides by clicking the Print button on the Standard toolbar. This method will bypass the Print dialog box and send your presentation as full pages of each slide directly to the printer.

- PowerPoint automatically prints information using the settings previously selected in the Print dialog box.

TRY *it* OUT *p1-9*

1. Open **1.2vienna** from the Data CD.

2. Click **File, Print.**
3. Click the **Print what** list arrow and select **Handouts.**
4. Click the **Slides per page** list arrow and select **4.**
5. Click the **Preview** button.
6. Click the **Close** button.
7. Click **File, Print.**
8. Click the **Slides per page** list arrow and select **6.**
9. Click the **Color/Grayscale** list arrow and select **Pure Black and White.**
10. Click **OK.**
11. Close the file; do not save.

GOAL

To open a presentation and change page setup and print options

SETTING THE STAGE/WRAPUP

File name: **1.2traveltips**

WHAT YOU NEED TO KNOW

- In this Rehearsal activity, you will open a presentation, change the slide orientation, and print the pages as handouts with six slides per page.

DIRECTIONS

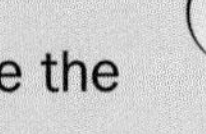

1. Open **1.2traveltips** from the Data CD.
2. Size the slides for overheads and change the orientation to portrait.
3. Switch to Slide show view and view the presentation.
4. Return to Normal view.
5. Print the slides in Pure Black and White as handouts with six slides per page.
6. Close the presentation; save the changes.

Cues for Reference

Change Views

- Click the desired view button:
  - Normal view 
  - Slide sorter view 
  - Slide show view  

or

1. Click **View.**
2. Choose a view option.

Run a Slide Show

1. Display Slide 1.
2. Click the **Slide Show View** button. 

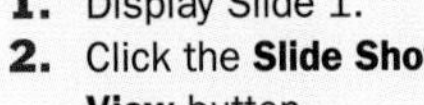

or

Click **View, Slide Show.**

Select Page Setup Options

1. Click **File.**
2. Click **Page Setup.**
3. Select the desired options.
4. Click **OK.**

View a Presentation in Grayscale or Black and White

1. Click the **Print Preview** button. 
2. Click **Options.**
3. Click **Color/Grayscale, Grayscale,** or **Pure Black and White.**
4. Click **Close** to return to the color settings.

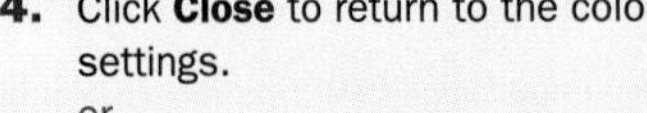

or

1. Click the **Color/Grayscale** button on the Standard toolbar. 
2. Click **Grayscale** or **Pure Black and White.**
3. Click the **Color/Grayscale** button.
4. Click the **Close Black and White View** button or **Close Grayscale View** button to return to the color settings.

Print a Presentation

- Click the **Print** button. 

or

1. Click **File.**
2. Click **Print.**
3. Select the desired options.
4. Click **OK.**

1
2
3

LESSON 2

Informative Presentations

In this lesson, you will learn to use PowerPoint features to create and enhance informative presentations.
Informative presentations either report or explain. A reporting presentation brings the audience up to date about an issue or a product. An explanatory presentation provides information on a specific topic. You will complete presentations on the following topics in this lesson:

- Marketing strategies for a new product
- Information about the care of plants
- Information about a company's services
- A new employee orientation
- Information about a travel destination

Upon completion of this lesson, you should have mastered the following skill sets:

- Create a presentation using blank slides
- Apply slide layouts
- Add slides to a presentation
- Work with placeholders
  - Add text to placeholders
  - Move, copy, delete, and size placeholders
  - Create a placeholder
  - Format a placeholder
- Create a presentation using a design template
- Change slide color scheme
- Change slide background
  - Create a custom background
- Replace fonts
- Move, copy, duplicate, and delete slides
- Work with clip art and photographs
  - Insert clip art and photographs
  - Edit clip art and photographs
- Apply slide transitions
- Apply animation schemes
- Check spelling and grammar

Terms

Software-related

Blank presentation
Slide layout
Placeholders
Handles
Rotate
Text box
Design template
Slide background
Clip art
Slide transition
Animation scheme

TRYOUT

TASK 1

GOAL

To practice using the following skill sets:

- Create a presentation using blank slides
- Apply slide layouts
- Add slides to a presentation
- Work with placeholders
  - Add text to placeholders
  - Edit placeholders
    - Move, copy, delete, size, and rotate
  - Create a placeholder
  - Format a placeholder

POWERPOINT

WHAT YOU NEED TO KNOW

Create a Presentation Using Blank Slides

- The *blank presentation* option lets you build your own unique presentation from blank slides that contain standard default formats and layouts.
- PowerPoint opens with a blank slide and the Getting Started task pane, as shown in Figure 2.1. "Presentation1" appears on the title bar as the presentation name until you provide a file name during the save process.

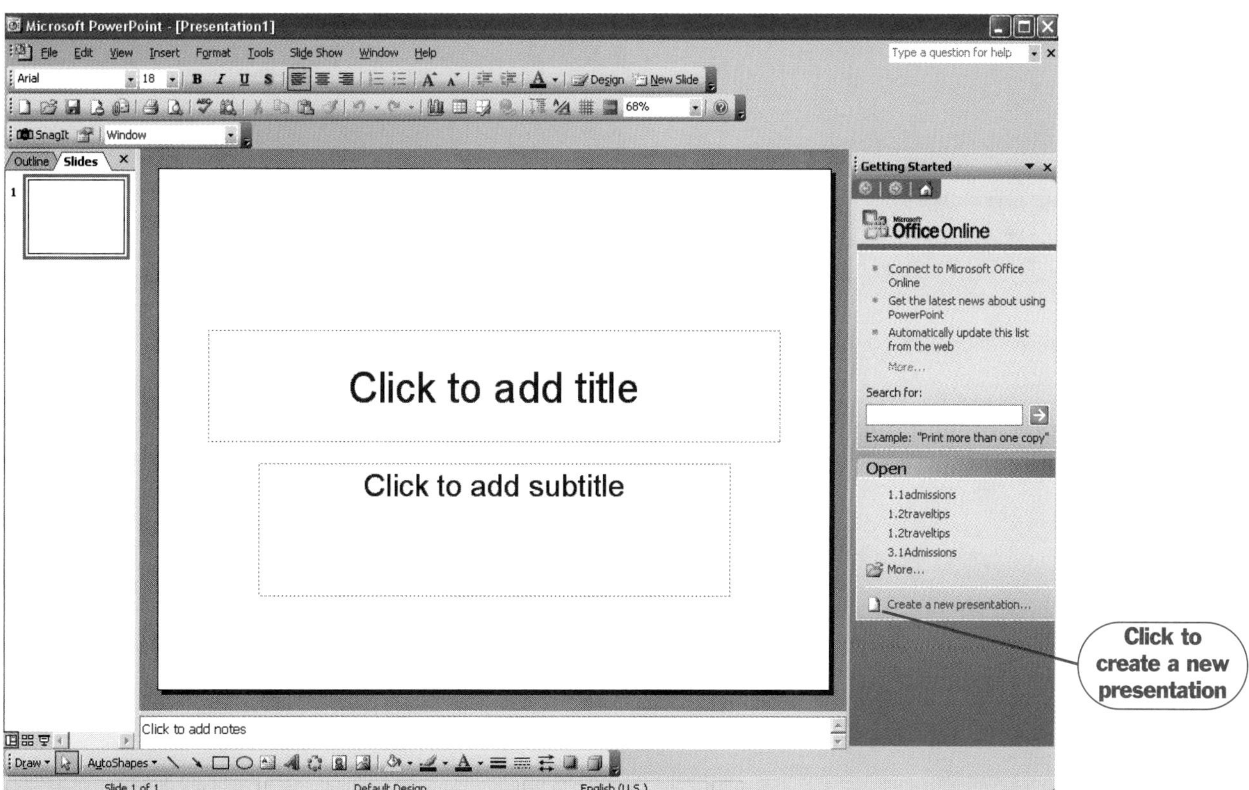

Figure 2.1 New presentation with Getting Started task pane displayed

- The first slide layout is formatted as a title slide (shown in Figure 2.1), which is generally the first slide in a presentation. There are, however, 26 other slide layouts from which to choose. (See the Slide Layouts task pane in Figure 2.3.)
- To start a new blank presentation once PowerPoint is started, use one of the following three methods:
   1. Click the Create a New Presentation button at the bottom of the Getting Started task pane. This displays the New Presentation task pane, as shown in Figure 2.2. Click the Blank presentation link, which displays a blank slide and the Slide Layout task pane. (See Figure 2.3.)

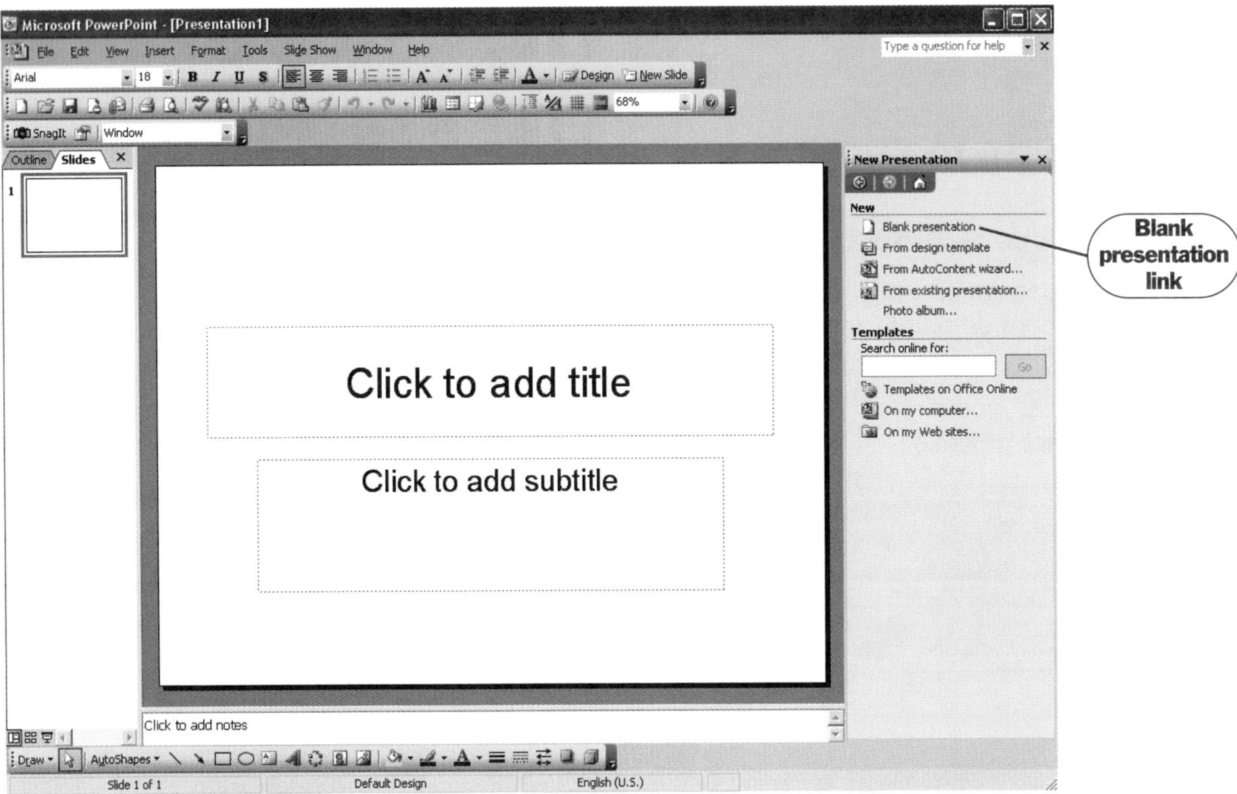

Figure 2.2 New presentation with New Presentation task pane displayed

   2. Click the New button on the Standard toolbar. This displays a new blank title slide and the Slide Layout task pane, as shown in Figure 2.3 

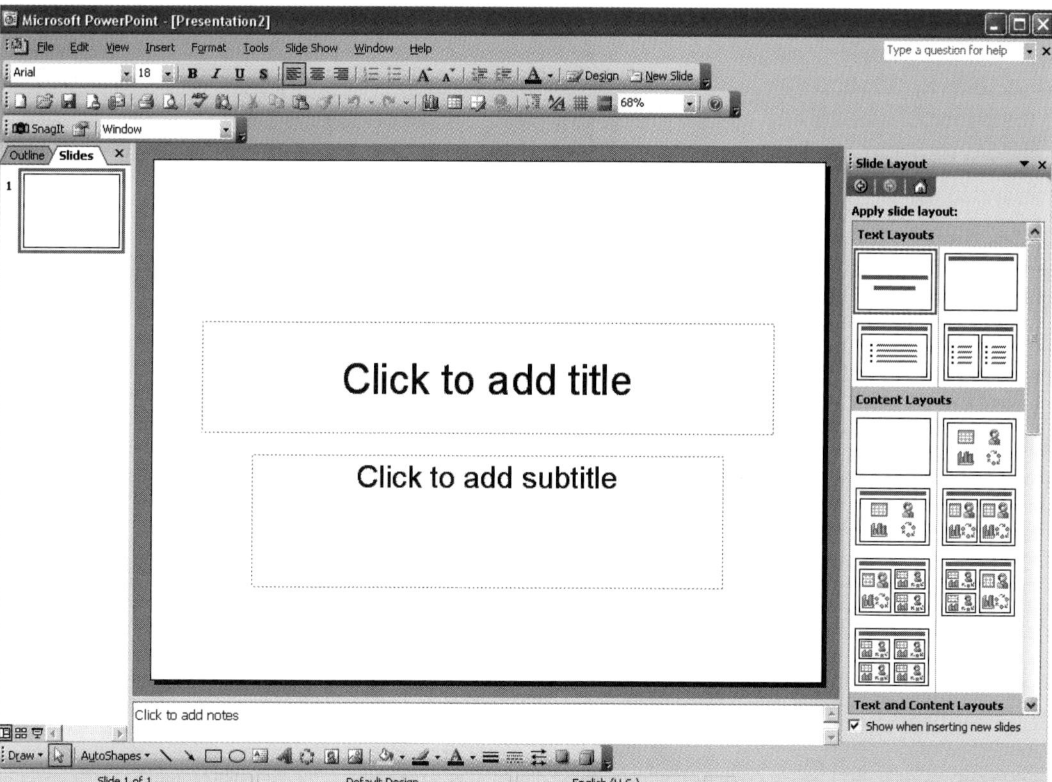

Figure 2.3 New presentation with Slide Layout task pane displayed

3. Click File, New. Like method 1, this displays the New Presentation task pane. Click the Blank Presentation link, which displays the blank slide and the Slide Layout task pane.

POWERPOINT

TRY*it* OUT *p2-1*

1. Click **Start, All Programs, Microsoft Office, Microsoft Office PowerPoint 2003** to start the program. A blank title slide and the Getting Started task pane appears, with "Presentation1" indicated on the title bar.
2. Click the **Create a new presentation** link on the Getting Started task pane.
3. Click the **Blank presentation** link on the New Presentation task pane (Presentation2 should be displayed on the title bar).
4. Click the **Close** button on the presentation window.

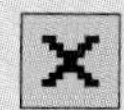

5. Click **File**, **New** on the menu. Click the **Blank presentation** link on the New Presentation task pane. Notice that another blank presentation has opened with "Presentation3" indicated on the title bar. Notice, too, that the Slide Layout task pane has replaced the New Presentation task pane.
6. Do not close the file.

Apply Slide Layouts

- The Slide Layout task pane, shown in Figure 2.4, displays 27 available slide layouts shown as thumbnail samples.
- A *slide layout* specifies how text or objects are positioned on the slide. PowerPoint classifies layouts as Text, Content, Text and Content, or Other. A pop-up description of the slide's layout appears when you place the mouse pointer over the thumbnail sample (see Figure 2.4).
- You can change the layout of the current slide by clicking the thumbnail sample layout on the Slide Layout task pane.
- To display the Slide Layout task pane, you can use one of the following methods:
  - Click the Other Task Panes list arrow on the task pane title bar and select Slide Layout, as shown in Figure 2.5.
  - Click Format, Slide Layout.
  - Right-click the slide outside a placeholder to display the shortcut menu, then select Slide Layout.

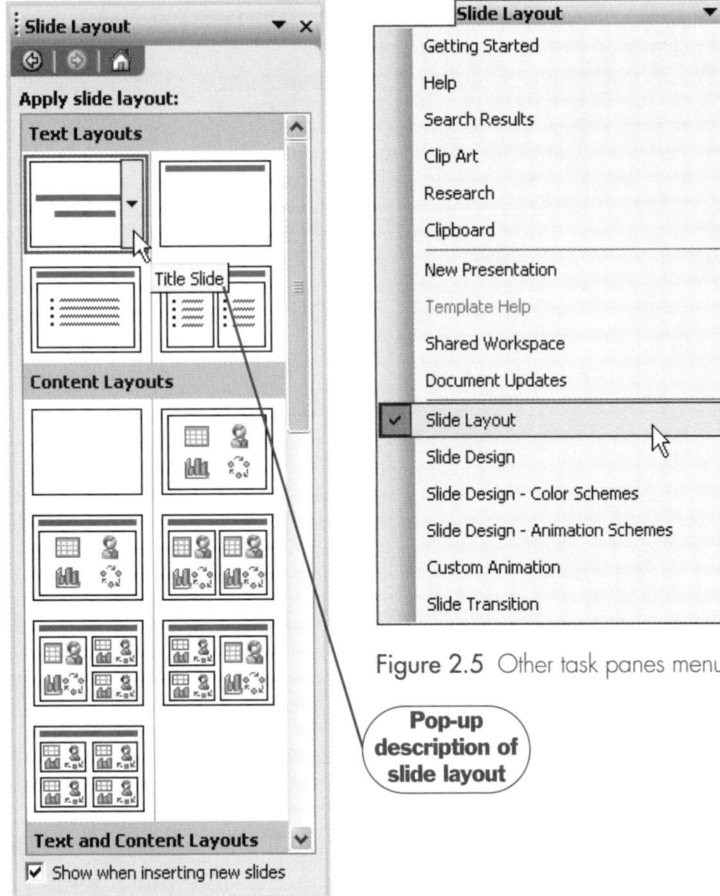

Figure 2.4 Slide Layout task pane

Figure 2.5 Other task panes menu

TRY *it* OUT *p2-2*

Note: A blank title slide and the Slide Layout task pane should be displayed. If the Slide Layout task pane is not displayed, right-click outside a placeholder to display the shortcut menu and select Slide Layout.

1. Click each layout below Text Layouts. Note that the title slide is replaced with the layout you select.
2. Click the **Title Slide** layout.
3. Do not close the presentation.

Add Slides to a Presentation

- You can easily add slides to a presentation using one of the following methods:
  - Click the New Slide button on the Formatting toolbar. 
  - Press the Ctrl + M keys.
  - Click Insert, New Slide.
  - Click the list arrow on the slide layout thumbnail and choose Insert New Slide as shown in Figure 2.6.
- PowerPoint places the new slide immediately after the slide that is displayed or selected at the time you create the new slide.
- The Title and Text slide, as shown in Figure 2.7, is the default layout for any added slide in a presentation. You can, however, change the layout of any slide in a presentation as explained previously. The number of slides is shown on the status bar (see Figure 2.7).
- You can apply the same slide layout to multiple slides. To do so, hold down the Ctrl key as you select slides displayed on the Slides tab. Once you select multiple slides, click the list arrow on the slide thumbnail you want in the Slide Layout task pane and choose Apply to Selected Slides (see Figure 2.6).

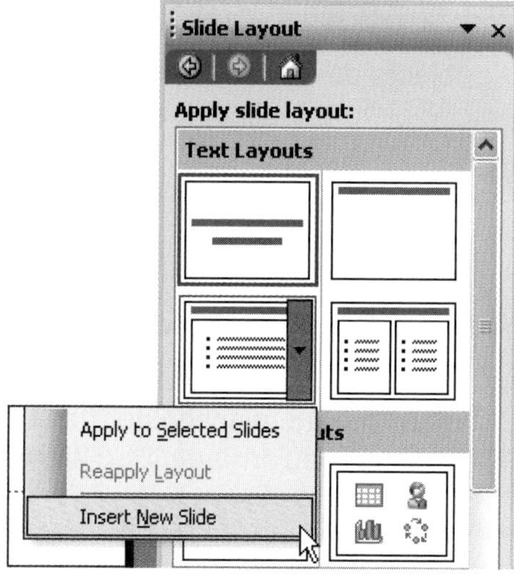

Figure 2.6 Insert new slide from slide layout thumbnail

Slide Title

- First bullet point
- Second bullet point
- Third bullet point

Figure 2.7 Title and Text slide layout

POWERPOINT

TRY *it* OUT *p2-3*

1. Click the **New Slide** button twice to add two new slides (Slides 2 and 3). Note that these are Title and Text layouts.
2. Click the **Title and 2-Column Text** layout option in the Slide Layout task pane to change the slide layout.
3. Click the list arrow on the Content slide layout thumbnail and click **Insert New Slide**.
4. Hold down the Ctrl key as you select all the slides in the pane.
5. Click the Title slide layout list arrow and choose **Apply to Selected Slides**. Scroll through the slides. Note that all the slides now have the Title slide layout.
6. Click **File**, **Close;** do not save.

Work with Placeholders

- PowerPoint slides contain *placeholders* (empty boxes), which identify the placement of text or objects on a slide, shown in Figure 2.8. Each placeholder contains instructions to help you complete the slide. Placeholders behave like text boxes (which you learned to use in Word).
- All title placeholders contain the formatting for title text, whereas all body text placeholders include formatting for subtitles or bulleted lists. You can add text, as well as manipulate and format placeholders, to create a customized look for your slides.

Add Text to Placeholders

- To enter text into a placeholder, click inside the placeholder. When *handles* appear to let you know that the placeholder has been activated, enter the new text. You can use the alignment tools on the Formatting toolbar to position text left, right, centered, or justified.

Figure 2.8 Selected text placeholder

- If you start typing without selecting a placeholder, PowerPoint automatically places the text in the first placeholder.
- Pressing the Enter key in a bulleted list automatically generates another bullet on a new line. To create bulleted sublevels, press the Tab key or click the Increase Indent button on the Formatting toolbar. Different bullet shapes identify each sublevel, as shown in Figure 2.9. To return to the previous level, press the Shift + Tab keys or click the Decrease Indent button on the Formatting toolbar.
- As you add text to a placeholder, PowerPoint adjusts the size of the text to fit within the space of the placeholder. The first time PowerPoint automatically resizes text, the AutoFit Options button appears on the side of the placeholder. Clicking this button provides you with options to turn the AutoFit feature on or off, as shown in Figure 2.10. If you turn the AutoFit feature off, you will have to resize the placeholder manually to fit the text within it.

- Level 1
  - Sublevel 2
    - Sublevel 3
      - Sublevel 4
        - » Sublevel 5

Figure 2.9 Bullet levels

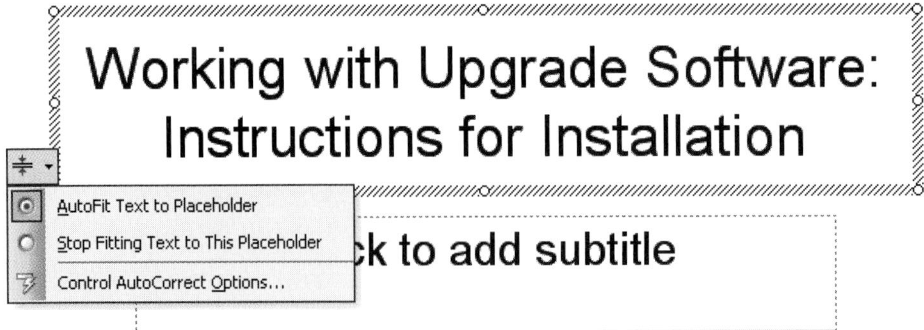

Figure 2.10 AutoFit options menu

TRY *it* OUT *p2-4*

1. Click the **New** button. A title slide should be displayed.
2. Click the **title placeholder** and enter: `Sales Overview: Developing Strategies for Successful Product Marketing.` Notice that PowerPoint resizes the text to fit the placeholder and the AutoFit options button displays.
3. Click the **subtitle placeholder** and enter your first and last name.
4. Click the **New Slide** button (Slide 2). Note that it is a Title and Text slide. 
5. Click the **title placeholder** and enter: `Agenda.`
6. Click the **text placeholder** and enter the following bullet points. Press the **Enter** key after each bullet point:
   - `Market by Market`
   - `New Products`
   - `Launch Dates`
   - `Next Steps`
   - `Conclusion`
7. Click the **New Slide** button to add a new slide (Slide 3). Note that it is a Title and Text slide.
8. Click the **Title and 2-Column Text** layout option in the Slide Layout task pane to change the slide layout.
9. Click the **title placeholder** and enter: `Market by Market.`
10. Click in the **column 1 text placeholder** and enter the following bullet points. Press **Enter** after each bullet point:
    - `New York`
    - `Los Angeles`
    - `Chicago`
    - `Philadelphia`
11. Click in the **column 2 text placeholder** and enter the following bullet points. Press the **Enter** key after each bullet point:
    - `San Francisco`
    - `Dallas`
    - `Atlanta`
    - `Houston`
12. Click the list arrow on the Content slide layout thumbnail and click **Insert New Slide** (Slide 4).
13. Save the file; name it **p2-4practice.yi** (yi = your initials). Close the file.

Edit Placeholders

- You can easily move, copy, delete, size, rotate, and format placeholders to create a customized look for your slides. To edit a placeholder, you must first click to select it. A selected placeholder displays handles, which means that the placeholder or object is in Edit mode (see Figure 2.8).

Move and Copy

- To move a placeholder and its contents, select it and place the mouse pointer on the border (not on a handle) until the pointer changes to a four-headed arrow. Click and hold down the mouse button while you drag the placeholder to the location you want.
- As you drag an object across a slide, a dotted box shows its new location, as shown in Figure 2.11.

Figure 2.11 Moving a placeholder

- To copy a placeholder, select it and hold down Ctrl while you drag the placeholder to the new location.

Delete

- To delete a text placeholder, select it to display its handles, click on a border (not on a handle), and press the Delete key twice (once if the placeholder is empty). (The first time you press the Delete key, the contents of the placeholder are deleted. The second time deletes the placeholder itself.)

Size

- To change the vertical size (height), drag a top- or bottom-middle handle, as shown in Figure 2.12. To change the horizontal size (width), drag a left- or right-middle handle. To change the size of the placeholder proportionally, drag a corner handle. The text within the placeholder will adjust to its new borders. You can also size the placeholder by a specific amount in the Format AutoShape dialog box. Right-click the placeholder, and click Format Placeholder. Click the Size tab and enter a height and width amount in the appropriate box, as shown in Figure 2.13.

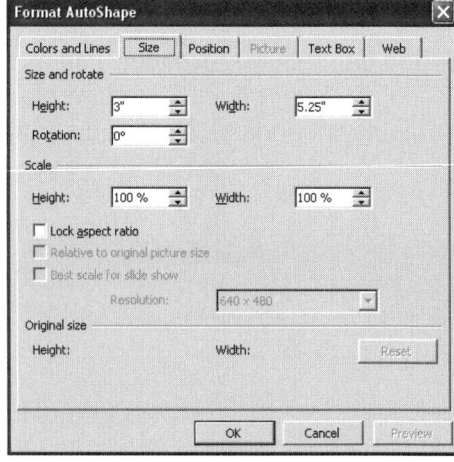

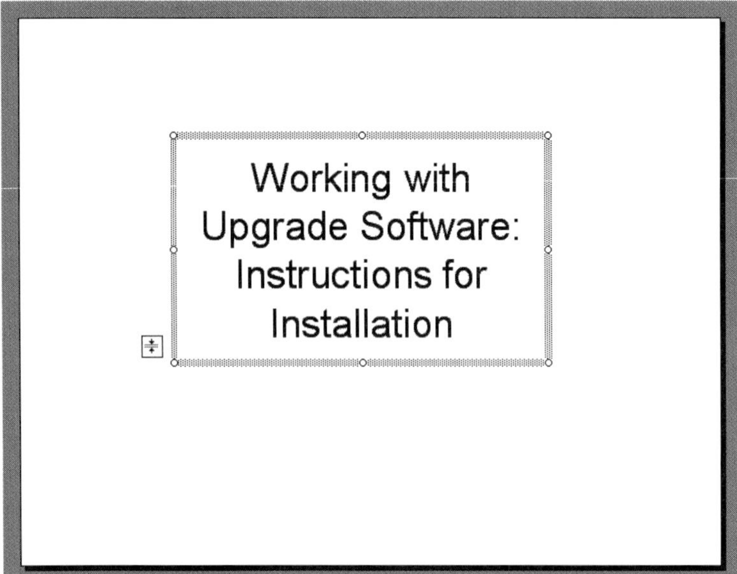

Figure 2.12 Sized placeholder

Figure 2.13 Format AutoShape dialog box

Rotate

▶ You can *rotate* a placeholder in 90-degree increments, or you can use the free rotate tool to rotate the box to any angle. To rotate a placeholder, select it, click the Draw button on the drawing toolbar, select Rotate or Flip, then click the Rotate option you want. If you choose the Free Rotate option, the placeholder will display green rotate handles. Click on a handle and rotate the box to any angle you want, as shown in Figure 2.14.

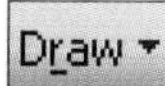

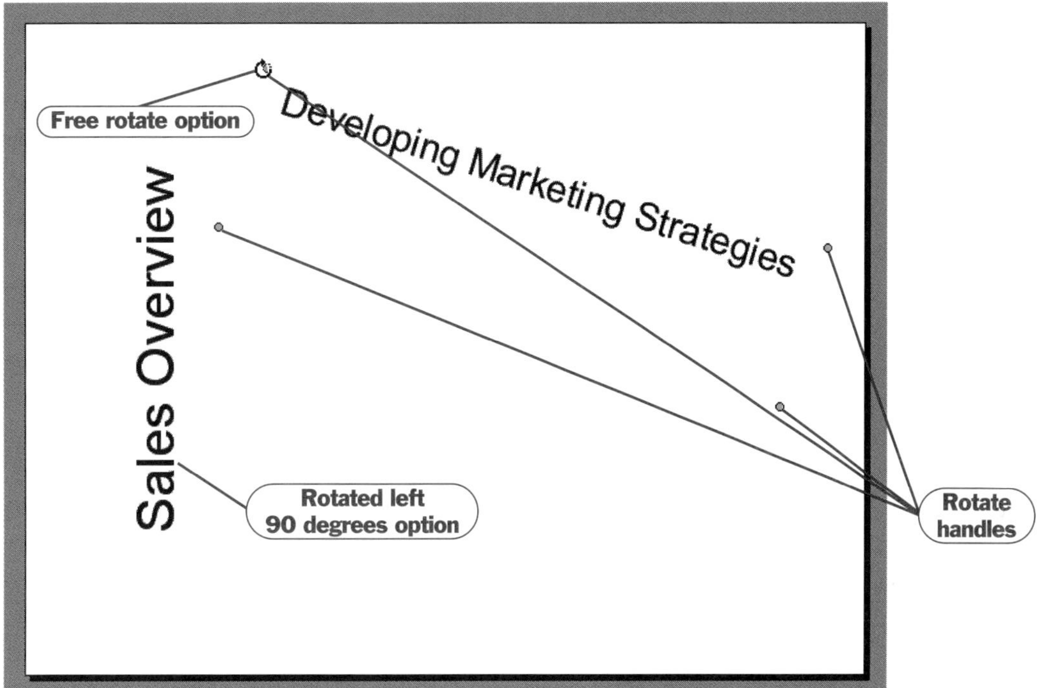

Figure 2.14 Rotate a placeholder

TRY *it* OUT *p2-5*

1. Click the **New** button to start a new presentation.
2. Click the **title placeholder** and enter: `Four Corners Realty.`
3. Click the **subtitle placeholder** and enter:
   `450 Flora Boulevard`
   `Hollywood, FL`
   `30025`
4. To edit the placeholders as shown at right, do the following:
   a. Right-click the subtitle placeholder and select **Format Placeholder.**
   b. Click the **Size** tab and enter **2"** in the Height box and **2"** in the Width box, then click **OK.** Move the placeholder to the top-right corner as shown.
   c. Select the title placeholder. Click **Draw, Rotate or Flip, Rotate Left 90°.** Size the placeholder to fit the height of the slide, then move it to the left of the slide as shown.
5. Do not close the file.

Create a Placeholder

- To add text to a slide in a location other than in a given placeholder, you can create a text box. A *text box* serves as a text placeholder, allowing you to insert text anywhere on a slide.
- You can create text boxes only in Normal view.
- To draw a text box, click the Text Box button on the Drawing toolbar. Click and drag the mouse diagonally on the slide to create the required box size. After releasing the mouse, enter the new text.

- The box displays with sizing handles and a green rotate handle.
- If the text box is not located were you want or is not at the size or angle you want, you can move, resize, or rotate it.

TRY *it* OUT *p2-6*

1. Click the **Text Box** button on the Drawing toolbar.

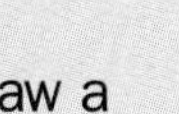

2. Click and drag the mouse to draw a text box.
3. Enter: `Finest Properties for Over 50 Years!`
4. Rotate and resize the box and place it as shown.
5. Do not close the file.

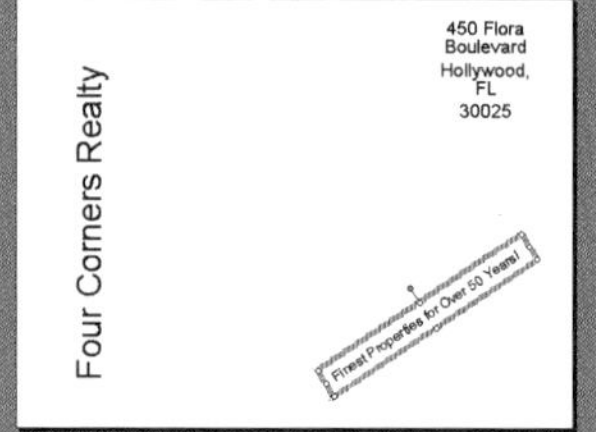

Format a Placeholder

- Like text boxes, you can add colorful border lines around the placeholder and/or fill the box with a color or pattern and/or add a 3-D or shadow effect (with or without the border line). Figure 2.15 shows a slide with various placeholder formats.

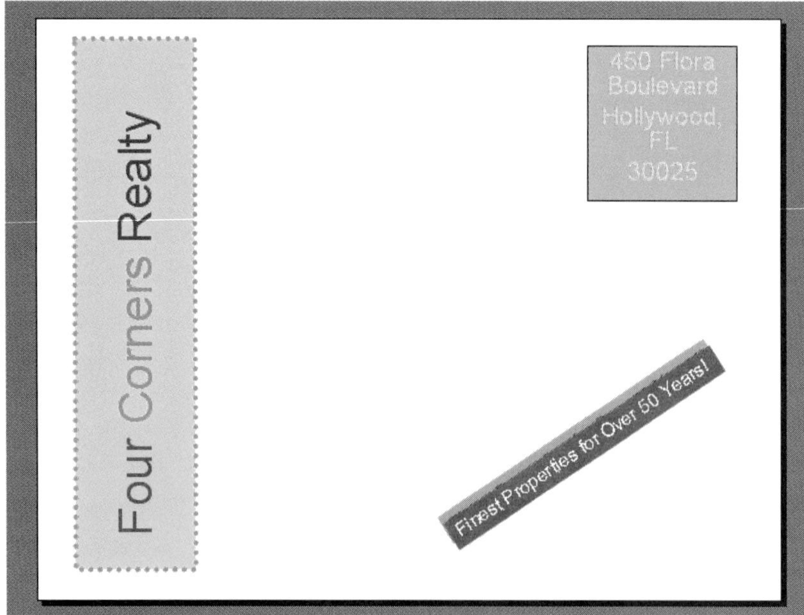

Figure 2.15 Placeholder format options

▶ To format a placeholder, right-click the placeholder and select Format placeholder from the shortcut menu. In the Format AutoShape dialog box, click the Colors and Lines tab shown in Figure 2.16, and make the selections you want. You can also use the Fill Color, Line Color, Font Color, Line Style, and Dash Style buttons on the Drawing toolbar as you did in Word.

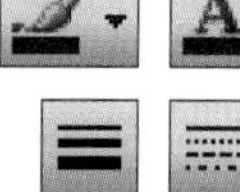

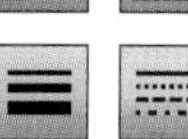

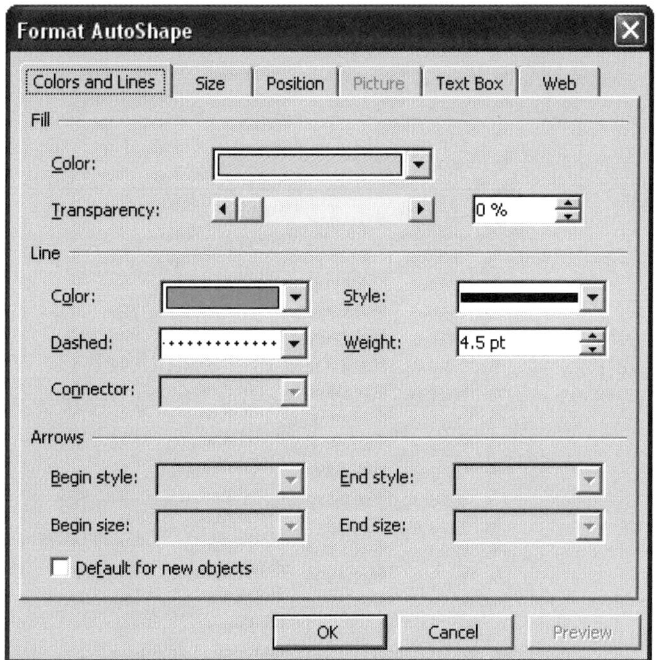

Figure 2.16 Colors and Lines tab in Format AutoShape dialog box

POWERPOINT

TRY*it*OUT *p2-7*

Refer to Figure 2.15 for this TryitOut.

1. Click in the text box that contains the words Four Corners Realty. Format it as follows:
   a. Click the **Fill Color** button list arrow on the Drawing toolbar, click **More Fill Colors**, and choose **yellow**.
   b. Click the **Dash Style** button on the Drawing toolbar and click the **Square Dot** option.
   c. Click the **Line Color** list arrow and choose a color from the Standard or Custom tab in the Colors dialog box, if necessary.
   d. Click the **Line Style** button and choose **4 ½ point**.
   e. For each word in the box, click the **Font Color** button and choose a font color as shown in Figure 2.15.
2. Click in the box that contains the address. Format it as follows:
   a. Click the **Line Color** list arrow and click **Black.**
   b. Click the **Fill Color** button, click **More Fill Colors**, and choose **green**.
   c. Select the text, click the **Font Color** button and choose **yellow**.
3. Click in the box that contains the text *Finest Properties for Over 50 Years!*
   a. Click the **Fill Color** button and choose **red**.
   b. Select the text, click the **Font Color** button and choose **white**.
   c. Click the **Shadow Style** button, and choose the first shadow style option.
4. Close the file; do not save.

GOAL
To create a presentation that informs employees of marketing strategies for launching a new product

SETTING THE STAGE/WRAPUP
File name: **2.1isstrategy**

WHAT YOU NEED TO KNOW

- When you develop a presentation, it is important to know your audience, why they are there, and to keep the presentation focused on your objective.
- Marketing strategies are well-thought-out plans to sell or promote a product, company, or service.
- In this Rehearsal activity, you will create a presentation that explains to the sales staff the marketing strategies that they will use to launch a new fitness center.

DIRECTIONS

1. Open a new blank presentation.
2. Accept the default title slide layout for the first slide.
3. Enter the title and subtitle as illustrated on the first slide shown on the facing page.
   - Rotate the title placeholder and format it as shown.
   - Size the subtitle placeholder to 1" high by 6" wide, move it to the bottom of the slide, and format it as shown.
4. Add new slides as indicated in the illustration and enter the text as shown.
5. Save the file as **2.1isstrategy.**
6. Run the presentation.
7. Close the presentation.

Marketing Strategies

In-Shape Fitness Center

1

Overview

- Marketing Goals
- Current Promotions/Publicity
- Other Marketing Ideas
- Next Steps

2

Marketing Goals

- Image
  - Hip
  - Cutting-edge classes and equipment
  - Not just a place to work out
- Acquire new members
  - Those without existing gym memberships
  - Those who are members at other gyms
- Garner as much publicity as possible
- Attain strong promotional partners

3

Current Promotions/Publicity

- Running ads in several local newspapers and magazines
- Features in
  - *US Health* magazine
  - *Get Fit* magazine
- Promotion with JUMP workout wear!
- Limited-time 2-for-1 membership incentive
- WNEW feature news segment on *What's New in New York!*

4

Other Marketing Ideas

- Food product cross-promotion
  - Protein bars
  - Bottled water
  - Other health foods
- More health news/magazine features
- New membership incentives
  - Free dumbbells with membership
  - Seasonal promotions
- Local online advertising

5

Next Steps

- Prep sales staff for opening day
- Meet with potential promotional partners
- Create premium items for giveaways
- Preliminary plans for launch party
- HAVE A GREAT DAY!

6

Cues for Reference

Create a Blank Presentation

1. Click **File.**
2. Click **New.**
3. Click the **Blank presentation** link on the task pane.

or

- Click the **New** button.

Office XP

- Click the **New Slide** button.

or

- Click the **Blank Presentation** link on the task pane.

Add Slides to a Presentation

- Click the **New Slide** button.

or

- Press **Ctrl + M.**

or

1. Click **Insert.**
2. Click **New Slide.**

Apply Slide Layout

1. Click **Format.**
2. Click **Slide Layout.**
3. Click the thumbnail of the appropriate layout.

or

1. Click the **Other Task Panes** list arrow.
2. Click **Slide Layout.**
3. Click the thumbnail of the appropriate layout.

or

1. Right-click on the slide outside any placeholders.
2. Click **Slide Layout.**
3. Click the thumbnail of the appropriate layout.

Create a Placeholder

1. Click the **Text Box** button on the Drawing toolbar.
2. Click on the slide and drag diagonally down to draw the box.
3. Enter the text.

Edit Placeholders

Click the placeholder or object to display its handles.

Move/Copy

1. Position the mouse pointer on a border (not a handle).
2. Click and drag the placeholder or object to the new location.

or

- Press **Ctrl** and click and drag the placeholder or object to the new location to copy it.

Delete

1. Click on a border (not a handle).
2. Press **Delete** (to delete the placeholder content).
3. Press **Delete** again (to delete the placeholder).

Rotate

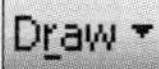

1. Click the **Draw** button
2. Select **Rotate** or **Flip.**
3. Click a rotate option.
4. If you select the Free Rotate option, drag the rotate handle to the appropriate position.

GOAL

To practice using the following skill sets:

- Create a presentation using a design template
- Change slide color scheme
  - Change slide background
  - Create a custom background
  - Replace fonts
- Move, copy, duplicate, and delete slides

WHAT YOU NEED TO KNOW

Create a Presentation Using a Design Template

- You can create slides that have been predesigned with colorful backgrounds, fonts, themes, and layouts. The *design template* option lets you choose from the numerous predesigned formats that are available with PowerPoint.
- To begin a new presentation using a design template, display the New Presentation task pane, as shown in Figure 2.17, and click the From design template link.
- The Slide Design task pane, as shown in Figure 2.18, displays the available design templates. A description of the design appears when you place the mouse pointer over the thumbnail sample. Click the slide design you want from those available.
- To display the Slide Design task pane, you can use one of the following methods:
  - Click the Slide Design button on the Formatting toolbar.
  - Click Format, Slide Design.
  - Right-click on the slide outside of any placeholders to display the shortcut menu and select Slide Design.
- To apply a design template to the current presentation, click the thumbnail in the Slide Design task pane of the design you want.

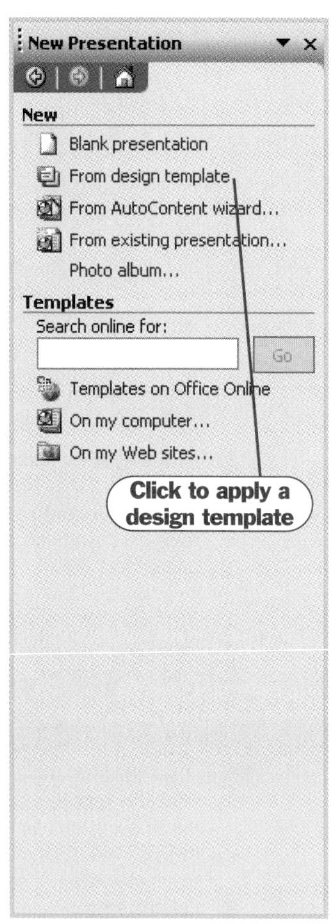

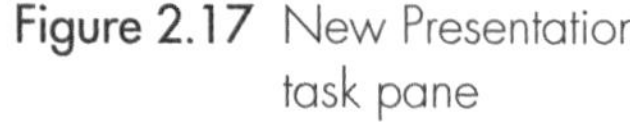

Figure 2.17 New Presentation task pane

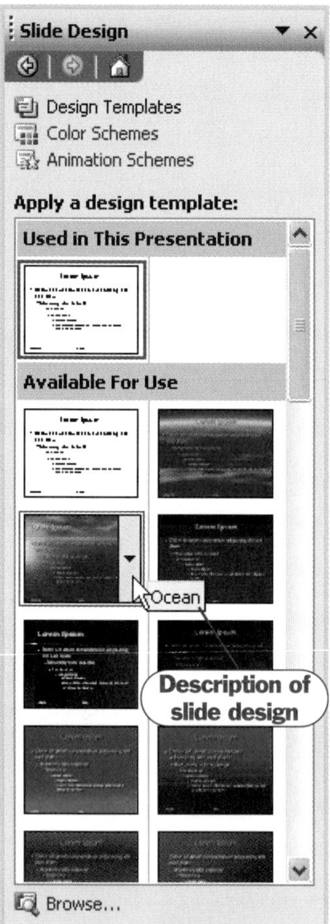

Figure 2.18 Slide Design task pane

TRY *it* OUT *p2-8*

1. Click the **New** button to create a new presentation.

2. Click the **Slide Design** button on the Formatting toolbar.
3. Click a design template in the Slide Design task pane.
4. Enter your first and last name in the title placeholder.
5. Enter today's date in the subtitle placeholder.
6. Click another design in the Slide Design task pane. Notice the new color scheme, font style, and formatting.
7. Apply two other designs and notice the effects of the formatting.
8. Close the file; do not save.

Change a Slide Color Scheme

- Each template design has a predefined color scheme that includes the slide background, title text, fills, lines, shadows, accents, and hyperlinks. PowerPoint lets you change the entire color scheme of your presentation or change individual parts (for example, line colors and slide background only). You may change the color scheme of one or all slides in a presentation.
- To change a slide's color scheme, click the Edit Color Schemes link on the Slide Design task pane, as shown in Figure 2.19. Design and Blank templates come with various alternative color schemes that automatically appear when you select the Color Schemes link. Click one of the slide thumbnails to apply a new color scheme to your presentation.
- If the preexisting color scheme does not meet your needs, you can modify it to your specifications. To do so, click the Edit Color Scheme link on the Slide Design task pane. In the Edit Color Scheme dialog box, as shown in Figure 2.20, click the Custom tab to make custom changes to individual slide parts. Select the item to change from the Scheme colors list, click the Change Color button to select from a palette of additional colors, and click OK. A preview window displays the results of your choices. Click Apply to apply the new color scheme to all slides. Once you make custom changes, click the Add As Standard Scheme button to save the new color scheme as a standard scheme that you can easily use again.

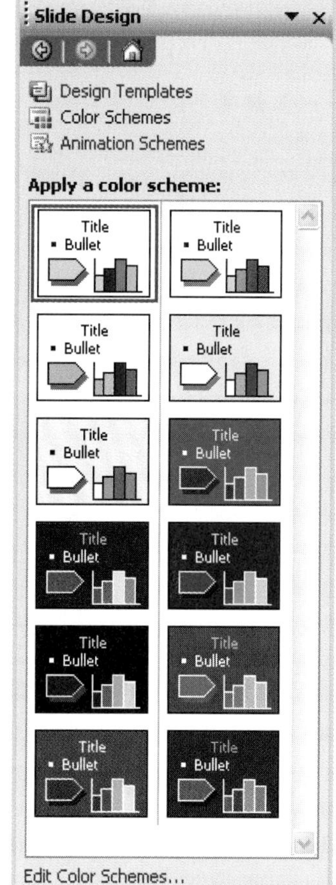

Figure 2.19 Slide Design task pane with Color Schemes displayed

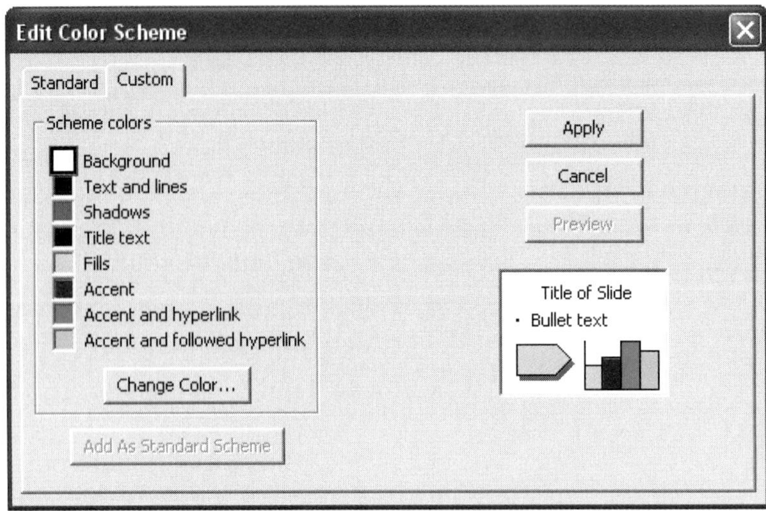

Figure 2.20 Edit Color Scheme dialog box

TRY*it*OUT *p2-9*

1. Open a new blank presentation.
2. Click the **Slide Design** button.
3. Click a slide thumbnail to apply any design template.
4. Click the **Color Schemes** link in the Slide Design task pane.
5. Click three different slide thumbnails to view different color schemes.
6. Click the **Edit Color Schemes** link at the bottom of the Slide Design task pane.
7. Click the **Title text** box.
8. Click **Change Color.**
9. Click the **Standard** tab.
10. Click any color.
11. Click **OK.**
12. Click **Apply.**
13. Close the file; do not save.

Change a Slide Background

- The *slide background* is the bottom portion of the slide's structure. Each template design has a predefined background color. You can change any of these elements. To do so, click Format, Background. In the Background dialog box that opens, shown in Figure 2.21, click the Background fill list arrow to select a new background color, and choose to apply the new background color to one or all slides.

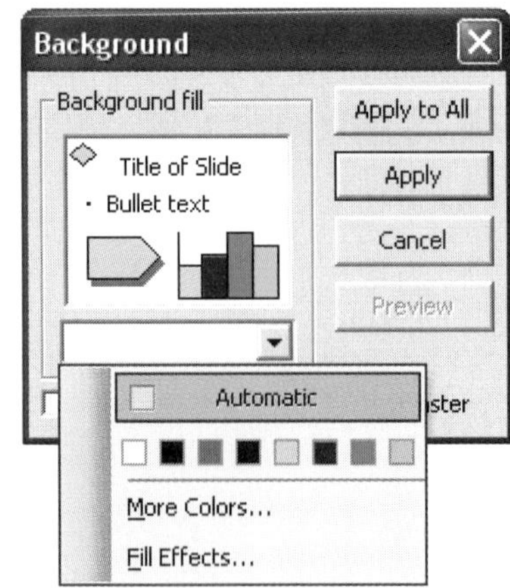

Figure 2.21 Background dialog box

Create Custom Backgrounds

- To apply a color gradient (blending of colors), texture, pattern, or picture as the slide background, click the Background fill list arrow on the Background dialog box and choose Fill Effects. In the Fill Effects dialog box that appears, as shown in Figure 2.22, click the appropriate tab and choose the options you want. A sample window displays the result of your selections.

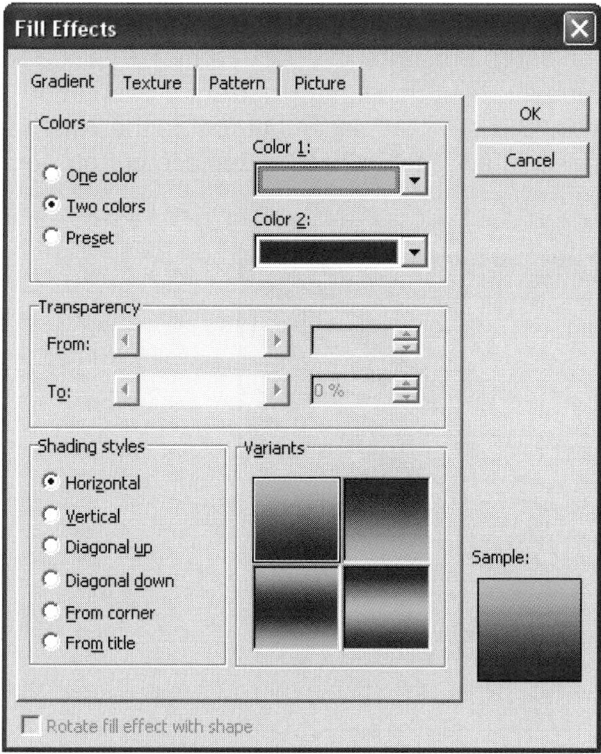

Figure 2.22 Fill Effects dialog box

▶ You can also customize a slide's background to include a scanned image, a downloaded picture, or any other graphic image that comes with Office. (Using images for slide backgrounds will be covered in Task 3.)

POWERPOINT

TRY *it* OUT *p2-10*

1. Open **p2.10latte** from the Data CD.
2. Click **Format, Background.**
3. Click the **Background fill** list arrow and choose **any color shown in the current color scheme.**
4. Click **Apply to All.**
5. Display the title slide, if necessary.
6. Click **Format, Background.**
7. Click the **Background Fill** list arrow and click **More Colors.**
8. Click the **Custom** tab.
9. Click the **bright yellow** hue area in the **Colors** palette.
10. Drag the arrow to display a **mustard-yellow** color, and click **OK.**
11. Click **Apply.**
12. Cycle through the slides to see the effect of the slide backgrounds.
13. Close the presentation; do not save.

Replace Fonts

- Each presentation design applies specific fonts, font styles, and font sizes for various components on the slide (slide titles, bulleted lists, etc.). You may like the design of the template, but not the font.
- To change the font throughout the entire presentation, click Format, Replace Fonts. In the Replace Font dialog box that opens, the font used in the current presentation is indicated in the Replace box, as shown in Figure 2.23. Enter a replacement font in the With box or click the list arrow and choose a font from those listed. Then, click the Replace button. Replacing a font does not affect the font style or size.

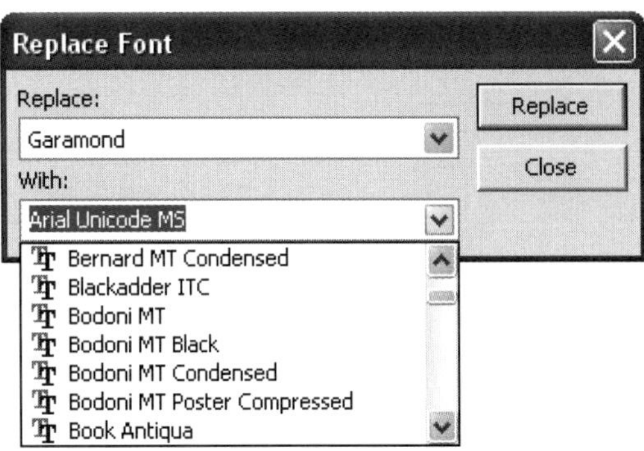

Figure 2.23 Replace Font dialog box

TRY *it* OUT *p2-11*

1. Open **p2.11entreport** from the Data CD.
2. Cycle through the slides and notice the slide fonts.
3. Click **Format**, **Replace Fonts.**
4. Click the **Replace** list arrow and select **Garamond**, if not already selected.
5. Click the **With** list arrow and click **Comic Sans MS**.
6. Click **Replace** and click **Close**.
7. Cycle through the presentation and notice the change.
8. Do not close the presentation.

Move, Copy, Duplicate, and Delete Slides

- You can move, copy, or delete slides in slide sorter view, on the Outline tab, or on the Slides tab. It is easiest and most efficient, however, to perform these tasks in Slide sorter view, because PowerPoint displays all slides as thumbnails and you can easily see the flow of the presentation as you move, copy, or delete slides.
- In Slide sorter view, click on the slide you want to move, copy, or delete. A dark border outlines selected slides, as shown in Figure 2.24. To select multiple slides to move, copy, or delete as a group, hold down the Ctrl key and click each slide you want to include.
- To move or copy a slide, select and drag it to a new location. When you move the slide, the mouse pointer arrow adds a slide icon (or a slide icon with a plus sign [+] when you copy) and a vertical bar identifies the new position of the slide. Figure 2.24 illustrates a slide that is being copied to a new location. When the bar appears in the position where you want to place the slide, release the mouse button.

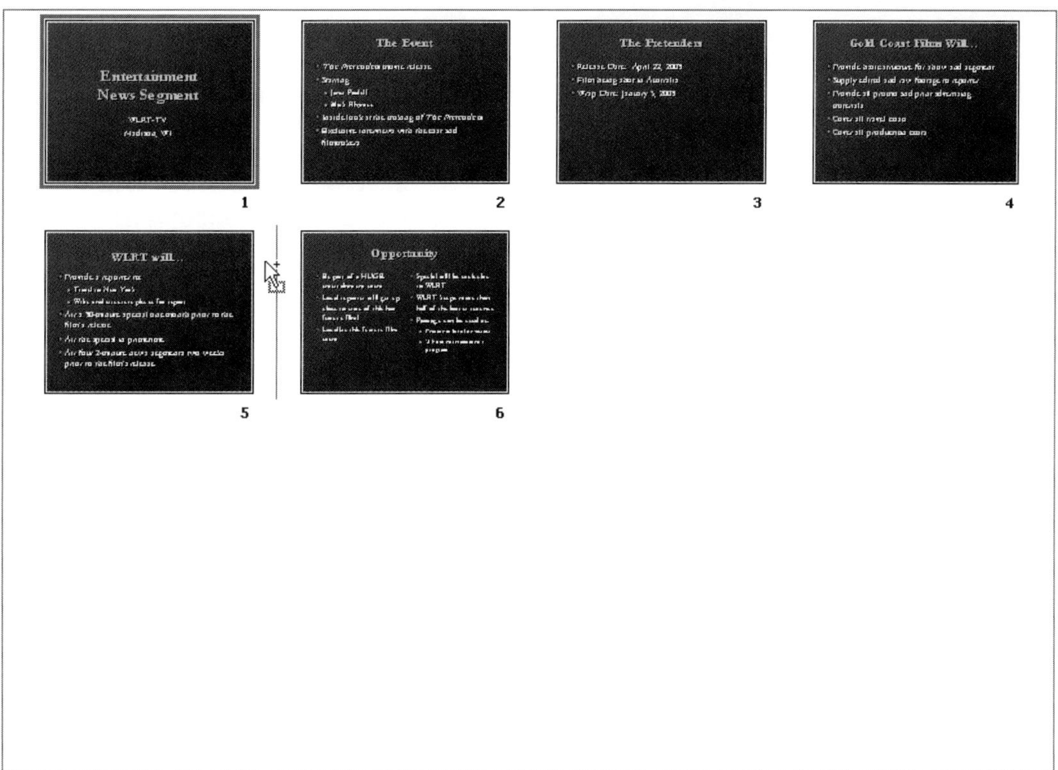

Figure 2.24 Copy a slide in Slide sorter view

- You can also use the Duplicate Slide command to copy a slide. Click Insert, Duplicate Slide. PowerPoint inserts the duplicate slide immediately after the original slide.
- To delete a slide, select the slide and press the Delete key.
- If you move, copy, or delete a slide and then change your mind, use the Undo command to reverse the action.

TRY *it* OUT *p2-12*

Note: The presentation from TryitOut 2-11 should be displayed.

1. Click the **Slide Sorter View** button.
2. Click **Slide 5** ("WLRT will...") and press the **Delete** key.
3. Click **Slide 4** ("Gold Coast Films Will...") and drag it to become Slide 2. Notice that PowerPoint has moved the slide.
4. Click **Slide 2** ("Gold Coast Films Will..."), hold down **Ctrl**, and drag Slide 2 so it becomes the last slide in the presentation. Notice that PowerPoint has copied the slide.
5. Double-click **Slide 6** to display it in Normal view. Click the **title placeholder** and enter `To Summarize,` before the word "Gold."
6. On the Slides tab, click **Slide 2** and press the **Delete** key.
7. On the Slides tab, move Slide 4 (Opportunity) to become Slide 3.
8. Save the file as **2.12entreport.yi** (yi = your initials); close the file.

POWERPOINT

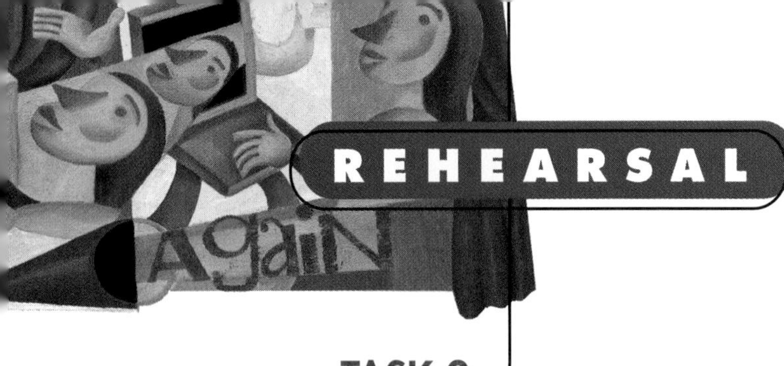

GOAL
To create a five-slide informative presentation that contains a title slide, four text slides, and an applied design

SETTING THE STAGE/WRAPUP
File name: **2.2houseplant**

WHAT YOU NEED TO KNOW

- In this Rehearsal activity, you will create a presentation that informs Green Brothers Gardening clients how to care for indoor plants.

DIRECTIONS

1. Open a new presentation and apply a template design that relates to the topic.
2. Accept the default title slide layout for the first slide.
3. Enter the title and subtitle as illustrated on the facing page.
4. Add new slides as indicated in the illustration and enter the text as shown.
5. Change the title slide background color. Note: You may choose any background color that complements the slide color scheme. The illustration is a guide.
6. Replace the fonts in the presentation with **Comic Sans MS**.
7. Move Slide 4 ("Growing Basics") to become Slide 2.
8. View the slides in Pure Black and White.
9. Print Slide 5 ("Featured Plant—The Orchid") in Pure Black and White.
10. Run the presentation.
11. Save the presentation; name it **2.2houseplant.**
12. Close the presentation.

Cues for Reference

Apply a Design Template

1. Click the **Slide Design** button.
2. Click the thumbnail of the appropriate layout.

or

1. Click **Format.**
2. Click **Slide Design.**
3. Click the thumbnail of the appropriate layout.

or

1. Right-click on the slide.
2. Click **Slide Design.**
3. Click the thumbnail of the appropriate layout.

Change Slide Color Scheme

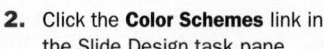

1. Click the **Slide Design** button. 
2. Click the **Color Schemes** link in the Slide Design task pane.
3. Click the thumbnail of the desired color scheme.

Change Slide Background

1. Click **Format.**
2. Click **Background.**
3. Click the **Background fill** list arrow.
4. Choose a new background fill color.
5. Click **Apply to All** or **Apply.**

Replace Fonts

1. Click **Format, Replace Fonts.**
2. Click **Replace** list arrow and select font to replace.
3. Click **With** list arrow and select replacement font.
4. Click **Replace.**

Move, Copy, or Delete Slides

In Slide sorter view

1. Select slide to move, copy, or delete.
2. Drag slide to new location to **move**; hold down **Ctrl** and drag to new location to **copy**; press the **Delete** key to delete.

Duplicate Slides

1. Select slide to duplicate.
2. Click **Insert.**
3. Click **Duplicate Slide.**

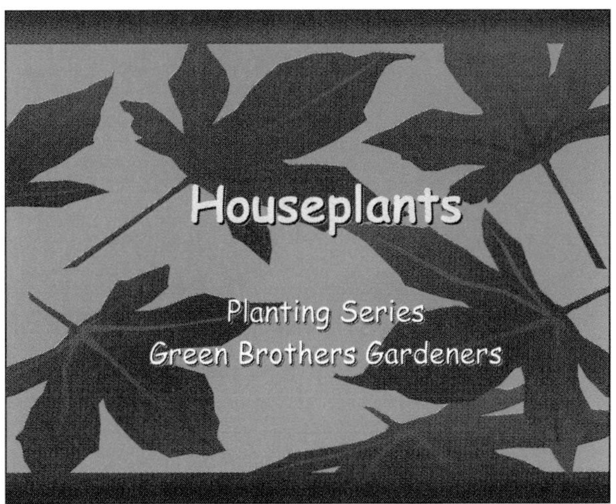

1

Types of Fertilizer

- Granulated
  - Economical
  - Reapply every few weeks
- Slow-release
  - Relatively expensive
  - Lasts several months
  - Rarely burns plants
- Water soluble
  - Takes effect quickly
  - Must be applied on a regular basis
- Organic
  - Slow-releasing
  - Very safe for plants
  - Expensive

2

Watering Tips

- Use warm water
- Water before plant wilts
- Know your plant, and water from above or below as necessary
- Soil should be thoroughly soaked, without overwatering

3

Growing Basics

- Bright light, but NOT direct sunlight
- 65 to 75 degrees Fahrenheit with relative humidity
  - Spray with water several times a day
  - Keep pot in a tray of damp pebbles
- Do not overwater
- Soil should be a mixture of dirt, peat, sand, and vermiculite
  - Good drainage
  - Air can circulate to roots
- Feed plants with fertilizer

4

Featured Plant—The Orchid

- Thousands of orchid species
- Phalaenopsis is the best indoor orchid
- The Pot
  - Should be free-draining
  - Water cannot accumulate around roots
- Light
  - Moderate light
  - Not direct sunlight, but not dark
- Temperature
  - 75 degrees Fahrenheit during the day
  - 55-60 degrees Fahrenheit at night
  - Humidity at 50%
- Water
  - Depends on plant species
  - Depends on light

5

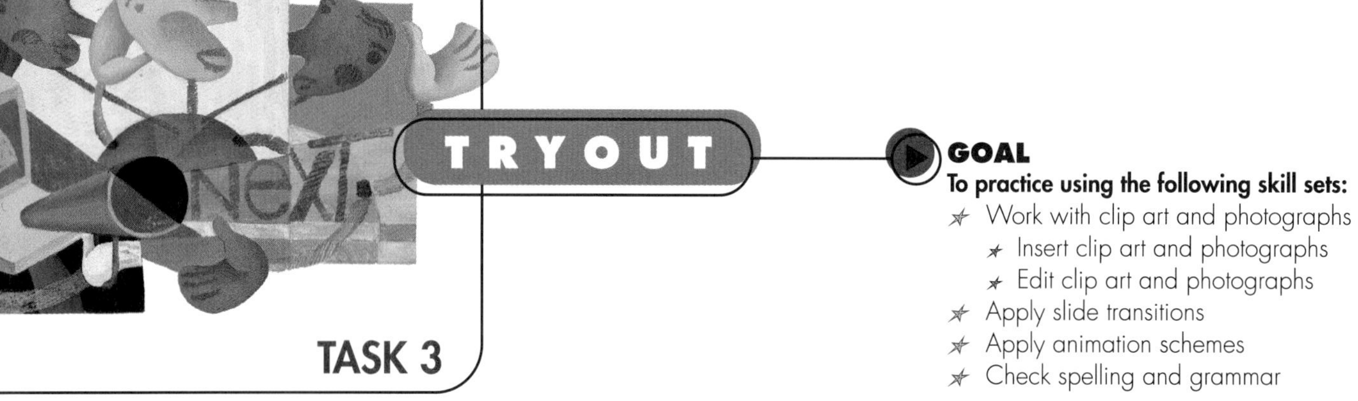

GOAL

To practice using the following skill sets:

- Work with clip art and photographs
  - Insert clip art and photographs
  - Edit clip art and photographs
- Apply slide transitions
- Apply animation schemes
- Check spelling and grammar

WHAT YOU NEED TO KNOW

Work with Clip Art and Photographs

- To enhance a slide visually, you can insert many different elements. The most frequently used element is *clip art,* which is a collection of ready-made drawings, illustrations, and photographs.
- As indicated in Task 1, there are numerous slide layouts. PowerPoint categorizes layouts by what will be placed on them. In addition to text placeholders, slides can contain object placeholders.
- An object placeholder can contain any type of object—clip art, a chart, a graph, a media clip, a table, an organization chart, a diagram, or a picture.
- Object placeholders appear on Content layouts, Text and Content layouts, and Other layouts. Figure 2.25 illustrates a Title, Text, and Content slide layout containing multiple object icons.

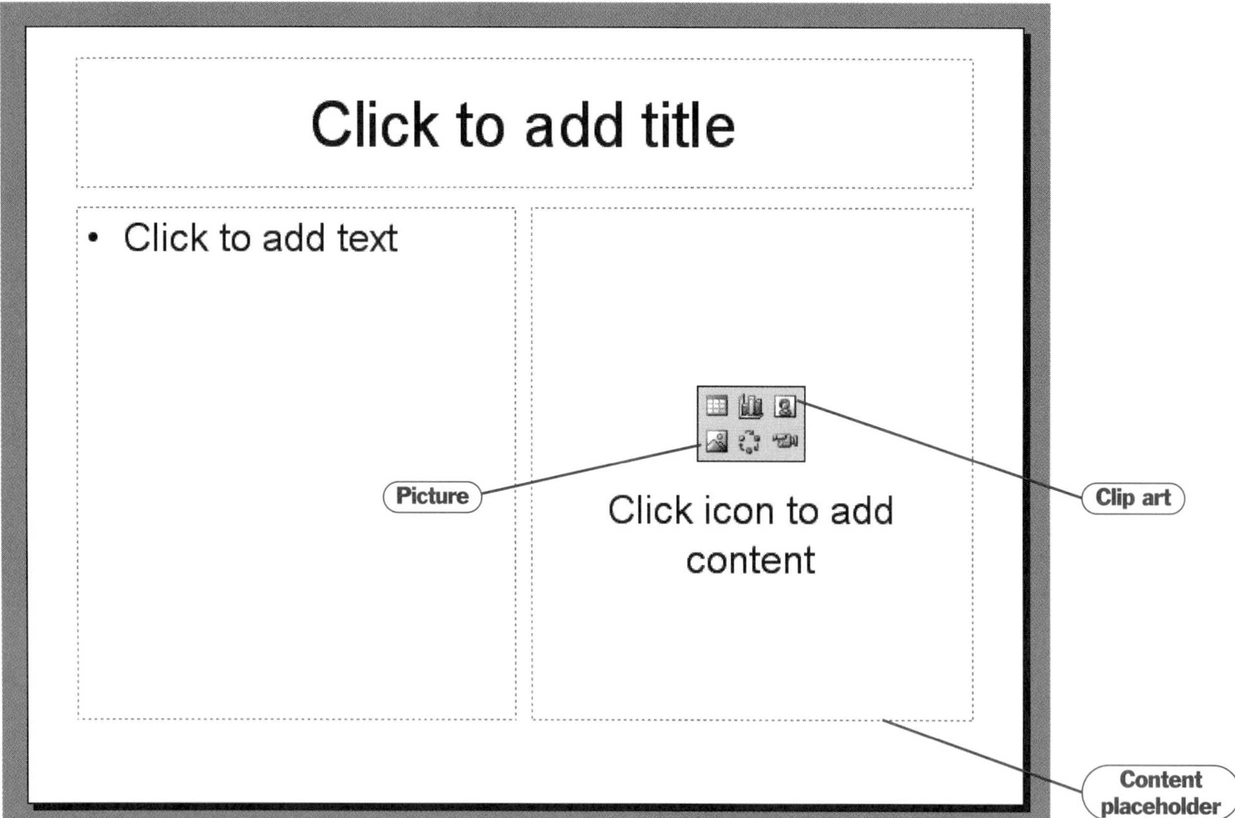

Figure 2.25 Title, Text, and Content slide layout

Insert Clip Art and Photographs

- To insert clip art, select a layout that contains the Insert Clip Art button.
- When the slide layout that you want displays, click the Insert Clip Art button, which will open the Select Picture dialog box, shown in Figure 2.26.
- Use the scroll bar to look through the clip art options. To find clip art by topic or theme, enter the topic or theme name in the Search text box and click the Go button. PowerPoint displays those images that match your search word. Double-click the clip art image to insert it on the slide.
- The image appears with sizing and rotate handles, as shown in Figure 2.27. Click off the clip art image to hide the handles.
- You can also place clip art on a slide without inserting it into a placeholder. To do so, click Insert, Picture, Clip Art, or click the Insert Clip Art button on the Drawing toolbar. The Clip Art task pane appears, shown in Figure 2.28, from which you can search for the clip art you want. If you want a specific type of media (clip art or photographs), click the Results should be list arrow and select the option or options you want.

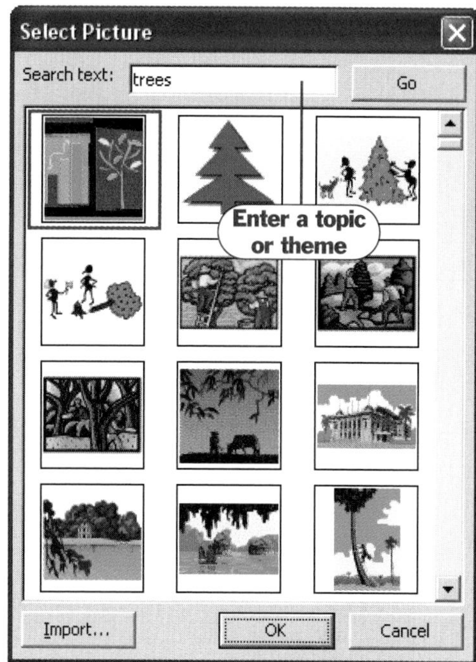

Figure 2.26 Select Picture dialog box

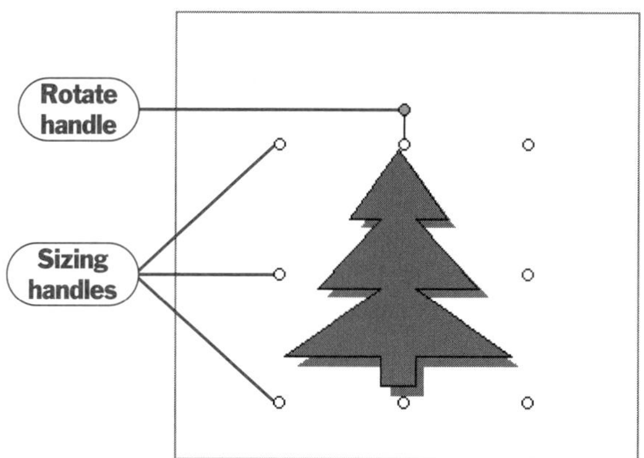

Figure 2.27 Clip art image

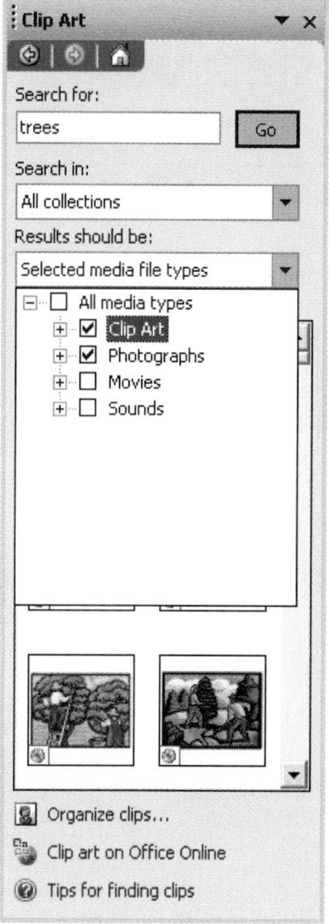

Figure 2.28 Clip Art task pane

POWERPOINT

- If PowerPoint does not have the clip art or photograph you want, you can download additional images from the Web or from a digital camera. You can also use scanned images. If you scan an image, or download one from a digital camera or from the Web, PowerPoint automatically saves the image in the My Pictures folder.
- To insert an image that has been saved as a file on your computer, click the Picture button on an object slide or click Insert, Picture, From File. This will open the Insert Picture dialog box, shown in Figure 2.29. Click the picture you want, then click Insert.

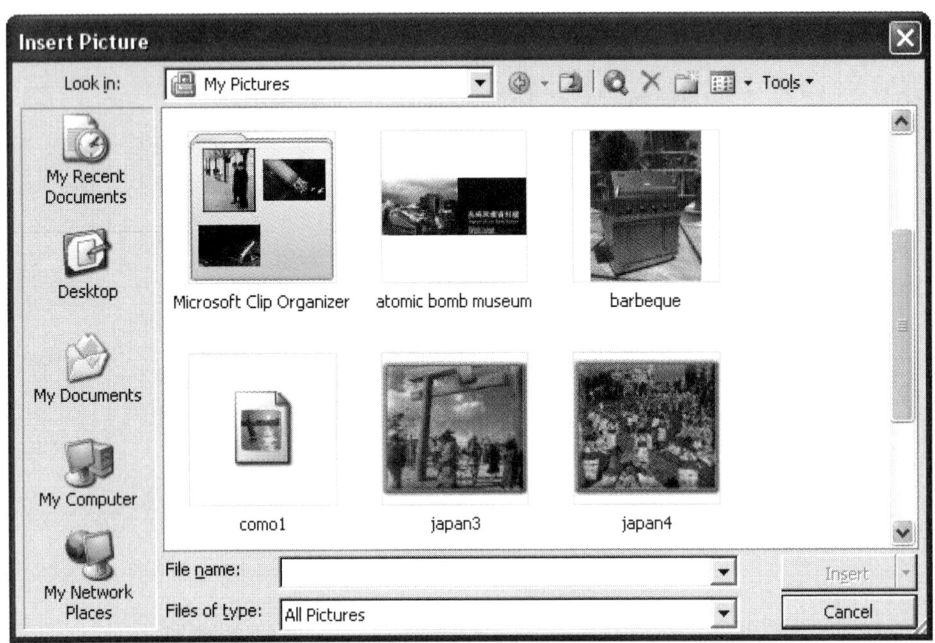

Figure 2.29 Insert Picture dialog box

TRY *it* OUT *p2-13*

1. Click the **New** button.
2. Select the **Title and Content** slide layout from the Content Layouts category.
3. Click the **Insert Clip Art** button.
4. Enter `Tree` in the Search text box and click **Go.**
5. Double-click the tree of your choice.
6. Click off the image to hide the sizing handles.
7. Click the **New Slide** button.

8. Click the **Blank** slide layout from the Content Layouts category.
9. Click **Insert, Picture, Clip Art.**

Note: If you are prompted to add clips to the Clip Organizer, click Later.

10. Enter `Plants` in the Search for text box. Click the **Results should be** list box and check **Photographs**, if necessary. Deselect all other options, then click **Go**.
11. Click any image to insert it.
12. Display Slide 1.
13. Do not close the file.

Edit Clip Art and Photographs

- You can edit clip art and photographs (move, copy, delete, size, and rotate) using the same techniques that you used when working with placeholders. Remember, you must first select the clip art or photograph before moving, copying, deleting, sizing, or rotating it.
- The Picture toolbar, shown in Figure 2.30, contains buttons that allow you to modify pictures and clip art objects. If the Picture toolbar is not displayed, click View, select Toolbars, and click Picture.

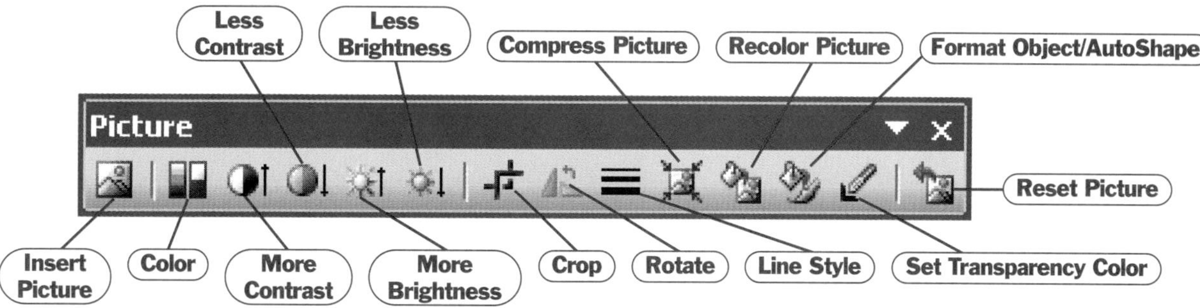

Figure 2.30 Picture toolbar

POWERPOINT

The table below describes each button on the Picture toolbar and when and how you might use it.

BUTTON	DESCRIPTION
Insert Picture	Opens the Insert Picture dialog box
Color	Changes color in a picture to various other color options.
More Contrast	Provides more contrast to a picture. Click as many times as necessary until the picture or clip art appears as you want it.
Less Contrast	Provides less contrast to a picture. Click as many times as necessary until the picture or clip art appears as you want it.
More Brightness	Provides more brightness to a picture. Click as many times as necessary until the picture or clip art appears as you want it.
Less Brightness	Provides less brightness to a picture. Click as many times as necessary until the picture or clip art appears as you want it.
Crop	Allows you to cut out any unwanted parts of a picture. While cropping makes the image look as if you resized it, its edges have actually been cut off. However, the image is not cut off permanently; it is hidden.
Rotate	Rotates the image left in 90-degree increments.
Line Style	Allows you to select a line style to insert around the image.
Compress Picture	Allows you to compress a picture's file size.
Recolor Picture	Allows you to recolor certain image file types.
Format Object / AutoShape	Opens the Format Object or AutoShape dialog box, which provides numerous editing options.
Set Transparent Color	Allows you to change a solid color in a picture to a transparent color. Position the pointer over a solid color and click.
Reset Picture	Returns the picture to its original setting.

TRY*it* OUT *p2-14*

Note: The slide containing the tree clip art image and the text box should be displayed.

1. Display the Picture toolbar, if it is not already displayed (View, Toolbars, Picture).
2. Create the slide shown as follows:

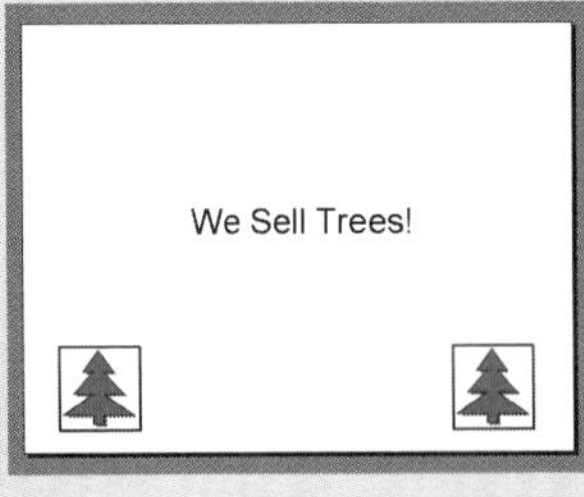

   a. Enter `We Sell Trees!` in the title placeholder.
   b. Click the **tree** graphic to display its handles.
   c. Position the mouse pointer on a corner handle until a two-headed arrow appears.
   d. Click and drag the handle inward to reduce the size of the graphic.
   e. Position the mouse pointer on the graphic until a four-headed arrow appears.
   f. Click and drag the graphic to move it to the bottom left of the slide.
   g. If the handles are not displayed, click to select the graphic. Hold down the **Ctrl** key and drag to copy the graphic to the middle of the slide. Repeat the process and copy the graphic to the bottom right of the slide.
   h. Click and drag the title placeholder to the middle of the slide.
3. Click to select the middle graphic; press the **Delete** key. *Note: The Content placeholder might reappear.*
4. For each remaining graphic: Click to select, then click the the **Line Style** button on the Picture toolbar. Choose a 3-point line.
5. Close the file; do not save.

Apply Slide Transitions

- *Slide transitions* control the way slides move on and off the screen during a slide show.
- You can add transitions to slides in all views. To add a transition to a slide, display or select the slide on which to add a transition and click Slide Show, Slide Transition.
- In the Slide Transition task pane that opens, as shown in Figure 2.31, select a transition. If you want to apply the same transition effect to all slides in the presentation, click Apply to All Slides.

- If the AutoPreview box is checked, the transition effect you click automatically plays on the slide. If it is not checked, click the Play button to preview the transition effect.
- You can modify the transition speed and/or add a transition sound by selecting the appropriate option in the Modify transition section of the Slide Transition task pane. The transition speed controls how fast or slow the slide moves on and off the screen; a transition sound adds a sound effect as the slide moves on and off the screen.
- The Advance slide options allow you to specify how you want to move on to the next slide—manually or automatically. If you choose to advance slides manually, click to select the On mouse click check box. To advance slides automatically, click to select the Automatically after check box and specify the amount of time to elapse between slides.

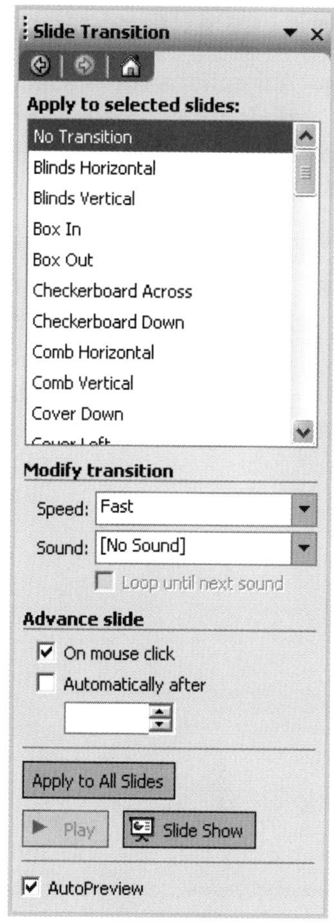

Figure 2.31 Slide Transition task pane

POWERPOINT

TRY *it* OUT *p2-15*

1. Open **p2.15neworleans** from the Data CD.
2. Click **Slide Show, Slide Transition.**
3. Click **Cover Down** in the Apply to selected slides list and press the **Page Down** key.
4. Click **Shape Diamond** in the Apply to selected slides list.
5. Click the **Speed** list arrow and click **Slow.**
6. Click the **Sound** list arrow and click **Voltage.** Press the **Page Down** key. *Note: Sound effects may not be installed on your computer. Click "Yes" if you are prompted to install this feature.*
7. Click **Dissolve** in the Apply to selected slides list.
8. Check the **Automatically after** check box and click the **up** increment arrow to display 2 seconds.
9. Drag the scroll bar to return to Slide 1.
10. Click the **Slide Show View** button.
11. Click the left mouse button to advance to the next slide.
12. Click the left mouse button again. *Note: Wait two seconds; the slide will automatically advance without your clicking the mouse button.*
13. Press the **Escape** key.
14. Close the file; do not save.

Apply Animation Schemes

- Animations are visual or sound effects that affect the way text and objects appear on a slide during a slide show. *Animation schemes* are preset animations that also include transition effects. Therefore, when you apply an animation scheme, you are also applying the scheme's transition effect.
- PowerPoint classifies animation schemes by how busy they are—from subtle to exciting.
- You can apply animation schemes to slides in any view. To apply an animation scheme, display or select the slide on which to apply the animation and click Slide Show, Animation Schemes. In the Slide Design Animation Schemes task pane that opens, as shown in Figure 2.32, click an animation scheme. You can choose to apply the animation scheme to the selected slide or to all slides.

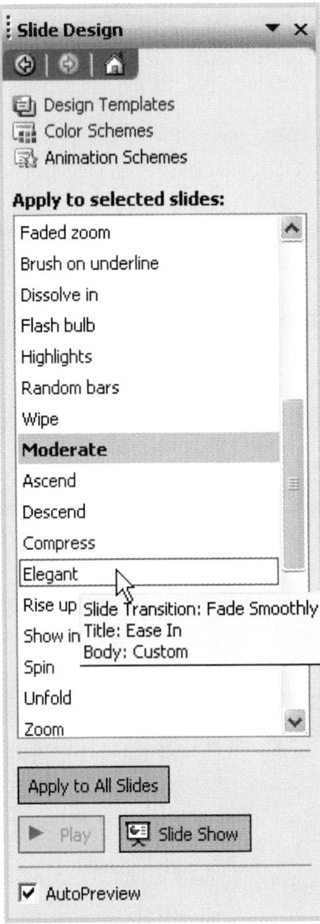

Figure 2.32 Slide Design Animation Schemes task pane

- In Slide sorter view, slides containing transitions are marked by a slide icon appearing below and to the left of the miniature slide image, as shown in Figure 2.33.

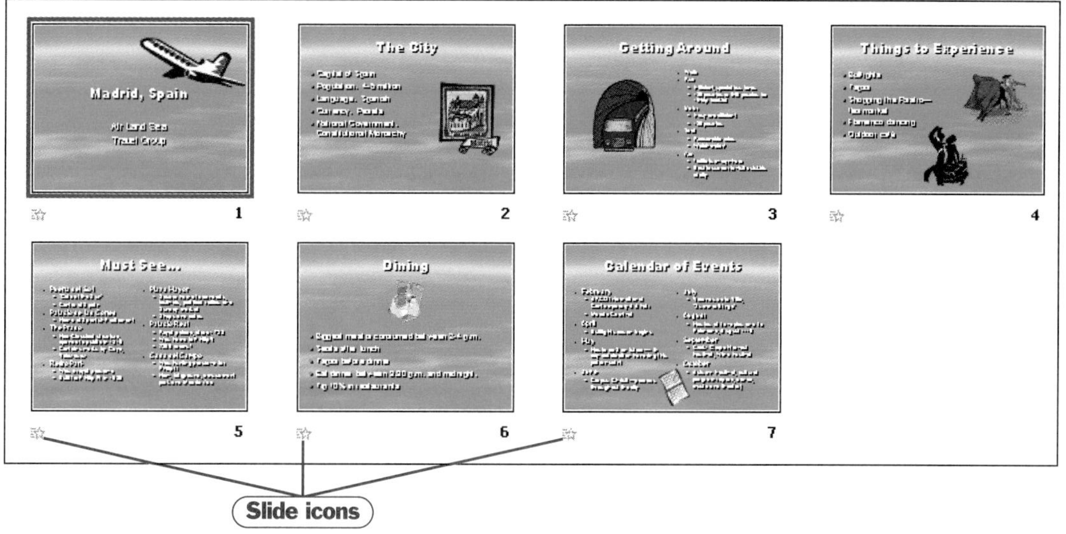

Figure 2.33 Marked Slides in Slide sorter view

POWERPOINT

TRY *it* OUT *p2-16*

1. Open **p2.16neworleans** from the Data CD.
2. Click **Slide Show, Animation Schemes.**
3. Click the **Compress** scheme, listed under the Moderate subheading in the task pane.
4. Click **Apply to All Slides.**
5. Click the **Slide Show View** button. 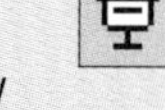
6. Continue to click the mouse to view the entire slide show.
7. Switch to Slide sorter view. Note that the slides containing an animation scheme are marked with a star icon.
8. Close the file; do not save.

Check Spelling and Grammar

- If automatic spell checking is activated, wavy red lines appear under words that PowerPoint recognizes as possible errors.
- The spelling and grammar feature may be used in PowerPoint as in other Office applications.
- After creating your presentation, click the Spelling button on the toolbar or select Spelling from the Tools menu. 

GOAL
To create a six-slide informative presentation that includes clip art and text layout slides

SETTING THE STAGE/WRAPUP
File name: **2.3overview**

WHAT YOU NEED TO KNOW

- Use clip art to enhance a presentation and make it more appealing. Pictures, if you use them correctly, can communicate an idea that words are unable to express. They can also help make the presentation, or idea within the presentation, more memorable.
- It is important to use visuals that are relevant to the slide's topic. Do not add graphics just to fill space.
- Transitions and animation schemes transform a dull presentation into one that heightens the audience's attention.
- Animation schemes allow you to introduce text bullet-by-bullet so that the audience does not jump ahead of you as you deliver your presentation.
- In this Rehearsal activity, you will create a presentation informing a new client about the services of Occasions Event Planning, a company that organizes, plans, and implements corporate and consumer events.

DIRECTIONS

1. Open a new presentation and apply an appropriate slide design.
2. Accept the default title slide layout for the first slide.
3. Enter the title and subtitle as illustrated on the facing page.
4. Add new slides as indicated in the illustration and enter the corresponding text.
5. Insert relevant clip art where shown.

   Note: For Slides 3 and 5, use a slide layout that contains clip art placeholders. For Slide 4, insert clip art directly on the slide.
6. On Slide 2, draw a text box and enter the text, `We work with you from concept to completion!`, as shown in the illustration. Use a 24-point font size and any desired font color. Position the text box as shown.
7. Apply a transition effect to Slide 1.
8. Apply the same Animation scheme to Slides 2-6.
9. Save the presentation; name it **2.3overview.**
10. Close the presentation.

Occasions Event Planning

Company Overview

1

What We Do

- Corporate Events
  - Holiday Parties
  - Product Promotions
  - Corporate Picnics
  - Conferences
  - Corporate Dinners/Lunches
- Consumer Events
  - Birthdays
  - Weddings
  - Bar/Bat Mitzvahs
  - Holiday Parties

We work with you from concept to completion!

2

Planning

- Budget
- Theme
- Location
- Invitations
- Entertainment
- Decorations
- Photographer/ Videographer

3

Themes and Entertainment

- Themes
  - Sports
  - Casino
  - Carnival
  - Broadway Shows
  - Beach Party
  - Mardi Gras
  - Decades—60's, 70's, 80's, etc.

- Entertainment
  - Music
    - DJ
    - Band
    - Orchestra
  - Fun Stuff
    - Magicians
    - Caricatures
    - Karaoke
    - Clowns
    - Palm Readers
    - Giveaways

4

The Guest List

- Invitations
  - Reply Cards
  - RSVP Line
- Out-of-town guests
  - Hotel
  - Welcome Gifts
  - Transportation to event

5

Some of Our Clients

- Trilogy Productions
- Sutton Investment Group
- In-Shape Fitness Centers
- Time Out Sporting Goods
- Air, Land, Sea Travel Group

6

POWERPOINT

Cues for Reference

Insert Clip Art

Into a Clip Art/Content Placeholder

1. Select a slide layout that contains a clip art or content placeholder.
2. Click the clip art icon on the slide.
3. Click desired clip art image.
4. Click **OK.**

Directly onto a Slide (Not into a Placeholder)

1. Click **Insert, Picture, Clip Art.**
2. Click the appropriate clip art image on the Clip Art task pane.
3. Click **OK.**

or

1. Click **Insert Clip Art** button.
2. Click the appropriate clip art image on the Clip Art task pane.
3. Click **OK.**

Add Slide Transitions

1. Display the slide on which the transition should be applied.
2. Click **Slide Show, Slide Transition.**
3. Click a transition in the Slide Transition task pane.
4. Click the **Speed** list arrow to modify transition speed.
5. Click the **Sound** list arrow to add a transition sound.
6. Click **Apply to All Slides** to apply the transition effect to all slides.
   or
   Display another slide and repeat the steps above to apply a different slide transition to it.

Advance Slides Automatically

1. Click the **Automatically after** check box.
2. Click the **up** or **down** increment arrows to specify a time after which the slide will advance to the next one.
3. Click **Apply to All Slides** to apply the transition effect to all slides.
   or
   Display another slide and repeat the steps above to apply a different transition to it.

Apply Preset Animations

1. Display the slide on which to apply a preset animation scheme.
2. Click **Slide Show, Animation Schemes.**
3. Click an animation scheme in the Slide Design Animation Scheme task pane.
4. Click **Apply to All Slides** to apply the animation to all slides.
   or
   Display another slide and repeat the steps above to apply a different animation to it.

PERFORMANCE

SETTING THE STAGE
- Act I File name: **pp2trilogy**
- Act II File name: **pp2madrid**

Act I

You are the internship coordinator at Trilogy Productions. Your company has just hired 20 interns for the summer. To orient the new interns to Trilogy Productions, you have been asked to create a presentation that informs new interns of each department's responsibilities. Use the following information to create this presentation.

Follow these guidelines:

- You may use the bold headings as slide titles and the italicized words as bullet points.
- Use an appropriate design template, a variety of slide layouts, clip art, and a text box. You may change the slide background, if you want.
- Apply animation schemes to all slides.
- Create a relevant title for the presentation itself. Save the presentation as **pp2trilogy.**

Fast Facts

CEO John Alan and CFO Andrew Martin founded Trilogy Productions *in 1990.* Trilogy maintains *offices in New York and Los Angeles* and currently *employs more than 500 people.* Since its founding, Trilogy has *released 50 feature films and 7 Emmy-winning television programs.*

Departments

Six departments provide the foundation for Trilogy's award-winning work: *Production, Distribution, Marketing/Publicity/Promotions, Television, Merchandising, and Interactive.*

Production

The Production Department is responsible for making the movies—from start to finish. The movie production process begins with *story and script development.* After a script is selected and purchased, *a budget is assigned and a production schedule is developed. A director and cast are then selected* and *preproduction begins.* After the movie is filmed, it goes into the final stage of *postproduction,* where the director and Trilogy agree on a final cut.

Distribution

The film is then ready to be distributed. The Distribution Department *books the theaters that will show the film.* As theaters are located all over the world, Trilogy has *domestic distribution offices in*

New York, Los Angeles, Chicago, and Atlanta and *international offices in London and Buenos Aires* to facilitate the distribution of the films. The Distribution Department also *calculates Trilogy's film grosses* (money earned on the films).

Marketing/Publicity/Promotions

The Marketing, Publicity, and Promotions Departments work to promote the films. They are responsible for *creating the movie trailers* (commercials/previews) that play on television and in theaters and the *movie posters* that appear on billboards or newspapers. The departments also *plan and coordinate movie premieres, create giveaway items, write press releases, coordinate talent appearances on* TV talk shows and entertainment news programs, and *develop sweepstakes opportunities.*

Television

Trilogy also has a strong Television Department that *develops programming* for *network, cable, and syndication* as well as *licenses movies* to these TV outlets. The Television Department also does its own *marketing and promotions for its current series.*

POWERPOINT

Merchandising

The Merchandising Department *works with various licensees to create products based on Trilogy's film and television properties. It distributes these products (which can be T-shirts, Halloween costumes, posters, toys, etc.) to retail stores.*

Interactive

Trilogy's Interactive Department *creates and maintains Web sites for current television series and movies.* It also *sends e-mails and e-newsletters to fans* to promote the films and TV shows. Finally, it *maintains an e-commerce site*, which sells many of the products developed by the Merchandising Department.

Act II

You are the tour coordinator for the Air Land Sea Travel Group. Your company has decided to offer a tour to Madrid, Spain. For the travel agents to sell this trip to potential travelers, they must be well informed about the city of Madrid. You asked one of your assistants to research the city and provide you with summary highlights.

Follow these guidelines:

- From the summary paragraphs on the next page, create slides that contain appropriate bulleted information. Create a title for each slide that summarizes slide information. Remember, the objective of this presentation is to inform travel agents about facts, highlights, and tourist attractions of Madrid.
- You will need to do research on the Internet to create the last slide, which describes seasonal events in Madrid. To get this information (which your assistant forgot to include) go to www.travelocity.com. Click in the Guides and Advice tab, enter `Madrid` in the Enter your destination here box and click Find. Then, click the Best Time to Visit link in the Destination Guide section of the Web page. Print the page and use the Calendar of Events information to list the annual events on the slide.

- Apply animation schemes to all slides.
- Save your presentation as **pp2madrid.**

Summary Paragraphs

- Madrid is the capital city of Spain, home to nearly 5 million people. The national government is a constitutional monarchy, the national language is Spanish, and the national currency is the Peseta.
- The city provides adequate public transportation. The bus system and the metro are the easiest and most efficient ways to get around. The fare for the bus or metro is 130 pesetas. The bus, however, offers a 10-trip booklet for 645 pesetas. Taxis are available at reasonable rates, but be sure to watch the meter, as taxi drivers might take advantage of tourists. *Do not* rent a car unless you plan to travel outside of the city. Traffic within Madrid is terrible. Overall, the best way to see the city is to walk.
- While in Spain you should experience the things for which Spain is known. You might see a bullfight, eat tapas, shop the Rastro (flea market), try or watch flamenco dancing, and spend some time at an outdoor café.

- There are so many sights in Madrid worth visiting; if you are limited for time, however, you should be sure to see the following places: The Puerta del Sol, or "Gate of the Sun," marks the center of Spain. The Palacio de las Cortes is the home of the Spanish Parliament. The Prado museum, which was opened to the public in 1819, is a spectacular neoclassical structure that houses works by the famous Spanish painters Goya and Velázquez, among many, many others. Near the Prado is Retiro Park, which was a royal preserve built in 1636 for Philip IV. Plaza Mayor is a square in the city that hosts concerts, festivals, political rallies, and a Sunday market. Many shops and cafés also surround it. The Palacio Real, or Royal Palace, was built in 1738, has 2,800 rooms, and was home to Philip V. Casa del Campo, once a hunting preserve for Philip II, is now a fairground and amusement park that houses the Madrid Zoo.
- The biggest meal of the day in Spain is consumed between 2 and 4 p.m., after which people take a siesta. Before dinner most Spaniards enjoy tapas, small dishes of food similar to appetizers. Dinner is eaten between 9:30 p.m. and midnight. When dining out, a gratuity is not usually included on the check, however, it is customary to tip about 10%.
- There are many annual events in Madrid, and, depending on when you visit, you might be able to experience one! *Go to the Web site mentioned in the directions and list the annual events on the slide.*

1
2
3

LESSON 3

Sales Presentations

In this lesson, you will learn to use PowerPoint features to create effective sales presentations. Businesses use sales presentations to sell a product, a service, or an idea.

Upon completion of this lesson, you should have mastered the following skill sets:

- Work with outlines
- Create a summary slide
- Hide a slide
- Link slides
- Format bullets
- Insert headers and footers
- Work with slide and title masters
- Save as a template
- Create a custom show
  - Link to a custom show
  - Link the table of contents slide to a custom show
- Work with objects
  - Create Shapes/AutoShapes
  - Create WordArt
  - Format objects
  - Layer objects
  - Group, ungroup, and regroup objects
  - Use grids and guides
  - Nudge objects
  - Align or distribute objects
  - Use Action buttons

Terms

Software-related

Outline
Footer
Custom show
Action buttons
Slide master
Title master
Template
Custom show
AutoShapes
WordArt
Grids
Guides
Grouping
Ungrouping
Regrouping
Action buttons

GOAL
To practice using the following skill sets:

- Work with outlines
- Create a summary slide
- Hide a slide
- Link slides

WHAT YOU NEED TO KNOW

Work with Outlines

- You can view slide content as an *outline* to see the flow of your presentation. To do so, click the Outline tab in the Outline and Slides tab pane, as shown in Figure 3.1. Slides are shown numbered down the left side of the screen, and slide icons identify the start of each new slide.

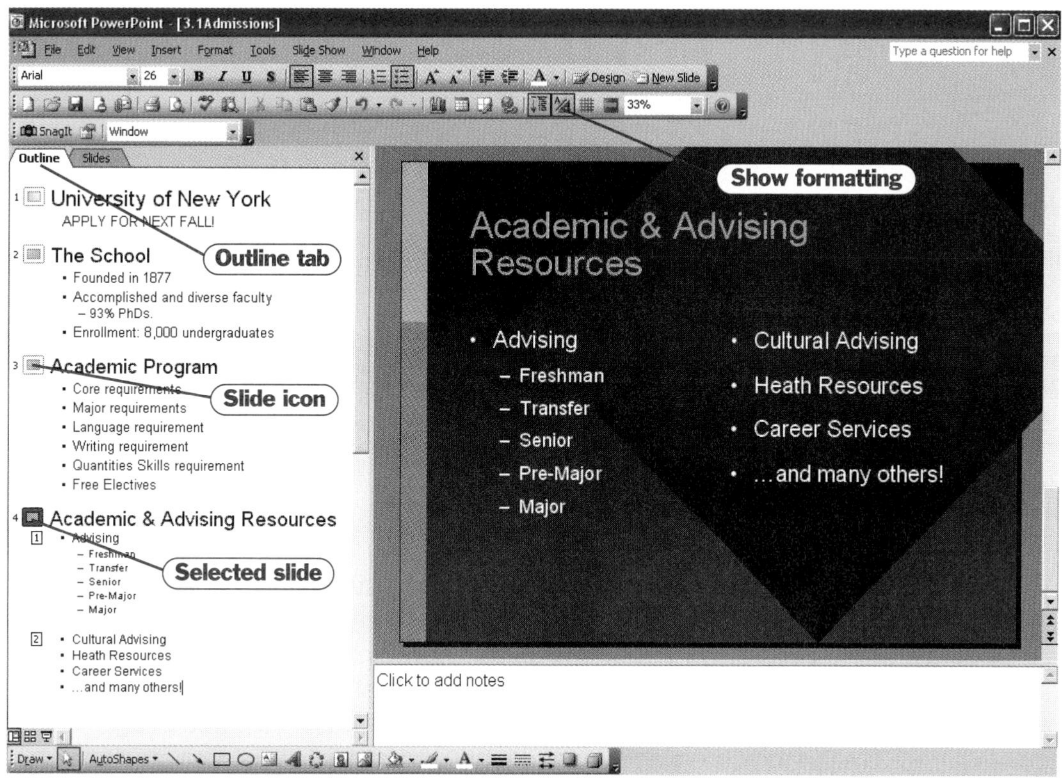

Figure 3.1 Outline tab pane

- On the Outline tab, slide content appears as plain text, without formatting or enhancements. To display text formatting and enhancements that appear on the slide, click the Show Formatting button on the Standard toolbar.
- You can also create a presentation as an outline or import an outline from Word to become a presentation. Importing an outline will be covered in Lesson 5.

TRY *it* OUT *p3-1*

1. Open **3.1Admissions** from the Data CD; save as **3.1Admissions1.yi** (yi = your initials).

2. Click the **Outline** tab, if necessary.
3. Click the **Slide 4** icon.
4. Click the **New Slide** button.

5. On the **Outline tab**, enter `Additional Programs` as the title for **Slide 5** and add the following bullet and subbullet points:
   - `Study Abroad`
   - `Exceptional Programs`
   - `Fall, Spring, or Summer`
   - `Undergraduate Research Opportunities`
   - `Individualized Majors`
   - `Honors Programs`
6. Click the **Slide 5** icon and drag it up to become **Slide 4.**
7. Click **View, Toolbars, Outlining.**
8. On **Slide 2** ("The School"), click the last bullet.
9. Click the **Move Up** button twice.

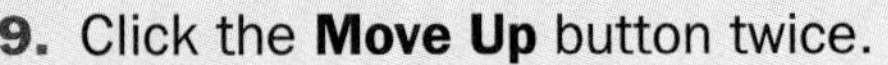

10. Click the **Slide 4** icon.
11. Click the **Collapse** button.

12. Click the **Expand All** button.

13. Click **File, Print.**
14. Select **outline view** in the Print what box and click **OK.**
15. Save; do not close the file.

▶ Outlines in PowerPoint behave the same way they did in Word. To edit slide content in an outline, use the Outlining toolbar shown in Figure 3.2.

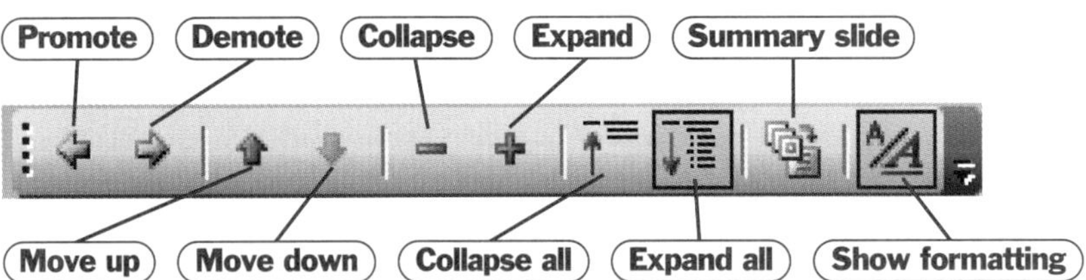

Figure 3.2 Outlining toolbar

▶ Outlines can serve as a table of contents or agenda that you can distribute to an audience. To create a table of contents, you would not display all of the subtext on each slide. To collapse or hide subtext on all slides so that only slide titles appear, as shown in Figure 3.3, click the Collapse All button on the Outlining toolbar. To redisplay subtext on all slides, click the Expand All button. To collapse text on one slide, double-click the slide icon or press the Alt + Shift key + minus sign (-). To expand text on one slide, double-click the slide icon or press the Alt + Shift key + plus sign (+).

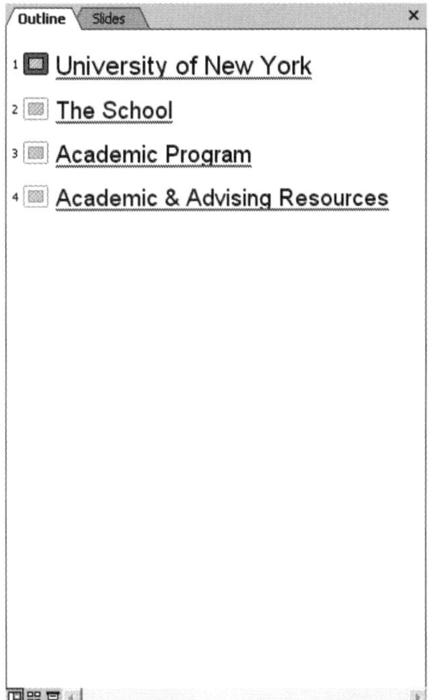

Figure 3.3 Text collapsed on all slides

▶ To print an outline, use the same procedures that you use to print slides, but in the Print dialog box you must select Outline View from the Print what list, as shown in Figure 3.4.

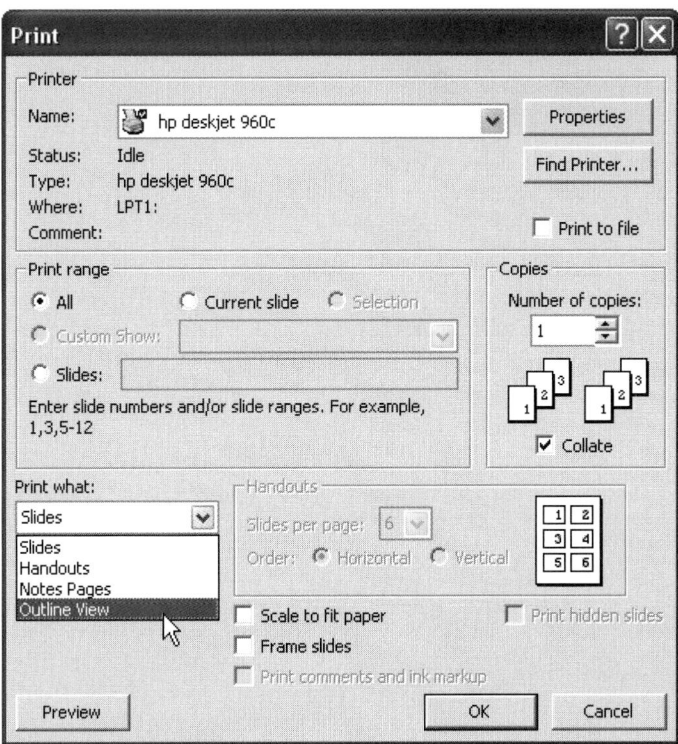

Figure 3.4 Print dialog box in outline view

POWERPOINT

Create a Summary Slide

- A summary slide creates a bulleted list of all the titles in a presentation. You can place it at the beginning of your presentation to act as a table of contents, or you can put it at the end to summarize the content of your slide show.
- To create a summary slide, use one of the following methods:
  - Switch to Slide sorter view and select the slides from which to create a summary slide. To select all slides, click Edit, Select All. To select specific slides, hold down the Ctrl key as you click the slides you want and click the Summary Slide button on the Slide Sorter toolbar.

  - In the Outline and Slides tab pane, click either the Slides or the Outline tab and display the Outlining toolbar. Select slides from which to create a summary slide and click the Summary Slide button on the Outlining toolbar.
- PowerPoint automatically places the summary slide, as shown in Figure 3.5, before the first selected slide, but you can move it as required (in Slide sorter view or on the Slides tab).

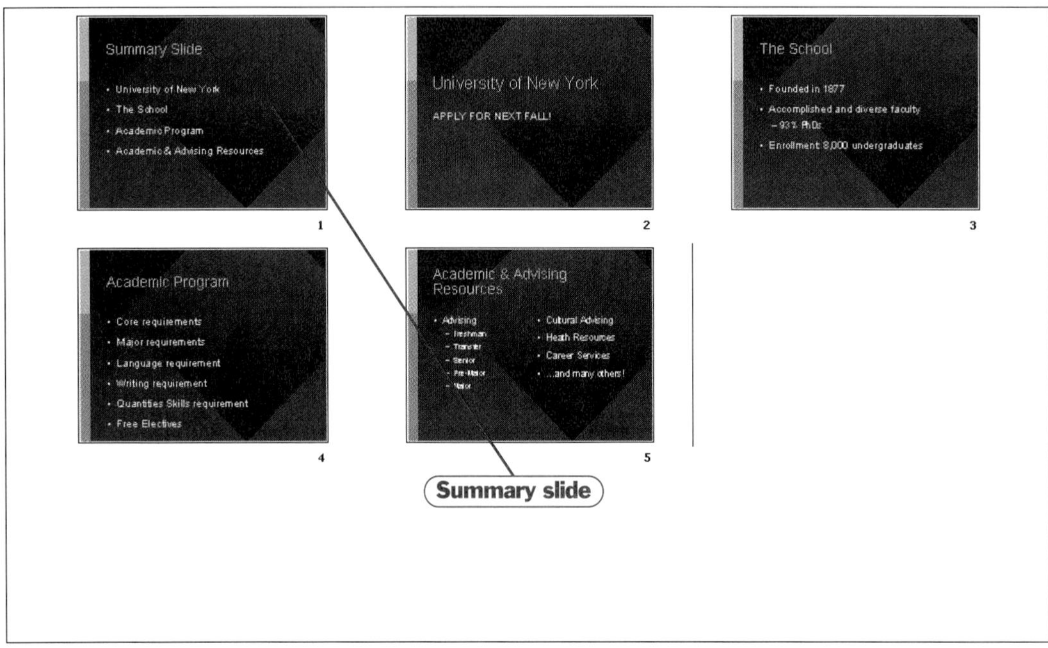

Figure 3.5 Summary slide

TRY it OUT *p3-2*

Note: ***3.1Admissions1.yi*** *should be on the screen.*

1. Click the **Slide Sorter View** button.

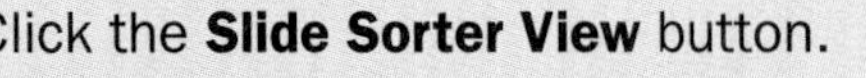

2. Press the **Ctrl** key and click **Slides 1, 2, 3,** and **4.**
3. Click the **Summary Slide** button.

4. Close the file; do not save.

Hide a Slide

- A slide presentation created for one audience may not be suitable for another. You can use the same presentation for different audiences by hiding slides that are not relevant. Hiding slides does not delete them; it hides them during the presentation.
- To hide a slide, select the slide in the Slides pane or in Slide sorter view. Then click Slide Show, Hide Slide. A diagonal bar across the slide number indicates that the slide is hidden, as shown in Figure 3.6.
- To unhide a slide, repeat the process you used to hide it. The diagonal bar will be removed from across the slide number.

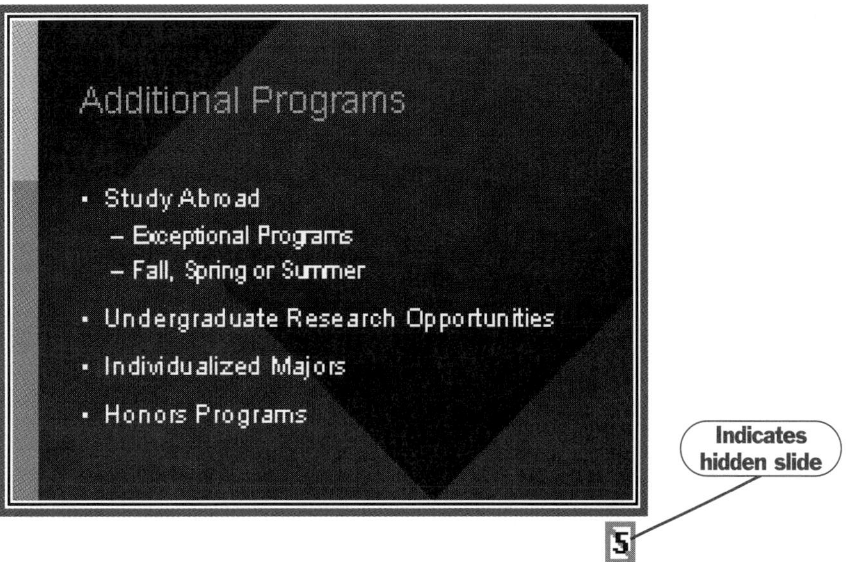

Figure 3.6 Hidden slide

TRY *it* OUT *p3-3*

1. Open **p3.3membership** from the Data CD.
2. Click the **Slides** tab.
3. Click the **Slide 4 miniature** on the Slides tab.
4. Click **Slide Show, Hide Slide.**
5. Click **Slide Show, View Show.**
6. Click the **mouse** button to advance through the entire presentation.
7. Notice that **Slide 4** ("The Membership") is hidden, and thus does not appear in the slide show.
8. Right-click the **Slide 4 miniature** on the Slides tab.
9. Click **Hide Slide,** to unhide the slide.
10. Close the presentation; do not save.

Link Slides

- A hyperlink is a shortcut that allows you to jump to another location. You can create a hyperlink on a slide to link to another slide within a presentation, a slide in another presentation, or a document in another software program. A hyperlink can also be created to link to a Web site. (PowerPoint and the Web will be covered in Lesson 5.)
- You can apply a hyperlink to text or objects. When you apply a hyperlink to text, the text appears underlined and in color. When you apply a hyperlink to an object, there is no visible change to the object.
- You can activate hyperlinks only in Slide show view. When you position the mouse pointer over text or an object that contains a hyperlink while in Slide show view, it changes to a hand, as shown in Figure 3.7. Clicking on a hyperlink activates the link and brings you to the linked slide or program.

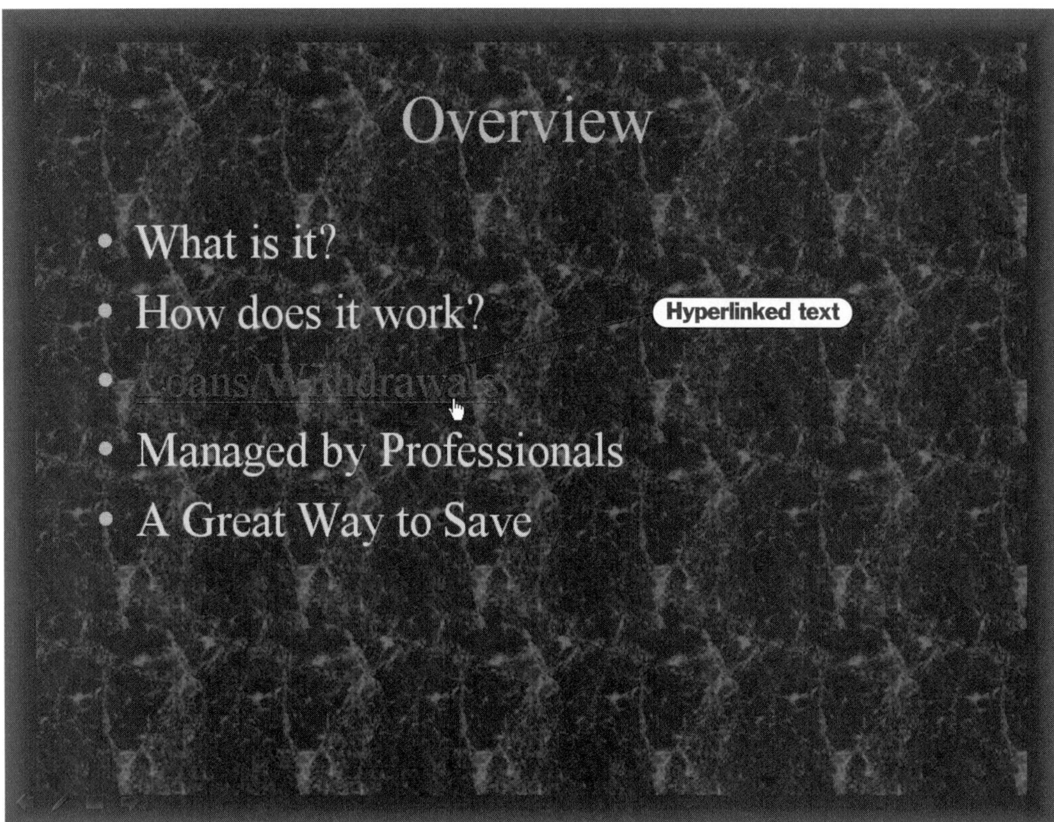

Figure 3.7 Hyperlinked text

- To create a hyperlink to link to another slide within a presentation, select the text or object on which to create the link and click Insert, Hyperlink, or click the Insert Hyperlink button on the Standard toolbar, or right-click and select Hyperlink. In the Insert Hyperlink dialog box that displays, as shown in Figure 3.8, click Place in This Document in the Link to section. This displays all of the slide titles within the presentation. In the Select a place in this document box, click the slide title of the slide to which you want to link.

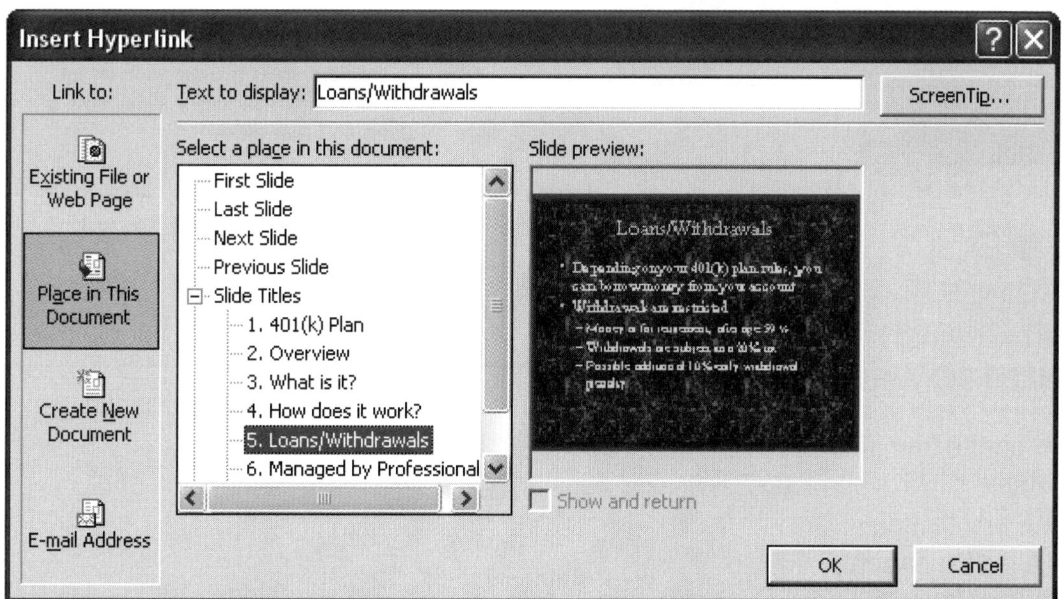

Figure 3.8 Insert Hyperlink dialog box

POWERPOINT

TRY *it* OUT *p3-4*

1. Open **p3.4retire401k** from the Data CD.
2. Display **Slide 2** ("Overview").
3. Select **Loans/Withdrawals.**
4. Click **Insert, Hyperlink.**
5. In the Link to section, click **Place in This Document.**
6. In the Select a place in this document box, click **5. Loans/Withdrawals.**
7. Click **OK.**
8. Click the **Slide Show View** button.

9. When you get to Slide 2, click the **Loans/Withdrawals** hyperlink.
10. Press the **Escape** key.
11. Close the file; do not save.

REHEARSAL

Again

TASK 1

GOAL

To create a sales presentation as an outline, add a summary slide, hide a slide, and link slides

SETTING THE STAGE/WRAPUP

File name: 3.1retire401k.ppt

WHAT YOU NEED TO KNOW

- Outlines serve as the framework for a presentation.
- The information in an outline should follow a logical pattern, beginning with an introduction, containing an explanation and discussion, and ending with a clear conclusion.
- A 401(k) is a type of retirement plan that a business offers to employees. The business deducts a percentage of each employee's salary every pay period and deposits it into a 401(k) investment account.
- In this Rehearsal activity, you will create and then modify a six-slide sales presentation. You will deliver this presentation to employees to convince them to contribute a percentage of their salaries to a 401(k) retirement fund.

DIRECTIONS

1. Open a new blank presentation.
2. Click the **Outline** tab.
3. Enter the titles for each slide as shown in Illustration A below.
4. Add the subtext as shown in Illustration B on the facing page.
5. Collapse all of the subtext.
6. Move **Slide 6** ("Managed by Professionals") to become **Slide 5.**
7. Create a summary slide that contains the titles of Slides 2 through 6.
8. Display **Slide 2** ("Summary Slide"), if necessary.
9. Replace the title "Summary Slide" with: `Overview.`
10. Apply an appropriate design template to the presentation.
11. Make all occurrences of "401(k)" boldface.
12. Expand all of the text.
13. Show the text formatting on the Outline tab.
14. Run the slide show.
15. Print one copy of the complete outline.
16. Save the file; name it **3.1retire401k.**

1 **401(k) Plan**
2 What Is It?
3 How Does It Work?
4 Loans/Withdrawals
5 A Great Way to Save
6 Managed by Professionals

Illustration A

1 **401(k)** Plan

Sutton Investment Group

2 What Is It?

- Type of retirement plan for employees of participating companies
- Save and invest money deducted from paycheck
- Established by federal government in 1981

3 How Does It Work?

- You decide how much to deduct from each paycheck
  - There is a legal maximum
  - Deductions are not taxed
- You decide how to invest the money

4 Loans/Withdrawals

- Depending on your **401(k)** plan rules, you can borrow money from your account
- Withdrawals are restricted
  - Money is for retirement, after age 59½
  - Withdrawals are subject to a 20% tax
  - Possible additional 10% early-withdrawal penalty

5 A Great Way to Save

- Increase your take-home salary
- Company match
  - Some companies contribute a certain amount into your account for every dollar that you contribute
- Automatic deductions force you to save!
- If need be, money can be accessed

6 Managed by Professionals

- Sutton Investment Group
  - Team of experienced investment professionals
  - Portfolio managers manage each fund
  - Global analysts provide comprehensive research

Illustration B

POWERPOINT

Cues for Reference

Switch to Outline View

- Click the **Outline** tab.

Add Slides in Outline View

- Click the **New Slide** button.

  or
- Press **Ctrl** + **M.**

  or
- Select **Insert, New Slide.**

Add Text in Outline View

1. Click **View, Toolbars, Outlining.**
2. Press **Enter** to add a bulleted item under the title line.
3. Click the **Demote** button to indent or add subitems, or the **Promote** button to go back one text or subitem level.

  or
- Click the **Increase Indent** button to indent or add subitems, or the **Decrease Indent** button to go back one text or subitem level.

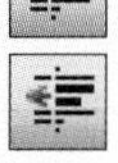

Create a Summary Slide

1. Click the **Slide Sorter View** button.
2. Press **Ctrl** and click the slides to include in the summary slide.
3. Click the **Summary Slide** button.

Hide/Unhide a Slide

1. Click **Slide** tab (in Outline/ Slides pane).
2. Click slide thumbnail of the slide you want to hide.
3. Click **Slide Show, Hide Slide.**
4. To unhide a slide, repeat Steps 1–3.

Link Slides

1. Select text on which to create a hyperlink.
2. Click **Insert, Hyperlink.**
3. Click **Place in This Document.**
4. Click slide to link to.
5. Click **OK.**

GOAL
To practice using the following skill sets:
- Format bullets
- Insert headers and footers
- Work with slide and title masters
- Save as a template

WHAT YOU NEED TO KNOW

Format Bullets

- Many slide layouts contain bulleted text. You can change the style, size, and color of bullets to add visual excitement to your presentation on individual slides, or keep them consisistent on all slides by working with the slide master. (Slide master will be covered later in this task.)
- To change the format of bullets, position the insertion point in the bulleted item or list level you want to change. Click Format, Bullets and Numbering or right-click the mouse and select Bullets and Numbering from the shortcut menu. In the Bullets and Numbering dialog box that opens, as shown in Figure 3.9, click the Bulleted tab and choose a desired bullet type, color, and size.

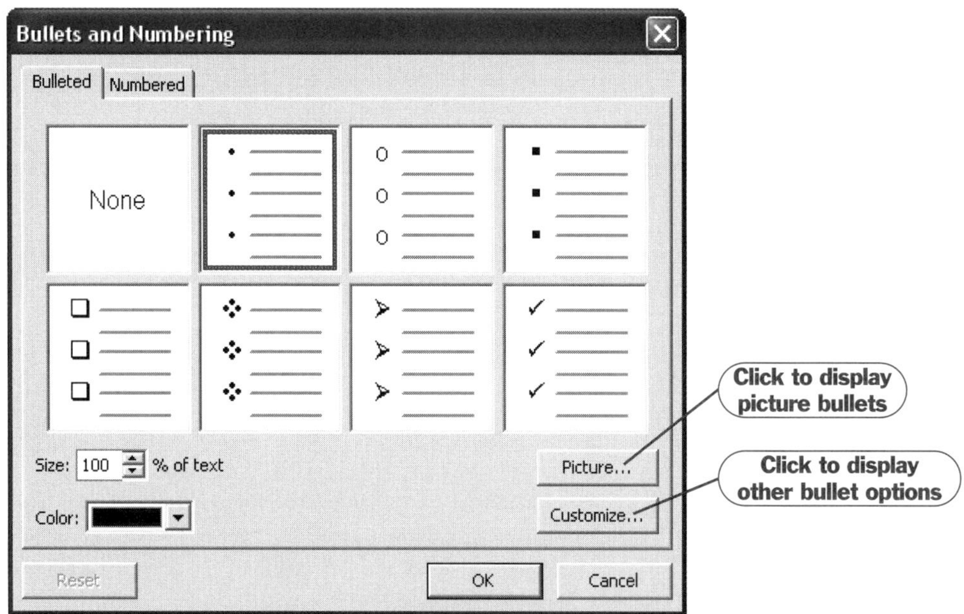

Figure 3.9 Bullets and Numbering dialog box

- To use symbols and graphical fonts as bullets, click the Customize button. In the Symbol dialog box that opens, as shown in Figure 3.10, click the Font list arrow and choose a symbol font. Then choose a bullet and click OK. The Symbol dialog box saves the last 16 custom bullets that you used.
- To use a decorative bullet, click the Picture button. Numerous decorative bullets appear in the Picture Bullet dialog box, as shown in Figure 3.11. Click the bullet you prefer, which will appear in the Bulleted tab of the Bullets and Numbering dialog box.

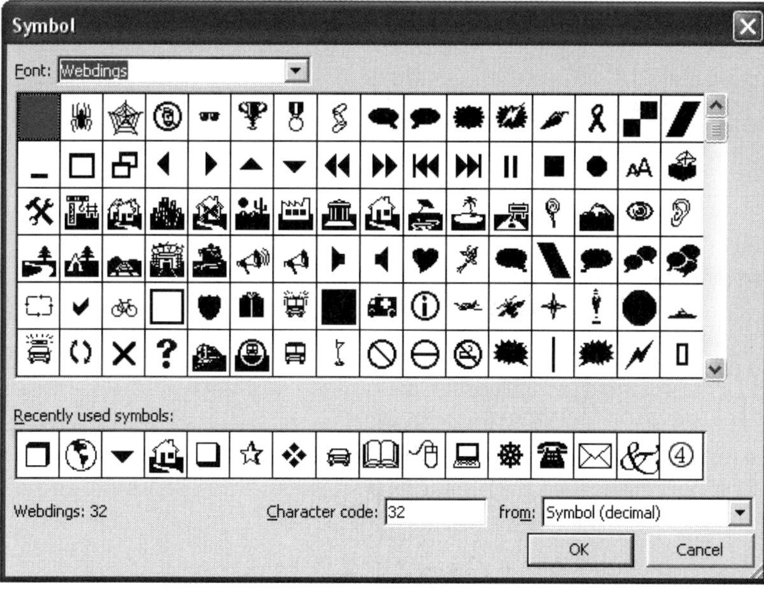

Figure 3.10 Symbol dialog box

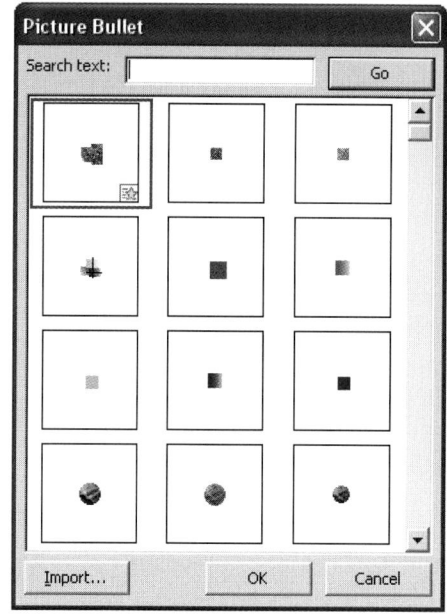

Figure 3.11 Picture Bullet dialog box

▶ To remove bullets, position the insertion point in the bulleted item or list level and click the Bullets button on the Formatting toolbar.

TRY *it* OUT *p3-5*

1. Start a new blank presentation.
2. Click the **New Slide** button to display a text slide layout.
3. Enter `Sales Overview` as the first bullet point.
4. Click **Format, Bullets and Numbering.**
5. Click a desired bulleted list style from those that are displayed.
6. Click **OK.**
7. Press the **Enter** key.
8. Press the **Tab** key.
9. Enter `Northeast` as the subbullet.
10. Right-click the mouse and select **Bullets and Numbering.**
11. Click **Customize.**
12. Select **Wingdings** from the Font list.
13. Click a bullet style.
14. Click **OK** twice.
15. Insert a new slide. Use a text slide layout.
16. Right-click the mouse in the text placeholder and select **Bullets and Numbering.**
17. Click **Picture.**
18. Click a bullet style, and click **OK.**
19. Enter `Marketing Strategies` as the bullet text for the first bullet.
20. Switch to Slide sorter view.
21. Delete **Slide 2.**
22. Display Normal view.
23. Do not close the presentation.

Insert Footers (Date and Time, Slide Numbers)

- A *footer* is the same text that appears at the bottom of every slide.
- You can include slide numbers, the date or time, and other text that you want in the footer area on individual or all slides.
- To insert a footer, click View, Header and Footer. In the Header and Footer dialog box that opens, as shown in Figure 3.12, click the appropriate check box to indicate whether you want to include the date and time, slide number, or footer. Enter the footer text in the appropriate box.

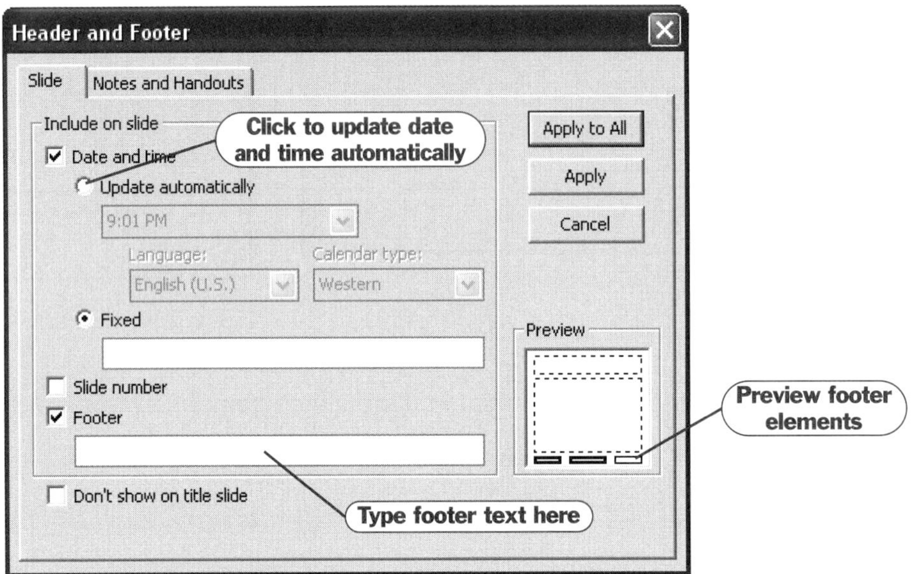

Figure 3.12 Header and Footer dialog box

- PowerPoint provides footer placeholders for this information. The date and time appear on the bottom left of the slide; footer text appears in the middle of the slide; and the slide number appears on the bottom right. You can move footer placeholders the same way you move any other placeholder (see preview window in Figure 3.12).
- To have the date or time update automatically each time you open the presentation, click the Update automatically option button. To insert a date or time that does not update automatically, click the Fixed option button and enter the date or time you want displayed.
- If you do not want your footer selections to appear on the title slide, click the Don't show on title slide check box.
- You can format the slide number, date and time, and footer text just like all other text within a placeholder.

TRY *it* OUT *p3-6*

Note: The first slide of the presentation from Try it Out 3-5 should be displayed.

1. Click **View, Header and Footer.**
2. On the **Slide** tab, click the **Date and time** check box to select it, if it is not already checked.
3. Click the **Fixed** option button, if necessary, and enter today's date in the Fixed text box.
4. Click the **Slide number** check box to select it.
5. Click the **Footer** check box to select it, if it is not already checked.
6. Enter your name in the Footer text box.
7. Click the **Don't show on title slide** check box.
8. Click **Apply to All.**
9. Run the slide show.
10. Close the file; do not save.

Work with the Slide and Title Master

- The *slide master* contains the default settings for all the slides in a presentation, except the title slide. The *title master* contains the default settings for the format of the title slide.
- By changing the content or formatting (font style, font size, color, position, tabs, indents, background, color scheme, or template) of text or object placeholders on the slide master, PowerPoint automatically reformats all slides throughout the active presentation. If you want to include clip art, your company's logo, or a saying or quote on all slides in your presentation, you can include it on the slide master. You can also include the date and time, footer text, and slide numbers on the slide master. Figure 3.13 shows a slide master.

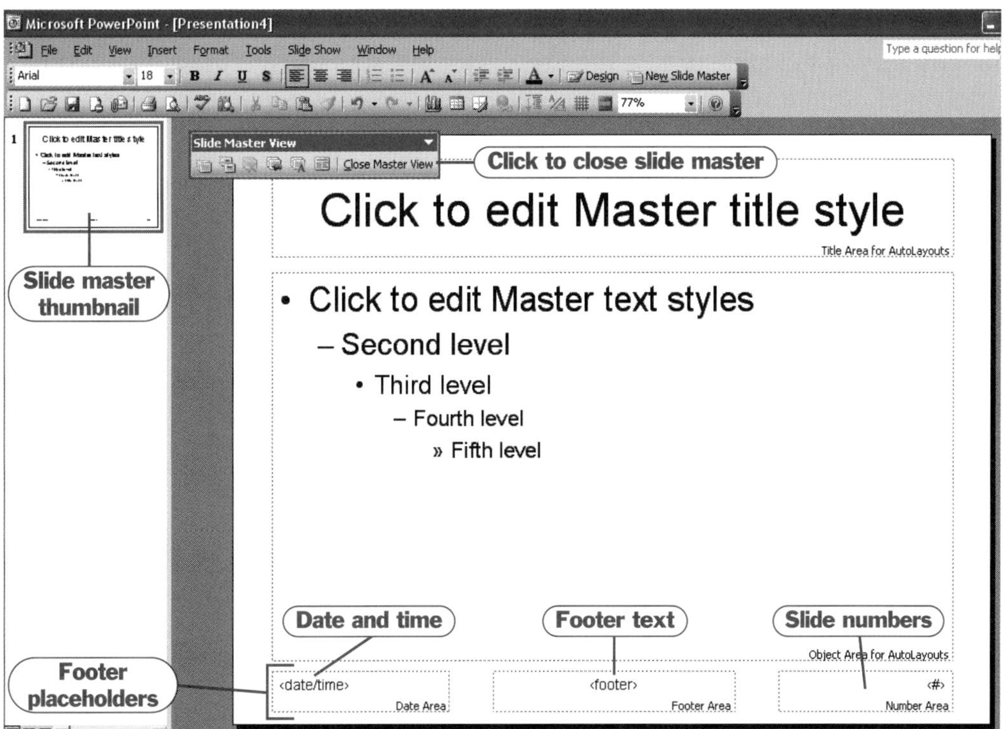

Figure 3.13 Slide master

- To access the slide master, click View, Master, Slide Master. A slide master thumbnail appears in a pane to the left of the slide master, replacing the Outline and Slides tab pane.
- Some design templates come with a slide and title master, whereas others come with only a slide master. You can, however, insert a title master to correspond with a slide master. To do so, click the Insert New Title Master button on the Slide Master View toolbar or right-click the slide master thumbnail and select New Title Master. A title master slide appears, on which you can make the changes you want.
- When you insert a title master, a gray line connects the title master thumbnail to its corresponding slide master thumbnail, forming a slide-title master pair, as shown in Figure 3.14.

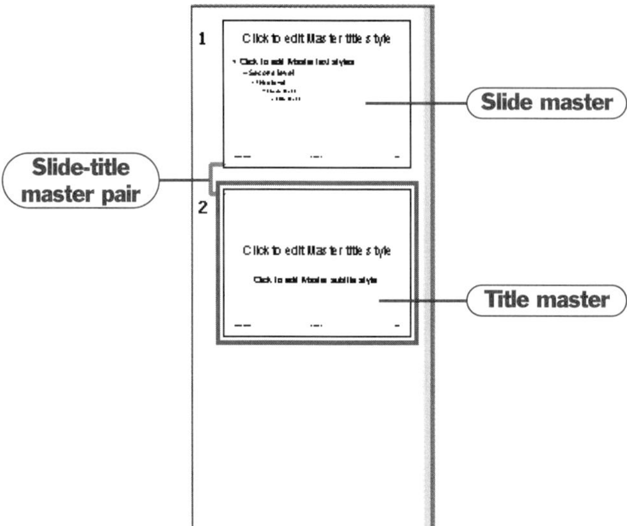

Figure 3.14 Slide-title master pair

- After making your changes to the slide or title master, click the Close Master View button on the Slide Master View toolbar to return to Normal view. The newly designed master appears as a thumbnail in the Slide Design task pane.
- Formatting changes you make to individual slides after you create the slide master override changes you made on the slide master. If you do not want slide master objects to appear on a particular slide, display the slide and click Format, Background. In the Background dialog box that opens, shown in Figure 3.15, click the Omit background graphics from master check box and click Apply.

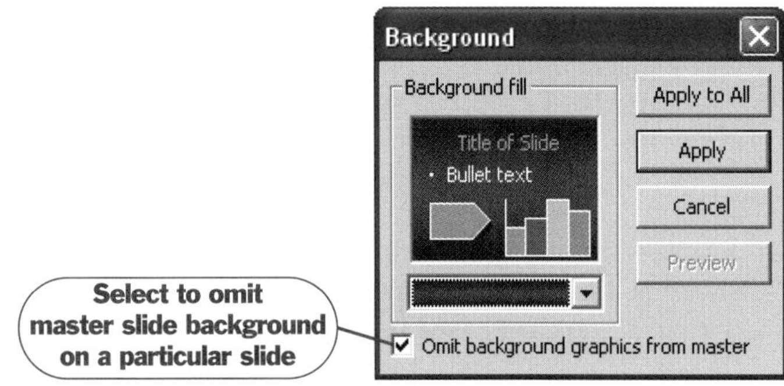

Figure 3.15 Background dialog box

- To delete a slide master or title master, select the master thumbnail in the left pane and click the Delete Master button on the Slide Master View toolbar. PowerPoint might automatically delete a slide master if, for example, slides that follow the master are deleted. To avoid losing a master while creating a presentation, select the master thumbnail you wish to preserve from the left pane and click the Preserve Master button on the Slide Master View toolbar.

TRY *it* OUT *p3-7*

1. Start a new blank presentation.
2. Click **View, Master,** and **Slide Master.**
3. Click **Click to edit the Master title style** and apply a green decorative font.
4. Click **Click to edit Master text styles** and apply a dark blue Times New Roman font.
5. Position the insertion point in the first bulleted item, if necessary.
6. Click **Format, Bullets and Numbering.**
7. Choose a different bullet symbol.
8. Click **OK.**
9. Click on the **Second level** text.
10. Click the **Italic** button.
11. Click the **Insert New Title Master** button.

12. Click the **Slide Master** thumbnail in the left pane.
13. Click **Insert, Picture, Clip Art.** Note: Be sure you have selected Clip Art in the Results should be list.
14. Enter `Tree` in the Search for text box, and click **Go.**
15. Click to select a graphic and place it in the bottom-right corner of the slide.
16. Click the **Close Master View** button.
17. Click the **New Slide** button.

18. Do not close the file.

Apply Multiple Slide Masters

- You can apply multiple slide designs within the same presentation. This is particularly useful if you want to differentiate or color-code certain sections or create custom shows within the presentation. (Using multiple slide masters within a custom show will be detailed in Task 3.)
- If you apply more than one design template to your presentation, several slide master pairs appear in the left pane—one for each slide design, as shown Figure 3.16.

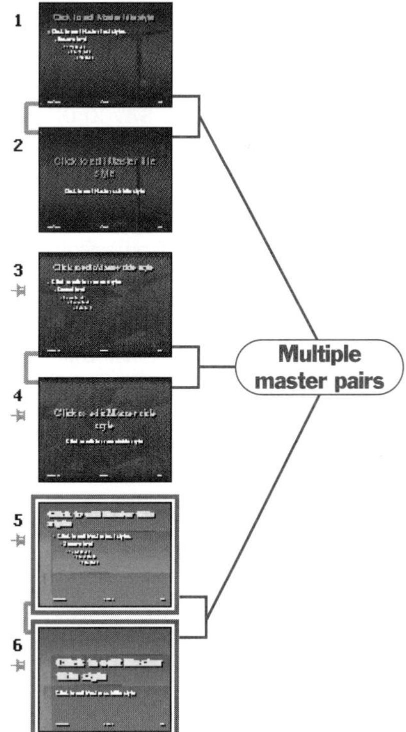

Figure 3.16 Multiple slide masters

TRY *it* OUT *p3-8*

Note: The presentation from Try it Out p3-7 should be displayed.

1. Click **View, Master,** and **Slide Master.**
2. Click the **Design** button.
3. Click the list arrow on the thumbnail of a design template displayed in the Slide Design task pane.
4. Click **Add Design.**
5. Click the list arrow on the thumbnail of another design template.
6. Click **Add Design.**
7. Click the **Close Master View** button.
8. Do not close the presentation.

Save as a Template

- You can save your presentation design or a slide master as a new *template*. You can then use the template to create new presentations or apply it to existing presentations.
- To save your presentation design as a template, click File, Save As. In the Save as dialog box that opens, as shown in Figure 3.17, enter a template name in the File name text box and select Design Template in the Save as type list box.
- If you have created multiple slide masters within a presentation and saved one of them as a template, PowerPoint saves all of the masters along with it. When you then apply the saved template, PowerPoint prompts you to copy either all of the masters into your presentation (they will all appear in the Slide Design task pane) or just the first master in the template.
- To apply a saved design template, click the Design button and click the Browse link at the bottom of the Slide Design task pane. In the Apply Design Template dialog box, double-click the desired template design, as shown in Figure 3.18. Once you apply your template design, it appears as a thumbnail in the Slide Design task pane, as shown in Figure 3.19.

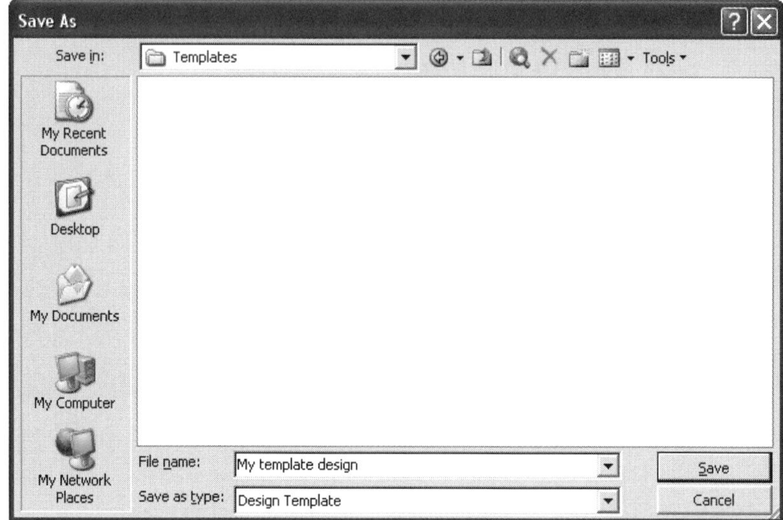

Figure 3.17 Save As dialog box

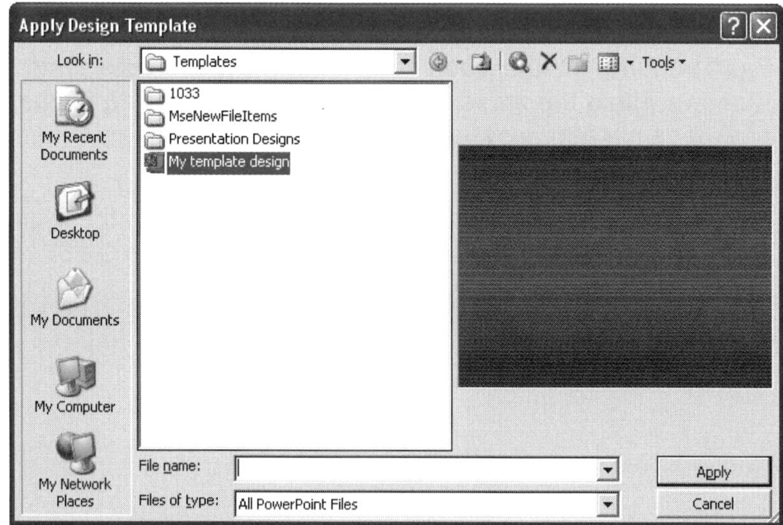

Figure 3.18 Apply Design Template dialog box

▶ You can apply multiple templates to a presentation so that slides appear with different slide designs. To do so, select the slides from the Slides tab or Slide sorter view on which to apply the particular template, click the slide thumbnail list arrow of the desired template design, as shown in Figure 3.20, and click Apply to Selected Slides.

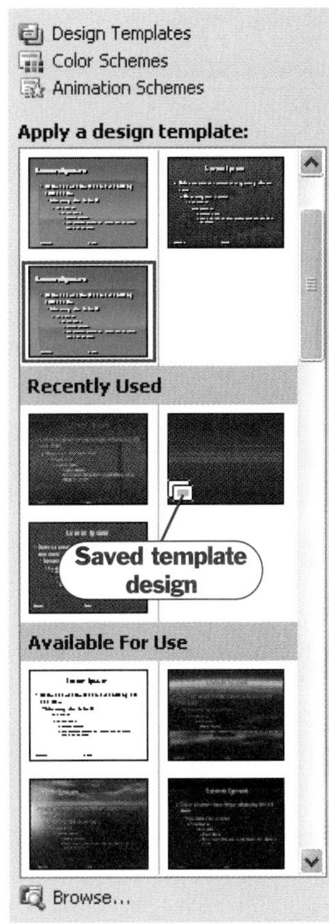

Figure 3.19 Slide design templates

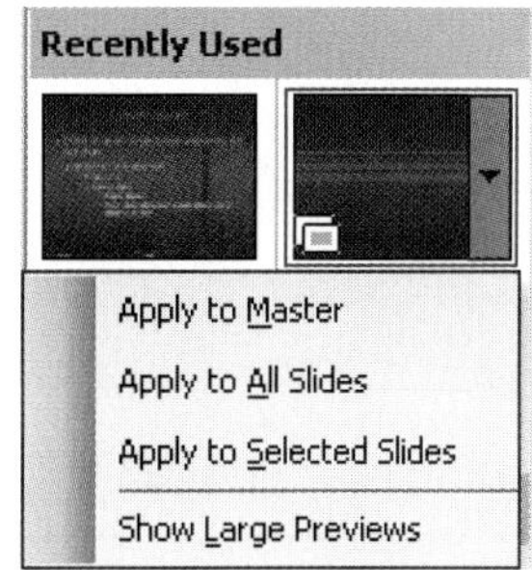

Figure 3.20 Apply template to selected slide

TRY *it* OUT *p3-9*

Note: The presentation from Try it Out p3-8 should be displayed.

1. Click **View, Master, Slide Master.**
2. Click the **slide master thumbnail** in the left pane of the master with the clip art that you selected in a previous exercise.
3. Click **File, Save As.**
4. Click the **Save as type** list arrow and choose **Design Template.**
5. Select the folder in which to place the template.
6. Enter `My Template` in the File name text box.
7. Click **Save.**
8. Close the presentation; do not save.
9. Start a new blank presentation.
10. Click the **Design** button.
11. Click the **Browse** link at the bottom of the Slide Design task pane.
12. Select the folder in which you saved My Template.
13. Click **My Template.**
14. Click **Apply.**
15. Click **Yes** when prompted to copy all of the masters into your presentation.
16. Click the **New Slide** button. 
17. Click the **Design** button.
18. Click the **Clouds** design template list arrow and click **Apply to Selected Slides.**
19. Close the file; do not save.

GOAL
To use the slide and title master to embellish a presentation, add fonts, change bullets, and save a custom template

SETTING THE STAGE/WRAPUP
File names:
3.2summerproposal.ppt
3.2summertemplate.pot

WHAT YOU NEED TO KNOW

- The title master defines the styles and layout for the title slide only. In addition to using the title slide as the first slide in a presentation, you can use it as a transition between presentation sections and/or as the last slide in a presentation.
- In this Rehearsal activity, you will edit the slide and title masters to enhance an existing sales presentation.

DIRECTIONS

1. Open **3.2summerproposal** from the Data CD.
2. View the slide master.
   a. Apply the Ocean design. Change the color scheme to turquoise blue.
   b. Insert a summer-related graphic in the top-right corner of the slide. Resize the title text placeholder if necessary.
   c. Change the master title font and color the new font dark blue.
   d. Change the bullet for the first level to a star; color it yellow.
   e. Change the bullet for the second level to a circle.
   f. Change the color of the third-level bullet to green.
   g. Enter `Proposal for Summer Event` as the footer text.
   h. Include the date in the footer to update automatically using the month, day, and year format (May 25, 2001) on all slides except the title slide.
3. Display Slide 8.
   a. Remove the graphic from the background for this slide only.
   b. Remove the bullet from the last line; center the text. Format the line spacing so that there is one line space between this line and the line before it.
4. View the title master.
   a. Insert a relevant graphic; place it and size it as required.
   b. Italicize the subtitle text.
5. Run the slide show, then print one copy of the presentation as handouts with four slides per page.
6. Save the presentation; name it **3.2summerproposal.yi** (yi = your initials) and save the presentation as a template; name it **3.2summertemplateyi** (yi = your initials) and close the file.
7. Start a new blank presentation and apply the **3.2summertemplateyi** design.

Continued on next page

8. Enter `Venture Investments Summer Outing` in the title placeholder.
9. Enter `Occasions Event Planning` in the subtitle placeholder.
10. Add a new text slide and apply the Ocean design template to Slide 2 only.
11. Enter `Getting Started` in the title placeholder. Enter the following in the bulleted text placeholder: **`Date, Approximate number of attendees, Budget, Venue, Menu, Entertainment.`**
12. Close the file; do not save.

POWERPOINT

1

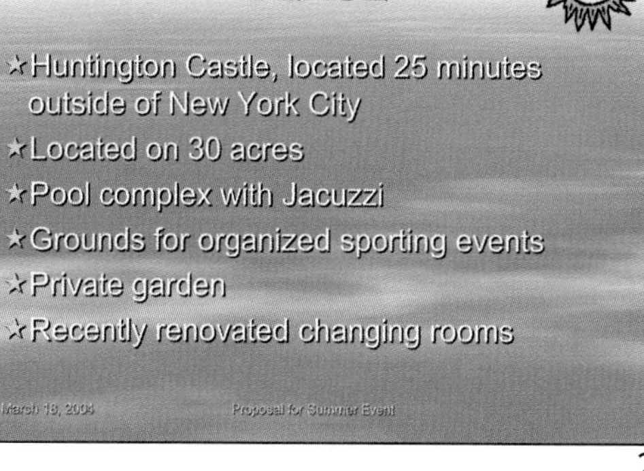

2

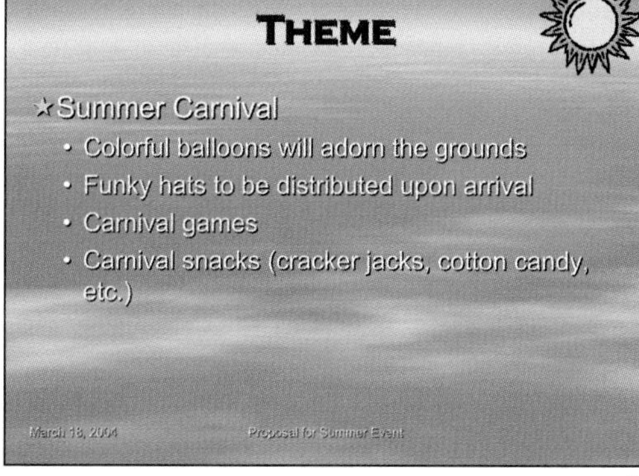

3

4

5

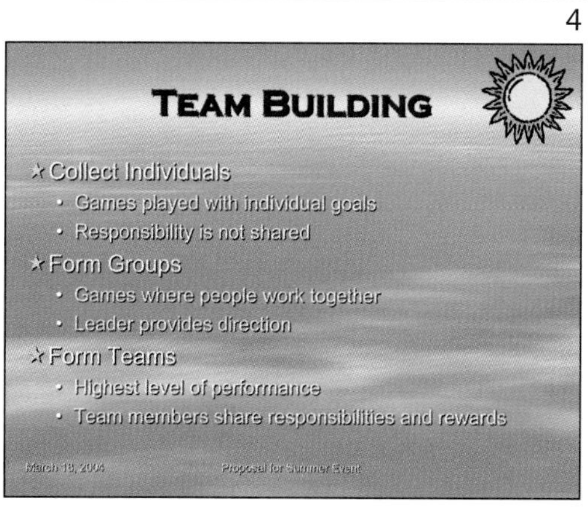

6

Next Steps

- Set date
- Exact number of attendees
- Calculate total costs and budgets
- Hire caterer
- Hire all aspects of entertainment
- Coordinate precise itinerary for the day

March 18, 2004 Proposal for Summer Event

7

Occasions Event Planners For Your Corporate Needs

- Top-notch service
- Proven record of success with Fortune 500 clients
- Flawless execution of events

"You say yes, we do the rest!"

March 18, 2004 Proposal for Summer Event

8

Cues for Reference

Format Bullets

1. Position the insertion point in the desired bulleted item or select several bulleted items.
2. Right-click and select **Bullets and Numbering** from the shortcut menu.

or

1. Click **Format.**
2. Click **Bullets and Numbering.**
3. Click a bulleted list style and click **OK.**

or

1. Click **Format.**
2. Click **Bullets and Numbering.**
3. Click **Customize.**
4. Click the **Font** list arrow.
5. Select a font.
6. Click a bullet style.
7. Click **OK** twice.

Turn Bullets On or Off

- Click the **Bullets** button.

Insert Page Numbers, Date and Time, and Other Footer Text

1. Click **View.**
2. Click **Header and Footer.**
3. Click the **Slide** tab.
4. Click **Date and time** to insert the date or time.
5. Click **Update automatically.**

   or

   a. Click **Fixed.**
   b. Click in the **Fixed** text box and enter the date and/or time.
6. Click **Slide number** to add slide numbers.
7. Click **Footer.**
8. Click in the **Footer** text box and enter the footer text.
9. Click **Don't show on title slide** to omit the footer from the title slide.
10. Click **Apply to All.**

    or

    Click **Apply.**

Use Slide and Title Master

1. Click **View.**
2. Click **Master.**
3. Click **Slide Master.**
4. Format font, size, alignment, slide background, color scheme, and other enhancements.
5. If necessary, click the **Insert New Title Master** button on the Slide Master View toolbar to add a corresponding title master.
6. Make the desired changes.
7. Click the **Close Master View** button.

Omit Master Slide Object

1. Display the slide on which to omit the Slide Master object.
2. Click **Format.**
3. Click **Background.**
4. Select **Omit background graphics from master.**
5. Click **Apply.**

Save as Template

1. Click **File.**
2. Click **Save As.**
3. Click the **Save as type** list arrow and select **Design Template.**
4. Click in the **File name** text box and enter the desired template file name.
5. Click **Save.**

Apply Saved Template

1. Click the **Design** button.
2. Click the **Browse** link.
3. Double-click the required template.

Apply Template to Selected Slides

1. Display the slide on which to apply the template.
2. Click the **Design** button.
3. Click the required template's slide thumbnail list arrow.
4. Click **Apply to Selected Slides.**

GOAL
To practice using the following skill sets:
- Create a custom show
  - Link to a custom show
  - Link a table of contents slide to a custom show

WHAT YOU NEED TO KNOW

Create a Custom Show

- A *custom show* is a group of related slides within a presentation that you can deliver independently of the entire presentation. Think of a custom show as a presentation within a presentation. Custom shows are useful if you want to show different audiences slides that pertain only to them.
- To create a custom show, open the presentation you want to customize. Then click Slide Show, Custom Shows. In the Custom Shows dialog box that opens, as shown in Figure 3.21, click the New button to specify a new custom show.

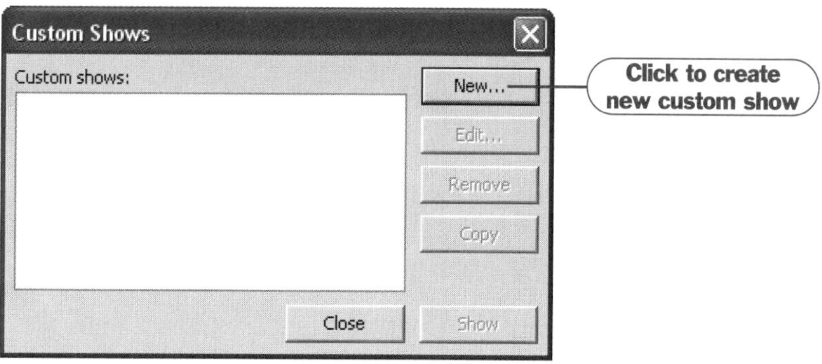

Figure 3.21 Custom Shows dialog box

- In the Define Custom Show dialog box that opens, as shown in Figure 3.22, all the slides in the presentation appear in the Slides in presentation box. Click each slide you want to include in the custom show and click the Add button. (To select multiple slides, hold down the Ctrl key as you click each slide.) Enter a name in the Slide show name box to name the custom show.
- You can change the order of the slides in the Slides in custom show box by selecting the slide to move and clicking the up or down arrow buttons. To remove a slide from the custom show, click the slide and click the Remove button.

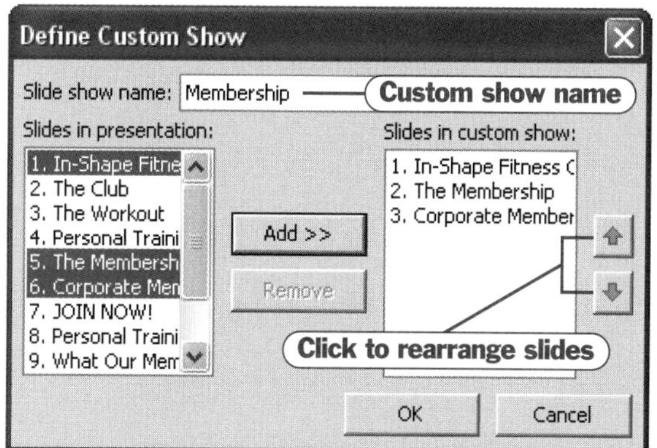

Figure 3.22 Define Custom Show dialog box

- Once you create a custom show, it appears in the Custom Shows dialog box, as shown in Figure 3.23. You can create multiple custom shows by repeating the procedures above.

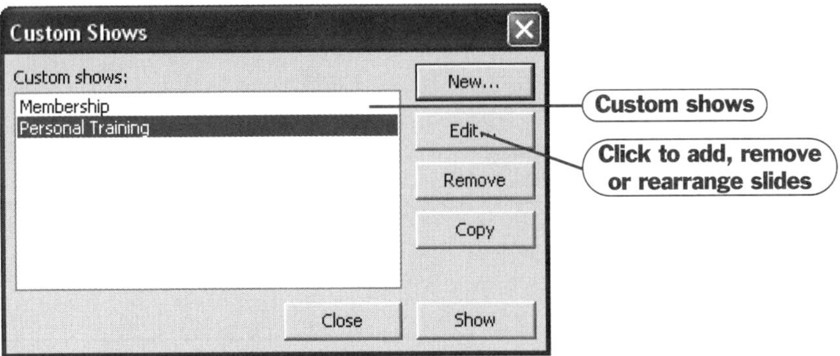

Figure 3.23 Custom Shows dialog box

- You can also add, remove, or rearrange slides in a previously created custom show. Click the custom show you want to edit in the Custom Shows dialog box, click the Edit button, as shown in Figure 3.23, and make any changes in the Define Custom Show dialog box.
- To delete a show, select the show to delete and click Remove.
- To preview the custom show from the dialog box, select the custom show, and click the Show button. This begins a slide show of only the slides in the specified custom show.
- To set up a slide show to run only the slides in a custom show rather than all the slides in the presentation, click Slide Show, Set Up Show. In the Set Up Show dialog box that opens, as shown in Figure 3.24, click the Custom show option, click the Custom show list arrow to select the custom show, and click OK. Then click the Slide Show View button to run the slide show. Note: The Custom Show option is only available if Custom Shows have been set up.
- You can also run a custom show at any time during a slide show. Click the Slide Show View button to run the slide show. Then, right-click the mouse, select Custom Show, and click the custom show you want to run, as shown in Figure 3.25. The slide show advances to the selected custom show and runs the slide show from that point forward.

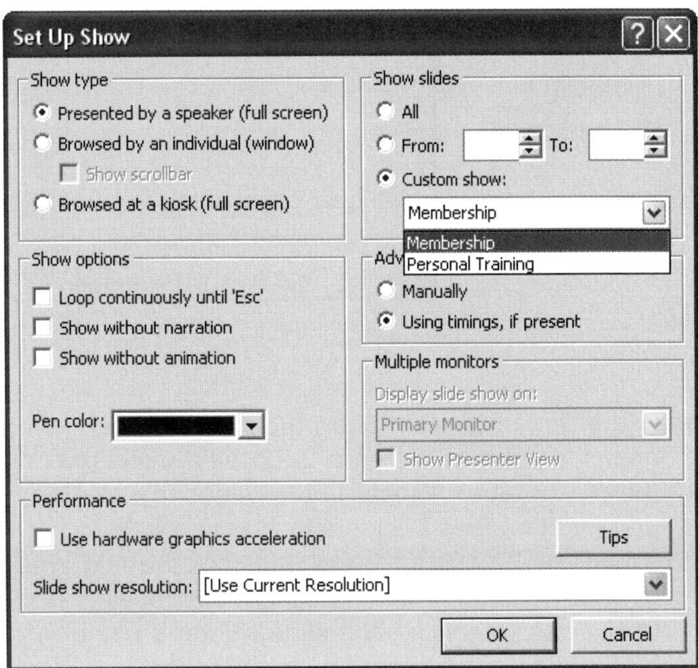

Figure 3.24 Set Up Show dialog box

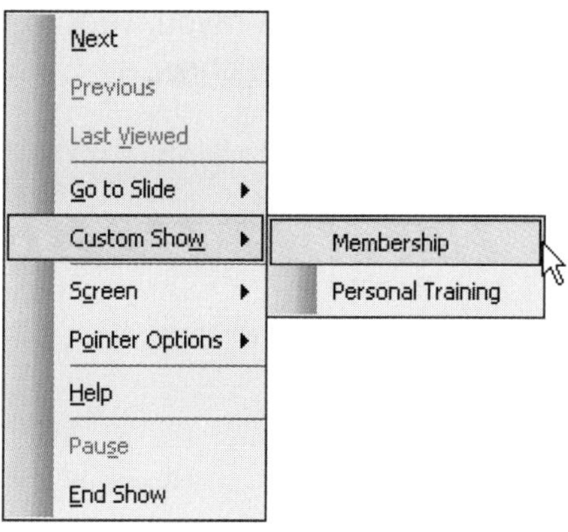

Figure 3.25 Run a custom show from Slide show view

POWERPOINT

TRY it OUT *p3-10*

1. Open **p3.10inshape** from the Data CD.
2. Click **Slide Show, Custom Shows.**
3. Click the **New** button, click in the **Slide show name** box, if necessary, and enter: `Membership.`
4. Press and hold down the **Ctrl** key while you click **Slides 1, 5,** and **6** in the Slides in presentation box.
5. Click the **Add** button and click **OK.**
6. Click the **Edit** button, click **Slide 2** in the Slides in custom show box, click the **down arrow** once, and click **OK.**
7. Click the **New** button, click in the **Slide show name** box if necessary, and enter: `Personal Training.`
8. Press and hold down the **Ctrl** key while you click **Slides 8-12** in the Slides in presentation box.
9. Click the **Add** button and click **OK.**
10. Click the **Membership** custom show and click the **Show** button. View all slides in the Membership custom show.
11. Click **Slide Show, Custom Shows.**
12. Click the **Membership** custom show if necessary, click the **Remove** button, and click **Close.**
13. Click the **Slide Show View** button, right-click the mouse, select **Custom Show,** and click **Personal Training.** View all slides in the Personal Training custom show.
14. Click **Slide Show, Set Up Show.**
15. Click the **Custom show** option, click the **Personal Training** custom show, and click **OK.**
16. Click the **Slide Show View** button and view all slides in the Personal Training custom show.
17. Close the presentation; do not save.

Link to a Custom Show

- A presentation might begin with generic slides containing information for all audiences and link to different custom shows with information for specific audiences.
- To create a hyperlink on text or objects to link to a custom show, you must first create the custom show using the procedures described above. Then, use the procedures learned previously to create the hyperlink. In the Insert Hyperlink dialog box, click the Place in This Document button, and select the custom show from the Select a place in this document box, as

shown in Figure 3.26. Select the Show and return option if you want to return automatically to the slide that contained the link after viewing the custom show.

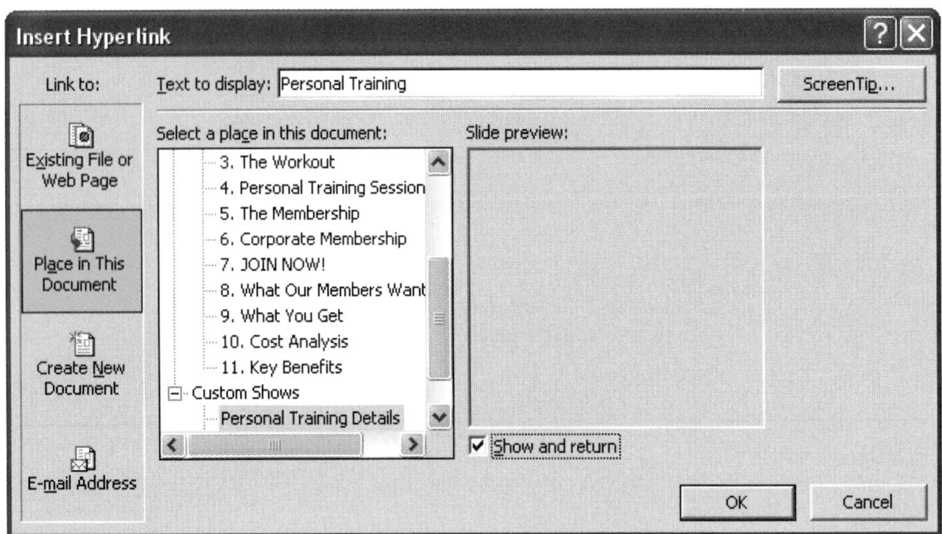

Figure 3.26 Insert Hyperlink dialog box

- Depending on the order in which you plan to present your slides and custom shows, you might have to hide the custom show slides so that they do not appear twice during the slide show (once with the custom show and once as slides in the presentation). Run the slide show and test the hyperlinks before determining whether or not you need to hide slides.

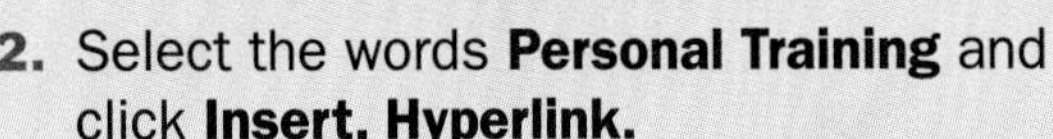

1. Open **p3.11customshows** from the Data CD and display **Slide 4 (Personal Training Sessions Will...).**
2. Select the words **Personal Training** and click **Insert, Hyperlink.**
3. Click the **Place in This Document** button and select the **Personal Training Details** custom show from the Select a place in this document box.
4. Click the **Show and return** option and click **OK.**
5. Display the **Slides** tab and select **Slides 8-11.**
6. Click **Slide Show, Hide Slide.**
7. Display **Slide 1.**
8. Click the **Slide Show View** button.

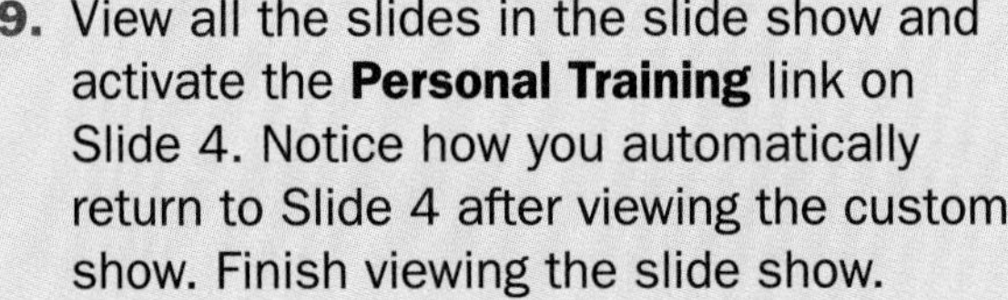

9. View all the slides in the slide show and activate the **Personal Training** link on Slide 4. Notice how you automatically return to Slide 4 after viewing the custom show. Finish viewing the slide show.
10. Close the presentation; do not save.

Link the Table of Contents Slide to a Custom Show

- As learned previously, you can use the Summary Slide feature to create a table of contents slide. This is useful when working with custom shows since you can list the main sections of your presentation and link each item in the contents slide to jump to a different custom show in your presentation. Figure 3.27 illustrates this concept.

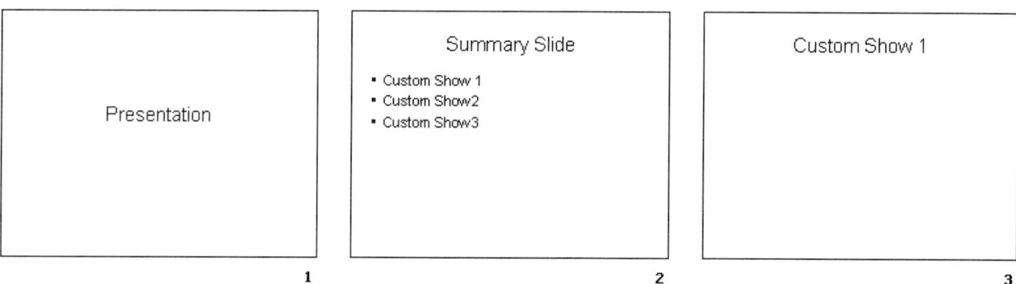

Figure 3.27 Links to custom shows from the table of contents slide

POWERPOINT

▶ To create a hyperlink from each table of contents item to its corresponding custom show and automatically return to the contents slide, select the item, and click Slide Show, Action Settings. In the Action Settings dialog box that opens, as shown in Figure 3.28, click the Hyperlink to button and select Custom Show from the Hyperlink to drop-down list. This opens the Link To Custom Show dialog box, as shown in Figure 3.29. Select the show to which you want to link, click the Show and return box, and click OK twice. You can also create a hyperlink from each bulleted item to its custom show by using the Insert, Hyperlink procedure.

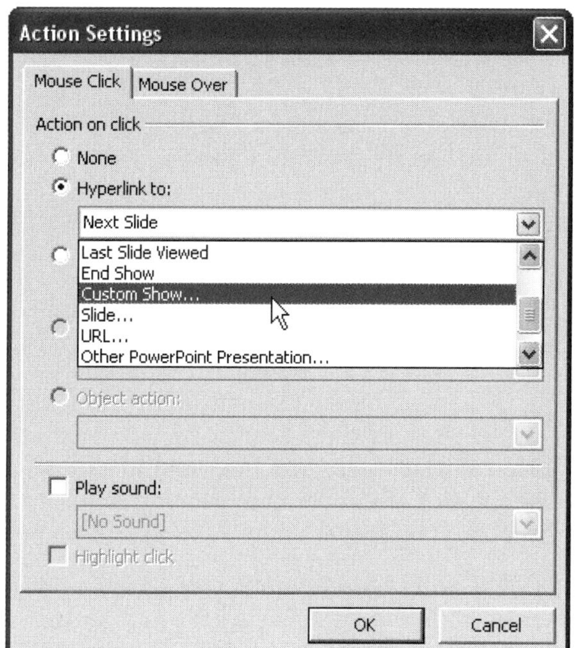

Figure 3.28 Action Settings dialog box

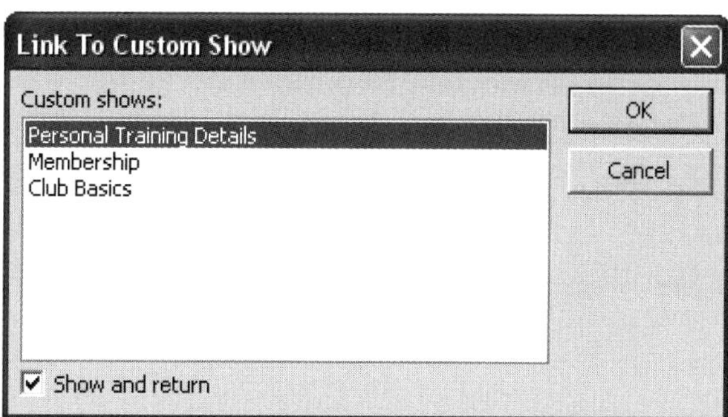

Figure 3.29 Link To Custom Show dialog box

▶ Create a table of contents slide after you complete the entire presentation.

TRY it OUT *p3-12*

1. Open **p3.12customshows** from the Data CD.
2. Click the **Slide Sorter View** button.
3. Click **Slide 2** and press and hold down the **Ctrl** key as you click **Slides 5** and **8.** Then click the **Summary Slide** button.

4. Double-click **Slide 2 (Summary Slide).**
5. Change the last bullet to read: `Personal Training.`
6. Move **The Membership** to become Bullet 3. When you do so, "Personal Training" should automatically become Bullet 2.
7. Select **The Club** and click **Slide Show, Action Settings.**
8. Click the **Hyperlink to** button and select **Custom Show** from the list.
9. Click the **Club Basics** custom show, click the **Show and return** box, and click **OK** twice.
10. Repeat the procedures in Steps 7 through 9 to link Personal Training to the Personal Training Details custom show and The Membership to the Membership custom show. Do not click the Show and return box when linking to the Membership custom show.
11. Click **Slide Show, Custom Shows.**
12. Click **Personal Training Details** and click the **Edit** button.
13. Click **Summary Slide** in the Slides in custom show box and click **Remove.** Then click **OK** and **Close.**
14. Display **Slide 1** and run the slide show.
15. On Slide 2 (the summary slide), click **The Club** link and play The Club custom show.
16. When you return to Slide 2, click the **Personal Training** link to play the Personal Training Details custom show.
17. When you return to Slide 2 again, play the **Membership** custom show.
18. Do not close the presentation.

Use Multiple Masters within a Custom Show

- As you learned previously, PowerPoint allows you to create multiple slide and title masters that you can apply within the same presentation. This is especially useful if you are creating different sections, or custom shows, in a presentation.
- Remember, to create more than one slide master, click View, select Master, and click Slide Master. On the Slide Master View toolbar that appears, shown in Figure 3.30, click the Insert New Slide Master button. A blank master appears in the left pane and you can format it as you want.

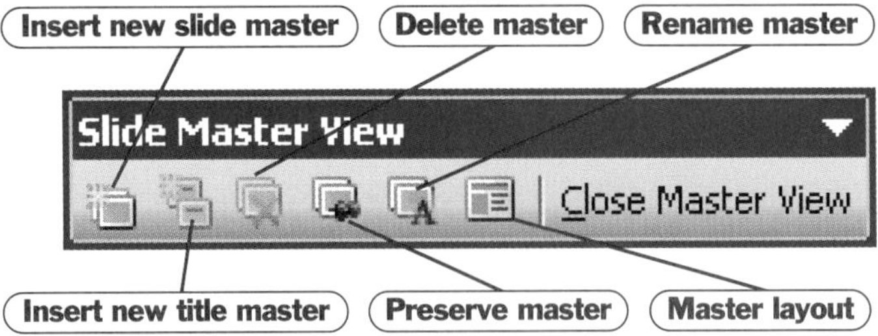

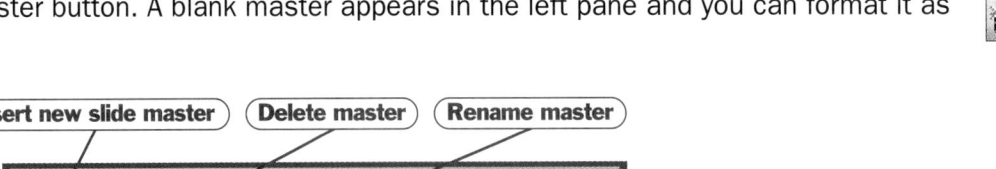

Figure 3.30 Slide Master View toolbar

TRY *it* OUT *p3-13*

Note: ***p3.12customshows*** *should still be open on your screen.*

1. Click **View, Master,** and **Slide Master.**
2. Click **Insert, Duplicate Slide Master.**
3. Right-click the **slide master** thumbnail of the new slide-title master pair and click **Slide Design.**
4. Click the **Color Schemes** link in the Slide Design task pane.
5. Click a thumbnail to apply a different color scheme.
6. Select the **Title** text on the new slide master and apply a new font style and font color to complement the color scheme.
7. Click the **Rename Master** button and name the master: `Personal Training.`
8. Click **Rename.**
9. Click **Close Master View.**
10. Click the **Slides** tab if necessary, and select **Slides 9, 10, 11,** and **12.**
11. Click the **Design Templates** link in the Slide Design task pane.
12. Click the **Personal Training** thumbnail list arrow and click **Apply to Selected Slides.**
13. Display **Slide 2,** run the slide show, and activate each link to its respective custom show.
14. Close the presentation; do not save.

REHEARSAL

Again

TASK 3

GOAL

To create a sales presentation using custom shows and multiple slide masters

SETTING THE STAGE/WRAPUP

File name: **3.3landscaping**

WHAT YOU NEED TO KNOW

- It is useful to create and apply multiple slide masters when you want to differentiate sections within a presentation.
- In this Rehearsal activity, you will create a 17-slide presentation to sell the services of Green Brothers Gardening to property owners.

DIRECTIONS

1. Start a new presentation and apply the Maple design template. (If the Maple design template is not available, select a template with a nature theme.)
2. Apply a green color scheme to the design template.
3. Display the **Slide Master.**
   a. Change the title font to a bright green sans serif font; change the subtitle text to a white sans-serif font.
   b. Change the Level 1 bullet to ❖, and color it pink; change the Level 2 bullet to • and color it light yellow.
   c. Insert today's date as fixed on all slides except the title slide.
   d. Create a text box and insert the words `Green Brothers` in any desired font; position it in the lower-right of the slide. Apply a pink border line and a light green fill color.
4. Create the slides shown in the following illustration.
5. Duplicate the original slide master.
   a. Rename the new master: `Garden Types.`
   b. Apply an orange color scheme to the new slide master.
   c. Color the title text a dark orange and the subtitle text white.
   d. Edit the Green Brothers text box on the master. Change the outline color to dark orange and the inside color to yellow.
   e. Change the color of the Levels 1 and 2 bullets to coordinate with the color scheme.
6. Create a custom show for Slides 5 through 10; name it: `Services.`
7. Create a custom show for Slides 11 through 16; name it: `Garden Types.`
8. Apply the Garden Types slide master to the Garden Types custom show (Slides 11 through 16).

Continued on next page

9. Display **Slide 4** ("What We Do").
   a. Create a hyperlink on the word **Services** to link to the **Services** custom show. Choose to show the custom show and return to the linked slide.
   b. Create a hyperlink on the words **Custom Gardening** to link to the **Garden Types** custom show. Choose to show the custom show and return to the linked slide.
   c. Create a hyperlink on the words **Contact us** to link to the last slide in the presentation.
10. Display **Slide 1** and run the slide show. Activate the links on Slide 4.
11. Save the presentation as **3.3landscaping**.

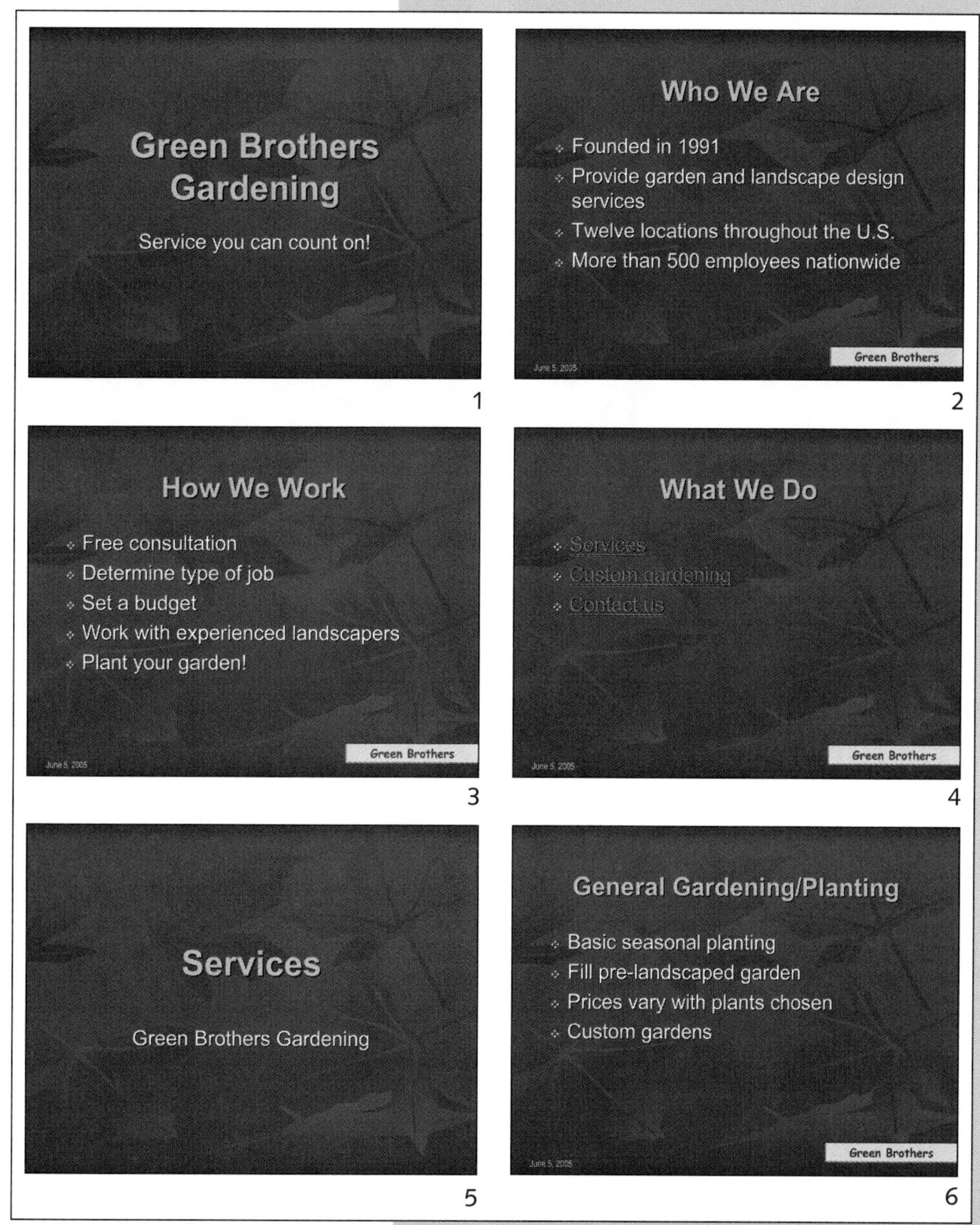

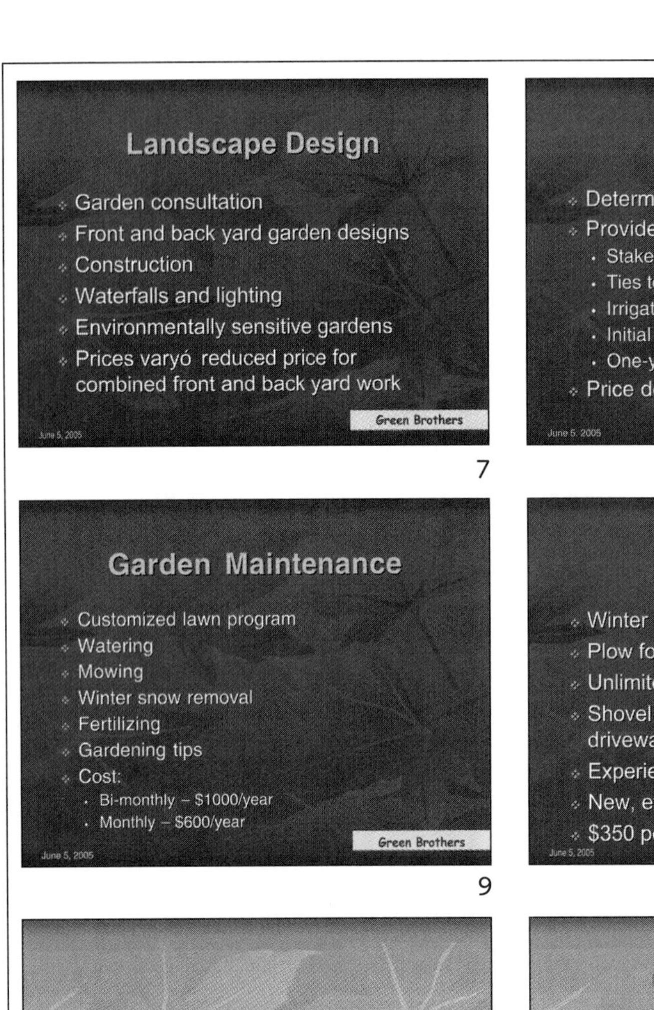

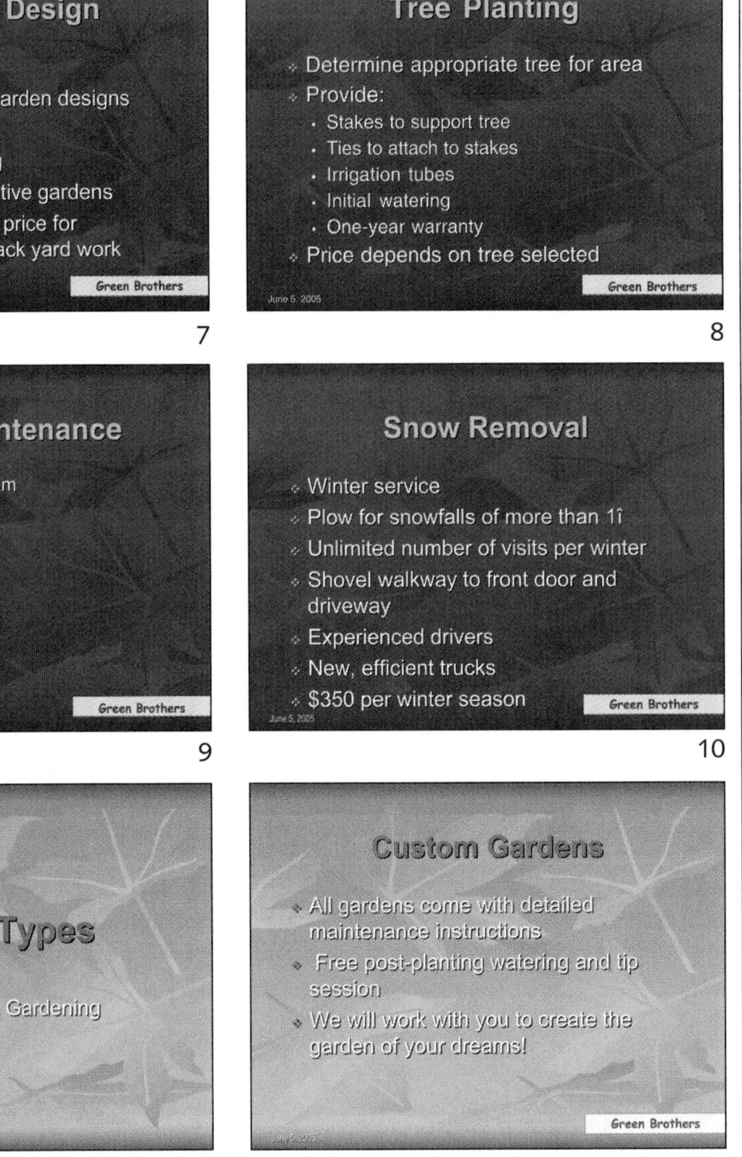

Landscape Design
Garden consultation
Front and back yard garden designs
Construction
Waterfalls and lighting
Environmentally sensitive gardens
Prices varyó reduced price for combined front and back yard work
Green Brothers
June 5, 2005
7
Tree Planting
Determine appropriate tree for area
Provide:
Stakes to support tree
Ties to attach to stakes
Irrigation tubes
Initial watering
One-year warranty
Price depends on tree selected
Green Brothers
June 5, 2005
8
Garden Maintenance
Customized lawn program
Watering
Mowing
Winter snow removal
Fertilizing
Gardening tips
Cost:
Bi-monthly – $1000/year
Monthly – $600/year
Green Brothers
June 5, 2005
9
Snow Removal
Winter service
Plow for snowfalls of more than 1î
Unlimited number of visits per winter
Shovel walkway to front door and driveway
Experienced drivers
New, efficient trucks
$350 per winter season
Green Brothers
June 5, 2005
10
Garden Types
Green Brothers Gardening
11
Custom Gardens
All gardens come with detailed maintenance instructions
Free post-planting watering and tip session
We will work with you to create the garden of your dreams!
Green Brothers
12

Summer Perennials

- Colorful arrangement of drifts
- Plant species selected for complementary colors and textures
- Tall plants in back, smaller plants in front
- Ideal locations:
  - Terrace
  - Pool
  - Lawnis edge

Green Brothers

13

Shade/Sun

Shade Garden

- Colorful species selected especially for shaded areas
- Perfect for the shady side of the pool or along a fence

Sunny Garden

- Colorful, with upright flowers and shrubs
- Perfect on a hillside, near rocky terrain, or near boulders

Green Brothers

14

Cutting Garden

- Perennials, bulbs, and annuals
- Plants to cut for your own floral arrangements
- Garden layout
  - Paths provide easy access to plants
  - Perennials and annuals grown separately

Green Brothers

15

Vegetable Garden

- Up to 30 different kinds of vegetables
- Special flowering plants to keep pests away
- Comes with customized recipes, depending on the vegetables you select for your garden
- Layout provides easy access to vegetables

Green Brothers

16

Arrange for your free consultation TODAY!

Call us at 703-555-0005

Green Brothers Gardening

17

Cues for Reference

Create a Custom Show

1. Open presentation you want to customize.
2. Click **Slide Show, Custom Shows.**
3. Click **New** button.
4. Click each slide to add to custom show and click **Add.**
5. Click in **Slide show name** box and enter name for custom show.
6. Click **OK.**
7. Click **Close.**

Link to a Custom Show

1. Select text or object to link to a custom show.
2. Click **Insert, Hyperlink.**
3. Click **Place in This Document** button.
4. Click custom show.
5. Click **Show and return** box to select it.
6. Click **OK.**

Create a Table of Contents Slide

1. Click **Slide Sorter View** button.
2. Press and hold down **Ctrl key** and click first slide of each custom show.
3. Click **Summary Slide** button.

POWERPOINT

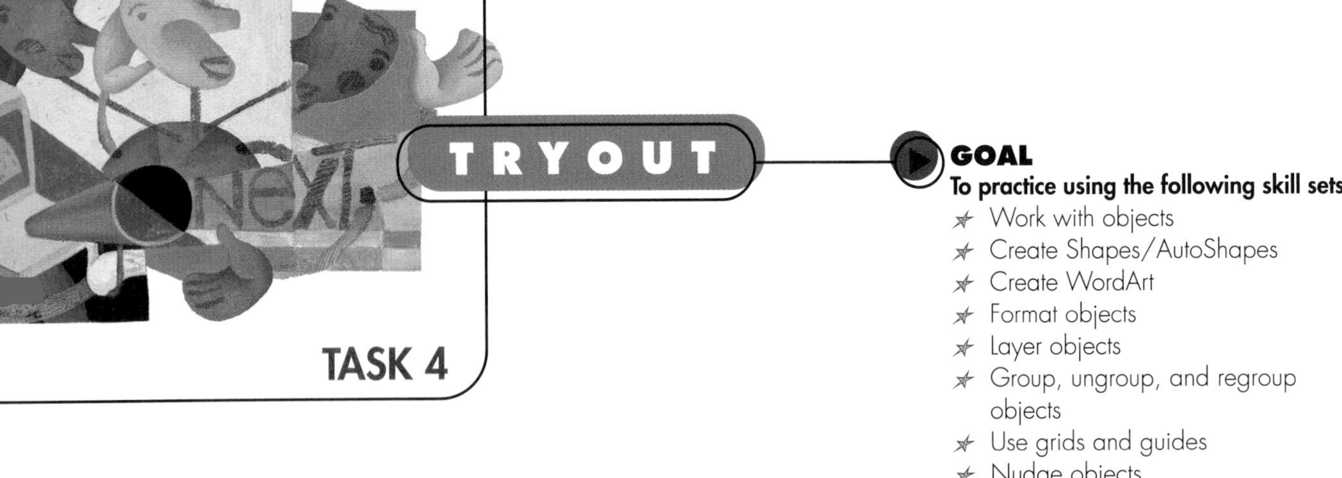

GOAL

To practice using the following skill sets:

- Work with objects
- Create Shapes/AutoShapes
- Create WordArt
- Format objects
- Layer objects
- Group, ungroup, and regroup objects
- Use grids and guides
- Nudge objects
- Align or distribute objects
- Use Action buttons

WHAT YOU NEED TO KNOW

Work with Objects

- As you learned in Word, objects include clip art, photographs, shapes, lines, charts, diagrams, tables, and video and sound clips. These same elements may be used on PowerPoint slides to visually and audibly enhance a presentation. You will learn to use tables, charts, diagrams, and media clips in Lesson 4.
- Objects generally behave the same way in every application. That is, you can edit (move, copy, delete, size, and rotate) and format (change fill and border lines) objects using the same techniques you learned previously.

Create Shapes and AutoShapes

- Use drawing tools to create simple objects or designs on your slides. Drawing tools are found on the Drawing toolbar, as shown in Figure 3.31, which appears only in Normal and Slide master views. To display the Drawing toolbar, click View, Toolbars, and Drawing.

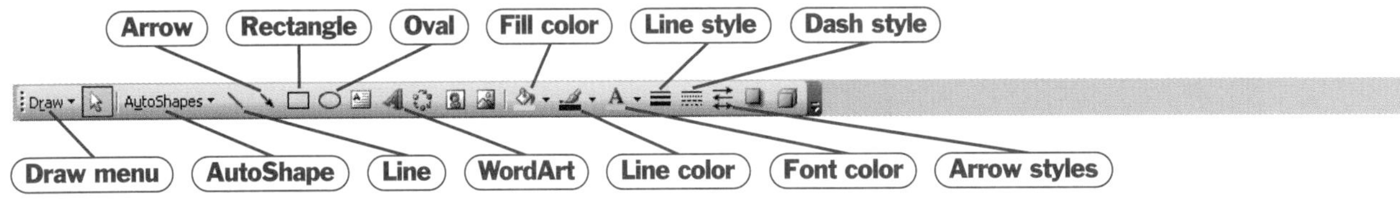

Figure 3.31 Drawing toolbar

- *AutoShapes* are predesigned shapes and symbols. When you click AutoShapes on the Drawing toolbar, several menus containing a variety of shapes and other objects appear, as shown in Figure 3.32. Each menu has a move handle that you can click and drag away from the pop-up menu to make it into its own floating toolbar.

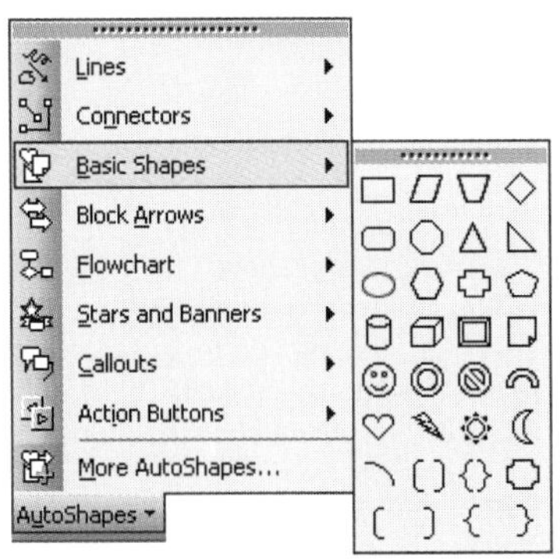

Figure 3.32 AutoShapes menu

▶ To draw an object, click the Drawing toolbar button for the object you want to draw. Click and drag the mouse pointer (now a crosshair) to the point where you want the object to end. Like clip art, the object appears with sizing and rotate handles.

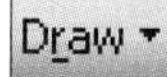

▶ Most drawing objects have an adjustment handle that allows you to alter the shape, but not the size, of the object, as shown in Figure 3.33.

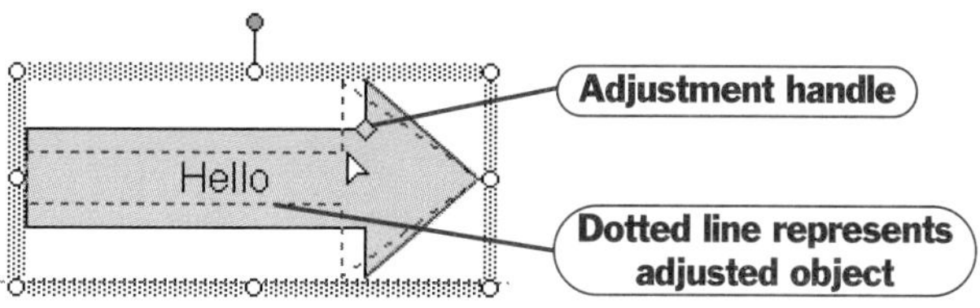

Figure 3.33 AutoShape with an adjustment handle

▶ You can add text to an AutoShape. The text attaches to the shape and moves or rotates with the shape. To add text to an AutoShape, click the shape and enter the text (see Figure 3.33).

POWERPOINT

TRY *it* OUT *p3-14*

1. Start a new blank presentation.
2. Click **View, Toolbars.** Click **Drawing** to display the Drawing toolbar, if it is not already displayed.
3. Click the **Blank** slide layout.
4. Click the **Rectangle** button.
5. Click and drag the mouse anywhere on the slide to draw a rectangle.
6. Click the **Oval** button.
7. Press the **Shift** key while you click and drag the mouse anywhere on the slide to draw a perfect circle.
8. Click the **Arrow** button.
9. Click and drag the mouse to draw an upward-pointing arrow.
10. Click the **AutoShapes** button.

11. Select **Stars and Banners.**
12. Drag the move handle to create a Stars and Banners floating toolbar.
13. Click the **Down Ribbon** object to select it, if necessary, and size it so that it is longer than it is wide.
14. Click and drag the **top adjustment handle** down to make the ribbon thinner.
15. Click the **Down Ribbon** object, if necessary, and enter: `Congratulations.`
16. Click the **Close** button on the Stars and Banners toolbar.
17. Close the file; do not save.

Create WordArt

- *WordArt* lets you create a graphic object with text.
- To create WordArt, click the Insert WordArt button on the Drawing toolbar. In the WordArt Gallery dialog box that appears, shown in Figure 3.34, click the effect that you want to apply to the text and click OK.

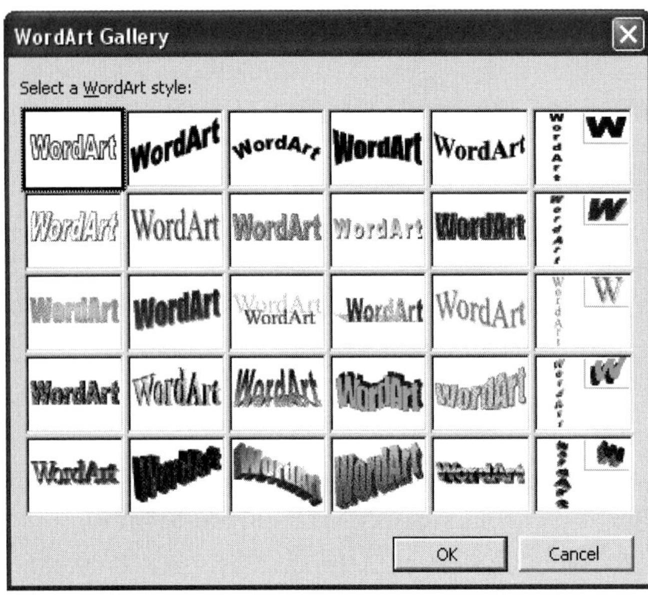

Figure 3.34 WordArt Gallery dialog box

- In the Edit WordArt Text dialog box that follows, shown in Figure 3.35, enter the WordArt text in the Text box and select a font, font size, and font style (bold or italic) and click OK.

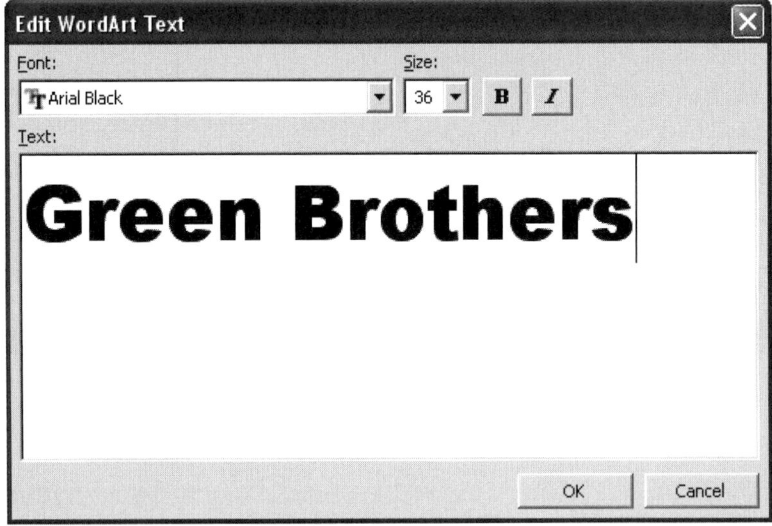

Figure 3.35 Edit WordArt Text dialog box

- Once WordArt is on the slide, you can edit it further by selecting the appropriate button on the WordArt toolbar. You can change the fill color, line color, width, and text size. In addition, you can change the WordArt shape and edit the size and spacing of the letters.

TRY *it* OUT *p3-15*

Note: Start a new blank presentation.

1. Display the Drawing toolbar if it is not already displayed.
2. Click the **New** button.
3. Click the **Blank** slide layout.
4. Click the **Insert WordArt** button on the Drawing toolbar.
5. Click any WordArt style and click **OK.**
6. Enter your first name in the Text box.
7. Click the **Font** list arrow and select **Arial** and click **OK.**
8. Click and drag the WordArt object to the top of the slide.
9. Click and drag a corner handle to make it larger.
10. Click the **Edit Text** button on the WordArt toolbar.

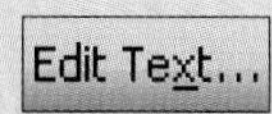

11. Move the insertion point to the end of your first name and press the **Enter** key.
12. Enter your last name and click **OK.**
13. Close the file; do not save.

Format Objects

- You can format objects in PowerPoint using the same techniques you used for placeholders and clip art. You can change a shape's fill color or pattern, or you can change the color, pattern, or thickness of the line around a shape as shown in Figure 3.36.

Figure 3.36 Object with new fill color and line style

- The table below reviews the formatting you can apply to objects in PowerPoint. Remember, there are several ways you can apply formatting. Regardless of the procedure you use, you must always select the object first before formatting it.
- You can use the menus (click Format AutoShape, or Object, or Textbox, etc., and make your changes in the dialog box). This method allows you to make several formatting selections at once.
- You can right-click the object and select formatting options from the shortcut menu.
- You can use the tools found on the Drawing toolbar to format the object.

FORMATTING OPTION	PROCEDURE
Fill Color or Pattern	Click the **Fill color** button on the Drawing toolbar or make change in the Format dialog box. The color choices that appear are those that complement the color scheme of the presentation. To choose a color other than those displayed, select More Fill Colors.
Font Color	Click the **Font color** button on the Drawing toolbar or make change in the Format dialog box.
Line Color	Click the **Line color** button on the Drawing toolbar or make change in the Format dialog box.
Line Thickness	Click the **Line style** button on the Drawing toolbar or make change in the Format dialog box.
Line Type (dotted, dashed, straight)	Click the **Dash style** button on the Drawing toolbar or make change in the Format dialog box.
Shadow	Click the **Shadow style** button on the Drawing toolbar or make change in the Format dialog box.
3-D Effect	Click the **3-D Style** button on the Drawing toolbar or make change in the Format dialog box.

TRY *it* OUT *p3-16*

1. Start a new blank presentation.
2. Click the **Blank** slide layout.
3. Click the **Rectangle** button.
4. Click and drag the mouse to draw a rectangle anywhere on the slide.
5. Click the **Fill Color** list arrow, and select a color.

6. Click the **Line Style** button, and choose the **6 pt** line style.

7. Click the **Line** button.

8. Click and drag the mouse to draw a line anywhere on the slide.
9. Click the **Dash Style** button, and select a dash style.
10. Click the **Arrow Style** button and select **Arrow Style 7.** Notice that when you place the mouse pointer over an arrow style, a description of it will appear.
11. Click the **Line Color** list arrow, and select **More Line Colors.**
12. Click the color **Red** and click **OK.**
13. Do not close the file.

Flip and Rotate Objects

- The Flip and Rotate features allow you to reposition or angle an object on a slide.
- The Flip feature allows you to change the direction of an object. You can flip it horizontally (left/right) or vertically (top/bottom). To flip an object, select the object, click the Draw button on the Drawing toolbar and select Rotate or Flip. Then, click either Flip Horizontal or Flip Vertical, as shown in Figures 3.37 and 3.38.

Figure 3.37 Flip Horizontal

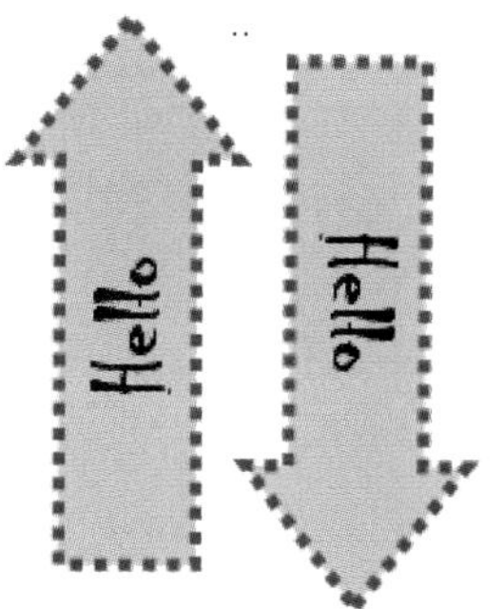

Figure 3.38 Flip Vertical

POWERPOINT

- The Rotate feature allows you to turn an object to a certain angle. To rotate an object, click the Draw button on the Drawing toolbar and select Rotate or Flip. Clicking the Free Rotate option changes the object's handles to green rotate handles, which you can drag to turn the object to any angle.
- To rotate an object by 90-degree increments, select the object, click the Draw button, select Rotate or Flip, and click Rotate Right or Rotate Left.

Layer Objects

- You can layer or stack shapes or objects on top of one another to create interesting effects.
- You may adjust the layers by moving objects behind others or bringing them forward in the stack. To do so, select the object, click the Draw button on the Drawing toolbar, click Order, then select an option. The Bring to Front option places the object on top of all other objects; the Send to Back option places the object beneath all other objects; the Bring Forward option moves the object up one layer in the stack; the Send Backward option moves the object down one layer in the stack, as shown in Figures 3.39 and 3.40.

Draw ▾

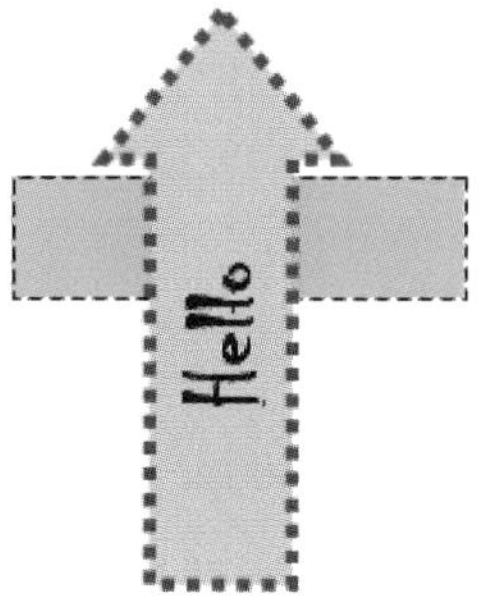

Figure 3.39 Arrow brought forward

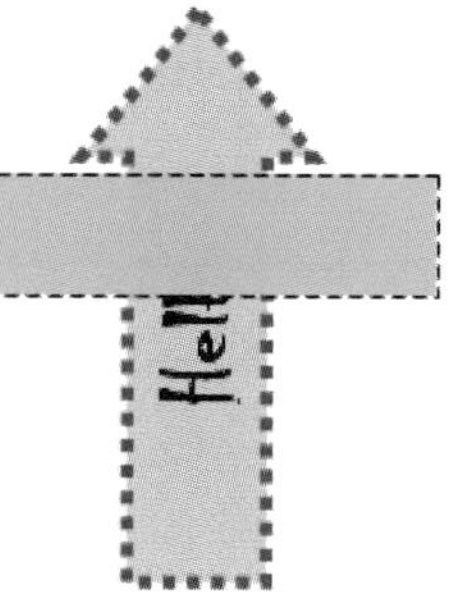

Figure 3.40 Arrow sent backward

TRY *it* OUT *p3-17*

Note: The presentation from Try it Out p3-16 should be displayed.

1. Click the **New Slide** button.

2. Click the **Blank Slide** layout.
3. Click **AutoShapes, Block Arrows, Right Arrow.** Click and drag the arrow anywhere on the slide.
4. Click **AutoShapes, Stars and Banners, 5-Point Star.** Click and drag to draw the star anywhere on the slide.

Continued on next page

TRY it OUT *p3-17 Continued*

5. Click the **Oval** button. Press the **Shift** key while you click and drag to draw a perfect circle anywhere on the slide.
6. Click the **Arrow** to select it.
7. Click **Draw, Rotate or Flip,** and **Rotate Left 90°.**
8. Click the **Star.**
9. Click **Draw, Rotate or Flip, Free Rotate.**
10. Click and drag any of the rotate handles to change the position of the star.
11. Click the **Line** button.

12. Draw a straight line over the circle.
13. Click **Draw, Order,** and **Send to Back.**
14. Click and drag the arrow over the circle.
15. With the Arrow selected, click **Draw, Order, Bring to Front.**
16. Do not close the file.

Group, Ungroup, and Regroup Objects

- When a drawing comprises several basic shapes, it is difficult to move, copy, or duplicate all the shapes as a single object. *Grouping* allows you to select all the shapes in the group and treat them as one object so that you can copy, duplicate, and move them in one operation.
- To group an object composed of individual shapes, press the Shift key as you select each shape, then click the Draw button on the Drawing toolbar and click Group. You can also right-click on the selected objects, then select Grouping, Group from the shortcut menu.

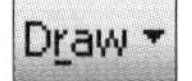

- *Ungrouping* allows you to separate grouped objects. To do so, select the grouped object, click the Draw button on the Drawing toolbar, then select Ungroup. You can also right-click the grouped object, then select Grouping, Ungroup from the shortcut menu.
- *Regrouping* allows you to regroup objects that you separated using the Ungroup command. To do so, click the Draw button on the Drawing toolbar, then select Regroup.

TRY it OUT *p3-18*

Note: The presentation from Try it Out 3-17 should be displayed.

1. Click the **New Slide** button.

2. Click the **Blank Slide** layout.
3. Click **AutoShapes, Basic Shapes,** and select the **Heart** shape.
4. Click and drag anywhere on the slide to draw a heart.
5. Click **AutoShapes, Basic Shapes,** and select the **Lightning Bolt** shape.
6. Click and drag the mouse to draw the shape diagonally through the heart.
7. Click the **Rectangle** button.
8. Draw a rectangle over the heart and arrow.
9. Click the **Fill Color** list button and color the rectangle yellow.
10. Right-click the rectangle and click **Order, Send to Back.** Deselect the rectangle.
11. Press and hold the **Shift** key while you click the **Heart, Lightning Bolt,** and **Rectangle.**
12. Click **Draw, Group.**
13. Click and drag the grouped object to the center of the slide.
14. While objects are still selected, click **Draw, Ungroup.**

Continued on next page

TRY it OUT *p3-18 Continued*

15. Click off the objects.
16. Click the **rectangle.**
17. Click the **Fill Color** list, then color the rectangle light blue. 
18. Click **Draw, Regroup.**
19. Close the presentation; do not save.

Use the Grid and Guides

POWERPOINT

- The Grid and Guides features allow you to position an object on a slide with more precision. A *grid* contains evenly spaced horizontal and vertical lines, which are hidden when you print a presentation, but appear on screen to help align objects. *Guides* are invisible vertical and horizontal lines, which you can also use to align objects.
- To display the grid or guides, click View, Grid and Guides. In the Grid and Guides dialog box that opens, as shown in Figure 3.41, click the appropriate check boxes to display the grid or drawing guides on screen. To set spacing between grid lines, click the Spacing list arrow and select a preset size.

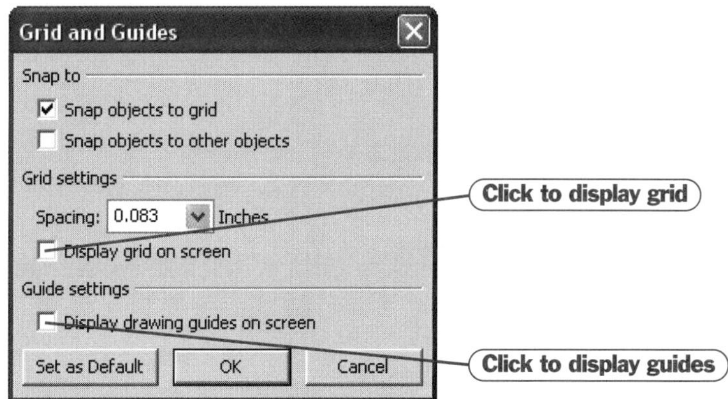

Figure 3.41 Grid and Guides dialog box

- The Snap objects to grid option allows you to position an object on the grid, regardless of whether or not you have chosen to display the grid. When you turn on the Snap objects to grid option and move an object, the object snaps to the nearest point on the grid. You can also choose to snap objects to other objects. This option aligns an object with another object as you move or draw it.
- You can also display or hide a grid by clicking the Show/Hide Grid button on the Standard toolbar. 
- To move a guide, click and drag it to a preferred position. The grid and guides do not print, nor do they appear during a slide show.

Nudge Objects

- The Nudge feature allows you to move objects slightly left, right, up, or down.
- To nudge an object, select the object, click the Draw button on the Drawing toolbar, and select Nudge. Then, click either the Up, Down, Left, or Right options, as shown in Figure 3.42. You can also select the object and press the directional keys on the keyboard to nudge the object in a particular direction.

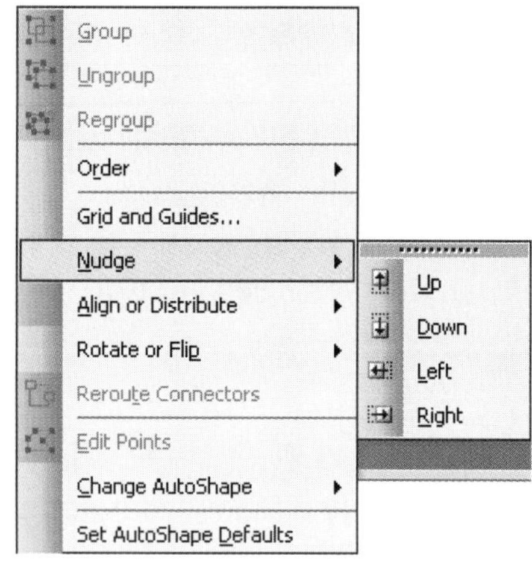

Figure 3.42 Nudge options

TRY *it* OUT *p3-19*

1. Start a new blank presentation and click the **Blank** content layout.
2. Click **View, Grid and Guides.**
3. Click **Display grid on screen.**
4. Click the **Spacing** list arrow and select **1".**
5. Click **OK.**
6. Click **AutoShapes, Stars and Banners,** and select the **5-Point Star** shape.
7. Click and drag on the slide to draw a star.
8. Drag the star along the slide and notice how it snaps to the grid; release the mouse button.
9. Click **View, Grid and Guides.**
10. Click **Snap objects to grid** to deselect this option. Click **OK.**
11. Drag the star and notice how it no longer snaps to the grid.
12. With the star still selected, click **Draw, Nudge,** and click **Up.**
13. Click **Draw, Nudge,** and click **Left.**

Note: If you do not deselect Snap objects to grid, the object snaps to the next grid mark when you nudge it.

14. Do not close the presentation.

Align or Distribute Objects

- The Align or Distribute feature allows you to align or distribute objects in relation to each other, or to distribute them evenly on the slide.
- To align or distribute objects, you must first select each object you want to align or distribute. To do so, press the Shift key while clicking each object. Then click Draw and select Align or Distribute. Click the preferred option from the menu, as shown in Figure 3.43. If you want to distribute objects evenly on the slide, you must select Relative to Slide before you select either Distribute Horizontally or Distribute Vertically. Figure 3.44 shows aligned and distributed objects.

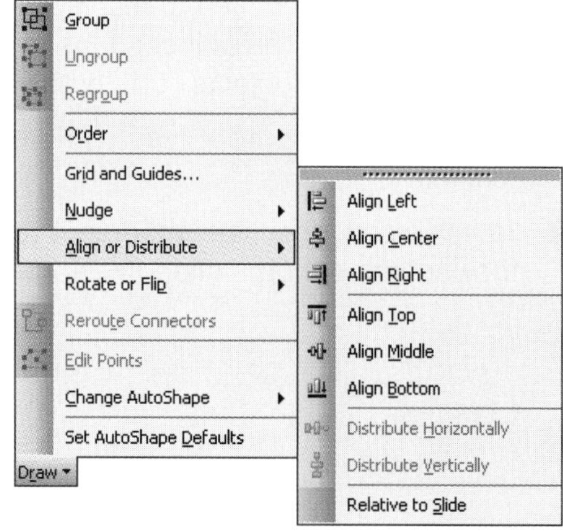

Figure 3.43 Align or Distribute menu options

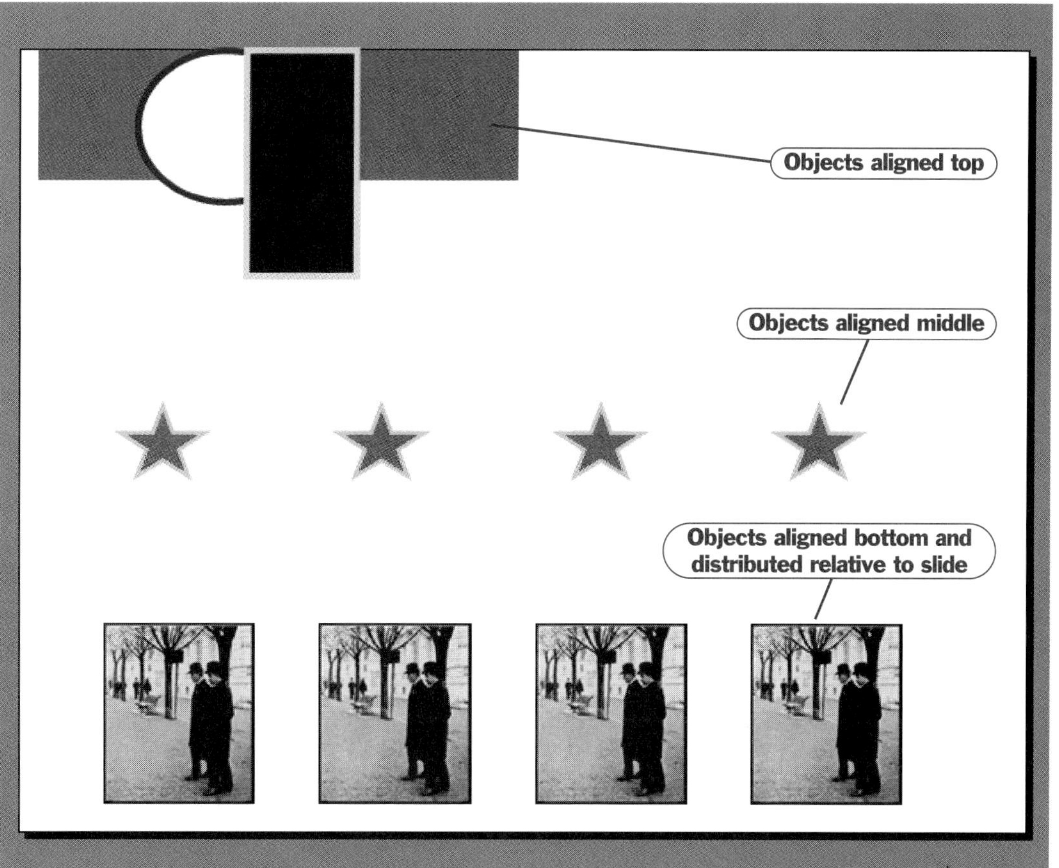

Figure 3.44 Aligned and distributed objects

POWERPOINT

TRY *it* OUT *p3-20*

Note: The presentation from Try it Out p3-19 should be displayed.

1. Click **View, Grid and Guides.**
2. Click to select the **Display grid on screen** check box, if it has not already been selected, then click **OK.**
3. Click the **Oval** button.
4. Click and drag anywhere on the slide to draw an oval.
5. Click **AutoShapes, Block Arrows,** and select the **Down Arrow** shape**.**
6. Click and drag anywhere on the slide to draw a downward-pointing arrow. Deselect the arrow.
7. Press and hold the **Shift** key while you click the **Star, Circle,** and **Arrow.** Release the **Shift** key.
8. Click **Draw,** select **Align or Distribute,** and click **Align Top.**
9. Click **Draw,** select **Align or Distribute,** and click **Relative to Slide.**
10. Click **Draw,** select **Align or Distribute,** and click **Distribute Horizontally.**
11. Click **View, Grid and Guides.**
12. Click to deselect the **Display grid on screen** check box.
13. Close the presentation; do not save.

Use Action Buttons

- You have already learned how to insert a hyperlink on text or objects to link to another slide in your presentation, another file, or a custom show. You can also place a hyperlink on an action button. *Action buttons* are ready-made buttons found in the AutoShapes menu that contain commonly understood symbols that indicate specific actions such as advancing to the next slide, returning to the first slide, and so forth.

- To insert an action button, click AutoShapes on the Drawing toolbar, select Action Buttons, and click an action button, as shown in Figure 3.45. Click the slide and drag the mouse diagonally to draw the button. (Press the Shift key as you drag the mouse to draw a perfect square.)

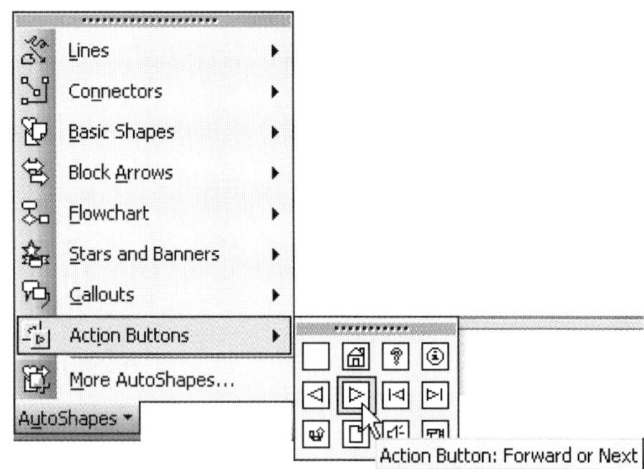

Figure 3.45 Action buttons

- When you release the mouse button, the Action Settings dialog box automatically opens, as shown in Figure 3.46. The setting options on the Mouse Click and Mouse Over tabs are identical. If you want an action button to activate when you click it, make your selections in the Mouse Click tab. If you want the action button to activate when you place the mouse pointer over it, make your selection in the Mouse Over tab.

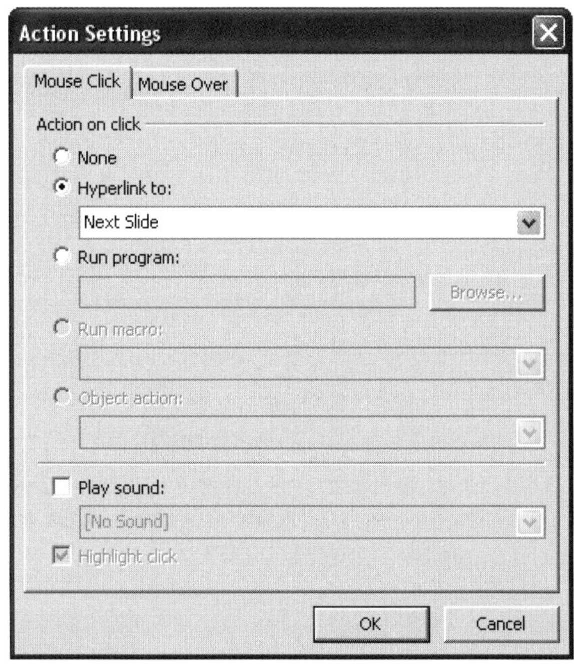

Figure 3.46 Action Settings dialog box

- To create a hyperlink on an action button, click the Hyperlink to button in the Action Settings dialog box. Click the Hyperlink to list arrow and select whether to link to another slide, a Web site, a custom show, or a file. If you insert one of the ready-made action buttons, the action settings reflect whatever the button indicates. For example, if you insert the Next Slide action button, the Action Settings dialog box is set so that clicking the action button advances you to the next slide.

- To play a sound when you activate an action button, click the Play Sound check box in the Action Settings dialog box, click the Play Sound list arrow, and select a sound effect.

- Like other AutoShapes, you can size, move, and format action buttons. The action button color complements the color scheme of the presentation, as shown in Figure 3.47. To change the color, right-click the button, click Format AutoShape, and make any changes in the Format AutoShape dialog box.

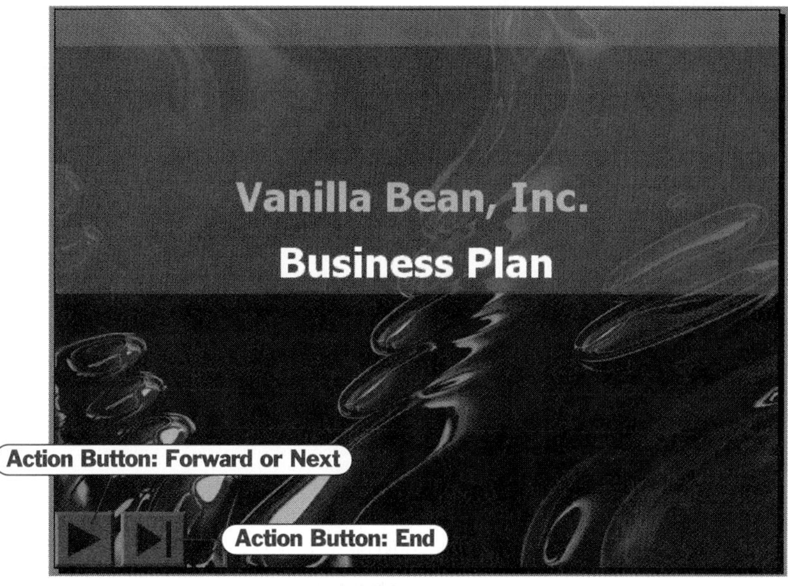

Figure 3.47 Slide with action buttons

POWERPOINT

▶ Action buttons become active when you run your presentation (in Slide show view). When you place the mouse over an action button, the mouse pointer changes to a hand. If you want the same action buttons to appear on all the slides of your presentation, insert the action buttons on the slide master.

TRY *it* OUT *p3-21*

1. Open **p3.21neworleans** from the Data CD.
2. Display **Slide 3.**
3. Click **AutoShapes, Action Buttons,** and select the **Back or Previous** button. 
4. Drag the mouse to draw a button in the bottom-right of the slide. *Note: Be sure to leave room for another button to the right of the Back or Previous button.*
5. Click the **Mouse Click** tab and click **OK** to accept that the action button will hyperlink to the previous slide.
6. Click the **adjustment handle** and drag right to make the arrow smaller.
7. Click **AutoShapes,** select **Action Buttons.** Click the **Forward or Next** button.
8. Drag the mouse to draw a button to the right of the Back or Previous button.
9. Click the **Mouse Over** tab, make sure **Hyperlink to** is selected, and choose **Next Slide** from the Hyperlink to list.
10. Click the **Play Sound** box, click the **Play Sound** list arrow, select **Chime,** and click **OK.** *Note: The Sound Effects feature may need to be installed.*
11. Click the **adjustment handle** and drag right to make the button appear like the one next to it.
12. Click the **Slide Show View** button. 
13. Place the mouse over the **Next** button to advance to the next slide. 
14. Press the **Backspace** key.
15. Click the **Back** button to view the previous slide. 
16. Press the **Esc** key.
17. Close the file; do not save the presentation.

REHEARSAL

TASK 4

GOALS
To use, edit, and work with AutoShapes, WordArt, and alignment techniques to create and enhance two presentations

SETTING THE STAGE/WRAPUP
File name: **3.4goldstar**
3.4creativesales

WHAT YOU NEED TO KNOW

- It is important that your presentation have a professional and readable layout. When placing objects, be sure that they don't interfere with text.
- In this Rehearsal activity, you will create a six-slide sales presentation for Green Brothers Gardeners to introduce a new plant fertilizer to landscapers. You will also create a six-slide presentation that outlines sales techniques used by Occasions Event Planning to attract business.

DIRECTIONS

Green Brothers Presentation

1. Start a new presentation; apply an appropriate design template. (You use Templates on Office Online, which you can access on the New Presentation task pane.)
2. Apply a green color scheme to your slides.
3. Create the slides shown on the facing page.
   a. On Slide 1, insert a relevant clip-art image and rotate it.
   b. On Slide 2, draw a spider as shown; color it Black and/or Gray. Copy the spider and place both spiders on the slide as shown.

Tip: To create the spider's body, draw a circle. Draw two ovals for the eyes. Create three legs using the free-form line AutoShape. Group the legs, then flip them horizontally. Attach them to the other side of the spider's body. Group all shapes.

   c. On Slide 3, insert a relevant clip art image.
   d. On Slide 5, insert a clip art image where indicated in the illustration; size, rotate, and/or flip it to fit appropriately.

4. View the slide master.
   a. Apply any font and font color to the title, then make it bold.
   b. Draw a star and place it at the bottom of the slide.
      - Size it wider than it is tall.
      - Apply any fill and line color.
   c. Copy the star twice.
   d. Layer the stars as shown.
   e. Group the three stars.
   f. Create a WordArt object with the words `Gold Star.`
      - Apply any color to the WordArt.
      - Position the WordArt on the gold star as shown.
   g. Group the stars and the WordArt.

Continued on next page

5. Create a summary slide displaying the titles of Slides 2 through 5.
6. Move the summary slide to be the last slide in the presentation (Slide 6).
7. On Slide 6, replace "Summary Slide" with `Recap.`
8. Adjust title placeholders to fit the title text on one line, if necessary.
9. Run the slide show.
10. Save the presentation as **3.4goldstar.**

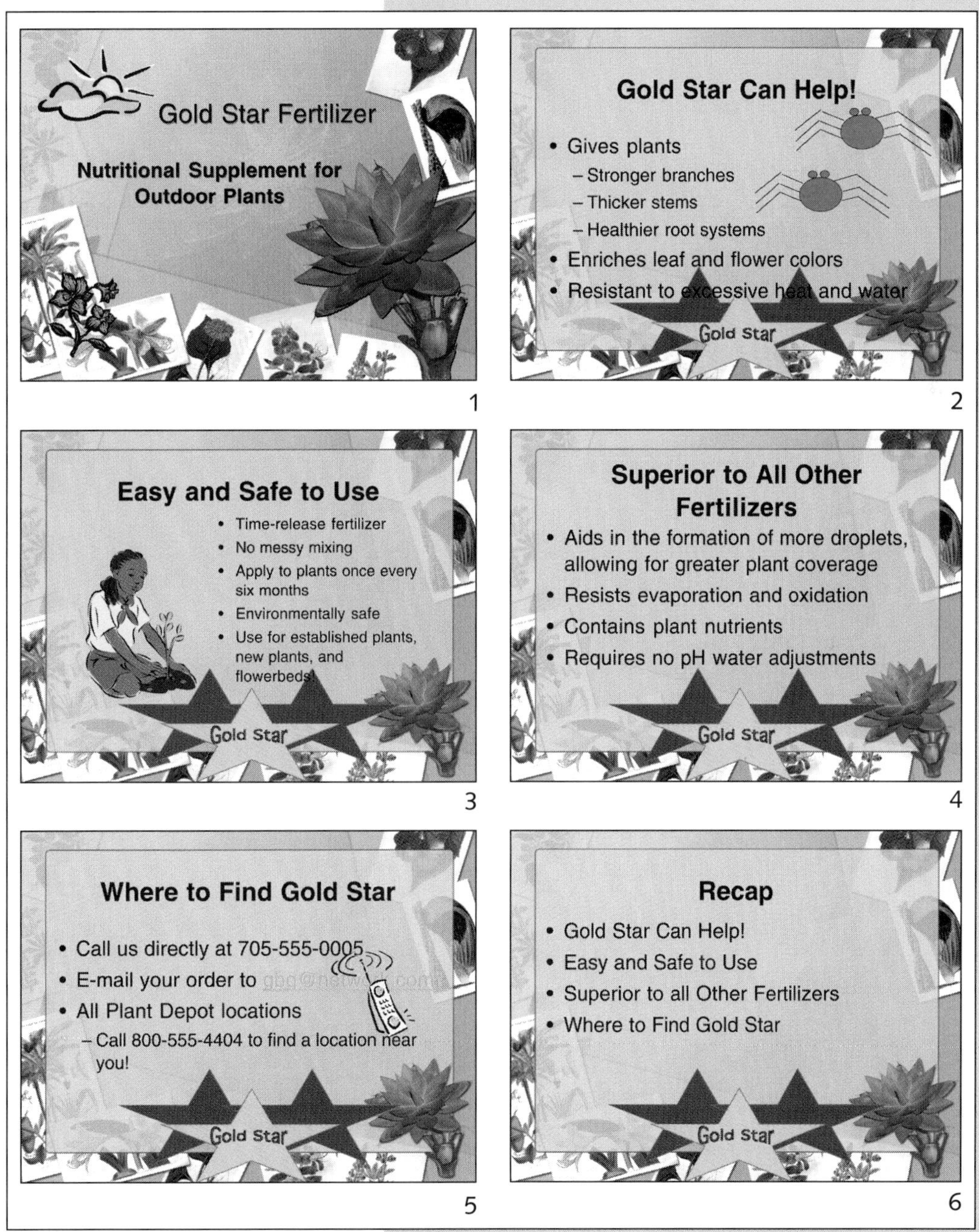

Continued on next page

Occasions Event Planning Presentation

1. Create the presentation as shown below and on the next page.
2. Customize the background for all slides using the picture **3.4agenda,** located on the Data CD. 
3. Display the slide master.
   a. Change the first level bullet to any preferred graphical bullet.
   b. Change the second level bullet to a blue hyphen.
   c. Change the third level bullet to a light blue circle.
   d. Apply any sans serif font to the bulleted text; color it dark pink.
   e. Apply a decorative font to the title text; color it dark blue.

Continued on next page

1

2

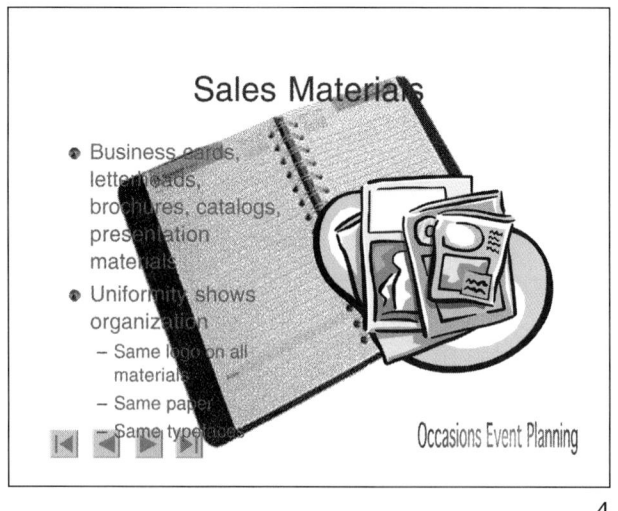

Sales Kits

- Tool for making initial client contact
- Guide for account executive
- Provides client with material to make an informed decision

Occasions Event Planning

3

Sales Materials

- Business cards, letterheads, brochures, catalogs, presentation materials
- Uniformity shows organization
  – Same logo on all materials
  – Same paper
  – Same typefaces

Occasions Event Planning

4

f. Create a WordArt object with the words: **Occasions Event Planning**. Use any font. Use a straight style.
   i. Apply a two-color gradient fill effect to the WordArt. Color 1 should be Aqua; color 2 should be Dark Blue. Click From center in the Shading styles box. Adjust size and location, if necessary.
   ii. Position the WordArt horizontally 7" from the top-left corner, and vertically 6.85" from the top-left corner.

g. Insert the following four action buttons on the bottom left of the slide, in this order: Beginning, Previous, Next, End. Select a fill and line color for the buttons that complements the slide design. Align and distribute the buttons at the bottom of the slide as shown.

POWERPOINT

5

6

Making the Presentation

- Use sales video, with clips of events
- Use sales materials to promote
  - Venues
  - Caterers
  - Entertainers
- Leave behind premium items
  - Samples of party favors
  - All contain Occasions logo

Occasions Event Planning

7

Continued on next page

4. Display Slide 1 ("Creative Sales").
   a. Use the following guidelines to create a balloon, as shown: 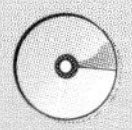
      i. Display the grid and set its spacing to 1/10" (0.101).
      ii. Draw an oval to fit inside one of the grid squares.
      iii. Draw a tiny triangle and send it behind the oval.
      iv. Use the Scribble AutoShape to draw the balloon's string.
      v. Color the oval and triangle the same color.
      vi. Group the oval, triangle, and scribble.
   b. Copy and paste the balloon three times.
   c. Color each balloon differently.
   d. Align the tops of the first and third balloons, relative to the slide.
   e. Position the second balloon slightly lower than the first one; then align the tops of the second and fourth balloons, relative to each other.
   f. Distribute the four balloons horizontally, relative to the slide.
5. Display Slide 2 ("Our Sales Strategy").
   a. Draw a star.
   b. Size it 2" high by 2" wide.
   c. Copy and paste it twice.
   d. Position the stars as shown.
   e. Distribute the stars vertically, relative to each other.
   f. Right-align the stars, relative to the slide.
   g. Color the top star a bright yellow, the middle star a lighter yellow, and the bottom star an even lighter yellow.
6. Display Slide 6 ("The Event Catalog").
   a. Insert the picture, **3.4wedcake**, located on the Data CD.
   b. Adjust the contrast and brightness of the picture, as you prefer.
   c. Crop the edges of the picture, so that the cake fills up the picture.
7. Display Slide 7 ("Making the Presentation").
   a. Insert the clip art image, **3.4present**, located on the Data CD.
   b. Ungroup the image and delete the Red background.
   c. Color the graph as shown in the illustration.
   d. Color the line of the legs of the easel Brown; use a white fill for the legs.
   e. Regroup all components of the image.

Continued on next page

8. Insert relevant clip art or pictures on Slides 3 and 4 as shown.
   a. Adjust the contrast and brightness of the object.
   b. Crop the object to delete any extraneous part of the picture or clip art.
9. Apply any animation scheme.
10. Run the slide show.
11. Save the file as **3.4creativesales.**

POWERPOINT

Cues for Reference

Draw AutoShapes
1. Click **AutoShapes** on the Drawing toolbar.
2. Click the appropriate shape category on the shortcut menu.
3. Click the appropriate shape.
4. Position a crosshair (+) where the shape will start.
5. Click and drag to appropriate end point.

Format AutoShapes
1. Click the **AutoShape** to select it.
2. Select **Format, AutoShape.**
   or
   Right-click the **AutoShape** and choose **Format AutoShape.**
3. Click the **Colors and Lines** tab.
4. Make desired fill, line, and/or arrow formatting changes.
5. Click **OK.**

Insert WordArt
1. Click the **Insert WordArt** button on the Drawing toolbar.
2. Click a WordArt style.
3. Click **OK.**
4. Enter the WordArt text.
5. Make desired font, font size, and font style changes.
6. Click **OK.**

Layer Objects
1. Right-click the object.
2. Click **Draw, Order.**
3. Select an option:
   - Bring to Front
   - Send to Back
   - Bring Forward
   - Send Backward

Group/Ungroup/Regroup Objects
Group Objects
1. Press and hold **Shift** and click each object to group.
2. Click **Draw.**
3. Click **Group.**

Ungroup Objects
1. Click the grouped object.
2. Click **Draw, Ungroup.**

Regroup Objects
1. Select all of the originally grouped objects
2. Click **Draw, Regroup.**

Display Grid and Guides
1. Click **View, Grid and Guides.**
2. Click **Display grid on screen.**
   and/or
   - Click **Display drawing guides on screen.**
3. Click **OK.**

Snap to Grid/Other Objects
1. Click **Draw, Grid and Guides.**
2. Click **Snap objects to grid.**
   and/or
   - Click **Snap objects to other objects.**
3. Click **OK.**

Nudge
1. Click object to move.
2. Click **Draw, Nudge.**
3. Click preferred direction or press direction keys on keyboard.

Align/Distribute Objects
1. Press and hold **Shift** and click each object to align or distribute.
2. Click **Draw, Align** or **Distribute.**
3. Click **Relative to Slide,** if objects should align in relation to slide.
   Note: A check mark indicates that Relative to Slide is selected.
4. Click preferred alignment option or click **Distribute Horizontally** or **Distribute Vertically.**

Flip and Rotate Objects
1. Click the object.
2. Click **Draw, Rotate, or Flip.**
3. Select a Rotate or Flip option.

Insert An Action Button
1. Click **AutoShapes, Action Buttons** and click desired action button.
2. Click on slide and drag mouse diagonally to draw button.
3. Click **Mouse Click** tab or **Click Mouse Over** tab.
4. Make selections, and click **OK.**

PERFORMANCE

SETTING THE STAGE
Act I File names:
pp3undercover.ppt
Act II File names:
pp3partnership.ppt

Act I

You are the assistant to the director of television sales at Trilogy Productions. Your boss must sell a new television series called *Undercover* to television stations. She has asked you to create a sales presentation for potential station buyers.

Follow these guidelines:

- Use an outline to create and organize the presentation content indicated in the following paragraphs.
- Each bold heading represents a title slide. The title slide will precede each informational slide; there will be 4 title slides all together. The paragraph below the heading contains the text of the informational slide. Summarize the information in the informational paragraph into bullet points for your slides.
- Apply a design template. Use your creativity to design the slides using slide masters, footers, clip art, AutoShapes, WordArt, text alignments, and any other embellishments.
- Create a logo for the new show Undercover, which you will place on all the title slides. These title slides will indicate new sections of the presentation.
- Create a relevant title for the presentation itself.
- Include a summary slide as the last slide in the presentation.
- Save your presentation; name it **pp3undercover.**

The Show

Undercover is a new action/adventure series about detectives from a New York City police department who go undercover to fight crime and injustice in the city streets. Each episode will bring exciting storylines, great action sequences, wit, irony, and romance. The show is set in New York City, the perfect backdrop for mystery, adventure, and lots of action, and will be a feature film-quality production with a budget of $1 million per episode.

The show features talented, young stars including John Wagner, whose recent film credits include *The Diaries* and *The Breakfast Bunch*. The show also stars Alison Tepper, Janet Fine, and Maurice Banks.

The Credits

Undercover has hired an outstanding production team to bring this exciting program to TV. Jeff Grant is the executive producer. His credits include *Home Sweet Home* (TV), *The Long*

Ride Away (film), and *Stalkers* (film). Susan Holmes is the director; her credits include *Wired* (film), *Crime Scenes* (TV), and *The Range* (TV). The head writer is Sloane Peterson, who has also written *Winter in Miami* (film), *The Wedding Fiasco* (film), and *Detective, Detective* (TV).

The Genre

Action/adventure programs do well with key demographics and are most successful with women and men age 25 to 54. Of all the programs on TV this year, every action hour placed in the top half of the rankings. Action/adventure programming is a staple genre that appeals to the masses.

Trilogy Productions has been successful with this genre. Our other two shows currently on the air are action/adventure programs, and they consistently rank among the top five in the genre. Our marketing campaigns and publicity stunts garner tremendous attention. Furthermore, every single one of our action/adventure films has been a blockbuster!

Perfect for Your Station

This show will play well in key time slots: early afternoons, evenings, and late at night. The show is advertiser-friendly and has flexible demographic appeal.

Act II

Odyssey Travel Gear believes that a good way to sell its products is to partner with various travel agencies. Odyssey has decided to create a sales presentation to propose this idea to travel agents who will attend a travel convention next month. You have been asked to create a nine-slide sales presentation.

Follow these guidelines:

- Use an outline to create and organize the presentation content indicated in the following paragraphs. Each bold heading represents a new slide; the paragraph below the heading contains the information to include on that slide. Summarize the information into bullet points for your slides.
- Apply a design template. Use your creativity to design the slides using slide masters, footers, clip art, AutoShapes, text alignments, and any other embellishments.
- Use WordArt to create Odyssey Travel Gear's motto: **`Whether you travel far or near, don't leave without Odyssey Travel Gear!`** Position the WordArt on Slide 1.
- Insert a summary slide as the second slide in the presentation; change its title to **`Overview`**.
- Use two slide masters for this presentation. Use the same design template for these masters but apply different color schemes to differentiate them. Apply one of the slide master designs to Slides 1 through 4; apply the other slide master design to Slides 5 through 9.
- Save your presentation; name it **pp3partnership.**

Odyssey Travel Gear

This partnership proposal will be delivered on October 30, 2005.

What We Do

We offer high-quality travel products that make travel easier and more comfortable. We supply a wide range of travel products to meet the needs of all travelers. We pride ourselves on providing outstanding customer service and offer our products at extremely low prices. We will match any competitor's price.

Our Success Speaks for Itself

Within the past year, our catalog and Internet sales have doubled, and we have opened five more retail stores. We are consistently featured in top travel magazines including *Travel and Tourism, Voyages,* and *Around the World.* Furthermore, our products and exceptional service have received rave reviews from top travel critics.

The Partnership

We are seeking a mutually beneficial partnership that will offer your clients discounted products from Odyssey Travel Gear.

Partner Benefits

This partnership will result in benefits for both Odyssey Travel Gear and your travel agency. Both parties will profit from new advertising, cross-promotion, global reach, and revenue opportunities.

Your Role

The travel agency's contribution to the partnership will be as follows: Advertise Odyssey Travel Gear to your clients as your exclusive travel gear supplier, distribute Odyssey catalogs in all of your travel agencies, include an Odyssey logo on all marketing materials generated by your agency, and include a link to Odyssey's Web site from your agency's Web site.

What We'll Offer

Odyssey's contribution to the partnership will be as follows: Product discounts of up to 25% to your travel clients only, links from our Web site to your agency's Web site, a *Travel Specials* insert in our catalog that includes travel deals from your agency, and client referrals.

Make It Happen

It's now up to you to make this partnership a reality. If you are interested in moving forward or have any questions, call president and CEO Jane McBride or marketing director Thomas Romano at 630-555-8888. You can also fax your name and agency information to 630-555-8787, and we'll contact you!

1
2
3

LESSON 4

Persuasive Presentations

In this lesson, you will learn to use PowerPoint features to create persuasive presentations. Persuasive presentations should generate understanding, change or form attitudes or opinions, and build consensus.

Upon completion of this lesson, you should be able to use the following skill sets:

- Use template presentations
- Use the AutoContent Wizard
- Work with tables, charts, and diagrams
- Work with media
- Use custom animations
- Use the annotation pen
- Work with a photo album
- Use handouts
- Use speaker notes
- Work with the Handout and Notes Master
- Rehearse timings

Terms

Software-related

- Template presentations
- AutoContent Wizard
- Looping
- Custom animations
- Annotation pen
- Photo album
- Handouts
- Speaker notes
- Handout master
- Notes master

GOAL

To practice using the following skill sets:

- Use template presentations
- Use the AutoContent Wizard
- Work with tables, charts, and diagrams
- Work with media

WHAT YOU NEED TO KNOW

Use Template Presentations

- *Template presentations* are predesigned sets of slides that relate to a particular topic. Slides within each template presentation include suggested text for the type of information that you enter on them.
- To access template presentations, click File, New. In the New Presentation task pane that displays, click the On my computer link below Templates, as shown in Figure 4.1.

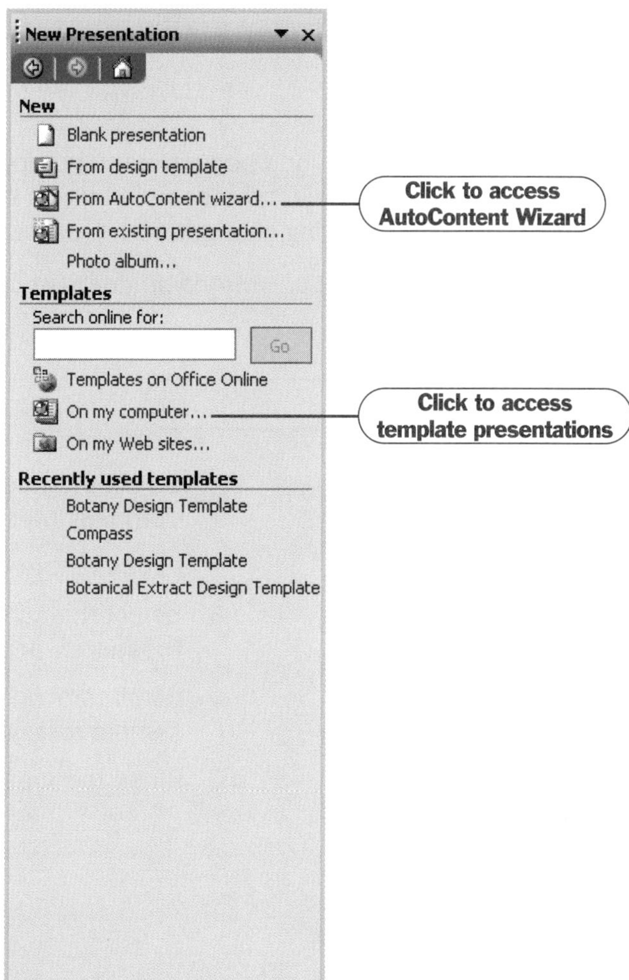

Figure 4.1 New Presentation task pane

- In the New Presentations dialog box that opens, click the Presentations tab and select the presentation template that corresponds to the subject of the presentation you are creating, as shown in Figure 4.2.

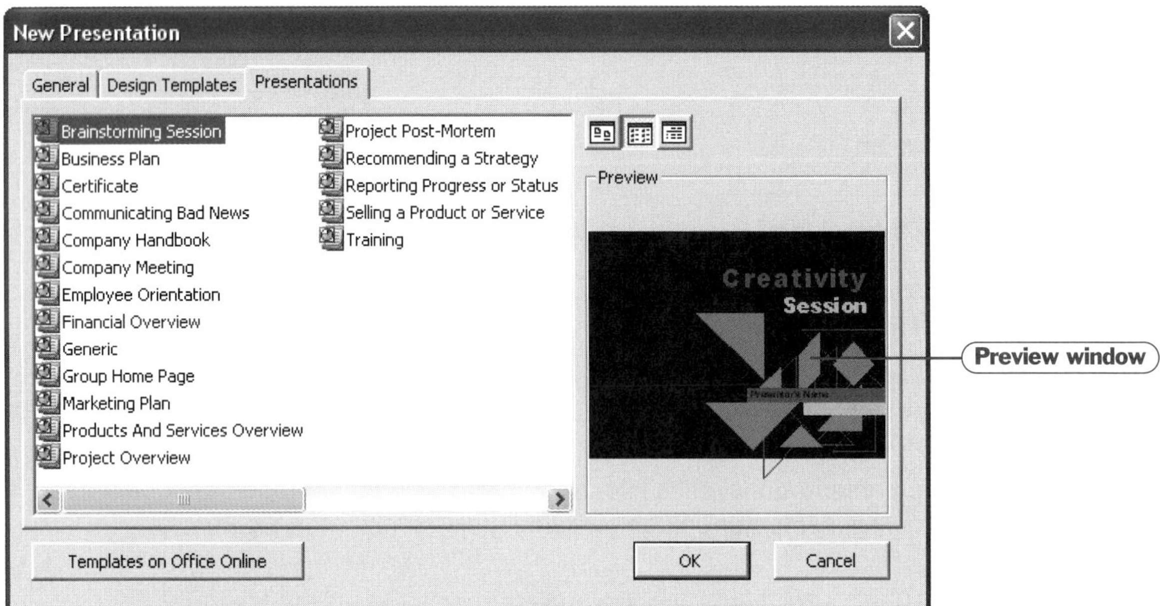

Figure 4.2 New Presentation dialog box

- After you choose a template, the presentation opens and the number of slides in the presentation appears on the status bar. Select the sample text on each slide and replace it with your own. You can make additional formatting changes to the presentation if necessary.

Note: Template presentations must be installed on your computer to complete this Try it Out.

TRY *it* OUT *p4-1*

1. Start PowerPoint.
2. Click **File, New** to display the New Presentation task pane.
3. Click the **On my computer** link.
4. Click the **Presentations** tab.
5. Click the **Company Meeting** template.
6. Click **OK.**
7. Select the title text on the first slide, **Company Meeting Title,** and enter:

   `Product Development Meeting`
8. Select the subtitle text on the first slide, **Presenter,** and enter your name.
9. Scroll through the slides and note the sample text on each slide.
10. Close the presentation; do not save.

Use the AutoContent Wizard

- The *AutoContent Wizard* walks you through the presentation development process to help you create presentations on a particular subject.
- To run the AutoContent Wizard, click the From AutoContent wizard link in the New Presentation task pane (see Figure 4.1).
- In the AutoContent Wizard dialog box that opens, as shown in Figure 4.3, follow the prompts and make the selections you want.

Figure 4.3 AutoContent Wizard dialog box

POWERPOINT

TRY *it* OUT *p4-2*

1. Click **File, New.**
2. Click the **From AutoContent wizard** link in the New Presentation task pane.
3. Click **Next.**
4. Click the **All** button to view all of the available presentation templates. Click each of the buttons to view the presentation templates by topic.
5. Click the **General** button.
6. Click the **Recommending a Strategy** presentation and click **Next.**
7. Click **On-screen presentation**, if necessary, and click **Next.**
8. Click in the **Presentation title** box and enter:

   `Marketing Strategies for New Age Vitamins`
9. Click in the **Footer** box and enter:

   `We're in a New Age!`
10. Check the **Date last updated** box, check the **Slide number** box, if necessary, and click **Next.**
11. Click **Finish.**
12. Scroll through the slides and note the sample text on each slide.
13. Close the file; do not save.

Work with Tables, Charts, and Diagrams

- Tables, charts, and diagrams are visual elements you can use to present and explain data.
- Content slides, which you used when working with clip art, contain placeholders to work with one or more of these visual elements. Figures 4.4 and 4.5 illustrate a Title and Content layout and a Title and Chart layout. The procedures you use to create and edit these elements are the same as those you used in Word.

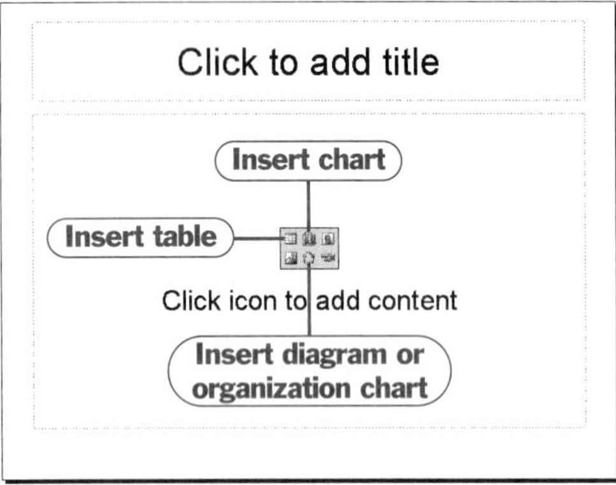

Figure 4.4 Title and Content slide layout

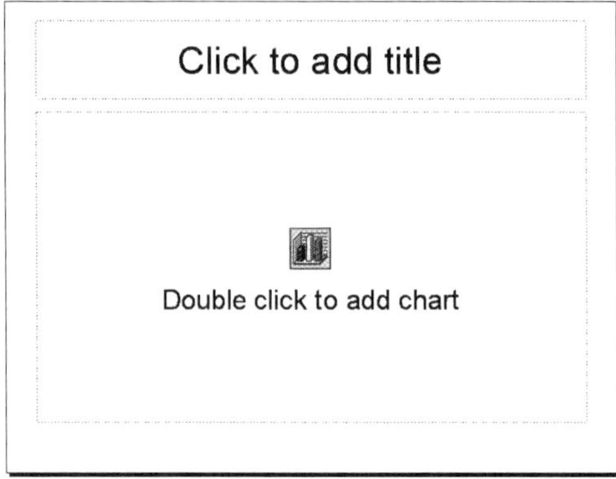

Figure 4.5 Title and Chart slide layout

Tables

- A table consists of rows, which run horizontally, and columns, which run vertically. The rows and columns intersect to form boxes, called cells.
- To create a table on a slide, use one of the following methods:
  - Apply a Content layout and click the Insert Table icon.
  - Apply the Title and Table layout and double-click the table placeholder.
- In the Insert Table dialog box that opens, as shown in Figure 4.6, enter the number of columns and rows in the table.
- You can also create a table on a slide that does not contain a content or table placeholder. To do so, click Insert, Table from the menu and enter the number of columns and rows in the dialog box in the Insert Table dialog box shown in Figure 4.6. The number of columns and rows you choose will automatically fill the slide area, as shown in Figure 4.7.

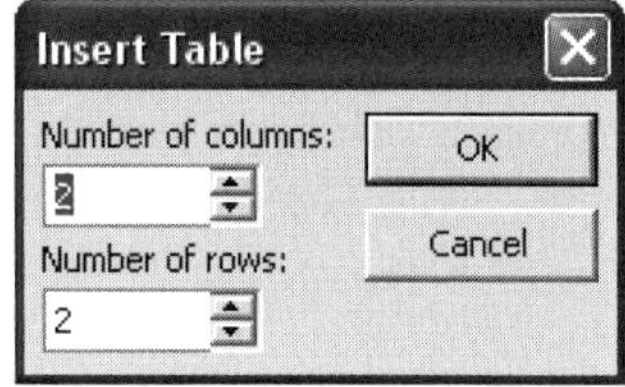

Figure 4.6 Insert Table dialog box

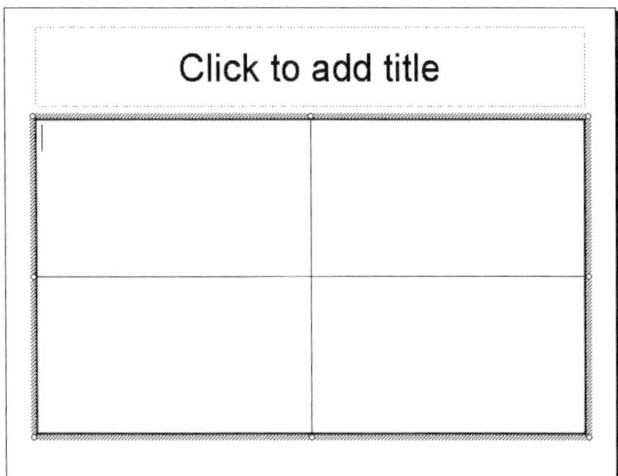

Figure 4.7 Slide with Table, 2 columns and 2 rows displayed

- You can add text to a table and move from cell to cell using the same techniques you learned in Word. Remember, pressing the tab key in the last cell of the right-most column creates a new row.
- To format a table, (change border style, add shading) use the appropriate buttons on the Tables and Borders toolbar, shown in Figure 4.8.

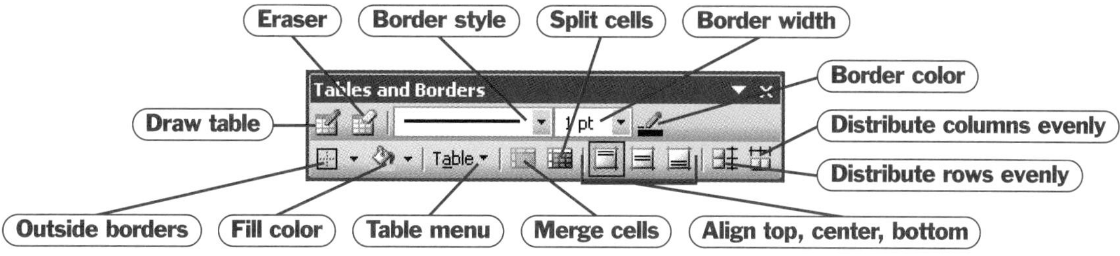

Figure 4.8 Tables and Borders toolbar

- You can insert and delete columns and rows using the same procedures you used in Word. Click the Table button on the Tables and Borders toolbar and choose an insert and/or delete option from the menu, as shown in Figure 4.9.

Table ▾

POWERPOINT

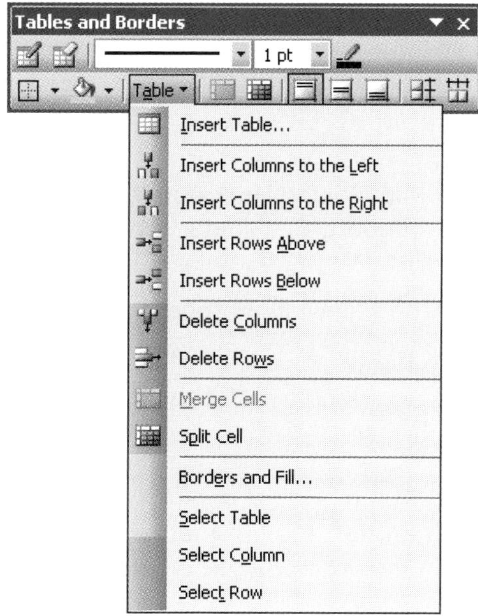

Figure 4.9 Table menu

TRY*it*OUT *p4-3*

1. Click the **New** button.
2. Click the **Content slide thumbnail** in the Slide Layout task pane.
3. Click the **Insert Table** icon.
4. Enter `4` in the Number of columns box. Enter `7` in the Number of rows box.
5. Click **OK.**
6. Click in the top-left cell, if necessary, and enter: `Course Offering.`
7. Press the **Tab** key.
8. Enter: `Professor.`
9. Press the **Tab** key.
10. Enter: `Credits.`
11. Drag the vertical border to widen the first column to fit the text, then widen the second column to fit the text.
12. Click **View, Toolbars,** and **Tables and Borders** to display the Tables and Borders toolbar (if not already displayed).
13. Click anywhere in Column 4.
14. Click the **Table** button and click **Delete Columns.** 

15. Click anywhere in the first row.
16. Right-click the mouse and select **Insert Rows.**
17. Click and drag the **table placeholder border** to center the table on the slide.
18. Close the file; do not save.

Charts

- A chart may be added to a PowerPoint slide by importing one that was already created in Excel, or creating one using the Chart feature. (Importing objects from other programs is covered in Lesson 5.)
- To create a chart on a slide, use one of the following methods:
  - Apply a Content slide layout and click the Insert Chart icon.
  - Apply the Title and Chart slide layout and double-click the chart icon.
  - Click Insert, Chart on the menu.
  - Click the Insert Chart button on the Standard toolbar. 
- A datasheet window appears, along with a Chart toolbar that replaces the Standard toolbar. Several charting features also appear on the Formatting toolbar, as shown in Figure 4.10.

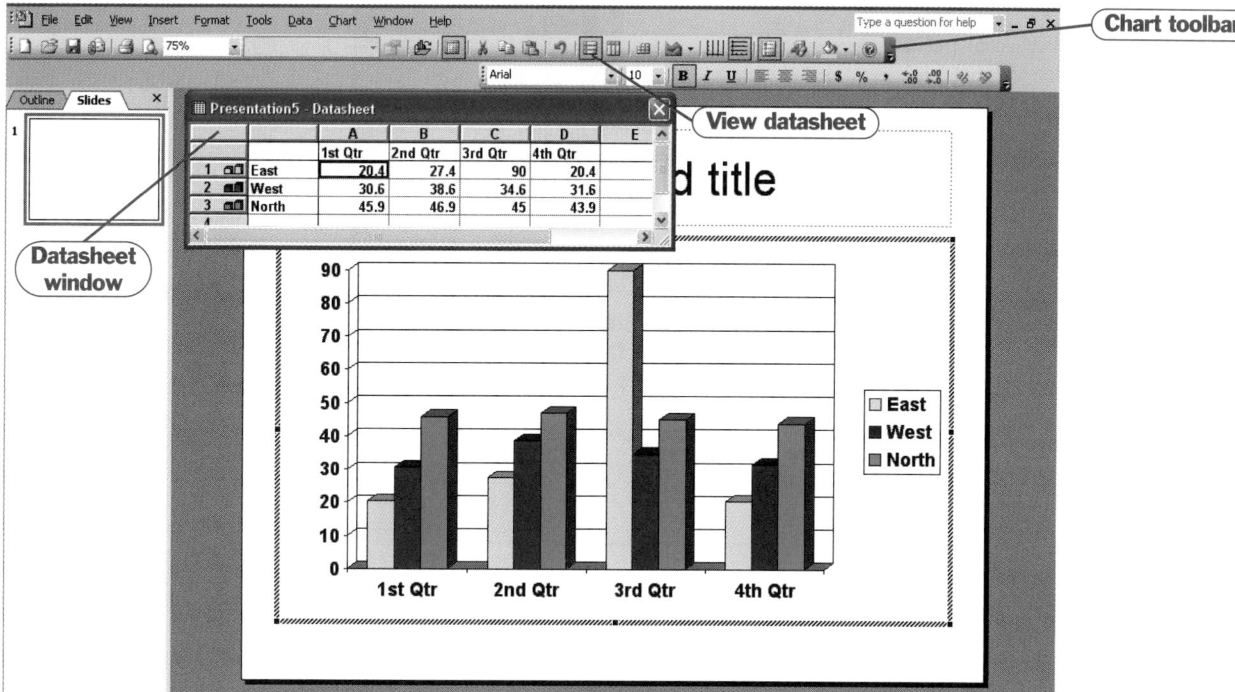

Figure 4.10 Chart and datasheet

▶ Delete the sample data in the datasheet, and then enter the data you want to chart. The chart reflects the new data. Click the View Datasheet button on the toolbar to hide the datasheet. Click it again to display the datasheet.

▶ The default chart type is 3-D column. To change the chart type, double-click the chart so that it is in Edit mode, then click Chart, Chart Type. In the Chart Type dialog box that opens, shown in Figure 4.11, click the Standard Types or Custom Types tab, then click a chart type. Or, click the Chart Type button on the Chart toolbar, then select a chart type from the pop-up menu.

▶ You can enhance your chart with a chart title, axes titles, and/or data labels. Data labels allow you to indicate the exact value of each data point. To add these features, select the chart to format, then click Chart, Chart Options. In the Chart Options dialog box that opens, shown in Figure 4.12, click a tab and make the desired enhancements.

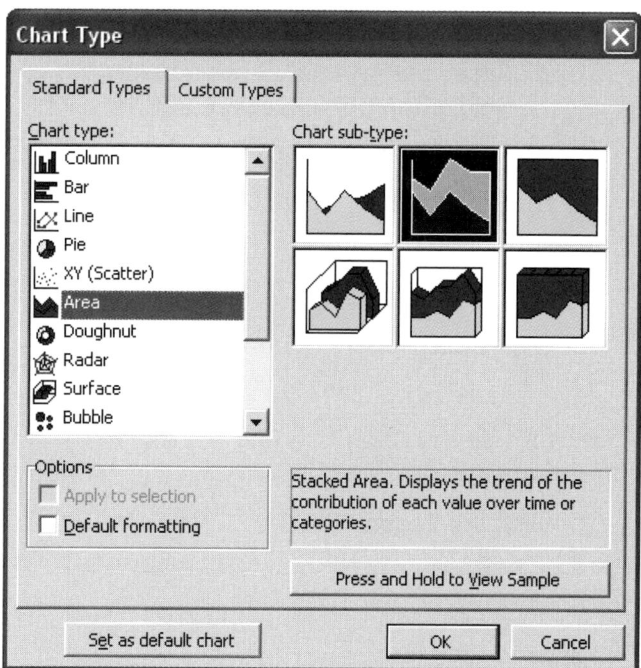

Figure 4.11 Chart Type dialog box

POWERPOINT

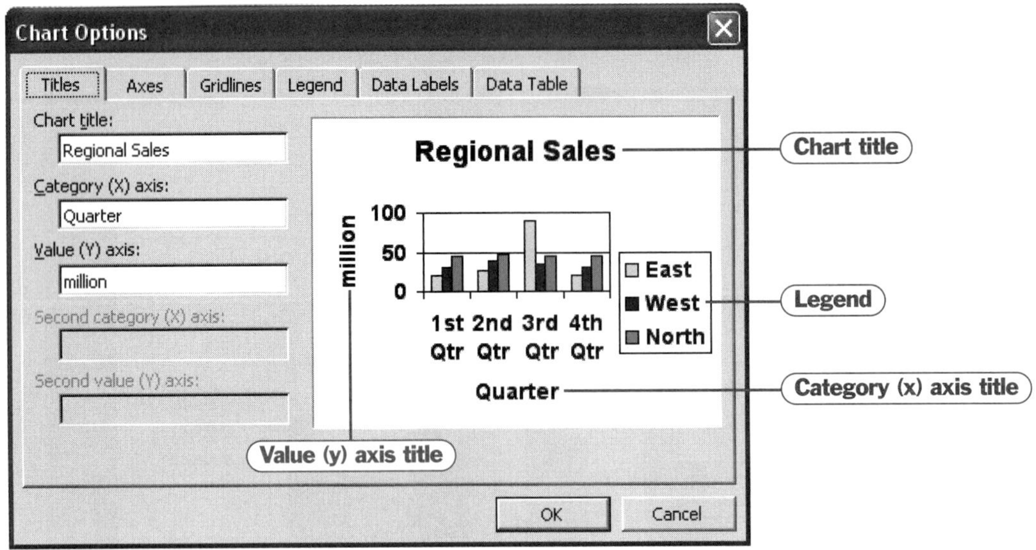

Figure 4.12 Chart Options dialog box

TRY *it* OUT *p4-4*

1. Click the **New** button.
2. Click the **Title and Chart** slide thumbnail in the Slide Layout task pane.
3. Double-click the **Chart** icon.
4. Delete the data from the datasheet and enter the new data shown below, then close the datasheet window.

	2000	2001	2002	2003
Internet	24%	30%	42%	55%
Catalog	50%	40%	30%	20%
Store	26%	30%	28%	25%

5. Click **Chart, Chart Options.**
6. Click the **Titles** tab (if not already displayed).
7. Click in the Chart title text box and enter: `Sales Analysis.`
8. Click the **Legend** tab.
9. Click **Bottom** to change the placement of the legend.
10. Click the **Data Labels** tab.
11. Click the **Value** check box to display category values and click **OK.**
12. Right-click a blank part of the chart, click **Chart Type,** and click **Bar** in the Chart Type box.
13. Click the **100% Stacked Bar** sample in the Chart sub-type box.
14. Click the **Press and Hold to View Sample** button.
15. Click **Cancel.**
16. Click the slide outside the chart placeholder.
17. Do not close the presentation.

Diagrams

▶ Diagrams show process flows and relationships. An organization chart is a type of diagram you can use to illustrate a hierarchy or structure. You can also use organization charts to show the flow of a project or a family tree.

- To create a diagram or organization chart on a slide, use one of the following methods:
  - Apply a Content slide layout, and click the Insert Diagram or Organization Chart icon. 
  - Apply the Diagram or Organization Chart slide layout and double-click the icon.
  - Click Insert, Diagram to add a diagram or organization chart to a slide that does not contain a specialized placeholder.
- In the Diagram Gallery dialog box that opens, as shown in Figure 4.13, click a diagram type.

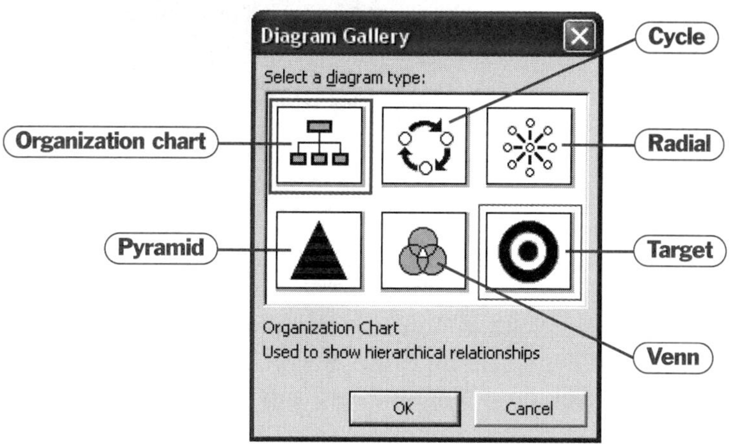

Figure 4.13 Diagram Gallery

- After selecting a diagram and clicking OK, the image appears with sizing handles and a nonprinting border. A toolbar also appears, to assist you with formatting options. Figure 4.14 shows an organization chart with an organization chart toolbar.

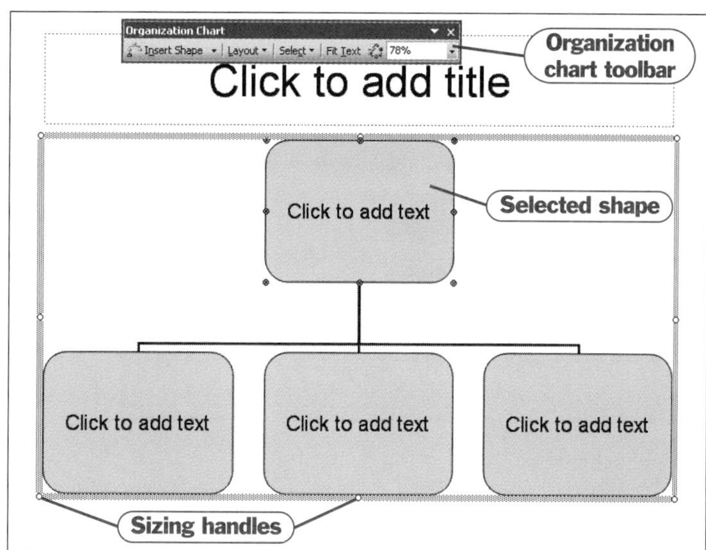

Figure 4.14 Organization chart

POWERPOINT

▶ As shown in Figure 4.14, an organization chart appears with four boxes. However, you can add or remove shapes from the chart as required. There are four shape types: Superior, Assistant, Subordinate, and Coworker. To add a shape, click the shape to which the new shape should attach, click the Insert Shape list arrow on the Organization Chart toolbar, as shown in Figure 4.15, then click the required box type. A diagram next to the box type indicates how the box attaches.

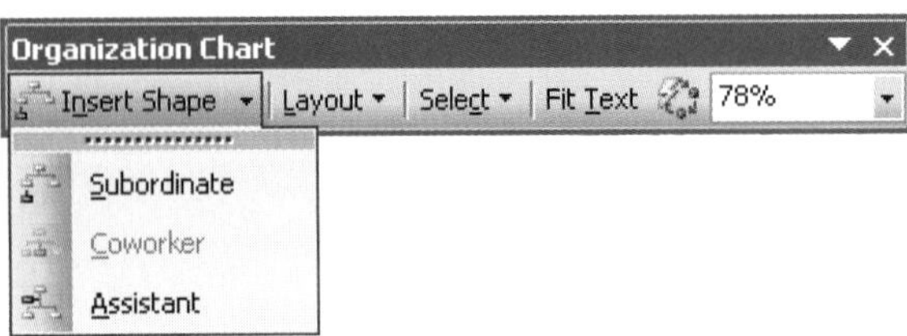

Figure 4.15 Organization Chart toolbar

▶ Shapes behave like text boxes. Use the same techniques to enter text or to format a shape that you used with text boxes. You can apply a preset style that comes with PowerPoint to organization charts. To apply a preset style, click the AutoFormat button on the Organization Chart toolbar and choose a style from the Organization Chart Style Gallery dialog box, as shown in Figure 4.16. You can also right-click on a diagram part and choose a format option from the shortcut menu.

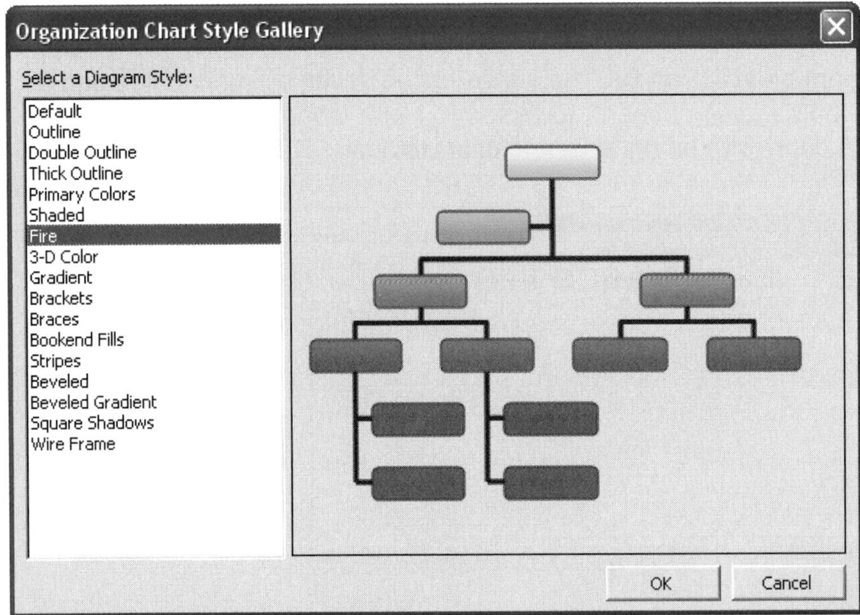

Figure 4.16 Organization Chart Style Gallery

TRY *it* OUT *p4-5*

Note: The presentation from Try it Out p4-4 should be displayed.

1. Click the **New Slide** button.
2. Click the **Content** slide thumbnail in the Slide Layout task pane.
3. Click the **Insert Diagram or Organization Chart** icon.
4. Click the **Organization Chart diagram** type and click **OK.**
5. Click in the top (superior) box and enter the following on two lines: `Jen Patton President.`
6. Click in the left subordinate box and enter the following on two lines: `Darren Wong Vice President.`
7. Click the middle subordinate coworker box and enter the following on two lines: `Denise Richards Vice President.`
8. Click the border of the right subordinate box and press **Delete.**
9. Click Darren Wong's box. Click the **Insert Shape** list arrow on the Organization Chart toolbar and click **Assistant.**
10. Click the **Assistant box** and enter the following on two lines: `Michelle Reiner Assistant.`
11. Click Darren Wong's box. Click the **Select** button on the Organization Chart toolbar and click **Level.**
12. Click **Format, AutoShape.** Click the **Colors and Lines** tab (if not already displayed).
13. Click the **Color** list arrow and select a different color.
14. Click **OK.**
15. Click and drag a corner size handle to reduce the size of the drawing canvas.
16. Click the slide outside the chart placeholder.
17. Close the presentation; do not save.

POWERPOINT

Work with Media

- Media include sound effects, music, video, or animated .gifs (pictures that have animation effects) that you can add to slides. The media becomes activiated during a slide show.
- You can add media clips to slides in the same way that you add clip-art images. Like clip art, media clips come preloaded with Office and are located in the Microsoft Clip Organizer.
- To add a media clip, use a slide layout that contains a media clip icon. Click (or double-click) the icon as indicated on the slide to open the Media Clip dialog box shown in Figure 4.17, then scroll or search for a sound, video clip, or animated .gif. (Video clips and animated .gifs are indicated by a "star" icon in the lower right of the thumbnail.) Click to select the clip, then click OK. PowerPoint prompts you to play the media clip automatically in the slide show when the slide appears. If you indicate no, the media clip will play only when you click to select it.

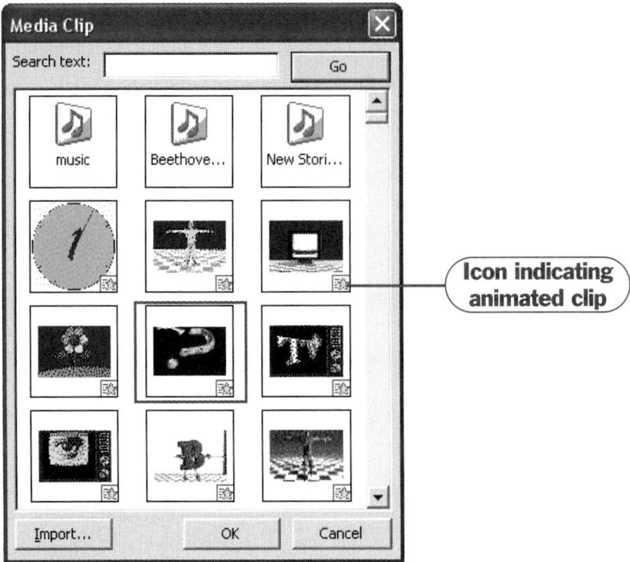

Figure 4.17 Media Clip dialog box

- You can also insert media clips on slides without media content placeholders. To do so, click Insert, Movies and Sounds, then select Movie or Sound from Clip Organizer. In the Clip Art task pane that opens, as shown in Figure 4.18, scroll to search for an existing video, sound, or animated .gif. Make sure that Movies and Sounds are checked in the Results should be list.

Figure 4.18 Clip Art task pane

▶ Media clips appear on slides as shown in Figure 4.19. To play a media clip, you must be in Slide Show view. You can, however, preview a media clip in Normal view by double-clicking it, or by right-clicking the media clip and selecting either Play Movie or Play Sound. An animated .gif plays automatically in Slide Show view.

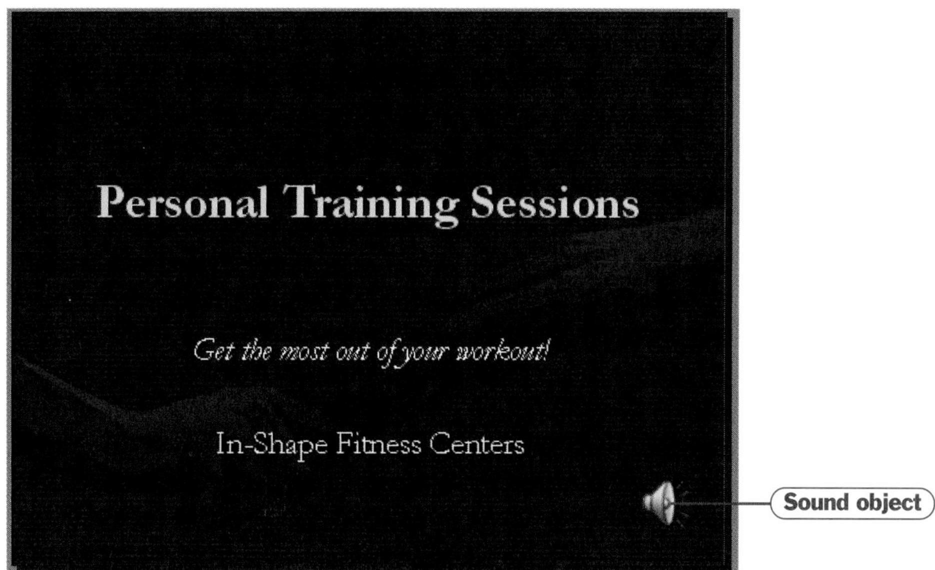

Figure 4.19 Media clips noted on a slide

POWERPOINT

Looping Media

▶ *Looping* allows you to play a sound or movie continuously until you advance to the next slide. To loop a sound or movie, right-click the media clip and select Edit Movie Object or Edit Sound Object. The Movie or Sound Options dialog box opens, as shown in Figures 4.20 and 4.21. Click the Loop until stopped check box.

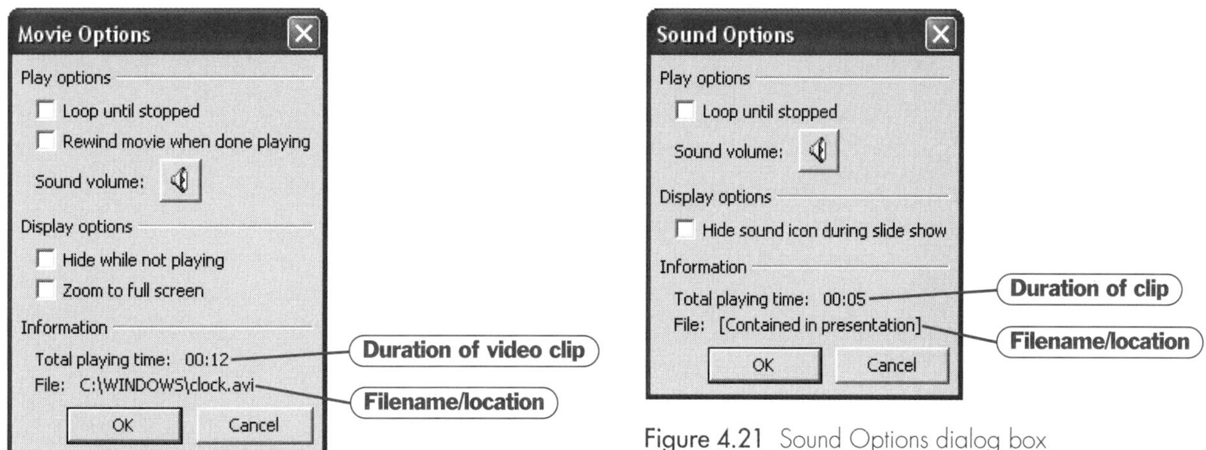

Figure 4.20 Movie Options dialog box

Figure 4.21 Sound Options dialog box

TRY*it*OUT *p4-6*

1. Start a new blank presentation.
2. Click **Format, Slide Layout.**
3. Click the **Content** slide thumbnail to apply it.
4. Click the **Insert Media Clip** icon. 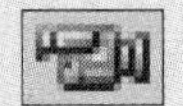
5. Scroll down to find an animated .gif. Click it and click **OK.**
6. Click the **Slide Show View** button.
7. Press the **Escape** key to end the slide show. 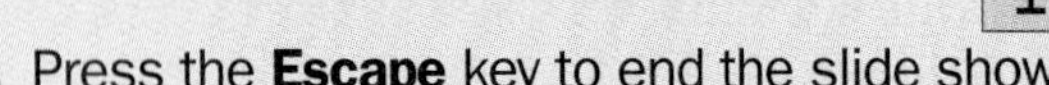
8. Click **Insert, Movies and Sounds,** and **Sound from Clip Organizer.**
9. Click a music clip.
10. Select the **When Clicked** option.
11. Click and drag the sound object to the lower right of the slide.
12. Click the **Slide Show View** button.
13. Click the **media clip** (sound object) to play it.
14. Click anywhere on the slide and press the **Esc** key to end the slide show.
15. Close the file; do not save.

Insert Music from a CD

▶ To enhance your presentation with music from a CD, insert a CD in the computer's CD-ROM drive. Display the slide on which you want the music to play, and click Insert, select Movies and Sound, and click Play CD Audio Track. In the Insert CD Audio dialog box that opens, shown in Figure 4.22, click in the Start at Track box, enter the track number of the song you want to play, click the Time box and enter the time of the starting point in the track. Click the End at Track box, enter the track number where the music will end, click the Time box, and enter the time of the ending point in the track. The dialog box shows the total playing time. If you want the music to repeat automatically when it is finished playing, click the Loop until stopped box.

Figure 4.22 Insert CD Audio dialog box

▶ Figure 4.22 shows a setting to play a CD from the beginning of Track 1 through the beginning of Track 2, with a total playing time of 25 seconds.

TRY *it* OUT *p4-7*

Note: You must have a music CD available to complete this Try it Out.

1. Open **p4.7training** from the Data CD. Display Slide 1 (if it is not already displayed).
2. Insert a CD into the CD-ROM drive.
3. Click **Insert,** select **Movies and Sounds,** and click **Play CD Audio Track.**
4. Click the **Start at Track** increment arrow to display Track 2 and click the **End at Track** increment arrow to display Track 3. Click **OK.**
5. Click the **Automatically** option.
6. Click and drag the **CD** icon to the bottom-right of the first slide.
7. Click the **Slide Show View** button. The music will begin automatically. Then click the mouse to advance to the next slide.
8. Press the **Esc** key. Close the presentation; do not save.

GOAL
To use the AutoContent Wizard to create a presentation containing charts, diagrams, and media

SETTING THE STAGE/WRAPUP
File name: 4.1realty

WHAT YOU NEED TO KNOW

- A persuasive presentation is used to convince the audience in some way.
- A persuasive presentation should clearly state your goals, your expectations, and the benefits of your proposal.
- Media clips can be used to get the audience's attention and emphasize points within your presentation. However, be sure they do not overshadow the presentation. The media clips that you select should complement the subject of the presentation.
- If you are using music from a CD in your presentation, you must give credit to the source of the material (in this case, the musician). Also, some music may be copyrighted, which means that, depending on how you plan to use the presentation, you may need to obtain permission to use the music.
- In this Rehearsal activity, you will use the AutoContent Wizard to create a presentation that persuades a real estate developer to hire Four Corners Realty Company as its exclusive sales agent. You will use charts, diagrams, hyperlinks, and media clips to enhance the presentation.

DIRECTIONS

1. Start the AutoContent Wizard.
   a. Apply the **Selling a Product or Service** presentation template. Note: Templates must be installed on your computer to complete this activity. You can also download templates from *www.microsoft.com*.
   b. Select the on-screen presentation delivery output.
   c. Enter the following presentation title: `Four Corners Realty.`
   d. Include the following footer on all slides: `Selling fine properties for more than 25 years...`
   e. Include the slide number, but not the date, on all slides.
2. Delete any preexisting template logo or footer that appears on the slides.
3. Enter the following subtitle on the title slide: `The Lake View Development`
4. Replace slide text as indicated in Illustration A. Notice the new text corresponds to this template slide text.

Continued on next page

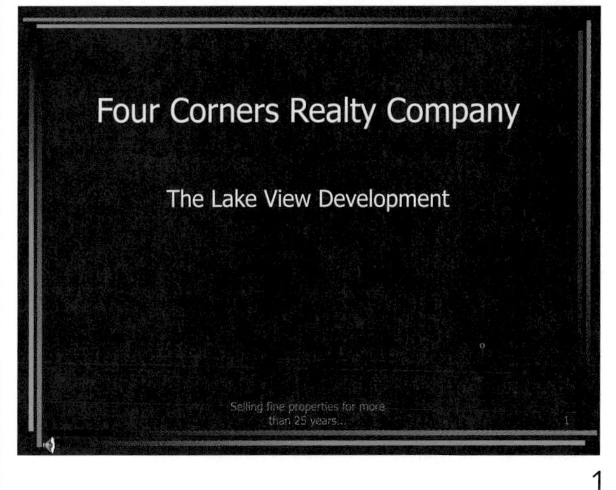
Four Corners Realty Company
The Lake View Development
Selling fine properties for more than 25 years...
1

1

We Work to Market and Sell Your Property

- Stellar history of residential on-site marketing
- Plan and implement strong marketing program
- Implement budgets based on sales and marketing strategy
- Assist developers in pricing strategies
- Help attain necessary financing
- Provide accurate market analysis

Selling fine properties for more than 25 years... 2

2

Action

- Target appropriate demo
  - Part-time residents
  - Retirees
- Provide incentives to sell property early
- Create and distribute comprehensive press kits

Selling fine properties for more than 25 years... 3

3

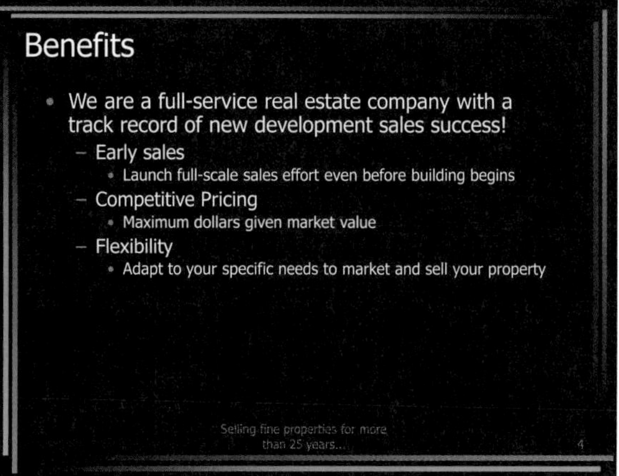
Benefits
We are a full-service real estate company with a track record of new development sales success!
Early sales
Launch full-scale sales effort even before building begins
Competitive Pricing
Maximum dollars given market value
Flexibility
Adapt to your specific needs to market and sell your property
Selling fine properties for more than 25 years...
4

4

Choose the Right Broker!

- Experience
- Outstanding Staff
- Proven Success
- Detailed and respected marketing plans

Selling fine properties for more than 25 years... 5

5

Illustration A

Continued on next page

5. Insert new slides as shown in Illustration B.
   a. On the Title, Text, and Content slide, delete the data from the datasheet and enter the new data shown here:

	2002	2003	2004
1 BR	98,000	105,000	119,000
2 BR	128,000	139,000	154,000
3 BR	187,000	210,000	222,000

   b. On the Title and Content slide, enter the managers' names and their titles, as indicated in Illustration B. Apply an AutoFormat.
   c. Add a summary slide as Slide 2, which contains the titles of Slides 2 through 6.
   d. Include hyperlinks where indicated in Illustration B, from the slide title to its corresponding slide.
6. On Slide 1, insert a sound clip to play classical music. The sound should play automatically when the slide show begins. Place the sound object in the bottom-left corner of the slide.
7. Run the slide show several times; activate the hyperlinks each time.
8. Print one copy of the presentation as handouts with six slides per page.
9. Save the file; name it **4.1realty.** Close the file.

Continued on next page

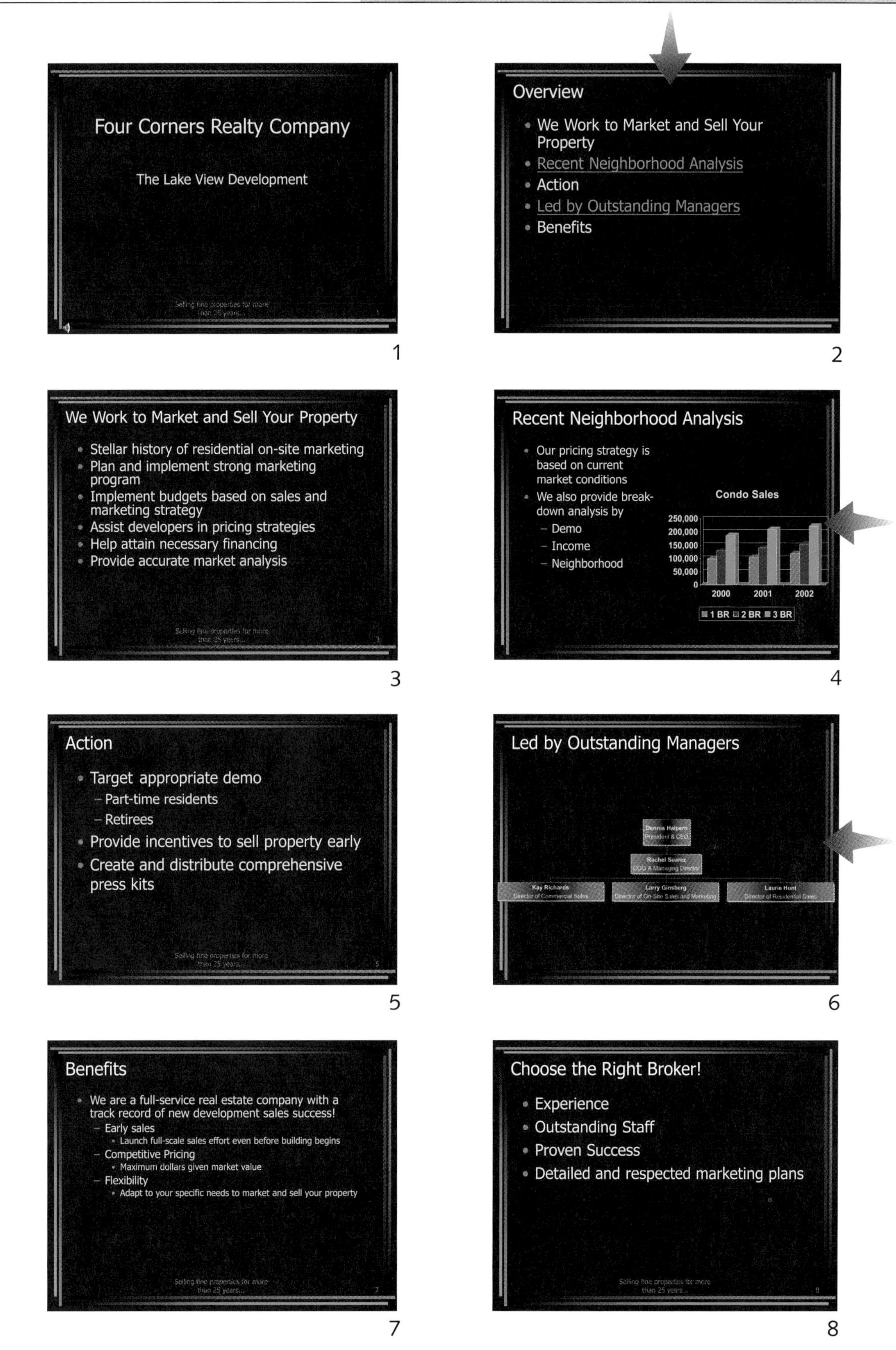

Four Corners Realty Company
The Lake View Development
1
Overview
We Work to Market and Sell Your Property
Recent Neighborhood Analysis
Action
Led by Outstanding Managers
Benefits
2
We Work to Market and Sell Your Property
Stellar history of residential on-site marketing
Plan and implement strong marketing program
Implement budgets based on sales and marketing strategy
Assist developers in pricing strategies
Help attain necessary financing
Provide accurate market analysis
3
Recent Neighborhood Analysis
Our pricing strategy is based on current market conditions
We also provide break-down analysis by
Demo
Income
Neighborhood
Condo Sales
250,000
200,000
150,000
100,000
50,000
0
2000
2001
2002
1 BR 2 BR 3 BR
4
Action
Target appropriate demo
Part-time residents
Retirees
Provide incentives to sell property early
Create and distribute comprehensive press kits
5
Led by Outstanding Managers
6
Benefits
We are a full-service real estate company with a track record of new development sales success!
Early sales
Launch full-scale sales effort even before building begins
Competitive Pricing
Maximum dollars given market value
Flexibility
Adapt to your specific needs to market and sell your property
7
Choose the Right Broker!
Experience
Outstanding Staff
Proven Success
Detailed and respected marketing plans
8

Illustration B

POWERPOINT

Cues for Reference

Open a Template Presentation

1. Click **File, New.**
2. Click the **On my computer** link in the New Presentation task pane.
3. Click the **Presentations** tab.
4. Click the presentation you want.
5. Click **OK.**

or

1. Click the **Templates on Office Online** link.
2. Enter **Presentations** in the search box.
3. Download the presentation you want from those listed.

Office XP

1. Click **File, New.**
2. Click the **From Design Template** link in the New Presentation task pane.
3. Click the **General Templates** link.
4. Click the **Presentations** tab.
5. Click required presentation.
6. Click **OK.**

Use AutoContent Wizard

1. Click **File, New.**
2. Click the **From AutoContent Wizard** link in the New Presentation task pane.
3. Follow the prompts to complete the presentation template.

Insert a Table

1. Click the **New Slide** button.
   or
   Right-click the mouse on the slide and click **Slide Layout.**
2. Click the thumbnail of a slide layout containing a content placeholder.
3. Click the **Insert Table** icon.
4. Enter the number of columns.
5. Press **Tab.**
6. Enter the number of rows.
7. Click **OK.**

Insert a Table without Using a Placeholder

1. Display the slide on which you want the table.
2. Click the **Insert Table** button on the Standard toolbar and drag to highlight the required number of columns or rows.

or

1. Click **Insert, Table.**
2. Enter the number of columns and rows.
3. Click **OK.**

Insert a Chart on a Slide

1. Click the **New Slide** button.
   or
   Right-click the mouse on the slide and click **Slide Layout.**
2. Click the thumbnail of a slide layout containing a content placeholder.
3. Click the **Insert Chart** icon. 
4. Delete the sample data and enter the data you want to chart in the datasheet.

Hide the Datasheet

- Click **View, Datasheet.**

Select a Chart Type

1. Click **Chart, Chart Type.**
2. Click the **Standard Types** tab or the **Custom Types** tab.
3. Click a chart type or subchart type (if necessary).
4. Click **OK.**

Insert a Diagram or an Organizaton Chart

1. Click the **New Slide** button.
   or
   Right-click the mouse on the slide and click **Slide Layout.**
2. Click the thumbnail of a slide layout containing a content placeholder.
3. Click the **Insert Diagram or Organization Chart** icon.
4. Click a diagram type.
5. Click **OK.**

Add Shapes to an Organization Chart

1. Click the box to which you want to attach a shape.
2. Click the **Insert Shape** list arrow on the Organization Chart toolbar.
3. Click an option: **Subordinate, Coworker,** or **Assistant.**

Add Media to Slides

1. Apply a content slide layout.
2. Click the **Insert Media Clip** icon. 
3. Click a sound, movie, or animated .gif.
4. Click **OK.**
5. Click **Automatically** or **When Clicked** when prompted to play the sound or video automatically in the slide show.

or

1. Click **Insert, Movies and Sounds, Sound or Movie from Clip Organizer** or **Sound or Movie from File.**
2. Click sound or movie clip.
3. Click **Automatically** or **When Clicked** and click **OK.**

Play Music from a CD

1. Click **Insert,** select **Movies and Sounds,** and click **Play CD Audio Track.**
2. Click **Start at Track** box and enter number of track on which to start playing.
3. Click **End at Track** box and enter number of track after which to stop playing.
4. Click **Loop until stopped** box to restart music automatically.
5. Click **OK.**

Loop Sound or Video Clips

1. Right-click the sound or video object.
2. Click **Edit Movie Object** or **Edit Sound Object.**
3. Click in the **Loop until stopped** check box.
4. Click **OK.**

Play Media Clips

1. Click the **Slide Show View** button. 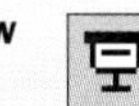
2. Click the sound or movie object to play it, if necessary.

GOAL
To practice using the following skill sets:
- Use custom animations
- Use the annotation pen
- Work with a photo album

WHAT YOU NEED TO KNOW

Use Custom Animations

- As you learned in Lesson 2, animations are visual or sound effects that you can add to text or objects during a slide show. In that lesson, you learned to apply preset animation schemes (preset animations include a transition effect). A customized animation scheme allows you to choose animation effects and combine them.
- To create a *custom animation,* you must be in Normal view. Display the slide on which you want to animate text or objects and click Slide Show, Custom Animation. This displays the Custom Animation task pane, as shown in Figure 4.23.
- Select the text or object you want to animate on the slide and click the Add Effect button in the task pane. Select one of the following animation options, as shown in Figure 4.24:
  - Entrance — animates an item as it enters the slide.
  - Emphasis — animates an item that is already displayed on the slide.
  - Exit — animates an item as it exits the slide.
  - Motion Paths — animates text or an object so it follows a specific path during the slide show.
- Each option displays a list of effects. The More Effects option displays an extensive list of effects ranging from subtle to exciting. You can add one or multiple animation effects to text or objects.
- The effect(s) appear(s) in the Custom Animation list in the task pane with a number, timing icon, and animation effect icon (a star), as shown in Figure 4.25.
  - The numbers indicate the order in which the animation will play; the timing icon indicates how the animation will be activated.
  - The animation effect icon indicates the animation type that you applied (Entrance, Emphasis, Exit, or Motion Paths).

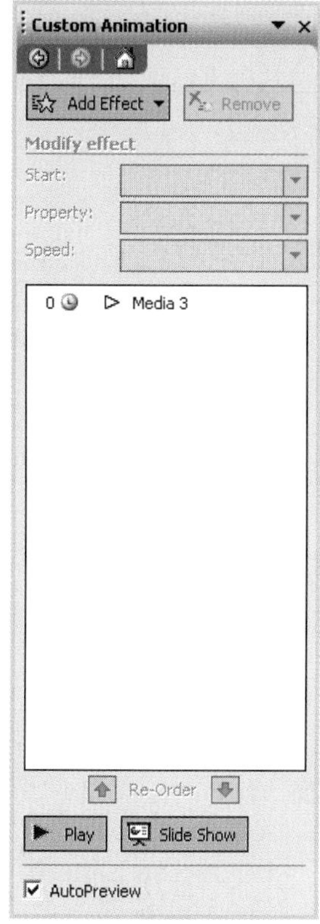

Figure 4.23 Custom Animation task pane

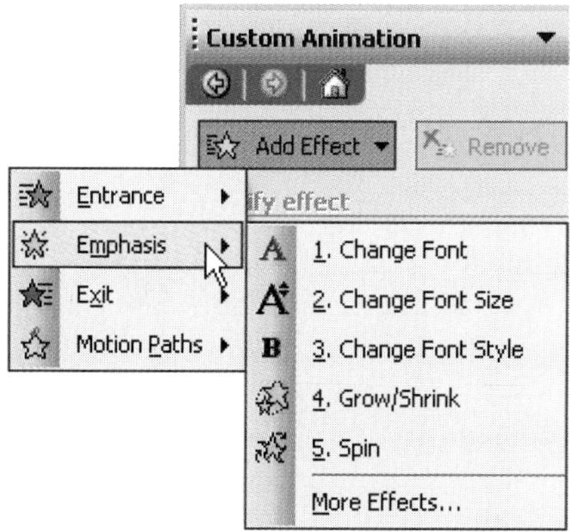

Figure 4.24 Add Effect menu button

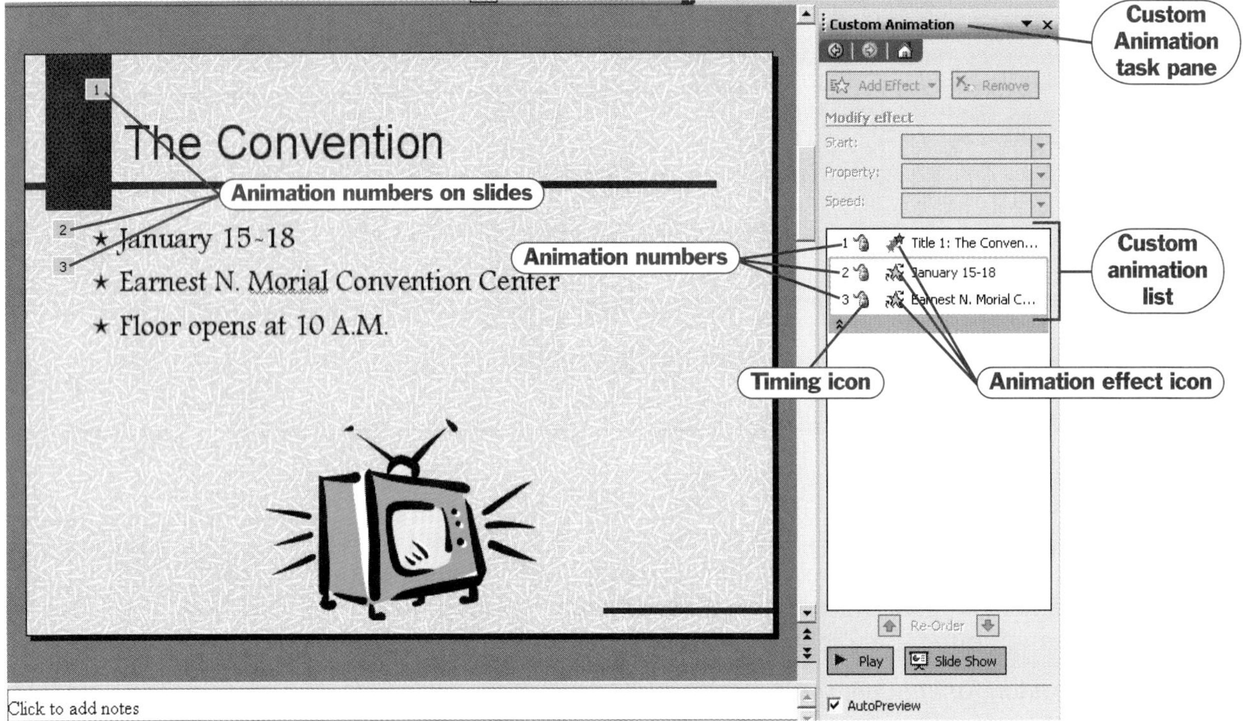

Figure 4.25 Apply custom animation

- Some animations provide Direction, Speed, or other custom options, as shown in Figure 4.26. For example, if you apply a Fly In text effect, you can also choose to have the text appear From Bottom and Fast. Click the Direction, Speed, or other custom option list arrow in the task pane and choose the effect(s) you want.
- When you apply an animation to text or objects on a slide, a star icon will appear next to the slide thumbnail on the Slides tab and below the slide thumbnail in Slide Sorter view, as shown in Figure 4.27.

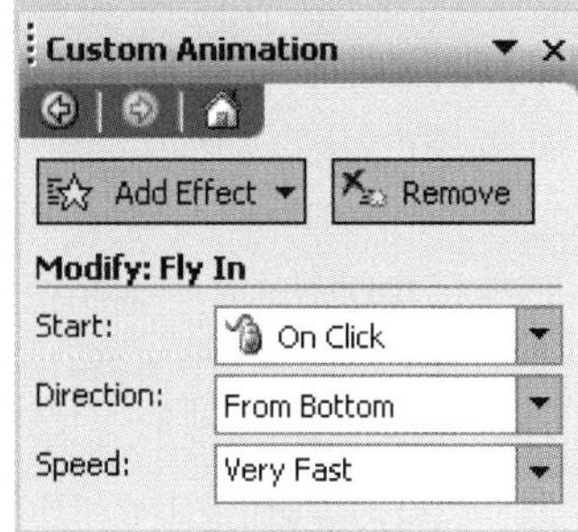

Figure 4.26 Modify custom animation

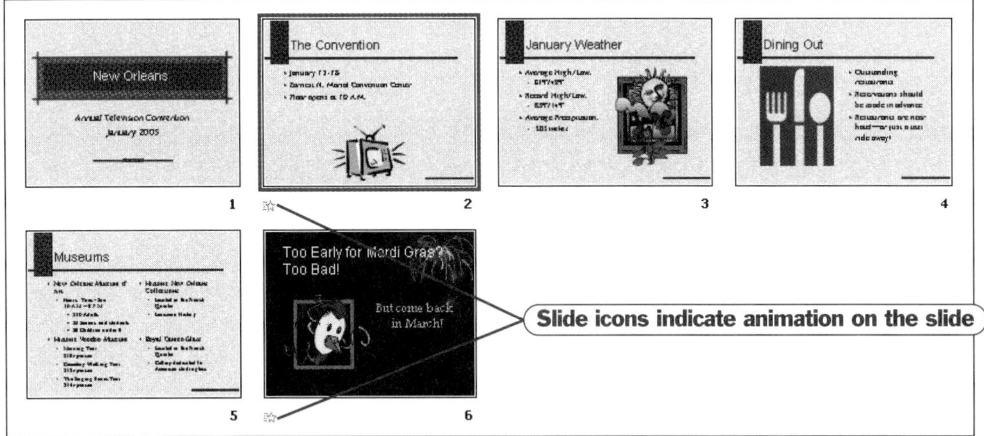

Figure 4.27 Animation icon on slide

TRY it OUT *p4-8*

1. Open **p4.8neworleans** from the Data CD.
2. Display **Slide 2** in Normal view and click the title, **The Convention.**
3. Click **Slide Show, Custom Animation.**
4. Click **Add Effect, Entrance,** and click **Fly In.**
5. Click the Direction list arrow and select **From Top.** Click the Speed list arrow and select **Medium.**
6. Click the bulleted text, click **Add Effect, Emphasis,** click **More Effects,** scroll down, then double-click **Blast** under the exciting category.
7. Click the **TV** clip art object, click **Add Effect, Entrance,** (More Effects, if necessary), and click **Appear,** then click **OK.**
8. Do not close the presentation.

POWERPOINT

Edit a Custom Animation

- To change an animation effect after you apply it, click the animation effect in the Custom Animation list. Then click the Change button and apply a new effect, or click the Remove button to delete it, as shown in Figure 4.28.

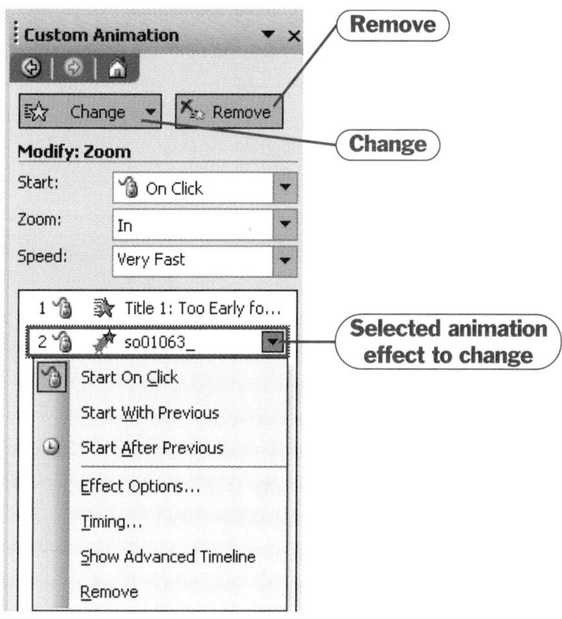

Figure 4.28 Change animation effect

- The animations play in the order in which they are numbered. The numbers also appear on the slide to help you visualize the order in which the animations will play. Multiple animations are indicated on the slide by either additional numbers next to the animated object or by an ellipsis (...) next to the original animation number, as shown in Figure 4.29.

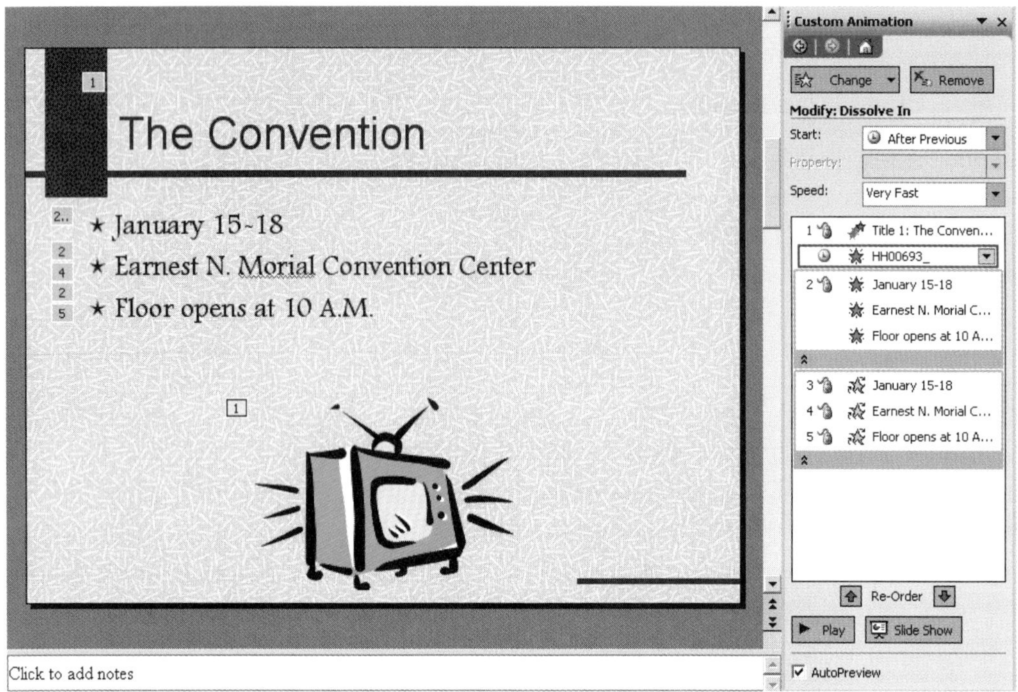

Figure 4.29 Multiple animation effects

- To change the play order, click the effect in the Custom Animation task pane list and click the up or down Re-Order buttons, as shown in Figure 4.30. To preview a slide's animation effects, display the slide and click the Play button in the Custom Animation task pane (see Figure 4.23). This also displays a timeline, shown in Figure 4.30, which shows the timing for each animation.

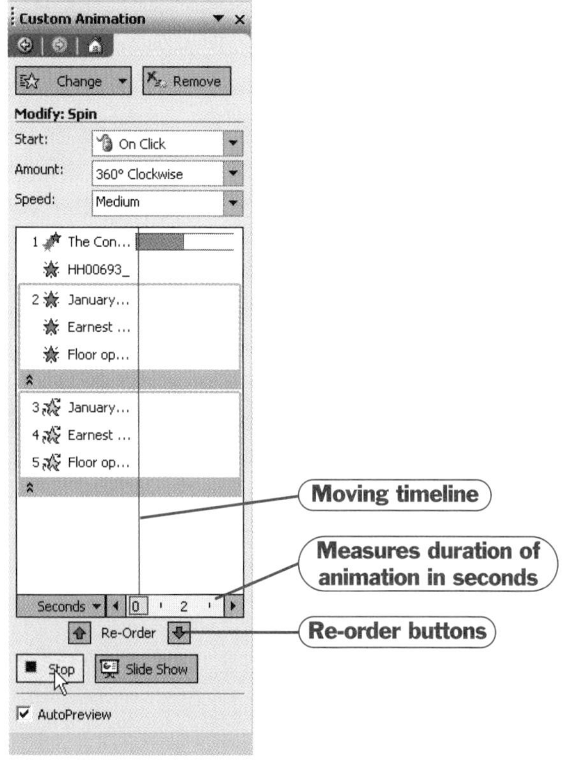

Figure 4.30 Play animation

▶ Use the slide master to apply the same animation effect to all titles or bulleted text throughout a presentation. If you are in Normal view and you try to reorder an animation effect that you created in slide master view, you must click the Master Animation list arrow in the Custom Animation list and click the Copy Effects to Slide option, as shown in Figure 4.31.

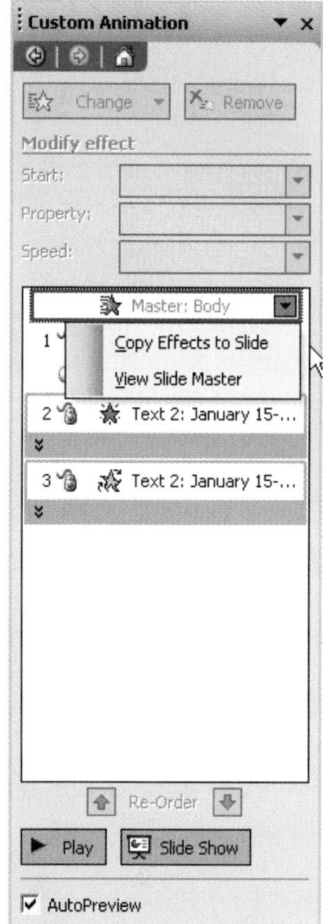

Figure 4.31 Copy slide master effects to a slide

POWERPOINT

TRY *it* OUT *p4-9*

Note: ***p4.8neworleans*** *should still be open on your screen.*

1. Display **Slide 2,** click **Animation #2 (Text 2)** in the Custom Animation list, click **Change, Entrance, More Effects,** and click **Appear.**
2. Click the bulleted text on the slide, click **Add Effect, Emphasis,** and click **Spin.**
3. Click **Animation #5 (TV clip art object)** in the Custom Animation list, click **Change, Entrance, Dissolve In,** and click **OK.**
4. Click **Animation #5 (TV clip art object)** and click the **Re-Order** up arrow button until it becomes Animation #2.
5. Click the **Play** button. 

6. Display **Slide 6** and click the clip art object.
7. In the Custom Animation task pane, click **Add Effect, Entrance, More Effects,** and double-click **Zoom** under the moderate category.
8. Do not close the presentation.

Apply Sound and Other Effects

- To apply sound effects, set timings, or change the way text is animated, click the Custom Animation list arrow of the animation effect you want to modify, and select Effect Options from the menu that appears, as shown in Figure 4.32.
- In the dialog box that opens (which displays the name of the applied effect), click the Effect tab, as shown in Figure 4.33, click the Sound list arrow, and select a sound effect that you want to add to your animation. If you download a sound effect from the Internet or have a sound effect on disk, click Other Sound from the bottom of the list and double-click the sound file. To change the volume of the sound effect, click the sound icon and drag the volume button up or down on the pop-up menu.
- You can add other enhancements to your animation on the Effect tab. Choose whether you want text or an object to dim or change color after it is animated by clicking the After animation list arrow and selecting a color. Animate text all at once, by word or letter, by clicking the Animate text list arrow and selecting an option. If you apply a sound effect and animate text letter-by-letter, each time a letter appears on screen, the sound effect will play.

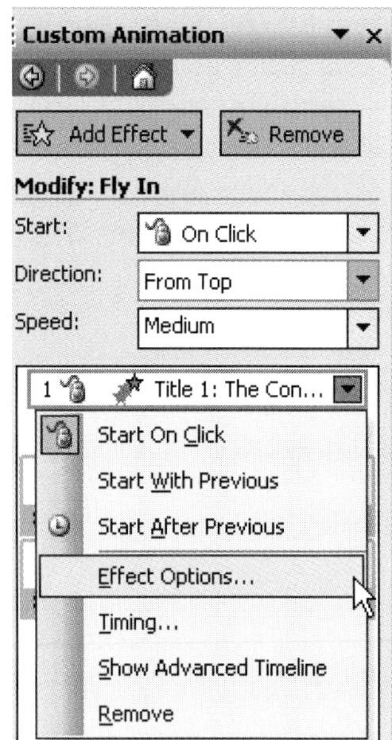

Figure 4.32 Custom Animation list arrow

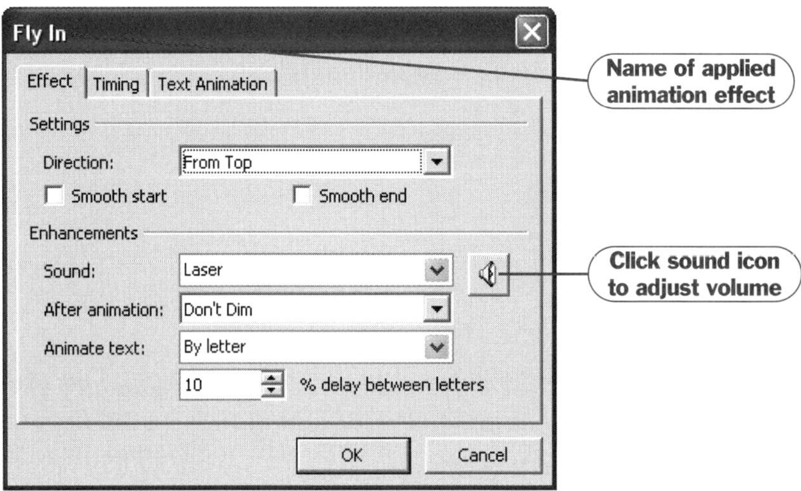

Figure 4.33 Effect tab

- You can apply a number of timing options to your animations to ensure that text and objects appear smoothly and look professional. These options include setting start times (including delays), speed or duration, and repeat effects. You can also set Triggers, an animation option that plays the animation when a specified item is clicked.

▶ Click the Timing tab, as shown in Figure 4.34, and select one or more of the following options to set animation timing effects shown in the table below.

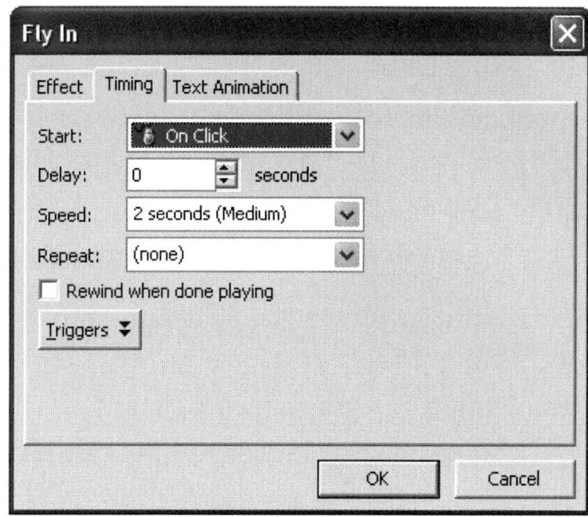

Figure 4.34 Timing tab

TO SET THIS TIMING EFFECT OPTION:	DO THIS:
Select a timing option	• Click the Start list arrow. • Select an option. *Note: to start the animation by clicking the slide, click the On Click option. To start the animation at the same time as the previous animation, click the With Previous option. To start the animation after the previous animation, click After Previous.*
Create a delay between the end of one animation and the start of another	• Click in the Delay box and enter the number of seconds by which to delay the animation.
Set the speed of an animation	• Click the Speed list arrow and select an option.
Loop an animation	• Click the Repeat list arrow and select an option.
Rewind an animation automatically after it plays	• Click the Rewind when done playing check box.
Set an animation to play when you click text or an object	• Click the Triggers button, select the Start effect on click of option, and select an item from the list.

▶ Click the Text Animation tab, as shown in Figure 4.35, to change the way text appears on screen and to set timings for animated paragraphs or bullets. Click the Group text list arrow to select how you want to group text when it appears on the slide. If you want paragraphs or bullets to display automatically without having to click the mouse, click Automatically after and indicate the number of seconds after which the next set of text should appear.

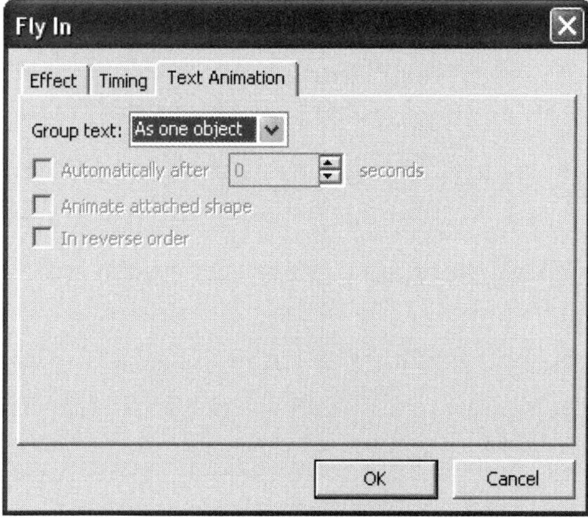

Figure 4.35 Text Animation tab

TRY it OUT *p4-10*

Note: ***p4.8neworleans*** *should still be open on your screen.*

1. Display **Slide 2.**
2. Select **Animation #1 (The Convention)**, click its list arrow in the Custom Animation list, and then click **Effect Options.**
3. Click the **Effect** tab, click the **Sound** list arrow, and select **Laser.** Click the **Animate text** list arrow, select **By letter,** and click **OK.** *Note: If sound clips are not available to you, they may need to be installed.*
4. Select **Animation #2 (TV clip art object)**, click its list arrow, and then click **Effect Options.**
5. Click the **Effect** tab, click the **Sound** list arrow, and select **Voltage.**
6. Click the **Timing** tab, click the **Start** list arrow, and select **After Previous.** Click the **Delay** box increment arrow to display **.5 seconds,** and click **OK.**
7. Select **Animation #3 (which is now Text 2),** click its list arrow, and then click **Effect Options.** Click the **Text Animation** tab, click the **Group text** list arrow, select **All paragraphs at once,** and click **OK.**
8. Click the **Slide Show View** button and display the text and objects on **Slide 2.** Then press the **Esc** key.
9. Close the presentation; save the file as **4.10neworleans.yi** (yi = your initials).

Animate Charts

- You can animate charts and diagrams using the same techniques used to animate text and objects. You can also animate individual sections of a chart or diagram to create an interesting effect or emphasize data.
- To animate a chart, select the chart and click Slide Show, Custom Animation. Click the Add Effect button and select the animation effect you want to apply. To animate individual sections of the chart, click the Animation list arrow and click Effect Options. In the Effect Options dialog box that opens, click the Chart Animation tab and select the element you want to animate from the Group chart list, as shown in Figure 4.36. Click the Animate grid and legend box if you want to animate that, as well.

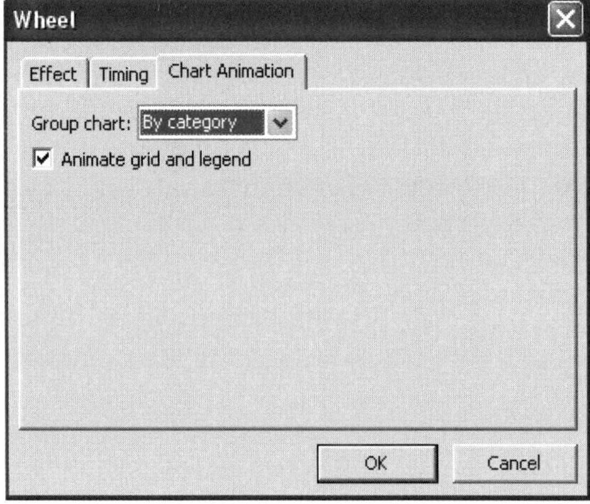

Figure 4.36 Chart Animation tab

TRY*it* OUT *p4-11*

1. Open **p4.11charts** from the Data CD.
2. Click the pie chart, click **Slide Show,** and click **Custom Animation.**
3. Click **Add Effect, Entrance,** and click **More Effects** and then choose **Dissolve In,** then click **OK.**
4. Click the **Animation #1 (Chart 2)** list arrow in the Custom Animation list, and click **Effect Options.**
5. Click the **Chart Animation** tab, click the **Group chart** list arrow, and click **By category.** Click in the **Animate grid and legend** box to select it, if necessary, and click **OK.**
6. Click the **Slide Show View** button.  
7. Do not close the file.

Animate Diagrams

▶ You can animate individual parts of a diagram or organization chart, just as you can animate sections of a chart. Select the diagram you want to animate and click Slide Show, Custom Animation. Click the Add Effect button and select the animation effect you want to apply. Then click the Animation list arrow and click Effect Options. In the Effect Options dialog box that opens, click the Diagram Animation tab and select how you want the diagram to animate from the Group diagram list, as shown in Figure 4.37.

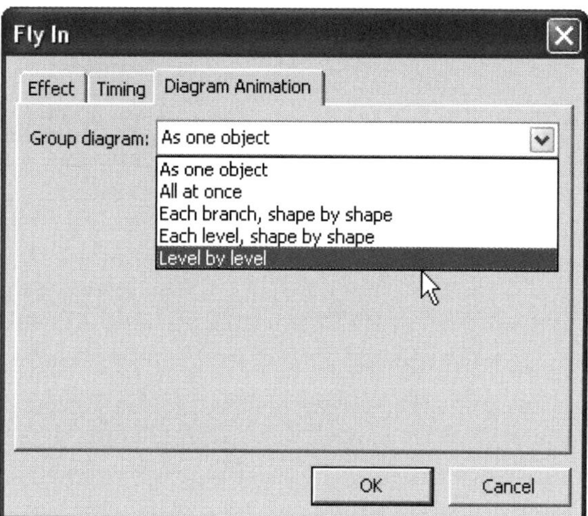

Figure 4.37 Diagram Animation tab

TRY*it* OUT *p4-12*

Note: ***p4.11charts*** *should still be open on your screen.*

1. Display **Slide 2.**
2. Click the organization chart to select it.
3. Click **Slide Show, Custom Animation** if the task pane is not displayed.
4. Click **Add Effect, Entrance,** and click **Fly In**.
5. Click the **Animation #1 (Organization Chart)** list arrow in the Custom Animation list and click **Effect Options.**
6. Click the **Diagram Animation** tab, click the **Group diagram** list arrow, click **Level by level,** and click **OK.**
7. Click the **Slide Show View** button and click the mouse to display the entire organization chart. 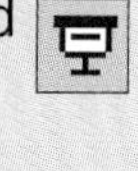
8. Close the file; do not save.

Create Self-Running Presentations

- You can set slide shows to run themselves, so that slides advance automatically and the presentation restarts when the slide show is finished. Self-running slide shows are particularly useful to display in a kiosk (a publicly accessed, freestanding computer terminal) at trade shows or on a sales counter.
- To create a self-running presentation, you must set slide transitions to run without having to click the mouse. As you have already learned, slide transitions control the way slides move on and off the screen during a slide show.
- When creating a self-running presentation, slide transition timings must be set to allow enough time for people to review the slide information. Click Slide Show, Slide Transition. In the Slide Transition task pane, click the Automatically after box, as shown in Figure 4.38, and set the number of seconds after which the slide advances to the next one. If both the On mouse click and Automatically after boxes are checked, the presentation advances to the next slide either on the mouse click or after the specified time—whichever comes first.

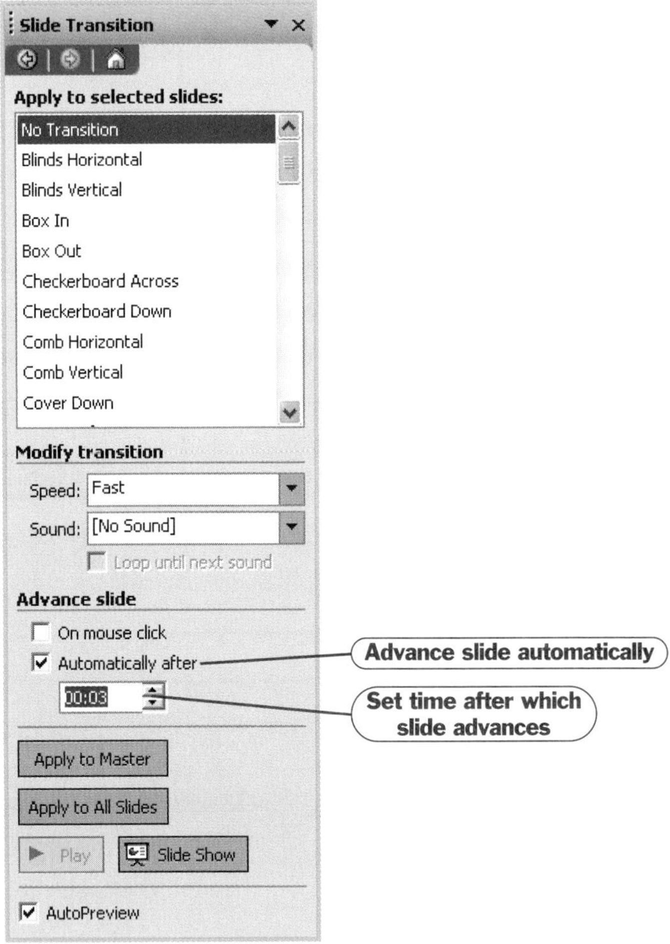

Figure 4.38 Slide Transition task pane

- When slide transitions advance slides automatically, objects on the slide animate automatically, whether or not they have been set to do so.

- You can set the slide show to restart automatically when it ends. Click Slide Show, Set Up Show. In the Set Up Show dialog box, as shown in Figure 4.39, click Loop continuously until 'Esc,' or click Browsed at a kiosk, which also sets the presentation to loop continuously.
- If you do not want animations to play at all during the slide show, click the Show without animation box in the Set Up Show dialog box.

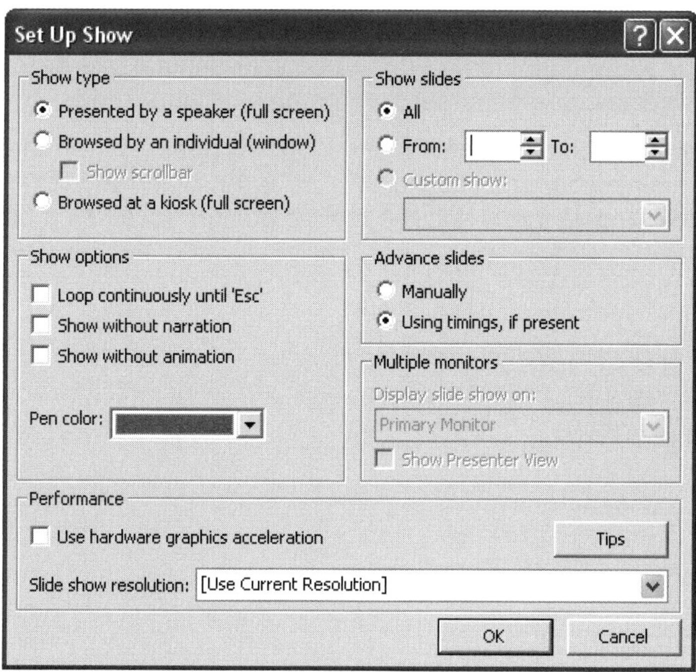

Figure 4.39 Set Up Show dialog box

TRY *it* OUT *p4-13*

1. Open **p4.13neworleans** from the Data CD.
2. Click **Slide Show, Slide Transition.**
3. Click the **Automatically after** box to select it. Click in the time box and set the time to `00:05`.
4. Click **Apply to All Slides.**
5. Click **Slide Show, Set Up Show.**
6. Click **Browsed at a kiosk** (notice that the Loop continuously until 'Esc' option becomes checked and dimmed) and click **OK.**
7. Click the **Slide Show View** button and view the slide show twice.
8. Close the file; do not save.

POWERPOINT

Use the Annotation Pen

- The *annotation pen,* or annotator, allows you to draw on slides during a slide show.
- Annotations made on the screen during a slide show do not alter the slide in any way and they disappear when you move on to another slide. PowerPoint suspends slide transition and animation timings when you are annotating; they begin again when you turn off the annotation pen.
- When you end the slide show, you will be prompted to Keep your annotations or Disgard them. You can click E on the keyboard to erase annotations from an individual slide.
- To access the annotation pen, click the Annotator menu icon, which appears in the lower-left corner of the screen during a slide show, as shown in Figure 4.40. When you click the icon, select the type of pen from the pop-up menu and the mouse pointer becomes a pen point so you can write on the slide.

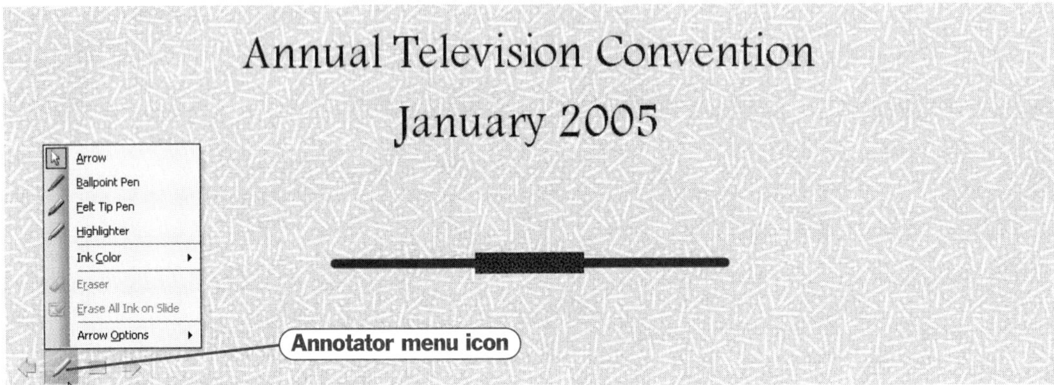

Figure 4.40 Annotator menu icon

- If you want to change the ink color, click the menu icon, select Ink Color, then select the color from the palette that displays.

TRY *it* OUT *p4-14*

1. Open **p4.14devon** from the Data CD. Display Slide 4.
2. Click the **Slide Show View** button.
3. Click the **Annotator Menu** icon. Note: The icon appears when the mouse is moved.
4. Click **Felt Tip Pen.**

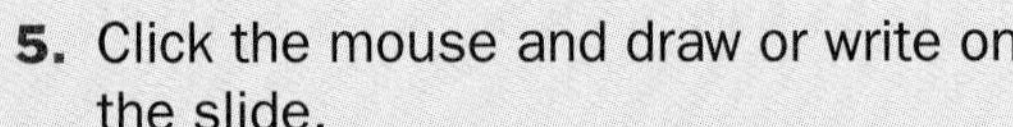

5. Click the mouse and draw or write on the slide.

Note: You might want to draw a line following the Fund's increase over the years.

6. Press the **E** key on the keyboard, which will erase your annotation on this slide.
7. Press the **Esc** key twice.
8. Close the file; do not save.

Work with Photo Albums

- A *photo album* is a collection of pictures that you can create from a variety of sources (file, disk, scanner, digital camera), which you can then customize with special layout options such as oval frames and captions. A photo album is an independent presentation that you can add to an existing presentation, publish to the Web, e-mail, and/or print.
- To create a photo album, click Insert, select Picture, and click New Photo Album. In the Photo Album dialog box that opens, as shown in Figure 4.41, you must indicate where your photos are coming from. Click the File/Disk button if your photos are saved on a file or disk. Select the folder or disk that contains the picture, click the picture, and click Insert. (To select multiple pictures, hold down the Ctrl key as you click each picture.)

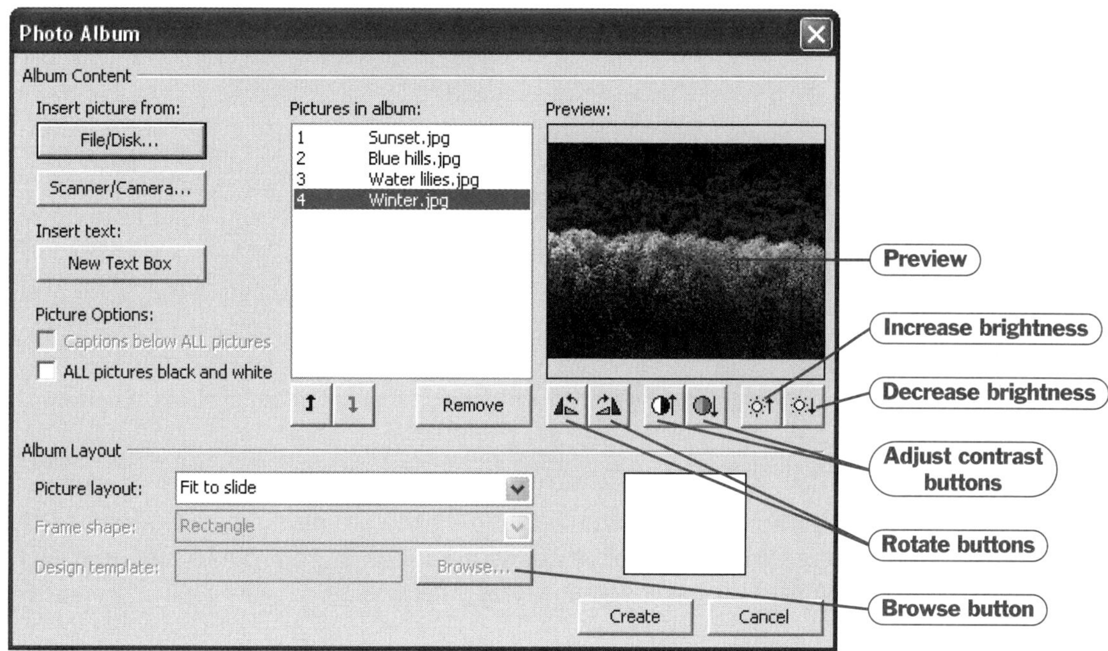

Figure 4.41 Photo Album dialog box

- If your images are coming from a scanner or digital camera, click the Scanner/Camera button and select the device you want to use. If your pictures are located in a digital camera, click Custom Insert and follow the prompts to insert the photos.
- After clicking Create to complete the album-creation process, a new presentation opens.
- You can customize the layout of the photo album pages (which are actually slides) to include frame options, captions, and/or text boxes. The layout you create applies to the entire photo album. You cannot customize individual pages.
- To include a text box placeholder as part of a photo album layout, click the New Text Box button in the Photo Album dialog box. The text box and picture file names that you are including in your photo album appear in the Pictures in album list box. When you select a picture, the preview window displays a thumbnail.
- To rotate the picture 90 degrees, click the rotate buttons. Click the appropriate buttons as many times as necessary to adjust the contrast and/or brightness of a picture. 

▶ You can specify the number of pictures on a slide by clicking the Picture layout list arrow, as shown in Figure 4.42, and selecting the number of pictures you want. The number on the left side of the Pictures in album list box indicates the slide on which the pictures will appear. The default is for one picture to fill an entire slide.

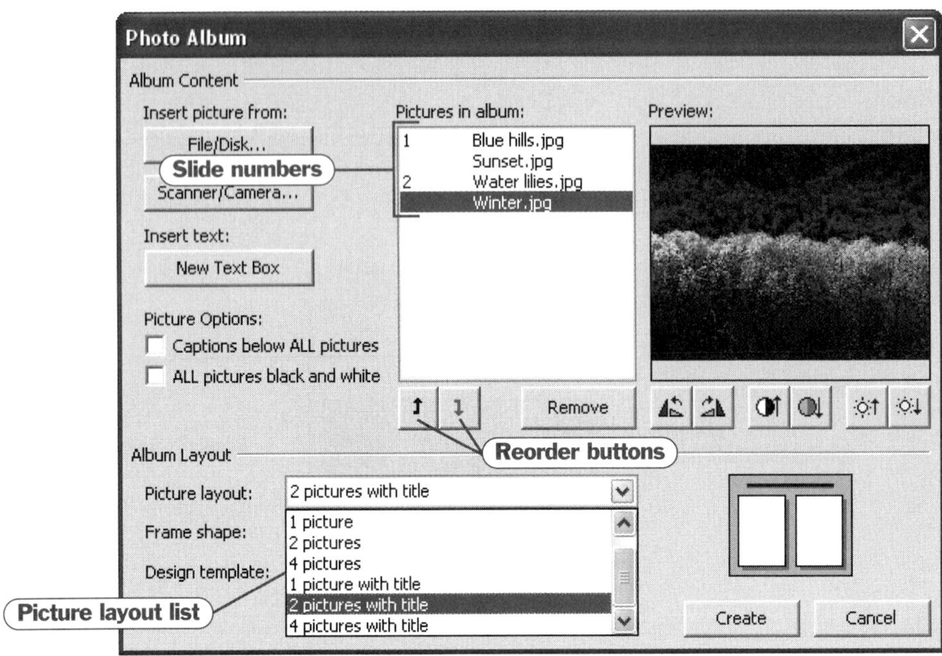

Figure 4.42 Change picture layout

▶ To change the frame that surrounds each picture, click the Frame shape list arrow and select an option, as shown in Figure 4.43. To apply a design template to your photo album, click the Browse button (see Figure 4.41), and select a template design.

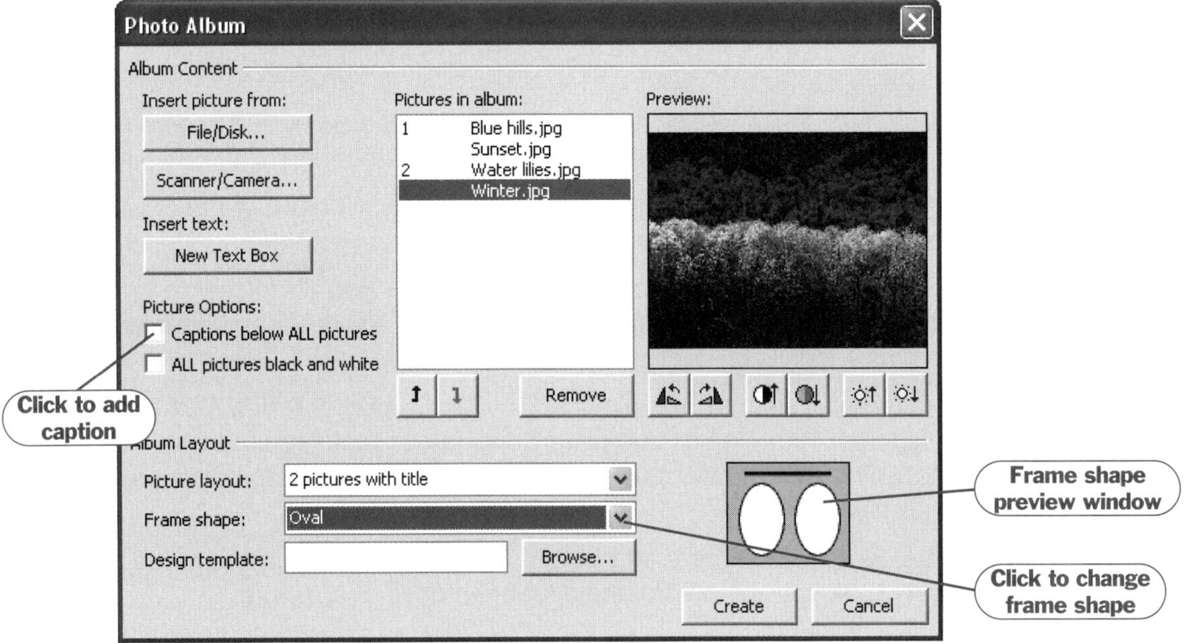

Figure 4.43 Change frame shape

▶ Click in the Captions below ALL pictures box to add a caption to each picture in the album. Your pictures will appear with a caption placeholder that contains the file name of the picture, as shown in Figure 4.44. Click the placeholder and enter your caption to replace the file name. To display pictures in black and white, click in the ALL pictures black and white box.

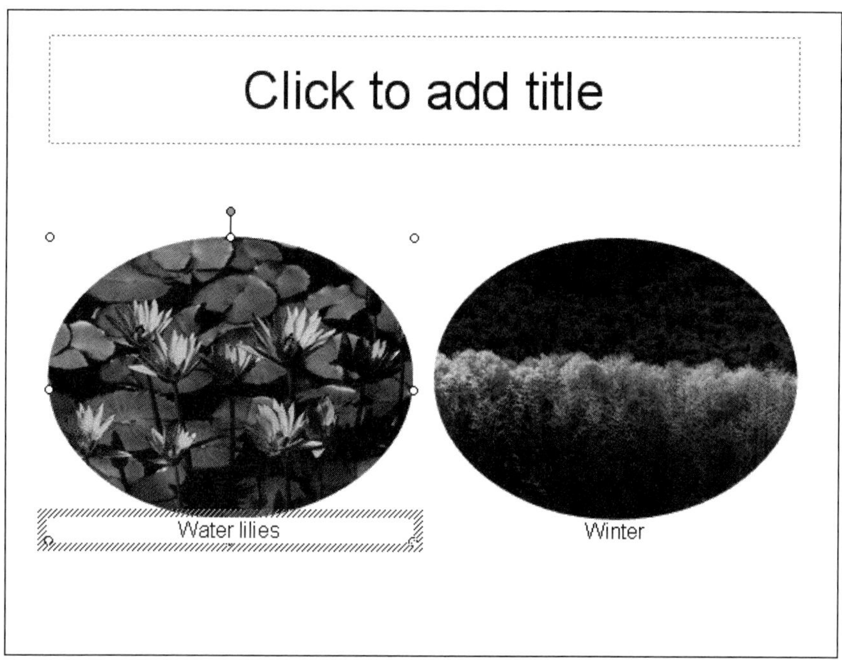

Figure 4.44 Album photos with captions

▶ After you select all appropriate options, click Create. The photo album automatically appears with a custom title slide, as shown in Figure 4.45. You can change the title and subtitle on the title slide as desired.

Figure 4.45 Title slide of photo album

POWERPOINT

▶ To insert a photo album into another presentation, you must first save and close the photo album. Then open the presentation in which you want to insert the photo album. Click Insert, Slides From Files, click the Browse button, double-click the photo album file, and click Insert All.

TRY *it* OUT *p4-15*

1. Click **Insert,** select **Picture,** and click **New Photo Album.**
2. Click the **File/Disk** button.
3. Click the **Look in** list arrow and select the **Data CD.**
4. Hold down the **Ctrl** key as you click **p4.15iceberg, p4.15paris,** and **p4.15wedcake.** Then click **Insert.**
5. Click the **New Text Box** button.
6. Click the **Picture layout** list arrow and click **2 pictures.**
7. Click the **Frame shape** list arrow and click **Oval.**
8. Reorder the items in the Pictures in album list box as follows: **p4.15wedcake, p4.15paris, Text Box, p4.15iceberg.**
9. Click in the **Captions below ALL pictures** box to select it.
10. Click **Browse** and select a template design to apply to the photo album.
11. Click **Create** and scroll through the slides to view the photo album.
12. Print one copy of the photo album.
13. Save the presentation as **4.15practicealbum.yi** (yi = your initials) and close it.

1
2
3

GOALS

To create and enhance a presentation using a table and diagrams

To create a self-running presentation that contains custom animations and a photo album

SETTING THE STAGE/WRAPUP

File names: **4.2training**
4.2broker
4.2photoalbum
4.2brokeralbum

WHAT YOU NEED TO KNOW

- In this Rehearsal activity, you will create three presentations as follows:
  - A presentation for In-Shape Fitness Centers, encouraging their members to buy personal training sessions. The fitness director has given you the information to include on each slide and has asked you to add a table and diagrams to it, as shown on the following pages. He has also asked you to make the presentation as exciting as possible, using sound, clip art, animated .gifs, transitions, and animation schemes.
  - A seven-slide presentation for potential clients of Four Corners Realty to persuade them to use Four Corners when they plan to buy or sell a home. Because Four Corners plans to run this presentation in a kiosk in the local mall, you must set the presentation to run continuously and loop it to restart automatically.
  - A photo album.

DIRECTIONS

In-Shape Fitness Centers

1. Create a new presentation as shown on the following pages.
2. Apply any template design.
3. View the Title master, then the Slide Master.
   - Insert the following four action buttons on the bottom-right of each slide, in this order:
     - Beginning
     - Previous
     - Next
     - End
   - Select a new fill color and line color for the buttons that complements the design template.
   - Use the **Align** or **Distribute** option to evenly space the buttons. Be sure that each button is the same size.
4. Add diagrams to Slides 4 and 6, as illustrated. Apply any font face and color.
5. Add a table to Slide 5, as illustrated. Change the font color of text in all cells to **Light Blue.**
6. Apply a transition effect to Slide 1.
7. Apply an Animation scheme (the same one) to slides 2 through 8.
8. Insert a sound clip on Slide 1 that plays automatically when the slide show begins.
9. Insert a sound clip on Slide 8. The sound should not play automatically. Loop the sound so that it plays continuously.
10. Insert clip art and/or animated .gifs, as illustrated.
11. Run the slide show; play the sound.
12. Save the presentation; name it **4.2training.**

Continued on next page

1

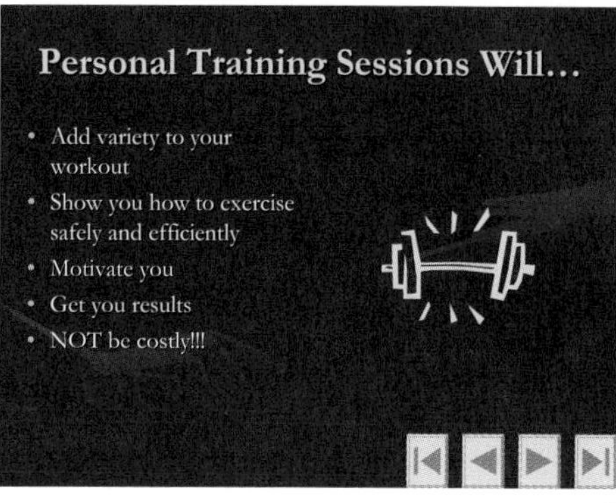

2

What Our Members Want

- Outstanding, personable and experienced personal trainers
- Low cost
- Noticeable results
- Convenience

3

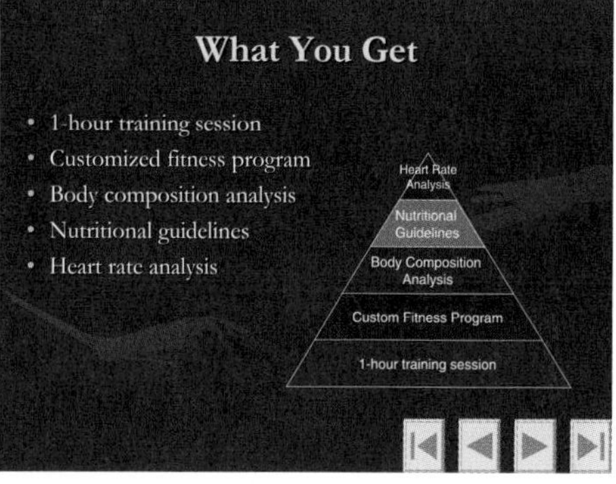

4

Cost Analysis

- The more you buy, the cheaper it gets
- Buy the 30-pack session and get a free massage!

# of sessions	Price
Individual Sessions	$75.00/session
10-pack	$70.00/session
20-pack	$65.00/session
30-pack	$60.00/session

5

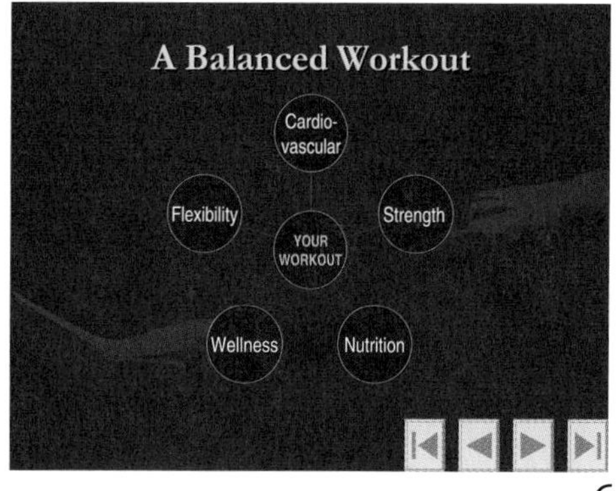

6

7

8

POWERPOINT

Four Corners Realty

1. Create a new presentation as shown on the facing page.
2. Apply any template design.
3. View the slide master.
   a. Apply any font styles and font colors.
   b. Apply the **Flip Entrance** animation effect to the title.
   c. Apply the **Zoom Entrance** animation effect to bulleted text.
4. Display Slide 1.
   a. Create a WordArt object for the following text: `Bringing People and Places Together for More Than 50 Years.` Apply the **Wipe from Left at Medium Speed** Entrance effect to the WordArt object.
   b. Apply a **Spin Emphasis** animation effect on the clip art object. Both animations should activate after the previous action.
5. Display Slide 4.
   a. Animate the bulleted text.
   b. Apply the **Wheel Entrance** animation effect to the diagram. Group the diagram so that each shape is introduced, one at a time, in the **Clockwise-Inward** direction with a **Chime** sound.
   c. Set the diagram to animate before the bulleted text.
6. Display Slide 6.
   a. Use the information in the table below to create a bar graph:

Year	1993	1994	1995	1996	1997
Houses Sold	100	110	100	130	150
Year	1998	1999	2000	2001	2002
Houses Sold	165	200	240	250	275

   b. Apply the **Wipe from Bottom Entrance** animation effect to the chart and group the chart by category. Animate the grid and legend. For the Year 2002, apply the Explosion sound effect.
7. Run the slide show.
8. Display Slide 1.
   a. Apply the **Shape Circle** transition effect to all slides.
   b. Set the transition for all slides to advance automatically after 10 seconds.
9. Set up the slide show to Loop continuously until 'Esc.'

Continued on next page

June 28, 2005

1

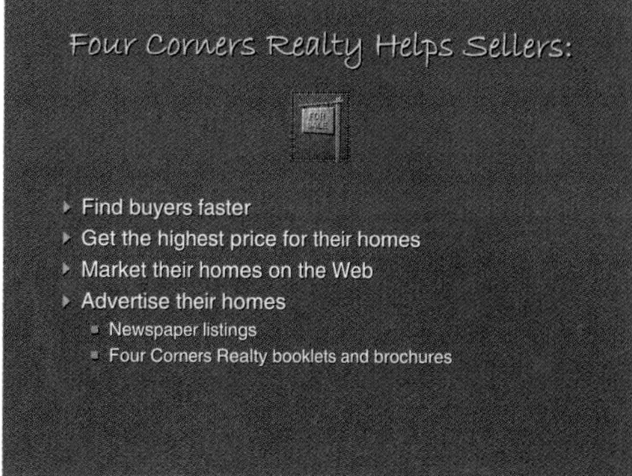

Four Corners Realty Helps Sellers:
Find buyers faster
Get the highest price for their homes
Market their homes on the Web
Advertise their homes
Newspaper listings
Four Corners Realty booklets and brochures

2

Four Corners Realty Helps Buyers:

- Find the right home for their needs
- Research the market to evaluate property values
- See homes in different neighborhoods and price ranges
- Find a mortgage broker

3

Four Corners Realty Markets Properties Through Different Media

- Four Corners Market Report
  - Research publication on the local real estate market
- www.FourCornersRealty.com
  - Online listings of properties
- Brochures
  - Specialty brochures feature unique properties
- Advertising
  - Promotions in newspapers and magazines are our primary vehicle for marketing

Market Report

Advertising

Marketing Options

Brochures

Web Site

4

FourCornersRealty.com Serves the Real Estate Needs of Buyers and Sellers

- Potential buyers can search for properties by location, size, and price range
- Buyers can view photos and floor plans, and take virtual tours
- Listings found in advertisements can be further researched online
- Sellers benefit from our online banner advertising on prominent national real estate sites
- Listing with Four Corners ensures that your home will be featured on our site for worldwide viewing

5

The Number of Houses Sold by Four Corners Has Grown Significantly over the Past Five Years

6

Let Four Corners Realty Find You the Home of Your Dreams

- Brokers available to show properties seven days a week
- Free consultations on buying and selling real estate
- Lowest brokerage fees in the business

7

POWERPOINT

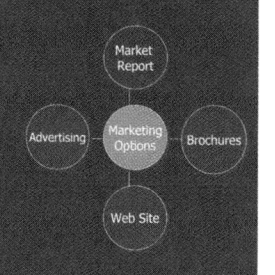

10. Run the Slide Show. When the show runs twice, press the **Esc** key.
11. Save the presentation as **4.2broker.yi** (yi = your initials) and close it.

Create the Photo Album

1. Go to: `www.realtor.com`. Search for homes in Hollywood, Florida (and its surrounding areas) that cost between $300,000 and $600,000.
   a. Save the photographs of nine different homes as .bmp images in a folder you create for this purpose.
2. Create a photo album using the nine photographs from the House Photos folder.
   a. Change the order of the slides in the album, if appropriate.
   b. Adjust each picture's contrast and brightness, if necessary.
   c. Place two pictures on a slide, each with a caption.
   d. Apply any frame shape and design template.
3. Insert slide titles and subtitles, as shown in the following illustration. Use the **Curved Down Ribbon** AutoShape for the subtitle text on Slide 1. Apply any font style, font color, and fill color to the titles and subtitle.
4. Replace the current filename captions below each photograph with captions describing the house and providing the price. Size each caption to fit below its picture.
5. Save the file as **4.2photoalbum.**
6. Swtich to Slide Sorter view. Copy all slides in the presentation.
7. Open **4.2broker.yi**. Switch to Slide Sorter view.
8. Copy all of the slides from **4.2photoalbum** as the last six slides in the presentation.
9. Save the newly created presentation as **4.2brokeralbum**.
10. Print one copy of the presentation as handouts with six slides per page.
11. Close the file; save the changes.

1

2

3

4

5

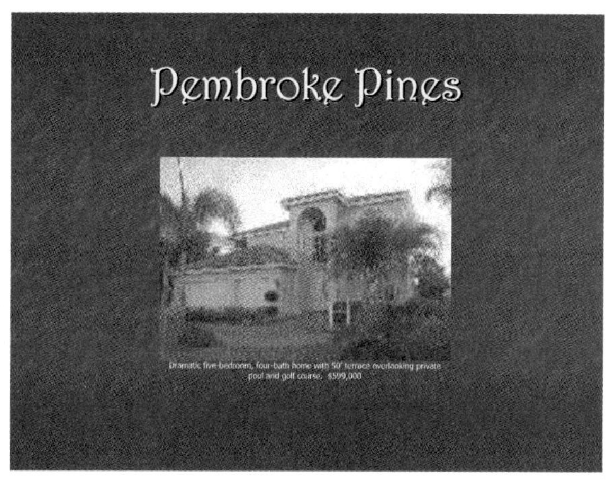

6

POWERPOINT

Cues for Reference

Use Custom Animations

1. Display slide on which to apply animation effect.
2. Click **Slide Show, Custom Animation.**
3. Click object to animate.
   or
   Right-click object to animate and click **Custom Animation.**
4. Click **Add Effect** button in Custom Animation task pane.
5. Click one of following animation options:
   - **Entrance**
   - **Emphasis**
   - **Exit**
   - **Motion Paths**
6. Click an animation.
   or
   Click **More Effects** to view other animation options and double-click an effect.

Time Animations

1. Display **Custom Animation** task pane.
2. Click animation in the Custom Animation list.
3. Click **Start** arrow in Custom Animation task pane and click either:
   a. **On Click,** to activate animation on the mouse click.
   b. **With Previous,** to activate animation at same time as previous one.
   c. **After Previous,** to activate animation after a previous animation has finished.

   or

   a. Click list arrow of animation in Custom Animation list and click **Timing.**
   b. Click **Start** list arrow and click when to activate animation.
   c. Click **Delay** increment arrow buttons to specify time lapse before animation is activated.
   d. Click **OK.**

Modify an Animation Effect

1. Click animation in Custom Animation list.
2. Click **Animation** list arrow and click **Effect Options.**
3. Make any changes and click **OK.**

Animate Charts and Diagrams

1. Click chart or diagram to animate.
2. Click **Slide Show, Custom Animation.**
3. Click **Add Effect,** click animation option, and select animation effect.
4. Click **Chart or Diagram** list arrow in Custom Animation list and click **Effect Options.**
5. Click **Chart Animation** or **Diagram Animation** tab and make appropriate selections.
6. Click **OK.**

Create Self-Running Presentations

1. Click **Slide Show, Slide Transition.**
2. Click **Automatically after** box to select it.
3. Click **Automatically after** up or down increment buttons to specify a time after which slides will advance.
4. Click **Apply to All Slides.**

Use the Annotation Pen

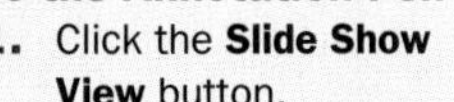

1. Click the **Slide Show View** button. 
2. Click the **Annotator Menu** icon.
3. Click a pointer type (Ballpoint Pen, Felt Tip Pen, Highlighter).
4. Click and drag the mouse to write on the slide.
5. Press **E** to erase the annotation from the slide.
   or
   Press the **Escape** key twice and click **Keep** or **Discard.**

Office XP

1. Click the **Slide Show View** button. 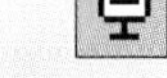
2. Click the **Annotator Menu** icon.
3. Click **Pointer Options, Pen.**
4. Click and drag the mouse to write on the slide.
5. Press **E** to erase the annotations.

Create a Photo Album

1. Click **Insert, Picture, New Photo Album.**
2. Click one of following buttons to insert a picture:
   - **File/Disk.**
   - **Scanner/Camera.**
3. Select photographs to insert, and click **Insert.**
4. Click appropriate rotate, contrast, and brightness buttons to adjust pictures.
5. Select picture options.
6. Click **Picture layout** list arrow and select layout.
7. Click **Frame shape** list arrow and select frame.
8. Click **Browse** button to select design template. Double-click template.
9. Click **Create.**

GOAL

To practice using the following skill sets:

- Use handouts
- Use speaker notes
- Use Handout Master and Notes Master
- Rehearse timings

POWERPOINT

WHAT YOU NEED TO KNOW

Use Handouts

- PowerPoint allows you to print your presentation as handouts with 1, 2, 3, 4, 6, or 9 slides on a page. You can distribute these *handouts* to the audience so that they can follow along with your on-screen presentation and have material to which they can refer at a later time.
- In previous exercises, you printed your presentation as handouts with six slides per page. To print handouts with a different number of slides per page, use the same procedure: Click File, Print. The Print dialog box opens, as shown in Figure 4.46. In the Print what list box, select Handouts; in the Slides per page list box, select the required number of slides per page, then click OK.

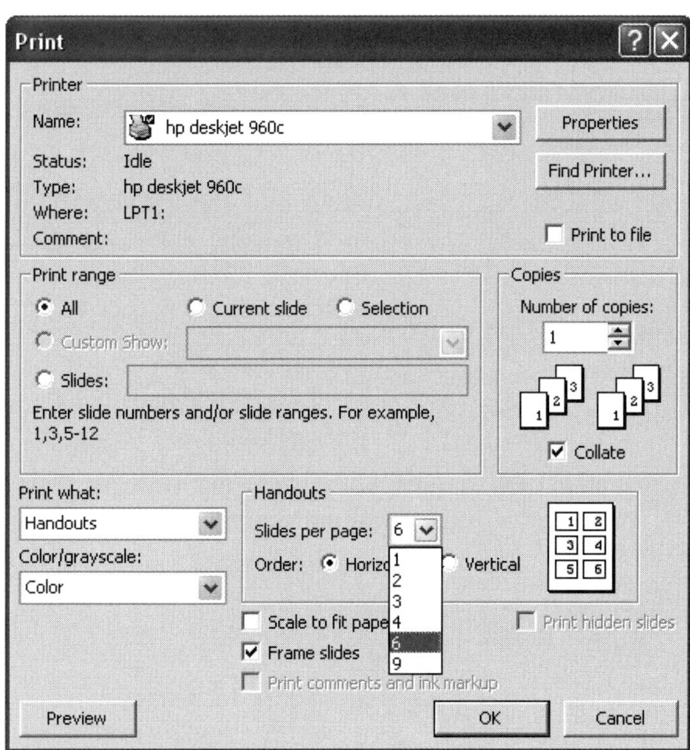

Figure 4.46 Print dialog box

Use Speaker Notes

- *Speaker notes* are used to assist the speaker in delivering a presentation. You can also distribute speaker notes to the audience, providing details of the information on each slide.
- Enter and format speaker notes in the notes pane in Normal view or in Notes Page view. To enter text in the notes pane, click in the notes pane and enter your notes. To display more of the notes pane, click and drag the top border of the pane.
- To enter text in Notes Page view, click View, Notes Page. A notes page, which contains a slide and a text placeholder, appears, as shown in Figure 4.47. Click in the text placeholder to enter and/or format your notes.
- Use the same procedures to print the notes pages that you use to print slides and handouts.

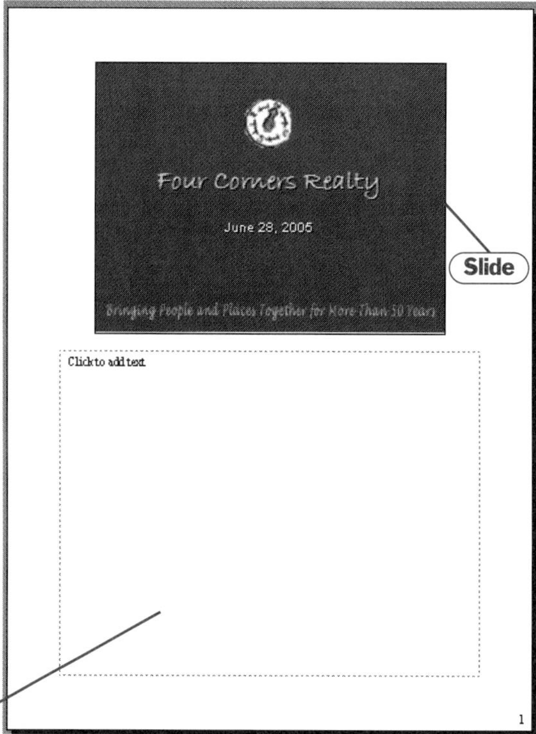

Figure 4.47 Notes Page view

TRY it OUT *p4-16*

1. Open **p4.16devon** from the Data CD.
2. Click in the notes pane.
3. Enter the following: `Introduce yourself. Briefly explain the purpose of the presentation.`
4. Drag the top border of the notes pane to expand it.
5. Display Slide 2.
6. Click **View, Notes Page.**
7. Click in the text placeholder.

Note: Zoom in, if necessary, to enlarge the text placeholder.

8. Enter the following: `Give examples of other funds that have not been performing as well in our unstable economy: -The Parker Fund -Westinghouse Fund Emphasize that despite downturns in the market, Devon has been profitable.`
9. Click **File, Print.**
10. Click the **Print what** list arrow and click **Notes Pages.**
11. Click the **Print what** list arrow and click **Handouts.**
12. Click the **Slides per page** list arrow and click **9.**
13. Click **Cancel.**
14. Save the file; name it **4.16devonnotes.yi** (yi = your initials).
15. Do not close the file.

Use Handout Master and Notes Master

- In Lesson 3, you learned to use the slide master to customize all slides of a presentation by adding text, objects, and/or color schemes to a master slide. Similarly, the *handout master* and the *notes master* allow you to customize your handouts and notes pages.
- To view the handout master, click View, Master, Handout Master. On the handout master that appears, as shown in Figure 4.48, you can change the number of slides per page and add headers, footers, objects, page numbers, the date, and color schemes.

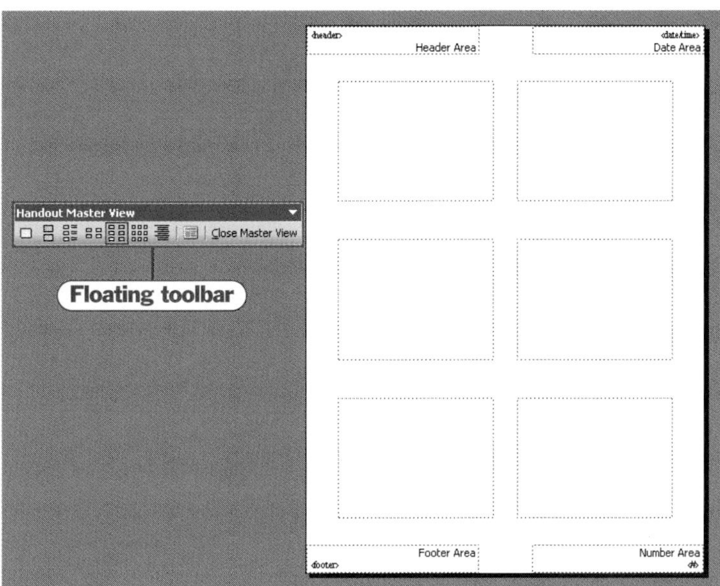

Figure 4.48 Handout master

- To view the notes master, click View, Master, Notes Master. On the notes master that appears, as shown in Figure 4.49, you can apply text styles to placeholder text and add headers, footers, objects, page numbers, the date, and color schemes.

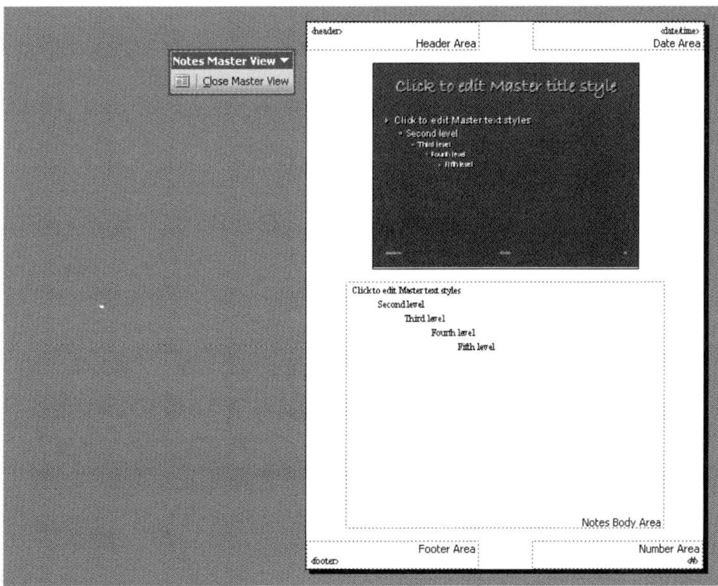

Figure 4.49 Notes master

- You can add headers and footers to the handout master and the notes master by clicking View, Header and Footer. In the Header and Footer dialog box, as shown in Figure 4.50, click the Notes and Handouts tab and make your selections.

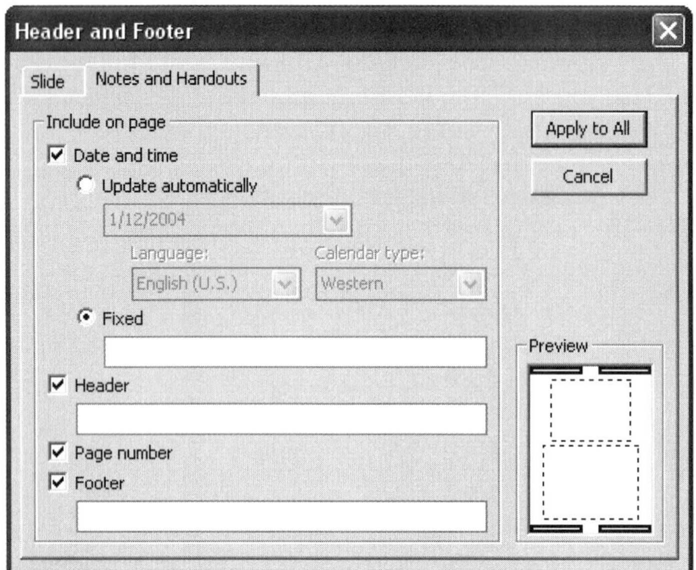

Figure 4.50 Header and Footer dialog box

TRY *it* OUT *p4-17*

Note: ***4.3devonnotes.yi*** *should be displayed.*

1. Click **View, Master,** and **Notes Master.**
2. Click **View, Header and Footer.**
3. Click the **Fixed option** button, if it is not already selected.
4. Click in the **Fixed text** box and enter today's date.
5. Click the **Header** check box, if not already selected.
6. Click in the Header text box and enter:

   `Devon Mutual Funds`
7. Click **Apply to All.**
8. Click **Format, Slide Design.**
9. Click the **Color Schemes** link.
10. Click the slide thumbnail of a color scheme.
11. Click the **Close Master View** button.
12. Click **File, Print Preview.**
13. Click the **Print What** list arrow.
14. Click **Notes Pages.**
15. Scroll down to view all pages.
16. Click **Close** to close the Print Preview screen.
17. Click **Close**; do not save.

Rehearse Timings

- If you have to deliver a presentation with time constraints, you can rehearse how long it takes for you to deliver it. To do so, click Slide Show, Rehearse Timings. This activates a slide show and opens the Rehearsal toolbar, as shown in Figure 4.51.

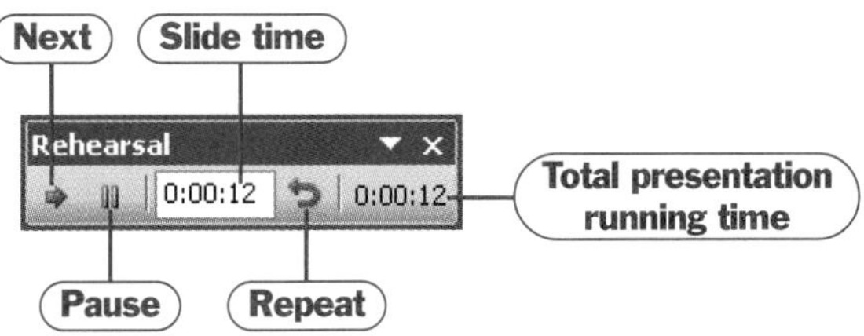

Figure 4.51 Rehearsal toolbar

- As soon as you start the slide show, the timer begins. When you finish narrating the first slide, click the Next button on the Rehearsal toolbar, or click on the slide to advance to the next slide. Notice that the clock in the Slide Time box resets (goes back to 00:00), while the clock measuring the presentation's total running time continues. Thus, each slide, as well as the entire presentation, is timed.
- If you want to reset the timing while you are narrating a slide, click the Repeat button on the toolbar. If you need to pause the timer during your rehearsal, click the Pause button.
- When you reach the end of the slide show, PowerPoint displays the total running time and prompts you to save the new timings. If you choose to save the timings, PowerPoint switches to Slide Sorter view and displays the individual slide timings below each slide, as shown in Figure 4.52.

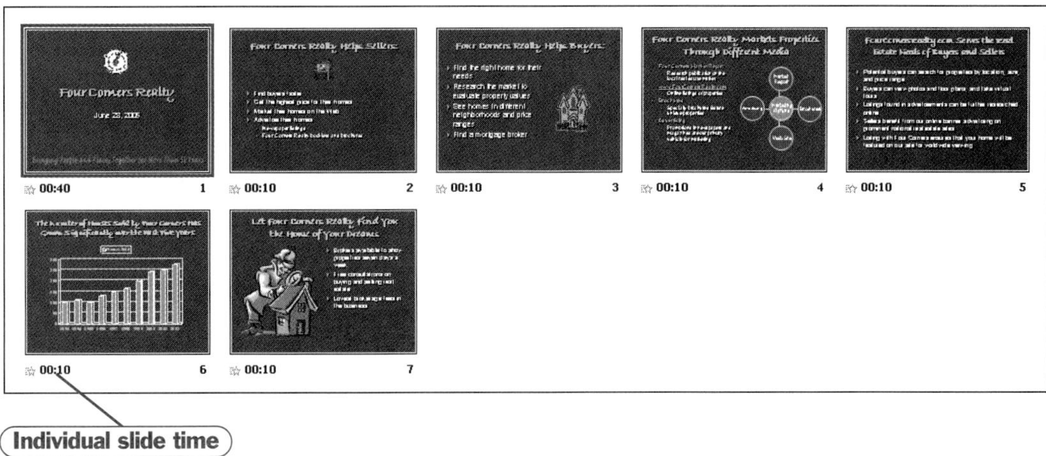

Figure 4.52 Slide timings in Slide Sorter view

- Use your notes pages to help you deliver the presentation. You might want to use the annotation pen during the rehearsal as you would during the actual presentation.

POWERPOINT

TRY *it* OUT *p4-18*

1. Open **4.2training,** which you created in Task 2.
2. Click **Slide Show, Rehearse Timings.**
3. Read the text on Slide1 as if you were presenting it.
4. Click the **Next** button on the Rehearsal toolbar.

5. Continue to deliver the presentation. Click each slide to advance to the next one.
6. Click **Yes** when prompted to save the new slide timings.
7. Close the file; do not save.

1
2
3

GOAL
To create a presentation with charts, speaker notes, and handout pages

SETTING THE STAGE/WRAPUP
File name: **4.3seniors**

WHAT YOU NEED TO KNOW

- Speaker notes can include quotes, statistics, or lists, which help to further explain an item on the slide.
- You generally distribute handouts to the audience so they can follow along with your presentation. You can also distribute handouts with plenty of white space so audience members can take notes.
- The best way to ensure that you do not exceed your time limit is to rehearse the presentation.
- In this Rehearsal activity, you will create a seven-slide presentation to college seniors, persuading them to invest their money in a Sutton Investment Group account. You will add notes as you create the presentation and will customize the handouts pages, which you will distribute to the audience. You will also rehearse the presentation to make sure that you do not exceed the five-minute time limit you were given.

DIRECTIONS

1. Start a new design template presentation.
2. Insert text and notes as illustrated on the facing page.
3. On Slide 2:
   a. Create a text box and enter a question mark.
   b. Size it to 400 pt., and color it Light Purple. Center it on the page and send it to the back.
4. On Slide 5, use the following information to create an Area chart:
   a. Year 1 $5,500 | Year 5 $16,000 | Year 10 $29,260
      Year 15 $42,460 | Year 20 $55,660 | Year 25 $68,860
   b. Insert the following title:
      `The Power of Saving and Investing`
   c. Format the y-axis to currency with no decimal points.
   d. Hide the legend.
   e. Format the x-axis titles to align at a 45-degree angle.
5. View the handout master.
   a. Set the page to display four slides per page.
   b. Include a header/footer on all slides with the date (to update automatically), the page number, and a footer that reads:
      `Sutton Investment Group`
   c. Format the handout background, and apply the Large grid pattern to all pages; color the foreground Aqua and the background White.
6. View the notes master. Apply to the notes page the same background that you used for the handouts pages.
7. Apply any animation scheme to all slides.
8. Print one copy of the notes pages.

Continued on next page

9. Rehearse and time the presentation using your notes, then discard them.
10. On Slide 5, use the annotation pen to point out the growth displayed on the chart.
11. Run the slide show.
12. Close the file; save the presentation; name it **4.3seniors.**

1

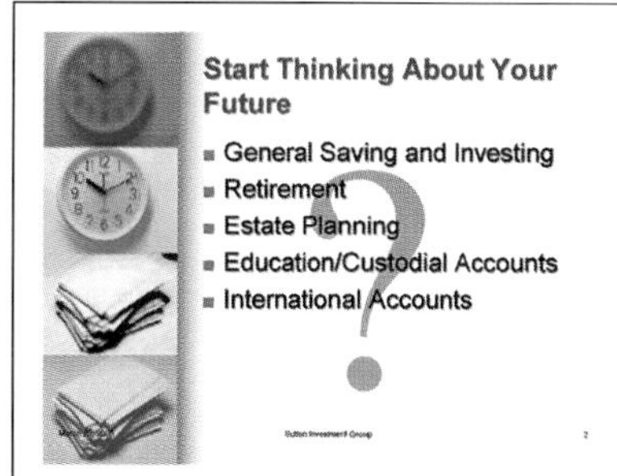

2

3

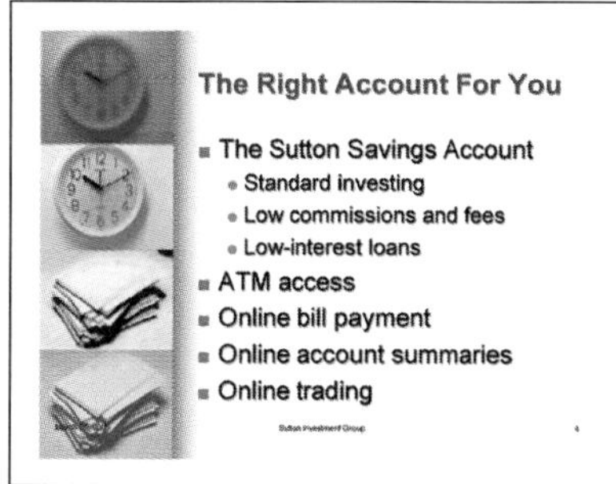

4

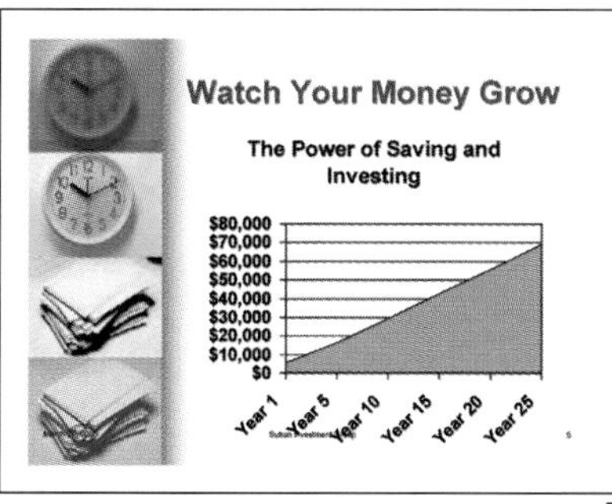

5

6

7

Cues for Reference

Print Handouts
1. Click **File, Print.**
2. Click the **Print what** list arrow.
3. Click **Handouts.**
4. Click the **Slides per page** list arrow and click the required number of slides per page.
5. Click **OK.**

Create Speaker Notes
- Click in the notes pane and enter your notes.

or
1. Click **View, Notes Page.**
2. Click in the text placeholder and enter your notes.

Print Notes Pages
1. Click **File, Print.**
2. Click the **Print what** list arrow.
3. Click **Notes Pages.**
4. Click **OK.**

Customize Handout Master
1. Click **View, Master,** and **Handout Master.**
2. Make the necessary changes.

To add headers/footers:
   a. Click **View, Header and Footer.**
   b. Click the **Notes and Handouts** tab.
   c. Make the necessary changes.
   d. Click **Apply to All.**

3. Click **Close Master View.**

Customize Notes Master
1. Click **View, Master,** and **Notes Master.**
2. Make the necessary changes.

To add headers/footers
   a. Click **View, Header and Footer.**
   b. Click the **Notes and Handouts** tab.
   c. Make the necessary changes.
   d. Click **Apply to All.**

3. Click **Close Master View.**

Rehearse Timings
1. Click **Slide Show.**
2. Click **Rehearse Timings.**
3. Click the **Next** button on the Rehearsal toolbar to advance to the next slide or animation. 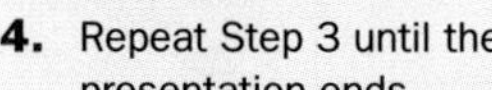
4. Repeat Step 3 until the presentation ends.
5. Click **Yes** or **No** when prompted to keep the new slide timings.

SETTING THE STAGE
Act I File name: pp4recruit
Act II File name:
pp4odysseyoutdoors

Act I

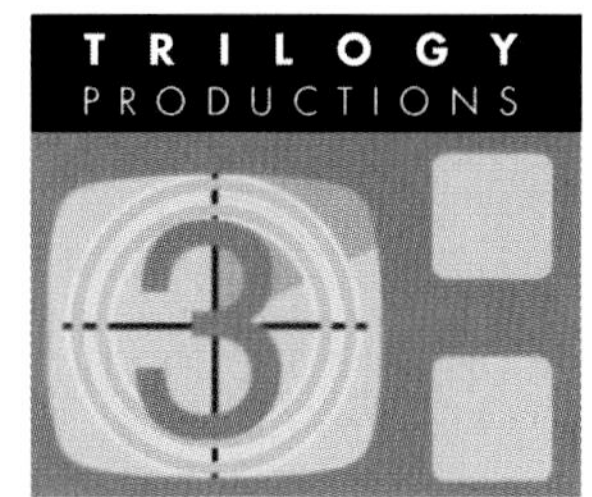

You are the human resources manager at Trilogy Productions. Trilogy has decided to visit several colleges to recruit future employees. You have been asked to create a 10- to 12-slide presentation to persuade college seniors to work at Trilogy. Use the information on the next page to develop your slides. The summary slide shown below will help you determine slide titles.

Follow these guidelines: The first three slides shown below are provided as a sample.

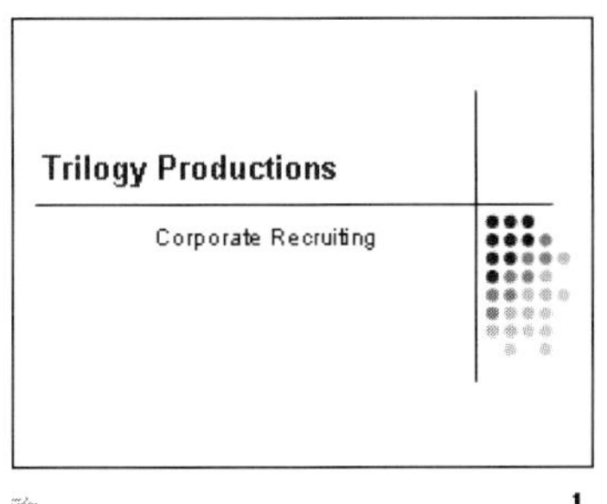

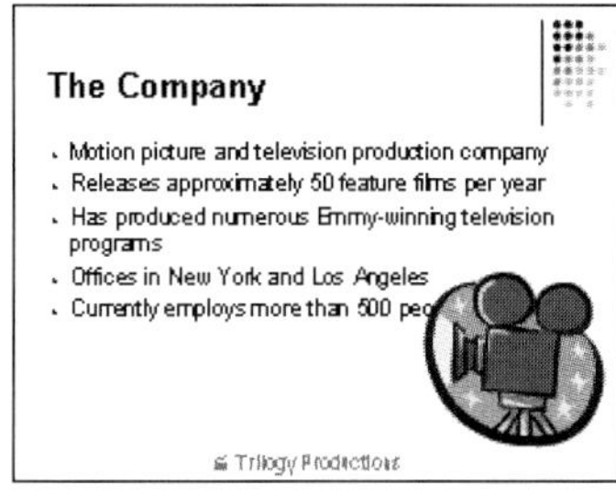

- Use any design template.
- Include a summary slide as Slide 2; add a hyperlink to each title on the slide to link it to its corresponding slide.
- Apply any transitions and/or animation schemes.
- Use Content slides, where appropriate.
- Use any clip art, media clips, color schemes, headers, footers, etc. to enhance the presentation.
- Search the Web for film/college/work-related images. Copy and paste, or download desired images from the Web, and include them on relevant slides in the presentation.
- Include a slide entitled Working in the Entertainment Industry. Go to www.bls.gov/oco/cg/cgs038.htm, which is a page from the Career Guide on the U.S. Department of Labor Statistics Web site. Read about careers in motion picture production and distribution and include any relevant information on the slide. You can create a hyperlink somewhere on the slide to link to this Web page. Also, use this page to write notes to yourself about the entertainment industry that you can share with potential employees.

- After you create the presentation, type notes that you think would help you deliver the presentation.
- Format the handout master to print four slides per page, and apply any background. Also include the date and a footer that says:

  `Trilogy Productions`

- Rehearse and time your delivery of the presentation using your notes and the annotation pen to explain the charts. (This will require that you print notes pages before the rehearsal.) Do not save timings.
- Deliver the presentation; try to stay within the rehearsed time.
- Print a copy of the presentation as handouts.
- Save the presentation; name it **pp4recruit.**

A Career at Trilogy Productions

Trilogy is a motion picture and television production company. We release approximately 50 feature films per year and have produced numerous Emmy-winning television programs. Our offices are located in New York and Los Angeles, and we currently employ more than 500 people.

Our corporate staff is as follows: John Alan is the president and CEO. Andrew Martin, CFO, reports to John. Reporting to Andrew are Christopher Manning, director of marketing and sales; Travis Haimes, director of interactive; Rachel D'Amato, director of distribution; and Jennifer Nastro, director of production. Anna Jennings is a manager of publicity and promotions, and she reports to Christopher.

Our growth over the past few years is a result of our philosophy. We produce movies and television programs to please our audiences. We foster a fun and challenging work environment. As a result, our films continue to break box-office records, and our television programs earn critical acclaim.

Trilogy offers a training program to a select group of individuals. This is a very rare opportunity—especially in the entertainment field. The program is well known throughout the industry and very well respected. The training is a 12-month program in which there is formal classroom training once a week. Trainees get rotational experience, thus giving them broad exposure before we place them permanently.

Just to give you an idea of how competitive the training program is, here are some statistics on last year's recruits. We received 2,578 résumés. Of those, we granted interviews to 100 candidates (3.5%). Of those interviewed, we offered jobs to 10 individuals (0.5%). All 10 accepted our offer.

We are looking for individuals who are energetic, articulate, creative, motivated, outgoing, and able to manage multiple projects.

Working at Trilogy is truly a unique opportunity. We are a top entertainment company, we offer the best possible training, and we provide outstanding medical, dental, and 401(k) benefits.

To apply for the training program, fax your resume to 212-555-8100. We look forward to meeting you!

Act II

Odyssey Travel Gear has decided to add a new line to its business. The company is planning to create a travel magazine for rugged sports enthusiasts called *Odyssey Outdoors*. The magazine will profile fun and exotic places to travel to engage in outdoor sporting activities.

To raise money to launch this new business, the people at Odyssey Travel Gear need to persuade potential investors that *Odyssey Outdoors* is a viable idea and business. Thus, they need to create a business plan. A business plan is a summary of the goals and objectives of a business and outlines how the business will operate and how resources will be organized. Visit the following Web sites to view sample business plans and get an idea of how business plans are structured: www.sba.gov and www.bplans.com.

Jane McBride, the president and CEO of Odyssey Travel Gear, has asked you to create a business plan for *Odyssey Outdoors* with information that she has provided on the next page. Your business plan should have at least 12 slides.

Follow these guidelines: The first three slides shown below are provided as a sample.

1

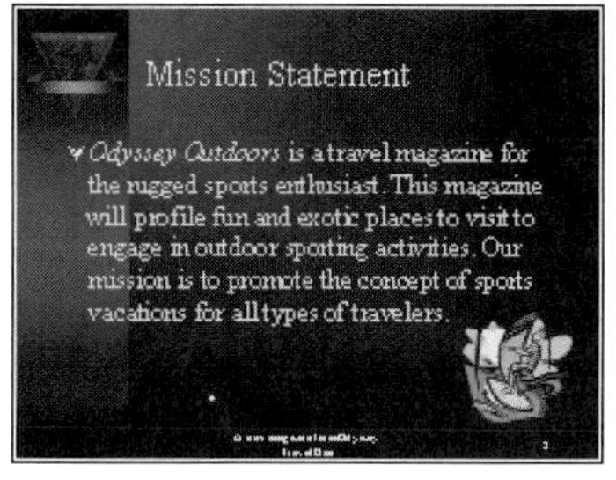

2

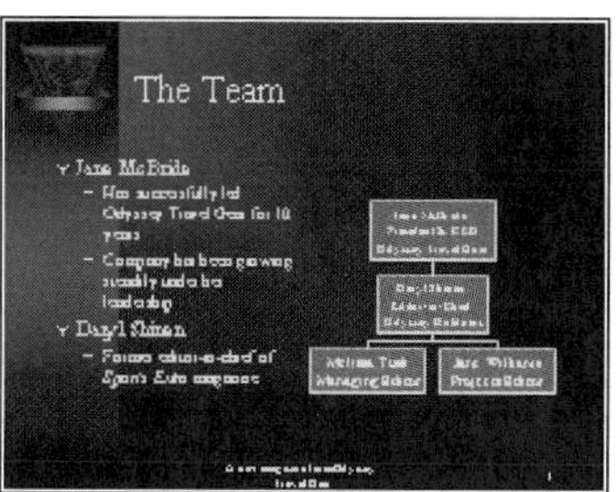

3

- Use the business plan template to create the presentation. Replace the sample template text with the information Ms. McBride has provided.
- Include an appropriate presentation title.
- Include a summary slide as Slide 2; add a hyperlink to each title on the slide to link it to its corresponding slide. Note: If the summary slide spans two slides, reduce the font size and consolidate the bullets onto one slide.
- Apply any transitions and/or animation schemes.
- Use object slides, where appropriate.
- Use any clip art, media clips, color schemes, headers, footers, etc. to enhance the presentation.
- Search the Web for sports/media/business-related images. Copy and paste, or download desired images from the Web, and include them on relevant slides in the presentation.
- Format the handout master to print six slides per page and apply any background. Also include the date and a footer that says:

```
Odyssey Outdoors
```

- After you write the presentation, enter notes that you think would help you deliver the presentation.
- Rehearse and time your delivery of the presentation, using your notes and the annotation pen to explain the charts. (This will require that you print notes pages before the rehearsal.)
- Deliver the presentation; try to stay within the rehearsed time.
- Print a copy of the presentation as handouts.
- Save the presentation; name it **pp4odysseyoutdoors.**

Odyssey Outdoors

Odyssey Outdoors is a travel magazine for the rugged sports enthusiast. This magazine will profile fun and exotic places to travel to engage in outdoor sporting activities. Our mission is to promote the concept of sports vacations for all types of travelers.

Jane McBride, president and CEO of Odyssey Travel Gear, will run the company. She has successfully led Odyssey Travel Gear for 10 years, during which time Odyssey has grown steadily. Reporting to her as the editor-in-chief of *Odyssey Outdoors* will be Daryl Shinen. He is the former editor-in-chief of Sports Extra magazine. Both Melissa Tusk (managing editor) and Jane Williams (projects editor) will report to Daryl.

Our target market is primarily Odyssey Travel Gear customers and outdoor sports enthusiasts. Sports interests define market segments, so our media strategy and execution will vary by segment.

Now is the time to launch this magazine, as opportunities in the market have presented themselves—people are increasingly health conscious, people are economically able to take trips, and there are hundreds of fun and exotic destinations, both warm and cold, to visit for active vacations.

Our business concept is as follows: Wc want to create a spin-off of the already existing and successful Odyssey Travel Gear. We are looking to serve a clearly defined niche market. We already have distribution channels and we already reach those who buy from Odyssey Travel Gear and those who receive the Odyssey Travel Gear catalog.

Odyssey Outdoors has a competitive advantage, as we already have a successful franchise and distribution channels. Furthermore, though there are sports magazines and travel magazines, there are no magazines that are a combination of the two.

Once established, our goals and objectives are to reach and inform our target market, cross-promote with Odyssey Travel Gear, and consistently increase the distribution and sales of *Odyssey Outdoors*.

Below is our sales forecast.

Sales Forecast

	Year 1	**Year 2**	**Year 3**
Subscriptions	$1,525,500	$1,876,000	$2,455,500
Newsstand	$55,935	$60,290	$65,325
Ad Revenue	$265,770	$275,000	$300,000
TOTAL	**$1,847,205**	**$2,211,290**	**$2,820,825**

Because we already print catalogs for Odyssey Travel Gear, our printing requirements are already fulfilled. We plan to hire 30 new employees to help run *Odyssey Outdoors*. These employees will work out of Odyssey Travel Gear's offices. We will, however, need to order additional technology resources as we see fit.

Finally, the key issues that are facing us as we start *Odyssey Outdoors* are twofold. We have near-term issues of initial funding and the hiring of new employees. Long term, we might face changes in the economy that could affect people's ability to go on vacation, the ability of people to get information on active vacations from the Internet, and the ever-present threat of new competition.

LESSON 5

Integration/PowerPoint and the Web

In this lesson, you will learn to use the features found in PowerPoint to integrate presentations with elements found in other applications. To enhance the visual composition of slides, you can import into PowerPoint charts and worksheets created in Excel and tables and outlines created in Word. You will also learn to use PowerPoint features to set up your presentation so you can deliver it from remote locations and to work with PowerPoint and the Web.

Upon completion of this lesson, you should be able to use the following skill sets:

- Import and export text and objects
  - Import a Word outline as a presentation
  - Export a presentation as an outline
  - Import an Excel chart or worksheet to a slide
  - Import a Word table to a slide
  - Import a slide from another presentation
- Add, edit, and delete comments
- Set up a review cycle (compare and merge documents)
- Embed fonts
- Package a presentation for CD
- Save a presentation as a Web page
- Preview a presentation as a Web page
- Publish a presentation to the Web
- Set up and schedule an online broadcast

Terms

Software-related

- Source document
- Destination document
- Embedded object
- Linked object
- Comments
- HTML
- Web server

GOAL

To practice using the following skill sets:

- Import and export text and objects
- Import a Word outline as a presentation
- Export a presentation as an outline
- Import an Excel chart or worksheet to a slide
- Import a Word table to a slide
- Import a slide from another presentation

POWERPOINT

WHAT YOU NEED TO KNOW

Import and Export Text and Objects

- As you learned previously, Office 2003 allows you to share data between applications. In PowerPoint, for example, you can import data created in Excel or Word to enhance your presentation.
- When importing and exporting files, it is important to know where the data originated and where the data is going. The *source document* is the file from which the data originates. The *destination document* is the file that receives the data.

Import a Word Outline as a Presentation

- You can use an outline created in Word as slides in a presentation. The source file is the Word document; the destination file is the PowerPoint slide.
- Each first-level heading of the outline translates into a slide title. Each second-level heading translates into bulleted items, as shown in Figures 5.1 and 5.2.

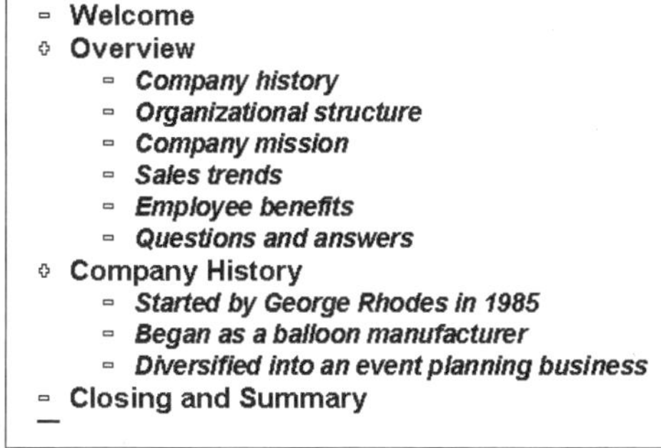

Figure 5.1 Outline text

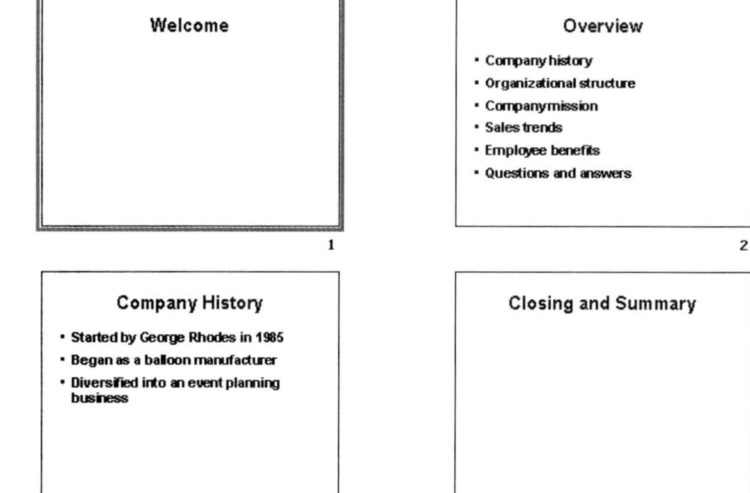

Figure 5.2 Outline text becomes slides

- To import a Word outline to become a new presentation, click File, Open while in PowerPoint. In the Open dialog box, as shown in Figure 5.3, click the Files of type list arrow and click All Outlines. Double-click the document you want to use. PowerPoint automatically opens the Word outline and converts it into PowerPoint slides.

Note: PowerPoint uses converters to import files in the correct format. These converters are installed when you load Office. If PowerPoint cannot open the file you want, open the file in the source program (Word, in this case), save it in Rich Text Format, then try importing it again.

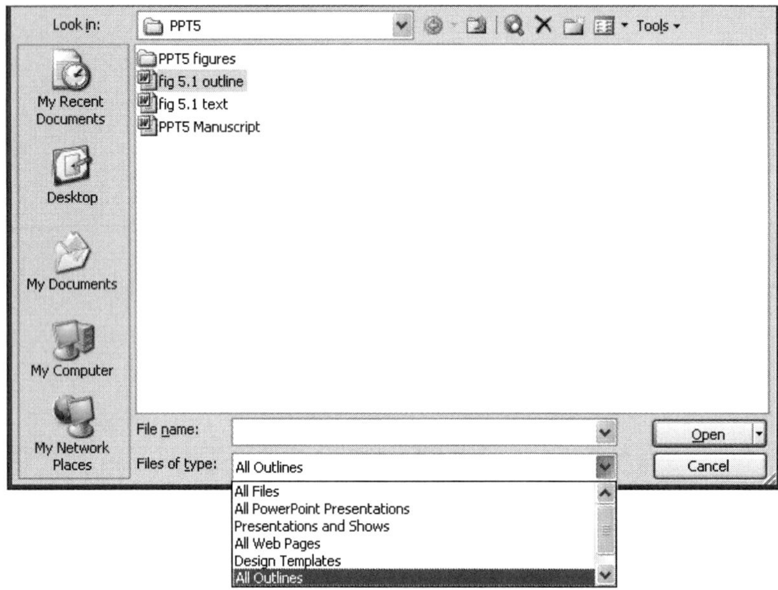

Figure 5.3 Open dialog box

- To import a Word outline to become slides in an existing presentation, display the Outline tab, click the slide icon above where the outline text should be inserted, as shown in Figure 5.4, and click Insert, Slides from Outline. In the Insert Outline dialog box that opens, select the file you want to use and click Insert.

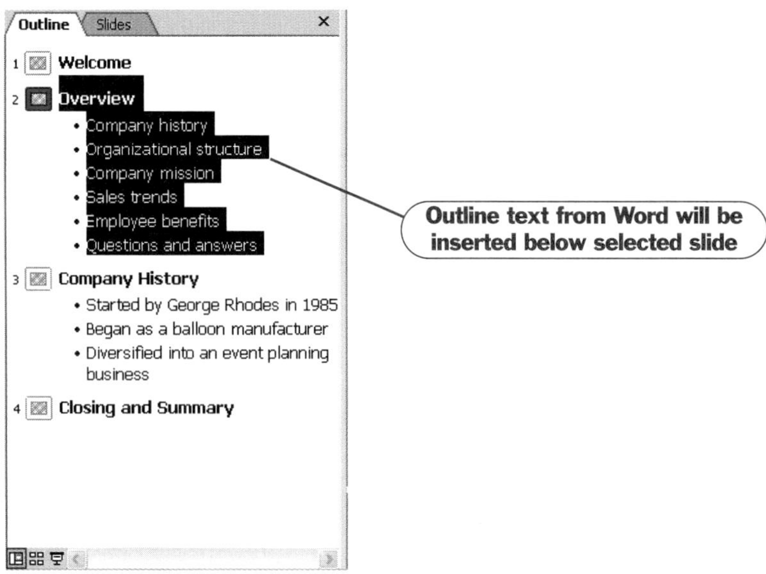

Figure 5.4 Import an outline into an existing presentation

TRY it OUT p5-1

To create a new presentation from a Word outline, do the following:

1. Open a new blank presentation.
2. Click the **Slides** tab (if it is not already selected).
3. Click **File, Open.**
4. Click the **Files of type** list arrow and click **All Outlines.**
5. Open **p5.1pfoutline** from the Data CD.
6. Click each slide.
7. Close the file; do not save.

To add a Word outline to an existing presentation, do the following:

1. Open **p5.1pfmeeting** from the Data CD. (This is a three-slide presentation.)
2. Click the **Outline** tab.
3. Click on the **Slide 2 icon.**
4. Click **Insert, Slides from Outline.**
5. Double-click **p5.1pfoutline** from the Data CD. 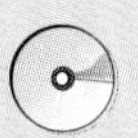
6. Close the file; do not save.

Export a Presentation as an Outline

- You can export slide text from a presentation to become an outline in Word. Each slide title translates into level 1 headings; bulleted lists translate into level 2 headings. This is a useful feature if you want to incorporate an outline into a document.
- To export a presentation, display the presentation. Click File, Send To, and Microsoft Office Word. In the Send to Microsoft Office Word dialog box that opens, as shown in Figure 5.5, click the Outline only option and click OK. Word starts automatically, and the slide text exports to a new document in outline format.

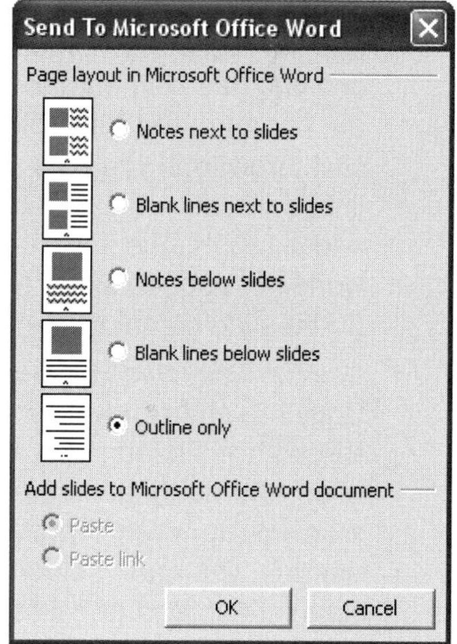

Figure 5.5 Send to Microsoft Office Word dialog box

TRY it OUT p5-2

1. Open **p5.2membership** from the Data CD. 
2. Click **File, Send To.**
3. Click **Microsoft Office Word.**
4. Click **Outline only.**
5. Click **OK.**
6. Print one copy of the outline.
7. Close the Word file; do not save.
8. Close the PowerPoint file.

Import an Excel Chart or Worksheet to a Slide

- In addition to creating a chart on a Content slide, you can import a chart or worksheet you created in Excel onto a slide.
- Imported charts and worksheets function like other objects; that is, you can size, copy, move, edit, or delete them.
- There are two ways to import an object; each has a different effect on data:
  - You can import a file and create an *embedded object*. With an embedded object, data in the destination file does not change if you modify the source file. Embedded objects become part of the destination file with no connection to the source file.
  - You can import a file and create a *linked object*. With a linked object, any change made to the source file is automatically updated in the destination file. The source and destination files are connected by the link.
- To import a chart or worksheet, display the slide on which you want to add the object, then use one of the following methods:
  - *Use the Insert, Object commands.* Click Insert, Object. In the Insert Object dialog box that opens, shown in Figure 5.6, click Create from file. In the File text box, enter the location and file name that contains the chart or worksheet you want to insert. If you are not sure where the file is located, click Browse. If you want to create a linked file, click the Link check box and click OK. The imported chart or worksheet appears in a placeholder (if the slide contains one).
  - *Use the Copy and Paste commands.* Copy the chart or worksheet from the source file and paste it onto the slide (the destination file). To create a linked file when copying and pasting, you must select Edit, Paste Special (instead of Paste). This opens the Paste Special dialog box, as shown in Figure 5.7, where you can select the Paste link option.

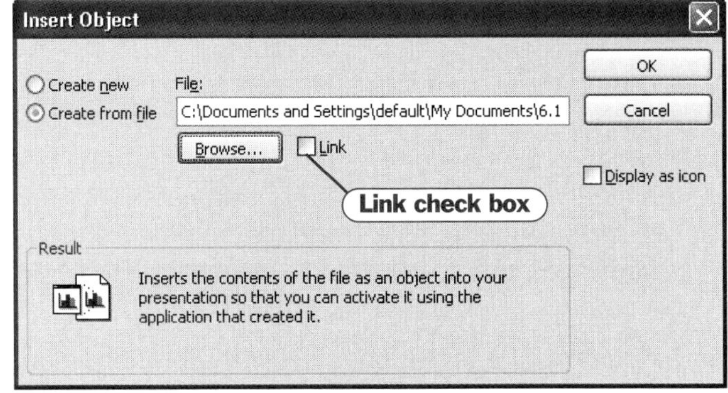

Figure 5.6 Insert Object dialog box

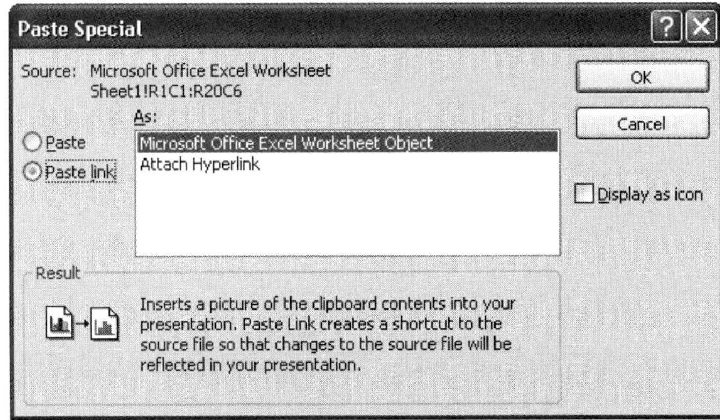

Figure 5.7 Paste Special dialog box

- To edit an imported chart or worksheet that was embedded, double-click it. You can edit the chart or worksheet directly on the slide.
- To edit an imported chart or worksheet that was linked, do one of the following:
  - Double-click it. This will open Excel as shown in Figure 5.8, where you can make your corrections.
  - Right-click the object and select Linked Worksheet Object, Open. This, too, will open Excel and allow you to make your corrections there.
- To return to PowerPoint, click File, Exit. Once you exit Excel, the corrections will be reflected on the slide.

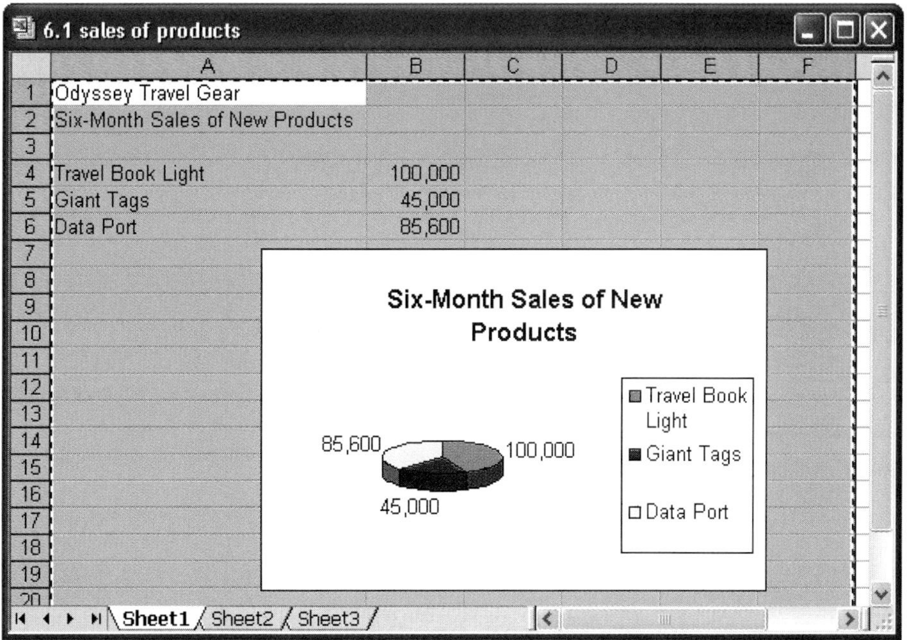

Figure 5.8 Imported Excel worksheet

- When you make a change to the source file, PowerPoint will prompt you to update the links the next time you open the destination file.

TRY *it* OUT *p5-3*

1. Open a new blank presentation.
2. Click to apply the **Title Only** slide layout. Click **Insert, Object.**
3. Click **Create from file**. Enter the Data CD location and **p5.3pfbudget** in the File text box (example: D:\p5.1pfbudget).
4. Click the **Link** option, and click OK.
5. Drag a corner handle to size the chart to fill the slide area. Click and drag the object to move it to the middle of the slide.
6. Double-click the object. Click to edit **Cell B5** (3,500) to become:

   `$2,550.00`
7. Click **File, Exit** to close Excel; click **Yes** to save the changes. Notice that the amount has been updated on the PowerPoint slide.
8. Right-click the worksheet, and then select **Linked Worksheet Object, Open.**
9. Click to edit **Cell B5** (Television) to become: `$1,550.00.`
10. Click **File, Exit** to close Excel; click **Yes** to save the changes. Notice that the amount has been updated again on the PowerPoint Slide.
11. Close the file; do not save.

POWERPOINT

Import a Word Table to a Slide

- Like charts and worksheets, you can import tables you created in Word onto a slide. Once imported, tables also function like other objects—you can size, copy, move, edit, or delete them.
- The procedure for importing a table as an embedded or linked object is the same as for charts and worksheets. Figure 5.9 shows an embedded table on a slide that was selected (double-clicked) for editing.

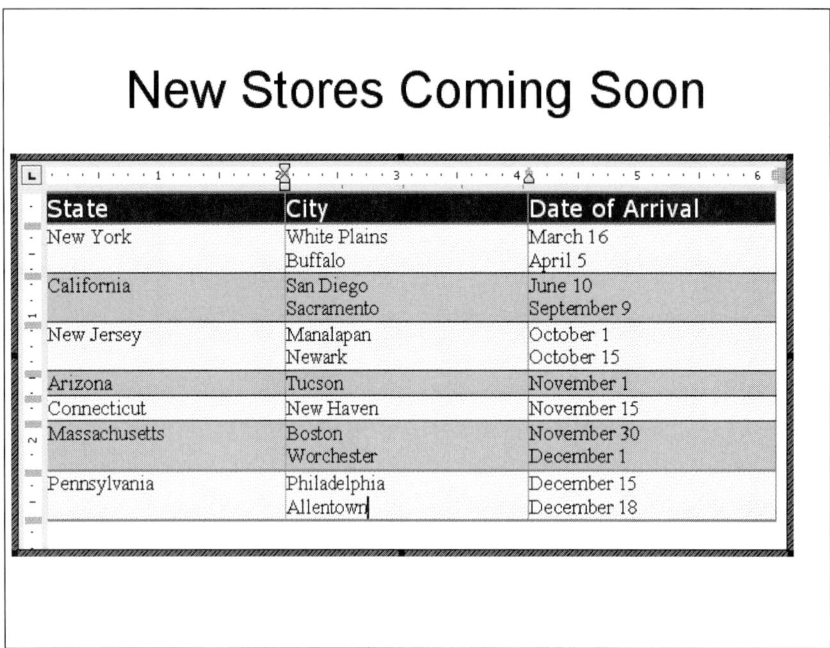

Figure 5.9 Editing an embedded Word table in PowerPoint

TRY*it*OUT *p5-4*

1. Click the **New** button to open a new blank presentation. 
2. Click to apply a **Title and Content** slide layout.
3. Click the **Title** placeholder and enter: `New Stores Coming Soon.`
4. Click **Insert, Object,** and click **Create from file.** 
5. Enter the Data CD location and **p5.4pftable** in the File text box, and click **OK.**
6. Right-click the object and select **Document Object, Open.**
7. Click to edit the White Plains Date of Arrival to: `March 22.`
8. Click **File, Close & Return to Presentation.**
9. Click the **New Slide** button. Click to apply a **Title Only** slide layout. 
10. Start Word and open **p5.4pftable** from the Data CD.
11. Select the **entire table.** Click **Edit, Copy.**
12. Switch to PowerPoint. Click **Edit, Paste Special,** then click **Paste link, OK.**
13. Double-click the **object.** Change the White Plains date of arrival to: `April 1.`
14. Click **File, Close.** When prompted to save changes, click **Yes.**
15. Return to PowerPoint. Notice that the changes were made in the destination document.
16. Double-click the object. Notice that the changes were made in the source document.
17. Close the files; do not save.

Import a Slide from Another Presentation

- You can insert one or more slides from another presentation (source) into your current presentation (destination). To do so, open the presentation in which you want to insert slides. Click Insert, Slides from Files. In the Slide Finder dialog box that opens, as shown in Figure 5.10, enter the location and presentation file name of your source file in the File text box. If you do not know the location of the presentation, click Browse. The slides display in the Slide Finder dialog box. Click the slide you want to insert and click Insert (or click Insert All to insert all the slides in the presentation). Use Slide Sorter view to rearrange the slides, if necessary.

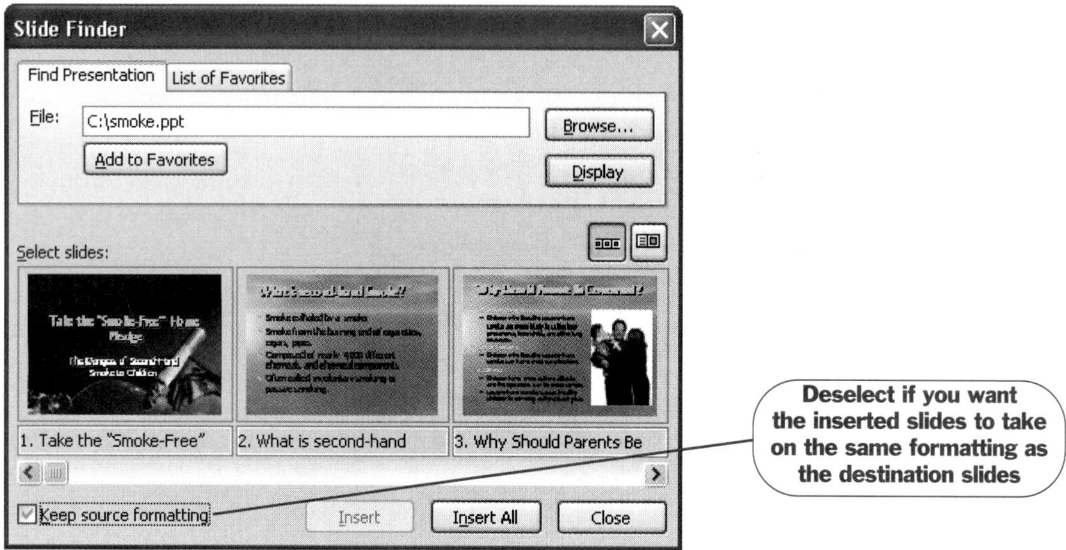

Figure 5.10 Slide Finder dialog box

- You must deselect the Keep source formatting check box if you want the inserted slide(s) to take on the same formatting as the destination presentation.

TRY *it* OUT *p5-5*

1. Open **p5.5pfundercover** from the Data CD.
2. Click the **Slides** tab.
3. Click the last slide in the presentation.
4. Click **Insert, Slides from Files.**
5. Enter the Data CD location and **p5.5pfstation** in the File text box.
6. If checked, click the **Keep source formatting** check box to deselect it.
7. Click **Insert All** and click **Close.**
8. Close the file; do not save.

1
2
3

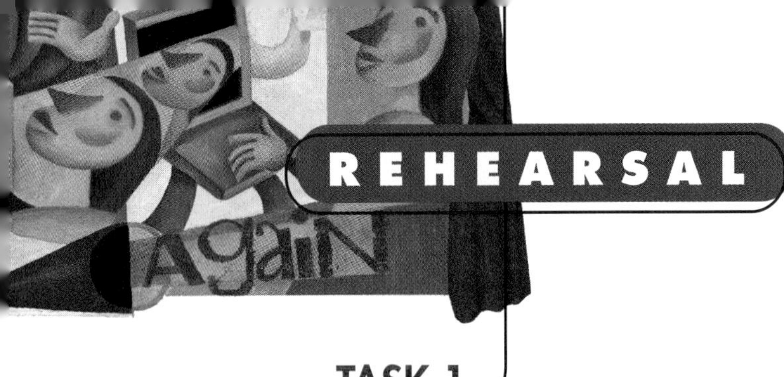

GOAL

To create a presentation from a Word outline and to enhance the presentation using an Excel chart and a Word table

SETTING THE STAGE/WRAPUP

File name: 5.1tofinancial

WHAT YOU NEED TO KNOW

- Importing a Word outline into PowerPoint allows you to take what may have started out as notes and transform it into a full-fledged presentation.
- Tables and charts support points made in your presentation. Linking them to their source prevents you from having to update each chart or table individually, thus narrowing the margin for error.
- In this Rehearsal activity, you work for Time Out Sporting Goods and have just received the year-end income statements for both of the Time Out Sporting Goods stores. Your boss has been asked to analyze these statements and then give a presentation to the CEO (chief executive officer) and CFO (chief financial officer) on Time Out's financial performance. After reviewing many documents, your boss created an outline in Word from which he wants you to create the presentation.
- You will import your boss's outline from Word and enhance the presentation using the income statements and a Word table that he provided. You will then import slides from another presentation to use as the last two slides in this presentation.

DIRECTIONS

Note: All files to be imported (and noted in bold) are on the Data CD.

1. Start a new blank presentation.
2. Import the Word outline, **5.1tooutline,** located on the Data CD, to PowerPoint.
3. Format the presentation as shown on the facing page.
   - a. Apply any design template.
   - b. Insert clip art images as shown.
   - c. On Slide 4, insert the table from the **5.1highlightstable** Word file located on the Data CD. Link the table.
   - d. On Slide 5, import the chart found on the Column Chart tab of the **5.1salechart** Excel workbook located on the Data CD.
   - e. On Slide 6, import and link the chart found on the Chart Data tab of the **5.1salechart** Excel workbook located on the Data CD.
   - f. Switch to Excel, and open the **5.1salechart** workbook. Click the **Chart Data** tab. Click **Cell D6** and change the Net Income to `92,000`. Save and close the spreadsheet, then switch to PowerPoint and notice that the pie chart on Slide 6 reflects the change.
   - g. On Slide 7, import the Consolidated Income Statement (beginning with row 6) from the Consolidated Income Statement worksheet of the **5.1salechart** Excel workbook located on the Data CD. *(Hint: Use the Paste Special feature and paste the income statement as an Excel Worksheet Object.)*
   - h. Format the slide master with any fonts, bullets, and headers/footers.
   - i. Apply any animation scheme.
4. Insert the slides from **5.1yearahead** on the Data CD as the last slides in the presentation. Deselect the option to keep the source formatting.

5. Create a summary slide as Slide 3, using the slide titles indicated in the illustration. Change the title of the summary slide to "Contents." Link each bulleted item to its corresponding slide.
6. Save the presentation; name it **5.1tofinancial.**
7. Run the slide show.
8. Exit Word; exit PowerPoint.

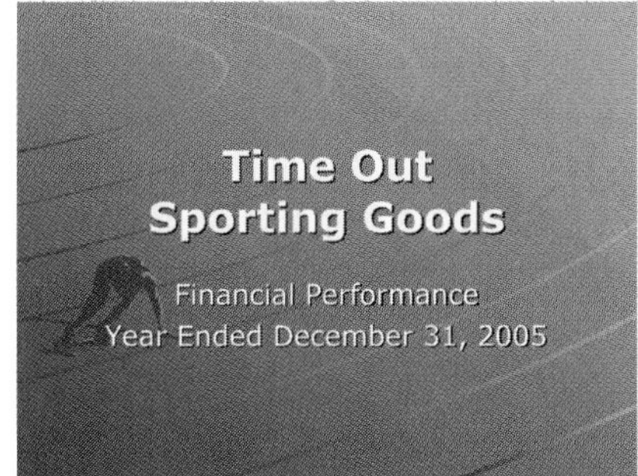

1

2

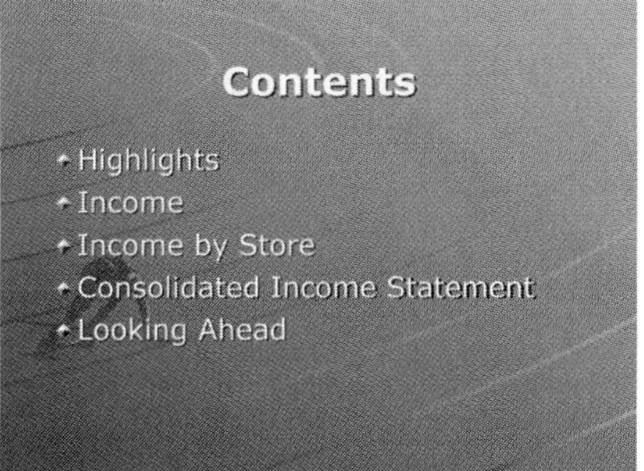

3

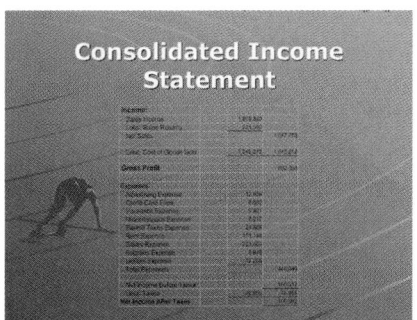

4

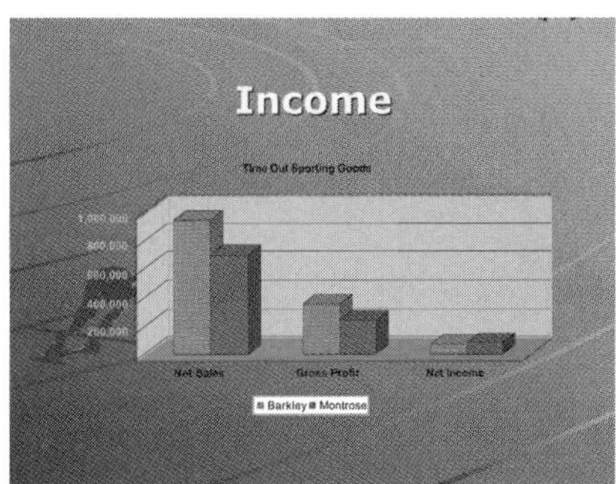

5

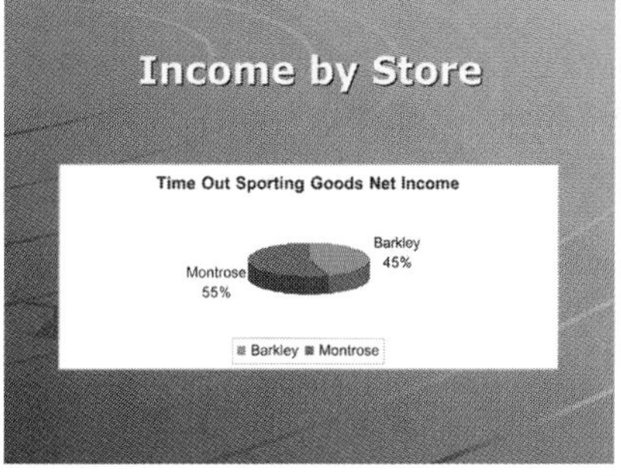

6

Consolidated Income Statement

7

8

POWERPOINT

Cues for Reference

Import a Word Outline as a New Presentation

1. Click **File, Open.**
2. Click the **Files of type** list arrow and click **All Outlines.**
3. Double-click the appropriate file.

Import an Outline to an Existing Presentation

1. Click the **Outline** tab.
2. Click the slide icon above where the outline text should appear.
3. Click **Insert, Slides from Outline.**
4. Double-click the appropriate file.

Export PowerPoint Slides to a Word Outline

1. Click **File, Send To,** and **Microsoft Office Word.**
2. Click **Outline only.**
3. Click **OK.**

Embed an Object from an Existing File

1. Display the slide on which to add a chart, table, or worksheet.
2. Click **Insert, Object.**
3. Click **Create from file.**
4. Click **Browse.**
5. Select the file that contains the appropriate chart, table, or worksheet.

or

1. Select the object to embed from the source file.
2. Right-click and select **Copy.**
3. Display the slide on which to place the object.
4. Right-click the slide and select **Paste.**

Link an Object

1. Select the object to link from the source file.
2. Click **Edit, Copy.**
3. Display the slide on which to place the object.
4. Click **Edit, Paste Special.**
5. Click **Paste link.**
6. Select the appropriate object from the As box.
7. Click **OK.**

Edit an Object

1. Double-click the object.

   or

   If a worksheet or chart object, right-click the object and select **Worksheet Object, Edit.**
   If a table object, right-click the object and select **Document Object, Edit.**
2. Make the necessary changes.
3. Click on the slide to exit edit mode.

Import a Slide from Another Presentation

1. Open the presentation in which you want to insert slides.
2. Click **Insert, Slides from Files.**
3. Click in the **File text** box, enter the file name, and click **Display.**

   or

   Click **Browse** and double-click the appropriate presentation.
4. Click the slides to insert and click **Insert.**

   or

   Click **Insert All** to insert all slides.
5. Click **Close.**

GOAL

To practice using the following skill sets:

- Add, edit, and delete comments
- Set up a review cycle (compare and merge documents)
- Embed fonts
- Package a presentation for CD

POWERPOINT

WHAT YOU NEED TO KNOW

Add, Edit, and Delete Comments

- *Comments* are hidden notes or annotations that you or a reviewer can add to a presentation (reviewing a presentation is covered later in this Task). You can read these comments on screen, hide them when you print the presentation, print them with the presentation, or incorporate them into the presentation.
- To add a comment, you must be in Normal view. Display the slide on which to add a comment and click Insert, Comment. You can also click the Insert Comment button on the Reviewing toolbar, as shown in Figure 5.11. (To display the Reviewing toolbar, click View, Toolbars, and Reviewing.) A comment box automatically appears in the top-left corner of the slide, and you can drag the comment anywhere on the slide. Enter your comment in the comment box, as shown in Figure 5.12. Click outside the comment box to resume working on the slide. By default, PowerPoint uses information in the User Information Profile to identify the author of the comments.

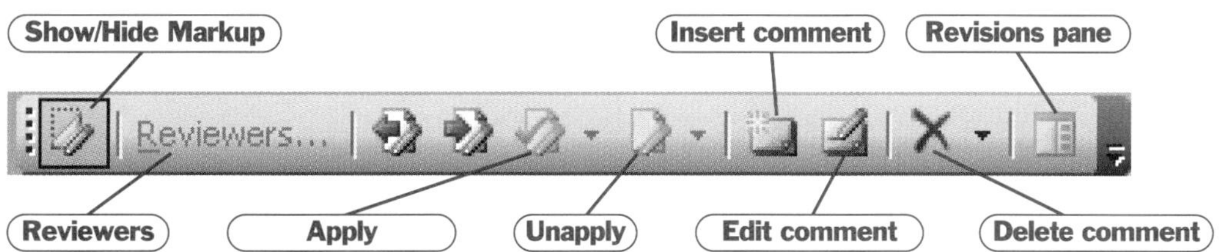

Figure 5.11 Reviewing toolbar

Figure 5.12 Insert comment

- To edit a comment, insert a new comment, or delete a comment, right-click the comment and select an option from the shortcut menu, as shown in Figure 5.13. You can also click the appropriate button on the Reviewing toolbar.

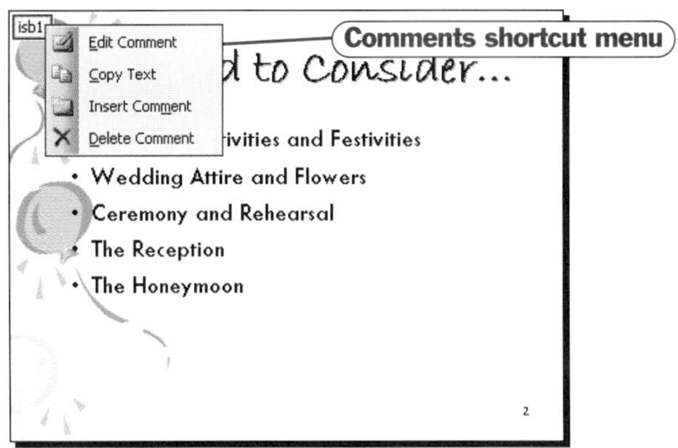

Figure 5.13 Comments shortcut menu

- Comments print with slides unless you choose to hide them. To hide a comment, click the Show/Hide Markup button on the Reviewing toolbar.
- To print comment pages, click File, Print. In the Print dialog box that opens, as shown in Figure 5.14, click the Print comments and ink markup check box. Figure 5.15 illustrates a printed comments page.

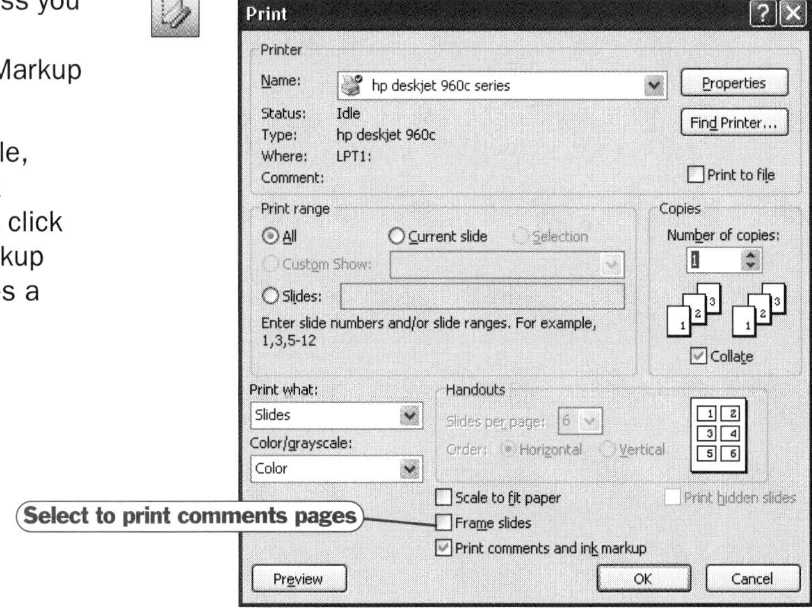

Figure 5.14 Print comments pages

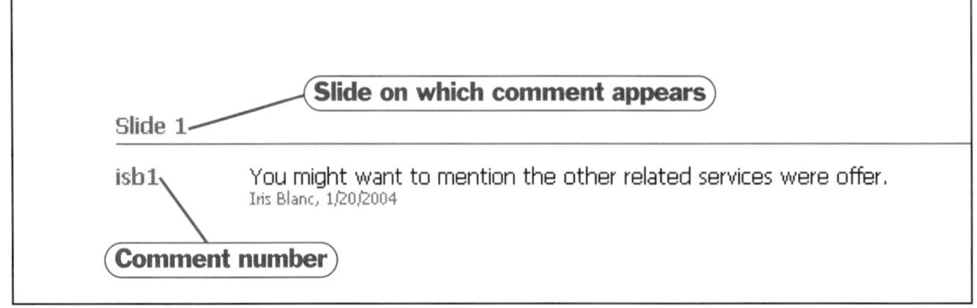

Figure 5.15 Comments page

TRY *it* OUT *p5-6*

1. Open **p5.6collegeplan** from the Data CD.
2. Display Slide 2 (The Basics).
3. Click **Insert, Comment.**
4. Enter the following in the comment box:

   `Make note that some colleges do not accept the ACT and that students should know which standardized test the college accepts before applying.`
5. Click on the slide to close the comment box.
6. Click and drag the comment and place it next to the bullet that says "Take the SAT and/or ACT."
7. Place the mouse pointer over the comment to view it.
8. Display Slide 3 (Find the RIGHT College).
9. Click **Insert, Comment.**
10. Enter the following in the comment box:

    `Insert a table showing the date, time, and location of upcoming college fairs. Also include a picture of a past college fair.`
11. Click on the slide to close the comment box.
12. Display Slide 2.
13. Right-click the comment and click **Edit Comment.**
14. Add the following to the comment:

    `Include a chart or table that compares and contrasts the ACT and SAT.`
15. Click on the slide to close the comment box.
16. Close the file; do not save.

POWERPOINT

Set up a Review Cycle

Send a Presentation for Review

▶ The Review feature allows reviewers to make changes and add notes on the electronic copy of a presentation, which the author can choose to accept or reject at a later time. Figure 5.16 illustrates a review cycle.

Figure 5.16 Review cycle

▶ You can send a presentation for review via e-mail, a shared folder (on a network), or a disk. To send a presentation for review using Microsoft Outlook, open the presentation and click File, Send To, and Mail Recipient (For Review). Enter the e-mail addresses of those whom you want to review the presentation, enter a short message if necessary, and click Send, as shown in Figure 5.17.

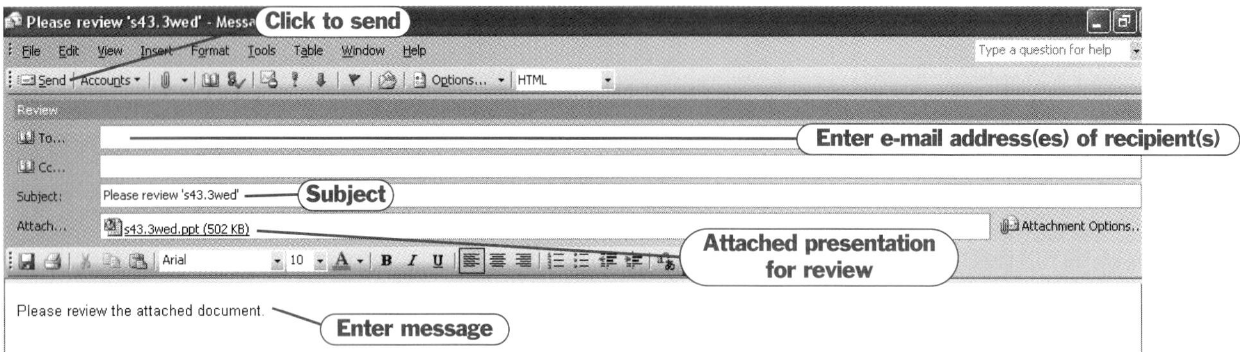

Figure 5.17 Send a presentation for review via Outlook

▶ To send a presentation for review using an e-mail program other than Outlook (and thus send the presentation as an attachment), a shared folder, or a disk, click File, Save As. In the Save as type list box, click Presentation for Review, as shown in Figure 5.18. Enter a file name in the File name text box and click Save.

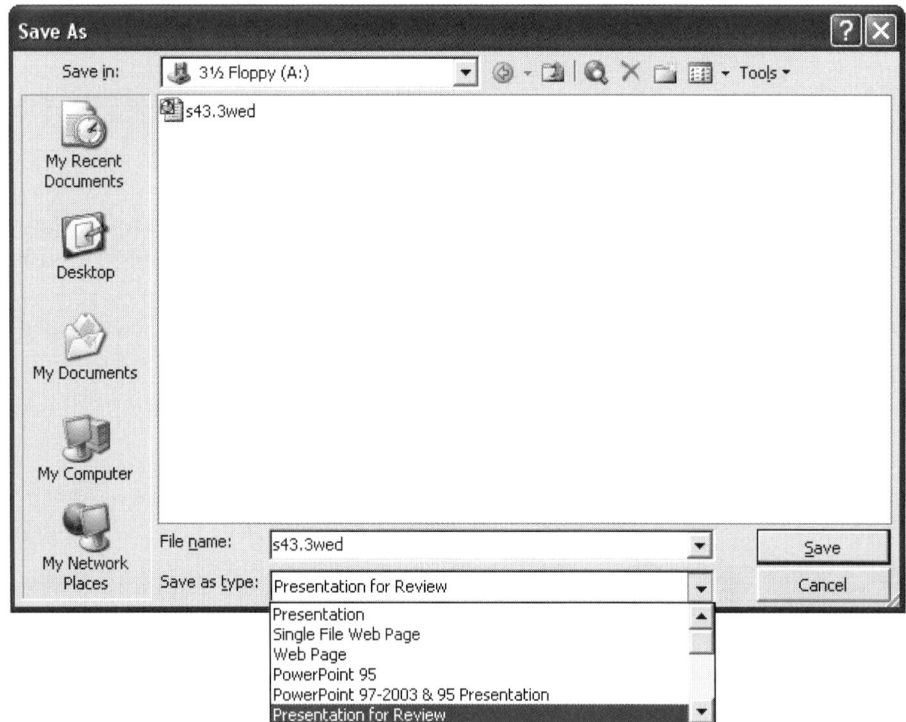

Figure 5.18 Save As dialog box

▶ When you send a presentation for review, you must remember to send all linked files as well.

Review a Presentation

- When a reviewer receives and opens the presentation, he or she can make any changes—formatting changes, changes to the slide master, and so on.
- The reviewer can also add comments to individual slides, using the procedures previously described.
- After changes are made, the reviewer will send it back to the author. These changes are recorded, but do not overwrite the author's original presentation.
- To send a reviewed presentation back to the author using Outlook, click File, Send To, and Original Sender. Always send the presentation back to the author the same way you received it.

Review Comments and Changes

POWERPOINT

- Once all reviewed presentations are received, the author can merge them into the original presentation and compare everyone's comments with the original. To merge the reviewed presentations with the original, open the original presentation and click Tools, Compare and Merge Presentations. In the Choose Files to Merge with Current Presentation dialog box, click the reviewed presentations you want to compare and click Merge, as shown in Figure 5.19. If you received the reviewed presentation via Outlook, you will be prompted to merge the presentations when you double-click the attachment.

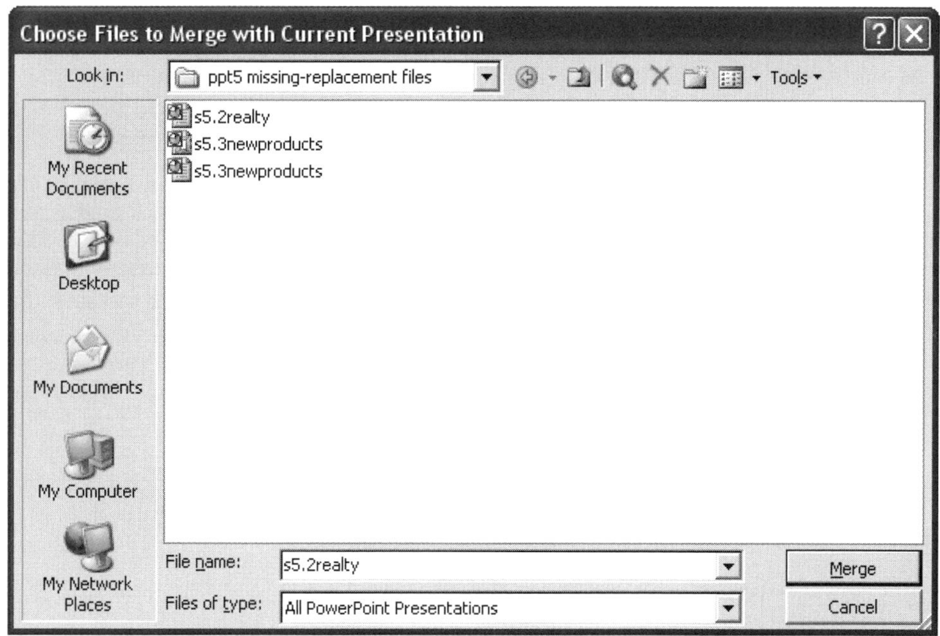

Figure 5.19 Choose Files to Merge with Current Presentation dialog box

- Once you have merged the presentations, a Markup button appears on the original presentation wherever a reviewer has made a change, as shown in Figure 5.20.

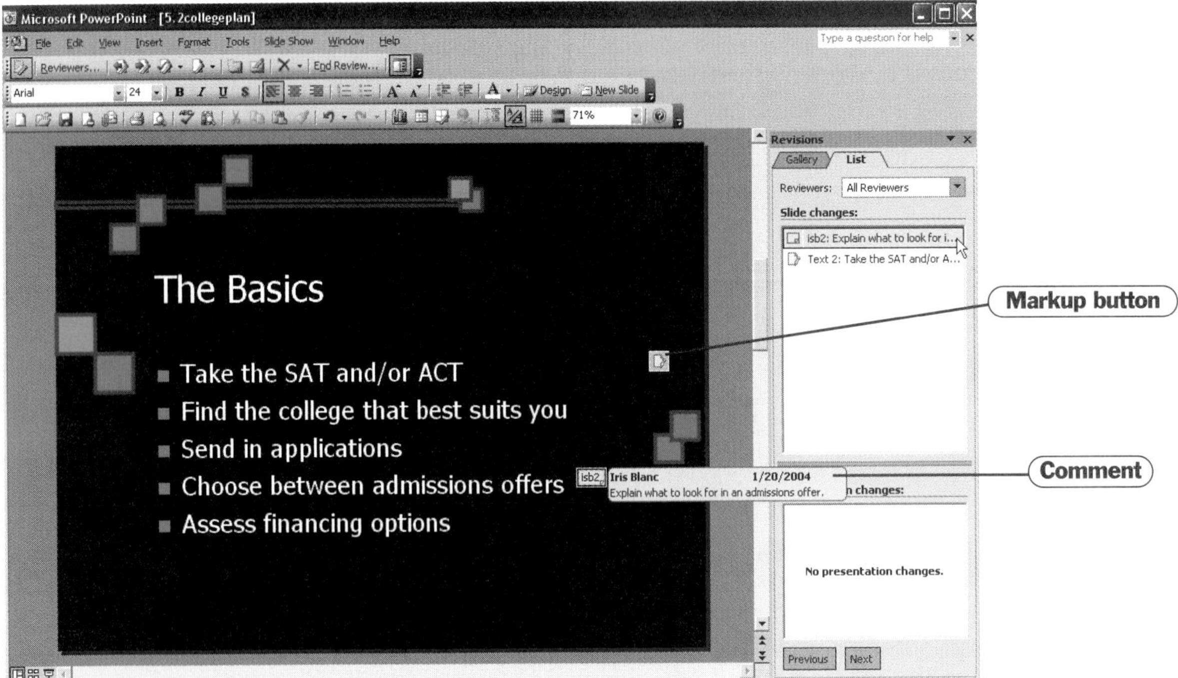

Figure 5.20 Merged presentations

- You can accept or reject changes by clicking the Markup button. In the menu that appears, click in a box to accept a change; leave a box unchecked to reject a change. If you do accept a change, the Markup button displays a checkmark, as shown in Figure 5.21.

- You can also view changes and comments, as well as accept or reject changes and comments, from the Revisions task pane, which appears when you combine presentations. When you select a reviewer's comment or change from the Slide changes box, the full comment or a description of the edits made appears on the slide, as shown in Figure 5.22. You can then accept or reject the change or delete the comment.

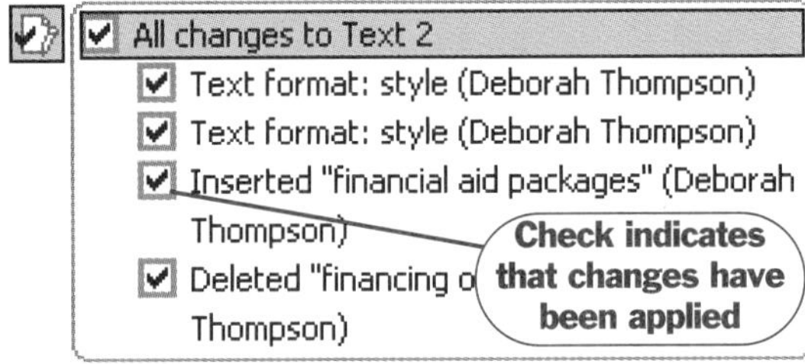

Figure 5.21 Apply changes

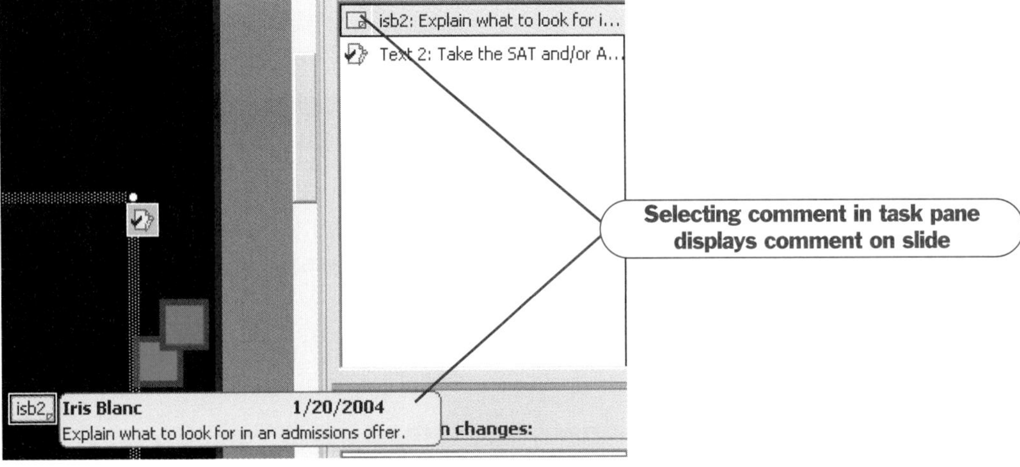

Figure 5.22 Revisions task pane with comment selected

- Clicking the Gallery tab in the Revisions task pane, as shown in Figure 5.23, allows you to see a thumbnail of a reviewer's slide next to the original slide in the slide pane. You can choose to accept or reject a reviewer's changes by clicking the list arrow on the thumbnail and selecting the option you want.

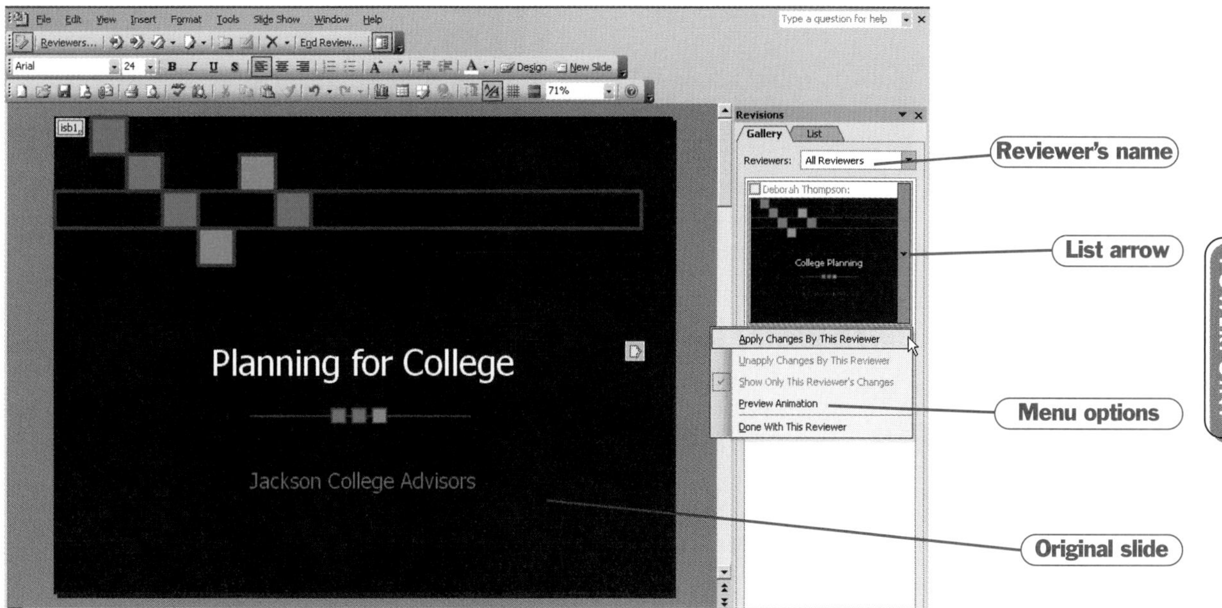

Figure 5.23 Gallery tab

POWERPOINT

- You can also accept or reject reviewer changes and comments using the Reviewing toolbar (see Figure 5.11).
- After reviewing your presentation (merging and comparing the original with the reviewed presentations), click the End Review button on the Reviewing toolbar. This will incorporate all the changes you accepted during the review process into your original file. Once you end a review, you will be unable to combine any future reviewed presentations with your original.

  End Review...

  In this Try it Out, you are the author, saving and sending your presentation for review.

TRY*it*OUT *p5-7*

1. Open **p5.7collegeplan** from the Data CD. *Note:* This is the author's original file.
2. Click **File, Save As.**
3. Click the **Save in** list arrow and select a folder in which to save the presentation for review.
4. Click the **Save as type** list arrow and click **Presentation for Review.**
5. Enter the file name `p5.7collegereview` in the File name text box and click **Save.**
6. Close **p5.7collegeplan.**

   You are now the reviewer, applying edits and comments.
7. Open **p5.7collegereview.** *Note:* You might be prompted to merge changes into the original file. If so, click **No.**
8. Display Slide 1 and replace the title "Planning for College" with: `College Planning.`
9. Display Slide 2.
   a. Make **SAT** and **ACT boldface.**
   b. Change the last bullet "Assess financing options" to: `Assess financial aid packages.`
   c. Click **Insert, Comment.**
   d. Enter `Explain what to look for in an admissions offer` in the comment box.
   e. Click on the slide to close the comment box.
   f. Click and drag the comment next to the bullet that says "Choose between admissions offers."
10. Click the **Save** button.
11. Close the file.

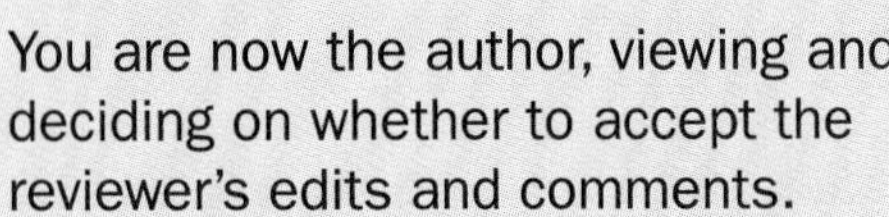

You are now the author, viewing and deciding on whether to accept the reviewer's edits and comments.

12. Open **p5.7collegeplan** from the Data CD.
13. Click **Tools, Compare and Merge Presentations.**
14. Click the **Look in** list arrow, select the folder that contains **p5.7collegereview,** and double-click the file.
15. On Slide 1, click the **Markup** button on the slide and click in the **All Changes to Title 1** box.

16. Click the **Next Item** button on the Reviewing toolbar.

17. Right-click the comment and click **Delete Comment.**
18. Click the **Markup** button on Slide 2.

19. Click in the **Inserted financial aid packages** box and click the **Deleted financing options** box.
20. Click the **End Review** button on the Reviewing toolbar and click **Yes** when prompted.

21. Scroll through the presentation and notice the reviewer's changes.
22. Close the file; save the changes.

Embed Fonts

- The Embed Fonts feature ensures that the fonts you use in a presentation are available no matter what computer you use to deliver it.
- You can choose to embed fonts when you save a presentation. To do so, click File, Save As. In the Save As dialog box, click Tools, Save Options. In the Save Options dialog box that opens, as shown in Figure 5.24, click the Embed TrueType fonts check box. To keep the file size to a minimum, you can choose to embed only the characters you use in the presentation. If you want all characters available to you, click Embed all characters.

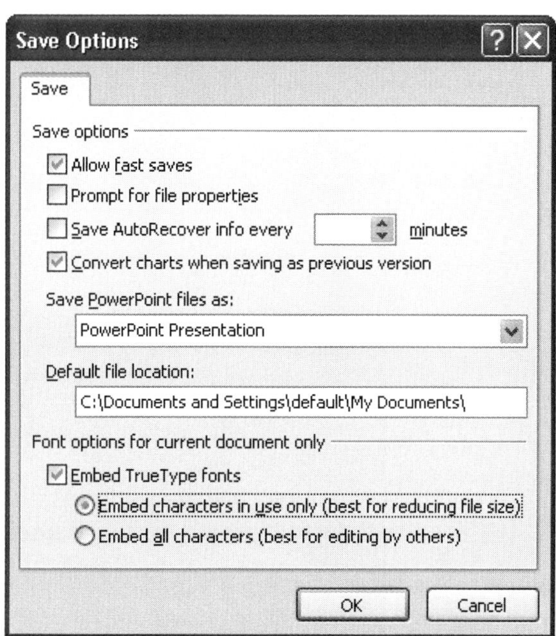

Figure 5.24 Save Options dialog box

TRY *it* OUT *p5-8*

1. Open **p5.8brand** from the Data CD.
2. Click **File, Save As.**
3. Click **Tools, Save Options.**
4. Click the **Embed TrueType fonts** check box.
5. Click **Embed all characters**, if necessary.
6. Click **OK.**
7. Click in the **File name** text box and enter: `brand.`
8. Click **Save.**
9. Close the presentation.

POWERPOINT

Packaging Presentations for Copying to CDs

- The Package for CD option lets you save your presentation to one of the following CDs: a blank recordable CD (CD-R), a blank rewritable CD (CD-RW), or a CD-RW with existing content that can be overwritten. *Note: If you use a CD-R, make sure you copy all the files you need onto the CD the first time. After the files are copied, you cannot add more files to the CD.*

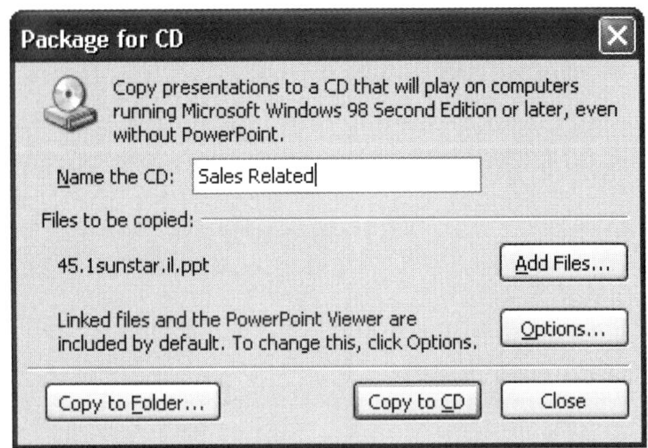

Figure 5.25 Package for CD dialog box

- When you copy a presentation with the Package for CD feature, you save PowerPoint Viewer along with it. PowerPoint Viewer is the program that allows you to view a presentation on a computer that does not have PowerPoint installed.
- To Package a presentation for CD, click File, Package for CD. In the Package for CD dialog box, shown in Figure 5.25, enter a CD name in the Name the CD box.
- To add more presentations or other files, click Add Files. Then, select the files you want to add and click Add. Presentations to be copied will display in the Files to be copied list, as shown in Figure 5.26.

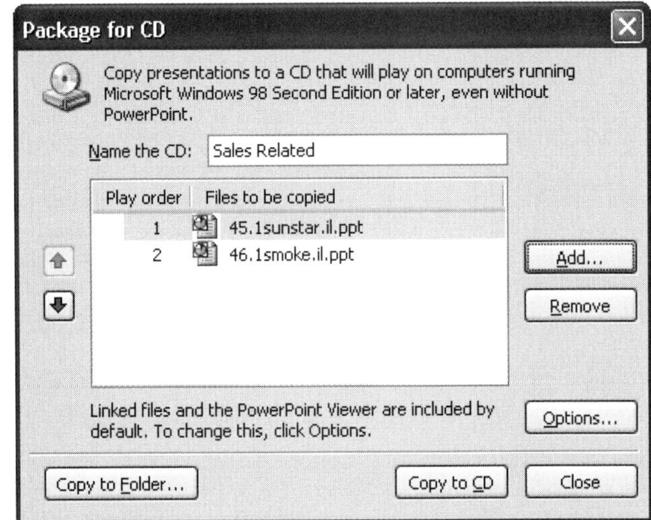

Figure 5.26 Files to be copied list

- By default, the presentation that is currently open is already in the Files to be Copied list and presentations are set up to run automatically in the order in which they are listed. You can, however, change that order by clicking the up or down arrow to move it to a new position in the list. Files linked to the presentation are included automatically and will not appear in the Files to be Copied list. Click the Options button to change default settings. When all the files you want to copy to the CD are listed, click Copy to CD.

TRY it OUT *p5-9*

Note: You must insert a blank CD in the CD drive to complete this Try it Out. If you do not have a CD, you can complete steps 1–8 only.

1. Open **p5.9collegeplan** from the Data CD.
2. Click **File, Package for CD.**
3. Enter `Sales Related` in the **Name the CD** box.
4. Click **Add Files.**
5. Select **p5.9brand** from the Data CD.
6. Click the **Options** button.

7. Deselect PowerPoint Viewer and click **OK.**
8. Click **Copy to CD** if you have a blank CD in the CD drive. Otherwise, click **Close.**
9. Close all files.

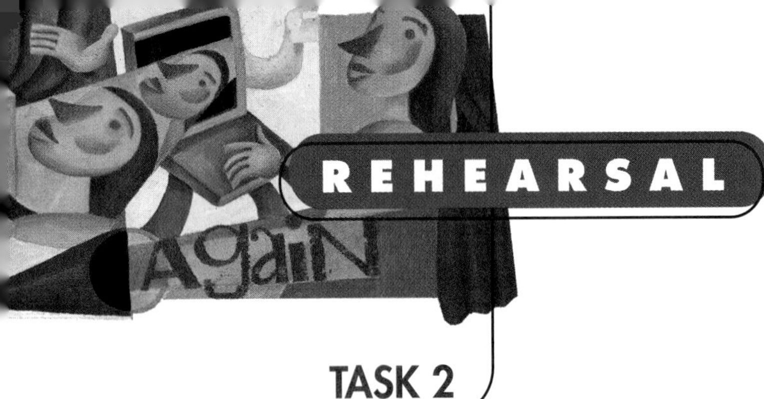

GOAL

To review and edit a presentation using comments and the compare and merge features, and to prepare the presentation for delivery from another computer by embedding fonts and packaging the presentation for copying to a CD

SETTING THE STAGE/WRAPUP

File name: **5.2realty**

WHAT YOU NEED TO KNOW

- Setting up a review cycle allows multiple people, located anywhere in the world, to collaborate on a presentation. Each person can make changes to an original presentation independently. These changes or comments can then be pieced together, resulting in a true collaboration.
- In this Rehearsal activity, you will send a presentation you previously created to a reviewer for comment. You will then use the compare and merge feature to edit the presentation for Four Corners Realty.

DIRECTIONS

1. Open **4.1realty,** which you created in Lesson 4. If this file is not available to you, open **5.2realty** from the Data CD.
2. Save the presentation for review; name it **5.2realtyreview.**
3. Make changes and add comments to **5.2realtyreview** as follows:
   a. On Slide 1: Add a comment that reads: `Create a footer using WordArt`. Use the Title and Slide Master to do so.
   b. On the remaining slides: Replace, delete, and/or add text so that your presentation matches the one on the facing pages.
4. Save and close **5.2realtyreview;** open **4.1realty** (or **5.2realty**), the original presentation.
5. Compare and merge the original and reviewed presentations.
6. Make changes to the slide master, as suggested by the comment on Slide 1, then delete the comment.
7. Accept all changes to Slides 2, 3, 4, 5, and 6 (Benefits).
8. Add clip art throughout the presentation, as shown in the illustration.
9. Print one copy of the presentation as handouts.
10. Save the file as **5.2realty** and embed the fonts.

Note: Some fonts have licensing restrictions and cannot be saved with a presentation. If you try to embed a font that has such a restriction, PowerPoint will prevent you from doing so. If this happens, click OK and embed just those fonts that are available.

11. Copy the presentation to a CD if a CD is available to you. Otherwise, skip this step.
    a. Include linked files and embed TrueType fonts.
    b. Do not pack PowerPoint Viewer.
12. Close the file; save the changes.

1

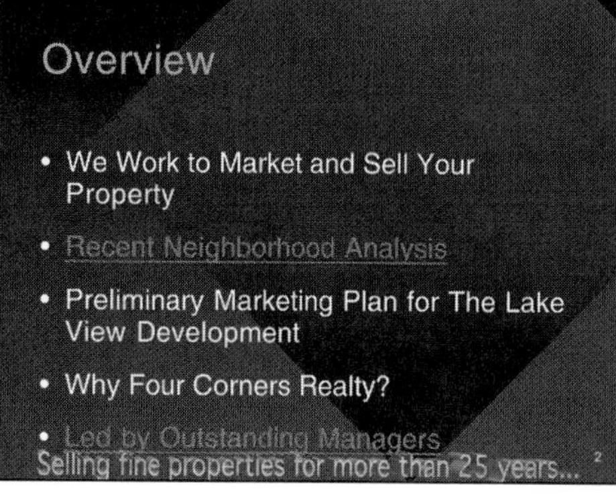

Overview
• We Work to Market and Sell Your Property
• Recent Neighborhood Analysis
• Preliminary Marketing Plan for The Lake View Development
• Why Four Corners Realty?
• Led by Outstanding Managers
Selling fine properties for more than 25 years...
2

2

POWERPOINT

We Work to Market and Sell Your Property
• Extensive experience with residential on-site marketing
• Stellar client list
• What we'll do:
– Plan and implement a strong marketing program
– Implement budgets based on sales and marketing strategy
– Assist developers in pricing strategies
– Help attain necessary financing
– Provide accurate market analysis
Selling fine properties for more than 25 years...
3

3

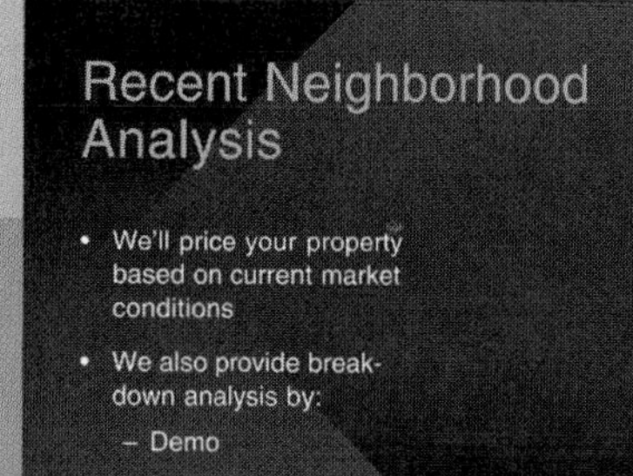

Recent Neighborhood Analysis
• We'll price your property based on current market conditions
• We also provide break-down analysis by:
– Demo
– Income
– Neighborhood
Selling fine properties for more than 25 years...
4

4

Preliminary Marketing Plan for the Lake View Development

• Target appropriate demo
  – Part-time residents
  – Retirees
• Provide incentives to sell property early
• Create and distribute comprehensive press kits

Selling fine properties for more than 25 years... 5

5

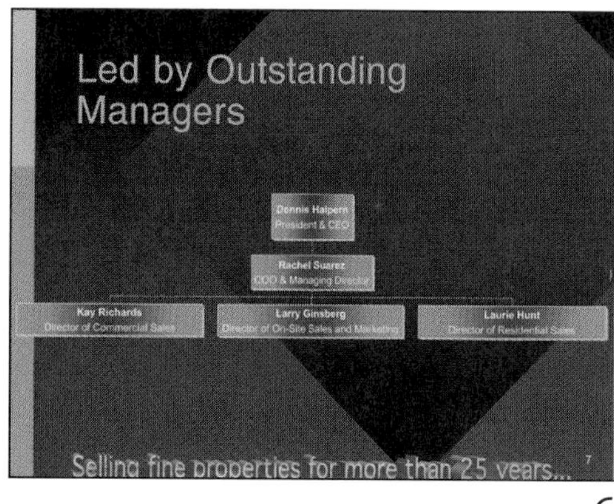

6

Why Four Corners Realty?

• We are a full-service real estate company with a track record of new development sales success!
  – Early sales
    • Launch full-scale sales effort even before building begins
  – Competitive pricing
    • Maximum dollars given market value
  – Flexibility
    • Adapt to your specific needs to market and sell your property

Selling fine properties for more than 25 years... 6

7

Choose the Right Broker!

• Experience
• Outstanding staff
• Proven success
• Detailed and respected marketing plans

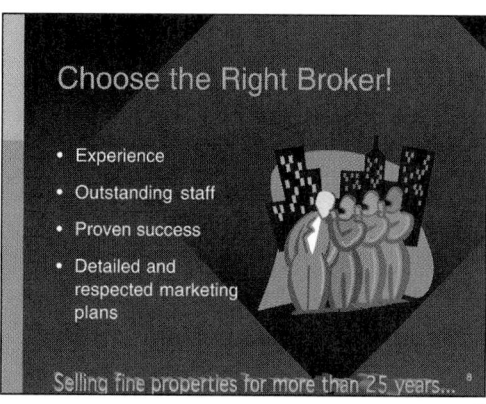

Selling fine properties for more than 25 years... 8

8

Cues for Reference

Insert Comments

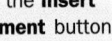

1. Display the slide on which to add a comment.
2. Click **Insert, Comment.**
   or
   a. Click **View, Toolbars, Reviewing.**
   b. Click the **Insert Comment** button. 
3. Enter the comment in the comment box.

Send a Presentation for Review Using Microsoft Outlook

1. Click **File, Send To,** and **Mail Recipient (For Review).**
2. Click in the **To** box and enter the e-mail address of the reviewer.
3. Click in the message window and enter a message, if necessary.
4. Click **Send.**

Use an E-mail Program Other than Outlook, a Shared Folder, or a Disk

1. Click **File, Save As.**
2. Click the **Save as type** list arrow and select **Presentation for Review.**
3. Click the **File name** text box and enter a file name.
4. Click **OK.**

Compare Original and Reviewed Presentations

1. Open the original presentation.
2. Click **Tools, Compare and Merge Presentations.**
3. Click the reviewed presentation to which you want to compare the original presentation.
4. Click **Merge.**

Embed Fonts

1. Click **File, Save As.**
2. Click **Tools, Save Options.**
3. Click the **Embed TrueType fonts** check box.
4. Click **Embed characters in use only**
   or
   Click **Embed all characters.**
5. Click **OK.**
6. Click in the **File name** text box and enter a file name.
7. Click **Save.**

Packaging Presentations for Copying to CDs

1. Insert a CD into the CD drive.
2. Click **File, Package for CD.**
3. Type the name for the CD in the **Name the CD** box.
4. To add more presentations or other files, click **Add Files.**
5. Select the files you want to add, and click **Add.**
6. Click **Copy to CD.**

GOAL
To practice using the following skill sets:
- Save a presentation as a Web page
- Preview a presentation as a Web page
- Publish a presentation to the Web
- Set up and schedule an online broadcast

POWERPOINT

WHAT YOU NEED TO KNOW

Save a Presentation as a Web Page

- You can save any presentation you create in PowerPoint as a Web page. Doing so saves the presentation in *HTML* format, a programming language that Web browsers use to interpret and display Web pages. It also automatically creates frames, which make navigating the presentation easier and more Web-friendly.
- To save a presentation as a Web page, click File, Save As Web Page. In the Save As dialog box that displays, shown in Figure 5.27, click the Change Title button to change the title of your Web page. This title appears in the title bar of the Web browser when you eventually publish the presentation to the Web. Click the File name text box, enter a file name, and click Save.

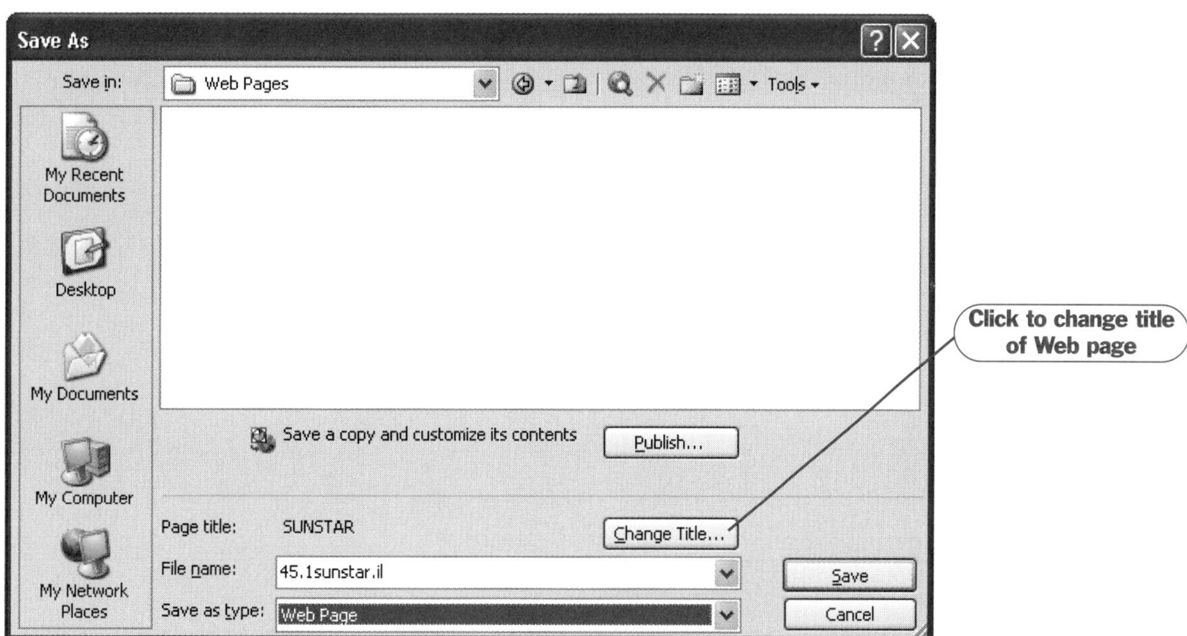

Figure 5.27 Save As dialog box

Preview a Presentation as a Web Page

- To preview your presentation as a Web page, click File, Web Page Preview. This opens your presentation in Internet Explorer, as shown in Figure 5.28. Internet Explorer is the Web browser that comes with the Microsoft Office suite. The presentation displays a slide and outline pane along with navigation buttons at the bottom of the window.

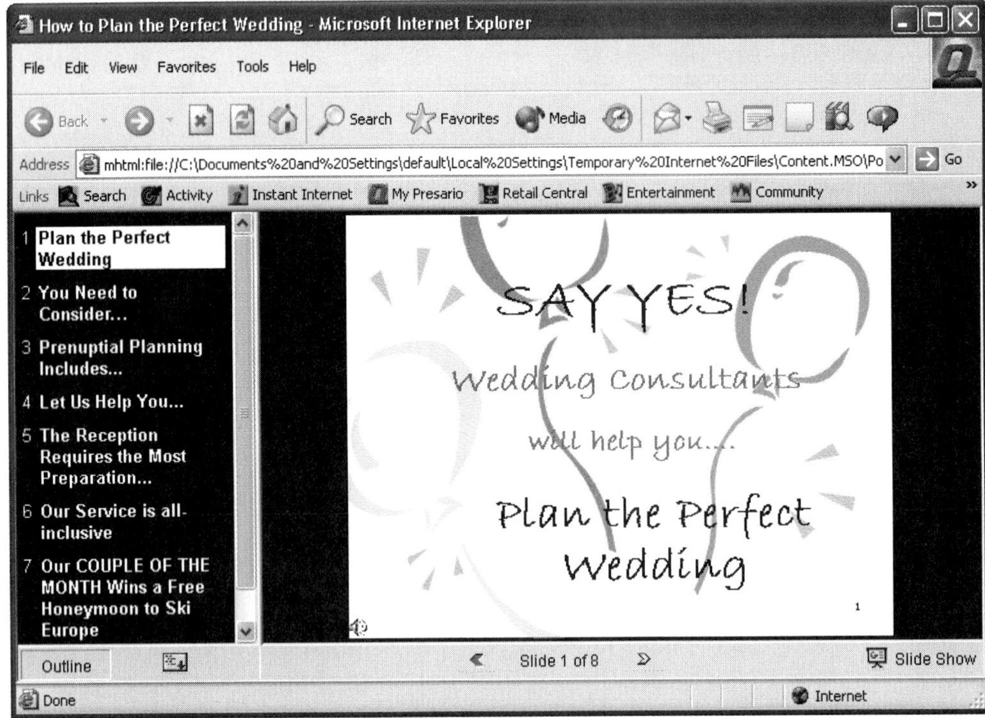

Figure 5.28 Web page preview

TRY it OUT *p5-10*

1. Open **p5.10devon** from the Data CD.
2. Click **File, Save as Web Page.**
3. Click the **Change Title** button and enter:

   `Devon Investments`
4. Click **OK.**
5. Click in the File name text box and enter:

   `devon`
6. Click **Save.**
7. Click **File, Web Page Preview.** Note the layout of the presentation in the browser.
8. Close the browser.
9. Close the file.

Publish a Presentation to the Web

- Publishing your presentation to the Web allows others to access it via a Web browser. This requires, however, that you contact your Internet Service Provider or that you install Web server software. A *Web server* is a computer with specialized software that manages Web sites. When you publish a presentation, you are actually publishing it to a Web server from which an audience can view it with a browser.
- To publish a presentation to the Web, click File, Save as Web Page. In the Save As dialog box, specify a file name and Web page title, as you did when saving a presentation as a Web page. Then, click the Publish button to display the Publish as Web Page dialog box, as shown in Figure 5.29.

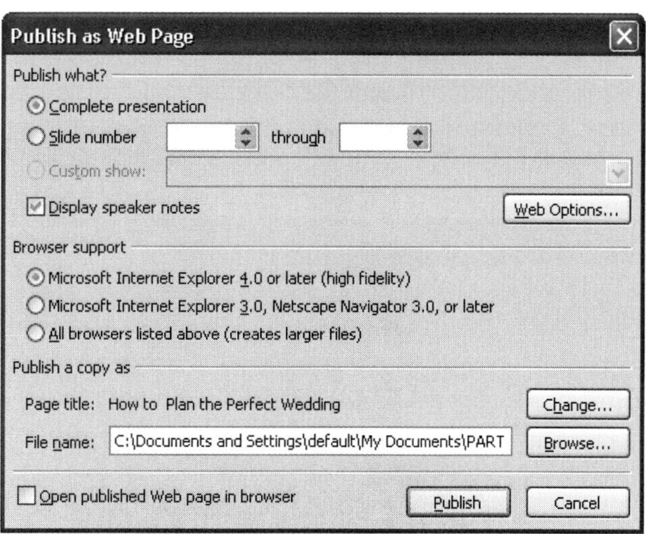

Figure 5.29 Publish as Web Page dialog box

- In the Publish as Web Page dialog box, identify a Web browser and make other specifications such as how much of the presentation to publish and whether to publish the speaker notes.
- After making your selections, you can view the Web page in a browser. Click the Open published Web page in browser check box and click Publish.

Set Up and Schedule an Online Broadcast

- If you want to deliver your presentation to audiences in different locations, you can do so by broadcasting it live over the Internet or an intranet. (An intranet is a network belonging to an organization or company that only those who work within the company can access.) Before you broadcast your presentation, you must set it up appropriately and notify audience members when the broadcast will occur.
- To broadcast your presentation, open it and select Slide Show, Online Broadcast, Schedule a Live Broadcast. (*Note:* If this option is not available on your Slide Show menu, you must download the presentation broadcast feature from Microsoft Office Online, then install it. See your instructor for help in downloading this, if necessary.) In the Schedule Presentation Broadcast dialog box that opens, as shown in Figure 5.30, enter information about the presentation, which will appear in your viewer's browser before the presentation broadcast begins.

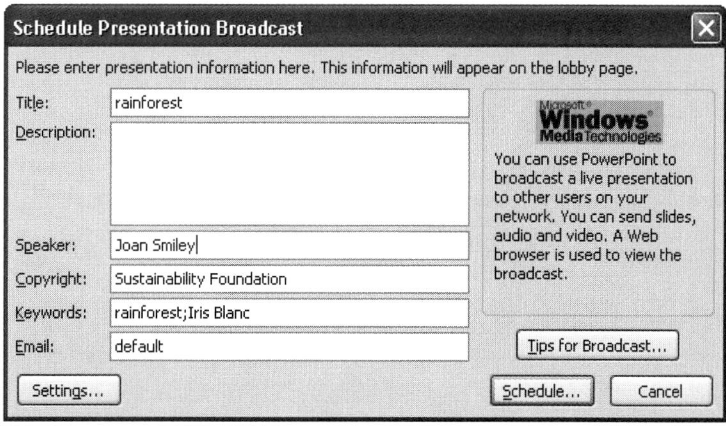

Figure 5.30 Schedule Presentation Broadcast dialog box

- Click the Settings button to display the Broadcast Settings dialog box, as shown in Figure 5.31, in which you can specify audio, video streaming, and chat options. You also have to indicate the server location to which the presentation files should be sent, as well as the name of the server that will stream any audio or video. Consult a network administrator or your Internet Service Provider to complete this part of the setup.

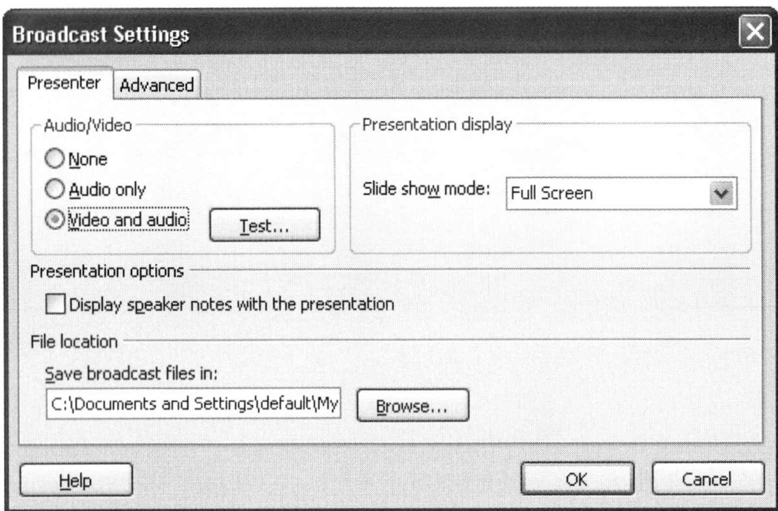

Figure 5.31 Broadcast Settings dialog box

- Once you have completed the setup, you can schedule the online broadcast. To do so, click the Schedule button in the Schedule Presentation Broadcast dialog box. This opens your e-mail program. If you have Outlook, you can use it to arrange a broadcast (see Outlook Help for information on this feature). If you do not have Outlook, include the date and time of the broadcast in your e-mail message. PowerPoint includes the URL of the broadcast site in the message.
- To view a broadcast presentation, all participants need a Web browser that supports advanced broadcasting features, such as Internet Explorer 4.0 or a later version.
- To begin broadcasting your presentation, click Slide Show, Online Broadcast, Start Live Broadcast Now, and follow the prompts to broadcast.

A
1
2
3

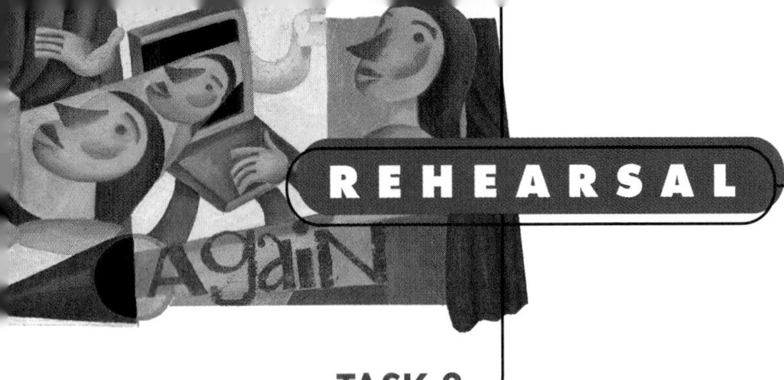

GOAL
To create and enhance a presentation, then save the presentation as a Web page

SETTING THE STAGE/WRAPUP
File name: **5.3newproducts**

WHAT YOU NEED TO KNOW

- Remember that many images on the Web are copyrighted and you may need permission to use them.
- In this Rehearsal activity, you will assume that you work in the Marketing Department at Green Brothers Gardeners. You have been asked to create a presentation to persuade gardening and landscaping retailers to carry two new software products that Green Brothers has recently developed. Enhance your presentation with relevant images (you may download images from the Web, if you want). You will also save your presentation as a Web page so that it can eventually be published to the Web.

DIRECTIONS

1. Start a new presentation; apply the Products And Services Overview presentation template. (Click On my computer on the task pane and select the Presentations tab.)
2. Create slide text as indicated on the following page.
   a. Include a table and clip art, as shown.
   b. For Slide 1, include a picture of a tree. You can create a logo using the tree, if necessary.
   c. On Slide 2, insert a hyperlink on the text "Two new software products," then link to the Word file **5.3greenbros** on the Data CD.
   d. On Slide 3:
      - Find a map of the U.S.A. and copy it onto the slide.
      - Insert a hyperlink on the word "Japanese" that links to www.jgarden.org.
      - Insert a hyperlink on the word "tropical" that links to www.htbg.com.
   e. For Slide 4, insert four different garden-related pictures on the slide as shown. If they are not available in your clip art collection, you may download them from the Web.
3. Apply any slide transitions and/or animation schemes you want.
4. View the Slide Master and change the first-level bullet to a three-leaf clover. Change the title font style and color.
5. Display Slide 8. Format the table with a solid gray fill color and green borders.
6. Save the file as a Web page.
   a. Change the Web page title to Green Brothers Gardeners.
   b. Name the file **5.3newproducts.**
7. Preview the presentation as a Web page.
8. Close the file.

1

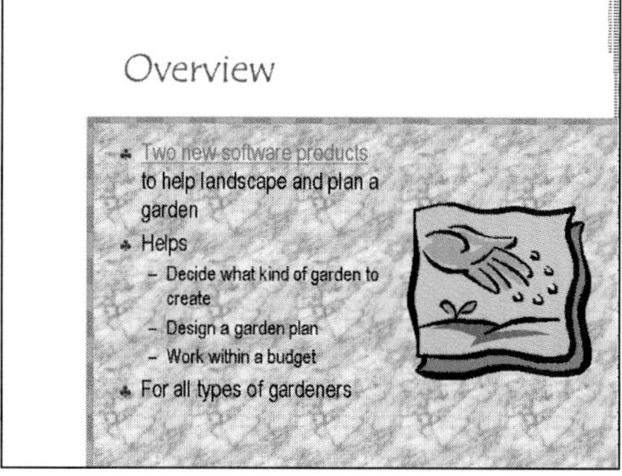

2

Features & Benefits

- **Landscape Helper**
  - Decide what kind of garden to create
    - Location (walkway, yard, along fence or house)
    - Specialty garden (rose, cut flowers, herbs/food)
    - Theme garden (, , seasonal, color)
  - Create a Garden Plan
    - Garden Size
    - Seeds or potted plants
    - Layout
  - How to care for a garden based on geographical conditions
    - Watering tips
    - Fertilizer and food
- **Garden Administrator**
  - How to stick to a gardening budget
  - Tools/Supplies needed and where to get them

3

Garden Ideas

4

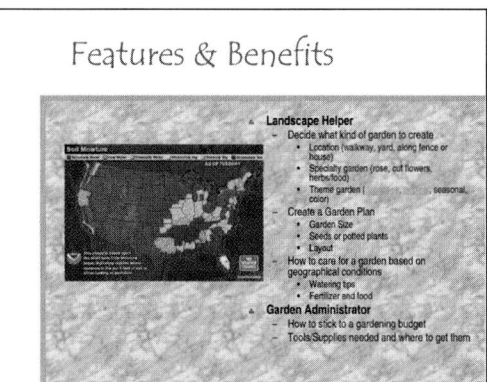

- Good for beginners
  - Makes gardening fun and easy
  - Provides helpful hints, especially for new gardeners
- Great for experienced gardeners
  - Used advanced features of software to
    - Design and plant various types of gardens
    - Strategically mix plant types
- Software provides pictures of most plant types and colors
- See your garden before it's planted!

5

Pricing

- Landscape Helper: $39.95
- Garden Administrator: $29.95
- Get **both** for **ONLY**: $59.95
- Buy both and get **10% off** first purchase of plants and/or planting tools at Green Brothers

6

Specifications

- Software available for PC or Mac
- Tutorial teaches basic features of software
- Easy to install
- Run off of a CD, disk or install

7

Availability

- Available now in all Green Brothers Stores
- Other distribution channels and rollout dates

Store	Availability Date
Garden Depot	May 15, 2003
Landscape Central	June 30, 2003
Bob's Better Home Store	July 15, 2003

8

POWERPOINT

Cues for Reference

Save as a Web Page

1. Click **File, Save as Web Page.**
2. Click the **Change Title** button.
3. Enter the **Page title** in the page title text box.
4. Click **OK.**
5. Click in the **File name** text box and enter a file name.
6. Click **Save.**

Preview a Presentation as a Web Page

1. Click **File, Web Page Preview.**
2. Click **File, Close** in the Web browser to exit Preview mode.

Publish a Presentation to the Web

1. Click **File, Save as Web Page.**
2. Click the **Change Title** button.
3. Enter the **Page title** in the page title text box.
4. Click **OK.**
5. Click in the **File name** text box and enter a file name.
6. Click the **Publish** button.
7. Make your selections.
8. Click **Publish.**

Set up and Schedule a Broadcast Presentation

1. Click **Slide Show, Online Broadcast,** and **Schedule a Live Broadcast.**
2. Enter the presentation information.
3. Click the **Settings** button.
4. Make your selections.
5. Click **OK.**
6. Click the **Schedule** button.
7. Enter the schedule information.
8. Send the e-mail message.

SETTING THE STAGE
Act I File name: **pp5trilogy**
Act II File name: **pp5airlandsea**

POWERPOINT

Act I

You work in the Marketing and Distribution Department at Trilogy Productions. This department decides which films to buy from outside producers. Once it buys or acquires films, Trilogy must then market and distribute them.

Your department is meeting with several producers who want to learn more about Trilogy's role as a distributor and marketer of films and TV shows. Your boss has asked you to create an informative presentation to convince producers that Trilogy Productions has the marketing and distribution expertise to make a hit movie.

Your boss has given you several files and notes to work with to create this presentation. Below are her notes, from which you can create the presentation. She would like you to include tables and charts that were created in other applications.

Follow these guidelines:

- Provide an appropriate title for the presentation.
- Each paragragh of notes contains information for one slide. Summarize the information into bullet points.
- Create appropriate titles for each slide.
- Apply any design template.
- Search the Web for movie images, then copy them to the appropriate slides.
- Apply transitions and an animation scheme.
- After you create and save the presentation, save a copy as **pp5trilogyreview** for review. Have a classmate or your teacher review (make changes and add comments to) your presentation, then compare the reviewed document with your original and accept or reject the changes.
- Make sure to embed the fonts in the presentation.
- Run the slide show. Deliver the presentation, if time permits, and use the annotation pen to explain the tables.
- Save the file; name it **pp5trilogy.**

Use the following notes to create your slides.

Trilogy Productions markets and distributes films and TV shows. We are known for our innovative marketing campaigns and promotions. In addition, we have extensive distribution channels, which are maintained by an outstanding sales force and our strong relationships in the industry.

Our experience in marketing and distribution speaks for itself. We market and distribute as many as 10 television shows and 30 films per year. Our products generate tremendous attention, and are consistently featured in trade publications and other print materials, as well as on television news and entertainment programs.

Our current television series, Undercover, is a top-ranked action hour. Since its season premiere, the national ratings of the show have grown significantly. Our success with this program is due to extensive promotions (sweepstakes, home video, and Internet cross-promotion) and publicity from sci-fi magazines and television appearances.

Note: Your boss has given you a ratings presentation for Undercover, located on the Data CD as **pp5undercover.** *It contains a slide with a table that ranks Undercover, as well as a slide with a chart showing national ratings growth. Create hyperlinks, where appropriate, to these specific slides. pp5undercover contains a slide entitled "Shown Growth Throughout the Season." Insert this slide into the presentation immediately after the slide that discusses Undercover's performance on TV.*

Our films, released this past year, did exceptionally well. Because of wide distribution, we experienced high box-office grosses and international recognition. Because of our marketing effort, we were able to heighten consumer awareness, thus increasing our box-office grosses.

Note: Your boss has given you a Word document, located on the Data CD as **pp5boxoffice,** *that contains a table with the past year's box office results. Add this table to the slide.*

Review this year's upcoming slate of films.

Note: Your boss has given you a Word document, located on the Data CD as **pp5releaseschedule,** *that contains a table with this year's upcoming films. Add this table to the slide.*

Finally, summarize the reasons why this producer should sell his movie to Trilogy. Emphasize that Trilogy has tremendous experience in marketing and distribution, our success has been proven over and over with our past and current products, we have the necessary relationships in the industry, and we are a fun, innovative company.

Act II

You work in the Accounting Department at Air Land Sea Travel Group. You and your colleagues have been asked to analyze the income statement for the quarter ended June 30 and recommend a strategy to increase the company's net income over the next few quarters. A copy of the income statement is located on the Data CD under the file name **pp5income**.

Use the information below to create a presentation to the CEO (chief executive officer) and CFO (chief financial officer) of the company. Your boss has given you notes on what to include in the presentation, as well as an outline of the recommended strategy, which is located on the Data CD under the file name **pp5outline**. You will create the first five slides using the notes below, and the last two slides by importing the Word outline.

POWERPOINT

Follow these guidelines:

- Give your presentation an appropriate title.
- Each paragragh of notes contains information for one slide. Summarize the information into bullet points.
- Create appropriate titles for the slides that are not imported from Word.
- Apply any design template.
- Include the date as a footer on the Slide Master.
- Search the Web for pictures of San Diego, New York, Boston, or San Francisco and copy them to the appropriate slides.
- Apply transitions and an animation scheme.
- Write notes for each slide to help you deliver the presentation.
- Save the file; name it **pp5airlandsea**.
- After you create and save the presentation, save a copy as **pp5salesreview** for review. Have a classmate or your teacher review your presentation (making changes and adding comments) and compare the reviewed document with your original and accept or reject the changes.
- Run the slide show.
- Save the presentation as **pp5airlandsea**.

Use the following notes to create your slides.

At Air Land Sea Travel Group, our vision is to provide our clients outstanding travel services at low commissions. With the increasing amount of online travel bookings, we must meet market demands and ensure that our bottom line continues to increase.

We are way ahead of our competition. In 2002, we had more travel bookings than any of the top agencies.

Note: Insert the chart on the Competition tab of **pp5competition**, *located on the Data CD. Insert a comment on this page that reads:* `Be sure to update these numbers before delivering the presentation.` *Insert a link to the chart.*

Overall, our agencies are profitable, but some are much more so than others.

Note: Insert Income Analysis Bar chart from **pp5income**.

Our current situation shows that our Boston location has the lowest total income, whereas San Diego has the lowest net income.

Note: Insert the Total Income pie chart and the Net Income pie chart from **pp5income**.

After analyzing the income statements of each of our locations, we recommend merging the Boston and New York offices and relocating our San Diego offices. Doing so will help reduce expenses and ultimately increase our net income.

Note: An explanation of our recommendation is outlined on the Data CD under the file name **pp5recommendation**. *Import this outline to be the last two slides in the presentation.*

You just received a copy of the 2005 Travel Review newsletter, which indicates that Air Land Sea actually booked 14,635 trips this year, and 4 Seasons Travel booked 2,345 trips.

Note: Update **pp5competition** *to reflect this change.*

1
2
3

1
2
3

SETTING THE STAGE/WRAPUP

File names: **Conference Details.doc**
chcomlet.doc
map.doc
data.xls
finalbud.xls
chofcom.mdb

FINAL PERFORMANCE

You are the assistant to Sara Vickers, the conference coordinator at Occasions Event Planning in New York, NY. Your New Jersey office has been hired by the New Jersey Small Business Development Association to assist in planning the 10th Annual Small Business Ownership Conference, which will be held on May 21, 2005, from 7:30 a.m. to 5:00 p.m. at the Teaneck Marriott at Glenpointe, a hotel and conference center in New Jersey.

The purpose of this conference is to give small business owners from the state the opportunity to attend workshops and exhibits that will provide the tools needed to grow their businesses and to provide networking opportunities with fellow entrepreneurs.

In preparation for this event, you will complete numerous projects that will require you to use various Office tools, as follows:

Internet

- Research and gather contact information for the New Jersey Chambers of Commerce
- Research the conference facility to locate the meeting floor layout

Excel

- Create an RSVP list, including fees collected
- Develop a budget
- Prepare a comparative income statement

Word

- Develop a Web site
- Create a logo
- Create a press release
- Design a flyer
- Send a merged letter to recipients
- Develop the conference program

PowerPoint

- Create a 10-12 slide multimedia presentation

Access

- Create and query a table

Outlook

- Schedule meetings

The next few pages will provide detailed information to assist you with finalizing these projects. The projects are divided into three parts and follow the sequence of events as they would occur if you were truly planning a conference.

Follow these Guidelines

1. Before starting any of the projects, you will need to read the "Conference Details" section on pages 3–7. This section provides facts that you will need to include in some of the projects.
2. Complete the projects in the order they are presented on pages 8–20.
3. For each project, do the following:
   a. Include your first and last name as a header.
   b. Keep all first drafts. Place all first drafts and final projects in a folder. These may be used as portfolio work samples.
   c. Print one copy.

Note: Data files needed to complete the projects are located on the Data CD. You can copy information contained in the **Conference Details** *Word data file and paste it into the project(s) where appropriate.*

Conference Details

- The conference will open with a keynote address by Thomas McLeod, president of the New Jersey Commerce Commission and a member of the governor's cabinet. Anthony Ericson, the president of the New Jersey Small Business Development Association, will make the closing remarks.
- The luncheon will include remarks by BBN-TV business reporter Marcie Thomas, who will recount local success stories.
- Throughout the day, there will be numerous one-hour breakout sessions. Attendees may choose to attend any one of the 10 sessions listed on the next page. Each session will be repeated three times throughout the day.

Below is the list of all sessions, the room in which each session will be held, the speaker's name, and a brief description of each session.

1. **Business Plans for Small Businesses** (Montclair Room) *Speaker: Pamela Areana* Looking for investment capital, loans, or a direction for your business? Create a simple business plan to formulate your ideas and detail your financial plans.
2. **Buying and Selling a Business** (Alpine Room) *Speaker: Joseph Kubiak* What are the considerations when buying an ongoing business or franchise? What steps should you take when you want to sell a business?
3. **E-Business for Small Businesses** (Morris Room) *Speaker: Gregory Martinez* How can your business profit by having a Web site? How can you use e-mail for advertising and marketing your product?
4. **Finance for Small Businesses** (East Ballroom, Section III) *Speaker: Ann McConnell* What software will help you maintain business records? What records are necessary? How can you minimize accounting service fees?
5. **How to Start Your Own Business** (East Ballroom, Section I) *Speaker: Norman Posner* What do you need to get started? What steps should you take?
6. **Interviewing and Hiring for Employee Retention** (Essex Room) *Speaker: Fran Suraci* Learn how to tailor your interviewing questions and how to interpret answers to select the ideal candidate.
7. **Managing Work, Life, and Family** (Palisades Room) *Speaker: Jonathan Lismore* Is balancing all your commitments creating stress in your life? Learn how to manage your business so that you have more time for life and family.
8. **Networking** (Hospitality Suite) *Hosts: Mary Ann Kingsley and Lawrence Treacy* Make business contacts by attending this brief get-acquainted session, which includes tips for networking. Most of the session will be free-form for meeting and greeting the participants.
9. **Your Professional Image: Entrepreneur** (Princeton Room) *Speaker: Robert Martinson* How do you create and promote your professional business image? Learn image-enhancing tips for company policies, promotions, publications, etc.
10. **Web Page Design for the Small Business** (East Ballroom, Section II) *Speaker: Gregory Lee* Keep up with the competition by getting on the Web! Learn the basics for creating your company's very own Web page and the advantages of doing so.

- Twenty-five local businesses will be exhibiting their products and services. These businesses include local banks, software vendors, accounting firms, human resource companies, business-to-business services, Web site designers, telecommunications companies, and financial planning companies. Conference exhibitors are listed below.
    - Areana Business Plan Consultants
    - Bergenfield Community College
    - Brandt and Brandt
    - Business Software, Ltd
    - Business Management Consultants, Inc
    - Commerce Bank
    - Computer Gurus
    - First State Bank
    - Financial Umbrella, Inc
    - Greg, Parsons, and Holtz
    - Human Resources Consulting, Inc
    - Ippolino Insurance Agency
    - Kerrigan Internet Consultants
    - Lee Web Site Design
    - Nunez Central Supply Company
    - Office Supplies Depot
    - PeopleSoft
    - Personnel Associates, Inc
    - PriceWaterhouseCoopers
    - Security Insurance Group
    - Software Solutions, Inc
    - State of New Jersey Economic Development Board
    - Tenafly Chamber of Commerce
    - Wassau Bank and Trust Company
    - Web Design Services, Inc

- Participants can register for the conference by completing and mailing the registration form on the flyer or from the Web site. The registration form is shown below.

Send or fax this form to:

SARA VICKERS, Conference Coordinator
Occasions Event Planning, NJ Office
1045 Palisades Avenue
Fort Lee, NJ 07024

Telephone: (201) 555-4322
Fax: (201) 555-4323

CONFERENCE REGISTRATION INCLUDES LUNCHEON AND ALL SESSIONS

Name____________________ Company____________________

Address____

City____________________ State________ Zip__________

❐ New Jersey Small Business Development Association Member: $60 ❐ Other: $85

❐ Check enclosed (made out to Small Business Ownership Conference)
❐ Charge my credit card: Amex, Discover, Visa, or MasterCard (circle one)

Acct #____________________ Exp. date____________________

Signature____

- The corporate sponsors, to be credited in the conference program, are listed below.

  Commerce Bank

  PeopleSoft

  Sam Malone Mercury

  Software Solutions, Inc

  State of New Jersey Economic Development Board

  Tenafly Chamber of Commerce

- The conference schedule and room assignments are as follows:

7:30–8:30	Conference registration/ Continental breakfast	Conference center lobby
8:30–9:15	Keynote address— *Speaker: Thomas McLeod*	Grand Ballroom, Section A
9:30	Exhibits open	Grand Ballroom, Section C
9:30–10:30	Breakout session #1	Various
10:45–11:45	Breakout session #2	Various
12:00–1:30	Luncheon— *Speaker: Marcie Thomas*	Grand Ballroom, Section B
1:45–2:45	Breakout session #3	Various
3:00	Exhibits close	Grand Ballroom, Section C
3:00–3:45	Closing session— *Speaker: Anthony Ericson*	Grand Ballroom, Section A
4:00–5:00	Networking and cocktail party	Grand Ballroom, Section B

- The room layout of the conference facility is on the hotel's Web site and is also shown below. To locate the hotel's conference facility layout, do the following:
  a. Go to www.marriotthotels.com.
  b. Click on Events & Meetings.
  c. Click on Find a Location.
  d. Click on Search Hotels.
  e. Choose New Jersey from the Select a State drop-down list.
  f. Enter 10 in the Number of Meeting Rooms text box and click Find.
  g. Select Teaneck Marriott at Glenpointe.
  h. Click the Meeting Space link, then click the View floor plans for this hotel link.

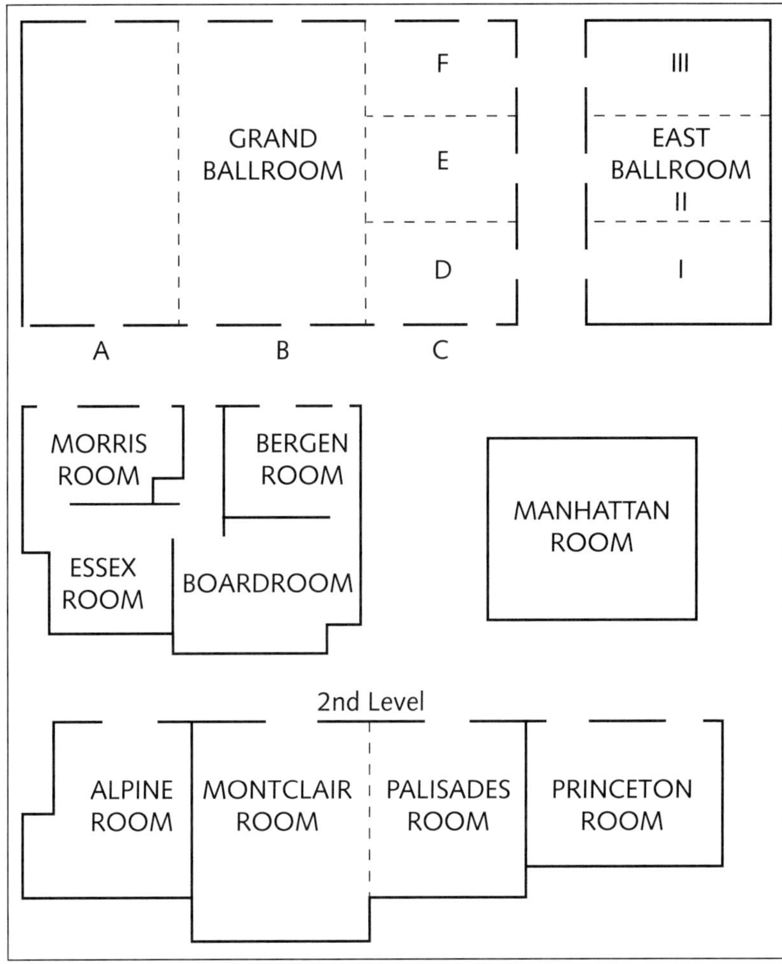

PROJECTS

Part I

The Logo

Create or locate a colorful logo for the 10th Annual Small Business Ownership Conference to use on the flyer, letter, conference program, Web site, and title slide of the presentation.

The Press Release

1. Create a press release.
2. It should be dated May 21, 2005, and should announce the 10th Annual Small Business Ownership Conference.
3. Indicate the highlights of this year's program (found in Conference Details).
   - Include a quote from the Conference Chairperson for the event, Wendy Pilgrim: "This year's 10th anniversary conference is sure to be our most successful one yet. We are excited to have such an extensive program with impressive and inspiring speakers."
   - Indicate that the announcement was made today by Anthony Ericson, President of the New Jersey Small Business Development association in Newark, the sponsoring organization for the conference.
4. The press contact is Christine Powell from the New Jersey Small Business Development Association, (973) 555-1272.

The Flyer

1. Design a one-page flyer, which will be mailed to New Jersey and New York Chambers of Commerce members, encouraging them to attend the conference. It will also be included in the letter sent to members of the New Jersey Small Business Development Association.
2. Include the conference logo, conference date, conference location, and the breakout session titles, as well as the keynote and closing speakers.

3. Include a tear-off with the registration form, so people can register by fax or mail. (You can find needed conference information in the Conference Details section.)

Note: The flyer shown below is a guide.

BREAKOUT SESSIONS:

10th Annual

Small Business Ownership Conference

May 21, 2005, 7:30 a.m. – 5:00 p.m.
Marriott Glenpointe Hotel, Teaneck, NJ

KEYNOTE SPEAKER: Thomas McLeod, President of the NJ Commerce
LUNCHEON SPEAKER: Marcie Thomas of BBN-TV

- Business Plans for Small Businesses
- Buying and Selling a Business
- E-Business for Small Businesses
- Finance for Small Businesses
- How to Start Your Own Business
- Interviewing and Hiring for Employee Retention
- Managing Work, Life, and Family
- Networking
- Your Professional Image: Entrepreneur Identity
- Web Page Design for the Small Business

CLOSING SPEAKER Anthony Ericson, President, NJ-SBDA

Send or fax this form to:
SARA VICKERS, Conference Coordinator
Occasions Event Planning-NJ Office
1045 Palisades Avenue
Fort Lee, NJ 07024

Telephone: 201-555-4322
Fax: 201-555-4323

CONFERENCE REGISTRATION INCLUDES LUNCHEON AND ALL SESSIONS

Name___________________________________Company____________________

Address____

City__________________________________State___________Zip______________

☐ NJ Small Business Development Assn. Member: ☐ $60 ☐ Other: $85
☐ Check Enclosed (made out to Small Business Ownership Conference)
☐ Charge my credit card: Amex, Discover, Visa or MasterCard (circle one)
Acct #________________ Exp. date_________
Signature_________________________________

Planning Meetings

Use Outlook to schedule the following meetings:

January 3 – Meeting with Hotel Event Planner and NJ Small Business Association representative at the Glenpointe Marriott – 11:00 a.m.

January 10 – Meet with corporate sponsor representatives at Occasions Event Planning NY office. 10:00 a.m.

Participants:

Commerce Bank

PeopleSoft

Sam Malone Mercury

Software Solutions, Inc

State of New Jersey Economic Development Board

Tenafly Chamber of Commerce

The Letter and Data File

You will send letters to members of the New Jersey Chambers of Commerce, who are also members of the New Jersey Small Business Development Association, inviting them to the conference. To complete the project, do the following:

1. Open the Access file, **chofcom,** from the Data CD. This data file contains a list of the members of the New Jersey and New York Chambers of Commerce Association. The Illustration below shows the **NYNJTable** within the chofcom database file.

	ID NO	Member	Chamber name	Address1	Address2	City	State	Zip	Telephone
▶	1	☑	Cape May County Chamber of Commerce	P.O. Box 74		Capo May Cour	NJ	08210	609-555-5181
	2	☑	North Jersey Regional Chamber of Comme	Northview Office Park	1033 Rt. 46 East	Clifton	NJ	07013	973-555-3243
	3	☑	Greater Atlantic City Chamber of Commerc	1125 Atlantic Ave. #105		Atlantic City	NJ	08401	609-555-1665
	4	☑	Bergenfield Chamber of Commerce	35 S. Washington		Bergenfield	NJ	07621	201-555-2323
	5	☐	Bound Brook Chamber of Commerce	309 W. Union Ave. PO Box 227		Bound Brook	NJ	08805	732-555-7273
	6	☑	Cherry Hill Regional Chamber of Commerc	1060 Kings Hwy. N. #200		Cherry Hil	NJ	08034	856-555-1600
	7	☑	East Brunswick Regional Chamber of Com	24 Brunswick Woods Drive	P.O. Box 56	East Brunswick	NJ	08816	732-555-3009
	8	☐	Edison Chamber of Commerce	PO Box 2103		Edison	NJ	08818	732-555-0300
	9	☑	Englewood Chamber of Commerce	2-10 N. Van Brunt Street		Englewood	NJ	07631	201-555-2381
	10	☑	Fort Lee Chamber of Commerce	2357 Lemoine Ave.		Fort Lee	NJ	07024	201-555-7575
	11	☑	Hackensack, New Jersey Chamber of Con	190 Main Street #305		Hackensack	NJ	07601	201-489-3700
	13	☐	Lakewood Chamber of Commerce	200 Clifton Ave		Lakewood	NJ	08701	732-555-0012
	14	☐	Manasquan, New Jersey Chamber of Com	PO Box 365		Manasquan	NJ	08736	732-444-8303
	15	☑	Morris County Chamber	10 Park Ave.		Morristown	NJ	07960	973-555-4332
	16	☑	Newark Area Regional Business Partnersh	744 Broad St.	26th. Floor	Newark	NJ	07012	973-444-6587
	17	☑	Paramus, New Jersey Chamber of Comme	58 Midland Ave.	PO Box 325	Paramus	NJ	07652	201-555-3344
	18	☑	Ridgefield Park, New Jersey Chamber of (	78 Mount Vernon Street		Ridgefield Park	NJ	07660	201-444-3880
	19	☑	Tenafly Chamber of Commerce	PO Box 163		Tenafly	NJ	07670	201-444-3504
	20	☑	Woodbridge, New Jersey Chamber of Cor	52 Main Street		Woodbridge	NJ	07095	732-555-4040
	21	☐	The County Chamber of Commerce	235 Mamaroneck Avenue		White Plains	NY	10605	914-555-2110
	22	☐	The Bronx Chamber	111 Calhoun Street		Bronx	NY	10465	718-555-4111
	23	☐	Brooklyn NY Chamber of Commerce	7 Metro Tech Center #2000		Brooklyn	NY	11201	718-555-1000
	24	☐	Fishkill, New York Chamber of Commerce	300 Westage Business Center #100		Fishkill	NY	12524	914-555-2067
	25	☐	The Chamber of Commerce of Orange Coı	154 Main Street		Goshen	NY	10924	914-555-8080
	26	☐	Hyde Park, New York Chamber of Comme	PO Box 17		Hyde Park	NY	12538	914-229-8612
	27	☐	Larchmont, New York Chamber of Comme	2005 Palmer Ave #201		Larchmont	NY	10538	914-555-2297
	28	☐	Rockville Centre, Chamber of Commerce	PO Box 226		Rockville Centre	NY	11571	516-666-0666
	29	☐	Yonkers, New York Chamber of Commerc	20 S. Broadway #1207		Yonkers	NY	10701	914-555-0223
	30	☐	Albany New York Region Chamber of Com	540 Broadway		Albany	NY	12207	518-555-3434
	31	☐	Greater Rochester Metro Chamber of Com	55 St. Paul St.		Rochester	NY	14604	716-555-2220
	32	☐	Syracuse, New York Chamber of Commer	572 Salina St.		Syracuse	NY	13202	315-555-4342
	33	☐	Staten Island, New York Chamber of Comr	130 Bay Street		Staten Island	NY	10301	718-555-2295
*	ıtoNumber)	▣							

2. Edit the table to include information for additional chambers of commerce who have joined the association.
   a. Create a form (using the **NYNJTable**) and add each chamber of commerce and the name of its president into the database as follows:
      - New Brunswick, Nat Zanardi
      - Toms River, Judy Gordon
      - Westfield, John Carling
   b. Search the U.S. Chambers of Commerce Directory on the Internet at www.2chambers.com to find the address, zip, telephone, and fax numbers of New Brunswick, Toms River, and Westfield chambers of commerce; add this information to the database using the form.

Note: This information does change often and may not match data in the solution files.

3. Create a query of only New Jersey members. (Query the database on the MEMBER and STATE fields and save the query.)
4. Complete the invitation letter. The letter, shown here and located on the Data CD as **chcomlet,** is not complete. You must insert merge codes and the conference logo. You can redesign the letterhead to accommodate the logo, if you want. You will note that the letter invites members of the New Jersey Chambers of Commerce, who are also members of the New Jersey Small Business Development Association, to the conference.
5. Merge the completed letter with the New Jersey members query table to produce your mailing.
6. Save the merged file, if you wish.

10TH ANNUAL SMALL BUSINESS OWNERSHIP CONFERENCE
May 21, 2005, 7:30 a.m. to 5:30 p.m.
Teaneck Marriott at Glenpointe

February 1, 2005

«Title» «First» «Last»
«Chamber_Name»
«Address1»
«Address2»
«City», «State» «Zip»

Dear «Title» «Last»:

We are happy to invite you and all the members of your Chamber to the 10th Annual Small Business Ownership Conference. This is an anniversary year and the events planned for this conference reflect goal to make this the biggest and best conference ever. This year, the conference will be held on May 21 at the Teaneck Marriott at Glenpointe, the hotel and conference center.

Please read the enclosed flyer, which highlights the day's keynote speaker and other impressive guests. We are confident that this year's convention is going to be a tremendous success, due to the informative sessions and the outstanding conference exhibitors that will be present. If there are any «Chamber_Name» members who are interested in reserving a booth for the conference, contact Wendy Pilgrim at the N.J. Small Business Development Association to receive all of the necessary exhibit information.

We are offering members of the N.J. Small Business Development Association a reduced registration fee of $45. All the members of your Chamber of Commerce are included at this rate. Please reproduce the flyer for your members and have them fax or mail the registrations as per the instructions on the flyer.

The Small Business Ownership Conference is, as always, a great opportunity to network, but this year the sessions, speakers and exhibitors make it a "must". We look forward to seeing you and the members of your group at our 10th Annual conference in May.

Cordially,

Anthony Ericson
President

ae/

Enclosure

New Jersey Small Business Development Association 134 Market Street Newark, NJ 07012
PHONE: 973-555-1232 FAX: 973-555-1233

The Web Site

1. Create a home page for the Small Business Ownership Conference. You may use a Web template if you want. Include the following on the home page:
   a. The name, date and time of the conference.
   b. The conference logo.
   c. A navigation bar that links to all pages (see step 2).
   d. A "welcome to the home page" statement.
   e. Location of the event, the Teaneck Marriott at Glenpointe. Create a hyperlink to the Teaneck Marriott's home page at www.marriott.com/property/propertyPage/EWRGP
   f. Contact Information
      - The Small Business Development Association
      - Wendy Pilgrim, Vice President and Event Coordinator
      - 134 Market Street, Newark, NJ 07012
      - Telephone: (973) 555-1232
      - Fax: (973) 555-1233
      - E-mail: pilgrim@sbda.net
2. Create additional Web pages for each of the following aspects of the conference that can be accessed by the navigation bars on all pages. Use the names below for the navigation bar and use each name as the respective page title. (The information for each of these pages can be found in the Conference Details section.)
   - Exhibitors
   - Schedule of Events
   - Breakout Sessions
   - Registration Information (Use the tear-off registration form here.)

Part II

The conference preparation is well under way, and responses are beginning to come in. As more people register for the conference, you will need to update various documents. Therefore, you need to complete the following projects at this time.

The RSVP List

1. A spreadsheet has been created to keep track of those who have responded so far and the amount of their checks. To complete the spreadsheet, open the Excel file **data.xls,** located on the Data CD, and select Sheet 2, titled **RSVP,** shown below.
2. Enter the fee for each respondent. (Remember, New Jersey Small Business Development Association members pay $60, while nonmembers pay $85.) To enter the fees, create an IF statement to test if the Member column contains a "Y." If it contains a "Y," enter 60.00; otherwise, enter 85.00.
3. After all fees are entered, total them in Cell E51, leaving room for additional respondents.
4. Alphabetize the RSVP list by last name.

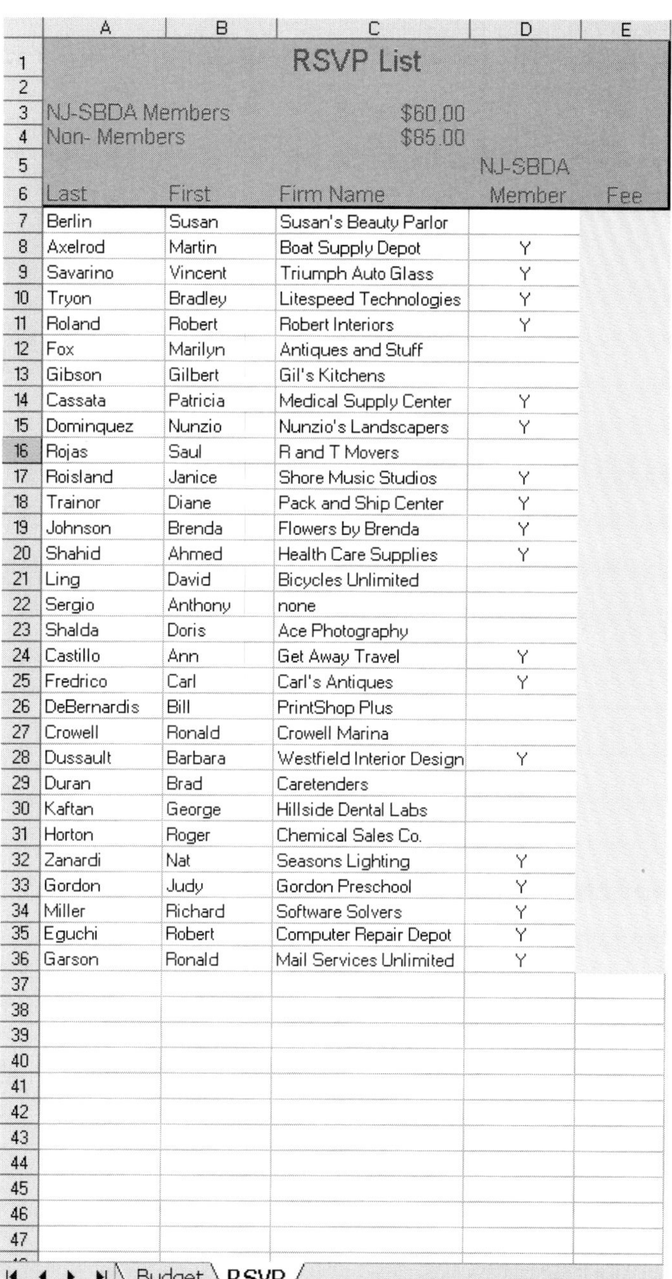

	A	B	C	D	E
1			RSVP List		
2					
3	NJ-SBDA Members		$60.00		
4	Non- Members		$85.00		
5				NJ-SBDA	
6	Last	First	Firm Name	Member	Fee
7	Berlin	Susan	Susan's Beauty Parlor		
8	Axelrod	Martin	Boat Supply Depot	Y	
9	Savarino	Vincent	Triumph Auto Glass	Y	
10	Tryon	Bradley	Litespeed Technologies	Y	
11	Roland	Robert	Robert Interiors	Y	
12	Fox	Marilyn	Antiques and Stuff		
13	Gibson	Gilbert	Gil's Kitchens		
14	Cassata	Patricia	Medical Supply Center	Y	
15	Dominquez	Nunzio	Nunzio's Landscapers	Y	
16	Rojas	Saul	R and T Movers		
17	Roisland	Janice	Shore Music Studios	Y	
18	Trainor	Diane	Pack and Ship Center	Y	
19	Johnson	Brenda	Flowers by Brenda	Y	
20	Shahid	Ahmed	Health Care Supplies	Y	
21	Ling	David	Bicycles Unlimited		
22	Sergio	Anthony	none		
23	Shalda	Doris	Ace Photography		
24	Castillo	Ann	Get Away Travel	Y	
25	Fredrico	Carl	Carl's Antiques	Y	
26	DeBernardis	Bill	PrintShop Plus		
27	Crowell	Ronald	Crowell Marina		
28	Dussault	Barbara	Westfield Interior Design	Y	
29	Duran	Brad	Caretenders		
30	Kaftan	George	Hillside Dental Labs		
31	Horton	Roger	Chemical Sales Co.		
32	Zanardi	Nat	Seasons Lighting	Y	
33	Gordon	Judy	Gordon Preschool	Y	
34	Miller	Richard	Software Solvers	Y	
35	Eguchi	Robert	Computer Repair Depot	Y	
36	Garson	Ronald	Mail Services Unlimited	Y	
37					
38					
39					
40					
41					
42					
43					
44					
45					
46					
47					

Budget RSVP

Budget Analysis

1. The actual budget and the estimated budget are compared on the Excel file, **data.xls,** Sheet 1, titled **Budget,** located on the Data CD, which is shown below.
2. Switch to Sheet 2, **RSVP.** Copy the total in Cell E51 and paste link it to the Actual Registration Fee cell on Sheet 1, **Budget.**

Note: The budget estimate was based on 100 attendees; the actual numbers are not known at this time. By creating a link, each time you update the RSVP list, the budget analysis page also changes.

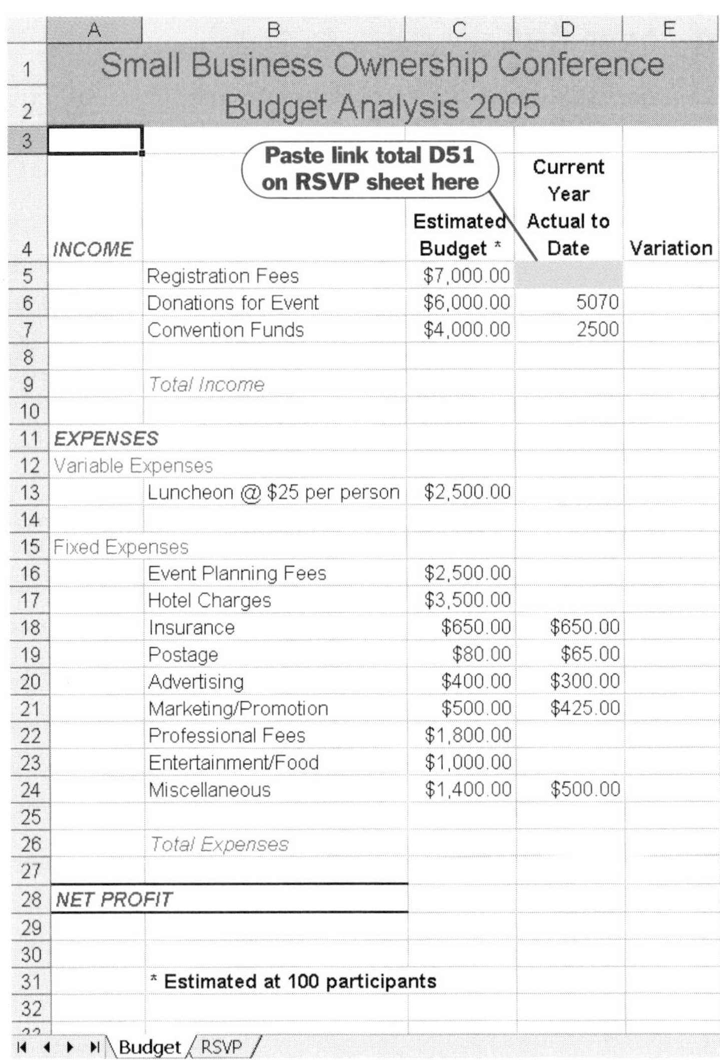

	A	B	C	D	E
1	Small Business Ownership Conference				
2	Budget Analysis 2005				
3					
4	*INCOME*		Estimated Budget *	Current Year Actual to Date	Variation
5		Registration Fees	$7,000.00		
6		Donations for Event	$6,000.00	5070	
7		Convention Funds	$4,000.00	2500	
8					
9		*Total Income*			
10					
11	***EXPENSES***				
12	Variable Expenses				
13		Luncheon @ $25 per person	$2,500.00		
14					
15	Fixed Expenses				
16		Event Planning Fees	$2,500.00		
17		Hotel Charges	$3,500.00		
18		Insurance	$650.00	$650.00	
19		Postage	$80.00	$65.00	
20		Advertising	$400.00	$300.00	
21		Marketing/Promotion	$500.00	$425.00	
22		Professional Fees	$1,800.00		
23		Entertainment/Food	$1,000.00		
24		Miscellaneous	$1,400.00	$500.00	
25					
26		*Total Expenses*			
27					
28	*NET PROFIT*				
29					
30					
31		* Estimated at 100 participants			
32					

Update the RSVP List

The following people have just responded. Add their names and the fees collected to the RSVP list. Those who have a Y next to their names are NJ-SBDA members. Note: The total is automatically updated when the fees are entered, and the increased total is reflected in the budget spreadsheet because of the link. After entering the fees, re-alphabetize the list by last name.

Mr. Tyrone Thompson, Newark Glass Associates, Y

Mr. John Vincenza, Gazebo Gardening Supply, Y

Mr. James Josephs, Josephs Medical Supplies

Ms. Connie Williams, Isolde Spa and Beauty Salon, Y

Mr. Larry Vasalotos, Vasalotos Insurance Agency, Y

Ms. Sally Ciratoz, no affiliation (enter "none" in the field)

Part III

It is now ten days before the conference and you will be finalizing all necessary documents.

The Conference Program

Now that the conference details are established, you can complete the conference program that will be distributed to all conference attendees.

You have been asked to work with a few members of your department on this project. Ask each member to plan a page by sketching the content on a plain sheet of paper. After discussing the layout and all the design elements you plan to use, you can start creating the document on the computer.

1. Design a conference program using the information found in the Conference Details section on pages 3–7. Enhance the program with clip art and any relevant design elements.
   a. The program should be in the form of an eight-page brochure.

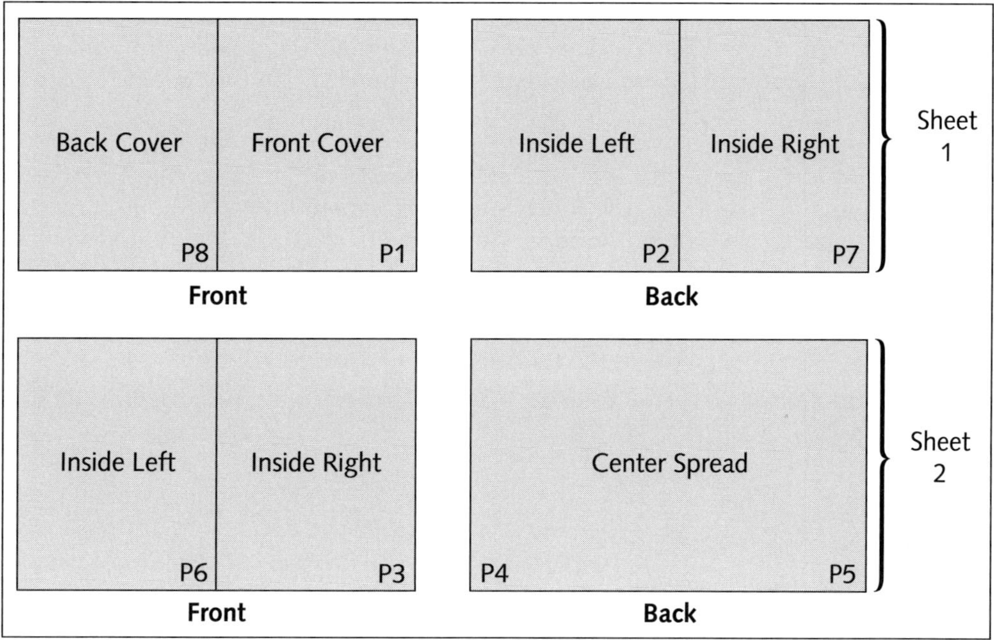

   b. Each page should contain the following information:
   - Sheet 1, Page 8, Back Cover
     - Insert a map showing the location of the Teaneck Marriott at Glenpointe. Both the map and the directions are on the hotel's Web site at: www.marriott.com/property/propertyPage/EWRGP. If you cannot obtain the map, use the **map.doc** file provided on the Data CD.
     - Insert the hotel name, address, telephone number, name of the sponsoring organization (New Jersey Small Business Development Association), and the conference title (Small Business Ownership Conference) at the bottom of the page.

- Sheet 1, Page 1, Front Cover
  - Insert the conference name, logo, date, and location.
- Sheet 1, Page 2, Inside Left
  - Insert the following text:

Welcome to the 10th Annual Small Business Ownership Conference!

The Association greets all the small business owners and their employees here today. We are happy to announce another increase in registration over last year's conference. Based upon last year's evaluations, we have added workshops in Web page design and business plan development.

This year's keynote speaker, Thomas McLeod, brings greetings from the governor of our state and will discuss the economic climate for small business in New Jersey.

Twenty-five local businesses are displaying and selling their products and services, including banks, accounting firms, office suppliers, software solution providers, Web designers, and financial planners.

Relax and visit with friends at the luncheon and networking session. Along with a wonderful luncheon, we will enjoy hearing from local BBN-TV reporter, Marcie Thomas, who will speak on local success stories.

Finally, Anthony Ericson, our president, will make the brief closing remarks and award attendee prizes.

Don't forget!! Enter your name in the drawing for a free weekend at the Marriott in New York City.

And enjoy your day!

- Sheet 1, Page 7, Inside Right
  - Insert the conference sponsors and exhibitors.
- Sheet 2, Page 6, Inside Left
  - Insert the room layout, found on the hotel Web site.
- Sheet 2, Page 3, Inside Right
  - Insert the conference schedule.
- Sheet 2, Page 4, Left Center Spread
  - Insert five breakout sessions and room assignments.
- Sheet 2, Page 5, Right Center Spread
  - Insert remaining breakout sessions and room assignments.

2. After creating the front and back of each sheet, print them back-to-back and fold them in half to create the brochure.

Budget Analysis

The final income and expense data is shown on the **Budget** sheet in the Excel file, **finalbud,** located on the Data CD, also shown below. To date, 120 participants have registered. The shaded areas require formulas as follows:

- Complete the actual variable expense data in D12. Enter a formula to calculate the luncheon expense based on 120 participants.
- Calculate the total income, total expenses, and net profit.
- Enter a formula to calculate the variations between the budgeted and actual values.
- Remove all shading from cells.

	A	B	C	D	E
1	Small Business Ownership Conference				
2	Budget Analysis 2005				
3	INCOME		**Estimated Budget**	**Actual**	**Variation**
4		Registration Fees	$7,000.00	$8,200.00	
5		Donations for Event	$6,000.00	$8,870.00	
6		Convention Funds	$4,000.00	$2,500.00	
7					
8		*Total Income*			
9					
10	***EXPENSES***				
11	Variable Expenses				
12		Luncheon @ $25 per person	$2,500.00		
13					
14	Fixed Expenses				
15		Event Planning Fees	$2,500.00	$3,000.00	
16		Hotel Charges	$3,500.00	$3,500.00	
17		Insurance	$650.00	$650.00	
18		Postage	$80.00	$70.00	
19		Advertising	$400.00	$300.00	
20		Marketing/Promotion	$500.00	$425.00	
21		Professional Fees	$1,800.00	$2,000.00	
22		Entertainment/Food	$1,000.00	$2,000.00	
23		Miscellaneous	$1,400.00	$1,500.00	
24					
25		*Total Expenses*			
26					
27	***NET PROFIT***				
28					
29					
30					
31					
32					
33					

Budget / Comparative IS

Use 120 for the number of actual lunches

Comparative Income Statement

1. Complete the comparative income statement in the Excel file, **finalbud,** located on the Data CD and shown below, to compare this year's income and expenses with last year's.

	A	B	C	D	E	F
1		Small Business Ownership Conference				
2		Comparative Income Statement				
3						
4				This Year	Last Year	
5		INCOME				
6			Registration Fees		$6,580.00	
7			Donations for Event		$5,225.00	
8			Convention Funds		$2,000.00	
9						
10			*Total Income*		$13,805.00	
11						
12		***EXPENSES***				
13		Variable Expenses				
14			Luncheon @ $25 per person		$1,800.00	
15						
16		Fixed Expenses				
17			Event Planning Fees		$2,000.00	
18			Hotel Charges		$2,100.00	
19			Insurance		$500.00	
20			Postage		$50.00	
21			Advertising		$200.00	
22			Marketing/Promotion		$225.00	
23			Professional Fees		$1,600.00	
24			Entertainment/Food		$1,500.00	
25			Miscellaneous		$1,250.00	
26						
27			*Total Expenses*		$11,225.00	
28						
29		***NET PROFIT***			**$2,580.00**	
30						
31						
32						
33						
34						

Budget | Comparative IS

Copy Actual column data from Budget sheet to this column

2. Copy the Actual column data from the **Budget** sheet and paste link it to the This Year column on the **Comparative IS** sheet. This will allow for updating if values are changed on the **Budget** worksheet.

3. Then, create a chart (as a separate chart sheet) comparing the income sections for this year and last year.

The Presentation

1. Create a 10- to 12-slide presentation that will be delivered to the New Jersey Small Business Development Association Conference Committee to inform them of what has been planned for the convention. The contents of some slides are very specific; other slides require you to rely on your creativity.

2. Include the following slides in the presentation:
   a. A title slide.
   b. An organization chart slide for the New Jersey Small Business Development Association Conference Organization.
      - Anthony Ericson is the president. Reporting to him: Sara Vickers is the conference coordinator at Occasions Event Planning and Wendy Pilgrim, who is the vice president and event coordinator for the Association. Christine Powell, press contact; Jonathan Kaufman, business development; and Michael Rondel, budget management, are assisting Wendy Pilgrim. Your name and title should be shown under Sara Vickers.

c. A slide outlining the date, time, place, and approximate number of attendees. Include the following link to the Teaneck Marriott at Glenpointe: www.marriott.com/property/propertyPage/EWRGP
d. A slide showing the day's events (the conference schedule).
e. A slide summarizing the highlights of the conference. Include the following information: there will be a keynote speaker, a luncheon speaker, exciting breakout sessions, and interesting exhibits.
f. A slide outlining the sessions and speakers.
g. A slide titled **The Budget**. Include the following bullet points:
   - Higher profit as compared to last year.
   - Donations from corporate sponsors provided cushion.
   - Details *(link the word "Details" on The Budget slide to the comparative income statement).*
h. A slide titled **Income Comparison**. Copy the chart created in the spreadsheet and paste link it on this slide.
i. A slide listing the exhibitors.
j. A summary slide.

3. Enhance your presentation as follows:
   a. Use a design template or custom background.
   b. Use relevant clip art, music, or video clips on slides where they will be most effective.
   c. Use transitions and animations.
   d. Include a footer on each slide that includes the conference title.

3-D references A cell reference in a formula that refers to calculating values in a cell or cells in the same location on a group of worksheets in a workbook.

Absolute cell reference In Excel, a reference to a particular cell or group of cells that must remain constant even if you copy the contents or formula in one cell to another cell.

Access provider See *ISP*.

Account An accounting form used to summarize increases and decreases in an item.

Account statement A monthly summary of the increases and decreases in an account.

Accounts payable Creditors to whom a business owes money.

Accounts receivable Customers that owe money to a business.

Active cell The cell in use or the cell that is ready to receive text or a formula.

Active cell reference The row and column location of the active cell, which appears in the name box.

Active document The document in use.

Address (e-mail) Internet mail location that identifies a user to whom e-mail can be sent.

Address Book A collection of names and e-mail addresses, created from the contacts in the Contacts folder in Outlook. Use it to find and select names and e-mail addresses when sending an e-mail message.

Agenda A plan or list of things to be done, events to occur, or matters to be brought before a committee, council, or board.

Aggregate function In Excel, used to calculate totals and includes functions such as Sum, Count, Average, or Variance.

Align center Text alignment in which text is centered between the margins.

Align left Text alignment in which text is even at the left margin and uneven at the right margin.

Align right Text alignment in which text is uneven at the left margin and even at the right margin.

Alignment The placement of text relative to the margins of a page, a cell, or a column.

Animation Adding sound or special effects to the way text and objects move on and off a slide during a slide show.

Annotation pen See *Annotator.*

Annotation A hidden note that is inserted as part of the Comments feature.

Annotator In presentations, an on-screen "pen" that allows the user to draw on slides during a slide show.

Annual interest Interest rate for the use of money expressed on an annual basis.

Append To add the data from a spreadsheet, database, or text file to an existing table.

Application program A specific set of instructions that tell a computer what to do (e.g., word processing, spreadsheet analysis, database organization).

Appointment In Outlook, an activity you schedule in your calendar that does not involve inviting other people or reserving resources.

Archive To store old files in another folder.

Ascending A sorting order to organize text alphabetically from A to Z or numbers/figures from smallest to largest.

ASP A file containing embedded server-side scripting, executed on a server, and sent to and displayed in a client Web browser as a standard HTML file.

Attachment A file that you select to send with an outgoing e-mail message.

AutoArchive An Outlook feature that automatically moves old Outlook items at scheduled intervals to the archive location, and discards items that have expired and are no longer valid.

AutoComplete The automatic completion of an entry in an Excel column using previously entered column data.

AutoContent Wizard A feature that guides the user through the presentation creation process.

AutoCorrect A feature that automatically replaces common capitalization, spelling, and grammatical errors with the correct text as you enter it.

AutoFill The Excel feature that allows you to drag, copy, and fill data.

AutoFit Feature to widen columns to fit the longest data in that column.

AutoForm A Forms feature in Access that automatically creates a form to display all the fields in a table one record at a time. There are five AutoForm Wizards: AutoForm: Columnar, AutoForm: Tabular, AutoForm: Datasheet, AutoForm: PivotTable, and AutoForm: PivotChart.

AutoFormat A feature that provides a predefined format applied to a report, a form, a worksheet, or a table.

AutoNumber Data Type Used to enter identification numbers automatically, in sequential (incrementing by one) or random order, when a record is added.

AutoPage An Access feature that automatically creates a basic Web page to display all the records and fields in a table or a query.

AutoPage: Columnar A shortcut that automatically creates a data access page in columnar format. Each field is displayed on a separate line with a label to its left.

AutoReport An Access tool available in Reports that automatically creates a basic report to display all the fields in a database table or a query.

AutoShapes Predesigned shapes and symbols which you can place and size, found on the Drawing toolbar.

AutoSum A feature that automatically adds the selected numbers in a column.

AutoText Frequently used text, graphics, fields, tables or bookmarks that are saved entries, then inserted into a document when needed using a unique name.

Balance sheet A financial report that shows the value of a business, its assets, liabilities, and capital on a specific date.

Balanced columns A column style in which text evens out as it is typed into the columns.

Bandwidth The amount of information that can be transmitted over a communication line.

Banner A page banner, used for Web page titles, that includes the styles and graphics of a theme and displays text that you can format.

Baud rate A measurement for data transmission speed.

Benefits statement Report by an employer stating benefits offered or provided to employees.

Bibliography Identifies sources used, quoted, or paraphrased within a document.

Bit The smallest unit of measurement for computer data.

Bitmap The graphics file format recognized by almost all Windows applications and commonly used for photographs and images. Bitmapped images and photographs are made up of a series of dots that create the image.

Bits per second A measurement used to describe how fast data is transmitted through a modem. This term is synonymous with *baud rate.*

Boilerplate Standardized or repetitive text.

Bold A text enhancement in which text is darkened.

Bookmark A placeholder that is created to mark specific text on a page, a page in a document, or a Web site so that the user can easily return to that place at a later time.

Boolean operators Words or symbols that modify the search for information on the Web or in a database.

Border A variety of line styles that surround the edge of a cell or page.

Bps See *Bits per second.*

Broadcasting The act of sending the same e-mail message to several users at once.

Browser See *Web browser.*

Budget An analysis of the projected income and expenses for a future period.

Bulleted list A list of items marked by a round dot or other symbol.

Bullets and Numbering A feature in Office that allows the user to create bulleted or numbered paragraphs.

Business form A document format that is developed for an activity that occurs repeatedly.

Byte A group of eight bits that represent one character. Computer storage is measured in bytes.

Cable modem See *Modem.*

Calculated control A field object in Access that uses data from a table and a formula or expression to generate its data. See *Calculated field.*

Calculated field A field defined in a query in Access that displays the result of an expression. Its content is not stored in the underlying table. The value is recalculated each time a value in the expression changes, and each time the query is opened.

Caption Explanatory text appearing above or below an object or chart.

Category A keyword or phrase that helps you keep track of items that are related but stored in different folders so you can easily find, sort, filter, or group them.

Category labels Identifies values in a chart data series as shown on the horizontal or x-axis.

CD-ROM See *Compact Disc-Read-Only Memory.*

Cell In spreadsheets, the intersection of a row and column.

Cell address The location of a cell as identified by the column letter and row number.

Cell comment A notation or documentation added to a cell in a worksheet.

Cell coordinate The column letter and row number given to a cell. For example, A1 is the coordinate for the cell in the first row, first column.

Cell cursor In spreadsheets, the heavy line that outlines a cell and indicates the active cell.

Center alignment The positioning of text and/or graphics between the left and right margins. See *Align center.*

Central Processing Unit The principal computer hardware device that controls the speed and processing of a computer.

Chart A visual representation of data. The terms graph and chart are interchangeable.

Chart sheet A separate sheet created to display a chart on a full page.

Chart Wizard A tool that helps you add a chart to a report, worksheet, or form, based on source data from a worksheet, table, or query.

Chat A system whereby users can "talk live" or exchange messages with other Internet users. Unlike e-mail, chat messages are sent and received as text is entered.

Citation A reference, usually made in the form of a footnote or endnote, to give credit to the source of any borrowed material used in a document, presentation, or report.

Click and type A feature found in Word whereby clicking the mouse button in a particular place in a document will relocate the insertion point to that location.

Clip Art Pictures and drawings that can be inserted into a document.

Clipboard A memory area of the computer where data is stored temporarily.

Close button A button (represented by an "X") that closes the document or program window.

Column Vertical area for data that is identified by letter across a spreadsheet grid.

Column chart Compares individual or sets of values using the proportional height of the columns.

Combination chart A custom chart that plots the data series using two different chart types.

Comments Hidden notes or annotations that a user or a reviewer can add to a document, worksheet, or presentation.

Compact Disc-Read-Only Memory A CD-ROM disk can store large amounts of information (moving images, sound, digital programs, and information files) that cannot be overwritten.

Complimentary close The closing of a letter, located directly above the signature line.

Computer An electronic device that can perform tasks and calculations to provide logical information based on the instructions given to it.

Consolidated income statement An income statement that is made up of data from various subsidiaries or divisions.

Controls Objects that display or organize data on a form.

Copy and paste A method of creating a duplicate of text or a graphic and placing it in another location in a document.

Copy formatting A feature that enables the user to copy formatting (font face, style, and size) from one part of text to another.

Count In spreadsheets and databases, a built-in formula that counts the cells in a range or data items in a field.

CPU See *Central Processing Unit.*

Criteria Restrictions you place on a query, in Access, to specify records with which you want to work. See also *Search criterion.*

Crop A drawing tool used to trim a graphic image.

Currency data type Used for monetary or currency values and displays two decimal places and a dollar sign.

Custom tabs A feature that allows the user to set special stopping points on the typing line. See *Tab.*

Cut and paste A method of moving text or a graphic. The "cut" procedure deletes text from a document and places it on the clipboard. The "paste" procedure retrieves text from the clipboard and allows the user to place it in another location in a document.

Cyberspace The navigation area or terrain that a user "travels" when surfing the Internet.

Data Information in the form of numbers or words.

Data access page A Web page that you use to view, input, edit, and manipulate data stored in an Access database.

Data labels Identify the values that each charted item represents.

Data series A group of values in a chart identified by a label.

Data source (document) The document used in the merge process that contains variable information (such as names, addresses, dates, and/or amounts).

Data type In a database, a classification of field information (e.g., text, currency, date).

Database A collection of data that is organized so that its contents can easily be accessed, managed, and updated. A database program is software used to organize and manage information.

Database design See *Database structure.*

Database management system Provides functions to store, search, filter, query, and report on the data in a database.

Database objects Tools you need to store, maintain, search, analyze, and report on data in a database.

Database structure The design of the database, which includes the field names, field sizes, and data types of the data files in the database.

Database window Where objects are organized, accessed, and maintained.

Datasheet Another name for a table.

Date/Time data type Used to define a field containing date and/or time information.

DAT See *Digital Audio Tape.*

Decimal tab A tab type in which data is aligned at a decimal point.

Default settings A preset condition of the software.

Delimited text file A data file where field values are separated by a character, such as a comma or tab.

Delivery address The address of the person to whom a letter is written.

Descending A sort order used to organize text alphabetically from Z to A or numbers/figures from largest to smallest.

Design view Used to create or modify the design of a new or existing database object.

Desktop Place on the computer screen where the user can work with applications and files.

Desktop publishing Using graphics and page design programs for publishing purposes.

Destination file The file that receives the data from another file.

Dialog box A box that contains options to carry out a command.

Digital Audio Tape A standard magnetic medium that has the ability to hold large amounts of information on a tape that is much smaller than an audiocassette.

Digital Video Disc A type of CD-ROM that holds a minimum of 4.7 gigabytes, enough for a full-length movie.

Display See *Monitor.*

Distribution list A distribution list is added to the Outlook Address Book or Contacts folder as one e-mail address; when you send a message to a distribution list, it goes to each address in the list.

Domain The name given to a computer on the Internet so one computer can find another.

Download The process to bring information from a remote computer "down" to your own.

Drafts An Outlook folder that stores unfinished messages.

Drag-and-drop A method of moving text using the mouse. Text is "dragged" from its original location and dropped into its new location.

Drop capital The first letter of a paragraph that is much larger and drops several lines below the paragraph text.

DVD See *Digital Video Disc.*

Edit mode Double-click a cell or press F2 to go into worksheet Edit mode.

Electronic mail (e-mail) Messages exchanged via the Internet.

Ellipsis marks Three periods following a menu item that indicate a dialog box is forthcoming.

E-mail address A unique address required to send and receive electronic mail; it typically includes a person's name, the domain name of the ISP, and an extension. See *Address (e-mail).*

Embed See *Embedded object.*

Embedded chart A chart object that is placed on a worksheet.

Embedded file An object placed into a destination file that becomes part of that file, but can be edited in its source application.

Embedded object An object that can be edited using the application in which it was created.

Enclosure notation A notation located at the bottom left of the letter that indicates that the letter has attachments.

Endnotes A list of citations located at the end of a document.

Expand indicator A button to expand or collapse groups of records. It displays the plus (+) or minus (–) sign.

Expense report A report of money spent by an employee on business travel or expenses.

Export To copy data and database objects from Access to another database, spreadsheet, or file.

Extensible Markup Language (XML) A standard format for delivering rich, structured data. It describes the content of a Web document.

Favorites folder A folder that allows the user to record frequently visited Web sites.

Fax A term derived from the word *facsimile*, which is a duplicate or copy, and means to send a copy electronically via a modem.

Field In database systems, categories of information that make up a record.

Field content Specific data in a field. A field's limit is 65,536 characters.

Field name A name that identifies a field.

Field properties Settings that you can modify to define how data is stored, manipulated, or displayed.

File A collection of information treated as an individual unit by a computer operating system.

File extension Three characters following a file name that identify the file type.

File name A name given to saved data.

File server Shared network computer providing access to files for users in a common environment.

File transfer protocol A protocol for transferring files across the Internet.

Fill handle The rectangular indicator at the bottom right corner of a cell that is used with AutoFill.

Fill series A feature used to quickly enter sequential numbers, dates, or times, in any increment, into a column or row.

Filter A feature that sets criteria to select or sort data. Only data that matches the criteria is allowed to pass through the filter.

Find and replace A feature that scans a document and searches for occurrences of specified text, symbols, or formatting and replaces it with other specified text, symbols, or formatting.

First-line indent A feature that allows you to set the amount of space the first line of each paragraph indents.

Fixed-width text file A data file containing fields with fixed widths.

Floppy disk A removable storage medium, 3.5" disks, that contains up to 1.4 megabytes each.

Flyer A one-page communication that is posted in public or distributed.

Folder A subdivision of a drive that you create to hold files that are related to each other.

Font The appearance of a character distinguished by typeface and size.

Font color Refers to the appearance of characters to which color has been applied.

Font face The design for a set of characters. Examples include Times New Roman, Arial, and Helvetica.

Font size The height of the characters, measured in points.

Font style Refers to the appearance of characters that have been emphasized. Bold, italic, and underline are the most common examples of font styles.

Footer The same text or graphic appearing at the bottom of every page or every other page in a document.

Footnote References that appear at the bottom of a page that give credit to the source of information.

Forecast function Used to project unknown data values based on a series of known values.

Foreign key In Access, a field in one or more tables that refers to the primary key field or fields in another table. The data in the foreign key and primary key fields must match.

Form detail Displays records in Access. You can either display one record on the screen or page, or you can display as many as will fit.

Form footer In Access, displays information that you want to show for every record. It appears at the bottom of the screen in Form view and after the last detail section on the last page when printed.

Form header In Access, displays information you want to show for every record, such as the form title. The header appears at the top of the screen in Form view and at the top of the first page when printed.

Form properties In Access, attributes that are stored in a form property sheet to define a form's characteristics.

Form sections In Access, the part of a form; they include the Form, Header, Footer, and Detail sections as well as the Page header and footer.

Form Wizard A wizard used in Access to create forms built on one or more tables.

Format Painter A feature that allows the user to copy formatting such as font face, style, and size from one part of text to another.

Forms A format that displays one record at a time; used to enter or update data.

Formula An instruction to the computer to calculate data in a certain way.

Formula bar The formula bar is under the toolbars, shows the entry of data, and provides formula assistance.

Freeze panes Used to keep headings or row data in view when scrolling through a large worksheet.

FTP See *File Transfer Protocol.*

Full block style letter A letter style in which all parts start at the left margin.

Function In spreadsheets, a built-in formula that performs special calculations automatically.

Function arguments The cell addresses that make up the data for the function formula.

FV (future value) function Used to calculate the future value of a series of equal payments, at a fixed interest rate, for a specific number of payments.

General ledger Contains the major accounts of a business.

GIF See *Graphics Interchange Format.*

Gigabyte 1,000 megabytes (or 1,000,000 bytes).

Global Address Book A feature of Microsoft Exchange Server that contains all user and distribution list e-mail addresses in your organization. The network administrator creates and maintains this address book.

Global chart A chart that displays data from all fields.

Graphic A line, circle, or box that has been created, or an image or illustration that is imported into a publication.

Graphics Interchange Format An image file format that can be viewed in a Web browser.

Grayscale Tones of gray to show the effects of color.

Grid In a table or worksheet, boxes that form as a result of the intersection of columns and rows.

Gridlines Lines that mark the boundaries of columns and rows in a table.

Group In desktop publishing, an option that allows a user to make one object from several selected objects.

Group footer Used to present information at the end of a group of records.

Group header Used to present information, such as a group title or total, at the beginning of a group of records.

Group sheets Selecting multiple worksheets as a group so that you can make entries on all sheets simultaneously.

Grouped data access page An interactive Web page that you can use to filter and see only the information you want to view. A grouped page efficiently presents a large amount of related data.

Grouping In a database, related records organized together, but set apart from other records. Grouped records are usually organized on the contents of a field.

Groupware Programming that supports people working together in a collective effort who are located remotely from each other.

Gutter space The space between columns.

Hacker (slang) A user who breaks into classified and secret computer systems for malicious purposes.

Handles Boxes surrounding an object indicating that it has been selected and that it is in an Edit mode.

Handouts A printout of a presentation in which slides are printed with two, three, four, six, or nine slides on a page, and given to an audience for future reference.

Hanging indent An indentation style in which all lines in a paragraph are indented except the first line.

Hard drive A storage device that usually resides inside the computer and holds huge amounts of information. Also known as a "fixed" disk.

Hard page break A term used to indicate a forced page break.

Hardware The actual physical computer and all the wires, cables, and peripherals surrounding it.

Header The same text appearing at the top of every page or every other page in a document.

History list A record of Web sites visited.

Home page The first page of a Web site that contains general information as well as links to other related pages.

Hot spot A geometric area of an image that acts like an image or text hyperlink.

HTML See *Hypertext Markup Language.*

Http See *Hypertext transfer protocol.*

Hyperlink A shortcut that allows you to jump to another location in another workbook, a file on your hard drive or network, or an internet address.

Hyperlink data type Used to link to a path to a file on a hard drive, a UNC (LAN server) path, or a URL (Internet address).

Hypertext Text formatted as a hyperlink.

Hypertext Markup Language (HTML) The programming language used to write content for the World Wide Web.

Hypertext transfer protocol (http) The data transmission rules used to transfer Web documents across the Internet.

Hyphenate The act of breaking up words (by syllable) at the end of a line to produce a tighter right margin.

IDC/HTX files Microsoft Internet Information Server uses an IDC file and an HTX file to retrieve data from an ODBC data source and format it as an HTML document.

IF statement A logical function (formula) that allows the user to set up a condition to test data and to perform calculations accordingly.

Import To copy data from a text file, spreadsheet, or database table into an Access table. The source of the data is not modified.

Inbox An Outlook folder that receives and stores e-mail messages.

Income statement A financial report that shows income, expenses, and profits for the period.

Indent A feature that sets temporary left, right, or left and right margins for paragraph text.

Information manager An application that lets you organize information, manage your time, and communicate with others. (Outlook.)

Inline graphic An imported or drawn graphic set in text, functioning as a text character.

Input devices Hardware that transports data into the computer.

Input Mask In Access, a pattern or template for a field.

Insert mode Mode that shifts existing characters to the right when new characters are inserted.

Insertion point The blinking vertical line that appears in a document window and indicates where the next character to be keyed will appear.

Inside address The address of the person to whom a letter is written.

Integrate The ability to share information between applications.

Integration The sharing or combining of data between Office applications.

Interactivity Allows the users to work in a worksheet published to the Web.

Intercasting The ability to surf the Web through the TV.

Internal citation A citation that is indicated directly after the quoted text. Only the author's last name and the year of publication is shown.

Internet A worldwide linked network of computers.

Internet address See *Internet protocol.*

Internet Explorer A Web browser that installs with the Microsoft Office suite.

Internet protocol A protocol that enables information on the Internet to be routed from one network to another.

Internet Service Provider (ISP) A business that provides access to the Internet for electronic mail or use of the World Wide Web.

Intranet An internal network confined within a specific location, usually one particular office or building.

IP address See *Internet protocol.*

ISP See *Internet Service Provider.*

Italics A text enhancement in which text is slanted.

Item The basic element that holds information in Outlook (similar to a file in other programs). Items include e-mail messages, appointments, contacts, tasks, journal entries, and notes.

Itinerary A day-by-day travel schedule or timetable, which includes times for arrival, meetings, and departures as well as contact information.

JPG See *Joint Photographic Experts Group.*

Joint Photographic Experts Group An image file format used to compress and store images that include thousands of colors. Most Web browsers support this format.

Journal A record of business transactions in chronological order.

Justify An alignment option in which text is even at the left and right margins.

Kerning A feature that slightly alters the spacing between pairs of letters.

Kilobyte 1,024 bytes.

Label In spreadsheets, a text entry.

Label alignment In spreadsheets, the alignment of a label entry (left-aligned by default).

Label prefix Numeric labels are entered with an apostrophe ('), which serves as the label prefix.

Label Wizard A tool that allows you to create mailing and other labels, in standard and custom sizes, based on the data in the database.

Landscape orientation A paper orientation that is wider than it is tall.

LAN See *Local Area Network.*

Laptop computers Portable computers, also known as notebooks.

Layout preview In Access, a Report view that displays a report's layout.

Leader A series of dots that connect one column to another to keep the reader's eye focused.

Leading The vertical line spacing between lines of text or data measured in points.

Left alignment To position text along the left margin. See *Align Left.*

Left/right indent See *Indent.*

Legend In spreadsheet charting, the information that identifies the data series.

Letter spacing The relative space between characters.

Line break A format applied to the end of a line. It ends a line of text without inserting a new paragraph at the end of the line.

Line chart Compares individual sets of values with lines connecting the points of data.

Line space The vertical spacing between lines of text or data.

Link See *Hyperlink.*

Link bar A set of hyperlinks used for navigating a Web site, also called navigation bar. It is usually placed on all pages of a Web.

Linked file A shortcut to source file data placed in a destination file. All data changes update in both locations.

Linking Connecting data between files so that a change made in one file automatically updates the other.

Local Area Network (LAN) A computer network that covers a small area.

Local Information Store Data file that stores your messages and other items on your computer.

Logo A symbol, picture, or saying that creates an image of a company.

Lookup Wizard A tool that automates the process of creating Lookup fields.

Lookup Wizard data type An option that starts a wizard to assist in defining a field that looks up values from another table or list of values.

Macro A symbol, name, or key that represents a list of commands or actions.

Mail merge A word processing and database feature that allows the user to mass-produce letters and other documents so they appear to be personalized.

Main document In the merge process, the document that contains elements that do not change. Sometimes referred to as the form document.

Mainframe A computer capable of storing and processing large amounts of data; it can have several hundred simultaneous users.

Manual A handbook, booklet, catalog, or guidebook that provides instruction and/or information to a particular audience.

Manuscript A document that provides information, research, and/or a writer's opinion about a topic.

Many-to-many relationship In Access, record in one table having many matching records in another, and a record in the second table having many matching records in the first.

Margins The parameters that are set to position data on a page.

Master Category List The list of categories supplied by Outlook that you can use to group items or to find them. Included are general categories such as Business, Personal, and Phone Calls.

Master slide In presentations, a slide that contains default settings that affect all the slides in a presentation.

Masthead The information included in the top portion of a newsletter: the newsletter's title, intended audience, division or organization publishing the document, volume and/or issue number, and the current date of the issue.

MAX In spreadsheets and databases, a built-in formula that returns the highest value in a range of cells or data items in a field.

Maximize button A button that enlarges a document or application to fill the screen.

Meeting An appointment for which you reserve resources or invite people to attend.

Memo data type Used for long text, such as notes or descriptions. Field limit is 65,536 characters.

Memorandum A written communication within a company.

Menu A list of related commands or options.

Merge A feature that combines a data document with a main document to mass-produce personalized letters or other documents.

Merge cells Removing the dividing lines between cells to create a single, larger cell. This is also referred to as joining cells.

Merge field names The name of a code for what is eventually inserted into that location during the mail merge process.

MHTML An encapsulated aggregate document that includes all the elements of a Web site in a single file.

MIN In spreadsheets and databases, a built-in formula that returns the lowest value in a range of cells or data items in a field.

Minicomputer A type of computer that supports multiple users, each with its own terminal.

Minimize button A button that reduces the window to an icon.

Minutes A summary of the discussions of a meeting.

Modem A device that lets your computer communicate through standard telephone lines or over TV cable lines for connection to the Internet, and/or other modems, and/or communication devices.

Monitor A hardware device that allows the user to view computer information. Also called a Video Display Terminal (VDT).

Mouse A hand-held device that controls the pointer and lets you select options from the screen.

Multimedia Combining text, graphics, video, animation, and sound in computer applications.

Name box In spreadsheets, the area to the left of the formula bar that identifies the cell reference of the active cell.

Navigation structure Sets the relationship between the home page and the other pages in the Web. The structure is used for link bar and navigation features.

Negative numbers Result of a calculation that is a value less than zero.

Network Computers that are connected. See *LAN*, *Internet*, or *Intranet*.

Newsletter A communication that allows people who share a common interest to exchange ideas, developments, and information on a regular basis.

Newspaper style column A column style in which text first fills one column, then the next column.

Node One particular computer on the Internet—also called a host computer or file server.

Nonadjacent selection A selection of worksheet data that is not contiguous accomplished using the Ctrl key.

Nonbreaking space A code inserted between words to prevent them from breaking during word-wrap.

Normal view The default view in Word and PowerPoint.

Notes Electronic notepaper that you can use to jot down questions, ideas, reminders, and other bits of information.

NPER Number of payments.

Number data type Used for numeric data that may be included in mathematical calculations, except calculations involving money.

Numbered list A list of items marked by a number or letter.

Numeric label In spreadsheets, text that begins with a number. Numeric labels cannot be calculated.

Object Item that can be selected and manipulated.

ODBC A standard way of sharing data between databases and programs.

ODBC driver A program file used to connect to a particular database. Each database program requires a different driver.

Office Shortcut Bar Displays buttons on the desktop that represent features found in Microsoft Office.

One-to-many relationship In Access, a record in one table that matches many records in a second table, with the second table having only one match to the first.

One-to-one relationship In Access, each record in one table that has only one matching record in a second table, with each record in the second table having only one matching record in the first table.

Online Connected and ready to receive and/or transmit data.

Operating system The software that runs on a computer and is responsible for file management, disks, printers, peripherals, and the general operation of the computer.

Order of mathematical operations Formulas are executed in the following order: parentheses, exponents, multiplication and division, and addition and subtraction.

Organization chart Illustrates a company's hierarchy.

Orientation The direction that text is printed on a page. Or, on charts, the plotting of data in a chart by row or column layout.

Orphan The last line of a paragraph appearing by itself at the top of a column or page.

Outbox An Outlook folder that stores messages that you have created and intend to send via e-mail.

Outline A list of topics and subtopics used to organize information before writing a report or delivering a speech.

Outline and Slides tab pane Window in PowerPoint to the left of the Slide pane that displays the presentation as an outline or as slide miniatures.

Outline view A view in Word and PowerPoint that displays text in an outline format.

Output device A device that allows the user to see or hear the information the computer compiles.

Over All In Access, a setting in the RunningSum property, used to display a running sum of values in the same group level. The value accumulates until the end of the report.

Overtype mode Mode that replaces existing text with new text.

Page break The location in a document where one page ends and another begins.

Page footer Displays information you want at the bottom of every printed page.

Page header Displays information you want at the top of every printed page.

Page Wizard Asks you questions about what information you want to include in a data access page and how you want to present and format it.

Pages A database object that enables you to create a Web page linked to an Access database.

Paragraph spacing A feature that allows the user to insert additional space between paragraphs, headings, or subheadings.

Parallel column A column style in which text moves from the left column to the right column. Parallel columns are used to create a list, script, itinerary, minutes of a meeting, or any other document in which text must be read horizontally.

Password A secret code used to keep messages or documents private.

Paste link Connecting the data from one location to another so that if the original data is changed, it updates in the linked location.

Paste values A paste option that allows you to paste only the values, but not the formulas of copied data.

Payroll register A worksheet that calculates employees' salary, taxes, and net pay.

PC See *Personal computer.*

Peripherals All secondary parts of a computer system, which assist in expandability, such as monitors, printers, modems, scanners, removable cartridge drives, and speakers.

Personal Address Book Used to store distribution lists you use frequently, such as a list of everyone on a committee. Personal Address Book files have a .pab extension and can be copied to disk.

Personal computer Computers small enough to fit on a desk that are relatively inexpensive and are designed for an individual user.

Photo Album In PowerPoint, the ability to create a presentation using multiple pictures from a hard disk, scanner, digital camera, or Web camera.

Pie chart Circular graphs used to show the relationship of each value in a data range to the total of the range.

Pixels Series of dots that make up a computer screen.

Placeholder In presentations, blank boxes that define the placement of text and other objects on a slide.

Placeholder (Web) A bookmarking procedure that allows the user to record a Web site he/she might revisit.

PMT (payment function) Used to calculate a loan payment based on the principal (present value of loan), interest rate, and number of payments.

Point size Measures the height of characters. A point is approximately 1/72 of an inch.

Portrait orientation A paper orientation that is taller than it is wide.

Portfolio A group of investments owned by a person or business.

Presentation The application component of Office that allows the user to create and save slides to use as slide shows.

Presentation software Software that allows the user to create a collection of slides that may be shown while an oral report is given, to help summarize data and emphasize report highlights.

Press release A document that is sent to various newspapers and magazines announcing a new product, a development, or an item of special interest.

Preview pane Displays items in a separate pane so you can view the list of items at the same time.

Primary key In a database, a field that uniquely identifies each record in a table.

Principal Present value of a loan.

Print queue The order in which documents wait to be printed.

Print titles Used to print row or column titles for a large worksheet that prints on more than one page.

Professional invoice An invoice or bill sent for services such as legal, accounting, or consulting services.

Programming The act of creating code using a computer language to make applications.

Protocol The rules that must be observed for two electronic devices to communicate with each other.

Pull quote Text art, generally in a box and in a larger size than the surrounding type, consisting of important, interesting, or provocative text from the body copy.

Purchase order A form sent by a firm to a vendor to request shipment of items listed on the order.

PV (present value) function Used to calculate the present value of a series of equal payments, at a fixed interest rate, for a specific number of payments.

Quarterly Every three months, or four times a year.

Queries A structured way to tell Access or Excel to retrieve data from one or more database tables, Web sites, or worksheets that meet certain criteria.

RAM See *Random Access Memory*.

Random Access Memory Main memory of the computer.

Range In spreadsheet applications, one or more contiguous cells.

Rate Interest rate per period.

Read-Only Memory Computer memory on which data has been prerecorded. Once data has been written on a ROM chip, it cannot be removed and can only be read.

Reading Layout View A view in Word that optimizes the reading experience by hiding all toolbars except for the reading layout.

Reciprocal Used to calculate the result of subtracting a percentage discount by multiplying by the percentage left after the discount is subtracted from 100%.

Record In a database, a record lists information about one person or one thing.

Record-bound A chart that shows data from the current record.

Record navigation toolbar Contains buttons to add, delete, save, undo changes, sort, filter, navigate between records, and use help for data access pages in Access.

Redo A feature that lets the user reverse the last undo action.

Referential integrity In Access, enforces rules to maintain the relationship between tables when you enter or delete records.

Regroup To group objects that have been separated using the Ungroup command.

Reimbursement A request to be repaid for money spent on business expenses.

Relational database A database that can work with data in two or more files at the same time.

Relational database management system Provides tools for linking databases containing related information in addition to data maintenance and storage.

Relative (cell) reference In spreadsheets, cell references that change relative to their new locations when a formula is copied.

Reminder A message that appears at a specified interval before an appointment, meeting, or task that announces when the activity is set to occur. Reminders appear any time Outlook is running, even if it is not your active program.

Re Part of a memorandum heading which means *in reference to* or *subject.*

Report detail section In Access, it displays the main body of a report.

Report footer In Access, it appears once at the end of the report. Displays data such as report totals.

Report header In Access, it appears at the top of the first page when printed or previewed. Displays information you want to show for every record, such as the form title.

Report section In Access, the section that includes the report header and footer, Group header and footer, page header and footer, and detail sections.

Report selector In Access, the box where the rulers meet in the upper-left corner of a report in Design view.

Report Wizard In Access, a tool that builds a report by asking you questions about what information you want to include and how you want to present and format it.

Reports In a database, objects that use data from tables and/or queries to create a presentation-quality printout.

Research Tools A task pane that provides resources for research.

Resolution Sharpness or depth of detail of an image, usually expressed in dots per inch.

Restore button A button to the right of the title bar that restores the window to its previous size.

Résumé A document that lists one's personal experience, skill, and abilities and is used to gain employment.

Return address The address of the person sending a letter.

Revenue Income or monies received by a business.

Reverse text A type style that changes black letters or lines to white.

Right alignment To position text along the right margin. See *Align right.*

Right-aligned tab A tab type in which text is right-aligned at a tab setting.

ROM See *Read-Only Memory.*

Router A hardware device that connects two networks together.

Row Horizontal area for data that is identified by a number along the side of a spreadsheet grid.

Row Source Type property In Access, it specifies the entries in a list to be used for field lookup.

Rules A term used in desktop publishing to apply to lines.

RunningSum property In Access, it is used to calculate record-by-record or group-by-group totals in a report.

S&P 500 Standard and Poor's 500 stock index is a weighted index, made up of the stock prices of 500 blue chip stocks, which reflects market trends.

Sales invoice A bill sent by a seller to a buyer, detailing the terms and items sold.

Sales journal A record of sales transactions.

Salutation The opening greeting of a letter (Dear Ms. Jones:).

Sans serif A font type that is straight-edged.

Scanner A digitizing input peripheral device.

Schedule of accounts payable A list, prepared monthly, of the balances of creditor accounts.

Schedule of accounts receivable A list, prepared monthly, of the balances of customer accounts.

ScreenTip Pop-up name that appears when the insertion point is positioned over a toolbar button or hyperlink.

Script A typeface that resembles handwriting.

Scroll The act of viewing all parts of a document.

Scroll box A box that you can drag a precise distance to see a different area of a document.

Scroll buttons Buttons with up, down, left, and right arrows used to scroll to different areas of a document.

Search criterion In a database, the information provided by the user so the software can locate a record.

Search engine A program that searches the documents on the Web for specified keywords and returns a list of the documents in which the keywords were found.

Section break A feature that allows the user to create multiple sections in a document so that they can be formatted differently.

Section selector In Access, the box to the left of a section bar. It selects the section and opens its property sheet.

Select query In Access, it asks a question about the data stored in one or more tables and returns a result set in the form of a datasheet.

Selecting text An action that highlights a character, word, or block of text/data.

Sent Items An Outlook folder that stores copies of e-mail messages that have been sent.

Serial value The numeric value of a date which allows you to use dates in formulas and represents the number of days from January to the date entered.

Series A list of numbers or text that is in a sequential arrangement that can be produced using AutoFill.

Series labels Identifies charted values and appears in the legend.

Serif A font type with lines or curves extending from the ends of the letters.

Server A computer that provides common access to files on a computer network.

Shading A feature that allows the user to add a tint or color to paragraph text and table cells.

Shared border A part of a Web site that appears the same on multiple pages.

Show/Hide codes A feature that allows the user to display or conceal document formatting codes.

Signature In Outlook, the name of a person who creates a message that is inserted at the end of an outgoing message.

Signature line The typed name of the person who has signed the letter. The signature is directly above the signature line.

Sizing handles See *Handles*.

Slide master Contains the default settings for all the slides in a presentation, except the title slide.

Slide pane Window in PowerPoint that contains the slide on which you can create your presentation.

Slide show view Displays slides as an on-screen presentation.

Slide sorter view Displays slides in miniature.

Slide transitions See *Transition*.

Slide views Ways in which a slide may be displayed.

Smart tags A set of buttons that are shared with other Office applications. These buttons provide options for changing a given action or error.

Soft page break A term used to indicate an automatic new page.

Software The most commonly used term to refer to computer applications.

Software program A detailed set of computer instructions that resides in the computer and tells the computer what to do.

Solver An add-in feature for Excel that provides "what-if" analysis tools.

Sorting Allows the user to rearrange the order of words or numbers in a list or records in a database.

Sorting and Grouping box In Access, it displays group properties and enables you to display, or not display, group headers or footers.

Source The file where data originates.

Source file Provides the data for integrating into another file.

Speaker notes The written notes that correspond to slides in a presentation. They help the speaker remember key points during a presentation.

Split cells Reversing the merge cells process and returning cells to their normal size.

Split windows The feature that allows the user to divide a window, thus display files in separate windows.

Spreadsheet A software application that is used for analysis and charting of numerical data.

Status bar The area in an application window which displays information about the current status of the document.

Structured data Formatted data that can be imported to Access from other programs and file formats, i.e., worksheets or tables.

Style A set of formatting characteristics that can be applied to a paragraph or selected text.

Subdatasheet A datasheet that is nested within another datasheet containing related data.

Subscript Characters that print below a line of type.

SUM In spreadsheet and database applications, a function used to add numbers in a range or values in a field.

Supercomputer The fastest type of computer. It can store data and perform numerous tasks simultaneously. It is also used for specialized tasks that require vast amounts of mathematical calculations such as weather forecasting or medical and weapons research.

Superscript Characters that print above a line of type.

Symbol In word processing, an ornamental font or special character.

System software Software that controls the way computer parts work together.

Tab A feature that allows the user to set a stopping point on the typing line.

Tab scrolling buttons Allow you to scroll hidden worksheets into view.

Table A series of columns and rows in which data is entered, formatted, and organized.

Table Wizard A tool to assist in creating tables. It provides 25 business and 20 personal samples containing predetermined fields that can be customized.

Tagged Image File Format An image file format used to compress and store color images. This format is recognized by most Windows applications, but is not recognized by Web browsers.

Tags Indicate how Web browsers should display page elements such as text and graphics, and how to respond to user actions.

Task A personal or work-related duty or errand that you want to track through to completion.

Task Manager A list of tasks in Outlook that is used to monitor important things that need to be completed.

Task pane Appears on the right side of the document/data/slide window on startup, and shows options pertinent to the task at hand.

Task request A request sent in an e-mail message, asking the recipient to complete a task from the sender.

Taskbar The area at the bottom of the Windows screen that allows you to switch easily between applications.

Tax status The number of dependents and marital status of employees, which is used for payroll tax calculations.

Telecommunications Communication between individual computer users, facilitated by the use of a computer, modem, and telephone line.

Template presentation Predesigned sets of slides that relate to a particular topic.

Template A designed and formatted document on which new documents are based.

Terms Credit terms given to a buyer that may involve discounts for early payment.

Text alignments Arranging text along or between the margins on a page.

Text art Graphic elements created from text (e.g., raised or drop capitals, text boxes, or rotated text).

Text box A box that contains text or graphics that can be positioned, sized, and edited.

Text data type Used for alpha characters or a mix of alpha and numeric characters (street addresses), or for numbers that will not be calculated (zip codes). Field size is up to 255 characters, default size is 50.

Text string A word, words, phrase, and/or operators that are used to search for documents, data, or other information.

Text-wrap An option for controlling whether and how text wraps around a graphic or other object.

Theme A format or design template for creating Web pages.

Thesaurus A feature that provides the user with synonyms for selected words.

TIFF See *Tagged Image File Format.*

Title bar The shaded bar at the top of a dialog box or application window that displays the title of the box, or the name of the file, and the application.

Title master Contains the default settings for the format of the title slide in a presentation.

Toolbar A collection of buttons located under the menu bar that displays icons which represent various commands.

Toolbox In Access, a form design feature that contains objects or tools used to design a form.

Transaction A business event or activity that changes the financial status of a business.

Transfer connect protocol/Internet protocol A set of communication rules that control the way data is transferred between computers on the Internet.

Transition A feature that can be applied in presentations to control the way slides move on and off the screen.

Trial balance A list of all the accounts in a business consisting of debit and credit balances, which must be equal to show that the books are in balance.

Type size Measurement of characters in points by vertical height.

Type style Modification of typefaces to add emphasis or contrast (e.g., bold or italic).

Typeface The design of a character.

Unbound control A field object not connected to a data source. Used to display information such as text, lines, rectangles, and pictures.

Undo A feature that lets the user reverse an action.

Ungroup The act of separating an object that has been grouped.

Uniform Resource Locator A Web address.

URL See *Uniform Resource Locator.*

Value On a worksheet, a numeric entry that is able to be calculated.

Variable Data that will change.

VDT See *Video Display Terminal.*

Vendor A supplier or merchant that provides your company with goods or services.

Vertical centering Text that is centered between the top and bottom margins.

Video Display Terminal See *Monitor.*

Virtual reality A computer simulation of three-dimensional real-world dynamics.

WAN See *Wide Area Network.*

Watermark Text or graphics used as a background image on printed documents.

Web browser A software program that displays information retrieved from the Internet in a readable format.

Web component Advanced content elements that you can place on a Web page, such as Photo Gallery, Link Bars, and Dynamic Effects.

Web Layout view The document view in Word that allows you to see how a document will look on the Web.

Web page A visual presentation of an idea using text, graphics, sound, and video, that is viewed over the Internet.

Web Page Preview A Page view that enables you to see how the data access page will appear as a Web page.

Web server A computer that is connected to the Internet 24 hours a day so that your Web site runs at all times.

Web site A collection of Web pages connected by hyperlinks.

Wide Area Network A computer network that links computers outside a local area.

Widow The first line of a paragraph appearing by itself at the bottom of a column or page.

Wildcard A character or symbol used in a search string to substitute for unknown characters.

Window control buttons See *Maximize, Minimize, and Restore buttons.*

Windows Explorer A Windows tool, in versions before Windows XP, that allows the user to look inside the computer and view its contents.

Windows Metafile An image file format, which is recognized by almost all Windows applications, but not recognized by Web browsers.

Wizard A feature that guides the user through the process of using a feature to create a document, or compile data.

WMF See *Windows Metafile.*

WordArt Text created as a graphic image.

Word count A feature that allows the user to calculate pages, characters, paragraphs, and lines in a document.

Word processing A software application that uses a computer and software to create, edit, and print text-based documents such as letters, reports, and memos.

Word underline A single line that appears below individual words.

Word-wrap A feature that automatically advances text to the next line without pressing the Enter key.

Workbook A spreadsheet file that contains many worksheets.

Working folder The default location for saving and opening files.

Worksheet See *Spreadsheet.*

World Wide Web See *Internet.*

WWW See *World Wide Web.*

X-axis In spreadsheet charting, the horizontal scale that typically displays the data series.

XML See *Extensible Markup Language.*

Y-axis In spreadsheet charting, the vertical scale that typically displays the scale values.

Yes/No data type Used for data that is one of two values, such as Yes/No, True/False, or On/Off.

Zip disks Removable disks that hold as much information as 80 floppy disks. A zip disk requires a zip drive, which can be connected inside or outside the computer.

Zoom Used to magnify (zoom in) or reduce (zoom out) the size of the document on screen.

A

B

C

D

E

F

G

H

I

J

K

L

M

N

O

P

Q

R

S

T

U

V

W

X

Y

Z

1
2
3